Microsoft
Visual
FoxPro® 6.0
Language
Reference

Microsoft Press

PUBLISHED BY
Microsoft Press
A Division of Microsoft Corporation
One Microsoft Way
Redmond, Washington 98052-6399

Library of Congress Cataloging-in-Publication Data
    Microsoft Visual FoxPro 6.0 Language Reference / Microsoft
        Corporation.
            p. cm.
        Includes index.
        ISBN 1-57231-870-8
        1. Visual FoxPro for Windows   2. Database management.
    I. Microsoft Corporation.
    QA76.9.D3M5739   1998
    005.75'65--dc21

98-7484
CIP

Printed and bound in the United States of America.

1 2 3 4 5 6 7 8 9   WCWC   3 2 1 0 9 8

Distributed in Canada by ITP Nelson, a division of Thomson Canada Limited.

A CIP catalogue record for this book is available from the British Library.

Microsoft Press books are available through booksellers and distributors worldwide. For further information about international editions, contact your local Microsoft Corporation office or contact Microsoft Press International directly at fax (425) 936-7329. Visit our Web site at mspress.microsoft.com.

Acquisitions Editor: Eric Stroo
Project Editor: Anne Taussig

Contents

Introduction

Welcome to Microsoft Visual FoxPro, the relational database system that simplifies data management and streamlines application development.

About This Book

- The Language Reference is an A to Z reference for the Visual FoxPro language. The following language elements are described in this book:

- Commands

- Functions

- Controls and Objects

- Properties

- Events

- Methods

Each language topic appears in alphabetical order and provides the following information:

- General description

- Syntax

- Arguments, parameters, and settings descriptions, plus additional remarks

- Code example

For an overview of how to use the Visual FoxPro programming language and its elements, see "Overview of the Language" in Help. For information on programming concepts, using classes, and manipulating objects using properties, events, and methods, see Part 1, "Programming in Visual FoxPro," in the *Microsoft Visual FoxPro 6.0 Programmer's Guide*.

Getting Help

The Visual FoxPro Help system gives you quick access to information about using the Visual FoxPro design tools and language elements.

Need Help? Press F1

If you are working with a command or keyword you need more information about, highlight the command or keyword in the Command window and press F1 to display a context-sensitive Help topic on that item. Note that to get Help you have to choose the MSDN Library option during setup.

Sample Files

A variety of sample applications, databases, and files are included with Visual FoxPro and the MSDN Library to demonstrate programming techniques. To find more information, see the "Welcome to Visual FoxPro" screen when you start Visual FoxPro.

Using Code Examples

Many language topics in Help contain code examples that you can run in a program window. You must install the sample files provided in Setup before you can run the program examples.

To run a code example

1. At the top of the Help topic, click the "Example" link.

2. Select the code you want to run and copy it to the Clipboard (CTRL+C).

3. Click the Command window in Visual FoxPro and type MODIFY COMMAND to open a program window, or choose New from the File menu in Visual FoxPro, click the Program option button in the New dialog box, then click the New File button.

4. Paste the code into the program window (CTRL+V).

5. Click the ! button to run the program.

6. Name and save the program when prompted. When saved, the program runs.

Document Conventions

The following typographic conventions are used in Visual FoxPro documentation:

Example	Convention
setup	Bold font indicates words, other than language commands, that you must type.
In the **Query Designer** toolbar, choose **Add Table**.	Bold font is also used in procedures to highlight interface elements such as the name of a window, menu, dialog box, toolbar, button, or option.
SET HELP TO	Capital letters denote commands and keywords, acronyms, constants, and device names.
Press the TAB key. Press SHIFT+F1.	Capital letters denote the names of keys on the keyboard. A plus sign (+) indicates a combination of keys.
Buttons.vcx	Initial capital letters indicate file names.
C:\My Computer\ Working Files\Document	Initial capital letters identify folders and directories. In a path, folders, directories, and file names are separated by backslashes.
http://www.microsoft.com/	Lowercase letters are used for URLs. Server, share, and file names are separated by forward slashes.
FontSize	Initial capital letters indicate the names of objects, properties, events, and methods. If the name consists of more than one word, the initial-capital words are concatenated.
event-driven	Italic letters denote defined terms the first time they occur in text. Defined terms are part of the product Glossary. Click on the italicized word to see the definition.

`IF StatusText() = "Test"`
`  = MESSAGEBOX( "OK" )`
`ENDIF`
	Monospace font indicates command lines you type, code examples, and references in text to the code examples.

`USE customer`	Lowercase letters indicate table and field names.
`nTotal, cName`	Lowercase letters prefix variable names and placeholders. The prefix indicates the data type of the variable: c for Character, n for Numeric, l for Logical, d for Date, t for DateTime, y for Currency, o for Object, and e for any expression.

In syntax, the following conventions are used:

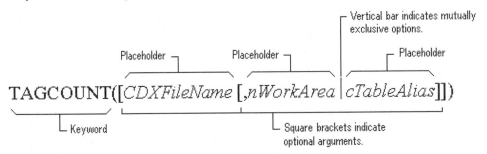

Example	Convention
DELETE VIEW *ViewName*	In syntax, words in italics are placeholders for information you supply.
[STYLE *cStyleName*]	In syntax, brackets enclose optional items.
SET BELL ON | OFF	In syntax, a vertical bar separates two mutually exclusive choices.
[, *WindowName2* …]	In syntax, an ellipsis indicates that an item can be repeated in a list any number of times. A comma separates the list items.

Alphabetic Reference

#DEFINE ... #UNDEF Preprocessor Directive

Creates and releases compile-time constants.

Syntax

#DEFINE *ConstantName eExpression*
...
#UNDEF *ConstantName*

Arguments

ConstantName
> Specifies a compile-time constant name. The constant name must be a legitimate Microsoft Visual FoxPro name that begins with a letter or an underscore and consists of up to 254 letters, digits, or underscores. To improve program readability and simplify debugging, capitalize your constant names and use a standard naming convention for them.
>
> > **Important** Do not use Visual FoxPro keywords for constant names.
>
> To stop text substitution for a constant created with #DEFINE, issue #UNDEF *ConstantName*.

eExpression
> Specifies the value of the compile-time constant. *eExpression* can be a name or an expression that evaluates to a character, numeric, currency, date, datetime, or logical value.
>
> > **Important** Do not use system variables for *eExpression*. System variables are not evaluated until run time.

Remarks

The #DEFINE and #UNDEF preprocessor directives are used to create compile-time constants in programs. By creating constants with #DEFINE instead of using variables, you can reduce memory consumption, increase performance, and simplify programs.

To create a constant with #DEFINE, specify the constant's name with *ConstantName* and its value with *eExpression*. When the program is compiled, text substitution is performed and the constant value expression is substituted for the constant name wherever it appears in the program. You can stop the substitution for the constant by issuing #UNDEF.

Substitution occurs only in program lines that follow the #DEFINE statement that creates the constant and that precede the #UNDEF statement for that constant. The constant is available only to the program that creates the constant.

If #DEFINE is placed within an event or method procedure in a form, the #DEFINE compile-time constant is available only within the event or method procedure. To make #DEFINE compile-time constants available to all event and method procedures in a form, choose the Include File menu item from the Form menu and specify a header file containing the #DEFINE compile-time constants.

Note that compile time constants are not recognized when placed within quotation marks.

Example

The following program creates a compile-time constant named MAXITEMS. This constant is used in a FOR ... NEXT loop to display the numbers 1 through 10.

```
#DEFINE MAXITEMS 10
CLEAR
FOR gnCount = 1 TO MAXITEMS
    ? gnCount
NEXT
```

See Also

COMPILE, #IF ... #ENDIF, #IFDEF | #IFNDEF ... #ENDIF

#IF ... #ENDIF Preprocessor Directive

Conditionally includes source code at compile-time.

Syntax

#IF *nExpression1* | *lExpression1*
    Commands
[#ELIF *nExpression2* | #ELIF *lExpression2*
    Commands
    ...
#ELIF *nExpressionN* | #ELIF *lExpressionN*
    Commands]
[#ELSE
    Commands]
#ENDIF

Arguments

#IF *nExpression1* | *lExpression1*
Commands
    nExpression1 specifies the numeric expression that is evaluated.

- If the expression is nonzero, the commands immediately following #IF are included in the compiled code. The #IF ... #ENDIF structure is exited, and the first program line following #ENDIF is then compiled.

- If the expression is 0, the commands immediately following #IF are not included in the compiled code. Any following #ELIF directives are evaluated.

lExpression1 specifies the logical expression that is evaluated.

- If the expression is true (.T.), the commands immediately following #IF are included in the compiled code. The #IF ... #ENDIF structure is exited, and the first program line following #ENDIF is then compiled.

- If the expression is false (.F.), the commands immediately following #IF are not included in the compiled code. Any following #ELIF directives are evaluated.

   Note Do not specify system variables for *nExpression1* or *lExpression1*. System variables are not evaluated until run time.

#ELIF *nExpression2* | #ELIF *lExpression2*
Commands

...

#ELIF *nExpressionN* | #ELIF *lExpressionN*
Commands

   If *nExpression1* is 0 or *lExpression1* is false (.F.), the #ELIF directives are evaluated. The first #ELIF expression *nExpression2* or *lExpression2*, if present, is evaluated. If *nExpression2* is nonzero or *lExpression2* is true (.T.), the commands following #ELIF are included in the compiled code. The #IF ... #ENDIF structure is exited, and the first program line following #ENDIF is then compiled.

   If *nExpression2* is 0 or *lExpression2* is false (.F.), the commands following #ELIF are not included in the compiled code. The next #ELIF directive is evaluated.

#ELSE *Commands*

   If no #ELIF directives are included, or if those that are included evaluate to 0 or false (.F.), the presence or absence of #ELSE determines whether any additional commands are included in the compiled code.:

- If #ELSE is included, the commands following #ELSE are included in the compiled code.

- If #ELSE is not included, none of the commands between #IF and #ENDIF are included in the compiled code. The #IF ... #ENDIF structure is exited, and compilation continues on the first program line following #ENDIF.

#ENDIF

   Indicates the end of the #IF statement.

Remarks

#IF ... #ENDIF can improve the readability of source code, reduce compiled program size, and, in some cases, improve performance.

When the #IF ... #ENDIF structure is compiled, successive logical or numeric expressions within the structure are evaluated. The evaluation results determine which set of Visual FoxPro commands (if any) are included in the compiled code.

Example

In the following example, the #IF ... #ENDIF structure determines which version of Visual FoxPro compiles the program and then displays the appropriate message.

```
#IF 'WINDOWS' $ UPPER(VERSION( ))
    ? 'This was compiled under Visual FoxPro for Windows'

#ELIF 'MAC' $ UPPER(VERSION( ))
    ? 'This was compiled under Visual FoxPro for Macintosh'

#ELIF 'UNIX' $ UPPER(VERSION( ))
    ? 'This was compiled under FoxPro for UNIX'

#ELSE
    ? 'This was compiled under FoxPro for MS-DOS'

#ENDIF
```

See Also

COMPILE, #DEFINE ... #UNDEF, #IFDEF | #IFNDEF ... #ENDIF

#IFDEF | #IFNDEF ... #ENDIF Preprocessor Directive

Conditionally includes a set of commands at compile time if a compile-time constant is defined.

Syntax

#IFDEF | #IFNDEF *ConstantName*
    Commands
[#ELSE
    Commands]
#ENDIF

Arguments

#IFDEF

Specifies that a set of commands is included at compile time when the *ConstantName* is defined.

The following describe how a set of commands is included at compile time when you include #IFDEF:

- If *ConstantName* is defined, the set of commands following #IFDEF and preceding #ELSE or #ENDIF (whichever occurs first) is included at compile time.

- If *ConstantName* is not defined and #ELSE is included, the set of commands following #ELSE and preceding #ENDIF is included at compile time.

- If *ConstantName* is not defined and #ELSE is not included, no commands within the #IFDEF ... #ENDIF structure are included at compile time.

#IFNDEF

Specifies that a set of commands is included at compile time when the *ConstantName* is not defined.

The following describe how a set of commands is included at compile time when you include #IFNDEF:

- If *ConstantName* is not defined, the set of commands following #IFNDEF and preceding #ELSE or #ENDIF (whichever occurs first) is included at compile time.

- If *ConstantName* is defined and #ELSE is included, the set of commands following #ELSE and preceding #ENDIF is included at compile time.

- If *ConstantName* is defined and #ELSE is not included, no commands within the #IFNDEF ... #ENDIF structure are included at compile time.

ConstantName

Specifies the compile-time constant whose existence determines whether a set of commands is included at compile time. Compile-time constants are defined with #DEFINE.

Commands

Specifies the set of commands that is included at compile time.

Remarks

You can nest an #IFDEF | #IFNDEF ... #ENDIF structure within another #IFDEF | #IFNDEF ... #ENDIF structure.

Comments can be placed on the same line after #IFDEF, #IFNDEF, #ELSE, and #ENDIF. These comments are ignored during compilation and program execution.

Example

The following example creates a compile-time constant named MYDEFINE.
#IFDEF ... #ENDIF displays a message if the compile-time constant has been defined.

```
#DEFINE MYDEFINE 1

#IFDEF MYDEFINE
   WAIT WINDOW "MYDEFINE exists"

#ELSE
   WAIT WINDOW "MYDEFINE does not exist"

#ENDIF
```

See Also

COMPILE, #DEFINE ... #UNDEF, #IF ... #ENDIF, #INCLUDE

#INCLUDE Preprocessor Directive

Tells the Visual FoxPro preprocessor to treat the contents of a specified header file as if it appeared in a Visual FoxPro program.

Syntax

#INCLUDE *FileName*

Arguments

FileName

Specifies the name of the header file that is merged into the program during compilation.

You can include a path with the header file name. When you include a path with the header file name, Visual FoxPro searches for the header file only in the specified location.

If you do not include a path with the header file name, Visual FoxPro searches for the header file in the default Visual FoxPro directory, and then along the Visual FoxPro path. The Visual FoxPro path is specified with SET PATH.

Remarks

You can create header files containing preprocessor directives and then use #INCLUDE to merge the contents of the header file into a program when the program is compiled. The contents of the header file are inserted into the program during compilation at the point where #INCLUDE appears in the program.

Only the #DEFINE ... #UNDEF and #IF ... #ENDIF preprocessor directives are recognized in a header file. Comments and Visual FoxPro commands included in a header file are ignored.

A program can contain any number of #INCLUDE directives. These directives can appear anywhere within the program. #INCLUDE directives can also appear in header files, allowing you to nest #INCLUDE directives.

Header files typically have an .h extension, although they can have any extension. A Visual FoxPro header file, Foxpro.h, is included. It contains many of the constants described throughout this documentation.

Example

In the following example, two files are used: Const.h, a header file, and Myprog.prg, a program file. The header file contains several #DEFINE directives that create compile-time constants. The program file uses #INCLUDE to merge the Const.h header file at compilation, making the compile-time constants in the header file available to the program.

```
*** Header file CONST.H ***
#DEFINE ERROR_NODISK      1
#DEFINE ERROR_DISKFULL  2
#DEFINE ERROR_UNKNOWN   3


*** Program file MYPROG.PRG ***

#INCLUDE CONST.H

FUNCTION chkerror
PARAMETER errcode
   DO CASE
   CASE errcode = ERROR_NODISK
   ?"Error - No Disk"
   CASE errcode = ERROR_DISKFULL
   ?"Error - Disk Full"
   CASE errcode = ERROR_UNKNOWN
   ?"Unknown Error"
   ENDCASE
RETURN
```

See Also

#DEFINE ... #UNDEF, #IF ... #ENDIF, #IFDEF | #IFNDEF ... #ENDIF, _INCLUDE

:: Scope Resolution Operator

Runs a parent class method from within a subclass method.

Syntax

cClassName::cMethod

Remarks

The :: operator is used to execute a parent class method from within a subclass method. When you create a subclass, the subclass methods are automatically inherited from the parent class. The :: operator lets you execute the parent class method in the subclass method and then perform additional processing for the subclass method. The subclass definitions in the example demonstrate how the :: operator is used to execute the parent class method within a subclass method.

For additional information about the :: scope resolution operator, see Chapter 3, "Object-Oriented Programming," in the *Microsoft Visual FoxPro 6.0 Programmer's Guide*.

Examples

The following example creates a form and adds two command buttons to the form. By clicking either button, you can exit the form — the second button, cmdAnotherButton, calls the Click procedure from cmdQuit. This action is possible because of subclassing. The scope resolution operator calls the parent class code for the subclassed object.

```
frmMyForm = CREATEOBJECT("Form")
frmMyForm.Width   = 450
frmMyForm.Height  = 100
frmMyForm.Caption = "Scope Resolution Example"
frmMyForm.AutoCenter =.T.
frmMyForm.AddObject("cmdQuit","cmdQuitButton")
frmMyForm.AddObject("cmdAnother","cmdAnotherButton")
frmMyForm.SHOW        && Display the form
READ EVENTS           && Start event processing
```

The following example defines two command buttons. The first button will be used to subclass the second button. The subclassing can be seen by the FontBold and ForeColor properties which are defined for cmdQuit, but never explicitly set for the cmdAnotherButton. We are defining cmdAnotherButton to be a subclass of the cmdQuitButton. As a result, this button will pick up all the attributes defined above for cmdQuitButton.

```
DEFINE CLASS cmdQuitButton AS CommandButton
   Caption = "\<Quit"   && Caption on command button
   Left   = 175     && Left edge of button
   Top    = 60      && Position for top of button
   Height = 25      && Button height
   Visible = .T.    && Show button on form
   FontItalic = .T.    && Turn on italic text
   ForeColor = RGB(0,0,255) && Change button text color

   PROCEDURE Click
   WAIT WINDOW "Executing the CLICK procedure for cmdQuit." TIMEOUT 1
   CLEAR EVENTS     && Stop event processing, close Form
ENDDEFINE
DEFINE CLASS cmdAnotherButton AS cmdQuitButton

   Caption = "Click to quit"
   Left   = 175
   Top    = 30
   Height = 25

   PROCEDURE Click
   WAIT WINDOW "Click event for button: cmdAnotherButton" TIMEOUT 1
   cmdQuitButton::Click
ENDDEFINE
```

See Also

ADD CLASS, CREATE CLASS, CREATE CLASSLIB, CREATEOBJECT( ), DEFINE CLASS, DODEFAULT( ), GETOBJECT( ), MODIFY CLASS, RELEASE CLASSLIB, SET CLASSLIB, WITH ... ENDWITH

$ Operator

Returns true (.T.) if a character expression is contained in another character expression; otherwise, returns false (.F.).

Syntax

cSearchFor $ *cSearchIn*

Returns

Logical

Arguments

cSearchFor
Specifies the expression looked for within *cSearchIn*.

cSearchIn
Specifies the expression that is searched to see if it contains *cSearchFor*.

If *cSearchFor* is found in *cSearchIn*, $ returns true (.T.); otherwise, it returns false (.F.). *cSearchFor* and *cSearchIn* can be character-type variables or array elements, character-type fields, character string literals, or memo fields of any length.

Memo fields can be manipulated like character expressions, fields in tables, variables, or array elements. For example, if MEMO_FLD is a memo field, the following is acceptable:

```
LIST FOR 'FOX' $ UPPER(memo_fld)
```

Remarks

If the character expression isn't found, false (.F.) is returned. The $ operator is case-sensitive and is not Rushmore optimizable.

Example

The following example creates a table called memotest containing one memo field. Three records are appended to the table. LIST is used to display the three records. The dollar sign ($) is used to list the records that contain the string "FOX." The files created for the example are then deleted.

```
CLOSE DATABASES
CLEAR
CREATE TABLE memotest (Text C(3), Memo M)
INSERT INTO  memotest (Text, Memo) VALUES ('Fox', 'Fox')
INSERT INTO  memotest (Text, Memo) VALUES ('Cat', 'Cat')
INSERT INTO  memotest (Text, Memo) VALUES ('FOX', 'FOX')
LIST FIELDS  Memo, Text FOR 'FOX' $ UPPER(Memo)
USE
DELETE FILE memotest.dbf
DELETE FILE memotest.fpt
```

See Also

AT( )

% Operator

Returns the remainder (modulus) obtained by dividing one numeric expression into another.

Syntax

nDividend % nDivisor

Arguments

nDividend
> Specifies the dividend (numeric expression being divided). The number of decimal places in *nDividend* determines the number of decimal places in the result.

nDivisor
> Specifies the divisor (the numeric expression dividing the dividend *nDividend*). A positive number is returned if *nDivisor* is positive; a negative number if *nDivisor* is negative. *nDivisor* cannot be zero.

Remarks

The modulus operator (%) and MOD( ) return identical results.

The modulus operator (%) is an arithmetic operator. Other arithmetic operators are: + (addition), – (subtraction), * (multiplication), / (division), and ^ (exponentiation). When these operators are combined in a numeric expression, % has the same precedence as * and /.

For a further discussion of operators and their order of precedence, see "Operators" in Help.

Example

```
? 36 % 10          && Displays 6
? (4*9) % (90/9)     && Displays 6
? 25.250 % 5.0     && Displays 0.250
? IIF(YEAR(DATE( )) % 4 = 0, 'Summer Olympics this year';
  , 'No Summer Olympics this year')
```

See Also

MOD( )

& Command

Performs macro substitution.

Syntax

& *VarName*[.*cExpression*]

Arguments

& VarName

Specifies the name of the variable or array element to reference in the macro substitution. Do not include the M. prefix that distinguishes variables from fields. Such inclusion causes a syntax error. The macro should not exceed the maximum statement length permitted in Visual FoxPro.

A variable cannot reference itself recursively in macro substitution. For example, the following generates an error message:

```
STORE '&gcX' TO gcX
? &gcX
```

Macro substitution statements that appear in DO WHILE, FOR, and SCAN are evaluated only at the start of the loop and are not reevaluated on subsequent iterations. Any changes to the variable or array element that occur within the loop are not recognized.

.cExpression

The optional period (.) delimiter and *.cExpression* are used to append additional characters to a macro. *cExpression* appended to the macro with *.cExpression* can also be a macro. If *cExpression* is a property name, include an extra period (*cExpression..PropertyName*).

Remarks

Macro substitution treats the contents of a variable or array element as a character string literal. When an ampersand (&) precedes a character-type variable or array element, the contents of the variable or element replace the macro reference. You can use macro substitution in any command or function that accepts a character string literal.

Tip   Whenever possible, use a name expression instead of macro substitution. A name expression operates like macro substitution. However, a name expression is limited to passing character strings as names. Use a name expression for significantly faster processing if a command or function accepts a name (a file name, window name, menu name, and so on).

For additional information on name expressions, see "Overview of the Language" in Help.

While the following commands are acceptable:

```
STORE 'customer' TO gcTableName
STORE 'company'  TO gcTagName
USE &gcTableName ORDER &gcTagName
```

use a name expression instead:

```
USE (gcTableName) ORDER (gcTagName)
```

Macro substitution is useful for substituting a keyword in a command. In the following example, the TALK setting is saved to a variable so the setting can be restored later in the program. The original TALK setting is restored with macro substitution.

Example

```
STORE SET('TALK') TO gcSaveTalk
SET TALK OFF
*
*  Additional program code
*
SET TALK &gcSaveTalk  && Restore original TALK setting
```

See Also

STORE

&& Command

Indicates the beginning of a nonexecuting inline comment in a program file.

Syntax

&& [*Comments*]

Arguments

Comments

Indicates that inline comments follow. For example:

```
STORE (20*12) TO gnPayments  && 20 years of monthly payments
```

Inserting inline comments to denote the end of the IF ... ENDIF, DO, and FOR ... ENDFOR structured programming commands greatly improves the readability of programs.

Remarks

Place a semicolon (;) at the end of each comment line that continues to a following line. You cannot place && and a comment after the semicolon used to continue a command line to an additional line.

Example

```
NOTE  Initialize the page number;
   variable.
STORE 1 to gnPageNum
* Set up the loop
DO WHILE gnPageNum <= 25  && loop 25 times
   gnPageNum = gnPageNum + 1
ENDDO  && DO WHILE gnPageNum <= 25
```

See Also

*, MODIFY COMMAND, MODIFY FILE, NOTE

* Command

Indicates the beginning of a nonexecuting comment line in a program file.

Syntax

* [*Comments*]

Arguments

Comments

> Specifies the comment in the comment line. For example:

```
*   This is a comment
```

Remarks

Place a semicolon (;) at the end of each comment line that continues to a following line.

Example

```
* Initialize the page number;
   variable.
STORE 1 to gnPageNum

* Set up the loop
DO WHILE gnPageNum <= 25  && loop 25 times
   gnPageNum = gnPageNum + 1
ENDDO  && DO WHILE gnPageNum <= 25
```

See Also

&&, MODIFY COMMAND, MODIFY FILE, NOTE

= Command

Evaluates one or more expressions.

Syntax

= *Expression1* [, *Expression2* ...]

Arguments

Expression1 [, *Expression2* ...]
    Specifies the expression or expressions that the = command evaluates.

Remarks

The = command evaluates one or more expressions, *Expression1*, *Expression2* ..., and discards the return values. This option is particularly useful when a Visual FoxPro function or a user-defined function has a desired effect, but there is no need to assign the function's return value to a variable, array element, or field.

For example, to turn insert mode on, you can issue the following command:

```
= INSMODE(.T.)
```

INSMODE normally returns a true (.T.) or false (.F.) value. In the example above, the function is executed but the return value is discarded.

If only one expression (*Expression1*) is included, the equal sign is optional.

> **Note**   There are two unrelated uses for the equal sign (=). It can be used as an operator in logical expressions to make a comparison, or to assign values to variables and array elements. In these two cases, the equal sign (=) is an operator and not a command. See "Relational Operators" in Help for more information about using the equal sign (=) as an operator in logical expressions. See STORE for more information about using the equal sign (=) to assign values to variables and array elements.

See Also

EVALUATE

\ | \\ Command

Prints or displays lines of text.

Syntax

TextLine

– or –

TextLine

Arguments

\TextLine

When you use \, the text line is preceded by a carriage return and a line feed.

\\TextLine

When you use \\, the text line is not preceded by a carriage return and a line feed.

Any spaces preceding \ and \\ are not included in the output line, but spaces following \ and \\ are included.

You can embed an expression in the text line. If the expression is enclosed in the text merge delimiters (<< >> by default) and SET TEXTMERGE is ON, the expression is evaluated and its value is output as text.

Remarks

The \ and \\ commands facilitate text merge in Visual FoxPro. Text merge lets you output text to a file to create form letters or programs.

Use \ and \\ to output a text line to the current text-merge output file and the screen. SET TEXTMERGE is used to specify the text merge output file. If text merge isn't directed to a file, the text line is output only to the main Visual FoxPro window or the active user-defined output window. SET TEXTMERGE NOSHOW suppresses output to the main Visual FoxPro window or the active user-defined window.

Example

```
CLOSE DATABASES
OPEN DATABASE (HOME(2) + 'Data\testdata')
USE Customer      && Open customer table
SET TEXTMERGE ON
SET TEXTMERGE TO letter.txt

\<<CDOW(DATE( ))>>, <<CMONTH(DATE( ))>>

\\ <<DAY(DATE( ))>>, <<YEAR(DATE( ))>>

\

\

\Dear <<contact>>

\Additional text

\

\Thank you,
```

```
\

\XYZ Corporation
CLOSE ALL
MODIFY FILE letter.txt NOEDIT
```

See Also

_PRETEXT, SET TEXTMERGE, SET TEXTMERGE DELIMITERS, _TEXT,
TEXT ... ENDTEXT

? | ?? Command

Evaluates expressions and displays the results.

Syntax

? | ?? *Expression1*
    [PICTURE *cFormatCodes*] | [FUNCTION *cFormatCodes*] | [V*nWidth*]
    [AT *nColumn*]
    [FONT *cFontName* [, *nFontSize*] [STYLE *cFontStyle* | *Expression2*]]
    [, *Expression3*] ...

Arguments

? *Expression1*
    Evaluates the expression specified by *Expression1* and sends a carriage return and line
    feed before the expression results. The results are displayed on the next line of the main
    Visual FoxPro window or the active user-defined window and printed at the left margin
    of a page, unless a function code *cFormatCodes* or the _ALIGNMENT system variable
    specifies otherwise.

    If you omit the expressions, a blank line is displayed or printed. A space is placed
    between expression results when multiple expressions are included.

?? *Expression1*
    Evaluates the expression specified by *Expression1* and displays the expression results
    on the current line at the current position of the main Visual FoxPro window, an active
    user-defined window, or the printer. A carriage return and line feed are not sent before
    the results.

PICTURE *cFormatCodes*
    Specifies a picture format in which the result of *Expression1* is displayed.
    cFormatCodes can consist of function codes, picture codes, or a combination of both.
    You can use the same codes available in the Format and InputMask properties.

Function codes affect the overall format of the result; picture codes act on individual characters in the result. If function codes are used in *cFormatCodes*, they must appear before the picture codes and they must be preceded by @. Multiple function codes with no embedded spaces can immediately follow @. The last function code must be followed by one or more spaces. The space or spaces signal the end of the function codes and the start of the picture codes.

FUNCTION *cFormatCodes*

Specifies a function code to include in ? and ?? output. If the function clause is included, do not precede the function codes with @. Function codes must be preceded by @ when included in PICTURE.

V*nWidth*

Specifies a special function code that enables the results of a character expression to stretch vertically within a limited number of columns. *nWidth* specifies the number of columns in the output.

```
? 'This is an example of how the V function code works.' ;
   FUNCTION 'V10'
```

AT *nColumn*

Specifies the column number where the output is displayed. This option lets you align output in columns to create a table. The numeric expression *nColumn* can be a user-defined function that returns a numeric value.

FONT *cFontName* [, *nFontSize*]

Specifies a font for ? | ?? output. *cFontName* specifies the name of the font, and *nFontSize* specifies the point size. For example, the following command displays the system date in 16-point Courier font:

```
? DATE( ) FONT 'Courier',16
```

If you include the FONT clause but omit the point size *nFontSize*, a 10-point font is used.

If you omit the FONT clause and ? | ?? output is placed in the main Visual FoxPro window, the main Visual FoxPro window font is used for the output. If you omit the FONT clause and ? | ?? output is placed in a user-defined window, the user-defined window font is used for the output.

Note If the font you specify is not available, a font with similar font characteristics is substituted.

STYLE *cFontStyle*

Specifies a font style for ? | ?? output. If you omit the STYLE clause, the Normal font style is used. If the font style you specify is not available, a font style with similar characteristics is substituted.

Note   You must include the FONT clause when you specify a font style with the
STYLE clause.

The font styles you can specify with *cFontStyle* are as follows:

Character	Font style
B	Bold
I	Italic
N	Normal
O	Outline
Q	Opaque
S	Shadow
–	Strikethrough
T	Transparent
U	Underline

You can include more than one character to specify a combination of font styles.
For example, the following command displays the system date in Courier Bold Italic:

```
? DATE( ) FONT 'COURIER' STYLE 'BI'
```

Remarks

? and ?? evaluate expressions and send the results to the main Visual FoxPro window,
an active user-defined window, or the printer.

If SET PRINTER is ON, the expression results are directed to the printer and the main
Visual FoxPro window or an active user-defined window. If SET PRINTER is ON and
SET CONSOLE is OFF, the results are directed only to the printer.

Example

```
? 15 * (10+10)

? 'Welcome to ' PICTURE '@!'

?? 'Visual FoxPro'
```

See Also

???, @ ... SAY, SET MEMOWIDTH, SET PRINTER, SET SPACE

??? Command

Sends output directly to the printer.

Syntax

??? cExpression

Arguments

cExpression
Specifies the characters that are sent to the printer.

Remarks

A group of three question marks bypasses the printer driver and sends the contents of *cExpression* directly to the printer. *cExpression* must contain valid printer codes.

Printer control codes allow you to reset the printer, change type styles and sizes, and enable or disable boldface printing. These codes can consist of any combination of printable or nonprintable characters that are specific to the printer you're using. You can direct control codes to the printer in several different ways:

- Use combinations of CHR( ) and quoted strings concatenated with + to send ASCII characters directly to the printer.

- Use quotation marks to send a string containing printer codes or ASCII characters.

- Codes can be sent to the printer before printing begins and after printing ends with the _PSCODE and _PECODE system variables. For more information, see _PSCODE and _PECODE.

Printer control codes vary from printer to printer. The best source for information about printer control codes is the manual that came with your printer.

See Also

? | ??, @ ... SAY, CHR( ), Print Dialog Box

@ ... BOX Command

Included for backward compatibility. Use the Shape control instead.

@ ... CLASS Command

Creates a control or object that can be activated with READ.

Syntax

@ nRow, nColumn CLASS ClassName NAME ObjectName

Arguments

@ nRow, nColumn

Specifies the position of the control or object. The height and width of the control or object is determined by the class default height and width values.

Rows are numbered from top to bottom. The first row is number 0 in the main Visual FoxPro window or in a user-defined window. Row 0 is the row immediately beneath the Visual FoxPro system menu bar.

Columns are numbered from left to right. The first column is number 0 in the main Microsoft Visual FoxPro window or in a user-defined window. When a control or object is placed in a user-defined window, the row and column coordinates are relative to the user-defined window, not to the main Visual FoxPro window.

A position in the main Visual FoxPro window or in a user-defined window is determined by the font of the window. Most fonts can be displayed in a wide variety of sizes; some are proportionally spaced. A row corresponds to the height of the current font; a column corresponds to the average width of a letter in the current font.

You can position the control or object using decimal fractions for row and column coordinates.

CLASS *ClassName*

Specifies the class of the control or object. *ClassName* can be a Visual FoxPro base class or a user-defined class. The following table lists the Visual FoxPro base classes you can specify for *ClassName*.

Base class names

CheckBox	Column	ComboBox
CommandButton	CommandGroup	Container
Control	Cursor	Custom
DataEnvironment	EditBox	Grid
Header	Image	Label
Line	ListBox	OLEBoundControl
OLEControl	OptionButton	OptionGroup
Page	PageFrame	Relation
Separator	Shape	Spinner
TextBox	Timer	

NAME *ObjectName*

Specifies the name of the object reference variable to create. The object-oriented properties, events, and methods of the control or object can be manipulated by referencing this variable.

Remarks

@ ... CLASS provides an intermediate step for converting programs and applications created in earlier versions of FoxPro to the preferred object-oriented programming methods of Visual FoxPro. For additional information about backward compatibility with FoxPro 2.x controls, see "Controls and Objects," later in this language reference.

For information about object-oriented programming in Visual FoxPro, see Chapter 3, "Object-Oriented Programming," in the *Microsoft Visual FoxPro 6.0 Programmer's Guide*.

Example

The following example demonstrates how @ ... CLASS can be used with programming techniques used in earlier FoxPro versions (in this example, use of READ to activate controls). @ ... CLASS is used to create a text box whose properties can be changed with the Visual FoxPro object-oriented programming techniques.

ON KEY LABEL is used to display the Windows Color dialog box when you press CTRL+I. The TextBox is placed on the main Visual FoxPro window using @ ... CLASS, and READ activates the text box.

```
CLEAR
ON KEY LABEL CTRL+I _SCREEN.PageFrame1.Page1.goFirstName.BackColor;
   = GETCOLOR( )
@ 2,2 SAY 'Press Ctrl+I to change the background color'

@ 4,2 CLASS TextBox NAME goFirstName
READ
CLEAR
```

See Also

CREATEOBJECT( ), DEFINE CLASS. READ, _SCREEN

@ ... CLEAR Command

Clears a portion of the main Visual FoxPro window or a user-defined window.

Syntax

@ *nRow1*, *nColumn1* [CLEAR | CLEAR TO *nRow2*, *nColumn2*]

Arguments

@ *nRow1*, *nColumn1* CLEAR

Clears a rectangular area whose upper-left corner begins at *nRow1* and *nColumn1* and continues to the lower-right corner of the main Visual FoxPro window or a user-defined window.

CLEAR TO *nRow2, nColumn2*

>Clears a rectangular area whose upper-left corner is at *nRow1* and *nColumn1* and whose lower-right corner is at *nRow2* and *nColumn2*.

Remarks

If you omit CLEAR or CLEAR TO, Visual FoxPro clears *nRow1* from *nColumn1* to the end of the row.

Example

The following example clears the screen, main Visual FoxPro window, or user-defined window from the second row to the bottom of the window.

```
@ 2,0 CLEAR
```

The following example clears a rectangular region. The area from row 10 and column 0 to row 20 and column 20 is cleared.

```
@ 10,0 CLEAR TO 20,20
```

See Also

CLEAR

@ ... EDIT – Edit Boxes Command

Included for backward compatibility. Use the EditBox control instead.

@ ... FILL Command

Changes the colors of existing text within an area of the screen.

Syntax

@ *nRow1, nColumn1* FILL TO *nRow2, nColumn2*
[COLOR SCHEME *nSchemeNumber* | COLOR *ColorPairList*]

Arguments

@ *nRow1, nColumn1*

>Specifies the upper-left corner of the area to change.

FILL TO *nRow2, nColumn2*

>Specifies the lower-right corner of the area to change.

COLOR SCHEME *nSchemeNumber*

>Specifies the color of the area. Only the first color pair in the specified color scheme determines the color of the area.

COLOR *ColorPairList*

    Specifies the color of the area. Only the first color pair in the specified color pair list determines the color of the area.

    If you omit the COLOR SCHEME or COLOR clauses, the rectangular portion is cleared. An area can also be cleared with @ ... CLEAR.

    For information about color schemes and color pairs, see "Colors Overview," later in this language reference.

Remarks

This command changes the colors of text within a rectangular area of the main Visual FoxPro window or the active user-defined window. You can set the foreground and background color attributes for existing text only. Any text output to the same area after you issue @ ... FILL appears in the default screen or window colors.

Example

The following example clears the main Visual FoxPro window and fills an area with color.

```
ACTIVATE SCREEN
CLEAR

@ 4,1 FILL TO 10, 8 COLOR GR+/B
```

See Also

@ ... SAY, Colors Overview

@ ... GET – Check Boxes Command

Included for backward compatibility. Use the CheckBox control instead.

@ ... GET – Combo Boxes Command

Included for backward compatibility. Use the ComboBox control instead.

@ ... GET – Command Buttons Command

Included for backward compatibility. Use the CommandButton control instead.

@ ... GET – List Boxes Command

Included for backward compatibility. Use the ListBox control instead.

@ ... GET – Option Buttons Command

Included for backward compatibility. Use the OptionGroup control instead.

@ ... GET – Spinners Command

Included for backward compatibility. Use the Spinner control instead.

@ ... GET – Text Boxes Command

Included for backward compatibility. Use the TextBox control instead.

@ ... GET – Transparent Buttons Command

Included for backward compatibility. Use the CommandButton control instead.

@ ... MENU Command

Included for backward compatibility. Use the Menu Designer and CREATE MENU instead.

@ ... PROMPT Command

Included for backward compatibility. Use the Menu Designer and CREATE MENU instead.

@ ... SAY Command

Included for backward compatibility. Use the Label control to display text and the TextBox control to display the contents of fields and variables.

@ ... SAY – Pictures & OLE Objects Command

Included for backward compatibility. Use the Image, OLE Bound, and OLE Container controls instead.

@ ... SCROLL Command

Moves an area of the main Microsoft Visual FoxPro window or a user-defined window up, down, left, or right.

Syntax

@ *nRow1, nColumn1* TO *nRow2, nColumn2* SCROLL
   [UP | DOWN | LEFT | RIGHT]
   [BY *nMoveAmount*]

Arguments

@ *nRow1, nColumn1* TO *nRow2, nColumn2* SCROLL
   Moves a rectangular area whose upper-left corner is at *nRow1, nColumn1* and lower-right corner is at *nRow2, nColumn2*.

UP | DOWN | LEFT | RIGHT
   Specifies the direction in which rectangular area is moved. If you omit a direction clause, the area is moved upward.

BY *nMoveAmount*
   Specifies the number of rows or columns the rectangular area is moved. If you omit BY *nMoveAmount*, the region is moved by one row or column.

See Also

SCROLL

@ ... TO Command

Included for backward compatibility. Use the Shape control instead.

ABS( ) Function

Returns the absolute value of the specified numeric expression.

Syntax

ABS(*nExpression*)

Returns

Numeric

Arguments

nExpression

Specifies the numeric expression whose absolute value ABS( ) returns.

Example

```
? ABS(-45)        && Displays 45
? ABS(10-30)      && Displays 20
? ABS(30-10)      && Displays 20
STORE 40 TO gnNumber1
STORE 2 TO gnNumber2
? ABS(gnNumber2-gnNumber1)      && Displays 38
```

See Also

INT( ), ROUND( ), SIGN( )

ACCEPT Command

Included for backward compatibility. Use the TextBox control instead.

ACLASS( ) Function

Places an object's class name and its ancestor class names into a variable array.

Syntax

ACLASS(*ArrayName*, *oExpression*)

Returns

Numeric

Arguments

ArrayName

Specifies the name of the array into which the class names are placed. If you specify the name of an array that doesn't exist, Microsoft Visual FoxPro automatically creates the array. If you specify the name of an existing array that isn't large enough to hold all the parent names, Visual FoxPro automatically increases the size of the array. If the array is larger than necessary, the array size is truncated. If you specify the name of an existing two-dimensional array, the array is redimensioned to a one-dimensional array.

oExpression

Specifies an object whose class name and ancestor class names are placed into the array. *oExpression* can be any object expression, such as an object reference, an object variable, or an object array element.

Remarks

ACLASS( ) creates a one-dimensional array containing the class name of the specified object and its ancestor class names. The first array element contains the class name of the object, the second element contains the name of the object's parent class, the third element contains the name of the object's grandparent class, and so on.

ACLASS( ) returns the number of class names in the array. ACLASS( ) returns 0 if the array cannot be created.

Example

The following example creates two custom classes named FormChild and FormGrandChild from the Visual FoxPro Form base class. ACLASS( ) is used to create an array named gaNewarray containing the class names, which are then displayed.

```
CLEAR
frmMyForm = CREATEOBJECT("FormGrandChild")
FOR nCount = 1 TO ACLASS(gaNewarray, frmMyForm)      && Creates an array
    ? gaNewarray(nCount)  && Displays the names of the classes
ENDFOR
RELEASE frmMyForm

DEFINE CLASS FormChild AS FORM
ENDDEFINE

DEFINE CLASS FormGrandChild AS FormChild
ENDDEFINE
```

See Also

ADD CLASS, AMEMBERS( ), CREATE CLASS, CREATE CLASSLIB, CREATEOBJECT( ), DEFINE CLASS

ACOPY( ) Function

Copies elements from one array to another array.

Syntax

ACOPY(*SourceArrayName, DestinationArrayName*
[, *nFirstSourceElement* [, *nNumberElements* [, *nFirstDestElement*]]])

Returns

Numeric

Arguments

SourceArrayName, DestinationArrayName

Specifies the source array *SourceArrayName* from which elements are copied one-to-one to the destination array *DestinationArrayName*. The elements in the source array replace the elements in the destination array.

The arrays can be one- or two-dimensional. If the destination array doesn't exist, Visual FoxPro automatically creates it. In such a case, the size of the destination array will be the same as that of the source array.

> **Note** You can refer to an element in a two-dimensional variable array in two ways: The first uses two subscripts to specify the row and column position of the element in the array; the other uses a single-element number. This function and others that manipulate two-dimensional arrays require single-element numbers (here, *nFirstSourceElement* and *nFirstDestElement*). Use AELEMENT( ) to return the proper element number for a two-dimensional array from its row and column subscripts.

nFirstSourceElement

Specifies the first element number in the source array to be copied; inclusive (element number *nFirstSourceElement* is included in the copying). If *nFirstSourceElement* isn't included, copying begins with the first element in the source array.

nNumberElements

Specifies the number of elements copied from the source array. If *nNumberElements* is –1, all elements of the source array beginning with element *nFirstSourceElement* are copied.

nFirstDestElement

Specifies the first element in the destination array to be replaced.

Remarks

ACOPY( ) returns the number of elements copied to the destination array.

Example

The following example creates an array from selected records in the `customer` table and then uses ACOPY( ) to create a new array.

```
CLOSE DATABASES
OPEN DATABASE (HOME(2) + 'data\testdata')
USE customer        && Open customer table

SELECT DISTINCT company ;
   FROM customer ;
   ORDER BY company ;
   WHERE country = 'Germany';
   INTO ARRAY gaCompanies
= ACOPY(gaCompanies, gaCompaniesTemp)   && Make a copy of the array
CLEAR
DISPLAY MEMORY LIKE gaCompaniesTemp
```

See Also

ADEL( ), AELEMENT( ), AINS( ), ASCAN( ), ASORT( ), DIMENSION

ACOS( ) Function

Returns the arc cosine of a specified numeric expression.

Syntax

ACOS(*nExpression*)

Returns

Numeric

Arguments

nExpression

Specifies a numeric expression whose arc cosine ACOS( ) returns. The value of *nExpression* can range from –1 through +1. The value returned by ACOS( ) ranges from 0 through pi (3.141592). The number of decimal places ACOS( ) returns is determined by SET DECIMALS.

Use RTOD( ) to convert radians to degrees.

Remarks

The arc cosine is returned in radians.

Example

```
CLEAR
? RTOD(ACOS(0))  && Displays 90.00
STORE -1 to gnArcAngle
? RTOD(ACOS(gnArcAngle))  && Displays 180.00
? RTOD(ACOS(SQRT(2)/2))  && Displays 45.00
```

See Also

ASIN( ), ATAN( ), ATN2( ), COS( ), DTOR( ), RTOD( ), SET DECIMALS, SIN( ), TAN( )

Activate Event

Occurs when a Form, FormSet, or Page object becomes active or when a Toolbar object is shown.

Syntax

PROCEDURE *Object*.Activate

Remarks

Triggers for this event depend on the type of object:

- A FormSet object is activated when a form in the form set receives the focus or when the Show method for the form set is called.

- A Form object is activated by a user action, such as clicking a form or a control or when the Show method for the Form object is called.

- A Page object is activated by user action, such as clicking the tab of the page or clicking a control contained in the page, or if the ActivePage property of the page frame containing it is set to the page's number.

- A ToolBar object is activated when the Show method for the ToolBar is called.

If you use the Show method for a form set, all forms with their Visible property set to true (.T.) are shown. The Activate event is triggered first for the form set, then for the form, and then for the page.

Applies To

Form, FormSet, Page, ToolBar

See Also

ActivePage Property, Deactivate Event, GotFocus Event, LostFocus Event, SetFocus Method, Show Method, Visible Property

ACTIVATE MENU Command

Displays and activates a menu bar.

Syntax

ACTIVATE MENU *MenuBarName*
   [NOWAIT]
   [PAD *MenuTitleName*]

Arguments

MenuBarName
   Specifies the name of the menu bar to activate.

NOWAIT
   Specifies that at run time the program should not wait for the user to choose a menu
   from the active menu bar or to press ESC. Instead, the program continues to execute. A
   menu activated with the NOWAIT option does not return program execution to the line
   following the ACTIVATE MENU command when DEACTIVATE MENU is issued.

PAD *MenuTitleName*
   Specifies the menu title name that is automatically selected when the menu bar is
   activated. If you don't specify a menu title name, the first menu title name in the
   activated menu bar is activated by default.

Remarks

Displays and activates the menu bar specified with *MenuBarName*. This command works
in conjunction with DEFINE MENU and DEFINE PAD.

   Tip When you include the Visual FoxPro system menu bar (_MSYSMENU) in
   an application, there is no need to activate the menu. Instead, issue SET SYSMENU
   AUTOMATIC.

Example

The following example uses ACTIVATE MENU to display and activate a user-defined
menu system. The current system menu bar is first saved to memory with SET SYSMENU
SAVE, and then all system menu titles are removed with SET SYSMENU TO.

Two menu titles are created with DEFINE PAD; DEFINE POPUP is used to create a
drop-down menu for each menu title. DEFINE BAR is used to create menu items on each
of the menus. When a menu title is chosen, ON PAD uses ACTIVATE POPUP to activate
the corresponding menu. ACTIVATE MENU displays and activates the menu bar.

When a menu item is chosen from a menu, the CHOICE procedure is executed. CHOICE
displays the name of the chosen item and the name of the menu containing the item.

```
*** Name this program ACTIMENU.PRG ***
CLEAR
SET SYSMENU SAVE
SET SYSMENU TO
ON KEY LABEL ESC KEYBOARD CHR(13)
DEFINE MENU example BAR AT LINE 1
DEFINE PAD convpad OF example PROMPT '\<Conversions' COLOR SCHEME 3 ;
   KEY ALT+C, ''
DEFINE PAD cardpad OF example PROMPT 'Card \<Info' COLOR SCHEME 3 ;
   KEY ALT+I, ''
ON PAD convpad OF example ACTIVATE POPUP conversion
ON PAD cardpad OF example ACTIVATE POPUP cardinfo
DEFINE POPUP conversion MARGIN RELATIVE COLOR SCHEME 4
DEFINE BAR 1 OF conversion PROMPT 'Ar\<ea' ;
   KEY CTRL+E, '^E'
DEFINE BAR 2 OF conversion PROMPT '\<Length' ;
   KEY CTRL+L, '^L'
DEFINE BAR 3 OF conversion PROMPT 'Ma\<ss' ;
   KEY CTRL+S, '^S'
DEFINE BAR 4 OF conversion PROMPT 'Spee\<d' ;
   KEY CTRL+D, '^D'
DEFINE BAR 5 OF conversion PROMPT '\<Temperature' ;
   KEY CTRL+T, '^T'
DEFINE BAR 6 OF conversion PROMPT 'T\<ime' ;
   KEY CTRL+I, '^I'
DEFINE BAR 7 OF conversion PROMPT 'Volu\<me' ;
   KEY CTRL+M, '^M'
ON SELECTION POPUP conversion DO choice IN actimenu;
   WITH PROMPT( ), POPUP( )
DEFINE POPUP cardinfo MARGIN RELATIVE COLOR SCHEME 4
DEFINE BAR 1 OF cardinfo PROMPT '\<View Charges' ;
   KEY ALT+V, ''
DEFINE BAR 2 OF cardinfo PROMPT 'View \<Payments' ;
   KEY ALT+P, ''
DEFINE BAR 3 OF cardinfo PROMPT 'Vie\<w Users' ;
   KEY ALT+W, ''
DEFINE BAR 4 OF cardinfo PROMPT '\-'
DEFINE BAR 5 OF cardinfo PROMPT '\<Charges ' ;
   KEY ALT+C, ''
ON SELECTION POPUP cardinfo;
   DO choice IN actimenu WITH PROMPT( ), POPUP( )

ACTIVATE MENU example
DEACTIVATE MENU example
RELEASE MENU example EXTENDED
SET SYSMENU TO DEFAULT
ON KEY LABEL ESC
PROCEDURE choice
PARAMETERS mprompt, mpopup
WAIT WINDOW 'You chose ' + mprompt + ' from popup ' + mpopup NOWAIT
```

See Also

CLEAR MENUS, CREATE MENU, DEACTIVATE MENU, DEFINE MENU, DEFINE PAD, HIDE MENU, SET SYSMENU, SHOW MENU

ACTIVATE POPUP Command

Displays and activates a menu.

Syntax

ACTIVATE POPUP *MenuName*
    [AT *nRow*, *nColumn*]
    [BAR *nMenuItemNumber*]
    [NOWAIT]
    [REST]

Arguments

MenuName
    Specifies the name of the menu to activate.

AT *nRow*, *nColumn*
    Specifies the position of the menu on the screen or in a user-defined window. The row and column coordinate applies to the upper-left corner of the menu. The position you specify with this argument takes precedence over a position you specify with the FROM argument in DEFINE POPUP.

BAR *nMenuItemNumber*
    Specifies the item in the menu that is selected when the menu is activated. For example, if *nMenuItemNumber* is 2, the second item is selected. The first item is selected if you omit BAR *nMenuItemNumber* or if *nMenuItemNumber* is greater than the number of items in the menu.

NOWAIT
    Specifies that, at run time, a program does not wait for the user to choose an item from the menu before continuing program execution. Instead, the program continues to execute.

REST
    A menu created with the PROMPT FIELD clause of DEFINE POPUP places records from a field into the menu. When the menu is activated, the first item in the menu is initially selected, even if the record pointer in the table containing the field is positioned on a record other than the first record.

    Include REST to specify that the item selected when the menu is activated corresponds to the current record pointer position in the table.

Remarks

ACTIVATE POPUP works in conjunction with DEFINE POPUP, used to create the menu, and DEFINE BAR, used to create the items on the menu.

Example

This example uses ACTIVATE POPUP with ON PAD to activate a menu when a menu title is chosen. The current system menu bar is first saved to memory with SET SYSMENU SAVE, and then all system menu titles are removed with SET SYSMENU TO.

Two new system menu titles are created with DEFINE PAD; DEFINE POPUP is used to create a menu for each menu title. DEFINE BAR is used to create menu items on each of the menus. When a menu title is chosen, ON PAD uses ACTIVATE POPUP to activate the corresponding menu.

When an item is chosen from a menu, the CHOICE procedure is executed. CHOICE displays the name of the chosen item and the name of the menu containing the item. If the Exit item is chosen from the Card Info menu, the original Visual FoxPro system menu is restored.

```
*** Name this program ACTIPOP.PRG ***
CLEAR
SET SYSMENU SAVE
SET SYSMENU TO
DEFINE PAD convpad OF _MSYSMENU PROMPT '\<Conversions' COLOR SCHEME 3 ;
   KEY ALT+C, ''
DEFINE PAD cardpad OF _MSYSMENU PROMPT 'Card \<Info' COLOR SCHEME 3 ;
   KEY ALT+I, ''
ON PAD convpad OF _MSYSMENU ACTIVATE POPUP conversion
ON PAD cardpad OF _MSYSMENU ACTIVATE POPUP cardinfo
DEFINE POPUP conversion MARGIN RELATIVE COLOR SCHEME 4
DEFINE BAR 1 OF conversion PROMPT 'Ar\<ea' KEY CTRL+E, '^E'
DEFINE BAR 2 OF conversion PROMPT '\<Length' ;
   KEY CTRL+L, '^L'
DEFINE BAR 3 OF conversion PROMPT 'Ma\<ss' ;
   KEY CTRL+S, '^S'
DEFINE BAR 4 OF conversion PROMPT 'Spee\<d' ;
   KEY CTRL+D, '^D'
DEFINE BAR 5 OF conversion PROMPT '\<Temperature' ;
   KEY CTRL+T, '^T'
DEFINE BAR 6 OF conversion PROMPT 'T\<ime' ;
   KEY CTRL+I, '^I'
DEFINE BAR 7 OF conversion PROMPT 'Volu\<me' ;
   KEY CTRL+M, '^M'
ON SELECTION POPUP conversion;
   DO choice IN actipop WITH PROMPT(), POPUP()
DEFINE POPUP cardinfo MARGIN RELATIVE COLOR SCHEME 4
```

```
DEFINE BAR 1 OF cardinfo PROMPT '\<View Charges' ;
    KEY ALT+V, ''
DEFINE BAR 2 OF cardinfo PROMPT 'View \<Payments' ;
    KEY ALT+P, ''
DEFINE BAR 3 OF cardinfo PROMPT 'Vie\<w Users' ;
    KEY ALT+W, ''
DEFINE BAR 4 OF cardinfo PROMPT '\-'
DEFINE BAR 5 OF cardinfo PROMPT '\<Charges' ;
    KEY ALT+C, ''
DEFINE BAR 6 OF cardinfo PROMPT '\-'
DEFINE BAR 7 OF cardinfo PROMPT 'E\<xit';
    KEY ALT+X, ''
ON SELECTION POPUP cardinfo;
DO choice IN actipop WITH PROMPT(),POPUP()

PROCEDURE choice
PARAMETERS mprompt, mpopup
WAIT WINDOW 'You chose ' + mprompt + ;
    ' from popup ' + mpopup NOWAIT
IF mprompt = 'Exit'
    SET SYSMENU TO DEFAULT
ENDIF
```

See Also

CLEAR POPUPS, CREATE MENU, DEACTIVATE POPUP, DEFINE BAR, DEFINE
POPUP, HIDE POPUP, MOVE POPUP, ON SELECTION POPUP, POP POPUP,
POPUP( ), PROMPT( ), PUSH POPUP, SHOW POPUP

ACTIVATE SCREEN Command

Sends all subsequent output to the main Visual FoxPro window instead of to the active
user-defined window.

Syntax

ACTIVATE SCREEN

Remarks

Use ACTIVATE WINDOW to direct output to a user-defined window.

See Also

ACTIVATE WINDOW, DEACTIVATE WINDOW, DEFINE WINDOW,
HIDE WINDOW, SHOW WINDOW

ACTIVATE WINDOW Command

Displays and activates one or more user-defined windows or Visual FoxPro system windows.

Syntax

ACTIVATE WINDOW *WindowName1* [, *WindowName2* ...]
    | ALL
    [IN [WINDOW] *WindowName3* | IN SCREEN
    [BOTTOM | TOP | SAME]
    [NOSHOW]

Arguments

WindowName1 [, *WindowName2* ...]
> Specifies the name of each window to activate. Separate the window names with commas. In Visual FoxPro, you can specify the name of a toolbar to activate. See SHOW WINDOW for a list of Visual FoxPro toolbar names.

ALL
> Specifies that all windows are activated. The last window activated is the active output window.

IN [WINDOW] *WindowName3*
> Specifies the name of the parent window within which the window is placed and activated. The activated window becomes a child window. A parent window can have multiple child windows. A child window activated inside a parent window cannot be moved outside the parent window. If the parent window is moved, the child window moves with it.
>
> > **Note** The parent window must be visible for any of its child windows to be visible.

IN SCREEN
> Places and activates a window in the main Visual FoxPro window. A window can be placed in a parent window by including IN WINDOW in DEFINE WINDOW when the window is created. Including the IN SCREEN clause in ACTIVATE WINDOW overrides the IN WINDOW clause in DEFINE WINDOW.

BOTTOM | TOP | SAME
> Specifies where windows are activated with respect to other previously activated windows. By default, a window becomes the window on top when it is activated. Including BOTTOM places a window behind all other windows. TOP places it in front of all other windows. SAME activates a window without affecting its front-to-back placement.

NOSHOW
> Activates and directs output to a window without displaying the window.

Remarks

User-defined windows are created with DEFINE WINDOW.

Activating a window makes it the window on top and directs all output to that window. Output can be directed to only one window at a time. A window remains the active output window until it is deactivated or released, or until another window or the main Visual FoxPro window is activated.

The names of user-defined windows appear in the bottom section of the Window menu. The name of the active user-defined window is marked with a check mark.

More than one window can be placed in the main Visual FoxPro window at one time, but output is directed only to the last window activated. When more than one window is open, deactivating the active output window removes it from the main Visual FoxPro window and sends subsequent output to another window. If there is no active output window, output is directed to the main Visual FoxPro window.

> **Note** To ensure output is directed to a specific window when you deactivate the active output window, you must explicitly activate the window you want to send output to with ACTIVATE WINDOW.

All activated windows are displayed until DEACTIVATE WINDOW or HIDE WINDOW is issued to remove them from view. Issuing either command removes windows from view but not from memory. Windows can be redisplayed by issuing ACTIVATE WINDOW or SHOW WINDOW.

To remove windows from view and from memory, use CLEAR WINDOWS, RELEASE WINDOWS, or CLEAR ALL. Windows that are removed from memory must be redefined to place them back in the main Visual FoxPro window.

You can use ACTIVATE WINDOW to place Visual FoxPro system windows in the main Visual FoxPro window or in a parent window.

The following system windows can be opened with ACTIVATE WINDOW:

- Command
- Call Stack
- Data Session
- Debug
- Debug Output
- Locals
- Trace
- Watch

To activate a system window and or a toolbar, enclose the entire system window or toolbar name in quotation marks. For example, to activate the Call Stack debugging window in Visual FoxPro, issue the following command:

```
ACTIVATE WINDOW "Call Stack"
```

Use HIDE WINDOW or RELEASE WINDOW to remove a system window from the main Visual FoxPro window or a parent window.

Example

The following example defines a window named output and activates it, placing it in the main Visual FoxPro window. The WAIT command pauses execution, the window is hidden, and then redisplayed.

```
CLEAR
DEFINE WINDOW output FROM 2,1 TO 13,75 TITLE 'Output' ;
   CLOSE FLOAT GROW ZOOM
ACTIVATE WINDOW output
WAIT WINDOW 'Press any key to hide window output'
HIDE WINDOW output
WAIT WINDOW 'Press any key to show window output'
SHOW WINDOW output
WAIT WINDOW 'Press any key to release window output'
RELEASE WINDOW output
```

See Also

CLEAR WINDOWS, DEACTIVATE WINDOW, DEFINE WINDOW, HIDE WINDOW, RELEASE WINDOWS, SHOW WINDOW

ActivateCell Method

Activates a cell in a Grid control.

Syntax

Grid.ActivateCell(*nRow, nCol*)

Arguments

nRow, nCol
   Specifies the row and the column that contain the active cell.

Applies To

Grid

See Also

ActiveColumn Property, ActiveRow Property, GridHitTest Method

ActiveColumn Property

Returns as an integer the column number that contains the active cell in a Grid control. Not available at design time; read-only at run time.

Syntax

Grid.ActiveColumn

Remarks

ActiveColumn returns zero if the grid doesn't have the focus.

Applies To

Grid

See Also

ActivateCell Method, ActiveRow Property, GridHitTest Method

ActiveControl Property

References the active control on an object. Not available at design time; read-only at run time.

Syntax

Object.ActiveControl.*Property*[= *Value*]

Arguments

Property
The property to return or set.

Value
The current or new property value.

Remarks

This property is not available if all controls on the specified object are invisible or disabled.

If the object is active, the ActiveControl property references the control that has the focus. If the object is not active, an error occurs.

Applies To

Container, Form, Page, _SCREEN, ToolBar

See Also

ActiveForm Property

ActiveDoc Object

Creates an Active Document that can be hosted in an Active Document container such as Microsoft Internet Explorer.

Syntax

ActiveDoc

Remarks

The ActiveDoc object allows programmatic access to events that occur when an Active Document is hosted, and provides access to the properties for the Active Document. It can also be used as the base class for an application from which a stand-alone .APP or .EXE is created.

For additional information about creating Active Documents, see "Active Documents" in Chapter 31, "Interoperability and the Internet," in the *Microsoft Visual FoxPro 6.0 Programmer's Guide*.

Properties

Application	BaseClass	Caption
ContainerReleaseType	Class	ClassLibrary
Comment	Name	Parent
ParentClass	Tag	

Events

CommandTargetExec	CommandTargetQuery	ContainerRelease
Destroy	Error	HideDoc
Init	Run	ShowDoc

Methods

AddProperty	ReadExpression	ReadMethod
ResetToDefault	SaveAsClass	WriteExpression

See Also

COMCLASSINFO( ), GETHOST( ), ISHOSTED( )

ActiveForm Property

References the active Form object in a form set or the _SCREEN object. Not available at design time; read-only at run time.

Syntax

Object.ActiveForm.*Property* [= *Setting*]

– or –

Object.ActiveForm.*Method*

Arguments

Property
> Specifies any property of the active form contained in the form set; for example, the Caption property.

Setting
> The existing or new setting of the *Property*.

Method
> Specifies any method of the active form contained in the form set; for example, the Move method.

Remarks

If the containing FormSet object is active, ActiveForm references the Form object that has the focus. If the containing FormSet object is not active, an error occurs.

Use the ActiveForm property to access the active Form object's properties and methods.

Applies To

Form, FormSet, _SCREEN

See Also

Activate Event, Deactivate Event

ActivePage Property

Returns the number of the active Page in a PageFrame object. Available at design time; read/write at run time.

Syntax

PageFrame.ActivePage

Applies To

PageFrame

See Also

Activate Event, GotFocus Event

ActiveProject Property

Contains an object reference to the Project object for the currently active Project Manager window. Read-only at design time and run time.

Syntax

Object.ActiveProject

Remarks

The ActiveProject property contains an object reference to the Project object for the foremost Project Manager window when more than one Project Manager window is open. An error is generated if you attempt to access the ActiveProject property when a Project Manager window isn't open.

For more information about projects, see "Project Manager Hooks" in Chapter 32, "Application Development and Developer Productivity," of the *Microsoft Visual FoxPro 6.0 Programmer's Guide*.

Applies To

Application Object, _VFP

See Also

File Object, Files Collection, Project Object, ProjectHook Object, Projects Collection, Server Object, Servers Collection

ActiveRow Property

Specifies the row that contains the active cell in a Grid control. Not available at design time; read-only at run time.

Syntax

Grid.ActiveRow

Remarks

The ActiveRow property does not return the same value as RECNO( ) in an indexed table. ActiveRow returns zero if the grid doesn't have the focus.

Applies To

Grid

See Also

ActivateCell Method, ActiveColumn Property, GridHitTest Method, RECNO( )

ADATABASES( ) Function

Places the names of all open databases and their paths into a variable array.

Syntax

ADATABASES(*ArrayName*)

Returns

Numeric

Arguments

ArrayName
> Specifies the name of the array. If the array you specify doesn't exist, Visual FoxPro automatically creates the array. If the array exists and isn't large enough to contain all the database information, Visual FoxPro automatically increases the size of the array to accommodate the information. If the array is larger than necessary, Visual FoxPro truncates the array. If the array exists and ADATABASES( ) returns 0 because no databases are open, an existing array remains unchanged. If the array doesn't exist, and ADATABASES( ) returns 0, the array is not created.

Remarks

The names of all open databases in the current data session are placed into a variable array.

ADATABASES( ) creates a two-dimensional array. The first column of the array contains the names of the open databases, and the second column contains the paths to the databases.

ADATABASES( ) returns the number of database names (rows) in the array. If no databases are open, ADATABASES( ) returns 0 and the array isn't created.

Example

The following example opens the `testdata` database, and then uses ADATABASES( ) to create an array named `gaDatabase` containing the names of all open databases.

```
SET PATH TO (HOME(2) + 'data\')     && Sets path to database
OPEN DATABASE testdata && Opens the database
CLEAR
? ADATABASES(gaDatabase)     && Creates an array of open databases
DISPLAY MEMORY LIKE gadatabase  && Displays the contents of the array
CLOSE DATABASES
```

See Also

CREATE DATABASE, DISPLAY DATABASE, LIST DATABASE, MODIFY DATABASE, OPEN DATABASE

ADBOBJECTS( ) Function

Places the names of named connections, relations, tables, or SQL views in the current database into a variable array.

Syntax

ADBOBJECTS(*ArrayName*, *cSetting*)

Returns

Numeric

Arguments

ArrayName

Specifies the name of the array in which the names are placed. If the array you specify doesn't exist, Visual FoxPro automatically creates the array. If the array exists and isn't large enough to contain all the names, Visual FoxPro automatically increases the size of the array to accommodate the names. If the array is larger than necessary, Visual FoxPro truncates the array. If the array exists and ADBOBJECTS( ) returns 0 because no names are found, the array remains unchanged. If the array doesn't exist, and ADBOBJECTS( ) returns 0, the array is not created.

A one-dimensional array is created when you specify CONNECTION, TABLE, or VIEW for *cSetting*. Each row in the one-dimensional array contains the name of a connection, table, or view in the database.

A two-dimensional array is created when you specify RELATION for *cSetting*. Each row in the two-dimensional array corresponds to a relationship in the database. The first column in an array row contains the name of the child table and the second column in an array row contains the name of the parent table. The third column contains the name of the index tag for the child table and the fourth column contains the name of the index tag for the parent table.

The fifth column in an array row contains referential integrity information. This column is empty if the relation has no referential integrity rules. If the relationship does have referential integrity rules, the column contains characters corresponding to the type of referential integrity rules for updates, deletions, and insertions.

The first character indicates the type of update rule, the second character indicates the type of deletion rule, and the third character indicates the type of insertion rule.

Possible values for updates and deletions are "C" for cascade, "R" for restrict, and "I" for ignore. Possible values for insertions are "R" for restrict, and "I" for ignore. For example, if a relation has cascaded updates, restricted deletions, and ignores insertion referential integrity rules, the column contains "CRI."

cSetting

Specifies the names to place in the variable array. The following table lists the values for *cSetting* and the corresponding names placed in the array:

cSetting	Names
CONNECTION	Connection names
RELATION	Table relationships
TABLE	Table names
VIEW	View names

The CONNECTION, RELATION, TABLE, and VIEW settings cannot be abbreviated.

Remarks

A database must be open and current when ADBOBJECTS( ) is issued; otherwise Visual FoxPro generates an error message.

Example

The following example opens the testdata database and uses ADBOBJECTS( ) to create an array named gaTables containing names of tables in the database. The tables names are then displayed.

```
* Close any open databases
CLOSE DATABASES

* Clear desktop to prepare for displaying the array
CLEAR

* Open sample testdata database
OPEN DATABASE (HOME(2) + 'Data\testdata')

* Function call with cSetting for table names
=ADBOBJECTS(gaTables, "TABLE")

* Displays array gaTables created by ADBOBJECTS( ) function
DISPLAY MEMORY LIKE gaTables
```

See Also

ADATABASES( ), CREATE, CREATE CONNECTION, CREATE DATABASE, CREATE SQL VIEW, CREATE TABLE – SQL, DISPLAY DATABASE, INDBC( ), LIST DATABASE, MODIFY DATABASE, SET DATABASE

Add Method

Adds a file to a project.

Syntax

Object.Add(*cFileName*)

Returns

Object

Arguments

cFileName

Specifies the name of the file to add to the project. An error is generated if the file you specify does not exist. The Project Manager window, if open, is refreshed after the file has been added.

Remarks

The Add method is a method for the files collection. When a file is added to a project with the Add method, a File object is created for the file, and the File object is added to the Files collection.

An object reference to the newly added file is returned if the file is successfully added to the project. The null value is returned if the file can't be added to the project.

The QueryAddFile event occurs just before a file is added to a project. If the QueryAddFile event returns true (.T.), the file is added to the project. The file isn't added to the project if the QueryAddFile event returns false (.F.) or includes NODEFAULT.

Applies To

Files Collection

See Also

File Object, QueryAddFile Event

ADD CLASS Command

Adds a class definition to a .vcx visual class library.

Syntax

ADD CLASS *ClassName* [OF *ClassLibraryName1*] TO *ClassLibraryName2*
    [OVERWRITE]

Arguments

ClassName
Specifies the name of the class definition added to the .vcx visual class library *ClassLibraryName2*.

If you omit the optional OF *ClassLibraryName1* clause, Visual FoxPro searches for the class definition in any .vcx visual class libraries opened with SET CLASSLIB.

Visual FoxPro generates an error if the class definition cannot be located or a class definition with the name you specify already exists in *ClassLibraryName2*.

OF *ClassLibraryName1*
Specifies a .vcx visual class library from which the class definition is copied.

TO *ClassLibraryName2*
Specifies the .vcx visual class library to which the class definition is added. If you specify a .vcx visual class library that does not exist, Visual FoxPro creates the visual class library and adds the class definition to the library.

OVERWRITE
Specifies that a class definition with the same name as the class definition you specify with *ClassName* is overwritten. An error message is generated if you omit OVERWRITE and a class definition with the same name as *ClassName* already exists in the .vcx visual class library.

Remarks

Use ADD CLASS to add a class definition to a class library, or to copy a class definition from one .vcx visual class library to another. A class definition cannot be added from a Visual FoxPro program or application (.prg or .app), or a procedure file.

See Also

ACLASS( ), AMEMBERS( ), CREATE CLASS, CREATE CLASSLIB, DEFINE CLASS, MODIFY CLASS, RELEASE CLASSLIB, REMOVE CLASS, RENAME CLASS, SET CLASSLIB

ADD TABLE Command

Adds a free table to the current database.

Syntax

ADD TABLE *TableName* | ?
    [NAME *LongTableName*]

Arguments

TableName
Specifies the name of the table added to the database.

?
>Displays the Open dialog box from which you can choose a table to add to the database.

NAME *LongTableName*
>Specifies a long name for the table. Long names can contain up to 128 characters and can be used in place of short file names that have a .dbf extension.

Remarks

After the table is added to the database, you can perform the same operations on it as you can on any other table.

Once the table is added to the database, it is no longer free. However, any table in the database can be made free by issuing REMOVE TABLE.

The table you are adding:

- Must be a valid .dbf file.

- Cannot have the same name as an existing table in the open database, unless you assign the table a unique long name.

- Cannot exist in another database. Use REMOVE TABLE to remove the table from another database.

The database to which you are adding a table cannot be involved in a transaction.

Example

The following example creates two databases named mydbc1 and mydbc2, and a table named table1. The table is added to mydbc1 when it is created. The table is then closed and removed from mydbc1. ADD TABLE is then used to add the table to mydbc2. RENAME TABLE is used to change the name of the table from table1 to table2.

```
CREATE DATABASE mydbc1
CREATE DATABASE mydbc2
SET DATABASE TO mydbc1
CREATE TABLE table1 (cField1 C(10), n N(10))  && Adds table to mydbc1
CLOSE TABLES     && A table must be closed to remove it from a database
REMOVE TABLE table1
SET DATABASE TO mydbc2
ADD TABLE table1
RENAME TABLE table1 TO table2
```

See Also

CLOSE DATABASES, CREATE DATABASE, DISPLAY TABLES, FREE TABLE, OPEN DATABASE, REMOVE TABLE

ADDBS( ) Function

Adds a backslash (if needed) to a path expression.

Syntax

ADDBS(*cPath*)

Returns

Character

Arguments

cPath Specifies the path name to which to add the backslash.

See Also

DEFAULTEXT( ), FILE( ), FORCEEXT( ), FORCEPATH( ), JUSTDRIVE( ), JUSTEXT( ), JUSTFNAME( ), JUSTPATH( ), JUSTSTEM( )

AddColumn Method

Adds a Column object to a Grid control.

Syntax

Grid.AddColumn(*nIndex*)

Arguments

nIndex
Specifies a number representing the position in the grid where the new Column is added.

Remarks

When AddColum( ) is called, existing columns are moved to the right, and their ColumnOrder properties are incremented accordingly. The grid's ColumnCount property is also increased.

The grid's Controls property array is enlarged by one element, and a reference to the new column is placed in the new element. The new column is assigned a unique name.

For example, to add a new column, then assign a new name to that column, you could do the following.

```
THISFORM.Grid1.AddColumn(1)    && Insert column at left.
THISFORM.Grid1.Columns(THISFORM.Grid1.ColumnCount).Name = "NewColumn"
THISFORM.Grid1.NewColumn.ControlSource = "Customer.CustID"
```

Applies To

Grid

See Also

AddObject Method, ColumnCount Property, DeleteColumn Method

AddItem Method

Adds a new item to a ComboBox or ListBox control, optionally allowing you to specify the item's index.

Syntax

*Control.*AddItem(*cItem* [, *nIndex*] [, *nColumn*])

Arguments

cItem

Specifies the string expression to add to the control.

nIndex

Specifies the position where the item is placed in the control. If you supply a valid value for the optional *nIndex*, *cItem* is placed at that position within the control. If you specify an *nIndex* that already exists, the item is inserted at that position and all items below that item are moved down one position in the list portion of the ComboBox or ListBox control.

If you omit *nIndex* and the Sorted property is set to true (.T.), *cItem* is added in alphabetic sort order. If you omit *nIndex* and the Sorted property is set to false (.F.), *cItem* is added to the end of the list portion of the ComboBox or ListBox control.

nColumn

Specifies the column of the control to which the new item is added. The default is 1.

Remarks

Use the AddItem method or AddListItem method when the RowSourceType property is set to 0 (None).

Each item added to a ComboBox or ListBox has two identification numbers assigned to it:

- *nItemID*, an integer corresponding to the unique ID of the item in the control: the first item corresponds to *nItemID* = 1, unless another *nItemID* is specified.

- *nIndex*, an integer corresponding to the order in which items are displayed by the control: the first item in the control corresponds to *nIndex* = 1.

Applies To

ComboBox, ListBox

See Also

AddListItem Method, Clear Method, ListIndex Property, ListItemID Property, RowSourceType Property, RemoveItem Method, Sorted Property

AddListItem Method

Adds a new item to a ComboBox or ListBox control, optionally allowing you to specify the item's item ID.

Syntax

*Control.*AddListItem(*cItem* [, *nItemID*] [, *nColumn*])

Arguments

cItem
>Specifies the item to add to the control.

nItemID
>Specifies an integer representing the unique ID of the item in the control. The maximum value you can specify for *nItemID* is 32,767.

>If you omit *nItemID* and the Sorted property is set to true (.T.), *cItem* is added in alphabetic sort order. If you omit *nItemID* and the Sorted property is set to false (.F.), *cItem* is added to the end of the list of the ComboBox or ListBox.

nColumn
>Specifies the column of the control to add the new item to. The default is 1.

Remarks

Use the AddItem method or AddListItem method when the RowSourceType property is set to 0 (None).

Each item added to a ComboBox or ListBox has two identification numbers assigned to it:

- *nItemID*, an integer corresponding to the unique ID of the item in the control: the first item corresponds to *nItemID* = 1, unless another *nItemID* is specified.

- *nIndex*, an integer corresponding to the order in which items are displayed by the control: the first item in the control corresponds to *nIndex* = 1.

Applies To

ComboBox, ListBox

See Also

AddItem Method, Clear Method, ListIndex Property, ListItemID Property, RowSourceType Property, RemoveItem Method, Sorted Property

AddObject Method

Adds an object to a Container object at run time.

Syntax

Object.AddObject(*cName*, *cClass* [, *cOLEClass*] [, *aInit1*, *aInit2* ...])

Arguments

cName
Specifies the name used to reference the new object.

cClass
Specifies the class of the object to add.

cOLEClass
Specifies the OLE class of the object to add.

aInit1, *aInit2*
Specifies parameters passed to the Init event of the new object.

Remarks

Calling the AddObject method triggers the Init event of the object being added. When a form is added to a form set, the Load event occurs before the Init event.

Note When you use AddObject to add an object to a container, the object's Visible property is set to false (.F.) so you can set the properties of the object without any awkward visual effects as the object's appearance changes.

Example

The following example demonstrates how the AddObject method can be used to add objects or controls to a form. AddObject is used to add a Line control and three command buttons to the form.

The Visible property is set to true (.T.) for the Line control and the command buttons. By default, objects and controls are not visible when they are added to a form.

```
frmMyForm = CREATEOBJECT('Form')  && Create a Form
frmMyForm.Closable = .F.  && Disable the Control menu box

frmMyForm.AddObject('shpLine','Line')  && Add a Line control to the form
frmMyForm.AddObject('cmdCmndBtn1','cmdMyCmndBtn1')  && Up Cmnd button
frmMyForm.AddObject('cmdCmndBtn2','cmdMyCmndBtn2')  && Down Cmnd button
frmMyForm.AddObject('cmdCmndBtn3','cmdMyCmndBtn3')  && Quit Cmnd button

frmMyForm.shpLine.Visible = .T.  && Make Line control visible
frmMyForm.shpLine.Top = 20  && Specify Line control row
frmMyForm.shpLine.Left = 125  && Specify Line control column
```

```
frmMyForm.cmdCmndBtn1.Visible =.T.  && Up Command button visible
frmMyForm.cmdCmndBtn2.Visible =.T.  && Down" Command button visible
frmMyForm.cmdCmndBtn3.Visible =.T.  && Quit Command button visible

frmMyForm.SHOW  && Display the form
READ EVENTS  && Start event processing

DEFINE CLASS cmdMyCmndBtn1 AS COMMANDBUTTON  && Create Command button
   Caption = 'Slant \<Up'  && Caption on the Command button
   Left = 50  && Command button column
   Top = 100  && Command button row
   Height = 25  && Command button height

   PROCEDURE Click
      ThisForm.shpLine.Visible = .F.  && Hide the Line control
      ThisForm.shpLine.LineSlant ='/'  && Slant up
      ThisForm.shpLine.Visible = .T.  && Show the Line control
ENDDEFINE

DEFINE CLASS cmdMyCmndBtn2 AS CommandButton  && Create Command button
   Caption = 'Slant \<Down'  && Caption on the Command button
   Left = 200  && Command button column
   Top = 100  && Command button row
   Height = 25  && Command button height

   PROCEDURE Click
      ThisForm.shpLine.Visible = .F.  && Hide the Line control
      ThisForm.shpLine.LineSlant ='\'  && Slant down
      ThisForm.shpLine.Visible = .T.  && Show the Line control
ENDDEFINE

DEFINE CLASS cmdMyCmndBtn3 AS CommandButton  && Create Command button
   Caption = '\<Quit'  && Caption on the Command button
   Cancel = .T.  && Default Cancel Command button (Esc)
   Left = 125  && Command button column
   Top = 150  && Command button row
   Height = 25  && Command button height

   PROCEDURE Click
      CLEAR EVENTS  && Stop event processing, close Form
ENDDEFINE
```

Applies To

Column, CommandGroup, Container Object, Custom, DataEnvironment, Form, FormSet, Grid, OptionGroup, Page, PageFrame, _SCREEN, ToolBar

See Also

Init Event, Load Event, RemoveObject Method, Visible Property

AddProperty Method

Adds a new property to an object.

Syntax

*Object.*AddProperty(*cPropertyName* [, *eNewValue*])

Returns

Logical

Arguments

cPropertyName
Specifies the name of the new property to add to the object.

eNewValue
Specifies the value to which the new property is set. If *eNewValue* is omitted, the value of the new property is unchanged if the property already exists or is set to false (.F.) for a new property.

Remarks

The AddProperty( ) method allows you to add a property to an object at runtime. The new property is added as a PUBLIC property.

You can also create property arrays for an object. Every element in the property array is initialized to *eNewValue* if it is included, otherwise every property array element contains false (.F.). The following code demonstrates how you can create a property array for an object:

```
oMyForm = CREATEOBJECT('Form')
oMyForm.AddProperty('MyArray(2)', 1)  && Add an array as a property
oMyForm.MyArray(2) = 'Two'
CLEAR
? oMyForm.MyArray(1)  && Displays 1
? oMyForm.MyArray(2)  && Displays 2
```

If a property with the name you specify doesn't exist, the property is created and a logical true (.T.) is returned.

If a property already exists with the name you specify, then AddProperty( ) returns the following:

- True (.T.) if the new property is an array property and the existing property is also an array property. The size of the array is re-dimensioned to that of the new array. If a value is specified with *eNewValue*, all the elements in the array are set to its value. If *eNewValue* is omitted, all the array elements are set to false (.F.).

- True (.T.) if the new property is not an array property and the existing property is an array property. The property remains an array property. If a value is specified with *eNewValue*, all the elements in the array are set to its value. If *eNewValue* is omitted, the array elements remain unchanged.

- True (.T.) if the new property is not an array property and the existing property is not an array property or is not a read-only Visual FoxPro native property. If a value is specified with *eNewValue*, the existing property is set to its value. If *eNewValue* is omitted, the existing property value remains unchanged.

- False (.F.) if the new property is an array property and the existing property is not an array property. The existing property remains unchanged.

- A "Property *<PropertyName>* is read-only" error is generated if the existing property is a read-only Visual FoxPro native property such as the BaseClass property.

- An "Incorrect property name" error is generated if the property name is not valid (the property name contains a space or other illegal characters).

Applies To

ActiveDoc, CheckBox, Column, ComboBox, CommandButton, CommandGroup, Container Object, Control Object, Cursor Object, Custom, DataEnvironment Object, EditBox, Form, FormSet, Grid, Header, Image, Label, Line, ListBox, OLE Bound Control, OLE Container Control, OptionButton, OptionGroup, Page, PageFrame, ProjectHook Object, Relation Object, _SCREEN, Separator Object, Shape, Spinner, TextBox, Timer, ToolBar

See Also

DEFINE CLASS, NewObject Method, SaveAs Method, SaveAsClass Method

AddToSCC Method

Adds a file in a project to source code control.

Syntax

Object.AddToSCC( )

Remarks

True (.T.) is returned if the file is successfully added to source code control. False (.F.) is returned if the file could not be added to source code control or the project is not under source code control.

Applies To

File Object

See Also

CheckIn Method, CheckOut Method, GetLatestVersion Method, RemoveFromSCC Method, UndoCheckOut Method

ADEL( ) Function

Deletes an element from a one-dimensional array, or a row or column from a two-dimensional array.

Syntax

ADEL(*ArrayName*, *nElementNumber* [, 2])

Returns

Numeric

Arguments

ArrayName
  Specifies the array from which the element, row, or column is deleted.

nElementNumber
  Specifies the number of the element, row, or column to delete from the array. You must include the optional 2 argument to delete a column from the array.

  For more information on how to reference elements in an array, see the DIMENSION Command, later in this language reference.

2
  Deletes a column from the array.

Remarks

Deleting an element, row, or column from an array doesn't change the size of the array; instead, the trailing elements, rows, or columns are moved towards the start of the array, and the last element, row, or column in the array is set to false (.F.).

If the element, row, or column is successfully deleted, 1 is returned.

Example

The following example creates and fills an array, then searches for a particular company name, which, if found, is removed from the array.

```
CLOSE DATABASES
OPEN DATABASE (HOME(2) + 'Data\testdata')
USE customer      && Open customer table
SELECT company FROM customer ;
   WHERE country = 'UK' ;
   INTO ARRAY gaCompanies
gnCount = _TALLY
gcName = 'Seven Seas Imports'
```

```
CLEAR
DISPLAY MEMORY LIKE gaCompanies
gnPos = ASCAN(gaCompanies, gcName)    && Search for company
IF gnPos != 0
   * Company found, remove it from the array
   = ADEL(gaCompanies, gnPos)
   gnCount = gnCount - 1
ENDIF
DISPLAY MEMORY LIKE gaCompanies
```

See Also

ACOPY( ), ADIR( ), AELEMENT( ), AFIELDS( ), AINS( ), ALEN( ), ASCAN( ),
ASORT( ), ASUBSCRIPT( ), DIMENSION

ADIR( ) Function

Places information about files into an array and then returns the number of files.

Syntax

ADIR(*ArrayName* [, *cFileSkeleton* [, *cAttribute*]])

Returns

Numeric

Arguments

ArrayName

Specifies the name of the array. If the array you include doesn't exist, Visual FoxPro
automatically creates the array. If the array exists and isn't large enough to contain
all the information, Visual FoxPro automatically increases the size of the array to
accommodate the information. If the array is larger than necessary, Visual FoxPro
truncates the array. If the array exists and ADIR( ) returns 0 because no matching
files are found, the array remains unchanged. If the array doesn't exist and ADIR( )
returns 0, the array isn't created.

The following table describes the contents and data type of each column in the array:

Column	Array contents	Data type
1	File names	Character
2	File sizes	Numeric
3	Dates last modified	Date
4	Times last modified	Character
5	File attributes	Character

The last array column contains the file attributes of the matching files. Each file attribute is expressed by a letter; a file can have more than one attribute. The following table indicates the file attribute represented by each letter:

Letter	Attribute
A	Archive – Read/Write
H	Hidden
R	Read-only
S	System
D	Directory

cFileSkeleton

Specifies a file skeleton so you can store information about files with names or extensions that match a search criterion. For example, the criterion can be all tables, all text files, all files with names that have A as their first letter, and so on. Such general searches are done by including the wildcards * and ? in *cFileSkeleton*. A question mark represents a single character; an asterisk represents any number of characters. You can use any number of wildcards in any position within the file skeleton.

You can specify a drive and/or directory to search in for matching file names. If you don't specify a drive and directory, Visual FoxPro places information about files in the current directory into the array.

cAttribute

Specifies the inclusion of subdirectories and hidden or system files.

cAttribute can contain any combination of D, H, and S. Including D returns subdirectory names of the current directory in addition to file names that match the file skeleton specified in *cFileSkeleton*. Including H returns information about hidden files that match the file skeleton specified in *cFileSkeleton*. Including S returns information about system files that match the file skeleton specified in *cFileSkeleton*.

Include an empty string in *cFileSkeleton* to return just subdirectory names, hidden files or system files.

You can include V in *cAttribute* to return the volume name of the current drive. Only the volume name is returned to the array if V is included with D, H, or S. The volume name is stored in the first array element and the remainder of the array is truncated.

Remarks

For each file, ADIR( ) places into the array the file name, size, date last modified, time last modified, and attributes.

Example

The following example uses ADIR( ) to create an array containing database information. The names of the databases are then displayed.

```
CLOSE DATABASES
SET PATH TO (HOME(2) + 'Data')

gnDbcnumber = ADIR(gaDatabase, '*.DBC')  && Create array

CLEAR
FOR nCount = 1 TO gnDbcnumber  && Loop for number of databases
   ? gaDatabase(nCount,1)  && Display database names
ENDFOR
SET PATH TO HOME( )  && Set path to Visual FoxPro directory
```

See Also

ADEL( ), AELEMENT( ), AFIELDS( ), AINS( ), ALEN( ), ANETRESOURCES( ), ASCAN( ), ASORT( ), ASUBSCRIPT( ), DIMENSION, DIR or DIRECTORY

AELEMENT( ) Function

Returns the number of an array element from the element's subscripts.

Syntax

AELEMENT(*ArrayName*, *nRowSubscript* [, *nColumnSubscript*])

Returns

Numeric

Arguments

ArrayName
Specifies the name of the array whose element number you want to return.

nRowSubscript
Specifies the row subscript. If the array is one-dimensional, AELEMENT( ) identically returns *nRowSubscript*.

If you include just *nRowSubscript*, and it is greater than the number of rows in the array, Visual FoxPro generates an error message.

nColumnSubscript
Specifies the column subscript. If the array is two-dimensional, include both *nRowSubscript* and *nColumnSubscript*.

Remarks

You can refer to an element in a two-dimensional array in one of two ways. The first method uses two subscripts to specify the row and column position of the element in the array, and the second method uses a single-element number. AELEMENT( ) returns the element number when supplied with an element's row and column subscripts.

The Visual FoxPro functions ADEL( ), ADIR( ), AFIELDS( ), AINS( ), ALEN( ), ASCAN( ), ASORT( ), and ASUBSCRIPT( ) can manipulate two-dimensional arrays, and require that elements be referred to by their element number. AELEMENT( ) facilitates conversion from subscripts to an element number for use by these functions. The corresponding row and column subscripts can be returned from an element number with ASUBSCRIPT( ).

The following example illustrates the creation of an array with two rows and three columns. DISPLAY MEMORY shows the contents of the elements of the array listed in element number order.

```
DIMENSION gaMyArray(2,3)
DISPLAY MEMORY LIKE gaMyArray
gaMyArray    Pub  A
   ( 1, 1)   L  .F. (element number 1)
   ( 1, 2)   L  .F. (element number 2)
   ( 1, 3)   L  .F. (element number 3)
   ( 2, 1)   L  .F. (element number 4)
   ( 2, 2)   L  .F. (element number 5)
   ( 2, 3)   L  .F. (element number 6)
```

An element can be referred to by its subscripts or its element number. The commands STORE 'INVOICE' TO gaMyArray(2, 1) and STORE 'INVOICE' TO gaMyArray(4) both store the character string INVOICE to the same array element.

In one-dimensional arrays, an element number is identical to its single-row subscript. It isn't necessary to use AELEMENT( ) with one-dimensional arrays.

See Also

ADEL( ), ADIR( ), AFIELDS( ), AINS( ), ALEN( ), ASCAN( ), ASORT( ), ASUBSCRIPT( ), DIMENSION, DISPLAY MEMORY

AERROR( ) Function

Creates a variable array containing information about the most recent Visual FoxPro, OLE, or ODBC error.

Syntax

AERROR(*ArrayName*)

Returns

Numeric

Arguments

ArrayName
    Specifies the name of the array that AERROR( ) creates.

Remarks

AERROR( ) creates an array with seven columns and returns the number of rows in the array. The type of error that occurred determines the number of rows in the array.

The following table describes the contents of each element when a Visual FoxPro error occurs. When a Visual FoxPro error occurs, the array contains one row.

Element number	Description
1	Numeric. The number of the error. Identical to the value returned by ERROR( ).
2	Character. The text of the error message. Identical to the value returned by MESSAGE( ).
3	The null value. However, if the error has an additional error parameter, contains the text of the error parameter. Identical to the value returned by SYS(2018).
4	The null value. However, as appropriate, contains the number of the work area in which the error occurred.
5	The null value. However, if a trigger failed (error 1539), contains one of the following numeric values: 1 – Insert trigger failed. 2 – Update trigger failed. 3 – Delete trigger failed.
6	The null value.
7	The null value.

The following table describes the contents of each element when OLE errors numbered 1427 or 1429 occur. When these OLE errors occur, the array contains one row.

Element number	Description
1	Numeric. Contains 1427 or 1429.
2	Character. The text of the Visual FoxPro error message.
3	Character. The text of the OLE error message.
4	Character. The application name (for example, Microsoft Excel).
5	The null value or Character. Contains the name of the application's Help file where more information about the error can be found if the information is available from the application; otherwise contains the null value.

(continued)

Element number	Description
6	The null value or Character. Contains the Help context ID for the appropriate Help topic if the information is available from the application; otherwise contains the null value.
7	Numeric. An OLE 2.0 exception number.

The following table describes the contents of each element when an ODBC error numbered 1526 occurs. When an ODBC error occurs, the array contains two or more rows; one row for each ODBC error.

Element number	Description
1	Numeric. Contains 1526.
2	Character. The text of the error message.
3	Character. The text of the ODBC error message.
4	Character. The current ODBC SQL state.
5	Numeric. The error number from the ODBC data source.
6	Numeric. The ODBC connection handle.
7	The null value.

Example

The following example uses ON ERROR to specify an error handling routine named errhand. An error is generated by issuing a misspelled command (BRWS). The errhand error handling routine uses AERROR( ) to create an array containing error information, and this information is then displayed.

```
ON ERROR DO errhand    && errhand is the error handler procedure

BRWS  && Causes a syntax error
ON ERROR  && Restore system error handler

PROCEDURE errhand
  = AERROR(aErrorArray)  && Data from most recent error
  CLEAR
  ? 'The error provided the following information'  && Display message
  FOR n = 1 TO 7  && Display all elements of the array
    ? aErrorArray(n)
  ENDFOR
```

See Also

COMRETURNERROR( ), CREATE TRIGGER, ERROR( ), MESSAGE( ), ON ERROR, SYS(2018) – Error Message Parameter

AFIELDS( ) Function

Places information about the structure of the current table into an array and returns the number of fields in the table.

Syntax

AFIELDS(*ArrayName* [, *nWorkArea* | *cTableAlias*])

Returns

Numeric

Arguments

ArrayName

Specifies an array into which information about the table structure is placed. If the array you include in AFIELDS( ) doesn't exist, Visual FoxPro automatically creates it. If the array exists and isn't large enough to contain all the information returned by AFIELDS( ), the size of the array is automatically increased to accommodate the information.

nWorkArea

Specifies the work area of the table for which structure information is placed into an array.

cTableAlias

Specifies the alias of the table for which structure information is placed into an array.

If you omit *nWorkArea* and *cTableAlias*, structure information is placed in an array for the table in the currently selected work area.

The following table describes the content of each column in the array and the data type of the information stored in each column. One row is created for each field in the table.

Column number	Field info	Data type
1	Field name	Character
2	Field type: C = Character D = Date L = Logical M = Memo N = Numeric F = Float I = Integer B = Double Y = Currency T = DateTime G = General	Character

(continued)

Column number	Field info	Data type
3	Field width	Numeric
4	Decimal places	Numeric
5	Null values allowed	Logical
6	Code page translation not allowed	Logical
7	Field validation expression	Character
8	Field validation text	Character
9	Field default value	Character
10	Table validation expression	Character
11	Table validation text	Character
12	Long table name	Character
13	Insert trigger expression	Character
14	Update trigger expression	Character
15	Delete trigger expression	Character
16	Table comment	Character

Remarks

AFIELDS( ) returns the number of fields in the table. The array contains 16 columns and the same number of rows as fields in the table.

You can use COPY STRUCTURE EXTENDED to place similar information into a table instead of an array.

Example

The following example creates an array named gaMyArray containing information about the fields in the customer table. The names of the fields are displayed.

```
CLOSE DATABASES
OPEN DATABASE (HOME(2) + 'Data\testdata')
USE Customer      && Open customer table

gnFieldcount = AFIELDS(gaMyArray)  && Create array
CLEAR
FOR nCount = 1 TO gnFieldcount
  ? gaMyArray(nCount,1)  && Display field names
ENDFOR
```

See Also

ADEL( ), ADIR( ), AELEMENT( ), AINS( ), ALEN( ), ALTER TABLE – SQL, ASCAN( ), ASORT( ), ASUBSCRIPT( ), COPY STRUCTURE EXTENDED, CREATE, CREATE TABLE, DIMENSION

AFONT( ) Function

Places information about available fonts into an array.

Syntax

AFONT(*ArrayName* [, *cFontName* [, *nFontSize*]])

Returns

Logical

Arguments

ArrayName

Specifies the variable array into which the names of available fonts are placed. If the array is not large enough to contain all the fonts, Visual FoxPro automatically increases the size of the array. If you specify an existing two-dimensional array, Visual FoxPro changes the array to a one-dimensional array.

If the array is successfully created, AFONT( ) returns true (.T.); otherwise, AFONT( ) returns false (.F.).

cFontName

Specifies a font for which information is placed into the array.

If the font you specify supports only discrete font sizes (8-point, 10-point, ...), the font sizes are stored to the array and AFONT( ) returns true (.T.). If the font you specify in *cFontName* is scalable (supports fractional font-size values), the array has a single element containing –1 and AFONT( ) returns true (.T.).

If the font you specify is not available, the array isn't created and AFONT( ) returns false (.F.).

nFontSize

Specifies a size for the font specified in *cFontName*.

If the font size *nFontSize* is available for the font specified in *cFontName,* the array has a single element containing a true (.T.) value and AFONT( ) returns true (.T.). If the font size is not available for the specified font, the array is not created and AFONT( ) returns false (.F.).

Remarks

AFONT( ) places the names of available fonts into an array. It can also be used to determine available font sizes or if a font is scalable. Use GETFONT( ) to display a dialog containing available fonts, font sizes, and styles.

Example

The following example uses AFONT( ) to create an array containing the names of all available fonts. The name of each font is displayed, along with an example of the font. If there are more than 10 fonts installed, only the first 10 are displayed.

```
CLEAR
=AFONT(gaFontArray)  && Array containing font names
gnNumFonts = ALEN(gaFontArray)  && Number of fonts
IF gnNumFonts > 10
   gnNumFonts = 10  && Display first 10 fonts
ENDIF

FOR nCount = 1 TO gnNumFonts
   ? ALLTRIM(gaFontArray(nCount))  && Display font name
   ?? ' This is an example of ' ;
      + ALLTRIM(gaFontArray(nCount)) FONT gaFontArray(nCount), 8
ENDFOR
```

See Also

FONTMETRIC( ), GETFONT( ), TXTWIDTH( ), SYSMETRIC( ), WFONT( )

AfterBuild Event

Occurs after a project is rebuilt or an application file (.app), dynamic link library (.dll), or executable file (.exe) is created from a project.

Syntax

PROCEDURE *Object.*AfterBuild
[LPARAMETERS *nError*]

Arguments

nError
> The Visual FoxPro error number returned after the project is rebuilt or an .app, .dll, or .exe is created. If *nError* is 0, no errors occurred when the project was rebuilt or the .app, .dll, or .exe was created.

Applies To

ProjectHook Object

See Also

BeforeBuild Event, Build Method

AfterCloseTables Event

Occurs after the tables or views specified in the data environment for a form, form set, or report are released.

Syntax

PROCEDURE *DataEnvironment*.AfterCloseTables

Remarks

For a form or form set, the AfterCloseTables event occurs after the form set's or form's Unload event occurs and after any tables or views that were opened by the data environment are closed.

For a report, the AfterCloseTables event occurs after any tables or views that were opened by the data environment are closed.

The AfterCloseTables event occurs whenever the CloseTables method is called. The Destroy event of the data environment and its associated objects occurs after the AfterCloseTables event.

Applies To

DataEnvironment

See Also

CloseTables Method, Destroy Event, Unload Event

AfterDock Event

Occurs after a ToolBar object is docked.

Syntax

PROCEDURE *ToolBar*.AfterDock
[LPARAMETERS *nIndex*]

Arguments

nIndex
　　Uniquely identifies a control if it is in a control array.

Remarks

The AfterDock event occurs when the user docks a ToolBar or when the Dock method is invoked.

Applies To

ToolBar

See Also

BeforeDock Event, Dock Method, Undock Event

AfterRowColChange Event

Occurs when the user moves to another row or column in the Grid, after the new cell gets the focus, and after the When event of the object in the new row or column. The AfterRowColChange event doesn't fire unless the When event of the object in the new row or column returns true (.T.).

Syntax

PROCEDURE *Grid*.AfterRowColChange
LPARAMETERS *nColIndex*

Arguments

nColIndex
Returns the index of the newly selected row or column.

Remarks

AfterRowColChange is triggered interactively by the mouse or keyboard, or programmatically, such as by calling the ActivateCell method.

Applies To

Grid

See Also

ActivateCell Method, BeforeRowColChange Event, When Event

AGETCLASS( ) Function

Displays class libraries in the Open dialog box and creates an array containing the name of the class library and class chosen.

Syntax

AGETCLASS(*ArrayName* [, *cLibraryName* [, *cClassName* [, *cTitleText*
  [, *cFileNameCaption* [, *cButtonCaption*]]]]])

Returns

Logical

Arguments

ArrayName

Specifies the name of the array in which the names of the class library and class are placed. If the array you specify doesn't exist, Visual FoxPro automatically creates the array. If the array exists and isn't large enough to contain the names of the class library and class, Visual FoxPro automatically increases the size of the array. If the array is larger than necessary, Visual FoxPro truncates the array. If the array exists and AGETCLASS( ) returns false (.F.) because the Class Library dialog box was closed by pressing ESC, choosing Cancel, or clicking the Close button, the array remains unchanged. If the array doesn't exist and AGETCLASS( ) returns false (.F.), the array isn't created.

The following table lists the contents of each element of the array created when you chose a class.

Element	Contents
1	File name of the class library chosen.
2	Name of the class chosen.

cLibraryName

Specifies the name of the class library initially selected when the Open dialog is displayed. The class library name you specify is displayed in the File name text box. An error is generated if the class library you specify doesn't exist or *cLibraryName* is the empty string or the null value.

cClassName

Specifies the name of the class initially selected in the Class name list when the Open dialog is displayed. If the class you specify doesn't exist, the first class in the Class name list is selected. An error is generated if you omit *cLibraryName* or *cClassName* is the null value.

cTitleText

Specifies the text displayed in the title bar of the Open dialog. By default, "Open" is the text displayed.

cFileNameCaption

Specifies the text displayed next to the File name text box. By default, "File name:" is the text displayed.

cButtonCaption

Specifies the caption for the OK button.

Remarks

If you chose a class, AGETCLASS( ) returns true (.T.) and creates a one-dimensional array containing two elements. The first element contains the file name of the class library chosen; the second element contains the name of the class chosen.

False (.F.) is returned if you exit the Class Library dialog box by pressing ESC, choosing Cancel, or clicking the Close button.

Example

The following example creates an array named aClassLib. The directory is changed to the Samples subdirectory containing the sample class libraries. AGETCLASS( ) is used to display a dialog with the Buttons class library and the VCR class selected. If you choose the Modify button, the name of the class library and class you select is stored in the array. The class is then opened in the Class designer.

```
LOCAL aClassLib(2)  && Create an array, initialized to .F.
cCurrentDir = CURDIR( )  && Save the current directory
CD HOME(2) + 'CLASSES'  && Switch directories

AGETCLASS(aClassLib, 'BUTTONS.VCX', 'VCR', 'Modify Class', ;
   'Class File:', 'Modify')  && Display the dialog
CD (cCurrentDir)  && Switch to the previous directory

IF TYPE('aClassLib(2)') = 'C'  && Class chosen?
   MODIFY CLASS (aClassLib(2)) OF (aClassLib(1))  && Open to modify
ENDIF
```

See Also

ACLASS( ), AMEMBERS( ), AVCXCLASSES( ), CREATE CLASS

AGETFILEVERSION( ) Function

Creates an array containing information about files with Windows version resources such as .exe, .dll, and .fll files, or automation servers created in Visual FoxPro.

Syntax

AGETFILEVERSION(*ArrayName*, *cFileName*)

Returns

Numeric

Arguments

ArrayName
Specifies the name of the array in which the file information is placed. If the array you specify doesn't exist, Visual FoxPro automatically creates the array. If the array exists and isn't large enough to contain the file information, Visual FoxPro automatically increases the size of the array. If the array is larger than necessary, Visual FoxPro truncates the array.

The following table lists the contents of each element of the array.

Element	Contents
1	Comments
2	Company Name
3	File Description
4	File Version
5	Internal Name
6	Legal Copyright
7	Legal Trademarks
8	Original File Name
9	Private Build
10	Product Name
11	Product Version
12	Special Build
13	OLE Self-Registration (contains "OLESelfRegister" if the file supports self-registration; otherwise contains the empty string)
14	Language (derived from the Translation Code)
15	Translation Code

For example, you can use the following code to determine the Locale ID for the Visual FoxPro executable file:

```
DIMENSION aFiles[1]
AGETFILEVERSION(aFiles,"VFP6.EXE")
? EVAL("0x"+LEFT(aFiles[15],4))
** Returns 1033 for US version
```

cFileName

Specifies the name file for which information is placed in the array. The class library name you specify is displayed in the File name text box. An error is generated if the class library you specify doesn't exist.

Remarks

AGETFILEVERSION( ) is typically used to get information about files with Windows version resources such as .exe, .dll, and .fll files, or automation servers created in Visual FoxPro. You must specify a value for at least one item in the EXE Version dialog Box for a Visual FoxPro automation server to have Windows version resources.

AGETFILEVERSION( ) returns the number of elements in the array. If the file you specify doesn't contain Windows version resources, zero is returned and the array (if already created) remains unchanged.

The minimum number of characters to which AGETFILEVERSION( ) can be abbreviated is five characters.

See Also

ADIR( ), DIR or DIRECTORY

AINS( ) Function

Inserts an element into a one-dimensional array, or a row or column into a two-dimensional array.

Syntax

AINS(*ArrayName*, *nElementNumber* [, 2])

Returns

Numeric

Arguments

ArrayName
Specifies the name of the array into which the element is inserted.

nElementNumber
Specifies where the new element, row, or column is inserted into the array.

To insert an element into a one-dimensional array, include *ArrayName* and the element *nElementNumber* where the insertion occurs. The new element is inserted just before element *nElementNumber*. To insert a row into a two-dimensional array, include *ArrayName* and the number of the row *nElementNumber* where the insertion occurs. The new row is inserted just before row *nElementNumber*.

For more information on referencing an array element by its subscripts, see the DIMENSION Command, later in this language reference.

2
Inserts a column into a two-dimensional array. The new column is inserted just before the column specified with *nElementNumber*.

Remarks

Inserting an element, row, or column into an array does not change the size of the array. The trailing elements, rows, or columns are shifted toward the end of the array and the last element, row, or column in the array is dropped from it. The newly inserted element, row, or column is initialized to false (.F.).

AINS( ) returns 1 if the element, row, or column is successfully inserted.

Example

The following example creates and fills an array with company names and scans the array for a specific company name. If the company name isn't found, it inserts the missing company name into the array.

```
CLOSE DATABASES
OPEN DATABASE (HOME(2) + 'Data\testdata')
USE customer        && Open customer table
SELECT company FROM customer ;
   WHERE country = 'Germany' ;
   INTO ARRAY gaCompanies

gnCount = _TALLY
gcName = 'Seven Seas Imports'
CLEAR
DISPLAY MEMORY LIKE gaCompanies

IF ASCAN(gaCompanies, gcName) = 0   && Search for company
*** Company not found-add it ***
   DIMENSION gaCompanies[gnCount+1,1]
   = AINS(gaCompanies, gnCount-1)
   gaCompanies[gnCount-1] = gcName
ENDIF
DISPLAY MEMORY LIKE gaCompanies
```

See Also

ACOPY( ), ADEL( ), ADIR( ), AELEMENT( ), AFIELDS( ), ALEN( ), ASCAN( ), ASORT( ), ASUBSCRIPT( ), DIMENSION

AINSTANCE( ) Function

Places instances of a class into a variable array and returns the number of instances placed in the array.

Syntax

AINSTANCE(*ArrayName*, *cClassName*)

Returns

Numeric

Arguments

ArrayName
Specifies the name of the array into which the instances are placed. If the array you specify doesn't exist, Visual FoxPro automatically creates the array. If the array exists and isn't large enough to contain all the instances, Visual FoxPro automatically increases the size of the array to accommodate the instances. If the array is larger than

necessary, Visual FoxPro truncates the array. If the array exists and AINSTANCE( ) returns 0 because no instances are found, the array remains unchanged. If the array doesn't exist and AINSTANCE( ) returns 0, the array is not created.

Only class instances assigned to variables and array elements with CREATEOBJECT( ) are placed into the array.

cClassName

Specifies a Visual FoxPro base class name or a user-defined class name. The following table lists the Visual FoxPro base classes you can specify for *cClassName*:

Base class names

ActiveDoc	CheckBox	Column
ComboBox	CommandButton	CommandGroup
Container	Control	Cursor
Custom	DataEnvironment	EditBox
Form	FormSet	Grid
Header	Hyperlink	Image
Label	Line	ListBox
OLEBoundControl	OLEControl	OptionButton
OptionGroup	Page	PageFrame
ProjectHook	Relation	Separator
Shape	Spinner	TextBox
Timer	ToolBar	

Example

In the following example, CREATEOBJECT( ) is used to create two instances of the Visual FoxPro Form base class. AINSTANCE( ) is used to create an array named gaMyArray that contains the variable references (goINSTANCE1 and goINSTANCE2) for each form instance. The contents of the array are then displayed.

```
CLEAR ALL
goINSTANCE1 = CREATEOBJECT('Form')
goINSTANCE2 = CREATEOBJECT('Form')

CLEAR
? AINSTANCE(gaMyArray, 'Form')  && Returns 2, two form instances
DISPLAY MEMORY LIKE gaMyArray  && Displays the references
```

See Also

ADD CLASS, AMEMBERS( ), CREATE CLASS, CREATE CLASSLIB, CREATEOBJECT( ), DEFINE CLASS

ALEN( ) Function

Returns the number of elements, rows, or columns in an array.

Syntax

ALEN(*ArrayName* [, *nArrayAttribute*])

Returns

Numeric

Arguments

ArrayName

Specifies the name of the array. If you include only the array name, ALEN( ) returns the number of elements in the array.

nArrayAttribute

Determines whether ALEN( ) returns the number of elements, rows or columns in the array according to the following values for *nArrayAttribute*:

0	Returns the number of elements in the array. Omitting *nArrayAttribute* is identical to specifying 0.
1	Returns the number of rows in the array.
2	Returns the number of columns in the array. If the array is a one-dimensional array, ALEN( ) returns 0 (no columns).

Example

The following example uses AFONT( ) to create an array containing the names of all available fonts. ALEN( ) is used to determine the number of rows in the array. The name of each font is displayed, along with an example of the font. If more than 10 fonts are installed, only the first 10 are displayed.

```
CLEAR
=AFONT(gaFontArray)  && Array containing font names
gnNumFonts= ALEN(gaFontArray)  && Number of fonts
IF gnNumFonts > 10
   gnNumFonts = 10  && Display first 10 fonts
ENDIF

FOR nCount = 1 TO gnNumFonts
   ? ALLTRIM(gaFontArray(nCount))  && Display font name
   ?? ' This is an example of ' ;
      + ALLTRIM(gaFontArray(nCount)) FONT gaFontArray(nCount), 8
ENDFOR
```

See Also

ADEL( ), ADIR( ), AELEMENT( ), AFIELDS( ), AINS( ), ASCAN( ), ASORT( ),
ASUBSCRIPT( ), DIMENSION, STORE

Alias Property

Specifies the alias used for each table or view associated with a Cursor object. Available at
design time and run time.

Syntax

DataEnvironment.Cursor.Alias[= *cText*]

Arguments

cText
   Specifies the alias used for the table or view associated with the Cursor object.

Remarks

When the data environment is loaded, each table or view associated with a Cursor object
is assigned an alias that is, by default, the same as the table or view name. Use the Alias
property to override the default alias name.

The Alias property mimics the behavior of the USE command's ALIAS clause.

Applies To

Cursor

See Also

USE

ALIAS( ) Function

Returns the table alias of the current or specified work area.

Syntax

ALIAS([*nWorkArea* | *cTableAlias*])

Returns

Character

Arguments

nWorkArea
   Specifies the work area number for which ALIAS( ) returns the table alias.

cTableAlias
> Specifies the table alias for which ALIAS( ) returns the table alias.

> If you omit *nWorkArea* or *cTableAlias*, ALIAS( ) returns the alias of the table open in the current work area. An empty string is returned if a table isn't open in the current or specified work area.

Example

The following example opens the customer table and displays its alias. The customer table is opened again in another work area, is assigned an alias of MyCustomer, and the alias is displayed.

```
CLOSE DATABASES
OPEN DATABASE (HOME(2) + 'Data\testdata')
USE customer      && Open customer table
CLEAR
? ALIAS( )  && Display the alias
SELECT 0
USE customer AGAIN ALIAS MyCustomer  && Different alias
? ALIAS( )  && Display the alias
```

See Also

DBF( ), SELECT( )

Align Property

Specifies the alignment of an ActiveX control (.ocx) on a form. Available at design time and run time.

Syntax

OLEContainerControl.Align[= *nAlign*]

Arguments

nAlign
> The settings for the Align property are:

Setting	Description
0	Standard alignment. The ActiveX control is placed in the same position as the OLE Container control on the form.
1	Top. The ActiveX control is placed at the top of the form.
2	Bottom. The ActiveX control is placed at the bottom of the form.
3	Left. The ActiveX control is placed at the left edge of the form.
4	Right. The ActiveX control is placed at the right edge of the form.

Remarks

An ActiveX control (.ocx file) is placed in OLE Container control.

The Align property is only available for ActiveX controls that support changes to their alignment. Insertable OLE objects such as Microsoft Excel worksheets do not support the Align property.

The Align property is available only for ActiveX controls that are placed on a form.

If two or more ActiveX controls have the same Align property setting, the controls are stacked on top of each other.

Applies To

OLE Container Control

See Also

OLE Container Control

Alignment Property

Specifies the alignment of text associated with a control. Available at design time and run time.

Syntax

Control.Alignment[= *nAlign*]

Arguments

nAlign
  For a CheckBox or OptionButton control, the settings for the Alignment property are:

Setting	Description
0	(Default) Left. Aligns control to the left with text on the right.
1	(Default for Middle Eastern versions of Windows) Right. Aligns control to the right with text on the left.

  For a ComboBox, EditBox, Header, Label, or Spinner control, the settings for the Alignment property are:

Setting	Description
0	(Default) Left. Aligns text flush left. The default for combo boxes, edit boxes, headers, and labels.
1	(Default for Middle Eastern versions of Windows) Right. Aligns text flush right. The default for spinners.

(continued)

(continued)

Setting	Description
2	Center. Aligns the text in the middle with equal spaces to the right and left.
3	Automatic. Aligns text based on the data type of the control source.

For a TextBox control, the settings for the Alignment property are:

Setting	Description
0	Left. Aligns the text flush left.
1	Right. Aligns the text flush right.
2	Center. Aligns the text in the middle with equal spaces to the right and left.
3	(Default) Automatic. For a TextBox control not contained in a Column, aligns text based on the data type of the control source. Numeric types (numeric, double, float, currency, integer) are right-aligned; controls with other data types are left-aligned. For a TextBox control contained in a column, the Alignment setting for the column determines alignment of text in the text box.

For a column, the settings for the Alignment property are:

Setting	Description
0	Middle Left. Aligns the text flush left and centers it vertically.
1	Middle Right. Aligns the text flush right and centers it vertically.
2	Middle Center. Aligns the text in the middle with equal spaces to the right and left and centers it vertically.
3	(Default) Automatic. Aligns text based on the data type of the control source. Numeric types (numeric, double, float, currency, integer) are right-aligned; controls with other data types are left-aligned.
4	Top Left. Aligns the text flush left at the top of the column.
5	Top Right. Aligns the text flush right at the top of the column.
6	Top Center. Aligns the text in the middle with equal spaces to the right and left, at the top of the column.
7	Bottom Left. Aligns the text flush left at the bottom of the column.
8	Bottom Right. Aligns the text flush right at the bottom of the column.
9	Bottom Center. Aligns the text in the middle with equal spaces to the right and left, at the bottom of the column.

Remarks

For a ComboBox, the Alignment property applies only when the Style property is set to 0.

Applies To

CheckBox, Column, ComboBox, EditBox, Header, Label, OptionButton, Spinner, TextBox

See Also

AutoSize Property, Caption Property

_ALIGNMENT System Variable

Included for backward compatibility. Use the Report Designer instead.

ALINES( ) Function

Copies each line in a character expression or memo field to a corresponding row in an array.

Syntax

ALINES(*ArrayName*, *cExpression* [, *lTrim*])

Returns

Numeric

Arguments

ArrayName
Specifies the name of the array to which the lines in the character expression or memo field are copied. If the array you specify doesn't exist, Visual FoxPro automatically creates the array. If the array exists and isn't large enough to contain all the lines in the memo field, Visual FoxPro automatically increases the size of the array. If the array is larger than necessary, Visual FoxPro truncates the array.

cExpression
Specifies the character expression or memo field containing the lines copied to the array. If *cExpression* is the empty string or the null value, an array with a single row is created and the row contains the empty string.

lTrim
Specifies that leading and trailing blanks are removed from the lines copied to the array. If *lTrim* is true (.T.), leading and trailing blanks are removed from the lines. If *lTrim* is false (.F.) or is omitted, leading and trailing blanks are not removed.

Remarks

ALINES( ) returns the number of rows in the array (or, identically, the number of lines in the character expression or memo field). The first line of the character expression or memo field is copied to the first row of the array, the second line of the character expression or memo field is copied to the second row of the array, and so on.

A line feed (CHR(10)) or carriage return (CHR(13)) character denotes the end of a line. The end of the line can also be denoted with either combination of these two characters (CHR(10) + CHR(13) or CHR(13) + CHR(10)).

ALINES( ) provides an easy way to parse lines in a character expression or memo field. While MLINES( ) can also be used to parse a character expression or memo field, ALINES( ) is faster and requires less programming. Also, ALINES( ) is not affected by the value of SET MEMOWIDTH.

You must have sufficient memory to copy the lines in a large memo field to an array. Visual FoxPro generates an error message if you lack sufficient memory.

Example

The following program opens the Employee table in the Testdata database. ALINES( ) is used to copy the lines in the Notes memo field to an array named aMyArray, and then the contents of the array is displayed.

In this example, ALINES( ) returns 1 because the employee description was typed into the memo field without pressing Enter after any of the sentences.

```
CLOSE DATABASES
CLEAR
SET TALK OFF
OPEN DATABASE (HOME(2) + 'data\testdata')
USE employee  && Open Employee table

? ALINES(aMyArray, employee.notes)  && Displays 1
? aMyArray(1)
```

See Also

MEMLINES( ), MLINE( ), _MLINE, SCATTER

AllowAddNew Property

Specifies whether new records can be added to a table from within a grid. Available at design time and run time.

Syntax

Grid.AllowAddNew[= *lExpr*]

Arguments

lExpr

One of the following:

Setting	Description
True (.T.)	New records can be added to a table from within a grid.
False (.F.)	(Default) New records cannot be added to a table from within a grid.

Remarks

If AllowAddNew is set to true (.T.), you can add a new record to a table in a grid by pressing the down arrow while positioned on the last record in the grid, as long as the grid is read/write. New records cannot be added from within the grid if the grid is read-only (if the RecordSourceType is a query, a table is read-only, and so on).

Applies To

Grid

See Also

APPEND

AllowHeaderSizing Property

Specifies whether the height of a grid's header can be changed at run time. Available at design time and run time.

Syntax

Grid.AllowHeaderSizing[= *lExpr*]

Arguments

lExpr

One of the following:

Setting	Description
True (.T.)	(Default) The height of the grid's header can be changed by dragging the header at run time.
False (.F.)	The height of the grid's header cannot be changed by dragging the header at run time.

Applies To

Grid

See Also

AllowRowSizing Property

AllowRowSizing Property

Specifies whether the height of records in a grid can be changed at run time. Available at design time and run time.

Syntax

Grid.AllowRowSizing[= *lExpr*]

Arguments

lExpr

One of the following:

Setting	Description
True (.T.)	(Default) The height of records in the grid can be changed by dragging at run time.
False (.F.)	The height of records in the grid cannot be changed by dragging at run time.

Applies To

Grid

See Also

AllowHeaderSizing Property

AllowTabs Property

Specifies whether tabs are allowed in an EditBox control.

Syntax

EditBox.AllowTabs[= *lExpr*]

Arguments

lExpr

The settings for the AllowTabs property are:

Setting	Description
True (.T.)	Tabs are allowed; press CTRL+TAB to exit the field.
False (.F.)	(Default) Tabs are not allowed in the EditBox; pressing the TAB key moves the focus to the next control in the tab order.

Applies To

EditBox

See Also

TabIndex Property, TabStop Property

ALLTRIM( ) Function

Removes leading and trailing blanks from the specified character expression and returns the trimmed expression as a character string.

Syntax

ALLTRIM(*cExpression*)

Returns

Character

Arguments

cExpression

Specifies the character expression from which leading and trailing blanks are removed.

Remarks

ALLTRIM( ) can be used to ensure that blanks are removed from data entered by a user.

Example

The following example uses AFONT( ) to create an array containing the names of all available fonts. ALLTRIM( ) is used to remove leading and trailing spaces from the font names. The trimmed name of each font is displayed, along with an example of the font. If more than 10 fonts are installed, only the first 10 are displayed.

```
CLEAR
=AFONT(gaFontArray)  && Array containing font names
gnNumFonts= ALEN(gaFontArray)  && Number of fonts
IF gnNumFonts > 10
   gnNumFonts = 10  && Display first 10 fonts
ENDIF

FOR nCount = 1 TO gnNumFonts
   ? ALLTRIM(gaFontArray(nCount))  && Display font name
   ?? ' This is an example of ' ;
      + ALLTRIM(gaFontArray(nCount)) FONT gaFontArray(nCount), 8
ENDFOR
```

See Also

LTRIM( ), RTRIM( ), TRIM( )

ALTER TABLE – SQL Command

Programmatically modifies the structure of a table.

Syntax

ALTER TABLE *TableName1*
    ADD I ALTER [COLUMN] *FieldName1*
        FieldType [(*nFieldWidth* [, *nPrecision*])]
        [NULL I NOT NULL]
        [CHECK *lExpression1* [ERROR *cMessageText1*]]
        [DEFAULT *eExpression1*]
        [PRIMARY KEY I UNIQUE]
        [REFERENCES *TableName2* [TAG *TagName1*]]
        [NOCPTRANS]

– or –

ALTER TABLE *TableName1*
    ALTER [COLUMN] *FieldName2*
        [NULL I NOT NULL]
        [SET DEFAULT *eExpression2*]
        [SET CHECK *lExpression2* [ERROR *cMessageText2*]]
        [DROP DEFAULT]
        [DROP CHECK]

– or –

ALTER TABLE *TableName1*
    [DROP [COLUMN] *FieldName3*]
    [SET CHECK *lExpression3* [ERROR *cMessageText3*]]
    [DROP CHECK]
    [ADD PRIMARY KEY *eExpression3* TAG *TagName2* [FOR *lExpression4*]]
    [DROP PRIMARY KEY]
    [ADD UNIQUE *eExpression4* [TAG *TagName3* [FOR *lExpression5*]]]
    [DROP UNIQUE TAG *TagName4*]
    [ADD FOREIGN KEY [*eExpression5*] TAG *TagName4* [FOR *lExpression6*]
        REFERENCES *TableName2* [TAG *TagName5*]]
    [DROP FOREIGN KEY TAG *TagName6* [SAVE]]
    [RENAME COLUMN *FieldName4* TO *FieldName5*]
    [NOVALIDATE]

Arguments

TableName1
    Specifies the name of the table whose structure is modified.

ADD [COLUMN] *FieldName1*
    Specifies the name of the field to add. A single table can contain up to 255 fields.
    If one or more fields allow null values, the limit is reduced by one to 254 fields.

ALTER [COLUMN] *FieldName1*

Specifies the name of an existing field to modify.

FieldType [(*nFieldWidth* [, *nPrecision*])]

Specifies the field type, field width, and field precision (number of decimal places) for a new or modified field.

FieldType is a single letter indicating the field's data type. Some field data types require that you specify *nFieldWidth* or *nPrecision* or both.

The following table lists the values for *FieldType* and indicates whether *nFieldWidth* and *nPrecision* are required:

FieldType	nFieldWidth	nPrecision	Description
C	n	–	Character field of width n
D	–	–	Date
T	–	–	DateTime
N	n	d	Numeric field of width n with d decimal places
F	n	d	Floating numeric field of width n with d decimal places
I	–	–	Integer
B	–	d	Double
Y	–	–	Currency
L	–	–	Logical
M	–	–	Memo
G	–	–	General
P	–	–	Picture

nFieldWidth and *nPrecision* are ignored for D, T, I, Y, L, M, G, and P types. *nPrecision* defaults to zero (no decimal places) if *nPrecision* isn't included for the N, F, or B types.

NULL | NOT NULL

Allows or precludes null values in the field. If one or more fields can contain null values, the maximum number of fields the table can contain is reduced by one, from 255 to 254.

If you omit NULL and NOT NULL, the current setting of SET NULL determines whether null values are allowed in the field. However, if you omit NULL and NOT NULL and include the PRIMARY KEY or UNIQUE clause, the current setting of SET NULL is ignored and the field defaults to NOT NULL.

CHECK *lExpression1*

> Specifies a validation rule for the field. *lExpression1* must evaluate to a logical expression; it can be a user-defined function or a stored procedure. When a blank record is appended, the validation rule is checked. An error is generated if the validation rule doesn't allow for a blank field value in an appended record.

ERROR *cMessageText1*

> Specifies the error message displayed when the field validation rule generates an error. The message is displayed only when data is changed within a Browse or Edit window.

DEFAULT *eExpression1*

> Specifies a default value for the field. The data type of *eExpression1* must be the same as the data type for the field.

PRIMARY KEY

> Creates a primary index tag. The index tag has the same name as the field.

UNIQUE

> Creates a candidate index tag with the same name as the field.

> For more information about candidate indexes, see Chapter 7, "Working with Tables," in the *Microsoft Visual FoxPro 6.0 Programmer's Guide*.

> **Note** Candidate indexes (created by including the UNIQUE option, provided for ANSI compatibility in ALTER TABLE or CREATE TABLE) are not the same as indexes created with the UNIQUE option in the INDEX command. An index created with UNIQUE in the INDEX command allows duplicate index keys; candidate indexes do not allow duplicate index keys.

> Null values and duplicate records are not permitted in a field used for a primary or candidate index.

> If you are creating a new field with ADD COLUMN, Microsoft Visual FoxPro will not generate an error if you create a primary or candidate index for a field that supports null values. However, Visual FoxPro will generate an error if you attempt to enter a null or duplicate value into a field used for a primary or candidate index.

> If you are modifying an existing field and the primary or candidate index expression consists of fields in the table, Visual FoxPro checks the fields to see if they contain null values or duplicate records. If they do, Visual FoxPro generates an error and the table is not altered.

REFERENCES *TableName2* TAG *TagName1*

> Specifies the parent table to which a persistent relationship is established. TAG *TagName1* specifies the parent table's index tag on which the relationship is based. Index tag names can contain up to 10 characters.

NOCPTRANS

Prevents translation to a different code page for character and memo fields. If the table is converted to another code page, the fields for which NOCPTRANS has been specified are not translated. NOCPTRANS can only be specified for character and memo fields.

The following example creates a table named MYTABLE containing two character fields and two memo fields. The second character field `char2` and the second memo field `memo2` include NOCPTRANS to prevent translation.

```
CREATE TABLE mytable (char1 C(10), char2 C(10) NOCPTRANS,;
    memo1 M, memo2 M NOCPTRANS)
```

ALTER [COLUMN] *FieldName2*

Specifies the name of an existing field to modify. Note that multiple ALTER COLUMN clauses are required to change more than one property of a field in a single ALTER TABLE command. See the ALTER TABLE examples to see how the ALTER COLUMN clauses are structured.

SET DEFAULT *eExpression2*

Specifies a new default value for an existing field. The data type of *eExpression2* must be the same as the data type for the field.

SET CHECK *lExpression2*

Specifies a new validation rule for an existing field. *lExpression2* must evaluate to a logical expression, and may be a user-defined function or a stored procedure.

ERROR *cMessageText2*

Specifies the error message displayed when the field validation rule generates an error. The message is displayed only when data is changed within a Browse or Edit window.

DROP DEFAULT

Removes the default value for an existing field.

DROP CHECK

Removes the validation rule for an existing field.

DROP [COLUMN] *FieldName3*

Specifies a field to remove from the table. Removing a field from the table also removes the field's default value setting and field validation rule.

If index key or trigger expressions reference the field, the expressions become invalid when the field is removed. In this case, an error isn't generated when the field is removed, but the invalid index key or trigger expressions will generate errors at run time.

SET CHECK *lExpression3*

Specifies the table validation rule. *lExpression3* must evaluate to a logical expression; it can be a user-defined function or a stored procedure.

ERROR *cMessageText3*

Specifies the error message displayed when the table validation rule generates an error. The message is displayed only when data is changed within a Browse or Edit window.

DROP CHECK

Removes the table's validation rule.

ADD PRIMARY KEY *eExpression3* TAG *TagName2* [FOR *lExpression4*]

Adds a primary index to the table. *eExpression3* specifies the primary index key expression; *TagName2* specifies the name of the primary index tag. Index tag names can contain up to 10 characters. If TAG *TagName2* is omitted and *eExpression3* is a single field, the primary index tag has the same name as the field specified in *eExpression3*.

Include FOR *lExpression4* to specify a condition whereby only records that satisfy the filter expression *lExpression4* are available for display and access; primary index keys are created in the index file for just those records matching the filter expression. Note that you should avoid using the FOR clause to create a primary index; the uniqueness of a primary key is only enforced for those records that match the condition specified with FOR *lExpression4*. Instead, use the INDEX command with a FOR clause to create a filtered index.

Rushmore optimizes an ALTER TABLE ... FOR *lExpression4* command if *lExpression4* is an optimizable expression. For best performance, use an optimizable expression in the FOR clause.

For more information, see the SET OPTIMIZE Command, later in this language reference, and "Understanding Rushmore Technology" in Chapter 15, "Optimizing Applications," in the *Microsoft Visual FoxPro 6.0 Programmer's Guide*.

DROP PRIMARY KEY

Removes the primary index and its index tag. Because a table can have only one primary key, it isn't necessary to specify the name of the primary key. Removing the primary index also deletes any persistent relations based on the primary key.

ADD UNIQUE *eExpression4* [TAG *TagName3* [FOR *lExpression5*]]

Adds a candidate index to the table. *eExpression4* specifies the candidate index key expression; *TagName3* specifies the name of the candidate index tag. Index tag names can contain up to 10 characters. If you omit TAG *TagName3,* and if *eExpression4* is a single field, the candidate index tag has the same name as the field specified in *eExpression4*.

Include FOR *lExpression5* to specify a condition whereby only records that satisfy the filter expression *lExpression5* are available for display and access; candidate index keys are created in the index file for just those records matching the filter expression.

Rushmore optimizes an ALTER TABLE ... FOR *lExpression5* command if *lExpression5* is an optimizable expression. For best performance, use an optimizable expression in the FOR clause.

For more information, see the SET OPTIMIZE Command, later in this language reference, and "Understanding Rushmore Technology" in Chapter 15, "Optimizing Applications," in the *Microsoft Visual FoxPro 6.0 Programmer's Guide*.

DROP UNIQUE TAG *TagName4*

Removes the candidate index and its index tag. Because a table can have multiple candidate keys, you must specify the name of the candidate index tag.

ADD FOREIGN KEY [*eExpression5*] **TAG** *TagName4* [FOR *lExpression6*]

Adds a foreign (non-primary) index to the table. *eExpression5* specifies the foreign index key expression and *TagName4* specifies the name of the foreign index tag. Index tag names can contain up to 10 characters.

Include FOR *lExpression6* to specify a condition whereby only records that satisfy the filter expression *lExpression6* are available for display and access; foreign index keys are created in the index file for just those records matching the filter expression.

Rushmore optimizes an ALTER TABLE ... FOR *lExpression6* command if *lExpression6* is an optimizable expression. For best performance, use an optimizable expression in the FOR clause.

For more information, see the SET OPTIMIZE Command, later in this language reference, and "Understanding Rushmore Technology" in Chapter 15, "Optimizing Applications," in the *Microsoft Visual FoxPro 6.0 Programmer's Guide*.

REFERENCES *TableName2* [TAG *TagName5*]

Specifies the parent table to which a persistent relationship is established. Include TAG *TagName5* to establish a relationship based on an existing index tag for the parent table. Index tag names can contain up to 10 characters. If you omit TAG *TagName5*, the relationship is established using the parent table's primary index tag.

DROP FOREIGN KEY TAG *TagName6* [SAVE]

Deletes a foreign key whose index tag is *TagName6*. If you omit SAVE, the index tag is deleted from the structural index. Include SAVE to prevent the index tag from being deleted from the structural index.

RENAME COLUMN *FieldName4* **TO** *FieldName5*

Allows you to change the name of a field in the table. *FieldName4* specifies the name of the field that is renamed. *FieldName5* specifies the new name of the field.

Caution Exercise care when renaming table fields — index expressions, field and table validation rules, commands, functions, and so on, may reference the original field names.

NOVALIDATE

Specifies that Visual FoxPro allows changes to be made to the structure of the table that may violate the integrity of the data in the table. By default, Visual FoxPro prevents ALTER TABLE from making changes to the structure of the table that violate the integrity of the data in the table. Include NOVALIDATE to override this default behavior.

Remarks

ALTER TABLE can be used to modify the structure of a table that has not been added to a database. However, Visual FoxPro generates an error if you include the DEFAULT, FOREIGN KEY, PRIMARY KEY, REFERENCES, or SET clauses when modifying a free table.

ALTER TABLE may rebuild the table by creating a new table header and appending records to the table header. For example, changing a field's type or width may cause the table to be rebuilt.

After a table is rebuilt, field validation rules are executed for any fields whose type or width is changed. If you change the type or width of any field in the table, the table rule is executed.

If you modify field or table validation rules for a table that has records, Visual FoxPro tests the new field or table validation rules against the existing data and issues a warning on the first occurrence of a field or table validation rule or of a trigger violation.

Examples

Example 1 adds a field called `fax` to the `customer` table and allows the field to have null values.

Example 2 makes the `cust_id` field the primary key of the `customer` table.

Example 3 adds a field validation rule to the `quantity` field of the `orders` table so that values in the `quantity` field must be non-negative.

Example 4 adds a one-to-many persistent relation between the `customer` and `orders` tables based on the primary key `cust_id` in the `customer` table and a new foreign key index `cust_id` in the `orders` table.

Example 5 removes the field validation rule from the `quantity` field in the `orders` table.

Example 6 removes the persistent relation between the `customer` and `orders` tables, but keeps the `cust_id` index tag in the `orders` table.

Example 7 adds a field called `fax2` to the `customer` table and prevents the field from containing null values. The new structure of the table is displayed. Two ALTER COLUMN clauses are used to allow the field to have null values and set the default value for the field to the null value. Note that multiple ALTER COLUMN clauses are required to change more than one property of a field in a single ALTER TABLE command. The new field is then removed from the table to restore the table to its original state.

```
* Example 1
SET PATH TO (HOME(2) + 'Data\')     && Sets path to table
ALTER TABLE customer ADD COLUMN fax c(20) NULL

* Example 2
ALTER TABLE customer ADD PRIMARY KEY cust_id TAG cust_id

ALTER TABLE customer ALTER COLUMN cust_id c(5) PRIMARY KEY
```

```
* Example 3
ALTER TABLE orders;
   ALTER COLUMN quantity SET CHECK quantity >= 0;
   ERROR "Quantities must be non-negative"

* Example 4
ALTER TABLE orders;
   ADD FOREIGN KEY cust_id TAG cust_id REFERENCES customer

* Example 5
ALTER TABLE orders ALTER COLUMN quantity DROP CHECK

* Example 6
ALTER TABLE orders DROP FOREIGN KEY TAG cust_id SAVE

* Example 7
CLEAR
ALTER TABLE customer ADD COLUMN fax2 c(20) NOT NULL
DISPLAY STRUCTURE

ALTER TABLE customer;
   ALTER COLUMN fax2 NULL;
   ALTER COLUMN fax2 SET DEFAULT .NULL.

ALTER TABLE customer DROP COLUMN fax2
```

See Also

CREATE TABLE – SQL, INDEX, MODIFY STRUCTURE, OPEN DATABASE

AlwaysOnTop Property

Prevents other windows from covering the form's window. Available at design time; read/write at run time.

Syntax

Object.AlwaysOnTop[= *lExpr*]

Arguments

lExpr
    The settings for the AlwaysOnTop property are:

Setting	Description
True (.T.)	The form is always on top (only another window with the AlwaysOnTop property set to true (.T.) can be on top of the form).
False (.F.)	(Default) The form can be covered by another window.

Remarks

Note that the AlwaysOnTop property only applies to MDI (multiple-document interface) forms, created when the ShowWindow property is set to 1 – In Top-Level Form.

Applies To

Form, _SCREEN

See Also

ShowWindow Property, ZOrder Method

AMEMBERS( ) Function

Places the names of properties, procedures, and member objects for an object into a variable array.

Syntax

AMEMBERS(*ArrayName*, *ObjectName* | *cClassName* [, 1 | 2])

Returns

Numeric

Arguments

ArrayName
　　Specifies the array into which the names of the member properties for *ObjectName* are placed. If you specify the name of an array that doesn't exist, the array is automatically created. If the array isn't large enough to contain all the names, Visual FoxPro automatically increases the size of the array.

ObjectName
　　Specifies the object whose member properties are placed in the variable array specified with *ArrayName*. *ObjectName* can be any expression that evaluates to an object, such as an object reference, an object variable, or an object array element.

cClassName
　　Specifies the class whose member properties are placed in the variable array specified with *ArrayName*.

1
　　Specifies that the array contains the properties of the object as well as the methods and member objects. The resulting array is two-dimensional with the second column specifying what type of member is listed in the first column. The possible values for the second column are Property, Event, Method, or Object.

2
　　Specifies that the array contains the names of the objects that are members of the object specified with *ObjectName*. The resulting array is one-dimensional.

This option provides a method to determine the names of all Form objects in a form set or controls in a form.

Remarks

AMEMBERS( ) returns the number of objects, properties, and procedures for the object, or 0 if the array cannot be created. If you omit the optional 1 and 2 arguments, a one-dimensional array is created containing the properties for *ObjectName*.

Example

The following example uses CREATEOBJECT( ) to create a Form object named `goForm1`. AMEMBERS( ) is used to create an array named `gaPropArray` containing the properties available for the form; the properties are then displayed.

```
CLEAR
goForm1 = CREATEOBJECT("Form")  && Creates a Form
= AMEMBERS(gaPropArray, goForm1, 1)  && Array containing Form properties
DISPLAY MEMORY LIKE gaPropArray  && Display the Form properties
```

See Also

ADD CLASS, AINSTANCE( ), CREATE CLASS, CREATE CLASSLIB, CREATEOBJECT( ), DEFINE CLASS

ANETRESOURCES( ) Function

Places the names of network shares or printers into an array and then returns the number of resources.

Syntax

ANETRESOURCES(*ArrayName*, *cNetworkName*, *nResourceType*)

Returns

Numeric

Arguments

ArrayName
Specifies the name of the array containing the network share or printer information. If the array you specify doesn't exist, Visual FoxPro automatically creates the array. If the array exists and isn't large enough to contain all the information, Visual FoxPro automatically increases the size of the array to accommodate the information. If the array is larger than necessary, Visual FoxPro truncates the array.

If the array exists and ANETRESOURCES( ) returns 0 because no network shares or printers are found, the array remains unchanged. If the array doesn't exist and ANETRESOURCES( ) returns 0, the array isn't created.

cNetworkName

    Specifies the name of the network for which share or printer information is returned. The network name should be in the format "\\NetworkName." You do not have to be connected to the network you specify, and specifying a network doesn't connect you to the network.

nResourceType

    Specifies the type of network resource for which information is returned. The names of shares on the network are returned if *nResourceType* evaluates to 1. The names of printers on the network are returned if *nResourceType* evaluates to 2.

Remarks

ANETRESOURCES( ) returns the number of network shares or printers found (identical to the number of rows in the array). ANETRESOURCES( ) returns zero if there are no shares or printers for the network of the type you specify, or the network you specify doesn't exist.

See Also

ADIR( )

AMOUSEOBJ( ) Function

Creates an array containing information about the mouse pointer position and the object over which the mouse pointer is positioned.

Syntax

AMOUSEOBJ(*ArrayName* [, 1])

Returns

Numeric

Arguments

ArrayName

    Specifies the name of the array containing the mouse pointer information. If the array you specify doesn't exist, Visual FoxPro automatically creates the array. If the array exists and isn't large enough to contain all the lines in the memo field, Visual FoxPro automatically increases the size of the array. If the array is larger than necessary, Visual FoxPro truncates the array.

    The array that is created contains four rows. The following table describes the contents of each row in the array:

Array row	Description
1	Contains an object reference to the object over which the mouse pointer is positioned when AMOUSEOBJ( ) is executed.
2	Contains an object reference to the container of the object over which the mouse pointer is positioned when AMOUSEOBJ( ) is executed.
3	Contains the horizontal (X) coordinate in pixels of the mouse pointer, relative to the container of the object over which the mouse pointer is positioned when AMOUSEOBJ( ) is executed.
4	Contains the vertical (Y) coordinate in pixels of the mouse pointer, relative to the container of the object over which the mouse pointer is positioned when AMOUSEOBJ( ) is executed.

Note that the first and second rows in the array can contain the same values if the mouse is positioned over a generic container such as a pageframe.

[, 1]

This optional parameter specifies that the mouse pointer information contained in the array is relative to the current form (THISFORM). If this option is included, the second array row always contains an object reference to the current form, and the third and fourth rows contain the mouse pointer coordinates relative to the current form.

Remarks

AMOUSEOBJ( ) can also be used to determine where the mouse pointer is positioned during design time. The following table lists the design time element and the values contained in each row of the array:

Design-time element	Array contents
Form and Class Designers	Row 1 – Object reference to the control. Row 2 – Object reference to the form. Row 3 – Mouse pointer horizontal (X) coordinate relative to the form. Row 4 – Mouse pointer vertical (Y) coordinate relative to the form.
Project Manager	Row 1 – Object reference to the project. Row 2 – Object reference to the project. Row 3 – Zero. Row 4 – Zero.
Visual FoxPro Desktop	Row 1 – Object reference to the desktop. Row 2 – Object reference to the desktop. Row 3 – Mouse pointer horizontal (X) coordinate relative to the desktop. Row 4 – Mouse pointer vertical (Y) coordinate relative to the desktop.

AMOUSEOBJ( ) returns 4 (the number of rows in the array) if the mouse pointer is positioned over an area listed above. If the mouse pointer is positioned over an area other than those listed above, AMOUSEOBJ( ) returns zero and if the array you specify already exists, it remains unchanged. If the array you specify doesn't exist, it isn't created.

See Also

MCOL( ), MROW( ), SYS(1270) – Object Location

ANSITOOEM( ) Function

Included for backward compatibility. Use GETCP( ) instead.

APPEND Command

Adds one or more new records to the end of a table.

Syntax

APPEND [BLANK]
    [IN *nWorkArea* | *cTableAlias*]
    [NOMENU]

Arguments

BLANK

    Adds one blank record to the end of the current table. Visual FoxPro does not open an editing window when you issue APPEND BLANK.

    You can edit the new record with BROWSE, CHANGE, or EDIT.

IN *nWorkArea*

    Specifies the work area of the table to which a new record is appended.

IN *cTableAlias*

    Specifies the alias of the table to which a new record is appended.

    If you omit *nWorkArea* and *cTableAlias*, a new record is appended to the table in the currently selected work area. If you issue APPEND, a blank record is added to the table you specify with *nWorkArea* or *cTableAlias* and the table is automatically selected. If you issue APPEND BLANK, a blank record is added to the table you specify with *nWorkArea* or *cTableAlias* and the table is not selected.

NOMENU

    Specifies that the Table menu title is removed from the system menu bar, preventing changes to the format of the editing window.

Remarks

When you issue APPEND or APPEND BLANK and a table isn't open in the currently selected work area, the Open dialog appears so that you can choose a table to which you can append records.

APPEND opens an editing window so you can enter data into one or more new records. When you add a new record, Visual FoxPro updates any indexes that are open.

Example

The following example uses APPEND BLANK to create a table with 10 records containing random values, then displays the maximum and minimum values in the table.

```
CLOSE DATABASES
CREATE TABLE Random (cValue N(3))
FOR nItem = 1 TO 10  && Append 10 records
   APPEND BLANK
   REPLACE cValue WITH 1 + 100 * RAND( )  && Insert random values
ENDFOR

CLEAR
LIST  && Display the values
gnMaximum = 1  && Initialize minimum value
gnMinimum = 100  && Initialize maximum value
SCAN
   gnMinimum = MIN(gnMinimum, cValue)
   gnMaximum = MAX(gnMaximum, cValue)
ENDSCAN
? 'The minimum value is: ', gnMinimum  && Display minimum value
? 'The maximum value is: ', gnMaximum  && Display maximum value
```

See Also

APPEND FROM ARRAY, BROWSE, CHANGE, EDIT, INSERT – SQL, REPLACE

APPEND FROM Command

Adds records to the end of the currently selected table from another file.

Syntax

APPEND FROM *FileName* | ?
    [FIELDS *FieldList*]
    [FOR *lExpression*]
    [[TYPE] [DELIMITED [WITH *Delimiter* | WITH BLANK | WITH TAB
    | WITH CHARACTER *Delimiter*]
    | DIF | FW2 | MOD | PDOX | RPD | SDF | SYLK
      | WK1 | WK3 | WKS | WR1 | WRK | CVS
      | XLS | XL5 [SHEET *cSheetName*] | XL8 [SHEET *cSheetName*]]]
    [AS *nCodePage*]

Arguments

FileName

Specifies the name of the file to append from. If you don't include a file name extension, a Visual FoxPro table and a default extension .dbf is assumed. If you are appending from a Visual FoxPro table, records in the table that are marked for deletion are appended, regardless of the SET DELETED setting.

?

Displays the Open dialog box, from which you can choose a table to append from.

FIELDS *FieldList*

Specifies to which fields data is appended.

FOR *lExpression*

Appends a new record for each record in the currently selected table for which *lExpression* evaluates to true (.T.). Records are appended until the end of the currently selected table is reached. If you omit FOR, the entire source file is appended to the currently selected table.

TYPE

Specifies the source file type of the file you are appending from. Although you must specify a file type if the file you are appending from isn't a Visual FoxPro table, you need not include the TYPE key word. You can append from a wide variety of different file types including delimited ASCII text files, in which you can specify a field delimiter.

If the source file you are appending from doesn't have the usual default file extension for that type of file, the source file name must include the file's extension. For example, Microsoft Excel worksheets normally have an .xls extension. If the Microsoft Excel worksheet you append from has an extension other than the expected .xls, be sure to specify the extension.

> **Note** When you are appending from a worksheet, the data in the worksheet must be stored in a row-major order rather than a column-major order. This allows the appended worksheet data to match the table structure.

DELIMITED

Specifies that the source file from which data is appended to the current Visual FoxPro table is a delimited file. A delimited file is an ASCII text file in which each record ends with a carriage return and line feed. Field contents are by default assumed to be separated from each other by commas (do not include extra spaces before or after the commas), and character field values to be additionally delimited by double quotation marks. For example:

```
"Smith",9999999,"TELEPHONE"
```

The file extension is assumed to be .txt for all delimited files.

You can import dates from delimited files if the dates are in proper date format. The date format defaults to mm/dd/yy. Including the century portion of a date is optional. Visual FoxPro will import a date, such as 12/25/95, that doesn't include the century and assumes the date is in the twentieth century. Date delimiters can be any non-numeric character except the delimiter that separates the fields in the delimited file.

Dates in other formats can be imported if their formats match date formats available in SET DATE. To import dates that are not in the default format, issue SET DATE with the proper date format before using APPEND FROM. To test whether a date format can be successfully imported, use it with CTOD( ). If the date is acceptable to CTOD( ), the date will import properly.

DELIMITED WITH *Delimiter*

Indicates that character fields are separated by a character other than the quotation mark.

DELIMITED WITH BLANK

Specifies files that contain fields separated by spaces instead of commas.

DELIMITED WITH TAB

Specifies files that contain fields separated by tabs rather than commas.

DELIMITED WITH CHARACTER *Delimiter*

Specifies files that contain fields all enclosed by the character specified with *Delimiter*. If *Delimiter* is a semicolon (the character used in Visual FoxPro to indicate command line continuation), enclose the semicolon in quotation marks. You can also specify the BLANK and TAB keywords for *Delimiter*.

The WITH *Delimiter* clause can be combined with the WITH CHARACTER clause. For example, the following command adds records from a text file with character fields enclosed by underscores and all fields delimited from each other with asterisks:

```
APPEND FROM mytxt.txt DELIMITED WITH _ ;
   WITH CHARACTER *
```

DIF

Include DIF to import data from a VisiCalc .dif (Data Interchange Format) file. Vectors (columns) become fields in the currently selected table and tuples (rows) become records. DIF file names are assumed to have a .dif extension.

FW2

Include FW2 to import data from a file created by Framework II. FW2 file names are assumed to have a .fw2 extension.

MOD

Include MOD to import data from a Microsoft Multiplan version 4.01 file. MOD files are created by Microsoft Multiplan version 4.01, and are assumed to have a .mod extension.

PDOX

> Include PDOX to import data from a Paradox version 3.5 or 4.0 database file. Paradox file names are assumed to have a .db extension.

RPD

> Include RPD to import data from a file created by RapidFile version 1.2. RapidFile file names are assumed to have an .rpd extension.

SDF

> Include SDF to import data from a System Data Format file. An SDF file is an ASCII text file in which records have a fixed length and end with a carriage return and line feed. Fields are not delimited. The file name extension is assumed to be .txt for SDF files.

SYLK

> Include SYLK to import data from a SYLK (Symbolic Link) interchange format file. SYLK files are used in Microsoft MultiPlan. Columns in the SYLK file become fields in the Visual FoxPro table and rows become records. SYLK file names have no extension.

WK1

> Include WK1 to import data from a Lotus 1-2-3 version 2.x spreadsheet. Each column from the spreadsheet becomes a field in the table; each spreadsheet row becomes a record in the table. A .WK1 file name extension is assigned to a spreadsheet created in Lotus 1-2-3 revision 2.x.

WK3

> Include WK3 to import data from a Lotus 1-2-3 spreadsheet. Each column from the spreadsheet becomes a field in the table; each spreadsheet row becomes a record in the table. A .wk3 file name extension is assigned to a spreadsheet created in Lotus 1-2-3 revision 3.x.

WKS

> Include WKS to import data from a Lotus 1-2-3 revision 1-A spreadsheet. Each column from the spreadsheet becomes a field in the table; each spreadsheet row becomes a record in the table. A .wks file name extension is assigned to a spreadsheet created in Lotus 1-2-3 revision 1-A.

WR1

> Include WR1 to import data from a Lotus Symphony version 1.1 or 1.2 spreadsheet. Each column from the spreadsheet becomes a field in the table and each spreadsheet row becomes a record in the table. A .wr1 file name extension is assigned to a spreadsheet created in Symphony versions 1.1 or 1.2.

WRK

> Include WRK to import data from a Lotus Symphony version 1.0 spreadsheet. Each column from the spreadsheet becomes a field in the table and each spreadsheet row becomes a record in the table. A .wrk file name extension is assigned to a spreadsheet created in Symphony version 1.0.

CVS

Include CVS to import data from a comma separated value file. A CSV file has field names as the first line in the file; the field names are ignored when the file is imported.

XLS

Include XLS to import data from a Microsoft Excel worksheet. Each column from the worksheet becomes a field in the table and each worksheet row becomes a record in the table. Worksheet files created in Microsoft Excel are given an .xls file name extension.

XL5

Include XL5 to import data from Microsoft Excel version 5.0. Columns from the worksheet become fields in the table; the worksheet rows become records in the table. Worksheet files created in Microsoft Excel have an .xls extension.

If you omit the SHEET clause, the data in Sheet1 is imported. To import data from a specific sheet, include the SHEET keyword and specify the sheet name with *cSheetName*.

XL8

Include XL8 to import data from Microsoft Excel 97. Columns from the worksheet become fields in the table; the worksheet rows become records in the table. Worksheet files created in Microsoft Excel have an .xls extension.

If you omit the SHEET clause, the data in Sheet1 is imported. To import data from a specific sheet, include the SHEET keyword and specify the sheet name with *cSheetName*.

AS *nCodePage*

Specifies the code page of the source table or file. Visual FoxPro copies the contents of the source table or file and, as it copies the data, automatically converts the data to the code page of the current table.

If you specify a value for *nCodePage* that is not supported, Visual FoxPro generates an error message. You can use GETCP( ) for *nCodePage* to display the Code Page dialog box, allowing you to specify a code page for the appended table or file.

If you omit AS *nCodePage* and Visual FoxPro cannot determine the code page of the source table or file, Visual FoxPro copies the contents of the source table or file. As it copies the data, it automatically converts the data to the current Visual FoxPro code page. If SET CPDIALOG is ON, the table in the currently selected work area is marked with a code page. If you're appending from a table not marked with a code page, the Code Page dialog is displayed, allowing you to choose the code page of the table from which you're appending. The current Visual FoxPro code page can be determined with CPCURRENT( ).

If you omit AS *nCodePage* and Visual FoxPro can determine the code page of the table or file being appended, Visual FoxPro copies the contents of the appended table or file. As it copies the data, it automatically converts the data to the code page of the currently selected table.

If *nCodePage* is 0, Visual FoxPro assumes that the code page of the table or file being appended is the same as the code page of the currently selected table. No conversion to the current Visual FoxPro code page occurs.

Remarks

If the file from which you append is a Visual FoxPro table or a table created in an earlier version of FoxPro, a .dbf extension is assumed. If the Visual FoxPro table or the table created in an earlier version of FoxPro doesn't have a .dbf extension, you must specify its extension. If the file is not a Visual FoxPro table or a table created in an earlier version of FoxPro, you must specify the type of file from which you append.

Before you can append from a table created in dBASE IV or dBASE V that contains a memo field, you must first open the table in Visual FoxPro with USE. When you are prompted to convert the file, choose Yes.

If you append from a Visual FoxPro table or a table created in an earlier version of FoxPro, the table you append from can be open in another work area. Records marked for deletion in the table you are appending from are unmarked once the records are appended.

Use the DBF( ) function to append from a temporary read-only cursor created by a SELECT – SQL command. Include the name of the cursor in the DBF( ) function as in the following example:

```
APPEND FROM DBF('<Cursor Name>')
```

Example

In the following example, the customer table is opened, its structure is copied to a table called backup, and backup is then opened. Visual FoxPro then appends all records from Finland from the customer table. These records are then copied to a new delimited file called TEMP.TXT.

```
CLOSE DATABASES
OPEN DATABASE (HOME(2) + 'Data\testdata')
USE customer   && Open customer table
COPY STRUCTURE TO backup
USE backup

APPEND FROM customer FOR country = 'Finland'
COPY TO temp TYPE DELIMITED
MODIFY FILE temp.txt
USE
DELETE FILE backup.dbf
DELETE FILE temp.txt
```

See Also

COPY FILE, COPY TO, EXPORT, GETCP( ), IMPORT

APPEND FROM ARRAY Command

Adds one record to the currently selected table for each row in an array and fills each record with data from the corresponding array row.

Syntax

APPEND FROM ARRAY *ArrayName*
    [FOR *lExpression*]
    [FIELDS *FieldList*
    | FIELDS LIKE *Skeleton*
    | FIELDS EXCEPT *Skeleton*]

Arguments

ArrayName
> Specifies the name of the array that contains the data to be copied to the new records. New records are added to the table until all rows in the array are appended.

FOR *lExpression*
> Specifies a condition for appending records from the array. *lExpression* must contain the name of a target field in its conditional expression.
>
> Before a row of the array is appended to a record in the table, the array element corresponding to the target field specified in *lExpression* is checked to determine whether that array element meets the condition in *lExpression*. If the array element satisfies the condition, a record is appended.
>
> If the array element does not satisfy the condition, the array row is not appended and the next row in the array is checked to determine whether it meets the condition.

FIELDS *FieldList*
> Specifies that only the fields in *FieldList* are updated from the array. The first field in the list is updated with the contents of the first element in the array, the second field is updated from the second element, and so on.

FIELDS LIKE *Skeleton*
> Specifies that fields that match the field skeleton *Skeleton* are updated from the array.

FIELDS EXCEPT *Skeleton*
> Specifies that all fields except those that match the field skeleton *Skeleton* are updated from the array.
>
> The field skeleton *Skeleton* supports wildcards. For example, to specify that all fields that begin with the letters A and P are updated from the array, use the following:

```
APPEND FROM ARRAY aMyArray FIELDS LIKE A*,P*
```

The LIKE clause can be combined with the EXCEPT clause:

```
APPEND FROM ARRAY aMyArray FIELDS LIKE A*,P* EXCEPT PARTNO*
```

Remarks

Memo and general fields are ignored in APPEND FROM ARRAY. When a table is open for shared use, APPEND FROM ARRAY locks the table header while records are being added.

If the array is one-dimensional, APPEND FROM ARRAY adds one record to the table. The contents of the first array element fill the first field of the newly added record, the contents of the second element of the array fill the second field of the record, and so on.

If the one-dimensional array has more elements than the table has fields, the additional elements are ignored. If the table has more fields than the array has elements, the additional fields are initialized to the default empty value. Here are the default empty values for each field type:

Field type	Default value
Character	Spaces
Numeric	0
Currency	0
Float	0
Integer	0
Double	0
Date	Empty Date (e.g. CTOD(""))
DateTime	Empty DateTime (e.g. CTOT(""))
Logical	False (.F.)
Memo	Empty (no contents)

If the array is two-dimensional, APPEND FROM ARRAY adds a new record to the table for each row in the array. For example, if the array has four rows, four new records are appended to the table.

The contents of the first array column fill the first field of the newly added records, the second array column fills the second field of the new records, and so on. For example, if the array has four rows and three columns, elements from the first array column fill the first field in each of the four new records appended to the table.

If the two-dimensional array has more columns than the table has fields, the additional columns are ignored. If the table has more fields than the array has columns, the additional fields are initialized to empty values.

APPEND FROM ARRAY can fill a field even if the data type of the corresponding array element doesn't match the data type of the field, provided that the array element data is compatible with the data type of the corresponding field. If the data isn't compatible, the field is initialized to an empty value.

Example

This example creates a table and then uses APPEND FROM ARRAY to append a record to the new table.

```
LOCAL ARRAY aNewRec(3)

* Create the table
CREATE TABLE Test FREE  (Object C(10), Color C(16), SqFt n(6,2))
SCATTER TO aNewRec BLANK  && Create a new array from the table
aNewRec[1]="Box"         && Fill the the array
aNewRec[2]="Red"
aNewRec[3]=12.5

APPEND FROM ARRAY aNewRec   && Add record containing array contents
            && to the table
```

See Also

APPEND, COPY TO ARRAY, DIMENSION, GATHER, SCATTER

APPEND GENERAL Command

Imports an OLE object from a file and places it into a general field.

Syntax

APPEND GENERAL *GeneralFieldName*
    [FROM *FileName*]
    [DATA *cExpression*]
    [LINK]
    [CLASS *OLEClassName*]

Arguments

GeneralFieldName
    Specifies the name of the general field in which the OLE object is placed. You can specify a general field in a table open in a noncurrent work area by including the table alias with the field name.

FROM *FileName*
    Specifies the file containing the OLE object. You must include the entire file name, including its extension. If the file is located in a directory other than the current default directory, include the path with the file name.

DATA *cExpression*
    Specifies a character expression that is evaluated and passed as a character string to the OLE object in the general field. The OLE object must be capable of receiving and processing the string. For example, you cannot send a character string to a graphics object such as one created using Paintbrush.

LINK
Creates a link between the OLE object and the file that contains the object. The OLE object appears in the general field but the object's definition remains in the file. If you omit LINK, the OLE object is embedded in the general field.

CLASS *OLEClassName*
Specifies an OLE class for an OLE object other than the default class.

> **Tip** You can determine the class for an OLE object by running REGEDIT and double-clicking the OLE object. The class name is listed under Identifier.

You can specify a class name when the file extension for the file containing the OLE object is different from the default extension and you want to force the behavior for the class. If the default extension can be used by multiple Automation servers, include the class to specify a particular server.

Remarks

If an OLE object already exists in the general field, it is replaced with the OLE object from the file. To remove an OLE object from a general field, issue APPEND GENERAL *GeneralFieldName* (*GeneralFieldName* is the name of the general field to clear) without any additional arguments.

For additional information about OLE objects in Visual FoxPro, see Chapter 16, "Adding OLE," in the *Microsoft Visual FoxPro 6.0 Programmer's Guide*.

Example

The following example imports a Microsoft Excel chart in the Excel directory to a general field named mygenfield.

```
CREATE TABLE MyGenTbl (mygenfield G)
APPEND BLANK  && Add a blank record

APPEND GENERAL mygenfield FROM C:\EXCEL\BOOK1.XLS CLASS EXCELCHART
```

See Also

@ ... SAY – Pictures & OLE Objects, MODIFY GENERAL, OLE Bound Control

APPEND MEMO Command

Copies the contents of a text file to a memo field.

Syntax

APPEND MEMO *MemoFieldName* FROM *FileName*
[OVERWRITE] [AS *nCodePage*]

Arguments

MemoFieldName
Specifies the name of the memo field to which the file is appended.

FROM *FileName*
> Specifies the text file whose contents are copied to the memo field. You must include the entire text file name, including its extension.

OVERWRITE
> Replaces the current contents of the memo field with the contents of the file.

AS *nCodePage*
> Specifies the code page of the text file copied to the memo field. Microsoft Visual FoxPro copies the contents of the text file and, as it copies the data to the memo field, automatically converts the data from the code page you specify to the code page of the table containing the memo field. If the table containing the memo field is not marked with a code page, Visual FoxPro automatically converts the data from the code page you specify to the current Visual FoxPro code page.

> If you specify a value for *nCodePage* that is not supported, Visual FoxPro generates an error message. You can use GETCP( ) for *nCodePage* to display the Code Page dialog box, allowing you to specify a code page for the appended table or file.

> If you omit the AS *nCodePage* clause or specify 0 for *nCodePage*, no code page conversion occurs for the text file.

Remarks

The entire text file is appended to the contents of the specified memo field in the current record if overwrite is omitted.

Example

In the following example, the contents of the memo field notes are copied to a file called Test.txt. Test.txt is then appended to the contents of the memo field. Finally, the contents of Test.txt replace the current contents of the memo field.

```
CLOSE DATABASES
OPEN DATABASE (HOME(2) + 'Data\testdata')
USE employee  && Open Employee table
WAIT WINDOW 'Employee notes memo field - press ESC' NOWAIT
MODIFY MEMO notes NOEDIT  && Open the notes memo field
COPY MEMO notes TO test.txt  && Create test file from memo field
WAIT WINDOW 'TEST.TXT text file - press ESC' NOWAIT
MODIFY FILE test.txt NOEDIT && Open the text file
WAIT WINDOW 'Employee notes now appended - press ESC' NOWAIT
APPEND MEMO notes FROM test.txt  && Add contents of text file
MODIFY MEMO notes NOEDIT  && Display memo field again
WAIT WINDOW 'Overwrite Employee notes- press ESC' NOWAIT
APPEND MEMO notes FROM test.txt OVERWRITE  && Replace notes
MODIFY MEMO notes NOEDIT NOWAIT
DELETE FILE test.txt
```

See Also

COPY MEMO, GETCP( )

APPEND PROCEDURES Command

Appends stored procedures in a text file to the stored procedures in the current database.

Syntax

APPEND PROCEDURES FROM *FileName*
   [AS *nCodePage*] [OVERWRITE]

Arguments

FileName
   Specifies the name of a text file from which the stored procedures are appended.

AS *nCodePage*
   Specifies the code page of the text file from which the stored procedures are appended. Visual FoxPro copies the contents of the text file and, as it does so, automatically converts the contents of the text file to the code page you specify.

   If you specify a value for *nCodePage* that is not supported, Visual FoxPro generates an error message. You can use GETCP( ) for *nCodePage* to display the Code Page dialog box, allowing you to specify a code page for the text file from which the stored procedures are appended.

   If you omit AS *nCodePage*, Visual FoxPro copies the contents of the text file from which the stored procedures are appended and, as it does so, automatically converts the contents of the text file to the current Visual FoxPro code page. The current Visual FoxPro code page can be determined with CPCURRENT( ).

   If *nCodePage* is 0, Visual FoxPro assumes that the code page of the text file from which the stored procedures are appended is the same as the code page of the current database, and that no conversion to the current Visual FoxPro code page occurs.

OVERWRITE
   Specifies that the current stored procedures in the database are overwritten by those in the text file. If you omit OVERWRITE, the current stored procedures in the database are not overwritten, and the stored procedures in the text file are appended to the current stored procedures.

Remarks

Use APPEND PROCEDURES to programmatically modify stored procedures in a database. A database must be open and current when APPEND PROCEDURES is issued; otherwise Visual FoxPro generates an error message.

Example

The following example opens the testdata database. A temporary table named mytable with a single memo field is created, and REPLACE is used to place a stored procedure named MyProcedure in the memo field. COPY MEMO is used to create a temporary text file named Mytemp.txt that contains the contents of the memo field.

APPEND PROCEDURES is used to append the stored procedure from the temporary text file to the database. DISPLAY PROCEDURES displays the stored procedures in the database and then the temporary table and text file are erased.

Note To view or edit stored procedures through the user interface, use the Database Designer.

```
CLOSE DATABASES
* Open the testdata database
OPEN DATABASE (HOME(2) + 'Data\testdata')

* Create a free, temporary table with one memo field called mProcedure
CREATE TABLE mytable FREE (mProcedure M)
APPEND BLANK           && Add a blank record to mytable

* Add PROCEDURE command, name, and carriage return/linefeed to
* memo field
REPLACE mProcedure WITH "PROCEDURE MyProcedure" + CHR(13) + CHR(10)

* Copy contents of memo field to temporary file
COPY MEMO mProcedure TO mytemp.txt
USE               && Close the temporary table

APPEND PROCEDURES FROM mytemp.txt   && Copy procedure to the database
CLEAR

* Display the procedures associated with the current database
DISPLAY PROCEDURES
DELETE FILE mytable.dbf     && Erase temporary table
DELETE FILE mytable.fpt     && Erase temporary table memo file
DELETE FILE mytemp.txt      && Erase temporary text file
```

See Also

COPY PROCEDURES, CREATE TRIGGER, DISPLAY PROCEDURES, MODIFY PROCEDURE, OPEN DATABASE, PROCEDURE, SET DATABASE

Application Object

An object created for each instance of Visual FoxPro that exposes a set of Visual FoxPro properties and methods.

Syntax

Application.*PropertyName*[= *eValue*]

– or –

Application.*Method*

Arguments

PropertyName
   Specifies a property for the application object.

eValue
   Specifies a value for the property.

Method
   Specifies a method to execute for the application object.

Remarks

Visual FoxPro is an automation server, allowing other applications such as Microsoft Excel or Visual Basic to remotely start and manipulate Visual FoxPro through properties and methods. The Application object is also available from within an instance of Visual FoxPro.

The syntax used by an application to create an instance of an automation server such as Visual FoxPro is typically unique to the application. Consult the application's documentation for the proper syntax to create an instance of an automation server and then manipulate the instance through the properties and methods.

Properties

ActiveForm	Application	AutoYield
Caption	DefaultFilePath	FullName
Height Property	Left	Name
OLERequestPendingTimeout	OLEServerBusyRaiseError	OLEServerBusyTimeout
Parent	StartMode	StatusBar
Top	Version	Visible
Width		

Methods

| DataToClip | DoCmd | Eval |
| Help | Quit | RequestData |

Example

You can start another instance of Visual FoxPro from within Visual FoxPro with the following command:

```
oNewInstance = CREATEOBJECT('VisualFoxPro.Application')
```

A new instance of Visual FoxPro is not visible when it is created; the following command makes the new instance visible:

```
oNewInstance.Visible = .T.
```

See Also

CREATEOBJECT( )

Application Property

Provides a reference to the Application object containing an object. Not available at design time; read-only at run time.

Syntax

Object.Application.*Property* [= *Setting*]

– or –

Object.Application.*Method*

Settings

Property
    Specifies any property of the Application object or the _VFP system variable; for example, the Caption property.

Setting
    The existing or new setting of the Property.

Method
    Specifies any method of the Application object or the _VFP system variable; for example, the DoCmd method.

Remarks

Use the Application property to access an Application object's properties and methods from an object contained by the application. The Application property can also be used with the _VFP system variable to access properties and methods for the current instance of Visual FoxPro.

Applies To

ActiveDoc, CheckBox, Column, ComboBox, CommandButton, CommandGroup, Container, Control, Cursor, Custom, DataEnvironment, EditBox, Form, FormSet, Grid, Header, Hyperlink, Image, Label, Line, ListBox, OLE Bound Control, OLE Container Control, OptionButton, OptionGroup, Page, PageFrame, ProjectHook Object, Relation, _SCREEN, Separator, Shape, Spinner, TextBox, Timer, ToolBar

See Also

CREATEOBJECT( )

APRINTERS( ) Function

Places the names of printers currently installed in the Windows Print Manager into a variable array.

Syntax

APRINTERS(*ArrayName*)

Returns

Numeric

Arguments

ArrayName

Specifies the name of the array containing the names of the installed printers and their ports. If the array you include doesn't exist, Visual FoxPro automatically creates the array. If the array exists and isn't large enough to contain all the printer information, Visual FoxPro automatically increases the size of the array to accommodate the information. If the array is larger than necessary, Visual FoxPro truncates the array. If the array exists and APRINTERS( ) returns 0 because no printers are installed, the array remains unchanged. If the array doesn't exist and APRINTERS( ) returns 0, the array isn't created.

Remarks

APRINTERS( ) creates a two-dimensional array. The first column of the array contains the names of the currently installed printers, and the second column contains the ports to which the printers are connected.

APRINTERS( ) returns the number of installed printers. If no printer is installed, it returns 0.

Visual FoxPro obtains the names of the installed printers and their ports from Windows. However, Visual FoxPro doesn't check to see if the printers are actually connected to your machine.

Example

The following example uses APRINTERS( ) to create an array named gaPrinters that contains the names and ports of installed printers. The printers and their ports are then displayed. If no printer is installed, a message is displayed.

```
IF APRINTERS(gaPrinters) > 0  && If there are installed printer drivers
    CLEAR  && Clear the main Visual FoxPro window
    DISPLAY MEMORY LIKE gaPrinters && Display the printers and ports
ELSE  && Otherwise, no printer are installed
    WAIT WINDOW 'No printers installed.'
ENDIF
```

See Also

GETPRINTER( ), PRINTSTATUS( ), PRTINFO( ), SET PRINTER

ASC( ) Function

Returns the ANSI value for the leftmost character in a character expression.

Syntax

ASC(*cExpression*)

Returns

Numeric

Arguments

cExpression
Specifies the character expression containing the character whose ANSI value ASC( ) returns. Any characters after the first character in *cExpression* are ignored by ASC( ).

Remarks

ASC( ) returns the position of the character in the character table of the current code page. Every character has a unique ANSI value in the range from 0 to 255.

Example

The following example displays the characters A through J and uses ASC( ) to display their corresponding ANSI values.

```
STORE 'ABCDEFGHIJ' TO gcANSI  && 10 characters
CLEAR
FOR nCOUNT = 1 TO 10
    ? SUBSTR(gcANSI, nCount,1)  && Display a character
    ?? ASC(SUBSTR(gcANSI, nCount)) && Display ANSI value
ENDFOR
```

See Also

CHR( )

ASCAN( ) Function

Searches an array for an element containing the same data and data type as an expression.

Syntax

ASCAN(*ArrayName*, *eExpression* [, *nStartElement* [, *nElementsSearched*]])

Returns

Numeric

Arguments

ArrayName
Specifies the name of the array to search.

eExpression
Specifies the general expression to search for.

nStartElement
Specifies the element number at which the search begins. The element number you specify is included in the search. If you omit *nStartElement*, the entire array is searched by default.

nElementsSearched
Specifies the number of elements that are searched. If you omit *nStartElement* and *nElementsSearched*, the search begins with the first array element and continues to the last array element.

> **Note** You can refer to an element in a two-dimensional variable array in one of two ways. The first method uses two subscripts to specify the row and column position of the element in the array; the other method uses an element number. This function and others that manipulate two-dimensional arrays require element numbers (*nStartElement* and *nElementsSearched*). Use AELEMENT( ) to return the element number from row and column subscripts in a two-dimensional array.

Remarks

If a match is found, ASCAN( ) returns the number of the element containing the expression. If a match cannot be found, ASCAN( ) returns 0.

The criteria for a successful match of character data are determined by the setting of SET EXACT. If SET EXACT is ON, an element must match the search expression character for character and have the same length. If SET EXACT is OFF, and an element and search expression match until the end of the expression is reached, the match is successful.

For more information on match criteria for character strings, see the string comparison table in the SET EXACT Command, later in this language reference.

Example

The following example creates and fills an array with company names, and then uses ASCAN( ) to search for a particular company name. If the company name is found, it is removed from the array.

```
CLOSE DATABASES
OPEN DATABASE (HOME(2) + 'Data\testdata')
USE customer       && Open customer table
SELECT company FROM customer ;
    WHERE country = 'UK' ;
    INTO ARRAY gaCompanies
gnCount = _TALLY
gcName = 'Seven Seas Imports'
CLEAR
DISPLAY MEMORY LIKE gaCompanies*
gnPos = ASCAN(gaCompanies, gcName) && Search for company
IF gnPos != 0
    *** Company found, remove it from the array ***
    = ADEL(gaCompanies, gnPos)
    gnCount = gnCount - 1
ENDIF
DISPLAY MEMORY LIKE gaCompanies
```

See Also

ACOPY( ), ADEL( ), ADIR( ), AELEMENT( ), AFIELDS( ), AINS( ), ASORT( ), ASUBSCRIPT( ), DIMENSION, SET EXACT

_ASCIICOLS System Variable

Specifies the number of columns in a text file created with REPORT ... TO FILE ASCII.

Syntax

_ASCIICOLS = *nExpression*

Arguments

nExpression
    Specifies the number of columns in the text file. The default value is 80.

Remarks

Include the TO FILE ASCII clause in REPORT to create a text file.

See Also

_ASCIIROWS, CREATE REPORT, MODIFY REPORT, REPORT

_ASCIIROWS System Variable

Specifies the number of rows in a text file created with REPORT ... TO FILE ASCII.

Syntax

_ASCIIROWS = *nExpression*

Arguments

nExpression
    Specifies the number of rows in the text file. The default value is 63.

Remarks

Include the TO FILE ASCII clause in REPORT to create a text file.

See Also

_ASCIICOLS, CREATE REPORT, MODIFY REPORT, REPORT

ASELOBJ( ) Function

Places object references to currently selected controls in the active Form Designer into a variable array.

Syntax

ASELOBJ(*ArrayName*, [1 | 2])

Returns

Numeric

Arguments

ArrayName
    Specifies the name of the array containing the object references of the
    currently selected controls. If the array you specify doesn't exist, Visual FoxPro
    automatically creates the array. If the array exists and isn't large enough to
    contain all the control information, Visual FoxPro automatically increases
    the size of the array to accommodate the information. If the array is larger
    than necessary, Visual FoxPro truncates the array. If the array exists and
    ASELOBJ( ) returns 0 because no controls are currently selected, the array
    remains unchanged. If the array doesn't exist and ASELOBJ( ) returns 0, the
    array isn't created.

1

Creates a one-element array containing an object reference to the container for the currently selected control. For example, if the currently selected control is a spinner on a form, the array contains an element with the value "FORM." Include 1 when issuing ASELOBJ( ) from within the Command window. Note that if a page frame is selected, ASELOBJ( ) returns the name of the current page.

2

Specifies that Visual FoxPro creates a one-element array containing an object reference to the DataEnvironment object for the form. The DataEnvironment object allows you to determine the data environment properties for the form.

Remarks

ASELOBJ( ) creates a one-dimensional array containing object references to the currently selected controls in the active Form Designer and returns the number of currently selected controls. If no controls are currently selected and the optional 1 argument is omitted, ASELOBJ( ) returns 0 and the array isn't created. ASELOBJ( ) does not recognize the form as the selected control if there are no controls on the form. If no controls are currently selected and the optional 1 argument is included, ASELOBJ( ) returns 1.

You can use ASELOBJ( ) to create your own control builders.

Example

Before running the following example, open a new form in the Form Designer and add one or more controls with Caption properties, such as a Label or CommandButton, to the form. Select a number of these controls and then run the example. ASELOBJ( ) displays the names of the selected controls, and then changes the captions of the selected controls.

```
gnobjects = ASELOBJ(gaSelected)      && Create array of control names
IF gnobjects > 0  && 0 indicates no controls selected
   CLEAR
   DISPLAY MEMORY LIKE gaSelected      && Displays selected controls
   FOR nCnt = 1 TO gnobjects
      ? gaSelected(nCnt).Caption + ' => New Caption ' ;
         + LTRIM(STR(nCnt))  && Display old and new caption
      gaSelected(nCnt).Caption = 'New Caption ' ;
         + ALLTRIM(STR(nCnt))  && Assign new caption
   NEXT
ENDIF
```

See Also

CREATE FORM, DataEnvironment Object

ASIN( ) Function

Returns in radians the arc sine of a numeric expression.

Syntax

ASIN(*nExpression*)

Returns

Numeric

Arguments

nExpression

Specifies the numeric expression whose arc sine ASIN( ) returns. The value of *nExpression* can range from +1 through –1, and the value ASIN( ) returns can range from –pi/2 through +pi/2 (–1.57079 to 1.57079). The number of decimal places in the display of the result can be specified with SET DECIMALS.

Remarks

Use RTOD( ) to convert radians to degrees.

Example

```
CLEAR
? RTOD(ASIN(0))  && Returns 0.00
STORE 1 to gnArcAngle
? RTOD(ASIN(gnArcAngle))  && Returns 90.00
? RTOD(ASIN(SQRT(2)/2))  && Returns 45.00
```

See Also

RTOD( ), SET DECIMALS, SIN( )

ASORT( ) Function

Sorts elements in an array in ascending or descending order.

Syntax

ASORT(*ArrayName* [, *nStartElement* [, *nNumberSorted* [, *nSortOrder*]]])

Returns

Numeric

Arguments

ArrayName

Specifies the name of the array to sort.

nStartElement

Specifies the starting element of the sort. If you omit *nStartElement*, the array is sorted starting with the first array element by default. If the array is one-dimensional, the sort includes *nStartElement*. If the array is two-dimensional, the starting element *nStartElement* determines both the row where the sort begins and the column that determines the sort order of the rows.

> **Note** You can refer to an element in a two-dimensional array in one of two ways. The first method uses two subscripts to specify the row and column position of the element in the array; the other method uses an element number. This function and others that manipulate two-dimensional arrays require element numbers (in ASORT( ) the numeric expressions *nStartElement* and *nNumberSorted*). You can use AELEMENT( ) to return the element number from row and column subscripts in a two-dimensional array.

The following example illustrates that the starting element *nStartElement* determines how the rows in a two-dimensional array are sorted. A small array named `gaArray` is created and sorted twice. The first sort begins with the first element of `gaArray`; the rows are sorted based on the values contained in the first column of the array. The second sort begins with the fourth element of `gaArray`; the rows are sorted based on the values contained in the second column.

The first sort begins with the first row. The second sort begins with the second row. You can use DISPLAY MEMORY to display the contents of the array; in these examples tables are used to graphically display the results of the sorts.

These commands create the array named `gaArray`:

```
DIMENSION gaArray(3,2)
gaArray(1) = 'G'
gaArray(2) = 'A'
gaArray(3) = 'C'
gaArray(4) = 'Z'
gaArray(5) = 'B'
gaArray(6) = 'N'
```

`gaArray` looks like this:

	Column 1	Column 2
Row 1	G	A
Row 2	C	Z
Row 3	B	N

The array is then sorted by ASORT( ) starting with the first element (1,1) in the array. The elements in the first column are placed in ascending order by rearranging the rows of the array.

```
=ASORT(gaArray,1)
```

Note the new order of the rows:

	Column 1	Column 2
Row 1	B	N
Row 2	C	Z
Row 3	G	A

The array is then sorted starting with the fourth element (2,2) in the array. The elements in the second column are placed in order by rearranging the array rows.

```
=ASORT(gaArray,4)
```

Note the difference in the order of the rows:

	Column 1	Column 2
Row 1	B	N
Row 2	G	A
Row 3	C	Z

nNumberSorted

Specifies the number of elements that are sorted in a one-dimensional array, or the number of rows that are sorted in a two-dimensional array. For example, if the array is one-dimensional and *nStartElement* is 2, indicating that the sort starts with the second array element, and *nNumberSorted* is 3, indicating that the sort should include three elements, the second, third and fourth array elements are sorted. If *nNumberSorted* is –1 or is omitted, all array elements from the starting element *nStartElement* through the last element in the array are sorted.

If the array is two-dimensional, *nNumberSorted* designates the number of rows to sort, beginning with the row containing the starting element *nStartElement*. For example, if *nStartElement* is 2 and *nNumberSorted* is 3, the row containing the second array element and the following two rows are sorted. If *nNumberSorted* is –1 or is omitted, all array rows beginning with the row containing the starting element *nStartElement* through the last array row are sorted.

nSortOrder

Specifies the sort order (ascending or descending) for the elements in the array. By default, array elements are sorted in ascending order. If *nSortOrder* is 0 or is omitted, the array elements are sorted in ascending order. If *nSortOrder* is 1 or any nonzero value, the array elements are sorted in descending order.

Remarks

All elements included in the sort must be of the same data type. One-dimensional arrays are sorted by their elements; two-dimensional arrays are sorted by their rows. When a two-dimensional array is sorted, the order of the rows in the array is changed so that the elements in a column of the array are in ascending or descending order.

If the sort is successful, 1 is returned; otherwise −1 is returned.

Example

The following example copies the contact field from the customer table to an array named gaContact. The first 20 contacts in the array are displayed, the array is sorted, and the contacts are displayed again in sorted order.

```
CLOSE DATABASES
OPEN DATABASE (HOME(2) + 'Data\testdata')
USE Customer  && Open customer table

COUNT TO gnCount  && Number of contacts
DIMENSION gaContact(gnCount,1)  && Create a contact array
COPY TO ARRAY gaContact FIELD contact    && Fill the array

CLEAR
? 'Contact names:'
?
FOR nCount = 1 TO 20
    ? gaContact(nCount)  && Display first 20 contacts
ENDFOR
= ASORT(gaContact)     && Sort the array

?
? 'Sorted Contact names:'
?
FOR nCount = 1 TO 20
    ? gaContact(nCount)  && Display first 20 contacts, sorted
ENDFOR
```

See Also

ACOPY( ), ADEL( ), ADIR( ), AELEMENT( ), AFIELDS( ), AINS( ), ALEN( ), ASCAN( )

ASSERT Command

Displays a message box when a logical expression evaluates to false (.F.).

Syntax

ASSERT *lExpression* [MESSAGE *cMessageText*]

Arguments

lExpression

Specifies the logical expression that is evaluated. If *lExpression* evaluates to a logical false (.F.), a debugging dialog box is displayed. If *lExpression* evaluates to a logical true (.T.), the dialog box is not displayed.

cMessageText

Specifies the text displayed in the debugging dialog box. If you omit *cMessageText*, the default text is displayed, indicating the line number on which the assertion failed and procedure containing the assertion.

Remarks

This command is ignored if the SET ASSERTS command is set to OFF.

The message box contains Cancel, Debug, Ignore and Ignore All buttons. The following table describes the action performed when each button is chosen.

Button	Action
Debug	Program execution is suspended and the Debugger window is displayed with the Trace window active.
Cancel	Program execution is ended.
Ignore	Program execution continues with the line following the ASSERT command.
Ignore All	Program execution continues with the line following the ASSERT command and ASSERTS is set to OFF. Subsequent ASSERT commands are ignored until ASSERTS is set to ON.

See Also

Debugger Window, SET ASSERTS

ASSIST Command

Included for backward compatibility. Use the DO Command instead.

_ASSIST System Variable

Included for backward compatibility. Use the DO Command instead.

ASUBSCRIPT( ) Function

Returns the row or column subscript of an element from the element's number.

Syntax

ASUBSCRIPT(*ArrayName*, *nElementNumber*, *nSubscript*)

Returns

Numeric

Arguments

ArrayName
Specifies the name of the array.

nElementNumber
Specifies the element number.

nSubscript
Determines if the row or column subscript is returned.

If the array is one-dimensional, include the element number in *nElementNumber* and 1 in *nSubscript*. ASUBSCRIPT( ) identically returns *nElementNumber*.

If the array is two-dimensional, include both the element number *nElementNumber* and a value of 1 or 2 in *nSubscript*. Specifying 1 in *nSubscript* returns the row subscript of the element, and specifying 2 returns the column subscript.

For more information on how to reference elements in an array, see the DIMENSION Command, later in this language reference.

Remarks

You can refer to elements in two-dimensional variable arrays in one of two ways. The first method uses two subscripts to specify the row and column position of the element in the array. The second method uses an element number. Use ASUBSCRIPT( ) to obtain an element's row or column subscript from the element's number.

In the following example, an array with two rows and three columns is created. DISPLAY MEMORY shows the contents of the elements of the array listed in element number order.

```
DIMENSION gaMyArray(2,3)
DISPLAY MEMORY LIKE gaMyArray
GAMYARRAY   Pub   A
    ( 1, 1)   L   .F. (element number 1)
    ( 1, 2)   L   .F. (element number 2)
    ( 1, 3)   L   .F. (element number 3)
    ( 2, 1)   L   .F. (element number 4)
    ( 2, 2)   L   .F. (element number 5)
    ( 2, 3)   L   .F. (element number 6)
```

Each of these commands stores the character string INVOICE to the same array element:

```
STORE 'INVOICE' TO gaMyArray(2, 1)
STORE 'INVOICE' TO gaMyArray(4)
```

In one-dimensional arrays, an element's number is identical to its single row subscript. It isn't necessary to use ASUBSCRIPT( ) with one-dimensional arrays.

See Also

ADEL( ), ADIR( ), AELEMENT( ), AFIELDS( ), AINS( ), ALEN( ), ASCAN( ), ASORT( ), DIMENSION, DISPLAY MEMORY

AT( ) Function

Returns the beginning numeric position of the first occurrence of a character expression or memo field within another character expression or memo field, counting from the leftmost character.

Syntax

AT(*cSearchExpression*, *cExpressionSearched* [, *nOccurrence*])

Returns

Numeric

Arguments

cSearchExpression
Specifies the character expression that AT( ) searches for in *cExpressionSearched*.

cExpressionSearched
Specifies the character expression *cSearchExpression* searches for.

Both *cSearchExpression* and *cExpressionSearched* can be memo fields of any size.

nOccurrence
    Specifies which occurrence (first, second, third, and so on) of *cSearchExpression* is searched for in *cExpressionSearched*. By default, AT( ) searches for the first occurrence of *cSearchExpression* (*nOccurrence* = 1). Including *nOccurrence* lets you search for additional occurrences of *cSearchExpression* in *cExpressionSearched*. AT( ) returns 0 if *nOccurrence* is greater than the number of times *cSearchExpression* occurs in *cExpressionSearched*.

Remarks

AT( ) searches the second character expression for the first occurrence of the first character expression. It then returns an integer indicating the position of the first character in the character expression found. If the character expression isn't found, AT( ) returns 0.

The search performed by AT( ) is case-sensitive. To perform a search that isn't case-sensitive, use ATC( ).

Example

```
STORE 'Now is the time for all good men' TO gcString
STORE 'is the' TO gcFindString
CLEAR
? AT(gcFindString,gcString)   && Displays 5
STORE 'IS' TO gcFindString
? AT(gcFindString,gcString)   && Displays 0, case-sensitive
```

See Also

AT_C( ), ATC( ), ATCLINE( ), ATLINE( ), LEFT( ), RAT( ), RATLINE( ), RIGHT( ), SUBSTR( )

AT_C( ) Function

Returns the beginning numeric position of the first occurrence of a character expression or memo field within another character expression or memo field, counting from the leftmost character.

Syntax

AT_C(*cSearchExpression*, *cExpressionSearched* [, *nOccurrence*])

Returns

Numeric

Arguments

cSearchExpression
    Specifies the character expression that AT_C( ) searches for in *cExpressionSearched*.

cExpressionSearched

Specifies the character expression *cSearchExpression* searches for.

Both *cSearchExpression* and *cExpressionSearched* can be memo fields of any size.

nOccurrence

Specifies which occurrence (first, second, third, and so on) of *cSearchExpression* is searched for in *cExpressionSearched*. By default, AT_C( ) searches for the first occurrence of *cSearchExpression* (*nOccurrence* = 1). Including *nOccurrence* lets you search for additional occurrences of *cSearchExpression* in *cExpressionSearched*. AT_C( ) returns 0 if *nOccurrence* is greater than the number of times *cSearchExpression* occurs in *cExpressionSearched*.

Remarks

AT_C( ) searches the second character expression for the first occurrence of the first character expression. It then returns an integer indicating the position of the first character in the character expression found. If the character expression isn't found, AT_C( ) returns 0.

AT_C( ) is designed for expressions containing double-byte characters. If the expression contains only single-byte characters, AT_C( ) is equivalent to AT( ).

The search performed by AT_C( ) is case-sensitive. To perform a search that isn't case-sensitive, use ATCC( ).

This function is useful for manipulating double-byte character sets for languages such as Hiragana and Katakana.

See Also

ATCC( ), LEFTC( ), RATC( ), RIGHTC( ), SUBSTRC( )

ATAN( ) Function

Returns in radians the arc tangent of a numeric expression.

Syntax

ATAN(*nExpression*)

Returns

Numeric

Arguments

nExpression

Specifies a numeric expression whose arc tangent ATAN( ) returns. *nExpression* can be any value. The value returned by ATAN( ) can range from –pi/2 through +pi/2 (–1.57079 to 1.57079). The number of decimal places displayed in the value returned by ATAN( ) is determined by SET DECIMALS.

Remarks

Use RTOD( ) to convert radians to degrees.

Example

```
CLEAR
? ATAN(0)  && Displays 0.00
STORE PI( )/2 to gnAngle
? ATAN(gnAngle)  && Displays 1.00
? ATAN(PI( )/2)  && Displays 1.00
? ATAN(DTOR(90))  && Displays 1.00
```

See Also

ATN2( ), RTOD( ), SET DECIMALS, TAN( )

ATC( ) Function

Returns the beginning numeric position of the first occurrence of a character expression or memo field within another character expression or memo field, without regard for the case of these two expressions.

Syntax

ATC(*cSearchExpression, cExpressionSearched* [, *nOccurrence*])

Returns

Numeric

Arguments

cSearchExpression
　　Specifies the character expression that ATC( ) searches for in *cExpressionSearched*.

cExpressionSearched
　　Specifies the character expression *cSearchExpression* searches for.

　　Both *cSearchExpression* and *cExpressionSearched* can be memo fields of any size.

nOccurrence
　　Specifies which occurrence (first, second, third, and so on) of *cSearchExpression* is searched for in *cExpressionSearched*. By default, ATC( ) searches for the first occurrence of *cSearchExpression* (*nOccurrence* = 1). Including *nOccurrence* lets you search for additional occurrences of *cSearchExpression* in *cExpressionSearched*.

Remarks

ATC( ) searches the second character expression for the occurrence of the first character expression, without concern for the case (upper or lower) of the characters in either expression. Use AT( ) to perform a case-sensitive search.

ATC( ) returns an integer corresponding to the position where the first character of the character expression is found. If the character expression isn't found, ATC( ) returns 0.

Example

```
STORE 'Now is the time for all good men ... ' TO gcString
STORE 'IS THE' TO gcFindString
CLEAR
? ATC(gcFindString, gcString)  && Displays 5
STORE 'is' TO gcFindString
? ATC(gcFindString, gcString)  && Displays 5
? ATC('now',gcString)  && Displays 1
```

See Also

AT( ), ATCC( ), ATCLINE( ), ATLINE( ), LEFT( ), RAT( ), RATLINE( ), RIGHT( ), SUBSTR( )

ATCC( ) Function

Returns the beginning numeric position of the first occurrence of a character expression or memo field within another character expression or memo field, without regard for the case of these two expressions.

Syntax

ATCC(*cSearchExpression, cExpressionSearched* [, *nOccurrence*])

Returns

Numeric

Arguments

cSearchExpression
    Specifies the character expression that ATCC( ) searches for in *cExpressionSearched*.

cExpressionSearched
    Specifies the character expression *cSearchExpression* searches for.

    Both *cSearchExpression* and *cExpressionSearched* can be memo fields of any size.

nOccurrence
    Specifies which occurrence (first, second, third, and so on) of *cSearchExpression* is searched for in *cExpressionSearched*. By default, ATCC( ) searches for the first occurrence of *cSearchExpression* (*nOccurrence* = 1). Including *nOccurrence* lets you search for additional occurrences of *cSearchExpression* in *cExpressionSearched*.

Remarks

ATCC( ) is designed for expressions containing double-byte characters. If the expression contains only single-byte characters, ATCC( ) is equivalent to ATC( ).

ATCC( ) searches the second character expression for the occurrence of the first character expression, without concern for the case (upper or lower) of the characters in either expression. Use AT_C( ) to perform a case-sensitive search.

ATCC( ) returns an integer corresponding to the position where the first character of the character expression is found. If the character expression isn't found, ATCC( ) returns 0.

This function is useful for manipulating double-byte character sets for languages such as Hiragana and Katakana.

See Also

AT_C( ), LEFTC( ), RATC( ), RIGHTC( ), SUBSTRC( )

ATCLINE( ) Function

Returns the line number of the first occurrence of a character expression or memo field within another character expression or memo field, without regard for the case (upper or lower) of the characters in either expression.

Syntax

ATCLINE(*cSearchExpression*, *cExpressionSearched*)

Returns

Numeric

Arguments

cSearchExpression
Specifies the character expression that ATCLINE( ) searches for in *cExpressionSearched*.

cExpressionSearched
Specifies the character expression *cSearchExpression* searches for.

Both *cSearchExpression* and *cExpressionSearched* can be memo fields of any size. Use MLINE( ) to return the line containing the matching character expression.

> **Tip** ATCLINE( ) offers a convenient way to search memo fields.

Remarks

If the search is successful, ATCLINE( ) returns the number of the line containing the first character expression. If the search is unsuccessful, ATCLINE( ) returns 0.

The line number that ATCLINE( ) returns is determined by the value of SET MEMOWIDTH, even if *cExpressionSearched* isn't a memo field. For more information, see SET MEMOWIDTH.

Use ATLINE( ) to perform a case-sensitive search.

Examples

Example 1 locates the first time a character string occurs in a memo field, displays the first and last names of the employee, and the line of the memo containing the character string.

Example 2 demonstrates how the memo width affects ATCLINE( ).

```
* Example 1
CLOSE DATABASES
OPEN DATABASE (HOME(2) + 'Data\testdata')
USE employee  && Open employee table

CLEAR
STORE 'JAPANESE' TO gcFindString  && Case insensitive
LOCATE FOR ATCLINE(gcFindString, notes) != 0
? First_Name
?? Last_Name
? MLINE(notes, ATCLINE(gcFindString, notes))

* Example 2
STORE '1234567890ABCDEFGHIJ' TO gcString
SET MEMOWIDTH TO 20
? ATCLINE('AB', gcString)  && Displays 1
SET MEMOWIDTH TO 10
? ATCLINE('AB', gcString)  && Displays 2
```

See Also

AT( ), ATC( ), ATLINE( ), MLINE( ), RAT( ), RATLINE( ), SET MEMOWIDTH

ATLINE( ) Function

Returns the line number of the first occurrence of a character expression or memo field within another character expression or memo field, counting from the first line.

Syntax

ATLINE(*cSearchExpression*, *cExpressionSearched*)

Returns

Numeric

Arguments

cSearchExpression
Specifies the character expression that Microsoft Visual FoxPro looks for in *cExpressionSearched*.

cExpressionSearched

Specifies the character expression that *cSearchExpression* searches for.

Both *cSearchExpression* and *cExpressionSearched* can be memo fields of any size.

Use MLINE( ) to return the line containing the matching character expression as a character string.

Tip ATLINE( ) offers a convenient way to search memo fields.

Remarks

ATLINE( ) searches the second character expression for the occurrence of the first character expression. ATLINE( ) performs a case-sensitive search. Use ATCLINE( ) to perform a search that isn't case-sensitive.

If the search is successful, ATLINE( ) returns the number of the line where the match occurs. If the search is unsuccessful, ATLINE( ) returns 0.

The line number that ATLINE( ) returns is determined by the value of SET MEMOWIDTH, even if *cExpressionSearched* isn't a memo field. For more information, see SET MEMOWIDTH.

Examples

Example 1 locates the first time a character string occurs in a memo field, displays the first and last names of the employee, and the line of the memo containing the character string.

Example 2 demonstrates how the memo width affects ATLINE( ).

```
* Example 1
CLOSE DATABASES
OPEN DATABASE (HOME(2) + 'Data\testdata')
USE employee  && Open employee table

CLEAR
STORE 'Japanese' TO gcFindString  && Case sensitive
LOCATE FOR ATLINE(gcFindString, notes) != 0
? First_Name
?? Last_Name
? MLINE(notes, ATLINE(gcFindString, notes))

* Example 2
STORE '1234567890ABCDEFGHIJ' TO gcString
SET MEMOWIDTH TO 20
? ATLINE('AB', gcString)  && Displays 1
SET MEMOWIDTH TO 10
? ATLINE('AB', gcString)  && Displays 2
```

See Also

AT( ), ATC( ), ATCLINE( ), MLINE( ), RAT( ), RATLINE( ), SET MEMOWIDTH

ATN2( ) Function

Returns the arc tangent in all four quadrants from specified values.

Syntax

ATN2(*nYCoordinate*, *nXCoordinate*)

Returns

Numeric

Arguments

nYCoordinate
   Specifies the y coordinate.

nXCoordinate
   Specifies the x coordinate.

Remarks

ATN2( ) returns the angle (in radians) between the line y = 0 and the line connecting the specified coordinates and the origin (0, 0) of the coordinate system.

ATN2( ) returns a value between $-$ pi/2 and +pi/2.

You can convert the value returned by ATN2( ) to degrees with RTOD( ). You can specify the number of decimal places that are displayed in the result with SET DECIMALS.

Example

```
CLEAR
? PI( )  && Displays 3.14
? ATN2(0,-1)  && Displays 3.14
STORE COS(PI( )) TO gnXCoord
STORE SIN(PI( )) TO gnYCoord
? ATN2(gnYCoord,gnXCoord)  && Displays 3.14
? ATN2(gnYCoord,gnXCoord)/PI( )  && Displays 1.00
```

See Also

ATAN( ), DTOR( ), RTOD( ), SET DECIMALS, TAN( )

AUSED( ) Function

Places table aliases and work areas for a data session into a variable array.

Syntax

AUSED(*ArrayName* [, *nDataSessionNumber*])

Returns

Numeric

Arguments

ArrayName
> Specifies the name of the array containing the table aliases and work areas for a data session. If the array you specify doesn't exist, Microsoft Visual FoxPro automatically creates the array. If the array exists and isn't large enough to contain all the table aliases and work areas, Visual FoxPro automatically increases the size of the array. If the array is larger than necessary, Visual FoxPro truncates the array. If the array exists and AUSED( ) returns 0 because no tables are open in the data session, the array remains unchanged. If the array doesn't exist and AUSED( ) returns 0, the array isn't created.

nDataSessionNumber
> Specifies the data session number for which AUSED( ) returns the table aliases and work areas. If you omit *nDataSessionNumber*, AUSED( ) returns information about the current data session. Use SET DATASESSION to specify the current data session.

Remarks

AUSED( ) returns the number of rows in the array, which is identical to the number of tables open in the data session.

AUSED( ) creates a two-dimensional array and places the aliases of tables open for the data session in the first column of the array. The second column of the array contains the tables' corresponding work area numbers.

Example

The following example uses AUSED( ) to create an array named `gaInuse` that contains the table aliases and work areas for tables open in the current data session. The number of open tables for the current data session is displayed, and the table aliases and work areas are then displayed.

```
OPEN DATABASE (HOME(2) + 'Data\testdata') EXCLUSIVE
USE Customer IN 0
CLEAR
? AUSED(gaInuse)
DISPLAY MEMORY LIKE gaInuse
CLOSE DATABASES
```

See Also

ALIAS( ), SET DATASESSION, USE

AutoActivate Property

Determines how an OLE Container control can be activated. Available at design time and run time.

Syntax

Control.AutoActivate[= *nValue*]

Arguments

nValue

The settings for the AutoActivate property are:

Setting	Description
0	Manual. The control isn't automatically activated. You can activate a control programmatically using the DoVerb method.
1	GotFocus. If the control contains an object, the application that provides the object is activated when the control receives the focus.
2	(Default) DoubleClick. If the control contains an object, the application that provides the object is activated when the user double-clicks the control or presses ENTER when the control has the focus.
3	Automatic. If the control contains an object, the application that provides the object is activated based on the object's normal method of activation (when the control receives the focus or when the user double-clicks the control).

Remarks

If an embedded object supports in-place activation, you can set AutoActivate to 1 (GotFocus) to activate an object when the control receives the focus.

Note   When AutoActivate is set to 2 (Double-Click), the DblClick event does not occur.

Applies To

OLE Bound Control, OLE Container Control

See Also

DoVerb Method

AutoCenter Property

Specifies whether the form object is automatically centered in the main Visual FoxPro window or on the desktop the first time it is displayed. Available at design time and run time.

Syntax

Object.AutoCenter [= *lExpr*]

Arguments

lExpr

Specifies whether the Form object is centered or placed according to the settings of the Top and Left properties. The settings for the AutoCenter property are:

Setting	Description
True (.T.)	The Form object is centered and the values of the Top and Left properties are set to the new position.
False (.F.)	(Default) The Form object is not centered and is placed at the coordinates specified by the Top and Left properties.

Remarks

Forms are displayed in the main window, so setting AutoCenter to true (.T.) centers the form within the main window.

Note Resetting AutoCenter to false (.F.) after it has been set to true (.T.) will not return the form to the original Top and Left position.

Applies To

Form, _SCREEN

See Also

Desktop Property, Left Property, Top Property

AutoCloseTables Property

Specifies whether the tables or views specified by the data environment are closed when the form set, form, or report is released. Available at design time; read-only at run time.

Syntax

DataEnvironment.AutoCloseTables[= *lExpr*]

Arguments

lExpr

The settings for the AutoCloseTables property are:

Setting	Description
True (.T.)	(Default) Closes the tables and views when the form set, form, or report is released.
False (.F.)	Tables and views remain open when the form set, form, or report is released.

Remarks

If AutoCloseTables is set to false (.F.) and the form set, form, or report is not running in a private data session, the tables and views associated with Cursors in the data environment remain open after the form set, form, or report is released. In all other cases, the tables and views associated with Cursors in the data environment are closed.

Applies To

DataEnvironment

See Also

AutoOpenTables Property, DataSession Property, DataSessionID Property

AutoIncrement Property

Specifies if the build version number of a project is automatically incremented each time a distributable .exe or in-process .dll is built.

Syntax

Object.AutoIncrement[= *lExpression*]

Arguments

lExpression
    The settings for the AutoIncrement property are:

Setting	Description
True (.T.)	The build version number of a project is automatically incremented each time a distributable .exe or in-process .dll is built.
False (.F.)	(Default) The build version number isn't automatically incremented.

Remarks

The build version number isn't incremented if AutoIncrement is set to false (.F.) or when the project is rebuilt or a distributable .app is built.

The value of the AutoIncrement property corresponds to the **Auto Increment** check box in the EXE Version dialog box. The build version number can be determined or set with the VersionNumber property.

Applies To

Project Object

See Also

BUILD APP, BUILD DLL, BUILD EXE, BUILD PROJECT, EXE Version Dialog Box, VersionNumber Property

AutoOpenTables Property

Determines whether the tables or views associated with a form set, form, or report's data environment are loaded automatically. Available at design time; read-only at run time.

Syntax

DataEnvironment.AutoOpenTables[= *lExpr*]

Arguments

lExpr

    The settings for the AutoOpenTables property are:

Setting	Description
True (.T.)	(Default) The form set, form, or report's tables and views are opened automatically.
False (.F.)	The tables and views are not opened automatically.

Remarks

If AutoOpenTables is set to false (.F.), you can call the data environment's OpenTables method to programmatically load the data environment.

Applies To

DataEnvironment

See Also

BeforeOpenTables Event, OpenTables Method, OpenViews Property

AutoRelease Property

Determines whether a form set is released when the last form in the form set is released. Available at design time; read/write at run time.

Syntax

FormSet.AutoRelease[= *lExpr*]

Arguments

lExpr

The settings for the AutoRelease property are:

Setting	Description
True (.T.)	The default in the Form Designer. The form set is released when the last form in the form set is released.
False (.F.)	The default in program code. The form set is not released when the last form in the form set is released.

Applies To

FormSet

See Also

Release Method, ReleaseType Property

AutoSize Property

Specifies whether a control is automatically resized to fit its contents. Available at design time and run time.

Syntax

*Control.*AutoSize[= *lExpr*]

Arguments

lExpr

Specifies whether a control is resized to fit its contents. The settings for the AutoSize property are:

Setting	Description
True (.T.)	The control is automatically resized to fit its contents.
False (.F.)	(Default) The contents are clipped when they exceed the area of the control.

Remarks

For OLE Container controls, Autosize applies only to OLE objects that support in-place editing. The Sizable property must be set to true (.T.) to change the size of an OLE object during in-place editing.

Applies To

CheckBox, CommandButton, CommandGroup, Label, OLE Bound Control, OLE Container Control, OptionButton, OptionGroup

See Also

Alignment Property, Height Property, Width Property

AutoVerbMenu Property

Specifies whether a shortcut menu containing an OLE object's verbs is displayed when the OLE object is clicked with the right mouse button. Available at run time only.

Syntax

Control.AutoVerbMenu[= *lExpr*]

Arguments

lExpr
One of the following:

Setting	Description
True (.T.)	(Default) The shortcut menu containing the OLE object's verbs is displayed when the OLE object is right-clicked.
False (.F.)	The shortcut menu containing the OLE object's verbs is not displayed when the OLE object is right-clicked.

Remarks

At run time, if the AutoVerbMenu and Enabled properties are set to true (.T.), right-clicking the OLE object displays the shortcut menu containing the verbs supported by the OLE object. If the AutoVerbMenu and Enabled properties are set to false (.F.) or the OLE object does not support verbs, the shortcut menu isn't displayed when you right-click the OLE object.

Applies To

Enabled Property, OLE Bound Control, OLE Container Control

See Also

DoVerb Method

AutoYield Property

Specifies whether an instance of Visual FoxPro processes pending Windows events between execution of each line of user program code.

Syntax

ApplicationObject.AutoYield[= *lExpr*]

Arguments

lExpr

Specifies whether an instance of Visual FoxPro processes Windows events between each line of user program code. *lExpr* can be one of the following logical values:

lExpr	Description
True (.T.)	(Default) The instance of Visual FoxPro processes pending Windows events between execution of each line of user program code.
	If *lExpr* is set to true (.T.), the instance of Visual FoxPro processes pending Windows events in the same manner as earlier versions of Visual FoxPro.
False (.F.)	The instance of Visual FoxPro does not process pending Windows events between each line of user program code.
	All pending Windows events are placed in a queue, and the events in the queue are processed when DOEVENTS is issued or a wait state occurs. A wait state occurs when Visual FoxPro is waiting for input from the user. The WAIT command does not create a wait state.

Remarks

The AutoYield property should be set to false (.F.) when a form contains an ActiveX control. Setting AutoYield to false (.F.) prevents events for an ActiveX control from executing between lines of user program code. For example, if AutoYield is set to true (.T.), clicking an ActiveX control while user program code is executing may cause an event for the ActiveX control to execute, ignoring the user program code for the event, producing undesirable or unpredictable results.

The following occurs when the AutoYield property is set to false (.F.):

- ActiveX controls cannot process events until a wait state occurs, so clicking an ActiveX control has no effect while user program code is executing. This is the same behavior for Visual FoxPro controls such as the Grid.

- ON KEY LABEL commands and mouse events are ignored while user program code is executing. The ON KEY LABEL commands and mouse events are placed in a queue and processed at the next wait state.

- Pressing Esc does not interrupt program execution. This is identical to setting ESCAPE to OFF. In this case you cannot exit infinite loops without shutting down the instance of Visual FoxPro.

- Queries cannot be interrupted.

- Switching to other applications is supported, but you cannot switch back to Visual FoxPro while Visual FoxPro user program code is executing.

Applies To

Application Object, _VFP System Variable

See Also

DOEVENTS Command

AVCXCLASSES( ) Function

Places the information about classes in a class library into an array.

Syntax

AVCXCLASSES(*ArrayName*, *cLibraryName*)

Returns

Numeric

Arguments

ArrayName

Specifies the name of the array in which the class information is placed. If the array you specify doesn't exist, Visual FoxPro automatically creates the array. If the array exists and isn't large enough to contain the class names and base classes, Visual FoxPro automatically increases the size of the array. If the array is larger than necessary, Visual FoxPro truncates the array.

The array contains a row for each class in the class library, and each row contains 11 columns containing information about the class. The following table lists the class information in each column.

Column	Class information	.vcx field name
1	Class name.	OBJNAME
2	Base class of the class.	BASECLASS
3	Parent class name of the class.	CLASS
4	Relative path and file name of the parent class library.	CLASSLOC
5	Relative path and file name of the bitmap for a custom class icon.	RESERVED4
6	Relative path and file name for a custom Project Manager or Class Browser class icon.	RESERVED5
7	ScaleMode of the class, Pixels or Foxels.	RESERVED6
8	Description of the class.	RESERVED7
9	Relative path and file name for the #INCLUDE file for the class.	RESERVED8
10	User-defined information for the class.	USER
11	Logical true (.T.) if the class is OLEPUBLIC, otherwise logical false (.F.).	RESERVED2

cLibraryName

Specifies the name of the class library for which AVCXCLASSES( ) places class information into the array specified with *ArrayName*. *cLibraryName* can contain a path to the class library. An error is generated if the class library you specify doesn't exist.

Remarks

AVCXCLASSES( ) returns the number of rows in the array (the number of classes in the class library).

Example

The following example uses AVCXCLASSES( ) to create and populate an array named aClasses with the names and base classes of the classes in the Buttons class library. DISPLAY MEMORY lists the contents of the array in the main Visual FoxPro window.

```
ACTIVATE SCREEN
CLEAR

? AVCXCLASSES(aClasses, '\VFP\SAMPLES\CLASSES\BUTTONS.VCX')
*** Displays 5

FOR nColCount = 1 TO ALEN(aClasses,2) && Loop through columns
    ? aClasses(1, nColCount) && Each column of the 1st class
NEXT

*** Displays the following:
*
* cmdCancel
* commandbutton
* cmdok
* buttons.vcx
* cancel.bmp
* cancel.bmp
* Pixels
* Release Form or Form Set
*
*
* .F.
```

See Also

ACLASS( ), AGETCLASS( ), AMEMBERS( ), CREATE CLASS

AVERAGE Command

Computes the arithmetic mean of numeric expressions or fields.

Syntax

AVERAGE [*ExpressionList*]
    [*Scope*] [FOR *lExpression1*] [WHILE *lExpression2*]
    [TO *VarList* I TO ARRAY *ArrayName*]
    [NOOPTIMIZE]

Arguments

ExpressionList

    Specifies the expressions to average. *ExpressionList* can be a list of fields from the table separated by commas, or numeric expressions involving fields from the table.

Scope

    Specifies the record or range of records to include in the average. Only the records that fall within the range of records specified by the scope are averaged. The scope clauses are: ALL, NEXT *nRecords*, RECORD *nRecordNumber*, and REST. The default scope for AVERAGE is ALL records.

    Commands that include *Scope* operate only on the table in the active work area.

FOR *lExpression1*

    Specifies a condition whereby only the records that satisfy the logical condition *lExpression* are included. This argument allows you to filter out undesired records.

    Rushmore optimizes an AVERAGE FOR query if *lExpression* is an optimizable expression. For best performance, use an optimizable expression in the FOR clause. For information on Rushmore optimizable expressions, see the SET OPTIMIZE Command, later in this language reference, and "Understanding Rushmore Technology" in Chapter 15, "Optimizing Applications," in the *Microsoft Visual FoxPro 6.0 Programmer's Guide*.

WHILE *lExpression2*

    Specifies that as long as the logical expression *lExpression2* evaluates to true (.T.), records are included in the average.

TO *VarList*

    Specifies the list of variables or array elements to which the results of the average are stored.

TO ARRAY *ArrayName*

    Specifies the one-dimensional array to which the results of the average are stored. The one-dimensional array can be created before the execution of AVERAGE.

If the array you include in AVERAGE doesn't exist, Visual FoxPro automatically creates it. If the array exists and isn't large enough to contain all the results, Visual FoxPro increases the size of the array automatically to accommodate the information.

NOOPTIMIZE

Disables Rushmore optimization of AVERAGE. For more information, see the SET OPTIMIZE Command, later in this language reference, and "Understanding Rushmore Technology" in Chapter 15, "Optimizing Applications," in the *Microsoft Visual FoxPro 6.0 Programmer's Guide*.

Remarks

All numeric fields in the selected table are averaged unless you include an optional expression list. The result is displayed on the screen if SET TALK is ON. If SET HEADINGS is ON, the field names or expression involving the field names are displayed above the results.

Example

```
CLOSE DATABASES
OPEN DATABASE (HOME(2) + 'Data\testdata')
USE orders  && Open order table

CLEAR
AVERAGE Order_Amt  && Calcuate averages of all orders
AVERAGE Order_Amt TO gnAvg  && Store average to memory variable
? 'Average order amount: '
?? gnAvg  && Display the average again
```

See Also

CALCULATE, DIMENSION, SET HEADINGS, SUM

BackColor, ForeColor Properties

Specifies the background or foreground color used to display text and graphics in an object. Available at design time and run time.

Syntax

Object.BackColor[= *nColor*]
Object.ForeColor[= *nColor*]

Arguments

nColor

Specifies a single color value.

The following table lists typical color values.

Color	RGB Values	*nColor* Value
White	255, 255, 255	16777215
Black	0, 0, 0	0
Gray	192, 192, 192	12632256
Dark gray	128, 128, 128	8421504
Red	255, 0, 0	255
Dark red	128, 0, 0	128
Yellow	255, 255, 0	65535
Dark yellow	128, 128, 0	32896
Green	0, 255, 0	65280
Dark green	0, 128, 0	32768
Cyan	0, 255, 255	16776960
Dark cyan	0, 128, 128	8421376
Blue	0, 0, 255	16711680
Dark blue	0, 0, 128	8388608
Magenta	255, 0 ,255	16711935
Dark magenta	128, 0, 128	8388736

Remarks

Visual FoxPro uses a red-green-blue (RGB) color scheme for colors. The red, green, and blue components are each represented by a number between 0 and 255. Use the RGB( ) function to convert the three component colors into one composite *nColor*.

Example

The following example demonstrates how the Shape control can be used to display a circle, ellipse, or square on a form, and how the BackColor property can be used to specify the color of each shape.

A form is created, and a set of option buttons and a command button are placed on the form. When you choose one of the option buttons, the corresponding shape is displayed on the form. The BackColor property is used to specify the color of each shape. The Height, Width, and Curvature properties of each shape determine the type of shape created.

```
frmMyForm = CREATEOBJECT('Form')  && Create a Form
frmMyForm.Closable = .F.  && Disable the Control menu box
```

```
frmMyForm.AddObject('cmdCommand1','cmdMyCmndBtn')  && Add Command button
frmMyForm.AddObject('opgOptionGroup1','opgMyOptGrp')  && Add Option Group
frmMyForm.AddObject('shpCircle1','shpMyCircle')  && Add Circle Shape
frmMyForm.AddObject('shpEllipse1','shpMyEllipse')  && Add Ellipse Shape
frmMyForm.AddObject('shpSquare','shpMySquare')  && Add Box Shape

frmMyForm.cmdCommand1.Visible =.T.  && "Quit" Command button visible

frmMyForm.opgOptionGroup1.Buttons(1).Caption = "\<Circle"
frmMyForm.opgOptionGroup1.Buttons(2).Caption = "\<Ellipse"
frmMyForm.opgOptionGroup1.Buttons(3).Caption = "\<Square"
frmMyForm.opgOptionGroup1.SetAll("Width", 100)  && Set Option group width
frmMyForm.opgOptionGroup1.Visible = .T.  && Option Group visible
frmMyForm.opgOptionGroup1.Click  && Show the circle

frmMyForm.SHOW  && Display the form
READ EVENTS  && Start event processing

DEFINE CLASS opgMyOptGrp AS OptionGroup  && Create an Option Group
   ButtonCount = 3  && Three Option buttons
   Top = 10
   Left = 10
   Height = 75
   Width = 100

   PROCEDURE Click
      ThisForm.shpCircle1.Visible = .F.  && Hide the circle
      ThisForm.shpEllipse1.Visible = .F.  && Hide the ellipse
      ThisForm.shpSquare.Visible = .F.  && Hide the square

      DO CASE
         CASE ThisForm.opgOptionGroup1.Value = 1
            ThisForm.shpCircle1.Visible = .T.  && Show the circle
         CASE ThisForm.opgOptionGroup1.Value = 2
            ThisForm.shpEllipse1.Visible = .T.  && Show the ellipse
         CASE ThisForm.opgOptionGroup1.Value = 3
            ThisForm.shpSquare.Visible = .T.  && Show the square
      ENDCASE
ENDDEFINE

DEFINE CLASS cmdMyCmndBtn AS CommandButton  && Create Command button
   Caption = '\<Quit'  && Caption on the Command button
   Cancel = .T.  && Default Cancel Command button (Esc)
   Left = 125  && Command button column
   Top = 210  && Command button row
   Height = 25  && Command button height
```

```
   PROCEDURE Click
      CLEAR EVENTS  && Stop event processing, close Form
ENDDEFINE

DEFINE CLASS shpMyCircle AS SHAPE  && Create a circle
   Top = 10
   Left = 200
   Width = 100
   Height = 100
   Curvature = 99
   BackColor = RGB(255,0,0)  && Red
ENDDEFINE

DEFINE CLASS shpMyEllipse AS SHAPE  && Create an ellipse
   Top = 35
   Left = 200
   Width = 100
   Height = 50
   Curvature = 99
   BackColor = RGB(0,128,0)  && Green
ENDDEFINE

DEFINE CLASS shpMySquare AS SHAPE  && Create a square
   Top = 10
   Left = 200
   Width = 100
   Height = 100
   Curvature = 0
   BackColor = RGB(0,0,255)  && Blue
ENDDEFINE
```

Applies To

CheckBox, Column, ComboBox, CommandButton, CommandGroup, Container Object,
Control Object, EditBox, Form, Grid, Header, Label, OptionButton, OptionGroup, Page,
_SCREEN, Shape, Spinner, TextBox, ToolBar

Note The BackColor property does not apply to the CommandButton control.
The ForeColor property does not apply to the CommandGroup, OptionGroup,
or Shape controls.

See Also

BackStyle Property, ColorScheme Property, Colors Overview, DisabledBackColor,
DisabledForeColor Properties, FillColor Property, FillStyle Property,
GETCOLOR( ), RGB( )

BackStyle Property

Specifies whether the background of an object is transparent or opaque. Available at design time and run time.

Syntax

Object.BackStyle[= *nStyle*]

Arguments

nStyle

The settings for the BackStyle property are:

Setting	Description
0	Transparent. Anything behind the object is visible.
1	(Default) Opaque. The object's BackColor fills the control and obscures any color or graphics behind it.

Remarks

You can use the BackStyle property to create transparent controls when you are using a background color on a Form object or when you want to place a control over a graphic. Use an opaque control when you want it to stand out on a busy background.

An object's BackColor property is ignored if the BackStyle property is set to 0 (Transparent).

For a Page object, the BackStyle property is read-only when the Tabs property is set to true (.T.) for the PageFrame containing the Page.

Applies To

CheckBox, CommandGroup, Container Object, Control Object, EditBox, Image, Label, OptionButton, OptionGroup, Page, Shape, TextBox

See Also

BackColor, ForeColor Properties

BAR( ) Function

Returns the number of the most recently chosen item from a menu defined with DEFINE POPUP or a menu item chosen from a Visual FoxPro menu.

Syntax

BAR( )

Returns

Numeric

Remarks

Each item on a menu is assigned a number with DEFINE BAR. When a menu item is chosen from the menu, BAR( ) returns the number assigned to that item. A program can branch to other routines based on the value that BAR( ) returns.

BAR( ) returns 0 if there is no active menu or if the user presses ESC to exit the menu.

Example

The following example uses BAR( ) to pass the number of a menu item to a procedure. The current system menu bar is saved to memory with SET SYSMENU SAVE, and then all system menu titles are removed with SET SYSMENU TO.

Two menu titles are created with DEFINE PAD; DEFINE POPUP is used to create a menu for each menu title. DEFINE BAR is used to create items on each menu. When you choose a menu title, ON PAD uses ACTIVATE POPUP to activate the corresponding menu.

When you choose an item from a menu, ON SELECTION POPUP uses BAR( ) and POPUP( ) to pass the item number and menu title to the choice procedure. The choice procedure displays the number of the chosen item and the name of the menu containing the item, and the original Visual FoxPro system menu is restored with SET SYSMENU TO DEFAULT.

```
*** Name this program BAR_EXAM.PRG ***
CLEAR
SET SYSMENU SAVE
SET SYSMENU TO
DEFINE PAD padConv OF _MSYSMENU ;
   PROMPT '\<Conversions' COLOR SCHEME 3 ;
   KEY ALT+C, ''
DEFINE PAD padCard OF _MSYSMENU ;
   PROMPT 'Card \<Info' COLOR SCHEME 3 ;
   KEY ALT+I, ''
ON PAD padConv OF _MSYSMENU ACTIVATE POPUP popConv
ON PAD padCard OF _MSYSMENU ACTIVATE POPUP popCard
DEFINE POPUP popConv MARGIN RELATIVE COLOR SCHEME 4
DEFINE BAR 1 OF popConv PROMPT 'Ar\<ea' KEY CTRL+E, '^E'
DEFINE BAR 2 OF popConv PROMPT '\<Length' ;
   KEY CTRL+L, '^L'
DEFINE BAR 3 OF popConv PROMPT 'Ma\<ss' ;
   KEY CTRL+S, '^S'
DEFINE BAR 4 OF popConv PROMPT 'Spee\<d' ;
   KEY CTRL+D, '^D'
DEFINE BAR 5 OF popConv PROMPT '\<Temperature' ;
   KEY CTRL+T, '^T'
```

```
DEFINE BAR 6 OF popConv PROMPT 'T\<ime' ;
   KEY CTRL+I, '^I'
DEFINE BAR 7 OF popConv PROMPT 'Volu\<me' ;
   KEY CTRL+M, '^M'
*** Here is where the POPCONV menu uses the BAR( ) function
*** to pass a bar number to the procedure called choice below.
ON SELECTION POPUP popConv;
   DO choice IN bar_exam WITH BAR( ), POPUP( )
DEFINE POPUP popCard MARGIN RELATIVE COLOR SCHEME 4
DEFINE BAR 1 OF popCard PROMPT '\<View Charges' ;
   KEY ALT+V, ''
DEFINE BAR 2 OF popCard PROMPT 'View \<Payments' ;
   KEY ALT+P, ''
DEFINE BAR 3 OF popCard PROMPT 'Vie\<w Users' ;
   KEY ALT+W, ''
DEFINE BAR 4 OF popCard PROMPT '\-'
DEFINE BAR 5 OF popCard PROMPT '\<Charges ';
   KEY ALT+C
DEFINE BAR 6 OF popCard PROMPT '\-'
DEFINE BAR 7 OF popCard PROMPT 'E\<xit ';
   KEY ALT+X
*** Here is where the POPCARD menu uses the BAR( ) function
*** to pass a bar number to the procedure called choice below.
ON SELECTION POPUP popCard;
   DO choice IN bar_exam WITH BAR( ), POPUP( )
*** The procedure choice uses the gnBar parameter
*** to contain the value passed by the BAR( ) function.
PROCEDURE choice
PARAMETERS gnBar, gcPopup
WAIT WINDOW 'You chose bar #' + LTRIM(STR(gnBar)) + ;
   ' from popup ' + gcPopup NOWAIT
SET SYSMENU TO DEFAULT
```

See Also

ACTIVATE POPUP, CNTBAR( ), DEFINE BAR, DEFINE POPUP, GETBAR( ), MRKBAR( ), ON BAR, ON SELECTION BAR, PRMBAR( )

BARCOUNT( ) Function

Included for compatibility with dBASE.

BARPROMPT( ) Function

Included for compatibility with dBASE.

BaseClass Property

Contains the name of the Visual FoxPro base class on which the referenced object is based. Read-only at design time and run time.

Syntax

Object.BaseClass

Arguments

cBaseClass
    Contains the Visual FoxPro base class on which the object is based.

Remarks

For a list of Visual FoxPro base classes, see "Controls and Objects," later in this language reference.

Applies To

ActiveDoc, CheckBox, Column, ComboBox, CommandButton, CommandGroup, Container Object, Control Object, Custom, EditBox, Form, FormSet, Grid, Header, Hyperlink, Image, Label, Line, ListBox, OLE Bound Control, OLE Container Control, OptionButton, OptionGroup, Page, PageFrame, ProjectHook, _SCREEN, Shape, Spinner, TextBox, Timer, ToolBar

See Also

Class Property

_BEAUTIFY System Variable

Specifies the beautification application for Visual FoxPro programs, is run when you choose the **Beautify** command on the **Tools** menu.

Syntax

_BEAUTIFY = *cProgramName*

Arguments

cProgramName
    Specifies a beautification application. If your beautification application is in a directory other than the current default directory, include a path with the application name.

    You can also specify a beautification application in your configuration file by including a line using this syntax:

```
_BEAUTIFY = cProgramName
```

Note that your beautification application must accept a single parameter, the name of the program to beautify. Your beautification application can modify the program, write the modifications to a temporary file, and then return the name of the temporary file to FoxPro. FoxPro reads the temporary file back into the editing session under the original FoxPro program name and then deletes the temporary file.

Remarks

The **Beautify** command appears on the **Tools** menu when you open a program or text file in an editing window.

See Also

Documenting Wizard

BeforeBuild Event

Occurs before a project is rebuilt or an application file (.app), dynamic link library (.dll), or executable file (.exe) is created from a project.

Syntax

PROCEDURE *Object*.BeforeBuild
[LPARAMETERS *cOutputName*, *nBuildAction*, *lRebuildAll*, *lShowErrors*, *lBuildNewGuids*]

Arguments

cOutputName
Specifies the name of the application, dynamic link library, or executable file that is created.

If *cOutputName* includes a file extension and *nBuildAction* is omitted, the file extension in *cOutputName* determines the type of file built. For example, if the extension in *cOutputName* is ".exe" an executable file is created.

nBuildAction
Specifies if the project is rebuilt or an application, dynamic link library, or executable file is created.

The following table lists the values for *nBuildAction* with a description of each.

nBuildAction	FoxPro.h constant	Description
1	BUILDACTION_REBUILD	Rebuilds the project.
2	BUILDACTION_BUILDAPP	Creates an .app.
3	BUILDACTION_BUILDEXE	Creates an .exe.
4	BUILDACTION_BUILDDLL	Creates a .dll.

nBuildAction takes precedence over the file extension specified in *cOutPutName*. For example, an executable file is created if *nBuildAction* is 3 and *cOutputName* doesn't specify an ".exe" extension.

lRebuildAll

Specifies if files in the project are recompiled before an .app, .dll, or .exe is created. If *lRebuildAll* is true (.T.), the following are recompiled:

- Program files.

- Format files.

- Source code in forms, labels, reports, and Visual class libraries.

- Stored procedures in databases.

If *lRebuildAll* is false (.F.) or is omitted, files in the project are not recompiled before the .app, .dll, or .exe is created.

lShowErrors

Specifies if compilation errors are displayed in an editing window after the build is complete. If *lShowErrors* is true (.T.), the errors are displayed. If *lShowErrors* is false (.F.) or is omitted, compilation errors aren't displayed.

lBuildNewGUIDs

Specifies if new registry GUIDs (globally unique identifiers) are generated when an executable file or dynamic link library is created. If *lBuildNewGUIDs* is true (.T.), new GUIDs are generated. If *lBuildNewGUIDs* is false (.F.) or is omitted, new GUIDs aren't generated. *lBuildNewGUIDs* is ignored if *nBuildAction* is less than 3.

Remarks

The parameters listed above are passed to the BeforeBuild event when you execute the Build method, when you issue the BUILD APP, BUILD DLL, BUILD EXE, or BUILD PROJECT commands, or when you choose **OK** in the Build Options dialog box. The parameters are passed by reference with the exception of the *nBuildAction* parameter, which is passed by value. You can change the values of these parameters within the BeforeBuild event to change how a project, .app, .dll, or .exe is created from the project.

Include NODEFAULT in the BeforeBuild event to prevent a project from being rebuilt or an application file (.app), dynamic link library (.dll), or executable file (.exe) from being created.

Applies To

ProjectHook Object

See Also

AfterBuild Event, Build Method

BeforeDock Event

Occurs before the ToolBar object is docked.

Syntax

PROCEDURE *ToolBar*.BeforeDock
LPARAMETERS [*nIndex*] , *nLocation*

Arguments

nIndex
    Uniquely identifies a control if it is in a control array.

nLocation
    Specifies where the ToolBar will be docked. The values for *nLocation* are:

Value	FOXPRO.H Constant	Description
−1	TOOL_NOTDOCKED	ToolBar will be undocked.
0	TOOL_TOP	ToolBar will be docked at the top of the main Visual FoxPro window.
1	TOOL_LEFT	ToolBar will be docked at the left side of the main Visual FoxPro window.
2	TOOL_RIGHT	ToolBar will be docked at the right side of the main Visual FoxPro window.
3	TOOL_BOTTOM	ToolBar will be docked at the bottom of the main Visual FoxPro window.

Remarks

The BeforeDock event occurs when the ToolBar is dragged to a docking region or when the Dock method is invoked.

BeforeDock is triggered before the ToolBar is redrawn, so you can change the appearance of the toolbar. This is useful if the ToolBar has a control, such as a ComboBox, that you want to replace with a control of different proportions, such as a CommandButton, when the ToolBar is docked.

Applies To

ToolBar

See Also

AfterDock Event, Dock Method, Undock Event

BeforeOpenTables Event

Occurs just before the tables and views associated with the data environment for a form set, form, or report are opened.

Syntax

PROCEDURE *DataEnvironment*.BeforeOpenTables

Remarks

For a form set or form, the BeforeOpenTables event occurs before the form set's or form's Load event.

Applies To

DataEnvironment

See Also

AfterCloseTables Event, CloseTables Method, Load Event, OpenTables Method, Unload Event

BeforeRowColChange Event

Occurs when the user changes the active row or column, before the new cell gets the focus. It also occurs before the Valid event of the current object in the grid column and any rules in the database. Use NODEFAULT to prevent the active row and column in the grid from changing.

Syntax

PROCEDURE *Grid*.BeforeRowColChange
LPARAMETERS *nColIndex*

Arguments

nColIndex
    Returns the index of the newly active row or column.

Remarks

BeforeRowColChange is triggered interactively using the mouse or keyboard or programmatically, such as calling the ActivateCell method.

Applies To

Grid

See Also

ActivateCell Method, AfterRowColChange Event, DEFINE CLASS [NODEFAULT], Valid Event

BEGIN TRANSACTION Command

Begins a transaction. Transactions are supported only for tables in a database. See the CREATE DATABASE and ADD TABLE Commands, in this language reference, for information on how to create and add tables to a database.

Syntax

BEGIN TRANSACTION

Remarks

To save any modifications you made and end the transaction, issue END TRANSACTION. If the transaction fails (the server fails, the workstation fails, or you exit Visual FoxPro without committing the transaction) or if you issue ROLLBACK, the file or files in the transaction are restored to their original state.

Transactions can be nested five levels deep. An error is generated if you attempt a sixth level of nesting.

When you modify records in a table that is part of a transaction, other users on the network do not have access (read or write) to the records until you end the transaction.

When other users on the network try to access records you have modified, they must wait until you end your transaction. They receive the message "Record not available ... please wait" until the records become available. Because of this, it is important to keep the length of the transaction to a minimum or conduct the transaction during times when others do not need access.

The following commands and functions are not supported during a transaction:

Commands and functions

ADD TABLE	APPEND PROCEDURES	CLEAR ALL
CLOSE ALL*	CLOSE DATABASES*	COPY INDEXES
COPY PROCEDURES	CREATE CONNECTION	CREATE DATABASE
CREATE TRIGGER	CREATE SQL VIEW	CREATE VIEW
DELETE CONNECTION	DELETE DATABASE	DELETE TRIGGER
DELETE VIEW	MODIFY CONNECTION	MODIFY DATABASE
MODIFY PROCEDURE	MODIFY VIEW	REMOVE TABLE
RENAME TABLE	REQUERY( )	

* If CLOSE ALL is issued while a transaction is in progress, all tables in all open databases are closed. However, the databases remain open. Issuing CLOSE DATABASES within a transaction closes all tables in the current database, but the database remains open.

Also, the following commands and functions cannot be issued for a specific table participating in a transaction:

Commands and functions

ALTER TABLE	CREATE TABLE	CURSORSETPROP( )
DELETE TAG	INDEX	INSERT
MODIFY STRUCTURE	PACK	REINDEX
TABLEREVERT( )	ZAP	

Example

In the following example, the customer table in the testdata database is opened. Optimistic table buffering is set for the customer table. The contents of the cust_id and company fields are displayed, and then the contents of the company field is replaced within the buffered data.

BEGIN TRANSACTION is issued to start a transaction. The TABLEUPDATE( ) function is used to write the changes to the table. The new contents are displayed, and ROLLBACK is issued to restore the original contents of the company field. The cust_id and company fields are displayed again with the company field containing its original values.

```
CLEAR
CLOSE DATABASES

* Transactions are only supported within a DBC
OPEN DATABASE (HOME(2) + 'Data\testdata')

SET MULTILOCKS ON  && Required for buffering

USE customer
=CURSORSETPROP("Buffering",5)
? 'The original company field'
LIST FIELDS cust_id, company NEXT 5
REPLACE ALL company WITH "***"  && Change field contents

BEGIN TRANSACTION
   =TABLEUPDATE(.T.)
   GO TOP
   ? 'The modified company field'
   LIST FIELDS cust_id, company NEXT 5
   ROLLBACK  && Restore original field contents

=TABLEREVERT(.T.)
GO TOP
? 'The restored company field'
LIST FIELDS cust_id, company NEXT 5
```

See Also

END TRANSACTION, ROLLBACK, TXNLEVEL( )

BETWEEN( ) Function

Determines whether the value of an expression lies between the values of two other expressions of the same data type.

Syntax

BETWEEN(*eTestValue*, *eLowValue*, *eHighValue*)

Returns

Logical or null value

Arguments

eTestValue

Specifies the expression whose value BETWEEN( ) tests. If the value of *eTestValue* is greater than or equal to the value of *eLowerValue* and less than or equal to the value of *eHighValue*, BETWEEN( ) returns true (.T.). Otherwise, BETWEEN( ) returns false (.F.). BETWEEN( ) returns the null value if either *eLowValue* or *eHighValue* are the null value.

eLowValue

Specifies the lower value in the range BETWEEN( ) evaluates.

eHighValue

Specifies the upper value in the range BETWEEN( ) evaluates.

Remarks

BETWEEN( ) returns a value of true (.T.) if the value of a character, date, datetime, numeric, float, integer, double, or currency expression lies between the values of two other expressions of the same data type. If the value of the expression doesn't lie between the values of two other expressions, BETWEEN( ) returns false (.F.). BETWEEN( ) returns the null value if either *eLowValue* or *eHighValue* is the null value.

Example

The following example scans the `orders` table for all records in the `order_amt` field with values between 950 and 1000 inclusive and displays the `cust_id` field and the `order_amt` field.

```
CLOSE DATABASES
OPEN DATABASE (HOME(2) + 'Data\testdata')
USE orders  && Open order table
```

```
CLEAR
SCAN FOR BETWEEN(order_amt,950,1000)
   ? cust_id, order_amt
ENDSCAN
```

See Also

MAX( ), MIN( )

BINTOC( ) Function

Converts an integer value to a binary character representation.

Syntax

BINTOC(*nExpression* [, *nSize*])

Returns

Character

Arguments

nExpression
　　Specifies the integer value to convert.

nSize
　　Specifies the length in characters of the returned character string.

　　nSize also determines the value you can specify for *nExpression*. The following table lists the permissible values for *nSize* and the corresponding range of values for *nExpression*:

nSize	nExpression Range
1	–128 to 127
2	–32,768 to 32,767
4 (default)	–2,147,483,648 to 2,147,483,647

　　If *nSize* is omitted, BINTOC( ) returns a character string composed of four characters.

Remarks

BINTOC( ) can be used to reduce the size of indexes for numeric fields containing integer data. For example, a numeric field named iPartCode might contain an integer value from 1 to 127 which corresponds to a parts classification code. BINTOC( ) lets you convert the value in the numeric field to a single character representation. For example, the following command creates an index with a one-character index key:

```
INDEX ON BINTOC(nPartCode,1) TAG PartCode
```

See Also

CTOBIN( ) Function

BITAND( ) Function

Returns the result of a bitwise AND operation performed on two numeric values.

Syntax

BITAND(*nExpression1*, *nExpression2*)

Returns

Numeric

Arguments

nExpression1, *nExpression2*
  Specifies the numeric values on which the bitwise AND operation is performed.
  If *nExpression1* and *nExpression2* are not integers, they are converted to integers
  before the bitwise AND operation is performed.

Remarks

BITAND( ) compares each bit in *nExpression1* to the corresponding bit in *nExpression2*.
If the bits in *nExpression1* and *nExpression2* are both 1, the corresponding result bit is set
to 1; otherwise, the corresponding result bit is set to 0.

The following table shows the result of a bitwise AND operation on corresponding
nExpression1 and *nExpression2* bits:

nExpression1 bit	*nExpression2* bit	Resulting bit
0	0	0
0	1	0
1	1	1
1	0	0

Example

```
x = 3   && 0011 binary
y = 6   && 0110 binary

? BITAND(x,y) && Returns 2, 0010 binary
```

See Also

BITCLEAR( ), BITLSHIFT( ), BITNOT( ), BITOR( ), BITRSHIFT( ), BITSET( ),
BITTEST( ), BITXOR( )

BITCLEAR( ) Function

Clears a specified bit (sets it to 0) in a numeric value and returns the resulting value.

Syntax

BITCLEAR(*nExpression1*, *nExpression2*)

Returns

Numeric

Arguments

nExpression1

Specifies the numeric value in which a bit is cleared. If *nExpression1* is not an integer, it is converted to an integer before its bit is set.

nExpression2

Specifies the bit position in *nExpression1* that is cleared. *nExpression2* can range from 0 to 31; 0 is the rightmost bit.

Example

```
x = 7  && 0111 binary
y = 1  && 2nd bit position (0 = 1st bit position)
? BITCLEAR(x,y) && Returns 5, 0101 binary
```

See Also

BITAND( ), BITLSHIFT( ), BITNOT( ), BITOR( ), BITRSHIFT( ), BITSET( ), BITTEST( ), BITXOR( )

BITLSHIFT( ) Function

Returns the result of shifting the bits of a numeric value to the left a specified number of positions.

Syntax

BITLSHIFT(*nExpression1*, *nExpression2*)

Returns

Numeric

Arguments

nExpression1

Specifies the numeric value whose bits are shifted to the left. If *nExpression1* is not an integer, it is converted to an integer before its bits are shifted.

nExpression2
> Specifies the number of bit positions to shift. If *nExpression2* is not an integer, it is converted to an integer.

Example

```
x = 5   && 0101 binary
y = 1   && Shift bits 1 position left

? BITLSHIFT(x,y) && Returns 10, 1010 binary
```

See Also

BITAND( ), BITCLEAR( ), BITNOT( ), BITOR( ), BITRSHIFT( ), BITSET( ), BITTEST( ), BITXOR( )

BITNOT( ) Function

Returns the result of a bitwise NOT operation performed on a numeric value.

Syntax

BITNOT(*nExpression*)

Returns

Numeric

Arguments

nExpression
> Specifies the numeric value on which the bitwise NOT operation is performed. If *nExpression* is not an integer, it is converted to an integer before its bits are shifted.

Remarks

BITNOT( ) returns the bitwise complement of *nExpression*. The numeric value returned by BITNOT( ) represents *nExpression* with each bit of value 0 switched to 1 and each bit of value 1 switched to 0.

The following table shows the result of a bitwise NOT operation on *nExpression*:

nExpression bit	Resulting bit
0	1
1	0

Example

```
x = 5   && 0101 binary
? BITNOT(x) && Returns -6
```

See Also

BITAND( ), BITCLEAR( ), BITLSHIFT( ), BITOR( ), BITRSHIFT( ), BITSET( ),
BITTEST( ), BITXOR( )

BITOR( ) Function

Returns the result of a bitwise inclusive OR operation performed on two numeric values.

Syntax

BITOR(*nExpression1*, *nExpression2*)

Returns

Numeric

Arguments

nExpression1, *nExpression2*
  Specifies the numeric values on which the bitwise inclusive OR operation is
  performed. If *nExpression1* and *nExpression2* are not integers, they are converted
  to integers before the bitwise inclusive OR operation is performed.

Remarks

BITOR( ) compares each bit in *nExpression1* to the corresponding bit in *nExpression2*.
If either bit in *nExpression1* or *nExpression2* is 1, the corresponding result bit is set to 1;
otherwise, the corresponding result bit is set to 0.

The following table shows the result of an inclusive OR operation on corresponding
nExpression1 and *nExpression2* bits:

nExpression1 bit	*nExpression2* bit	Resulting bit
0	0	0
0	1	1
1	0	1
1	1	1

Example

```
x = 5  && 0101 binary
y = 6  && 0110 binary

? BITOR(x,y) && Returns 7, 0111 binary
```

See Also

BITAND( ), BITCLEAR( ), BITLSHIFT( ), BITNOT( ), BITRSHIFT( ), BITSET( ), BITTEST( ), BITXOR( )

BITRSHIFT( ) Function

Returns the result of shifting the bits of a numeric value to the right a specified number of positions.

Syntax

BITRSHIFT(*nExpression1*, *nExpression2*)

Returns

Numeric

Arguments

nExpression1

Specifies the numeric value whose bits are shifted to the right. If *nExpression1* is not an integer, it is converted to an integer before its bits are shifted.

nExpression2

Specifies the number of bit positions to shift. If *nExpression2* is not an integer, it is converted to an integer.

Example

```
x = 5   && 0101 binary
y = 1   && Shift bits 1 position right

? BITRSHIFT(x,y) && Returns 2, 0010 binary
```

See Also

BITAND( ), BITCLEAR( ), BITLSHIFT( ), BITNOT( ), BITOR( ), BITSET( ), BITTEST( ), BITXOR( )

BITSET( ) Function

Sets the bit to 1 in a numeric value and returns the resulting value.

Syntax

BITSET(*nExpression1*, *nExpression2*)

Returns

Numeric

Arguments

nExpression1

Specifies the numeric value in which a bit is set. If *nExpression1* is not an integer, it is converted to an integer before its bit is set.

nExpression2

Specifies the bit position in *nExpression1* that is set to 1. *nExpression2* can range from 0 to 31; 0 is the rightmost bit.

Example

```
x = 5    && 0101 binary
y = 1    && 2nd bit position (0 = 1st bit position)
? BITSET(x,y) && Returns 7, 0111 binary
```

See Also

BITAND( ), BITCLEAR( ), BITLSHIFT( ), BITNOT( ), BITOR( ), BITRSHIFT( ), BITTEST( ), BITXOR( )

BITTEST( ) Function

Returns true (.T.) if a specified bit in a numeric value is set to 1; otherwise, returns false (.F.).

Syntax

BITTEST(*nExpression1*, *nExpression2*)

Returns

Logical

Arguments

nExpression1

Specifies the numeric value in which a bit is checked. If *nExpression1* is not an integer, it is converted to an integer before its bit is checked.

nExpression2

Specifies the bit position in *nExpression1* that is checked. *nExpression2* can range from 0 to 31; 0 is the rightmost bit.

Example

The following example uses BITTEST( ) to determine whether a series of integers are even. If an integer is even, the function IsEven returns true (.T.); otherwise, it returns false (.F.).

```
CLEAR
? '2 even? '
?? IsEven(2)   && Even, .T. returned
? '3 even? '
?? IsEven(3)   && Not even, .F. returned
? '0 even? '
?? IsEven(0)   && Even, .T. returned
? '-13 even? '
?? IsEven(-13)  && Not even, .F. returned

Function IsEven
   PARAMETER nInteger
   RETURN NOT BITTEST(nInteger, 0)
```

See Also

BITAND( ), BITCLEAR( ), BITLSHIFT( ), BITNOT( ), BITOR( ), BITRSHIFT( ), BITSET( ), BITXOR( )

BITXOR( ) Function

Returns the result of a bitwise exclusive OR operation performed on two numeric values.

Syntax

BITXOR(*nExpression1*, *nExpression2*)

Returns

Numeric

Arguments

nExpression1, *nExpression2*

Specifies the numeric values on which the bitwise exclusive OR operation is performed. If *nExpression1* and *nExpression2* are not integers, they are converted to integers before the bitwise exclusive OR operation is performed.

Remarks

BITXOR( ) compares each bit in *nExpression1* to the corresponding bit in *nExpression2*. If one bit is 0 and the other bit is 1, the corresponding result bit is set to 1. Otherwise, the corresponding result bit is set to 0.

The following table shows the result of an exclusive OR operation on corresponding *nExpression1* and *nExpression2* bits:

nExpression1 bit	nExpression2 bit	Result bit
0	0	0
0	1	1
1	0	1
1	1	0

Example

```
x = 5  && 0101 binary
y = 6  && 0110 binary

? BITXOR(x,y) && Returns 3, 0011 binary
```

See Also

BITAND( ), BITCLEAR( ), BITLSHIFT( ), BITNOT( ), BITOR( ), BITRSHIFT( ), BITSET( ), BITTEST( )

BLANK Command

Clears data from all fields in the current record when issued without additional arguments.

Syntax

BLANK
    [FIELDS *FieldList*]
    [*Scope*]
    [FOR *lExpression1*]
    [WHILE *lExpression2*]
    [NOOPTIMIZE]

Arguments

FIELDS *FieldList*
    Clears only the fields you specify with *FieldList*. If you omit the FIELDS clause, all fields in a record are cleared by default. Any field you specify in an unselected work area must be prefaced with the alias of the work area.

        Important   BLANK does not clear field data of a record in another related work area if the record pointer is at the end of the file in the current work area. The record pointer must be on a record in the current work area in order for BLANK to act on the fields in the related record.

Scope

Specifies a range of records to clear. Only the records that fall within the range are cleared. The scope clauses are: ALL, NEXT *nRecords*, RECORD *nRecordNumber*, and REST.

For more information on scope clauses, see "Scope Clauses" and "Overview of the Language" in Help. Commands which include *Scope* operate only on the table in the active work area.

The default scope for BLANK is the current record (NEXT 1).

FOR *lExpression1*

Clears field data in records for which *lExpression1* evaluates to true (.T.). Rushmore optimizes BLANK FOR if *lExpression1* is an optimizable expression. A discussion of Rushmore optimization appears in "Understanding Rushmore Technology" in Chapter 15, "Optimizing Applications," in the *Microsoft Visual FoxPro 6.0 Programmer's Guide*.

WHILE *lExpression2*

Specifies a condition whereby field data in records is cleared as long as the logical expression *lExpression2* evaluates to true (.T.).

NOOPTIMIZE

Prevents Rushmore optimization of BLANK. For more information see the SET OPTIMIZE Command, later in this language reference, and "Understanding Rushmore Technology" in Chapter 15, "Optimizing Applications," in the *Microsoft Visual FoxPro 6.0 Programmer's Guide*.

Remarks

Use APPEND BLANK to add a new blank record to the end of a table. Use ISBLANK( ) to determine if a field in a record is blank.

Example

The following example opens the `customer` table in the `testdata` database. The contents of the first record are displayed. SCATTER is used to save the contents of the record to an array. The record is cleared with BLANK, and the contents of the record are displayed again. GATHER is used to restore the original record contents, and the restored record contents are displayed again.

```
CLOSE DATABASES
OPEN DATABASE (HOME(2) + 'data\testdata')
USE customer  && Open customer table

CLEAR
DISPLAY  && Displays the current record
SCATTER TO gaCustomer  && Create array with record contents
BLANK  && Clear the record
```

```
DISPLAY  && Displays the blank record
GATHER FROM gaCustomer  && Restore original record contents
DISPLAY  && Display the restored record
```

See Also

APPEND, EMPTY( ), ISBLANK( ), REPLACE, SET OPTIMIZE

BOF( ) Function

Determines whether the record pointer is positioned at the beginning of a table.

Syntax

BOF([*nWorkArea* | *cTableAlias*])

Returns

Logical

Arguments

nWorkArea
    Specifies the work area number for a table open in another work area.

cTableAlias
    Specifies the table alias for a table open in another work area.

    If the table you want to test for a beginning-of-file condition is open in a work area
    other than the currently selected work area, use these optional arguments to specify the
    work area number or table alias for the table. If a table isn't open in the work area you
    specify, BOF( ) returns false (.F.).

Remarks

Use BOF( ) to test for a beginning-of-file condition for a table. BOF( ) returns true (.T.) if
you have tried to move the record pointer to a position before the first record in the table.

Example

The following example opens the customer table and lists the company name one page at a
time, starting with the last record in the table. The listing continues until the beginning of
the file is reached or until you choose Cancel.

```
CLOSE DATABASES
CLEAR
OPEN DATABASE (HOME() + "samples\data\testdata")
USE customer
GO BOTTOM
local recCtr, btnValue
recCtr = 0
btnValue = 1
```

```
DO WHILE btnValue = 1 AND NOT BOF()
    ? "Company : " + company
    recCtr = recCtr + 1
    if (recCtr % 20) = 0 then
        btnValue =MESSAGEBOX ("Click OK to continue, Cancel to quit.",33)
        clear
    endif
    Skip -1     && Move up one record
ENDDO
=MESSAGEBOX("Listing complete.",48)
```

See Also

EOF( )

BorderColor Property

Specifies the border color of an object. Available at design time and run time.

Syntax

*Object.*BorderColor[= *nColor*]

Arguments

nColor

Specifies the border color value.

The following table lists typical color values:

Color	RGB values	*nColor* value
White	255, 255, 255	16777215
Black	0, 0, 0	0
Gray	192, 192, 192	12632256
Dark gray	128, 128, 128	8421504
Red	255, 0, 0	255
Dark red	128, 0, 0	128
Yellow	255, 255, 0	65535
Dark yellow	128, 128, 0	32896
Green	0, 255, 0	65280
Dark green	0, 128, 0	32768
Cyan	0, 255, 255	16776960

(continued)

Color	RGB values	*nColor* value
Dark cyan	0, 128, 128	8421376
Blue	0, 0, 255	16711680
Dark blue	0, 0, 128	8388608
Magenta	255, 0 ,255	16711935
Dark magenta	128, 0, 128	8388736

Remarks

BorderColor applies only to a text box or edit box when the SpecialEffect property is set to 1 – Plain.

Use the RGB( ) function to convert the three component colors into one composite *nColor*.

Applies To

ComboBox, CommandGroup, Container Object, Control Object, EditBox, Image, Line, ListBox, OptionGroup, PageFrame, Shape, TextBox

See Also

BackColor Property, Colors Overview, GetColor( ), RGB( ), SpecialEffect Property

BorderStyle Property

Specifies the border style of an object. Available at design time and run time.

Syntax

Object.BorderStyle[= *nStyle*]

Arguments

nStyle
For a CommandGroup, EditBox, Image, Label, OptionGroup, or TextBox control, the settings for the BorderStyle property are:

Setting	Description
0	None. Default for Image and Label controls.
1	Fixed Single. Default for CommandGroup, EditBox, OptionGroup, and TextBox controls.

For a line or shape, the settings for the BorderStyle property are:

Setting	Description
0	Transparent
1	(Default) Solid. The outer edge of the border is the outer edge of the Shape control.
2	Dash
3	Dot
4	Dash-Dot
5	Dash-Dot-Dot
6	Inside Solid

For a Form object, the settings for the BorderStyle property are:

Setting	Description
0	No border
1	Fixed Single
2	Fixed Dialog
3	(Default) Sizable

Remarks

If the BorderWidth property setting is greater than 1, regardless of the BorderStyle setting, a solid border is drawn. If BorderWidth is set to 1, BorderStyle produces the effects described in the tables above.

Applies To

ComboBox, CommandGroup, EditBox, Form, Image, Label, Line, OptionGroup, _SCREEN, Shape, TextBox, Spinner

See Also

BorderColor Property, BorderWidth Property, DrawStyle Property, DrawWidth Property

BorderWidth Property

Specifies the width of a control's border. Available at design time and run time.

Syntax

Control.BorderWidth[= *nWidth*]

Arguments

nWidth

Specifies the width, which can range from 0 to 8192.

> **Note** If the BorderWidth setting is greater than 1, the BorderStyle property setting is ignored.

Remarks

When BorderWidth is set to 0, the control appears to have no border. You cannot change the BorderWidth setting for the PageFrame control.

Applies To

Container Object, Control Object, Line, PageFrame, Shape

See Also

BorderStyle Property

Bound Property

Determines whether a control in a Column object is bound to the control source for the Column. Available at design time and run time.

Syntax

Column.Bound[= *lExpr*]

Arguments

lExpr

The settings for the Bound property are:

Setting	Description
True (.T.)	(Default) The control is bound to the column's control source.
False (.F.)	The control is not bound to the column's control source.

Remarks

If a column's Bound property is set to true (.T.), the column's ControlSource property setting applies to the column and any controls contained in it. If you attempt to set the contained control's ControlSource property, an error occurs. If a column's Bound property is set to false (.F.), you can set the ControlSource property of a contained control directly. If you subsequently set the ControlSource setting of the column, it overrides the ControlSource setting of the contained control.

Typically, the following controls are bound to the corresponding data types:

Column control base class	Typical column data types
CheckBox	Logical, Numeric
ComboBox	Character, Numeric
CommandButton	Character, Numeric
EditBox	Character
ListBox	Character, Numeric
OptionButton	Character, Numeric
Spinner	Currency, Numeric
TextBox	Any data type except General or Memo

Note You cannot bind a control to a column whose data type is General or Memo.

Applies To

Column

See Also

AddObject Method, ControlSource Property, CurrentControl Property, Sparse Property

BoundColumn Property

Determines which column of a multicolumn list box or combo box is bound to the Value property of the control. Available at design time and run time.

Syntax

*Control.*BoundColumn[= *nCol*]

Arguments

nCol
Specifies the number of the column that is bound to the Value property. The default for *nCol* is 1.

Remarks

Use BoundColumn when the list box or combo box has multiple columns and when you want the data in a column other than the first column to be stored in the control's Value property.

Applies To

ComboBox, ListBox

See Also

Value Property

BoundTo Property

Specifies whether the Value property of a combo box or list box is determined by the List or the ListIndex properties. Available at design time and run time.

Syntax

[*Form.*]*Control*.BoundTo[= *lExpression*]

Arguments

lExpression
    The settings for the BoundTo property are:

Setting	Description
.T.	The Value property is determined by the List property.
.F.	(Default) The Value property is determined by data type of the variable or field specified in the ControlSource property.

If the variable or field specified in the ControlSource property setting is of character type, the Value property is determined by the List property.

If the variable or field specified in the ControlSource property setting is of numeric type, the Value property uses the index number from the ListIndex property.

This setting provides compatibility with Microsoft Visual FoxPro 3.0 and 2.x versions of FoxPro.

Remarks

In Visual FoxPro 3.0, if the ControlSource property for a combo box or list box is numeric, the ListIndex property value of the selected item is stored in the variable or field to which the control is bound. Set the BoundTo property to true (.T.) to store the value of the List property in the variable or field to which the control is bound.

Applies To

ComboBox, ListBox

See Also

ControlSource Property, ListIndex Property, Value Property

Box Method

Draws a rectangle on a Form object.

Syntax

Object.Box(*nXCoord1*, *nYCoord1*, *nXCoord2*, *nYCoord2*)

– or –

Object.Box(*nXCoord2*, *nYCoord2*)

Arguments

nXCoord1, *nYCoord1*

Specifies the coordinates of the starting point for the rectangle. The ScaleMode method of the form determines the unit of measurement used. If you omit these arguments, the value of CurrentX and CurrentY are used.

nXCoord2, *nYCoord2*

Specifies the endpoint of the rectangle.

Remarks

The width of the lines drawn depends on the DrawWidth property setting. How a rectangle is drawn on the background depends on the settings of the DrawMode and DrawStyle properties. When the Box method is called, the CurrentX and CurrentY properties are set to the endpoint specified by the last two arguments.

Applies To

Form, _SCREEN

See Also

CurrentX, CurrentY Properties, DrawMode Property, DrawStyle Property, DrawWidth Property, ScaleMode Property

_BOX System Variable

Included for backward compatibility. Use the Report Designer instead.

BROWSE Command

Opens the Browse window and displays records from the current or selected table.

Syntax

BROWSE
    [FIELDS *FieldList*]
    [FONT *cFontName* [, *nFontSize*]]
    [STYLE *cFontStyle*]
    [FOR *lExpression1* [REST]]
    [FORMAT]
    [FREEZE *FieldName*]
    [KEY *eExpression1* [, *eExpression2*]]
    [LAST | NOINIT]
    [LOCK *nNumberOfFields*]
    [LPARTITION]
    [NAME *ObjectName*]
    [NOAPPEND]
    [NODELETE]
    [NOEDIT | NOMODIFY]
    [NOLGRID] [NORGRID]
    [NOLINK]
    [NOMENU]
    [NOOPTIMIZE]
    [NOREFRESH]
    [NORMAL]
    [NOWAIT]
    [PARTITION *nColumnNumber* [LEDIT] [REDIT]]
    [PREFERENCE *PreferenceName*]
    [SAVE]
    [TIMEOUT *nSeconds*]
    [TITLE *cTitleText*]
    [VALID [:F] *lExpression2* [ERROR *cMessageText*]]
    [WHEN *lExpression3*]
    [WIDTH *nFieldWidth*]
    [WINDOW *WindowName1*]
    [IN [WINDOW] *WindowName2* | IN SCREEN]
    [COLOR SCHEME *nSchemeNumber*]

Arguments

FIELDS *FieldList*

Specifies the fields that appear in the Browse window. The fields are displayed in the order specified in *FieldList*. You can include fields from other related tables in the field list. When you include a field from a related table, preface the field name with its table alias and a period.

If you omit FIELDS, all the fields in the table are displayed in the order they appear in the table structure.

FONT *cFontName* [, *nFontSize*]

Specifies the Browse window's font and font size. The character expression *cFontName* specifies the name of the font, and the numeric expression *nFontSize* specifies the font size. For example, the following clause specifies 16-point Courier font for the fields displayed in a Browse window:

```
FONT 'Courier',16
```

If you include the FONT clause but omit the font size *nFontSize*, a 10-point font is used in the Browse window. If you omit the FONT clause, 8-point MS Sans Serif is used.

If the font you specify is not available, a font with similar font characteristics is substituted.

STYLE *cFontStyle*

Specifies the Browse window's font style. If you omit the STYLE clause, the Normal font style is used

If the font style you specify is not available, a font style with similar characteristics is substituted or the Normal font style is used.

Character	Font style
B	Bold
I	Italic
N	Normal
O	Outline
Q	Opaque
S	Shadow
–	Strikeout
T	Transparent
U	Underline

You can include more than one character to specify a combination of font styles. The following example opens a Browse window and uses an underlined font:

```
CLOSE DATABASES
OPEN DATABASE (HOME(2) + 'data\testdata')
USE customer   && Open customer table
IF _WINDOWS
   BROWSE FIELDS contact FONT 'System', 15  STYLE 'NU'
ENDIF
IF _MAC
BROWSE FIELDS contact FONT 'Geneva', 14  STYLE 'NU'
ENDIF
```

FOR *lExpression1*

Specifies a condition whereby only records for which *lExpression1* is true are displayed in the Browse window.

Rushmore optimizes a query specified with a BROWSE FOR if *lExpression1* is an optimizable expression. For best performance, use an optimizable expression in the FOR clause. For information on Rushmore optimizable expressions, see the SET OPTIMIZE Command, later in this language reference, and "Understanding Rushmore Technology" in Chapter 15, "Optimizing Applications," in the *Microsoft Visual FoxPro 6.0 Programmer's Guide*.

Include FOR to move the record pointer to the first record meeting the condition. Include REST to keep the record pointer at its current position.

REST

Prevents the record pointer from being moved from its current position to the top of the table when a Browse window is opened with the FOR clause. Otherwise, BROWSE positions the record pointer at the top of the table by default.

FORMAT

Specifies the use of a format file to control the display and data-entry format in a Browse window. The format file must first be opened with SET FORMAT. The following information is extracted from the format file and applied to the Browse window:

- The list of fields to browse

- All VALID clauses

- All WHEN clauses

- All RANGE clauses

- Field sizes (as specified in PICTURE clauses)

- All SAY expressions (included as calculated BROWSE fields)

The following example uses a format file to validate data entered into a Browse window. Positions specified with @ ... GET are ignored.

The first line creates a BROWSE field (`cust_id`) that is 5 characters wide and allows the entry of letters and digits only. The second line creates a BROWSE field (`company`) that cannot contain a blank value and can contain a maximum of 20 alphabetic characters.

The third line creates a BROWSE field (`contact`) into which you enter data only when the field is blank.

Here are the contents of the Custentr.fmt format file, which is used to validate data entered into the `customer` table:

```
@ 3,0 GET cust_id PICTURE 'NNNNN'
@ 3,0 GET company VALID company != SPACE(40) ;
   PICTURE 'AAAAAAAAAAAAAAAAAAAA'
@ 3,0 GET contact WHEN contact = SPACE(40)


* This is the program that uses the format file
CLOSE DATABASES
OPEN DATABASE (HOME(2) + 'data\testdata')
USE customer   && Open customer table
SET FORMAT TO custentr.fmt
BROWSE FORMAT
```

FREEZE *FieldName*

Permits changes to be made to only one field in the Browse window. You specify this field with *FieldName*. The remaining fields are displayed but cannot be edited.

```
CLOSE DATABASES
OPEN DATABASE (HOME(2) + 'data\testdata')
USE customer   && Open customer table
BROWSE FIELDS phone :H = 'Phone Number:' , ;
   company :H = 'Company:' ;
   FREEZE phone
```

KEY *eExpression1* [, *eExpression2*]

Limits the scope of records that are displayed in the Browse window. With KEY you can specify an index key value (*eExpression1*) or a range of key values (*eExpression1*, *eExpression2*) for the records that are displayed in the Browse window. The table you browse must be indexed, and the index key value or values included in the KEY clause must be the same data type as the index expression of the master index file or tag.

For example, the `customer` table includes a character field containing postal codes. If the table is indexed on the postal code field, you can specify a range of postal codes in the KEY clause.

In the following example, only records with postal codes falling within the range of 10,000 to 30,000 are displayed in the Browse window:

```
CLOSE DATABASES
OPEN DATABASE (HOME(2) + 'data\testdata')
USE customer  && Open customer table
SET ORDER TO postalcode
BROWSE KEY '10000', '30000'
```

LAST | NOINIT

Saves any configuration changes made to the appearance of a Browse window. The changes are saved in the FOXUSER file and can include changes to the field list, the size of each field, and the location and size of the Browse window.

If you issue BROWSE with the LAST or NOINIT clause, the Browse window opens in the same configuration that was last saved in the FOXUSER file if SET RESOURCE is ON. This restores the Browse window configuration created with the last BROWSE command. If the last BROWSE issued in the Command window included a long list of clauses, issue BROWSE with the LAST or NOINIT option to avoid having to retype the command. For more information on the FOXUSER file, see the SET RESOURCE Command, later in this language reference.

If the last Browse window was opened with a BROWSE that included a PREFERENCE clause, BROWSE LAST won't restore the preference.

Any Browse window configuration changes you make in the current session aren't saved if you exit BROWSE by pressing CTRL+Q.

The LAST and NOINIT clauses are identical; NOINIT provides dBASE compatibility.

LOCK *nNumberOfFields*

Specifies the number of fields you can see in the left partition of the Browse window without tabbing or scrolling. The left partition sizes automatically to be able to display the number of fields you specify with *nNumberOfFields*.

LPARTITION

Specifies that the cursor is placed in the first field in the left Browse window partition. By default, the cursor is placed in the first field in the right partition when the Browse window is opened.

NAME *ObjectName*

Creates an object reference for the Browse window, allowing you to manipulate the Browse window with object-oriented properties available for the Grid control. For additional information about object-oriented programming in Visual FoxPro, see Chapter 3, "Object-Oriented Programming," in the *Microsoft Visual FoxPro 6.0 Programmer's Guide*. For additional information about the Grid control properties that you can specify for a Browse window created with the NAME clause, see "Grid Control," later in this language reference.

NOAPPEND

Prevents the user from adding records to the table by pressing CTRL+Y or by choosing Append Record from the Table menu.

> **Important** Including NOAPPEND doesn't prevent you from appending a record from within a routine (created with VALID, WHEN, or ON KEY LABEL) while in the Browse window.

NODELETE

Prevents records from being marked for deletion from within a Browse window. By default, a record can be marked for deletion by pressing CTRL+T, choosing Toggle Delete from the Table menu, or by clicking in the leftmost column of the record to be deleted.

NOEDIT | NOMODIFY

Prevents a user from modifying the table. NOEDIT and NOMODIFY are identical. If you include either clause, you can browse or search the table, but you cannot edit it. However, you can append and delete records.

NOLGRID

Removes the field gridlines in the left partition of the Browse window.

NORGRID

Removes the field gridlines in the right partition of the Browse window.

NOLINK

Unlinks the partitions in a Browse window. By default, the left and right partitions of the Browse window are linked together so that when you scroll through one partition, the other partition scrolls.

NOMENU

Removes the Table menu title from the system menu bar, preventing access to the Browse menu.

NOOPTIMIZE

Disables Rushmore optimization of BROWSE. For more information, see the SET OPTIMIZE Command, later in this language reference, and "Understanding Rushmore Technology" in Chapter 15, "Optimizing Applications," in the *Microsoft Visual FoxPro 6.0 Programmer's Guide*.

NOREFRESH

Prevents the Browse window from being refreshed. Browse windows are refreshed at the rate determined by SET REFRESH. NOREFRESH is useful with read-only files and improves performance.

NORMAL

Opens the Browse window with its normal default settings, such as its colors, size, position, title, and control options (GROW, FLOAT, ZOOM, and so on). If you omit NORMAL and the current output window is a user-defined window with its own settings, the Browse window assumes those user-defined settings also.

NOWAIT

Continues program execution immediately after the Browse window is opened. The program doesn't wait for the Browse window to be closed but continues executing on the program line immediately following the program line containing BROWSE NOWAIT. If you omit NOWAIT when BROWSE is issued from within a program, a Browse window is opened and program execution pauses until the Browse window is closed.

NOWAIT is available only from within a program. Including NOWAIT when issuing BROWSE from the Command window has no effect.

PARTITION *nColumnNumber*

Splits a Browse window into left and right partitions with *nColumnNumber* specifying the column number of the split bar. For example, if *nColumnNumber* is 20, the split bar is placed in column 20 of the Browse window.

LEDIT

Specifies that the left partition of the Browse window appears in Edit mode.

REDIT

Specifies that the right partition of the Browse window appears in Edit mode. This example opens a Browse window with the split bar placed in column 20 and the right partition open in Edit mode.

Include both keywords to open both partitions in Edit mode.

```
CLOSE DATABASES
OPEN DATABASE (HOME(2) + 'data\testdata')
USE customer  && Open customer table
BROWSE PARTITION 20 REDIT
```

PREFERENCE *PreferenceName*

Saves a Browse window's attributes and options for later use. Unlike LAST, which restores the Browse window as it appeared in the previous session, PREFERENCE saves a Browse window's attributes indefinitely in the FOXUSER resource file. Preferences can be retrieved at any time.

Issuing BROWSE with the specified preference name for the first time creates an entry in the FOXUSER file that saves the Browse window configuration. Issuing BROWSE later with the same preference name restores the Browse window to that preference state. When the Browse window is closed, the preference is updated.

Preference names can be up to 10 characters long, must begin with a letter or an underscore, and can contain any combination of letters, numbers and underscores.

Once you have a preference the way you like it, you can prevent it from being changed. Close the Browse window, issue SET RESOURCE OFF, open the FOXUSER file as a table, and change the record containing the preference to read-only by changing the value of the logical field READONLY to true (.T.).

For more information about the FOXUSER resource file, see the SET RESOURCE Command, later in this language reference.

If you exit a Browse window by pressing CTRL+Q, no Browse window changes are saved to the resource file.

SAVE

Keeps the Browse window and any of its memo field text-editing windows active and visible (open). You can then return to the Browse window after cycling through other open windows with the keyboard or the mouse.

SAVE is available only from within a program. SAVE has no effect when included with BROWSE in the Command window because BROWSE SAVE is always the default in the interactive mode.

TIMEOUT *nSeconds*

Specifies how long a Browse window waits for input. The numeric expression *nSeconds* specifies how many seconds can elapse without any input before the Browse window automatically closes.

TIMEOUT is available only from within a program; it has no effect when you issue BROWSE from the Command window. In the following example, the Browse window is closed if no input occurs in 10 seconds.

```
DEFINE WINDOW wBrowse FROM 1,1 TO 24,40 ;
    CLOSE ;
    GROW ;
    COLOR SCHEME 10
CLOSE DATABASES
OPEN DATABASE (HOME(2) + 'data\testdata')
USE customer  && Open customer table
BROWSE WINDOW wBrowse ;
    FIELDS phone :H = 'Phone Number:' , ;
    company :H = 'Company:' ;
    TIMEOUT 10
RELEASE WINDOW wBrowse
```

TITLE *cTitleText*

Overrides the default table name or alias that appears in the Browse window title bar with the title you specify with *cTitleText*. Otherwise, the name or alias of the table being browsed appears in the title bar.

If you issue BROWSE WINDOW to place the Browse window in a user-defined window, the Browse window's title replaces the user-defined window's title.

```
CLOSE DATABASES
OPEN DATABASE (HOME(2) + 'data\testdata')
USE customer  && Open customer table
```

```
BROWSE;
    TITLE 'My Browse Window' ;
    FIELDS phone :H = 'Phone Number' , ;
    company :H = 'Company:'
```

VALID *lExpression2*

Performs record-level validation in a Browse window. The VALID clause is executed only if a change is made to the record and you attempt to move the cursor to another record. The VALID clause is not executed if the only change is to a memo field.

If VALID returns a value that is true (.T.), the user can move the cursor to another record. If VALID returns a false value (.F.), the cursor remains in the current field and Visual FoxPro generates an error message. If VALID returns 0, the cursor remains in the current field, and an error message isn't displayed.

The VALID clause shouldn't be confused with the verify option (:V), which enables field-level validation.

:F

Forces the VALID clause to execute before the user moves the cursor to the next record. In this case, VALID is executed even if the record isn't changed.

ERROR *cMessageText*

Specifies an error message that overrides the system default error message. Visual FoxPro displays *cMessageText* when VALID returns false (.F.).

WHEN *lExpression3*

Evaluates a condition when the user moves the cursor to another record. If *lExpression3* evaluates to true (.T.), the user can modify the record moved to. If *lExpression3* evaluates to false (.F.) or 0, the record the user moves to becomes read-only and cannot be modified.

The WHEN clause isn't executed when another window is activated.

WIDTH *nFieldWidth*

Limits the number of characters displayed for all fields in a Browse window to *nFieldWidth*. The contents of a field can be scrolled horizontally using the Left and Right Arrow keys or the horizontal scroll bar. Including the WIDTH clause doesn't change the size of fields in the table; it alters only the way the fields are displayed in the Browse window. If a width has been specified for an individual field with the FIELDS clause, it overrides the width specified with the WIDTH clause for that field.

WINDOW *WindowName1*

Specifies a user-defined window whose characteristics the Browse window assumes. For example, if the user-defined window is created with the FLOAT clause, the Browse window can be moved. The specified window doesn't have to be active or visible, but it must be defined.

IN [WINDOW] *WindowName2*

Specifies the parent window within which the Browse window is opened. The Browse window doesn't assume the characteristics of the parent window. A Browse window activated inside a parent window cannot be moved outside the parent window. If the parent window is moved, the Browse window moves with it.

To access the Browse window, the parent window must first be defined with DEFINE WINDOW and must be active and visible.

IN SCREEN

Explicitly places a Browse window on the main Visual FoxPro window when a user-defined window is active.

COLOR SCHEME *nSchemeNumber*

Specifies the number of a color scheme used for the Browse window's colors.

The Browse window assumes the color scheme established using the Windows Color Control Panel.

Remarks

A Browse window allows you to view records in a table, edit those records, and append additional records. Visual FoxPro allows you to have several Browse windows open at the same time.

If you press ESC to exit a Browse window, changes made to the last field you modified are discarded. However, if you move to another record after modifying a field, your changes to the field are saved.

For information on navigating in the Browse window, see Chapter 2, "Creating Tables and Indexes," in the *User's Guide* in Help.

The field list can specify any combination of fields or calculated fields.

The syntax of the field list is:

```
FieldName1
   [:R]
   [:nColumnWidth]
   [:V = lExpression1 [:F] [:E = cMessageText]]
   [:P = cFormatCodes]
   [:B = eLowerBound, eUpperBound [:F]]
   [:H = cHeadingText]
   [:W = lExpression2]
   [, FieldName2 [:R]...]
```

Calculated Fields...   The field list can contain statements for creating calculated fields. A calculated field contains read-only data created with an expression. The expression can take any form, but it must be a valid Visual FoxPro expression.

The format of the statement you use to create a calculated field is:

CalculatedFieldName = eExpression

The following example creates a calculated field called location:

```
CLOSE DATABASES
OPEN DATABASE (HOME(2) + 'data\testdata')
USE customer  && Open customer table
BROWSE FIELDS location = ALLTRIM(city) + ', ' + country
```

city and country are the names of fields from the currently selected table.

The FIELDS clause field list includes options that enable special handling of fields displayed in a Browse window:

:R

Specifies that the field is read-only. The data it contains can be viewed but not edited.

In the following example, a Browse window is opened with the cust_id and company fields. The cust_id field is read-only and cannot be changed.

```
CLOSE DATABASES
OPEN DATABASE (HOME(2) + 'data\testdata')
USE customer  && Open customer table
BROWSE FIELDS cust_id:R, company
```

:nColumnWidth

Specifies the display size for a field in columns. The value of *:nColumnWidth* doesn't affect the size of the field in the table; it only alters the way the field appears in the Browse window.

:V = *lExpression1* [:F] [:E = *cMessageText*]

Lets you perform field-level data validation within the Browse window. If *lExpression1* evaluates to true (.T.) when you move the cursor from a field, the data input into the field is considered correct and the cursor moves to the next field.

If *lExpression1* evaluates to false (.F.), the data input is considered incorrect, the cursor remains in the field and a message appears. If *lExpression1* evaluates to 0, the data input is considered incorrect and the cursor remains in the field but no error message appears.

The verify option is not executed for memo fields.

By default, *lExpression1* is evaluated only when the field is modified. To force verification, include the :F option.

You can display your own error message by including the :E option described below.

:F

Determines whether the expression in the verify option is evaluated when you move the cursor out of a field or another window is activated. If :F is not included, *lExpression1* is evaluated only if changes are made to the field. If :F is included, *lExpression1* is evaluated even if the field isn't modified.

:E = *cMessageText*

If the validation expression :V = *lExpression1* evaluates to true (.T.), the cursor leaves the field normally. If the expression evaluates to false (.F.), the cursor remains in the field, and Visual FoxPro generates an error message.

If the error option (:E) is included, *cMessageText* appears instead of the system error message. *cMessageText* appears only if SET NOTIFY is ON. The bell is sounded if SET BELL is ON.

If :V = *lExpression1* evaluates to 0, no message appears and the cursor remains in the field being validated. This option lets you display your own error messages in validation routines.

The following example opens the `products` table and displays the `product_id` and `prod_name` fields. The `product_id` field is a numeric field that will accept up to five numbers. For purposes of this example, we consider a `product_id` greater than 100 to be invalid.

:V specifies the validation criteria. :F forces the validation check to be performed whether the data is changed or not. :E replaces the Visual FoxPro system error message with a user-defined error message. In Visual FoxPro, the error message appears in the status bar at the bottom of the main Visual FoxPro window.

Press ESC to close the Browse window.

```
CLOSE DATABASES
OPEN DATABASE (HOME(2) + 'data\testdata')
USE products   && Open products table
IF _WINDOWS OR _MAC
   SET STATUS BAR ON
ENDIF
USE products
BROWSE FIELDS in_stock :V = in_stock < 100 ;
   :F ;
   :E = 'The stock amount must be less than 100'
```

:P = *cFormatCodes*

If you include a FIELDS clause, you can also specify a picture option (:P) for each field in the list. The picture option lets you create a list of codes that controls the display and input of data for each field in a Browse window. *cFormatCodes* is the list of codes.

The following example uses the picture option to allow only numeric data in a specific format to be entered in the `unit_price` field:

```
CLOSE DATABASES
OPEN DATABASE (HOME(2) + 'data\testdata')
USE products   && Open products table
BROWSE FIELDS unit_price :P = '99,999.99'
```

See the Format and InputMask Properties, later in this language reference, for more information about picture option codes.

:B = *eLowerBound*, *eUpperBound* [:F]

Specifies a set of boundaries between which data in a field must fall. The boundary expressions *eLowerBound* and *eUpperBound* must match the data type of the field. They cannot be user-defined functions. If the data entered doesn't fall between *eLowerBound* and *eUpperBound*, a system error message appears indicating the range within which the data must fall.

By default, the data you enter is checked against the boundary values only if you make a change to the contents of the field. To force checking against the boundary values, include the forced validation option (:F).

The following example ensures that the value in the `in_stock` field falls between 1 and 100. Press ESC to close the Browse window.

```
CLOSE DATABASES
OPEN DATABASE (HOME(2) + 'data\testdata')
USE products  && Open products table
BROWSE FIELDS in_stock :B = 1, 100    :F
```

:H = *cHeadingText*

Replaces the default field names with your own headings, which you specify with *cHeadingText*. By default, field names are used as the column headings in the Browse window.

The following example provides user-defined headings for the displayed fields.

```
CLOSE DATABASES
OPEN DATABASE (HOME(2) + 'data\testdata')
USE products  && Open products table
BROWSE FIELDS prod_name :H = 'Product Name:', ;
    unit_price :H = 'Price per Unit:'
```

:W = *lExpression2*

Determines whether the cursor can be moved to a field. If *lExpression2* evaluates to false (.F.), moving the cursor to the field is prohibited. If *lExpression2* evaluates to true (.T.), the cursor can be moved to the field. User-defined functions are supported in *lExpression2*.

If moving the cursor to all fields is prohibited, the current record is marked read-only. This occurs only when every field contains a WHEN clause that evaluates to false.

SET SKIP Support... SET SKIP lets you establish a one-to-many relationship between two tables. For each record in the parent table, there can be multiple related records in the child table. If you create a one-to-many relationship, you may use BROWSE to view records from both the parent and child tables.

The parent record appears once, along with the first matching record from the child table. Any subsequent matching records are displayed in the rows following the parent record and first matching child record. The fill character for repeated parent information depends on the current Browse window font.

If the record pointer is positioned on a parent record, you can move the pointer through the parent records in the Browse window by pressing CTRL+DOWN ARROW to move to the next parent record or CTRL+UP ARROW to move to the previous parent record. For more information on creating one-to-many relationships, see the SET SKIP Command, later in this language reference.

The FIELDS clause field list contains records from both the parent and child tables. The names of fields are prefaced with their table alias (orders or customer) and a period.

```
CLEAR
CLOSE DATABASES
OPEN DATABASE (HOME(2) + 'data\testdata')
USE customer ORDER cust_id IN 0   && Parent table
USE orders ORDER cust_id IN 0  && Child table
SELECT customer     && Back to parent work area
SET RELATION TO cust_id INTO orders     && Establish relationship
SET SKIP TO orders  && One-to-many relationship
WAIT WINDOW 'Scroll to see shipping dates for each customer' NOWAIT
BROWSE FIELDS customer.cust_id :H='Customer Number', ;
    customer.city :H='Customer City', orders.shipped_on
```

Useful Functions...   Several Visual FoxPro functions return useful information about a Browse window.

Function	Description
VARREAD( )	Returns the name of the field the cursor is in for the active Browse window.
RECNO( )	Returns the record number of the selected record in the active Browse window.

See Also

CHANGE, EDIT, Grid Control, SET SKIP, WTITLE( )

_BROWSER System Variable

Contains the name of the class browser application.

Syntax

_BROWSER = *cProgramName*

Arguments

cProgramName

Specifies a class browser application. _BROWSER contains Browser.app if you have installed the class browser application.

If the class browser is in a directory other than the current default, include a path with the class browser application name.

If the class browser is in a folder other than the current default, include a path with the class browser application name.

You can also specify a class browser application in your Visual FoxPro configuration file by including a line using this syntax:

```
_BROWSER = cProgramName
```

A different class browser application can be specified by storing the new application name in _BROWSER from within the Command window or a program.

Remarks

Browser.app displays the relationships between classes in a visual class library (.vcx) and is installed by default in the directory in which Visual FoxPro is installed.

You can run the class browser by issuing the following command:

```
DO (_BROWSER)
```

Issuing this command adds a class browser menu item in the Tools menu and starts the class browser. The class browser can be run again by choosing the class browser menu item.

To add the class browser menu item to the Tools menu without starting the class browser, issue the following command:

```
DO (_BROWSER) WITH 0
```

You can also run the class browser for a specific visual class library or an object reference, and you can optionally include the name of a class that is initially selected. For example, the following command starts the class browser, opens the Buttons visual class library, and selects the VCR class:

```
DO (_BROWSER) WITH HOME( ) + '\SAMPLES\CONTROLS\BUTTONS.VCX', 'VCR'
```

For additional information about the Visual FoxPro Class Browser, see "Managing Classes with the Class Browser."

See Also

CREATE CLASS, CREATE CLASSLIB, CREATE FORM, CREATEOBJECT( ), DEFINE CLASS, System Variables Overview

BufferMode Property

Specifies whether records are updated pessimistically or optimistically. Available at design time and run time.

Syntax

Object.BufferMode[= *nValue*]

Arguments

nValue

The settings for the BufferMode property are:

Setting	Description
0	(Default) None. Records are locked when editing begins and fields are written when the record pointer moves. Mimics FoxPro 2.x behavior.
1	Pessimistic. Records are locked when editing begins and fields are written when the record pointer moves. You can use TABLEREVERT( ) to undo your changes to the current record.
2	Optimistic. Records are not locked when edited and Visual FoxPro attempts to lock the records when they are written to disk with TABLEUPDATE( ).

Remarks

If BufferMode is set to 1 or 2, any cursor used by a Grid control is enabled for table buffering. Any other control bound to data uses row buffering.

Applies To

Form, FormSet, _SCREEN

See Also

BufferModeOverride Property, TABLEREVERT( ), TABLEUPDATE ( )

BufferModeOverride Property

Specifies whether to override the BufferMode property set at the form or form set level. Available at design time and run time.

Syntax

DataEnvironment.Cursor.BufferModeOverride[= *nValue*]

Arguments

nValue

The settings for the BufferModeOverride property are listed in the following table:

Setting	Description
0	None. No buffering is done.
1	(Default) Use form Setting. Uses the BufferMode property set at the form or form set level.
2	Pessimistic row buffering. Locks the record and buffers the changes until the record pointer moves. You can use TABLEREVERT( ) to undo your changes.
3	Optimistic row buffering. Allows edits to a single record and locks the record only when it is written to disk. You can use TABLEREVERT( ) to undo your changes.
4	Pessimistic table buffering. Locks each record edited, but records are not written to disk until TABLEUPDATE( ) is called. You can use TABLEREVERT( ) to undo your changes.
5	Optimistic table buffering. Allows edits to all records and does not lock them until the records are written to disk with TABLEUPDATE( ). You can use TABLEREVERT( ) to undo your changes.

Remarks

If the cursor is based on a local or remote view, the only BufferModeOverride settings available are 3 and 5. If the form set or form's BufferMode property is set to 1 (Pessimistic), the default setting for BufferModeOverride is 3 (Optimistic row buffering) for cursors based on views.

Applies To

Cursor

See Also

BufferMode Property, TABLEREVERT( ), TABLEUPDATE ( )

BUILD APP Command

Creates an application file with an .APP file name extension using information from a project file.

Syntax

BUILD APP *APPFileName* FROM *ProjectName* [RECOMPILE]

Arguments

APPFileName
  Specifies the file name of the application to build. The default file name extension is .app.

FROM *ProjectName*
  Specifies the name of the project from which the application is built.

RECOMPILE

Specifies that the project is compiled before the application file is built. All program and format files; form, label, report, and visual class library source code; and stored procedures in databases in the project are compiled.

Remarks

You create a project file with CREATE PROJECT or MODIFY PROJECT. A project file is a table that uses the file extensions .pjx (table file) and .pjt (memo file).

Before using BUILD APP, be sure that the project file contains all of the files needed in the application. If required files are missing during the build, Visual FoxPro generates an error. These and other compile-time errors are stored in an error file with an .ERR file extension. The first eight characters of the error file name are the same as the first eight characters of your project name.

For more information on building projects, see Chapter 13, "Compiling an Application," in the *Microsoft Visual FoxPro 6.0 Programmer's Guide*.

See Also

BUILD EXE, Build Method, BUILD PROJECT, CREATE PROJECT, MODIFY PROJECT

BUILD DLL Command

Creates a Dynamic Link Library (DLL) with a .dll file name extension using class information from a project file.

Syntax

BUILD DLL *DLLFileName* FROM *ProjectName* [RECOMPILE]

Arguments

DLLFileName

Specifies the file name of the dynamic link library to build. The default file name extension is .dll.

FROM *ProjectName*

Specifies the name of the project from which the dynamic link library is built.

The project must contain a class designated as OLEPUBLIC or an error message is displayed. To designate a class as OLEPUBLIC in program code, include the OLEPUBLIC keyword in DEFINE CLASS. To designate a class as OLEPUBLIC in the Class Designer, choose Class Info from the Class Menu and select the OLE Public check box.

RECOMPILE

Specifies that the project is compiled before the dynamic link library is built. All program and format files; form, label, report, and visual class library source code; and stored procedures in databases in the project are compiled.

Remarks

BUILD DLL automatically registers the servers in the Server Classes list box on the Servers tab of the Project Information dialog box.

For information about creating custom Automation servers, see "Creating Automation Servers" in Chapter 16, "Adding OLE," of the *Microsoft Visual FoxPro 6.0 Programmer's Guide*.

See Also

BUILD EXE, Build Method, BUILD PROJECT, CREATE PROJECT, MODIFY PROJECT

BUILD EXE Command

Creates an executable file from a project.

Syntax

BUILD EXE *EXEFileName* FROM *ProjectName* [RECOMPILE]

Arguments

EXEFileName
Specifies the name of the executable file to create. If an .app application file with the same root file name as the stand-alone executable file exists, it is deleted. If an executable file exists and you create an .app file with the same name, the executable file is deleted.

FROM *ProjectName*
Specifies the name of the project from which the executable file is built.

RECOMPILE
Specifies that the project is compiled before the executable file is built. All program and format files; form, label, report, and visual class library source code; and stored procedures in databases in the project are compiled.

Remarks

For additional information about creating executable files, see Chapter 25, "Building an Application for Distribution," in the *Microsoft Visual FoxPro 6.0 Programmer's Guide*.

An executable file created with BUILD EXE requires two support files: Vfp6r.dll and Vfp6renu.dll (en denotes the English version). These files must be placed in the same directory as the executable file or along the MS-DOS path.

If the executable file contains OLEPUBLIC class definitions, BUILD EXE automatically registers the OLEPUBLIC class definitions in the system registry. OLEPUBLIC class definitions appear in the Server Classes list box on the Servers tab of the Project Information dialog box.

BUILD EXE also creates .vbr (registration) and .tlb (type library) files with the same name as the executable file. The .vbr file allow you to register the class definitions in the system registry when the executable file is moved to a different computer. The .tlb file is for use with object browsers.

For more information about registering OLEPUBLIC class definitions in an executable file, see Chapter 16, "Adding OLE" in the *Microsoft Visual FoxPro 6.0 Programmer's Guide*.

See Also

BUILD APP, Build Method, BUILD PROJECT

Build Method

Rebuilds a project, or creates an application file (.app), dynamic link library (.dll), or executable file (.exe) from a project.

Syntax

Object.Build([*cOutputName*] [, *nBuildAction*] [, *lRebuildAll*]
   [, *lShowErrors*] [, *lBuildNewGUIDs*])

Arguments

cOutputName
   Specifies the name of the application, dynamic link library, or executable file that is created.

   If *cOutputName* includes a file extension and *nBuildAction* is omitted, the file extension in *cOutputName* determines the type of file built. For example, if the extension in *cOutputName* is ".exe" an executable file is created.

nBuildAction
   Specifies if the project is rebuilt or an application, dynamic link library, or executable file is created.

   The following table lists the values for *nBuildAction* with a description of each.

nBuildAction	FoxPro.H Constant	Description
1	BUILDACTION_REBUILD	(Default) Rebuilds the project.
2	BUILDACTION_BUILDAPP	Creates an .app.
3	BUILDACTION_BUILDEXE	Creates an .exe.
4	BUILDACTION_BUILDDLL	Creates a .dll.

If *cOutPutName* doesn't include an extension, the appropriate extension is added.

lRebuildAll

Specifies if files in the project are recompiled before an .app, .dll, or .exe is created. If *lRebuildAll* is true (.T.), the following are recompiled:

- Program files.

- Format files.

- Source code in forms, labels, reports, and visual class libraries.

- Stored procedures in databases.

If If *lRebuildAll* is false (.F.) or is omitted, files in the project are not recompiled before the .app, .dll, or .exe is created.

lShowErrors

Specifies if compilation errors are displayed in an editing window after the build is complete. If *lShowErrors* is true (.T.), the errors are displayed. If If *lShowErrors* is false (.F.) or is omitted, compilation errors aren't displayed.

lBuildNewGUIDs

Specifies if new registry GUIDs (globally unique identifiers) are generated when an executable file or dynamic link library is created. If *lBuildNewGUIDs* is true (.T.), new GUIDs are generated. If *lBuildNewGUIDs* is false (.F.) or is omitted, new GUIDs aren't generated. *lBuildNewGUIDs* is ignored if *nBuildAction* is less than 3.

Remarks

A logical true (.T.) is returned if the project is successfully rebuilt or an .app, .dll, or .exe is successfully created without errors; otherwise false (.F.) is returned.

Applies To

Project Object

See Also

BUILD APP, BUILD DLL, BUILD EXE, BUILD PROJECT, CREATE PROJECT, MODIFY PROJECT, Refresh Method

BUILD PROJECT Command

Creates and builds a project file.

Syntax

BUILD PROJECT *ProjectFileName* [RECOMPILE]
    [FROM *ProgramName1* | *MenuName1* | *ReportName1* | *LabelName1*
      | *FormName1* | *LibraryName1*
    [, *ProgramName2* | *MenuName2* | *ReportName2* | *LabelName2*
      | *FormName2* | *LibraryName2* ...]]

Arguments

ProjectFileName
Specifies the name of the project table to be created.

RECOMPILE
Compiles all files in the project. If RECOMPILE is omitted, only the files that have been modified are compiled when the project is built.

FROM *ProgramName1* | *MenuName1* | *ReportName1* | *LabelName1* | *FormName1* | *LibraryName1*
Specifies the files to include in the project. You can specify one or more program, menu, report, label, form, or library files and the project will keep track of these files, as well as the dependencies, references, and connections among them.

The first executable program or menu file in the FROM clause is the master program file in the project by default.

Remarks

BUILD PROJECT automatically creates a project table with a .pjx file name extension by opening and processing one or more program, menu, report, label, form, or library files that you specify. You can use the project file to create one of two program types: an application file with an .app extension or an executable file with an .exe extension. The project table keeps track of all the files required to create an application, as well as the dependencies, references, and connections among the files. Once you specify the pieces in the project, Visual FoxPro makes sure that the application is based on the latest source files.

For more information on building projects, see Chapter 13, "Compiling an Application," in the *Microsoft Visual FoxPro 6.0 Programmer's Guide*.

When Visual FoxPro encounters a program, menu, or form file while creating a project file from BUILD PROJECT, it finds its compiled file and compares the time and date stamp of the two files. If the time and date stamp of the source file is later than that of the compiled file, Visual FoxPro recompiles the source file.

Each project file contains a time and date stamp so you can refresh the project file when you make changes to files in the project or when dependencies change. This practice helps to guarantee that any applications created from a project file will always use the most recent source files. To refresh a project file, issue BUILD PROJECT without the optional FROM clause. Visual FoxPro then updates the specified project.

When you issue BUILD PROJECT, unresolved references and other errors are reported but do not prevent the project file from being created. This enables you to build a project even when all the necessary pieces aren't actually created or available at the time the project is built. Unresolved references or other problems can be corrected by refreshing the project file at a later date, or by manually modifying the information stored in the project file with MODIFY PROJECT.

See Also

BUILD APP, BUILD EXE, Build Method, BuildDateTime Property, CREATE PROJECT, EXTERNAL, MODIFY PROJECT

BuildDateTime Property

Contains the last build date and time for a project. Read-only.

Syntax

Object.BuildDateTime

Remarks

A project is built with BUILD PROJECT or by choosing **Rebuild Project** in the Build Options dialog box.

BuildDateTime contains the empty DateTime if the project has not been built.

Applies To

Project Object

See Also

Build Options, BUILD PROJECT

_BUILDER System Variable

Contains the name of the Visual FoxPro builder application.

Syntax

_BUILDER = *cProgramName*

Arguments

cProgramName
　　Specifies a builder application. If your builder application is in a directory other than the current Visual FoxPro default directory, include a path with the application name.

Remarks

The _BUILDER system variable contains the name of the application that Visual FoxPro uses when you choose a builder in the Form Designer. By default, _BUILDER contains BUILDER.APP, installed in your Visual FoxPro directory. You can specify a different name for the builder application.

See Also

System Variables Overview

ButtonCount Property

Specifies the number of buttons in a CommandGroup or OptionGroup. Available at design time and run time.

Syntax

*Control.*ButtonCount[= *nNumber*]

Arguments

nNumber
    Specifies the number of buttons for the control.

Remarks

Use the ButtonCount property to dynamically set the number of buttons contained in a CommandGroup or OptionGroup.

If you change the number of buttons at run time, names are automatically assigned to the new buttons. The buttons are assigned the name Command*N* for a CommandGroup or Option*N* for an OptionGroup where *N* is the number of the button added. For example, if there are four buttons in the CommandGroup and the Buttons property setting is changed to 5, the new button is named Command5.

Example

The following example creates an OptionGroup control and places the control on a form. The OptionGroup control has three buttons; depending on the option button you click, a circle, ellipse, or square appears. The ButtonCount property is used to specify the number of buttons in the OptionGroup. The Buttons and Caption properties specify the text displayed next to each option button.

The Shape control is used to create the circle, ellipse, and square. The OptionGroup control's Click event uses a DO CASE ... ENDCASE structure and the Value property to display the appropriate shape when you click an option button.

```
frmMyForm = CREATEOBJECT('Form')  && Create a Form
frmMyForm.Closable = .F.  && Disable the Control menu box

frmMyForm.AddObject('cmdCommand1','cmdMyCmndBtn')  && Add Command button
frmMyForm.AddObject('opgOptionGroup1','opgMyOptGrp') && Add Option Group
frmMyForm.AddObject('shpCircle1','shpMyCircle')  && Add Circle Shape
frmMyForm.AddObject('shpEllipse1','shpMyEllipse')  && Add Ellipse Shape
frmMyForm.AddObject('shpSquare','shpMySquare')  && Add Box Shape

frmMyForm.cmdCommand1.Visible =.T.  && "Quit" Command button visible

frmMyForm.opgOptionGroup1.Buttons(1).Caption = "\<Circle"
frmMyForm.opgOptionGroup1.Buttons(2).Caption = "\<Ellipse"
```

```
frmMyForm.opgOptionGroup1.Buttons(3).Caption = "\<Square"
frmMyForm.opgOptionGroup1.SetAll("Width", 100) && Set Option group width
frmMyForm.opgOptionGroup1.Visible = .T.  && Option Group visible
frmMyForm.opgOptionGroup1.Click  && Show the circle

frmMyForm.SHOW  && Display the form
READ EVENTS  && Start event processing

DEFINE CLASS opgMyOptGrp AS OptionGroup  && Create an Option Group
   ButtonCount = 3  && Three Option buttons
   Top = 10
   Left = 10
   Height = 75
   Width = 100

   PROCEDURE Click
      ThisForm.shpCircle1.Visible = .F.  && Hide the circle
      ThisForm.shpEllipse1.Visible = .F.  && Hide the ellipse
      ThisForm.shpSquare.Visible = .F.  && Hide the square

      DO CASE
         CASE ThisForm.opgOptionGroup1.Value = 1
            ThisForm.shpCircle1.Visible = .T. && Show the circle
         CASE ThisForm.opgOptionGroup1.Value = 2
            ThisForm.shpEllipse1.Visible = .T.  && Show the ellipse
         CASE ThisForm.opgOptionGroup1.Value = 3
            ThisForm.shpSquare.Visible = .T.  && Show the square
      ENDCASE
ENDDEFINE

DEFINE CLASS cmdMyCmndBtn AS CommandButton  && Create Command button
   Caption = '\<Quit'  && Caption on the Command button
   Cancel = .T.  && Default Cancel Command button (Esc)
   Left = 125  && Command button column
   Top = 210  && Command button row
   Height = 25  && Command button height

   PROCEDURE Click
      CLEAR EVENTS  && Stop event processing, close Form
ENDDEFINE

DEFINE CLASS shpMyCircle AS SHAPE  && Create a circle
   Top = 10
   Left = 200
   Width = 100
   Height = 100
   Curvature = 99
   BackColor = RGB(255,0,0)  && Red
ENDDEFINE
```

```
DEFINE CLASS shpMyEllipse AS SHAPE  && Create an ellipse
   Top = 35
   Left = 200
   Width = 100
   Height = 50
   Curvature = 99
   BackColor = RGB(0,128,0)  && Green
ENDDEFINE

DEFINE CLASS shpMySquare AS SHAPE  && Create a square
   Top = 10
   Left = 200
   Width = 100
   Height = 100
   Curvature = 0
   BackColor = RGB(0,0,255)  && Blue
ENDDEFINE
```

Applies To

CommandGroup, OptionGroup

See Also

Buttons Property

Buttons Property

An array for accessing every button in a group. Not available at design time.

Syntax

Control.Buttons (*nIndex*).*Property* = *Value*

– or –

Control.Buttons (*nIndex*).*Method*

Arguments

nIndex

An integer between 1 and the number of buttons specified in the ButtonCount property for *Control*.

Property

A property of a CommandButton or OptionButton.

Value

The value of *Property*.

Method

A method of a CommandButton or OptionButton.

Remarks

You can use the Buttons property to set properties and call methods for all the buttons in the group. The Buttons property is an array that is created when the button group is created.

Applies To

CommandGroup, OptionGroup

See Also

ButtonCount Property, SetAll Method

Example

The following example creates an OptionGroup control and places the control on a form. The OptionGroup control has three buttons; depending on the option button you click, a circle, ellipse, or square appears. The ButtonCount property specifies the number of buttons in the OptionGroup. The Buttons and Caption properties specify the text displayed next to each option button.

The Shape control is used to create the circle, ellipse, and square. The OptionGroup control's Click event uses a DO CASE ... ENDCASE structure and the Value property to display the appropriate shape when you click an option button.

```
frmMyForm = CREATEOBJECT('Form')  && Create a Form
frmMyForm.Closable = .F.  && Disable the Control menu box

frmMyForm.AddObject('cmdCommand1','cmdMyCmndBtn')  && Add Command button
frmMyForm.AddObject('opgOptionGroup1','opgMyOptGrp') && Add Option Group
frmMyForm.AddObject('shpCircle1','shpMyCircle')  && Add Circle Shape
frmMyForm.AddObject('shpEllipse1','shpMyEllipse')  && Add Ellipse Shape
frmMyForm.AddObject('shpSquare','shpMySquare')  && Add Box Shape

frmMyForm.cmdCommand1.Visible =.T.  && "Quit" Command button visible

frmMyForm.opgOptionGroup1.Buttons(1).Caption = "\<Circle"
frmMyForm.opgOptionGroup1.Buttons(2).Caption = "\<Ellipse"
frmMyForm.opgOptionGroup1.Buttons(3).Caption = "\<Square"
frmMyForm.opgOptionGroup1.SetAll("Width", 100) && Set Option group width
frmMyForm.opgOptionGroup1.Visible = .T.  && Option Group visible
frmMyForm.opgOptionGroup1.Click  && Show the circle

frmMyForm.SHOW  && Display the form
READ EVENTS  && Start event processing

DEFINE CLASS opgMyOptGrp AS OptionGroup  && Create an Option Group
   ButtonCount = 3  && Three Option buttons
   Top = 10
   Left = 10
   Height = 75
   Width = 100
```

```
      PROCEDURE Click
         ThisForm.shpCircle1.Visible = .F.  && Hide the circle
         ThisForm.shpEllipse1.Visible = .F.  && Hide the ellipse
         ThisForm.shpSquare.Visible = .F.   && Hide the square

         DO CASE
            CASE ThisForm.opgOptionGroup1.Value = 1
               ThisForm.shpCircle1.Visible = .T. && Show the circle
            CASE ThisForm.opgOptionGroup1.Value = 2
               ThisForm.shpEllipse1.Visible = .T.  && Show the ellipse
            CASE ThisForm.opgOptionGroup1.Value = 3
               ThisForm.shpSquare.Visible = .T.  && Show the square
         ENDCASE
ENDDEFINE

DEFINE CLASS cmdMyCmndBtn AS CommandButton  && Create Command button
   Caption = '\<Quit'  && Caption on the Command button
   Cancel = .T.  && Default Cancel Command button (Esc)
   Left = 125  && Command button column
   Top = 210  && Command button row
   Height = 25  && Command button height

   PROCEDURE Click
      CLEAR EVENTS  && Stop event processing, close Form
ENDDEFINE

DEFINE CLASS shpMyCircle AS SHAPE  && Create a circle
   Top = 10
   Left = 200
   Width = 100
   Height = 100
   Curvature = 99
   BackColor = RGB(255,0,0)  && Red
ENDDEFINE

DEFINE CLASS shpMyEllipse AS SHAPE  && Create an ellipse
   Top = 35
   Left = 200
   Width = 100
   Height = 50
   Curvature = 99
   BackColor = RGB(0,128,0)  && Green
ENDDEFINE

DEFINE CLASS shpMySquare AS SHAPE  && Create a square
   Top = 10
   Left = 200
   Width = 100
   Height = 100
   Curvature = 0
   BackColor = RGB(0,0,255)  && Blue
ENDDEFINE
```

_CALCMEM System Variable

Contains the numeric value that Microsoft Visual FoxPro stores in the Calculator's memory.

Syntax

_CALCMEM = *nCalculatorValue*

Arguments

nCalculatorValue
    Specifies the numeric value that _CALCMEM stores in memory.

Remarks

You can save the result of a calculation in the Calculator's memory and return the result to a program, or you can place a specific value in the Calculator's memory before using the Calculator.

To initialize the Calculator's memory, store a numeric value to _CALCMEM with STORE or the = assignment operator. When you use the Calculator, its memory contains the value you specified.

Example

The following program example stores the numeric constant 1234 to _CALCMEM. The program then displays the Calculator and stuffs the keyboard with the letter R. The keystroke R displays the value stored in the Calculator's memory.

```
STORE 1234 TO _CALCMEM
ACTIVATE WINDOW calculator
CLEAR TYPEAHEAD
KEYBOARD CHR(82)
```

See Also

ACTIVATE WINDOW, _CALCVALUE, STORE

CALCULATE Command

Performs financial and statistical operations on fields in a table or on expressions involving fields.

Syntax

CALCULATE *eExpressionList*
    [*Scope*] [FOR *lExpression1*] [WHILE *lExpression2*]
    [TO *VarList* | TO ARRAY *ArrayName*],
    [NOOPTIMIZE]

Arguments

eExpressionList

Specifies the expressions that can contain any combination of the following functions:

AVG(*nExpression*)

CNT( )

MAX(*eExpression*)

MIN(*eExpression*)

NPV(*nExpression1*, *nExpression2* [, *nExpression3*])

STD(*nExpression*)

SUM(*nExpression*)

VAR(*nExpression*)

Functions in the expression list *eExpressionList* are separated by commas. These functions are specific to CALCULATE and are described in detail later in this section. They should not be confused with similarly named independent functions. For example, CALCULATE MIN( ) is not the same as MIN( ).

Scope

Specifies a range of records used in the calculation. Only the records that fall within the range of records are included in the calculation. The scope clauses are: ALL, NEXT *nRecords*, RECORD *nRecordNumber*, and REST. For more information on scope clauses, see "Scope Clauses" in Help. Commands that include *Scope* operate only on the table in the active work area.

The default scope for CALCULATE is ALL records.

FOR *lExpression1*

Specifies that only the records that satisfy the logical condition *lExpression1* are included in the calculation. Including a FOR clause conditionally includes records in the calculation, filtering out undesired records.

Rushmore optimizes a CALCULATE ... FOR query if *lExpression1* is an optimizable expression. For best performance, use an optimizable expression in the FOR clause. For information on Rushmore optimizable expressions, see the SET OPTIMIZE Command, later in this language reference, and "Understanding Rushmore Technology" in Chapter 15, "Optimizing Applications," in the *Microsoft Visual FoxPro 6.0 Programmer's Guide*.

WHILE *lExpression2*

Specifies a condition whereby records are included in the calculation as long as the logical expression *lExpression2* evaluates to true (.T.).

TO *VarList*

Specifies one or more variables to which the results of the calculation are stored. If a variable you specify does not exist, Visual FoxPro automatically creates the variable with the name you specify.

TO ARRAY *ArrayName*

Specifies an array name to which the results of the calculation can be stored. If the array name you specify does not exist, Visual FoxPro automatically creates an array with the name you specify. If the array exists and isn't large enough to contain all the results of the calculation, Visual FoxPro automatically increases the size of the array to accommodate the information. If an existing array is larger than necessary, additional elements are left unchanged. Results are stored to the array elements in the order they are specified in the CALCULATE command.

NOOPTIMIZE

Disables Rushmore optimization of CALCULATE. For more information, see the SET OPTIMIZE Command, later in this language reference, and "Understanding Rushmore Technology" in Chapter 15, "Optimizing Applications," in the *Microsoft Visual FoxPro 6.0 Programmer's Guide*.

AVG(*nExpression*)

Computes the arithmetic mean of *nExpression*. Only records meeting the *Scope* and/or optional FOR or WHILE conditions are included in the result.

CNT( )

Returns the number of records in the table. Only records meeting the *Scope* and/or optional FOR or WHILE conditions are included in the result.

MAX(*eExpression*)

Returns the highest or latest value of *eExpression*. Within the MAX( ) clause, you can specify any character, date, datetime, numeric, float, integer, double, or currency field, or any expression using fields of these types. Only records meeting the *Scope* and/or optional FOR or WHILE conditions are included in the result.

MIN(*eExpression*)

Returns the lowest or earliest value of *eExpression*. Any character, date, datetime, numeric, float, integer, double, or currency field, or any valid expression using fields of these types, can be included in *eExpression*. Only records meeting the *Scope* and/or optional FOR or WHILE conditions are included in the result.

NPV(*nExpression1*, *nExpression2* [, *nExpression3*])

Computes the net present value of a series of future cash flows discounted at a constant periodic interest rate.

nExpression1 specifies the interest rate expressed as a decimal value.

nExpression2 specifies a field, field expression, or a numeric expression representing a series of cash flows. Each cash flow can be either positive or negative. In cases where *nExpression2* is a field, the value for each record in the field is considered a cash flow.

nExpression3 specifies an optional initial investment. If the initial investment isn't included, then the initial investment is assumed to occur at the end of the first period. This initial investment is the first record in the field and is negative to represent a cash outflow.

Only records meeting the *Scope* and/or optional FOR or WHILE conditions are included in the result.

STD(*nExpression*)

Computes the standard deviation of *nExpression*. The standard deviation measures the degree to which the values of fields or expressions involving fields differ from the average of all the values. The smaller the standard deviation, the less the values vary from the average. Only records meeting the *Scope* and/or optional FOR or WHILE conditions are included in the result.

SUM(*nExpression*)

Totals the values of *nExpression*. Only records meeting the *Scope* and/or optional FOR or WHILE conditions are included in the result.

VAR(*nExpression*)

Computes the variance from the average of *nExpression*. The variance is the standard deviation squared. The smaller the variance, the less the values vary from the average. Only records meeting the *Scope* and/or optional FOR or WHILE conditions are included in the result.

Remarks

Records containing the null value are not included in the operations that CALCULATE performs.

Example

```
CLOSE DATABASES
OPEN DATABASE (HOME(2) + 'data\testdata')
USE orders   && Open Orders table

SET TALK ON
CLEAR

CALCULATE AVG(order_amt), MIN(order_amt), MAX(order_amt)

CALCULATE STD(order_amt), VAR(order_amt) TO gnStd, gnVar
```

See Also

AVERAGE, COUNT, DIMENSION, FV( ), MAX( ), MIN( ), PAYMENT( ), PV( ), SUM

_CALCVALUE System Variable

Contains the numeric value that the Calculator displays.

Syntax

_CALCVALUE = *nCalculatorDisplayValue*

Arguments

nCalculatorDisplayValue
    Specifies the numeric value that the Calculator displays.

Remarks

You can return the result of a calculation to a program or you can place a specific value in the Calculator's display before using the Calculator.

To initialize the Calculator's display, store a numeric value to _CALCVALUE with STORE or the = assignment operator. When you use the Calculator, it displays the value you specified.

Example

In the following example, the numeric value 1234 is stored to _CALCVALUE. The Calculator then displays the value 1234.

```
STORE 1234 TO _CALCVALUE
ACTIVATE WINDOW calculator
```

See Also

ACTIVATE WINDOW, _CALCMEM, STORE

CALL Command

Included for backward compatibility. Use SET LIBRARY instead.

CANCEL Command

Ends execution of the current Visual FoxPro program file.

Syntax

CANCEL

Remarks

Control returns to the Command window when Visual FoxPro is being used interactively.

If a distributed run-time application is running, CANCEL terminates the application and control returns to Windows. If a program is executing in Visual FoxPro during design time, CANCEL terminates the program and control returns to the Command window.

Executing CANCEL releases all private variables.

Example

The following example simulates a program execution loop. Each time through the loop you are asked if you want to continue. If you press the Cancel button, CANCEL stops program execution.

```
DO WHILE .T.
   IF MESSAGEBOX("Do you want to continue?",36) <> 6
      CANCEL
   ENDIF
ENDDO
```

See Also

QUIT, RESUME, RETURN, SUSPEND

Cancel Property

Specifies whether a CommandButton or OLE Container control is the Cancel button; that is, if the user presses the ESC key, the Cancel button's Click event will occur. Available at design time and run time.

Syntax

Object.Cancel[= *lExpr*]

Arguments

lExpr

The settings for the Cancel property are:

Setting	Description
True (.T.)	The CommandButton or OLE Container control is the Cancel button.
False (.F.)	(Default) The CommandButton or OLE Container control is not the Cancel button.

Remarks

The Cancel property applies only to an OLE Container control that contains an "Acts like a Button" ActiveX control (.ocx).

Example

The following example creates a command button and an OptionGroup control and places them on a form. The Cancel property is used to assign the command button as the Cancel button. If the ESC key is pressed, the Command button's Click event occurs and the Click event procedure executes CLEAR EVENTS to close the form and stop event processing.

The OptionGroup control has three buttons; depending on the option button you click, a circle, ellipse, or square is displayed. The Shape Control is used to create the circle, ellipse, and square. The OptionGroup control's Click event uses a DO CASE ... ENDCASE structure and the Value property to display the appropriate shape when you click an option button.

```
frmMyForm = CREATEOBJECT('Form')  && Create a Form
frmMyForm.Closable = .F.  && Disable the Control menu box

frmMyForm.AddObject('cmdCommand1','cmdMyCmndBtn')  && Add Command button
frmMyForm.AddObject('opgOptionGroup1','opgMyOptGrp') && Add Option Group
frmMyForm.AddObject('shpCircle1','shpMyCircle')  && Add Circle Shape
frmMyForm.AddObject('shpEllipse1','shpMyEllipse')  && Add Ellipse Shape
frmMyForm.AddObject('shpSquare','shpMySquare')  && Add Box Shape

frmMyForm.cmdCommand1.Visible =.T.  && "Quit" Command button visible

frmMyForm.opgOptionGroup1.Buttons(1).Caption = "\<Circle"
frmMyForm.opgOptionGroup1.Buttons(2).Caption = "\<Ellipse"
frmMyForm.opgOptionGroup1.Buttons(3).Caption = "\<Square"
frmMyForm.opgOptionGroup1.SetAll("Width", 100) && Set Option group width
frmMyForm.opgOptionGroup1.Visible = .T.  && Option Group visible
frmMyForm.opgOptionGroup1.Click  && Show the circle

frmMyForm.SHOW  && Display the form
READ EVENTS  && Start event processing

DEFINE CLASS opgMyOptGrp AS OptionGroup  && Create an Option Group
   ButtonCount = 3  && Three Option buttons
   Top = 10
   Left = 10
   Height = 75
   Width = 100

   PROCEDURE Click
      ThisForm.shpCircle1.Visible = .F.  && Hide the circle
      ThisForm.shpEllipse1.Visible = .F.  && Hide the ellipse
      ThisForm.shpSquare.Visible = .F.  && Hide the square
```

```
        DO CASE
          CASE ThisForm.opgOptionGroup1.Value = 1
             ThisForm.shpCircle1.Visible = .T. && Show the circle
          CASE ThisForm.opgOptionGroup1.Value = 2
             ThisForm.shpEllipse1.Visible = .T.  && Show the ellipse
          CASE ThisForm.opgOptionGroup1.Value = 3
             ThisForm.shpSquare.Visible = .T.  && Show the square
        ENDCASE
ENDDEFINE

DEFINE CLASS cmdMyCmndBtn AS CommandButton  && Create Command button
   Caption = '\<Quit'  && Caption on the Command button
   Cancel = .T.  && Default Cancel Command button (Esc)
   Left = 125  && Command button column
   Top = 210  && Command button row
   Height = 25  && Command button height

   PROCEDURE Click
      CLEAR EVENTS  && Stop event processing, close Form
ENDDEFINE

DEFINE CLASS shpMyCircle AS SHAPE  && Create a circle
   Top = 10
   Left = 200
   Width = 100
   Height = 100
   Curvature = 99
   BackColor = RGB(255,0,0)  && Red
ENDDEFINE

DEFINE CLASS shpMyEllipse AS SHAPE  && Create an ellipse
   Top = 35
   Left = 200
   Width = 100
   Height = 50
   Curvature = 99
   BackColor = RGB(0,128,0)  && Green
ENDDEFINE

DEFINE CLASS shpMySquare AS SHAPE  && Create a square
   Top = 10
   Left = 200
   Width = 100
   Height = 100
   Curvature = 0
   BackColor = RGB(0,0,255)  && Blue
ENDDEFINE
```

Applies To

CommandButton, OLE Container Control

See Also

Click Event, Default Property

CANDIDATE( ) Function

Returns true (.T.) if an index tag is a candidate index tag; otherwise, returns false (.F.).

Syntax

CANDIDATE([*nIndexNumber*] [, *nWorkArea* | *cTableAlias*])

Returns

Logical

Arguments

nIndexNumber

Specifies the number of the index tag for which CANDIDATE( ) returns the candidate status. CANDIDATE( ) returns the candidate status in the following order as *nIndexNumber* increases from 1 to the total number of structural compound and independent compound index tags:

1. Candidate status for each tag in the structural compound index (if one is present) is returned first. The candidate status is returned for the tags in the order in which the tags are created in the structural index.

2. Candidate status for each tag in any open independent compound indexes is returned last. The candidate status is returned for the tags in the order in which the tags are created in the independent compound indexes.

If you omit *nIndexNumber*, CANDIDATE( ) checks the master controlling index tag to see if it's a candidate index tag. If there is no master controlling index tag, CANDIDATE( ) returns false (.F.).

nWorkArea

Specifies the work area of the index tag specified with *nIndexNumber*.

cTableAlias

Specifies the work area of the index tag specified with *nIndexNumber*.

If you omit *nWorkArea* and *cTableAlias*, CANDIDATE( ) checks the index tag in the currently selected work area to see if it's a candidate index tag.

Remarks

A candidate index tag is an index tag that can become the primary index tag because it doesn't contain null or duplicate values.

Example

The following example opens the `customer` table in the `testdata` database.
FOR ... ENDFOR is used to create a loop in which the candidate status of each index tag in the `customer` structural index is checked. The name of each structural index tag is displayed with its candidate status.

```
CLOSE DATABASES
OPEN DATABASE (HOME(2) + 'data\testdata')
USE customer      && Open customer table

FOR nCount = 1 TO 254
   IF !EMPTY(TAG(nCount))  && Checks for tags in the index
   ? TAG(nCount)  && Display tag name
   ? CANDIDATE(nCount)  && Display candidate status
   ELSE
      EXIT  && Exit the loop when no more tags are found
   ENDIF
ENDFOR
```

See Also

ALTER TABLE – SQL, CREATE TABLE – SQL, INDEX, PRIMARY( )

CAPSLOCK( ) Function

Returns the current mode of the CAPS LOCK key or sets the CAPS LOCK key mode on or off.

Syntax

CAPSLOCK([*lExpression*])

Returns

Logical

Arguments

lExpression
> Include to turn the CAPS LOCK key on or off. CAPSLOCK(.T.) turns CAPS LOCK on and CAPSLOCK(.F.) turns CAPS LOCK off. A logical value is returned corresponding to the CAPS LOCK setting before CAPSLOCK(.T.) or CAPSLOCK(.F.) is issued.

Remarks

Issuing CAPSLOCK( ) with no argument returns true (.T.) if CAPS LOCK is on, or false (.F.) if CAPS LOCK is off.

Example

The following code stores the state of CAPSLOCK( ) to a system variable. The = command executes the CAPSLOCK( ) function to set CAPS LOCK on. Then the = command executes the CAPSLOCK( ) function to set CAPS LOCK to its previous state.

```
glOldLock = CAPSLOCK( )     && Save original setting
= CAPSLOCK(.T.)      && Turn CAPS LOCK on

*** Perform any number of statements ***

= CAPSLOCK(glOldLock)  && Return to original setting

*** or, toggle CapsLock to the opposite value and back ***

= CAPSLOCK(!CAPSLOCK( ))
WAIT WINDOW
= CAPSLOCK(!CAPSLOCK( ))
WAIT WINDOW
= CAPSLOCK(glOldLock)  && Return to original setting
```

See Also

INSMODE( ), NUMLOCK( )

Caption Property

Specifies the text displayed in an object's caption. Available at design time and run time.

Syntax

Object.Caption[= *cText*]

Arguments

cText
Specifies text displayed with an object.

Remarks

Captions are displayed differently depending on the object:

- For forms, the Caption property specifies the text displayed in the form's title bar. When the form is minimized, this text is displayed below the form's icon.

- For pages of a PageFrame object, the Caption property specifies the text displayed on the tab of each page.

- For controls, the Caption property specifies the text displayed on or next to a control.

- For controls with the Style property set to 1 (Graphical), and for forms that are minimized, the caption is displayed under the icon.

- For Active Documents, the Caption property determines the text that is displayed on the Active Document's Help menu item when the Active Document's Help menu is merged with the Help menu of its container. The text on the Active Document's Help menu item is followed by "Help." For example, if the Caption property is set to "My Application," the Active Document's Help menu item displays as "My Application Help." The default Caption property value is "ActiveDoc1." If the Caption property is set to the empty string, "Microsoft Visual FoxPro" is displayed as the Help menu item.

When you create a new form or control, its default caption is the same as the default Name property setting. This default caption includes the object class and an integer, such as Command1, Combo1, or Form1.

The Name property is the way to refer to an object in code; the Caption property is what appears on the screen to identify the control. These two properties start out with the same value, but are set independently thereafter.

If there is no Width property setting specified for the control, the control is automatically sized to hold the caption.

For CommandGroup and OptionGroup objects, the caption is displayed only if the BorderStyle property is set to 1 (Fixed Single).

For a Label control, set the AutoSize property to true (.T.) to automatically resize the control to fit its caption. The maximum number of characters for the Caption property for a Label control is 256.

To assign an access key to a control, include a backslash and a less-than sign (\<) in the caption immediately preceding the character you want to designate as the access key. A user can then press ALT and the specified character to move the focus to that control. If the control is a command button, check box, or option button, pressing ALT and the specified character also has the effect of clicking the control.

Access keys are available only if KEYCOMP has been set to WINDOWS. If KEYCOMP is set to MAC, access keys are not available, and the access key letter in a caption is not underlined.

Applies To

ActiveDoc Object, CheckBox, CommandButton, Form, Header, Label, OptionButton, Page, _SCREEN, ToolBar

See Also

AutoSize Property, BorderStyle Property, Name Property, Style Property, Width Property

CD | CHDIR Command

Changes the default Visual FoxPro directory to the directory you specify.

Syntax

CD *cPath* | CHDIR *cPath*

Arguments

cPath

Specifies one of the following:

- A drive designator.

- A drive designator with a directory.

- A child directory.

- Any of the above using MSDOS shorthand notation (\ or ..). When you include ..
  to change to the parent directory, you must include a space between CD or CHDIR
  and the two periods.

Remarks

Use CD or CHDIR to specify the default Visual FoxPro directory. Visual FoxPro searches
for files in the default Visual FoxPro directory. If Visual FoxPro cannot find a file in the
default directory, it then searches the Visual FoxPro path if one has been specified. Use
SET PATH to specify the Visual FoxPro path.

If you create a file and don't specify where to place it, the file is placed in the default
Visual FoxPro directory.

Example

The following example uses MKDIR to create a new directory named mytstdir, then
CHDIR is used to change to the new directory. GETDIR( ) is used to display the directory
structure, and then RMDIR is used to remove the newly created directory GETDIR( ) is
used to display the directory structure again.

```
SET DEFAULT TO HOME( )  && Restore Visual FoxPro directory
MKDIR mytstdir  && Create a new directory

CHDIR mytstdir  && Change to the new directory
= GETDIR( )  && Display the Select Directory dialog box
SET DEFAULT TO HOME( )  && Restore Visual FoxPro directory
RMDIR mytstdir  && Remove the new directory
= GETDIR( )  && Display the Select Directory dialog box
```

See Also

DIRECTORY, DIRECTORY( ), GETDIR( ), HOME( ), MD I MKDIR, RD I RMDIR, SET DEFAULT, SET PATH, SYS(5) – Default Drive, SYS(2003) – Current Directory, SYS(2004) – Visual FoxPro Start Directory

CDOW( ) Function

Returns the day of the week from a given Date or DateTime expression.

Syntax

CDOW(*dExpression* I *tExpression*)

Returns

Character

Arguments

dExpression
> Specifies the date from which CDOW( ) returns the day.

tExpression
> Specifies the datetime from which CDOW( ) returns the day.

Remarks

CDOW( ) returns the name of the day of the week as a string in proper noun format.

Example

```
STORE {^1998-02-16} TO gdDate
CLEAR
? CDOW(gdDate)  && Displays Monday
```

See Also

DAY( ), DOW( ), SET FDOW, SET FWEEK, SYS( ) Functions Overview

CDX( ) Function

Returns the names of the open compound index (.cdx) file that has the specified index position number.

Syntax

CDX(*nIndexNumber* [, *nWorkArea* I *cTableAlias*])

Returns

Character

Arguments

nIndexNumber

The following apply to a table with a structural compound index and one or more compound indexes:

nIndexNumber	Description
1	Returns the name of the structural index file (which is always the same as the name of the table).
2	Returns the first compound index file name specified in the INDEX clause of USE or in SET INDEX.
3	Returns the second compound index file name, if any, and so on.
Greater than the number of open .cdx files	Returns the empty string.

The following apply to a table with no structural compound index and one or more compound indexes:

nIndexNumber	Description
1	Returns the first compound index file name specified in the INDEX clause of USE or in SET INDEX.
2	Returns the second compound index file name, if any, and so on.
Greater than the number of open .cdx files	Returns the empty string.

nWorkArea

Specifies the work area number of a table whose open compound index file names you want CDX( ) to return.

cTableAlias

Specifies the alias of a table whose open compound index file names you want CDX( ) to return.

If you omit *nWorkArea* and *cTableAlias*, names of compound index files are returned for the table in the currently selected work area.

Remarks

The CDX( ) function is identical to the MDX( ) function.

A .cdx (compound) index consists of one physical file containing many index tags. Each index tag is an index order reference for the associated table.

There are two types of .cdx files: standard compound index (.cdx) and structural .cdx. A standard compound index (.cdx) may have a different name from its associated table and can reside in a different directory from its associated table. A table can have multiple compound index files. You open a compound index with the INDEX clause of USE or with SET INDEX.

A structural .cdx must have the same name as its associated table and reside in the same directory. A table can have only one structural index file. Structural .cdx files are automatically opened and updated when the associated table is opened with USE.

CDX( ) ignores any .idx (Microsoft FoxBASE+ and FoxPro 1.0 compatible index) files specified in USE or SET INDEX.

Use TAG( ) to return individual tag names contained in a .cdx, and NDX( ) to return the name of open .idx files.

When SET FULLPATH is ON, CDX( ) returns the path and name of the .cdx. When SET FULLPATH is OFF, CDX( ) returns the drive and name of the .cdx.

Example

The following example opens the `customer` table in the `testdata` database. FOR ... ENDFOR is used to create a loop in which the name of each structural index is displayed.

```
CLOSE DATABASES
OPEN DATABASE (HOME(2) + 'data\testdata')
USE customer        && Open customer table

CLEAR
FOR nCount = 1 TO 254
   IF !EMPTY(TAG(nCount))  && Checks for tags in the index
   ? CDX(nCount)      && Display structural index names
   ELSE
      EXIT  && Exit the loop when no more tags are found
   ENDIF
ENDFOR
```

See Also

INDEX, MDX( ), NDX( ), SET FULLPATH, SET INDEX, SYS(14) – Index Expression, SYS(21) – Controlling Index Number, SYS(22) – Controlling Tag or Index Name, SYS(2021) – Filtered Index Expression, TAG( ), USE

CEILING( ) Function

Returns the next highest integer that is greater than or equal to the specified numeric expression.

Syntax

CEILING(*nExpression*)

Returns

Numeric

Arguments

nExpression
    Specifies the number whose next highest integer CEILING( ) returns.

Remarks

CEILING rounds a number with a fractional portion to the next highest integer.

Example

```
STORE 10.1 TO num1
STORE -10.9 TO num2
? CEILING(num1)  && Displays 11
? CEILING(num2)  && Displays -10
? CEILING(10.0)  && Displays 10
? CEILING(-10.0) && Displays -10
```

See Also

FLOOR( ), ROUND( )

Century Property

Specifies whether the century portion of a date is displayed in a text box. Available at design time and run time.

Syntax

Object.Century[= *nValue*]

Arguments

nValue

One of the following settings:

Setting	Description
0	Off. The century portion of the date is not displayed.
1	(Default) On. The century portion of the date is displayed.
2	The SET CENTURY setting determines if the century portion of the date is displayed. If SET CENTURY is ON, the century portion of the date is displayed. If SET CENTURY is OFF, the century portion of the date is not displayed.

Remarks

The Century property setting is ignored if the DateFormat property is set to Short or Long.

Note that in earlier versions of Visual FoxPro the default for the Century property is 2.

Applies To

TextBox

See Also

DateFormat Property, DateMark Property, Hours Property, Seconds Property, SET CENTURY, StrictDateEntry Property

CHANGE Command

Displays fields for editing.

Syntax

CHANGE
    [FIELDS *FieldList*]
    [*Scope*] [FOR *lExpression1*] [WHILE *lExpression2*]
    [FONT *cFontName* [, *nFontSize*]]
    [STYLE *cFontStyle*]
    [FREEZE *FieldName*]
    [KEY *eExpression1* [, *eExpression2*]]
    [LAST | NOINIT]
    [LPARTITION]
    [NAME *ObjectName*]
    [NOAPPEND]
    [NOCLEAR]
    [NODELETE]
    [NOEDIT | NOMODIFY]
    [NOLINK]

[NOMENU]
[NOOPTIMIZE]
[NORMAL]
[NOWAIT]
[PARTITION *nColumnNumber* [LEDIT] [REDIT]]
[PREFERENCE *PreferenceName*]
[REST]
[SAVE]
[TIMEOUT *nSeconds*]
[TITLE *cTitleText*]
[VALID [:F] *lExpression3* [ERROR *cMessageText*]]
[WHEN *lExpression4*]
[WIDTH *nFieldWidth*]
[WINDOW *WindowName1*]
[IN [WINDOW] *WindowNam2* | IN SCREEN | IN MACDESKTOP]]
[COLOR SCHEME *nSchemeNumber*
| COLOR *ColorPairList*]

Arguments

The arguments for CHANGE are the same as those for EDIT. See the EDIT Command, later in this language reference.

Remarks

CHANGE works just like EDIT.

See Also

BROWSE, EDIT, WTITLE( )

CheckBox Control

Creates a check box.

Syntax

CheckBox

Remarks

A check box is used to toggle between two states, such as true (.T.) and false (.F.) or yes and no. When a condition is true, a checkmark appears in the check box.

Use the Caption property to specify the text that appears next to a check box. Use the Picture property to specify a picture for a check box.

For additional information about CheckBox controls, see Chapter 10, "Using Controls," in the *Microsoft Visual FoxPro 6.0 Programmer's Guide*.

Properties

Alignment	Application	AutoSize
BackColor	BackStyle	BaseClass
Caption	Class	ClassLibrary
ColorScheme	ColorSource	Comment
ControlSource	DisabledBackColor	DisabledForeColor
DisabledPicture	DownPicture	DragIcon
DragMode	Enabled	FontBold
FontCondense	FontExtend	FontItalic
FontName	FontOutline	FontShadow
FontSize	FontStrikeThru	FontUnderline
ForeColor	Height	HelpContextID
Left	MouseIcon	MousePointer
Name	OLEDragMode	OLEDragPicture
OLEDropEffects	OLEDropHasData Property	OLEDropMode
Parent	ParentClass	Picture
ReadOnly	RightToLeft	SpecialEffect
StatusBarText	Style	TabIndex
TabStop	Tag	TerminateRead
ToolTipText	Top	Value
Visible	WhatsThisHelpID	Width

Events

Click	DblClick	Destroy
DragDrop	DragOver	Error
ErrorMessage	GotFocus	Init
InteractiveChange	KeyPress	LostFocus

Message	MiddleClick	MouseDown
MouseMove	MouseUp	MouseWheel
OLECompleteDrag	OLEDragDrop	OLEDragOver
OLEGiveFeedBack	OLESetData	OLEStartDrag
ProgrammaticChange	RightClick	UIEnable
Valid	When	

Methods

AddProperty	CloneObject	Drag
Move	OLEDrag	ReadExpression
ReadMethod	Refresh	ResetToDefault
SaveAsClass	SetFocus	ShowWhatsThis
WriteExpression	WriteMethod	ZOrder

See Also

CREATE CLASS, CREATE FORM, DEFINE CLASS

CheckIn Method

Checks in changes made to a file in a project under source code control.

Syntax

Object.CheckIn( )

Remarks

True (.T.) is returned if the file is successfully checked in. False (.F.) is returned if the file could not be checked into source code control or the project is not under source code control.

Applies To

File Object

See Also

AddToSCC Method, CheckOut Method, GetLatestVersion Method, RemoveFromSCC Method, UndoCheckOut Method

CheckOut Method

Checks out a file in a project under source code control, allowing you to make changes to the file.

Syntax

Object.CheckOut( )

Remarks

True (.T.) is returned if the file is successfully checked out of source code control. False (.F.) is returned if the file could not be checked out or the project is not under source code control.

Applies To

File Object

See Also

AddToSCC Method, CheckIn Method, GetLatestVersion Method, RemoveFromSCC Method, UndoCheckOut Method

ChildAlias Property

Specifies the alias of the child table. Read-only at design time and run time.

Syntax

DataEnvironment.Relation.ChildAlias[= *cText*]

Arguments

cText
    Specifies the alias of the child table in the relation.

Remarks

The ChildAlias property setting must be the same name as the Alias property setting for the Cursor object that represents the child table.

Applies To

Relation

See Also

Alias Property, ParentAlias Property

ChildOrder Property

Specifies the index tag for the record source of the Grid control or Relation object. Available at design time and read-only at run time.

Syntax

Object.ChildOrder[= *cTagName*]

Arguments

cTagName
    Specifies an existing index tag name.

Remarks

If the ChildOrder property is set, the Order property of the Cursor for the child table is ignored.

Use this property to link two tables that have a one-to-many relationship. For example, a customer table containing one record per customer links to an order table containing multiple orders per customer. For this one-to-many relationship, set the ChildOrder property to the customer ID index tag field.

The ChildOrder property mimics the behavior of SET ORDER.

Applies To

Grid, Relation

See Also

ControlSource Property, LinkMaster Property, SET ORDER

CHR( ) Function

Returns the character associated with the specified numeric ANSI code.

Syntax

CHR(*nANSICode*)

Returns

Character

Arguments

nANSICode
    Specifies a number between 0 and 255 whose equivalent ANSI character CHR( ) returns.

    Use ASC( ) to return the ANSI value for a specified character.

Remarks

CHR( ) returns a single character corresponding to the numeric position of the character in the character table of the current code page. CHR( ) can be used to send printer control codes to a printer.

Example

The following example displays the numbers 65 through 75 and uses CHR( ) to display their corresponding character values A through K.

```
CLEAR
FOR nCOUNT = 65 TO 75
   ? nCount && Display numeric value
   ?? ' ' + CHR(nCount) && Display character
ENDFOR
```

See Also

ASC( ), INKEY( )

CHRSAW( ) Function

Determines whether or not a character is present in the keyboard buffer.

Syntax

CHRSAW([*nSeconds*])

Returns

Logical

Arguments

nSeconds

Specifies the time in seconds that CHRSAW( ) waits before checking the keyboard buffer. The keyboard buffer is checked immediately if you omit *nSeconds*.

Including *nSeconds* lets you use CHRSAW( ) for a variety of timed activities. For example, your program can close an application if a key hasn't been pressed for a specific number of seconds.

Remarks

CHRSAW( ) returns true (.T.) if a character is present in the keyboard buffer, and false (.F.) if not. CHRSAW( ) doesn't affect the keyboard buffer contents.

Example

In the following example, the system displays a window containing input fields created with @ ... GET commands, and waits 5 seconds for keyboard input. If a key isn't pressed in this time period, CHRSAW( ) returns false (.F.) and the program terminates.

```
SET TALK OFF
DEFINE WINDOW wEnter FROM 7,10 to 13,70 PANEL
ACTIVATE WINDOW wEnter
@ 1,3 SAY 'Customer: '   GET gcCustomer  DEFAULT SPACE(40)
@ 3,3 SAY 'Address:  '   GET gcAddress  DEFAULT SPACE(40)
WAIT WINDOW 'Waiting for input' NOWAIT
IF NOT CHRSAW(5)
   DEACTIVATE WINDOW wEnter
   CLEAR GETS
ELSE
   READ
   DEACTIVATE WINDOW wEnter
ENDIF
RELEASE WINDOW wEnter
WAIT
CLEAR
```

See Also

INKEY( ), KEYBOARD, READKEY( )

CHRTRAN( ) Function

Replaces each character in a character expression that matches a character in a second character expression with the corresponding character in a third character expression.

Syntax

CHRTRAN(*cSearchedExpression*, *cSearchExpression*, *cReplacementExpression*)

Returns

Character

Arguments

cSearchedExpression
Specifies the expression in which CHRTRAN( ) replaces characters.

cSearchExpression
Specifies the expression containing the characters CHRTRAN( ) looks for in *cSearchedExpression*.

cReplacementExpression

Specifies the expression containing the replacement characters.

If a character in *cSearchExpression* is found in *cSearchedExpression*, the character in *cSearchedExpression* is replaced by a character from *cReplacementExpression* that's in the same position in *cReplacementExpression* as the respective character in *cSearchExpression*.

If *cReplacementExpression* has fewer characters than *cSearchExpression*, the additional characters in *cSearchExpression* are deleted from *cSearchedExpression*. If *cReplacementExpression* has more characters than *cSearchExpression*, the additional characters in *cReplacementExpression* are ignored.

Remarks

CHRTRAN( ) translates the character expression *cSearchedExpression* using the translation expressions *cSearchExpression* and *cReplacementExpression* and returns the resulting character string.

Example

```
? CHRTRAN('ABCDEF', 'ACE', 'XYZ')  && Displays XBYDZF
? CHRTRAN('ABCD', 'ABC', 'YZ')  && Displays YZD
? CHRTRAN('ABCDEF', 'ACE', 'XYZQRST')  && Displays XBYDZF
```

See Also

CHRTRANC( ), SYS(15) – Character Translation

CHRTRANC( ) Function

Replaces each character in a character expression that matches a character in a second character expression with the corresponding character in a third character expression.

Syntax

CHRTRANC(*cSearched*, *cSearchFor*, *cReplacement*)

Returns

Character

Arguments

cSearched

Specifies the expression in which CHRTRANC( ) replaces characters.

cSearchFor

Specifies the expression containing the characters CHRTRANC( ) looks for in *cSearched*.

cReplacement

Specifies the expression containing the replacement characters.

If a character in *cSearchFor* is found in *cSearched*, the character in *cSearched* is replaced by a character from *cReplacement* that's in the same position in *cReplacement* as the respective character in *cSearchFor*.

If *cReplacement* has fewer characters than *cSearchFor*, the additional characters in *cSearchFor* are deleted from *cSearched*. If *cReplacement* has more characters than *cSearchFor*, the additional characters in *cReplacement* are ignored.

Remarks

CHRTRANC( ) is designed to facilitate working with expressions that contain double-byte characters. Use CHRTRANC( ) to replace single-byte characters with double-byte characters or double-byte characters with single-byte characters. If the expressions contains only single-byte characters, CHRTRANC( ) is equivalent to CHRTRAN( ).

This function is useful for manipulating double-byte character sets for languages such as Hiragana and Katakana.

See Also

CHRTRAN( ), STRCONV( )

Circle Method

Draws a circle or ellipse on a form.

Syntax

Object.Circle (*nRadius* [, *nXCoord*, *nYCoord* [, *nAspect*]])

Arguments

nRadius

Specifies the radius of the circle or ellipse. The ScaleMode property of the form determines the unit of measurement used.

nXCoord, nYCoord

Specifies the coordinates for the center point of the circle or ellipse. The ScaleMode property of the form determines the units of measurement used.

nAspect

Specifies the aspect ratio of the circle. The default value is 1.0, which produces a perfect (nonelliptical) circle. Values greater than 1.0 produce a vertical ellipse; values less than 1.0 produce a horizontal ellipse.

Remarks

To control the width of the line used to draw the circle or ellipse, set the DrawWidth property.

To control the way the circle is drawn in the background, set the DrawMode and DrawStyle properties.

To fill a circle, set the FillColor and FillStyle properties of the form.

When the Circle method is invoked, CurrentX and CurrentY are set to the center point arguments, *nXCoord, nYCoord*.

Applies To

Form, _SCREEN

See Also

BackColor Property, CurrentX, CurrentY Properties, DrawMode Property, DrawStyle Property, DrawWidth Property, FillColor Property, FillStyle Property, ForeColor Property, ScaleMode Property

Class Property

Returns the name of the class on which an object is based. Read-only at design time and run time.

Syntax

Object.Class

Remarks

In the Class Designer, the Class property returns the actual name of the class.

Applies To

ActiveDoc Object, CheckBox, Column, ComboBox, CommandButton, CommandGroup, Container Object, Control Object, Custom, EditBox, Form, FormSet, Grid, Header, Image, Label, Line, ListBox, OLE Bound Control, OLE Container Control, OptionButton, OptionGroup, Page, PageFrame, ProjectHook Object, Shape, _SCREEN, Spinner, TextBox, Timer, ToolBar

See Also

AddObject Method, BaseClass Property

ClassLibrary Property

Specifies the file name of the user-defined class library that contains the object's class. Read-only at design time and run time.

Syntax

Object.ClassLibrary

Remarks

Visual FoxPro base class objects are built into the product and have no ClassLibrary setting.

Applies To

ActiveDoc Object, CheckBox, Column, ComboBox, CommandButton, CommandGroup, Container Object, Control Object, Custom, EditBox, Form, FormSet, Grid, Header, Image, Label, Line, ListBox, OLE Bound Control, OLE Container Control, OptionButton, OptionGroup, Page, PageFrame, ProjectHook Object, _SCREEN, Shape, Spinner, TextBox, Timer, ToolBar

See Also

BaseClass Property

CleanUp Method

Cleans up a project table by removing records marked for deletion and packing memo fields.

Syntax

Object.CleanUp(*lRemoveObjectCode*)

Arguments

lRemoveObjectCode
Specifies if object code stored in the OBJECT field of the project table is removed. If *lRemoveObjectCode* is true (.T.), the object code is removed from the table. If *lRemoveObjectCode* is false (.F.) or is omitted, the object code isn't removed.

The OBJECT field contains object code for program (.prg), menu (.mnx), and query (.qpr) files in the project. If the object code stored in the OBJECT field of the project table is removed, the next time the project is rebuilt the source code is compiled and the object code is stored in the OBJECT field again.

Remarks

Every project has a corresponding table that contains project information. Use the CleanUp method to reduce the size of the table by removing records marked for deletion and packing memo fields. Cleaning up a project table reduces the time it takes to rebuild a large project or create an application file (.app), dynamic link library (.dll), or executable file (.exe) from a large project.

Applies To

Project Object

See Also

BUILD APP, BUILD DLL, BUILD EXE, Build Method, BUILD PROJECT, CREATE PROJECT, MODIFY PROJECT

CLEAR Commands

Releases the specified item or items from memory.

Syntax

CLEAR

    [ALL | CLASS *ClassName* | CLASSLIB *ClassLibraryName* | DEBUG
    | DLLS | EVENTS | FIELDS | GETS | MACROS | MEMORY
    | MENUS | POPUPS | PROGRAM | PROMPT | READ [ALL]
    | RESOURCES [*FileName*] | TYPEAHEAD | WINDOWS]

Arguments

ALL

    Releases from memory all variables and arrays and the definitions of all user-defined menu bars, menus, and windows. CLOSE ALL also closes any tables, including all associated index, format and memo files, and selects work area 1. CLEAR ALL also releases from memory all external shared library functions registered with DECLARE – DLL.

    CLEAR ALL does not release system variables, and does not clear the compiled program buffer. Use CLEAR PROGRAM to clear the compiled program buffer.

    Issuing CLEAR ALL within an event or method for an active control or object generates a Visual FoxPro error message. An object type variable cannot be released from memory when its associated control or object is active.

CLASS *ClassName*

    Clears a class definition from memory. When an instance of a class is created, Visual FoxPro keeps the class definition in memory after the instance is released. Use CLEAR CLASS to clear a class definition from memory after its instance is released.

CLASSLIB *ClassLibraryName*

    Clears from memory all class definitions contained in a visual class library. If instances of classes in the class library exist, the class definitions are not cleared from memory. However, all class definitions that do not have instances are cleared from memory.

DEBUG

    Clears all breakpoints in the Debugger and restores the Debugger windows (Call Stack, Trace, Watch, etc.) to their default positions.

    If Clear Debug is issued when the Debugger is closed, the Debugger is opened with the Debugger windows in their default positions.

    Works in either fox or debugger frame mode.

DLLS

Clears from memory all external shared libraries registered with DECLARE – DLL. See the DECLARE – DLL Command, later in this language reference, for more information about registering external shared library functions.

EVENTS

Stops event processing started with READ EVENTS. When CLEAR EVENTS is executed, program execution continues on the program line immediately following READ EVENTS.

FIELDS

Releases a list created with SET FIELDS and executes SET FIELDS OFF. CLEAR FIELDS differs from SET FIELDS TO in that it releases all field lists for all work areas, not just the field list for the current work area. Also, SET FIELDS TO does not implicitly issue a SET FIELDS OFF.

GETS

Releases all pending @ ... GET controls. Issuing CLEAR also releases all pending @ ... GET controls.

MACROS

Releases from memory all keyboard macros, including any SET FUNCTION key assignments. Macros can be saved to a macro file or to a memo field with SAVE MACROS and restored later with RESTORE MACROS. You can also restore the default macros with RESTORE MACROS.

MEMORY

Releases from memory all public and private memory variables and arrays. System variables aren't released.

MENUS

Releases all menu bar definitions from memory.

POPUPS

Releases from memory all menu definitions created with DEFINE POPUP.

PROGRAM

Clears the compiled program buffer. Visual FoxPro keeps a buffer of the most recently executed programs. In rare cases, Visual FoxPro might not recognize changes made to program files on disk. CLEAR PROGRAM forces Visual FoxPro to read the programs from disk, rather than from the program buffer. The most common reason Visual FoxPro might not recognize changes made to program files is your using an external or terminate-and-stay-resident (TSR) editor to modify a program file. With this exception, you should not have to use CLEAR PROGRAM.

PROMPT

Releases menu items created with @ ... PROMPT.

READ [ALL]

Included for backward compatibility. Use CLEAR EVENTS instead.

RESOURCES [*FileName*]

Specifies the name of a cached bitmap, picture, font, cursor, or icon file to be cleared from memory. If no file name is specified, all bitmap, picture, font, cursor and icon files are removed from memory.

When Visual FoxPro displays a bitmap, picture, cursor, icon, or font resource, the resource is cached to optimized performance. If a resource of the same name is used (for example, a different bitmap with the same name as one already cached), Visual FoxPro does not reload the resource.

Clearing a resource file is therefore particularly useful for removing a graphic image from memory and forcing Visual FoxPro to reload an image of the same name from disk. For example, a report might display graphic images from a database, all of which are named TEMP; however, because they all have the same name, Visual FoxPro will not reload each new graphic unless the existing one has been cleared from memory using the CLEAR RESOURCES command.

TYPEAHEAD

Clears the keyboard type-ahead buffer. CLEAR TYPEAHEAD is useful when you want to prevent input into a field or prevent a response to a prompt before the field or prompt is displayed.

WINDOWS

Releases from memory all user-defined window definitions and clears the windows from the main Visual FoxPro window or the active user-defined window. Use SAVE WINDOW to save window definitions in a file or memo field for later use.

Issuing CLEAR WINDOWS releases any system variable references to forms. For example, the following commands create a system variable reference for a form, and then displays information about the variable:

```
goMyForm = CREATEOBJECT('FORM')
DISPLAY MEMORY LIKE goMyForm  && Displays GOMYFORM  O  FORM
```

Issuing CLEAR WINDOWS releases the system variable reference and the variable now contains the null value:

```
CLEAR WINDOWS
DISPLAY MEMORY LIKE goMyForm  && Displays GOMYFORM  O  .NULL.
```

Remarks

CLEAR erases the main Visual FoxPro window or the current user-defined window, and releases from memory all pending @ ... GET controls. You can include CLEAR in format files.

See Also

@ ... CLEAR, CLOSE, DECLARE –DLL, READ, READ EVENTS, RELEASE, RELEASE CLASSLIB, RELEASE WINDOWS

Clear Method

Clears the contents of a ComboBox or ListBox control.

Syntax

Object.Clear

Remarks

For the Clear method to have an effect, the RowSourceType property must be set to 0 (None).

Applies To

ComboBox, ListBox

See Also

AddItem Method, RemoveItem Method

ClearData Method

Clears all data and data formats from the OLE drag-and-drop DataObject object. Available at run time only.

Syntax

oDataObject.ClearData

Remarks

The ClearData method can only be executed in the OLEStartDrag event; calling the ClearData method from the OLEDragDrop or OLE DragOver events generates an error.

Applies To

DataObject Object

See Also

GetData Method, GetFormat Method, OLE drag-and-drop Overview, SetData Method, SetFormat Method

Click Event

Occurs when you include code in a program that triggers the event, or when the user presses and releases the left mouse button while the pointer is over a control, changes the value of certain controls, or clicks in a blank area of a form.

Syntax

PROCEDURE *Object*.Click
[LPARAMETERS *nIndex*]

Arguments

nIndex
Uniquely identifies a control if it is in a control array.

Remarks

The Click event occurs when the user:

- Clicks a check box, command button, combo box, list box, or option button with the left mouse button.

- Presses the SPACEBAR when a command button, option button, or check box has the focus.

- Presses ENTER when a form has a command button with its Default property set to true (.T.).

- Presses the access key for a control. For example, if the caption of a command button is "\<Go", pressing ALT+G triggers the Click event.

- Clicks a blank area of a form. Click events on a form do not occur when the pointer is over the title bar, the Window menu icon, or the window borders.

- Clicks the text entry area of a spinner.

- Clicks a disabled control. The Click event occurs for the form on which the disabled control is placed.

The Click event also occurs as a result of code you include that issues the MOUSE command.

Example

The following example creates an OptionGroup control and places the control on a form. The OptionGroup control has three buttons, and depending on the option button you click, a circle, ellipse, or square appears. The ButtonCount property is used to specify the number of buttons in the OptionGroup. The Buttons and Caption properties are used to specify the text displayed next to each option button.

The Shape control is used to create the circle, ellipse, and square. The OptionGroup control's Click event uses a DO CASE ... ENDCASE structure and the Value property to display the appropriate shape when you click an option button.

```
frmMyForm = CREATEOBJECT('Form')  && Create a Form
frmMyForm.Closable = .F.  && Disable the window pop-up menu

frmMyForm.AddObject('cmdCommand1','cmdMyCmndBtn')  && Add Command button
frmMyForm.AddObject('opgOptionGroup1','opgMyOptGrp') && Add Option Group
frmMyForm.AddObject('shpCircle1','shpMyCircle')  && Add Circle Shape
frmMyForm.AddObject('shpEllipse1','shpMyEllipse')  && Add Ellipse Shape
frmMyForm.AddObject('shpSquare','shpMySquare')  && Add Box Shape

frmMyForm.cmdCommand1.Visible =.T.  && "Quit" Command button visible

frmMyForm.opgOptionGroup1.Buttons(1).Caption = "\<Circle"
frmMyForm.opgOptionGroup1.Buttons(2).Caption = "\<Ellipse"
frmMyForm.opgOptionGroup1.Buttons(3).Caption = "\<Square"
frmMyForm.opgOptionGroup1.SetAll("Width", 100) && Set Option group width
frmMyForm.opgOptionGroup1.Visible = .T.  && Option Group visible
frmMyForm.opgOptionGroup1.Click  && Show the circle

frmMyForm.SHOW  && Display the form
READ EVENTS  && Start event processing

DEFINE CLASS opgMyOptGrp AS OptionGroup  && Create an Option Group
   ButtonCount = 3  && Three Option buttons
   Top = 10
   Left = 10
   Height = 75
   Width = 100

   PROCEDURE Click
      ThisForm.shpCircle1.Visible = .F.  && Hide the circle
      ThisForm.shpEllipse1.Visible = .F.  && Hide the ellipse
      ThisForm.shpSquare.Visible = .F.  && Hide the square

      DO CASE
         CASE ThisForm.opgOptionGroup1.Value = 1
            ThisForm.shpCircle1.Visible = .T. && Show the circle
         CASE ThisForm.opgOptionGroup1.Value = 2
            ThisForm.shpEllipse1.Visible = .T.  && Show the ellipse
         CASE ThisForm.opgOptionGroup1.Value = 3
            ThisForm.shpSquare.Visible = .T.  && Show the square
      ENDCASE
ENDDEFINE
```

```
DEFINE CLASS cmdMyCmndBtn AS CommandButton  && Create Command button
   Caption = '\<Quit'  && Caption on the Command button
   Cancel = .T.  && Default Cancel Command button (Esc)
   Left = 125  && Command button column
   Top = 210  && Command button row
   Height = 25  && Command button height

   PROCEDURE Click
      CLEAR EVENTS  && Stop event processing, close Form
ENDDEFINE

DEFINE CLASS shpMyCircle AS SHAPE  && Create a circle
   Top = 10
   Left = 200
   Width = 100
   Height = 100
   Curvature = 99
   BackColor = RGB(255,0,0)  && Red
ENDDEFINE

DEFINE CLASS shpMyEllipse AS SHAPE  && Create an ellipse
   Top = 35
   Left = 200
   Width = 100
   Height = 50
   Curvature = 99
   BackColor = RGB(0,128,0)  && Green
ENDDEFINE

DEFINE CLASS shpMySquare AS SHAPE  && Create a square
   Top = 10
   Left = 200
   Width = 100
   Height = 100
   Curvature = 0
   BackColor = RGB(0,0,255)  && Blue
ENDDEFINE
```

Applies To

CheckBox, ComboBox, CommandButton, CommandGroup, Container Object, Control Object, EditBox, Form, Grid, Header, Image, Label, Line, ListBox, OptionButton, OptionGroup, Page, PageFrame, Shape, Spinner, TextBox, ToolBar

See Also

DblClick Event, MiddleClick Event, MOUSE, MouseDown Event, MouseUp Event, MouseWheel Event, Value Property

ClipControls Property

Determines whether graphics methods in Paint events repaint the entire object or only newly exposed areas. Also determines whether the graphical operating environment creates a clipping region that excludes nongraphical controls contained by the object. Available at design time and run time.

Syntax

Object.ClipControls[= *lExpr*]

Arguments

lExpr

The settings for the ClipControls property are:

Setting	Description
True (.T.)	(Default) Graphics methods in Paint events repaint the entire object. A clipping region is created around nongraphical controls on a form before a Paint event.
False (.F.)	Graphics methods in Paint events repaint only newly exposed areas. A clipping region is not created around nongraphical controls.

Applies To

Form, _SCREEN

See Also

Paint Event

_CLIPTEXT System Variable

Contains the contents of the Clipboard.

Syntax

_CLIPTEXT = *cExpression*

Arguments

cExpression

Specifies the character expression to store in the Clipboard.

Remarks

You can place a character expression *cExpression* on the Clipboard with STORE or the = assignment operator.

See Also

PRIVATE, PUBLIC, STORE

CloneObject Method

Duplicates an object, including all the object's properties, events, and methods.
Available only at design time.

Syntax

Object.CloneObject(*NewName*)

Arguments

NewName
    Specifies the name of the new, or duplicate, object.

Applies To

CheckBox, ComboBox, CommandButton, CommandGroup, Custom, EditBox, Grid,
Image, Label, Line, ListBox, OLE Bound Control, OLE Container Control, OptionButton,
OptionGroup, Page, PageFrame, Shape, Spinner, TextBox, Timer, ToolBar

See Also

SaveAs Method, SaveAsClass Method

Closable Property

Specifies whether the form can be closed by double-clicking the window pop-up menu
icon, choosing Close from the window pop-up menu, or by clicking the Close button.
Available at design time and run time.

Syntax

Object.Closable[= *lExpr*]

Arguments

lExpr
    The settings for the Closable property are:

Setting	Description
True (.T.)	(Default) The Close item is added to the window pop-up menu.
False (.F.)	The form cannot be closed by double-clicking the window pop-up menu icon, and the Close item is removed from the window pop-up menu.

Example

The following example demonstrates how the Closable property is set to false (.F.) to
prevent a form from being closed using the window pop-up menu or the Close button.

If the form's Closable property is set to true (.T.) and the form is closed using the window pop-up menu, CLEAR EVENTS must be issued to stop event processing and exit the program.

```
frmMyForm = CREATEOBJECT('Form')  && Create a Form
frmMyForm.Closable = .F.  && Disable the window pop-up menu
                          && and Close button

frmMyForm.AddObject('shpLine','Line')  && Add a Line control to the form
frmMyForm.AddObject('cmdCmndBtn1','cmdMyCmndBtn1')  && Up Cmnd button
frmMyForm.AddObject('cmdCmndBtn2','cmdMyCmndBtn2')  && Down Cmnd button
frmMyForm.AddObject('cmdCmndBtn3','cmdMyCmndBtn3')  && Quit Cmnd button

frmMyForm.shpLine.Visible = .T.  && Make Line control visible
frmMyForm.shpLine.Top = 20  && Specify Line control row
frmMyForm.shpLine.Left = 125  && Specify Line control column

frmMyForm.cmdCmndBtn1.Visible =.T.  && Up Command button visible
frmMyForm.cmdCmndBtn2.Visible =.T.  && Down" Command button visible
frmMyForm.cmdCmndBtn3.Visible =.T.  && Quit Command button visible

frmMyForm.SHOW  && Display the form
READ EVENTS  && Start event processing

DEFINE CLASS cmdMyCmndBtn1 AS COMMANDBUTTON  && Create Command button
   Caption = 'Slant \<Up'  && Caption on the Command button
   Left = 50  && Command button column
   Top = 100  && Command button row
   Height = 25  && Command button height

   PROCEDURE Click
      ThisForm.shpLine.Visible = .F.  && Hide the Line control
      ThisForm.shpLine.LineSlant ='/'  && Slant up
      ThisForm.shpLine.Visible = .T.  && Show the Line control
ENDDEFINE

DEFINE CLASS cmdMyCmndBtn2 AS CommandButton  && Create Command button
   Caption = 'Slant \<Down'  && Caption on the Command button
   Left = 200  && Command button column
   Top = 100  && Command button row
   Height = 25  && Command button height

   PROCEDURE Click
      ThisForm.shpLine.Visible = .F.  && Hide the Line control
      ThisForm.shpLine.LineSlant ='\'  && Slant down
      ThisForm.shpLine.Visible = .T.  && Show the Line control
ENDDEFINE
```

```
DEFINE CLASS cmdMyCmndBtn3 AS CommandButton  && Create Command button
   Caption = '\<Quit'  && Caption on the Command button
   Cancel = .T.  && Default Cancel Command button (Esc)
   Left = 125  && Command button column
   Top = 150  && Command button row
   Height = 25  && Command button height

   PROCEDURE Click
      CLEAR EVENTS  && Stop event processing, close Form
ENDDEFINE
```

Applies To

Form, _SCREEN

See Also

ControlBox Property, TitleBar Property

CLOSE Commands

Closes various file types.

Syntax

CLOSE
    [ALL | ALTERNATE | DATABASES [ALL] | DEBUGGER
    | FORMAT | INDEXES | PROCEDURE | TABLES [ALL]]

Arguments

ALL

    Closes all open databases, tables, and indexes in all work areas and selects work area 1. CLOSE ALL also closes any files opened with the FCREATE( ) and FOPEN( ) low-level file functions. CLOSE ALL does not close a file opened with SET PRINT.

    CLOSE ALL also closes the following:

- Form Designer

- Project Manager

- Label Designer

- Report Designer

- Query Designer

    CLOSE ALL does not close these:

- Command window

- Debug window

- Help

- Trace window

CLOSE ALTERNATE

Closes an alternate file opened with SET ALTERNATE.

CLOSE DATABASES [ALL]

Closes the current database and its tables. If there is no current database, all open free tables, indexes, and format files in all work areas are closed and work area 1 is selected.

ALL

Specifies that the following are closed:

- All open databases and their tables.

- All open free tables.

- All indexes and format files in all work areas.

Work area 1 is selected.

CLOSE DEBUGGER

Closes the Visual FoxPro debugger.

CLOSE FORMAT

Closes a format file in the current work area opened with SET FORMAT.

CLOSE INDEXES

Closes all open index files (both single-entry .idx and independent compound .cdx files) in the current work area. A structural compound index (a .cdx file automatically opened with the table) is not closed.

CLOSE PROCEDURE

Closes a procedure file opened with SET PROCEDURE.

CLOSE TABLES [ALL]

Closes all tables in the currently selected database. CLOSE TABLES closes all free tables in all work areas if a database isn't open.

Include ALL to close all tables in all databases, and all free tables. All databases remain open.

CLOSE TABLES should not be issued when a transaction is in progress; Visual FoxPro will generate an error message.

See Also

ADD TABLE, CLOSE MEMO, CREATE DATABASE

Close Method

Closes a project and releases the project's ProjectHook and Project objects.

Syntax

Object.Close( )

Remarks

Executing the Close method causes the project's ProjectHook.Destroy event to occur. After the ProjectHook.Destroy event occurs, the ProjectHook object is released, and then the Project object is released.

Applies To

Project Object

See Also

CLOSE Commands, Destroy Event

CLOSE MEMO Command

Closes one or more memo editing windows.

Syntax

CLOSE MEMO *MemoFieldName1* [, *MemoFieldName2* ...] | ALL

Arguments

MemoFieldName1 [, *MemoFieldName2* ...]
Specifies the name of the memo field whose memo editing window you want to close. To close a set of memo editing windows, include a list of memo field names with the field names separated by commas. You can close the memo editing window of a memo field in a table open in another work area by including the table alias.

ALL
Closes all memo editing windows for all memo fields in any open tables.

Remarks

CLOSE MEMO closes memo editing windows opened with MODIFY MEMO, or opened from a Browse window or Edit window. CLOSE MEMO saves any changes you made to the memo fields.

Closing a table containing the memo field or fields also saves any changes you made and closes the memo windows.

BROWSE, MODIFY MEMO

CloseTables Method

Causes the tables and views associated with the data environment to close.

Syntax

DataEnvironment.CloseTables

Remarks

Closes the tables and views associated with Cursor objects in the data environment. You can reopen the tables and views by calling the OpenTables method.

Applies To

DataEnvironment

See Also

AfterCloseTables Event, AutoCloseTables Property, BeforeOpenTables Event, OpenTables Method

Cls Method

Clears graphics and text from a form.

Syntax

Object.Cls

Remarks

Cls clears text and graphics generated at run time with graphics and printing statements. Background bitmaps created using the Picture property and controls placed on the form at design time are not affected by the Cls method.

The Cls method resets the CurrentX and CurrentY properties to 0.

Applies To

Form, _SCREEN

See Also

Circle Method, CurrentX, CurrentY Properties, Line Method, Picture Property

CLSID Property

Contains the registered CLSID (Class Identifier) for a server in a project. Read-only at design time and run time.

Syntax

Object.CLSID

Remarks

A CLSID is created in the Windows registry for a server when you build an executable file (.exe) or dynamic link library (.dll) from a project.

Applies To

Server Object

See Also

CREATEOBJECTEX( ), ProgID Property, TypeLibCLSID Property, TypeLibDesc Property, TypeLibName Property

CMONTH( ) Function

Returns the name of the month from a given date or DateTime expression.

Syntax

CMONTH(*dExpression* | *tExpression*)

Returns

Character

Arguments

dExpression
Specifies the date expression from which CMONTH( ) returns the name of the month.

tExpression
Specifies the DateTime expression from which CMONTH( ) returns the name of the month.

Remarks

CMONTH( ) returns the name of the month as a string in proper noun format.

Example

```
? CMONTH(DATE( ))
STORE {^1998-02-16} TO gdDueDate
? 'Your payment was due in ', CMONTH(gdDueDate)
STORE gdDueDate+60 TO gdFinalDate
? 'You must pay by ', CMONTH(gdFinalDate)
```

See Also

DMY( ), MDY( ), MONTH( )

CNTBAR( ) Function

Returns the number of menu items on a user-defined menu or the Visual FoxPro system menu.

Syntax

CNTBAR(*cMenuName*)

Returns

Numeric

Arguments

cMenuName

Specifies the name of the menu for which CNTBAR( ) returns the number of menu items. For a list of the Visual FoxPro system menu names, see "System Menu Names," later in this language reference.

Remarks

If a user-defined menu is created with the PROMPT option in DEFINE POPUP, Visual FoxPro evaluates the number of menu items when you issue ACTIVATE POPUP. For such a menu, CNTBAR( ) returns a meaningful value only after you activate the menu. However, if the menu items in the menu are created with DEFINE BAR, CNTBAR( ) can determine the number of menu items before you issue ACTIVATE POPUP.

Example

In the following program example, named CNTBAR.PRG, a menu title is added to the system menu. The menu popEnv is created with four menu items. The program places a mark character by each item when the item is selected. CNTBAR( ) is used within a loop to initially display marks next to the appropriate menu items.

```
*** You must name this program CNTBAR.PRG ***
CLEAR
SET TALK OFF
DEFINE PAD padEnv OF _MSYSMENU PROMPT 'E\<nvironment';
   KEY ALT+R, 'ALT+R'
```

```
ON PAD padEnv OF _MSYSMENU ACTIVATE POPUP popEnv
DEFINE POPUP popEnv MARGIN RELATIVE COLOR SCHEME 4
DEFINE BAR 1 OF popEnv PROMPT '\<Status Bar'
DEFINE BAR 2 OF popEnv PROMPT '\<Clock'
DEFINE BAR 3 OF popEnv PROMPT '\<Extended Video'
DEFINE BAR 4 OF popEnv PROMPT 'St\<icky'
ON SELECTION POPUP popEnv DO enviropop IN cntbar.prg
FOR i = 1 TO CNTBAR('popEnv')
   DO CASE
      CASE PRMBAR('popEnv', i) = 'Status Bar'
         IF _WINDOWS or _MAC
            SET MARK OF BAR i OF popEnv TO SET('STATUS BAR') = 'ON'
         ELSE
            SET MARK OF BAR i OF popEnv TO SET('STATUS') = 'ON'
         ENDIF
      CASE PRMBAR('popEnv', i) = 'Clock'
         SET MARK OF BAR i OF popEnv TO  SET('CLOCK') = 'ON'
      CASE PRMBAR('popEnv', i) = 'Extended Video'
         SET MARK OF BAR i OF popEnv TO  SROW( ) > 25
      CASE PRMBAR('popEnv', i) = 'Sticky'
         SET MARK OF BAR i OF popEnv TO  SET('STICKY') = 'ON'
   ENDCASE
ENDFOR
PROCEDURE enviropop
DO CASE
   CASE PROMPT() = 'Status'
      IF mrkbar('popEnv', BAR( ))
         DO CASE
            CASE _WINDOWS OR _MAC
               SET STATUS BAR OFF
            CASE _DOS
               SET STATUS OFF
            OTHERWISE
         ENDCASE
         SET MARK OF BAR BAR( ) OF popEnv TO .F.
      ELSE
         DO CASE
            CASE _WINDOWS OR _MAC
               SET STATUS BAR ON
            CASE _DOS
               SET STATUS ON
            OTHERWISE
         ENDCASE
         SET MARK OF BAR BAR( ) OF popEnv TO .T.
      ENDIF
```

```
CASE PROMPT( ) = 'Clock'
   IF mrkbar('popEnv', BAR( ))
      SET CLOCK OFF
      SET MARK OF BAR BAR( ) OF popEnv TO .F.
   ELSE
      DO CASE
         CASE _WINDOWS OR _MAC
            SET STATUS BAR ON
            SET CLOCK STATUS
         CASE _DOS
            SET CLOCK ON
         OTHERWISE
      ENDCASE
      SET MARK OF BAR BAR( ) OF popEnv TO .T.
   ENDIF
CASE PROMPT( ) = 'Extended Video'
   IF MRKBAR('popEnv', BAR( ))
      SET DISPLAY TO VGA25
      SET MARK OF BAR BAR( ) OF popEnv TO .F.
   ELSE
      SET DISPLAY TO VGA50
      SET MARK OF BAR BAR( ) OF popEnv TO .T.
   ENDIF
CASE PROMPT( ) = 'Sticky'
   IF MRKBAR('popEnv', BAR( ))
      DO CASE
         CASE _WINDOWS OR _MAC
            WAIT WINDOW 'STICKY is always on in this Visual FoxPro version'
         CASE _DOS
            SET STICKY OFF
         OTHERWISE
      ENDCASE
      SET MARK OF BAR BAR( ) OF popEnv TO .F.
   ELSE
      DO CASE
         CASE _WINDOWS OR _MAC
            WAIT WINDOW 'STICKY is always ON in Visual FoxPro'
         CASE _DOS
            SET STICKY ON
         OTHERWISE
      ENDCASE
      SET MARK OF BAR BAR( ) OF popEnv TO .T.
   ENDIF
ENDCASE
```

See Also

ACTIVATE POPUP, CNTPAD( ), CREATE MENU, DEFINE BAR, DEFINE POPUP, GETBAR( ), MRKBAR( ), ON BAR, ON SELECTION BAR, PRMBAR( )

CNTPAD( ) Function

Returns the number of menu titles on a user-defined menu bar or the Visual FoxPro system menu bar.

Syntax

CNTPAD(*cMenuBarName*)

Returns

Numeric

Arguments

cMenuBarName

Specifies the name of the menu bar for which CNTPAD( ) returns the number of menu titles.

Example

The following command uses CNTPAD( ) to display the number of menu titles in the Visual FoxPro system menu bar.

```
? CNTPAD('_MSYSMENU')
```

See Also

ACTIVATE MENU, CNTBAR( ), CREATE MENU, DEFINE PAD, DEFINE MENU, GETPAD( ), MRKPAD( ), ON PAD, ON SELECTION PAD, PRMPAD( )

CodePage Property

Contains the code page of a file in a project. Read-only at design time and run time.

Syntax

Object.CodePage

Remarks

The code page is a numeric value indicating the character set used for the file. Code pages usually correspond to different platforms and languages and are used in international applications.

Applies To

File Object

See Also

CPCONVERT( ), CPCURRENT( ), CPDBF( )

COL( ) Function

Included for backward compatibility. Use the CurrentX property.

Colors Overview

Visual FoxPro offers a sophisticated set of commands for full control of colors.

By default, Visual FoxPro takes its colors from the operating system's Control Panel settings. At startup, the Control Panel colors are mapped to the Visual FoxPro default color schemes. You can set colors directly with the SET COLOR commands or interactively in the Control Panel. Refer to your Windows documentation for more information about setting colors with the Control Panel.

Not all Visual FoxPro interface elements can be controlled by color schemes — for example, system elements such as the Data Session window and Command window, the system menu bar, and so on.

Color Terms

The following color terms are used throughout the FoxPro documentation.

Color Pair

A color pair contains two color codes that specify the foreground and background colors. A color pair consists of a set of two letters separated by a forward slash; the first letter specifying the foreground color and the second letter specifying the background color.

For example, the following color pair specifies a red foreground on a white background:

```
R/W
```

The following table lists the available colors and their codes.

Color	Code
Black	N
Blank	X
Blue	B
Brown	GR
Cyan	BG
Green	G
Inverse	I
Magenta	RB
Red	R
White	W
Yellow	GR+
Underlined	U

An asterisk (*) placed immediately after a color code can be used to denote blinking or bright (depending on your video hardware and the setting for SET BLINK) for the background color. In Visual FoxPro, including an asterisk makes the background bright rather than blinking. A plus sign (+) placed immediately after a color code can be used to denote high intensity for the foreground color.

On monochrome monitors, only four colors are available: white (W), black (N), underlined (U), and inverse video (I). The blank (X) color is useful for entering passwords.

RGB Color Pairs

A color pair can also be specified with a set of six RGB (red, green, and blue) color values separated by commas. These values range from 0 (lowest intensity or no color) to 255 (high intensity or bright color). Each foreground and background color requires three values, one for red, one for green, and one for blue. A color pair, therefore, requires six values, three for the foreground and three for the background.

Here is the RGB color code for red on dark gray (high intensity black):

```
RGB(255,0,0,64,64,64)
```

The first three values in the RGB expression above set the foreground color to red and the second three values set the background color to dark gray.

The following is a table of the colors that are available in Visual FoxPro, including the color codes and the corresponding RGB values.

Color	Color code	RGB value
White	W+	255,255,255
Black	N	0,0,0
Dark Gray	N+	64,64,64 (25% gray)
Gray	W	192,192,192
Red	R+	255,0,0
Dark Red	R	128,0,0
Yellow	GR+	255,255,0
Dark Yellow	GR	128,128,0
Green	G+	0,255,0
Dark Green	G	0,128,0
Cyan	BG+	0,255,255
Dark Cyan	BG	0,128,128
Blue	B+	0,0,255
Dark Blue	B	0,0,128
Magenta	RB+	255,0,255
Dark Magenta	RB	128,0,128
Blank	X	N/A

When using RGB values, the following rules determine the color:

- When all three color values (R, G or B) are below 32, the color is black.

- When all three color values (R, G or B) are between 32 and 64, the character code is dark gray.

- When all three color values (R, G or B) are between 65 and 191, the character code is gray.

- When any of the three color values (R, G or B) are above 191, the color is high intensity (+ or *).

Color Pair List

A color-pair list consists of one to ten color pairs separated by commas. For example:

```
W+/B, W+/BG, GR+/B, GR+/B, R+/B, W+/GR, GR+/RB, N+/N, GR+/B, R+/B
```

A color-pair list for a monochrome monitor might look like this:

```
W/N, N+/W, W+/N, W+/N, W/N, U+/N, W+/N, -, W+/N, W/N
```

Color-pair lists for monochrome monitors might have a dash (-) in the eighth color-pair location to indicate that a shadow isn't present.

Color pairs can also be specified as a set of RGB (red, green, and blue) values. A set of RGB color values looks like this:

```
RGB(0,255,0,255,0,0), RGB(127,255,0,0,0,0), ...
```

Color Scheme

A color scheme is a set of 10 color pairs. Use SCHEME( ) or RGBSCHEME( ) to return the color pairs for a color scheme.

Color schemes control the colors of interface elements such as system windows, user-defined windows, menus, and so on. In Visual FoxPro, the color of some interface elements are not controlled by a color scheme. For example, the colors of the Data Session window and Command window, the system menu bar, and so on cannot be controlled by a color scheme.

In your configuration file, you can specify your own startup color schemes. Include the following line for each color scheme you want to change:

```
COLOR OF SCHEME nScheme = Colorpairlist
```

> **Note** In Visual FoxPro, color schemes 13 through 15 are reserved for internal use. In FoxPro for Windows, color schemes 13 and 14 are reserved for internal use. In FoxPro for Macintosh, color schemes 13 through 16 are reserved for internal use. Do not use these color schemes.

Color Set

A color set consists of 24 color schemes. You can save the complete color environment in a color set. Color sets are not supported in FoxPro for Macintosh.

Color sets, like keyboard macros and memory variables, can be saved for later use. A color set can be saved with CREATE COLOR SET. Color sets are stored in the Foxuser.dbf resource file.

You can load a color set with SET COLOR SET.

When Visual FoxPro is first started, the Control Panel color settings are loaded into the default color set. To specify a startup color set in your configuration file, include the following line:

```
COLOR SET = ColorSetName
```

See Also

CREATE COLOR SET, GETCOLOR( ), RGB( ), RGBSCHEME( ), SET COLOR OF SCHEME, SET COLOR SET, SET COLOR TO

ColorScheme Property

Included for backward compatibility. Use the BackColor, ForeColor properties instead.

ColorSource Property

Determines how a control's colors are set. Available at design time and run time.

Syntax

Object.ColorSource[= *nSource*]

Arguments

nSource

The settings for *nSource* are:

Setting	Description
0	Object's Color Properties. The control uses its color property settings (ForeColor, BackColor, and so on). This setting is available for the following controls and objects:
	CheckBox, ComboBox, CommandButton, CommandGroup, Container, Control, EditBox, Form, Image, Label, Line, ListBox, OptionButton, OptionGroup, Page, PageFrame, Shape, Spinner, TextBox, and Toolbar.
1	Form's Color Scheme. The control uses the color scheme of the form in which it is placed. This setting is available for the following controls and objects:
	CheckBox, ComboBox, CommandButton, EditBox, Label, ListBox, OptionButton, Shape, Spinner, and TextBox.
2	ColorScheme Property Scheme. The control uses the color scheme specified in its ColorScheme property. This setting is available for the following controls and objects:
	CheckBox, ComboBox, CommandButton, EditBox, Label, ListBox, OptionButton, Shape, Spinner, and TextBox.
3	Default Scheme. The control uses its default color scheme. For most controls, the default color scheme is the form's color scheme; for EditBoxes and ListBoxes, the default color scheme is Scheme 2, User Menus. This setting is available for the following controls and objects:
	CheckBox, ComboBox, CommandButton, EditBox, Label, ListBox, OptionButton, Shape, Spinner, and TextBox.

(continued)

(continued)

Setting	Description
4	Windows Control Panel (3D Colors) (Default). The control uses the 3D color settings specified in the Windows Control Panel. This setting is available for the following controls and objects:
	CheckBox, ComboBox, CommandButton, CommandGroup, Container, Control, EditBox, Form, Image, Label, Line, ListBox, OptionButton, OptionGroup, Page, PageFrame, Shape, Spinner, TextBox, and Toolbar.
5	Windows Control Panel (Windows Colors). The control uses the color settings specified in the Windows Control Panel. This setting is available only for the Form object.

Remarks

Setting a color property (ForeColor, BackColor, SelectedForeColor, and so on) for an object overrides the ColorSource property setting. If a color property is not set for an object, the object's colors are determined by the ColorSource property setting.

Applies To

CheckBox, ComboBox, CommandButton, CommandGroup, Container, Control, EditBox, Form, Image, Label, Line, ListBox, OptionButton, OptionGroup, Page, PageFrame, Shape, Spinner, TextBox, Toolbar

See Also

ColorScheme Property

Column Object

Creates a Column in a Grid.

Syntax

Column

Remarks

The number of Columns in a Grid is specified with the Grid's ColumnCount property.

A Column in a Grid can contain data from a field in a table, or the value of an expression. Use the DataSource property to specify the data that appears in the Column.

A Column can also contain controls. Controls are added to a Column in a Grid with the AddObject method in the Init event for the form containing the Grid. Use the column's CurrentControl property to set the active control in the Grid's column. Set the control's ControlSource property to specify the source of the control's data.

Note that headers and controls for a Column cannot be accessed until the Init event for the Grid occurs.

For additional information about creating Columns in a Grid, see the Grid Control, later in this language reference, and Chapter 10, "Using Controls," in the *Microsoft Visual FoxPro 6.0 Programmer's Guide*.

Properties

Alignment	Application	BackColor
BaseClass	Bound	Class
ClassLibrary	ColumnOrder	Comment
ControlCount	Controls	ControlSource
CurrentControl	DynamicAlignment	DynamicBackColor
DynamicCurrentControl	DynamicFontBold	DynamicFontItalic
DynamicFontName	DynamicFontOutline	DynamicFontShadow
DynamicFontSize	DynamicFontStrikeThru	DynamicFontUnderline
DynamicForeColor	DynamicInputMask	Enabled
FontBold	FontCondense	FontExtend
FontItalic	FontName	FontOutline
FontShadow	FontSize	FontStrikeThru
FontUnderline	ForeColor	Format
InputMask	Movable	Name
Parent	ParentClass	ReadOnly
Resizable	SelectOnEntry	Sparse
Tag	Visible	Width

Events

MouseMove	MouseWheel	Moved
Resize		

Methods

AddObject	AddProperty	Move
ReadExpression	ReadMethod	Refresh
RemoveObject	ResetToDefault	SaveAsClass
SetAll	SetFocus	WriteExpression
WriteMethod	ZOrder	

See Also

CREATE CLASS, CREATE FORM, DEFINE CLASS, Grid Control, Header Object

ColumnCount Property

Specifies the number of Column objects in a Grid, ComboBox, or ListBox control. For a grid, available at design time and read/write at run time. For a combo box or list box, available at design time and run time.

Syntax

Object.ColumnCount[= *nCol*]

Arguments

nCol

For a Grid control, specifies the number of columns to display. The default is –1, which specifies that the Grid control should contain enough columns to accommodate all the fields in the grid's record source. The maximum number of columns is 255. If you create a specific number of columns by setting *nCol* to a positive value, specify the data to display in a particular column by setting that column's ControlSource property. (If ControlSource is not specified for a column, the Grid control displays the next available undisplayed field of the grid's record source.)

For a ComboBox or ListBox control, *nCol* specifies the number of columns the control contains. If you set ColumnCount to 0, the first column is displayed based on the RowSource property or on the items added with the AddItem method.

Remarks

For a grid, use the AddColumn method to increase the number of columns.

Applies To

ComboBox, Grid, ListBox

See Also

AddColumn Method, Order Property

ColumnLines Property

Shows or hides the lines between columns. Available at design time and run time.

Syntax

Control.ColumnLines[= *lExpr*]

Arguments

lExpr

Specifies whether lines separating columns are displayed. The settings for the ColumnLines property are:

Setting	Description
True (.T.)	(Default) The lines between columns are visible.
False (.F.)	The lines between columns are hidden.

Applies To

ComboBox, ListBox

See Also

ColumnWidths Property

ColumnOrder Property

Specifies the relative order of column objects in a Grid control. Available at design time and run time.

Syntax

Column.ColumnOrder[= *nExpr*]

Arguments

nExpr

Specifies the order of a column relative to other columns in the grid.

Remarks

If a Grid contains five columns and you want the third column displayed last, set the ColumnOrder property of the third column to 5. The ColumnOrder setting for the fourth column becomes 3, the ColumnOrder setting for the fifth column becomes 4, and so on.

> **Note** ColumnOrder settings do not have to be sequential. There can be gaps. For example, if a Grid contains three columns, you can add a fourth and set its ColumnOrder property to 10.

Applies To

Column

See Also

Activate Event, Deactivate Event, ZOrder Method

Columns Property

An array for accessing individual Column objects in the Grid control by column number. Available at design time and read-only at run time.

Syntax

Grid.Columns(*nCol*).*Property* [= *Setting*]

Arguments

nCol
> Specifies the column in agGrid whose property is referenced. The far left Column is number 1.

Property
> Specifies the column's property to access.

Setting
> Specifies the new property setting for all cells specified with *nCol*.

Remarks

Use the Columns property to access the properties of a particular Column in a Grid. For example, SpecialGrid.Column(1).BackColor = RGB(255,0,0) changes the BackColor property of all the cells in Column 1 to bright red.

Applies To

Grid

See Also

Column Object, ColumnCount Property, SetAll Method

ColumnWidths Property

Specifies the width of columns for a ComboBox or ListBox control. Available at design time and run time.

Syntax

Control.ColumnWidths[= "*cCol1Width, cCol2Width, ... cColnWidth*"]

Arguments

"*cCol1Width, cCol2Width, ... cColnWidth*"
> Specifies the width of a column or series of columns in the ComboBox or ListBox. For example, *cColumnWidths* = "5, 7, 9" specifies that the first column is 5 units wide, the second column is 7 units wide, and the third column is 9 units wide, in the

unit of measurement specified by the ScaleMode property of the form. Use commas to separate each width number. You can specify the number of columns with the ColumnCount property.

Applies To

ComboBox, ListBox

See Also

ColumnCount Property, ScaleMode Property, Width Property

ComboBox Control

Creates a combo box.

Syntax

ComboBox

Remarks

When selected, the ComboBox control opens, displaying a list of items from which you can choose one. A ComboBox control combines the features of a TextBox control and a ListBox control. You can enter information in the text box portion or select an item from the list box portion of the control.

An item in a ComboBox control can be disabled by placing a backslash (\) before the item. If the item begins with a backslash and should not be disabled, add an additional backslash.

The Style property determines the ComboBox control type. If the Style property is set to 0, a drop-down ComboBox control is created. If the Style property is set to 2, a drop-down list box is created.

For additional information about ComboBox controls, see "Form Designer" in Help, and Chapter 10, "Using Controls," in the *Microsoft Visual FoxPro 6.0 Programmer's Guide*.

Properties

Alignment	Application	BackColor
BaseClass	BorderColor	BorderStyle
BoundColumn	BoundTo	Class
ClassLibrary	ColorScheme	ColorSource
ColumnCount	ColumnLines	ColumnWidths
Comment	ControlSource	DisabledBackColor

DisabledForeColor	DisabledItemBackColor	DisabledItemForeColor
DisplayCount Property	DisplayValue	DragIcon
DragMode	Enabled	FirstElement
FontBold	FontCondense	FontExtend
FontItalic	FontName	FontOutline
FontShadow	FontSize	FontStrikeThru
FontUnderline	ForeColor	Format
Height	HelpContextID	HideSelection
IMEMode	IncrementalSearch	InputMask
ItemBackColor	ItemData	ItemForeColor
ItemIDData	ItemTips	Left
List	ListCount	ListIndex
ListItem	ListItemID	Margin
MouseIcon	MousePointer	Name
NewIndex	NewItemID	NullDisplay
NumberOfElements	OLEDragMode	OLEDragPicture
OLEDropEffects	OLEDropHasData Property	OLEDropMode
OLEDropTextInsertion	Parent	ParentClass
Picture	ReadOnly	RightToLeft
RowSource	RowSourceType	Selected
SelectedBackColor	SelectedForeColor	SelectedID
SelectedItemBackColor	SelectedItemForeColor	SelectOnEntry
SelLength	SelStart	SelText
Sorted	SpecialEffect	StatusBarText
Style	TabIndex	TabStop
Tag	Text Property	TerminateRead
ToolTipText	Top	TopIndex
TopItemID	Value	Visible
WhatsThisHelpID	Width	

Events

Click	DblClick	Destroy
DownClick	DragDrop	DragOver
DropDown	Error	ErrorMessage
GotFocus	Init	InteractiveChange
KeyPress	LostFocus	Message
MiddleClick Event	MouseDown	MouseMove
MouseUp	MouseWheel	OLECompleteDrag
OLEDragDrop	OLEDragOver	OLEGiveFeedBack
OLESetData	OLEStartDrag	ProgrammaticChange
RangeHigh	RangeLow	RightClick
UIEnable	UpClick	Valid
When		

Methods

AddItem	AddListItem	AddProperty
Clear	CloneObject	Drag
IndexToItemID	ItemIDToIndex	Move
OLEDrag	ReadExpression	ReadMethod
Refresh	RemoveItem	RemoveListItem
Requery	ResetToDefault	SaveAsClass
SetFocus	SetViewPort	ShowWhatsThis
WriteExpression	WriteMethod	ZOrder

See Also

CREATE CLASS, CREATE FORM, DEFINE CLASS

COMARRAY( ) Function

Specifies how arrays are passed to COM objects.

Syntax

COMARRAY(*oObject* [, *nNewValue*])

Returns

Numeric

Arguments

oObject
An object reference to the COM object.

nNewValue
Specifies how an array is passed to the COM object specified with *oObject*. The following table lists the settings for *nNewValue* and how the array is passed to the COM object.

nNewValue	Description
0	The array is a zero based array, and it is passed by value.
1 (Default)	The array is a one based array, and it is passed by value. Compatible with earlier versions of Visual FoxPro.
10	The array is a zero based array, and it is passed by reference.
11	The array is a one based array, and it is passed by reference.

Issue COMARRAY( ) without the *nNewValue* argument to return the current setting.

Remarks

Earlier versions of Visual FoxPro can only pass arrays to COM objects by value. Also, the array passed to the COM object is assumed be a one-based array, meaning that the first element, row, and column in the array is referenced with 1.

However, some COM objects require that arrays passed to them be passed by reference, or the array passed is zero-based (the first element, row, and column in the array is referenced with 0), or both. COMARRAY( ) lets you specify how the array is passed to the COM object, and assumes you know how the array should be passed to the COM object.

Note that COMARRAY( ) is only used when arrays are passed to COM objects using the following syntax:

```
oComObject.Method(@MyArray)
```

If the @ token is omitted, only the first element of the array is passed to the COM object and COMARRAY( ) has no effect.

See Also

COMCLASSINFO( ), CREATEOBJECT( ), GETOBJECT( )

COMCLASSINFO( ) Function

Returns registry information about a COM object such as a Visual FoxPro automation server.

Syntax

COMCLASSINFO(*oObject* [, *nInfoType*])

Returns

Character

Arguments

oObject
An object reference to a COM or OLE object.

nInfoType
Specifies the type of information to return. The following table lists the values for *nInfoType* and the information returned.

nInfoType	Information returned
1 (Default)	The object's programmatic identifier (ProgID).
A	ProgID is a registry entry that can be associated with a CLSID.
2	The object's VersionIndependentProgID.
	The VersionIndependentProgID associates a ProgID with a CLSID. It is used to determine the latest version of an object application, refers to the application's class, and does not change from version to version.
3	The object's friendly name.
4	The object's class identifier (CLSID). A CLSID is a globally unique identifier that identifies a COM class object.

Remarks

COMCLASSINFO( ) returns the empty string if registry information isn't available for the object you specify. Visual FoxPro automation servers are COM objects, both .exe executable files and .dll dynamic link libraries you can create in the Project Manager.

See Also

COMARRAY( ), CREATE PROJECT, CREATEOBJECT( ), GETOBJECT( )

CommandButton Control

Creates a single command button.

Syntax

CommandButton

Remarks

A command button is typically used to start an event that performs an action such as closing a form, moving to a different record, printing a report, and so on. Use the CommandGroup control to create a set of command buttons that you can manipulate individually or as a group.

Use the Caption property to specify the text that appears on a command button. Use the Picture property to specify a picture for a command button.

You can choose a command button by clicking it, and, if the Default property is set to true (.T.), by pressing the ENTER key when the command button is selected. If the Cancel property of the command button is set to true (.T.), you can choose the command button by pressing the ESC key.

For additional information about command buttons, see "Form Designer" in Help, and Chapter 10, "Using Controls," in the *Microsoft Visual FoxPro 6.0 Programmer's Guide*.

Properties

Application	AutoSize	BaseClass
Cancel	Caption	ClassLibrary
Class	ColorScheme	ColorSource
Comment	Default	DisabledForeColor
DisabledPicture	DownPicture	DragIcon
DragMode	Enabled	FontBold
FontCondense	FontExtend	FontItalic
FontName	FontOutline	FontShadow
FontSize	FontStrikeThru	FontUnderline
ForeColor	Height	HelpContextID
Left	MouseIcon	MousePointer
Name	OLEDragMode	OLEDragPicture

OLEDropEffects	OLEDropHasData Property	OLEDropMode
Parent	ParentClass	Picture
RightToLeft	SpecialEffect	StatusBarText
Style	TabIndex	TabStop
Tag	TerminateRead	ToolTipText
Top	Visible	WhatsThisHelpID
Width	WordWrap	

Events

Click	Destroy	DragDrop
DragOver	Error	ErrorMessage
GotFocus	Init	KeyPress
LostFocus	Message	MiddleClick Event
MouseDown	MouseMove	MouseUp
MouseWheel	OLECompleteDrag	OLEDragDrop
OLEDragOver	OLEGiveFeedBack	OLESetData
OLEStartDrag	RightClick	UIEnable
Valid	When	

Methods

AddProperty	CloneObject	Drag
Move	OLEDrag	ReadExpression
ReadMethod	Refresh	ResetToDefault
SaveAsClass	SetFocus	ShowWhatsThis
WriteExpression	WriteMethod	ZOrder

Example

The following example demonstrates how command buttons can be added to a form. The Caption property is used to specify the text on the command buttons and the text indicating each button's access key sequence. The Cancel property is used to specify a button that is chosen when you press ESC.

The AddObject method is used to add three command buttons to the form, allowing you to change the direction in which a Line control slants or to close the form.

```
frmMyForm = CREATEOBJECT('Form')  && Create a Form
frmMyForm.Closable = .F.  && Disable the Control menu box

frmMyForm.AddObject('shpLine','Line')  && Add a Line control to the form
frmMyForm.AddObject('cmdCmndBtn1','cmdMyCmndBtn1')  && Up Cmnd button
frmMyForm.AddObject('cmdCmndBtn2','cmdMyCmndBtn2')  && Down Cmnd button
frmMyForm.AddObject('cmdCmndBtn3','cmdMyCmndBtn3')  && Quit Cmnd button

frmMyForm.shpLine.Visible = .T.  && Make Line control visible
frmMyForm.shpLine.Top = 20  && Specify Line control row
frmMyForm.shpLine.Left = 125  && Specify Line control column

frmMyForm.cmdCmndBtn1.Visible =.T.  && Up Command button visible
frmMyForm.cmdCmndBtn2.Visible =.T.  && Down" Command button visible
frmMyForm.cmdCmndBtn3.Visible =.T.  && Quit Command button visible

frmMyForm.SHOW  && Display the form
READ EVENTS  && Start event processing

DEFINE CLASS cmdMyCmndBtn1 AS CommandButton  && Create Command button
    Caption = 'Slant \<Up'  && Caption on the Command button
    Left = 50  && Command button column
    Top = 100  && Command button row
    Height = 25  && Command button height

    PROCEDURE Click
        ThisForm.shpLine.Visible = .F.  && Hide the Line control
        ThisForm.shpLine.LineSlant ='/'  && Slant up
        ThisForm.shpLine.Visible = .T.  && Show the Line control
ENDDEFINE

DEFINE CLASS cmdMyCmndBtn2 AS CommandButton  && Create Command button
    Caption = 'Slant \<Down'  && Caption on the Command button
    Left = 200  && Command button column
    Top = 100  && Command button row
    Height = 25  && Command button height

    PROCEDURE Click
        ThisForm.shpLine.Visible = .F.  && Hide the Line control
        ThisForm.shpLine.LineSlant ='\'  && Slant down
        ThisForm.shpLine.Visible = .T.  && Show the Line control
ENDDEFINE

DEFINE CLASS cmdMyCmndBtn3 AS CommandButton  && Create Command button
    Caption = '\<Quit'  && Caption on the Command button
    Cancel = .T.  && Default Cancel Command button (Esc)
    Left = 125  && Command button column
    Top = 150  && Command button row
    Height = 25  && Command button height
```

```
    PROCEDURE Click
        CLEAR EVENTS  && Stop event processing, close Form
ENDDEFINE
```

See Also

CommandGroup Control, CREATE CLASS, CREATE FORM, DEFINE CLASS

CommandGroup Control

Creates a group of command buttons.

Syntax

CommandGroup

Remarks

Use the CommandGroup control to create a set of command buttons that you can manipulate individually or as a group. Use the CommandButton control to create an individual command button.

Use the ButtonCount property to specify the number of command buttons in the group, and the Caption property to specify a label for the command button group.

For additional information about command button groups, see "Form Designer" in Help, and Chapter 10, "Using Controls," in the *Microsoft Visual FoxPro 6.0 Programmer's Guide*.

Properties

Application	AutoSize	BackColor
BackStyle	BaseClass	BorderColor
BorderStyle	ButtonCount	Buttons
Class	ClassLibrary	ColorSource
Comment	ControlSource	DragIcon
DragMode	Enabled	Height
HelpContextID	Left	MouseIcon
MousePointer	Name	OLEDragMode
OLEDragPicture	OLEDropEffects	OLEDropHasData Property
OLEDropMode	Parent	ParentClass

SpecialEffect	TabIndex	Tag
TerminateRead	Top	Value
Visible	WhatsThisHelpID	Width

Events

Click	DblClick	DragDrop
DragOver	Error	ErrorMessage
Init	InteractiveChange	Message
MiddleClick Event	MouseDown	MouseMove
MouseUp	MouseWheel	OLECompleteDrag
OLEDragDrop	OLEDragOver	OLEGiveFeedBack
OLESetData	OLEStartDrag	ProgrammaticChange
RightClick	UIEnable	Valid
When		

Methods

AddObject	AddProperty	CloneObject
Drag	Move	NewObject
OLEDrag	ReadExpression	ReadMethod
Refresh	RemoveObject	ResetToDefault
SaveAsClass	SetAll	ShowWhatsThis
WriteExpression	WriteMethod	ZOrder

See Also

CommandButton Control, CREATE CLASS, CREATE FORM, DEFINE CLASS

CommandTargetExec Event

Occurs when an Active Document host notifies an Active Document of the command to be executed.

Syntax

PROCEDURE *Object*.CommandTargetExec
[LPARAMETERS *nCommandID*, *nExecOption*, *eArgIn*, *eArgOut*]

Arguments

nCommandID

A parameter passed by the Active Document's host to the CommandTargetExec event that indicates the command to be executed. The following table lists the values passed to the event that Visual FoxPro can process and the corresponding command to be executed.

nCommandID	FOXPRO.H Constant	Command
1	CMDID_OPEN	File menu **Open** command.
2	CMDID_NEW	File menu **New** command.
3	CMDID_SAVE	File menu **Save** command.
4	CMDID_SAVEAS	File menu **Save As** command.
5	CMDID_SAVECOPYAS	File menu **Save Copy As** command.
6	CMDID_PRINT	File menu **Print** command.
7	CMDID_PRINTPREVIEW	File menu **Print Preview** command.
8	CMDID_PAGESETUP	File menu **Page Setup** command.
9	CMDID_SPELL	Tools menu **Spelling** command.
10	CMDID_PROPERTIES	File menu **Properties** command.
11	CMDID_CUT	Edit menu **Cut** command.
12	CMDID_COPY	Edit menu **Copy** command.
13	CMDID_PASTE	Edit menu **Paste** command.
14	CMDID_PASTESPECIAL	Edit menu **Paste Special** command.
15	CMDID_UNDO	Edit menu **Undo** command.
16	CMDID_REDO	Edit menu **Redo** command.
17	CMDID_SELECTALL	Edit menu **Select All** command.
18	CMDID_CLEARSELECTION	Edit menu **Clear** command.
19	CMDID_ZOOM	View menu **Zoom** command.
20	CMDID_GETZOOMRANGE	Retrieves zoom range applicable to the View menu **Zoom** command.
21	CMDID_UPDATECOMMANDS	Notifies the Active Document of state changes.
22	CMDID_REFRESH	Asks the Active Document to refresh its display. Implemented by the Active Document.

(continued)

(continued)

nCommandID	FOXPRO.H Constant	Command
23	CMDID_STOP	Asks the Active Document to stop its processing.
24	CMDID_HIDETOOLBARS	Asks the Active Document to hide its toolbars. Implemented by the Active Document.
25	CMDID_SETPROGRESSMAX	Sets the maximum value of the progress indicator.
26	CMDID_SETPROGRESSPOS	Sets the current value of the progress indicator.
27	CMDID_PROGRESSTEXT	Sets the text contained in the progress indicator.
28	CMDID_SETTITLE	Sets the title bar text.
29	CMDID_DOWNLOADSTATE	Sent by the host when its download state changes.
30	CMDID_STOPDOWNLOAD	Stops the download when executed.
31	CMDID_ONTOOLBARACTIVATED	One of the container's toolbars has received the focus.
36	CMDID_ENABLE_INTERACTION	Sent by the Active Document host to tell the Active Document to either pause or resume any multimedia (audio or animation) in the Active Document.
		Returns a true (.T.) value to *eArgIn* if a multimedia file running in a control in the Active Document should be resumed, or false (.F.) if the multimedia file should be paused.
		Internet Explorer 4.0 uses this command to inform an Active Document when it is minimized or completely covered by another window so that the Active Document can pause playing of multimedia information.
37	CMDID_ONUNLOAD	Sent by the Active Document host before navigation to another site is initiated or the host is closed. Set *eArgOut* to false (.F.) to prevent an Active Document from being closed by its host. Set *eArgOut* to true (.T.) to allow an Active Document to be closed by its host.

nExecOption

A parameter passed to the CommandTargetExec event that indicates the default action desired for the specified command.

The following table lists the values for *nExecOption* and the actions that are performed.

nExecOption	FOXPRO.H Constant	Action
0	CMDEXECOPT_DODEFAULT	Use the default behavior, whether prompting the user for input or not.
1	CMDEXECOPT_PROMPTUSER	Execute the command after obtaining user input.
2	CMDEXECOPT_DONTPROMPTUSER	Execute the command without prompting the user. For example, clicking the Print toolbar button causes a document to be immediately printed without user input
3	CMDEXECOPT_SHOWHELP	Show help for the corresponding command, but do not actually execute the command.

eArgIn

A parameter passed from the Active Document host to the CommandTargetExec event. This parameter is typically the null value, with the notable exception of when *nCommandID* is 36. When *nCommandID* is 36, *eArgIn* contains a value. See the table in the *nCommandID* parameter description above for more information about the logical value passed to *eArgIn*.

eArgOut

An output parameter returned from the CommandTargetExec event to Active Document host. This parameter is typically the null value, with the notable exception of when *nCommandID* is 37. When *nCommandID* is 37 (indicating the Active Document host is about to close or navigate to another site), you can set *eArgOut* to false (.F.) to prevent the Active Document from being closed by its host. Set *eArgOut* to true (.T.) to allow the Active Document to be closed by its host.

Remarks

The CommandTargetExec event allows an Active Document to perform custom actions based on commands sent to the Active Document by its host. These commands may be sent in response to the user choosing a menu or toolbar item or triggering an event in the Active Document host. The value returned from the CommandTargetExec event notifies the Active Document host if you handled the command. If you didn't handle the command, the Active Document host may perform its own default processing of the command.

The following table lists the appropriate values to return from the CommandTargetExec event.

Return Value	FOXPRO.H Constant	Command Action
0	CMD_OK	Command handled okay by the Active Document.
		Return this value when the Active Document has handled the command identified with *nCommandID*. For example, if the Open command on the File menu on the host is chosen, your Active Document can determine in its CommandTargetExec event that *nCommandID* is 1 and then execute its own Open file routine, perhaps using the Visual FoxPro GETFILE( ) function.
2	CMD_NOTSUPPORTED	Command not supported by the Active Document.
		Return this value when the command identified with *nCommandID* is not recognized as a command that can be handled by the Active Document.
3	CMD_DISABLED	Command disabled for the Active Document.
		Return this value when the command identified with *nCommandID* is currently disabled and cannot be executed by the Active Document.
4	CMD_NOHELP	No help available for the command from the Active Document.
		Return this value when the Active Document doesn't support help for the command identified with *nCommandID*.
5	CMD_CANCELED	The user canceled the execution of command.
		Return this value when the Active Document attempted to handle the command identified with *nCommandID* but the user canceled the operation.

If the CommandTargetExec event contains no user code, 2 (command not supported by the Active Document) is returned to the Active Document host. If the CommandTargetExec event contains user code but doesn't include a RETURN statement, 0 (command handled okay by the Active Document) is returned to the Active Document host.

Visual FoxPro utilizes the IOleCommandTarget interface for the CommandTargetExec and CommandTargetQuery events. Search for IOleCommandTarget in the MSDN library for additional information about how these events are implemented.

Applies To

ActiveDoc Object

See Also

CommandTargetQuery Event

CommandTargetQuery Event

Occurs when an Active Document host updates its user interface.

Syntax

PROCEDURE *Object*.CommandTargetQuery
[LPARAMETERS *aCommands*, *nCommandTextFlag*, *cCommandTextOut*]

Arguments

aCommands

A two-dimensional array containing a list of commands supported by the Active Document host.

The first column of the array contains numeric values that correspond to the commands supported by the Active Document host. For a list of the commands and their numeric values, see the *nCommandID* parameter in CommandTargetExec Event.

The second column of the array contains numeric values that correspond to the support status for each of the commands. The following table lists the values that the second column can contain and the corresponding support status for the commands.

Value	FOXPRO.H Constant	Description
0	CMDF_NOTSUPPORTED	The command is not supported by this object.
1	CMDF_SUPPORTED	The command is supported by this object.
2	CMDF_ENABLED	The command is available and enabled.
4	CMDF_LATCHED	The command is an on-off toggle and is currently on.
8	CMDF_NINCHED	The command is an on-off toggle but the state cannot be determined because the attribute of this command is found in both on and off states in the relevant selection. This state corresponds to an "indeterminate" state of a 3-state check box, for example.

The second column of the array initially contains zero for each command. Your event code should store a value to the second column to indicate the level of support provided by the Active Document for each command. You can add any combination of these values together to specify additional levels of support. For example, your Active Document procedure for a command is supported (1), and available and enabled (2), store 3 (1 + 2) to the second column for the corresponding command.

nCommandTextFlag

A parameter passed from the Active Document host to the CommandTargetExec event. *nCommandTextFlag* indicates the type of command information to pass to the Active Document host via the *cCommandTextOut* parameter. The following table lists the values for *nCommandTextFlag* and the corresponding command information to pass to the Active Document host.

nCommandTextFlag	Command Information
0	No extra information is requested.
1	The Active Document should provide the localized name for the command.
2	The Active Document should provide a localized status bar string for the command.

cCommandTextOut

A parameter passed from the CommandTargetExec event to Active Document host. *cCommandTextOut* is the text that is displayed for a command, usually in the Active Document host's status bar. *cCommandTextOut* applies to the command in the first row of the array.

Remarks

The CommandTargetQuery event lets you notify an Active Document's host which commands the Active Document can support, and what type of support is available for each command. You can also specify the text that is displayed when a command (typically a menu item) is selected.

Visual FoxPro utilizes the IOleCommandTarget interface for the CommandTargetExec and CommandTargetQuery events. Search for IOleCommandTarget in the MSDN library for additional information about how these events are implemented.

Note that Internet Explorer versions 3 and 4 typically don't request the command text via *cCommandTextOut*. Therefore, *nCommandTextFlag* is typically zero and *cCommandTextOut* typically contains the null value. These parameters are included for future compatibility with the IOleCommandTarget interface, and can be safely ignored in your applications.

Applies To

ActiveDoc Object

See Also

CommandTargetExec Event

Comment Property

Stores information about an object. Available at design time and run time.

Syntax

Object.Comment[= *cTextString*]

Arguments

cTextString
    Specifies a text string.

Remarks

Unlike other properties, the value of the Comment property is not used by Visual FoxPro; you can use this property to identify or describe objects.

You can use this property to assign an identification string to an object without affecting any of its other property settings. The Comment property is useful for checking the identity of a control or form that is passed as a variable to a procedure.

By default, the Comment property is set to a zero-length string ("").

> **Tip** When you create a new instance of a form, assign a unique value to the Comment property.

Applies To

ActiveDoc, CheckBox, ComboBox, CommandButton, CommandGroup, Container Object, Control Object, Custom, EditBox, Form, FormSet, Grid, Image, Label, Line, ListBox, OLE Bound Control, OLE Container Control, OptionButton, OptionGroup, Page, PageFrame, ProjectHook Object, _SCREEN, Shape, Spinner, TextBox, Timer, ToolBar

See Also

Caption Property, Name Property

COMPILE Command

Compiles one or more source files and creates an object file for each source file.

Syntax

COMPILE [CLASSLIB | LABEL | REPORT] *FileName* | *FileSkeleton* | ?
    [ENCRYPT] [NODEBUG]
    [AS *nCodePage*]

Arguments

CLASSLIB

Specifies that the file to compile is a visual class library (.vcx). Visual class library source code is stored in memo fields in the visual class library table. COMPILE CLASSLIB compiles these memo fields into object code that is stored in an additional memo field.

LABEL

Specifies that the file to compile is a label definition file (.lbx). Source code for the data environment saved with the label definition file is compiled and stored in an additional memo field.

REPORT

Specifies that the file to compile is a report definition file (.frx). Source code for the data environment saved with the report definition file is compiled and stored in an additional memo field.

FileName | FileSkeleton

Specifies for compilation a single file *FileName* or a set of files that match a file skeleton *FileSkeleton* containing wildcards such as * and ?. For example, to compile all program files with the extension .prg in the current directory or folder, issue COMPILE *.PRG.

?

Displays the Compile dialog box, allowing you to choose a file to compile.

ENCRYPT

Encrypts your compiled Visual FoxPro programs. Cannot be used with the CLASSLIB, LABEL, and REPORT keywords. This prevents any access to your original source programs. For additional source code protection, always include this option when compiling programs intended for distribution.

NODEBUG

Reduces the size of your compiled file by 2 bytes per source file line. Cannot be used with the CLASSLIB, LABEL, and REPORT keywords. These two bytes in the compiled file are a reference to the corresponding line in the source file. Removing these two bytes doesn't affect the program's performance, but it does reduce your compiled file size, and conserves disk space.

When you include NODEBUG, you cannot view a program's execution in the Trace window or use MESSAGE(1) to return the source code for a line that causes an error.

AS *nCodePage*

Specifies the code page for which the program is compiled. Cannot be used with the CLASSLIB, LABEL, and REPORT keywords. The compilation code page you specify with this clause overrides the global compilation code page specified with SET CPCOMPILE.

Remarks

Visual FoxPro executes only object files, so if a source file hasn't been compiled it is automatically compiled when you run the program. The source file remains unchanged. A separate compiled file is created with the same root name as the source file, but with a different extension. The following table lists the source and compiled file extensions for each file type:

File type	Source extension	Compiled extension
Program file	.prg	.fxp
Form code	.spr	.spx
Menu code	.mpr	.mpx
Query	.qpr	.qpx
Format	.fmt	.prx

The compiler detects any syntax errors in the source file. Compilation error messages are saved to a text file if SET LOGERRORS is ON when the file is compiled. The error log file has the same root name as the compiled file, and has an .err extension. If SET LOGERRORS is OFF, the error log file isn't created.

See Also

BUILD APP, BUILD PROJECT, #DEFINE ... #UNDEF, #IF ... #ENDIF, #IFDEF | #IFNDEF... #ENDIF, #INCLUDE, MODIFY COMMAND, MODIFY PROJECT, SET CPCOMPILE, SET LOGERRORS

COMPILE DATABASE Command

Compiles stored procedures in a database.

Syntax

COMPILE DATABASE *DatabaseName*

Arguments

DatabaseName
    Specifies the name of the database containing the stored procedures to compile. You can compile stored procedures in a database that is not open.

Remarks

Use COMPILE DATABASE to compile stored procedures outside the Database Designer. Stored procedures can be created and modified interactively with MODIFY PROCEDURES, or programmatically with APPEND PROCEDURES.

COMPILE DATABASE packs memo fields in the .dct memo file for the database to remove unused space from the memo file. Records marked for deletion in the database table aren't removed from the table.

Example

The following example compiles all stored procedures in the testdata database.

```
CLOSE DATABASES
COMPILE DATABASE (HOME(2) + 'data\testdata')
```

See Also

APPEND PROCEDURES, COPY PROCEDURES, CREATE TRIGGER, DISPLAY PROCEDURES, MODIFY PROCEDURE, OPEN DATABASE

COMPILE FORM Command

Compiles one or more Form objects.

Syntax

COMPILE FORM *FormName* | *cFileSkeleton* [ALL]

Arguments

FormName
Specifies the name of the form to compile.

cFileSkeleton
Specifies a subset of form files to compile. *cFileSkeleton* is a file specification skeleton that supports wildcards. For example, to compile all Form objects that begin with A, use the following command:

```
COMPILE FORM A*
```

ALL
Compiles all records for all Visual FoxPro platforms in the Form table. If you omit ALL, only records for the current Visual FoxPro platform are compiled.

Remarks

Forms are automatically compiled when they are saved in the Form Designer. Use COMPILE FORM to compile a form outside the Form Designer.

Form source code is stored in memo fields in the Form table. COMPILE FORM compiles these memo fields into object code that is stored in an additional memo field. The object code in this additional field is executed when you issue DO FORM.

Note that if a form has an include (.h) file and the include file is moved from its original directory, a compilation error occurs and is listed in the .err error log file. The form can be run, but cannot be saved if modified until you correct the path to the include file. To correct the path to the include file, open the form with MODIFY FORM, choose Include File from the Form menu, and specify the include file with its new path in the Include File dialog box.

See Also

CREATE FORM, DO FORM, MODIFY FORM

COMPOBJ( ) Function

Compares the properties of two objects and returns true (.T.) if their properties and property values are identical.

Syntax

COMPOBJ(*oExpression1*, *oExpression2*)

Arguments

oExpression1, *oExpression2*
Specifies the objects to compare. *oExpression1* and *oExpression2* can be any expressions that evaluate to objects, such as object references, object variables, or object array elements.

Returns

Logical

Remarks

COMPOBJ( ) returns false (.F.) if an object has a property that the other object doesn't have, or if the objects have identical properties but the values of one or more properties differ.

Example

In the following example, two ListBoxes named lstMyList1 and lstMyList2 and a ComboBox named cmbMyCombo are created. The Name property of each ListBox is displayed.

COMPOBJ( ) is used to compare the properties of the first ListBox with the properties of the ComboBox. Because many of the properties are different, .F. is displayed. COMPOBJ( ) is then used to compare the properties of the first ListBox with the properties of the second ListBox. Because the Names properties are different, .T. is displayed. The second ListBox lstMyList2 is replaced with the first ListBox lstMyList1, and COMPOBJ( ) is used to compare the properties. Because their properties are identical, .T. is displayed.

```
lstMyList1 = CREATEOBJ('ListBox')  && Creates a ListBox
lstMyList2 = CREATEOBJ('ListBox')  && Creates a second ListBox
cmbMyCombo = CREATEOBJ('ComboBox')  && Creates a ComboBox

CLEAR
? lstMyList1.Name  && Displays List1 Name property
? lstMyList2.Name  && Displays List2 Name property

? COMPOBJ(lstMyList1, cmbMyCombo)      && Displays .F.
? COMPOBJ(lstMyList1, lstMyList2)      && Displays .F., different Names
lstMyList2.Name = lstMyList1.Name
? COMPOBJ(lstMyList1, lstMyList2)      && Displays .T., same properties
```

See Also

CREATEOBJECT( ), DEFINE CLASS, GETOBJECT( ), SET CLASSLIB

COMRETURNERROR( ) Function

Populates the COM exception structure with information that Automation clients can use to determine the source of Automation errors.

Syntax

COMRETURNERROR(*cExceptionSource*, *cExceptionText*)

Arguments

cExceptionSource
   Specifies the text for the source of the exception.

cExceptionText
   Specifies the text for the description of the exception.

Remarks

COMRETURNERROR( ) allows Visual FoxPro Automation servers to populate the COM exception structure so that Automation clients can determine the cause of an error on the Automation server.

Executing COMRETURNERROR( ) places the specified text on the COM exception structure and returns control to the client. Program execution on the Automation server is terminated from the point where COMRETURNERROR( ) is executed. The Automation server remains in memory and program execution on the Automation server resumes at the next method called by the client.

Visual FoxPro clients can use AERROR( ) to view the text placed on the COM exception structure.

See Also

AERROR( ), ON ERROR

Container Object

Creates an object that can contain other objects.

Syntax

Container

Remarks

Container objects can contain other objects and allow access to the objects contained within them. For example, if you create a container object that contains two list boxes and two command buttons, and then add the container object to a form, the list boxes and command buttons can be manipulated at design time and at run time.

For more information about container objects and how they differ from other objects and controls, see Chapter 3, "Object-Oriented Programming," in the *Microsoft Visual FoxPro 6.0 Programmer's Guide*.

Properties

ActiveControl	Application	BackColor
BackStyle	BaseClass	BorderColor
BorderWidth	Class	ClassLibrary
ColorSource	Comment	ControlCount
Controls	DragIcon	DragMode
Enabled	ForeColor	Height
HelpContextID	Left	MouseIcon
MousePointer	Name	Objects
OLEDragMode	OLEDragPicture	OLEDropEffects
OLEDropHasData Property	OLEDropMode	Parent
ParentClass	Picture	SpecialEffect
TabIndex	TabStop	Tag
Top	Visible	WhatsThisHelpID
Width		

Events

Click	DblClick	Destroy
DragDrop	DragOver	Error
GotFocus	Init	LostFocus
MiddleClick Event	MouseDown	MouseMove
MouseUp	MouseWheel	Moved
OLECompleteDrag	OLEDragDrop	OLEDragOver
OLEGiveFeedBack	OLESetData	OLEStartDrag
Resize	RightClick	UIEnable

Methods

AddObject	AddProperty	Drag
Draw	Move	NewObject
OLEDrag	ReadExpression	ReadMethod
Refresh	RemoveObject	ResetToDefault
SaveAsClass	SetAll	SetFocus
ShowWhatsThis	WriteExpression	Zorder

See Also

CREATE CLASS, CREATE FORM, DEFINE CLASS

ContainerRelease Event

Occurs when an Active Document is released by its host.

Syntax

PROCEDURE *Object*.ContainerRelease

Remarks

An Active Document can be released by its host when the host is shut down, when the Active Document is dropped from the host's cache, or when you navigate from the Active Document. For example, Microsoft Internet Explorer 4.0 for Windows releases an Active Document when you navigate from the Active Document. Microsoft Internet Explorer 3.0 for Windows releases an Active Document when it is dropped from its cache of four pages.

The ContainerReleaseType property can be set in this event; Visual FoxPro checks its value after this event occurs to determine if the Active Document is opened in the Visual FoxPro runtime.

Applies To

ActiveDoc Object

See Also

ContainerReleaseType Property

ContainerReleaseType Property

Specifies if an Active Document is opened in the Visual FoxPro runtime when the Active Document is released by its host. Available at design time and run time.

Syntax

Object.ContainerReleaseType[= *nExpression*]

Arguments

nExpression
The settings for *nExpression* are:

Setting	Description
0	(Default) The Active Document is opened in the Visual FoxPro runtime when it is released by its host. The Active Document continues to run in the main Visual FoxPro window of the runtime.
1	The Active Document isn't opened in the Visual FoxPro runtime, and the Active Document is shut down.

Remarks

The ContainerRelease event occurs when an Active Document is released by its host. You can query the value of the ContainerReleaseType property in this event; if its value is 1, you can perform shutdown procedures such as closing open files and cleaning up the Visual FoxPro environment. Note that when ContainerReleaseType is set to 1 and the Active Document is closed, an instance of the Visual FoxPro runtime, Vfp6r.exe, remains until the Active Document host is also closed.

An Active Document can be released by its host when the host is shut down, when the Active Document is dropped from the host's cache, or when you navigate from the Active Document. For example, Microsoft Internet Explorer 4.0 for Windows releases an Active Document when you navigate from the Active Document. Microsoft Internet Explorer 3.0 for Windows releases an Active Document when it is dropped from its cache of four pages.

You can set this property in the ContainerRelease event to specify if the Active Document is opened in the Visual FoxPro runtime when it is released from its host.

Applies To

ActiveDoc Object

See Also

ContainerRelease Event

CONTINUE Command

Continues the previous LOCATE.

Syntax

CONTINUE

Remarks

CONTINUE is used after LOCATE succeeds in finding a record, to continue the LOCATE operation. CONTINUE moves the record pointer to the next record for which the logical expression specified in the previous LOCATE evaluates to true (.T.).

CONTINUE can be repeated until the end of the file is encountered, or until the end of the scope you specified with LOCATE is reached.

If CONTINUE succeeds in finding a record, RECNO( ) returns the record number of the record, FOUND( ) returns a value of true (.T.), and EOF( ) returns a value of false (.F.).

If CONTINUE doesn't succeed in finding a record, RECNO( ) returns the number of records in the table plus one, FOUND( ) returns false (.F.), and EOF( ) returns true (.T.).

Example

In the following example, all customers from France are counted and the total is displayed. All records are found using one LOCATE command followed by a CONTINUE command within a loop.

```
CLOSE DATABASES
OPEN DATABASE (HOME(2) + 'Data\testdata')
USE customer   && Opens Customer table
SET TALK OFF
STORE 0 TO gnCount

LOCATE FOR ALLTRIM(UPPER(country)) = 'FRANCE'
DO WHILE FOUND( )
   gnCount = gnCount + 1
   CONTINUE
ENDDO
? 'Total customers from France: '+ LTRIM(STR(gnCount))
```

See Also

EOF( ), FOUND( ), LOCATE, SEEK

ContinuousScroll Property

Specifies if scrolling within a form is continuous, or if scrolling occurs only when a scroll box is released. Available at design time and run time.

Syntax

Object.ContinuousScroll[= *lExpression*]

Arguments

lExpression
The settings for *lExpression* are:

Setting	Description
True (.T.)	(Default) Scrolling is continuous within the form.
	The form scrolls continuously as the scroll boxes are moved. The Scrolled event occurs continuously as the form is scrolled.
False (.F.)	Scrolling only occurs when a scroll box is released.
	The form is stationary until a scroll box is released, and then the form is redrawn in its new position. The Scrolled event occurs after the form is redrawn.

Remarks

The Scrollbars property determines if a form has scroll bars.

Applies To

Form

See Also

ScrollBars Property, Scrolled Event

Control Object

Creates a control object that can contain other protected objects.

Syntax

Control

Remarks

Control objects can contain other objects, but, unlike container objects, do not allow access to the objects contained within them. For example, if you create a control object that consists of two ListBoxes and two CommandButtons, and then add the control object to a form, the ListBoxes and CommandButtons cannot be manipulated individually at design time or at run time.

For more information about control objects and how they differ from other objects and controls, see Chapter 3, "Object-Oriented Programming," in the *Microsoft Visual FoxPro 6.0 Programmer's Guide*.

Properties

ActiveControl	Application	BackColor
BackStyle	BaseClass	BorderColor
BorderWidth	Class	ClassLibrary
ColorSource	Comment	ControlCount
Controls	DragIcon	DragMode
Enabled	ForeColor	Height
HelpContextID	Left	MouseIcon
MousePointer	Name	Objects Property
OLEDragMode	OLEDragPicture	OLEDropEffects
OLEDropHasData Property	OLEDropMode	Parent
ParentClass	Picture	SpecialEffect
TabIndex	TabStop	Tag
Top	Visible	WhatsThisHelpID
Width		

Events

Click	DblClick	Destroy
DragDrop	DragOver	Error
GotFocus	Init	LostFocus
MiddleClick Event	MouseDown	MouseMove
MouseUp	MouseWheel	Moved
OLECompleteDrag	OLEDragDrop	OLEDragOver
OLEGiveFeedBack	OLESetData	OLEStartDrag
Resize	RightClick	UIEnable

Methods

AddProperty	Drag	Draw
Move	OLEDrag	ReadExpression
ReadMethod	Refresh	ResetToDefault
SaveAsClass	SetFocus	ShowWhatsThis
WriteExpression	ZOrder	

See Also

CREATE CLASS, CREATE FORM, DEFINE CLASS

ControlBox Property

Specifies whether a pop-up menu icon appears in the upper-left corner of a form or toolbar at run time. Available at design time and run time.

Syntax

Object.ControlBox[= *lExpr*]

Arguments

lExpr

The settings for the ControlBox property are:

Setting	Description
True (.T.)	(Default) Displays a pop-up menu icon.
False (.F.)	Does not display a pop-up menu icon.

Remarks

Both modal and modeless forms and toolbars can include a pop-up menu icon. The menu commands available at run time depend on the settings for related properties. For example, setting MaxButton and MinButton to false (.F.) disables the Maximize and Minimize menu commands on the pop-up menu, but the Move and Close menu commands remain available.

Note Settings you specify for ControlBox, BorderStyle, MaxButton, and MinButton are not reflected in the form's appearance until run time.

Applies To

Form, _SCREEN, ToolBar

See Also

BorderStyle Property, Closable Property, MaxButton Property, MinButton Property

ControlCount Property

Specifies the number of controls in a container object. Not available at design time; read-only at run time.

Syntax

*Object.*ControlCount

Remarks

You can use this property to cycle through all the controls on a container and perform an operation on each.

Applies To

Column, Container Object, Control Object, Form, Page, _SCREEN, ToolBar

See Also

Controls Property

Controls and Objects

This topic describes support for controls and objects created in earlier FoxPro versions and new controls added to Visual FoxPro.

The easiest way to create controls and objects is by using the Form Designer. For more information about creating controls with the Form Designer, see Chapter 9, "Creating Forms," in the *Microsoft Visual FoxPro 6.0 Programmer's Guide.*

You can also create controls and objects programmatically. See the DEFINE CLASS Command, later in this language reference, for more information about creating controls programmatically from the Visual FoxPro base classes, and Chapter 3, "Object-Oriented Programming," in the *Microsoft Visual FoxPro 6.0 Programmer's Guide.*

Some controls behave slightly differently depending on whether you are using Visual FoxPro for Windows or Visual FoxPro for Macintosh; by default, controls in Visual FoxPro for Macintosh follow user interface conventions common to Macintosh applications. For example, by default the CheckBox, ComboBox, and OptionButton controls cannot receive the focus in Visual FoxPro for Macintosh. For more details about differences in control behavior, see the SET KEYCOMP Command, later in this language reference.

In Visual FoxPro, a NAME clause has been added to each of the controls created in previous FoxPro versions. The NAME clause creates an object reference for controls created with @ ... GET and @ ... EDIT, allowing you to manipulate the controls with Visual FoxPro properties, events, and methods. The NAME clause provides an intermediate step to upgrade your applications using Visual FoxPro object-oriented programming techniques.

Compatibility with FoxPro 2.x Controls

The following table lists the controls available in earlier FoxPro versions and the base class you can use to programmatically create the same control in Visual FoxPro.

FoxPro 2.x controls	Equivalent Visual FoxPro controls	Visual FoxPro base class names
@ ... GET – Check Boxes	CheckBox Control	CheckBox
@ ... GET – Lists	ListBox Control	ListBox
@ ... GET – Popups	ComboBox Control	ComboBox
@ ... GET – Push Buttons	CommandButton Control	CommandButton
@ ... GET – Radio Buttons	OptionButton Control	OptionButton
@ ... GET – Spinners	Spinner Control	Spinner
@ ... GET – Text Boxes	TextBox Control	TextBox
@ ... EDIT – Text Edit Regions	EditBox Control	EditBox

Visual FoxPro Base Classes

In addition, the following controls and objects are new to Visual FoxPro and can be created programmatically only from their Visual FoxPro base classes.

Controls and objects	Base class names	Description
ActiveDoc Object	ActiveDoc	Creates an Active Document that can be hosted in an Active Document container such as the Microsoft Office Binder and Internet Explorer.
Column Object	Column	Creates a column in a grid.
CommandGroup Control	CommandGroup	Creates a group of command buttons.
Container Object	Container	Creates an object that can contain other objects.
Control Object	Control	Creates a control object that can contain other protected objects.
Cursor Object	Cursor	Created when a table or view is added to the data environment for a form, form set, or report.
Custom Object	Custom	Creates a custom, user-defined object.
DataEnvironment Object	DataEnvironment	Created when a form, form set, or report is opened.

(continued)

(continued)

Controls and objects	Base class names	Description
Form Object	Form	Creates a form.
FormSet Object	FormSet	Creates a form set.
Grid Control	Grid	Creates a Grid control.
Header Object	Header	Creates a Header for a Column in a Grid.
Hyperlink Object	HyperLink	Creates a hyperlink object, allowing you to jump to a URL (Uniform Resource Locator).
Image Control	Image	Creates an Image control that displays a .bmp or PICT picture.
Label Control	Label	Creates a Label control that displays text.
Line Control	Line	Creates a Line control that displays a horizontal, vertical, or diagonal line.
OLE Container Control	OLEControl	Creates an OLE Container control.
OLE Bound Control	OLEBoundControl	Creates an OLE Bound control.
OptionGroup Control	OptionGroup	Creates a group of option buttons.
Page Object	Page	Creates a page in a page frame.
PageFrame Control	PageFrame	Creates a page frame to contain pages.
ProjectHook Object	ProjectHook	Instantiated whenever a project is opened, providing programmatic access to project events.
Relation Object	Relation	Created when you establish relationships from within the Data Environment Designer for a form, form set, or report.
Separator Object	Separator	Creates a Separator object that places space between controls in a toolbar.
Shape Control	Shape	Creates a Shape control that displays a box, circle, or ellipse.
Timer Control	Timer	Creates a Timer control that can execute code at regular intervals.
ToolBar Object	Toolbar	Creates a toolbar on which controls can be placed.

See Also

CREATE CLASS, CREATE FORM, DEFINE CLASS

Controls Property

An array for accessing the controls in a container object. Available at run time.

Syntax

ContainerObject.Controls*(Index).Property*[= *Expr*]

Arguments

Expr
    Specifies a property value for a control contained in *ContainerObject*.

Remarks

Use the Controls property to access the properties of contained objects.

Applies To

Column, Container Object, Control Object, Form, Page, _SCREEN, ToolBar

See Also

ControlCount Property

ControlSource Property

Specifies the source of data to which an object is bound. Available at design time and run time.

Syntax

Object.ControlSource[= *cName*]

Arguments

cName
    For controls, *cName* is a variable or field.

Remarks

Once the ControlSource property is set to a field or variable, the Value property always has the same data value and the same data type as the variable or field to which the ControlSource property is set.

For TextBox controls, *cName* is typically a field.

In a Grid control, if you do not specify a ControlSource setting for a column, the column displays the next available undisplayed field of the grid's record source.

If a Column's Bound property is set to true (.T.), the Column's ControlSource property setting applies to the column and any controls contained in it. If you attempt to set the contained control's ControlSource property, an error occurs. If a Column's Bound property is set to false (.F.), you can set the ControlSource property of a contained control directly. If you subsequently set the ControlSource setting of the Column, it overrides the ControlSource setting of the contained control.

Applies To

CheckBox, Column, ComboBox, CommandGroup, EditBox, ListBox, OLE Bound Control, OptionButton, OptionGroup, Spinner, TextBox

See Also

Bound Property, Order Property, RecordSourceType Property, Value Property

_CONVERTER System Variable

Contains the name of the Microsoft Visual FoxPro converter application.

Syntax

_CONVERTER = *cProgramName*

Arguments

cProgramName

Specifies a converter application. If your converter application is in a directory other than the current Visual FoxPro default directory, include a path with the application name.

You can also specify a converter application in your Visual FoxPro configuration file by including a line using the following syntax:

```
_CONVERTER = cProgramName
```

Remarks

The _CONVERTER system memory variable contains the name of the application that Visual FoxPro uses when you attempt to open a screen, report, or project created in an earlier FoxPro version. By default, _CONVERTER contains Convert.app, installed in your Visual FoxPro directory. You can specify a different name for the converter application.

See Also

System Variables Overview

COPY FILE Command

Duplicates any type of file.

Syntax

COPY FILE *FileName1* TO *FileName2*

Remarks

COPY FILE creates a duplicate of the file whose name is specified in *FileName1*. You can use COPY FILE to copy any type of file. The file to be copied cannot be open. You must include the extensions for both the source file name *FileName1* and destination file name *FileName2*.

FileName1 and *FileName2* can contain wildcard characters such as * and ?. For example, to create backup copies of all program files with the extension .prg in the current directory, issue COPY FILE *.prg TO *.bak.

If you use COPY FILE to create a backup of a table that has a memo field, a structural index or both, be sure to copy the .fpt and .cdx files as well.

See Also

DELETE FILE, RENAME, RENAME TABLE

COPY INDEXES Command

Creates compound index tags from single-entry .idx index files.

Syntax

COPY INDEXES *IndexFileList* | ALL
    [TO *CDXFileName*]

Arguments

IndexFileList
    Specifies the single-entry .idx index files whose index expressions are used to create the tags. Separate the index file names with commas. The name assigned to each tag is the root name of the corresponding single-entry index file. If you create a tag from an index file that has the same name as an existing tag, a dialog is displayed (if SAFETY is ON) asking if you would like to overwrite the tag.

ALL
    Specifies to create index tags from all open single-entry index files.

TO *CDXFileName*
    Creates tags in a non-structural compound index file. Specify the name of the non-structural compound index file with *CDXFileName*. If a non-structural compound index file with the specified name doesn't exist, Visual FoxPro automatically creates it.

Remarks

A compound index file is an index file containing separate index entries called *tags*. Each tag is identified by its unique tag name. The default extension for a compound index file is .cdx.

You must first open the table and single-entry index files before using COPY INDEXES. The index expressions from the single-entry index files are used to create the new tags.

If you omit the TO clause, the new tags are added to the structural compound index file that is automatically opened with the table. If a structural compound index file doesn't exist for the table, COPY INDEXES creates one.

Use COPY TAG to create a single-entry index file from compound index file tags.

See Also

CDX( ), COPY TAG, DELETE TAG, INDEX, TAG( ), USE

COPY MEMO Command

Copies the contents of the specified memo field in the current record to a text file.

Syntax

COPY MEMO *MemoFieldName* TO *FileName*
    [ADDITIVE]
    [AS *nCodePage*]

Arguments

MemoFieldName
    Specifies the name of the memo field copied to the text file.

TO *FileName*
    Specifies the name of a new or existing text file to which the memo field is copied. If you do not provide an extension in *FileName*, a .txt extension is assigned. You can also include a path with the file name.

ADDITIVE
    Appends the contents of the memo field to the end of the specified text file. If you omit ADDITIVE, the memo field contents replace the contents of the text file.

AS *nCodePage*
    Specifies the code page for the text file COPY MEMO creates. Visual FoxPro copies the contents of the specified memo field, and, as it copies the data, automatically converts the data to the code page you specify for the text file.

    If you specify a value for *nCodePage* that is not supported, Visual FoxPro generates an error message. You can use GETCP( ) for *nCodePage* to display the Code Page dialog box, allowing you to specify a code page for the file Visual FoxPro creates.

    If AS *nCodePage* is omitted or is 0, no code page conversion occurs.

Example

In the following example, the contents of the memo field named `notes` are copied to a file called Test.txt. The memo field is then copied again and appended to the end of the text file.

```
CLOSE DATABASES
OPEN DATABASE (HOME(2) + 'Data\testdata')
USE employee && Opens Employee table
COPY MEMO notes TO test.txt
WAIT WINDOW 'Memo contents now in test.txt' NOWAIT
MODIFY FILE test.txt
COPY MEMO notes TO test.txt ADDITIVE
WAIT WINDOW 'Memo contents added again to test.txt' NOWAIT
MODIFY FILE test.txt
DELETE FILE test.txt
```

See Also

APPEND MEMO, COPY FILE, COPY TO, MODIFY MEMO

COPY PROCEDURES Command

Copies stored procedures in the current database to a text file.

Syntax

COPY PROCEDURES TO *FileName*
    [AS *nCodePage*] [ADDITIVE]

Arguments

FileName
    Specifies the name of a text file to which the stored procedures are copied. If the file doesn't exist, Visual FoxPro automatically creates it.

AS *nCodePage*
    Specifies the code page for the text file to which the stored procedures are copied. Visual FoxPro copies the stored procedures, and, as it does so, automatically converts the stored procedures to the code page you specify.

    If you specify a value for *nCodePage* that is not supported, Visual FoxPro generates an error message. You can use GETCP( ) for *nCodePage* to display the Code Page dialog box, allowing you to specify a code page for the text file to which the stored procedures are copied.

    If you omit AS *nCodePage* or if AS *nCodePage* is 0, no code page conversion occurs.

ADDITIVE
    Appends the stored procedures to the end of the specified text file. If you omit ADDITIVE, the stored procedures replace the contents of the text file.

Remarks

Use COPY PROCEDURES with APPEND PROCEDURES to programmatically modify stored procedures in a database. A database must be open and current when COPY PROCEDURES is issued; otherwise Visual FoxPro generates an error message.

Example

The following example opens the testdata database, and uses COPY PROCEDURES to copy the procedures to a temporary text file named Myproc.txt. MODIFY FILE is used to open the temporary text file, which will be empty if there are no stored procedures in the database.

If there are no stored procedures in the database, you can run the example for APPEND PROCEDURES to add a procedure to database.

```
CLOSE DATABASES
OPEN DATABASE (HOME(2) + 'data\testdata')

COPY PROCEDURES TO myproc.txt && Copy stored procedures to a file
MODIFY FILE myproc.txt  && Open the file
DELETE FILE myproc.txt  && Erase the file
```

See Also

APPEND PROCEDURES, CREATE TRIGGER, DISPLAY PROCEDURES, MODIFY PROCEDURE, SET DATABASE

COPY STRUCTURE Command

Creates a new, empty free table with the same structure as the currently selected table.

Syntax

COPY STRUCTURE TO *TableName*
    [FIELDS *FieldList*] [[WITH] CDX | [WITH] PRODUCTION]
    [DATABASE *cDatabaseName* [NAME *cTableName*]]

Arguments

TableName
    Specifies the name of the new, empty table to create.

    In Visual FoxPro, null value support and the code page for the new, free table are identical to the currently selected table.

FIELDS *FieldList*
    Specifies that only the fields whose names are specified in the *FieldList* are copied to the new table. If you omit FIELDS *FieldList*, all fields are copied to the new table.

[WITH] CDX | [WITH] PRODUCTION
Creates a structural index file for the new table that is identical to the structural index file of the existing table. The tags and index expressions from the original structural index file are copied to the new structural index file.

The CDX and PRODUCTION clauses are identical.

In Visual FoxPro, a primary index for the currently selected table is converted to a candidate index for the new empty table.

DATABASE *cDatabaseName*
Specifies the name of an existing database to which the new table is added. Note that the table and field properties are not copied to the database.

NAME *cTableName*
Specifies the name of the table as it appears in the database.

Example

In the following example, the `customer` table is opened, its structure is copied to a table called `backup` and `backup` is opened. APPEND FROM then appends records to the `backup` table from the `customer` table, and a Browse window is opened for the `backup` table.

```
CLOSE DATABASES
OPEN DATABASE (HOME(2) + 'Data\testdata')
USE customer  && Opens Customer table

COPY STRUCTURE TO backup
USE backup
APPEND FROM customer FOR country = 'UK'
BROWSE FIELDS contact, country
USE
DELETE FILE backup.dbf
```

See Also

COPY STRUCTURE EXTENDED, CREATE, DISPLAY STRUCTURE

COPY STRUCTURE EXTENDED Command

Creates a new table with fields containing the structure of the currently selected table.

Syntax

COPY STRUCTURE EXTENDED TO *FileName*
[DATABASE *DatabaseName* [NAME *LongTableName*]]
[FIELDS *FieldList*]

Arguments

FileName
> Specifies the new table to create.

DATABASE *DatabaseName*
> Specifies a database to which the new table is added.

NAME *LongTableName*
> Specifies a long name for the new table. Long names can contain up to 128 characters and can be used in place of short file names in the database.

FIELDS *FieldList*
> Specifies that only the fields specified in *FieldList* are included in a record in the new table. If you omit FIELDS *FieldList*, all fields have a record in the new table.

Remarks

Information about each field in the currently selected table is copied to a record in the new table. The structure of the new table is fixed in format and consists of sixteen fields. The following table lists the names of the 16 fields and their contents.

Field	Field type	Contents
FIELD_NAME	Character	Field names from selected table (128 characters wide)
FIELD_TYPE	Character	Field types: C = Character Y = Currency N = Numeric F = Float I = Integer B = Double D = Date T = DateTime L = Logical M = Memo G = General
FIELD_LEN	Numeric	Field widths
FIELD_DEC	Numeric	Number of decimal places in numeric fields
FIELD_NULL	Logical	Field null value support
FIELD_NOCP	Logical	Code page translation not allowed (character and memo fields only)
FIELD_DEFA	Memo	Field default values
FIELD_RULE	Memo	Field validation rules
FIELD_ERR	Memo	Field validation text

(continued)

Field	Field type	Contents
TABLE_RULE	Memo	Table validation rule
TABLE_ERR	Memo	Table validation text
TABLE_NAME	Character	Long table name (first record only)
INS_TRIG	Memo	Insert trigger expression (first record only)
UPD_TRIG	Memo	Update trigger expression (first record only)
DEL_TRIG	Memo	Delete trigger expression (first record only)
TABLE_CMT	Memo	Table comment (first record only)

You can modify the newly created table and then use CREATE FROM to create a new table with a different structure. COPY STRUCTURE and CREATE FROM allow you to programmatically change the structure of a table.

The width of the FIELD_NAME field is 10 characters in previous versions of Visual FoxPro, FoxPro for Windows, and FoxPro for MS-DOS. To use CREATE FROM with a table created by COPY STRUCTURE EXTENDED in Visual FoxPro 5.0 and earlier, you must change the width of the FIELD_NAME field to 10 characters. Note that some field types are not supported in Visual FoxPro 3.0 and earlier versions.

Example

The following example displays the structure of the orders table, copies the structure extended to a temp table, browses temp, creates a backup table from temp, and displays the structure of backup.

```
CLOSE DATABASES
OPEN DATABASE (HOME(2) + 'Data\testdata')
USE orders   && Opens Orders table
CLEAR
DISPLAY STRUCTURE

WAIT WINDOW 'Structure of the orders table' NOWAIT
COPY STRUCTURE EXTENDED TO temp
USE temp
WAIT WINDOW 'The temp table - 1 row per field in orders' NOWAIT
BROWSE
CREATE backup FROM temp
USE backup
DISPLAY STRUCTURE
WAIT WINDOW 'Backup.dbf has the same structure as orders' NOWAIT
USE
DELETE FILE temp.dbf
DELETE FILE backup.dbf
```

See Also

AFIELDS( ), CREATE FROM

COPY TAG Command

Creates a single-entry index (.idx) file from a tag in a compound index file.

Syntax

COPY TAG *TagName* [OF *CDXFileName*]
    TO *IndexFileName*

Arguments

TagName
    Specifies the tag used to create the single-entry .idx file.

OF *CDXFileName*
    Specifies the compound index file containing the tag. Include this clause if there are tags with the same names in the open compound index files. If you omit OF *CDXFileName*, Visual FoxPro looks for the tag first in the structural index file. If it isn't found there, Visual FoxPro searches all the open non-structural compound index files.

TO *IndexFileName*
    Specifies the name of the single-entry .idx file to create.

Remarks

Use COPY TAG to create a new single-entry .idx file from a tag in a .cdx compound index file.

The compound index file from which you create the single-entry .idx file must be open. Structural compound index files are automatically opened when you open a table. Non-structural compound indexes must be explicitly opened with USE ... INDEX or SET INDEX. For more information about compound index files, see the INDEX Command, later in this language reference.

Use COPY INDEX to create tags in compound index files from single-entry .idx files.

See Also

CDX( ), COPY INDEXES, DELETE TAG, INDEX, TAG( ), USE

COPY TO Command

Creates a new file from the contents of the currently selected table.

Syntax

COPY TO *FileName*
    [DATABASE *DatabaseName* [NAME *LongTableName*]]
    [FIELDS *FieldList*
    | FIELDS LIKE *Skeleton*
    | FIELDS EXCEPT *Skeleton*]
    [*Scope*] [FOR *lExpression1*] [WHILE *lExpression2*]
    [[WITH] CDX] | [[WITH] PRODUCTION]
    [NOOPTIMIZE]
    [[TYPE] [FOXPLUS | FOX2X | DIF | MOD
    | SDF | SYLK | WK1 | WKS | WR1 | WRK | CVS | | XLS | XL5
    | DELIMITED [WITH *Delimiter* | WITH BLANK | WITH TAB
    | WITH CHARACTER *Delimiter*]]]
    [AS *nCodePage*]

Arguments

FileName
    Specifies the name of the new file COPY TO creates. If you do not include an extension with the file name, the default extension for the specified file type is assigned. If you do not specify a file type, COPY TO creates a new Visual FoxPro table and assigns the table file name the default extension .dbf.

DATABASE *DatabaseName*
    Specifies a database to which the new table is added.

NAME *LongTableName*
    Specifies a long name for the new table. Long names can contain up to 128 characters and can be used in place of short file names in the database.

FIELDS *FieldList*
    Specifies which fields are copied to the new file. If you omit FIELDS *FieldList*, all fields are copied to the file. If the file you are creating is not a table, memo fields are not copied to the new file, even if memo field names are included in the field list.

FIELDS LIKE *Skeleton*
    Specifies that fields from the original table that match the field skeleton *Skeleton* are included in the new file that COPY TO creates.

FIELDS EXCEPT *Skeleton*

Specifies that all fields except those that match the field skeleton *Skeleton* are included in the new file that COPY TO creates.

The field skeleton *Skeleton* supports wildcards. For example, to specify that all fields that begin with the letters A and P are included in the new file, use the following:

```
COPY TO mytable FIELDS LIKE A*,P*
```

The LIKE clause can be combined with the EXCEPT clause:

```
COPY TO mytable FIELDS LIKE A*,P* EXCEPT PARTNO*
```

Scope

Specifies a range of records to copy to a file. Only the records within the range are copied. The scope clauses are: ALL, NEXT *nRecords*, RECORD *nRecordNumber*, and REST. For more information on scope clauses, see "Scope Clauses" in Help.

FOR *lExpression1*

Specifies that only the records for which the logical condition *lExpression1* evaluates to true (.T.) are copied to the file. Include FOR *lExpression1* to conditionally copy records, filtering out undesired records.

Rushmore optimizes COPY TO with a FOR *lExpression1* clause if *lExpression1* is an optimizable expression. For best performance, use an optimizable expression in the FOR *lExpression1* clause.

For information on Rushmore optimizable expressions, see the SET OPTIMIZE Command, later in this language reference, and "Understanding Rushmore Technology" in Chapter 15, "Optimizing Applications," in the *Microsoft Visual FoxPro 6.0 Programmer's Guide*.

WHILE *lExpression2*

Specifies a condition whereby records are copied for as long as the logical expression *lExpression2* evaluates to true (.T.).

[WITH] CDX | [WITH] PRODUCTION

Creates a structural index file for the new table that is identical to the structural index file of the existing table. The tags and index expressions from the original structural index file are copied to the new structural index file. The CDX and PRODUCTION clauses are identical.

Do not include CDX or PRODUCTION if you are copying to a file other than a new Visual FoxPro table.

NOOPTIMIZE

Disables Rushmore optimization of COPY TO.

For more information, see the SET OPTIMIZE Command, later in this language reference, and "Understanding Rushmore Technology" in Chapter 15, "Optimizing Applications," in the *Microsoft Visual FoxPro 6.0 Programmer's Guide*.

TYPE

Specifies the file type if the file you create isn't a Visual FoxPro table. Although you must specify a file type, you need not include the TYPE keyword.

FOXPLUS

Visual FoxPro memo files have a different structure than Microsoft FoxBASE+ memo files. If your source Visual FoxPro table contains a memo field, include the FOXPLUS clause to create a table that can be used in FoxBASE+. The Visual FoxPro memo field cannot contain binary data because FoxBASE+ does not support binary data in memo fields.

FOX2X

Creates a new table that can be opened in earlier versions of FoxPro (versions 2.0, 2.5, and 2.6).

For Numeric, Float, Integer, Double, and Currency type fields, null values in the source table are converted to zero in the new table. For other field types, null values in the source table are converted to blanks in the new table. For further information about blank values, see the ISBLANK( ) Function, later in this language reference.

The following table lists the Visual FoxPro fields types that are converted to different field types in the new table when the FOX2X argument is included.

Visual FoxPro field type	FoxPro 2.x field type
Currency	Float
DateTime	Date
Double	Float
Integer	Numeric

DIF

Creates a VisiCalc .dif (Data Interchange Format) file. Fields from the Visual FoxPro table become vectors (columns) and records become tuples (rows). The new file name is assigned a .dif extension if you do not include an extension in *FileName*.

Creates a Microsoft Multiplan version 4.01 file. The new Microsoft Multiplan file name is assigned an .mod extension if an extension isn't included.

Creates an SDF (System Data Format) file. An SDF file is an ASCII text file in which records have a fixed length and end with a carriage return and line feed. Fields aren't delimited. The SDF file name is assigned a .txt file extension if you do not include an extension. Note that the SET CENTURY setting is ignored when creating SDF files with COPY TO.

Creates a SYLK (Symbolic Link) interchange file. SYLK files are used in Microsoft MultiPlan. Each field from the currently selected table becomes a column in the spreadsheet and each record becomes a row. SYLK file names have no extension.

Creates a Lotus 1-2-3 version 2.x spreadsheet file. Each field from the currently selected table becomes a column in the spreadsheet and each record becomes a row. A .wk1 file name extension is assigned to the new spreadsheet.

WKS

Creates a Lotus 1-2-3 version 1a spreadsheet file. Each field from the currently selected table becomes a column in the spreadsheet and each record becomes a row. A .wks file name extension is assigned to the new spreadsheet.

Creates a Lotus Symphony version 1.1 or 1.2 spreadsheet file. Each field from the currently selected table becomes a column in the spreadsheet and each record becomes a row. A .wr1 file name extension is assigned to the new spreadsheet.

WRK

Creates a Lotus Symphony version 1.0 spreadsheet file. Each field from the currently selected table becomes a column in the spreadsheet and each record becomes a row. A .wr1 file name extension is assigned to the new spreadsheet.

CVS

Creates a comma separated value file. A CSV file has the field names as the first line in the file, and the field values in the remainder of the file are separated with commas.

Creates a Microsoft Excel version 2.0 worksheet file. Each field from the currently selected table becomes a column in the spreadsheet and each record becomes a row. An .xls extension is assigned to the new worksheet if you do not include a file extension.

XL5

Creates a Microsoft Excel version 5.0 worksheet file. Each field from the currently selected table becomes a column in the spreadsheet and each record becomes a row. An .xls extension is assigned to the new worksheet if you do not include a file extension.

Creates a delimited file. A delimited file is an ASCII text file in which each record ends with a carriage return and linefeed. The default field separator is a comma. Since character data may include commas, character fields are additionally delimited with double quotation marks.

Unless you specify otherwise, a .txt extension is assigned to all newly created DELIMITED files.

DELIMITED WITH *Delimiter*

Creates a delimited file with character fields delimited by a character other than a quotation mark. The character that delimits character fields is specified with *Delimiter*.

DELIMITED WITH BLANK

Creates a delimited file with fields separated by spaces instead of commas.

DELIMITED WITH TAB

Creates a delimited file with fields separated by tabs instead of commas.

DELIMITED WITH CHARACTER *Delimiter*

Creates a delimited file with all fields enclosed by the character specified with *Delimiter*. If *Delimiter* is a semicolon (the character used in Visual FoxPro to indicate command line continuation), enclose the semicolon in quotation marks. You can also specify the BLANK and TAB keywords for *Delimiter*.

Note that the WITH *Delimiter* clause can be combined with the WITH CHARACTER clause. For example, the following command creates a text file with character fields enclosed by underscores and all fields delimited from each other with semicolons:

```
COPY TO mytxt.txt DELIMITED WITH _ WITH CHARACTER ';'
```

AS *nCodePage*

Specifies the code page for the table or file COPY TO creates. Visual FoxPro copies the contents of the currently selected table, and, as it copies the data, automatically converts the data to the code page you specify for the new table or file. If possible, Visual FoxPro marks the newly created table or file with the code page you specify.

If you specify a value for *nCodePage* that is not supported, Visual FoxPro generates an error message. You can use GETCP( ) for *nCodePage* to display the Code Page dialog box, allowing you to specify a code page for the table or file Visual FoxPro creates.

If you omit AS *nCodePage*, the newly created table or file is converted to the current Visual FoxPro code page.

If *nCodePage* is 0, no code page conversion occurs and the newly created table or file is not marked with a code page.

Remarks

If an index order is set, records are copied in master index order.

Example

In the following example, the `customer` table is opened and the next three records are copied to a new DELIMITED data file called TEMP.TXT.

```
CLOSE DATABASES
OPEN DATABASE (HOME(2) + 'Data\testdata')
USE customer  && Opens Customer table

COPY NEXT 3 TO temp TYPE DELIMITED
WAIT WINDOW 'This is the delimited text file' NOWAIT
MODIFY FILE temp.txt
DELETE FILE temp.txt
```

See Also

APPEND FROM, COPY FILE, GETCP( ), EXPORT, IMPORT, RENAME TABLE

COPY TO ARRAY Command

Copies data from the currently selected table to an array.

Syntax

COPY TO ARRAY *ArrayName*
    [FIELDS *FieldList*]
    [*Scope*] [FOR *lExpression1*] [WHILE *lExpression2*]
    [NOOPTIMIZE]

Arguments

ArrayName
    Specifies the array to which data from the table is copied.

FIELDS *FieldList*
    Specifies that only the fields specified in *FieldList* are copied to the array. If you omit FIELDS *FieldList*, all fields are copied to the array if the array has enough columns.

Scope
    Specifies a range of records copied to the array. Only the records within the range are copied. The scope clauses are: ALL, NEXT *nRecords*, RECORD *nRecordNumber*, and REST.

    For more information on scope clauses, see "Scope Clauses" in Help.

    The default scope for COPY TO ARRAY is ALL records.

FOR *lExpression1*
    Specifies that only the records that satisfy the logical condition *lExpression1* are copied to the array. Including FOR lets you conditionally copy records to the array, filtering out undesired records.

    Rushmore optimizes a COPY TO ARRAY query that includes FOR *lExpression1* if *lExpression1* is an optimizable expression. For best performance, use an optimizable expression in the FOR clause.

    For information on Rushmore optimizable expressions, see the SET OPTIMIZE Command, later in this language reference, and "Understanding Rushmore Technology" in Chapter 15, "Optimizing Applications," in the *Microsoft Visual FoxPro 6.0 Programmer's Guide*.

WHILE *lExpression2*
    Specifies a condition whereby records are copied to the array as long as the logical expression *lExpression2* evaluates to true (.T.).

NOOPTIMIZE

Disables Rushmore optimization of COPY TO ARRAY. For more information, see the SET OPTIMIZE Command, later in this language reference, and "Understanding Rushmore Technology" in Chapter 15, "Optimizing Applications," in the *Microsoft Visual FoxPro 6.0 Programmer's Guide*.

Remarks

COPY TO ARRAY and SCATTER are similar. COPY TO ARRAY copies multiple records to an array while SCATTER copies just one record into an array or a set of memory variables. Both COPY TO ARRAY and SCATTER create a new array if an array with the name you specify doesn't exist.

To copy a single record to an array you can specify a one-dimensional array. The one-dimensional array you specify should have the same number of elements as fields in the table, not counting memo fields. Memo fields are ignored in COPY TO ARRAY.

If you specify a one-dimensional array, the first field of a record is stored to the first element of the array, the second field is stored to the second element of the array, and so on. If the one-dimensional array has more elements than the table has fields, any remaining elements remain unchanged. If the array has fewer elements than the table has fields, any remaining fields are ignored.

To copy multiple records or an entire table to an array, specify a two-dimensional array. The number of rows in the array is the number of records the array can hold, and the number of columns in the array is the number of fields the array can hold.

Each record is stored in one row of the array, and each field of the record is stored in one column of the array. For each record, the first field is stored to the first column of the array, the second field is stored to the second column of the array, and so on. If the array has more columns than the table has fields, any remaining columns aren't changed. If the array has fewer columns than the table has fields, any remaining fields aren't stored to the array.

Each successive row in the array is filled with the contents of the next record in the table. If the array has more rows than the table has records, any remaining rows aren't changed. If the array has fewer rows than the table has records, any remaining records aren't stored to the array.

Data can be copied from arrays to new table records with APPEND FROM ARRAY. Data can also be copied from either an array or a set of memory variables to records in a table with GATHER.

Example

In the following example, the `customer` table is opened. A two-dimensional array is then created and the first three records from `customer` are copied to the array. DISPLAY MEMORY shows the data stored in the array.

```
CLOSE DATABASES
OPEN DATABASE (HOME(2) + 'Data\testdata')
USE customer   && Opens Customer table

DIMENSION gaTemp(3,10)
COPY NEXT 3 TO ARRAY gaTemp
DISPLAY MEMORY LIKE gaTemp
```

See Also

APPEND FROM ARRAY, DECLARE, DIMENSION GATHER, PUBLIC, SCATTER, STORE

COS( ) Function

Returns the cosine of a numeric expression.

Syntax

COS(*nExpression*)

Returns

Numeric

Arguments

nExpression
Specifies a numeric expression whose cosine COS( ) returns. *nExpression* can be any value.

Remarks

COS( ) returns the cosine of *nExpression* in radians. Use DTOR( ) to convert an angle from degrees to radians. The number of decimal places that COS( ) returns can be specified with SET DECIMALS. The value COS( ) returns ranges between –1 and 1.

Example

```
CLEAR
? COS(0)  && Displays 1.00
? COS(PI( ))  && Displays -1.00
? COS(DTOR(180))  && Displays -1.00
STORE PI( ) * 3 TO gnAngle
? COS(gnAngle)  && Displays -1.00
```

See Also

ACOS( ), DTOR( ), RTOD( ), SET DECIMALS, SIN( )

COUNT Command

Counts table records.

Syntax

COUNT
[*Scope*] [FOR *lExpression1*] [WHILE *lExpression2*]
[TO *VarName*]
[NOOPTIMIZE]

Arguments

Scope
Specifies a range of records to be included in the count. The scope clauses are: ALL, NEXT *nRecords*, RECORD *nRecordNumber*, and REST. For more information on scope clauses, see "Scope Clauses" in Help. Commands that include *Scope* operate only on the table in the active work area.

The default scope for COUNT is ALL records.

FOR *lExpression1*
Specifies that only the records that satisfy the logical condition *lExpression1* are counted. Including FOR lets you conditionally count records, filtering out undesired records.

Rushmore will optimize a COUNT FOR query if *lExpression1* is an optimizable expression. For best performance, use an optimizable expression in the FOR clause.

For more information on optimizable expressions, see the SET OPTIMIZE Command, later in this language reference, and "Understanding Rushmore Technology" in Chapter 15, "Optimizing Applications," in the *Microsoft Visual FoxPro 6.0 Programmer's Guide*.

WHILE *lExpression2*
Specifies a condition whereby records are counted for as long as the logical expression *lExpression2* evaluates to true (.T.).

TO *VarName*
Specifies the variable or array to which the record count is stored. If the variable you specify doesn't exist, Visual FoxPro creates it.

NOOPTIMIZE
Disables Rushmore optimization of COUNT. For more information see the SET OPTIMIZE Command, later in this language reference, and "Understanding Rushmore Technology" in Chapter 15, "Optimizing Applications," in the *Microsoft Visual FoxPro 6.0 Programmer's Guide*.

Remarks

COUNT counts the records within a scope of records for which the FOR or WHILE conditions are true. If SET TALK is ON, the record count is displayed.

Records marked for deletion are included in the count if SET DELETE is OFF.

For a discussion of how null values affect COUNT, see "Overview of the Language" in Help.

Example

The following example counts and displays the number of customers in Paris.

```
CLOSE DATABASES
OPEN DATABASE (HOME(2) + 'Data\testdata')
USE customer  && Opens Customer table

CLEAR
COUNT FOR UPPER(city) = 'PARIS'
DISPLAY FIELDS company, contact FOR UPPER(city) = 'PARIS'
```

See Also

CALCULATE, SET DELETED, SET TALK

Count Property

Contains a count of the number of project, file, or server objects in a project, file, or server collection. Read-only at design time and run time.

Syntax

Object.Count

Remarks

For a projects collection, the Count property contains zero if there are no instances of the Project Manager. For a file or server collection, the Count property contains zero if there are no files or servers in the file or server collection.

Applies To

Files Collection, Projects Collection, Servers Collection

See Also

Item Method

_COVERAGE System Variable

Contains the name of the Visual FoxPro application that creates the Debugger coverage and profiler output.

Syntax

_COVERAGE = *cProgramName*

Arguments

cProgramName

Specifies a coverage output application. If your coverage output application is in a directory other than the current Visual FoxPro default directory, include a path with the application name.

You can also specify a coverage output application in your Visual FoxPro configuration file by including a line using this syntax:

```
_COVERAGE = cProgramName
```

Remarks

By default, _COVERAGE contains Coverage.app, installed in your Visual FoxPro directory. You can specify a different name for the coverage output application.

See Also

SET COVERAGE, SET EVENTTRACKING

CPCONVERT( ) Function

Converts character or memo fields or character expressions to another code page.

Syntax

CPCONVERT(*nCurrentCodePage*, *nNewCodePage*, *cExpression*)

Arguments

nCurrentCodePage

Specifies the code page that *cExpression* is being converted from.

nNewCodePage

Specifies the code page to which *cExpression* is converted.

cExpression

Specifies the character expression that's converted.

Remarks

Note that CPCONVERT( ) isn't required for normal cross-platform functioning of the product. It is used strictly to access the underlying translation facilities of Visual FoxPro.

For example, if the variable `gcCharExpr` contains a character that looks like ä on the Macintosh (in code page 10000) then CPCONVERT( ) will return a character that looks like ä in Microsoft Windows (code page 1252):

```
CPCONVERT(10000, 1252, gcCharExpr)
```

For additional information on code pages and Visual FoxPro's international support, see "Code Pages Supported by Visual FoxPro" in Chapter 18, "Developing International Applications," in the *Microsoft Visual FoxPro 6.0 Programmer's Guide*.

See Also

CPCURRENT( ), CPDBF( ), MODIFY COMMAND, MODIFY FILE, SET NOCPTRANS

CPCURRENT( ) Function

Returns the code page setting (if any) in your Visual FoxPro configuration file, or returns the current operating system code page.

Syntax

CPCURRENT([1 | 2])

Remarks

CPCURRENT( ) returns one of the following:

- In Visual FoxPro, the current operating system code page if the CODEPAGE configuration item isn't included in your configuration file. In previous versions of FoxPro, 0 is returned if the CODEPAGE configuration item isn't included in your configuration file.

- The code page number specified in the CODEPAGE configuration item. For example, CPCURRENT( ) returns 852 if the following line is included in your configuration file:

```
CODEPAGE = 852
```

- The current operating system code page if you have included the following line in your configuration file:

```
CODEPAGE = AUTO
```

In Visual FoxPro, CPCURRENT(1) returns the current operating system code page, regardless of your configuration CODEPAGE setting.

CPCURRENT(2) always returns the underlying operating system code page, regardless of your configuration CODEPAGE setting. For example, if you're running Windows, CPCURRENT(2) returns the MS-DOS code page.

For additional information on code pages and Visual FoxPro's international support, see "Code Pages Supported by Visual FoxPro" in Chapter 18, "Developing International Applications," in the *Microsoft Visual FoxPro 6.0 Programmer's Guide*.

See Also

CPCONVERT( ), CPDBF( ), MODIFY COMMAND, MODIFY FILE, SET NOCPTRANS

CPDBF( ) Function

Returns the code page with which an open table has been marked.

Syntax

CPDBF([*nWorkArea* | *cTableAlias*])

Arguments

nWorkArea
   Specifies the work area number.

cTableAlias
   Specifies the table alias.

   Include *nWorkArea* or *cTableAlias* to specify a table open in a work area other than the current work area. CPDBF( ) returns 0 if a table isn't open in the work area you specify. If a table doesn't have the alias you specify with *cTableAlias*, Visual FoxPro generates an error message.

Remarks

DISPLAY STRUCTURE also displays the code page with which an open table has been marked.

For additional information on code pages and Visual FoxPro's international support, see "Code Pages Supported by Visual FoxPro," and Chapter 18, "Developing International Applications," in the *Microsoft Visual FoxPro 6.0 Programmer's Guide*.

See Also

CPCONVERT( ), CPCURRENT( ), MODIFY COMMAND, MODIFY FILE, SET NOCPTRANS

CREATE Command

Builds a new Visual FoxPro table.

Syntax

CREATE [*FileName* | ?]

Arguments

FileName
Specifies the name of the table to create.

?
Displays the Create dialog box that prompts you to name the table being created.

Remarks

In Visual FoxPro, if a database is open when you create a table, the table is automatically added to the database.

When running on the Windows operating system, you cannot create a table with the name of an MS-DOS device, such as CON, NUL, PRN, and COM1. You should avoid using hyphens in a table name because hyphenated table names don't appear in the Data Session window, and can cause confusion with the alias pointer (–>).

A table is created by defining the name, type, and size of each field. Once the structure of the table is created, you can then add records to the table. For more information on tables, see Chapter 3, "Creating Tables," in the *User's Guide* in Help.

See Also

ADD TABLE, ALTER TABLE – SQL, CREATE DATABASE, CREATE TABLE – SQL, MODIFY STRUCTURE

CREATE CLASS Command

Opens the Class Designer, allowing you to create a new class definition.

Syntax

CREATE CLASS *ClassName* | ? [OF *ClassLibraryName1* | ?]
    [AS *cBaseClassName* [FROM *ClassLibraryName2*]] [NOWAIT]

Arguments

ClassName
Specifies the name of the class definition to create.

?

Displays the New Class dialog box, from which you can specify the name of the class definition to create.

OF *ClassLibraryName1*

Specifies the name of the .vcx visual class library to create. If the .vcx visual class library already exists, the class definition is added to it.

A .vcx file extension is assumed for the visual class library. Be sure to include the file extension if the visual class library you specify has a file extension other than .vcx.

?

Displays the New Class dialog box, from which you can specify the name of a new or existing .vcx visual class library to which the class definition is added.

AS *cBaseClassName*

Specifies the class on which the class definition is based. *cBaseClassName* can be any Visual FoxPro base class except Column, Cursor, DataEnvironment, Header, Page, and Relation. You can also specify a user-defined class for *cBaseClassName* if you include the FROM *ClassLibraryName2* clause that specifies the name of the .vcx visual class library containing the user-defined class.

If you omit AS *cBaseClassName*, the class definition is based on the Visual FoxPro FormSet base class.

FROM *ClassLibraryName2*

Specifies the name of the .vcx visual class library containing the user-defined class specified with *cBaseClassName*.

NOWAIT

Continues program execution after the Class Designer has been opened. The program doesn't wait for the Class Designer to be closed, but continues execution on the program line immediately following the line that contains CREATE CLASS NOWAIT. If you omit NOWAIT, when CREATE CLASS is issued in a program, the Class Designer is opened and program execution pauses until the Class Designer is closed.

Including NOWAIT has no effect on CREATE CLASS when it is issued in the Command window.

Remarks

Use CREATE CLASS to create a class definition and save it in a .vcx visual class library. You can open the .vcx visual class library with SET CLASSLIB, allowing you to access the class definitions within the .vcx visual class library.

See Also

ADD CLASS, _BROWSER, CREATE CLASSLIB, DEFINE CLASS, _INCLUDE, MODIFY CLASS, RELEASE CLASSLIB, SET CLASSLIB

CREATE CLASSLIB Command

Creates a new, empty visual class library (.vcx) file.

Syntax

CREATE CLASSLIB *ClassLibraryName*

Arguments

ClassLibraryName

Specifies the name of the visual class library to create. If a visual class library with the name you specify already exists and SET SAFETY is ON, Visual FoxPro asks if you'd like to overwrite the existing visual class library. If SET SAFETY is OFF, the existing file is automatically overwritten.

If you don't specify an extension for the file name, Visual FoxPro automatically assigns a .vcx extension.

Remarks

Class definitions can be added to a visual class library with ADD CLASS and CREATE CLASS.

Example

The following example uses CREATE CLASSLIB to create a visual class library named `myclslib`. A class named `myform` based on the Visual FoxPro Form base class is created and is stored in the `myclslib` visual class library. SET CLASSLIB is used to open the `myclslib` visual class library so that classes within it can be used.

```
CREATE CLASSLIB myclslib      && Creates a new .VCX visual class library
CREATE CLASS myform OF myclslib AS "Form"  && Creates new class
SET CLASSLIB TO myclslib ADDITIVE      && Opens MyClsLib.VCX
```

See Also

ADD CLASS, _BROWSER, CREATE CLASS, DEFINE CLASS, MODIFY CLASS, RELEASE CLASSLIB, SET CLASS

CREATE COLOR SET Command

Creates a color set from the current color settings.

Syntax

CREATE COLOR SET *ColorSetName*

Arguments

ColorSetName

Specifies the name of the color set to create.

Remarks

Every color pair in every color scheme is saved in the color set you create. A color set name can be up to 24 characters long in Visual FoxPro, (10 characters in earlier FoxPro versions) and can contain numbers and underscores, but it cannot begin with a number.

Once you have created a color set, you can load it with SET COLOR SET.

Color sets are saved in the Visual FoxPro resource file. If a color set exists with the same name you specify, it is overwritten.

For more information on color schemes and color pairs, see "Colors Overview," earlier in this language reference.

See Also

SET COLOR OF SCHEME, SET COLOR SET, SET COLOR TO

CREATE CONNECTION Command

Creates a named connection and stores it in the current database.

Syntax

CREATE CONNECTION [*ConnectionName* | ?]
    [DATASOURCE *cDataSourceName*]
    [USERID *cUserID*] [PASSWORD *cPassWord*]
    [DATABASE *cDatabaseName*]
    | CONNSTRING *cConnectionString*]

Arguments

ConnectionName
    Specifies the name of the connection to create.

?
    Displays the Connection Designer from which you can create and save a connection.

DATASOURCE *cDataSourceName*
    Specifies the name of the ODBC data source for the connection.

USERID *cUserID*
    Specifies your user identification for the ODBC data source.

PASSWORD *cPassWord*
    Specifies your password for the ODBC data source.

DATABASE *cDatabaseName*
    Specifies a database on the server to which the connection is made.

CONNSTRING *cConnectionString*
    Specifies a connection string for the ODBC data source. The connection string can be used instead of explicitly including the ODBC data source, the user identification, and the password.

Remarks

If you omit the optional arguments, the Connection Designer appears, allowing you to interactively create a connection.

Example

The following example assumes an ODBC data source called MyFoxSQLNT is available, and the user ID for the data source is "sa." The testdata database is opened, and a connection named Myconn is created. DISPLAY CONNECTIONS is used to display the named connections in the database. The connection is then removed from the database with DELETE CONNECTION.

```
CLOSE DATABASES
OPEN DATABASE (HOME(2) + 'data\testdata')
CREATE CONNECTION Myconn DATASOURCE "MyFoxSQLNT" USERID "sa"

CLEAR
DISPLAY CONNECTIONS  && Displays named connections in the database
DELETE CONNECTION Myconn  && Removes the connection just created
```

See Also

DELETE CONNECTION, DBGETPROP( ), DISPLAY CONNECTIONS, LIST CONNECTIONS, MODIFY CONNECTION, OPEN DATABASE, RENAME CONNECTION

CREATE CURSOR – SQL Command

Creates a temporary table.

Syntax

CREATE CURSOR *alias_name*
    (*fname1 type* [(*precision* [, *scale*])
       [NULL | NOT NULL]
       [CHECK *lExpression* [ERROR *cMessageText*]]
       [DEFAULT *eExpression*]
       [UNIQUE]
       [NOCPTRANS]]
    [, *fname2* ...])
    | FROM ARRAY *ArrayName*

Arguments

alias_name
> Specifies the name of the temporary table to create. *alias_name* can be a name expression.

fname
> Specifies the name of a field in the temporary table. Each *fname* can be a name expression.

type
> Specifies a single letter indicating the data type for the field.

precision
> Specifies the width of the field specified with *fname*. Some data types require that you specify a *precision*.

scale
> Specifies the number of decimal places for the specified data type. Some data types require that you specify a *scale*.

The following table shows what *type*, *precision*, and *scale* can be:

FieldType	nFieldWidth	nPrecision	Description
C	n	–	Character field of width *n*
D	–	–	Date
T	–	–	Datetime
N	n	d	Numeric field of width *n* with *d* decimal places
F	n	d	Floating numeric field of width *n* with *d* decimal places
I	–	–	Integer
B	–	d	Double
Y	–	–	Currency
L	–	–	Logical
M	–	–	Memo
G	–	–	General
P	–	–	Picture

nFieldWidth and *nPrecision* are ignored for D, T, Y, L, M, G, and P types. *nPrecision* defaults to zero (no decimal places) if *nPrecision* isn't included for the N, F, or B types.

NULL

Allows null values in the field.

NOT NULL

Prevents null values in the field.

If you omit NULL and NOT NULL, the current setting of SET NULL determines if null values are allowed in the field. However, if you omit NULL and NOT NULL and include the PRIMARY KEY or UNIQUE clause, the current setting of SET NULL is ignored and the field defaults to NOT NULL.

CHECK *lExpression*

Specifies a validation rule for the field. *lExpression* can be a user-defined function.

ERROR *cMessageText*

Specifies the error message Visual FoxPro displays when the field validation rule generates an error. The message is displayed only when data is changed within a Browse window or Edit window.

DEFAULT *eExpression*

Specifies a default value for the field. The data type of *eExpression* must be the same as the field's data type.

UNIQUE

Creates a candidate index for the field. The candidate index tag has the same name as the field.

For more information about candidate indexes, see "Indexing Tables" in Chapter 7, "Working with Tables," in the *Microsoft Visual FoxPro 6.0 Programmer's Guide*.

> **Note** Candidate indexes (created by including the UNIQUE option) are not the same as indexes created with the UNIQUE option in the INDEX command. An index created with the UNIQUE option in the INDEX command allows duplicate index keys; candidate indexes do not allow duplicate index keys.

Null values and duplicate records are not permitted in a field used for a candidate index. However, Microsoft Visual FoxPro will not generate an error if you create a candidate index for a field that supports null values. Visual FoxPro will generate an error if you attempt to enter a null or duplicate value into a field used for a candidate index.

NOCPTRANS

Prevents translation to a different code page for character and memo fields. If the cursor is converted to another code page, the fields for which NOCPTRANS has been specified are not translated. NOCPTRANS can be specified only for character and memo fields.

The following example creates a cursor named MYCURSOR containing two character fields and two memo fields. The second character field CHAR2 and the second memo field MEMO2 include NOCPTRANS to prevent translation.

```
CREATE CURSOR mycursor (char1 C(10), char2 C(10) NOCPTRANS,;
    memo1 M, memo2 M NOCPTRANS)
```

FROM ARRAY *ArrayName*

Specifies the name of an existing array whose contents are the name, type, precision, and scale for each field in the temporary table. See the AFIELDS( ) Function, earlier in this language reference, for the proper format for the contents of the array.

Remarks

CREATE CURSOR creates a temporary table that exists only until it is closed. A temporary table created with **CREATE CURSOR** can be manipulated like any other table — it can be browsed and indexed, and you can append and modify records.

The temporary table is opened in the lowest available work area, and can be accessed by its alias. Each field in the temporary table is defined with a name, type, precision, and scale. These definitions can be obtained from the command itself or from an array. The temporary table is opened exclusively regardless of the setting of SET EXCLUSIVE.

Example

The following example creates a cursor with the alias employee. A blank record is appended, filled, and displayed with the BROWSE command.

```
CLOSE DATABASES
CLEAR
CREATE CURSOR employee ;
    (EmpID N(5), Name C(20), Address C(30), City C(30), ;
    PostalCode C(10), OfficeNo C(8) NULL, Specialty M)
DISPLAY STRUCTURE
WAIT WINDOW "Press a key to add a record."

INSERT INTO employee (EmpId, Name, Address, City, PostalCode, ;
    OfficeNo, Specialty);
    VALUES (1002, "Dr. Bonnie Doren", "University of Oregon", "Eugene", ;
        "98403", "", "Secondary Special Education")
BROWSE

* At this point you could copy this record to a permanent table
CLOSE ALL   && Once the cursor is closed, all data is flushed
    && from memory
CLEAR
```

See Also

AFIELDS( ), CREATE, CREATE QUERY, CREATE TABLE – SQL, INSERT – SQL, MODIFY QUERY, SELECT – SQL

CREATE DATABASE Command

Creates a database and opens it.

Syntax

CREATE DATABASE [*DatabaseName* | ?]

Arguments

DatabaseName

Specifies the name of the database to create.

If SAFETY is set to ON and the database name you specify has the same path and name as an existing database, Visual FoxPro displays a warning dialog box that prompts you to specify a new path or name for the database.

?

Displays the Create dialog box from which you can specify the name of the database to create.

Remarks

A database file has a .dbc extension. The associated database memo files have a .dct extension, and the associated index files have a .dcx extension.

The database is opened exclusively, regardless of the setting of SET EXCLUSIVE. Because CREATE DATABASE opens the database after it has been created, you do not have to issue a subsequent OPEN DATABASE command.

If CREATE DATABASE is issued without any of its optional arguments, the Create dialog box is displayed, allowing you to specify a name for the database.

Example

This example creates a database named `people`. A table named `friends` is created and is automatically added to the database. DISPLAY TABLES is used to display the tables in the database, and DISPLAY DATABASES is used to display information about the tables in the database.

```
CREATE DATABASE people
CREATE TABLE friends (FirstName C(20), LastName C(20))
CLEAR
DISPLAY TABLES  && Displays tables in the database
DISPLAY DATABASES  && Displays table information
```

See Also

ADD TABLE, CLOSE DATABASES, DBC( ), DBGETPROP( ), DBSETPROP( ), DELETE DATABASE, DISPLAY TABLES, FREE TABLE, MODIFY DATABASE, OPEN DATABASE, PACK DATABASE, REMOVE TABLE, SET DATABASE, VALIDATE DATABASE

CREATE FORM Command

Opens the Form Designer.

Syntax

CREATE FORM [*FormName* | ?]
    [AS *cClassName* FROM *cClassLibraryName* | ?]
    [NOWAIT] [SAVE] [DEFAULT]
    [[WINDOW *WindowName1*]
    [IN [WINDOW] *WindowName2* | IN SCREEN]]

Arguments

FormName

Specifies the file name for the form. If you don't specify an extension for the file name, Visual FoxPro automatically assigns an .scx extension. If a form file with the name you specify already exists, you are asked if you want to overwrite the existing file (if SET SAFETY is set to ON).

?

Displays the Create dialog box from which you can choose a form or enter the name of a new form to create.

AS *cClassName* FROM *cClassLibraryName* | ?

Creates a new form from a form class in a .vcx visual class library. *cClassName* specifies the name of the user-defined form class from which the new form is created. An error is generated if *cClassName* isn't based on a form. *cClassLibraryName* specifies the name of the .vcx visual class library containing the form class specified with *cClassName*. Include ? to display the Open dialog box, allowing you to specify the visual class library.

NOWAIT

Continues program execution after the Form Designer has been opened. The program doesn't wait for the Form Designer to be closed, but continues execution on the program line immediately following the line that contains CREATE FORM NOWAIT. If you omit NOWAIT, when CREATE FORM is issued in a program, the Form Designer is opened and program execution pauses until the Form Designer is closed.

Including NOWAIT has no effect on CREATE FORM when it is issued in the Command window.

SAVE

When issued in a program, leaves the Form Designer open after another window is brought forward. Including the SAVE option has no effect when issued from the Command window.

DEFAULT

Specifies that the Form Designer is opened with the default Visual FoxPro form template, overriding a default form template specified on the Forms tab of the Options dialog.

For additional information about form templates, see Chapter 9, "Creating Forms," in the *Microsoft Visual FoxPro 6.0 Programmer's Guide*.

WINDOW *WindowName1*

Specifies a window whose characteristics the Form Designer takes on. For example, if the window is created with the FLOAT option of DEFINE WINDOW, the Form Designer can be moved. The window need not be active or visible, but it must be defined.

The Form Designer has a default size that can be larger than the window from which it takes its characteristics. In this case, the Form Designer still assumes the characteristics of the window in which it is placed. The upper-left corner of the Form Designer is placed at the same coordinates as the upper-left corner of the window, and extends beyond the window's borders.

IN [WINDOW] *WindowName2*

Specifies a parent window in which the Form Designer is opened. The Form Designer doesn't assume the characteristics of the parent window and cannot be moved outside the parent window. If the parent window is moved, the Form Designer moves with it.

The parent window must first be defined with DEFINE WINDOW, and must be visible, to access the Form Designer.

IN SCREEN

Specifies that the Form Designer is explicitly opened in the main Visual FoxPro window, after the Form Designer has been placed in a parent window. The Form Designer is placed in a parent window by including the IN WINDOW clause.

Remarks

Issuing CREATE FORM without any additional arguments opens a new form in the Form Designer. When you exit the Form Designer, you are prompted to save the form with a different name.

See Also

_BROWSER, COMPILE FORM, DO FORM, GETPEM( ), _INCLUDE, MODIFY FORM, PEMSTATUS( ), SYS(1269) – Property Information, SYS(1270) – Object Location, SYS(1271) – Object's .SCX File, SYS(1272) – Object Hierarchy

CREATE FROM Command

Creates a table from a COPY STRUCTURE EXTENDED file.

Syntax

CREATE
  [*FileName1* [DATABASE *DatabaseName* [NAME *LongTableName*]]]
  FROM [*FileName2*]

Arguments

FileName1
  Specifies the name of the new table to create.

DATABASE *DatabaseName*
  Specifies a database to which the new table is added.

NAME *LongTableName*
  Specifies a long name for the new table. Long names can contain up to 128 characters and can be used in place of short file names in the database.

FileName2
  Specifies the table (created either with COPY STRUCTURE EXTENDED or manually) from which the new table is created.

Remarks

This variation of CREATE assumes that the table specified in *FileName2* has been created either with COPY STRUCTURE EXTENDED or manually. A new table *FileName1* is created with the structure described in *FileName2*. The newly created table becomes the active table.

If you don't include either *FileName1* or *FileName2* or both, a dialog box is displayed. In this dialog, you can specify the file to be created, or the FROM file, or both.

Note that all records in *FileName2*, including those marked for deletion, are used to created *FileName1*.

Example

The following example displays the structure of the `orders` table, copies the structure extended to the `temp` table, browses `temp`, creates a table called `backup` from `temp`, and displays the structure of `backup`.

```
CLOSE DATABASES
CLEAR
SET PATH TO (HOME(2) + 'Data\')      && Sets path to database
USE orders
DISPLAY STRUCTURE
WAIT WINDOW 'Structure of the orders table' NOWAIT
```

```
COPY STRUCTURE EXTENDED TO temp
USE temp
WAIT WINDOW 'Temp table has 1 row per field in ORDERS' NOWAIT
BROWSE
CREATE backup FROM temp
USE backup
DISPLAY STRUCTURE
WAIT WINDOW 'Backup.dbf has the same structure as ORDERS' NOWAIT
USE
DELETE FILE temp.dbf
DELETE FILE backup.dbf
```

See Also

COPY STRUCTURE EXTENDED

CREATE LABEL Command

Opens the Label Designer so you can create a label.

Syntax

CREATE LABEL [*FileName* | ?]
    [NOWAIT] [SAVE]
    [WINDOW *WindowName1*]
    [IN [WINDOW] *WindowName2* | IN SCREEN

Arguments

FileName

Specifies the file name for the label. If you don't specify an extension for the file name, Visual FoxPro automatically assigns an .lbx extension.

?

Displays the Create dialog box that prompts you to name the label being created.

NOWAIT

Continues program execution after the Label Designer is opened. The program doesn't wait for the Label Designer to be closed, but continues execution on the program line immediately following the line that contains CREATE LABEL NOWAIT. If you omit NOWAIT when CREATE LABEL is issued in a program, the Label Designer is opened and program execution pauses until the Label Designer is closed.

Including the NOWAIT option has no effect on the CREATE LABEL command when issued from the Command window.

SAVE

Leaves the Label Designer open after another window is activated. If you omit SAVE, the Label Designer is closed when another window is activated.

Including SAVE has no effect when issued from the Command window.

WINDOW *WindowName1*

Specifies a window whose characteristics the Label Designer takes on. For example, if the window is created with the FLOAT option of DEFINE WINDOW, the Label Designer can be moved. The window doesn't have to be active or visible, but it must be defined.

The Label Designer has a default size that can be larger than the window from which it takes its characteristics. In this case, the Label Designer still assumes the characteristics of the window in which it is placed. The upper-left corner of the Label Designer is placed at the same coordinates as the upper-left corner of the window, and extends beyond the window's borders.

IN [WINDOW] *WindowName2*

Specifies a parent window in which the Label Designer is opened. The Label Designer doesn't assume the characteristics of the parent window and cannot be moved outside the parent window. If the parent window is moved, the Label Designer moves with it.

The parent window must first be defined with DEFINE WINDOW, and must be visible to access the Label Designer.

IN SCREEN

Specifies that the Label Designer is explicitly opened in the main Visual FoxPro window, after the Label Designer has been placed in a parent window. A Label Designer is placed in a parent window by including the IN WINDOW clause.

Remarks

CREATE LABEL lets you create labels in standard label formats or design your own custom labels. You can also use the Label Wizard to create labels.

For more information on creating labels, see Chapter 7, "Designing Reports and Labels," in the *User's Guide* in Help.

See Also

LABEL, MODIFY LABEL

CREATE MENU Command

Opens the Menu Designer in Visual FoxPro.

Syntax

CREATE MENU [*FileName* | ?]
   [NOWAIT] [SAVE]
   [WINDOW *WindowName1*]
   [IN [WINDOW] *WindowName2* | IN SCREEN

Arguments

FileName

Specifies the file name for the menu table. If you don't specify an extension for the file name, Visual FoxPro automatically assigns an .mnx extension.

?

Displays the Create dialog box that prompts you to name the menu being created.

NOWAIT

Continues program execution after the Menu Designer is opened. The program doesn't wait for the Menu Designer to be closed, but continues execution on the program line immediately following the line that contains CREATE MENU NOWAIT. If you omit NOWAIT, when CREATE MENU is issued in a program, the Menu Designer is opened and program execution pauses until the Menu Designer is closed.

If you issue CREATE MENU from the Command window and include NOWAIT, the New Menu dialog is not displayed. The New Menu dialog lets you specify the type of menu (standard or shortcut) created.

SAVE

Leaves the Menu Designer open after another window is activated. If you omit SAVE, the Menu Designer is closed when another window is activated. Including SAVE has no effect when issued from the Command window.

WINDOW *WindowName1*

Specifies a window whose characteristics the Menu Designer takes on. For example, if the window is created with the FLOAT option of DEFINE WINDOW, the Menu Designer can be moved. The window need not be active or visible, but it must be defined.

The Menu Designer has a default size that can be larger than the window from which it takes its characteristics. In this case, the Menu Designer still assumes the characteristics of the window in which it is placed. The upper-left corner of the Menu Designer is placed at the same coordinates as the upper-left corner of the window, and extends beyond the window's borders.

IN [WINDOW] *WindowName2*

Specifies a parent window in which the Menu Designer is opened. The Menu Designer doesn't assume the characteristics of the parent window and cannot be moved outside the parent window. If the parent window is moved, the Menu Designer moves with it.

The parent window must first be defined with DEFINE WINDOW, and must be visible, to access the Menu Designer.

IN SCREEN

Specifies that the Menu Designer is opened explicitly in the main Visual FoxPro window, after the Menu Designer has been placed in a parent window. The Menu Designer is placed in a parent window by including the IN WINDOW clause.

Remarks

Issuing CREATE MENU without any additional arguments opens the Menu Designer within which you can define a menu system. The name MENU1 is temporarily assigned to the menu definition table. When you exit the Menu Designer, you can save the menu definition under a different name.

For more information on creating menus, see Chapter 11, "Designing Menus and Toolbars," in the *Microsoft Visual FoxPro 6.0 Programmer's Guide.*

See Also

DEFINE MENU, MODIFY MENU

CREATE PROJECT Command

Opens the Project Manager so you can create a project.

Syntax

CREATE PROJECT [*FileName* | ?]
    [NOWAIT] [SAVE]
    [WINDOW *WindowName1*]
    [IN [WINDOW] *WindowName2* | IN SCREEN
    [NOSHOW] [NOPROJECTHOOK]

Arguments

FileName
    Specifies the file name for the project table. If you don't specify an extension for the file name, Visual FoxPro automatically assigns a .pjx extension.

?
    Displays the Create dialog box that prompts you to name the project being created.

NOWAIT
    Continues program execution after the Project Manager is opened. The program doesn't wait for the Project Manager to be closed, but continues execution on the program line immediately following the line that contains CREATE PROJECT NOWAIT. If you omit NOWAIT when CREATE PROJECT is issued in a program, the Project Manager is opened and program execution pauses until the Project Manager is closed.

    Including NOWAIT has no effect on CREATE PROJECT when it is issued in the Command window.

SAVE
    Leaves the Project Manager open after another window is activated. If you omit SAVE, the Project Manager is closed when another window is activated.

    Including SAVE has no effect when issued from the Command window.

WINDOW *WindowName1*

Specifies a window whose characteristics the Project Manager takes on. For example, if the window is created with the FLOAT option of DEFINE WINDOW, the Project Manager can be moved. The window need not be active or visible, but it must be defined.

The Project Manager has a default size that can be larger than the window from which it takes its characteristics. In this case, the Project Manager still assumes the characteristics of the window in which it is placed. The upper-left corner of the Project Manager is placed at the same coordinates as the upper-left corner of the window, and extends beyond the window's borders.

IN [WINDOW] *WindowName2*

Specifies a parent window in which the Project Manager is opened. The Project Manager doesn't assume the characteristics of the parent window and cannot be moved outside the parent window. If the parent window is moved, the Project Manager moves with it.

The parent window must first be defined with DEFINE WINDOW, and must be visible, to access the Project Manager.

IN SCREEN

Specifies that the Project Manager is explicitly opened in the main Visual FoxPro window, after the Project Manager has been placed in a parent window. The Project Manager is placed in a parent window by including the IN WINDOW clause.

NOSHOW

Specifies that the Project Manager is hidden (its Visible property is set to false (.F.)) when it is opened. To display the Project Manager, set the Project Manager's Visible property to true (.T.). NOSHOW allows you to manipulate a project before displaying it in the Project Manager. Note that to avoid confusion with the NOSHADOW keyword, you cannot abbreviate NOSHOW to less than five characters.

NOPROJECTHOOK

Specifies that a ProjectHook object isn't created when the Project Manager is opened. Include NOPROJECTHOOK for projects that will not be manipulated programmatically through the Project Manager hooks. Note that a Project object is still created whenever a project file (.pjx) is opened.

Remarks

A project is a table that keeps track of all files that are required to create an application, as well as all dependencies, references, and connections among the files. A project table has a .pjx extension and an associated memo file with a .pjt extension. In a project, you specify all the pieces that are required for an application, and Visual FoxPro ensures that compiled files are based on the latest source files.

A project table can be opened with USE and manipulated like any other Visual FoxPro table.

Issuing the command CREATE PROJECT without any additional arguments displays the Create dialog, allowing you to specify a name for the project.

For more information on building projects, see Chapter 13, "Compiling an Application," in the *Microsoft Visual FoxPro 6.0 Programmer's Guide*.

See Also

BUILD APP, BUILD PROJECT, MODIFY PROJECT

CREATE QUERY Command

Opens the Query Designer.

Syntax

CREATE QUERY [*FileName* | ?]
    [NOWAIT]

Arguments

FileName
> Specifies the file name for the query. If you don't specify an extension for the file name, Visual FoxPro automatically assigns a .qpr extension.

?
> Displays the Create dialog box that prompts you to name the query being created.

NOWAIT
> Continues program execution after the Query Designer is opened. The program doesn't wait for the Query Designer to be closed, but continues execution on the program line immediately following the line that contains CREATE QUERY NOWAIT. If you omit NOWAIT when CREATE QUERY is issued in a program, the Query Designer is opened and program execution pauses until the Query Designer is closed.
>
> NOWAIT is effective only from within a program. It has no effect on CREATE QUERY when issued from the Command window.

Remarks

CREATE QUERY opens the Query Designer so you can interactively create a query.

A SQL SELECT command is used to retrieve data from tables. SELECT is very powerful and can replace a series of Visual FoxPro commands. Because one SQL SELECT performs the function of a series of Visual FoxPro commands, SELECT optimizes program performance.

Think of SELECT as a way to pose a query to Visual FoxPro to obtain information from tables. SELECT allows you to specify the information you want without telling Visual FoxPro how to retrieve the information. Visual FoxPro determines the best way to retrieve the information.

After you create a query, the query is stored as a Visual FoxPro program file with a .qpr extension. A query program can be executed with DO. You must include the query file extension when executing a query with DO, as shown in the following example.

```
DO my_query.qpr
```

Issuing the command CREATE QUERY without any additional arguments opens a new query window. The name QUERY1 is assigned to the query. When you exit the Query window, you can save the query with a different name.

For more information about creating queries, see "Creating a Query" in Chapter 4, "Retrieving Data," in the *User's Guide* in Help.

See Also

MODIFY QUERY, SELECT – SQL

CREATE REPORT Command

Opens a report in a Report Designer.

Syntax

CREATE REPORT [*FileName* | ?]
    [NOWAIT] [SAVE]
    [WINDOW *WindowName1*]
    [IN [WINDOW] *WindowName2* | IN SCREEN

Arguments

FileName

Specifies the file name for the report. If you don't specify an extension for the file name, Visual FoxPro automatically assigns an .frx extension. If a report file with the name you specify already exists, you are asked if you want to overwrite the existing file (if SET SAFETY is ON).

?

Displays the Create dialog box that prompts you to name the report being created.

NOWAIT

Continues program execution after the Report Designer is opened. The program doesn't wait for the Report Designer to be closed, but continues execution on the program line immediately following the line that contains CREATE REPORT NOWAIT. If you omit NOWAIT when CREATE REPORT is issued in a program, the Report Designer is opened and program execution pauses until the Report Designer is closed.

Including NOWAIT has no effect on CREATE REPORT when it is issued in the Command window.

SAVE

Leaves the Report Designer open after another window is activated. If you omit SAVE, the Report Designer is closed when another window is activated.

Including SAVE has no effect when issued from the Command window.

WINDOW *WindowName1*

Specifies a window whose characteristics the Report Designer takes on. For example, if the window is created with the FLOAT option of DEFINE WINDOW, the Report Designer can be moved. The window need not be active or visible, but it must be defined.

The Report Designer has a default size that can be larger than the window from which it takes its characteristics. In this case, the Report Designer still assumes the characteristics of the window in which it is placed. The upper-left corner of the Report Designer is placed at the same coordinates as the upper-left corner of the window, and extends beyond the window's borders.

IN [WINDOW] *WindowName2*

Specifies a parent window in which the Report Designer is opened. The Report Designer doesn't assume the characteristics of the parent window and cannot be moved outside the parent window. If the parent window is moved, the Report Designer moves with it.

The parent window must first be defined with DEFINE WINDOW, and must be visible, to access the Report Designer.

IN SCREEN

Specifies that the Report Designer is opened explicitly in the main Visual FoxPro window, after the Report Designer has been placed in a parent window. The Report Designer is placed in a parent window by including the IN WINDOW clause.

Remarks

Issuing CREATE REPORT without any additional arguments opens a new Report Designer. The name REPORT1 is assigned to the report definition. When you exit the Report Designer, you are prompted to save the report definition with a different name.

CREATE REPORT can also be used to generate a quick report without opening the Report Designer. For more information, see the following command, CREATE REPORT – Quick Report.

For additional information on reports and labels, see Chapter 7, "Designing Reports and Labels," in the *User's Guide* in Help.

See Also

_ASCIICOLS, _ASCIIROWS, CREATE REPORT – Quick Report, MODIFY REPORT, REPORT

CREATE REPORT – Quick Report Command

Programmatically creates a report.

Syntax

CREATE REPORT *FileName1* | *?* FROM *FileName2*
    [FORM | COLUMN] [FIELDS *FieldList*] [ALIAS]
    [NOOVERWRITE] [WIDTH *nColumns*]

Arguments

FileName1
> Specifies the file name for the report. If you don't specify an extension for the file name, Visual FoxPro automatically assigns an .frx extension.

?
> Displays the Create dialog box that prompts you to name the report being created.

FROM *FileName2*
> Specifies the name of the table from which the report is created. The table doesn't have to be open.

FORM
> Specifies that the report is created with the fields and their names arranged from top to bottom in the Detail band.

COLUMN
> Specifies that the report is created with the fields arranged from left to right across the page in the Detail band. The field names are placed in the Page Header band. If you omit FORM and COLUMN, the report defaults to the COLUMN format.

FIELDS *FieldList*
> Specifies the fields from the table that appear in the report. Separate the fields in *FieldList* with commas.

ALIAS
> Specifies that the table alias is added to the field names in the report.

NOOVERWRITE
> Specifies that an existing report isn't overwritten. If a report already exists with the name specified with *FileName1*, the report isn't created.

WIDTH *nColumns*
> Specifies the width of the report page in columns.

Remarks

This form of CREATE REPORT creates a quick report without opening the Report Designer. The report is created as if you chose Quick Report from the Report menu.

Another form of CREATE REPORT, discussed in the previous topic, opens the Report Designer to let you interactively create a report.

For additional information on reports and labels, see Chapter 7, "Designing Reports and Labels," in the *User's Guide* in Help.

See Also

CREATE REPORT, MODIFY REPORT, REPORT

CREATE SCREEN – Quick Screen Command

Included for backward compatibility. Use the Form Designer instead.

CREATE SCREEN Command

Included for backward compatibility. Use CREATE FORM instead.

CREATE SQL VIEW Command

Displays the View Designer, allowing you to create a SQL view.

Syntax

CREATE SQL VIEW [*ViewName*] [REMOTE]
    [CONNECTION *ConnectionName* [SHARE]
    | CONNECTION *DataSourceName*]
    [AS *SQLSELECTStatement*]

Arguments

ViewName
    Specifies the name of the view to create.

REMOTE
    Specifies that a remote view using remote tables is created. If you omit REMOTE, you can create a view using local tables.

CONNECTION *ConnectionName* [SHARE]

Specifies a named connection to establish when the view is opened. If you include the SHARE clause, Microsoft Visual FoxPro will use a shared connection if one is available. If a shared connection isn't available, a unique connection is created when the view is opened and cannot be shared with other views.

CONNECTION *DataSourceName*

Specifies an existing datasource to which a connection is established.

AS *SQLSELECTStatement*

Specifies the view definition. *SQLSELECTStatement* must be a valid SQL SELECT statement, and should not be enclosed in quotation marks. For local views, preface the view or table name with the name of the database and an exclamation point (!). For example, the following command creates a SQL view called `mysqlview` that selects all fields in the `orders` table in the `customer` database:

```
CREATE SQL VIEW mysqlview AS SELECT * FROM customer!orders
```

For additional information about SQL SELECT statements, see the SELECT – SQL Command, later in this language reference.

You can limit the scope of a view without creating a separate view for each subset of records by creating a parameterized view. A parameterized view uses a WHERE clause that limits the records downloaded to only those records by supplying a value as a parameter.

For example, you can create a SQL view that allows you to download records for any country, simply by supplying the country's name when you use the view.

The parameter you supply is evaluated as a Visual FoxPro expression. If the evaluation fails, Visual FoxPro prompts for the parameter value. For example, if the `customer` table from the Testdata database is located on a remote server, the following example creates a parameterized remote view that limits the view to those customers whose country matches the value supplied for the `?cCountry` parameter:

```
OPEN DATABASE testdata
CREATE SQL VIEW customer_remote_view CONNECTION remote_01 ;
   AS SELECT * FROM customer WHERE customer.country = ?cCountry
```

Tip If your parameter is an expression, enclose the parameter expression in parentheses. This allows the entire expression to be evaluated as part of the parameter.

For additional information about parameterized views, see Chapter 8, "Creating Views," in the *Microsoft Visual FoxPro 6.0 Programmer's Guide*.

Remarks

A SQL view allows you to extract specific fields and records from one or more related tables, and treat the resulting data set as a table that you can update. Views are a powerful means of providing customized access to selected portions of your database, combining the flexibility of a query with the ability to update data.

Example

The following example opens the testdata database. CREATE SQL VIEW is used to create a local SQL view named myview which is created from a SELECT – SQL statement that selects all records from the customer table. The View Designer is displayed, allowing you to modify the SQL view. After the View Designer is closed, the SQL view is erased.

```
CLOSE DATABASES
* Open testdata database
OPEN DATABASE (HOME(2) + 'data\testdata')

* Create view with initial select criteria from customer table
CREATE SQL VIEW myview AS SELECT * FROM testdata!customer;
   WHERE country="Mexico"

* Activate View Designer to modify or run query
MODIFY VIEW myview  &&Activates View Designer

* Delete view after View Designer closes
DELETE VIEW myview
```

See Also

CREATE DATABASE, CREATE VIEW, DELETE VIEW, DISPLAY VIEWS, LIST VIEWS, MODIFY VIEW, OPEN DATABASE, RENAME VIEW, SELECT – SQL, USE

CREATE TABLE – SQL Command

Creates a table having the specified fields.

Syntax

CREATE TABLE | DBF *TableName1* [NAME *LongTableName*] [FREE]
    (*FieldName1 FieldType* [(*nFieldWidth* [, *nPrecision*])])
        [NULL | NOT NULL]
        [CHECK *lExpression1* [ERROR *cMessageText1*]]
        [DEFAULT *eExpression1*]
        [PRIMARY KEY | UNIQUE]
        [REFERENCES *TableName2* [TAG *TagName1*]]
        [NOCPTRANS]
    [, *FieldName2* ...]
        [, PRIMARY KEY *eExpression2* TAG *TagName2*
        |, UNIQUE *eExpression3* TAG *TagName3*]
        [, FOREIGN KEY *eExpression4* TAG *TagName4* [NODUP]
            REFERENCES *TableName3* [TAG *TagName5*]]
        [, CHECK *lExpression2* [ERROR *cMessageText2*]])
| FROM ARRAY *ArrayName*

Arguments

TableName1

Specifies the name of the table to create. The TABLE and DBF options are identical.

NAME *LongTableName*

Specifies a long name for the table. A long table name can be specified only when a database is open because long table names are stored in databases.

Long names can contain up to 128 characters and can be used in place of short file names in the database.

FREE

Specifies that the table will not be added to an open database. FREE isn't required if a database isn't open.

(FieldName1 FieldType [(*nFieldWidth* [, *nPrecision*])]*)*

Specifies the field name, field type, field width, and field precision (number of decimal places), respectively.

A single table can contain up to 255 fields. If one or more fields allow null values, the limit is reduced by one to 254 fields.

FieldType is a single letter indicating the field's data type. Some field data types require that you specify *nFieldWidth* or *nPrecision,* or both.

The following table lists the values for *FieldType* and whether *nFieldWidth* and *nPrecision* are required.

FieldType	*nFieldWidth*	*nPrecision*	**Description**
C	n	–	Character field of width *n*
D	–	–	Date
T	–	–	DateTime
N	n	d	Numeric field of width *n* with *d* decimal places
F	n	d	Floating numeric field of width *n* with *d* decimal places
I	–	–	Integer
B	–	d	Double
Y	–	–	Currency
L	–	–	Logical
M	–	–	Memo
G	–	–	General

nFieldWidth and *nPrecision* are ignored for D, T, I, Y, L, M, G, and P types. *nPrecision* defaults to zero (no decimal places) if *nPrecision* isn't included for the N or F types. *nPrecision* defaults to the number of decimal places specified by the SET DECIMAL setting if *nPrecision* isn't included for the B type.

NULL

Allows null values in the field. If one or more fields can contain null values, the maximum number of fields the table can contain is reduced by one, from 255 to 254.

NOT NULL

Prevents null values in the field.

If you omit NULL and NOT NULL, the current setting of SET NULL determines if null values are allowed in the field. However, if you omit NULL and NOT NULL and include the PRIMARY KEY or UNIQUE clause, the current setting of SET NULL is ignored and the field defaults to NOT NULL.

CHECK *lExpression1*

Specifies a validation rule for the field. *lExpression1* can be a user-defined function. Note that when a blank record is appended, the validation rule is checked. An error is generated if the validation rule doesn't allow for a blank field value in an appended record.

ERROR *cMessageText1*

Specifies the error message Visual FoxPro displays when the validation rule specified with CHECK generates an error. The message is displayed only when data is changed within a Browse window or Edit window.

DEFAULT *eExpression1*

Specifies a default value for the field. The data type of *eExpression1* must be the same as the field's data type.

PRIMARY KEY

Creates a primary index for the field. The primary index tag has the same name as the field.

UNIQUE

Creates a candidate index for the field. The candidate index tag has the same name as the field. For more information about candidate indexes, see "Indexing Tables" in Chapter 7, "Working with Tables," in the *Microsoft Visual FoxPro 6.0 Programmer's Guide*.

> **Note** Candidate indexes (created by including the UNIQUE option in CREATE TABLE or ALTER TABLE – SQL) are not the same as indexes created with the UNIQUE option in the INDEX command. An index created with the UNIQUE option in the INDEX command allows duplicate index keys; candidate indexes do not allow duplicate index keys. See the INDEX Command, later in this language reference, for additional information on its UNIQUE option.

Null values and duplicate records are not permitted in a field used for a primary or candidate index. However, Visual FoxPro will not generate an error if you create a primary or candidate index for a field that supports null values. Visual FoxPro will generate an error if you attempt to enter a null or duplicate value into a field used for a primary or candidate index.

REFERENCES *TableName2* [TAG *TagName1*]

Specifies the parent table to which a persistent relationship is established. If you omit TAG *TagName1*, the relationship is established using the primary index key of the parent table. If the parent table does not have a primary index, Visual FoxPro generates an error.

Include TAG *TagName1* to establish a relation based on an existing index tag for the parent table. Index tag names can contain up to 10 characters.

The parent table cannot be a free table.

NOCPTRANS

Prevents translation to a different code page for character and memo fields. If the table is converted to another code page, the fields for which NOCPTRANS has been specified are not translated. NOCPTRANS can only be specified for character and memo fields.

The following example creates a table named MYTABLE containing two character fields and two memo fields. The second character field CHAR2 and the second memo field MEMO2 include NOCPTRANS to prevent translation.

```
CREATE TABLE mytable (char1 C(10), char2 C(10) NOCPTRANS,;
   memo1 M, memo2 M NOCPTRANS)
```

PRIMARY KEY *eExpression2* TAG *TagName2*

Specifies a primary index to create. *eExpression2* specifies any field or combination of fields in the table. TAG *TagName2* specifies the name for the primary index tag that is created. Index tag names can contain up to 10 characters.

Because a table can have only one primary index, you cannot include this clause if you have already created a primary index for a field. Visual FoxPro generates an error if you include more than one PRIMARY KEY clause in CREATE TABLE.

UNIQUE *eExpression3* TAG *TagName3*

Creates a candidate index. *eExpression3* specifies any field or combination of fields in the table. However, if you have created a primary index with one of the PRIMARY KEY options, you cannot include the field that was specified for the primary index. TAG *TagName3* specifies a tag name for the candidate index tag that is created. Index tag names can contain up to 10 characters.

A table can have multiple candidate indexes.

FOREIGN KEY *eExpression4* **TAG** *TagName4* **[NODUP]**

Creates a foreign (non-primary) index, and establishes a relationship to a parent table. *eExpression4* specifies the foreign index key expression and *TagName4* specifies the name of the foreign index key tag that is created. Index tag names can contain up to 10 characters. Include NODUP to create a candidate foreign index.

You can create multiple foreign indexes for the table, but the foreign index expressions must specify different fields in the table.

REFERENCES *TableName3* **[TAG** *TagName5*]

Specifies the parent table to which a persistent relationship is established. Include TAG *TagName5* to establish a relation based on an index tag for the parent table. Index tag names can contain up to 10 characters. If you omit TAG *TagName5*, the relationship is established using the parent table's primary index key by default.

CHECK *eExpression2* **[ERROR** *cMessageText2*]

Specifies the table validation rule. ERROR *cMessageText2* specifies the error message Visual FoxPro displays when the table validation rule is executed. The message is displayed only when data is changed within a Browse window or Edit window.

FROM ARRAY *ArrayName*

Specifies the name of an existing array whose contents are the name, type, precision, and scale for each field in the table. The contents of the array can be defined with the AFIELDS( ) function.

Remarks

The new table is opened in the lowest available work area, and can be accessed by its alias. The new table is opened exclusively, regardless of the current setting of SET EXCLUSIVE.

If a database is open and you don't include the FREE clause, the new table is added to the database. You cannot create a new table with the same name as a table in the database.

If a database isn't open when you create the new table, including the NAME, CHECK, DEFAULT, FOREIGN KEY, PRIMARY KEY, or REFERENCES clauses generates an error.

Note that the CREATE TABLE syntax uses commas to separate certain CREATE TABLE options. Also, the NULL, NOT NULL, CHECK, DEFAULT, PRIMARY KEY and UNIQUE clause must be placed within the parentheses containing the column definitions.

Example

The following example creates a new database named `Mydata1`. CREATE TABLE is used to create three tables (`Salesman`, `Customer`, and `Orders`). The FOREIGN KEY and REFERENCES clauses in the second CREATE TABLE command create a persistent one-to-many relationship between the `Salesman` and `Customer` tables. The DEFAULT clauses in the third CREATE TABLE command establish default values, and the CHECK and ERROR clauses establish business rules for entering data into specific fields. The MODIFY DATABASE is used to display the relationship between the three tables.

```
CLOSE DATABASES
CLEAR

* Create mydata database in the current directory or folder
CREATE DATABASE mydata1

* Create a salesman table with a primary key
CREATE TABLE salesman ;
   (SalesID c(6) PRIMARY KEY, ;
   SaleName C(20))

* Create a customer table and relate it to the salesman table.
CREATE TABLE customer ;
   (SalesID c(6), ;
   CustId i PRIMARY KEY, ;
   CustName c(20) UNIQUE,    ;
   SalesBranch c(3), ;
   FOREIGN KEY SalesId TAG SalesId REFERENCES salesman)

* Create an orders table related to customer with its own primary
* key and some business rules such as defaults & checks.
CREATE TABLE orders ;
   (OrderId i PRIMARY KEY, ;
      CustId i REFERENCES customer TAG CustId, ;
      OrderAmt y(4), ;
      OrderQty i ;
      DEFAULT 10 ;
      CHECK (OrderQty > 9) ;
      ERROR "Order Quantity must be at least 10", ;
         DiscPercent n(6,2) NULL ;
      DEFAULT .NULL., ;
      CHECK (OrderAmt > 0) ERROR "Order Amount Must be > 0" )

* Display new database, tables, and relationships
MODIFY DATABASE

* Delete example files
SET SAFETY OFF && To suppress verification message
CLOSE DATABASES     && Close database before deleting
DELETE DATABASE mydata1 DELETETABLES
```

See Also

AFIELDS( ), ALTER TABLE – SQL, CREATE, CREATE QUERY, INSERT – SQL,
MODIFY QUERY, MODIFY STRUCTURE, OPEN DATABASE, SELECT – SQL,
SET NOCPTRANS, SQL Commands Overview

CREATE TRIGGER Command

Creates a Delete, Insert, or Update trigger for a table.

Syntax

CREATE TRIGGER ON *TableName*
    FOR DELETE | INSERT | UPDATE AS *lExpression*

Arguments

TableName
    Specifies the table in the current database for which a trigger is created.

FOR DELETE | INSERT | UPDATE
    Specifies the type of trigger Visual FoxPro creates.

    If a trigger of the type you specify already exists and SET SAFETY is ON,
    Visual FoxPro asks you if you'd like to overwrite the existing trigger. If SET
    SAFETY is OFF, the existing trigger is automatically overwritten.

AS *lExpression*
    Specifies the logical expression evaluated when the trigger occurs. *lExpression* can
    be a user-defined function or a stored procedure that returns a logical value. Stored
    procedures are created for a table with MODIFY PROCEDURE.

    A user-defined function or a stored procedure can use AERROR( ) to determine the
    name of the table for which the trigger occurred and the trigger type.

    If *lExpression* evaluates to true (.T.), the command or event that caused the trigger
    to occur is executed.

    If *lExpression* evaluates to false (.F.), the command or event that caused the trigger
    to occur isn't executed. If an ON ERROR procedure is in effect, the ON ERROR
    procedure is executed instead of the command or event. If an ON ERROR procedure
    is not in effect, the command or event isn't executed and Visual FoxPro generates
    an error message.

Remarks

Use CREATE TRIGGER to trap for events that cause records in a table to be deleted,
added, or changed. Delete, Insert, or Update triggers can be created only for a table that
has been added to a database. Use CREATE DATABASE to create a database, and
ADD TABLE to add a table to a database.

The following lists describe the events that cause a Delete, Insert, or Update trigger
to occur.

Delete Trigger

- DELETE is issued.

- A record is marked for deletion from the Table Menu in a Browse window or Edit window.

- Note that issuing ZAP does not cause the Delete trigger to occur.

Insert Trigger

- APPEND FROM is issued.

- APPEND FROM ARRAY is issued.

- APPEND BLANK is issued.

- A record is appended from the Table Menu in a Browse window or Edit window.

- IMPORT is issued.

- INSERT – SQL is issued.

- RECALL is issued.

- A record is recalled from the Table Menu in a Browse window or Edit window.

Update Trigger

- GATHER is issued.

- REPLACE is issued.

- REPLACE FROM ARRAY is issued.

- UPDATE – SQL is issued.

- Other event that causes a record to be modified, such as when a Form changes the contents of a field.

The following rules apply to triggers created with CREATE TRIGGER:

- INSERT cannot be issued for a table with a trigger. However, INSERT – SQL can be used.

- Issuing PACK doesn't cause any triggers to occur.

- Issuing ZAP doesn't cause a Delete trigger to occur.

- No trigger occurs if you update a record marked for deletion.

- A trigger may not occur immediately, depending on the current buffering mode:

If table buffering is in effect, the Update trigger occurs when TABLEUPDATE( ) is issued and each buffered record is updated in the table.

Example

The following examples creates an Update trigger which prevents values greater than 50 from being entered in the maxordamt field in the customer table. An error message is generated when the first REPLACE command is executed because the value for the maxordamt field is greater than 50. The second REPLACE command does not generate an error because the value for the maxordamt field is less than or equal to 50.

```
CLOSE DATABASES

OPEN DATABASE (HOME(2) + 'data\testdata')
USE customer  && Open customer table

* Set trigger on maxordamt field to fail with values <= 50
CREATE TRIGGER ON customer FOR UPDATE AS maxordamt <= 50

ON ERROR  && Restore the system error handler

WAIT WINDOW "Press a key to test trigger with value of 60"+CHR(13);
 +"When you get the error message, press Ignore."
REPLACE maxordamt WITH 60    && Displays an error message
? maxordamt

WAIT WINDOW "Press a key to test with value of 50."
REPLACE maxordamt WITH 50    && Value is accepted
? maxordamt
DELETE TRIGGER ON customer FOR UPDATE  && Remove the trigger
```

See Also

ADD TABLE, AERROR( ), CREATE DATABASE, DELETE TRIGGER, DISPLAY DATABASE, LIST DATABASE, OPEN DATABASE

CREATE VIEW Command

Creates a view file from the Visual FoxPro environment.

Syntax

CREATE VIEW *FileName*

Arguments

FileName
    Specifies the name of the view file to create.

Remarks

CREATE VIEW builds a new view file containing information about the Visual FoxPro environment. SET VIEW restores the environment saved to a view file by CREATE VIEW. View files created with CREATE VIEW are assigned a .vue extension.

The information saved in a view file includes:

- All tables, index, alternate files, and format files currently open in all work areas
- All fields contained in the SET FIELDS list
- All established relations between open tables
- All filters in effect for open tables
- The DEFAULT and PATH settings
- The procedure file setting
- The current Help file
- The current resource file
- The SET SKIP status
- The status bar state (ON or OFF)

View files are useful both in programs and while debugging. Only one command, SET VIEW TO *FileName*, needs to be executed to restore the entire environment. While debugging, the environment settings can be saved in a view file, testing can be performed, and the environment can be restored to continue program execution.

See Also

CREATE SQL VIEW, SET VIEW

CREATEBINARY( ) Function

Converts character type data created in Visual FoxPro to a binary type character string you can pass to an ActiveX control or automation object.

Syntax

CREATEBINARY(*cExpression*)

Returns

Character

Arguments

cExpression
Specifies the character expression for which a binary type character string is returned.

Remarks

Visual FoxPro character strings can contain binary data. However, an ActiveX control or automation object character string (OLE VT_BSTR type data) cannot contain binary data. An ActiveX control or automation object passes binary data to applications such as Visual FoxPro as an array of VT_UI1 type data.

Visual FoxPro automatically converts binary data passed from an ActiveX control or automation object as an array of VT_UI1 type data to a Visual FoxPro character string. Visual FoxPro internally marks this character string as binary data passed from an ActiveX control or automation object. When the character string is passed back to an ActiveX control or automation object, Visual FoxPro automatically converts the character string to an array of VT_UI1 type data the ActiveX control or automation object expects.

Use CREATEBINARY( ) to convert character type data created in Visual FoxPro to a binary type character string you can pass to an ActiveX control or automation object. The minimum number of characters to which CREATEBINARY( ) can be abbreviated is 7.

For more information about ActiveX controls and automation objects, see Chapter 16, "Adding OLE," in the *Microsoft Visual FoxPro 6.0 Programmer's Guide*.

See Also

OLE Bound Control, OLE Container Control

CREATEOBJECT( ) Function

Creates an object from a class definition or an Automation-enabled application.

Syntax

CREATEOBJECT(*ClassName* [, *eParameter1*, *eParameter2*, ...])

Returns

Object

Arguments

ClassName
Specifies the class or OLE object from which the new object is created. Visual FoxPro searches for the class or OLE object in the following order:

1. Visual FoxPro base classes.

2. User-defined class definitions in memory in the order they were loaded.

3. Classes in the current program.

4. Classes in .vcx class libraries opened with SET CLASSLIB.

5. Classes in procedure files opened with SET PROCEDURE.

6. Classes in the Visual FoxPro program execution chain.

7. The OLE registry if SET OLEOBJECT is ON.

OLE objects are created using the following syntax for *ClassName*:

```
ApplicationName.Class
```

For example, to create a Microsoft Excel worksheet (which supports Automation), you can use the following syntax:

```
x = CREATEOBJECT('Excel.Sheet')
```

When this code is run, Microsoft Excel is started (if not already running), and a new worksheet is created.

A class library can have an alias. To specify an object in a class library with an alias, include the class library alias followed by a period and the object name.

Note that *ClassName* cannot be the Visual FoxPro OLE Container control base class.

eParameter1, eParameter2, ...
> These optional parameters are used to pass values to the Init event procedure for the class. The Init event is executed when you issue CREATEOBJECT( ) and allows you to initialize the object.

Remarks

Use CREATEOBJECT( ) to create an object from a class definition or an application that supports Automation, and assign a reference to the object to a system variable or array element.

Before you can create an object from a user-defined class, the user-defined class must first be created with DEFINE CLASS, or it must be available in a .vcx visual class library opened with SET CLASSLIB.

Use = or STORE to assign a reference to the object to a system variable or array element. If an object assigned to a system variable or array element is released, the system variable or array element contains the null value. Use RELEASE to remove the system variable or array element from memory.

Example

The following example uses DEFINE CLASS and CREATEOBJECT( ) to create two custom classes named FormChild and FormGrandChild from the Visual FoxPro Form base class. ACLASS( ) is used to create an array named `gaNewarray` containing the class names, which are then displayed.

```
CLEAR

* Verify current class library setting
cCurClassLib=SET("CLASSLIB")
IF LEN(ALLTRIM(cCurClassLib))=0
   cCurClassLib="None"
ENDIF
```

```
WAIT WINDOW "Current class library is: " + cCurClassLib + CHR(13);
   + "Press any key to continue..."

frmMyForm = CREATEOBJECT("FormGrandChild")

* Create an array
FOR nCount = 1 TO ACLASS(gaNewarray, frmMyForm)
   ? gaNewarray(nCount)  && Display the names of the classes
ENDFOR

RELEASE frmMyForm

* Create FormChild from FORM baseclass
DEFINE CLASS FormChild AS FORM
ENDDEFINE

* Create FormGrandChild from user-defined FormChild class
DEFINE CLASS FormGrandChild AS FormChild
ENDDEFINE
```

See Also

_BROWSER, COMCLASSINFO( ), CREATEOBJECTEX( ), DEFINE CLASS,
GETOBJECT( ), RELEASE, SET CLASSLIB, SET OLEOBJECT

CREATEOBJECTEX( ) Function

Creates an instance of a registered COM object (such as a Visual FoxPro Automation
server) on a remote computer.

Syntax

CREATEOBJECTEX(*cCLSID | cPROGID*, *cComputerName*)

Returns

Object

Arguments

cCLSID | cPROGID

Specifies the CLSID (Class Identifier) or PROGID (Programmatic Identifier) for the
COM object to instantiate. If you include a CLSID, the COM object must be registered
on the remote server you specify with *cComputerName*. If you include a PROGID,
the COM object must be registered on both the your local computer and the remote
computer you specify with *cComputerName*. Attempting to use a PROGID without
first registering the server on your local computer will generate the OLE error Code
0x800401f3, "Invalid Class String."

For Visual FoxPro automation servers created on your local machine, you can use the server object CLSID and PROGID properties to determine the local CLSID and PROGID values.

cComputerName

Specifies the remote computer on which the COM object is instantiated.

If *cComputerName* is the empty string, the COM object is instantiated on the local computer or a redirected machine as specified in the registry. Use Clireg32.exe or Racmgr32.exe to redirect the local machine to another machine through the registry.

cComputerName supports UNC (Universal Naming Convention) names such as "\\myserver" and "myserver," and DNS (Domain Name System) names such as "myserver.com," "www.microsoft.com," and "207.68.137.56."

Remarks

CREATEOBJECTEX( ) returns an object reference to the COM object if it is successfully instantiated. CREATEOBJECTEX( ) cannot be used to instantiate Visual FoxPro classes such as forms — use CREATEOBJECT( ) to instantiate Visual FoxPro classes. Note that you can only abbreviate CREATEOBJECTEX( ) to a minimum of 13 characters, distinguishing it from the CREATEOBJECT( ) function.

CREATEOBJECTEX( ) requires Windows NT 4.0 or later, or Windows 95 with DCOM95 installed.

For additional information about using Visual FoxPro to create Automation servers, see Chapter 16, "Adding OLE," in the *Microsoft Visual FoxPro 6.0 Programmer's Guide*.

See Also

CLSID Property, CREATEOBJECT( ) Function, ProgID Property, Server Object

CREATEOFFLINE( ) Function

Takes an existing view offline.

Syntax

CREATEOFFLINE(*ViewName* [, *cPath*])

Returns

Logical

Arguments

ViewName

Specifies the name of the existing view to take offline. The database containing the existing view must be open before you can take the existing view offline.

cPath
Specifies the directory in which the offline view is placed and the name of the offline view.

Remarks

CREATEOFFLINE( ) returns a logical true (.T.) if the existing view is successfully taken offline; otherwise false (.F.) is returned.

An offline view is opened with USE. When an offline view is open, you can append records or make changes to records in the offline view. However, you cannot use the CREATE TRIGGER, INSERT, PACK or ZAP commands in an offline view. After making changes to the offline view, you can update the data on the server with your changes by opening the offline view with USE and including the ONLINE clause.

You cannot refresh the contents of an offline view with data from the server until the offline view has been opened with USE and the ONLINE clause.

Use DROPOFFLINE( ) to take the offline view back online.

See Also

DROPOFFLINE( ), USE

CTOD( ) Function

Converts a character expression to a date expression.

Syntax

CTOD(*cExpression*)

Returns

Date

Arguments

cExpression
Specifies a character expression for which CTOD( ) returns a Date-type value.

Remarks

Note that CTOD( ) can create ambiguous Date values, and generates a compilation error when SET STRICTDATE is set to 2. Use DATE( ) instead to create nonambiguous Date values. For more information about ambiguous dates, see "Year 2000 Date Support" in Chapter 33, "Programming Improvements," in the *Microsoft Visual FoxPro 6.0 Programmer's Guide*.

See Also

DATE( ), SET STRICTDATE

CTOBIN( ) Function

Converts a binary character representation to an integer value.

Syntax

CTOBIN(*cExpression*)

Returns

Numeric

Arguments

cExpression
Specifies the binary character representation to convert.

Remarks

Use CTOBIN( ) to convert a binary character representation created with BINTOC( ) back to its integer value.

See Also

BINTOC( ) Function

CTOT( ) Function

Returns a DateTime value from a character expression.

Syntax

CTOT(*cCharacterExpression*)

Returns

DateTime

Arguments

cCharacterExpression
Specifies the character expression from which a DateTime value is returned.

Remarks

Note that CTOT( ) can create ambiguous DateTime values, and generates a compilation error when SET STRICTDATE is set to 2. Use DATETIME( ) instead to create nonambiguous Date values. For more information about ambiguous dates, see "Year 2000 Date Support" in Chapter 33, "Programming Improvements," in the *Microsoft Visual FoxPro 6.0 Programmer's Guide*.

See Also

DATETIME( ), SET STRICTDATE

CURDIR( ) Function

Returns the current directory.

Syntax

CURDIR([*cExpression*])

Returns

Character

Arguments

cExpression
Specifies the drive or volume for which CURDIR( ) returns the current directory or folder. If you omit *cExpression*, the current default drive or volume is assumed. The empty string is returned if the drive or volume you specify in *cExpression* doesn't exist. Note that this argument is only included for earlier versions of Visual FoxPro and FoxPro running under Window 3.1 or MS-DOS.

Remarks

CURDIR( ) returns, as a character string, the current MS-DOS directory on a specified drive.

Example

The following example stores the current directory to a variable, sets the default to the directory Visual FoxPro was started in, displays the new directory, returns the default to the original directory, and displays the original directory.

```
CLEAR
? 'Current directory: ', CURDIR( )
gcOldDir = SET('DEFAULT') + SYS(2003)
SET DEFAULT TO (HOME( ))
? 'Visual FoxPro directory: ', CURDIR( )
SET DEFAULT TO (gcOldDir)
? 'Current directory: ', CURDIR( )
```

See Also

FULLPATH( ), HOME( )

_CUROBJ System Variable

Included for backward compatibility. Use the ActiveControl property for new forms instead.

CurrentControl Property

Specifies which control contained in a Column object is used to display the values of the active cell. Available at design time; read/write at run time.

Syntax

Column.CurrentControl[= *cName*]

Arguments

cName

Specifies the name of the control that displays and accepts data for the active cell in a Column object.

Remarks

The default control is a TextBox having Text1 as the Name property. Use the AddObject method to add other controls.

If the Column's Sparse property is set to true (.T.), only the active cell in the Column uses the object specified in the CurrentControl property; the other cells display data using a TextBox. If the Sparse property is set to false (.F.), all cells in the Column use the CurrentControl property to display data.

Note You can add an unlimited number of controls to a Column object using the AddObject method. However, you can set the CurrentControl property for only one control at any given time.

Applies To

Column

See Also

AddObject Method, Bound Property, RemoveObject Method, Sparse Property

CurrentX, CurrentY Properties

Specifies the horizontal (X) and vertical (Y) coordinates for the next drawing method. Not available at design time; read/write at run time.

Syntax

Object.CurrentX[= *nXCoord*]
Object.CurrentY[= *nYCoord*]

Arguments

nXCoord

Specifies the horizontal coordinate of the form, in the unit of measurement specified by the ScaleMode property of the form.

nYCoord
> Specifies the vertical coordinate of the form, in the unit of measurement specified by the ScaleMode property of the form.

Remarks

Coordinates are measured from the upper-left corner of an object. CurrentX is 0 at an object's left edge and CurrentY is 0 at its top edge. Coordinates are expressed in foxels or the current unit of measurement defined by the ScaleMode property.

When you use the following graphics methods, the CurrentX and CurrentY settings are changed as indicated.

Method	CurrentX, CurrentY set to
Box	The endpoint of the box as specified by the last two arguments.
Circle	The center of the object.
Cls	0, 0.
Line	The endpoint of the line.
Print	The next print position.
Pset	The point drawn.

Applies To

Form, _SCREEN

See Also

Box Method, Circle Method, Cls Method, DrawMode Property, DrawStyle Property, Left Property, Line Method, PSet Method, ScaleMode Property, SYS(1270) – Object Location, Top Property

Cursor Object

Created when a table or view is added to the data environment for a form, form set, or report.

Syntax

Cursor

Remarks

The cursor object allows you to specify or determine properties for the table or view when the form, FormSet or report is run.

Note that setting a cursor object property at run time generates an error (with the exception of the Filter and Order properties, which can be set at run time). For a new property setting to take effect, you must call the CloseTables and OpenTables methods for the data environment. Also, if you change the Order property at run time of a cursor that is involved in a one-to-many relationship, the one-to-many relationship is broken.

For more information about the data environment for forms and form sets, see "Setting the Data Environment" in Chapter 9, "Creating Forms," in the *Microsoft Visual FoxPro 6.0 Programmer's Guide*.

For more information about the data environment for reports, see Chapter 12, "Adding Queries and Reports," in the *Microsoft Visual FoxPro 6.0 Programmer's Guide*.

Properties

Alias	Application	BufferModeOverride
CursorSource	Comment	Database
Exclusive	Filter	Name
NoDataOnLoad	Order	ReadOnly
Tag		

Events

Destroy	Error	Init

Methods

AddProperty	ReadExpression	ReadMethod
ResetToDefault	WriteExpression	

See Also

DataEnvironment Object, Relation Object

CURSORGETPROP( ) Function

Returns the current property settings for a Visual FoxPro table or a cursor.

Syntax

CURSORGETPROP(*cProperty* [, *nWorkArea* | *cTableAlias*])

Returns

Character, Numeric, or Logical

Arguments

cProperty
　　Specifies the property setting to return.

The following table includes a list of properties whose settings can be returned, the data type of the return value, and a description of the return value.

cProperty	Type	Description
BatchUpdateCount*	N	The number of update statements sent to the remote data source for buffered tables. 1 is the default. Adjusting this value can greatly increase update performance. Read/Write.
Buffering	N	1 – (Default) Row and table buffering is off. 2 – Pessimistic row buffering is on. 3 – Optimistic row buffering is on. 4 – Pessimistic table buffering is on. 5 – Optimistic table buffering is on. Read/Write.
CompareMemo	L	Contains true (.T.) (default) if memo fields (of type Memo, General, or Picture) are included in the WHERE clause for updates; otherwise, contains false (.F.). For views only. Read/Write.
ConnectHandle	N	The connection handle. This property is valid only when the data source contains a remote table. Read-Only.
ConnectName	C	The named connection used when the cursor is created. This property is valid only when the data source contains a remote table. Read-Only.
Database	C	The name of the database in which the table or view is contained. If a table is a free table, contains the empty string. Read-Only.
FetchAsNeeded	L	Contains true (.T.) if data is fetched as needed; otherwise, contains false (.F.) (default). For views only. Read/Write.
FetchMemo*	L	Contains true (.T.) if memo fields are fetched with the view results; otherwise, contains false (.F.) (default). Read/Write.
FetchSize*	N	The number of rows progressively fetched from the table result set. 100 rows is the default. Setting FetchSize to –1 retrieves the complete result set (limited by the MaxRecords setting). Read/Write.

(continued)

(continued)

cProperty	Type	Description
KeyFieldList	C	Comma delimited list of primary fields for the cursor. Read/Write.
MaxRecords*	N	The maximum number of rows fetched when result sets are returned. The default is –1 (all rows are returned). A value of 0 specifies that the view is executed but no results are fetched. Read/Write.
Prepared	L	Contains true (.T.) if SQL statements are prepared for subsequent REQUERY( ) function calls; otherwise, contains false (.F.) (default). REQUERY( ) is used to retrieve data again for a SQL view. See the SQLPREPARE( ) Function, later in this language reference, for additional information about preparing SQL statements. For views only. Read/Write.
SendUpdates	L	Contains true (.T.) if a SQL update query is sent to update tables when an update is made using the view; otherwise, contains false (.F.) (default). Read/Write.
SourceName	C	Contains the long name for a SQL view or a table in a database, or the file path and table name for a free table. Read-Only.
SourceType	N	1 – Specifies that the data source is a local SQL view. 2 – Specifies that the data source is a remote SQL view. 3 – Specifies that the data source is a table. Read-Only.
SQL	C	The SQL statement executed when the cursor is created. Read-Only.
Tables	C	A comma delimited list of the names of tables. Read/Write.
UpdatableFieldList	C	Comma delimited list of field names and the local field names assigned to the cursor. Use this option to specify valid Visual FoxPro names for fields in the cursor that have invalid Visual FoxPro field names. Read/Write.

(continued)

cProperty	Type	Description
UpdateNameList	C	Comma delimited list of fields in the view. This list can include fields from local and remote tables. Read/Write.
UpdateType	N	1 – Specifies that old data is updated with the new data (the default). 2 – Specifies that updates occur by deleting the old data and inserting the new data. Read/Write.
UseMemoSize*	N	The minimum size (in bytes) for which result columns are returned in memo fields. For example, if the width of a column result is greater than the value of UseMemoSize, the column result is stored in a memo field. UseMemoSize may vary from 1 to 255; the default value is 255. Read/Write.
WhereType	N	The WHERE clause for updates to tables. WhereType may assume the following values: 1 or DB_KEY (from FOXPRO.H). The WHERE clause used to update tables consists of only the primary fields specified with the KeyFieldList property. 2 or DB_KEYANDUPDATABLE (from FOXPRO.H). The WHERE clause used to update tables consists of the primary fields specified with the KeyFieldList property and any updatable fields. 3 or DB_KEYANDMODIFIED (from FOXPRO.H) (default). The WHERE clause used to update tables consists of the primary fields specified with the KeyFieldList property and any other fields that are modified. 4 or DB_KEYANDTIMESTAMP (from FOXPRO.H). The WHERE clause used to update tables consists of the primary fields specified with the KeyFieldList property and a comparison of the time stamps. Read/Write.

* The value returned by this property is significant only for remote views; if you get this property for local views, the CURSORGETPROP function returns the default value.

The following table includes a list of properties whose settings can be returned, the data type of the return value, and a description of the return value.

cProperty	Type	Description
BatchUpdateCount*	N	The number of update statements sent to the remote data source for buffered tables. 1 is the default. Adjusting this value can greatly increase update performance. Read/Write.
Buffering	N	1 – (Default) Row and table buffering is off. 2 – Pessimistic row buffering is on. 3 – Optimistic row buffering is on. 4 – Pessimistic table buffering is on. 5 – Optimistic table buffering is on. Read/Write.
CompareMemo	L	Contains true (.T.) (default) if memo fields (of type Memo, General, or Picture) are included in the WHERE clause for updates; otherwise, contains false (.F.). For views only. Read/Write.
ConnectHandle	N	The connection handle. This property is valid only when the data source contains a remote table. Read-Only.
ConnectName	C	The named connection used when the cursor is created. This property is valid only when the data source contains a remote table. Read-Only.
Database	C	The name of the database in which the table or view is contained. If a table is a free table, contains the empty string. Read-Only.
FetchAsNeeded	L	Contains true (.T.) if data is fetched as needed; otherwise, contains false (.F.) (default). For views only. Read/Write.
FetchMemo*	L	Contains true (.T.) if memo fields are fetched with the view results; otherwise, contains false (.F.) (default). Read/Write.
FetchSize*	N	The number of rows progressively fetched from the table result set. 100 rows is the default. Setting FetchSize to –1 retrieves the complete result set (limited by the MaxRecords setting). Read/Write.
KeyFieldList	C	Comma delimited list of primary fields for the cursor. Read/Write.

(continued)

cProperty	Type	Description
MaxRecords*	N	The maximum number of rows fetched when result sets are returned. The default is –1 (all rows are returned). A value of 0 specifies that the view is executed but no results are fetched. Read/Write.
Prepared	L	Contains true (.T.) if SQL statements are prepared for subsequent REQUERY( ) function calls; otherwise, contains false (.F.) (default). REQUERY( ) is used to retrieve data again for a SQL view. See the SQLPREPARE( ) Function, later in this language reference, for additional information about preparing SQL statements. For views only. Read/Write.
SendUpdates	L	Contains true (.T.) if a SQL update query is sent to update tables when an update is made using the view; otherwise, contains false (.F.) (default). Read/Write.
SourceName	C	Contains the long name for a SQL view or a table in a database, or the file path and table name for a free table. Read-Only.
SourceType	N	1 – Specifies that the data source is a local SQL view. 2 – Specifies that the data source is a remote SQL view. 3 – Specifies that the data source is a table. Read-Only.
SQL	C	The SQL statement executed when the cursor is created. Read-Only.
Tables	C	A comma delimited list of the names of tables. Read/Write.
UpdatableFieldList	C	Comma delimited list of field names and the local field names assigned to the cursor. Use this option to specify valid Visual FoxPro names for fields in the cursor that have invalid Visual FoxPro field names. Read/Write.
UpdateNameList	C	Comma delimited list of fields in the view. This list can include fields from local and remote tables. Read/Write.

(continued)

(continued)

cProperty	Type	Description
UpdateType	N	1 – Specifies that old data is updated with the new data (the default). 2 – Specifies that updates occur by deleting the old data and inserting the new data. Read/Write.
UseMemoSize*	N	The minimum size (in bytes) for which result columns are returned in memo fields. For example, if the width of a column result is greater than the value of UseMemoSize, the column result is stored in a memo field. UseMemoSize may vary from 1 to 255; the default value is 255. Read/Write.
WhereType	N	The WHERE clause for updates to tables. WhereType may assume the following values:
		1 or DB_KEY (from FOXPRO.H). The WHERE clause used to update tables consists of only the primary fields specified with the KeyFieldList property.
		2 or DB_KEYANDUPDATABLE (from FOXPRO.H). The WHERE clause used to update tables consists of the primary fields specified with the KeyFieldList property and any updatable fields.
		3 or DB_KEYANDMODIFIED (from FOXPRO.H) (default). The WHERE clause used to update tables consists of the primary fields specified with the KeyFieldList property and any other fields that are modified.
		4 or DB_KEYANDTIMESTAMP (from FOXPRO.H). The WHERE clause used to update tables consists of the primary fields specified with the KeyFieldList property and a comparison of the time stamps.
		Read/Write.

* The value returned by this property is significant only for remote views; if you get this property for local views, the CURSORGETPROP function returns the default value.

nWorkArea

Specifies the work area of the table or cursor from which the property setting is returned. If you specify 0 for *nWorkArea*, CURSORGETPROP( ) returns the environment setting.

cTableAlias

Specifies the alias of the table or cursor from which the property setting is returned.

Remarks

Use CURSORSETPROP( ) to set a specific property for a Visual FoxPro table or a cursor. See the following function, CURSORSETPROP( ), for additional information about each of the properties and their settings.

The current property settings are returned for the table or cursor open in the currently selected work area if CURSORGETPROP( ) is issued without the optional *cTableAlias* or *nWorkArea* arguments.

Example

The following example opens the `customer` table in the `testdata` database. CURSORGETPROP( ) is then used to display the buffering mode for the table and the name of the database in which the table is contained.

```
CLOSE DATABASES
CLEAR

OPEN DATABASE (HOME(2) + 'data\testdata')
USE customer      && Open customer table

? CURSORGETPROP("Buffering") && Displays buffering mode
? CURSORGETPROP("Database")  && Displays database name
```

See Also

CURSORSETPROP( ), SQLGETPROP( ), SQLSETPROP( )

CURSORSETPROP( ) Function

Specifies property settings for a Visual FoxPro table or a cursor.

Syntax

CURSORSETPROP(*cProperty* [, *eExpression*] [, *cTableAlias* | *nWorkArea*])

Returns

Logical

Arguments

cProperty
  Specifies the table or cursor property to set. Note that Buffering is the only property you can specify for a Visual FoxPro table.

eExpression
  Specifies the value for the property you specify with *cProperty*. If you omit *eExpression*, the property is set to its default value.

The following table lists the properties you can specify for *cProperty* and a description of the values *eExpression* can assume.

Property	*eExpression* values
BatchUpdateCount*	The number of update statements sent to the remote data source for buffered tables. 1 is the default. Adjusting this value can greatly increase update performance.
Buffering	1 – Sets row and table buffering off. Record locking and data writing are identical to earlier FoxPro versions. (the default). 2 – Sets pessimistic row buffering on. 3 – Sets optimistic row buffering on. 4 – Sets pessimistic table buffering on. 5 – Sets optimistic table buffering on. SET MULTILOCKS must be ON for all Buffering modes except 1 (off).
CompareMemo	.T. – Memo fields (of type Memo, General, or Picture) are included in the WHERE clause for updates. .F. – Memo fields are not included in the WHERE clause for updates.
FetchAsNeeded	.T. – Records are fetched as needed. .F. – For remote views, the number of records fetched is determined by the MaxRecord property. For local views, all records are fetched.
FetchMemo*	.T. – Memo fields are fetched with the view results. .F. – Memo fields are not fetched with the view results.
FetchSize*	Number of rows progressively fetched from the remote table result set. The default is 100 rows. Setting FetchSize to –1 retrieves the complete result set (limited by the MaxRecords setting).
KeyFieldList	Comma delimited list of primary fields for the cursor. No default. You must include a list of field names for updates to work.
MaxRecords*	The maximum number of rows fetched when result sets are returned. The default is –1 (all rows are returned). A value of 0 specifies that the view is executed but no results are fetched.
Prepared	Specify true (.T.) to prepare SQL statements for subsequent REQUERY( ) function calls. REQUERY( ) is used to retrieve data again for a SQL view. See the SQLPREPARE( ) Function, later in this language reference, for additional information about preparing SQL statements. The default is false (.F.).
SendUpdates	.T. – Specifies that a SQL update query is sent to update tables when an update is made using the view. .F. – Specifies that a SQL update query is not sent to update tables.
Tables	Comma delimited list of the names of remote tables. No default. You must include a list of table names for updates to work.

(continued)

Property	*eExpression* values
UpdatableFieldList	Comma delimited list of remote field names and the local field names assigned to the cursor. Use this option to specify valid Visual FoxPro names for fields in the cursor that have invalid Visual FoxPro field names.
UpdateNameList	Comma delimited list of fields in the view. This list can include fields from local and remote tables. You must include a list of fields for updates to work.
UpdateType	1 – Specifies that old data is updated with the new data (the default). 2 – Specifies that updates occur by deleting the old data and inserting the new data.
UseMemoSize*	Specifies the minimum size (in bytes) for which result columns are returned in memo fields. For example, if the width of a column result is greater than the value of UseMemoSize, the column result is stored in a memo field. UseMemoSize may vary from 1 to 255; the default value is 255.
WhereType	The WHERE clause for updates to remote tables. WhereType may assume the following values: 1 or DB_KEY (from FOXPRO.H). The WHERE clause used to update remote tables consists of only the primary fields specified with the KeyFieldList property. 2 or DB_KEYANDUPDATABLE (from FOXPRO.H). The WHERE clause used to update remote tables consists of the primary fields specified with the KeyFieldList property and any updatable fields. 3 or DB_KEYANDMODIFIED (from FOXPRO.H) (default). The WHERE clause used to update remote tables consists of the primary fields specified with the KeyFieldList property and any other fields that are modified. 4 or DB_KEYANDTIMESTAMP (from FOXPRO.H). The WHERE clause used to update remote tables consists of the primary fields specified with the KeyFieldList property and a comparison of the time stamps.

* This property is primarily used for remote views; setting it has no effect on local views. However, you can preset this property for local views that will be upsized.

cTableAlias
Specifies the alias of the table or cursor for which the property is set.

nWorkArea
Specifies the work area of the table or cursor for which the property is set. If you specify 0 for *nWorkArea*, CURSORSETPROP( ) sets the environment setting used for all subsequent tables or cursors.

Remarks

CURSORSETPROP( ) returns true (.T.) if Visual FoxPro successfully sets the property you specify. Visual FoxPro generates an error if the property you specify cannot be set.

The setting of the CURSORSETPROP( ) Buffering property determines how Visual FoxPro performs record locking and update buffering. For additional information on record locking and update buffering, see "Buffering Data" in Chapter 17, "Programming for Shared Access," in the *Microsoft Visual FoxPro 6.0 Programmer's Guide*.

The setting of the CURSORSETPROP( ) WhereType property determines how updates are performed on remote tables. For additional information about remote table updates, see Chapter 6, "Creating Databases," in the *Microsoft Visual FoxPro 6.0 Programmer's Guide*.

You can use CURSORSETPROP( ) to override the FetchSize SQLSETPROP( ) property for a cursor. This property is inherited from the cursor's connection handle by default.

Use CURSORGETPROP( ) to return the current property settings for a Visual FoxPro table or a cursor created for a table.

The property setting is specified for the table or cursor open in the currently selected work area if CURSORSETPROP( ) is issued without the optional *cTableAlias* or *nWorkArea* arguments.

Example

The following example demonstrates how you can enable optimistic table buffering with CURSORSETPROP( ). MULTILOCKS is set to ON, a requirement for table buffering. The customer table in the testdata database is opened, and CURSORSETPROP( ) is then used to set the buffering mode to optimistic table buffering (5). A message box is displayed showing the result of the operation.

```
CLOSE DATABASES
CLEAR

SET MULTILOCKS ON
OPEN DATABASE (HOME(2) + 'data\testdata')
USE customer      && Open customer table

* Set buffering mode and store logical result
lSuccess=CURSORSETPROP("Buffering", 5, "customer")
IF lSuccess = .T.
   =MESSAGEBOX("Operation successful!",0,"Operation Status")
ELSE
   =MESSAGEBOX("Operation NOT successful!",0,"Operation Status")
ENDIF
```

See Also

CURSORGETPROP( ), SET MULTILOCKS, SQLGETPROP( ), SQLSETPROP( )

CursorSource Property

Specifies the name of the table or view associated with a Cursor object. Read-only at design time; read/write at run time.

Syntax

DataEnvironment.Cursor.CursorSource[= *cText*]

Arguments

cText

For views, specifies the name of the view in a database. For tables in a database, specifies the long table name. For free tables, specifies the full path to the free table.

Applies To

Cursor Object

See Also

Database Property

CURVAL( ) Function

Returns field values directly from disk for a table or a remote data source.

Syntax

CURVAL(*cExpression* [, *cTableAlias* | *nWorkArea*])

Returns

Character, Currency, Date, DateTime, Double, Float, Logical, Numeric, or Memo

Arguments

cExpression

Specifies an expression whose value CURVAL( ) returns from a table or a remote data source. *cExpression* is typically a field or an expression consisting of a set of fields from the table or remote data source.

cTableAlias

Specifies the alias of the table from which the field values are returned from disk for a table or a remote data source.

nWorkArea

Specifies the work area of the table from which the field values are returned from disk for a table or a remote data source.

Remarks

The field values returned by CURVAL( ) and OLDVAL( ) can be compared to determine if another user on a network changed the field values while the fields were being edited. CURVAL( ) and OLDVAL( ) can only return different values when optimistic row or table buffering is enabled. Optimistic row or table buffering is enabled with CURSORSETPROP( ).

> **Note** If you are working with a view in a multiuser environment, the values returned by CURVAL( ) might not be up to date unless you call the REFRESH( ) function first. Data returned by a view is buffered, and the CURVAL( ) function reads values from the buffer. However, if other users have changed data in the underlying tables for the view, the buffered data is not updated until the REFRESH( ) function is called.

CURVAL( ) returns field values for the current record, and the return value data type is determined by the expression you specify with *cExpression*.

The value is returned for the table or cursor open in the currently selected work area if CURVAL( ) is issued without the optional *cTableAlias* or *nWorkArea* arguments.

Example

This example creates a free table named mytable, and a value of "One" is inserted into the cDigit field. Optimistic table buffering is enabled with SET MULTILOCKS ON and CURSORSETPROP( ).

A value of "Two" is then inserted into the cDigit field, and CURVAL( ) and OLDVAL( ) are used to display the original cDigit values. TABLEUPDATE( ) is used to commit the changes to the table, and CURVAL( ) and OLDVAL( ) are used to display the new cDigit values. Note that because this is a single user example, CURVAL( ) and OLDVAL( ) return the identical values.

```
CLOSE DATABASES
CLEAR

CREATE TABLE mytable FREE (cDigit C(10))
* Store original value
INSERT INTO mytable (cDigit) VALUES ("One")
SET MULTILOCKS ON        && Allow optimistic table buffering
= CURSORSETPROP("Buffering",5)   && Optimistic table buffering on
REPLACE cDigit WITH "Two"    && New value

? "Current value: " + CURVAL("cDigit", "mytable")
? "Old value: " + OLDVAL("cDigit", "mytable")
= TABLEUPDATE(.T.)        && Commit changes made to table
? "Table changes committed"
? "New current value: " + CURVAL("cDigit", "mytable")
? "New old value: " + OLDVAL("cDigit", "mytable")
```

See Also

GETFLDSTATE( ), OLDVAL( ), TABLEREVERT( ), TABLEUPDATE( ),
CURSORSETPROP( )

Curvature Property

Specifies the curvature of a Shape control's corners. Available at design time and run time.

Syntax

Shape.Curvature[= *nCurve*]

Arguments

nCurve

The settings for the Curvature property are:

Setting	Description
0	Specifies no curvature, creating square corners.
1 through 98	Specifies progressively rounded corners. A higher number increases the curvature.
99	Specifies maximum curvature and creates a circle or ellipse.

Example

The following example demonstrates how the Curvature property can be used with the Shape control to display a circle, ellipse, or square on a form.

A form is created, and a set of option buttons and a command button are placed on the form. When you click one of the option buttons, the corresponding shape is displayed on the form. The Height, Width, and Curvature properties of each shape determine the type of shape (circle, ellipse, or square) created. The Curvature property is set to 99 to create the circle and ellipse.

```
frmMyForm = CREATEOBJECT('Form')  && Create a Form
frmMyForm.Closable = .F.  && Disable the Control menu box

frmMyForm.AddObject('cmdCommand1','cmdMyCmndBtn')  && Add Command button
frmMyForm.AddObject('opgOptionGroup1','opgMyOptGrp') && Add Option Group
frmMyForm.AddObject('shpCircle1','shpMyCircle')  && Add Circle Shape
frmMyForm.AddObject('shpEllipse1','shpMyEllipse')  && Add Ellipse Shape
frmMyForm.AddObject('shpSquare','shpMySquare')  && Add Box Shape

frmMyForm.cmdCommand1.Visible =.T.  && "Quit" Command button visible

frmMyForm.opgOptionGroup1.Buttons(1).Caption = "\<Circle"
frmMyForm.opgOptionGroup1.Buttons(2).Caption = "\<Ellipse"
frmMyForm.opgOptionGroup1.Buttons(3).Caption = "\<Square"
```

```
frmMyForm.opgOptionGroup1.SetAll("Width", 100) && Set Option group width
frmMyForm.opgOptionGroup1.Visible = .T.  && Option Group visible
frmMyForm.opgOptionGroup1.Click  && Show the circle

frmMyForm.SHOW  && Display the form
READ EVENTS  && Start event processing

DEFINE CLASS opgMyOptGrp AS OptionGroup  && Create an Option Group
    ButtonCount = 3  && Three Option buttons
    Top = 10
    Left = 10
    Height = 75
    Width = 100

    PROCEDURE Click
        ThisForm.shpCircle1.Visible = .F.  && Hide the circle
        ThisForm.shpEllipse1.Visible = .F.  && Hide the ellipse
        ThisForm.shpSquare.Visible = .F.  && Hide the square

        DO CASE
           CASE ThisForm.opgOptionGroup1.Value = 1
              ThisForm.shpCircle1.Visible = .T. && Show the circle
           CASE ThisForm.opgOptionGroup1.Value = 2
              ThisForm.shpEllipse1.Visible = .T.  && Show the ellipse
           CASE ThisForm.opgOptionGroup1.Value = 3
              ThisForm.shpSquare.Visible = .T.  && Show the square
        ENDCASE
ENDDEFINE

DEFINE CLASS cmdMyCmndBtn AS CommandButton  && Create Command button
    Caption = '\<Quit'  && Caption on the Command button
    Cancel = .T.  && Default Cancel Command button (Esc)
    Left = 125  && Command button column
    Top = 210  && Command button row
    Height = 25  && Command button height

    PROCEDURE Click
        CLEAR EVENTS  && Stop event processing, close Form
ENDDEFINE

DEFINE CLASS shpMyCircle AS SHAPE  && Create a circle
    Top = 10
    Left = 200
    Width = 100
    Height = 100
    Curvature = 99
    BackColor = RGB(255,0,0)  && Red
ENDDEFINE
```

```
DEFINE CLASS shpMyEllipse AS SHAPE  && Create an ellipse
   Top = 35
   Left = 200
   Width = 100
   Height = 50
   Curvature = 99
   BackColor = RGB(0,128,0)  && Green
ENDDEFINE

DEFINE CLASS shpMySquare AS SHAPE  && Create a square
   Top = 10
   Left = 200
   Width = 100
   Height = 100
   Curvature = 0
   BackColor = RGB(0,0,255)  && Blue
ENDDEFINE
```

Applies To

Shape

See Also

Shape Control

Custom Object

Creates a custom, user-defined object.

Syntax

Custom

Remarks

A custom, user-defined class can be created with DEFINE CLASS, or with the Class Designer. Issue CREATE CLASS to display the class designer.

Custom, user-defined classes are classes with properties, events, and methods, but with no visual representation. The same general rules that apply to defining other types of classes apply to defining custom classes.

See Chapter 3, "Object-Oriented Programming," in the *Microsoft Visual FoxPro 6.0 Programmer's Guide* for additional information about creating custom objects as non-visual classes.

Properties

Application	BaseClass	Class
ClassLibrary	Comment	ControlCount
Controls	Height	HelpContextID
Left	Name	Object
Parent	ParentClass	Picture
Tag	Top	WhatsThisHelpID
Width		

Events

Destroy	Error	Init

Methods

AddObject	AddProperty	NewObject
ReadExpression	ReadMethod	RemoveObject
ResetToDefault	SaveAsClass	ShowWhatsThis
WriteExpression Method	WriteMethod Method	

See Also

CREATE CLASS, CREATE FORM, DEFINE CLASS

Database Property

Specifies the path to the database that contains the table or view associated with the Cursor object. Read-only at design time; read/write at run time.

Syntax

DataEnvironment.Cursor.Database[= *cPath*]

Arguments

cPath
Specifies the full path to the database (.dbc) file.

Remarks

Note   When the Cursor object is accessed using CURSORSETPROP( ), the Database property is read-only at run time.

If the Cursor is based on a free table, this property returns an empty string ("").

Applies To

Cursor

See Also

CursorSource Property

DataEnvironment Object

Created when a form, form set, or report is created.

Syntax

DataEnvironment

Remarks

The DataEnvironment object is a container object for the Cursor and Relation objects associated with the form, form set, or report.

Note that setting a DataEnvironment object property at run time generates an error. For a new property setting to take effect, you must call the CloseTables and OpenTables methods for the DataEnvironment object.

For more information about the data environment for forms and form sets, see Chapter 9, "Creating Forms," in the *Microsoft Visual FoxPro 6.0 Programmer's Guide*.

For more information about the data environment for reports, see Chapter 12, "Adding Queries and Reports," in the *Microsoft Visual FoxPro 6.0 Programmer's Guide*.

Properties

Application	AutoCloseTables	AutoOpenTables
Comment	InitialSelectedAlias	Name
OpenViews	Tag	

Events

AfterCloseTables	BeforeOpenTables	Destroy
Error	Init	

Methods

AddObject	AddProperty	CloseTables
OpenTables	ReadExpression	ReadMethod
RemoveObject	ResetToDefault	SaveAsClass
WriteExpression		

See Also

Cursor Object, Relation Object

DataEnvironment Property

Provides a reference to the object's data environment. Read-only at design time and run time.

Syntax

Object.DataEnvironment

Applies To

Form, FormSet

See Also

DataEnvironment Object

DataObject Object

Container for data being transferred from an OLE drag source to an OLE drop target. Available at run time only.

Syntax

oDataObject

Remarks

The DataObject object is a container for data being transferred from an OLE drag source to an OLE drop target, and exists only for the duration of an OLE drag-and-drop event. The DataObject object cannot be created programmatically and references to it become invalid once the OLE drag-and-drop operation is complete. The DataObject is passed as the oDataObject parameter in the OLEDragDrop, OLEDragOver, OLESetData, and OLEStartDrag events.

The DataObject can store multiple sets of data, each in a different format. Use the GetFormat and GetData methods to determine the data formats and data on the DataObject. Use the SetFormat, SetData, or ClearData methods to add data formats and data to the DataObject, or clear all data formats and data from the DataObject.

Methods

ClearData	GetData	GetFormat
SetData	SetFormat	

See Also

OLE Drag-and-Drop Overview, OLEDragDrop Event, OLEDragOver Event, OLESetData
Event, OLEStartDrag Event

DataSession Property

Specifies whether a form, form set, or toolbar can run in its own data session and has a
separate data environment. Available at design time; read-only at run time.

Syntax

Object.DataSession[= *nSession*]

Arguments

nSession

The settings for the DataSession property are:

Setting	Description
1	(Default) Default data session.
2	Private data session. Creates a new data session for each instance of the form, form set, or toolbar that is created.

Applies To

Form, FormSet, _SCREEN, ToolBar

See Also

DataSessionID Property

DataSessionID Property

Returns the data session ID that identifies the private data session for the form set, form,
or toolbar. Read-only at design time; read/write at run time.

If the DataSession property of the form, form set, or toolbar is set to 1 (Default Data
Session), returns the default data session ID.

Syntax

Object.DataSessionID

Remarks

Available only if the form set, form, or toolbar's DataSession property is set to 2
(Private data session).

You can use SET DATASESSION with the DataSessionID property to change data
sessions.

When you set DataSessionID, the setting affects the working data session for the object and all the objects it contains. The DataSessionID property setting does not affect noncontained objects or objects created using CREATEOBJECT( ).

Changing the DataSessionID property setting increments the reference count of the data session changed to and decrements the reference count of the data session changed from. However, if a data session is created by setting the DataSession property to 2 (Private data session), changing the DataSessionID property setting does not release the initial data session. In such case, the object must be released to free the initial session.

For more information on multiple data sessions, see Chapter 17, "Programming for Shared Access," in the *Microsoft Visual FoxPro 6.0 Programmer's Guide*.

Caution   Changing the DataSessionID property setting of an object that contains data-bound controls causes the controls to lose their original data sources. In general, use DataSessionID on objects that do not contain data-bound controls.

Applies To

Form, FormSet, _SCREEN, ToolBar

See Also

CREATEOBJECT( ), DataSession Property, SET DATASESSION

DataToClip Method

Copies a set of records as text to the Clipboard.

Syntax

ApplicationObject.DataToClip([*nWorkArea* | *cTableAlias*]
[, *nRecords*] [, *nClipFormat*])

Arguments

nWorkArea
Specifies the work area number of the table for which records are copied to the Clipboard. If you omit *cTableAlias* and *nWorkArea*, records are copied to the Clipboard for the table open in the current work area.

cTableAlias
Specifies the alias of the table for which the records are copied to the Clipboard.

nRecords
Specifies the number of records copied to the Clipboard. If *nRecords* is greater than the number of remaining records in the table, all the remaining records are copied to the Clipboard. If *nRecords* and *nClipFormat* are omitted, the current record and all remaining records are copied to the Clipboard.

nClipFormat

Specifies how fields are delimited. The settings for *nClipFormat* are:

nClipFormat	Description
1	(Default) Fields delimited with spaces
3	Fields delimited with tabs

If *nClipFormat* is omitted, fields are delimited with spaces.

Remarks

The field names appear as the first line of the text copied to the Clipboard, followed by a separate line for each record.

Applies To

Application Object, _VFP System Variable

See Also

Eval Method, SetVar Method

DATE( ) Function

Returns the current system date, which is controlled by the operating system, or creates a year 2000-compliant Date value.

Syntax

DATE([*nYear*, *nMonth*, *nDay*])

Returns

Date

Arguments

nYear

Specifies the year returned in the year 2000-compliant Date value. *nYear* can be a value from 100 to 9999.

nMonth

Specifies the month returned in the year 2000-compliant Date value. *nMonth* can be a value from 1 to 12.

nDay

Specifies the day returned in the year 2000-compliant Date value. *nDay* can be a value from 1 to 31.

Remarks

DATE( ) returns the current system date if it is issued without the optional arguments. Include the optional arguments to return a year 2000-compliant Date value. For more information about creating year 2000-compliant Date values, see "Year 2000 Date Support" in Chapter 33, "Programming Improvements," in the *Microsoft Visual FoxPro 6.0 Programmer's Guide*.

No Microsoft Visual FoxPro commands or functions can directly change the system date.

Example

The following example displays the current system date with and without the century, and then displays a year 2000-compliant date.

```
CLEAR
SET CENTURY OFF
? DATE( )  && Displays today's date without the century
SET CENTURY ON
? DATE( )  && Displays today's date with the century
? DATE(1998, 02, 16)  && Displays a year 2000-compliant Date value
```

See Also

CTOD( ), DATETIME( ), DTOC( ), SET CENTURY, SET DATE, SET MARK TO, SYS( ) Functions Overview

DateFormat Property

Specifies the format for Date and DateTime values displayed in a text box. Available at design time and run time.

Syntax

Object.DateFormat[= *nValue*]

Arguments

nValue
One of the following settings:

Setting	Description	Format
0	(Default) The displayed date format is determined by the setting of SET DATE.	Determined by SET DATE
1	American	mm/dd/yy

(continued)

Setting	Description	Format
2	ANSI	yy.mm.dd
3	British	dd/mm/yy
4	Italian	dd-mm-yy
5	French	dd/mm/yy
6	German	dd.mm.yy
7	Japan	yy/mm/dd
8	Taiwan	yy/mm/dd
9	USA	mm-dd-yy
10	MDY	mm/dd/yy
11	DMY	dd/mm/yy
12	YMD	yy/mm/dd
13	Short	Determined by the Windows Control Panel short date setting
14	Long	Determined by the Windows Control Panel long date setting

Remarks

A Date or DateTime value displayed in a text box may be displayed in a different format when the text box does not have the focus. Certain short and long date formats that you can specify in the Windows Control Panel do not correspond to valid Visual FoxPro formats, and are displayed in a default format.

The Format property overrides the DateFormat property when the YS, YL, E, or D settings are specified for the Format property.

Applies To

TextBox

See Also

Century Property, DateMark Property, Hours Property, Seconds Property, SET DATE, StrictDateEntry Property

DateMark Property

Specifies the delimiter for Date and DateTime values displayed in a text box. Available at design time and run time.

Syntax

Object.DateMark[= *cDateMarkCharacter*]

Arguments

cDateMarkCharacter

Specifies the Date and DateTime value delimiter. If *cDateMarkCharacter* is the empty string, the delimiter is determined by the setting of SET MARK. If *cDateMarkCharacter* is a space, the delimiter for the current setting of the text box's DateFormat property is used.

In the Properties window, use the = command to specify the empty string (= "") or a space (= " ") for the DateMark property.

Remarks

The DateMark property setting is ignored if the DateFormat property is set to Short or Long.

Applies To

TextBox

See Also

Century Property, DateFormat Property, Hours Property, Seconds Property, SET MARK TO, StrictDateEntry Property

DATETIME( ) Function

Returns the current date and time as a DateTime value, or creates a year 2000-compliant DateTime value.

Syntax

DATETIME([*nYear, nMonth, nDay* [, *nHours* [, *nMinutes* [, *nSeconds*]]]])

Returns

DateTime

Arguments

nYear

Specifies the year returned in the year 2000-compliant DateTime value. *nYear* can be a value from 100 to 9999.

nMonth

Specifies the month returned in the year 2000-compliant DateTime value. *nMonth* can be a value from 1 to 12.

nDay

Specifies the day returned in the year 2000-compliant DateTime value. *nDay* can be a value from 1 to 31.

nHours

Specifies the hours returned in the year 2000-compliant DateTime value. *nHours* can be a value from 0 (midnight) to 23 (11 P.M). Defaults to 0 if omitted.

nMinutes

Specifies the minutes returned in the year 2000-compliant DateTime value. *nMinutes* can be a value from 0 to 59. Defaults to 0 if omitted.

nSeconds

Specifies the seconds returned in the year 2000-compliant DateTime value. *nSeconds* can be a value from 0 to 59. Defaults to 0 if omitted.

Remarks

DATETIME( ) returns the current system DateTime if it is issued without the optional arguments.

Include the optional arguments to return a year 2000-compliant DateTime value. For more information about creating year 2000-compliant DateTimes, see "Year 2000 Date Support" in Chapter 33, "Programming Improvements," in the *Microsoft Visual FoxPro 6.0 Programmer's Guide*.

Example

This first example stores the Datetime for the New Year to a variable named `tNewyear`, and stores the current Datetime to a variable named `tToday`. The number of seconds between the current Datetime and the New Year is then displayed.

The second example uses DATETIME( ) to create a year 2000-compliant DateTime value.

```
tNewyear = DATETIME(YEAR(DATE( ) ) + 1, 1, 1)  && Next New Year
tToday = DATETIME( )
nSecondstonewyear = tNewyear - tToday
CLEAR
? "There are " + ALLTRIM (STR(nSecondstonewyear)) ;
  + " seconds to the next New Year."
```

```
CLEAR
SET CENTURY ON
SET DATE TO AMERICAN
? DATETIME(1998, 02, 16, 12, 34, 56) && Displays 02/16/1998 12:34:56 PM
```

See Also

CTOT( ), DATE( ), DTOT( ) HOUR( ), SEC( ), SECONDS( ), SET SECONDS, SET SYSFORMATS, TIME( ), TTOC( ), TTOD( )

DAY( ) Function

Returns the numeric day of the month for a given Date or DateTime expression.

Syntax

DAY(*dExpression* | *tExpression*)

Returns

Numeric

Arguments

dExpression

Specifies a date from which DAY( ) returns a day of the month. *dExpression* can be a date literal, a Date-type variable, an array element, or a date field.

tExpression

Specifies a date or time from which DAY( ) returns a day of the month. *dExpression* can be a DateTime literal, a DateTime-type variable, an array element, or a DateTime field.

Remarks

DAY( ) returns a number from 1 through 31.

Example

```
STORE {^1998-03-05} TO gdBDate

CLEAR
? CDOW(gdBDate)  && Displays Thursday
? DAY(gdBDate) && Displays 5
? 'That date is ', CMONTH(gdBDate), STR(DAY(gdBDate),2)
```

See Also

CDOW( ), DOW( ), SET FDOW, SET FWEEK, SYS( ) Functions Overview

DBC( ) Function

Returns the name and path of the current database.

Syntax

DBC( )

Returns

Character

Remarks

DBC( ) returns the empty string if there is no current database.

Use SET DATABASE to specify the current database.

Example

The following example opens the testdata database and uses DBC( ) to display information about the database.

```
CLOSE DATABASES
OPEN DATABASE (HOME(2) + 'data\testdata')  && Opens the DBC.

CLEAR
? DBC( )  && Displays the path and name of the database
```

See Also

ADD TABLE, CLOSE DATABASES, CREATE DATABASE, DISPLAY TABLES, OPEN DATABASE, REMOVE TABLE, SET DATABASE

DBF( ) Function

Returns the name of a table open in a specified work area or a table name from a table alias.

Syntax

DBF([*cTableAlias* | *nWorkArea*])

Returns

Character

Arguments

cTableAlias
    Specifies the table alias.

nWorkArea

Specifies the work area number.

If you omit *cTableAlias* and *nWorkArea*, DBF( ) returns the name of the table open in the current work area. DBF( ) returns an empty string if a table isn't open in the work area you specify. If a table doesn't have the alias you specify with *cTableAlias*, Visual FoxPro generates an error message.

For information on creating an alias for a table, see the USE Command, later in this language reference.

Remarks

When SET FULLPATH is ON, DBF( ) returns the path to the table with the table name. When SET FULLPATH is OFF, DBF( ) returns the drive on which the table resides with the table name.

Example

The following example returns the name of a table from its work area and its alias, and returns the empty string after all tables have been closed.

```
CLOSE DATABASES
OPEN DATABASE (HOME(2) + 'Data\testdata')
USE customer IN 2 ALIAS mycust
CLEAR
? DBF(2)  && Displays customer.dbf with its path
? DBF('mycust')  && Displays customer.dbf with its path
CLOSE DATABASES
? DBF( )      && Displays the empty string
```

See Also

CDX( ), FIELD( ), NDX( ), SET FULLPATH, USE

DBGETPROP( ) Function

Returns a property for the current database or for fields, named connections, tables, or views in the current database.

Syntax

DBGETPROP(*cName*, *cType*, *cProperty*)

Returns

Character, Numeric, or Logical

Arguments

cName

Specifies the name of the database, field, named connection, table, or view for which DBGETPROP( ) returns information.

To return information about a field in a table or a view, preface the name of the field with the name of the table or view containing the field. For example, to return information about the `custid` field in the `customer` table, specify the following for *cName*:

```
customer.custid
```

cType

Specifies whether *cName* is the current database, or a field, named connection, table, or view in the current database. The following table lists the values you can specify for *cType*:

cType	Description
CONNECTION	*cName* is a named connection in the current database.
DATABASE	*cName* is the current database.
FIELD	*cName* is a field in the current database.
TABLE	*cName* is a table in the current database.
VIEW	*cName* is a view in the current database.

cProperty

Specifies the name of the property for which DBGETPROP( ) returns information.

The following tables list the values you can specify for *cProperty*, the return value types, and descriptions of each property. Each description includes the read and write privileges for each property. If a property is read-only, its value cannot be changed with DBSETPROP( ). For more information about changing property values, see the DBSETPROP( ) Function, later in this language reference.

Connection properties

cProperty	Type	Description
Asynchronous	L	The connection mode.
		(Default) False (.F.) specifies a synchronous connection.
		True (.T.) specifies an asynchronous connection.
		Read/Write.
BatchMode	L	The batch processing mode.
		(Default) True (.T.) specifies the connection that operates in batch mode.
		Read/Write.

(continued)

Connection properties *(continued)*

cProperty	Type	Description
Comment	C	The text of the connection comment.
		Read/Write.
ConnectString	C	The login connection string.
		Read/Write.
ConnectTimeout	N	The connection timeout interval in seconds. The default is 0 (wait indefinitely).
		Read/Write.
Database	C	The name of the server database specified with the DATABASE clause in the CREATE CONNECTION command or in the Connection Designer.
		Read/Write.
DataSource	C	The name of the data source as defined in the Odbc.ini file.
		Read/Write.
DispLogin	N	Contains a numeric value that determines when the ODBC Login dialog box is displayed. DispLogin may assume the following values:
		1 or DB_PROMPTCOMPLETE (from Foxpro.h).
		1 is the default.
		2 or DB_PROMPTALWAYS (from Foxpro.h).
		3 or DB_PROMPTNEVER (from Foxpro.h).
		If 1 or DB_PROMPTCOMPLETE is specified, Microsoft Visual FoxPro displays the ODBC Login dialog box only if any required information is missing.
		If 2 or DB_PROMPTALWAYS is specified, the ODBC Login dialog box is always displayed, allowing you to change settings before connecting.
		If 3 or DB_PROMPTNEVER is specified, the ODBC Login dialog box is not displayed and Visual FoxPro generates an error if the required login information isn't available.
		Read/Write.

Connection properties *(continued)*

cProperty	Type	Description
DispWarnings	L	Contains a logical value that determines if non-trappable warnings from the remote table, ODBC, or Visual FoxPro are displayed.
		(Default) True (.T.) specifies that non-trappable errors are displayed.
		Read/Write.
IdleTimeout	N	The idle timeout interval in seconds. Active connections are deactivated after the specified time interval. The default value is 0 (wait indefinitely).
		Read/Write.
PacketSize	N	The size of the network packet used by the connection. Adjusting this value can improve performance. The default value is 4096 bytes (4K).
		Read/Write
PassWord	C	The connection password.
		Read/Write.
QueryTimeout	N	The query timeout interval in seconds. The default value is 0 (wait indefinitely).
		Read/Write.
Transactions	N	Contains a numeric value that determines how the connection manages transactions on the remote table. Transactions may assume the following values:
		1 or DB_TRANSAUTO (from Foxpro.h).
		1 is the default. Transaction processing for the remote table is handled automatically.
		2 or DB_TRANSMANUAL (from Foxpro.h).
		Transaction processing is handled manually through SQLCOMMIT( ) and SQLROLLBACK( ).
		Read/Write.
UserId	C	The user identification.
		Read/Write.
WaitTime	N	The amount of time in milliseconds that elapses before Visual FoxPro checks whether the SQL statement has completed executing. The default is 100 milliseconds.
		Read/Write.

Database properties

cProperty	Type	Description
Comment	C	The text of the database comment.
		Read/Write.
Version	N	The database version number.
		Read-Only.

Field properties for tables

cProperty	Type	Description
Caption	C	The field caption.
		Read/Write.
Comment	C	The text of the field comment.
		Read/Write.
DefaultValue	C	The field default value.
		Read-Only.
DisplayClass	C	Name of the class used for field mapping.
		Read/Write.
DisplayClassLibrary	C	Path to the class library specified with the DisplayClass property.
		Read/Write.
Format	C	The field display format. See the Format Property, later in this language reference, for a list of format settings.
		Read/Write.
InputMask	C	The field input format. See the InputMask Property, later in this language reference, for a list of input mask settings.
		Read/Write.
RuleExpression	C	The field rule expression.
		Read-Only.
RuleText	C	The field rule error text.
		Read-Only.

Field properties for views

cProperty	Type	Description
Caption	C	The field caption.
		Read/Write.
Comment	C	The text of the field comment.
		Read/Write.
DataType	C	The data type for a field in a view. Initially set to the data type for the field in the data source.
		To specify a different data type for a field with DBSETPROP( ), use the syntax for creating fields in CREATE TABLE – SQL.
		For example, to change the data type of an integer field named iCost in a table named Mytable to numeric type with width 4 and 2 decimal places, use
		DBSETPROP('mytable.icost', 'field', ; 'DataType', 'N(4,2)')
		You can also include the NOCPTRANS clause to prevent translation of character and memo fields to a different code page.
		Read/Write for remote views.
		Ignored for local views.
DefaultValue	C	The field default value.
		Read/Write.
KeyField	L	Contains true (.T.) if the field is specified in an index key expression; otherwise, contains false (.F.).
		Read/Write.
RuleExpression	C	The field rule expression.
		Read/Write.
RuleText	C	The field rule error text.
		Read/Write.
Updatable	L	Contains true (.T.) if the field can be updated; otherwise, contains false (.F.).
		Read/Write.
UpdateName	C	The name of the field used when data in the field is updated to the remote table. By default, the remote table field name.
		Read/Write.

Table properties

cProperty	Type	Description
Comment	C	The text of the table comment. Read/Write.
DeleteTrigger	C	The Delete trigger expression. Read-Only.
InsertTrigger	C	The Insert trigger expression. Read-Only.
Path	C	The path to the table. Read-Only.
PrimaryKey	C	The tag name of the primary key. Read-Only.
RuleExpression	C	The row rule expression. Read-Only.
RuleText	C	The row rule error text. Read-Only.
UpdateTrigger	C	The Update trigger expression. Read-Only.

View properties

cProperty	Type	Description
BatchUpdateCount	N	The number of update statements sent to the back end for views. 1 is the default. Adjusting this value can greatly increase update performance. Read/Write.
Comment	C	The text of the view comment. Read/Write.
CompareMemo	L	Contains true (.T.) (default) if memo fields (of type Memo, General, or Picture) are included in the WHERE clause for updates; otherwise, contains false (.F.). Read/Write.
ConnectName	C	The named connection used when the view is opened. Read-Only.

View properties *(continued)*

cProperty	Type	Description
FetchAsNeeded	L	Contains true (.T.) if data is fetched as needed; otherwise, contains false (.F.) (default). Read/Write.
FetchMemo	L	Contains true (.T.) (the default) if memo and general fields are fetched with the view results; otherwise, contains false (.F.). Read/Write.
FetchSize	N	The number of records fetched at a time from the remote tables (when progressive fetches are enabled). The default is 100 records. Setting FetchSize to –1 retrieves the complete result set (limited by the MaxRecords setting). Read/Write.
MaxRecords	N	The maximum number of records fetched when result sets are returned. The default is –1 (all rows are returned). A value of 0 specifies that the view is executed but no results are fetched. Read/Write.
Offline	L	Contains true (.T.) if the view is an offline view. Read-only.

ParameterList	C	The WHERE clause parameters. The format for the parameters is "*ParameterName1*, '*Type1*'; *ParameterName2*, '*Type2*'; ..." where *Type* is a one of the following characters specifying the parameter type:
		
		    C – Character
		    D – Date
		    T – DateTime
		    N – Numeric
		    F – Floating
		    B – Double
		    I – Integer
		    Y – Currency
		    L – Logical
		
		For example, "MyParam1, 'C' " specifies a single character type parameter named MyParam1.
		
		For more information about creating parameterized views, see Chapter 8, "Creating Views," in the *Microsoft Visual FoxPro 6.0 Programmer's Guide*.
		
		Read/Write.

(continued)

View properties *(continued)*

cProperty	Type	Description
Prepared	L	Contains true (.T.) if SQL statements are prepared for subsequent REQUERY( ) function calls. REQUERY( ) is used to retrieve data again for a SQL view. See the SQLPREPARE( ) Function, later in this language reference, for additional information about preparing SQL statements.
		The default is false (.F.).
		Read/Write.
RuleExpression	C	The row rule expression.
		Read/Write.
RuleText	C	The rule text expression displayed when an error occurs when data is edited in a Browse or Edit window.
		Read/Write.
SendUpdates	L	Contains true (.T.) if a SQL update query is sent to update remote tables; otherwise, contains false (.F.) (default).
		Read/Write.
ShareConnection	L	Contains true (.T.) if the view can share its connection handle with other connections; otherwise, contains false (.F.).
		Read/Write.
SourceType	N	The view source. SourceType may assume the following values:
		1. The view uses local tables. 2. The view uses remote tables.
		Read-Only.
SQL	C	The SQL statement executed when the view is opened.
		Read-Only.
Tables	C	A comma-delimited list of the names of the tables.
		Read/Write.
UpdateType	N	The update type. Valid values are:
		1 or DB_UPDATE (from Foxpro.h). The old data is updated with the new data (default).
		2 or DB_DELETEINSERT (from Foxpro.h). The old data is deleted and the new data is inserted.
		Read/Write.

View properties *(continued)*

cProperty	Type	Description
UseMemoSize	N	The minimum size (in bytes) for which result columns are returned in memo fields. For example, if the width of a column result is greater than the value of UseMemoSize, the column result is stored in a memo field. UseMemoSize may vary from 1 to 255; the default value is 255. Read/Write.
WhereType	N	The WHERE clause for updates to remote tables. WhereType may assume the following values: 1 or DB_KEY (from Foxpro.h). The WHERE clause used to update remote tables consists of only the primary fields specified with the KeyFieldList property. 2 or DB_KEYANDUPDATABLE (from Foxpro.h). The WHERE clause used to update remote tables consists of the primary fields specified with the KeyFieldList property and any updatable fields. 3 or DB_KEYANDMODIFIED (from Foxpro.h) (default). The WHERE clause used to update remote tables consists of the primary fields specified with the KeyFieldList property and any other fields that are modified. 4 or DB_KEYANDTIMESTAMP (from Foxpro.h). The WHERE clause used to update remote tables consists of the primary fields specified with the KeyFieldList property and a comparison of the time stamps. For more information about the WhereType property, see Chapter 8, "Creating Views," in the *Microsoft Visual FoxPro 6.0 Programmer's Guide*. Read/Write.

Remarks

A database must be opened before you can get its properties or those of its connections, tables, views, or fields. You do not need to execute the USE command to open a table or view before getting its properties.

For more details about the properties you can get for connections, databases, fields, tables, and views, refer to the topics listed in the following table.

For details about	Refer to this section	In this chapter of the *Microsoft Visual FoxPro 6.0 Programmer's Guide*
Database properties	"Viewing and Setting Database Properties"	Chapter 6, "Creating Databases"
Connections	"Accessing Remote Data"	Chapter 8, "Creating Views"
Views		Chapter 8, "Creating Views"
Triggers	"Using Triggers"	Chapter 7, "Working with Tables"
Captions	"Creating Captions for Fields"	Chapter 7, "Working with Tables"
Default values	"Creating Default Field Values"	Chapter 7, "Working with Tables"
	"Creating Default Values for View Fields"	Chapter 8, "Creating Views"
Comments	"Adding Comments to Fields"	Chapter 7, "Working with Tables"
	"Viewing and Setting Database Properties"	Chapter 6, "Creating Databases"
Primary key	"Controlling Duplicate Values"	Chapter 7, "Working with Tables"
Rules	"Enforcing Business Rules"	Chapter 7, "Working with Tables"
	"Setting or Changing Field-level or Table Rules"	Chapter 7, "Working with Tables"
	"Creating Rules on View Fields and Rows"	Chapter 8, "Creating Views"

Example

The following example displays the name of the primary key field for the customer table. It then displays the field comments for the cust_id field in the customer table. If there are no comments for the field, a message is displayed indicating there are no field comments. To add comments, see the example for the DBSETPROP( ) Function, later in this language reference.

```
CLOSE DATABASES
CLEAR

OPEN DATABASE (HOME(2) + 'Data\testdata')

* Displays the primary key field
cResults = DBGETPROP("customer", "Table", "PrimaryKey")
=MESSAGEBOX(cResults)   && Displays    'cust_id'

* Displays comments for the field 'cust_id'
cResults = DBGETPROP("customer.cust_id", "Field", "Comment")
IF LEN(ALLTRIM(cResults)) = 0
   =MESSAGEBOX("No Comment for this field." + CHR(13) + ;
     CHR (13) + "Use DBSETPROP( ) to add comments.")
```

```
ELSE
   =MESSAGEBOX("Cust_id field comments: " + cRESULTS)
ENDIF
```

See Also

ADD TABLE, CREATE CONNECTION, CREATE DATABASE, CREATE SQL VIEW, CURSORGETPROP( ), CURSORSETPROP( ), DBSETPROP( ), DISPLAY DATABASE, LIST DATABASE, RENAME CONNECTION, SQLCOMMIT( ), SQLROLLBACK( )

DblClick Event

Occurs when the user presses and releases the mouse button twice in quick succession.

Syntax

PROCEDURE *Object*.DblClick
[LPARAMETERS *nIndex*]

Arguments

nIndex
Uniquely identifies a control if it is in a control array.

Remarks

The DblClick event also occurs when you select an item in a list box or a combo box and press ENTER.

If DblClick doesn't occur within the system's double-click time limit, the object recognizes another Click event. Therefore, when you attach procedures for these related events, make sure that their actions do not conflict. Controls that don't receive DblClick events may receive two single clicks instead of a double-click.

Note If the mouse has more than one button, you can distinguish between the left, right, and middle mouse buttons using the MouseDown and MouseUp events.

Applies To

CheckBox, ComboBox, CommandGroup, Container Object, Control Object, EditBox, Form, Grid, Header, Image, Label, Line, ListBox, OptionButton, OptionGroup, Page, PageFrame, Shape, Spinner, TextBox, ToolBar

See Also

Click Event, MouseDown Event, MouseUp Event

_DBLCLICK System Variable

Specifies the time interval between double and triple mouse clicks.

Syntax

_DBLCLICK = *nTicks*

Arguments

nTicks

Specifies the time interval in seconds. Internal timing is measured in clock "ticks," which are each about 1/18th of a second. If you store an integer or decimal value to _DBLCLICK, Visual FoxPro may store it as a slightly different value due to rounding to ticks. The default value for _DBLCLICK is 0.5 seconds. _DBLCLICK can range from 0.05 to 5.5 seconds (1 to 100 ticks).

Remarks

The _DBLCLICK setting overrides the setting specified in the Mouse dialog box in the Window Control Panel.

_DBLCLICK contains a numeric value that determines the time interval Visual FoxPro uses to check for a double or triple mouse click. _DBLCLICK is the time interval between mouse clicks. For example, if _DBLCLICK is set to 0.5 seconds, you have a 1/2 second to click twice for a double-click, and 1 second to click three times for a triple-click.

The larger the value of _DBLCLICK, the longer you can wait between the first and second click for Visual FoxPro to interpret the two clicks as a double-click. If _DBLCLICK is set to a very small value, even quick double (or triple) clicks may be interpreted as two (or three) single clicks.

See Also

INKEY( )

DBSETPROP( ) Function

Sets a property for the current database or for fields, named connections, tables, or views in the current database.

Syntax

DBSETPROP(*cName*, *cType*, *cProperty*, *ePropertyValue*)

Returns

Logical

Arguments

cName

Specifies the name of the database, field, named connection, table, or view for which a property is set.

To set a property for a field in a table or a view, preface the name of the field with the name of the table or view containing the field. For example, to set a property for the custid field in the customer table, specify the following for *cName*:

```
customer.custid
```

cType

Specifies whether *cName* is the current database or for a field, named connection, table, or view in the current database.

The following table lists the values you can specify for *cType*:

cType	Description
CONNECTION	*cName* is a named connection in the current database.
DATABASE	*cName* is the current database.
FIELD	*cName* is a field in the current database.
TABLE	*cName* is a table in the current database.
VIEW	*cName* is a view in the current database.

cProperty

Specifies the name of the property to set. If a property is read-only, its value cannot be changed with DBSETPROP( ). If you attempt to set a property that is read-only, Visual FoxPro generates an error message.

For more information on properties you can specify with *cProperty*, including their data types, see the DBGETPROP( ) Function, earlier in this language reference.

ePropertyValue

Specifies the value to which *cProperty* is set. *ePropertyValue* must be the same data type as the property's data type.

Caution   Visual FoxPro does not verify that the value you specify is valid for the property. Thus, it is possible to set a property to an invalid value with DBSETPROP( ). For example, DBSETPROP( ) can be used to set a field rule expression to an expression that isn't valid for the field, and Visual FoxPro will not generate an error.

Remarks

Use DBSETPROP( ) to set properties for the current database, or fields, named connections, tables, or views in the current database. Use DBGETPROP( ) to determine the current property values.

DBSETPROP( ) returns true (.T.) if Visual FoxPro successfully sets the property you specify. Visual FoxPro generates an error if the property you specify cannot be set.

For more details about the properties you can get for connections, databases, fields, tables, and views, refer to the topics listed in the following table.

For details about	Refer to this section	In this chapter of the *Microsoft Visual FoxPro 6.0 Programmer's Guide*
Database properties	"Viewing and Setting Database Properties"	Chapter 6, "Creating Databases"
Connections	"Accessing Remote Data"	Chapter 8, "Creating Views"
Views		Chapter 8, "Creating Views"
Triggers	"Using Triggers"	Chapter 7, "Working with Tables"
Captions	"Creating Captions for Fields"	Chapter 7, "Working with Tables"
Default values	"Creating Default Field Values"	Chapter 7, "Working with Tables"
	"Creating Default Values for View Fields"	Chapter 8, "Creating Views"
Comments	"Adding Comments to Fields"	Chapter 7, "Working with Tables"
	"Viewing and Setting Database Properties"	Chapter 6, "Creating Databases"
Primary key	"Controlling Duplicate Values"	Chapter 7, "Working with Tables"
Rules	"Enforcing Business Rules"	Chapter 7, "Working with Tables"
	"Setting or Changing Field-level or Table Rules"	Chapter 7, "Working with Tables"
	"Creating Rules on View Fields and Rows"	Chapter 8, "Creating Views"

Example

The following example uses DBSETPROP( ) to specify a comment for the cust_id field in the customer table. DBGETPROP( ) is used to display the comment.

```
CLOSE DATABASES
CLEAR

OPEN DATABASE (HOME(2) + 'data\testdata')
USE customer      && Open customer table

= DBSETPROP("customer.cust_id", "Field", "Comment", ;
  "Property has been set by DBSETPROP.")  && New field comments
```

```
cRESULTS = DBGETPROP("customer.cust_id", "Field", "Comment")
WAIT WINDOW "Cust_id field comments: "+ cRESULTS  && Display comments
```

See Also

ADD TABLE, CREATE DATABASE, CURSORGETPROP( ), CURSORSETPROP( ),
DBGETPROP( ), DISPLAY DATABASE, LIST DATABASE, OPEN DATABASE,
SQLCOMMIT( ), SQLROLLBACK( )

DBUSED( ) Function

Returns true (.T.) if the specified database is open.

Syntax

DBUSED(*cDatabaseName*)

Returns

Logical

Arguments

cDatabaseName
Specifies the name of the database for which DBUSED( ) returns a logical value
indicating whether or not the database is open.

Remarks

DBUSED( ) returns true (.T.) if the specified database is open; otherwise, it returns
false (.F.).

Example

The following example opens the TESTDATA database, and then uses DBUSED( )
to determine if the TESTDATA database and a database named TEST are open.

```
CLOSE DATABASES
OPEN DATABASE (HOME(2) + 'Data\testdata')

CLEAR
? 'Testdata database open? '
?? DBUSED('testdata')     && Displays .T.
? 'Test database open? '
?? DBUSED('test')     && Displays .F.
```

See Also

CLOSE DATABASES, CREATE DATABASE, OPEN DATABASE

DDE Functions

Exchange data between Visual FoxPro and other Microsoft Windows-based applications.

Remarks

Visual FoxPro can act as both a server and a client to send and receive data to and from other Microsoft Windows-based applications.

The following naming conventions are used in applications that support DDE (dynamic data exchange).

Name	Description
Service Name	A name that the server responds to when a client tries to access the server. A server can support many service names.
Topic Name	A name that specifies a logical set of data. For file-based applications, topic names are usually file names. In other applications, topic names are application-specific. To access the server, the client must specify a topic name in addition to the server's service name.
Item Name	A name that specifies a unit of data that the server can pass to the client requesting the data.

To request data from another application, create a Visual FoxPro program that establishes Visual FoxPro as a client. Here is a brief outline for creating a simple Visual FoxPro program that requests data from another application:

- Establish a link to the server application with DDEInitiate( ).

- If the link is successfully established, use DDERequest( ) to request data from the server application. DDERequest( ) can be issued repeatedly to request additional data.

- After the data has been received, issue DDETerminate( ) to terminate the link to the server application to free up system resources.

The functions above establish a cold link. A cold link exists when the client initiates all the communications between the applications. For a discussion of other types of links, see the DDEAdvise( ) Function, later in this language reference.

The following is a brief outline for a program that establishes Visual FoxPro as a server:

- Use DDESetService( ) to create a service and specify the type of service.

- Use DDESetTopic( ) to create a service topic and specify the procedure to execute when the topic is specified in a client request.

- Create the procedure specified in DDESetTopic( ) to accept the parameters passed to the procedure.

- Within the procedure, process the request and, if appropriate, return the requested data to the client.

Note that these DDE functions differ from previous Visual FoxPro function conventions in the following ways:

- The first four characters of these functions are not unique.

- The function names exceed 10 characters and cannot be abbreviated.

DDE Function	Description
DDEAbortTrans( )	Ends an asynchronous DDE transaction.
DDEAdvise( )	Creates a notify link or an automatic link used in DDE.
DDEEnabled( )	Enables or disables DDE processing or returns the status of DDE processing.
DDEExecute( )	Using DDE, sends a command to another application.
DDEInitiate( )	Establishes a DDE channel between Visual FoxPro and another Microsoft Windows-based application.
DDELastError( )	Returns an error number for the last DDE function.
DDEPoke( )	Sends data between client and server applications in a DDE conversation.
DDERequest( )	Requests data from a server application in a dynamic DDE conversation.
DDESetOption( )	Changes or returns DDE settings.
DDESetService( )	Creates, releases, or modifies service names and settings in Visual FoxPro.
DDESetTopic( )	In a DDE conversation, creates or releases a topic name from a service name.
DDETerminate( )	Closes a DDE channel established with DDEInitiate( ).

See Also

DDEAbortTrans( ), DDEAdvise( ), DDEEnabled( ), DDEExecute( ), DDEInitiate( ), DDELastError( ), DDEPoke( ), DDERequest( ), DDESetOption( ), DDESetService( ), DDESetTopic( ), DDETerminate( )

DDEAbortTrans( ) Function

Ends an asynchronous dynamic data exchange (DDE) transaction.

Syntax

DDEAbortTrans(*nTransactionNumber*)

Returns

Logical

Arguments

nTransactionNumber
Specifies the transaction number returned by DDEExecute( ), DDEPoke( ), or DDERequest( ) when the transaction is sent to the server application.

Remarks

An asynchronous transaction allows Visual FoxPro program execution to continue without waiting for the server application to respond to a data request.

DDEExecute( ), DDEPoke( ), and DDERequest( ) wait for the period specified by DDESetOption( ) for a server application to respond, unless you specify a user-defined function to execute when the server application responds. Specifying a user-defined function to execute in these functions creates an asynchronous transaction.

If DDEAbortTrans( ) is called before the server has processed the request, the user-defined function won't be called for the transaction.

DDEAbortTrans( ) returns true (.T.) if the asynchronous transaction is successfully ended and returns false (.F.) if the asynchronous transaction cannot be ended. Use DDELastError( ) to determine why the transaction couldn't be ended.

See Also

DDEExecute( ), DDELastError( ), DDEPoke( ), DDERequest( )

DDEAdvise( ) Function

Creates a notify link or an automatic link used in a dynamic data exchange (DDE).

Syntax

DDEAdvise(*nChannelNumber*, *cItemName*, *cUDFName*, *nLinkType*)

Returns

Logical

Arguments

nChannelNumber
Specifies the channel number.

cItemName
Specifies the item name. For example, Microsoft Excel uses row and column notation to refer to cells in a worksheet. The item name R1C1 designates the cell in the first row and first column of the worksheet.

cUDFName
Specifies the user-defined function that is executed when a notify link or an automatic link is established and the item *cItemName* is modified. When the user-defined function is executed, it is passed the following six parameters in the order given below:

Parameter	Contents
Channel Number	The channel number of the server application.
Action	ADVISE or TERMINATE.
Item	The item name; for example, R1C1 for a Microsoft Excel worksheet cell.
Data	The new data (automatic link) or the empty string (notify link).
Format	The data format; for example, CF_TEXT.
Advise Status	The link type (0 = manual, 1 = notify, 2 = automatic).

The user-defined function should have six parameters in its LPARAMETER or PARAMETER statement to accept the values passed from the server application. If a notify link is established, the user-defined function is executed and the empty string is passed in the Data parameter. You can issue DDERequest( ) later to retrieve the data. If an automatic link is established, the user-defined function is executed and the data is passed in the Data parameter.

The Action parameter contains ADVISE when the link is being updated by the server. The user-defined function is called, and the Action parameter contains TERMINATE when the link is closed by the client or server.

Any value returned by the user-defined function is ignored.

nLinkType
Specifies the link type in the following way:

nLinkType	Link type
0	Manual
1	Notify
2	Automatic

You can turn off notification from the server application by specifying 0 for *nLinkType*. If the item changes, the user-defined function isn't executed.

Remarks

DDEAdvise( ) is used to create a notify link or an automatic link to an item name in a server application. When a notify link is created with DDEAdvise( ), the server application notifies Visual FoxPro that the item name has been modified. If an automatic link is created, the server application notifies Visual FoxPro that the item name has been modified and passes the new data to Visual FoxPro.

Before you can create a link, you must establish a channel to the server application with DDEInitiate( ).

You can also use DDEAdvise( ) to turn off notification from the server.

DDEAdvise( ) returns a true value (.T.) if it executes successfully; otherwise, it returns false (.F.).

Example

The following example demonstrates how you can establish a DDE channel to a Microsoft Excel worksheet named Sheet1. DDEAdvise( ) is used to establish two links to data in two worksheet cells (R1C1 and R1C2). The user-defined function NEWDATA is executed when data in either of the cells changes. The user-defined function tests the item and advise parameters to determine which item changed and what kind of link has been established.

```
PUBLIC mchannum
mchannum = DDEInitiate('Excel', 'Sheet1')
IF mchannum != -1
   = DDEAdvise(mchannum, 'R1C1', 'newdata', 1)      && Notify link
   = DDEAdvise(mchannum, 'R1C2', 'newdata', 2)      && Automatic link
   WAIT WINDOW 'Enter data in first two cells in Excel.'
ENDIF
PROCEDURE newdata
PARAMETERS channel, action, item, data, format, advise
IF action = 'ADVISE'
   DO CASE
      CASE item = 'R1C1'    && Notify link
         newvalue = DDERequest(channel, item)
         ? 'R1C1 notify link: ' + newvalue
      CASE item = 'R1C2'    && Automatic link
         newvalue = data
         ? 'R1C2 automatic link: ' + newvalue
   ENDCASE
ELSE
   IF action != "TERMINATE"
      = DDETerminate(mchannum)
   ENDIF
ENDIF
```

See Also

DDEInitiate( ), DDELastError( ), DDESetOption( ), DDETerminate( )

DDEEnabled( ) Function

Enables or disables dynamic data exchange (DDE) processing or returns the status of DDE processing.

Syntax

DDEEnabled([*lExpression1* | *nChannelNumber* [, *lExpression2*]])

Returns

Logical

Arguments

lExpression1

Specify true (.T.) or false (.F.) to globally enable or disable DDE processing. DDEEnabled( ) returns true (.T.) if DDE processing is successfully enabled or disabled; otherwise false (.F.) is returned.

nChannelNumber

Specifies the channel number for the channel whose DDE processing status DDEEnabled( ) returns. DDEEnabled( ) returns true (.T.) if DDE processing is enabled for the specified channel and returns false (.F.) if DDE processing is disabled.

lExpression2

To enable DDE processing for a specific channel, include the channel number (*nChannelNumber*) and specify true (.T.) for *lExpression2*. To disable DDE processing for a specific channel, include the channel number (*nChannelNumber*) and specify false (.F.) for *lExpression2*.

Remarks

Using DDEEnabled( ), you can globally enable or disable processing. You can also enable or disable DDE processing for specific channels.

DDEEnabled( ) can be used to protect critical code or disable links for short periods. When DDE processing is disabled, client requests are queued until DDE processing is enabled.

If DDEEnabled( ) is issued without any of its optional arguments, the global DDE processing status is returned. DDEEnabled( ) returns true (.T.) if DDE processing has been globally enabled and false (.F.) if DDE processing has been globally disabled.

See Also

DDEAbortTrans( ), DDEAdvise( ), DDEExecute( ), DDEInitiate( ), DDELastError( ), DDEPoke( ), DDERequest( ), DDESetOption( ), DDESetService( ), DDESetTopic( ), DDETerminate( )

DDEExecute( ) Function

Sends a command to another application, using dynamic data exchange (DDE).

Syntax

DDEExecute(*nChannelNumber*, *cCommand* [, *cUDFName*])

Returns

Logical

Arguments

nChannelNumber
Specifies the channel number.

cCommand
Specifies the command you want to send to the other application. The format of the command is determined by the application you are sending it to. Consult the application's documentation for the correct syntax.

cUDFName
Allows asynchronous command execution requests. If you omit *cUDFName*, a client application waits for the period specified with DDESetOption( ). If you specify a user-defined function with *cUDFName*, client program execution continues immediately after the command execution request is made.

When the server application finishes executing the command, the user-defined function you specify with *cUDFName* is executed. The user-defined function is passed six parameters in the order shown in the following table.

Parameter	Contents
Channel Number	The channel number of the server application.
Action	XACTCOMPLETE (successful execution). XACTFAIL (failed command execution).
Item	The item name; for example, R1C1 for a Microsoft Excel worksheet cell.
Data	The new data (REQUEST) or data passed (POKE or EXECUTED).
Format	The data format; for example, CF_TEXT.
Transaction Number	The transaction number returned by DDEExecute( ).

Use DDEAbortTrans( ) to cancel an uncompleted transaction. If the transaction fails, you can use DDELastError( ) to determine why it failed.

When you include *cUDFName*, DDEExecute( ) doesn't return a logical value. Instead, a transaction number is returned; if an error occurs, –1 is returned.

Remarks

The command sent with DDEExecute( ) must be understood by the application. Before you can execute the command, you must establish a channel to the server application with DDEInitiate( ).

For example, Microsoft Excel has an extensive set of macro commands, including DDE commands that let you request data from Visual FoxPro from within Microsoft Excel. If you establish a channel to Microsoft Excel, you can then use DDEExecute( ) to send macro commands to Microsoft Excel from within Visual FoxPro.

If the receiving application successfully executes the command, DDEExecute( ) returns true (.T.). If the receiving application cannot successfully execute the command or if the channel number you include is not valid, DDEExecute( ) returns false (.F.). If the optional asynchronous user-defined function *cUDFName* is included, a transaction number is returned. If an error occurs, DDEExecute( ) returns –1.

Example

The following example uses DDEInitiate( ) to establish a DDE channel between Visual FoxPro and the Microsoft Excel worksheet Sheet1. DDEExecute( ) is used to execute a Microsoft Excel command that maximizes the Microsoft Excel window.

```
gnChanNum = DDEInitiate('Excel', 'Sheet1')
IF gnChanNum != -1
   glExecute = DDEExecute(gnChanNum, '[App.Maximize]')
   IF glExecute != .F.
      WAIT WINDOW 'EXCEL window has been zoomed out.'
   ENDIF
   = DDETerminate(gnChanNum)    && Close the channel
ENDIF
```

See Also

DDEAbortTrans( ), DDEInitiate( ), DDELastError( ), DDESetOption( ), DDETerminate( )

DDEInitiate( ) Function

Establishes a dynamic data exchange (DDE) channel between Visual FoxPro and another Microsoft Windows-based application.

Syntax

DDEInitiate(*cServiceName*, *cTopicName*)

Returns

Numeric

Arguments

cServiceName

Specifies the service name of the server application which, in most cases, is the name of the executable file without its extension. The default service name for Visual FoxPro is Visual FoxPro. If you are establishing a channel to Microsoft Excel, *cServiceName* is Excel.

cTopicName

Specifies the topic name. The topic is application-specific and must be understood by the application. For example, one topic supplied by most DDE servers is the System topic. See the application documentation for the service and topic names supported by the application.

Remarks

DDEInitiate( ) establishes a DDE channel between Visual FoxPro and a DDE server application. Once a channel is established, Visual FoxPro can request data from the server by referring to the channel in subsequent DDE functions. Visual FoxPro acts as the client, requesting data from the server application through the channel.

If the channel is successfully established, DDEInitiate( ) returns the channel number. Channel numbers are non-negative, and the number of channels you can establish is limited only by your system resources.

DDEInitiate( ) returns –1 if the channel cannot be established. If the server application isn't open, Visual FoxPro asks if you would like to open it. If you choose Yes, Visual FoxPro attempts to open the application. (You can use DDELastError( ) to determine why a channel cannot be established.)

To avoid being asked whether you want to open the application, set the DDESetOption( ) SAFETY option. You can also use RUN with the /N option to start the application.

A channel can be closed with DDETerminate( ).

Example

The following example uses DDEInitiate( ) to establish a DDE channel between Visual FoxPro and a Microsoft Excel worksheet named Sheet1. 'Excel' is the service name, and 'Sheet1' is the topic name. The channel number is stored to the memory variable mchannum for use in subsequent DDE functions.

```
mchannum = DDEInitiate('Excel', 'Sheet1')
IF mchannum != -1
   * Process client actions
   = DDETerminate(mchannum)  && Close the channel
ENDIF
```

See Also

DDEAdvise( ), DDEEnabled( ), DDEExecute( ), DDELastError( ), DDEPoke( ), DDERequest( ), DDESetOption( ), DDETerminate( ), RUN | !

DDELastError( ) Function

Returns an error number for the last dynamic data exchange (DDE) function.

Syntax

DDELastError( )

Returns

Numeric

Remarks

You can use DDELastError( ) to help determine the cause of an error when a DDE function doesn't execute successfully.

DDELastError( ) returns 0 if the last DDE function executed successfully. It returns a nonzero value if the last DDE function was unsuccessful. The following table lists the error numbers and their descriptions.

Error number	Description
1	Service busy
2	Topic busy
3	Channel busy
4	No such service
5	No such topic
6	Bad channel
7	Insufficient memory
8	Acknowledge timeout
9	Request timeout
10	No DDEInitiate( )
11	Client attempted server transaction
12	Execute timeout
13	Bad parameter
14	Low memory
15	Memory error
16	Connect failure

(continued)

(continued)

Error number	Description
17	Request failure
18	Poke timeout
19	Could not display message
20	Multiple synchronous transactions
21	Server died
22	Internal DDE error
23	Advise timeout
24	Invalid transaction identifier
25	Unknown

See Also

DDEAbortTrans( ), DDEAdvise( ), DDEEnabled( ), DDEExecute( ), DDEInitiate( ), DDEPoke( ), DDERequest( ), DDESetOption( ), DDESetService( ), DDESetTopic( ), DDETerminate( )

DDEPoke( ) Function

Sends data between client and server applications in a dynamic data exchange (DDE) conversation.

Syntax

DDEPoke(*nChannelNumber, cItemName, cDataSent*
  [, *cDataFormat* [, *cUDFName*]])

Returns

Logical

Arguments

nChannelNumber

Specifies the channel number of the application data is sent to. If the channel number is a server channel, DDEPoke( ) sends the data in response to a request or a previously established notify or automatic link.

cItemName

Specifies the item name to which data is sent. The item name is application-specific and must be understood by the application. For example, Microsoft Excel supports R1C1 as a valid item name that refers to the first cell in a worksheet.

cDataSent

Specifies the data sent to the item name specified with *cItemName*.

cDataFormat

Specifies the format used to send the data. The default format is CF_TEXT. In this format, fields are delimited with tabs and records are delimited with a carriage return and a linefeed.

cUDFName

Allows asynchronous data transfer. If *cUDFName* is omitted, a client waits for the period specified with DDESetOption( ). If you specify the name of a user-defined function with *cUDFName*, client program execution continues immediately after the request is made.

When the data is available from the server application, the user-defined function specified with *cUDFName* is executed. The user-defined function is passed six parameters in this order:

Parameter	Contents
Channel Number	The channel number of the server application.
Action	XACTCOMPLETE (successful transaction). XACTFAIL (failed transaction).
Item	The item name; for example, R1C1 for a Microsoft Excel worksheet cell.
Data	The new data (REQUEST) or data passed (POKE or EXECUTED).
Format	The data format; for example, CF_TEXT.
Transaction Number	The transaction number returned by DDEPoke( ).

Use DDEAbortTrans( ) to cancel an uncompleted transaction. If the transaction fails, you can use DDELastError( ) to determine why it failed.

When you include *cUDFName*, DDEPoke( ) returns a transaction number if successful or –1 if an error occurs.

Remarks

DDEPoke( ) sends data as a character string to the item name in the application specified by the channel number.

If the data is successfully sent, DDEPoke( ) returns true (.T.). If the data cannot be sent, DDEPoke( ) returns false (.F.). If the asynchronous user-defined function *cUDFName* is included, DDEPoke( ) returns a transaction number; if an error occurs, DDEPoke( ) returns –1.

See Also

DDEAbortTrans( ), DDEInitiate( ), DDELastError( ), DDESetOption( ), DDETerminate( )

DDERequest( ) Function

Requests data from a server application in a dynamic data exchange (DDE) conversation.

Syntax

DDERequest(*nChannelNumber, cItemName* [, *cDataFormat* [, *cUDFName*]])

Returns

Character

Arguments

nChannelNumber
Specifies the channel number of the server application.

cItemName
Specifies the item name. The item name is application-specific and must be understood by the application. For example, Microsoft Excel uses row and column notation to refer to cells in a worksheet. The item name R1C1 designates the cell in the first row and first column of the worksheet.

cDataFormat
Specifies a format for the data requested. The default format is CF_TEXT. In this format, fields are delimited with tabs and records are delimited with a carriage return and a line feed.

cUDFName
Allows an asynchronous data transfer. If you omit *cUDFName*, Visual FoxPro waits for the data from the server for the period specified with DDESetOption( ). If you specify the name of a user-defined function with *cUDFName*, Visual FoxPro continues program execution immediately after the request is made.

When the data is available from the server application, the user-defined function specified with *cUDFName* is executed. The user-defined function is passed six parameters in this order:

Parameter	Contents
Channel Number	The channel number of the server application.
Action	XACTCOMPLETE (successful transaction). XACTFAIL (failed transaction).
Item	The item name; for example, R1C1 for a Microsoft Excel worksheet cell.
Data	The new data (REQUEST) or data passed (POKE or EXECUTED).
Format	The data format; for example, CF_TEXT.
Transaction Number	The transaction number returned by DDERequest( ).

Use DDEAbortTrans( ) to cancel an uncompleted transaction. If the transaction fails, you can use DDELastError( ) to determine why it failed.

When you include *cUDFName*, DDERequest( ) returns a transaction number equal to or greater than 0 if successful, or –1 if an error occurs.

Remarks

Before you can request data using DDERequest( ), you must establish a channel to the server application with DDEInitiate( ).

If the request for data is successful, DDERequest( ) returns the data as a character string. If the request fails, DDERequest( ) returns an empty string and DDELastError( ) returns a nonzero value. If you include the asynchronous user-defined function *cUDFName*, DDERequest( ) returns a transaction number if successful, or –1 if an error occurs.

Example

The following example uses DDEInitiate( ) to establish a DDE channel between Visual FoxPro and a Microsoft Excel worksheet named Sheet1. 'Excel' is the service name, and 'Sheet1' is the topic name. The channel number is stored to the memory variable mchannum for use in subsequent DDE functions.

DDERequest( ) requests the item name R1C1, the data in the first row and column of the Sheet1 spreadsheet.

```
mchannum = DDEInitiate('Excel', 'Sheet1')
IF mchannum != -1
   mrequest = DDERequest(mchannum, 'R1C1')
   IF !EMPTY(mrequest) AND DDELastError( ) = 0        && Successful
      WAIT WINDOW 'R1C1 contents: ' + mrequest
   ENDIF
   = DDETerminate(mchannum)                && Close the channel
ENDIF
```

See Also

DDEAbortTrans( ), DDEInitiate( ), DDELastError( ), DDESetOption( ), DDETerminate( )

DDESetOption( ) Function

Changes or returns dynamic data exchange (DDE) settings.

Syntax

DDESetOption(*cOption* [, *nTimeoutValue* | *lExpression*])

Returns

Logical or Numeric

Arguments

cOption

Specifies the setting options.

cOption	Setting	Default	Description
TIMEOUT	*nTimeoutValue* (number of milliseconds)	2000	The number of milliseconds DDE functions wait for the server application to respond; the current TIMEOUT value is returned if you omit *nTimeoutValue*.
SAFETY	*lExpression* (true (.T.) or false (.F.))	.T.	Specifies whether a dialog is displayed when you use DDEInitiate( ) to establish a channel to a server application and the application doesn't respond; the current SAFETY setting is returned if you omit *lExpression*.

nTimeoutValue

Specifies the timeout value.

lExpression

Enables or disables dialog display.

Remarks

Use DDESetOption( ) to change or return DDE settings. Two options, TIMEOUT and SAFETY, are available.

See Also

DDEAdvise( ), DDEEnabled( ), DDEExecute( ), DDEInitiate( ), DDEPoke( ), DDERequest( ), DDESetService( ), DDETerminate( )

DDESetService( ) Function

Creates, releases, or modifies DDE service names and settings.

Syntax

DDESetService(*cServiceName*, *cOption* [, *cDataFormat* | *lExpression*])

Returns

Logical

Arguments

cServiceName

Specifies the service name to create, release, modify, or return information about.

cOption

Specifies to create, release or modify a service name or to return information about a service name. The following table lists the options you can specify with *cOption*, the default values for the options and a description of each option.

Option	Default value	Description
DEFINE	–	Creates a new service name.
RELEASE	–	Releases an existing service name.
ADVISE	.F.	Enables or disables client notification of changes to item names.
EXECUTE	.F.	Enables or disables command execution.
POKE	.F.	Enables or disables client pokes to the service.
REQUEST	.T.	Enables or disables requests to the service name.
FORMATS	CF_TEXT	Specifies supported data formats.

DEFINE

Creates a new service name. For example, the following command creates the service name myservice:

```
glNewService = DDESetService('myservice', 'DEFINE')
```

RELEASE

Releases an existing service name to free up system resources. When a service name is released, all of the service's topic names are also released.

The following command releases the service name created in the previous example:

```
glRelease = DDESetService('myservice', 'RELEASE')
```

To release the default Visual FoxPro service, issue this command:

```
glRelFox = DDESetService('FoxPro', 'RELEASE')
```

ADVISE

Specifies whether a client is notified when data changes in an item name or specifies to return the current advise status for a service name. Refer to DDEAdvise( ) for additional information about advising clients.

To enable client notification, specify true (.T.) for *lExpression*. Specifying false (.F.) for *lExpression* disables client notification.

To return the current client notification status for the service name, omit *lExpression*. DDESetService( ) returns true if client notification is enabled for the service name; it returns false if client notification is disabled.

EXECUTE

Allows you to enable or disable command execution requests to a service name or to determine the current execute status for a service name.

To enable client requests to execute a command, specify true (.T.) for *lExpression*. Specifying false (.F.) for *lExpression* disables client requests to execute a command. .F. is the default value.

To return the current command execution status for the service name, omit *lExpression*. DDESetService( ) returns true if client command execution requests are enabled for the service name; otherwise, it returns false.

The following commands enable command execution and disable data requests from client applications for the service name myservice. The current command execution status for myservice is then displayed:

```
glExecute = DDESetService('myservice', 'EXECUTE', .T.)
glRequest = DDESetService('myservice', 'REQUEST', .F.)
? DDESetService('myservice', 'EXECUTE')
```

POKE

Allows you to enable or disable poke requests to the service name. You can also determine the current poke status for a service name. Refer to DDEPoke( ) for additional information about poking data to a server or a client.

To enable client poke requests, specify true (.T.) for *lExpression*. Specifying false (.F.) for *lExpression* disables client poke requests. .F. is the default value.

To return the current poke status for the service name, omit *lExpression*. DDESetService( ) returns true if poke requests are enabled for a service name; it returns false if poke requests are disabled.

REQUEST

Use REQUEST to enable or disable client requests to a service name or to return the current request status for the service name.

To enable client requests to the service name, specify true (.T.) for *lExpression*. Specifying false (.F.) disables client requests to the service name. True (.T.) is the default value.

To return the current request status for a service name, omit *lExpression*. DDESetService( ) returns true if client requests are enabled for the service name; it returns false if client requests are disabled.

The following commands disable requests from client applications to the service name myservice and display the current request status for myservice:

```
glRequest = DDESetService('myservice', 'REQUEST', .F.)
? DDESetService('myservice', 'REQUEST')
```

FORMATS [*cDataFormat*]

Specifies the data formats supported by the service name. Server requests for formats not specified with *cDataFormat* are rejected. When specifying data formats, include a list of the supported formats separated by commas. For example:

```
=DDESetService('myservice', 'FORMATS', 'CF_TEXT, CF_SYLK')
```

If you omit *cDataFormat*, only the CF_TEXT format is supported.

lExpression

Specifies the state of the REQUEST, EXECUTE, POKE, or ADVISE options. Specify true (.T.) for *lExpression* to enable the option or false (.F.) to disable it.

Remarks

Visual FoxPro can act as a dynamic data exchange (DDE) server to send data to client Microsoft Windows-based applications. DDESetService( ) is used to create, release, or modify service names and settings in Visual FoxPro. Each service name can have a set of topic names created with DDESetTopic( ). Client applications request data from DDE topic names.

DDESetService( ) returns true (.T.) if the service name is successfully created, released, or modified. If the service name cannot be created, released, or modified, DDESetService( ) returns false (.F.).

DDESetService( ) can also be used to return information about a service name. Visual FoxPro has the default service name FoxPro. The Visual FoxPro service name has one topic name called System. The following table lists all the item names supported by the System topic.

Item name	Item
Topics	A list of available topic names
Formats	A list of supported formats
Status	Busy or Ready
SysItems	A list of item names

You can use DDESetTopic( ) to modify the FoxPro service name or to release it. For information about manipulating Visual FoxPro service names, see the following function, DDESetTopic( ).

See Also

DDEEnabled( ), DDELastError( ), DDEPoke( ), DDESetTopic( )

DDESetTopic( ) Function

Creates or releases a topic name from a service name in a dynamic data exchange (DDE) conversation.

Syntax

DDESetTopic(*cServiceName*, *cTopicName* [, *cUDFName*])

Returns

Logical

Arguments

cServiceName

Specifies the service name. Additional service names can be created with DDESetService( ).

cTopicName

Specifies the topic name to create or release. If you include *cUDFName*, DDESetTopic( ) creates the topic name *cTopicName*. If you omit *cUDFName*, the topic name *cTopicName* is released. If *cTopicName* is an empty string, the user-defined function specified with *cUDFName* is executed for any topic name that isn't explicitly declared.

cUDFName

Specifies the name of the user-defined function executed when a client application makes a request to the topic name. If you omit *cUDFName*, the topic name *cTopicName* is released from the service name.

When the user-defined function is executed, it is passed the following six parameters in the order given below:

Parameter	Contents
Channel Number	The client channel number.
Action	ADVISE, EXECUTE, INITIATE, POKE, REQUEST, or TERMINATE.
Item	The item name; for example, R1C1 for a Microsoft Excel worksheet cell.
Data	Data from the client.
Format	The data format; for example, CF_TEXT.
Advise Status	The link type (0 = manual, 2 = notify or automatic).

The values of the Item, Data, and Advise Status parameters depend on the Action parameter. The following table lists the Action parameter values and the values contained in the Item, Data, and Advise Status parameters. A dash (–) indicates that the parameter value is the empty string.

Action value	Item value	Data value	Advise status
INITIATE	–	Topic name	–
TERMINATE	–	–	–
POKE	Item name	New data	–
REQUEST	Item name	–	–
EXECUTE	–	New command	–
ADVISE	Item name	–	Link type

If the user-defined function successfully handles the client request, the user-defined function should return true (.T.). If the request can't be handled or an error occurs, the user-defined function should return false (.F.). If false is returned when the Action parameter value is INITIATE, the client topic name request is rejected. If false is returned when the value is POKE, REQUEST, or EXECUTE, the request is ignored. If false is returned when the value is ADVISE, the client request for a notify or automatic link is rejected.

Remarks

After a topic name is created, any client requests to the topic name cause Visual FoxPro to execute the user-defined function specified with *cUDFName*. The user-defined function is passed a set of parameters whose values are determined by the client request. The user-defined function return value is passed to the client with DDEPoke( ). The return value is a logical value indicating whether the topic name can provide the service requested by the client.

DDESetTopic( ) returns true (.T.) if it successfully creates or releases the topic name. It returns false (.F.) if the topic name cannot be created or released. Use DDELastError( ) to determine why a topic name cannot be created or released.

Example

The following example creates a basic sample server called `myserver` that supports Visual FoxPro command execution from a client application. The client application makes requests to `myserver` through the DO topic, and macro substitution is used to execute the client's command.

```
*** Set Visual FoxPro up as a DDE server ***
= DDESetService('myserver', 'DEFINE')
= DDESetService('myserver', 'EXECUTE', .T.)
= DDESetTopic('myserver', 'DO', 'DOTOPIC')
WAIT WINDOW 'Server portion service setup ... ' NOWAIT
```

```
*** Use Visual FoxPro as a DDE client ***
gnChannel = DDEInitiate('myserver','DO')
=DDEExecute(gnChannel, 'WAIT WINDOW "Command Executed ... "')
=DDETerminate(gnChannel)
PROCEDURE dotopic
PARAMETERS gnChannel, gcAction, gcItem, gData, gcFormat, gnAdvise
glResult = .F.
*** It's necessary to return .T. from an    ***
*** INITIATE action or no connection is made ***
IF gcAction = 'INITIATE'
   glResult = .T.
ENDIF
IF gcAction = 'EXECUTE'
   &gData
   glResult = .T.
ENDIF
IF gcAction = 'TERMINATE'
   WAIT WINDOW 'Goodbye ... ' NOWAIT
   glResult = .T.
ENDIF
RETURN glResult
```

After running this example program, you have set up Visual FoxPro service, which other applications can access. If you have Microsoft Excel, you can run the following Excel macro:

```
gnMyChan = INITIATE("myserver","DO")
=EXECUTE(MyChan,"WAIT WINDOW 'Hi, this is EXCEL speaking'")
=RETURN( )
```

See Also

DDEEnabled( ), DDELastError( ), DDEPoke( ), DDESetService( )

DDETerminate( ) Function

Closes a dynamic data exchange (DDE) channel established with DDEInitiate( ).

Syntax

DDETerminate(*nChannelNumber* | *cServiceName*)

Returns

Logical

Arguments

nChannelNumber
Specifies the channel number to close.

cServiceName
Specifies the service name to close.

Remarks

If the channel is successfully closed, DDETerminate( ) returns true (.T.). If the channel cannot be closed, DDETerminate( ) returns false (.F.).

Be sure to close channels as soon as they are no longer needed to conserve system resources.

All channels are automatically closed if you exit Visual FoxPro by choosing Exit from the File menu or by issuing QUIT in the Command window or from within a program.

See Also

DDEAbortTrans( ), DDEAdvise( ), DDEExecute( ), DDEInitiate( ), DDELastError( ), DDEPoke( ), DDERequest( ), DDESetOption( )

Deactivate Event

Occurs when a container object, such as a form, is no longer active because none of its contained objects has the focus. For a toolbar, occurs when the toolbar is hidden using the Hide method.

Syntax

PROCEDURE *Object*.Deactivate

Remarks

The Activate and Deactivate events occur only when you are moving the focus within an application. Moving the focus to or from a form in another application doesn't trigger either event. The Deactivate event doesn't occur when unloading a form.

Whenever a new object is activated, either programmatically or interactively, the Deactivate event for the object previously active is triggered and the Activate event for the new object is triggered.

Applies To

Form, FormSet, Page, ToolBar

See Also

Activate Event, Hide Method, LostFocus Event, Show Method, Visible Property

DEACTIVATE MENU Command

Deactivates a user-defined menu bar and removes it from the screen; but doesn't remove the menu-bar definition from memory.

Syntax

DEACTIVATE MENU *MenuName1* [, *MenuName2* ...] | ALL

Arguments

MenuName1 [, *MenuName2* ...]
Specifies the names of the menu bars to deactivate. You can deactivate a set of menu bars by including a list of menu bar names separated by commas.

ALL
Deactivates all active menus.

Remarks

DEACTIVATE MENU removes an active menu bar or set of menu bars from the main Visual FoxPro window or a user-defined window without removing the menu bar definition from memory. A menu bar can be reactivated with ACTIVATE MENU and the menu bar name.

> **Tip** When you include the system menu bar (_MSYSMENU) in an application, you don't need to define, activate, or deactivate the menu bar. Instead, issue SET SYSMENU AUTOMATIC.

To release a specific menu bar or a set of menu bars from memory, use RELEASE MENUS. You can release all menu bars from memory with CLEAR MENUS or CLEAR ALL.

Program control is returned to the program line immediately following the line that activated the menu bar unless DEFINE MENU BAR is used to create the menu bar or ACTIVATE MENU NOWAIT is used to activate the menu bar.

Example

The following example uses DEACTIVATE MENU to deactivate a menu and remove it from the screen. The current system menu bar is saved to memory with SET SYSMENU SAVE, and all the system menu titles are removed with SET SYSMENU TO.

Two menu titles are created with DEFINE PAD, and DEFINE POPUP creates a menu for each menu title. DEFINE BAR creates menu items on each of the menus. When a menu title is chosen, ON PAD uses ACTIVATE POPUP to activate the corresponding menu. ACTIVATE MENU displays and activates the menu bar.

When an item is chosen from a menu, the CHOICE procedure is executed. CHOICE displays the name of the chosen item and the name of the menu containing the item. Program control continues on the line after ACTIVATE MENU.

Finally, the menu is deactivated and removed from the screen and is then released from memory with RELEASE MENUS EXTENDED.

```
*** Name this program DEACMENU.PRG ***
CLEAR
SET SYSMENU SAVE
SET SYSMENU TO
ON KEY LABEL ESC KEYBOARD CHR(13)
DEFINE MENU example BAR AT LINE 1
DEFINE PAD convpad OF example PROMPT '\<Conversions' COLOR SCHEME 3 ;
   KEY ALT+C, ''
DEFINE PAD cardpad OF example PROMPT 'Card \<Info' COLOR SCHEME 3 ;
   KEY ALT+I, ''
ON PAD convpad OF example ACTIVATE POPUP conversion
ON PAD cardpad OF example ACTIVATE POPUP cardinfo
DEFINE POPUP conversion MARGIN RELATIVE COLOR SCHEME 4
DEFINE BAR 1 OF conversion PROMPT 'Ar\<ea' ;
   KEY CTRL+E, '^E'
DEFINE BAR 2 OF conversion PROMPT '\<Length' ;
   KEY CTRL+L, '^L'
DEFINE BAR 3 OF conversion PROMPT 'Ma\<ss' ;
   KEY CTRL+S, '^S'
DEFINE BAR 4 OF conversion PROMPT 'Spee\<d' ;
   KEY CTRL+D, '^D'
DEFINE BAR 5 OF conversion PROMPT '\<Temperature' ;
   KEY CTRL+T, '^T'
DEFINE BAR 6 OF conversion PROMPT 'T\<ime' ;
   KEY CTRL+I, '^I'
DEFINE BAR 7 OF conversion PROMPT 'Volu\<me' ;
   KEY CTRL+M, '^M'
ON SELECTION POPUP conversion DO choice IN deacmenu WITH PROMPT( ), POPUP( )
DEFINE POPUP cardinfo MARGIN RELATIVE COLOR SCHEME 4
DEFINE BAR 1 OF cardinfo PROMPT '\<View Charges' ;
   KEY ALT+V, ''
DEFINE BAR 2 OF cardinfo PROMPT 'View \<Payments' ;
   KEY ALT+P, ''
DEFINE BAR 3 OF cardinfo PROMPT 'Vie\<w Users' ;
   KEY ALT+W, ''
DEFINE BAR 4 OF cardinfo PROMPT '\-'
DEFINE BAR 5 OF cardinfo PROMPT '\<Charges '
ON SELECTION POPUP cardinfo;
   DO choice IN deacmenu WITH PROMPT( ), POPUP( )

ACTIVATE MENU example
DEACTIVATE MENU example
RELEASE MENU example EXTENDED
SET SYSMENU NOSAVE
SET SYSMENU TO DEFAULT
ON KEY LABEL ESC
```

```
PROCEDURE choice
PARAMETERS mprompt, mpopup
WAIT WINDOW 'You chose ' + mprompt + ;
   ' from popup ' + mpopup NOWAIT
```

See Also

ACTIVATE MENU, CLEAR ALL, CLEAR MENUS, CREATE MENU, DEFINE MENU, HIDE MENU, RELEASE, SHOW MENU

DEACTIVATE POPUP Command

Deactivates a menu created with DEFINE POPUP.

Syntax

DEACTIVATE POPUP *MenuName1* [, *MenuName2* ...] | ALL

Arguments

MenuName1 [, *MenuName2* ...]

Specifies the names of the menu or menus to deactivate. You can deactivate a set of menus by including a list of menu names separated by commas.

ALL

Deactivates all active menus.

Remarks

DEACTIVATE POPUP removes an active menu or set of menus from the main Visual FoxPro window or a user-defined window without removing the menu definition from memory. A menu can be reactivated by using ACTIVATE POPUP and the menu name.

Use RELEASE POPUPS with the menu name to release a specific menu or a set of menus from memory. You can release all menus from memory with CLEAR POPUPS or CLEAR ALL.

Program control is returned to the line immediately following the line that activated the menu unless ACTIVATE POPUP NOWAIT is used to activate the menu.

See Also

ACTIVATE POPUP, CLEAR ALL CLEAR POPUPS, CREATE MENU, DEFINE POPUP, HIDE POPUP, RELEASE POPUPS, SHOW POPUP

DEACTIVATE WINDOW Command

Deactivates user-defined windows or Visual FoxPro system windows and removes them from the screen, but not from memory.

Syntax

DEACTIVATE WINDOW *WindowName1* [, *WindowName2* ...] | ALL

Arguments

WindowName1 [, *WindowName2* ...]
Specifies one or more windows to deactivate. You can specify Visual FoxPro system windows such as the Command window or a Browse window.

ALL
Deactivates all active windows.

To display the main FoxPro window again, choose Visual FoxPro Screen from the Window menu or issue ACTIVATE WINDOW SCREEN or SHOW WINDOW SCREEN.

Remarks

More than one user-defined window can be placed in the main Visual FoxPro window at the same time, but output is directed only to the most recently activated user-defined window. When more than one user-defined window is present, deactivating the current user-defined output window clears the contents of the window, removes the window from the screen and sends subsequent output to the previously activated user-defined window. If there is no output window, output is directed to the main Visual FoxPro window.

Use CLEAR WINDOWS or RELEASE WINDOWS to remove windows from both the screen and memory.

To deactivate a system window and or a toolbar (in Visual FoxPro), enclose the entire system window or toolbar name in quotation marks. For example, to deactivate the Report Controls toolbar in Visual FoxPro, issue the following command:

```
DEACTIVATE WINDOW "Report Controls"
```

Example

In the following example, a window named wOutput1 is defined and activated. After a record from the customer table is displayed, the program waits for the user to press a key and then deactivates the window.

```
CLOSE DATABASES
OPEN DATABASE (HOME(2) + 'Data\testdata')
USE customer  && Opens Customer table

CLEAR
DEFINE WINDOW wOutput1 FROM 2,1 TO 13,75 TITLE 'Output' ;
   CLOSE FLOAT GROW ZOOM
ACTIVATE WINDOW wOutput1

DISPLAY
WAIT WINDOW 'Press a key to deactivate the window'
DEACTIVATE WINDOW wOutput1
RELEASE WINDOW wOutput1
```

See Also

ACTIVATE WINDOW, CLEAR WINDOWS DEFINE WINDOW, HIDE WINDOW, RELEASE WINDOWS, SHOW WINDOW

DEBUG Command

Opens the Visual FoxPro debugger.

Syntax

DEBUG

Remarks

The debugger Environment setting (**FoxPro Frame** or **Debugger Frame**) determines if the debugger is placed on the Visual FoxPro desktop or in a separate window. Toggle this setting in the **Debugging** tab of the **Options** dialog box.

If you issue DEBUG when the debugger is open, the debugger becomes the active window.

See Also

CLOSE DEBUGGER, Debugging Tab, Options Dialog Box, DEBUGOUT, SET DEBUG

Debug Property

Specifies if debugging information is included with compiled source code in a project.

Syntax

Object.Debug[= *lExpression*]

Settings

lExpression
    The settings for the Debug property are:

Setting	Description
True (.T.)	(Default) Debugging information is included with the compiled source code.
False (.F.)	Debugging information isn't included and you cannot view a program's execution in the Trace window or use MESSAGE(1) to return the source code for a line that causes an error. Setting *lExpression* to false (.F.) is identical to including the NODEBUG argument in the COMPILE command.

Remarks

Source code in a project includes program and format files, source code in form, label, report, and Visual class libraries, and stored procedures in databases. The Debug property corresponds to the **Debug info** check box on the Project tab of the Project Information dialog box.

Applies To

Project Object

See Also

COMPILE, Project Information Dialog Box

DEBUGOUT Command

Directs the result of an expression to the Debug Output window.

Syntax

DEBUGOUT *eExpression*

Arguments

eExpression
Specifies an expression to evaluate and display in the **Debug Output** window.

Remarks

Use DEBUGOUT to identify when a procedure or function is executed. For example, you can place DEBUGOUT at the beginning of a procedure to display a message in the Debug Output window, indicating that the procedure has begun executing.

Note that you can only abbreviate DEBUGOUT to a minimum of 6 characters, distinguishing it from the DEBUG command.

See Also

DEBUG, Debug Output Window, SET DEBUG

DECLARE Command

Creates a one- or two-dimensional array.

Syntax

DECLARE *ArrayName1* (*nRows1* [, *nColumns1*])
    [, *ArrayName2* (*nRows2* [, *nColumns2*])] ...

Remarks

DECLARE is identical in operation and syntax to DIMENSION. For more information, see the DIMENSION Command, later in this language reference.

See Also

APPEND FROM ARRAY, COPY TO ARRAY DIMENSION, GATHER, PRIVATE, PUBLIC, SCATTER, SET COMPATIBLE, STORE

DECLARE – DLL Command

Registers a function in an external shared library. Libraries are 32-bit dynamic link library (.DLL) files.

Syntax

DECLARE [*cFunctionType*] *FunctionName* IN *LibraryName* [AS *AliasName*]
    [*cParamType1* [@] *ParamName1*,
        cParamType2 [@] *ParamName2*, ...]

Arguments

cFunctionType
    Indicates the data type of the return value from the shared library, if any. If the function does not return a value, omit *cFunctionType*.

    cFunctionType can assume the following values:

cFunctionType	Description
SHORT	16-bit integer
INTEGER	32-bit integer
SINGLE	32-bit floating point
DOUBLE	64-bit floating point
LONG	32-bit long integer
STRING	Character string

FunctionName

    Specifies the name of the shared library function to register in Visual FoxPro. Function names passed in this parameter are case-sensitive.

    Note A DLL function name may not be the same as stated in the Win32 API manual. For example, the MessageBox function should be named MessageBoxA (for single-byte character), and MessageBoxW (for UNICODE). If Visual FoxPro cannot locate the DLL function you specify with *FunctionName*, the letter A is appended to the end of the function name and Visual FoxPro searches again for the function with the new name.

    If the shared library function you specify has the same name as a Visual FoxPro function or is not a legal Visual FoxPro name, use the AS clause to assign an alias to the function when you register it, as described later in this topic.

IN *LibraryName*

    Specifies the name of the external shared library containing the function specified with *FunctionName*.

    If you specify WIN32API for the *LibraryName*, Visual FoxPro searches for the 32-bit Windows .dll function in Kernel32.dll, Gdi32.dll, User32.dll, Mpr.dll, and Advapi32.dll.

AS *AliasName*

    Specifies an alias name for a shared library function name that has the same name as a Visual FoxPro function or is not a legal Visual FoxPro name. *AliasName* should not be a Visual FoxPro reserved word or the name of a shared library function already registered with Visual FoxPro.

    If you assign alias to the function, use the alias when calling the shared library function. *AliasName* is not case-sensitive.

cParameterType1 [@] *ParamName1*, *cParameterType2* [@] *ParamName2*, ...

    Specifies the parameter types passed to the shared library function.

    cParameterType is required and specifies the data type of any parameters that the shared library function expects to have passed to it. *cParameterType* may be one of the following:

cParameterType	Description
INTEGER	32-bit integer
SINGLE	32-bit floating point
DOUBLE	64-bit floating point
LONG	32-bit long integer
STRING	Character string

Visual FoxPro generates an error if the parameters are not of the type the shared library function expects. Null values can be passed as empty character strings.

To pass a parameter by reference when you call the function, you must include @ after the parameter *cParameterType* in this command, and before the corresponding variable in the calling function. If you don't include @ in DECLARE, in the calling function, or in both, the parameter is passed by value. For information about shared library functions that require @ to pass parameters by reference, see the programmer's guide for your operating system or environment (for example, refer to the *Microsoft Win32 Programmer's Guide* for information on passing parameters to Windows DLLs).

Note The parameter names *ParamName1*, *ParamName2,* and so on, are optional, and are not used by Visual FoxPro or the shared library function. You can include them as a reminder of the names and types of parameters the function receives.

Remarks

Before you can call a shared library function from within Visual FoxPro, you must issue DECLARE with the name of the function, the name of the shared library containing the function, and the parameter types the function expects to receive.

For backward compatibility, Visual FoxPro allows calls to external API libraries using the SET LIBRARY command. (Using SET LIBRARY, you can access functions in Foxtools.fll). However, using DECLARE is the preferred method to register shared library functions.

For further information about calling shared library functions, see the programmer's guide for your operating system or environment (for example, refer to the *Microsoft Win32 Programmer's Guide* for information on calling DLLs).

Issue DISPLAY STATUS or LIST STATUS to display the names of registered functions. Issue CLEAR ALL or CLEAR DLLS to remove registered functions from memory.

Example

This example for Windows returns the window handle for Visual FoxPro or izero if you switch to another Windows application. When the WAIT window is displayed, you have 5 seconds to press ALT+TAB to switch to a different Windows application, or you can leave Visual FoxPro as the active application.

```
CLEAR
DECLARE INTEGER GetActiveWindow IN win32api
WAIT WINDOW "You can switch to another application now" TIMEOUT 5
? GetActiveWindow( )
```

See Also

CALL, CLEAR, DISPLAY DLLS, DISPLAY STATUS, LIST DLLS, LOAD, SET LIBRARY

Default Property

Specifies which command button or OLE Container control responds to the ENTER key being pressed when there are two or more command buttons on an active form. Available at design time and run time.

Syntax

Object.Default[= *lExpr*]

Arguments

lExpr

The settings for the Default property are:

Setting	Description
True (.T.)	When the button's Default property is set to true (.T.) and its parent form is active, the user can execute the button's command by pressing ENTER. (If the focus is in an edit box, the user can press CTRL+ENTER.)
	If KEYCOMP is set to WINDOWS, the default button's command is not executed if the focus has been moved to another command button. In that case, pressing ENTER affects the button with the focus instead of the default button.
False (.F.)	(Default) The button is not the default button.

Remarks

The Default property only applies to an OLE Container control that contains an "Acts like a Button" ActiveX control (.ocx).

Only one command button or OLE Container control on a form can be the default command button. When the Default property is set to true (.T.) for one command button or OLE Container control, it is automatically set to false (.F.) for all other command buttons or OLE Container controls on the form. You cannot create a default command button or OLE Container control in a toolbar.

Applies To

CommandButton, OLE Container Control

See Also

Enabled Property, KeyPress Event

DEFAULTEXT( ) Function

Returns a file name with a new extension if one doesn't already exist.

Syntax

DEFAULTEXT(*cFileName, cDefault*)

Returns

Character

Arguments

cFileName
   Specifies the filename (with or without a path or extension) to be returned.

cDefault
   Specifies the default extension without a period.

See Also

ADDBS( ), FILE( ), FORCEEXT( ), FORCEPATH( ), JUSTDRIVE( ), JUSTEXT( ), JUSTFNAME( ), JUSTPATH( ), JUSTSTEM( )

DefaultFilePath Property

Specifies the default drive and directory used by an Application object. Available at run time.

Syntax

ApplicationObject.DefaultFilePath[= *cPath*]

Arguments

cPath
   Specifies one of the following:

   - A drive designator.

   - A drive designator with a directory name.

   - A child directory name.

   - Any of the above using MS–DOS shorthand notation (\ or ..).

Remarks

The DefaultFilePath property is similar to SET DEFAULT.

Visual FoxPro searches for a file in the default Visual FoxPro directory. The default directory is the one from which you start Visual FoxPro. However, you can use the DefaultFilePath property to specify a different default directory. If Visual FoxPro cannot find a file in the default directory, it then searches the Visual FoxPro path if one has been specified. Use SET PATH to specify the Visual FoxPro path.

Applies To

Application Object, _VFP System Variable

See Also

SET DEFAULT, SET PATH

DEFINE BAR Command

Creates a menu item on a menu created with DEFINE POPUP.

Syntax

DEFINE BAR *nMenuItemNumber1* | *SystemItemName*
OF *MenuName* PROMPT *cMenuItemText*
    [BEFORE *nMenuItemNumber2* | AFTER *nMenuItemNumber3*]
    [FONT *cFontName* [, *nFontSize*]]
    [STYLE *cFontStyle*]
    [KEY *KeyLabel* [, *cKeyText*]]
    [MARK *cMarkCharacter*]
    [MESSAGE *cMessageText*]
    [SKIP [FOR *lExpression*]]
    [COLOR SCHEME *nSchemeNumber*
    | COLOR *ColorPairList*]

Arguments

nMenuItemNumber1
    Specifies the menu item number. The menu item number allows you to reference the menu item in other commands and functions.

SystemItemName
    Specifies a menu item on the Visual FoxPro system menu. For example, to provide access to the Print menu item, issue the following:

```
DEFINE BAR _MFI_PRINT OF popMyPopup PROMPT "Print..."
```

    Not all Visual FoxPro system menu items are available. Use SYS(2013) to return a list of the Visual FoxPro system menu names that are available.

OF *MenuName*
    Specifies the name of the menu on which the menu items are placed.

PROMPT *cMenuItemText*

Specifies the caption that appears on the menu item.

You can create a separator bar by specifying a backslash and a dash (\–) for *cMenuItemText*. A separator bar is used to separate item groups on a menu. For example, including the following command in a menu definition creates a separator bar between the third and fifth menu items:

```
DEFINE BAR 4 OF popMyPopup PROMPT '\-'
```

You can create multi-column menus by specifying a backslash and a vertical bar (\|) at the beginning of *cMenuItemText*. The menu item starts a new column, and subsequent menu items are placed in the same column until another menu item beginning with \| is encountered. For example, including the following command in a menu definition creates a new column in the menu:

```
DEFINE BAR 4 OF popMyPopup PROMPT '\|Start a new column'
```

You can create an access key for a menu item by placing a backslash and a less-than sign (\<) before the character to be the access key. For example:

```
DEFINE POPUP popReceive
DEFINE BAR 1 OF popReceive PROMPT '\<Invoices'
DEFINE BAR 2 OF popReceive PROMPT 'In\<quiry'
ACTIVATE POPUP popReceive
```

The user can press the I key to choose Invoices from the Receive menu and press the Q key to choose Inquiry from the same menu.

BEFORE *nMenuItemNumber2*

Places a menu item before the menu item specified with *nMenuItemNumber2*.

AFTER *nMenuItemNumber3*

Places a menu item after the menu item specified with *nMenuItemNumber3*.

> **Note** In order for BEFORE or AFTER to have an effect, you must include the RELATIVE clause when you create the menu with DEFINE POPUP.

You can also include _MFIRST and _MLAST in the BEFORE and AFTER clauses. If you include_MFIRST in the BEFORE clause, the menu item is the first item on the menu. If you include_MFIRST in the AFTER clause, the menu item is the second item on the menu. If you include_MLAST in the AFTER clause, the menu item is the last item on the menu. If you include_MLAST in the BEFORE clause, the menu item is the next-to-last item on the menu.

Menus created with DEFINE POPUP RELATIVE don't reserve space for undefined menu items. For example, if you define items 1, 2, 4, and 5 on a menu, a space for item 3 is not reserved. You can later insert item 3. The menu expands to accommodate it.

Run the following program examples and note the differences in the order and placement of the items on each menu:

```
*** RELATIVE Example ***
DEFINE POPUP popRelatYes RELATIVE FROM 1,1
DEFINE BAR 4  OF popRelatYes PROMPT '4444'
DEFINE BAR 3  OF popRelatYes PROMPT '3333'
DEFINE BAR 2  OF popRelatYes PROMPT '2222'
DEFINE BAR 1  OF popRelatYes PROMPT '1111'
DEFINE BAR 6  OF popRelatYes PROMPT '6666' BEFORE 4
ACTIVATE POPUP popRelatYes

*** NON-RELATIVE Example ***
DEFINE POPUP popRelatNo FROM 1,10
DEFINE BAR 4 OF popRelatNo PROMPT '4444'
DEFINE BAR 3 OF popRelatNo PROMPT '3333'
DEFINE BAR 2 OF popRelatNo PROMPT '2222'
DEFINE BAR 1 OF popRelatNo PROMPT '1111'
DEFINE BAR 6 OF popRelatNo PROMPT '6666'
ACTIVATE POPUP popRelatNo
```

FONT *cFontName* [, *nFontSize*]

Specifies a font for the menu item. *cFontName* specifies the name of the font, and *nFontSize* specifies the point size. For example, the following command creates a menu item in 12-point Courier font:

```
DEFINE BAR 1 OF popReceive PROMPT '\<Invoices' FONT 'Courier', 12
```

If the font you specify is not available, a font with similar font characteristics is substituted. If you include the FONT clause but omit the point size *nFontSize*, a 10-point font is used.

STYLE *cFontStyle*

Specifies a font style for the menu item. If you omit the STYLE clause, the normal font style is used. If the font style you specify is not available, the normal font style is used.

The font styles you can specify with *cFontStyle* are as follows:

Character	Font style
B	Bold
I	Italic
N	Normal
Q	Opaque
–	Strikeout
T	Transparent
U	Underline

You can include more than one character to specify a combination of font styles. For example, the following command specifies Bold Italic:

```
DEFINE BAR 1 OF popReceive PROMPT '\<Invoices' STYLE 'BI'
```

KEY *KeyLabel* [, *cKeyText*]

Specifies an access key or key combination for a menu item. The menu does not have to be activated in order for the menu item to be chosen, unlike when you assign an access key using a backslash and a less-than sign (\<).

For a list of available keys and key combinations and their key label names, see the ON KEY LABEL Command, later in this language reference.

> **Note** If a keyboard macro is already defined with the same key label, the keyboard macro takes precedence, and the menu item cannot be chosen with the specified key or key combination.

Include *cKeyText* to replace the key label with your own text. You can use any character in the *cKeyText* parameter; for example, you can use the text "^B" to indicate a key label of CTRL+B. For example, including KEY CTRL+B places the text CTRL+B on the menu to the right of the menu item name, but specifying KEY CTRL+B, "^B" places the text ^B on the menu. You can suppress the display of a key label by specifying an empty string for *cKeyText*.

MARK *cMarkCharacter*

Specifies a mark character that appears to the left of the menu item. MARK can be included to change the default mark character to a character specified with *cMarkCharacter*. If *cMarkCharacter* includes more than one character, only the first character is used as the mark character.

The default mark character is a check.

The MARK clause is ignored and the default mark character is used if the menu containing the menu item is integrated into the Visual FoxPro system menu. Also, the MARK clause is ignored if FoxFont isn't the font for the main Visual FoxPro window or the user-defined window in which the menu containing the menu item is placed.

> **Note** Specifying a mark character doesn't mark a menu item. Use SET MARK OF to mark a menu item.

Mark characters specified in DEFINE BAR take precedence over mark characters specified with MARK in DEFINE POPUP. SET MARK OF is used to toggle mark characters on or off, and can also be used to specify a mark character for an individual menu item or for all menu items.

MESSAGE *cMessageText*

Displays a message when the user selects a menu item. The message is placed in the graphical status bar. If the graphical status bar is turned off with SET STATUS BAR OFF, the message is centered on the last line of the main Visual FoxPro window.

SKIP [FOR *lExpression*]

Specifies a condition whereby if *lExpression* evaluates to true (.T.), the menu item is disabled, preventing the user from choosing it; if false (.F.), the menu item is enabled. A disabled menu item appears in the disabled colors.

You can also disable a menu item by placing a backslash (\) before the text of the prompt. For example:

```
DEFINE BAR 1 OF popReceive PROMPT '\Invoices'
```

A menu item disabled with SKIP or \ cannot be selected. Menus you create that include SKIP FOR expressions may not behave properly when the spelling checker or wizards are active.

SKIP FOR expressions typically depend on the value of skip variables, but the skip variables are not visible to your menus when the spelling checker or wizards are active. In the initialization code of the spelling checker and wizard applications (SPELLCHK.APP and GENGRAPH.APP respectively), PRIVATE ALL is intentionally issued. This hides skip variables from user-defined menus and causes an error message when you choose a menu.

To correct this situation, the following code is placed at the beginning of the spelling checker and wizard applications:

```
IF TYPE("_memvarmask") = "C" and !EMPTY(_memvarmask)
    PRIVATE ALL EXCEPT &_memvarmask
ELSE
    PRIVATE ALL
ENDIF
```

Suppose a certain menu item should be skipped when the variable named "skipvar" evaluates to true. You should include the following lines in your menu startup code to take advantage of the _MEMVARMASK variable:

```
PUBLIC _memvarmask
_memvarmask = "skipvar"
STORE .T. TO skipvar      && Skip initially.
```

To create a set of skip variables, include the following lines in your menu startup code:

```
PUBLIC _memvarmask
_memvarmask = "skip*"
STORE .T. TO skipthis, skipthat  && Skip initially.
```

When you run the spelling checker and wizards, they don't hide variables in SKIP FOR expressions, preventing the error messages you may experience when the spelling checker or wizards are active.

Note that _MEMVARMASK isn't a system variable.

COLOR SCHEME *nSchemeNumber*

> Specifies the colors for an individual menu item, overriding the default colors or the colors specified with DEFINE POPUP.

COLOR *ColorPairList*

> Specifies the colors for an individual menu item, overriding the default colors or the colors specified with DEFINE POPUP. You can specify the colors of all menu items, mark characters, and messages.
>
> By default, the colors of menu items are determined by color scheme 2 of the current color set.
>
> For more information on color schemes and color pairs, see "Colors Overview," earlier in this language reference.

Remarks

DEFINE BAR is used with DEFINE POPUP to create menus. A menu is created and assigned a name with DEFINE POPUP. Menu items are placed on the menu with a series of DEFINE BAR commands.

If you use the Menu Designer to create your menu, you may not have to use these commands at all. The Menu Designer automatically creates the commands for your menu. The Menu Designer uses the Visual FoxPro system menu, which you can then modify by adding your own menu items. For more information on creating menus, see "Creating a Menu System" in Chapter 11, "Designing Menus and Toolbars," in the *Microsoft Visual FoxPro 6.0 Programmer's Guide*.

You can also create a menu that contains records or fields from a table or a list of files available on disk. For more information, see the PROMPT FIELD, PROMPT STRUCTURE and PROMPT FILES clauses in the DEFINE POPUP Command, later in this language reference.

Use ON BAR to create a cascading submenu for a menu item.

Example

The following example uses DEFINE BAR to create items on menus. The current system menu bar is first saved to memory with SET SYSMENU SAVE, and then all system menu titles are removed with SET SYSMENU TO.

Two new system menu titles are created with DEFINE PAD, and DEFINE POPUP is used to create a drop-down menu for each menu title. DEFINE BAR is used to create items on each of the menus. When a menu title is chosen, ON PAD uses ACTIVATE POPUP to activate the corresponding menu.

When an item is chosen from a menu, ON SELECTION POPUP uses PROMPT( ) and POPUP( ) to pass the item number and menu name to the CHOICE procedure. CHOICE displays the prompt of the chosen item and the name of the menu containing the item. If Exit is chosen from the Card Info menu, the original Visual FoxPro system menu is restored.

```
*** Name this program DEFINBAR.PRG ***
CLEAR
SET SYSMENU SAVE
SET SYSMENU TO
DEFINE PAD convpad OF _MSYSMENU PROMPT '\<Conversions' COLOR SCHEME 3 ;
   KEY ALT+C, ''
DEFINE PAD cardpad OF _MSYSMENU PROMPT 'Card \<Info' COLOR SCHEME 3 ;
   KEY ALT+I, ''
ON PAD convpad OF _MSYSMENU ACTIVATE POPUP conversion
ON PAD cardpad OF _MSYSMENU ACTIVATE POPUP cardinfo
DEFINE POPUP conversion MARGIN RELATIVE COLOR SCHEME 4
DEFINE BAR 1 OF conversion PROMPT 'Ar\<ea' KEY CTRL+E, '^E'
DEFINE BAR 2 OF conversion PROMPT '\<Length' ;
   KEY CTRL+L, '^L'
DEFINE BAR 3 OF conversion PROMPT 'Ma\<ss' ;
   KEY CTRL+S, '^S'
DEFINE BAR 4 OF conversion PROMPT 'Spee\<d' ;
   KEY CTRL+D, '^D'
DEFINE BAR 5 OF conversion PROMPT '\<Temperature' ;
   KEY CTRL+T, '^T'
DEFINE BAR 6 OF conversion PROMPT 'T\<ime' ;
   KEY CTRL+I, '^I'
DEFINE BAR 7 OF conversion PROMPT 'Volu\<me' ;
   KEY CTRL+M, '^M'
ON SELECTION POPUP conversion;
   DO choice IN definbar WITH PROMPT( ), POPUP( )
DEFINE POPUP cardinfo MARGIN RELATIVE COLOR SCHEME 4
DEFINE BAR 1 OF cardinfo PROMPT '\<View Charges' ;
   KEY ALT+V, ''
DEFINE BAR 2 OF cardinfo PROMPT 'View \<Payments' ;
   KEY ALT+P, ''
DEFINE BAR 3 OF cardinfo PROMPT 'Vie\<w Users' KEY ALT+W, ''
DEFINE BAR 4 OF cardinfo PROMPT '\-'
DEFINE BAR 5 OF cardinfo PROMPT '\<Charges '
DEFINE BAR 6 OF cardinfo PROMPT '\-'
DEFINE BAR 7 OF cardinfo PROMPT 'E\<xit '
ON SELECTION POPUP cardinfo;
   DO choice IN definbar WITH PROMPT( ), POPUP( )
PROCEDURE choice
PARAMETERS mprompt, mpopup
WAIT WINDOW 'You chose ' + mprompt + ;
   ' from popup ' + mpopup NOWAIT
IF mprompt = 'Exit'
   SET SYSMENU TO DEFAULT
ENDIF
```

See Also

ACTIVATE POPUP, DEACTIVATE POPUP, DEFINE POPUP, HIDE POPUP,
RELEASE BAR, SET MESSAGE, SHOW POPUP

DEFINE BOX Command

Included for backward compatibility. Use the Report Designer instead.

DEFINE CLASS Command

Creates a user-defined class or subclass and specifies the properties, events, and methods for the class or subclass.

Syntax

DEFINE CLASS *ClassName1* AS *ParentClass* [OLEPUBLIC]
    [[PROTECTED | HIDDEN *PropertyName1*, *PropertyName2* ...]
       [Object.]*PropertyName* = *eExpression* ...]
    [ADD OBJECT [PROTECTED] *ObjectName* AS *ClassName2* [NOINIT]
       [WITH *cPropertylist*]]...
    [[PROTECTED | HIDDEN] FUNCTION | PROCEDURE *Name*[_ACCESS | _ASSIGN]
    | THIS_ACCESS [NODEFAULT]
       cStatements
    [ENDFUNC | ENDPROC]]...
ENDDEFINE

Arguments

ClassName1
    Specifies the name of the class to create.

AS *ParentClass*
    Specifies the parent class on which a class or subclass is based. The parent class can be a Visual FoxPro base class, such as the Form class, or another user-defined class or subclass.

    The following table lists the Visual FoxPro base classes:

Base class names

ActiveDoc	CheckBox	Column
ComboBox	CommandButton	CommandGroup
Container	Control	Cursor
Custom	DataEnvironment	EditBox
Form	FormSet	Grid
Header	Hyperlink	Image
ProjectHook	Label	Line

ListBox	OLEBoundControl	OLEControl
OptionButton	OptionGroup	Page
PageFrame	Relation	Separator
Shape	Spinner	TextBox
Timer	ToolBar	

A non-visual user-defined class is created by specifying Custom for *ParentClass*.

In the following example, a subclass named MyForm is created, based on the Form base class. A Click method is created that displays a dialog box when MyForm is clicked.

```
DEFINE CLASS MyForm AS Form
   PROCEDURE Click
     = MESSAGEBOX('MyForm has been clicked!')
   ENDPROC
ENDDEFINE
```

OLEPUBLIC

Specifies that the class in an Automation server can be accessed by an Automation client.

If a program containing an OLEPUBLIC class definition is added to a project, an executable (.exe) file or a dynamic link library (.dll) containing the class can be created interactively in the Project Manager or with BUILD EXE or BUILD DLL. The EXE or DLL is automatically registered with the operating system, and becomes available to any Automation client.

For information about creating custom Automation servers, see "Creating Automation Servers" in Chapter 16, "Adding OLE," in the *Microsoft Visual FoxPro 6.0 Programmer's Guide*.

[PROTECTED | HIDDEN *PropertyName1, PropertyName2 ...*]
[*Object.*]*PropertyName = eExpression ...* Creates a class or subclass property and assigns a default value to the property. Properties are named attributes of the class and define characteristics and behaviors for the class. Classes and subclasses can have multiple properties.

Use = to assign a value to the property. The following example creates a user-defined class named MyClass and creates two properties called Name and Version. The Name property is initialized to the empty string and the Version property is initialized to the character string 1.0.

```
DEFINE CLASS MyClass AS Custom
   Name = ''
   Version = '1.0'
ENDDEFINE
```

A property can be accessed outside the class or subclass definition after the object is created with **CREATEOBJECT( )**:

```
MyOjbect = CREATEOBJECT('MyClass')
```

Properties are accessed with the following syntax:

```
ObjectName.Property
```

The *.Object* keyword indicates to Visual FoxPro that the property value should be applied when the ActiveX control is created.

The following example adds the Outline ActiveX control to a form. The Object keyword is used to specify a property for the Outline control before it is created.

```
PUBLIC frmOLETest
frmOLETest = CREATEOBJECT('Form')
frmOLETest.Visible = .T.

frmOLETest.ADDOBJECT('OCXTest', 'BlueOLEControl', ;
    'MSOutl.Outline')
frmOLETest.OCXTest.AddItem('Item One')
frmOLETest.OCXTest.AddItem('Item Two')

DEFINE CLASS BlueOLEControl AS OLEControl

    * Set a property of the ActiveX control
    .Object.Backcolor = 16776960

    * Set properties of the OLE Container Control
    Visible = .T.
    Height = 100
    Width = 200
ENDDEFINE
```

Include PROTECTED and a list of property names to prevent access and changes to the properties from outside of the class or subclass definition. Methods and events within the class or subclass definition can access the protected properties.

In the following example, the Version property is protected, preventing it from being accessed and changed outside of the class definition. However, the Name property is not protected and can be accessed and changed.

```
DEFINE CLASS MyClass AS Custom
    PROTECTED Version
    Name = ''
    Version = '1.0'
ENDDEFINE
```

Include HIDDEN and a list of property names to prevent access and changes to the properties from outside of the class definition. Only methods and events within the class definition can access the hidden properties. While protected properties can be accessed by subclasses of the class definition, hidden properties can only be accessed from with the class definition.

ADD OBJECT

Adds an object to a class or subclass definition from a Visual FoxPro base class, user-defined class or subclass, or ActiveX custom control.

PROTECTED

Prevents access and changes to the object's properties from outside the class or subclass definition. The PROTECTED keyword must be placed immediately before *ObjectName* or FoxPro generates a syntax error.

ObjectName

Specifies the name of the object and is used to reference the object from within the class or subclass definition after an object is created from the class or subclass definition.

AS *ClassName2*

Specifies the name of the class or subclass containing the object you add to the class definition. For example, the following class definition adds a command button from the CommandButton base class and a list box from the ListBox base class.

```
DEFINE CLASS MyClass AS Custom
    ADD OBJECT CB1 AS CommandButton
    ADD OBJECT LIST1 AS ListBox
ENDDEFINE
```

NOINIT

Specifies that an object's Init method is not executed when the object is added.

WITH *cPropertyList*

Specifies a list of properties and property values for the object you add to the class or subclass definition. For example, the following class definition creates a class called `MyClass`, adds a command button to the class definition, and specifies the Caption and BackColor properties for the command button.

```
DEFINE CLASS MyClass AS CUSTOM
    ADD OBJECT CB1 AS CommandButton;
        WITH Caption = 'Cancel', BackColor = 2
ENDDEFINE
```

FUNCTION | PROCEDURE *Name*[_ACCESS | _ASSIGN] | THIS_ACCESS

Create events and methods for the class or subclass. Events and methods are created as a set of functions or procedures.

You can create an event function or procedure within a class or subclass definition to respond to an event. An event is an action such as a mouse click that is recognized by an object created with a class or subclass definition. For additional information about Visual FoxPro event processing, see "The Core Events" in Chapter 4, "Understanding the Event Model," in the *Microsoft Visual FoxPro 6.0 Programmer's Guide*.

Events are called with the following syntax:

```
ObjectName.Event
```

You can also create a method function or procedure within a class or subclass definition. A method is a procedure that acts upon the object created with the class or subclass definition. Methods are called with this syntax:

```
ObjectName.Method
```

The _ACCESS and _ASSIGN suffixes can be added to a procedure or function name to create an Access or Assign method for a property of the same name. The code in an Access method is executed whenever the property is queried. The code in an Assign method is executed whenever you attempt to change the value of the property.

In addition, you can create a THIS_ACCESS procedure or function that is executed whenever you attempt to change the value of a member of an object or a member of an object is queried.

For more information about creating Access and Assign methods with DEFINE CLASS, see "Access and Assign Methods" in Chapter 33, "Programming Improvements," in the *Microsoft Visual FoxPro 6.0 Programmer's Guide*.

NODEFAULT

Prevents Visual FoxPro from performing its default event or method processing for Visual FoxPro events and methods. For example, if the KeyPress event occurs, including NODEFAULT in the KeyPress procedure or function prevents Visual FoxPro from placing the key press into the Visual FoxPro keyboard buffer. This allows you to create a KeyPress procedure that lets you test which key is pressed before the key is sent to the keyboard buffer.

NODEFAULT may be placed anywhere within the event or method procedure. Note that NODEFAULT may also be placed within an event or method procedure in the Form Designer.

cStatements

[ENDFUNC | ENDPROC]]...
ENDDEFINE
cStatements are the Visual FoxPro commands that are executed when an event or method is executed.

Event and method functions and procedures can accept values by including a PARAMETERS or LPARAMETERS statement as the first executable line of the function or procedure.

Unlike most Visual FoxPro keywords, you cannot abbreviate ENDFUNC and ENDPROC. This prevents conflicts with the ENDFOR and ENDPRINTJOB keywords.

The following example demonstrates how to create an event procedure that displays a message when the command button is clicked. This event procedure overrides the default command button Click event.

```
DEFINE CLASS MyClass AS Custom
    ADD OBJECT MyButton AS CommandButton
    ADD OBJECT MyList AS ListBox
    PROCEDURE MyButton.Click
      = MESSAGEBOX('This is my click event procedure')
    ENDPROC
ENDDEFINE
```

Remarks

User-defined classes are a set of commands placed in a program file, similar to a procedure. The commands that follow the class or subclass definition define the properties, events, and methods for the class or subclass.

> **Note** You cannot have normal executable program code included in a program file after procedures; only class definitions, procedures, and user-defined functions can follow the first DEFINE CLASS, PROCEDURE or FUNCTION command in the file.

Class and subclass definitions created with DEFINE CLASS cannot be placed within structured programming commands, such as IF ... ENDIF or DO CASE ... ENDCASE. Nor can they be placed in loops, such as DO WHILE ... ENDDO or FOR ... ENDFOR.

To create an object from a class or subclass definition, issue CREATEOBJECT( ) with the class or subclass name.

Example

The following example uses DEFINE CLASS and CREATEOBJECT( ) to create two custom classes named FormChild and FormGrandChild from the Visual FoxPro Form base class. ACLASS( ) is used to create an array named gaNewarray containing the class names, which are then displayed.

```
CLEAR
frmMyForm = CREATEOBJECT("FormGrandChild")
FOR nCount = 1 TO ACLASS(gaNewarray, frmMyForm)     && Creates an array
   ? gaNewarray(nCount)  && Displays the names of the classes
ENDFOR
RELEASE frmMyForm

DEFINE CLASS FormChild AS FORM
ENDDEFINE

DEFINE CLASS FormGrandChild AS FormChild
ENDDEFINE
```

See Also

:: Scope Resolution Operator, ADD CLASS, _BROWSER, CREATE CLASS, CREATE CLASSLIB, CREATEOBJECT( ), DODEFAULT( ), GETOBJECT( ), MODIFY CLASS, RELEASE CLASSLIB, SET CLASSLIB, WITH ... ENDWITH

DEFINE MENU Command

Creates a menu bar.

Syntax

DEFINE MENU *MenuBarName*
    [BAR [AT LINE *nRow*]]
    [IN [WINDOW] *WindowName* | IN SCREEN]
    [FONT *cFontName* [, *nFontSize*]]
    [STYLE *cFontStyle*]
    [KEY *KeyLabel*]
    [MARK *cMarkCharacter*]
    [MESSAGE *cMessageText*]
    [NOMARGIN]
    [COLOR SCHEME *nSchemeNumber*
    | COLOR *ColorPairList*]

Arguments

MenuBarName
Specifies the name of the menu bar to create. The menu bar name allows you to reference the menu bar in other commands and functions.

BAR [AT LINE *nRow*]
Creates a menu bar that behaves like the Visual FoxPro system menu bar. The menu bar has these characteristics:

- A horizontal menu bar one line high is drawn across the width of the main Visual FoxPro window or the user-defined window it is placed in.

- The placement of the menu titles on the menu bar is handled automatically.

- If the size or number of menu titles you define exceeds the size of the screen or a window in which the menu bar is placed, the menu bar scrolls.

The row number is specified with *nRow*.

IN [WINDOW] *WindowName*
Places a menu bar in a user-defined window. Specify the name of the window in which you want to place the menu bar with *WindowName*. If you omit IN WINDOW, the menu bar is placed in the main Visual FoxPro window by default unless there is an active user-defined window. If there is an active user-defined window, the menu bar is placed in the active window.

IN SCREEN

Explicitly places the menu bar in the main Visual FoxPro window.

FONT *cFontName* [, *nFontSize*]

Specifies a default font for all menu titles in the menu bar. You can override the default font for an individual menu title by including the FONT clause in DEFINE PAD.

cFontName specifies the name of the font, and *nFontSize* specifies the point size. For example, the following command creates a menu bar with menu titles in 12-point Courier font:

```
DEFINE MENU mnuExample FONT 'Courier', 12
```

If the font you specify is not available, a font with similar font characteristics is substituted. If you include the FONT clause but omit the point size *nFontSize*, a 10-point font is used.

The FONT clause is ignored for menu titles added to the Visual FoxPro system menu _MSYSMENU. Note that the Menu Designer uses the Visual FoxPro system menu.

STYLE *cFontStyle*

Specifies a default font style for all the menu titles in the menu bar. You can override the default style for individual menu titles by including the STYLE clause in DEFINE PAD.

If you omit the STYLE clause, or if the font style you specify is not available, the Normal font style is used.

The font styles you can specify with *cFontStyle* are as follows:

Character	Font style
B	Bold
I	Italic
N	Normal
Q	Opaque
–	Strikeout
T	Transparent
U	Underline

You can include more than one character to specify a combination of font styles. For example, the following command specifies Bold Italic:

```
DEFINE MENU mnuExample STYLE 'BI'
```

The STYLE clause is ignored for menu titles added to the Visual FoxPro system menu _MSYSMENU. The Menu Designer uses the Visual FoxPro system menu.

KEY *KeyLabel*

Specifies the key or key combination used to activate the menu bar. For a list of available keys and key combinations and their key label names, see the ON KEY LABEL Command, later in this language reference.

Including the KEY clause is equivalent to issuing the following command:

```
ON KEY LABEL KeyLabel ACTIVATE MENU MenuName
```

> **Note** If a keyboard macro is already defined with the same key label, the keyboard macro takes precedence, and the menu bar cannot be activated with the specified key or key combination.

MARK *cMarkCharacter*

Specifies a mark character that appears to the left of the menu titles on the menu bar. MARK can be included to change the default mark character to a character specified with *cMarkCharacter*. If *cMarkCharacter* includes more than one character, only the first character is used as the mark character.

The default mark character is a check. The MARK clause is ignored and the default mark character is used if the menu bar is the Visual FoxPro system menu. Also, the MARK clause is ignored if FoxFont isn't the font for the main Visual FoxPro window or the user-defined window in which the menu bar is placed.

> **Note** Specifying a mark character doesn't mark the menu names on a menu bar. Use SET MARK OF to mark the menu titles on a menu bar with the character you specify.

Mark characters specified with DEFINE PAD take precedence over mark characters specified with the MARK clause in DEFINE MENU. SET MARK OF is used to toggle mark characters on or off, and can also be used to specify a mark character for an individual menu item or for all menu items.

MESSAGE *cMessageText*

Displays a message when the user selects a menu title. The message is placed in the graphical status bar. If the graphical status bar is turned off with SET STATUS BAR OFF, the message is centered on the last line of the main Visual FoxPro window.

NOMARGIN

Removes the spaces that are placed to the left and right of each menu name by default.

COLOR SCHEME *nSchemeNumber*

Specifies the colors for an individual menu bar.

COLOR *ColorPairList*

Specifies the colors for an individual menu bar. By default, the colors of menu items are determined by color scheme 2 of the current color set.

For more information on color schemes and color pairs, see "Colors Overview," earlier in this language reference.

Remarks

Use DEFINE MENU to create the menu bar for your application's menu system. Use DEFINE PAD to create each of the menu titles (pads) on the menu bar. Use ON PAD ... ACTIVATE to specify which menu is displayed under each menu title. Use DEFINE POPUP to create the menus under each menu title. Use ACTIVATE MENU to activate the entire menu system.

If you use the Menu Designer to create your menu, you may not have to use these commands at all. The Menu Designer automatically creates the commands for your menu. The Menu Designer uses the Visual FoxPro system menu, which you can then modify by adding your own menu items.

For more information on creating menus, see "Creating a Menu System" in Chapter 11, "Designing Menus and Toolbars," in the *Microsoft Visual FoxPro 6.0 Programmer's Guide.*

Example

The following example uses DEFINE MENU to create a user-defined menu system. The current system menu bar is first saved to memory with SET SYSMENU SAVE, and then the system menu titles are cleared with SET SYSMENU TO.

DEFINE MENU creates the menu bar, and two menu titles are created with DEFINE PAD. DEFINE POPUP creates a menu for each menu title. DEFINE BAR creates items on each of the menus. When a menu title is chosen, ON PAD uses ACTIVATE POPUP to activate the corresponding menu. ACTIVATE MENU displays and activates the menu bar.

When an item is chosen from a menu, the CHOICE procedure is executed. CHOICE displays the name of the chosen item and the name of the menu containing the item.

```
*** Name this program DEFIMENU.PRG ***
CLEAR
SET SYSMENU SAVE
SET SYSMENU TO
ON KEY LABEL ESC KEYBOARD CHR(13)
DEFINE MENU example BAR AT LINE 1
DEFINE PAD convpad OF example PROMPT '\<Conversions' COLOR SCHEME 3 ;
   KEY ALT+C, ''
DEFINE PAD cardpad OF example PROMPT 'Card \<Info' COLOR SCHEME 3 ;
   KEY ALT+I, ''
ON PAD convpad OF example ACTIVATE POPUP conversion
ON PAD cardpad OF example ACTIVATE POPUP cardinfo
DEFINE POPUP conversion MARGIN RELATIVE COLOR SCHEME 4
DEFINE BAR 1 OF conversion PROMPT 'Ar\<ea' ;
   KEY CTRL+E, '^E'
DEFINE BAR 2 OF conversion PROMPT '\<Length' ;
   KEY CTRL+L, '^L'
DEFINE BAR 3 OF conversion PROMPT 'Ma\<ss' ;
   KEY CTRL+S, '^S'
```

```
DEFINE BAR 4 OF conversion PROMPT 'Spee\<d' ;
   KEY CTRL+D, '^D'
DEFINE BAR 5 OF conversion PROMPT '\<Temperature' ;
   KEY CTRL+T, '^T'
DEFINE BAR 6 OF conversion PROMPT 'T\<ime' ;
   KEY CTRL+I, '^I'
DEFINE BAR 7 OF conversion PROMPT 'Volu\<me' ;
   KEY CTRL+M, '^M'
ON SELECTION POPUP conversion DO choice IN defimenu WITH PROMPT( ), POPUP( )
DEFINE POPUP cardinfo MARGIN RELATIVE COLOR SCHEME 4
DEFINE BAR 1 OF cardinfo PROMPT '\<View Charges' ;
   KEY ALT+V, ''
DEFINE BAR 2 OF cardinfo PROMPT 'View \<Payments' ;
   KEY ALT+P, ''
DEFINE BAR 3 OF cardinfo PROMPT 'Vie\<w Users' ;
   KEY ALT+W, ''
DEFINE BAR 4 OF cardinfo PROMPT '\-'
DEFINE BAR 5 OF cardinfo PROMPT '\<Charges '
ON SELECTION POPUP cardinfo;
   DO choice IN defimenu WITH PROMPT( ), POPUP( )

ACTIVATE MENU example
DEACTIVATE MENU example
RELEASE MENU example EXTENDED
SET SYSMENU TO DEFAULT
ON KEY LABEL ESC
PROCEDURE choice
PARAMETERS mprompt, mpopup
WAIT WINDOW 'You chose ' + mprompt + ;
    ' from popup ' + mpopup NOWAIT
```

See Also

ACTIVATE MENU, CNTPAD( ), CREATE MENU, DEACTIVATE MENU, DEFINE PAD, GETPAD( ), HIDE MENU, MRKPAD( ), ON PAD, ON SELECTION PAD, PRMPAD( ), RELEASE MENUS, RELEASE PAD, SET MARK OF, SET SYSMENU, SHOW MENU

DEFINE PAD Command

Creates a menu title (pad) on a user-defined menu bar or the Visual FoxPro system menu bar.

Syntax

DEFINE PAD *MenuTitle1* OF *MenuBarName* PROMPT *cMenuTitleText*
    [AT *nRow, nColumn*]
    [BEFORE *MenuName2* | AFTER *MenuName3*]

[NEGOTIATE *cContainerPosition* [, *cObjectPosition*]]
[FONT *cFontName* [, *nFontSize*]]
[STYLE *cFontStyle*]
[KEY *KeyLabel* [, *cKeyText*]]
[MARK *cMarkCharacter*]
[SKIP [FOR *lExpression*]]
[MESSAGE *cMessageText*]
[COLOR SCHEME *nSchemeNumber*
| COLOR *ColorPairList*]

Arguments

MenuTitle1

Specifies the menu title to create. The menu title allows you to reference the menu title in other commands and functions.

OF *MenuBarName*

Specifies the name of the menu bar in which the menu title is placed.

PROMPT *cMenuTitleText*

Specifies the text that appears in the menu title.

You can create an access key for a menu title by placing a backslash and a less-than sign (\<) before the character you would like to be the access key. In the following example, the user can press the I key to choose Invoices from the Receive menu and press the Q key to choose Inquiry from the same menu:

```
DEFINE MENU mnuReceive
DEFINE PAD padInvoice OF mnureceive PROMPT "\<Invoices"
DEFINE PAD padInquire OF mnureceive PROMPT "In\<quiry"
ACTIVATE MENU mnuReceive
```

AT *nRow*, *nColumn*

Specifies where the menu title appears on the menu bar. *nRow*, *nColumn* are the coordinates of the left side of the menu title in the main Visual FoxPro window or in a user-defined window.

If you omit the AT clause, the left side of the first menu title is placed in row 0 of the main Visual FoxPro window or user-defined window. The next menu title is placed to the right of the first name on row 0, and so on.

Note You cannot include AT to specify a location for menu titles in menu bars created with the BAR clause in DEFINE MENU.

BEFORE *MenuName2*

Places the menu title on the menu bar to the left of the menu title specified with *MenuName2*. The order the menu titles are accessed from the keyboard corresponds to the location of the menu titles in the menu bar.

AFTER *MenuName3*

Places the menu title on the menu bar to the right of the menu title specified with *MenuName3*. The order the menu titles are accessed from the keyboard corresponds to the location of the menu titles in the menu bar.

You must first create the menu title you specify in a BEFORE or AFTER clause. If you don't create the menu title first, the placement of the menu title on the menu bar is determined by the order in which it is created or by a location specified with the AT clause.

For menu bars created without BAR, BEFORE or AFTER determines the order the menu titles are accessed from the keyboard. The location of a menu title is determined by the location specified with the AT clause.

Run the following two examples and note the differences in menu title placement and access order when menu titles are defined with and without the AT clause:

```
*** Program Example 1 without ATs ***
DEFINE MENU mnuBefAft
DEFINE PAD padOne OF mnuBefAft PROMPT '1111'
DEFINE PAD padTwo OF mnuBefAft PROMPT '2222'
DEFINE PAD padThree OF mnuBefAft PROMPT '3333'
DEFINE PAD padFour  OF mnuBefAft PROMPT '4444' BEFORE padTwo
ACTIVATE MENU mnuBefAft
```

```
*** Program Example 2 with ATs ***
DEFINE MENU mnuBefAft
DEFINE PAD padOne OF mnuBefAft PROMPT '1111' AT 1,5
DEFINE PAD padTwo OF mnuBefAft PROMPT '2222' AT 1,15
DEFINE PAD padThree OF mnuBefAft PROMPT '3333' AT 1,25
DEFINE PAD padFour  OF mnuBefAft PROMPT '4444' BEFORE padTwo AT 1,35
WAIT WINDOW 'Press ESC to erase menu' NOWAIT
ACTIVATE MENU mnuBefAft
```

NEGOTIATE *cContainerPosition* [, *cObjectPosition*]

cContainerPosition specifies the location of the menu title in the Visual FoxPro menu bar when OLE Visual editing occurs for an ActiveX control contained in a Visual FoxPro form.

cObjectPosition specifies the location of the menu title in the menu bar of an Active Document's host.

The settings for *cContainerPosition* are:

Setting	Description
NONE	The menu title is not displayed.
LEFT	The menu title is placed to the left of the File Group.
MIDDLE	The menu title is placed to the left of the Container Group, after the Edit menu.
RIGHT	The menu title is placed to the left of the Window Group.

The settings for *cObjectPosition* are:

Setting	Description
NONE	The menu title is not displayed.
LEFT	The menu title is placed to the right of the File Group.
MIDDLE	The menu title is placed to the right of the Container Group, after the Edit menu.
RIGHT	The menu title is placed on the Help menu.

Note that there can be only one RIGHT menu title in an Active Document application. If more than one RIGHT menu title is specified, then all the menu titles are placed to the left of the Help menu.

If you omit the NEGOTIATE clause, the menu title is removed from the menu bar when OLE visual editing occurs; NONE is the default for both *cContainerPosition* and *cObjectPosition*.

FONT *cFontName* [, *nFontSize*]

Specifies a font for the menu title. *cFontName* specifies the name of the font, and *nFontSize* specifies the point size. For example, the following command creates a menu title in 12-point Courier font:

```
DEFINE PAD padPageAccts OF mnuReceive FONT 'Courier', 12
```

If the font you specify is not available, a font with similar font characteristics is substituted. If you include the FONT clause but omit the point size *nFontSize*, a 10-point font is used.

The FONT clause is ignored for menu titles added to the Visual FoxPro system menu _MSYSMENU. Note that the Menu Designer uses the Visual FoxPro system menu.

STYLE *cFontStyle*

Specifies a font style for the menu title. If you omit the STYLE clause, or if the font style you specify is not available, the Normal font style is used.

The font styles you can specify with *cFontStyle* are as follows:

Character	Font style
B	Bold
I	Italic
N	Normal
Q	Opaque
–	Strikeout
T	Transparent
U	Underline

You can include more than one character to specify a combination of font styles. For example, the following command specifies Bold Italic:

```
DEFINE PAD padPageAccts OF mnuReceive STYLE 'BI'
```

The STYLE clause is ignored for menu titles added to the Visual FoxPro system menu _MSYSMENU. Note that the Menu Designer uses the Visual FoxPro system menu.

KEY *KeyLabel* [, *cKeyText*]

Specifies an access key or key combination for a menu title. For a list of available keys and key combinations and their key label names, see the ON KEY LABEL Command, later in this language reference.

Note If a keyboard macro is already defined with the same key label, the keyboard macro takes precedence, and the menu title cannot be chosen with the specified key or key combination.

The key label is placed to the right of menu titles in menu bars created without the BAR clause. The key label isn't displayed in menu bars created with the BAR clause or for menu titles in the Visual FoxPro system menu bar.

Include *cKeyText* to replace the key label with your own text. You can use any character in the *cKeyText* parameter; for example, you can use the text "^B" to indicate a key label of CTRL+B. For example, including KEY CTRL+B places the text CTRL+B on the menu to the right of the menu item name, but specifying KEY CTRL+B, "^B" places the text ^B on the menu. You can suppress the display of a key label by specifying an empty string for *cKeyText*.

MARK *cMarkCharacter*

Specifies a mark character that appears to the left of the menu title. MARK can be included to change the default mark character to a character specified with *cMarkCharacter*. If *cMarkCharacter* includes more than one character, only the first character is used as the mark character.

The default mark character is a check. The MARK clause is ignored and the default mark character is used if the menu bar containing the menu title is the Visual FoxPro system menu. Also, the MARK clause is ignored if FoxFont isn't the font for the main Visual FoxPro window or the user-defined window in which the menu bar containing the menu title is placed.

Mark characters specified with DEFINE PAD take precedence over mark characters specified with the MARK clause in DEFINE MENU. SET MARK OF is used to toggle marks on or off and can also be used to specify a mark character for an individual menu title or for all menu titles.

Note Specifying a mark character doesn't mark the menu title. Use SET MARK OF to mark a menu title with the character you specify.

SKIP [FOR *lExpression*]

Specifies a condition whereby if *lExpression* evaluates to true (.T.), the menu title is disabled, preventing the user form choosing it. If *lExpression* evaluates to false (.F.), the menu title is enabled.

You can also disable a menu item by placing a backslash (\) before the text of the menu title text. For example:

```
DEFINE PAD padPageAccts OF mnuReceive PROMPT '\Age Accounts'
```

The menu title `padPageAccts` is displayed dimmed, indicating that it cannot be chosen.

A disabled menu title can be displayed but can't be selected. However, a message specified with the MESSAGE clause is displayed.

MESSAGE *cMessageText*

Displays a message when the user selects a menu title. The message is placed in the graphical status bar. If the graphical status bar is turned off with SET STATUS BAR OFF, the message is centered on the last line of the main Visual FoxPro window.

COLOR SCHEME *nSchemeNumber*

Specifies the colors for an individual menu title, overriding the default colors or the colors specified with DEFINE MENU.

COLOR *ColorPairList*

Specifies the colors for an individual menu title, overriding the default colors or the colors specified with DEFINE MENU.

By default, the colors of menu titles in menu bars are determined by color scheme 2 of the current color set.

For more information on color schemes and color pairs, see "Colors Overview," earlier in this language reference.

Remarks

You must create each menu title placed on the menu bar with its own DEFINE PAD command. A menu bar must be defined with DEFINE MENU before you can place menu titles on it, and you must include the menu bar name in DEFINE PAD.

If you use the Menu Designer to create your menu, you may not have to use these commands at all. The Menu Designer automatically creates the commands for your menu. The Menu Designer uses the Visual FoxPro system menu, which you can then modify by adding your own menu items. For more information on creating menus, see "Creating a Menu System" in Chapter 11, "Designing Menus and Toolbars," in the *Microsoft Visual FoxPro 6.0 Programmer's Guide*.

Example

The following example uses DEFINE PAD to place menu titles in the Visual FoxPro system menu bar. The current system menu bar is first saved to memory with SET SYSMENU SAVE, and then all system menu titles are removed with SET SYSMENU TO.

Several system menu titles are created with DEFINE PAD. When a menu title is chosen, the CHOICE procedure is executed. CHOICE displays the name of the chosen menu title and the name of the menu bar, and toggles the menu titles' mark character on and off. If the Exit menu title is chosen, the original Visual FoxPro system menu is restored.

```
*** Name this program DEFINPAD.PRG ***
CLEAR
SET TALK OFF
SET SYSMENU SAVE
SET SYSMENU TO
PUBLIC markpad
markpad = .T.
DEFINE PAD syspad  OF _MSYSMENU PROMPT '\<System'  COLOR SCHEME 3 ;
   KEY ALT+S, ''
DEFINE PAD editpad OF _MSYSMENU PROMPT '\<Edit'  COLOR SCHEME 3 ;
   KEY ALT+E, ''
DEFINE PAD recordpad OF _MSYSMENU PROMPT '\<Record'  COLOR SCHEME 3 KEY ALT+R, ''
DEFINE PAD windowpad OF _MSYSMENU PROMPT '\<Window'  COLOR SCHEME 3 ;
   KEY ALT+W, ''
DEFINE PAD reportpad OF _MSYSMENU PROMPT 'Re\<ports' COLOR SCHEME 3 ;
   KEY ALT+P, ''
DEFINE PAD exitpad OF _MSYSMENU PROMPT 'E\<xit'  COLOR SCHEME 3 ;
   KEY ALT+X, ''
ON SELECTION MENU _MSYSMENU ;
   DO choice IN definpad WITH PAD( ), MENU( )
PROCEDURE choice
PARAMETER mpad, mmenu
WAIT WINDOW 'You chose ' + mpad + ;
   ' from menu ' + mmenu NOWAIT
SET MARK OF PAD (mpad) OF _MSYSMENU TO ;
   ! MRKPAD('_MSYSMENU', mpad)
markpad = ! markpad
IF mpad = 'EXITPAD'
   SET SYSMENU TO DEFAULT
ENDIF
```

See Also

ACTIVATE MENU, CREATE MENU, DEACTIVATE MENU, DEFINE MENU, GETPAD( ), HIDE MENU, MRKPAD( ), ON PAD, ON SELECTION PAD, PRMPAD( ), RELEASE PAD, SET MARK OF, SET MESSAGE, SET SYSMENU, SHOW MENU

DEFINE POPUP Command

Creates a menu.

Syntax

DEFINE POPUP *MenuName*
    [FROM *nRow1, nColumn1*]
    [TO *nRow2, nColumn2*]
    [IN [WINDOW] *WindowName* I IN SCREEN]
    [FONT *cFontName* [, *nFontSize*]]
    [STYLE *cFontStyle*]
    [FOOTER *cFooterText*]
    [KEY *KeyLabel*]
    [MARGIN]
    [MARK *cMarkCharacter*]
    [MESSAGE *cMessageText*]
    [MOVER]
    [MULTISELECT]
    [PROMPT FIELD *FieldName* I PROMPT FILES [LIKE *FileSkeleton*]
      I PROMPT STRUCTURE]
    [RELATIVE]
    [SCROLL]
    [SHORTCUT]
    [TITLE *cMenuTitleText*]
    [COLOR SCHEME *nSchemeNumber*
    I COLOR *ColorPairList*]

Arguments

MenuName
    Specifies the name of the menu to create.

FROM *nRow1, nColumn1* TO *nRow2, nColumn2*
    Specifies where the menu is placed. *nRow1, nColumn1* specifies coordinates for the upper-left corner of the menu. If you omit the FROM clause, Visual FoxPro places the upper-left corner of the menu in the first row and first column of the main Visual FoxPro window or a user-defined window.

    To create a menu with a specific size, you can also include TO *nRow2, nColumn2* to specify the location of the lower-right corner of the menu. If you include FROM *nRow1, nColumn1* and omit TO *nRow2, nColumn2*, Visual FoxPro automatically sizes the menu. The menu is as wide as the longest menu item in it (if the items are created with DEFINE BAR) and as long as needed to display all of the menu items. The menu length is limited by the size of the main Visual FoxPro window or user-defined window in which the menu is placed. If a menu isn't large enough to contain all of the menu items, a scroll bar appears so that you can scroll through the menu items.

IN [WINDOW] *WindowName*

Places a menu in a user-defined window you specify with *WindowName*. If you omit this clause, the menu is placed on the main Visual FoxPro window by default unless there is an active user-defined window. If there is an active user-defined window, the menu is placed in the active window.

IN SCREEN

Explicitly places a menu in the main Visual FoxPro window.

FONT *cFontName* [, *nFontSize*]

Specifies a default font for the menu. You can override the default font for an individual menu item by including the FONT clause in DEFINE BAR.

cFontName specifies the name of the font, and *nFontSize* specifies the point size. For example, the following command creates a menu in 12-point Courier font:

```
DEFINE POPUP popMyPopup FONT 'Courier', 12
```

If the font you specify is not available, a font with similar font characteristics is substituted. If you include the FONT clause but omit the point size *nFontSize*, a 10-point font is used.

STYLE *cFontStyle*

Specifies a default font style for the menu. You can override the default style for an individual menu item by including the FONT clause in DEFINE BAR.

If you omit the STYLE clause, or if the font style you specify is not available, the Normal font style is used.

The font styles you can specify with *cFontStyle* are listed in the following table:

Character	Font style
B	Bold
I	Italic
N	Normal
Q	Opaque
–	Strikeout
T	Transparent
U	Underline

You can include more than one character to specify a combination of font styles. For example, the following command specifies Bold Italic:

```
DEFINE MENU popMyPopup STYLE 'BI'
```

FOOTER *cFooterText*

Creates a footer with the text specified with *cFooterText* centered in the bottom border of the menu.

KEY *KeyLabel*

Specifies an access key or key combination for a menu. For a list of available keys and key combinations and their key label names, see the ON KEY LABEL Command, later in this language reference.

Including KEY is equivalent to issuing the following command:

```
ON KEY LABEL KeyLabel ACTIVATE POPUP MenuName
```

> **Note** If a keyboard macro is already defined with the same key label, the keyboard macro takes precedence, and the menu cannot be activated with the specified key or key combination.

MARGIN

Places an extra space to the left and right of each menu item. Mark characters are displayed in the space to the left of an item, and arrows indicating additional cascading submenus are available and are displayed to the right of menu items. If you omit MARGIN, the mark characters overwrite the first character of the menu item names; hierarchical arrows overwrite the last character of the menu items.

MARK *cMarkCharacter*

Specifies a character that appears to the left of an item on the menu. The default mark character is a check mark. The MARK clause is ignored and the default mark character is used if the menu is integrated into the Visual FoxPro system menu. Also, the MARK clause is ignored if FoxFont isn't the font for the main FoxPro window or the user-defined window in which the menu is placed.

MARK can be included to change the default mark character to a character specified with *cMarkCharacter*. If *cMarkCharacter* includes more than one character, only the first character is used as the mark character.

> **Note** Specifying a mark character doesn't mark a menu item. Use SET MARK OF to mark a menu item.

The MARK clause sets the mark character for all items on the menu. Mark characters specified with DEFINE BAR commands take precedence over mark characters specified with the MARK clause in DEFINE POPUP. SET MARK OF is used to toggle mark characters on or off and can also be used to specify a mark character for an individual menu item or for all menu items.

MESSAGE *cMessageText*

Displays a message when you select a menu item. The message is placed in the graphical status bar. If the character-based status bar is turned on with SET STATUS ON, the message is centered on the last line of the main Visual FoxPro window.

MOVER

Places a double-headed arrow (↕) in the Mover box to the left of the selected item in the menu. You can drag the double-headed arrow to move an item to another position on the menu. GETBAR( ) can be used to determine where each item is positioned on the menu.

You cannot rearrange items in a menu created with a PROMPT clause.

MULTISELECT

Allows the user to select multiple items from a menu at the same time. When the user chooses an item from a menu, the mark character is placed to the left of the item.

You cannot make multiple selections from a menu created with a PROMPT clause.

MRKBAR( ) can be used to determine which items are chosen from the menu.

If you include MULTISELECT in DEFINE POPUP, you can include MARGIN to reserve space in each item for the mark character.

In the following example, a menu named popFruits is created. MULTISELECT is included to create a menu that allows multiple items to be chosen.

Each of the four items has a different mark character. When a user chooses items from the menu, the items are marked and a routine named yourchoice displays the chosen items.

```
CLEAR
IF NOT _DOS
   MODIFY WINDOW SCREEN FONT 'foxfont', 12
ENDIF
ACTIVATE SCREEN
DEFINE POPUP popFruits FROM 5,5 ;
   MULTISELECT MARGIN            && Create multi-choice menu
DEFINE BAR 1 OF popFruits ;
   PROMPT '\<Apples'  MARK CHR(3)    && First item
DEFINE BAR 2 OF popFruits ;
   PROMPT '\<Bananas' MARK CHR(4)    && Second item
DEFINE BAR 3 OF popFruits ;
   PROMPT '\<Grapes'  MARK CHR(5) && Third item
DEFINE BAR 4 OF popFruits ;
   PROMPT '\<Lemons'  MARK CHR(6)    && Fourth item
@ 12,5 SAY 'Your choices:'
ON SELECTION POPUP popFruits DO yourchoice    && Choice routine
ACTIVATE POPUP popFruits
PROCEDURE yourchoice            && Executed when choice is made
@ 13,5 CLEAR
FOR gnCount = 1 TO CNTBAR('popFruits')       && Loop for # of items
   IF MRKBAR('popFruits', gnCount) = .T.     && Option is marked,
      ? PRMBAR('popFruits', gnCount) AT 5    && display caption
   ENDIF
NEXT
```

PROMPT FIELD *FieldName*

Specifies the field name from an open table whose records become the items on the menu. The menu contains an item for each record in the table. When the menu is activated, the tables' work area is selected.

> **Tip** You can take advantage of Rushmore optimization if you set a filter on the field specified with PROMPT FIELD used in the menu.
>
> For more information on Rushmore optimization, see the SET OPTIMIZE Command, later in this language reference, and "Understanding Rushmore Technology" in Chapter 15, "Optimizing Applications," in the *Microsoft Visual FoxPro 6.0 Programmer's Guide*.

FieldName can also contain multiple field names and expressions concatenated with the addition operator (+). *FieldName* can also be the name of the field in a table open in another work area or a user-defined function.

There is no limit to the number of entries that can appear in a menu created with PROMPT FIELD.

PROMPT FILES [LIKE *FileSkeleton*]

Creates a menu that displays the names of files available in the current directory.

LIKE *FileSkeleton* allows you to specify the files that are displayed in the menu using wildcards. For example, to create a menu that displays the names of tables in the default drive and directory, include the following command:

```
PROMPT FILES LIKE *.DBF
```

You can create a menu that displays the names of files on other drives and in other directories or folders by including a drive or volume specification, a directory specification, or both. For example, to create a menu that displays the names of program files in a directorycalled PROGRAMS on drive C, include the following command:

```
PROMPT FILES LIKE C:\PROGRAMS\*.PRG
```

PROMPT STRUCTURE

Displays the names of the fields in the current table on the menu according to the table's field structure. When the menu is activated, the table's work area is selected.

RELATIVE

Specifies the order in which items are placed on a menu. If you create a menu without the RELATIVE clause, an item is positioned on a menu in an order dictated by the item's bar number. Space on the menu is reserved for undefined items. For example, if the first and third items are defined and the menu is activated, a blank line reserved for the second item is placed on the menu.

If you create a menu with RELATIVE, the items appear on the menu in the order in which they are defined. Space in the menu isn't reserved for undefined items.

Defining a menu with RELATIVE also lets you make use of BEFORE and AFTER clauses in DEFINE BAR to position items on a menu relative to other items. If a menu is created without RELATIVE, including BEFORE or AFTER in DEFINE BAR generates an error.

Run the following two program examples and compare the placement of the items on each menu.

```
*** RELATIVE Example  ***
DEFINE POPUP popRelatYes RELATIVE FROM 1,1
DEFINE BAR 4  OF popRelatYes PROMPT '4444'
DEFINE BAR 3  OF popRelatYes PROMPT '3333'
DEFINE BAR 2  OF popRelatYes PROMPT '2222'
DEFINE BAR 1  OF popRelatYes PROMPT '1111'
DEFINE BAR 6  OF popRelatYes PROMPT '6666' BEFORE 4
ACTIVATE POPUP popRelatYes
*** NON-RELATIVE Example ***
DEFINE POPUP popRelatNo FROM 1,1
DEFINE BAR 4  OF popRelatNo PROMPT '4444'
DEFINE BAR 3  OF popRelatNo PROMPT '3333'
DEFINE BAR 2  OF popRelatNo PROMPT '2222'
DEFINE BAR 1  OF popRelatNo PROMPT '1111'
DEFINE BAR 6  OF popRelatNo PROMPT '6666'
ACTIVATE POPUP popRelatNo
```

SCROLL

Places a scroll bar to the right of the menu you create. The scroll bar is displayed only when there are more items than can fit on the menu, or if the menu is too long to fit in the main Visual FoxPro window or the user-defined window in which it is placed.

SHORTCUT

Creates a shortcut menu. A shortcut menu typically appears when a selection, toolbar, or taskbar button is clicked with the right mouse button. The shortcut menu lists commands that pertain to the screen region on which the mouse was right-clicked.

You can include MROW( ) and MCOL( ) in the FROM clause to activate the popup at the location where the mouse is clicked.

TITLE *cMenuTitleText*

Displays a title in the center of the top border of the menu. *cTitleText* specifies the menu title.

COLOR SCHEME *nSchemeNumber*

Specifies the colors for all elements of a menu. By default, the colors of menus created with DEFINE POPUP are controlled by color scheme 2.

COLOR *ColorPairList*

Specifies the colors for all elements of a menu.

For more information on color schemes and color pairs, see "Colors Overview," earlier in this language reference.

Remarks

To place a set of menu items that you define on a menu, use a series of DEFINE BAR commands. To place records, files, or fields in a menu, use the PROMPT FIELD, PROMPT FILES, or PROMPT STRUCTURE options of DEFINE POPUP.

When the menu is displayed and activated with ACTIVATE POPUP, you can choose one of the items on the menu. Depending on the item chosen, a routine can be executed or another menu can be displayed and activated. A menu that displays another menu when an item is chosen is called a cascading submenu. For more information on creating submenus, see the ON BAR Command, later in this language reference.

If you use the Menu Designer to create your menu, you may not have to use these commands at all. The Menu Designer automatically creates the commands for your menu. The Menu Designer uses the Visual FoxPro system menu, which you can then modify by adding your own menu items.

For more information on creating menus, see "Creating a Menu System" in Chapter 11, "Designing Menus and Toolbars," in the *Microsoft Visual FoxPro 6.0 Programmer's Guide*.

Example

The following example uses DEFINE POPUP to create menus that are activated when a menu title in the menu bar is chosen. The current system menu bar is first saved to memory with SET SYSMENU SAVE, and then all system menu titles are removed with SET SYSMENU TO.

Two new system menu titles are created with DEFINE PAD, and DEFINE POPUP creates a drop-down menu for each menu title. DEFINE BAR creates items on each of the menus. When a menu title is chosen, ON PAD uses ACTIVATE POPUP to activate the corresponding menu.

When an item is chosen from a menu, ON SELECTION POPUP uses PROMPT( ) and POPUP( ) to pass the item number and menu name to the CHOICE procedure. CHOICE displays the text of the chosen item and the name of the menu containing the item. If the Exit item is chosen from the Card Info menu, the original Visual FoxPro system menu is restored.

```
*** Name this program DEFINPOP.PRG ***
CLEAR
SET SYSMENU SAVE
SET SYSMENU TO
DEFINE PAD convpad OF _MSYSMENU PROMPT '\<Conversions' COLOR SCHEME 3 ;
   KEY ALT+C, ''
DEFINE PAD cardpad OF _MSYSMENU PROMPT 'Card \<Info' COLOR SCHEME 3 ;
   KEY ALT+I, ''
```

```
ON PAD convpad OF _MSYSMENU ACTIVATE POPUP conversion
ON PAD cardpad OF _MSYSMENU ACTIVATE POPUP cardinfo
DEFINE POPUP conversion MARGIN RELATIVE COLOR SCHEME 4
DEFINE BAR 1 OF conversion PROMPT 'Ar\<ea' KEY CTRL+E, '^E'
DEFINE BAR 2 OF conversion PROMPT '\<Length' ;
   KEY CTRL+L, '^L'
DEFINE BAR 3 OF conversion PROMPT 'Ma\<ss' ;
   KEY CTRL+S, '^S'
DEFINE BAR 4 OF conversion PROMPT 'Spee\<d' ;
   KEY CTRL+D, '^D'
DEFINE BAR 5 OF conversion PROMPT '\<Temperature' ;
   KEY CTRL+T, '^T'
DEFINE BAR 6 OF conversion PROMPT 'T\<ime' ;
   KEY CTRL+I, '^I'
DEFINE BAR 7 OF conversion PROMPT 'Volu\<me' ;
   KEY CTRL+M, '^M'
ON SELECTION POPUP conversion;
   DO choice IN definpop WITH PROMPT( ), POPUP( )
DEFINE POPUP cardinfo MARGIN RELATIVE COLOR SCHEME 4
DEFINE BAR 1 OF cardinfo PROMPT '\<View Charges' ;
   KEY ALT+V, ''
DEFINE BAR 2 OF cardinfo PROMPT 'View \<Payments' ;
   KEY ALT+P, ''
DEFINE BAR 3 OF cardinfo PROMPT 'Vie\<w Users' ;
   KEY ALT+W, ''
DEFINE BAR 4 OF cardinfo PROMPT '\-'
DEFINE BAR 5 OF cardinfo PROMPT '\<Charges '
DEFINE BAR 6 OF cardinfo PROMPT '\-'
DEFINE BAR 7 OF cardinfo PROMPT 'E\<xit '
ON SELECTION POPUP cardinfo;
   DO choice IN definpop WITH PROMPT( ), POPUP( )
PROCEDURE choice
PARAMETERS mprompt, mpopup
WAIT WINDOW 'You chose ' + mprompt + ;
   ' from popup ' + mpopup NOWAIT
IF mprompt = 'Exit'
   SET SYSMENU TO DEFAULT
ENDIF
```

See Also

ACTIVATE POPUP, CNTBAR( ) CREATE MENU, DEFINE BAR, GETBAR( ) HIDE POPUP, MOVE POPUP, MRKBAR( ), ON BAR, ON SELECTION BAR POPUP( ), PRMBAR( ), PROMPT( ), RELEASE POPUPS, SET MARK OF SET MESSAGE SIZE POPUP SHOW POPUP

DEFINE WINDOW Command

Creates a window and specifies its attributes.

Syntax

DEFINE WINDOW *WindowName1*
    FROM *nRow1, nColumn1* TO *nRow2, nColumn2*
    | AT *nRow3, nColumn3* SIZE *nRow4, nColumn4*
    [IN [WINDOW] *WindowName2* | IN SCREEN | IN DESKTOP
    [NAME *ObjectName*]
    [FONT *cFontName* [, *nFontSize*]]
    [STYLE *cFontStyle*]
    [FOOTER *cFooterText*]
    [TITLE *cTitleText*]
    [HALFHEIGHT]
    [DOUBLE | PANEL | NONE | SYSTEM | *cBorderString*]
    [CLOSE | NOCLOSE]
    [FLOAT | NOFLOAT]
    [GROW | NOGROW]
    [MDI | NOMDI]
    [MINIMIZE | NOMINIMIZE]
    [ZOOM | NOZOOM]
    [ICON FILE *FileName1*]
    [FILL *cFillCharacter* | FILL FILE *FileName2*]
    [COLOR SCHEME *nSchemeNumber*
    | COLOR *ColorPairList*]

Arguments

WindowName1

Specifies the name of the window to create. Window names can be up to 254 characters long in Visual FoxPro. They must begin with a letter or underscore, and cannot begin with a number. They can contain any combination of letters, numbers and underscores.

FROM *nRow1, nColumn1* TO *nRow2, nColumn2*

Specifies the position and size of the user-defined window on the main Visual FoxPro window. FROM *nRow1, nColumn1* specifies the position of the upper-left corner of the user-defined window on the main Visual FoxPro window. TO *nRow2, nColumn2* specifies the position of the lower-right corner of the user-defined window on the main Visual FoxPro window.

A window can be defined with coordinates that lie outside the Visual FoxPro window border and can be larger than the main Visual FoxPro window.

The window's location and size are determined by the font of the window's parent. The window's parent can be another user-defined window or the main Visual FoxPro window.

AT *nRow3*, *nColumn3* SIZE *nRow4*, *nColumn4*
Specifies the position and size of a user-defined window.

AT *nRow3*, *nColumn3* specifies the position of the upper-left corner of the user defined window on the main Visual FoxPro window. This position is determined by the current font of the window's parent. Because the AT clause is identical to the FROM clause in all respects, the two clauses can be used interchangeably.

SIZE *nRow4*, *nColumn4* specifies in rows and columns the size of the user-defined window and ensures that text displayed in a specific font will fit in the window you create.

You can specify a font and font style for a user-defined window by including the FONT and STYLE clauses. If you specify a font for the window and include the SIZE clause, its size is determined by the window's font height and width. If you don't specify a font for a window, the window's font is the default system font, 10-point FoxFont.

IN [WINDOW] *WindowName2*
Places a user-defined window in a parent window. The user-defined window becomes a child window and cannot be moved outside the parent window. If the parent window is moved, the child window moves with it.

When a child window is placed in a parent window, the child window coordinates specified with the FROM and TO clauses or the AT and SIZE clauses are relative to the parent window, not the main Visual FoxPro window.

In the following example, a parent window, wParent, is created. A child window, wChild, is placed in the parent window.

```
CLEAR
DEFINE WINDOW wParent ;
   FROM 1, 1 TO 20, 30 ;
   TITLE "Parent"          && Parent window.
ACTIVATE WINDOW wParent
DEFINE WINDOW wChild ;
   FROM 1, 1 TO 20, 20 ;
   TITLE "Child" ;
   IN WINDOW wParent       && Child window.
ACTIVATE WINDOW wChild
ACTIVATE SCREEN
WAIT WINDOW 'Press a key to clear the windows'
RELEASE WINDOW wParent, wChild
CLEAR
```

IN SCREEN

Explicitly places a user-defined window on the main Visual FoxPro window. If you omit IN SCREEN, the user-defined window is placed on the main Visual FoxPro window by default.

You can include the IN WINDOW clause in ACTIVATE WINDOW to place the window in another user-defined window and override this IN SCREEN clause.

IN DESKTOP

Places a user-defined window on the Microsoft Windows desktop, outside the main Visual FoxPro window. The position of the window is relative to the Windows desktop, and the current font of the main Visual FoxPro window.

NAME *ObjectName*

Creates an object reference for the window, allowing you to manipulate the window with object-oriented properties available for the form object.

For additional information about object-oriented programming in Visual FoxPro, see Chapter 3, "Object-Oriented Programming," in the *Microsoft Visual FoxPro 6.0 Programmer's Guide*. For additional information about the form object properties you can specify for a window created with the NAME clause, see "Form Object," later in this language reference.

FONT *cFontName* [, *nFontSize*]

Specifies a font for text placed in the window. *cFontName* specifies the name of the font and *nFontSize* specifies the point size. If you omit *nFontSize*, a 9-point font is used.

For example, this command creates a window that displays output directed to the window in a 16-point Courier font:

```
DEFINE WINDOW wDisplayFont FROM 2,2 TO 12,22 FONT 'Courier', 16
```

If you omit the FONT clause, a 10-point FoxFont is used. If the font you specify is not available, a font with similar font characteristics is substituted.

STYLE *cFontStyle*

Specifies a font style for text placed in the window. *cFontStyle* specifies the font. If you omit the STYLE clause, or if the font style you specify is not available, the Normal font style is used.

The following table lists font styles and their corresponding characters.

Character	Font style
B	Bold
I	Italic
N	Normal
Q	Opaque

(continued)

(continued)

Character	Font style
–	Strikeout
T	Transparent
U	Underline

You can include more than one character to specify a combination of font styles. In Visual FoxPro, the following commands specify the style Bold Italic:

```
DEFINE WINDOW wDisplayStyle FROM 2, 2 TO 12, 22 STYLE 'BI'
```

TITLE *cTitleText*

Assigns a title with the TITLE clause. *cTitleText* specifies the title's text and is centered in the top border of the window. If the title is wider than the window, the title is truncated.

HALFHEIGHT

Creates a window with a half-height title bar. This provides compatibility for windows created in previous versions of FoxPro that are imported into Visual FoxPro.

When you use DEFINE WINDOW to create a window, a half-height title bar is used, unless you include the SYSTEM keyword or you include a FONT clause.

If you include the HALFHEIGHT keyword, a half-height title bar is used regardless of whether the SYSTEM or FONT clause is included.

DOUBLE | PANEL | NONE | SYSTEM | *cBorderString*

Specifies a border style for a user-defined window. The default border is a single line.

Argument	Description
DOUBLE	Specifies a double-line border around the window.
PANEL	Specifies a wide border around the window.
NONE	Suppresses the border entirely.
SYSTEM	Specifies the user-defined window to look like a system window. When you include certain other clauses (GROW, ZOOM, and so on), the appropriate window controls are placed in the window's border.
cBorderString	Specifies a custom border. For more information on defining a custom border, see the SET BORDER Command, later in this language reference.

Including DOUBLE or a custom border string creates a window with the PANEL border. Including the CLOSE, FLOAT, GROW, ZOOM, or MINIMIZE clauses places the appropriate controls on the window even if the SYSTEM window definition clause is not included.

CLOSE

Allows the user to close a user-defined window using the keyboard or mouse. Closing a window removes it from the main Visual FoxPro window or a parent user-defined window and removes its definition from memory. If you omit CLOSE, you cannot close the window using the interface; the window must be closed using a command in a program or in the Command window.

NOCLOSE

Prevents the window from being closed except by a command in a program or in the Command window.

FLOAT

Allows the window to be moved using the keyboard or mouse. If you omit FLOAT, you cannot move the window except using the MOVE WINDOW command in a program or in the Command window.

NOFLOAT

Prevents the window from being moved except by using the MOVE WINDOW command in a program or in the Command window.

GROW

Allows you to resize a user-defined window using the keyboard or mouse. If you omit GROW, you cannot size the window except using the SIZE WINDOW command in a program or in the Command window.

NOGROW

Prevents the window from being resized except by the SIZE WINDOW command in a program or in the Command window.

MDI

Creates a user-defined window that is MDI-compliant. MDI (multiple document interface) is a specification that allows multiple document windows and determines their structure and behavior. If you omit MDI, the window you create isn't MDI-compliant.

When an MDI-compliant window is maximized:

- The window assumes the size of the main Visual FoxPro window. The window's controls disappear and its pop-up menu icon appears in the Visual FoxPro system menu bar. The window's Restore button is also placed in the Visual FoxPro system menu bar.

- The window title is placed in the Visual FoxPro title bar and is separated from the Visual FoxPro title by a hyphen.

- If you activate another MDI-compliant window, it is automatically maximized.

NOMDI

Creates a window that isn't MDI-compliant.

MINIMIZE

Allows you to minimize a user-defined window using the keyboard or mouse.

NOMINIMIZE

Prevents the window from being minimized.

ZOOM

Allows the window to be maximized using the keyboard or mouse. You can also restore the window to its original size.

NOZOOM

Prevents the window from being maximized.

ICON FILE *FileName*

Specifies the icon that displays when the window is minimized. You must include the MINIMIZE keyword in DEFINE WINDOW. You can specify only an icon (.ico) file; you cannot specify a bitmap (.bmp) file.

FILL FILE *FileName2*

Specifies a wallpaper (the background) for the window. The window is tiled with the specified *FileName2*. You specify a .bmp bitmap file.

COLOR SCHEME *nSchemeNumber*

Specifies the colors for the user-defined window. By default, the colors of windows created with DEFINE WINDOW are controlled by color scheme 1.

COLOR *ColorPairList*

Specifies the colors for the user-defined window.

For more information on color schemes and color pairs, see "Colors Overview," earlier in this language reference.

Remarks

After user-defined windows are created with DEFINE WINDOW, they can be displayed in the main Visual FoxPro window with ACTIVATE WINDOW or SHOW WINDOW. The number of user-defined windows you can create is limited only by the amount of available memory and system resources.

Activated windows remain in the main Visual FoxPro window until DEACTIVATE WINDOW or HIDE WINDOW is issued. DEACTIVATE WINDOW and HIDE WINDOW remove windows from the main Visual FoxPro window but don't remove the window definitions from memory. Windows can be placed back in the main Visual FoxPro window with ACTIVATE WINDOW or SHOW WINDOW.

Use CLEAR WINDOWS or RELEASE WINDOWS to remove windows from the main Visual FoxPro window and window definitions from memory. Windows whose definitions have been removed from memory must be recreated with DEFINE WINDOW in order to be redisplayed.

Example

In the following example, a window named `output` is created and activated. The program waits for you to press a key and then hides the window. The program waits for you to press a key again and then redisplays the window.

```
CLEAR
DEFINE WINDOW output FROM 2,1 TO 13,75 TITLE 'Output' ;
   CLOSE FLOAT GROW ZOOM
ACTIVATE WINDOW output
WAIT WINDOW 'press any key to hide window output'
HIDE WINDOW output
WAIT WINDOW 'press any key to show window output'
SHOW WINDOW output
WAIT WINDOW 'press any key to release window output'
RELEASE WINDOW  output
```

See Also

ACTIVATE WINDOW, DEACTIVATE WINDOW Fonts Overview, Form Object, HIDE WINDOW, MODIFY WINDOW MOVE WINDOW, RELEASE WINDOWS, SET BORDER, SHOW WINDOW

DefOLELCID Property

Specifies the default OLE Locale ID for a form or the main Visual FoxPro window. Available at design time and run time.

Syntax

Form.DefOLELCID[= *nValue*]

Arguments

nValue
>   Specifies a default OLE Locale ID value for a form or the main Visual FoxPro window. This default value determines the Locale ID for OLE Bound controls and OLE Container controls when they are placed on the form or the main Visual FoxPro window.

Remarks

If the default OLE Locale ID value for a form or the main Visual FoxPro window is changed to a new value, OLE Bound controls and OLE Container controls placed on the form or the main Visual FoxPro window after the new default Locale ID value is in effect use the new value.

If DefOLELCID is set to zero for a form or the main Visual FoxPro window, SYS(3004) determines the default Locale ID for OLE Bound controls and OLE Container controls placed on the form or the main Visual FoxPro window.

See SYS(3005), later in this language reference, for a listing of Locale IDs.

Note The DefOLELCID property only affects the language of the user interface, which OLE controls display, and not the language of the Automation commands. The Automation command language is affected only by the Global LocaleID, set with SYS(3005).

Applies To

Form, _SCREEN

See Also

OLELCID Property, SYS(3005) – Set Locale ID

DELETE Command

Marks records for deletion.

Syntax

DELETE
    [*Scope*] [FOR *lExpression1*] [WHILE *lExpression2*]
    [IN *nWorkArea | cTableAlias*]
    [NOOPTIMIZE]

Arguments

Scope

Specifies a range of records to mark for deletion. The scope clauses are: ALL, NEXT *nRecords*, RECORD *nRecordNumber*, and REST.

For more information on scope clauses, see "Scope Clauses" and "Overview of the Language," in Help.

The default scope for DELETE is the current record (NEXT 1).

FOR *lExpression1*

Specifies a condition whereby only the records that satisfy the logical condition *lExpression1* are marked for deletion.

Rushmore optimizes a query created with DELETE ... FOR if *lExpression1* is an optimizable expression and the table is indexed on DELETED( ). For best performance, use an optimizable expression in the FOR clause.

For information on Rushmore optimizable expressions, see the SET OPTIMIZE Command, later in this language reference, and "Understanding Rushmore Technology" in Chapter 15, "Optimizing Applications," in the *Microsoft Visual FoxPro 6.0 Programmer's Guide*.

WHILE *lExpression2*

Specifies a condition whereby records are marked for deletion for as long as *lExpression2* evaluates to true (.T.).

IN *nWorkArea*
> Specifies the work area of the table in which records are marked for deletion.

IN *cTableAlias*
> Specifies the alias of the table in which records are marked for deletion.

> If you omit *nWorkArea* and *cTableAlias*, records are marked for deletion in the table in the currently selected work area.

NOOPTIMIZE
> Disables Rushmore optimization of DELETE.

Remarks

Records marked for deletion aren't physically removed from the table until PACK is issued. Records marked for deletion can be recalled (unmarked) with RECALL.

Example

The following example opens the `customer` table in the `testdata` database. DELETE is used to mark all records for deletion where the `country` field contains USA. All the records marked for deletion are displayed. RECALL ALL is used to unmark all the records marked for deletion.

```
CLOSE DATABASES
OPEN DATABASE (HOME(2) + 'Data\testdata')
USE customer  && Opens Customer table

DELETE FOR country = 'USA'  && Mark for deletion
CLEAR
LIST FIELDS company, country FOR DELETED( ) && List marked records
RECALL ALL  && Unmark all records marked for deletion
```

See Also

DELETE – SQL, DELETED( ), PACK RECALL, SET DELETED

DELETE – SQL Command

Marks records for deletion.

Syntax

DELETE FROM [*DatabaseName!*]*TableName*
  [WHERE *FilterCondition1* [AND | OR *FilterCondition2* ...]]

Arguments

FROM [*DatabaseName!*]*TableName*
> Specifies the table in which records are marked for deletion.

DatabaseName! specifies the name of a non-current database containing the table. You must include the name of a database containing the table if the database is not the current database. Include the exclamation point (!) delimiter after the database name and before the table name.

WHERE *FilterCondition1* [AND I OR *FilterCondition2* ...]
Specifies that Visual FoxPro marks only certain records for deletion.

FilterCondition specifies the criteria that records must meet to be marked for deletion. You can include as many filter conditions as you like, connecting them with the AND or OR operator. You can also use the NOT operator to reverse the value of a logical expression, or use EMPTY( ) to check for an empty field.

Remarks

Records marked for deletion aren't physically removed from the table until PACK is issued. Records marked for deletion can be recalled (unmarked) with RECALL.

If SET DELETED is set to ON, records marked for deletion are ignored by all commands that include a scope.

Unlike DELETE, DELETE – SQL uses record locking when marking multiple records for deletion in tables opened for shared access. This reduces record contention in multiuser situations, but may reduce performance. For maximum performance, open the table for exclusive use or use FLOCK( ) to lock the table.

Example

The following example opens the `customer` table in the `testdata` database. DELETE – SQL is used to mark all records for deletion where the `country` field contains USA. All the records marked for deletion are displayed. RECALL ALL is used to unmark all the records marked for deletion.

```
CLOSE DATABASES
CLEAR

OPEN DATABASE HOME(2)+"Data\testdata"
USE customer  && Open Customer table

DELETE FROM customer WHERE country = "USA"   && Mark for deletion

CLEAR
LIST FIELDS company, country FOR DELETED( )  && List marked records
* If the file were packed at this point the records would be deleted
WAIT WINDOW "Records currently marked for deletion"+CHR(13) + ;
   "Press any key to revert..."

* Unmark all records marked for deletion
RECALL ALL
CLEAR
```

```
* Verify reverted records
COUNT FOR DELETED( )=.T. TO nDeleted

* Convert nDeleted to a character string and display information
WAIT WINDOW ALLTRIM(STR(nDeleted)) + " records marked for deletion."
```

See Also

DELETE, DELETED( ), PACK, RECALL, SET DELETED

DELETE CONNECTION Command

Deletes a named connection from the current database.

Syntax

DELETE CONNECTION *ConnectionName*

Arguments

ConnectionName
Specifies the name of the named connection to delete from the current database.

Remarks

Deleting a named connection definition does not close any active connections.

DELETE CONNECTION requires exclusive use of the database. To open a database for exclusive use, include EXCLUSIVE in OPEN DATABASE.

Example

The following example assumes an ODBC data source called MyFoxSQLNT is available, and the user ID for the data source is "sa." The testdata database is opened, and a connection named Myconn is created. DISPLAY CONNECTIONS is used to display the named connections in the database. The connection is then removed from the database with DELETE CONNECTION.

```
CLOSE DATABASES
OPEN DATABASE (HOME(2) + 'Data\testdata')

CREATE CONNECTION Myconn DATASOURCE "MyFoxSQLNT" USERID "sa"
DISPLAY CONNECTIONS    && Displays named connections in the database
DELETE CONNECTION Myconn  && Removes the connection just created
```

See Also

CREATE CONNECTION, MODIFY CONNECTION, RENAME CONNECTION

DELETE DATABASE Command

Deletes a database from disk.

Syntax

DELETE DATABASE *DatabaseName* | ?
  [DELETETABLES] [RECYCLE]

Arguments

DatabaseName
> Specifies the name of the database to delete from disk. The database you specify
> cannot be open. *DatabaseName* can include the path to the database with the database
> name.

?
> Displays the Delete dialog box from which you can specify the name of the database
> to delete from disk.

DELETETABLES
> Deletes the tables contained in the database from disk and the database containing the
> tables.

RECYCLE
> Specifies that the database isn't immediately deleted from disk and is placed in the
> Windows 95 Recycle Bin.

Remarks

Always use DELETE DATABASE to delete a database from disk. Unlike the file
manipulation utility of the operating system, DELETE DATABASE removes references
to the database from the tables in the database.

If SET SAFETY is ON, Visual FoxPro asks if you'd like to delete the database you
specify. If SET SAFETY is OFF, the database is automatically deleted from disk.

Example

This example creates a database named people. A table named friends is created and is
automatically added to the database. DISPLAY TABLES is used to display the tables in
the database, and DISPLAY DATABASES is used to display information about the tables
in the database.

DELETE DATABASE is used with the DELETETABLES option to remove the database
and its friends table from disk.

```
CLOSE ALL
CREATE DATABASE people
CREATE TABLE friends (FirstName C(20), LastName C(20))
CLEAR
```

```
DISPLAY TABLES  && Displays tables in the database
DISPLAY DATABASES  && Displays table information
CLOSE ALL
DELETE DATABASE people DELETETABLES
```

See Also

ADD TABLE, CLOSE DATABASES, DBC( ), DBGETPROP( ), DBSETPROP( ),
DISPLAY TABLES, OPEN DATABASE, REMOVE TABLE

DELETE FILE Command

Deletes a file from a disk.

Syntax

DELETE FILE [*FileName* | ?] [RECYCLE]

Arguments

FileName
Specifies the file to delete. *FileName* can contain wildcard characters such as * and ?.
For example, to delete backup files with the extension .bak in the current directory,
issue DELETE FILE *.bak.

?
Displays the Delete dialog from which you can choose a file to delete.

RECYCLE
Specifies that the file isn't immediately deleted from disk and is placed in the
Windows 95 Recycle Bin.

> **Caution** Any file deleted with this command cannot be retrieved. Even if SET
> SAFETY is ON, you are not warned before the file is deleted.

Remarks

The file you want to delete cannot be open when DELETE FILE is issued. The file name
must include a path if it is on a different drive or volume, or in a different directory from
the default, and the file name extension must be included. The file name cannot contain
wildcards.

Before you delete a table in a database, issue REMOVE TABLE with the table name
to remove references to the table from the database. If you delete a table that has an
associated .fpt memo file, be sure to delete the memo file.

Example

In the following example, the structure of Customer.dbf and all records in which the
country is USA are copied to a table named backup. The data in backup is then copied
to a text file, temp, which is opened and then deleted when it is closed.

```
CLOSE DATABASES
OPEN DATABASE (HOME(2) + 'Data\testdata')
USE customer  && Opens Customer table

COPY STRUCTURE TO backup
USE backup
APPEND FROM customer FOR country = 'USA'
COPY TO temp TYPE DELIMITED

WAIT WINDOW 'Press Esc to close and erase temp.txt' NOWAIT
MODIFY FILE temp.txt NOEDIT
DELETE FILE temp.txt
? IIF(FILE('temp.txt'),'File not deleted','File deleted')
USE
DELETE FILE backup.dbf
```

See Also

ERASE, REMOVE TABLE, SET SAFETY

DELETE TAG Command

Removes a tag or tags from a compound index (.cdx) file.

Syntax

DELETE TAG *TagName1* [OF *CDXFileName1*]
   [, *TagName2* [OF *CDXFileName2*]] ...

– or –

DELETE TAG ALL [OF *CDXFileName*]

Arguments

TagName1 [OF *CDXFileName1*] [, *TagName2* [OF *CDXFileName2*]] ...
   Specifies a tag to remove from a compound index file. You can delete multiple tags
   with one DELETE TAG by including a list of tag names separated by commas. If two
   or more tags with the same name exist in the open index files, you can remove a tag
   from a specific index file by including OF *CDXFileName*.

ALL [OF *CDXFileName*]
   Removes every tag from a compound index file. If the current table has a structural
   compound index file, all tags are removed from the index file, the index file is deleted
   from the disk, and the flag in the table's header indicating the presence of an associated
   structural compound index file is removed. Use ALL with OF *CDXFileName* to
   remove all tags from an open compound index file other than the structural compound
   index file.

Remarks

Compound index files, created with INDEX, contain tags corresponding to index entries. DELETE TAG is used to remove a tag or tags from open compound index files. You can delete only tags from compound index files open in the current work area. If you remove all the tags from a compound index file, the file is deleted from the disk.

Visual FoxPro looks first for a tag in the structural compound index file (if one is open). If the tag isn't in the structural compound index file, Visual FoxPro then looks for the tag in the other open compound index files.

Visual FoxPro issues a warning if you attempt to delete a primary or candidate index tag and SET SAFETY is ON.

See Also

COPY INDEXES, COPY TAG, INDEX, TAG( )

DELETE TRIGGER Command

Removes a Delete, Insert, or Update trigger for a table from the current database.

Syntax

DELETE TRIGGER ON *TableName* FOR DELETE | INSERT | UPDATE

Arguments

TableName
Specifies the name of table for which the trigger is deleted.

FOR DELETE | INSERT | UPDATE
Specifies the trigger to delete. Include FOR DELETE to remove the Delete trigger, FOR INSERT to remove the Insert trigger, and FOR UPDATE to remove the Update trigger.

Remarks

Use CREATE TRIGGER to create a Delete, Insert, or Update trigger for a table.

Example

The following examples creates an Update trigger which prevents values greater than 50 from being entered in the maxordamt field in the customer table. DISPLAY DATABASE is used to display the Update trigger. DELETE TRIGGER is then used to remove the Update trigger, and DISPLAY DATABASE is issued again to verify the removal of the Update trigger.

```
CLOSE DATABASES
OPEN DATABASE (HOME(2) + 'Data\testdata')  && Open testdata database
USE CUSTOMER  && Open customer table
```

```
CREATE TRIGGER ON customer FOR UPDATE AS maxordamt <= 50
CLEAR
DISPLAY DATABASE
DELETE TRIGGER ON customer FOR UPDATE
DISPLAY DATABASE
```

See Also

ADD TABLE, AERROR( ), CREATE DATABASE, CREATE TRIGGER, DISPLAY DATABASE, LIST DATABASE, OPEN DATABASE

DELETE VIEW Command

Deletes a SQL view from the current database.

Syntax

DELETE VIEW *ViewName*

Arguments

ViewName
Specifies the name of the view deleted from the current database.

Remarks

Use CREATE SQL VIEW to create a SQL view and add the view to the current database. If a SQL view is opened and then deleted, the cursors containing the SQL view results are not closed.

DELETE VIEW requires exclusive use of the database. To open a database for exclusive use, include EXCLUSIVE in OPEN DATABASE.

Example

The following example opens the testdata database. CREATE SQL VIEW is used to create a local SQL view named myview. The View Designer is displayed, allowing you to specify tables and conditions for the SQL view. After you save the SQL view, DISPLAY DATABASE is used to display information about the SQL view. DELETE VIEW is then used to delete the local SQL view named myview.

```
CLOSE DATABASES
OPEN DATABASE (HOME(2) + 'Data\testdata')

CREATE SQL VIEW myview
CLEAR
DISPLAY DATABASE
DELETE VIEW myview
```

See Also

CREATE SQL VIEW, OPEN DATABASE

DeleteColumn Method

Removes a Column object from a Grid control.

Syntax

Grid.DeleteColumn[(*nIndex*)]

Arguments

nIndex
Specifies a number referencing the order of Columns in a Grid. If *nIndex* is not specified, the last Column in the Grid is removed.

Applies To

Grid

See Also

AddColumn Method, AddObject Method, RemoveObject Method

Deleted Event

Occurs when the user marks a record for deletion, unmarks a record marked for deletion, or when DELETE is issued.

Syntax

PROCEDURE *Grid*.Deleted
LPARAMETERS *nRecNo*

Arguments

nRecNo
Returns the record number of the row being deleted.

Applies To

Grid

See Also

DELETE, DeleteMark Property

DELETED( ) Function

Returns a logical value that indicates whether the current record is marked for deletion.

Syntax

DELETED([*cTableAlias* | *nWorkArea*])

Returns

Logical

Arguments

cTableAlias | *nWorkArea*

You can check the status of the current record in a table open in another work area by specifying the work area number with *nWorkArea* or the table alias with *cTableAlias*. If a table isn't open in the work area you specify, DELETED( ) returns false.

If you omit *cTableAlias* and *nWorkArea*, the deleted status is returned for the current record in the current work area.

Remarks

If the record is marked for deletion, DELETED( ) returns true (.T.); otherwise, DELETED( ) returns false (.F.).

Records can be marked for deletion with DELETE and DELETE – SQL, and they can be unmarked with RECALL.

Rushmore optimizes queries that test the deleted status of records if the table is indexed on DELETED( ).

For information on using Rushmore to optimize queries, see the SET OPTIMIZE Command, later in this language reference, and "Understanding Rushmore Technology" in Chapter 15, "Optimizing Applications," in the *Microsoft Visual FoxPro 6.0 Programmer's Guide*.

Example

The following example opens the customer table in the testdata database. DELETE – SQL is used to mark all records for deletion where the country field contains USA. DELETED( ) is used to display all the records marked for deletion. RECALL ALL is used to unmark all the records marked for deletion.

```
CLOSE DATABASES
OPEN DATABASE (HOME(2) + 'Data\testdata')
USE customer   && Opens Customer table

DELETE FROM customer WHERE country = 'USA'   && Mark for deletion
CLEAR
LIST FIELDS company, country FOR DELETED( ) && List marked records
RECALL ALL   && Unmark all records marked for deletion
```

See Also

DELETE, DELETE – SQL, PACK, RECALL, SET DELETED

DeleteMark Property

Specifies whether the delete mark column appears in a Grid control. Available at design time and run time.

Syntax

Grid.DeleteMark[= *lExpr*]

Arguments

lExpr

   The settings for the DeleteMark property are:

Setting	Description
True (.T.)	(Default) The delete mark column appears on the Grid at the far left column.
False (.F.)	The delete mark column does not appear.

Remarks

The delete mark column enables the user to mark records for deletion. The user clicks in the delete column at the record to delete.

Applies To

Grid

See Also

DELETE, Deleted Event

DESCENDING( ) Function

Returns a logical value that indicates whether an index tag was created with the DESCENDING keyword or whether the DESCENDING keyword was included in USE, SET INDEX, or SET ORDER.

Syntax

DESCENDING([*CDXFileName*,] *nIndexNumber* [, *nWorkArea* | *cTableAlias*])

Returns

Logical

Arguments

CDXFileName

Specifies the name of a compound index file with *CDXFileName*. The compound index file you specify can be the structural compound index file automatically opened with the table or an independent compound index file.

nIndexNumber

Specifies which index tag or index file DESCENDING( ) tests. *nIndexNumber* is typically an integer that starts at 1 and is increased by 1 to return additional values for each index tag.

If *nIndexNumber* is 1, a value for the master single-entry .idx index file or master index tag (if one is present) is returned.

As *nIndexNumber* increases, values for each tag in the structural compound index (if one is present) are returned. The values are returned for the tags in the order in which the tags were created in the structural compound index.

After values for all the tags in the structural compound index are returned, values for each tag in any open independent compound indexes are then returned. The values are returned from the tags in the order in which the tags are created in the independent compound indexes.

The empty string is returned if *nIndexNumber* is greater than the total number of open, single-entry .idx files and structural compound and independent compound index tags.

nWorkArea | cTableAlias

Returns values for index files or tags open in a work area other than the current work area. *nWorkArea* specifies the work area number and *cTableAlias* specifies the table alias.

If no table has the alias you specify, Visual FoxPro generates an error message.

Remarks

You can order records in a table in descending order in two ways:

- You can include the DESCENDING keyword in the INDEX command to create a descending order index tag in a compound .cdx.

- You can include the DESCENDING keyword in USE, SET INDEX or SET ORDER to specify a descending order for the master index tag or the master single-entry index (.idx) file.

DESCENDING( ) can determine if an index tag was created in descending order. DESCENDING( ) returns true (.T.) if the index tag you specify was created with the DESCENDING keyword.

DESCENDING( ) can also determine if the master index tag or master index file is in descending order. DESCENDING( ) returns true (.T.) if the DESCENDING keyword was included in USE, SET INDEX, or SET ORDER for the master index tag or a single-entry index (.idx) file you specify.

If you don't include any of the optional arguments, DESCENDING( ) returns a value for the master index tag or master index file. If you don't include any of the optional arguments and a master index tag or .idx file isn't in effect (for example, you've issued SET ORDER TO to place the table in physical record order), DESCENDING( ) returns false (.F.).

Example

The following example opens the customer table in the testdata database. FOR ... ENDFOR is used to create a loop in which the descending status of each index tag in the customer structural index is checked. The name of each structural index tag is displayed with its descending status.

```
CLOSE DATABASES
OPEN DATABASE (HOME(2) + 'Data\testdata')
USE Customer      && Open customer table
CLEAR

FOR nCount = 1 TO 254
   IF !EMPTY(TAG(nCount))  && Checks for tags in the index
   ? TAG(nCount) + ' Descending? ' && Display tag name
   ?? DESCENDING(nCount)  && Display descending status
   ELSE
      EXIT  && Exit the loop when no more tags are found
   ENDIF
ENDFOR
```

See Also

INDEX, SET INDEX, SET ORDER, USE

Description Property

For a File object, the description for the file. For a Server object, the description of the server class. Available at design time and run time.

Syntax

Object.Description[= *cExpression*]

Arguments

cExpression
Specifies the description for the File or Server object.

For a File object, the default value is the empty string. You can also specify a description for a file in a project by choosing **Edit Description** from the Project menu.

For a Server, the default value is the name of the server class. You can also specify a description for a server in the Server tab of the **Project Information** dialog box. The Server object description also appears for the server in the Registry.

Applies To

File Object, Server Object

See Also

Name Property

Desktop Property

Specifies whether a form can appear anywhere on the Windows desktop or is contained in the main Visual FoxPro window. Available at design time; read-only at run time.

Syntax

Object.Desktop[= *lExpr*]

Arguments

lExpr

The settings for the Desktop property are:

Setting	Description
True (.T.)	The form can be anywhere on the Windows desktop.
False (.F.)	(Default) The form is contained in the main Visual FoxPro window.

Remarks

The Desktop property is ignored if the ShowWindow property is set to 2 – As Top-Level form.

Applies To

Form, _SCREEN

See Also

AlwaysOnTop Property, AutoCenter Property, MaxHeight Property, MaxLeft Property, MaxTop Property, MaxWidth Property, MinHeight Property, MinWidth Property, ShowWindow Property

Destroy Event

Occurs when an object is released.

Syntax

PROCEDURE *Object*.Destroy
[LPARAMETERS *nIndex*]

Arguments

nIndex
   Uniquely identifies a control if it is in a control array.

Remarks

The Destroy event for a container object triggers before the Destroy event for any of its contained objects; the container's Destroy event can refer to its contained objects before they are released.

Applies To

ActiveDoc Object, CheckBox, ComboBox, CommandButton, Container Object, Control Object, Cursor, Custom, DataEnvironment, EditBox, Form, FormSet, Grid, Image, Label, Line, ListBox, OLE Bound Control, OLE Container Control, OptionButton, Page, PageFrame, ProjectHook Object, Relation, Shape, Spinner, TextBox, Timer, ToolBar

See Also

AddObject Method, CREATEOBJECT( ), Init Event, RELEASE

_DIARYDATE System Variable

Contains the current date in the Calendar/Diary.

Syntax

_DIARYDATE = *dExpression*

Arguments

dExpression
   Specifies the date for the Calendar/Diary.

Remarks

With _DIARYDATE, you can display the Calendar/Diary with a specific date selected, or you can return the selected Calendar/Diary date.

By default, the current date is stored in _DIARYDATE. When you open the Calendar/Diary, the current date is selected. You can store a different date to _DIARYDATE so that the Calendar/Diary opens with this new date selected.

Selecting a new date when the Calendar/Diary is open causes the new date to be stored to _DIARYDATE. When you close the Calendar/Diary, _DIARYDATE contains the last selected date.

Example

In the following program example, the Calendar/Diary opens with March 28, 2001, selected and the value of _DIARYDATE appears below. July 4, 1776, is then stored to _DIARYDATE and _DIARYDATE displays again. The program then uses the DATE( ) function to select the current date, and displays _DIARYDATE.

```
SET CENTURY ON
STORE {^2001-03-28} TO _DIARYDATE
=MESSAGEBOX(DTOC(_DIARYDATE),64)
ACTIVATE WINDOW calendar
=MESSAGEBOX("Change date to July 4, 1776",48))
STORE {^1776-07-04} TO _DIARYDATE
=MESSAGEBOX(DTOC(_DIARYDATE),64)
=MESSAGEBOX("Change date to today's date",48)
STORE DATE( ) TO _DIARYDATE
=MESSAGEBOX(DTOC(_DIARYDATE),64)
RELEASE WINDOW calendar
```

See Also

STORE

DIFFERENCE( ) Function

Returns an integer, 0 through 4, which represents the relative phonetic difference between two character expressions.

Syntax

DIFFERENCE(*cExpression1*, *cExpression2*)

Returns

Numeric

Arguments

cExpression1, *cExpression2*
   Specifies the character expressions that DIFFERENCE( ) compares.

Remarks

DIFFERENCE( ) is useful for searching tables when the exact spelling of an entry isn't known.

The more alike the two expressions are spelled, the higher the number DIFFERENCE( ) returns. If the character expressions are spelled very similarly, DIFFERENCE( ) returns 4. For two character expressions with little in common phonetically, DIFFERENCE( ) returns 0.

Example

```
STORE 'Smith' TO gcName1
STORE 'Smythe'  TO gcName2
STORE 'Smittie' TO gcName3
STORE '' TO gcName4
CLEAR
? DIFFERENCE(gcName1, gcName2)  && Displays 4
? DIFFERENCE(gcName1, gcName3)  && Displays 4
? DIFFERENCE(gcName1, gcName4)  && Displays 1
```

See Also

SOUNDEX( )

DIMENSION Command

Creates a one- or two-dimensional array of variables.

Syntax

DIMENSION *ArrayName1(nRows1* [, *nColumns1*])
  [, *ArrayName2(nRows2* [, *nColumns2*])] ...

Arguments

ArrayName1
  Specifies the name of the array. Multiple arrays can be created with a single
  DIMENSION command by including additional array names (*ArrayName2*,
  ArrayName3, and so on).

nRows1 [, *nColumns1*]
  Specifies the size of the array to create. If you include just *nRows1*, a one-dimensional
  array is created. One-dimensional arrays have one column and *nRows1* rows. For
  example, the following command creates a one-dimensional array named gaArrayOne
  that contains one column and ten rows.

  ```
  DIMENSION gaArrayOne(10)
  ```

  To create a two-dimensional array, include both *nRows1* and *nColumns1*. *nRows1*
  specifies the number of rows in the array, and *nColumns1* specifies the number of
  columns. The following example creates a two-dimensional array named gaArrayTwo
  containing two rows and four columns:

  ```
  DIMENSION gaArrayTwo(2,4)
  ```

  You must specify a size for each array you create with DIMENSION. In the following
  example, three arrays are created: gaArrayOne and gaArrayTwo from the previous
  examples and a third array called gaArrayThree:

  ```
  DIMENSION gaArrayOne(10), gaArrayTwo(2,4), gaArrayThree(3,3)
  ```

You can use either brackets or parentheses to enclose the expressions in DIMENSION or DECLARE. For example, the following two commands create identical arrays:

```
DIMENSION gaArrayOne(10), gaArrayTwo[2,4], gaArrayThree(3,3)
DIMENSION gaArrayOne[10], gaArrayTwo(2,4), gaArrayThree[3,3]
```

Remarks

DIMENSION is identical in operation and syntax to DECLARE.

Array Elements...   The size of an array determines how many elements it can contain. Each element in an array can store a single piece of information. To determine how many elements an array contains and how much information it can store, multiply the number of rows (*nRows1*) in the array by the number of columns (*nColumns1*) in the array.

Array elements can contain any type of data and are initialized to false (.F.) when the array is first created. You can initialize all the elements in an array to the same value with STORE if SET COMPATIBLE is FOXPLUS or OFF (the default setting). For example:

```
DIMENSION gaArray(10,3)
STORE 'initial' TO gaArray
```

Array Subscripts...   Elements in an array are referenced by their subscripts. Each array element has a unique numeric subscript that identifies it. If the array is one-dimensional, an element's subscript is the same as its row number. For example, the subscript for the element in the third row of a one-dimensional array is 3.

Elements in two-dimensional arrays are referenced by two subscripts. The first subscript indicates the row location of the element, and the second subscript indicates the column location. For example, the subscripts for the element in the third row and fourth column of a two-dimensional array are 3,4. For a further discussion of array element subscripts, see the ASUBSCRIPT( ) Function, earlier in this language reference.

The subscript or subscripts for the first element in an array always start with 1. If an array is two-dimensional, it can also be referenced by a single subscript. Use AELEMENT( ) to return the single subscript from a pair of array row and column subscripts. Use ASUBSCRIPT( ) to return the row and column subscripts from a single subscript.

Redimensioning Arrays...   You can change the size and dimensions of an array by issuing DIMENSION again. The size of an array can be increased or decreased; one-dimensional arrays can be converted to two dimensions, and two-dimensional arrays can be reduced to one dimension.

If the number of elements in an array is increased, the contents of all the elements in the original array are copied to the newly redimensioned array. The additional array elements are initialized to false (.F.).

Examples

Example 1 demonstrates the result of increasing the size of a one-dimensional array. (Note that if you type these commands in the Command window the array will be PUBLIC, but it will be PRIVATE if you copy them into a program and run it.)

If the number of elements in an array is decreased, the elements and any data they contain are deleted. When a one-dimensional array is redimensioned to two dimensions, the contents of the original one-dimensional array are copied to the new array in an element-to-row order.

In Example 2, a one-dimensional array is converted to a two-dimensional array. The contents of the elements of the one-dimensional array are copied to the first row of the new array, followed by the second row and so on. The additional elements are initialized to false (.F.).

When a two-dimensional array is converted to one dimension, the contents of the original two-dimensional array are copied to the new array in a row-to-element order. The first element in the first row becomes the first element in the one-dimensional array, the second element in the first row becomes the second element, and so on.

Use ADEL( ) or AINS( ) to delete or insert array elements, rows and columns. Use APPEND FROM ARRAY, COPY TO ARRAY, SCATTER and GATHER to transfer data between table records and arrays.

In Example 3, a two-dimensional array is created and loaded with data. The array elements and the data they contain are displayed.

```
* Example 1
DIMENSION marray(2)
STORE 'A' TO marray(1)
STORE 'B' TO marray(2)
CLEAR
DISPLAY MEMORY LIKE marray
DIMENSION marray(4)
DISPLAY MEMORY LIKE marray
WAIT WINDOW

* Example 2
DIMENSION marrayone(4)
STORE 'E' TO marrayone(1)
STORE 'F' TO marrayone(2)
STORE 'G' TO marrayone(3)
STORE 'H' TO marrayone(4)
CLEAR
DISPLAY MEMORY LIKE marrayone
DIMENSION marrayone(2,3)
DISPLAY MEMORY LIKE marrayone
WAIT WINDOW
```

```
* Example 3
DIMENSION sample(2,3)
STORE 'Goodbye' TO sample(1,2)
STORE 'Hello' TO sample(2,2)
STORE 99 TO sample(6)
STORE .T. TO sample(1)
CLEAR
DISPLAY MEMORY LIKE sample
```

See Also

ACOPY( ), ADEL( ), ADIR( ), AELEMENT( ), AFIELDS( ), AFONT( ), AINS( ), ALEN( ), APPEND FROM ARRAY, ASCAN( ), ASORT( ), ASUBSCRIPT( ), COPY TO ARRAY, DECLARE, EXTERNAL, GATHER, PRIVATE, PUBLIC, SCATTER, SET COMPATIBLE, STORE

DIR or DIRECTORY Command

Displays information about the files in a directory.

Syntax

DIR | DIRECTORY [ON *Drive*]
    [[LIKE] [*Path*] [*FileSkeleton*]]
    [TO PRINTER [PROMPT] | TO FILE *FileName*]

Arguments

ON *Drive*
    Specifies the name of the drive on which the directory is located.

[LIKE] [*Path*] [*FileSkeleton*]
    Specifies the path to the directory containing the files. The path can include the drive name if you omit ON *Drive*.

    Include *FileSkeleton* to display information about file types other than tables. *FileSkeleton* is a file specification skeleton that supports wildcards. For example, to list all program files in the current directory, issue the following command:

```
DIR *.PRG
```

    In Visual FoxPro, you can issue the following command to list all files without extensions:

```
DIR *.
```

TO PRINTER [PROMPT]

Directs output from DIRECTORY to a printer.

In Microsoft Visual FoxPro, you can include the optional PROMPT clause to display a print dialog box before printing starts. In this dialog box you can adjust printer settings, including the number of copies and page numbers to print. The printer settings that you can adjust depend on the currently installed printer driver. Place the PROMPT keyword immediately after TO PRINTER.

TO FILE *FileName*

Directs output from DIRECTORY to the file specified with *FileName*. If the file already exists and SET SAFETY is ON, you are asked if you want to overwrite the file.

Remarks

Use DIR to display information about files.

DIR without the LIKE clause or a skeleton displays the following:

- Names of all tables in the directory.

- Number of records in each table.

- Date each table was last updated.

- Size of each table in bytes (tables in the original Microsoft FoxBASE format are noted as such).

- If each table is part of a database.

- The total size in bytes the tables occupy on disk (not including associated .fpt memo files).

- Number of tables displayed.

- Total number of bytes remaining on the disk.

The table information for the default drive and directory is displayed unless otherwise specified with *Drive* or *Path* or both.

Example

```
CLEAR
DIR  && Display tables in the current directory
DIR *.CDX && Display index files in the current directory
DIR A*.DBF  && Display tables that begin with A
DIR *.*  && Display all files, including those without extensions
```

See Also

DISPLAY FILES

DIRECTORY( ) Function

Returns true (.T.) if the specified directory is found on disk.

Syntax

DIRECTORY(*cDirectoryName*)

Returns

Logical

Arguments

cDirectoryName
Specifies the name of the directory to locate. If you do not include an absolute path for the directory you specify, Visual FoxPro searches for the directory relative to the Visual FoxPro default directory.

Remarks

The Visual FoxPro default directory is specified with SET DEFAULT.

See Also

FILE( ), GETDIR( ), GETFILE( ), SET DEFAULT

DisabledBackColor, DisabledForeColor Properties

Specifies the background and foreground colors for a disabled control. Available at design time and run time.

Syntax

Control.DisabledBackColor[= *nColor*]

– or –

Control.DisabledBackColor = RGB(*nRedValue, nGreenValue, nBlueValue*)
Control.DisabledForeColor[= *nColor*]

– or –

Control.DisabledForeColor = RGB(*nRedValue, nGreenValue, nBlueValue*)

Arguments

nColor
Specifies a single number to represent the color.

nRedValue, nGreenValue, nBlueValue
> Specifies three separate color intensities that compose the control's foreground color or background color; must be used with RGB( ) to consolidate the three color components into one number.

Remarks

The color you specify is dithered with gray.

> **Note** In the Properties window, you can double-click any of the color properties to display the Color dialog box. You can choose or define colors from this dialog box. The red, green, and blue intensities that correspond to the color you choose become the settings for these properties after you close the Color dialog box.

Applies To

CheckBox, ComboBox, CommandButton, EditBox, Label, ListBox, OptionButton, Spinner, TextBox

> **Note** The DisabledBackColor property does not apply to CommandButton controls.

See Also

BackColor, ForeColor Properties, Colors Overview

DisabledItemBackColor, DisabledItemForeColor Properties

Specifies the background or foreground color for the disabled items in a ComboBox or ListBox control. Available at design time and run time.

Syntax

Control.DisabledItemBackColor[= *nColor*]

– or –

Control.DisabledItemBackColor RGB(*nRedValue, nGreenValue, nBlueValue*)
Control.DisabledItemForeColor[= *nColor*]

– or –

Control.DisabledItemForeColor RGB(*nRedValue, nGreenValue, nBlueValue*)

Arguments

nColor
> Specifies a single number to represent the color.

Note In the Properties window, you can double-click any of the color properties to display the Color dialog box. You can choose or define colors from this dialog box. The red, green, and blue intensities that correspond to the color you choose become the settings for these properties after you close the Color dialog box.

For more information, see the color table in "BackColor, ForeColor Properties," earlier in this language reference.

Applies To

ComboBox, ListBox

See Also

BackColor, ForeColor Properties, DisabledForeColor, DisabledBackColor Properties, RGB( ), SelectedBackColor, SelectedForeColor Properties, SelectedItemBackColor, SelectedItemForeColor Properties

DisabledPicture Property

Specifies the graphic to display when the control is disabled. Available at design time and run time.

Syntax

Control.DisabledPicture[= *cPicture*]

Arguments

cPicture
Specifies either a complete path and file name of a bitmap or the name of a general field in a database table.

Remarks

If you set the DisabledPicture property at design time and the file you specify does not exist, Visual FoxPro displays an error message, but the property remains set to the file you specified. Visual FoxPro ignores the DisabledPicture property at run time if it is set to a file that does not exist.

If you do not set the DisabledPicture property, Visual FoxPro uses the Picture property setting to determine the graphic displayed when the control is disabled.

For CommandButton controls, the Style property must be set to 0 (Standard) for the bitmap to be displayed on the control; For CheckBox and OptionButton controls, the Style property must be set to 1 (Graphical).

Applies To

CheckBox, CommandButton, OptionButton

See Also

DownPicture Property, Enabled Property, Picture Property, Style Property

DISKSPACE( ) Function

Returns the number of bytes available on the default or specified disk drive or volume.

Syntax

DISKSPACE([*cVolumeName*])

Returns

Numeric

Arguments

cVolumeName
Specifies the name of the disk drive or volume for which the available space is returned. If *cVolumeName* is omitted, the available space is returned for the default disk drive or volume.

Remarks

This function is useful for determining whether sufficient space is available to back up files or to execute commands such as SORT that require additional disk space for temporary work files.

The default disk drive or volume is specified with SET DEFAULT.

DISKSPACE( ) returns –1 if there is an error reading the disk drive or volume. On some networks, the value returned by DISKSPACE( ) may not be accurate for large network drives.

Example

The following example uses DISKSPACE( ) to determine whether sufficient disk space is available to perform a sort.

```
*** Check DISKSPACE before sort ***
CLOSE DATABASES
OPEN DATABASE (HOME(2) + 'Data\testdata')
USE customer  && Opens Customer table

*** Get size of table header ***
gnTableHead = HEADER( )

*** Calculate size of table ***
gnFileSize = gnTableHead + (RECSIZE( ) * RECCOUNT( ) + 1)
IF DISKSPACE( ) > (gnFileSize * 3)
   WAIT WINDOW 'Sufficient diskspace to sort.'
ELSE
   WAIT WINDOW 'Insufficient diskspace. Sort cannot be done.'
ENDIF
```

See Also

HEADER( ), RECSIZE( ), SET DEFAULT

DISPLAY Command

Displays information about the current table in the main Visual FoxPro window or in the user-defined window.

Syntax

DISPLAY
    [[FIELDS] *FieldList*]
    [*Scope*] [FOR *lExpression1*] [WHILE *lExpression2*]
    [OFF]
    [NOCONSOLE]
    [NOOPTIMIZE]
    [TO PRINTER [PROMPT] | TO FILE *FileName*]

Arguments

FIELDS *FieldList*

Specifies the fields to display. If you omit FIELDS *FieldList*, all fields from the table are displayed by default.

Memo field contents aren't displayed unless the memo field name is explicitly included in the field list. The displayed width of memo fields is determined by SET MEMOWIDTH.

Scope

Specifies the range of records to display. Only the records that fall within the range are displayed. The scope clauses are: ALL, NEXT *nRecords*, RECORD *nRecordNumber*, and REST. Commands that include *Scope* operate only on the table in the active work area.

For more information on scope clauses, see "Scope Clauses" in Help.

The default scope for DISPLAY is the current record (NEXT 1).

FOR *lExpression1*

Specifies that only the records that satisfy the logical condition *lExpression1* are displayed. This allows you to filter out undesired records.

Rushmore optimizes a query created with DISPLAY ... FOR if *lExpression1* is an optimizable expression. For best performance, use an optimizable expression in the FOR clause.

For more information, see the SET OPTIMIZE Command, later in this language reference, and "Understanding Rushmore Technology" in Chapter 15, "Optimizing Applications," in the *Microsoft Visual FoxPro 6.0 Programmer's Guide*.

WHILE *lExpression2*
>Specifies a condition whereby records are displayed for as long as the logical expression *lExpression2* evaluates to true (.T.).

OFF
>Suppresses the display of record numbers. If you omit OFF, the record number is displayed before each record.

NOCONSOLE
>Suppresses output to the main Visual FoxPro window or to the active user-defined window.

NOOPTIMIZE
>Disables Rushmore optimization of DISPLAY.

>For more information, see the SET OPTIMIZE Command, later in this language reference, and "Understanding Rushmore Technology" in Chapter 15, "Optimizing Applications," in the *Microsoft Visual FoxPro 6.0 Programmer's Guide*.

TO PRINTER [PROMPT]
>Directs output from DISPLAY to a printer.

>In Visual FoxPro you can include the optional PROMPT clause to display a dialog box before printing starts. In this dialog box, you can adjust printer settings, including the number of copies and page numbers to print. The printer settings that you can adjust depend on the currently installed printer driver. Place PROMPT immediately after TO PRINTER.

TO FILE *FileName*
>Directs output from DISPLAY to the file specified with *FileName*. If the file already exists and SET SAFETY is ON, you are asked if you want to overwrite the file.

Remarks

DISPLAY displays the contents of records and the results of expressions for the current table. If there is more information than can be displayed in the window, the first screen of information is displayed and Visual FoxPro pauses. Press any key or click anywhere to see the next screen of information. DISPLAY is similar to LIST, except that LIST displays the same information in a continuous stream without pausing.

DISPLAY can also be used to display the results of expressions, which can consist of combinations of literals, memory variables, array elements, fields, and memo fields. Field names and expressions are displayed if SET HEADINGS is ON.

Example

The following example opens the `customer` table in the `testdata` database. The contents of the first record are displayed.

```
CLOSE DATABASES
OPEN DATABASE (HOME(2) + 'Data\testdata')
USE customer  && Opens Customer table

CLEAR
DISPLAY FIELD cust_id, company, contact OFF NEXT 10
```

See Also

LIST, SET HEADINGS, SET MEMOWIDTH

DISPLAY CONNECTIONS Command

Displays information about the named connections in the current database.

Syntax

DISPLAY CONNECTIONS
[TO PRINTER [PROMPT] | TO FILE *FileName*]
[NOCONSOLE]

Arguments

TO PRINTER [PROMPT]
Directs output from DISPLAY CONNECTIONS to a printer.

In Visual FoxPro, you can include the optional PROMPT clause to display a Print dialog box before printing starts. Place PROMPT immediately after TO PRINTER.

TO FILE *FileName*
Directs output from DISPLAY CONNECTIONS to the file specified with *FileName*. If the file already exists and SET SAFETY is ON, Visual FoxPro displays a prompt asking if you want to overwrite the file.

NOCONSOLE
Suppresses output to the main Visual FoxPro window or to the active user-defined window.

Remarks

DISPLAY CONNECTIONS displays the connection names, datasource, and connection string in the current database. Use DBGETPROP( ) to return additional information about connections in the current database.

Example

The following example assumes an ODBC data source called MyFoxSQLNT is available, and the user ID for the data source is "sa." The testdata database is opened, and a connection named Myconn is created. DISPLAY CONNECTIONS is used to display the named connections in the database.

```
CLOSE DATABASES
OPEN DATABASE (HOME(2) + 'data\testdata')

CREATE CONNECTION Myconn DATASOURCE "MyFoxSQLNT" USERID "sa"
CLEAR
DISPLAY CONNECTIONS      && Displays named connections in the database
```

See Also

CREATE CONNECTION, DELETE CONNECTION, DBGETPROP( ),
LIST CONNECTIONS, RENAME CONNECTION

DISPLAY DATABASE Command

Displays information about the current database or fields, named connections, tables, or views in the current database.

Syntax

DISPLAY DATABASE
    [TO PRINTER [PROMPT] | TO FILE *FileName*]
    [NOCONSOLE]

Arguments

TO PRINTER [PROMPT]
    Directs output from DISPLAY DATABASE to a printer.

    In Visual FoxPro, you can include the optional PROMPT clause to display a Print dialog box before printing starts. Place PROMPT immediately after TO PRINTER.

TO FILE *FileName*
    Directs output from DISPLAY DATABASE to the file specified with *FileName*. If the file already exists and SET SAFETY is ON, Visual FoxPro displays a prompt asking if you want to overwrite the file.

NOCONSOLE
    Suppresses output to the main Visual FoxPro window or to the active user-defined window.

Remarks

Use DBGETPROP( ) to return additional information about the current database.

Example

The following example creates a database named `people`. A table named `friends` is created and is automatically added to the database. DISPLAY TABLES is used to display the tables in the database, and DISPLAY DATABASES is used to display information about the tables in the database.

```
CREATE DATABASE people
CREATE TABLE friends (FirstName C(20), LastName C(20))
CLEAR
DISPLAY TABLES  && Displays tables in the database
DISPLAY DATABASES  && Displays table information
```

See Also

LIST DATABASE

DISPLAY DLLS Command

Displays information about shared library functions registered in Visual FoxPro with DECLARE – DLL.

Syntax

DISPLAY DLLS
    [TO PRINTER [PROMPT] | TO FILE *FileName*]
    [NOCONSOLE]

Arguments

TO PRINTER [PROMPT]
    Directs output from DISPLAY DLLS to a printer.

    In Visual FoxPro, you can include the optional PROMPT clause to display a Print dialog box before printing starts. Place PROMPT immediately after TO PRINTER.

TO FILE *FileName*
    Directs output from DISPLAY DLLS to the file specified with *FileName*. If the file already exists and SET SAFETY is ON, Visual FoxPro displays a prompt asking if you want to overwrite the file.

NOCONSOLE
    Suppresses output to the main Visual FoxPro window or to the active user-defined window.

See Also

DECLARE – DLL, LIST DLLS

DISPLAY FILES Command

Displays information about files.

Syntax

DISPLAY FILES
    [ON *Drive*]
    [LIKE *FileSkeleton*]
    [TO PRINTER [PROMPT] | TO FILE *FileName*]

Arguments

ON *Drive*
    Specifies the drive or volume on which the files reside.

LIKE *FileSkeleton*
    Specifies a condition whereby Visual FoxPro displays information only about files that match the skeleton pattern *FileSkeleton*. The skeleton pattern can contain wildcards such as ? and *.

TO PRINTER [PROMPT]
    Directs output from DISPLAY FILES to a printer.

    In Visual FoxPro, you can include the optional PROMPT clause to display a dialog box before printing starts. In this dialog box, you can adjust printer settings, including the number of copies and page numbers to print. The printer settings that you can adjust depend on the currently installed printer driver. Place the PROMPT keyword immediately after TO PRINTER.

TO FILE *FileName*
    Directs output from DISPLAY FILES to the file specified with *FileName*. If the file already exists and SET SAFETY is ON, you are asked if you want to overwrite the file.

Remarks

Use DISPLAY FILES to display information about files residing on a disk. You can display information about all files on a specified drive, volume, directory, or folder, or only files that match a skeleton pattern containing wildcards such as ? and *.

Issuing DISPLAY FILES without any arguments displays information about tables in the current directory. The information displayed includes the following:

- Table name.
- Number of records in the table.
- Date and time of the last update to the table.
- The size of each table in bytes.
- If each table is part of a database.

Example

The following example displays the names of the databases in the …\Samples\Vfp98\Data directory.

```
CLOSE DATABASES
OPEN DATABASE (HOME(2) + 'Data\testdata')

CLEAR
DISPLAY FILES LIKE *.DBC
```

See Also

DIR or DIRECTORY, LIST

DISPLAY MEMORY Command

Displays the current contents of variables and arrays.

Syntax

DISPLAY MEMORY
    [LIKE *FileSkeleton*]
    [TO PRINTER [PROMPT] | TO FILE *FileName*]
    [NOCONSOLE]

Arguments

LIKE *FileSkeleton*

    Displays information about variables and arrays that match the skeleton pattern *FileSkeleton*. If you include LIKE *FileSkeleton*, Microsoft Visual FoxPro displays only the contents of variables and arrays that match *FileSkeleton*. *FileSkeleton* supports wildcards such as ? and *. For example, to display all variables that begin with the letter A, issue:

```
DISPLAY MEMORY LIKE A*
```

TO PRINTER [PROMPT]

    Directs output from DISPLAY MEMORY to a printer.

    You can include the optional PROMPT clause to display a dialog box before printing starts. In this dialog box, you can adjust printer settings, including the number of copies and page numbers to print. The printer settings that you can adjust depend on the currently installed printer driver. Place the PROMPT keyword immediately after TO PRINTER.

TO FILE *FileName*

    Directs output from DISPLAY MEMORY to the file specified with *FileName*. If the file already exists and SET SAFETY is ON, you are asked if you want to overwrite the file.

NOCONSOLE
Suppresses output to the main Visual FoxPro window or to the active user-defined window.

Remarks

DISPLAY MEMORY shows the name, type, contents, and status of all currently defined variables and variable arrays. It also displays the number of variables defined, the number of bytes used, and the number of additional variables available. Note that the number of bytes used represents memory used by character type variables. Character type variables are the only type of variables that require additional memory beyond that allocated by the variable count specified with the MVCOUNT configuration item.

Information about system variables, menus, menu bars, menu titles, and windows is also displayed.

Example

In the following example, several variables are created and assigned values. DISPLAY MEMORY first displays all variables that begin with "sam" and then displays all variables that contain five letters and end with "exit."

```
STORE 'Goodbye' TO sample1
STORE 'Hello' TO sample2
STORE .T. TO texit
STORE .F. TO mexit

CLEAR
DISPLAY MEMORY LIKE sam*
DISPLAY MEMORY LIKE ?exit
```

See Also

DECLARE, DIMENSION, LIST, STORE

DISPLAY OBJECTS Command

Displays information about an object or a group of objects.

Syntax

DISPLAY OBJECTS
    [LIKE *cObjectSkeleton*]
    [TO PRINTER [PROMPT] | TO FILE *FileName*]
    [NOCONSOLE]

Arguments

LIKE *cObjectSkeleton*

> Displays information about a subset of objects. *cObjectSkeleton* is an object specification skeleton that supports wildcards (* and ?). For example, to display all objects that begin with A, use the following command:

```
DISPLAY OBJECTS LIKE A*
```

TO PRINTER [PROMPT]

> Directs output from DISPLAY OBJECTS to a printer.

> You can include the optional PROMPT clause to display a Print dialog box before printing starts. Place the PROMPT keyword immediately after TO PRINTER.

TO FILE *FileName*

> Directs output from DISPLAY OBJECTS to the file specified with *FileName*. If the file already exists and SET SAFETY is ON, Visual FoxPro displays a prompt asking if you want to overwrite the file.

NOCONSOLE

> Suppresses output to the main Visual FoxPro window or to the active user-defined window.

Remarks

DISPLAY OBJECTS displays the following information about all existing objects:

- Properties and their values.

- Methods.

- Member objects and the class or subclass on which they are based.

- Class or subclass on which objects are based.

- Class hierarchy for the objects.

DISPLAY OBJECTS fills the entire main Visual FoxPro window or user-defined window with information and then pauses. Press any key or click anywhere to see the next set of information. DISPLAY is similar to LIST, except that LIST displays the same information in a continuous stream without pausing.

Example

The following example uses DEFINE CLASS and CREATEOBJECT( ) to create two custom classes named FormChild and FormGrandChild from the Visual FoxPro Form base class. DISPLAY OBJECTS displays information about the objects and their properties.

```
CLEAR
frmMyForm = CREATEOBJECT("FormGrandChild")
DISPLAY OBJECTS LIKE frm*
RELEASE frmMyForm

DEFINE CLASS FormChild AS FORM
ENDDEFINE

DEFINE CLASS FormGrandChild AS FormChild
ENDDEFINE
```

See Also

LIST OBJECTS

DISPLAY PROCEDURES Command

Displays the names of procedures stored in the current database.

Syntax

DISPLAY PROCEDURES
    [TO PRINTER [PROMPT] | TO FILE *FileName*]
    [NOCONSOLE]

Arguments

TO PRINTER [PROMPT]
    Directs information returned from DISPLAY PROCEDURES to a printer.

    You can include PROMPT to display a Print dialog box before printing starts.
    Place the PROMPT keyword immediately after TO PRINTER.

TO FILE *FileName*
    Directs output from DISPLAY PROCEDURES to the file specified with *FileName*.
    If the file already exists and SET SAFETY is ON, Visual FoxPro displays a prompt
    asking if you want to overwrite the file.

NOCONSOLE
    Suppresses output to the main Visual FoxPro window or to the active user-defined
    window.

Remarks

Stored procedures are created with APPEND PROCEDURES, COPY PROCEDURES,
or MODIFY PROCEDURE.

Example

The following example opens the `testdata` database, and uses DISPLAY PROCEDURES to display the stored procedures (if any) in the database. If there are no stored procedures in the database, you can run the example for APPEND PROCEDURES to add a procedure to the database.

```
CLOSE DATABASES
OPEN DATABASE (HOME(2) + 'Data\testdata')

CLEAR
DISPLAY PROCEDURES  && Displays stored procedures in the database
```

See Also

APPEND PROCEDURES, COPY PROCEDURES, CREATE DATABASE, DISPLAY DATABASE, LIST PROCEDURES, MODIFY PROCEDURE

DISPLAY STATUS Command

Displays the status of the Visual FoxPro environment.

Syntax

DISPLAY STATUS
  [TO PRINTER [PROMPT] | TO FILE *FileName*]
  [NOCONSOLE]

Arguments

TO PRINTER [PROMPT]
  Directs output from DISPLAY STATUS to a printer.

  You can include the optional PROMPT clause to display a print dialog box before printing starts. In this dialog box, you can adjust printer settings, including the number of copies and page numbers to print. The printer settings that you can adjust depend on the currently installed printer driver. Place the PROMPT keyword immediately after TO PRINTER.

TO FILE *FileName*
  Directs output from DISPLAY STATUS to the file specified with *FileName*. If the file already exists and SET SAFETY is ON, you are asked if you want to overwrite the file.

NOCONSOLE
  Suppresses output to the main Visual FoxPro window or to the active user-defined window.

Remarks

This form of DISPLAY lists information about the current Visual FoxPro environment. The categories of information and the information in each category are as follows.

Table and index file information:

- Open tables
- Open memo files
- Table aliases
- Table code pages
- Table relations
- Active indexes
- Index file keys
- The controlling index file or tag
- Open structural compound files
- Open compound index tags
- The shared attribute status of each open table
- The currently locked records in each table
- The EXCLUSIVE use setting
- The LOCK setting
- The MULTILOCKS setting
- The SET REFRESH value
- The SET REPROCESS value

Open low-level file information:

- Open low-level files
- The file handle number for each low-level file
- The file pointer position for each low-level file
- Read/write attributes for each low-level file

Additional Visual FoxPro environment information:

- The procedure file in use
- The processor type
- The Visual FoxPro path

- The Visual FoxPro default directory
- The print destination
- The margin setting
- The current work area
- SET command settings
- Binary modules currently loaded
- DDE information in Visual FoxPro
- Current code page
- Current collating sequence
- Compiler code page
- Current date format
- Keyboard macro key combination
- How UDF parameters are passed
- Textmerge options
- External registered shared library functions (DLLs)

See Also

LIST

DISPLAY STRUCTURE Command

Displays the structure of a table file.

Syntax

DISPLAY STRUCTURE
    [IN *nWorkArea* | *cTableAlias*]
    [TO PRINTER [PROMPT] | TO FILE *FileName*]
    [NOCONSOLE]

Arguments

IN *nWorkArea* | *cTableAlias*
    Displays the structure of the table in a work area other than the current work areas.
    nWorkArea specifies the work area number and *cTableAlias* specifies the table alias.

TO PRINTER [PROMPT]
    Directs output from DISPLAY STRUCTURE to a printer.

You can include the optional PROMPT clause to display a dialog box before printing starts. In this dialog box, you can adjust printer settings, including the number of copies and page numbers to print. The printer settings that you can adjust depend on the currently installed printer driver. Place the PROMPT keyword immediately after TO PRINTER.

TO FILE *FileName*

Directs output from DISPLAY STRUCTURE to the file specified with *FileName*. If the file already exists and SET SAFETY is ON, you are asked if you want to overwrite the file.

NOCONSOLE

Suppresses output to the main Visual FoxPro window or to the active user-defined window.

Remarks

Use DISPLAY STRUCTURE to display the field structure of a table. The name of each field in the table is displayed with its type and width. If a field is a Numeric, Double, or Float type field, the number of decimal places in the field is displayed. Null value support for each field is also displayed.

DISPLAY STRUCTURE also displays the current number of records in the table and the date it was last updated. If the table has an associated memo field, the memo field block size is shown. The total width of all fields is also displayed, as is the table's code page.

The table can have a structural compound index that is opened with the table. If a tag in the structural compound index has the same name as a field in the table, the order of the tag (ascending or descending) and the tag's collation sequence is displayed next to the field name.

If SET FIELDS is used to limit access to fields in the table, an angle bracket (>) appears beside the names of fields that can be accessed.

Example

In the following example, the `customer` table in the `testdata` database is opened. DISPLAY STRUCTURE is used to display the table structure.

```
CLOSE DATABASES
OPEN DATABASE (HOME(2) + 'Data\testdata')
USE customer  && Opens Customer table

CLEAR
DISPLAY STRUCTURE
```

See Also

LIST

DISPLAY TABLES Command

Displays names and information about all the tables contained in the current database.

Syntax

DISPLAY TABLES
    [TO PRINTER [PROMPT] | TO FILE *FileName*]
    [NOCONSOLE]

Arguments

TO PRINTER [PROMPT]
    Directs output from DISPLAY TABLES to a printer.

    You can include PROMPT to display a Print dialog box before printing starts. Place the PROMPT keyword immediately after TO PRINTER.

TO FILE *FileName*
    Directs output from DISPLAY TABLES to the file specified with *FileName*. If the file already exists and SET SAFETY is ON, Visual FoxPro displays a prompt asking if you want to overwrite the file.

NOCONSOLE
    Suppresses output to the main Visual FoxPro window or to the active user-defined window.

Remarks

The information returned is a subset of the information shown using DISPLAY STATUS. However, the information displayed using DISPLAY TABLES contains only table-related information and displays the information regardless of whether the tables are open or not.

The following information is displayed:

- Table name

- Table path

Example

The following example opens the customer table in the testdata database. DISPLAY TABLES is used to display information about the tables in the database.

```
CLOSE DATABASES
SET PATH TO (HOME(2) + 'Data\')   && Sets path to database
OPEN DATABASE testdata   && Open testdata database

CLEAR
DISPLAY TABLES   && Displays information about tables in the database
```

See Also

ADD TABLE, CLOSE DATABASES, CREATE DATABASE, LIST TABLES, OPEN DATABASE, REMOVE TABLE

DISPLAY VIEWS Command

Displays information about SQL views in the current database and indicates whether the SQL views are based on local or remote tables.

Syntax

DISPLAY VIEWS
    [TO PRINTER [PROMPT] | TO FILE *FileName*]
    [NOCONSOLE]

Arguments

TO PRINTER [PROMPT]
    Directs output from DISPLAY VIEWS to a printer.

    You can include PROMPT to display the Print dialog box before printing starts. Place the PROMPT keyword immediately after TO PRINTER.

TO FILE *FileName*
    Directs output from DISPLAY VIEWS to the file specified with *FileName*. If the file already exists and SET SAFETY is ON, Visual FoxPro displays a prompt asking if you want to overwrite the file.

NOCONSOLE
    Suppresses output to the main Visual FoxPro window or to the active user-defined window.

Remarks

Use DBGETPROP( ) to return additional information about SQL views in the current database.

SQL views are created with CREATE SQL VIEW.

Example

The following example opens the `testdata` database. CREATE SQL VIEW is used to create a local SQL view named `myview`. The View Designer is displayed, allowing you to specify tables and conditions for the SQL view. After you save the SQL view you create, information about the SQL views in the database is displayed.

```
CLOSE DATABASES
OPEN DATABASE (HOME(2) + 'Data\testdata')
CREATE SQL VIEW myview
```

```
CLEAR
DISPLAY VIEWS
```

See Also

CREATE DATABASE, CREATE SQL VIEW, DBGETPROP( ), DISPLAY DATABASE, LIST VIEWS

DisplayCount Property

Specifies the maximum number of items displayed in the list portion of a ComboBox control.

Syntax

Object.DisplayCount[= *nExpression*]

Arguments

nExpression

Specifies the maximum number of items displayed in the list portion of the ComboBox control. The default value is zero; if *nExpression* is zero, a maximum of 7 items are displayed in the list.

Scroll arrows are not displayed in the list portion of a ComboBox control if *nExpression* is one.

Applies To

ComboBox

See Also

ColumnCount Property, DisplayValue Property

DisplayValue Property

Specifies the contents of the first column of the selected item in a ListBox or ComboBox control. Available at design time and run time.

Syntax

[*Form.*]*Control*.DisplayValue[= *Expr*]

Arguments

Expr

If DisplayValue is a character string, specifies the value of the first column of the selected item. If DisplayValue is numeric, specifies the index of the selected item.

Remarks

Use the DisplayValue property when a ComboBox or ListBox has more than one column and the control's BoundColumn property is set to a value greater than 1. The text displayed in the text box portion of the ComboBox is specified by DisplayValue when DisplayValue is a character string.

Note When a ComboBox or ListBox has only one column, the DisplayValue property and Value property of the control have the same setting if both contain character strings.

Applies To

ComboBox, ListBox

See Also

BoundColumn Property, Value Property

DMY( ) Function

Returns a character expression in day-month-year format (for example, 31 May 1998) from a Date or DateTime expression. The month name isn't abbreviated.

Syntax

DMY(*dExpression* | *tExpression*)

Returns

Character

Arguments

dExpression
　　Specifies the Date expression from which DMY( ) returns a character string in day-month-year format.

tExpression
　　Specifies the DateTime expression from which DMY( ) returns a character string in day-month-year format.

Remarks

If SET CENTURY is OFF, DMY( ) returns a character string in a dd-Month-yy format (for example, 16 February 98). If SET CENTURY is ON, the format is dd-Month-yyyy (for example, 16 February 1998).

Example

```
CLEAR
SET CENTURY OFF
? DMY(DATE( ))
```

```
SET CENTURY ON
? DMY(DATE( ))
```

See Also

MDY( ), SET CENTURY, SET DATE

DO Command

Executes a Visual FoxPro program or procedure.

Syntax

DO *ProgramName1* | *ProcedureName*
    [IN *ProgramName2*]
    [WITH *ParameterList*]

Arguments

ProgramName1

Specifies the name of the program to execute.

If you don't include an extension with the program you execute, Visual FoxPro looks for and executes these versions of the program in the following order:

- .exe (executable version)

- .app (an application)

- .fxp (compiled version)

- .prg (program)

To use DO to execute a specific menu program, form program, or query, you must include its extension (.mpr, .spr, or .qpr).

ProcedureName

Specifies the name of the procedure to execute. Visual FoxPro first looks for the procedure in the currently executing program. If the procedure is not located there, Visual FoxPro then looks for the procedure in the procedure files opened with SET PROCEDURE.

You can include the IN *ProgramName2* clause to tell Visual FoxPro to look for the procedure in a file you specify.

Multiple procedures within an executable (.exe) version or an application (.app) can have the same name. When you use DO to start a procedure in an executable version or in an application, Visual FoxPro searches only the main program of the executable version or application for the specified procedure.

IN *ProgramName2*

Executes a procedure in the program file specified with *ProgramName2*.

When the file is located, the procedure is executed. If the program file cannot be located, the message "File does not exist" appears. If the program file is located but the specified procedure isn't in the program file, the message "Procedure is not found" appears.

WITH *ParameterList*

Specifies parameters to pass to the program or procedure. The parameters listed in *ParameterList* can be expressions, memory variables, literals, fields, or user-defined functions. By default, parameters are passed to programs and procedures by reference. You can pass a parameter by value by placing it in parentheses.

See the SET UDFPARMS Command, later in this language reference, for a discussion of passing parameters by value or reference. The maximum number of parameters you can pass to a program or procedure is 27. For more information on parameter passing, see the LPARAMETERS and PARAMETERS Commands, later in this language reference.

Remarks

DO executes a Visual FoxPro program or procedure in a program or procedure file. A program file can itself contain additional DO commands, allowing you to nest DO commands up to 128 levels.

When you use DO to run a program, the commands contained in the program file are executed until one of the following occurs:

- RETURN is encountered.

- CANCEL is executed.

- Another DO is issued.

- The end of the file is reached.

- QUIT is executed.

When program execution is complete, control is returned to one of the following:

- The calling program.

- The Command window.

- The operating system.

If you choose Do from the Program menu and execute a program in a directory on a drive other than the current directory or drive, Visual FoxPro automatically changes the default directory and drive to the directory and drive containing the program.

See Also

CLEAR, LPARAMETERS, PARAMETERS, PARAMETERS( ), PRIVATE, PROCEDURE, PUBLIC, SET DEFAULT, SET DEVELOPMENT, SET PATH, SET PROCEDURE

DO CASE ... ENDCASE Command

Executes the first set of commands whose conditional expression evaluates to true (.T.).

Syntax

DO CASE
    CASE *lExpression1*
        Commands
    [CASE *lExpression2*
        Commands

      ...

    CASE *lExpressionN*
        Commands]
    [OTHERWISE
        Commands]
ENDCASE

Arguments

CASE *lExpression1 Commands* ...

When the first true (.T.) CASE expression is encountered, the set of commands following it is executed. Execution of the set of commands continues until the next CASE or ENDCASE is reached. Execution then resumes with the first command following ENDCASE.

If a CASE expression is false (.F.), the set of commands following it up to the next CASE clause is ignored.

Only one set of commands is executed. These are the first commands whose CASE expression evaluates to true (.T.). Any succeeding true (.T.) CASE expressions are ignored.

OTHERWISE *Commands*

If all of the CASE expressions evaluate to false (.F.), OTHERWISE determines if an additional set of commands is executed.

- If you include OTHERWISE, the commands following OTHERWISE are executed and execution skips to the first command following ENDCASE.

- If you omit OTHERWISE, execution skips to the first command following ENDCASE.

Remarks

DO CASE is used to execute a set of Visual FoxPro commands based on the value of a logical expression. When DO CASE is executed, successive logical expressions are evaluated; the values of the expressions determine which set of commands is executed.

Comments can be placed after DO CASE and ENDCASE on the same line. The comments are ignored during program compilation and execution.

Example

In this example, Visual FoxPro evaluates each CASE clause until the MONTH variable is found in one of the lists. The appropriate string is stored to the variable `rpt_title` and the DO CASE structure is exited.

```
STORE CMONTH(DATE( )) TO month  && The month today

DO CASE  && Begins loop

   CASE INLIST(month,'January','February','March')
      STORE 'First Quarter Earnings' TO rpt_title

   CASE INLIST(month,'April','May','June')
      STORE 'Second Quarter Earnings' TO rpt_title

   CASE INLIST(month,'July','August','September')
      STORE 'Third Quarter Earnings' TO rpt_title

   OTHERWISE
      STORE 'Fourth Quarter Earnings' TO rpt_title
ENDCASE  && Ends loop
WAIT WINDOW rpt_title NOWAIT
```

See Also

DO WHILE ... ENDDO, EXIT, FOR ... ENDFOR, IF ... ENDIF, IIF( ),
SCAN ... ENDSCAN

DoCmd Method

Executes a Visual FoxPro command for an instance of the Visual FoxPro application automation server.

Syntax

ApplicationObject.DoCmd(*cCommand*)

Arguments

cCommand
   Specifies the Visual FoxPro command to execute.

Remarks

cCommand must evaluate to a legal Visual FoxPro command.

Applies To

Application Object, _VFP System Variable

See Also

DO, Eval Method, SetVar Method

DODEFAULT( ) Function

Executes, from within a subclass, the parent class event or method of the same name.

Syntax

DODEFAULT([*eParameter1* [, *eParameter2*] ...])

Returns

Character, Numeric, Currency, Date, DateTime, Logical, or Memo

Arguments

eParameter1 [, *eParameter2*] ...
  Specifies parameters that are passed to the parent class event or method.

Remarks

DODEFAULT( ) executes, from within a subclass, the parent class event or method of the same name. For example, if DODEFAULT( ) is placed in the Click event of a subclass, the Click event of the parent class is executed. The :: scope resolution operator, unlike DODEFAULT( ), executes a parent class event or method of a different name.

The value DODEFAULT( ) returns is determined by the return value of the event or method.

Note that DODEFAULT( ) can be placed only within an event or method.

See Also

:: Scope Resolution Operator

DOEVENTS Command

Executes all pending Windows events.

Syntax

DOEVENTS

Remarks

Window events are placed in a queue when the AutoYield property is set to false (.F.) and program code is executing. DOEVENTS executes all pending Windows events and processes any user code associated with the Windows events.

See Also

AutoYield Property

DO FORM Command

Runs a compiled form or form set created with the Form Designer.

Syntax

DO FORM *FormName* | ?
    [NAME *VarName* [LINKED]]
    [WITH *cParameterList*]
    [TO *VarName*]
    [NOREAD] [NOSHOW]

Arguments

FormName
    Specifies the name of the form or form set to run.

?

    Displays the Do dialog box from which you can choose a form or form set to run.

NAME *VarName* [LINKED]
    Specifies a variable or array element with which you can reference the form or form set. If you specify a variable that doesn't exist, Microsoft Visual FoxPro automatically creates it. If you specify an array element, the array must exist before you issue DO FORM. If the variable or array element you specify already exists, its contents are overwritten.

    If you omit the NAME clause, Visual FoxPro creates an object type variable with the same name as the form or form set file.

    Include LINKED to link the form to the variable associated with it so that the form is released when the variable goes out of scope. If you don't include LINKED, a form can still be active, even though there is no object variable associated with the form.

WITH *cParameterList*
    Specifies the parameters passed to the form or form set.

    If a form is run, the parameters are passed to the form's Init method.

    If a form set is run, the parameters are passed to the form set's Init method if the form set's WindowType property is set to ModeLess (0) or Modal (1). The parameters are passed to the Setup1 method if the form set's WindowType property is set to Read (2) or ReadModal (3).

TO *VarName*

Specifies a variable to hold a value returned from the form. If the variable doesn't exist, Visual FoxPro automatically creates it. Use the RETURN command in the Unload event procedure of the form to specify the return value. If you do not include a return value, the default value of true (.T.) is returned. If you use TO, the WindowType property of the form must be set to 1 (Modal).

NOREAD

Specifies that the form set is created and displayed, even though controls are not activated until READ is issued. NOREAD is ignored if the form set object's WindowType property is not set to 2 (Read).

NOSHOW

Specifies that the form's Show method isn't called when the form is run. When you include NOSHOW and run the form, the form is not visible until the form's Visible property is set to true (.T.) or the form's Show method is called.

Remarks

DO FORM executes the Show method for the form or form set.

Example

The following example runs the stop watch (Swatch.scx) control sample.

```
DO FORM (HOME(2) + 'Solution\Controls\Timer\Swatch.scx')
```

See Also

COMPILE FORM, CREATE FORM, MODIFY FORM

DO WHILE ... ENDDO Command

Executes a set of commands within a conditional loop.

Syntax

DO WHILE *lExpression*
    Commands
    [LOOP]
    [EXIT]
ENDDO

Arguments

lExpression

Specifies a logical expression whose value determines whether the commands between DO WHILE and ENDDO are executed. As long as *lExpression* evaluates to true (.T.), the set of commands are executed.

Commands

Specifies the set of Visual FoxPro commands to be executed as long as *lExpression* evaluates to true (.T.).

LOOP

Returns program control directly back to DO WHILE. LOOP can be placed anywhere between DO WHILE and ENDDO.

EXIT

Transfers program control from within the DO WHILE loop to the first command following ENDDO. EXIT can be placed anywhere between DO WHILE and ENDDO.

Remarks

Commands between DO WHILE and ENDDO are executed for as long as the logical expression *lExpression* remains true (.T.). Each DO WHILE statement must have a corresponding ENDDO statement.

Comments can be placed after DO WHILE and ENDDO on the same line. The comments are ignored during program compilation and execution.

Example

In the following example, the number of products in stock priced over $20 is totaled in the DO WHILE loop until the end of the file (EOF) is encountered. The DO WHILE loop is exited and the total is displayed.

```
CLOSE DATABASES
OPEN DATABASE (HOME(2) + 'Data\testdata')
USE products  && Opens Products table
SET TALK OFF
gnStockTot = 0

DO WHILE .T.  && Begins loop
   IF EOF( )
      EXIT
   ENDIF
   IF unit_price < 20
      SKIP
      LOOP
   ENDIF
   gnStockTot = gnStockTot + in_stock
   SKIP

ENDDO     && Ends loop

CLEAR
? 'Total items in stock valued over 20 dollars:'
?? gnStockTot
```

See Also

DO CASE ... ENDCASE, FOR ... ENDFOR, IF ... ENDIF, IIF( ), SCAN ... ENDSCAN

Dock Method

Docks the ToolBar object along a border of the main Visual FoxPro window or along a side of the desktop.

Syntax

ToolBar.Dock(*nLocation* [, *X*, *Y*])

Arguments

nLocation

Specifies where the toolbar is docked. The values for *nLocation* are:

Value	Constant	Description
−1	TOOL_NOTDOCKED	Undocks the toolbar.
0	TOOL_TOP	Docks the toolbar at the top of the main Visual FoxPro window.
1	TOOL_LEFT	Docks the toolbar at the left side of the main Visual FoxPro window.
2	TOOL_RIGHT	Docks the toolbar at the right side of the main Visual FoxPro window.
3	TOOL_BOTTOM	Docks the toolbar at the bottom of the main Visual FoxPro window.

X, Y

Specifies the horizontal and vertical coordinates respectively of the docked position of the toolbar.

Remarks

Toolbars are docked along the borders of the main window. When a toolbar is docked, its title bar is hidden and its border is changed to a single line. The toolbar is also resized to a single row of buttons. The window is resized so that the toolbar does not obscure any information on the screen. For example, if the toolbar is docked at the top, the screen is moved down by the height of the toolbar.

Use the Move method to undock a toolbar. When using the Move method, the coordinates specified must be outside the dock area.

Applies To

ToolBar

See Also

AfterDock Event, BeforeDock Event, Docked Property, Undock Event

Docked Property

Contains a logical value indicating whether a user-defined ToolBar object is docked.
Read-only at design time and run time.

Syntax

ToolBar.Docked[= *lExpr*]

Arguments

lExpr

The settings for the Docked property are:

Setting	Description
True (.T.)	The toolbar is docked.
False (.F.)	The toolbar is not docked.

Applies To

ToolBar

See Also

DockPosition Property

DockPosition Property

Specifies the position where a user-defined ToolBar object is docked. Read-only at
design time and run time.

Syntax

ToolBar.DockPosition[= *nPosition*]

Arguments

nPosition

The values for *nPosition* are:

Setting	Position
−1	Undocked
0	Top
1	Left
2	Right
3	Bottom

Applies To

ToolBar

See Also

Docked Property

DocumentFile Property

Returns the name of the file from which a linked OLE object was created. At design time, specifies the name of the linked file. Read-only at design time and run time for an existing object, but can be set for an object when creating it.

Syntax

Object.DocumentFile[= *cFileName*]

Arguments

cFileName
> The name of the file to which the object is linked. The name includes the full path of the file.

Remarks

DocumentFile contains the empty string for embedded (not linked) objects.

You set the DocumentFile property of a linked OLE object using the Insert Object dialog box when you initially add an OLE container to a form. You can also set this property when creating an OLE object using the APPEND GENERAL command or when defining the object in code as part of a class definition.

Before specifying the contents of an OLE object using the DocumentFile property, specify the Automation server application by setting the object's OLEClass.

Example

The following example adds an OLE Container control to a form, and uses the DocumentFile and OleClass properties to specify a Microsoft Excel worksheet as the file to edit and Microsoft Excel as the Automation server.

The DocumentFile property specifies a worksheet named Book1.xls in the EXCEL directory on drive C. This example will not work properly if the file and directory specified in the DocumentFile property do not exist; it may be necessary to modify the DocumentFile property to specify an existing directory and worksheet file.

The DoVerb method is used to activate the worksheet for editing.

```
frmMyForm = CREATEOBJECT('form')  && Create a form
frmMyForm.Closable = .F.  && Disable the Control menu box
```

```
frmMyForm.AddObject('cmdCommand1','cmdMyCmdBtn')  && Add Command button
frmMyForm.AddObject("oleObject","oleExcelObject")  && Add OLE object

frmMyForm.cmdCommand1.Visible=.T.  && Display the "Quit" Command button

frmMyForm.oleObject.Visible=.T.  && Display the OLE control
frmMyForm.oleObject.Height = 50  && OLE control height

frmMyForm.Show  && Display the form

frmMyForm.oleObject.DoVerb(-1)  && -1 for Edit

READ EVENTS  && Start event processing

DEFINE CLASS oleExcelObject as OLEControl
   OleClass ="Excel.Sheet"  && Server name
   DocumentFile = "C:\EXCEL\BOOK1.XLS"  && This file must exist
ENDDEFINE

DEFINE CLASS cmdMyCmdBtn AS CommandButton  && Create Command button
   Caption = '\<Quit'  && Caption on the Command button
   Cancel = .T.  && Default Cancel Command button (Esc)
   Left = 125  && Command button column
   Top = 210  && Command button row
   Height = 25  && Command button height

   PROCEDURE Click
      CLEAR EVENTS  && Stop event processing, close form
ENDDEFINE
```

Applies To

OLE Bound Control, OLE Container Control

See Also

APPEND GENERAL, CREATEOBJECT( ), OLEClass

_DOS System Variable

Contains true (.T.) if you are using FoxPro for MS-DOS. Contains false (.F.) if you are using a different platform version of FoxPro or Visual FoxPro.

Syntax

_DOS = *lExpression*

Remarks

The value contained in _DOS cannot be changed with STORE or =.

See Also

_MAC, _UNIX, VERSION( ), _WINDOWS

DoScroll Method

Scrolls the Grid control to simulate a user clicking the scroll bars.

Syntax

Grid.DoScroll(*nDirection*)

Arguments

nDirection
   The settings for *nDirection* are:

Scroll command	Scroll action
0	Scroll up
1	Scroll down
2	Scroll page up
3	Scroll page down
4	Scroll left
5	Scroll right
6	Scroll page left
7	Scroll page right

Remarks

The Scrolled event is triggered after the DoScroll method.

Applies To

Grid

See Also

Scrolled Event

DoVerb Method

Executes a verb on the specified object.

Syntax

Object.DoVerb[(*Verb*)]

Arguments

Verb

The verb to execute on the object within the OLE container control. If not specified, the default verb is executed. The value of this argument can be one of the standard verbs supported by all objects or an index of the ObjectVerbs property array. Each object can support its own set of verbs.

The following values represent standard verbs supported by every object:

Value	Action
0	The default action for the object.
−1	Activates the object for editing. If the application that created the object supports in-place activation, the object is activated within the OLE container control.
−2	Opens the object in a separate application window. If the application that created the object supports in-place activation, the object is activated in its own window.
−3	For embedded objects, hides the application that created the object.
−4	If the object supports in-place activation, activates the object for in-place activation and shows any user interface tools. If the object doesn't support in-place activation, the object doesn't activate, and an error occurs.
−5	If the user moves the focus to the OLE container control, creates a window for the object and prepares the object to be edited. An error occurs if the object doesn't support activation on a single mouse click.
−6	Used when the object is activated for editing to discard all record of changes that the object's application can undo.

Remarks

If you set the AutoActivate property to 2 (DoubleClick), the OLE container control automatically activates the current object when the user double-clicks the control.

Tip Although you can use the name of the verb (edit, open, play, and so on) to specify the verb to use with DoVerb, it is much faster to use the index (0, 1, 2, and so on).

Example

The following example adds an OLE Container control to a form, and uses the OleClass and DocumentFile properties to specify Microsoft Excel as the Automation server and a Microsoft Excel worksheet as the file to edit.

The DocumentFile property specifies a worksheet named Book1.xls in the EXCEL directory on drive C. This example will not work properly if the file and directory specified in the DocumentFile property do not exist; it may be necessary to modify the DocumentFile property to specify an existing directory and worksheet file.

The DoVerb method is used to activate the worksheet for editing.

```
*frmMyForm = CREATEOBJECT('form')  && Create a form
*frmMyForm.Closable = .F.  && Disable the Control menu box

frmMyForm.AddObject('cmdCommand1','cmdMyCmdBtn')  && Add Command button
frmMyForm.AddObject("oleObject","oleExcelObject")  && Add OLE object

frmMyForm.cmdCommand1.Visible=.T.  && Display the "Quit" Command button

frmMyForm.oleObject.Visible=.T.  && Display the OLE control
frmMyForm.oleObject.Height = 50  && OLE control height

frmMyForm.Show  && Display the form

frmMyForm.oleObject.DoVerb(-1)  && -1 for Edit

READ EVENTS  && Start event processing

DEFINE CLASS oleExcelObject as OLEControl
   OleClass ="Excel.Sheet"  && Server name
   DocumentFile = "C:\EXCEL\BOOK1.XLS"  && This file must exist
ENDDEFINE

DEFINE CLASS cmdMyCmdBtn AS CommandButton  && Create Command button
   Caption = '\<Quit'  && Caption on the Command button
   Cancel = .T.  && Default Cancel Command button (Esc)
   Left = 125  && Command button column
   Top = 210  && Command button row
   Height = 25  && Command button height

   PROCEDURE Click
      CLEAR EVENTS  && Stop event processing, close form
ENDDEFINE
```

Applies To

OLE Bound Control, OLE Container Control

See Also

OLE Bound Control, OLE Container Control

DOW( ) Function

Returns a numeric day-of-the-week value from a Date or DateTime expression.

Syntax

DOW(dExpression | tExpression [, nFirstDayOfWeek])

Returns

Numeric

Arguments

dExpression
    Specifies the Date expression from which DOW( ) returns the day number.

tExpression
    Specifies the DateTime expression from which DOW( ) returns the day number.

nFirstDayOfWeek
    Specifies the first day of the week. *nFirstDayOfWeek* may be one of the following
    values.

nFirstDayOfWeek	Description
0	DOW( ) uses whatever day is currently selected in the Week Starts On list box, which appears on the Regional Tab in the Options dialog box.
1	Sunday. This is the default when *nFirstDayOfWeek* is omitted, and is the first day of the week used in earlier FoxPro versions.
2	Monday
3	Tuesday
4	Wednesday
5	Thursday
6	Friday
7	Saturday

Example

```
STORE DATE( ) TO gdDayNum
CLEAR
? DOW(gdDayNum)
? CDOW(gdDayNum)
```

See Also

CDOW( ), DAY( ), SET FDOW, SET FWEEK, SYS( ) Functions Overview, WEEK( )

DownClick Event

Occurs when the down arrow on a control is clicked.

Syntax

PROCEDURE *Control*.DownClick
[LPARAMETERS *nIndex*]

Arguments

nIndex
Uniquely identifies a control if it is in a control array.

Applies To

ComboBox, Spinner

See Also

UpClick Event

DownPicture Property

Specifies the graphic displayed when the control is selected. Available at design time and run time.

Syntax

Control.DownPicture[= *cPicture*]

Arguments

cPicture
Specifies either a complete path and file name of a bitmap or the name of a general field in a table.

Remarks

If you set the DownPicture property at design time and the file you specify does not exist, Microsoft Visual FoxPro displays an error message, but the property remains set to the file you specified. Visual FoxPro ignores the DownPicture property at run time if it is set to a file that does not exist.

If you do not specify a setting for the DownPicture property, Visual FoxPro uses the graphic specified by the Picture property when the control is selected.

For CommandButton controls, the Style property must be set to 0 (Standard) for the bitmap to be displayed on the control; For CheckBox and OptionButton controls, the Style property must be set to 1 (Graphical).

Applies To

CheckBox, CommandButton, OptionButton

See Also

DisabledPicture Property, Enabled Property, Picture Property, Style Property

Drag Method

Begins, ends, or cancels a drag operation.

Syntax

Control.Drag [(*nAction*)]

Arguments

nAction

Indicates the action to perform. If you omit *nAction*, *nAction* is set to 1.

The settings for the Drag method are:

Setting	Description
0	Cancel drag operation; restore original position of control.
1	(Default) Begin dragging the control.
2	End dragging — that is, drop the control.

Remarks

Usually, the MouseDown event procedure calls the Drag method to begin the dragging operation.

It's necessary to use the Drag method to control dragging only when the DragMode property of the control is set to 0 (Manual). You can use Drag on a control whose DragMode property is set to 1 (Automatic), but the MouseDown and MouseUp events are not triggered.

If you want the mouse pointer to change while the control is being dragged, use either the DragIcon property or the MousePointer property to define the pointer. The MousePointer property only has an effect if the DragIcon property is not set.

Applies To

CheckBox, ComboBox, CommandButton, CommandGroup, Container Object, Control Object, EditBox, Grid, Image, Label, Line, ListBox, OLE Bound Control, OLE Container Control, OptionButton, OptionGroup, Page, PageFrame, Shape, Spinner, TextBox

See Also

DragDrop Event, DragIcon Property, DragMode Property, MousePointer Property, Move Method

DragDrop Event

Occurs when a drag-and-drop operation is completed.

Syntax

PROCEDURE *Object*.DragDrop
LPARAMETERS [*nIndex,*] *oSource, nXCoord, nYCoord*

Arguments

You must include an **LPARAMETERS** or **PARAMETERS** statement in the event procedure and specify a name for each parameter. Visual FoxPro passes the DragDrop event three or four parameters in the following order:

nIndex
Uniquely identifies a control if it is in a control array.

oSource
References the control being dragged. You can refer to properties and methods of the control with this parameter.

nXCoord, nYCoord
Contains the current horizontal (*nXCoord*) and vertical (*nYCoord*) coordinates of the mouse pointer within the target form or control. These coordinates are always expressed in terms of the target's coordinate system in the unit of measurement determined by the ScaleMode property.

Remarks

A drag-and-drop operation is completed when a control is dragged over another control or form and the mouse button is released, or when the Drag method with its *nAction* argument set to 2 (Drop) is called for the control.

Use a DragDrop event to control what happens after a drag operation is complete. For example, you can move the source control to a new location or copy a file from one location to another.

Note The DragDrop event involves two objects, a control being dragged and a target object. The DragDrop event is triggered for the target object, not the control being dragged.

Use the DragMode property and Drag method to specify how dragging is to be initiated. Once dragging is initiated, you can handle events that precede a DragDrop event with a DragOver event.

Applies To

CheckBox, ComboBox, CommandButton, CommandGroup, Container Object, Control Object, EditBox, Form, Grid, Image, Label, Line, ListBox, OLE Bound Control, OLE Container Control, OptionButton, OptionGroup, Page, PageFrame, Shape, Spinner, TextBox, ToolBar

See Also

Drag Method, DragIcon Property, DragMode Property, DragOver Event, MouseDown Event, MouseUp Event, MouseMove Event

DragIcon Property

Specifies the icon displayed as the pointer during a drag-and-drop operation. Available at design time and run time.

Syntax

Control.DragIcon[= *cIcon*]

Arguments

cIcon

Specifies the file that contains the icon to use as the mouse pointer. Typically, you specify the icon file using the Properties window at design time. The file you specify must have the .cur extension and be saved in VGA-Mono 2-Color 32 x 32 format. If you try to use a color .cur file, an error message is generated. You can use ImageEdit, to create a two-color .cur file. If you omit *cIcon*, an arrow pointer inside a rectangle is used.

Remarks

DragIcon is useful for providing visual feedback during a drag operation — for instance, to indicate that the source control is over an appropriate target. DragIcon takes effect when the user initiates dragging. Typically, you set DragIcon during a MouseDown or DragOver event.

If you set the DragIcon property at design time and the file you specify does not exist, Visual FoxPro displays an error message, but the property remains set to the file you specified. Visual FoxPro ignores the DragIcon property at run time if it is set to a file that does not exist.

Applies To

CheckBox, ComboBox, CommandButton, CommandGroup, Container Object, Control Object, EditBox, Grid, Image, Label, Line, ListBox, OLE Bound Control, OLE Container Control, OptionButton, OptionGroup, Page, Shape, Spinner, TextBox

See Also

Drag Method, DragDrop Event, DragMode Property, MouseDown Event, MouseMove Event, MousePointer Property, MouseUp Event

DragMode Property

Specifies manual or automatic drag mode for a drag-and-drop operation. Available at design time and run time.

Syntax

Control.DragMode[= *nMode*]

Arguments

nMode

The settings for the DragMode property are:

Setting	Description
0	(Default) Manual. Requires using the Drag method to initiate dragging of the source control.
1	Automatic. Clicking the source control automatically initiates dragging.

Remarks

When DragMode is set to 0 (Manual), the control responds to mouse events and the Drag method must be used to begin drag operations.

When DragMode is set to 1 (Automatic), the control does not respond to mouse events, and drag operations begin automatically when the user presses and holds the primary (left) mouse button over the control.

Releasing the mouse button while the mouse pointer is over a target control or form during a drag operation generates a DragDrop event for the target object and ends the drag operation. Dragging can also trigger a DragOver event.

> **Note** While a control is being dragged, it does not receive other user-initiated mouse or keyboard events (KeyPress, MouseDown, MouseMove, or MouseUp).

Applies To

CheckBox, ComboBox, CommandButton, CommandGroup, Container Object, Control Object, EditBox, Grid, Image, Label, Line, ListBox, OLE Bound Control, OLE Container Control, OptionButton, OptionGroup, Page, PageFrame, Shape, Spinner, TextBox

See Also

DragDrop Event, DragIcon Property, DragOver Event, KeyPress Event, MouseDown Event, MouseMove Event, MouseUp Event, OLEDragMode Property

DragOver Event

Occurs when a control is being dragged over a target object.

Syntax

PROCEDURE *Object*.DragOver
LPARAMETERS [*nIndex,*] *oSource, nXCoord, nYCoord, nState*

Arguments

You must include an LPARAMETERS or PARAMETERS statement in the event procedure and specify a name for each parameter; otherwise an error occurs.
Visual FoxPro passes the DragOver event four or five parameters in the following order:

nIndex
Uniquely identifies a control if it is in a control array.

oSource
Contains a reference to the control being dragged. You can refer to properties and methods of the control with this parameter.

nXCoord, nYCoord
Contains the current horizontal (*nXCoord*) and vertical (*nYCoord*) position of the mouse pointer within the target form or control. The coordinates are always expressed in terms of the target's coordinate system in the unit of measurement determined by the ScaleMode property.

nState
Contains a number that represents the transition state of the control being dragged in relation to the target object:

Setting	Description
0	Enter. The control is being dragged within the range of a target.
1	Leave. The control is being dragged out of the range of a target.
2	Over. The control has moved from one position in the target to another.

Use *nState* to determine actions at key transition points. For example, you can highlight a possible target on *nState* = 0 (Enter) and restore the object's appearance on *nState* = 1 (Leave).

When an object receives a DragOver event with *nState* = 0 (Enter):

- A DragDrop event is triggered if the source control is dropped on a target object.

- Another DragOver event is triggered with *nState* = 1 (Leave) if the source control is not dropped on a valid target.

Remarks

The object under the drag icon is the target object and responds to the DragOver event. You can use this event to monitor when the mouse pointer enters, leaves, or is directly over a target object.

Use a DragOver event to determine what happens after dragging is initiated and before a control is dropped onto a target. For example, you can verify a valid target range by highlighting the target, by setting the BackColor, or ForeColor property or by displaying a special pointer.

Applies To

CheckBox, ComboBox, CommandButton, CommandGroup, Control Object, EditBox, Form, Grid, Image, Label, Line, ListBox, OLE Bound Control, OLE Container Control, OptionButton, OptionGroup, Page, PageFrame, Shape, Spinner, TextBox, ToolBar

See Also

Drag Method, DragDrop Event, DragIcon Property, DragMode Property, MouseDown Event, MouseUp Event, MouseMove Event

Draw Method

Repaints a Form object.

Syntax

Object.Draw

Applies To

Form, _SCREEN

See Also

Paint Event

DrawMode Property

Determines, in conjunction with the color properties, how a shape or line is displayed on screen. Available at design time and run time.

Syntax

Object.DrawMode[= *nMode*]

Arguments

nMode
    The settings for the DrawMode property are:

Setting	Description
1	Blackness Pen. Shape is drawn black.
2	NotMerge Pen. Inverse of setting 15.
3	Mask Not Pen. Combination of the colors common to the BackColor and the inverse of the ForeColor.
4	Not Copy Pen. Inverse of setting 13.
5	Mask Pen Not. Combination of the colors common to both the ForeColor and the inverse of the BackColor.
6	Invert. Inverse of the BackColor.
7	XOR Pen. Combination of the colors in the ForeColor and in the BackColor, but not in both.
8	Not Mask Pen. Inverse of setting 9.
9	Mask Pen. Combination of the colors common to both the ForeColor and the BackColor.
10	Not XOR Pen. Inverse of setting 7.
11	NOP. No operation. Output remains unchanged. In effect, this setting turns drawing off.
12	Merge Not Pen. Combination of the BackColor and the inverse of the ForeColor.
13	(Default). Copy Pen. Color specified by the ForeColor property.
14	Merge Pen Not. Combination of the ForeColor and the inverse of the BackColor.
15	Merge Pen. Combination of the ForeColor and the BackColor.
16	Whiteness Pen. Shape is drawn white.

Remarks

Use the DrawMode property to produce visual effects with Shape or Line controls or when drawing with graphics methods. As a new shape is drawn, Visual FoxPro compares each pixel in the pattern with the corresponding pixel in the existing background and then applies bitwise operations. For example, setting 7 uses the exclusive OR operator (XOR) to combine a drawing pattern pixel with the background pixel.

The exact effect of the DrawMode property setting depends on how the color of a line drawn at run time combines with colors already on the screen. Settings 1, 6, 7, 11, 13, and 16 yield the most predictable results.

Applies To

Form, Line, _SCREEN, Shape

See Also

Box Method, Circle Method, DrawWidth Property, DrawStyle Property, FillColor Property, FillStyle Property, Line Method, Pset Method

DrawStyle Property

Specifies the line style to use when drawing with graphics methods. Available at design time and run time.

Syntax

Object.DrawStyle[= *nStyle*]

Arguments

nStyle

The settings for the DrawStyle property are:

Setting	Description
0	(Default) Solid
1	Dash
2	Dot
3	Dash-Dot
4	Dash-Dot-Dot
5	Transparent
6	Inside Solid

Note   If DrawWidth is set to 1, DrawStyle produces the effect described in the preceding table for each setting. But if DrawWidth is set to a value greater than 1, settings 1 through 4 produce a solid line.

Applies To

Form, _SCREEN

See Also

Circle Method, DrawMode Property, DrawWidth Property, FillColor Property, FillStyle Property, ForeColor Property, Line Method, PSet Method

DrawWidth Property

Specifies the line width for output from graphics methods. Available at design time and run time.

Syntax

Object.DrawWidth[= *nSize*]

Arguments

nSize
Specifies the width of the line in pixels. You can set DrawWidth to a value of 1 through 32,767. The default value is 1 pixel wide.

Increase the value of this property to increase the width of the line.

Applies To

Form, _SCREEN

See Also

Circle Method, DrawMode Property, DrawStyle Property, FillColor Property, FillStyle Property, ForeColor Property

DRIVETYPE( ) Function

Returns the type of the specified drive.

Syntax

DRIVETYPE(*cDrive*)

Returns

Numeric

Arguments

cDrive
The drive designator. The colon in drive names (for example, "C:") is optional.

Remarks

The following table explains the number DRIVETYPE( ) returns and the corresponding drive type description.

Number	Drive Type
1	No type
2	Floppy disk
3	Hard disk
4	Removable drive or network drive
5	CD-ROM
6	RAM disk*

* Because there are many different types of RAM disks, you might get inconsistent return results.

See Also

SYS(5) – Default Drive or Volume

DROP TABLE Command

Removes a table from the current database and deletes it from disk.

Syntax

DROP TABLE *TableName* | *FileName* | *?* [RECYCLE]

Arguments

TableName
Specifies the table to remove from the current database and delete from disk.

FileName
Specifies a free table to delete from disk.

?
Displays the Remove dialog from which you can choose a table to remove from the current database and delete from disk.

RECYCLE
Specifies that the table isn't immediately deleted from disk and is placed in the Microsoft Windows Recycle Bin.

Remarks

When DROP TABLE is issued, all primary indexes, default values, and validation rules associated with the table are also removed. DROP TABLE also affects other tables in the current database if those tables have rules or relations associated with the table being removed. The rules and relations are no longer valid when the table is removed from the database.

Any table deleted with this command cannot be retrieved. Even if SET SAFETY is set to ON, you are not warned before the table is deleted.

See Also

ADD TABLE, CLOSE DATABASES, CREATE DATABASE, FREE TABLE, OPEN DATABASE

DROP VIEW Command

Deletes a SQL view from the current database.

Syntax

DROP VIEW *ViewName*

Arguments

ViewName
    Specifies the name of the view deleted from the current database.

Remarks

DROP VIEW is identical to DELETE VIEW; DROP VIEW is the ANSI SQL standard syntax for deleting a SQL view.

Use CREATE SQL VIEW to create a SQL view and add the view to the current database. If a SQL view is opened and then deleted, the cursors containing the SQL view results are not closed.

See Also

CREATE SQL VIEW, DELETE VIEW, OPEN DATABASE

DropDown Event

Occurs when the list portion of a ComboBox control is about to drop down after the drop-down arrow is clicked.

Syntax

PROCEDURE *ComboBox*.DropDown
[LPARAMETERS *nIndex*]

Arguments

You must include an LPARAMETERS or PARAMETERS statement in the event procedure and specify a name for each parameter; otherwise an error occurs. Visual FoxPro passes the DropDown event the following parameter:

nIndex
    Contains a number that uniquely identifies a control if it is in a control array.

Remarks

Use a DropDown event procedure to make final updates to the list portion of a ComboBox before the user makes a selection. This enables you to add or remove items from the list using the AddItem or RemoveItem method. This flexibility is useful if you want controls to interact at run time. For example, what you want to appear in the list portion of a ComboBox depends on what the user chooses in an OptionGroup.

Applies To

ComboBox

See Also

AddItem Method, DownClick Event, RemoveItem Method

DROPOFFLINE( ) Function

Discards all changes made to an offline view and takes the offline view back online.

Syntax

DROPOFFLINE(c*ViewName*)

Returns

Logical

Arguments

cViewName
    Specifies the name of the offline view to take back online.

Remarks

DROPOFFLINE( ) returns a logical true (.T.) if the offline view is successfully taken back online; otherwise it returns false (.F.).

See Also

CREATEOFFLINE( ), DROP VIEW, USE

DTOC( ) Function

Returns a Character-type date from a Date or DateTime expression.

Syntax

DTOC(*dExpression* | *tExpression* [, 1])

Returns

Character

Arguments

dExpression

Specifies a Date-type variable, array element, or field for which DTOC( ) returns a Character-type date.

tExpression

Specifies a DateTime-type variable, array element, or field for which DTOC( ) returns a Character-type date.

1

Returns the date in a format suitable for indexing. This is particularly useful for maintaining the table records in chronological sequence.

For example, to order table records in entry sequence, you could issue this command:

```
INDEX ON DTOC(gdInvDate, 1) + gnInvTime TAG Timeindx
```

`gdInvDate` and `gnInvTime` are fields containing the date and time when the data was entered in the record.

Remarks

DTOC( ) returns a character string corresponding to a Date or DateTime expression. The date format is determined by SET CENTURY and SET DATE.

Example

```
SET STRICTDATE TO 1
STORE CTOD({^1998-10-31}) TO gdThisDate
CLEAR
? DTOC(gdThisDate)
STORE DTOC({^1998-10-31}+90) TO gcExpireDate
? 'Your 90-day warranty expires ', gcExpireDate
? DTOC({^1998-10-31},1)
```

See Also

CTOD( ), SET CENTURY, SET DATE, SYS( ) Functions Overview, TTOC( )

DTOR( ) Function

Converts degrees to radians.

Syntax

DTOR(*nExpression*)

Returns

Numeric

Arguments

nExpression
> Specifies the numeric expression whose value you want to convert to radians. An angle expressed in a degree:minute:second format should be converted to its decimal equivalent.

Remarks

DTOR( ) converts the value of a numeric expression given in degrees to an equivalent value in radians. DTOR( ) is useful for working with the Microsoft Visual FoxPro trigonometric functions: ACOS( ), ASIN( ), COS( ), SIN( ), TAN( ).

Use RTOD( ) to convert radians to degrees.

Example

```
CLEAR
? DTOR(0)    && Displays 0.00
? DTOR(45)   && Displays 0.79
? DTOR(90)   && Displays 1.57
? DTOR(180)  && Displays 3.14
? COS(DTOR(90))  && Displays 0.00
```

See Also

ACOS( ), ASIN( ), COS( ), RTOD( ), SIN( ), TAN( )

DTOS( ) Function

Returns a character-string date in a yyyymmdd format from a specified Date or DateTime expression.

Syntax

DTOS(*dExpression* | *tExpression*)

Returns

Character

Arguments

dExpression
> Specifies the Date expression DTOS( ) converts to an eight-digit character string.

tExpression
> Specifies the DateTime expression DTOS( ) converts to an eight-digit character string.

Remarks

This function is useful for indexing tables on a Date or DateTime field. It is equivalent to DTOC( ) when its optional 1 argument is included.

The character string returned by DTOS( ) isn't affected by SET DATE or SET CENTURY.

Example

```
CLEAR
? DTOS(DATE( ))
```

See Also

DATE( ), DATETIME( ), CTOD( ), DTOC( )

DTOT( ) Function

Returns a DateTime value from a Date expression.

Syntax

DTOT(*dDateExpression*)

Returns

DateTime

Arguments

dDateExpression
    Specifies the Date expression from which a DateTime value is returned.

Remarks

The format of the DateTime value DTOT( ) returns depends on the current SET DATE and SET MARK settings. If a century isn't supplied, the twentieth century is assumed.

DTOT( ) adds a default time of midnight (12:00:00 A.M.) to the date to produce a valid DateTime value.

Example

```
? DTOT({^1998-02-16}) && Displays 02/16/1998 12:00:00am
```

See Also

CTOT( ), DATE( ), SEC( ), SECONDS( ), SET SECONDS, TIME( )

DynamicAlignment Property

Specifies the alignment of text and controls in a Column object. The alignment is re-evaluated at run time each time the Grid control is refreshed. Available at design time; read/write at run time.

Syntax

Column.DynamicAlignment[= *cAlign*]

Arguments

cAlign
> Specifies a character string expression that is re-evaluated at run time and results in one of the following values:

Setting	Description
0	Middle Left. Aligns the text flush left and centered vertically.
1	Middle Right. Aligns the text flush right and centered vertically.
2	Middle Center. Aligns the text in the middle with equal spaces to the right and left and centered vertically.
3	(Default) Automatic. Aligns text based on the data type of the control source. Numeric types (numeric, double, float, currency, integer) are right-aligned; controls with other data types are left-aligned.
4	Top Left. Aligns the text flush left and at the top of the column.
5	Top Right. Aligns the text flush right and at the top of the column.
6	Top Center. Aligns the text in the middle with equal spaces to the right and left and at the top of the column.
7	Bottom Left. Aligns the text flush left and at the bottom of the column.
8	Bottom Right. Aligns the text flush right and at the bottom of the column.
9	Bottom Center. Aligns the text in the middle with equal spaces to the right and left and at the bottom of the column.

Applies To

Column

See Also

Alignment Property

DynamicBackColor, DynamicForeColor Properties

Specifies the background and foreground colors of a Column object. The colors are re-evaluated at run time each time the Grid control is refreshed. Available at design time; read/write at run time.

Syntax

Column.DynamicBackColor[= *cExpression*]
Column.DynamicForeColor[= *cExpression*]

Arguments

cExpression
Specifies an expression in quotation marks that is re-evaluated at run time whenever the Grid control is refreshed. The run-time evaluation must result in a single color value.

Remarks

You can use the DynamicBackColor and DynamicForeColor properties to create special effects, such as displaying the odd-numbered rows in green and the even-numbered rows in gray.

Example

The following example uses the DynamicBackColor property and the SetAll method to specify the background colors for the records in a Grid control. If the number of a record displayed in the Grid is even, the record's DynamicBackColor is white, otherwise its DynamicBackColor is green.

A Grid control is placed on a form, and the `customer` table is opened and its contents displayed in the Grid. The Caption property is used to specify a different header caption (Customer ID) for the CUST_ID field. A command button is placed on the form to close the form.

```
CLOSE ALL  && Close tables and databases
OPEN DATABASE (HOME(2) + 'Data\testdata')

USE customer  IN 0  && Opens Customer table

frmMyForm = CREATEOBJECT('Form')  && Create a Form
frmMyForm.Closable = .f.  && Disable the Control menu box

frmMyForm.AddObject('cmdCommand1','cmdMyCmdBtn')  && Add Command button
frmMyForm.AddObject('grdGrid1','Grid')  && Add Grid control
```

```
frmMyForm.grdGrid1.Left = 25  && Adjust Grid position

frmMyForm.grdGrid1.SetAll("DynamicBackColor", ;
   "IIF(MOD(RECNO( ), 2)=0, RGB(255,255,255) ;
   , RGB(0,255,0))", "Column")  && Alternate white and green records

frmMyForm.grdGrid1.Visible = .T.  && Grid control visible
frmMyForm.cmdCommand1.Visible =.T.  && "Quit" Command button visible
frmMyForm.grdGrid1.Column1.Header1.Caption = 'Customer ID'

frmMyForm.SHOW  && Display the form
READ EVENTS  && Start event processing

DEFINE CLASS cmdMyCmdBtn AS CommandButton  && Create Command button
   Caption = '\<Quit'  && Caption on the Command button
   Cancel = .T.  && Default Cancel Command button (Esc)
   Left = 125  && Command button column
   Top = 210  && Command button row
   Height = 25  && Command button height

   PROCEDURE Click
      CLEAR EVENTS  && Stop event processing, close Form
      CLOSE ALL  && Close table and database
ENDDEFINE
```

Applies To

Column

See Also

BackColor_ForeColor Properties

DynamicCurrentControl Property

Specifies which control contained in a Column object is used to display the values of the active cell. The name of the control is re-evaluated each time the Grid control is refreshed. Available at design time; read/write at run time.

Syntax

Column.DynamicCurrentControl[= *cExpression*]

Arguments

cExpression
> Evaluates at run time to the name of the control that displays and accepts data for the active cell in *Column*.

Remarks

The default control is a TextBox having Text1 as the Name property. Use the AddObject method to add other controls.

If the Column's Sparse property is set to true (.T.), only the active cell in the Column uses the object specified in the DynamicCurrentControl property setting to display data; the other cells display data using a TextBox. If the Sparse property is set to false (.F.), all cells in the Column use the object specified in the DynamicCurrentControl property setting to display data.

Applies To

Column

See Also

AddObject Method, CurrentControl Property

DynamicFontBold, DynamicFontItalic, DynamicFontStrikethru, DynamicFontUnderline Properties

Specifies that text displayed in a Column object has one or more of the following styles: **Bold**, *Italic*, ~~Strikethru~~, or Underline. The logical expression is re-evaluated each time the Grid control is refreshed. Available at design time; read/write at run time.

Syntax

Column.DynamicFontBold[= "*lExpr*"]
Column.DynamicFontItalic[= "*lExpr*"]
Column.DynamicFontStrikeThru[= "*lExpr*"]
Column.DynamicFontUnderline[= "*lExpr*"]

Arguments

"*lExpr*"
    Evaluates to either true (.T.) or false (.F.). The settings for the dynamic font properties are:

Setting	Description
True (.T.)	Font style is bold, italic, strikethru, or underline.
False (.F.)	(Default except for DynamicFontBold) Font style is not bold, italic, strikethru, or underline.

Remarks

Use these properties to control the appearance of text based on data values at run time. For example, you can set DynamicFontUnderline to indicate names of new members in an organization.

Applies To

Column

See Also

DynamicFontSize Property

DynamicFontName Property

Specifies the name of the font used to display text in a Column object. The logical expression is re-evaluated at run time each time the Grid control is refreshed. Available at design time; read/write at run time.

Syntax

Column.DynamicFontName[= *cName*]

Arguments

cName
    Evaluates to the name of a font.

Remarks

At design time, a list of available fonts is displayed when you select the FontName property in the Properties window and click the down arrow to the right of the Properties Settings box.

Applies To

Column

See Also

FontName Property

DynamicFontOutline Property

Specifies whether the text associated with a Column object is outlined. The logical expression is re-evaluated at run time each time the Grid control is refreshed. Available at design time and run time.

Syntax

Column.DynamicFontOutline[= "*lExpr*"]

Arguments

"*lExpr*"

Evaluates to either true (.T.) or false (.F.). The settings for the DynamicFontOutline property are:

Setting	Description
True (.T.)	The text is outlined.
False (.F.)	(Default) The text is not outlined.

Applies To

Column

See Also

FontOutline Property, DynamicFontShadow Property

DynamicFontShadow Property

Specifies whether the text associated with a Column object is shadowed. The logical expression is re-evaluated at run time each time the Grid control is refreshed. Available at design time and run time.

Syntax

Column.DynamicFontShadow[= "*lExpr*"]

Arguments

"*lExpr*"

Evaluates to either true (.T.) or false (.F.). The settings for the DynamicFontShadow property are:

Setting	Description
True (.T.)	The text is shadowed.
False (.F.)	(Default) The text is not shadowed.

Applies To

Column

See Also

FontShadow Property, DynamicFontOutline Property

DynamicFontSize Property

Specifies the font size of text displayed in a Column object. The font size is re-evaluated at run time each time the Grid control is refreshed. Available at design time; read/write at run time.

Syntax

Column.FontSize[= "*nSize*"]

Arguments

"*nSize*"
    Evaluates to a font size. The default font size is 10 points.

Remarks

The maximum value for *nSize* is 2,048 points. There are 72 points in 1 inch.

Use this property to change the font size of a row.

Applies To

Column

See Also

DynamicAlignment Property, DynamicFontName Property

DynamicInputMask Property

Specifies how data is entered and displayed in a Column object. Re-evaluated at run time each time the Grid control is refreshed. Available at design time; read/write at run time.

Syntax

Column.DynamicInputMask[= *cInputMask*]

Arguments

cInputMask
    Specifies the dynamic format of text and controls in a column. *cInputMask* must evaluate to a character string of the following format:

    [@cFunction] [cMask]

The following demonstrates a typical format for *cInputMask*:

    Column1.DynamicInputMask = "@R$ ###,###,###.##"

For additional information about the format of *cFunction* and cMask, see the "Format" and "InputMask" properties, later in this language reference.

Remarks

The DynamicInputMask property takes precedence over the Format and InputMask properties.

If the control specified by the column's CurrentControl property is a text box, spinner, or combo box, the Format and InputMask portions of the DynamicInputMask expression are passed to the Format and InputMask properties for the text box, spinner, or combo box.

Applies To

Column

See Also

Format Property, InputMask Property

EDIT Command

Displays fields for editing.

Syntax

EDIT
    [FIELDS *FieldList*]
    [*Scope*] [FOR *lExpression1*] [WHILE *lExpression2*]
    [FONT *cFontName* [, *nFontSize*]]
    [STYLE *cFontStyle*]
    [FREEZE *FieldName*]
    [KEY *eExpression1* [, *eExpression2*]]
    [LAST | NOINIT]
    [LPARTITION]
    [NAME *ObjectName*]
    [NOAPPEND]
    [NODELETE]
    [NOEDIT | NOMODIFY]
    [NOLINK]
    [NOMENU]
    [NOOPTIMIZE]
    [NORMAL]
    [NOWAIT]
    [PARTITION *nColumnNumber* [LEDIT] [REDIT]]
    [PREFERENCE *PreferenceName*]
    [REST]
    [SAVE]
    [TIMEOUT *nSeconds*]

[TITLE *cTitleText*]
[VALID [:F] *lExpression3* [ERROR *cMessageText*]]
[WHEN *lExpression4*]
[WIDTH *nFieldWidth*]
[WINDOW *WindowName1*]
[IN [WINDOW] *WindowName2* | IN SCREEN
[COLOR SCHEME *nSchemeNumber*]

Arguments

FIELDS *FieldList*

Specifies the fields that appear in the Edit window. The fields are displayed in the order specified in *FieldList*. You can include fields from other related tables in the field list. When you include a field from a related table, preface the field name with its table alias and a period.

If you omit FIELDS, all fields in the table are displayed in the order they appear in the table structure.

The field list can specify any combination of fields or calculated fields, including fields from tables open in other work areas. The syntax of the field list is:

```
FieldName1
   [:R]
   [:nColumnWidth]
   [:V = lExpression1 [:F] [:E = cMessageText]]
   [:P = cFormatCodes]
   [:B = eLowerBound, eUpperBound [:F]]
   [:H = cHeadingText]
   [:W = lExpression2]
   [, FieldName2 [:R]...]
```

Calculated Fields

The field list can contain statements for creating calculated fields. A calculated field contains read-only data created with an expression. This expression may take any form but it must be a valid Visual FoxPro expression.

The syntax of the statement you use to create a calculated field is:

CalculatedFieldName = eExpression

This example creates a calculated field called location:

```
CLOSE DATABASES
OPEN DATABASE (HOME(2) + 'data\testdata')
USE customer  && Open customer table
EDIT FIELDS location = ALLTRIM(city) + ', ' + country
```

The FIELDS clause field list includes eight options, which enable special handling of fields displayed in the Edit window.

:nColumnWidth

Specifies the display size for a field in columns. The value of *:nColumnWidth* doesn't affect the size of the field in the table; it alters only the way the field appears in the Edit window.

:R

In the following example, an Edit window is opened with the `cust_id` and `company` fields. The `cust_id` field is read-only and cannot be changed.

```
CLOSE DATABASES
OPEN DATABASE (HOME(2) + 'data\testdata')
USE customer  && Open customer table
EDIT FIELDS cust_id:R, company
```

:V = *lExpression1*

Specifies a verify option that performs field-level data validation within the Edit window. If *lExpression1* evaluates to true (.T.) when you move the cursor from the field, the data input into the field is considered correct and the cursor moves to the next field.

If *lExpression1* evaluates to false (.F.), the data input is considered incorrect, the cursor remains in the field and a message is displayed. If *lExpression1* evaluates to 0, the data input is considered incorrect and the cursor remains in the field, but no error message is displayed.

By default, *lExpression1* is evaluated only when the field is modified. To force verification, include the :F option.

You can display your own error message by including the :E option.

The verify option isn't executed for memo fields.

:F

Specifies a forced validation option that determines if the expression in the verify option (*lExpression1*) is evaluated when you move the cursor from a field or another window is activated. If :F is not included, *lExpression1* is evaluated only if changes are made to the field. If :F is included, *lExpression1* is evaluated, even if the field isn't modified.

:E = *cMessageText*

Displays an error message specified with *cMessageText* instead of the default system message.

If the validation expression :V = *lExpression1* evaluates to true (.T.), the cursor leaves the field normally. If the expression evaluates to false (.F.), the cursor remains in the field and the error message appears.

If the validation expression :V = *lExpression1* evaluates to 0, no message is displayed and the cursor remains in the field being validated. This lets you display your own error messages in validation routines.

The error message is displayed only if SET NOTIFY is ON. The bell is sounded if SET BELL is ON.

The following example opens the products table and displays the product_id and prod_name fields. Enter a value greater than 100 in the product_id field to perform the field validation.

:V specifies the validation criteria. :F forces the validation check to be performed whether the data is changed or not. :E replaces the Visual FoxPro system error message with a user-defined error message.

In Visual FoxPro, the error message is displayed in the status bar at the bottom of the main Visual FoxPro window.

Press ESC to close the Edit window.

```
CLOSE DATABASES
OPEN DATABASE (HOME(2) + 'data\testdata')
USE products  && Open products table
IF _WINDOWS OR _MAC
   SET STATUS BAR ON
ENDIF
USE products
EDIT FIELDS in_stock :V = in_stock < 100 ;
   :F ;
   :E = 'The stock amount must be less than 100'
```

:P = *cFormatCodes*

Specifies a picture option that lets you create an editing template specified with *cFormatCodes* that controls the display and input of data for each field in an Edit window.

For more information on using picture editing codes, see the "Format" and "InputMask" properties, later in this language reference.

The following example uses the picture option to allow only numeric data in a specific format to be entered in the unit_price field:

```
CLOSE DATABASES
OPEN DATABASE (HOME(2) + 'data\testdata')
USE products  && Open products table
EDIT FIELDS unit_price :P = '99,999.99'
```

:B = *eLowerBound, eUpperBound* [:F]

Specifies a set of boundaries between which data must fall. The boundary expressions *eLowerBound* and *eUpperBound* must match the data type of the field and cannot be the names of user-defined functions. If the data entered doesn't fall between *eLowerBound* and *eUpperBound*, a system message is displayed indicating the range between which the data must fall.

By default, the data you enter is checked against the boundary values only if you make a change to the contents of the field. To force checking against the boundary values, include the forced validation option (:F).

The following example ensures that the value in the in_stock field is between 1 and 100. Press ESC to close the Edit window.

```
CLOSE DATABASES
OPEN DATABASE (HOME(2) + 'data\testdata')
USE products  && Open products table
EDIT FIELDS in_stock :B = 1, 100 :F
```

:H = *cHeadingText*

Specifies a heading option (:H) that allows you to replace the default field names with your own headings, which you specify with *cHeadingText*. By default, field names are placed to the left side of the fields in the Edit window.

The following example provides user-defined headings for the displayed fields.

```
CLOSE DATABASES
OPEN DATABASE (HOME(2) + 'data\testdata')
USE products  && Open products table
EDIT FIELDS prod_name :H = 'Product Name:', ;
    unit_price :H = 'Price per Unit:'
```

:W = *lExpression2*

Specifies a WHEN option that allows you to conditionally prohibit the cursor from being moved to a field based on the value of the logical expression *lExpression*. (:W) evaluates *lExpression*. If *lExpression2* evaluates to false (.F.), you can't move the cursor to the field. If *lExpression2* evaluates to true (.T.), you can move the cursor to the field. User-defined functions are supported in *lExpression2*.

Moving the cursor to all fields is prohibited if the current field is marked read-only. This occurs only when every field contains a WHEN clause that evaluates to false.

Scope

Specifies a range of records that are displayed in the Edit window. The scope clauses are: ALL, NEXT *nRecords*, RECORD *nRecordNumber*, and REST. Commands that include *Scope* operate only on the table in the active work area. The default scope for EDIT is ALL records.

For more information, see "Scope Clauses," in Help.

FOR *lExpression1*

Specifies that only the records that satisfy the logical condition *lExpression1* are displayed in the Edit window. Using this argument allows you to filter out undesired records.

Rushmore optimizes an EDIT FOR query if *lExpression1* is an optimizable expression. For best performance, use an optimizable expression in the FOR clause.

For more information, see the SET OPTIMIZE Command, later in this language reference, and "Understanding Rushmore Technology" in Chapter 15, "Optimizing Applications," in the *Microsoft Visual FoxPro 6.0 Programmer's Guide*.

WHILE *lExpression2*

Specifies a condition whereby records are displayed in the Edit window for as long as the logical expression *lExpression2* evaluates to true (.T.).

FONT *cFontName* [, *nFontSize*]

Specifies the Edit window's font and font size. The character expression *cFontName* specifies the name of the font, and the numeric expression *nFontSize* specifies the font size. For example, the following clause specifies 16-point Courier font for the fields displayed in an Edit window:

```
FONT 'Courier',16
```

If you include the FONT clause but omit the font size *nFontSize*, a 10-point font is used in the Edit window.

If you omit the FONT clause, 8-point MS Sans Serif is used. If the font you specify is not available, a font with similar font characteristics is substituted.

STYLE *cFontStyle*

Specifies the Edit window's font style in Visual FoxPro. If you omit the STYLE clause, the Normal font style is used.

If the font style you specify is not available, a font style with similar characteristics is substituted.

Character	Font style
B	Bold
I	Italic
N	Normal
O	Outline
Q	Opaque
S	Shadow
–	Strikeout
T	Transparent
U	Underline

You can include more than one character to specify a combination of font styles. The following example opens an Edit window and uses an underlined font:

```
CLOSE DATABASES
OPEN DATABASE (HOME(2) + 'data\testdata')
USE customer  && Opens customer table
```

```
IF _WINDOWS
   EDIT FIELDS contact FONT 'System', 15  STYLE 'NU'
ENDIF
IF _MAC
   EDIT FIELDS contact FONT 'Geneva', 14  STYLE 'NU'
ENDIF
```

FREEZE *FieldName*

Allows changes to be made to only one field specified with *FieldName* in the Edit window. The remaining fields are displayed and cannot be edited.

KEY *eExpression1* [, *eExpression2*]

Limits the scope of records that are displayed in the Edit window. With KEY, you can specify an index key value (*eExpression1*) or a range of key values (*eExpression1* , *eExpression2*) for the records displayed in the Edit window. The table must be indexed, and the index key value or values included in the KEY clause must be the same data type as the index expression of the master index file or master tag.

In the following example, only records with postal codes falling within the range of 10,000 to 30,000 are displayed in the Edit window:

```
CLOSE DATABASES
OPEN DATABASE (HOME(2) + 'data\testdata')
USE customer  && Open customer table
SET ORDER TO postalcode
EDIT KEY '10000', '30000'
```

LAST | NOINIT

Saves any configuration changes made to the appearance of an Edit window. The changes are saved in the FOXUSER file and can include changes to the field list, the size of each field, and the location and size of the Edit window. For more information on this file, see the SET RESOURCE Command, later in this language reference.

If you issue EDIT with the LAST clause, the Edit window opens in the same configuration that was last saved in the FOXUSER file. This restores the previous Edit window configuration created with the last EDIT. If the last EDIT command issued in the Command window included a long list of clauses, issue EDIT LAST to avoid having to retype the command.

Any Edit window configuration changes you make in the current session aren't saved if you exit EDIT by pressing CTRL+Q.

LPARTITION

Places the cursor in the first field in the left partition of the Edit window. An Edit window can be split into left and right partitions by including the PARTITION clause. By default, the cursor is placed in the first field in the right partition when the Edit window is opened.

The cursor is placed in the right partition of the Edit window if you include LPARTITION without the PARTITION clause.

NAME *ObjectName*

Creates an object reference for the Edit window, allowing you to manipulate the Edit window with object-oriented properties available for the Grid control.

For additional information about object-oriented programming in Visual FoxPro, see Chapter 3, "Object-Oriented Programming," in the *Microsoft Visual FoxPro 6.0 Programmer's Guide*. For additional information about the Grid control properties that you can specify for an Edit window created with the NAME clause, see "Grid Control," later in this language reference.

NOAPPEND

Prevents the user from adding records to the table by pressing CTRL+Y or choosing Append Mode from the View menu.

> **Important** Including NOAPPEND doesn't prevent you from appending a record from within a routine (created with VALID, WHEN, or ON KEY LABEL) while in the Edit window.

NODELETE

Prevents records from being marked for deletion from within an Edit window. By default, a record can be marked for deletion by pressing CTRL+T, choosing Toggle Deletion Mark from the Table menu or clicking in the leftmost column of the record to be deleted.

> **Important** Including NODELETE doesn't prevent you from marking a record for deletion from within a routine (created with VALID, WHEN or ON KEY LABEL) while in the Edit window.

NOEDIT | NOMODIFY

Prevents a user from modifying the table. NOEDIT and NOMODIFY are identical. If you include either clause, you can browse or search the table, but you cannot edit it. However, you can append and delete records.

NOLINK

Unlinks partitions in the Edit window. By default, the left and right partitions of the Edit window are linked; when you scroll through one partition, the other partition scrolls.

NOMENU

Removes the Table menu title in Visual FoxPro from the system menu bar, preventing access to the Edit menu.

NOOPTIMIZE

Disables Rushmore optimization of EDIT.

For more information, see the SET OPTIMIZE Command, later in this language reference, and "Understanding Rushmore Technology" in Chapter 15, "Optimizing Applications," in the *Microsoft Visual FoxPro 6.0 Programmer's Guide.*

NORMAL

Opens the Edit window with its normal default settings, such as its colors, size, position, title, and control options (GROW, FLOAT, ZOOM, and so on). If you omit NORMAL and the current output window is a user-defined window with its own settings, the Edit window assumes those user-defined settings as well.

NOWAIT

Continues program execution immediately after the Edit window is opened. The program doesn't wait for the Edit window to be closed but continues executing on the program line immediately following the program line containing EDIT NOWAIT. If you omit NOWAIT, when EDIT is issued from within a program, an Edit window is opened and program execution pauses until the Edit window is closed.

NOWAIT is available only from within a program. Including NOWAIT when issuing EDIT from the Command window has no effect.

PARTITION *nColumnNumber*

Splits an Edit window into left and right partitions with *nColumnNumber* specifying the column number of the split bar. For example, if *nColumnNumber* is 20, the split bar is placed in column 20 of the Edit window.

LEDIT

Specifies that the left partition of the Edit window appears in Browse mode.

REDIT

Specifies that the right partition of the Edit window appears in Browse mode. The following examples opens an Edit window with the split bar placed in column 20 and the right partition open in Browse mode.

Include both keywords to open both partitions in Browse mode.

```
CLOSE DATABASES
OPEN DATABASE (HOME(2) + 'data\testdata')
USE customer  && Opens customer table

EDIT PARTITION 30 REDIT
```

PREFERENCE *PreferenceName*

Saves an Edit window's attributes and options for later use. Unlike LAST, which restores the Edit window as it appeared in the previous session, PREFERENCE saves an Edit window's attributes indefinitely in the FOXUSER resource file. Preferences can be retrieved at any time. For more information about the FOXUSER resource file, see the SET RESOURCE Command, later in this language reference.

Issuing EDIT with the specified preference name *PreferenceName* for the first time creates an entry in the FOXUSER file that saves the Edit window configuration. Issuing EDIT later with the same preference name restores the Edit window to that preference state. When the Edit window is closed, the preference state is updated.

Preference names can be up to 10 characters long, must begin with a letter or an underscore, and can contain any combination of letters, numbers, and underscores.

Once you have a preference the way you like it, you can prevent it from being changed. Close the Edit window, issue SET RESOURCE OFF, open the FOXUSER file as a table, and change the field containing the preference to read-only by changing the value of the logical field READONLY to true (.T.).

For more information about the FOXUSER resource file, see the SET RESOURCE Command, later in this language reference.

REST

Prevents the record pointer from being moved from its current position to the top of the table. By default, EDIT positions the record pointer at the top of the table.

SAVE

Keeps the Edit window and any of its memo field text-editing windows active and visible (open). You can then return to the Edit window after cycling through other open windows with the keyboard or the mouse.

SAVE is available only from within a program. SAVE has no effect when included with EDIT in the Command window because EDIT SAVE is always the default in the interactive mode.

TIMEOUT *nSeconds*

Specifies how long an Edit window waits for input. The numeric expression *nSeconds* specifies how many seconds can elapse without any input before the Edit window automatically closes.

TIMEOUT is available only from within a program; it has no effect when you issue EDIT from the Command window. In the following example, the Edit window is closed if no input occurs in 10 seconds.

```
DEFINE WINDOW wEdit FROM 1,1 TO 24,40 ;
    CLOSE ;
    GROW ;
    COLOR SCHEME 10
CLOSE DATABASES
OPEN DATABASE (HOME(2) + 'data\testdata')
USE customer  && Open customer table
EDIT WINDOW wEdit ;
    FIELDS phone :H = 'Phone Number:' , ;
    company :H = 'Company:' ;
    TIMEOUT 10
RELEASE WINDOW wEdit
```

TITLE *cTitleText*

Overrides the default table name or alias that appears in the Edit window title bar with the title you specify with *cTitleText*. Otherwise, the name or alias of the table being browsed appears in the title bar.

If you issue EDIT WINDOW to place the Edit window in a user-defined window, the Edit window's title replaces the user-defined window's title.

```
CLOSE DATABASES
OPEN DATABASE (HOME(2) + 'data\testdata')
USE customer  && Open customer table
EDIT;
    TITLE 'My Edit Window' ;
    FIELDS phone :H = 'Phone Number' , ;
    company :H = 'Company:'
```

VALID *lExpression3*

Performs record-level validation in an Edit window. The VALID clause is executed only if a change is made to the record and you move the cursor to another record. The VALID clause is not executed if the only change is to a memo field.

If VALID returns true (.T.), you can move the cursor to another record. If VALID returns false (.F.), the cursor remains in the current field and Visual FoxPro displays an error message. You can display your own error message when VALID returns false by including the ERROR clause. The character expression *cMessageText* is displayed as the error message. If VALID returns 0, the cursor remains in the current field, and an error message isn't displayed.

The VALID clause shouldn't be confused with the verify option (:V), which enables field-level validation.

:F

Forces the VALID clause to execute before the user moves the cursor to the next record. In this case, VALID is executed even if the record isn't changed.

ERROR *cMessageText*

Specifies an error message that overrides the system default and whose contents you define with *cMessageText*. Visual FoxPro displays your error message when VALID returns false (.F.).

WHEN *lExpression4*

Evaluates a condition when the user moves the cursor to another record. If *lExpression4* evaluates to true (.T.), the user can modify the record moved to. If *lExpression4* evaluates to false (.F.) or 0, the record the user moves to becomes read-only and cannot be modified.

The WHEN clause isn't executed when another window is activated.

WIDTH *nFieldWidth*

Limits the number of characters displayed for all fields in a partition of the Edit window to *nFieldWidth*. Including the WIDTH clause doesn't change the size of fields in the table itself; it alters only the way the fields are displayed in the Edit window. If a width has been specified for an individual field with the FIELDS clause, it overrides the width specified with the WIDTH clause for that field.

WINDOW *WindowName1*

Specifies a user-defined window whose characteristics the Edit window assumes. For example, if the user-defined window is created with the FLOAT clause, the Edit window can be moved. The specified window doesn't have to be active or visible, but it must be defined.

IN [WINDOW] *WindowName2*

Specifies the parent window within which the Edit window is opened. The Edit window doesn't assume the characteristics of the parent window. An Edit window activated inside a parent window cannot be moved outside the parent window. If the parent window is moved, the Edit window moves with it.

To access the Edit window, the parent window must first be defined with DEFINE WINDOW and must be active and visible.

IN SCREEN

Explicitly places an Edit window in the main Visual FoxPro window when a user-defined window is active.

COLOR SCHEME *nSchemeNumber*

Specifies the number of a color scheme used for the Edit window's colors. In Visual FoxPro, the Edit window assumes the color scheme established using the Color Control Panel.

Remarks

EDIT allows you to edit the selected table within a window. EDIT behaves identically to CHANGE.

If you press ESC to exit the Edit window, changes made to the last field you modified are discarded. However, if you move to another record after modifying a field, your changes to the field are saved.

In a program, use DEACTIVATE WINDOW to save your changes and close an Edit window. Include the name of the Edit window in DEACTIVATE WINDOW. For more information on Edit window names, see the WTITLE( ) Function, later in this language reference.

SET SKIP Support

SET SKIP lets you establish a one-to-many relationship between two tables (see the example). For each record in the parent table, there can be multiple related records in the child table. If you create a one-to-many relationship, you can use EDIT to view records from both the parent and child tables.

The parent record appears once, along with the first matching record from the child table. Any subsequent matching records are displayed in the rows following the parent record and first matching child record. In FoxPro for MS-DOS, shaded blocks are displayed in any column containing information from the parent table beyond the first matching record. In Visual FoxPro, the fill character for repeated parent information depends on the current Edit window font.

For more information, see the SET SKIP Command, later in this language reference.

COL( ) and ROW( ) Support

Use COL( ) and ROW( ) to return the current screen row and column position of the cursor in an Edit window. If an Edit window is opened in the main Visual FoxPro window, the returned cursor position is relative to the main Visual FoxPro window, not to the Edit window itself. If an Edit window is opened in a user-defined window, COL( ) and ROW( ) return the cursor position relative to the user-defined window.

Example

The following example uses SET SKIP to create a one-to-many relationship between two tables. There is a single record in the parent table (customer) for each invoice created. The child table (orders) contains multiple records for each record in the parent table.

After the relationship is created, an Edit window displaying records from both the parent and child tables is opened.

```
CLEAR
CLOSE DATABASES
OPEN DATABASE (HOME(2) + 'data\testdata')
USE customer ORDER cust_id IN 0   && Parent table
USE orders ORDER cust_id IN 0  && Child table
SELECT customer     && Back to parent work area
SET RELATION TO cust_id INTO orders     && Establish relationship
SET SKIP TO orders  && One-to-many relationship
WAIT WINDOW 'Scroll to see shipping dates for each customer' NOWAIT
EDIT FIELDS customer.cust_id :H='Customer Number', ;
   customer.city :H='Customer City', orders.shipped_on
```

See Also

BROWSE, Grid Control, SET SKIP, WTITLE( )

EditBox Control

Creates an edit box.

Syntax

EditBox

Remarks

Use the EditBox control for editing a Character-type variable, array element, field, or memo field.

All standard Visual FoxPro editing features, such as cut, copy, and paste, are available for the edit box. The text in the edit box scrolls vertically and words are wrapped horizontally.

For additional information about creating edit boxes, see Chapter 10, "Using Controls," in the *Microsoft Visual FoxPro 6.0 Programmer's Guide*.

Properties

Alignment	AllowTabs	Application
BackColor	BackStyle	BaseClass
BorderColor	BorderStyle	Class
ClassLibrary	ColorScheme	ColorSource
Comment	ControlSource	DisabledBackColor
DisabledForeColor	DragIcon	DragMode
Enabled	FontBold	FontCondense
FontExtend	FontItalic	FontName
FontOutline	FontShadow	FontSize
FontStrikeThru	FontUnderline	ForeColor
Format	Height	HelpContextID
HideSelection	IMEMode	IntegralHeight
Left	Margin	MaxLength
MouseIcon	MousePointer	Name
NullDisplay	OLEDragMode	OLEDragPicture

OLEDropEffects	OLEDropHasData Property	OLEDropMode
OLEDropTextInsertion	Parent	ParentClass
PasswordChar	ReadOnly	RightToLeft
ScrollBars	SelectedBackColor	SelectedForeColor
SelectOnEntry	SelLength	SelStart
SelText	SpecialEffect	StatusBarText
TabIndex	TabStop	Tag
TerminateRead	Text	ToolTipText
Top	Value	Visible
WhatsThisHelpID	Width	

Events

Click	DblClick	Destroy
DragDrop	DragOver	Error
ErrorMessage	GotFocus	Init
InteractiveChange	KeyPress	LostFocus
Message	MiddleClick Event	MouseDown
MouseMove	MouseUp	MouseWheel
OLECompleteDrag	OLEDragDrop	OLEDragOver
OLEGiveFeedBack	OLESetData	OLEStartDrag
ProgrammaticChange	RightClick	UIEnable
Valid	When	

Methods

AddProperty	CloneObject	Drag
Move	OLEDrag	ReadExpression
ReadMethod	Refresh	ResetToDefault
SaveAsClass	SetFocus	ShowWhatsThis
WriteExpression	WriteMethod	ZOrder

See Also

CREATE CLASS, CREATE FORM, DEFINE CLASS

EJECT Command

Sends a formfeed to the printer.

Syntax

EJECT

Remarks

EJECT advances the printer to the top of the next page. EJECT sends a formfeed to the printer if the _PADVANCE system memory variable is set to FORMFEED. If _PADVANCE is set to LINEFEEDS, EJECT issues linefeeds to advance to the top of the next page.

EJECT resets PCOL( ) and PROW( ) values to the current column and row position of the printer's print head, but doesn't affect the value of the _PAGENO or _PLINENO system variables.

Example

In the following example, the company and phone fields in the customer table are printed. (Make sure a printer is attached and turned on for this example.) When the number of rows printed is greater than 62, the page is ejected.

```
CLOSE DATABASES
OPEN DATABASE (HOME(2) + 'data\testdata')
USE customer  && Opens customer table

SET DEVICE TO PRINTER
SET PRINT ON
DO WHILE NOT EOF( )
   @ PROW( )+1,10 SAY 'Company: ' + company
   @ PROW( )+1,10 SAY 'Phone: ' + phone
   @ PROW( )+1,1  SAY ''
   IF PROW( ) > 62
      EJECT
   ENDIF
   SKIP
ENDDO
SET PRINT OFF
SET DEVICE TO SCREEN
```

See Also

EJECT PAGE, ON PAGE, SET DEVICE, SET PRINTER, PCOL( ), PROW( ), System Variables Overview

EJECT PAGE Command

Sends a conditional page advance to the printer.

Syntax

EJECT PAGE

Remarks

Use EJECT PAGE to advance streaming output. The advance depends on the value of _PADVANCE and if an ON PAGE routine is in effect.

If _PADVANCE is set to FORMFEED and an ON PAGE routine isn't in effect, EJECT PAGE performs the following:

- Sends a formfeed to the printer if the printer is online.

- Sends linefeeds, as determined by the system memory variables _PLENGTH and _PLINENO, to the screen or to an alternate file or to both.

- Increments _PAGENO by 1.

- Sets _PLINENO to 0.

- If the system memory variable _PADVANCE is set to LINEFEEDS, and if an ON PAGE routine is in effect and _PLINENO is less than the page line number specified in the ON PAGE routine, EJECT PAGE sends to the printer, to the main Visual FoxPro window, or to an alternate file or to both, as many linefeeds as needed to advance to the top of the next page.

If an ON PAGE routine is not in effect, or if _PADVANCE is set to LINEFEEDS and _PLINENO is greater than the page line number specified with ON PAGE, EJECT PAGE does the following:

- Sends linefeeds, as determined by the system memory variables _PLENGTH and _PLINENO, to the printer, the main Visual FoxPro window, or to the alternate file or to both.

- Increments _PAGENO by 1.

- Sets _PLINENO to 0.

See Also

EJECT, ON PAGE, SET ALTERNATE, SET DEVICE, SET PRINTER, PCOL( ), PROW( ), System Variables Overview

EMPTY( ) Function

Determines whether an expression evaluates to empty.

Syntax

EMPTY(*eExpression*)

Returns

Logical

Arguments

eExpression

Specifies the expression that EMPTY( ) evaluates.

The expression you include can be a character, numeric, date, or logical expression, or the name of a memo or general field in an open table. EMPTY( ) returns true (.T.) when expressions evaluate to the following:

Expression type	Evaluates to
Character	The empty string, spaces, tabs, carriage returns, linefeeds, or any combination of these.
Numeric	0
Currency	0
Float	0
Integer	0
Double	0
Date	Empty (e.g. CTOD(''))
DateTime	Empty (e.g. CTOT(''))
Logical	False (.F.)
Memo	Empty (no contents)
General	Empty (no OLE object)
Picture	Empty (no picture)

EMPTY( ) cannot be used to determine if a variable object reference is empty. For example, a variable can contain an object reference for a form. If the form is closed by clicking Close from the form's pop-up menu or by issuing CLEAR WINDOWS, the variable contains the null value.

The following program example demonstrates how to use TYPE( ) and ISNULL( ) to determine if a variable object reference is valid.

```
goMyForm = CREATEOBJECT('Form')
WAIT WINDOW IIF(TYPE('goMyForm') = 'O' AND !ISNULL(goMyForm), ;
    'goMyForm has valid object reference',;
    'goMyForm does not have valid object reference')
```

Remarks

EMPTY( ) returns true (.T.) if the expression *eExpression* evaluates to empty; otherwise, EMPTY( ) returns false (.F.).

Example

The following example opens the customer table in the testdata database. FOR ... ENDFOR is used to create a loop in which EMPTY( ) s used to determine if TAG( ) returns the empty string. The name of each structural index tag is displayed with its candidate status.

```
CLOSE DATABASES
OPEN DATABASE (HOME(2) + 'data\testdata')
USE customer       && Open customer table

FOR nCount = 1 TO 254
   IF !EMPTY(TAG(nCount))  && Checks for empty string
   ? TAG(nCount)  && Display tag name
   ? CANDIDATE(nCount)  && Display candidate status
   ELSE
      EXIT  && Exit the loop when no more tags are found
   ENDIF
ENDFOR
```

See Also

LEN( )

Enabled Property

Specifies whether an object can respond to user-generated events. Available at design time and run time.

Syntax

Object.Enabled[= *lExpr*]

Arguments

lExpr

The settings for the Enabled property are:

Setting	Description
True (.T.)	(Default) An object responds to events.
False (.F.)	An object does not respond to events.

Remarks

The Enabled property allows objects to be enabled or disabled at run time. For example, you can disable objects that do not apply to the current state of the application. You can also disable a control to restrict its use — for example, an edit box can be disabled to display read-only information. If a control is disabled, it cannot be selected.

When a container object has its enabled property set to false (.F.), all of its contained controls are disabled, too. If the user clicks on any of the controls contained in a disabled Form, for example, no events are triggered.

Disabling a Timer control by setting Enabled to false (.F.) cancels the countdown specified by the Timer control's Interval property.

Applies To

CheckBox, Column, ComboBox, CommandButton, CommandGroup, Container Object, Control Object, EditBox, Form, Grid, Image, Label, Line, ListBox, OLE Bound Control, OLE Container Control, OptionButton, OptionGroup, Page, PageFrame, _SCREEN, Shape, Spinner, TextBox, Timer, ToolBar

See Also

Click Event, DblClick Event, DragDrop Event, DragOver Event, DropDown Event, KeyPress Event, MouseDown Event, MouseMove Event, MouseUp Event, RightClick Event, Scrolled Event, Undock Event

Encrypted Property

Specifies if compiled source code in a project is encrypted.

Syntax

Object.Encrypted[= *lExpression*]

Arguments

lExpression

The settings for the Encrypted property are:

Setting	Description
True (.T.)	The compiled source code is encrypted. Setting *lExpression* to true (.T.) provides additional protection for your source code, and is identical to including the ENCRYPT argument in the COMPILE command.
False (.F.)	(Default) The compiled source code isn't encrypted.

Remarks

Source code in a project includes program and format files, source code in form, label, report, and visual class libraries, and stored procedures in databases. The Encrypted property corresponds to the **Encrypted** check box on the **Project** tab of the Project Information dialog box.

Applies To

Project Object

See Also

COMPILE, Project Information Dialog Box

END TRANSACTION Command

Ends the current transaction and saves any changes made to tables, table memo files, or index files included in a transaction.

Syntax

END TRANSACTION

Remarks

Any updates to the database that were made between the previous BEGIN TRANSACTION and the END TRANSACTION are committed. If the transaction is the first or only transaction (that is, the transaction isn't nested), the changes are written to disk.

If a transaction is nested, END TRANSACTION causes all cached updates to be folded into the next higher transaction level. Nesting transactions has the potential to overwrite changes made to data at a higher transaction level.

If END TRANSACTION generates an error (for example, there is insufficient disk space to write changes to disk), changes made during the transaction are cancelled and the transaction ends.

See Also

BEGIN TRANSACTION, ROLLBACK, TXNLEVEL( )

EOF( ) Function

Determines whether the record pointer is positioned past the last record in the current or specified table.

Syntax

EOF([*nWorkArea* | *cTableAlias*])

Returns

Logical

Arguments

nWorkArea

Specifies the work area number of the table.

cTableAlias

Specifies the alias of the table.

EOF( ) returns false (.F.) if a table isn't open in the work area you specify.

If you do not specify a work area or alias, the table that is open in the currently selected work area is tested for the end of the table condition.

Remarks

EOF( ) returns true (.T.) if the record pointer reaches the end of the table file (EOF). The end of the table is reached when the record pointer passes the last record in the table. For example, when a FIND, LOCATE, or SEEK is unsuccessful, Visual FoxPro moves the record pointer past the last record, and EOF( ) returns true (.T.). EOF( ) returns false (.F.) if the record pointer isn't at the end of the table.

Example

The following example opens the `customer` table and lists the company name one page at a time until the end of the file is reached or you until you choose Cancel.

```
CLOSE DATABASES
CLEAR
OPEN DATABASE (HOME() + "samples\data\testdata")
USE customer
GO TOP
local recCtr, btnValue
recCtr = 0
btnValue = 1
```

```
DO WHILE btnValue = 1 AND NOT EOF()
   ? "Company : " + company
   recCtr = recCtr + 1
   if (recCtr % 20) = 0 then
      btnValue =MESSAGEBOX ("Click OK to continue, ;
         Cancel to quit.",33)
      clear
   endif
   Skip 1    && Move down one record
ENDDO
=MESSAGEBOX("Listing complete.",48)
```

See Also

BOF( ), GO | GOTO, SKIP

ERASE Command

Erases a file from disk.

Syntax

ERASE *FileNa*me | ? [RECYCLE]

Arguments

FileName

Specifies the file to be erased. Include the path with the file name if the file is on a different drive or directory from the current drive or directory.

FileName can contain wildcard characters such as * and ?. For example, to erase backup files, use ERASE *.bak.

?

Displays the Delete dialog box, from which you can choose a file to erase.

RECYCLE

Specifies that the file isn't immediately deleted from disk and is placed in the Microsoft Windows Recycle Bin.

Caution Exercise caution when using ERASE. Any file erased with this command cannot be retrieved. You aren't warned before the file is erased, even if SET SAFETY is ON.

Example

In the following example, the structure of CUSTOMER.DBF and all records in which the country is USA are copied to a table named backup. The data in backup is then copied to a text file, temp, which is opened and then deleted when it is closed.

```
CLOSE DATABASES
OPEN DATABASE (HOME(2) + 'data\testdata')
USE customer  && Opens customer table

COPY STRUCTURE TO backup
USE backup
APPEND FROM customer FOR country = 'USA'
COPY TO temp TYPE DELIMITED

WAIT WINDOW 'Press Esc to close and erase temp.txt' NOWAIT
MODIFY FILE temp.txt NOEDIT
ERASE temp.txt
? IIF(FILE('temp.txt'),'File not deleted','File deleted')
USE
ERASE backup.dbf
```

See Also

DELETE FILE

ERROR Command

Generates a Visual FoxPro error.

Syntax

ERROR *nErrorNumber*
| *nErrorNumber, cMessageText1*
| [*cMessageText2*]

Arguments

nErrorNumber

Specifies the number of the error to generate. The standard Visual FoxPro error message is used when an error number is specified.

For a list of Visual FoxPro error messages and their error numbers, see the Error Messages in online help.

cMessageText1

Specifies the text displayed in an error message that supplies additional information about the error. For example, if you reference a memory variable that doesn't exist, Visual FoxPro supplies the name of the memory variable in the error message.

cMessageText2

Specifies the text displayed in the error message. When *cMessageText2* is specified instead of *nErrorNumber*, Visual FoxPro error number 1098 (user-defined error) is generated. Use a carriage return (CHR(13)) in *cMessageText2* to move a portion of the error message to the next line.

Remarks

ERROR can be used to test error handling routines or to display custom error messages.

If an ON ERROR error handling routine is in effect when ERROR is issued, Visual FoxPro executes the ON ERROR routine. If an error occurs for an object, the object's Error event is executed.

If you issue ERROR from the Command window and an ON ERROR error handling routine is not in effect, Visual FoxPro displays the error message. If ERROR is issued in a program and an ON ERROR error handling routine is not in effect, Visual FoxPro displays the error message and allows you to cancel or suspend the program or ignore the error.

Example

The following example generates three error messages. The first error message is the Visual FoxPro error message "Variable not found" (error number 12). The second error message again generates error 12, and includes a variable name of Myvariable. The last error message is a user-defined error message (error number 1089) "My error message."

```
ERROR 12  && Generates the Visual FoxPro error "Variable not found"
ERROR 12, 'Myvariable'  && Variable 'Myvariable' not found error
ERROR 'My error message'  && Generates 'My error message' error
```

See Also

ON ERROR

Error Event

Occurs when there is a run-time error in a method.

Syntax

PROCEDURE *Object*.Error
LPARAMETERS [*nIndex*,] *nError*, *cMethod*, *nLine*

Arguments

Visual FoxPro passes the Error event three or four parameters in the following order:

nIndex
> Uniquely identifies a control if it is in a control array.

nError
> Contains the Visual FoxPro error number.

cMethod
> Contains the name of the method that caused the error. However, if a method calls a user-defined function, and an error occurs within that function, *cMethod* contains the name of the user-defined function, rather than the name of the method that called the function.

nLine

> Contains the line number within the method or user-defined function that caused the error.

Remarks

The Error event allows an object to handle errors. This event overrides the current ON ERROR routine and allows each object to trap and handle errors internally.

Important   The Error event is called only when the error occurs in code.

Applies To

ActiveDoc Object, CheckBox, ComboBox, CommandButton, CommandGroup, Container Object, Control Object, Cursor, Custom, DataEnvironment, EditBox, Form, FormSet, Grid, Image, Label, Line, ListBox, OLE Bound Control, OLE Container Control, OptionButton, OptionGroup, Page, PageFrame, ProjectHook Object, Relation, Shape, Spinner, TextBox, Timer, ToolBar

See Also

ON ERROR

ERROR( ) Function

Returns the error number for the error that triggered an ON ERROR routine.

Syntax

ERROR( )

Returns

Numeric

Remarks

ERROR( ) returns the number of the most recent error. An ON ERROR routine must be active for ERROR( ) to return a value other than 0.

When an error is trapped during program execution, the error type can be returned by ERROR( ) in an ON ERROR routine. The corresponding error message can be returned by MESSAGE( ).

The value ERROR( ) returns is reset by RETURN or RETRY.

Example

The following example demonstrates a simple error-handling routine that displays a message when an error occurs.

```
CLEAR
ON ERROR DO errhand WITH ERROR( ), MESSAGE( )

*** The next line generates an error - there is no BRWSE command

BRWSE
ON ERROR
RETURN

*** Error handler ***

PROCEDURE errhand
PARAMETER errnum,message
? Message
? 'Error number: '+ ALLTRIM(STR(Errnum))
RETURN
```

See Also

MESSAGE( ), ON ERROR, RETRY, RETURN

ErrorMessage Event

Included for backward compatibility with FoxPro 2.x. Use the Valid Event instead.

Eval Method

Evaluates an expression and returns the result for an instance of the Visual FoxPro application automation server.

Syntax

ApplicationObject.Eval(*cExpression*)

Returns

Character, Numeric, Currency, Date, or Logical

Arguments

cExpression
Specifies the expression to evaluate. *cExpression* can be a literal character string, or a valid Visual FoxPro expression, variable, array element, or field of any data type, enclosed in quotation marks.

Remarks

cExpression must be a legal Visual FoxPro character expression.

Applies To

Application Object, _VFP System Variable

See Also

DoCmd Method, SetVar Method

EVALUATE( ) Function

Evaluates a character expression and returns the result.

Syntax

EVALUATE(*cExpression*)

Returns

Character, Numeric, Currency, Date, DateTime, Logical, or Memo

Arguments

cExpression

Specifies the expression to evaluate. *cExpression* can be a literal character string, or a valid Visual FoxPro expression, variable, array element, or field of any data type, enclosed in quotation marks. *cExpression* cannot exceed 255 characters.

Whenever possible, use EVALUATE( ) or a name expression to replace macro substitution using &. EVALUATE and name expressions execute faster than macro substitution.

Remarks

EVALUATE( ) is similar to TYPE( ) but returns the result of an expression instead of the expression type. An expression containing EVALUATE( ) cannot be optimized by Rushmore.

See Also

TYPE( )

Exclude Property

Specifies if a file is excluded from an application (.app), dynamic link library (.dll), or executable file (.exe) when it is built from a project. Available at design time and run time.

Syntax

Object.Exclude[= *lExpression*]

Arguments

lExpression

Specifies if the file is excluded from an .app, .dll, or .exe when it is built. If *lExpression* is true (.T.), the file is excluded; otherwise the file is included.

The file type determines the default value for *lExpression*. For example, tables are automatically excluded when added to a project.

Remarks

Excluded files appear with a slashed circle before their names in the Project Manager. Excluded files are listed in the Project Manager window for your reference, but you must manually distribute them if the application needs them. You can also exclude a file by choosing **Exclude** in the Project menu.

Applies To

File Object

See Also

Build Method

Exclusive Property

Specifies whether a table associated with a Cursor object is opened exclusively. Available at design time; read/write at run time.

Syntax

DataEnvironment.Cursor.Exclusive[= *lExpr*]

Arguments

lExpr

The settings for the Exclusive property are:

Setting	Description
True (.T.)	(Default) The table associated with the Cursor is opened exclusively when the data environment is loaded.
False (.F.)	The table associated with the cursor is not opened exclusively when the data environment is loaded.

Remarks

Note When the Cursor object is accessed using CURSORSETPROP( ), the Exclusive property is read-only at run time.

When the data environment is loaded, each table associated with a Cursor can be opened exclusively (no other user in a multiuser environment can access the table) or in shared mode. Use the Exclusive property to specify how the table is accessed.

Note If you set the DataSession property to 2 (Private Data Session), the default setting of the Exclusive property for all Cursor objects in the data environment is changed to false (.F.).

For views, the View object itself is always opened in shared mode. However, the tables that define the view are affected by the Exclusive property. For local views, the Visual FoxPro tables that define the view are opened in exclusive or shared mode, depending on the setting of the Exclusive property. The Exclusive property has no effect on remote views.

The Exclusive property mimics the behavior of the USE command's EXCLUSIVE and SHARE clauses.

Applies To

Cursor

See Also

DataSession Property, SET EXCLUSIVE, USE

EXIT Command

Exits a DO WHILE, FOR, or SCAN loop.

Syntax

EXIT

Remarks

EXIT transfers control from within a DO WHILE ... ENDDO, FOR ... ENDFOR, or SCAN ... ENDSCAN loop to the command immediately following ENDDO, ENDFOR, or ENDSCAN.

Example

In the following example, the number of products in stock priced over 20 dollars is totaled in the DO WHILE loop until the end of the file (EOF) is encountered. The DO WHILE loop is exited and the total is displayed.

```
CLOSE DATABASES
OPEN DATABASE (HOME(2) + 'Data\testdata')
USE products  && Opens Products table
SET TALK OFF
gnStockTot = 0
```

```
DO WHILE .T.  && Beginning of loop
   IF EOF( )
      EXIT
   ENDIF
   IF unit_price < 20
      SKIP
      LOOP
   ENDIF
   gnStockTot = gnStockTot + in_stock
   SKIP
ENDDO  && End of loop

CLEAR
? 'Total items in stock valued over 20 dollars:'
?? gnStockTot
```

See Also

DO WHILE … ENDDO, FOR … ENDFOR, SCAN … ENDSCAN

EXP( ) Function

Returns the value of e^x where x is a specified numeric expression.

Syntax

EXP(*nExpression*)

Returns

Numeric

Arguments

nExpression
   Specifies the exponent, x, in the exponential expression e^x.

Remarks

The value of e, the base of natural logarithms, is approximately 2.71828. The number of decimal places returned by EXP( ) is specified with SET DECIMALS.

Example

```
? EXP(0)  && Displays 1.00
? EXP(1)  && Displays 2.72
```

See Also

LOG( ), SET DECIMALS

EXPORT Command

Copies data from a Visual FoxPro table to a file in a different format.

Syntax

EXPORT TO *FileName*
    [TYPE] DIF | MOD | SYLK
    | WK1 | WKS | WR1 | WRK | XLS | XL5
    [FIELDS *FieldList*]
    [*Scope*]
    [FOR *lExpression1*]
    [WHILE *lExpression2*]
    [NOOPTIMIZE]
    [AS *nCodePage*]

Arguments

FileName

Specifies the name of the file to which Visual FoxPro exports data. If you do not include an extension with the file name, the default extension for the specified file type is assigned.

TYPE

Specifies the type of file to be created. The TYPE keyword is optional, but you must specify one of the following file types.

File type	Description
DIF	Each field from a Visual FoxPro table becomes a vector (column) and each record becomes a tuple (row) in a DIF (Data Interchange Format) file, used by VisiCalc. The new file name is assigned a .DIF extension if an extension isn't included in *FileName*.
MOD	Use the MOD clause to export to a file in Microsoft Multiplan version 4.01 MOD format. The new file name is assigned a .MOD extension if you don't include an extension in *FileName*.
SYLK	A Symbolic Link interchange format (used by Microsoft Multiplan) in which each field from a Visual FoxPro table becomes a column in the spreadsheet and each record becomes a row. By default, SYLK file names have no extension.
WK1	Include this option to create a Lotus 1-2-3 spreadsheet from a Visual FoxPro table. A .WK1 extension is assigned to the spreadsheet file name for use with Lotus 1-2-3 revision 2.x. Each field from the table becomes a column in the new spreadsheet, and each record in the table becomes a spreadsheet row.
WKS	Include this option to create a Lotus 1-2-3 spreadsheet from a Visual FoxPro table. A .WKS extension is assigned to the spreadsheet file name for use with Lotus 1-2-3 revision 1-A. Each field from the table becomes a column in the new spreadsheet, and each record becomes a row in the spreadsheet.

(continued)

File type	Description
WR1	Include this option to create a Lotus Symphony spreadsheet from a Visual FoxPro table. A .WR1 extension is assigned to the spreadsheet for use with Symphony version 1.01. Each field from the table becomes a column in the new spreadsheet, and each record in the table becomes a row in the spreadsheet.
WRK	Include this option to create a Lotus Symphony spreadsheet from a Visual FoxPro table. A .WRK extension is assigned to the spreadsheet file name for use with Symphony version 1.10. Each field from the table becomes a column in the new spreadsheet, and each record in the table becomes a row in the spreadsheet.
XLS	Include this option to create a Microsoft Excel worksheet from a Visual FoxPro table. Each field in the selected table becomes a column in the worksheet, and each table record becomes a row. An .XLS file name extension is assigned to the newly created worksheet file unless you specify a different extension.
XL5	Include this option to create a Microsoft Excel version 5.0 worksheet file from a Visual FoxPro table. Each field from the currently selected table becomes a column in the spreadsheet and each record becomes a row. An .XLS extension is assigned to the new worksheet if you do not include a file extension.

FIELDS *FieldList*

Specifies which fields are copied to the new file. If you omit the FIELDS clause, all fields are copied to the new file. Memo and general fields are not copied to the new file even if their names are included in the field list.

Scope

Specifies a range of records to copy to the new file. *Scope* Specifies a range of records to copy to the new file. Only the records that fall within the range are copied to the new file. The scope clauses are: ALL, NEXT *nRecords*, RECORD *nRecordNumber*, and REST.

For more information on scope clauses, see "Scope Clauses," in Help. Commands that include *Scope* operate only on the table in the active work area.

The default scope for EXPORT is all records.

FOR *lExpression1*

Specifies that only records that satisfy the logical condition *lExpression1* are copied to the new file. Using this argument allows you to filter out undesired records.

Rushmore optimizes an EXPORT ... FOR *lExpression1* command if *lExpression1* is an optimizable expression. For best performance, use an optimizable expression in the FOR clause.

For more information, see the SET OPTIMIZE Command, later in this language reference, and "Understanding Rushmore Technology" in Chapter 15, "Optimizing Applications," in the *Microsoft Visual FoxPro 6.0 Programmer's Guide*.

WHILE *lExpression2*
> Specifies a condition whereby records are copied to the new file for as long as the logical expression *lExpression2* evaluates to true (.T.).

NOOPTIMIZE
> Disables Rushmore optimization of EXPORT.

> For more information, see the SET OPTIMIZE Command, later in this language reference, and "Understanding Rushmore Technology" in Chapter 15, "Optimizing Applications," in the *Microsoft Visual FoxPro 6.0 Programmer's Guide*.

AS *nCodePage*
> Specifies the code page for the file EXPORT creates. Visual FoxPro copies the contents of the currently selected table, and, as it copies the data, automatically converts the data to the code page you specify for the new file. If possible, Visual FoxPro marks the newly created file with the code page you specify.

> If you specify a value for *nCodePage* that is not supported, Visual FoxPro generates an error message. You can use GETCP( ) for *nCodePage* to display the Code Page dialog box, allowing you to specify a code page for the file Visual FoxPro creates.

> If you omit AS *nCodePage*, no code page conversion occurs. If possible, Visual FoxPro marks the newly created file with the code page of the table from which the data is copied.

> If *nCodePage* is 0, no code page conversion occurs and the newly created file is not marked with a code page.

Remarks

Use EXPORT to use Visual FoxPro data in other software packages.

If the table you are exporting from is indexed, the new file is created in the indexed order.

See Also

APPEND FROM, COPY TO, GETCP( ), IMPORT

EXTERNAL Command

Alerts the Project Manager to an undefined reference.

Syntax

EXTERNAL FILE *FileList* | ARRAY *ArrayList*
> | CLASS | FORM | LABEL | LIBRARY | MENU
> | PROCEDURE | QUERY | REPORT | SCREEN | TABLE

Arguments

FILE *FileList*
> Specifies that the file you include in an indirect file reference or macro substitution is a stand-alone file, such as a text file, .BMP bitmap file, and so on. *FileList* may contain a list of file names separated by commas.

ARRAY *ArrayList*

When an array is created in a program and then used in a lower-level program, include ARRAY with the array name in the lower-level program. *ArrayList* may contain a list of array names separated by commas.

In the following example, the first program creates an array named gaInvoice. The array is initialized and a lower-level program named dispinvo is called. dispinvo displays the contents of the array created in the higher-level program. The command **EXTERNAL ARRAY GAINVOICE** is included to alert the Project Manager.

```
DIMENSION gaInvoice(4)
STORE 'Paid' TO gaInvoice
DO dispinvo
*** Program dispinvo ***
PROCEDURE dispinvo
EXTERNAL ARRAY gaInvoice
? gaInvoice(1)
? gaInvoice(2)
? gaInvoice(3)
? gaInvoice(4)
RETURN
*** End of dispinvo program ***
```

When an array is passed to a user-defined function or procedure, the corresponding array in the user-defined function or procedure must be identified to the Project Manager. Include the ARRAY option with the name of the array included in the PARAMETER statement.

```
DIMENSION gaArrayOne(2)      && Create an array
EXTERNAL ARRAY gaArrayTwo    && Name of the array used in the UDF
SET TALK OFF
STORE 10 TO gaArrayOne(1)
STORE  2 TO gaArrayOne(2)
= ADDTWO(@gaArrayOne)        && Pass the array by reference to a UDF
FUNCTION ADDTWO
PARAMETER gaArrayTwo
CLEAR
gaArrayTwo(1) = gaArrayTwo(1) + 2
gaArrayTwo(2) = gaArrayTwo(2) + 2
? gaArrayTwo(1)
? gaArrayTwo(2)
```

CLASS

Specifies that the file you include in an indirect file reference or macro substitution is a visual class library.

```
EXTERNAL CLASS myvclass  && CLASS myvclass must exist
STORE 'myvclass' TO gcClassFile
MODIFY CLASS (gcClassFile)
```

FORM

If a Form definition file is included in an indirect file reference or macro substitution, include FORM and the Form file name. FORM is identical to SCREEN.

```
EXTERNAL FORM dataentr  && FORM dataentr must exist
STORE 'dataentr' TO gcFormFile
DO FORM (gcFormFile)
```

LABEL

Specifies that the file you include in an indirect file reference or macro substitution is a label definition file.

```
EXTERNAL LABEL Maillabl     && LABEL FORM Maillabl must exist
STORE 'Maillabl' TO gcLabelFile
LABEL FORM (gcLabelFile) PREVIEW
```

LIBRARY

Include LIBRARY when a library file is referenced by indirect file referencing or macro substitution in SET LIBRARY.

```
EXTERNAL LIBRARY regress  && LIBRARY regress must exist
STORE 'regress' TO gcStatFunc
SET LIBRARY TO (gcStatFunc)
```

MENU

If a menu definition file is included in an indirect file reference or macro substitution, include MENU and the menu file name.

```
EXTERNAL MENU pickfile  && MENU pickfile must exist
STORE 'pickfile' TO gcSysMenPad
MODIFY MENU (gcSysMenPad)
```

PROCEDURE

Identifies an external procedure or user-defined function.

```
EXTERNAL PROCEDURE delblank     && PROCEDURE delblank must exist
STORE 'delblank' TO gcTrimBlanks
DO (gcTrimBlanks) WITH 'A B C D E'
```

QUERY

Specifies that the file you include in an indirect file reference or macro substitution is a query file.

```
EXTERNAL QUERY sales  && QUERY sales must exist
STORE 'sales.qpr' TO gcSalesFile
DO (gcSalesFile)
```

REPORT

Specifies that the file you include in an indirect file reference or macro substitution is a report definition file.

```
EXTERNAL REPORT overdue      && REPORT overdue must exist
STORE 'overdue' TO gcReportFile
REPORT FORM (gcReportFile) PREVIEW
```

SCREEN

If a form definition file is included in an indirect file reference or macro substitution, include SCREEN and the screen file name. SCREEN is identical to FORM.

```
EXTERNAL SCREEN dataentr  && SCREEN dataentr must exist
STORE 'dataentr' TO gcScreenFile
MODIFY SCREEN (gcScreenFile)
```

TABLE

Specifies that the file you include in an indirect file reference or macro substitution is a Visual FoxPro table.

```
EXTERNAL TABLE customer && Table customer must exist
STORE 'customer' TO gcMyTable
USE (gcMyTable)
```

Remarks

Use EXTERNAL to include files and to resolve undefined references in a project created by the Project Manager. EXTERNAL is used only by the Project Manager and is ignored during program execution.

For more information on creating projects with the Project Manager, see "Using the Project Manager" in Chapter 15, "Compiling an Application," in the *Microsoft Visual FoxPro 6.0 Programmer's Guide*.

Files whose names you specify with EXTERNAL are included in a project by the Project Manager. You must include CLASS, FILE, FORM, LABEL, LIBRARY, MENU, PROCEDURE, QUERY, REPORT, SCREEN, or TABLE before the file name or a set of file names separated with commas to tell the Project Manager the type of files to include in the project.

The Project Manager must also be alerted to file names contained in a name expression or macro substitution. This ensures that all necessary files are included in a project when the project is built. It must also be alerted to arrays that are created in another procedure or user-defined function.

For more information on name expressions and macro substitution, see the & Command, earlier in this language reference. Whenever possible, use a name expression instead of macro substitution to improve performance.

See Also

BUILD APP, BUILD PROJECT

FCHSIZE( ) Function

Changes the size of a file opened with a low-level file function.

Syntax

FCHSIZE(*nFileHandle*, *nNewFileSize*)

Returns

Numeric

Arguments

nFileHandle

Specifies the file handle of the file whose size you wish to change. The file handle is returned by FOPEN( ) when you open the file or by FCREATE( ) when you create the file. If a file is opened with FOPEN( ), it must be opened with write or read/write privileges to be able to change its size.

nNewFileSize

Specifies the new file size in bytes. If *nNewFileSize* is less than the original file size, the file is truncated. If *nNewFileSize* is greater than the original file size, the file size is increased.

Remarks

Use FCHSIZE( ) to increase the file's size or truncate the file after a specified byte.

When a file's size is increased, Microsoft Visual FoxPro allocates sectors for the file on the drive where the file is opened. Since FCHSIZE( ) doesn't initialize the new file space, the space can contain previous data. Be sure to manage the new file space.

The final size of the file in bytes is returned. Visual FoxPro returns –1 if FCHSIZE( ) is unable to change the file size if, for example, an invalid file handle is specified because of insufficient disk space, or if the file is read-only.

Tip   This function can be used to truncate a file to length 0.

See Also

FCLOSE( ), FCREATE( ), FEOF( ), FFLUSH( ), FGETS( ), FOPEN( ), FPUTS( ), FREAD( ), FSEEK( ), FWRITE( )

FCLOSE( ) Function

Flushes and closes a file or communication port opened with a low-level file function.

Syntax

FCLOSE(*nFileHandle*)

Returns

Logical

Arguments

nFileHandle

Specifies the file handle of the low-level file to close. The numeric file handle is returned when you create the file with FCREATE( ) or open the file with FOPEN( ).

Remarks

If the file is successfully closed, FCLOSE( ) returns true (.T.) and releases the file handle. If the file cannot be closed, FCLOSE( ) returns false (.F.).

CLOSE ALL also closes low-level files.

See Also

CLOSE ALL, FCHSIZE( ), FCREATE( ), FEOF( ), FFLUSH( ), FGETS( ), FOPEN( ), FPUTS( ), FREAD( ), FSEEK( ), FWRITE( )

FCOUNT( ) Function

Returns the number of fields in a table.

Syntax

FCOUNT([*nWorkArea* | *cTableAlias*])

Returns

Numeric

Arguments

nWorkArea

Specifies the work area of the table for which FCOUNT( ) returns the number of fields.

FCOUNT( ) returns 0 if a table isn't open in the work area you specify.

cTableAlias

Specifies the alias of the table for which FCOUNT( ) returns the number of fields.

Visual FoxPro generates an error message if you specify a table alias that doesn't exist.

Remarks

If you omit the optional arguments, FCOUNT( ) returns the number of fields in the table open in the currently selected work area.

Example

```
CLOSE DATABASES
OPEN DATABASE (HOME(2) + 'Data\testdata')
USE customer  && Opens Customer table
SELECT 0
USE employee  && Opens employee table

CLEAR
? FCOUNT('CUSTOMER')   && Displays 13, # of fields in Customer
? FCOUNT('EMPLOYEE')   && Displays 22, # of fields in Employee
```

See Also

DBF( ), FIELD( ), FSIZE( )

FCREATE( ) Function

Creates and opens a low-level file.

Syntax

FCREATE(*cFileName* [, *nFileAttribute*])

Returns

Numeric

Arguments

cFileName
> Specifies the name of the file to create. You can include a drive designator and path with the file name. If a drive designator or path isn't included, the file is created in the default directory.

> **Note** Visual FoxPro will not recognize a path name properly if a disk or directory name contains an exclamation point (!).

nFileAttribute
> Specifies the attributes of the file created. The following table lists the file attributes you can specify.

nFileAttribute	File attributes
0	(Default) Read/Write
1	Read-Only
2	Hidden
3	Read-Only/Hidden
4	System
5	Read-Only/System
6	System/Hidden
7	Read-Only/Hidden/System

Note that a file created with *nFileAttribute* other than 0 cannot be written to with FPUTS( ) or FWRITE( ) until the file is closed and opened again.

Use DISPLAY STATUS or LIST STATUS to display or print information about files created and opened with FCREATE( ). DISPLAY STATUS and LIST STATUS give the following information about each file opened or created with a low-level file function:

- The drive, directory, and file name
- The file handle number
- The file pointer position
- The read/write attributes

Remarks

If a file with the name you specify already exists, it is overwritten without warning.

FCREATE( ) assigns a file handle number to the file, which you can use to identify the file in other Visual FoxPro low-level file functions. FCREATE( ) returns the file handle number when a file is created, or returns –1 if the file cannot be created.

Tip Assign the file handle number to a memory variable so you can access the file by the variable in other low-level file functions.

Example

```
IF FILE('errors.txt')  && Does file exist?
   gnErrFile = FOPEN('errors.txt',12)  && If so, open read-write
ELSE
   gnErrFile = FCREATE('errors.txt')  && If not create it
ENDIF
IF gnErrFile < 0    && Check for error opening file
   WAIT 'Cannot open or create output file' WINDOW NOWAIT
```

```
ELSE  && If no error, write to file
   =FWRITE(gnErrFile , 'Error information to be written here')
ENDIF
=FCLOSE(gnErrFile )     && Close file
IF gnErrFile > 0
MODIFY FILE errors.txt NOWAIT  && Open file in edit window
ENDIF
```

See Also

CLOSE ALL, FCHSIZE( ), FCREATE( ), FEOF( ), FFLUSH( ), FGETS( ), FOPEN( ),
FPUTS( ), FREAD( ), FSEEK( ), FWRITE( )

FDATE( ) Function

Returns the last modification Date or DateTime for a file.

Syntax

FDATE(*cFileName* [, *nType*])

Returns

Date

Arguments

cFileName

Specifies the name of the file whose last modification date FDATE( ) returns.
cFileName can include a path with the file name. If a path is not included with the file
name, Visual FoxPro searches for the file in the default directory and in any directories
or folders specified with SET PATH.

nType

Specifies that FDATE( ) returns the last modification date or DateTime of the file
specified with *cFileName*. If *nType* is 0, the last modification date is returned.
Including 0 is identical to omitting *nType*. If *nType* is 1, the last modification DateTime
is returned.

Remarks

The Date or DateTime value that FDATE( ) returns is assigned to the file by the operating
system.

Use LUPDATE( ) to determine the last modification date for an open table.

Example

The following example uses FDATE( ) to display the last modification DateTime for
Foxuser.dbf, the Visual FoxPro resource file.

```
? FDATE('FOXUSER.DBF', 1)  && Displays the last modification DateTime
```

See Also

FTIME( ), LUPDATE( )

FEOF( ) Function

Determines whether the file pointer is positioned at the end of a file.

Syntax

FEOF(*nFileHandle*)

Returns

Logical

Arguments

nFileHandle

Specifies the file handle number of the file to check for the end-of-file condition. FEOF( ) always returns true (.T.) if you specify a file handle number of a communication port opened with FOPEN( ).

Remarks

This low-level file function returns true (.T.) if the file pointer is positioned at the end of a file opened with a low-level file function. FEOF( ) returns false (.F.) if the file pointer isn't at the end of the file.

Example

```
*** Open the file test.txt ***

gnFileHandle = FOPEN('test.txt')

*** Move the file pointer to BOF ***

gnPosition = FSEEK(gnFileHandle, 0)

*** If file pointer is at BOF and EOF, the file is empty ***
*** Otherwise the file must have something in it ***

IF FEOF(gnFileHandle)
   WAIT WINDOW 'This file is empty!' NOWAIT
ELSE
   WAIT WINDOW 'This file has something in it!' NOWAIT
ENDIF
= FCLOSE(gnFileHandle)
```

See Also

FCHSIZE( ), FCLOSE( ), FCREATE( ), FGETS( ), FOPEN( ), FPUTS( ), FREAD( ), FSEEK( ), FWRITE( )

FERROR( ) Function

Returns a number corresponding to the most recent low-level file function error.

Syntax

FERROR( )

Returns

Numeric

Remarks

FERROR( ) returns 0 if a low-level file function executes successfully. A positive value is returned if a function doesn't execute successfully. The following table lists each error number returned by FERROR( ) and the cause of the error.

Error number	Error cause
2	File not found
4	Too many files open (out of file handles)
5	Access denied
6	Invalid file handle given
8	Out of memory
25	Seek error (can't seek before the start of a file)
29	Disk full
31	Error opening file

See Also

FCHSIZE( ), FCLOSE( ), FCREATE( ), FEOF( ), FFLUSH( ), FGETS( ), FOPEN( ), FPUTS( ), FREAD( ), FSEEK( ), FWRITE( )

FFLUSH( ) Function

Flushes to disk a file opened with a low-level function.

Syntax

FFLUSH(*nFileHandle*)

Returns

Logical

Arguments

nFileHandle
   Specifies the file handle of the file to flush to disk.

Remarks

FFLUSH( ) also releases the memory used by the file's buffer.

FLUSH is different from the FFLUSH( ) function. FLUSH doesn't operate on low-level files but rather on tables and indexes.

Example

The following example opens and writes to a file named Input.dat. After writing the first two strings, the program flushes the buffers to ensure that the strings are written to disk. It then writes the next two strings, flushes the buffers again and closes the file.

```
IF FILE('input.dat')
   gnTestFile = FOPEN('input.dat',2)
ELSE
   gnTestFile = FCREATE('input.dat')
ENDIF
gnIOBytes = FWRITE(gnTestFile,'Test output')
gnIOBytes = FWRITE(gnTestFile,' for low-level file I/O')
glFlushOk = FFLUSH(gnTestFile)
gnIOBytes = FWRITE(gnTestFile,'Test output2')
gnIOBytes = FWRITE(gnTestFile,' for low-level file I/O')
glFlushOk = FFLUSH(gnTestFile)
glCloseOk = FCLOSE(gnTestFile)
MODIFY FILE input.dat NOWAIT NOEDIT
```

See Also

FCHSIZE( ), FCLOSE( ), FCREATE( ), FEOF( ), FGETS( ), FOPEN( ), FPUTS( ), FREAD( ), FSEEK( ), FWRITE( )

FGETS( ) Function

Returns a series of bytes from a file or a communication port opened with a low-level file function until it encounters a carriage return.

Syntax

FGETS(*nFileHandle* [, *nBytes*])

Returns

Character

Arguments

nFileHandle

Specifies the numeric file handle of the file or communication port from which FGETS( ) returns data.

nBytes

Specifies the number of bytes FGETS( ) returns. FGETS( ) returns *nBytes* bytes unless a carriage return is encountered first. FGETS( ) returns data between the starting file-pointer position and the carriage return if a carriage return is encountered within *nBytes* bytes.

If you omit *nBytes*, FGETS( ) returns a maximum of 254 bytes by default.

Remarks

You can read a file line by line by issuing a series of FGETS( ).

FGETS( ) returns a series of bytes as a character string. Data is returned starting from the current file's pointer position and continuing until a carriage return is encountered. The file pointer is then positioned on the byte immediately following the carriage return. The carriage return isn't returned as part of the string, and line feeds are discarded.

Example

```
*** TEST.TXT must exist ***
STORE FOPEN('test.txt') TO gnFileHandle  && Open the file
STORE FSEEK(gnFileHandle, 0, 2) TO gnEnd && Move pointer to EOF
STORE FSEEK(gnFileHandle, 0) TO gnTop  && Move pointer to BOF
IF gnEnd <= 0  && Is file empty?
   WAIT WINDOW 'This file is empty!' NOWAIT
ELSE  && If not
   gcString = FGETS(gnFileHandle, gnEnd)  && Store contents
   ? gcString
ENDIF
= FCLOSE(gnFileHandle)  && Close the file
```

See Also

FCHSIZE( ), FCLOSE( ), FCREATE( ), FEOF( ), FFLUSH( ), FILETOSTR( ), FOPEN( ), FPUTS( ), FREAD( ), FSEEK( ), FWRITE( )

FIELD( ) Function

Returns the name of a field, referenced by number, in a table.

Syntax

FIELD(*nFieldNumber* [, *nWorkArea* | *cTableAlias*])

Returns

Character

Arguments

nFieldNumber

Specifies the field number. If *nFieldNumber* is 1, the name of the first field in the table is returned; if *nFieldNumber* is 2, the name of the second field is returned, and so on. The empty string is returned if *nFieldNumber* is greater than the number of fields. Field names are returned in upper case.

nWorkArea

Specifies the work area of the table for which FIELD( ) returns field names.

FIELD( ) returns the empty string if a table isn't open in the work area you specify.

cTableAlias

Specifies the alias of the table for which FIELD( ) returns field names.

Visual FoxPro generates an error message if you specify a table alias that doesn't exist.

Remarks

If you omit the optional arguments, FIELD( ) returns the names of the fields in the table open in the currently selected work area.

Example

```
CLOSE DATABASES
OPEN DATABASE (HOME(2) + 'Data\testdata')
USE customer  && Opens Customer table

CLEAR
FOR gnCount = 1 TO FCOUNT( )  && Loop for number of fields
   ? FIELD(gnCount)  && Display each field
NEXT
?
? 'Number of fields: ' + ALLTRIM(STR(gnCount -1))
```

See Also

DISPLAY STRUCTURE, FCOUNT( ), FSIZE( )

FILE( ) Function

Returns true (.T.) if the specified file is found on disk.

Syntax

FILE(*cFileName*)

Returns

Logical

Arguments

cFileName

Specifies the name of the file to locate. *cFileName* must include the file's extension. Visual FoxPro looks in the default directory for the file. If the file cannot be found in the default directory, Visual FoxPro searches along the Visual FoxPro path which is established with SET PATH.

You can include a path with the file name to search for a file in a directory or on a drive other than the current directory or drive.

Remarks

Use FILE( ) to find a file on disk. FILE( ) returns true (.T.) if the file can be found; otherwise FILE( ) returns false (.F.).

Example

The following example displays a message indicating if the Visual FoxPro resource file is present in the Visual FoxPro start up directory.

```
SET PATH TO HOME( )
CLEAR
IF FILE('foxuser.dbf')
   WAIT WINDOW 'Visual FoxPro resource file present'
ELSE
   WAIT WINDOW 'Visual FoxPro resource file not present'
ENDIF
```

See Also

FULLPATH( ), GETFILE( ), LOCFILE( )

FileClass Property

Contains the name of the form class on which a form in a project is based. Read-only at design time and run time.

Syntax

Object.FileClass

Remarks

The FileClass property applies only to forms in a project, and contains the empty string for other file types.

Applies To

File Object

See Also

FileClassLibrary Property, Type Property

FileClassLibrary Property

Contains the name of the class library containing the class on which a form in a project is based. Read-only at design time and run time.

Syntax

Object.FileClassLibrary

Remarks

The FileClassLibrary property applies only to forms in a project, and contains the empty string for other file types.

Applies To

File Object

See Also

FileClass Property, Type Property

File Object

Instantiated when a file is added to a project.

Syntax

File

Remarks

A file object is created and instantiated for each file added to a project. A file object provides an object reference to the file in the project, and allows you to determine information about the file and manipulate it through the File object properties and methods.

A project's files collection is composed of all the file objects in the project.

Note that a file object is a COM object, so assigning a file object reference to a memory variable creates a memory variable of class "Unknown Type."

Properties

CodePage	Description	Exclude
FileClass	FileClassLibrary	LastModified
Name	ReadOnly	SCCStatus
Type		

Methods

AddToSCC	CheckIn	CheckOut
GetLatestVersion	Modify	Remove
RemoveFromSCC	Run	UndoCheckOut

See Also

Files Collection

Files Collection

A collection of file objects in a project.

Syntax

Files

Remarks

The files collection consists of all the files in a project. Each file is an object that can be manipulated with the file object properties and methods.

Files in a file collection can be referenced by index number or name. For example, the following code opens the file that was first added to a project:

```
_VFP.ActiveProject.Files(1).Modify( )
```

The following code opens an editing window for Main.prg:

```
_VFP.ActiveProject.Files('Main.prg').Modify( )
```

Note that it isn't necessary to include the path with a file name.

For more information about the files collection and projects, see "Project Manager Hooks" in Chapter 32, "Application Development and Developer Productivity," of the *Microsoft Visual FoxPro 6.0 Programmer's Guide*.

Properties

Count

Methods

Add   Item

See Also

File Object

FILETOSTR( ) Function

Returns the contents of a file as a character string.

Syntax

FILETOSTR(*cFileName*)

Returns

Character

Arguments

cFileName
Specifies the name of the file whose contents are returned as a character string. If the file is in a directory other than the current default directory, include a path with the file name.

Remarks

Note that the size of the character string FILETOSTR( ) returns can be very large. The amount of available memory or disk space determines if you can store the character string to a memory variable, array element, or memo field. Also, character fields in

Visual FoxPro are limited to 254 characters. See "Visual FoxPro System Capacities" in Help, for more information about limitations on character type data.

See Also

FGETS( ), FREAD( ), STRTOFILE( )

FillColor Property

Specifies the color used to fill shapes drawn on an object by graphics routines. Available at design time and run time.

Syntax

Object.FillColor[= *nColor*]
Object.FillColor[= RGB(*nRedValue, nGreenValue, nBlueValue*)]

Arguments

nColor

Specifies a single number to represent the color. By default, FillColor is set to 0 (Black). For more information on color settings, see "BackColor, ForeColor Properties," earlier in this language reference

nRedValue, nGreenValue, nBlueValue

Specifies three separate color intensities that compose the fill color; must be used with the RGB( ) function to consolidate the three color components into one number, which is what the FillColor property is.

Note In the Properties window, you can double-click any of the color properties to display the Color dialog box. You can choose or define colors from this dialog box. The red, green, and blue intensities that correspond to the color you choose become the settings for these properties after you close the Color dialog box.

Remarks

When the FillStyle property is set to its default, 1 (Transparent), the FillColor setting is ignored.

Only an enclosed shape, such as a circle, box, or ellipse can be filled.

Shape objects use the BackColor property to specify the fill color.

Applies To

Form, _SCREEN, Shape

See Also

BackColor Property, Box Method, Circle Method, FillStyle Property, ForeColor, Property, GETCOLOR( ), RGB( )

FillStyle Property

Specifies the pattern used to fill shapes and figures created with the Circle and Box graphics methods. Available at design time and run time.

Syntax

Object.FillStyle[= *nStyle*]

Arguments

nStyle
Specifies the pattern used to fill a shape or figure. The settings for the FillStyle property are:

Setting	Description
0	Solid.
1	(Default) Transparent. The FillColor property is ignored.
2	Horizontal Line.
3	Vertical Line.
4	Upward Diagonal. Upward diagonal lines from upper left to lower right.
5	Downward Diagonal. Downward diagonal from lower left to upper right.
6	Cross. Crossed vertical and horizontal lines forming squares.
7	Diagonal Cross.

Applies To

Form, _SCREEN, Shape

See Also

BorderStyle Property, Box Method, Circle Method, DrawMode Property, DrawStyle Property, DrawWidth Property, FillColor Property

Filter Property

Excludes records that do not meet the criteria in the specified expression. Available at design time; read/write at run time.

Syntax

DataEnvironment.Cursor.Filter[= *cExpr*]

Arguments

cExpr
Any Visual FoxPro expression, typically an expression that operates on a set of records.

Remarks

Mimics the behavior of SET FILTER.

> **Note** When the Cursor object is accessed using CURSORSETPROP( ), the Filter property is read-only at run time.

Applies To

Cursor

See Also

SET FILTER

FILTER( ) Function

Returns the table filter expression specified in SET FILTER.

Syntax

FILTER([*nWorkArea* | *cTableAlias*])

Returns

Character

Arguments

nWorkArea

Specifies the work area of the table for which FILTER( ) returns the filter expression.

FILTER( ) returns the empty string if a table isn't open in the work area you specify.

cTableAlias

Specifies the alias of the table for which FILTER( ) returns the filter expression.

Visual FoxPro generates an error message if you specify a table alias that doesn't exist.

Remarks

If you omit the optional arguments, FILTER( ) returns the filter expression for the table open in the currently selected work area. For more information about creating a filter, see the SET FILTER Command, later in this language reference.

Example

```
CLOSE DATABASES
OPEN DATABASE (HOME(2) + 'Data\testdata')
USE customer   && Opens Customer table
SET TALK ON
SET FILTER TO SUBSTR(cust_id,1) = 'B'
```

```
CLEAR
? FILTER( )  && Display filter expression
STORE FILTER('customer') TO gcOldFilter   && Save filter expression
SET FILTER TO country = 'USA'
? FILTER( )  && Display filter expression
SET FILTER TO &gcOldFilter  && Restore filter expression
? FILTER( )  && Display filter expression

LIST FIELDS cust_id, contact  && Demonstrate filter condition
```

See Also

SET FILTER

FIND Command

Included for backward compatibility. Use SEEK instead.

FirstElement Property

Specifies the first element of an array to display in a ComboBox or ListBox control. Available at design time and run time.

Syntax

*Control.*FirstElement[= *nElement*]

Arguments

nElement
    Specifies which element in the array is displayed as the first element in the list.

Remarks

This property is available only when the RowSource is an array (RowSourceType = 5). Note that the FirstElement property only applies to ComboBoxes and ListBoxes with one column.

Applies To

ComboBox, ListBox

See Also

NumberOfElements Property, RowSource Property

FKLABEL( ) Function

Returns the name of the function key (F1, F2, F3 ...) from the key's corresponding function key number.

Syntax

FKLABEL(*nFunctionKeyNumber*)

Returns

Character

Arguments

nFunctionKeyNumber

Specifies the function key number. The value of *nFunctionKeyNumber* should be from 0 through the number of function keys minus 1. FKLABEL( ) returns the empty string if *nFunctionKeyNumber* is greater than the number of function keys minus 1. The number of function keys can be determined with FKMAX( ).

Remarks

Function keys can be programmed with SET FUNCTION.

The value returned by FKLABEL( ) is affected by SET COMPATIBLE. When COMPATIBLE is set to FOXPLUS (the default), FKLABEL( ) returns the function keys. When COMPATIBLE is set to DB4, FKLABEL( ) returns the function key and function key combinations (F1, CTRL+F1, SHIFT+F1, F2, CTRL+F2, SHIFT+F2, ...).

Example

```
CLEAR
SET COMPATIBLE OFF
? 'COMPATIBLE OFF'
?
FOR nCount = 1 TO FKMAX( )  && Loop for # of function keys
   ? FKLABEL(nCount)  && Display programmable function keys
ENDFOR
SET COMPATIBLE ON

?
? 'COMPATIBLE ON'
?
FOR nCount = 1 TO FKMAX( )  && Loop for # of function keys
   ? FKLABEL(nCount)  && Display programmable function keys
ENDFOR
```

See Also

FKMAX( ), SET COMPATIBLE, SET FUNCTION

FKMAX( ) Function

Returns the number of programmable function keys or function key combinations on your keyboard.

Syntax

FKMAX( )

Returns

Numeric

Remarks

The value returned by FKMAX( ) is affected by SET COMPATIBLE. When SET COMPATIBLE is set to FOXPLUS (the default), FKMAX( ) returns the number of function keys. When SET COMPATIBLE is set to DB4, FKMAX( ) returns the number of function key and function key combinations (F1, CTRL+F1, SHIFT+F1, F2, CTRL+F2, SHIFT+F2, ...).

Example

```
CLEAR
SET COMPATIBLE OFF
? 'COMPATIBLE OFF'
?
FOR nCount = 1 TO FKMAX( )  && Loop for # of function keys
   ? FKLABEL(nCount)  && Display programmable function keys
ENDFOR
SET COMPATIBLE ON

?
? 'COMPATIBLE ON'
?
FOR nCount = 1 TO FKMAX( )  && Loop for # of function keys
   ? FKLABEL(nCount)  && Display programmable function keys
ENDFOR
```

See Also

FKLABEL( ), SET COMPATIBLE, SET FUNCTION

FLDLIST( ) Function

Included for compatibility with dBASE.

FLOCK( ) Function

Attempts to lock the current or specified table.

Syntax

FLOCK([*nWorkArea* | *cTableAlias*])

Returns

Logical

Arguments

nWorkArea

Specifies the work area of the table that FLOCK( ) attempts to lock.

FLOCK( ) returns false (.F.) if a table isn't open in the work area you specify.

cTableAlias

Specifies the alias of the table that FLOCK( ) attempts to lock.

Microsoft Visual FoxPro generates an error message if you specify a table alias that doesn't exist.

Remarks

FLOCK( ) returns true (.T.) if the table is successfully locked and returns false (.F.) if the table or a record in the table is already locked by another user.

If you omit the optional arguments, FLOCK( ) attempts to lock the table open in the currently selected work area.

> **Note** If FLOCK( ) fails to lock a table, it returns false (.F.) and does not generate an error. As a result, you can't use FLOCK( ) to trigger an ON ERROR routine.

When a table is locked, the table is available for both read and write access by the user who placed the lock. Other users on the network have read-only access to the table. For information on how to lock a table and prevent access to it by other users, see the SET EXCLUSIVE and USE Commands, later in this language reference.

A table remains locked until it is unlocked by the user who placed the lock. The table can be unlocked by issuing UNLOCK, closing the table, or quitting Visual FoxPro. Tables can be closed with USE, CLEAR ALL, or CLOSE DATABASES.

By default, FLOCK( ) attempts to lock a table once. Use SET REPROCESS to automatically retry a table lock when the first attempt fails. SET REPROCESS determines the number of lock attempts, or the length of time during which lock attempts are made when the initial lock attempt is unsuccessful. For more information, see the SET REPROCESS Command, later in this language reference.

You can establish relations between two or more tables with SET RELATION. Placing a file lock on a table that is related to one or more tables doesn't place a file lock on the related tables. You must explicitly place and remove locks on the related tables.

For additional information about record and file locking and sharing tables on a network, see Chapter 17, "Programming for Shared Access," in the *Microsoft Visual FoxPro 6.0 Programmer's Guide*.

Example

```
CLOSE DATABASES
OPEN DATABASE (HOME(2) + 'Data\testdata')
USE products   && Opens products table
SET REPROCESS TO 3 SECONDS
SELECT * FROM products INTO TABLE newprods

IF FLOCK( )
   *** New product initialization ***
   REPLACE ALL in_stock  WITH 0.00
   REPLACE ALL on_order WITH 0.00
   WAIT 'Initialization Complete' WINDOW NOWAIT
ELSE
   *** File is locked, warn user ***
   WAIT WINDOW 'Unable to open products file; try again later!' NOWAIT
ENDIF

BROWSE FIELDS in_stock, on_order && Displays newprods table
USE
ERASE newprods.dbf
```

See Also

LOCK( ), RLOCK( ), SET REPROCESS, SET RELATION, UNLOCK, USE, SET EXCLUSIVE

FLOOR( ) Function

Returns the nearest integer that is less than or equal to the specified numeric expression.

Syntax

FLOOR(*nExpression*)

Returns

Numeric

Arguments

nExpression

Specifies the numeric expression for which FLOOR( ) returns the nearest integer that is less than or equal to the numeric expression.

Example

```
STORE  10.9 TO gnNumber1
STORE -10.1 TO gnNumber2

CLEAR
? FLOOR(gnNumber1)  && Displays 10
? FLOOR(gnNumber2)  && Displays -11
? FLOOR(10.0)  && Displays 10
? FLOOR(-10.0)  && Displays -10
```

See Also

CEILING( ), INT( ), ROUND( )

FLUSH Command

Saves table and index modifications to disk.

Syntax

FLUSH

Remarks

FLUSH ensures that modifications you make to all open tables and indexes are saved to disk.

Visual FoxPro automatically saves changes to disk when:

- You close a table with USE, CLOSE ALL, or CLOSE DATABASES. Only information for the file or files you close is flushed to disk.

- You unlock a record or file. Only information for the record or file unlocked is flushed to disk.

See Also

CLOSE DATABASES, FFLUSH( ), SET AUTOSAVE

Fonts Overview

Visual FoxPro can use the fonts you have installed. Fonts determine the appearance of displayed or printed text. In addition, fonts determine the position and size of controls.

Font Control Size and Position

In Visual FoxPro, the ScaleMode property for the Form on which a control is placed determines the control's size and position. If ScaleMode is set to Pixels (3), the size of a control is specified in pixels. If ScaleMode is set to Foxels (0), the size of a control is determined by the Form's current font and font size.

Foxel is a Visual FoxPro term that corresponds to the maximum height and average width of a character in the current font. The row height corresponds to the maximum height of a letter in the current font; the column width corresponds to the average width of a letter in the current font.

In Visual FoxPro, you can use decimal fractions for row and column coordinates to facilitate precise positioning of controls and output. In FoxPro for MS-DOS, fractional portions of row and column coordinates are ignored.

In Visual FoxPro, to determine or change the font for the main Visual FoxPro window, press SHIFT while you display the Format menu, then choose the Screen Font option. The font for a user-defined window can be specified by including the FONT clause when you create the window with DEFINE WINDOW.

Font Substitution

If you specify a font that is not available, Windows substitutes a font with similar font characteristics. Windows considers the point size, serif characteristics and the pitch of the font you request. A TrueType font is typically substituted. A raster or vector font is only substituted when the characteristics of the font you request closely match those of the raster or vector font.

Font Functions

Several functions can be used to return information about fonts and text in a specific font.

These functions include:

Function	Description
AFONT( )	Places information about available fonts into an array.
FONTMETRIC( )	Returns font attributes for installed fonts.
GETFONT( )	Displays the Font dialog and returns the name of the font you choose.
SYSMETRIC( )	Returns the size of a display element.

(continued)

(continued)

Function	Description
SCOLS( )	Returns the number of columns available in the main Visual FoxPro window. Useful when centering text or controls in the main Visual FoxPro window.
SROWS( )	Returns the number of rows available in the main Visual FoxPro window. Useful when centering text or controls in the main Visual FoxPro window.
WCOLS( )	Returns the number of columns within the specified window. Useful when centering text or controls in a user-defined window.
WFONT( )	Returns the name, size or style of the current font for a window.
WROWS( )	Returns the number of columns within the specified window. Useful when centering text or controls in a user-defined window.

See Also

AFONT( ), FONTMETRIC( ), GETFONT( ), SYSMETRIC( ), ScaleMode Property, SCOLS( ), SROWS( ), WCOLS( ), WFONT( ), WROWS( )

FontBold, FontItalic, FontStrikethru, FontUnderline Properties

Specifies whether text has one or more of the following styles: **Bold**, *Italic*, ~~Strikethru~~, or Underline. Available at design time and run time.

Syntax

Object.FontBold[= *lExpr*]
Object.FontItalic[= *lExpr*]
Object.FontStrikeThru[= *lExpr*]
Object.FontUnderline[= *lExpr*]

Arguments

lExpr
   The settings for the font properties are:

Setting	Description
True (.T.)	Font style is bold, italic, strikethru, or underline.
False (.F.)	(Default except for FontBold) Font style is not bold, italic, strikethru, or underline.

Remarks

In general, change the FontName property before you set size and style attributes with the FontSize, FontBold, FontItalic, FontStrikethru, and FontUnderline properties. However, when you set TrueType fonts to smaller than 8 points, you should set the point size with the FontSize property, next set the FontName property, and then set the size again with the FontSize property. Windows uses a different font for TrueType fonts that are smaller than 8 points.

Note Fonts that are available vary according to your system configuration, display devices, and printing devices. Font-related properties can be set only to values for which actual fonts exist.

Applies To

CheckBox, Column, ComboBox, CommandButton, EditBox, Form, Grid, Header, Label, ListBox, OptionButton, Page, _SCREEN, Spinner, TextBox

Note The FontBold property does not apply to the Page object.

See Also

FontName Property, FontSize Property, SetAll Method

FontCondense, FontExtend Properties

Available in Visual FoxPro for Macintosh only.

FONTMETRIC( ) Function

Returns font attributes for the current installed operating system fonts.

Syntax

FONTMETRIC(*nAttribute* [, *cFontName*, *nFontSize* [, *cFontStyle*]])

Returns

Numeric

Arguments

nAttribute
Determines the font attribute FONTMETRIC( ) returns. If you omit *cFontName*, *nFontSize*, and *cFontStyle*, FONTMETRIC( ) returns the attribute for the current font in the active output window.

The following table lists values for *nAttribute* and the corresponding font attributes returned.

nAttribute	Attribute
1	Character height in pixels
2	Character ascent (units above baseline) in pixels
3	Character descent (units below baseline) in pixels
4	Leading (space between lines) in pixels
5	Extra leading in pixels
6	Average character width in pixels
7	Maximum character width in pixels
8	Font weight.
9	Italic (0 = no, nonzero = yes)
10	Underlined (0 = no, nonzero = yes)
11	Strikeout (0 = no, nonzero = yes)
12	First character defined in font
13	Last character defined in font
14	Default character (substituted for characters not in font)
15	Word-break character
16	Pitch and family
17	Character set
18	Overhang (extra added width)
19	Horizontal aspect for font device
20	Vertical aspect for font device

For more information about the numeric values returned by FONTMETRIC( ), see the TEXTMETRIC function in the *Microsoft Windows Programmer's Reference*.

cFontName
Specifies the name of an installed font.

nFontSize
Specifies the point size of the font specified with *cFontName*.

cFontStyle
Specifies a font style code for the font specified with *cFontName*. If you omit *cFontStyle*, FONTMETRIC( ) returns the attribute for the Normal font style.

cFontStyle can be a character or a combination of characters listed in the following font style table. For example, the combination BI specifies the Bold Italic font style.

Character	Font style
B	Bold
I	Italic
N	Normal
O	Outline
Q	Opaque
S	Shadow
–	Strikeout
T	Transparent
U	Underline

Remarks

FONTMETRIC( ) returns font attributes for the current font for the active output window. WFONT( ) can be used to determine the current window font.

See Also

AFONT( ), Fonts Overview, GETFONT( ), SYSMETRIC( ), TXTWIDTH( ), WFONT( )

FontName Property

Specifies the name of the font used to display text. Available at design time and run time.

Syntax

Object.FontName[= *cName*]

Arguments

cName
    Specifies the name of the font. The default is Arial.

Remarks

The default FontSize property setting is 9 points. Available fonts vary according to your system configuration. Font-related properties can be set only to values for which fonts exist. At design time, a list of available fonts is displayed when you select the FontName property in the Properties window and click the down arrow to the right of the Property Settings box.

In general, change FontName before setting size and style attributes with the FontSize, FontBold, FontItalic, FontStrikethru, and FontUnderline properties.

Applies To

CheckBox, Column, ComboBox, CommandButton, EditBox, Form, Grid, Header, Label, ListBox, OptionButton, Page, _SCREEN, Spinner, TextBox

See Also

FontBold Property, FontItalic Property, FontStrikethru Property, FontUnderline Property, FontSize Property

FontOutline Property

Included for compatibility with the Macintosh.

FontShadow Property

Included for compatibility with the Macintosh.

FontSize Property

Specifies the font size for text displayed with an object. Available at design time and run time.

Syntax

Object.FontSize[= *nSize*]

Arguments

nSize
    Specifies the size of the font in points. The default font size is 9 points.

Remarks

The maximum value for *nSize* is 127 points. There are 72 points in 1 inch.

In general, you should change the FontName property before you set size and style attributes with the FontSize, FontBold, FontItalic, FontStrikethru, and FontUnderline properties. However, when you set TrueType fonts to smaller than 8 points, you should set the point size with the FontSize property, next set the FontName property, and then set the size again with the FontSize property. The Windows environment uses a different font for TrueType fonts that are smaller than 8 points.

> **Note** Available fonts vary according to your system configuration and printing devices. Font-related properties can be set only to values for which fonts exist.

Applies To

CheckBox, Column, ComboBox, CommandButton, EditBox, Form, Grid, Header, Label, ListBox, OptionButton, Page, _SCREEN, Spinner, TextBox

See Also

FontBold Property, FontItalic Property, FontStrikethru Property, FontUnderline Property

FOPEN( ) Function

Opens a file for use with low-level file functions.

Syntax

FOPEN(*cFileName* [, *nAttribute*])

Returns

Numeric

Arguments

cFileName

Specifies the name of the file to open. *cFileName* can include a path to open files in directories, folders, drives, or volumes not in the current Microsoft Visual FoxPro search path. If a path isn't included, Visual FoxPro searches for the file in the following locations:

- Default directory

- Path established with SET PATH

    Note Visual FoxPro will not recognize a path name properly if a disk or directory name contains an exclamation point (!).

nAttribute

Specifies read/write privileges or a buffering scheme for the file you open. The following table lists each number you can include in *nAttribute*, and the read/write file privileges and buffering scheme it establishes.

nAttribute	Read/Write privileges	Buffered/unbuffered
0	(Default) Read-Only	Buffered
1	Write-Only	Buffered
2	Read and Write	Buffered
10	Read-Only	Unbuffered
11	Write-Only	Unbuffered
12	Read and Write	Unbuffered

If *nAttribute* isn't included, or if *nAttribute* evaluates to 0, the file is opened as read-only and is buffered.

Note Visual FoxPro will not recognize a path name properly if a disk or directory name contains an exclamation point (!).

Remarks

If FOPEN( ) successfully opens the file, the file handle number of the file is returned. FOPEN( ) returns –1 if the file cannot be opened.

Tip Assign the file handle number to a memory variable so you can access the file by the memory variable in other low-level file functions.

The following information about files opened with FOPEN( ) can be displayed or sent to a printer with DISPLAY STATUS or LIST STATUS.

- Drive and directory or volume and folder, and file name

- File handle number

- File pointer position

- Read/write attributes

Example

```
IF FILE('errors.txt')  && Does file exist?
   gnErrFile = FOPEN('errors.txt',12)  && If so, open read-write
ELSE
   gnErrFile = FCREATE('errors.txt')  && If not, create it
ENDIF
IF gnErrFile < 0  && Check for error opening file
   WAIT 'Cannot open or create output file' WINDOW NOWAIT
ELSE  && If no error, write to file
   =FWRITE(gnErrFile, 'Error information to be written here')
ENDIF
=FCLOSE(gnErrFile)  && Close file
MODIFY FILE errors.txt NOWAIT  && Open file in edit window
```

See Also

CLOSE ALL, FCHSIZE( ), FCLOSE( ), FCREATE( ), FEOF( ), FFLUSH( ), FGETS( ), FPUTS( ), FREAD( ), FSEEK( ), FWRITE( )

FOR ... ENDFOR Command

Executes a set of commands a specified number of times.

Syntax

FOR *Var* = *nInitialValue* TO *nFinalValue* [STEP *nIncrement*]
   Commands
   [EXIT]
   [LOOP]
ENDFOR | NEXT

Arguments

Var

   Specifies a variable or an array element that acts as the counter. The variable or array element doesn't have to exist before FOR ... ENDFOR is executed.

nInitialValue TO *nFinalValue*

   nInitialValue is the initial value of the counter; *nFinalValue* is the final value of the counter.

STEP *nIncrement*

   nIncrement is the amount the counter is incremented or decremented. If *nIncrement* is negative, the counter is decremented. If you omit STEP, the counter is incremented by 1.

Commands

   Specifies the Visual FoxPro commands to be executed. *Commands* can include any number of commands.

EXIT

   Transfers control from within the FOR ... ENDFOR loop to the command immediately following ENDFOR. You can place EXIT anywhere between FOR and ENDFOR.

LOOP

   Returns control directly back to the FOR clause without executing the statements between LOOP and ENDFOR. The counter is incremented or decremented as if ENDFOR were reached. LOOP can be placed anywhere between FOR and ENDFOR.

Remarks

A variable or an array element is used as a counter to specify how many times the Visual FoxPro commands inside the FOR ... ENDFOR loop are executed.

The Visual FoxPro commands after FOR are executed until ENDFOR or NEXT is reached. The counter *MemVarName* is then incremented by the value of *nIncrement*. If you omit the STEP clause, the counter is incremented by 1. The counter is then compared with *nFinalValue*. If the counter is less than or equal to *nFinalValue*, the commands following the FOR clause are executed again. If the counter is greater than *nFinalValue*, the FOR ... ENDFOR loop is exited and program execution continues with the first command following ENDFOR or NEXT.

Note The values of *nInitialValue*, *nFinalValue*, and *nIncrement* are only read initially. However, changing the value of the counter *MemVarName* inside the loop affects the number of times the loop is executed.

If the value of *nIncrement* is negative and the initial value *nInitialValue* is greater than the final value *nFinalValue*, the counter is decremented each time through the loop.

Examples

In Example 1, the numbers 1 through 10 are displayed.

Example 2 uses memory variables for the initial, final, and STEP values to display all even-numbered records from 2 through 10 in `customer`.

```
* Example 1
CLEAR
FOR gnCount = 1 TO 10
   ? gnCount
ENDFOR

* Example 2
SET TALK OFF
CLOSE DATABASES
OPEN DATABASE (HOME(2) + 'Data\testdata')
USE customer  && Opens Customer table
STORE 2 TO gnI  && Initial value
STORE 10 TO gnJ  && Final value
STORE 2 TO K  && Step value
FOR gnCount = gnI TO gnJ STEP K
   GOTO gnCount  && Move record pointer
   DISPLAY company && Display company name
ENDFOR
```

See Also

DO CASE ... ENDCASE, DO WHILE ... ENDDO, IF ... ENDIF, SCAN ... ENDSCAN

FOR EACH ... ENDFOR Command

Executes a set of commands for each element in a Visual FoxPro array or collection.

Syntax

FOR EACH *Var* IN *Group*
    Commands
    [EXIT]
    [LOOP]
ENDFOR | NEXT [*Var*]

Arguments

Var

A variable or array element used to iterate through the elements of *Group*.

Group

A Visual FoxPro array, an OLE array, a Visual FoxPro collection, or an OLE collection.

Commands

Specifies the Visual FoxPro commands to be executed for each element in *Group*. *Commands* can include any number of commands.

EXIT

Transfers control from within the FOR EACH ... ENDFOR loop to the command immediately following ENDFOR. You can place EXIT anywhere between FOR EACH and ENDFOR.

LOOP

Returns control directly back to the FOR EACH clause without executing the statements between LOOP and ENDFOR. LOOP can be placed anywhere between FOR EACH and ENDFOR.

Examples

The following examples demonstrate how FOR EACH is used to enumerate elements in a Visual FoxPro array, an OLE array, and a set command buttons assigned to an object array.

In the following example, a Visual FoxPro variable array is created and FOR EACH is used to display the contents of each element in the array.

```
DIMENSION cMyArray(3)
cMyArray[1] = 'A'
cMyArray[2] = 'B'
cMyArray[3] = 'C'
```

```
FOR EACH cMyVar IN cMyArray
   ? cMyVar
ENDFOR
```

In the following example, an instance of Microsoft Excel is created, and a new workbook is added. FOR EACH is used to display the name of each worksheet in the workbook. This example requires that Microsoft Excel be properly installed on the machine on which the example is run.

```
oExcel = CREATE("Excel.Application")
oExcel.Workbooks.ADD

FOR EACH oMyVar IN oExcel.sheets
   ? oMyVar.name
NEXT oMyVar
```

In the following example, five command buttons are placed on a form. FOR EACH is used to display the buttons on the form and specify the captions, font styles and positions of each button.

```
PUBLIC oMyObject
oMyObject = CREATEOBJECT("frmTest")
oMyObject.SHOW

DEFINE CLASS frmTest AS FORM
Height = 200
DIMENSION MyArray[5]
   PROCEDURE Init

      FOR i = 1 to 5
         THIS.AddObject('THIS.MyArray[i]',;
            'COMMANDBUTTON')
      ENDFOR

      ****** FOR EACH - NEXT ******
      FOR EACH oButton IN THIS.MyArray
         oButton.Visible = .T.
      NEXT

      ****** FOR EACH - NEXT element  ******
      FOR EACH oButton IN THIS.MyArray
         oButton.FontBold = .T.
      NEXT obutton

      j = 1
      ****** FOR EACH - ENDFOR ******
      FOR EACH oButton IN THIS.MyArray
         oButton.top = j * 30
         j = j + 1
      ENDFOR
```

```
        ****** FOR EACH - ENDFOR element ******
        FOR EACH oButton IN THIS.MyArray
           oButton.FontItalic = .T.
        ENDFOR obutton

        j = 1
        ****** EXIT  ******
        FOR EACH oButton IN THIS.MyArray
           oButton.Caption = "test" + str(j)
           j = j+1
           IF j > 3
              EXIT
           ENDIF
        NEXT

        j = 1
        ****** LOOP  ******
        FOR EACH oButton IN THIS.MyArray
           IF j > 3
              LOOP
           ENDIF
           j = j + 1
           oButton.Left = 25
        NEXT
     ENDPROC
ENDDEFINE
```

See Also

FOR ... ENDFOR

FOR( ) Function

Returns the index filter expression of an open single-entry index (.idx) file or an index tag.

Syntax

FOR([*nIndexNumber* [, *nWorkArea* | *cTableAlias*]])

Returns

Character

Arguments

If you don't include any of the optional arguments, FOR( ) returns the index filter expression for the master index file or index tag. If a master index file or index tag isn't in effect (for example, you've issued SET ORDER TO to place the table in physical record order), FOR( ) returns the empty string.

nIndexNumber

Specifies the index file or tag for which the filter expression is returned. FOR( ) returns filter expressions in the following order as *nIndexNumber* increases from 1 to the total number of open single-entry files and structural compound and independent compound index tags:

1. Filter expressions from single-entry index files (if any are open) are returned first. The order the single-entry index files are included in USE or SET INDEX determines the order in which the filter expressions are returned.

2. Filter expressions for each tag in the structural compound index (if one is present) are returned next. The filter expressions are returned from the tags in the order the tags are created in the structural index.

3. Filter expressions for each tag in any open independent compound indexes are returned last. The filter expressions are returned from the tags in the order in which the tags are created in the independent compound indexes.

The empty string is returned if an index or index tag is created without a FOR clause or if *nIndexNumber* is greater than the total number of open single-entry files and structural compound and independent compound index tags.

nWorkArea

Specifies the work area of the table for which FOR( ) returns the index filter expressions.

FOR( ) returns the empty string if a table isn't open in the work area you specify.

cTableAlias

Specifies the alias of the table for which FOR( ) returns the index filter expressions.

Visual FoxPro generates an error message if you specify a table alias that doesn't exist.

Remarks

You can create filtered indexes in Visual FoxPro. If you include the optional FOR *lExpression* clause in INDEX, the index file acts as a filter on the table. Only records that match the filter expression *lExpression* are available for display and access. Index keys are created in the index file for just those records matching the filter expression.

USE and SET INDEX both support an index file name list that lets you open multiple index files for a table. Any combination of single-entry index file names, structural compound, or independent compound index file names can be included in the index file name list. FOR( ) is identical to SYS(2021) and is provided for compatibility with dBASE IV.

See Also

INDEX

FORCEEXT( ) Function

Returns a string with the old file name extension replaced by a new extension.

Syntax

FORCEEXT(*cFileName, cExtension*)

Returns

Character

Arguments

cFileName
Specifies the file name (with or without a path or extension) which will get a new extension.

cExtension
Specifies the new extension (without a period) for *cFileName*.

See Also

ADDBS( ), DEFAULTEXT( ), FILE( ), FORCEPATH( ), JUSTDRIVE( ), JUSTEXT( ), JUSTFNAME( ), JUSTPATH( ), JUSTSTEM( )

FORCEPATH( ) Function

Returns a file name with a new path name substituted for the old one.

Syntax

FORCEPATH(*cFileName, cPath*)

Returns

Character

Arguments

cFileName
Specifies the file name (with or without a path or extension) which will get a new path.

cPath
Specifies the new path for *cFileName*.

See Also

ADDBS( ), DEFAULTEXT( ), FILE( ), FORCEEXT( ), JUSTDRIVE( ), JUSTEXT( ), JUSTFNAME( ), JUSTPATH( ), JUSTSTEM( )

Form Object

Creates a form.

Syntax

Form

Remarks

Use the Form object to create a form to which you can add controls. You can also use the Form Designer. Forms have properties that determine their appearance, such as position, size, and color, as well as aspects of their behavior, such as whether they are sizable.

Forms can also respond to events initiated by a user or triggered by the system. For example, you can write code in a form's Click event procedure that changes the color of the form when you click it.

In addition to properties and events, you can use methods to manipulate Forms. For example, you can use the Move method to change a form's location and size.

When designing Forms, use the BorderStyle property to specify a form's border, and the Caption property to specify the text in the title bar. Setting BorderStyle to 0 removes the border. From within a program, you can use the Hide and Show methods to make Forms transparent or visible at run time.

For additional information about creating Forms, see Chapter 9, "Creating Forms," in the *Microsoft Visual FoxPro 6.0 Programmer's Guide*.

Properties

ActiveControl	ActiveForm	AlwaysOnTop
Application	AutoCenter	BackColor
BaseClass	BorderStyle	BufferMode
Caption	Class	ClassLibrary
ClipControls	Closable	ColorSource
Comment	ContinuousScroll Property	ControlBox
ControlCount	Controls	CurrentX
CurrentY	DataEnvironment	DataSession
DataSessionID	DefOLELCID Property	Desktop
DrawMode	DrawStyle	DrawWidth
Enabled	FillColor	FillStyle
FontBold	FontCondense	FontExtend

FontItalic	FontName	FontOutline
FontShadow	FontSize	FontStrikeThru
FontUnderline	ForeColor	HalfHeightCaption
Height	HelpContextID	HscrollSmallChange Property
Icon	KeyPreview	Left
LockScreen	MaxButton	MaxHeight
MaxLeft	MaxTop	MaxWidth
MDIForm	MinButton	MinHeight
MinWidth	MouseIcon	MousePointer
Movable	Name	Objects
OLEDragMode	OLEDragPicture	OLEDropEffects
OLEDropHasData Property	OLEDropMode	Parent
ParentClass	Picture	ReleaseType
RightToLeft	ScaleMode	ScrollBars
ShowTips	ShowWindow	SizeBox
TabIndex	TabStop	Tag
TitleBar Property	Top	ViewPortHeight Property
ViewPortLeft Property	ViewPortTop Property	ViewPortWidth Property
Visible	VscrollSmallChange Property	WhatsThisButton
WhatsThisHelp	WhatsThisHelpID	Width
WindowState	WindowType	ZoomBox

Events

Activate	Click	DblClick
Deactivate	Destroy	DragDrop
DragOver	Error	GotFocus
Init	KeyPress	Load
LostFocus	MiddleClick Event	MouseDown
MouseMove	MouseUp	MouseWheel
Moved	OLECompleteDrag	OLEDragDrop
OLEDragOver	OLEGiveFeedBack	OLESetData

OLEStartDrag	Paint	QueryUnload
Resize	RightClick	Scrolled
Unload		

Methods

AddObject	AddProperty	Box
Circle	Cls	Draw
Hide	Line	Move
NewObject	OLEDrag	Point
Print	PSet	ReadExpression
ReadMethod	Refresh	Release
RemoveObject	ResetToDefault	SaveAs
SaveAsClass	SetAll	SetViewPort
Show	ShowWhatsThis	TextHeight
TextWidth	WhatsThisMode	WriteExpression
WriteMethod	ZOrder	

See Also

CREATE CLASS, CREATE FORM, DEFINE CLASS, FormSet Object

Format Property

Specifies the input and output formatting of a control's Value property. Available at design time and run time.

Syntax

Control.Format[= *cFunction*]

Arguments

cFunction

Specifies the character constraints for data entry and formatting for display.

The valid *cFunction* settings for an EditBox control are:

Setting	Description
K	Selects all the text when the control gets the focus.

The valid *cFunction* settings for a Spinner control are:

Setting	Description
$	Displays the currency symbol.
^	Displays numeric data using scientific notation.
K	Selects all the text when the control gets the focus.
L	Displays leading zeros (instead of spaces) in the text box.
R	Displays the format mask for the text box that is specified in the InputMask property. The mask formats data for easier entry and clearer display (for example, if the mask is 99–999, the number 12345 is displayed as 12–345), but is not stored as part of the data. Use only with character or numeric data.
Z	Displays the value as blank if it is 0, except when the control has the focus.

The valid *cFunction* settings for a TextBox control and Column object are:

Setting	Description
!	Converts alphabetic characters to uppercase. Use with Character data only.
$	Displays the currency symbol. The ControlSource property must specify a numeric source for the text box.
^	Displays numeric data using scientific notation. The ControlSource property must specify a numeric source for the text box.
A	Allows alphabetic characters only (no spaces or punctuation marks).
D	Uses the current SET DATE format.
E	Edits Date values as British dates.
K	Selects all the text when the control gets the focus.
L	Displays leading zeros (instead of spaces) in the text box. The ControlSource property must specify a numeric source for the text box.
M	Included for backward compatibility.
R	Displays the format mask for the text box that is specified in the InputMask property. The mask formats data for easier entry and clearer display (for example, if the mask is 99–999, the number 12345 is displayed as 12–345), but is not stored as part of the data. Use only with character or numeric data.
T	Trims leading and trailing blanks from the input field.
YS	Displays Date values in a short date format determined by the Windows Control Panel short date setting.
YL	Displays Date values in a long date format determined by the Windows Control Panel long date setting.

Remarks

The Format property mimics the behavior of the FUNCTION clause for the @ ... GET and @ ... EDIT commands.

The Format property specifies a behavior for the entire input field. You can mix several Format codes, but they always affect everything in the input field. This property contrasts to the InputMask property in which each entry in the input mask corresponds to an entry in the input field.

Applies To

Column, ComboBox, EditBox, Spinner, TextBox

See Also

DynamicInputMask Property, InputMask Property

FormCount Property

Contains the number of forms in a form set. Not available at design time; read-only at run time.

Syntax

Object.FormCount

Remarks

You can use this property to cycle through all the forms in a form set and do some action.

Applies To

FormSet, _SCREEN

See Also

Forms Property

Forms Property

An array to access individual forms in a form set. Not available at design time; read-only at run time.

Syntax

Object.Forms(*nIndex*)

Arguments

nIndex
Uniquely identifies a form in a form set.

Remarks

Use the Forms property to change the property settings of forms in a form set without using the Name property of the forms. You can use the Forms property in conjunction with the FormCount property to step through all the forms in a form set and perform an action. For example, the following code changes the captions of all the forms in a form set:

```
FOR x = 1 TO THISFORMSET.FormCount
   THISFORMSET.Forms(x).Caption = THISFORMSET.Forms(x).Caption;
      + "[Read Only]"
ENDFOR
```

Applies To

FormSet, _SCREEN

See Also

FormCount Property

FormSet Object

Creates a form set.

Syntax

FormSet

Remarks

A form set is a container object that contains a set of forms. Form sets are similar to screen sets used in previous FoxPro versions.

For additional information about creating form sets, see "Creating a New Form Set" in Chapter 9, "Creating Forms," in the *Microsoft Visual FoxPro 6.0 Programmer's Guide*.

Properties

ActiveForm	Application	AutoRelease
BaseClass	Buffermode	Class
ClassLibrary	Comment	DataEnvironment
DataSession	DataSessionID	FormCount
Forms	Name	Parent
ParentClass	ReadBackColor	ReadCycle
ReadForeColor	ReadLock	ReadMouse
ReadSave	ReadTimeOut	Tag
Visible	WindowList	WindowType

Events

Activate	Deactivate	Destroy
Error	Init	Load
ReadActivate	ReadDeactivate	ReadShow
ReadValid	ReadWhen	Unload

Methods

AddObject	AddProperty	Hide
NewObject	ReadExpression	ReadMethod
Refresh	Release	RemoveObject
ResetToDefault	SaveAs	SaveAsClass
SetAll	Show	WriteExpression
WriteMethod		

See Also

CREATE CLASS, CREATE FORM, DEFINE CLASS, Form Object

FOUND( ) Function

Returns true (.T.) if CONTINUE, FIND, INDEXSEEK( ), LOCATE, or SEEK is successful.

Syntax

FOUND([*nWorkArea* | *cTableAlias*])

Returns

Logical

Arguments

nWorkArea

Specifies the work area of the table for which FOUND( ) returns a value indicating the success of the last CONTINUE, FIND, INDEXSEEK( ), LOCATE, or SEEK.

FOUND( ) returns false (.F.) if a table isn't open in the work area you specify.

cTableAlias

Specifies the alias of the table for which FOUND( ) returns a value indicating the success of the last CONTINUE, FIND, INDEXSEEK( ), LOCATE, or SEEK.

Visual FoxPro generates an error message if you specify a table alias that doesn't exist.

Remarks

FOUND( ) returns a logical value that indicates whether the most recently executed CONTINUE, FIND, INDEXSEEK( ), LOCATE, or SEEK was successful, or if the record pointer was moved in a related table. FOUND( ) returns true (.T.) if the search is successful; otherwise FOUND( ) returns false (.F.).

If you omit the optional arguments, FOUND( ) returns a value indicating the success of the last CONTINUE, FIND, INDEXSEEK( ), LOCATE, or SEEK for the table open in the currently selected work area.

Tip This function can be used to determine if a child table has a record that matches the parent record.

Example

In the following example, all customers from Germany are counted.

```
SET TALK OFF
CLOSE DATABASES
OPEN DATABASE (HOME(2) + 'Data\testdata')
USE customer  && Opens Customer table

STORE 0 TO gnCount
LOCATE FOR UPPER(country) = 'GERMANY'
DO WHILE FOUND( )
   gnCount = gnCount + 1
   CONTINUE
ENDDO
WAIT WINDOW 'Total customers from Germany: ' ;
   + LTRIM(STR(gnCount)) NOWAIT
```

See Also

CONTINUE, EOF( ), FIND, INDEXSEEK( ), LOCATE, SEEK

_FOXDOC System Variable

Included for backward compatibility. Use the Documenting Wizard instead.

FPUTS( ) Function

Writes a character string, carriage return, and line feed to a file opened with a low-level file function.

Syntax

FPUTS(*nFileHandle*, *cExpression* [, *nCharactersWritten*])

Returns

Numeric

Arguments

nFileHandle
> Specifies the file handle number for the file to which FPUTS( ) writes data.

cExpression
> Specifies the character expression that FPUTS( ) writes to the file.

nCharactersWritten
> Specifies the number of characters in *cExpression* to write to the file.

> FPUTS( ) writes the entire character expression *cExpression* to the file if you omit *nCharactersWritten*. If you include *nCharactersWritten*, *nCharactersWritten* characters are written to the file. If *nCharactersWritten* is less than the number of characters in *cExpression*, only *nCharactersWritten* characters are written to the file. All of *cExpression* is written to the file if *nCharactersWritten* is equal to or greater than the number of characters in *cExpression*.

Remarks

FPUTS( ) returns the number of bytes written to the file. Zero is returned if FPUTS( ) can't write to the file for any reason.

See Also

FCHSIZE( ), FCLOSE( ), FCREATE( ), FEOF( ), FFLUSH( ), FGETS( ), FOPEN( ), FREAD( ), FSEEK( ), FWRITE( )

FREAD( ) Function

Returns a specified number of bytes from a file opened with a low-level function.

Syntax

FREAD(*nFileHandle*, *nBytes*)

Returns

Character

Arguments

nFileHandle
> Specifies the file handle number for the file from which FREAD( ) returns data.

nBytes
> Specifies the number of bytes returned by FREAD( ). FREAD( ) returns data starting from the current file pointer position and continues until it returns *nBytes* bytes or until it encounters the end of the file.

Example

The following example uses FREAD( ) to display the contents of a file. If the file is empty, a message is displayed.

```
* TEST.TXT must exist -- you can create this file
* using Notepad.

Local gnFileHandle,nSize,cString
gnFileHandle = FOPEN("test.txt")
* Seek to end of file to determine the number of bytes in the file
nSize = FSEEK(gnFileHandle, 0, 2)        && Move pointer to EOF
IF nSize <= 0
   * If the file is empty, display an error message
   WAIT WINDOW "This file is empty!" NOWAIT
ELSE
   * If file is not empty, the program stores its contents
   * in memory, then displays the text on the main Visual FoxPro window
   = FSEEK(ggnFileHandle, 0, 0)        && Move pointer to BOF
   cString = FREAD(gnFileHandle, nSize)
   ? cString
ENDIF
= FCLOSE(gnFileHandle)           && Close the file
```

See Also

FCHSIZE( ), FCLOSE( ), FCREATE( ), FEOF( ), FFLUSH( ), FGETS( ), FILETOSTR( ), FOPEN( ), FPUTS( ), FSEEK( ), FWRITE( )

FREE TABLE Command

Removes a database reference from a table.

Syntax

FREE TABLE *TableName*

Arguments

TableName
    Specifies the name of the table from which the database reference is removed.

Remarks

If a database is accidentally deleted from disk, references to the database remain in the tables formerly contained in the database. FREE TABLE removes the database references from a table, allowing you to open the table or add the table to a different database.

Note FREE TABLE should never be issued to remove a table from a database if the database exists on disk. If the database exists on disk, FREE TABLE may render the database unusable. Use REMOVE TABLE instead. Unlike FREE TABLE, REMOVE TABLE removes all references from the database to primary indexes, default values, and validation rules associated with the table.

See Also

ADD TABLE, CREATE DATABASE, OPEN DATABASE, REMOVE TABLE

FSEEK( ) Function

Moves the file pointer in a file opened with a low-level file function.

Syntax

FSEEK(*nFileHandle*, *nBytesMoved* [, *nRelativePosition*])

Returns

Numeric

Arguments

nFileHandle

Specifies the file handle for the file in which FSEEK( ) moves the file pointer. A file handle number is returned by FCREATE( ) or FOPEN( ) when the file is created or opened.

nBytesMoved

Specifies the number of bytes to move the file pointer. The file pointer is moved toward the end of the file if *nBytesMoved* is positive. The file pointer is moved toward the beginning of the file if *nBytesMoved* is negative.

nRelativePosition

Moves the file pointer to a relative position in the file. By default, the file pointer is moved relative to the beginning of the file. You can also move the file pointer relative to the current file pointer or the end of the file by including *nRelativePosition*. The following table lists values for *nRelativePosition* and from where the file pointer is moved.

nRelativePosition	Moves the file pointer relative to
0	(Default) The beginning of the file.
1	The current file pointer position.
2	The end of the file.

Remarks

After moving the file pointer, FSEEK( ) returns the number of bytes the file pointer is positioned from the beginning of the file. The file pointer can also be moved with FREAD( ) and FWRITE( ).

Example

The following user-defined function uses FSEEK( ) to return the size of a file. If you don't pass parameters to the user-defined function, it returns –2. If the file cannot be found, the user-defined function returns –1.

```
FUNCTION fsize2
PARAMETERS gcFileName  && File to be checked
PRIVATE pnHandle,pnSize
IF PARAMETERS( ) = 0
   RETURN -2  && Return -2 if no parameter passed
ELSE
   IF !FILE(gcFileName)
      RETURN -1  && Return -1 if file does not exist
   ENDIF
ENDIF
pnHandle = FOPEN(gcFileName)   && Open file
pnSize = FSEEK(pnHandle,0,2)    && Determine file size, assign to pnSize
=FCLOSE(pnHandle)  && Close file
RETURN pnSize  && Return value
```

See Also

FCHSIZE( ), FCLOSE( ), FCREATE( ), FEOF( ), FFLUSH( ), FGETS( ), FOPEN( ), FPUTS( ), FREAD( ), FWRITE( )

FSIZE( ) Function

Returns the size in bytes of a specified field or file.

Syntax

FSIZE(*cFieldName* [, *nWorkArea* | *cTableAlias*] | *cFileName*)

Returns

Numeric

Arguments

cFieldName
 Specifies the name of the field.

nWorkArea
 Specifies the work area of the table for which FSIZE( ) returns a field size.

 FSIZE( ) returns 0 if a table isn't open in the work area you specify.

cTableAlias

Specifies the alias of the table for which FSIZE( ) returns a field size.

Visual FoxPro generates an error message if you specify a table alias that doesn't exist.

cFileName

Specifies a file for which FSIZE( ) returns the size in bytes.

Remarks

The current setting of SET COMPATIBLE determines if FSIZE( ) returns the size of a field or a file. If SET COMPATIBLE is set to OFF or FOXPLUS (the default), FSIZE( ) returns the size of a field. If SET COMPATIBLE is set to ON or DB4, FSIZE( ) returns the size of a file.

The following table shows the default size (in bytes) for each fixed-length field type.

Field type	Default field size(in bytes)
Currency	8
Date	8
DateTime	8
Double	8
Integer	4
Logical	1
Memo	4
General	4

The size of a field can be displayed with DISPLAY STRUCTURE and LIST STRUCTURE.

If you omit the optional *nWorkArea* and *cTableAlias* arguments, FSIZE( ) returns the field size for a field in the current table and work area.

Example

The following example uses FSIZE( ) to return the size of two fields in the customer table.

```
SET COMPATIBLE OFF
CLOSE DATABASES
OPEN DATABASE (HOME(2) + 'Data\testdata')
USE customer  && Open Customer table

CLEAR
? FSIZE('contact')  && Displays 30
? FSIZE('cust_id')  && Displays 6
```

See Also

DISPLAY STRUCTURE, FCOUNT( ), LIST

FTIME( ) Function

Returns the last modification time for a file.

Syntax

FTIME(*cFileName*)

Returns

Character

Arguments

cFileName

Specifies the name of the file whose last modification time FTIME( ) returns. *cFileName* can include a path with the file name. If a path is not included with the file name, Visual FoxPro searches for the file in the default directory and in any directories or folders specified with SET PATH.

Remarks

The time that FTIME( ) returns is assigned to the file by the operating system.

Example

The following example uses FTIME( ) to display the last modification time for FOXUSER.DBF, the Visual FoxPro resource file.

```
? FTIME('FOXUSER.DBF')  && Displays the last modification time
```

See Also

FDATE( ), LUPDATE( )

FullName Property

Contains the file name of an instance of Visual FoxPro and the name of the directory from which the instance of Visual FoxPro was started. Read-only at run time.

Syntax

ApplicationObject.FullName

Remarks

Use the FullName property to determine the directory from which an instance of Visual FoxPro was started.

Applies To

Application Object, _VFP System Variable

See Also

HOME( )

FULLPATH( ) Function

Returns the path to a specified file or the path relative to another file.

Syntax

FULLPATH(*cFileName1* [, *nMSDOSPath* | *cFileName2*])

Returns

Character

Arguments

cFileName1

Specifies the file for which Visual FoxPro searches. Be sure to include the file name extension.

If the file is located in the Visual FoxPro path, the path is returned with the file name. The Visual FoxPro path can be specified with SET PATH.

nMSDOSPath

Specifies that the MS-DOS path is searched instead of the Visual FoxPro path. *nMSDOSPath* can have any numeric value. If the file can't be located in the MS-DOS path, a path and the file name are returned as if the file had been found in the current default directory.

cFileName2

Specifies a second file name to search for. Be sure to include the file name extension. FULLPATH( ) returns the path for the first file relative to the second file.

See Also

DBF( ), FILE( ), LOCFILE( ), SYS(2014) – Minimum Path

FUNCTION Command

Identifies the start of a definition for a user-defined function.

Syntax

FUNCTION *FunctionName*
    Commands
    [RETURN [*eExpression*]]
ENDFUNC

Arguments

FunctionName

In Visual FoxPro, function names can be up to 254 characters long.

To distinguish a program file name with more than 10 characters from a function beginning with the same 10 characters in these two products, surround the program file name with quotation marks or include an extension after the program file name.

Remarks

In many programs, certain routines are frequently repeated. Defining commonly used routines as separate functions reduces program size and complexity and facilitates program maintenance.

FUNCTION *FunctionName* is a statement within a program. It designates the beginning of a function in a program and identifies the function by name.

FUNCTION *FunctionName* is followed by a series of Visual FoxPro commands that make up the function. You can include RETURN anywhere in the function to return control to the calling program or to another program, and to define a value returned by the user-defined function. If you do not include a RETURN command, an implicit RETURN is automatically executed when the function quits. If the RETURN command does not include a return value (or if an implicit RETURN is executed), Visual FoxPro assigns .T. (True) as the return value.

The function ends with the ENDFUNC command. This command is optional; the function quits when it encounters another FUNCTION command, a PROCEDURE command, or the end of the program file.

Comments can be placed on the same line after FUNCTION and ENDFUNC. These comments are ignored during compilation and program execution.

You cannot have normal executable program code included in a program file after user-defined functions; only user-defined functions, procedures, and class definitions can follow the first FUNCTION or PROCEDURE command in the file.

When you issue DO with a function name, Visual FoxPro searches for the function in a specific order as follows:

1. Visual FoxPro searches the file containing the DO command.

2. If the function isn't found there, Visual FoxPro searches the open procedure files. Procedure files are opened with SET PROCEDURE.

3. If the function isn't found in an open procedure file, Visual FoxPro searches the programs in the execution chain. Program files are searched from the most recently executed program through the first program executed.

4. If the function is still not found, Visual FoxPro searches for a stand-alone program. If a matching program file is found, the program is executed. Otherwise, Visual FoxPro generates an error message.

Include the IN clause in DO to execute a function in a specific file.

By default, parameters are passed to functions by value. For information on passing parameters to functions by reference, see the SET UDFPARMS Command, later in this language reference. A maximum of 27 parameters can be passed to a function. Parameters can be passed to a function by including a PARAMETERS or LPARAMETERS statement in the function, or by placing a list of parameters immediately after FUNCTION *FunctionName*. Enclose the list of parameters in a set of parentheses, and separate the parameters with commas.

Example

This example creates a custom object class called Hello and adds a function method called SayHello. The SayHello method returns the character string "Hello World" which is displayed by the MESSAGEBOX function. Note: The class definition code is placed after the program code that instantiates the object.

```
Local oHello
oHello=CREATEOBJECT("Hello")
=MESSAGEBOX(oHello.SayHello(),48)
RELEASE oHello

* Class definition code
DEFINE CLASS Hello AS CUSTOM
    FUNCTION SayHello
        RETURN "Hello World"
    ENDFUNC
ENDDEFINE
```

See Also

LPARAMETERS, PARAMETERS, PARAMETERS( ), PRIVATE, PROCEDURE, PUBLIC, RETURN, SET PROCEDURE, SET UDFPARMS

FV( ) Function

Returns the future value of a financial investment.

Syntax

FV(*nPayment*, *nInterestRate*, *nPeriods*)

Returns

Numeric

Arguments

nPayment
> Specifies the constant periodic payment (which can be negative or positive).

nInterestRate
> Specifies the periodic interest rate. If the interest rate is annual but the payments are made monthly, divide the annual interest rate by 12.

nPeriods
> Specifies the number of periods over which payments are made. FV( ) assumes that the periodic payments are made at the end of each period.

Remarks

FV( ) computes the future value of a series of constant periodic payments earning fixed compound interest. The future value is the total of all payments and the interest.

Example

```
STORE 500 TO gnPayment  && Monthly payment
STORE .075/12 TO gnInterest    && 7.5% annual interest rate
STORE 48 TO gnPeriods  && Four years (48 months)

CLEAR
? FV(gnPayment, gnInterest, gnPeriods)    && Displays 27887.93
```

See Also

CALCULATE, PV( )

FWRITE( ) Function

Writes a character string to a file opened with a low-level file function.

Syntax

FWRITE(*nFileHandle*, *cExpression* [, *nCharactersWritten*])

Returns

Numeric

Arguments

nFileHandle
> Specifies the file handle number for the file to which FWRITE( ) writes.

cExpression

Specifies the character expression that FWRITE( ) writes to the file specified with *nFileHandle*.

nCharactersWritten

FWRITE( ) writes the entire character expression to the file unless you include *nCharactersWritten*. When you include *nCharactersWritten*, *nCharactersWritten* characters are written to the file. If *nCharactersWritten* is less than the number of characters in *cExpression*, only *nCharactersWritten* characters are written to the file. All of the characters in *cExpression* are written to the file if *nCharactersWritten* is equal to or greater than the number of characters in *cExpression*.

Remarks

Unlike FPUTS( ), FWRITE( ) doesn't place a carriage return and a line feed at the end of the character string.

FWRITE( ) returns the number of bytes written to the file. If FWRITE( ) can't write to the file for any reason, 0 is returned.

See Also

FCHSIZE( ), FCLOSE( ), FCREATE( ), FEOF( ), FFLUSH( ), FGETS( ), FOPEN( ), FPUTS( ), FREAD( ), FSEEK( ), STRTOFILE( )

_GALLERY System Variable

Specifies the program that is executed when you choose Component Gallery from the Tools menu.

Syntax

_GALLERY = *ProgramName*

Arguments

ProgramName

Specifies a program. If your program is in a directory other than the current default directory, include a path with the program name.

Remarks

_GALLERY contains GALLERY.APP by default. For more information about the Component Gallery, see "Component Gallery" in Chapter 32, "Application Development and Developer Productivity," in the *Microsoft Visual FoxPro 6.0 Programmer's Guide*.

GATHER Command

Replaces the data in the current record of the currently selected table with data from an array, a set of variables, or an object.

Syntax

GATHER FROM *ArrayName* | MEMVAR | NAME *ObjectName*
    [FIELDS *FieldList* | FIELDS LIKE *Skeleton* | FIELDS EXCEPT *Skeleton*]
    [MEMO]

Arguments

FROM *ArrayName*

Specifies the array whose data replaces the data in the current record. The contents of the elements of the array, starting with the first element, replace the contents of the corresponding fields of the record. The contents of the first array element replace the first field of the record; the contents of the second array element replace the second field, and so on.

If the array has fewer elements than the table has fields, the additional fields are ignored. If the array has more elements than the table has fields, the additional array elements are ignored.

MEMVAR

Specifies the variables or array from which data is copied to the current record. Data is transferred from the variable to the field that has the same name as the variable. The contents of a field are not replaced if a variable doesn't exist with the same name as the field.

    Tip You can create variables with the same names as fields by including MEMVAR or BLANK in SCATTER.

NAME *ObjectName*

Specifies an object whose properties have the same names as fields in the table. The contents of each field are replaced by the value of the property with the same names as the fields. The contents of a field are not replaced if a property doesn't exist with the same name as the field.

FIELDS *FieldList*

Specifies the fields whose contents are replaced by the contents of the array elements or variables. Only the field specified with *FieldList* has its contents replaced.

FIELDS LIKE *Skeleton* | FIELDS EXCEPT *Skeleton*

You can selectively replace fields with the contents of array elements or variables by including the LIKE or EXCEPT clause or both. If you include LIKE *Skeleton*, Visual FoxPro replaces the fields that match *Skeleton*. If you include EXCEPT *Skeleton*, Visual FoxPro replaces all fields except those that match *Skeleton*.

Skeleton supports wildcards (* and ?). For example, to replace all fields that begin with the letters A and P, use:

```
GATHER FROM gamyarray FIELDS LIKE A*,P*
```

MEMO

Specifies that the contents of memo fields are replaced with the contents or array elements or variables. If you omit MEMO, memo fields are skipped when GATHER replaces the contents of fields with the contents of an array or variable. General and picture fields are always ignored in GATHER, even if you include the MEMO keyword.

Examples

Example 1

This example uses GATHER to copy data to a new record in a table. After the table Test is created, SCATTER is used to create a set of variables based on the fields in the table. Each field is then assigned a value and a new blank record is added to the table.

```
CREATE TABLE Test FREE ;
   (Object C(10), Color C(16), SqFt n(6,2))
SCATTER MEMVAR BLANK
m.Object="Box"
m.Color="Red"
m.SqFt=12.5
APPEND BLANK
GATHER MEMVAR
BROWSE
```

Example 2

This example uses GATHER along with the NAME clause to copy data to a new record in a table. After the table Test is created, SCATTER is used to create an object with properties based on the fields in the table. The object's properties are then assigned values and a new blank record is added to the table.

```
CREATE TABLE Test FREE ;
   (Object C(10), Color C(16), SqFt n(6,2))

SCATTER NAME oTest BLANK
oTest.Object="Box"
oTest.Color="Red"
oTest.SqFt=12.5
APPEND BLANK
GATHER NAME oTest
RELEASE oTest
BROWSE
```

See Also

APPEND FROM ARRAY, COPY TO ARRAY, DIMENSION, SCATTER

_GENGRAPH System Variable

Included for backward compatibility. Use the Graph Wizard instead.

_GENHTML System Variable

Specifies an HTML (Hypertext Markup Language) generation program.

Syntax

_GENHTML = *ProgramName*

Arguments

ProgramName
Specifies a program that generates HTML. If your HTML generation program is in a directory other than the current default directory, include a path with the program name.

Remarks

_GENHTML contains Genhtml.prg by default. Genhtml.prg is executed when you choose **Save As HTML** from the File menu. A text file that contains a hypertext markup language version of the form, menu, report, or table is created. The Save As HTML option is available only when the Form, Menu, or Report designers are active and the form, menu, or report has been saved, or when a Browse window is open.

See Also

CREATE FORM, CREATE MENU, CREATE REPORT, File menu, USE

_GENMENU System Variable

Specifies a menu generation program.

Syntax

_GENMENU = *ProgramName*

Arguments

ProgramName
Specifies a program that previous versions used to generate menu code from an .mnx menu definition table. If your program is in a directory other than the current default directory, include a path with the program name.

Remarks

_GENMENU contains Genmenu.prg by default.

See Also

CREATE MENU, _GENSCRN

_GENPD System Variable

Included for backward compatibility. Use the TO FILE ASCII argument in REPORT.

_GENSCRN System Variable

Included for backward compatibility. Use the Form Designer instead.

_GENXTAB System Variable

Included for backward compatibility. Use the Cross-tab Wizard instead.

GETBAR( ) Function

Returns the number of an item on a menu defined with DEFINE POPUP or the Visual FoxPro system menu.

Syntax

GETBAR(*MenuItemName*, *nMenuPosition*)

Returns

Numeric

Arguments

MenuItemName
Specifies the menu item.

nMenuPosition
Specifies a position on the menu. *nMenuPosition* can range from 1 through the number of items within the menu. 1 corresponds to the first item on the menu, 2 to the second item, and so on.

Remarks

Use GETBAR( ) to determine which item occupies a specific position on a menu. This function is useful when items on a menu are added, removed, or rearranged. Use DEFINE BAR to add an item to a menu or RELEASE BAR to remove an item. The position of items in a menu can be changed if MOVER is included when the menu is created with DEFINE POPUP.

Example

The following example creates a menu named popDemo. The MOVER keyword is included so the items in the menu can be rearranged. For information about rearranging menu items, see the MOVER clause in the DEFINE POPUP Command, earlier in this language reference.

The menu is activated, and a series of GETBAR( ) functions are used in PRMBAR( ) to return captions of each item. After you rearrange the items, press CTRL+Z to display the new item order.

```
CLEAR
ON KEY LABEL CTRL+Z DO showorder
WAIT WINDOW "Press CTRL+Z to refresh." NOWAIT

DEFINE POPUP popDemo MOVER FROM 2,2
DEFINE BAR 1 OF popDemo PROMPT 'One'
DEFINE BAR 2 OF popDemo PROMPT 'Two'
DEFINE BAR 3 OF popDemo PROMPT 'Three'
DEFINE BAR 4 OF popDemo PROMPT 'Four'

DO showorder
ACTIVATE POPUP popDemo

PROCEDURE showorder
CLEAR
@ 3,12 SAY  '1 ' + PRMBAR('popDemo', GETBAR('popDemo',1))
@ 4,12 SAY  '2 ' + PRMBAR('popDemo', GETBAR('popDemo',2))
@ 5,12 SAY  '3 ' + PRMBAR('popDemo', GETBAR('popDemo',3))
@ 6,12 SAY  '4 ' + PRMBAR('popDemo', GETBAR('popDemo',4))
RETURN
```

See Also

DEFINE BAR, DEFINE POPUP, RELEASE BAR

GETCOLOR( ) Function

Displays the Windows Color dialog box and returns the color number of the chosen color.

Syntax

GETCOLOR([*nDefaultColorNumber*])

Returns

Numeric

Arguments

nDefaultColorNumber

Specifies the color that is initially selected when the Color dialog box is displayed. If *nDefaultColorNumber* doesn't correspond to a color in the Color dialog box, the first color in the Color dialog box is selected. If you omit *nDefaultColorNumber*, black is selected.

Remarks

GETCOLOR( ) returns –1 if you exit the Color dialog box by pressing ESC, choosing the Cancel button, or choosing Close from the Control menu.

Example

The following example displays the Windows Color dialog box with the color red selected. A number corresponding to the color you choose is displayed when you exit the dialog box.

```
CLEAR
? GETCOLOR(255)
```

See Also

GETPICT( ), RGB( )

GETCP( ) Function

Prompts for a code page by displaying the Code Page dialog box, and then returns the number of the code page chosen.

Syntax

GETCP([*nCodePage*] [, *cText*] [, *cDialogTitle*])

Returns

Numeric

Arguments

nCodePage

Specifies the number of the code page that is initially selected when the Code Page dialog box is displayed. If *nCodePage* is 0 or if you omit *nCodePage*, a code page isn't selected when the Code Page dialog box is displayed.

cText

Specifies the text displayed in the Code Page dialog box. If you omit *cText*, Visual FoxPro displays the following text: "Please select a code page for cross-platform data sharing."

cDialogTitle

Specifies the title that appears in the Code Page dialog box title bar. If you omit *cDialogTitle*, the title "Code Page" is displayed.

Remarks

GETCP( ) returns 0 if you exit the Code Page dialog box by pressing ESC, choosing the Cancel button, or choosing Close from the Control menu.

The code pages listed in the Code Page dialog box are determined by FOXPRO.INT, the Visual FoxPro International code page support file.

You can include GETCP( ) in commands such as MODIFY COMMAND, APPEND FROM, and COPY TO that support the AS *nCodePage* clause. The Code Page dialog box is displayed, allowing you to specify the code page of the file opened, appended, or created. Because no code page 0 exists, you must trap for 0 in case the user chooses ESC, the Cancel button, or Close from the Control menu.

Example

The following example displays the Code Page dialog box with code page 1252 (Windows ANSI) selected. "Select a Code Page" is displayed as the caption in the Code Page dialog box, and "Code Page Selection" is displayed in the Code Page dialog box title bar.

```
? GETCP(1252, "Select a Code Page", "Code Page Selection")
```

See Also

APPEND FROM, COPY TO, EXPORT, IMPORT, MODIFY COMMAND, MODIFY FILE, MODIFY QUERY

GetData Method

Retrieves data from the OLE drag-and-drop DataObject object. Available at run time only.

Syntax

oDataObject.GetData(*nFormat* | *cFormat* [, *@ArrayName*])

Arguments

nFormat | *cFormat*

Specifies the format of the data to retrieve. The following table lists the values for each data format and a description of each format. The DataObject automatically supports the following formats (more formats are available, but these may require additional programming to use). For more information about the data formats available, see the documentation for Visual C++ on the Microsoft Developer Network.

Data format*	*nFormat* | *cFormat*	Description
CF_TEXT	1	Text format.
CF_OEMTEXT	7	Text format containing characters in the OEM character set.
CF_UNICODETEXT	13	Unicode text format, available only under Windows NT.
CF_FILES or CF_HDROP	15	A handle that identifies a list of files, such as a set of files dragged from the Windows Explorer.
CF_LOCALE	16	A handle to the locale identifier associated with text on the clipboard.
CFSTR_OLEVARIANTARRAY	"OLE Variant Array"	A Visual FoxPro array. Multiple values can be transferred in a single drag and drop operation with this format.
		For example, this format can be used to drag a set of items in a list box to another list box.
CFSTR_OLEVARIANT	"OLE Variant"	A Visual FoxPro variant. All data types in Visual FoxPro are represented as variants. This format can be used to drag and drop Visual FoxPro data without losing the data type.
CFSTR_VFPSOURCEOBJECT	"VFP Source Object"	A reference to a Visual FoxPro object.

* Defined in FOXPRO.H.

@ArrayName

Specifies the name of the array in which the data is stored when the data can contain multiple values. The only data formats in which the data can contain multiple values are CF_FILES, CF_HDROP, and CFSTR_OLEVARIANTARRAY. For example, you can drag a set of files from the Windows Explorer onto a Visual FoxPro list box. Use the GetData method in the OLEDragDrop event of the list box to place the names of the files into an array, then use the AddItem method in a FOR … ENDFOR loop to add the contents of the array to the list box.

The array must exist before you can specify its name in the GetData method. If the array exists and isn't large enough to contain the data, Visual FoxPro automatically increases the size of the array. If the array is larger than necessary, Visual FoxPro truncates the array.

Remarks

The value returned by the GetData method is determined by the format of the data specified with *nFormat* or *cFormat*. False (.F.) is returned if the DataObject doesn't contain data in the format you specify with *nFormat* or *cFormat*. True (.T.) is returned when the data is in a multiple value format such as CF_FILES, CF_HDROP, or CFSTR_OLEVARIANTARRAY. The data on the DataObject is returned when the data is in a single value format such as CF_TEXT, CFSTR_OLEVARIANT, or CFSTR_VFPSOURCEOBJECT.

The OLESetData event for a drag source is triggered if the data format you specify with *nFormat* or *cFormat* exists, but there is no data in the DataObject for that format. (The SetFormat method can be used to specify a data format before the corresponding data is placed on the DataObject with the SetData method.)

Applies To

DataObject Object

See Also

ClearData Method, GetFormat Method, OLE drag-and-drop Overview, OLESetData Event, SetData Method, SetFormat Method

GETDIR( ) Function

Displays the Select Directory dialog box from which you can choose a directory.

Syntax

GETDIR([*cDirectory* [, *cText*]])

Returns

Character

Arguments

cDirectory
Specifies the directory that is initially displayed in the dialog box. When *cDirectory* is not specified, the dialog box opens with the Visual FoxPro default directory displayed.

cText
Specifies the text for the directory list in the dialog box. In Windows 3.1, the text appears as the caption in the title bar of the dialog box. In Windows 95, the text appears below the title bar inside the dialog box.

Remarks

GETDIR( ) returns as a character string the name of the directory you choose.

If you do not choose a directory (you click Cancel, press ESC, or choose Close from the window menu), GETDIR( ) returns the empty string.

See Also

DIRECTORY, DIRECTORY( ), GETEXPR, GETFILE( )

GETENV( ) Function

Returns the contents of the specified MS-DOS environment variable.

Syntax

GETENV(*cVariableName*)

Returns

Character

Arguments

cVariableName

Specifies the name of the MS-DOS environment variable. The empty string is returned if the MS-DOS environment variable you specify doesn't exist.

You can locate the Windows directory with the WINDIR environmental variable, which Windows sets when it starts.

Remarks

Two environment variables are always available: COMSPEC and PATH. You can create your own environment variables with the MS-DOS SET command.

For additional information on creating environment variables, see your MS-DOS manual.

Example

```
CLEAR
? GETENV('PATH')  && Displays the MS-DOS path
```

See Also

DISKSPACE( ), OS( ), VERSION( )

GETEXPR Command

Displays the Expression Builder dialog box so you can create an expression and store the expression to a variable or array element.

Syntax

GETEXPR [*cCaptionText*] TO *MemVarName*
    [TYPE *cExpressionType* [; *cErrorMessageText*]]
    [DEFAULT *cDefaultExpression*]

Arguments

cCaptionText

Specifies the caption that appears in the Expression Builder. The caption can be used to remind the user of what kind of expression to build.

TO *MemVarName*

Specifies the variable or array element in which the expression is stored. If the variable doesn't already exist, Visual FoxPro creates it. GETEXPR won't create an array element.

If you exit the Expression Builder by pressing ESC or by choosing Cancel, the empty string is stored to the variable or array element. If a default expression is created with the DEFAULT clause, the default expression is stored to the variable if you exit the Expression Builder by pressing ESC or choosing Cancel.

TYPE *cExpressionType* [; *cErrorMessageText*]

Specifies the expression type. The following table lists the character to specify in *cExpressionType* for each expression type:

cExpressionType	Expression type
C	Character
D	Date
T	DateTime
N	Numeric
F	Float
I	Integer
B	Double
Y	Currency
L	Logical

You can specify the error message *cErrorMessageText* to be displayed if the expression isn't valid. If *cErrorMessageText* is included with *cExpressionType*, *cExpressionType* and *cErrorMessageText* must be separated by a semicolon (;). The combination of *cExpressionType*, the semicolon, and *cErrorMessageText* must be enclosed in single or double quotes in matching pairs.

DEFAULT *cDefaultExpression*

Allows you to display the initial default expression in the Expression Builder. You can accept the default expression or overwrite it with your own expression specified with *cDefaultExpression*. *cDefaultExpression* is stored to the variable or array element if you exit the Expression Builder by pressing ESC or choosing Cancel.

Example

In the following example, GETEXPR is used to get a LOCATE expression of the proper type. If LOCATE is successful, the company name is displayed; otherwise, a message is displayed.

```
CLOSE DATABASES
OPEN DATABASE (HOME(2) + 'Data\testdata')
USE customer   && Opens Customer table

GETEXPR 'Enter condition to locate ' TO gcTemp;
   TYPE 'L' DEFAULT 'COMPANY = ""'
LOCATE FOR &gcTemp
IF FOUND( )
   DISPLAY
ELSE
   ? 'Condition ' + gcTemp + ' was not found '
ENDIF
```

See Also

_GETEXPR, GETFILE( ), GETPICT( ), LOCFILE( ), PUTFILE( )

_GETEXPR System Variable

Specifies the program that is executed when you issue the GETEXPR command or invoke the Expression Builder dialog box from within Visual FoxPro.

Syntax

_GETEXPR = *ProgramName*

Arguments

ProgramName
Specifies a program that is executed when you issue the GETEXPR command or invoke the Expression Builder dialog box from within Visual FoxPro. If your program is in a directory other than the current default directory, include a path with the program name.

Remarks

_GETEXPR contains the empty string by default; the empty string indicates that the standard Visual FoxPro Expression Builder dialog box is displayed when the GETEXPR command is executed or when you invoke the Expression Builder dialog box from within Visual FoxPro.

You can create your own Expression Builder program that is executed when the GETEXPR command is executed or when you invoke the Expression Builder dialog box from within Visual FoxPro. Your Expression Builder program must contain an LPARAMETERS or PARAMETERS statement as the first executable line of the program to accept four parameters that Visual FoxPro passes to the program. The parameters are listed below in the order they passed:

Parameter	Description
cExpressionType	Specifies the expression type.
cErrorMessageText	Specifies the error message displayed if the expression isn't valid.
cDefaultExpression	Specifies the initial default expression in the Expression Builder.
cCaptionText	Specifies the caption that appears in the Expression Builder.

For example, the following could be the first executable line of your Expression Builder program:

```
LPARAMETERS cExpressionType, cErrorMessageText, ;
   cDefaultExpression, cCaptionText
```

If your Expression Builder program is executed when the Expression Builder dialog box is invoked from within Visual FoxPro, the first three parameters contain the empty string and the fourth parameter contains *cCaptionText*, the caption that appears in the Expression Builder.

Note that the Visual FoxPro Expression Builder is a modal dialog. Your Expression Builder program should set its form properties to the following values to create a modal dialog:

Form property	Property value
AlwaysOnTop	True (.T.)
Desktop	True (.T.)
WindowType	1 – Modal

See Also

GETEXPR

GETFILE( ) Function

Displays the **Open** dialog box and returns the name of the file you chose.

Syntax

GETFILE([*cFileExtensions*] [, *cText*] [, *cOpenButtonCaption*]
   [, *nButtonType*] [, *cTitleBarCaption*])

Returns

Character

Arguments

cFileExtensions

Specifies the file extensions of the files displayed in the scrollable list when the **All Files** menu item isn't chosen. If passing a value as a literal, enclose it in quotation marks. Do not include a period (.) in front of file extensions.

cFileExtensions can take a variety of forms:

- If *cFileExtensions* contains a single extension (for example, "PRG"), only files with that extension are displayed.

- If *cFileExtensions* is the empty string, all files in the current directory are displayed if *cCreatorType* is not included.

- *cFileExtensions* can also contain wildcards (* and ?). All files with extensions that meet the wildcard criteria are displayed. For example, if *cFileExtensions* is "?X?," all files with the extension .fxp, .exe, and .txt are displayed.

- In Visual FoxPro for Windows, *cFileExtensions* can contain a file description followed by a file extension or a list of file extensions separated with commas. The file description appears in the Files of Type list box. Separate the file description from the file extension or list of file extensions with a colon (:). Separate multiple file descriptions and their file extensions with a semicolon (;).

  For example, if *cFileExtensions* is "Text:TXT" the file description "Text" appears in the Files of Type list box and all files with a .txt extension are displayed.

  If *cFileExtensions* is "Tables:DBF; Files:TXT,BAK" the file descriptions "Tables" and "Files" appear in the Files of Type list box. When "Tables" is chosen from the Files of Type list box, all files with a .dbf extension are displayed. When "Files" is chosen from the Files of Type list box, all files with .txt and .bak extensions are displayed.

- If *cFileExtensions* contains just a semicolon (";"), all files without extensions are displayed.

cText

Specifies the text for the directory list in the Open dialog box. In Windows 95, the text appears below the list of files and long text strings may be truncated.

cOpenButtonCaption

Specifies a caption for the OK button.

nButtonType
Specifies the number and type of buttons that appear in the Open dialog box.
The following buttons appear in the dialog box when *nButtonType* is 0, 1, or 2.

nButtonType	Buttons
0 (or omitted)	OK Cancel
1	OK New Cancel
2	OK None Cancel

"Untitled" is returned with the path specified in the Open dialog box if *nButtonType* is 1 and the user chooses the New button. The empty string is returned if *nButtonType* is 2 and the user chooses the None button.

cTitleBarCaption
Specifies the title bar caption.

Remarks

GETFILE( ) returns the empty string if you exit the Open dialog box by pressing ESC, choosing Cancel, or choosing Close from the Control menu.

Example

```
CLOSE DATABASES
SELECT 0

gcTable = GETFILE('DBF', 'Browse or Create a .DBF:', 'Browse', 1;
   'Browse or Create')
DO CASE
   CASE 'Untitled' $ gcTable
      CREATE (gcTable)
   CASE EMPTY(gcTable)
      RETURN
   OTHERWISE
      USE (gcTable)
      BROWSE
ENDCASE
```

See Also

FULLPATH( ), GETEXPR, GETPICT( ), LOCFILE( ), PUTFILE( )

GETFLDSTATE( ) Function

Returns a numeric value indicating if a field in a table or cursor has been edited or had a record appended, or if the deleted status of the current record has been changed.

Syntax

GETFLDSTATE(*cFieldName* | *nFieldNumber* [, *cTableAlias* | *nWorkArea*])

Returns

Numeric

Arguments

cFieldName | *nFieldNumber*

Specifies the name of the field or the number of the field for which the edit status is returned. The field number *nFieldNumber* corresponds to the position of the field in the table or cursor structure. DISPLAY STRUCTURE or FIELD( ) can be used to determine a field's number.

You can specify –1 for *nFieldNumber* to return a character string consisting of deletion and edit status values for all fields in the table or cursor. For example, if a table has five fields and only the first field has been edited, GETFLDSTATE( ) returns the following:

121111

The 1 in the first position indicates the deletion status has not been changed.

You can also include 0 for *nFieldNumber* to determine if the deletion status of the current record has changed since the table or cursor was opened.

> **Note** Using GETFLDSTATE( ) only determines if the deletion status of the current record has changed. For example, if you mark a record for deletion and then recall it, GETFLDSTATE( ) indicates the deletion status has changed even though the record's deletion status has returned to its original state. Use DELETED( ) to determine the current deletion status of a record.

cTableAlias

Specifies the alias of the table or cursor for which the field edit or record deletion status is returned.

nWorkArea

Specifies the work area of the table or cursor for which the field edit or record deletion status is returned.

If you do not specify an alias or work area, GETFLDSTATE( ) returns a value for a field in the currently selected table or cursor.

Remarks

The following table lists the character return values and the corresponding edit or deletion status.

Return value	Edit or deletion status
1	Field has not been edited or deletion status has not changed.
2	Field has been edited or deletion status has changed.
3	Field in an appended record has not been edited or deletion status has not changed for the appended record.
4	Field in an appended record has been edited or deletion status has changed for the appended record.

Row or table buffering must first be enabled with CURSORSETPROP( ) for GETFLDSTATE( ) to operate on local tables.

The edit or deletion status is returned for the table or cursor open in the currently selected work area if GETFLDSTATE( ) is issued without the optional *cTableAlias* or *nWorkArea* arguments.

Example

The following example demonstrates how you can use GETFLDSTATE( ) to determine if the contents of a field have changed. MULTILOCKS is set to ON, a requirement for table buffering. The customer table in the testdata database is opened, and CURSORSETPROP( ) is then used to set the buffering mode to optimistic table buffering (5).

GETFLDSTATE( ) is issued to display a value (1) corresponding to the unmodified state of the cust_id field before it is modified. The cust_id field is modified with REPLACE, and GETFLDSTATE( ) is issued again to display a value (2) corresponding to the modified state of the cust_id field. TABLEREVERT( ) is used to return the table to its original state, and GETFLDSTATE( ) is issued again to display a value (1) corresponding to the original state of the cust_id field.

```
CLOSE DATABASES
CLEAR

SET MULTILOCKS ON          && Allow table buffering
OPEN DATABASE (HOME(2) + 'data\testdata')
USE Customer               && Open customer table
=CURSORSETPROP("Buffering",5,"customer")  && Enable table buffering

* Get field state on original cust_id field and display state
nState=GETFLDSTATE("cust_id")
DO DisplayState WITH nState
```

```
* Change field contents and display state
REPLACE cust_id    WITH "***"
nState=GETFLDSTATE("cust_id")
DO DisplayState WITH nState

* Discard table changes and display state
= TABLEREVERT(.T.)          && Discard all table changes
nState=GETFLDSTATE("cust_id")
DO DisplayState WITH nState

PROCEDURE DisplayState
PARAMETER nState
DO CASE
   CASE nState=1
      =MESSAGEBOX("Field has not been modified",0,"Results")
   OTHERWISE
      =MESSAGEBOX("Field has been modified",0,"Results")
ENDCASE
```

See Also

CURVAL( ), DELETED( ), FIELD( ), OLDVAL( ), CURSORSETPROP( ),
SETFLDSTATE( )

GETFONT( ) Function

Displays the Font dialog box and returns the name of the font you choose.

Syntax

GETFONT(*cFontName* [, *nFontSize* [, *cFontStyle*)

Returns

Character

Arguments

cFontName

Specifies the name of the font initially selected in the Font dialog box. If the font you
specify hasn't been installed, the default font is initially selected.

nFontSize

Specifies the font size initially selected in the Font dialog box. If the font size you
specify isn't supported, the default font size is initially selected. The font size defaults
to 10 point if *nFontSize* is less than or equal to zero or you omit *nFontSize*.

cFontStyle
>Specifies the font style initially selected in the Font dialog box. If the font style you specify isn't supported, the default font style is initially selected. *cFontStyle* is one or two characters that specify the font style. The following table lists the characters that you can specify for *cFontStyle* and the corresponding font style.

Character	Font style
B	Bold
I	Italic
BI	Bold Italic

Remarks

GETFONT( ) returns the name, size, and style of the font you choose. Your choice is returned as a character string with the font name, size, and style separated by commas.

GETFONT( ) returns the empty string if you exit the Font dialog box by choosing Cancel, choosing Close from the Control menu, or pressing ESC.

```
cMyFont = GETFONT( , , 'B')
```

>**Note** Visual FoxPro commands and functions can be abbreviated to four characters. In the case of GETFONT( ) and GETFILE( ), which both begin with the same four letters, precedence is given to GETFILE( ). Issuing GETF( ) displays the Open dialog box.

See Also

FONTMETRIC( ), SYSMETRIC( ), TXTWIDTH( ), WFONT( )

GetFormat Method

Determines if data in a specified format is available on the OLE drag-and-drop DataObject. Available at run time only.

Syntax

oDataObject.GetFormat(*nFormat* | *cFormat*)

Arguments

nFormat | *cFormat*
>Specifies the format of the data to retrieve. The following table lists some of the formats with a description of each format. For more information about the data formats available, see the documentation for Visual C++ on the Microsoft Developer Network. You can also create your own format by specifying a unique character string for *cFormat*.

Data Format*	nFormat	cFormat	Description
CF_TEXT	1	Text format.
CF_OEMTEXT	7	Text format containing characters in the OEM character set.
CF_UNICODETEXT	13	Unicode text format, available only under Windows NT.
CF_FILES or CF_HDROP	15	A handle that identifies a list of files, such as a set of files dragged from the Windows Explorer.
CFSTR_OLEVARIANTARRAY	"OLE Variant Array"	An array. Multiple values can be transferred in a single drag and drop operation with this format.
		For example, this format can be used to drag a set of items in a list box to another list box.
CFSTR_OLEVARIANT	"OLE Variant"	A variant. All data types in Visual FoxPro are represented as variants. This format can be used to drag and drop Visual FoxPro data without losing the data type.
CFSTR_VFPSOURCEOBJECT	"VFP Source Object"	A reference to the Visual FoxPro drag source object.

* Defined in FOXPRO.H.

Remarks

The GetFormat method returns true (.T.) if the DataObject contains data in the format you specify with *nFormat* or *cFormat*; otherwise returns false (.F.).

Applies To

DataObject Object

See Also

ClearData Method, GetData Method, OLE drag-and-drop Overview, SetData Method, SetFormat Method

GETHOST( ) Function

Returns an object reference to the container of an Active Document.

Syntax

GETHOST( )

Returns

Object

Remarks

Use GETHOST( ) to determine the container of an Active Document. The Name property can be used to determine the name of the container (such as Microsoft Internet Explorer) from the object reference.

GETHOST( ) returns the null value if the container cannot be determined or the Active Document isn't running in a container (for example, the Active Document is running in an interactive Visual FoxPro session or within the Visual FoxPro runtime).

See Also

ISHOSTED( ), Name Property

GetLatestVersion Method

Gets the latest version of a file in a project from source code control and copies a read-only version to your local drive.

Syntax

Object.GetLatestVersion( )

Remarks

The GetLatestVersion method does not check the file out.

True (.T.) is returned if source code control can successfully get the file. False (.F.) is returned if source code control cannot get the file or the project is not under source code control.

Applies To

File Object

See Also

AddToSCC Method, CheckIn Method, CheckOut Method, RemoveFromSCC Method, UndoCheckOut Method

GETNEXTMODIFIED( ) Function

Returns the record number for the next modified record in a buffered table or cursor.

Syntax

GETNEXTMODIFIED(*nRecordNumber* [, *cTableAlias* | *nWorkArea*])

Returns

Numeric

Arguments

nRecordNumber

Specifies the record number after which GETNEXTMODIFIED( ) searches for the next modified record. Specify 0 for *nRecordNumber* to determine the first record in the table or cursor that has been modified.

cTableAlias

Specifies the alias of the table or cursor for which GETNEXTMODIFIED( ) returns the number of the next modified record.

nWorkArea

Specifies the work area of the table or cursor for which GETNEXTMODIFIED( ) returns the number of the next modified record.

If you do not specify an alias or work area, GETNEXTMODIFIED( ) returns the record number for the next modified record in the currently selected table or cursor.

Remarks

GETNEXTMODIFIED( ) returns 0 if there are no modified records after the record you specify. A record is considered modified if the contents of any of its fields are changed in any way (even if the original field contents are restored) or the record's deletion status is changed.

GETNEXTMODIFIED( ) can operate only on tables and cursors for which table buffering is enabled. Table buffering is enabled with CURSORSETPROP( ).

Example

The following example demonstrates how you can use GETNEXTMODIFIED( ) to determine which records in a table have been changed. MULTILOCKS is set to ON, a requirement for table buffering. The customer table in the testdata database is opened, and CURSORSETPROP( ) is then used to set the buffering mode to optimistic table buffering (5).

SKIP is issued to move the record pointer to the second record, and the cust_id field is modified with REPLACE. GETNEXTMODIFIED(0) is used to display the record number of the next modified record (2, the second record), starting from the beginning of the table. TABLEREVERT( ) is used to return the table to its original state, and GETNEXTMODIFIED(0) is used again to display the record number of the next modified record (0, indicating that no records have been modified).

```
CLOSE DATABASES
CLEAR

OPEN DATABASE SYS (HOME(2) + 'data\testdata')
SET MULTILOCKS ON  && Allow table buffering
USE Customer      && Open customer table
=CURSORSETPROP("Buffering", 5, "customer")  && Enable table buffering

SKIP  && Move record pointer to the second record

* Change field contents
REPLACE cust_id WITH "***"

* Call MESSAGEBOX function with results of GETNEXTMODIFIED
=MESSAGEBOX("Record " + ALLTRIM(STR(GETNEXTMODIFIED(0))) + ;
   " has changed.",0,"Results")

* Revert table and display results with MESSAGEBOX
=TABLEREVERT(.T.)  && Discard all table changes
nChange=GETNEXTMODIFIED(0)
IF nChange=0
   =MESSAGEBOX("Record(s) have been reverted.",0,"Results")
ELSE
   =MESSAGEBOX("Record " + ALLTRIM(STR(GETNEXTMODIFIED(0))) + ;
   " has changed.",0,"Results")
ENDIF
```

See Also

CURSORSETPROP( ), CURVAL( ), GETFLDSTATE( ), OLDVAL( )

GETOBJECT( ) Function

Activates an Automation object and creates a reference to the object.

Syntax

GETOBJECT(*FileName* [, *ClassName*])

Returns

Object

Arguments

FileName

Specifies the full path and name of the file to activate. The application does not need to be specified, because the OLE dynamic link libraries determine the application to start based on the file name you provide.

For example, the following code launches Microsoft Excel, opens a file named BUDGET.XLS, and creates a reference through an object variable named MBUDVAR:

```
MBUDVAR = GETOBJECT('C:\EXCEL\WORK\BUDGET.XLS')
```

ClassName

Specifies the class name of the object to retrieve. Some applications can store more than one object type in the same file, allowing you to use the class name to specify the object to activate. For example, if a word processing application stores its documents, macro definitions, and ToolBar objects in the same file, you can create a reference to the document file with the following command:

```
MDOCFILE = GETOBJECT('C:\WRDPROC\MYDOC.DOC','WrdProc.Document')
  'WrdProc.Document')
```

With some server applications, each time you issue GETOBJECT( ), an additional instance of the application is started, using additional memory. If the application is already running, you can prevent additional instances of the application from starting by omitting *FileName* and including *ClassName*, as in this example:

```
oleApp = GETOBJECT(, "Excel.Application")
```

Remarks

Use GETOBJECT( ) to activate an Automation object from a file and to assign a reference to the object through a memory variable or array element.

If you specify an invalid file or class name, an OLE error is displayed, and the GETOBJECT( ) function returns an empty string.

See Also

COMCLASSINFO( ), CREATEOBJECT( ), DEFINE CLASS, SET OLEOBJECT

GETPAD( ) Function

Returns the menu title for a given position on the menu bar.

Syntax

GETPAD(*cMenuBarName*, *nMenuBarPosition*)

Returns

Character

Arguments

cMenuBarName
Specifies the menu bar name.

nMenuBarPosition
Specifies a position on the menu bar. *nMenuPosition* can range from 1 (the leftmost menu title on the menu bar) through the number of menu titles on the menu bar.

Remarks

Menu names on a titles bar can be added, removed, or rearranged. Use DEFINE PAD to add a menu name to a title bar or RELEASE PAD to remove a menu title.

Example

The following program uses GETPAD( ) to test if the Edit menu name is on the Visual FoxPro system menu bar. If it is, GETPAD( ) returns the menu name. (To restore the Edit menu bar to its default state, issue the command SET SYSMENU TO DEFAULT.)

```
FOR gnCount = 1 TO CNTPAD('_msysmenu')        && Number of pads
   IF PRMPAD('_msysmenu', GETPAD('_msysmenu', gnCount)) = 'Edit'
      RELEASE PAD (GETPAD('_msysmenu', gnCount)) OF _msysmenu
      EXIT
   ENDIF
ENDFOR
```

See Also

DEFINE MENU, DEFINE PAD, RELEASE PAD

GETPEM( ) Function

Returns the current value for a property or program code for an event or method at design time.

Syntax

GETPEM(*oObjectName* | *cClassName*, *cProperty* | *cEvent* | *cMethod*)

Returns

Character, Currency, Date, DateTime, Numeric, or Logical

Arguments

oObjectName

Specifies the object for which a property value or event or method program code is returned. *oObjectName* can be any expression that evaluates to an object, such as an object reference, an object memory variable, or an object array element.

cClassName

Specifies the class for which a property value or event or method program code is returned.

cProperty

Specifies the property whose value is returned.

cEvent

Specifies the event for which program code is returned.

cMethod

Specifies the method for which program code is returned.

Remarks

GETPEM( ) is supported only during an interactive Visual FoxPro session.

See Also

CREATE FORM, PEMSTATUS( ), SYS(1269) – Property Information, SYS(1270) – Object Location, SYS(1271) – Object's .SCX File, SYS(1272) – Object Hierarchy

GETPICT( ) Function

Displays the Open Picture dialog box and returns the name of the picture file you chose.

Syntax

GETPICT([*cFileExtensions*] [, *cFileNameCaption*] [, *cOpenButtonCaption*])

Returns

Character

Arguments

cFileExtensions

Specifies the file extensions of the picture files displayed in the scrollable list when the All Files menu item isn't chosen.

cFileExtensions can take the following forms:

- If *cFileExtensions* contains a single extension (for example, .bmp), only files with that extension are displayed.

- *cFileExtensions* can also contain wildcards (* and ?). All files with extensions that meet the wildcard criteria are displayed. For example, if *cFileExtensions* is ?X?, all files with the extension .fxp, .exe, and .txt are displayed.

- If *cFileExtensions* contains an empty string (""), files with the extensions .bmp and .dib are displayed.

cFileNameCaption

Specifies the caption displayed above the File Name text box. *cFileNameCaption* replaces "File Name" that appears when *cFileNameCaption* is omitted.

cOpenButtonCaption

Specifies a caption for the OK button.

Remarks

GETPICT( ) returns the empty string if you exit the Open Picture dialog box by pressing ESC, choosing the Cancel button, or clicking the Close button.

See Also

GETFILE( ), GETEXPR, LOCFILE( ), PUTFILE( )

GETPRINTER( ) Function

Displays the Print dialog box and returns the name of the printer you select.

Syntax

GETPRINTER( )

Returns

Character

Remarks

GETPRINTER( ) returns an empty string if you exit the Print dialog box by pressing ESC, choosing the Cancel button, or clicking the Close button.

Example

```
CLEAR
cPrinter = GETPRINTER( ) && Displays the Windows Printer Dialog
*** Displays the name of the printer chosen ***
WAIT WINDOW IIF(EMPTY(cPrinter), 'No printer chosen', cPrinter)
```

See Also

APRINTERS( ), SET PRINTER

GO | GOTO Command

Moves the record pointer to the specified record number.

Syntax

GO [RECORD] *nRecordNumber* [IN *nWorkArea* | IN *cTableAlias*]

– or –

GO TOP | BOTTOM [IN *nWorkArea* | IN *cTableAlias*]

– or –

GOTO [RECORD] *nRecordNumber* [IN *nWorkArea* | IN *cTableAlias*]

– or –

GOTO TOP | BOTTOM [IN *nWorkArea* | IN *cTableAlias*]

Arguments

RECORD *nRecordNumber*

Specifies the physical record number to move the record pointer to. You can omit GO or GOTO entirely and specify just the record number. If you specify just the record number, you can move the record pointer only within the current work area.

IN *nWorkArea*

Specifies the work area of the table in which the record pointer is moved.

IN *cTableAlias*

Specifies the alias of the table in which the record pointer is moved.

TOP

Positions the record pointer on the first record in the table. If the table has an ascending index in use, the first record is the record with the lowest key value. If the index is in descending order, the first record is the record with the highest key value.

BOTTOM

Positions the record pointer on the last record in the table. If the table has an ascending index in use, the last record is the record with the highest key value. If the index is in descending order, the last record is the record with the lowest key value.

Remarks

GO and GOTO can be used interchangeably. These commands operate on the table in the current work area unless you specify another work area with the IN clause.

Example

```
CLOSE DATABASES
OPEN DATABASE (HOME(2) + 'data\testdata')
USE products   && Opens Products table
USE customer IN 0  && Opens Customer table
GO BOTTOM IN products
CLEAR
? RECNO('products')
GO TOP
? RECNO( )       && Displays 1
GO 5
? RECNO( )       && Displays 5
```

See Also

RECNO( ), SELECT, SKIP

GoBack Method

Navigates backwards in the history list of an Active Document host.

Syntax

HyperLink.GoBack( )

Remarks

The GoBack method is supported only when an Active Documents is hosted in an Active Document container.

The GoBack method is ignored when executed outside of an Active Document host. For example, it is ignored when an Active Document is run in the Visual FoxPro runtime or in an interactive Visual FoxPro session.

Applies To

Hyperlink Object

See Also

GoForward Method, NavigateTo Method

GoForward Method

Navigates forwards in the history list of an Active Document host.

Syntax

HyperLink.GoForward( )

Remarks

The GoForward method is supported only when an Active Documents is hosted in an Active Document container.

The GoForward method is ignored when executed outside of an Active Document host. For example, it is ignored when an Active Document is run in the Visual FoxPro runtime or in an interactive Visual FoxPro session.

Applies To

Hyperlink Object

See Also

GoBack Method, NavigateTo Method

GOMONTH( ) Function

Returns the date that is a specified number of months before or after a given Date or DateTime expression.

Syntax

GOMONTH(*dExpression* | *tExpression*, *nNumberOfMonths*)

Returns

Date

Arguments

dExpression
  Specifies a date expression for which GOMONTH( ) returns the date.

tExpression
  Specifies a datetime expression for which GOMONTH( ) returns the date.

nNumberOfMonths
  Specifies the number of months from the date or datetime. If *nNumberOfMonths* is positive, GOMONTH( ) returns a date that is *nNumberOfMonths* months after the date or datetime. If *nNumberOfMonths* is negative, GOMONTH( ) returns a date that is *nNumberOfMonths* months before the date or datetime.

Example

```
SET CENTURY ON
STORE GOMONTH({^1998-02-16}, 5) TO gdDeadLine

CLEAR
? gdDeadLine  && Displays 07/16/1998
? GOMONTH({^1998-12-31}, 2)  && Displays 02/28/1999
? GOMONTH({^1998-12-31}, -2)  && Displays 10/31/1998
```

See Also

CMONTH( )

GotFocus Event

Occurs when an object receives the focus, either by user action or through code.

Syntax

PROCEDURE *Object.*GotFocus
[LPARAMETERS *nIndex*]

Arguments

nIndex
Uniquely identifies a control if it is in a control array.

Remarks

Use the GotFocus event to specify actions to occur when an object receives the focus. For example, by attaching a GotFocus event to each control on a Form, you can guide a user by displaying brief instructions or status bar messages. You can also provide visual cues by enabling, disabling, or showing other controls that depend on the control that has the focus.

A control receives the focus by user action, such as a mouse click, or when the SetFocus method is called in code.

> **Note** An object can receive the focus only if its Enabled and Visible properties are set to true (.T.). To customize the keyboard interface for moving the focus, set the tab order or specify access keys for controls on a form.

The GotFocus event occurs after the Activate event for the control's container.

Applies To

CheckBox, ComboBox, CommandButton, Container Object, Control Object, EditBox, Form, ListBox, OLE Bound Control, OLE Container Control, OptionButton, Spinner, TextBox

See Also

Activate Event, ActiveControl Property, Click Event, Deactivate Event, Enabled Property, LostFocus Event, SetFocus Method, TabIndex Property, TabStop Property, Visible Property

Grid Control

Creates a grid.

Syntax

Grid

Remarks

A grid is a container object that displays data in rows and columns, and is similar in appearance to a Browse window. A grid is also a container object that contains column objects. A column can contain a Header object and controls. Because a grid and its columns, headers, and controls each have their own set of properties, you have complete control over each element of the grid. You can create a grid interactively using the Grid Builder.

For additional information about creating grids, see Chapter 10, "Using Controls," in the *Microsoft Visual FoxPro 6.0 Programmer's Guide*.

Properties

ActiveColumn	ActiveRow	AllowAddNew
AllowHeaderSizing	AllowRowSizing	Application
BackColor	BaseClass	ChildOrder
Class	ClassLibrary	ColumnCount
Columns	Comment	DeleteMark
DragIcon	DragMode	Enabled
FontBold	FontCondense	FontExtend
FontItalic	FontName	FontOutline
FontShadow	FontSize	FontStrikeThru
FontUnderline	ForeColor	GridLineColor
GridLines	GridLineWidth	HeaderHeight
Height	HelpContextID	HighLight
HighLightRow	Left	LeftColumn
LinkMaster	MouseIcon	MousePointer
Name	OLEDragMode	OLEDragPicture

OLEDropEffects	OLEDropHasData Property	OLEDropMode
Panel	PanelLink	Parent
ParentClass	Partition	ReadOnly
RecordMark	RecordSource	RecordSourceType
RelationalExpr	RelativeColumn	RelativeRow
RightToLeft	RowHeight	ScrollBars
SplitBar	StatusBarText	TabIndex
TabStop	Tag	ToolTipText
Top	Value	View
Visible	WhatsThisHelpID	Width

Events

AfterRowColChange	BeforeRowColChange	Click
DblClick	Deleted	Destroy
DragDrop	DragOver	Error
Init	MiddleClick Event	MouseDown
MouseMove	MouseUp	MouseWheel
OLECompleteDrag	OLEDragDrop	OLEDragOver
OLEGiveFeedBack	OLESetData	OLEStartDrag
Resize	RightClick	Moved
Scrolled	UIEnable	Valid
When		

Methods

ActivateCell	AddColumn	AddObject
AddProperty	CloneObject	DeleteColumn
DoScroll	Drag	GridHitTest
Move	OLEDrag	ReadExpression
ReadMethod	Refresh	RemoveObject
ResetToDefault	SaveAsClass	SetAll
SetFocus	WriteExpression	WriteMethod
ZOrder		

Example

The following example places a Grid control on a form. The `customer` table is opened and its contents are displayed in the grid. The Caption property is used to specify a different header caption (Customer ID) for the CUST_ID field. A command button is placed on the form to close the form.

The SetAll method is used with the DynamicBackColor property to specify the background colors for the records. If the number of a record displayed in the grid is even, the record's DynamicBackColor is white, otherwise its DynamicBackColor is green.

```
CLOSE ALL  && Close tables and databases
OPEN DATABASE (HOME(2) + 'data\testdata')

USE customer  IN 0  && Opens Customer table

frmMyForm = CREATEOBJECT('Form')  && Create a Form
frmMyForm.Closable = .F.  && Disable the window pop-up menu

frmMyForm.AddObject('cmdCommand1','cmdMyCmdBtn')  && Add Command button
frmMyForm.AddObject('grdGrid1','Grid')  && Add Grid control

frmMyForm.grdGrid1.Left = 25  && Adjust Grid position

frmMyForm.grdGrid1.SetAll("DynamicBackColor", ;
   "IIF(MOD(RECNO( ), 2)=0, RGB(255,255,255) ;
   , RGB(0,255,0))", "Column")  && Alternate white and green records

frmMyForm.grdGrid1.Visible = .T.  && Grid control visible
frmMyForm.cmdCommand1.Visible =.T.  && "Quit" Command button visible
frmMyForm.grdGrid1.Column1.Header1.Caption = 'Customer ID'

frmMyForm.SHOW  && Display the form
READ EVENTS  && Start event processing

DEFINE CLASS cmdMyCmdBtn AS CommandButton  && Create Command button
   Caption = '\<Quit'  && Caption on the Command button
   Cancel = .T.  && Default Cancel Command button (Esc)
   Left = 125  && Command button column
   Top = 210  && Command button row
   Height = 25  && Command button height

   PROCEDURE Click
      CLEAR EVENTS  && Stop event processing, close form
      CLOSE ALL  && Close table and database
ENDDEFINE
```

See Also

Column Object, CREATE CLASS, CREATE FORM, DEFINE CLASS, Header Object

GridHitTest Method

Returns, as output parameters, the components of a grid control corresponding to specified horizontal (X) and vertical (Y) coordinates.

Syntax

Grid.GridHitTest(*nXCoord_In, nYCoord_In*
    [, *nWhere_Out* [, *nRelRow_Out* [, *nRelCol_Out* [, *nView_Out*]]]])

Arguments

nXCoord_In
    Specifies the horizontal (X) position in pixels within the form containing the grid.

nYCoord_In
    Specifies the vertical (Y) position in pixels within the form containing the grid.

nWhere_Out
    An output parameter that contains a value corresponding to the grid component at the position specified with *nXCoord_In* and *nYCoord_In*. The following table lists the values for @*nWhere_Out* and the corresponding grid component.

@*nWhere_Out*	Grid component
0	A grid component that cannot be determined.
1	Column header.
2	Between column headers.
3	Cell.
4	Reserved.
5	SplitBar.
6	Record deletion marker.
7	Reserved
8	Reserved.
9	Reserved.
10	Reserved.
11	Box in upper left corner.
12	Record marker.
13	Column header sizing area.
14	Row sizing area.

(continued)

(continued)

@nWhere_Out	Grid component
15	Reserved.
16	Horizontal scrollbar.
17	Vertical scrollbar.

nRelRow_Out
An output parameter containing the relative grid row at the specified point.

nRelCol_Out
An output parameter containing the relative grid column at the specified point.

nView_Out
An output parameter containing a value corresponding to the grid pane containing the specified point. If the grid is split into two panes, this parameter contains 0 if the specified point is in the left pane, and contains 1 if the specified point is in the right pane. If the grid isn't split into separate panes, this parameter contains 1.

Remarks

The GridHitTest( ) method returns true (.T.) if the specified point is within the grid; otherwise false (.F.) is returned.

The GridHitTest( ) method can be used during mouse events or OLE drop target events to determine where the mouse pointer is positioned over the grid. The *nRelRow_Out* and *nRelCol_Out* parameters can be passed to the ActivateCell( ) method to activate a specific cell in the grid.

Applies To

Grid Control

See Also

ActivateCell Method, ActiveColumn Property, ActiveRow Property, MCOL( ), MROW( )

GridLineColor Property

Specifies the color of the lines separating cells in a Grid control. Available at design time; read/write at run time.

Syntax

Grid.GridLineColor[= *nColor*]
Grid.GridLineColor = RGB(*nRedValue, nGreenValue, nBlueValue*)

Arguments

nColor
 Specifies a single number to represent the color. By default, GridLineColor is set to 0 (Black).

nRedValue, nGreenValue, nBlueValue
 Specifies three separate color intensities that compose the Grid's line color; must be used with the RGB( ) function to consolidate the three color components into one number, which is what the GridLineColor property is.

 Note the Properties window, you can double-click any of the color properties to display the Color dialog box. You can choose or define colors from this dialog box. The red, green, and blue intensities that correspond to the color you choose become the settings for these properties after you close the Color dialog box.

Applies To

Grid

See Also

GridLines Property, GridLineWidth Property

GridLines Property

Determines whether horizontal and vertical lines are displayed in the Grid control. Available at design time; read/write at run time.

Syntax

Grid.GridLines[= *nSetting*]

Arguments

nSetting
 The settings for the GridLines property are:

Setting	Description
0	None. No grid lines.
1	Horizontal. Horizontal grid lines only.
2	Vertical. Vertical grid lines only.
3	(Default) Both. Both horizontal and vertical grid lines.

Applies To

Grid

See Also

GridLineColor Property, GridLineWidth Property

GridLineWidth Property

Specifies the thickness, in pixels, of the lines separating cells in a Grid control. Available at design time; read/write at run time.

Syntax

Grid.GridLineWidth[= *nWidth*]

Arguments

nWidth
    Specifies the thickness of the line separating cells in a Grid control.

Applies To

Grid

See Also

GridLineColor Property, GridLines Property

HalfHeightCaption Property

Specifies whether the caption of a form is half the normal height. Available at design time and run time.

Syntax

Object.HalfHeightCaption[= *lExpr*]

Arguments

lExpr
    The settings for the HalfHeightCaption property are:

Setting	Description
True (.T.)	The form's caption is half the normal height.
False (.F.)	(Default) The form's caption is normal height.

Applies To

Form, _SCREEN

See Also

Caption Property

Header Object

Creates a header for a column in a Grid control.

Syntax

Header

Remarks

Each column in a grid contains a header. A header displays the caption at the top of a column, and can respond to events.

For additional information about creating headers in grids, see Chapter 10, "Using Controls," in the *Microsoft Visual FoxPro 6.0 Programmer's Guide*.

Properties

Alignment	Application	BackColor
BaseClass	Caption	Class
ClassLibrary	Comment	FontBold
FontCondense	FontExtend	FontItalic
FontName	FontOutline	FontShadow
FontSize	FontStrikeThru	FontUnderline
ForeColor	Name	Parent
ParentClass	Tag	

Events

Click	DblClick	MiddleClick Event
MouseDown	MouseMove	MouseUp
MouseWheel	RightClick	

Methods

AddProperty	ReadExpression	ReadMethod
Refresh	ResetToDefault	SaveAsClass
WriteExpression	WriteMethod	

Example

The following example uses the Header object with the Caption property to change the caption of the first header in a grid.

A Grid control is placed on a form and the customer table is opened and its contents displayed in the grid. The Header object and the Caption property are used to specify a different header caption (Customer ID) for the first header in the grid.

The SetAll method is used with the DynamicBackColor property to specify the background colors for the records. If the number of a record displayed in the grid is even, the record's DynamicBackColor is white, otherwise its DynamicBackColor is green. A command button is placed on the form to close the form.

```
CLOSE ALL  && Close tables and databases
OPEN DATABASE (HOME(2) + 'data\testdata')

USE customer  IN 0  && Opens Customer table

frmMyForm = CREATEOBJECT('form')  && Create a form
frmMyForm.Closable = .f.  && Disable the window pop-up menu

frmMyForm.AddObject('cmdCommand1','cmdMyCmdBtn')  && Add Command button
frmMyForm.AddObject('grdGrid1','Grid')  && Add Grid control

frmMyForm.grdGrid1.Left = 25  && Adjust Grid position

frmMyForm.grdGrid1.SetAll("DynamicBackColor", ;
   "IIF(MOD(RECNO( ), 2)=0, RGB(255,255,255) ;
   , RGB(0,255,0))", "Column")  && Alternate white and green records

frmMyForm.grdGrid1.Visible = .T.  && Grid control visible
frmMyForm.cmdCommand1.Visible =.T.  && "Quit" Command button visible
frmMyForm.grdGrid1.Column1.Header1.Caption = 'Customer ID'

frmMyForm.SHOW  && Display the form
READ EVENTS  && Start event processing

DEFINE CLASS cmdMyCmdBtn AS CommandButton  && Create Command button
   Caption = '\<Quit'  && Caption on the Command button
   Cancel = .T.  && Default Cancel Command button (Esc)
   Left = 125  && Command button column
   Top = 210  && Command button row
   Height = 25  && Command button height

   PROCEDURE Click
      CLEAR EVENTS  && Stop event processing, close form
      CLOSE ALL  && Close table and database
ENDDEFINE
```

See Also

Column Object, CREATE FORM, CREATE CLASS, DEFINE CLASS, Grid Control

HEADER( ) Function

Returns the number of bytes in the header of the current or specified table file.

Syntax

HEADER([*nWorkArea* | *cTableAlias*])

Returns

Numeric

Arguments

nWorkArea | *cTableAlias*

Returns the header size for a table open in another work area. *nWorkArea* specifies the work area number and *cTableAlias* specifies the table alias. If you omit the work area and alias, HEADER( ) returns the size of the header for the table open in the current work area.

HEADER( ) returns 0 if a table isn't open in the work area you specify. If a table doesn't have the alias you specify, Microsoft Visual FoxPro displays an error message.

Remarks

A table header contains information about the table itself, such as the field names and sizes and the presence of a memo file or structural index.

See Also

FSIZE( ), RECSIZE( )

HeaderHeight Property

Specifies the height of column headers in the Grid control. Available at design time; read/write at run time.

Syntax

Header.HeaderHeight[= *nHeight*]

Arguments

nHeight

The height of the header, specified in pixels.

Applies To

Grid

See Also

ScaleMode Property

Height Property

Specifies the height of an object on the screen. Available at design time and run time.

Syntax

Object.Height[= *nHeight*]

Arguments

nHeight

Specifies the object's height measured in the unit of measurement specified by the ScaleMode property of the form.

Remarks

For forms, the Height measurement does not include the borders and title bar.

For controls, the height is measured from the outside of the control's border.

The value for this property changes as the object is sized by the user or by code.

Use the Height and Width properties for calculations based on an object's total area.

Note The Height property is read-only when it applies to a control contained in a Column object.

Example

The following example demonstrates how the Height property is used specify the height of three command buttons on a form.

The AddObject method is used to add a Line control and three command buttons to a form. The Height property specifies the vertical height of each command button.

```
frmMyForm = CREATEOBJECT('form')  && Create a form
frmMyForm.Closable = .F.  && Disable the Control menu box

frmMyForm.AddObject('shpLine','Line')  && Add a Line control to the form
frmMyForm.AddObject('cmdCmndBtn1','cmdMyCmndBtn1')  && Up Cmnd button
frmMyForm.AddObject('cmdCmndBtn2','cmdMyCmndBtn2')  && Down Cmnd button
frmMyForm.AddObject('cmdCmndBtn3','cmdMyCmndBtn3')  && Quit Cmnd button

frmMyForm.shpLine.Visible = .T.  && Make Line control visible
frmMyForm.shpLine.Top = 20  && Specify Line control row
frmMyForm.shpLine.Left = 125  && Specify Line control column

frmMyForm.cmdCmndBtn1.Visible =.T.  && Up Command button visible
frmMyForm.cmdCmndBtn2.Visible =.T.  && Down" Command button visible
frmMyForm.cmdCmndBtn3.Visible =.T.  && Quit Command button visible
```

```
frmMyForm.SHOW  && Display the form
READ EVENTS  && Start event processing

DEFINE CLASS cmdMyCmndBtn1 AS COMMANDBUTTON  && Create Command button
    Caption = 'Slant \<Up'  && Caption on the Command button
    Left = 50  && Command button column
    Top = 100  && Command button row
    Height = 25  && Command button height

    PROCEDURE Click
        ThisForm.shpLine.Visible = .F.  && Hide the Line control
        ThisForm.shpLine.LineSlant ='/'  && Slant up
        ThisForm.shpLine.Visible = .T.  && Show the Line control
ENDDEFINE

DEFINE CLASS cmdMyCmndBtn2 AS CommandButton  && Create Command button
    Caption = 'Slant \<Down'  && Caption on the Command button
    Left = 200  && Command button column
    Top = 100  && Command button row
    Height = 25  && Command button height

    PROCEDURE Click
        ThisForm.shpLine.Visible = .F.  && Hide the Line control
        ThisForm.shpLine.LineSlant ='\'  && Slant down
        ThisForm.shpLine.Visible = .T.  && Show the Line control
ENDDEFINE

DEFINE CLASS cmdMyCmndBtn3 AS CommandButton  && Create Command button
    Caption = '\<Quit'  && Caption on the Command button
    Cancel = .T.  && Default Cancel Command button (Esc)
    Left = 125  && Command button column
    Top = 150  && Command button row
    Height = 25  && Command button height

    PROCEDURE Click
        CLEAR EVENTS  && Stop event processing, close form
ENDDEFINE
```

Applies To

CheckBox, ComboBox, CommandButton, CommandGroup, Container Object, Control Object, Custom, EditBox, Form, Grid, Image, Label, Line, ListBox, OLE Bound Control, OLE Container Control, OptionButton, OptionGroup, PageFrame, _SCREEN, Shape, Spinner, TextBox, Timer, ToolBar

See Also

Left Property, Move Method, ScaleMode Property, Top Property, Width Property

HELP Command

Opens the Help window.

Syntax

HELP
> [*Topic* | ID *nContextID*]
> [IN [WINDOW] *WindowName* | IN [WINDOW] SCREEN | IN [WINDOW] [NOWAIT]

Arguments

Topic
> Specifies the Help topic to display. If you include just a partial spelling of a topic title, Visual FoxPro opens the Help window and displays the topic with the closest matching title.

ID *nContextID*
> Specifies the Help topic to display, based on the topic's context ID.
>
> When you are using .dbf-style Help, *nContextID* is a value in the `Contextid` field of the help table. The `Contextid` field must be the first field in the table.
>
> When you are using graphical style Help, *nContextID* is a context number in the MAP section of the help project file.

IN [WINDOW] *WindowName*
> Opens the Help window within a parent window. The Help window doesn't assume the characteristics of the parent window it is placed in. If the Help window is activated inside a parent window, it cannot be moved outside the parent window. If the parent window is moved, the Help window moves with it. Before you can open the Help window from within a parent window, the parent window must first be defined with DEFINE WINDOW.

IN [WINDOW] SCREEN
> Explicitly places the Help window on the main Visual FoxPro window.

NOWAIT
> In .dbf-style Help, specifies that program execution should continue after the Help window is opened. If you omit NOWAIT when using .dbf-style Help, program execution is suspended at the line containing the HELP command until the Help window is closed.
>
> In graphical style Help, the NOWAIT argument has no effect, and program execution always continues after the HELP command has been issued.

Remarks

For more information on creating your own Help system, see Part 7, "Creating Help Files," in the *Microsoft Visual FoxPro 6.0 Programmer's Guide*.

See Also

SET HELP, SET HELPFILTER, SET TOPIC

Help Method

Opens the Help window.

Syntax

ApplicationObject.Help([*cFileName*] [, *nContextID*] [, *cHelpTopic*])

Arguments

cFileName
Specifies the name of the Help file open. Include a path with the Help file name if the Help file isn't in the default directory.

nContextID
Specifies the Help topic to display, based on the topic's context ID. *nContextID* is a context number in the MAP section of the help project file.

cHelpTopic
Specifies the Help topic to display. If you include just a partial spelling of a topic title, Visual FoxPro opens the Help window and displays the topic with the closest matching title.

Remarks

If none of the optional arguments are included, the main Help topic is displayed. This method does not support .dbf-style Help.

Applies To

Application Object, _VFP System Variable

See Also

HELP, SET HELP

HelpContextID Property

Specifies a context ID for a topic in a Help file to provide context-sensitive Help for the object. Available at design time and run time.

Syntax

Object.HelpContextID[= *nContextID*]

Arguments

nContextID
Specifies the context ID number of a topic in a graphical-style or .dbf-style Help file. The valid range for context ID numbers is range 0 to 268,435,455.

Remarks

To create context-sensitive Help for an object in your application, you must assign the same context number to both the object and the associated Help topic when you create the Help file.

If you have created graphical-style or .dbf-style Help for your application, Visual FoxPro calls the Help file and requests the topic identified by the current context ID number. You can specify a Help file with SET HELP TO, and you can specify a key to activate the Help file with ON KEY LABEL. The Help compiler required to create graphical-style help is included with Visual FoxPro.

The current context ID number is the setting of the HelpContextID property for the object that has the focus. If a nonzero current context number is not found, the main contents screen of the Help file is displayed.

For a server object, the HelpContextID property specifies the context ID for the type library created for the server. The ServerHelpFile property specifies the Help file containing the help topic corresponding to the context ID.

Applies To

CheckBox, ComboBox, CommandButton, CommandGroup, EditBox, Form, Grid, Image, Label, Line, ListBox, OLE Bound Control, OLE Container Control, OptionButton, OptionGroup, Page, _SCREEN, Server Object, Shape, Spinner, TextBox, ToolBar

See Also

ServerHelpFile Property, SET HELP, SET TOPIC

HIDE MENU Command

Hides one or more active user-defined menu bars.

Syntax

HIDE MENU *MenuBarName1* [, *MenuBarName2* ...] | ALL
    [SAVE]

Arguments

MenuBarName1 [, *MenuBarName2* ...]
    Specifies the name of the menu bar or a list of menu bars (separated by commas) to hide.

ALL
    Hides all defined menu bars.

SAVE

Places an image of a menu bar on the screen or in a window. Placing an image of a menu bar on the screen is useful during program development and testing. Menu bar images can be cleared from the main Visual FoxPro window or a user-defined window with CLEAR.

Remarks

HIDE MENU removes the specified menu bar, a set of menu bars, or all menu bars from the main Visual FoxPro window or from a user-defined window without removing the menu definition from memory. Before a menu bar can be hidden, it must first be created with DEFINE MENU. Hiding a menu bar isn't the same as deactivating it. When a menu bar is hidden, it stays resident in memory and can be displayed in the main Visual FoxPro window or in a user-defined window with ACTIVATE MENU or SHOW MENU.

See Also

ACTIVATE MENU, DEFINE MENU, DEFINE PAD, SHOW MENU

Hide Method

Hides a form, form set, or toolbar by setting the Visible property to false (.F.).

Syntax

Object.Hide

Remarks

Controls on a hidden form are not accessible to the user, but are still available and can be accessed in code. Although they are not visible, controls contained in an invisible form retain their own Visible property setting.

When the Visible property of the form set is set to false (.F.), the user cannot see the Forms it contains. Forms in a hidden form set are not accessible to the user, but are still available and can be accessed in code. The Hide method for a form set does not set the Visible property of its child Forms, so when a form is contained in a form set, you must check the Visible property settings of both the form and form set to determine if the form is visible.

After a form set is hidden, Visual FoxPro activates the last active object. If no objects were active before the form set, the main Visual FoxPro window becomes active.

Calling the Hide Method for the _SCREEN system variable has no effect.

Applies To

Form, FormSet, _SCREEN, ToolBar

See Also

Activate Event, Deactivate Event, Enabled Property, GotFocus Event, Show Method, Visible Property

HIDE POPUP Command

Hides one or more active menus created with DEFINE POPUP.

Syntax

HIDE POPUP *MenuName1* [, *MenuName2* ...] | ALL
[SAVE]

Arguments

MenuName1 [, *MenuName2* ...]
Specifies the name of the menu or a list of menus (separated by commas) to hide.

ALL
Hides all defined menus.

SAVE
Places an image of a menu in the main Visual FoxPro window or in a user-defined window. Placing an image of a menu on the screen is useful during program development and testing. Menu images can be cleared from the main Visual FoxPro window or from a user-defined window with CLEAR.

Remarks

HIDE POPUP removes the specified menu, a set of menus, or all menus from the main Visual FoxPro window or from a user-defined window without removing the menu definitions from memory. Before a menu can be hidden, it must first be created with DEFINE POPUP. Hiding a menu isn't the same as deactivating it. When a menu is hidden, it stays resident in memory and can be displayed in the main Visual FoxPro window or in a user-defined window with ACTIVATE POPUP or SHOW POPUP.

See Also

ACTIVATE POPUP, DEFINE BAR, DEFINE POPUP, SHOW POPUP

HIDE WINDOW Command

Hides an active user-defined window or Microsoft Visual FoxPro system window.

Syntax

HIDE WINDOW *WindowName1* [, *WindowName2* ...] | ALL | SCREEN
[IN [WINDOW] *WindowNameN* | IN [WINDOW] SCREEN
| IN [WINDOW]
[BOTTOM | TOP | SAME]

Arguments

WindowName1 [, *WindowName2* ...]

Specifies the name of the window or a list of windows (separated by commas) to hide. If you issue HIDE WINDOW without any arguments, the active window is hidden. In Visual FoxPro, you can specify the name of a toolbar to hide. See the SHOW WINDOW Command, later in this language reference, for a list of Visual FoxPro toolbar names.

ALL

Hides all windows.

SCREEN

Hides the main Visual FoxPro window. To display the main Visual FoxPro window again, issue ACTIVATE WINDOW SCREEN or SHOW WINDOW SCREEN.

IN [WINDOW] *WindowNameN*

Hides the window within a parent window.

IN [WINDOW] SCREEN

Explicitly hides a window in the main Visual FoxPro window.

BOTTOM | TOP | SAME

Specifies where windows are hidden with respect to other windows. BOTTOM places a window behind all other windows. TOP (the default) places a window in front of all other windows. SAME hides a window without affecting its front-to-back placement. To preserve the relative positions of multiple hidden windows when they are redisplayed with SHOW WINDOW ALL, include the SAME keyword when you hide the windows.

Remarks

HIDE WINDOW removes a window or a set of windows from the main Visual FoxPro window or from a user-defined window. You can use HIDE WINDOW to hide system windows, such as the Command window, the Data Session window, and so on.

Hiding a window isn't the same as closing it. When a window is hidden, it stays resident in memory and remains active. Output can be sent to a hidden window, but you cannot see it.

Releasing a window removes it from memory. Windows removed from memory must be defined again to be redisplayed. A window can be displayed with ACTIVATE WINDOW or SHOW WINDOW.

To hide a system window and or a toolbar (in Visual FoxPro), enclose the entire system window or toolbar name in quotation marks. For example, to hide the Report Controls toolbar in Visual FoxPro, issue the following command:

```
HIDE WINDOW "Report Controls"
```

Example

In the following example, a window named wOutput1 is defined and activated. The program waits for you to press a key and then hides the window. The program waits for you to press a key again and then displays the window. Pressing a key a third time removes the window from the screen and from memory.

```
DEFINE WINDOW wOutput1 FROM 6,1 TO 19,75 TITLE 'Output' ;
    CLOSE FLOAT GROW ZOOM
ACTIVATE WINDOW wOutput1

WAIT WINDOW 'Press a key to hide this window'
HIDE WINDOW wOutput1

WAIT WINDOW 'Press a key to see the window again'
SHOW WINDOW wOutput1

WAIT WINDOW 'Press a key to remove the window from memory'
DEACTIVATE WINDOW wOutput1
RELEASE WINDOW wOutput1
```

See Also

ACTIVATE WINDOW, DEACTIVATE WINDOW, DEFINE WINDOW, RELEASE WINDOW, SHOW WINDOW

HideDoc Event

Occurs when you navigate from an Active Document.

Syntax

PROCEDURE *Object*.HideDoc

Remarks

The HideDoc event occurs when you navigate from an Active Document to another document or the Active Document's container is closed.

The HideDoc event doesn't occur when the Active Document's container is minimized or when the container is restored to its original size.

Applies To

ActiveDoc Object

See Also

ShowDoc Event

HideSelection Property

Specifies whether selected text appears selected when a control loses focus. Available at design time and run time.

Syntax

Control.HideSelection[= *lExpr*]

Arguments

lExpr

The settings for the HideSelection property are:

Setting	Description
True (.T.)	(Default) Selected text does not appear selected when the control loses the focus.
False (.F.)	Selected text appears selected when the control loses the focus.

Remarks

You can use this property to indicate the text that is selected while another form or a dialog box has the focus — for example, in a spelling-check routine.

Applies To

ComboBox, EditBox, Spinner, TextBox

See Also

DisabledBackColor, DisabledForeColor Properties, GotFocus Event, LostFocus Event

Highlight Property

Specifies whether the cell with the focus in the Grid control appears selected. Available at design time; read/write at run time.

Syntax

Grid.Highlight[= *lExpr*]

Arguments

lExpr

The settings for the Highlight property are:

Setting	Description
True (.T.)	(Default) Selected cell is selected.
False (.F.)	Selected cell is not selected.

Remarks

If the HighLight property is set to true (.T.), you can use it in conjunction with a Column's SelectOnEntry property to determine if the entire cell appears selected. If you set the HighLight property to false (.F.), the SelectOnEntry property is ignored.

Applies To

Grid

See Also

HighlightRow Property, SelectOnEntry Property

HighlightRow Property

Specifies whether the current row and cell in a Grid control is highlighted. Available at design time; read/write at run time.

Syntax

Grid.HighlightRow[= *lExpr*]

Arguments

lExpr
> The settings for the HighlightRow property are:

Setting	Description
True (.T.)	(Default) Current row and cell are highlighted.
False (.F.)	Current row and cell are not highlighted.

Applies To

Grid

See Also

Highlight Property

HOME( ) Function

Returns the names of the Visual FoxPro and Visual Studio directories.

Syntax

HOME([*nLocation*])

Returns

Character

Arguments

nLocation

Specifies that HOME( ) returns the name of a specific Visual FoxPro or Visual Studio directory. Note that omitting *nLocation* is identical to HOME(0).

The following table lists the values for *nLocation* and the directory the HOME( ) returns. The directories listed below assume that you chose the default installation directory when you installed Visual FoxPro or Visual Studio.

nLocation	Directory
0 or omitted	The directory from which Visual FoxPro was started.
1	The Visual FoxPro installation root directory.
2	The directory containing the Visual FoxPro samples. This directory is identical to the samples directory in the _SAMPLES system variable.
3	The Visual Studio Common directory.
4	The Visual Studio Common\Graphics directory.
5	The Visual Studio and MSDN samples directory.
6	The Visual Studio Common\Tools directory.

Remarks

HOME( ) is similar to SYS(2004) and is provided for compatibility with dBASE IV.

Example

```
CLEAR
? 'Visual FoxPro startup directory:        ', HOME( )
? 'Visual FoxPro installation directory:  ', HOME(1)
? 'Visual FoxPro samples directory:        ', HOME(2)
? 'Visual Studio common directory:         ', HOME(3)
? 'Visual Studio graphics directory:       ', HOME(4)
? 'Visual Studio samples directory:        ', HOME(5)
? 'Visual Studio tools directory:          ', HOME(6)
```

See Also

_SAMPLES System Variable, SYS( ) Functions Overview, SYS(2004) – Visual FoxPro Start Directory

HomeDir Property

Specifies the home directory for a project.

Syntax

Object.HomeDir[= *cDirectory*]

Arguments

cDirectory

Specifies the home directory for the project. The default value is the directory in which the project file (.pjx) is located.

Remarks

The home directory for a project is the relative path for all the files in the project. The HomeDir property corresponds to the directory in the **Home** text box on the **Project** tab of the Project Information dialog box.

Applies To

Project Object

See Also

CURDIR( ), Project Information Dialog Box

HostName Property

Returns or sets the user-readable host name of your Visual FoxPro application. Available at design time; read/write at run time.

Syntax

Control.HostName [= *cName*]

Arguments

cName

Returns or sets a string expression specifying the host name.

Remarks

When editing an object, the HostName property setting can be displayed in the object's window title. However, some applications that provide objects do not display the HostName.

Applies To

OLE Bound Control, OLE Container Control

See Also

DocumentFile Property

HOUR( ) Function

Returns the hour portion from a DateTime expression.

Syntax

HOUR(*tExpression*)

Arguments

tExpression
    Specifies a DateTime expression from which HOUR( ) returns the hour.

Returns

Numeric

Remarks

HOUR( ) returns a numeric value based on a 24 hour format, and is not affected by the current setting of SET HOURS. For example, if SET HOURS is 12 or 24, the following command returns 13:

```
? HOUR({^1998-02-16 1:00p})
```

Example

The following example displays the hour portion of the current time and the hour portion of a specific time.

```
CLEAR
? HOUR(DATETIME( ))
? HOUR({^1998-02-16 10:42a})   && Displays 10
```

See Also

CTOT( ), DATE( ), DATETIME( ), DTOT( ), MINUTE( ), SEC( ), SECONDS( ), SET SECONDS, TIME( )

Hours Property

Specifies whether the hours portion of a DateTime value is displayed in 12- or 24-hour time format. Available at design time and run time.

Syntax

Object.Hours[= *nValue*]

Arguments

nValue

One of the following settings:

Setting	Description
0	(Default) The SET HOURS setting determines whether the hours portion of a DateTime value is displayed in 12- or 24-hour time format. If SET HOURS is 12, the hours portion of a DateTime value is displayed in 12-hour time format. If SET HOURS is 24, the hours portion of a DateTime value is displayed in 24-hour time format.
12	The hour portion of the DateTime value is displayed in a 12-hour time format.
24	The hour portion of the DateTime value is displayed in a 24-hour time format.

Remarks

The Hours property setting is ignored if the DateFormat property is set to Short or Long.

Applies To

TextBox

See Also

Century Property, DateFormat Property, DateMark Property, Seconds Property, SET HOURS, StrictDateEntry Property

HScrollSmallChange Property

Specifies the increment a form scrolls in the horizontal direction when you click on a horizontal scroll arrow. Available at design time and run time.

Syntax

Object.HScrollSmallChange[= *nExpression*]

Arguments

nExpression

Specifies the increment for horizontal scrolling. The unit of measure is determined by the Scalemode property setting. The default increment is 10 pixels when the Scalemode property is set to 3-Pixels.

Applies To

Form

See Also

ScaleMode Property, ScrollBars Property, VScrollSmallChange Property

Hyperlink Object

Creates a Hyperlink object.

Syntax

Hyperlink

Remarks

A Hyperlink object provides navigational capabilities for Visual FoxPro applications and Active Documents hosted in containers such as Microsoft Internet Explorer. Using the Hyperlink object, Visual FoxPro applications can request an Active Document container to jump to a given URL (Uniform Resource Locator).

A Hyperlink object has no user interface. The HyperLink object's NavigateTo method allows you to jump to a specific URL, and the GoBack and GoForward methods allow you to move backward or forward within the container's history list.

Note that the Hyperlink object is supported only in Microsoft Internet Explorer. Use the Visual FoxPro Hyperlink Button, Hyperlink Image, or Hyperlink Label foundation classes in the Component Gallery for browser independent navigational capabilities.

Properties

Application	BaseClass	Class
ClassLibrary	Comment	Name
Parent	ParentClass	Tag

Events

Destroy	Error	Init

Methods

AddProperty	GoBack Method	GoFoward Method
NavigateTo Method	ReadExpression	ReadMethod
ResetToDefault	SaveAsClass	WriteExpression

See Also

ActiveDoc Object

Icon Property

For forms, specifies the icon displayed for a form at run time when the form is minimized. Available at design time and run time.

For a project object, specifies the icon displayed for a distributed .exe application.

Syntax

Object.Icon[= *cFileName*]

Arguments

cFileName

For a form, specifies the file name and path of the icon to display when the form is minimized. For a distributed .exe application, specifies the file name and path of the icon displayed for the application.

Remarks

For forms, use the Icon property to specify a custom icon for any form that the user can minimize at run time. For example, you can assign a unique icon to a form to indicate the form's function. Enter the file name of the icon in the Properties window at design time. The file name you enter must have the .ico extension and icon format. If you do not specify a custom icon, the Visual FoxPro default icon for forms is used.

You can use the Microsoft Visual FoxPro Icon Library in the Graphics\Icons subdirectory as a source for icons.

> **Note** If you set the Icon property at design time and the file you specify does not exist, Visual FoxPro displays an error message, but the property remains set to the file you specified. Visual FoxPro ignores the Icon property at run time if it is set to a file that does not exist.

For a project object, use the Icon property to specify the icon displayed for a distributed .exe application. You cannot specify an icon for a distributed Visual FoxPro .app application.

Applies To

Form, Project Object, _SCREEN

See Also

Caption Property, Picture Property

IDXCOLLATE( ) Function

Returns the collation sequence for an index or index tag.

Syntax

IDXCOLLATE([*cCDXFileName*,] *nIndexNumber* [, *nWorkArea* | *cTableAlias*])

Returns

Character

Arguments

cCDXFileName
> Specifies the name of the compound index file. The compound index file you specify can be the structural compound index file automatically opened with the table or an independent compound index file.

nIndexNumber
> Specifies the index or index tag for which IDXCOLLATE( ) returns the collation sequence. IDXCOLLATE( ) returns the collation sequence for indexes and index tags in the following order as *nIndexNumber* increases from 1 to the total number of open index files and index tags:

> 1. Collation sequences for single-entry .idx index files (if any are open) are returned first. The order in which the single-entry index files are included in USE or SET INDEX determines how the collation sequences are returned.

> 2. Collation sequences for tags in the structural compound index (if one is present) are returned next. The collation sequences are returned for the tags in the order in which the tags are created in the structural compound index.

> 3. Collation sequences for tags in any open independent compound indexes are returned last. The collation sequences are returned for the tags in the order in which the tags are created in the independent compound indexes.

> The empty string is returned if *nIndexNumber* is greater than the total number of open single-entry .idx files and structural compound and independent compound index tags.

nWorkArea
> Specifies the work area of the table for which IDXCOLLATE( ) returns index file and index tag collation sequences.

> IDXCOLLATE( ) returns the empty string if a table isn't open in the work area you specify.

cTableAlias
> Specifies the alias of the table for which IDXCOLLATE( ) returns index file and index tag collation sequences.

> Visual FoxPro generates an error message if you specify a table alias that doesn't exist.

Remarks

IDXCOLLATE( ) can be used to return the collation sequence for each tag in multiple-entry compound index files, allowing you to completely delete an index file and rebuild it correctly, using a series of SET COLLATE and INDEX commands.

Note that IDXCOLLATE( ) isn't required for the proper functioning of REINDEX, because the collation sequence information is present in existing indexes and index tags.

For additional information about Visual FoxPro's international support, see Chapter 18, "Developing International Applications," in the *Microsoft Visual FoxPro 6.0 Programmer's Guide*.

Example

The following example opens the customer table in the testdata database.
FOR ... ENDFOR is used to create a loop in which IDXCOLLATE( ) is used to display the collation sequence of each index tag in the customer structural index. The name of each structural index tag is displayed with its collation sequence.

```
CLOSE DATABASES
OPEN DATABASE (HOME(2) + 'Data\testdata')
USE Customer      && Open customer table
CLEAR

FOR nCount = 1 TO 254
    IF !EMPTY(TAG(nCount))  && Checks for tags in the index
    ? TAG(nCount) + ' '  && Display tag name
    ?? IDXCOLLATE(nCount)  && Display collation sequence
    ELSE
        EXIT  && Exit the loop when no more tags are found
    ENDIF
ENDFOR
```

See Also

SET COLLATE

IF ... ENDIF Command

Conditionally executes a set of commands based on the value of a logical expression.

Syntax

IF *lExpression* [THEN]
   Commands
[ELSE
   Commands]
ENDIF

Arguments

lExpression

Specifies the logical expression that is evaluated. If *lExpression* evaluates to true (.T.), any commands following IF or THEN and preceding ELSE or ENDIF (whichever occurs first) are executed.

- If *lExpression* is false (.F.) and ELSE is included, any commands after ELSE and before ENDIF are executed.

- If *lExpression* is false (.F.) and ELSE isn't included, all commands between IF and ENDIF are ignored. In this case, program execution continues with the first command following ENDIF.

Remarks

You can nest an IF ... ENDIF block within another IF ... ENDIF block.

Comments preceded by && can be placed on the same line after IF, THEN, ELSE, and ENDIF. These comments are ignored during compilation and program execution.

Example

```
CLOSE DATABASES
OPEN DATABASE (HOME(2) + 'Data\testdata')
USE Customer      && Open customer table

GETEXPR 'Enter condition to locate ' TO gcTemp;
   TYPE 'L' DEFAULT 'COMPANY = ""'
LOCATE FOR &gcTemp  && Enter LOCATE expression
IF FOUND( )  && Was it found?
   DISPLAY  && If so, display the record
ELSE  && If not found
   ? 'Condition ' + gcTemp + ' was not found '   && Display a message
ENDIF
USE
```

See Also

DO CASE ... ENDCASE, DO WHILE ... ENDDO, FOR ... ENDFOR, IIF( ), SCAN ... ENDSCAN

IIF( ) Function

Returns one of two values depending on the value of a logical expression.

Syntax

IIF(*lExpression*, *eExpression1*, *eExpression2*)

Returns

Character, Numeric, Currency, Date, or DateTime

Arguments

lExpression
Specifies the logical expression that IIF( ) evaluates.

eExpression1, *eExpression2*
If *lExpression* evaluates to true (.T.), *eExpression1* is returned. If *lExpression* evaluates to false (.F.), *eExpression2* is returned.

Remarks

This function, also known as Immediate IF, evaluates a logical expression and then returns one of two expressions. If the logical expression evaluates to true (.T.), IIF( ) returns the first expression. If the logical expression evaluates to false (.F.), IIF( ) returns the second expression.

> **Tip** This function can be used in place of IF ... ENDIF for simple conditional expressions, and is especially useful in report and label expressions that conditionally specify field contents. The IIF( ) function also executes faster than an equivalent IF ... ENDIF.

Example

The following example uses IIF( ) to check if the notes field in the employee table is empty. If it is empty, "No description" is displayed; otherwise, the contents of the memo field are displayed.

```
CLOSE DATABASES
OPEN DATABASE (HOME(2) + 'Data\testdata')
USE employee  && Open Employee table
CLEAR

SCAN
   ? IIF(EMPTY(notes), 'No notes', notes)     && Empty memo field?
ENDSCAN
```

See Also

IF ... ENDIF

Image Control

Creates an Image control that displays a .bmp picture.

Syntax

Image

Remarks

An Image control is a graphical control that displays bitmaps that can't be changed directly. However, because an Image control has a full set of properties, events, and methods that other controls have, an Image control can respond to events and can be changed dynamically at run time.

For additional information about creating Images, see Chapter 10, "Using Controls," in the *Microsoft Visual FoxPro 6.0 Programmer's Guide*.

Properties

Application	BackStyle	BaseClass
BorderColor	BorderStyle	Class
ClassLibrary	ColorSource	Comment
DragIcon	DragMode	Enabled
Height	HelpContextID	Left
MousePointer	Name	OLEDragMode
OLEDragPicture	OLEDropEffects	OLEDropHasData Property
OLEDropMode	Parent	ParentClass
Picture	Stretch	Tag
ToolTipText	Top	Visible
WhatsThisHelpID	Width	

Events

Click	DblClick	Destroy
DragDrop	DragOver	Error
Init	MiddleClick Event	MouseDown
MouseMove	MouseUp	MouseWheel
OLECompleteDrag	OLEDragDrop	OLEDragOver
OLEGiveFeedBack	OLESetData	OLEStartDrag
RightClick	UIEnable	

Methods

AddProperty	CloneObject	Drag
Move	OLEDrag	ReadExpression
ReadMethod	ResetToDefault	SaveAsClass
WriteExpression	WriteMethod	Zorder

See Also

CREATE CLASS, CREATE FORM, DEFINE CLASS

IMEMode Property

Specifies the Input Method Editor (IME) window setting for an individual control. Available at design time and run time.

Syntax

Object.IMEMode[= *nExpression*]

Arguments

nExpression
    One of the following settings:

nExpression	IME window action
0	(Default) No Control. The operating system determines if the IME window is opened when the control has the focus. If the IME window is closed when the control has the focus, the IME window can be opened by pressing THE KEY COMBINATION THAT ACTIVATES THE IME WINDOW.
1	Open IME. The IME window is opened when the control has the focus.
2	Close IME. The IME window is closed when the control has the focus. The IME window can be opened by pressing the key combination that activates the IME window.

Remarks

This property is ignored unless you are running a Far East version of Microsoft Windows 95 or Windows NT.

Applies To

ComboBox, EditBox, TextBox

See Also

IMESTATUS( ), SET BROWSEIME

IMESTATUS( ) Function

Turns the IME (Input Method Editor) window on or off or returns the current IME status.

Syntax

IMESTATUS([*nExpression*])

Returns

Numeric

Arguments

nExpression

Turns the IME window on or off. The following table lists the values for *nExpression* and the corresponding state of the IME window.

nExpression	IME window action
0	Turns the IME window off.
1	Turns the IME window on.

If *nExpression* is omitted, IMESTATUS( ) returns the current IME status. The following table lists the values returned for the IME status. Use VERSION(3) to determine the current locale.

The following table lists the values returned for the IME status in the Japanese locale.

Return value	IME status
0	No IME installed
1	IME on
2	IME off
3	IME disabled
4	Hiragana mode (double-byte)
5	Katakana mode (double-byte)
6	Katakana mode (single-byte)
7	Alphanumeric mode (double-byte)
8	Alphanumeric mode (single-byte)

The following table lists the values returned for the IME status in the Korean locale.

Return value	IME status
0	No IME installed
1	Hangul mode (single-byte)
2	English mode (single-byte)
11	English mode (double-byte)
15	Hangul mode (double-byte)
23	Hanja conversion mode (Hangul + single-byte mode)
31	Hanja conversion mode (Hangul + double-byte mode)

Remarks

For more information, see "Entering International Characters" in Chapter 18, "Developing International Applications," in the *Microsoft Visual FoxPro 6.0 Programmer's Guide*.

This function is useful for manipulating double-byte character sets for languages such as Hiragana and Katakana.

See Also

SET BROWSEIME, IMEMode Property, ISLEADBYTE( ), STRCONV( )

IMPORT Command

Imports data from an external file format to create a new Visual FoxPro table.

Syntax

IMPORT FROM *FileName*
    [DATABASE *DatabaseName* [NAME *LongTableName*]]
    [TYPE] FW2 I MOD I PDOX I RPD I WK1
    I WK3 I WKS I WR1 I WRK I XLS
    I XL5 [SHEET *cSheetName*]
    I XL8 [SHEET *cSheetName*]
    [AS *nCodePage*]

Arguments

FileName
    Specifies the name of the file from which to import data. If you don't include an extension with the file name, the default extension for the specified file type is assumed.

DATABASE *DatabaseName*
    Specifies a database to which the new table is added.

NAME *LongTableName*

Specifies a long name for the new table. Long names can contain up to 128 characters and can be used in place of short file names in the database.

TYPE

The keyword TYPE is optional, but you must include one of the following file types:

File type	Description
FW2	Include FW2 to import FW2 files, created by Framework II.
MOD	Include MOD to import MOD files, created by Microsoft Multiplan version 4.1.
PDOX	Include PDOX to import Paradox files. Database files in Paradox versions 3.5 and 4.0 by Borland can be imported by including the PDOX option.
RPD	Include RPD to import RPD files, created by RapidFile.
WK1 | WK3 | WKS	Include WK1 to import data from a Lotus 1-2-3 spreadsheet. Columns from the spreadsheet become fields in the table and the spreadsheet rows become records in the table. A WK1 extension is assigned to spreadsheets created in Lotus 1-2-3 revision 2.x; a WK3 extension is assigned to spreadsheets created in Lotus 1-2-3 revision 3.x; and a .wks extension is assigned to spreadsheets created in Lotus 1-2-3 revision 1-A.
WR1 | WRK	Include WR1 to import data from a Lotus Symphony spreadsheet. Columns from the spreadsheet become fields in the table and the spreadsheet rows become records in the table. A WR1 extension is assigned to spreadsheets created in Symphony version 1.10, and a .wrk extension is assigned to spreadsheets created in Symphony version 1.1.
XLS	Include XLS to import data from Microsoft Excel worksheets versions 2.0, 3.0, and 4.0. Columns from the worksheet become fields in the table and the worksheet rows become records in the table. Worksheet files created in Microsoft Excel have an .xls extension.
XL5 [SHEET *cSheetName*]	Include XL5 to import data from Microsoft Excel version 5.0. Columns from the worksheet become fields in the table and the worksheet rows become records in the table. Worksheet files created in Microsoft Excel have an .xls extension.
	If you omit the SHEET clause, the data in Sheet1 is imported. To import data from a specific sheet, include the SHEET keyword and specify the sheet name with *cSheetName*.
XL8 [SHEET *cSheetName*]	Include XL8 to import data from Microsoft Excel 97. Columns from the worksheet become fields in the table and the worksheet rows become records in the table. Worksheet files created in Microsoft Excel have an .xls extension.
	If you omit the SHEET clause, the data in Sheet1 is imported. To import data from a specific sheet, include the SHEET keyword and specify the sheet name with *cSheetName*.

AS *nCodePage*

>Specifies the code page of the imported file. Visual FoxPro copies the contents of the imported file and, as it copies the data, automatically converts the data to the current Visual FoxPro code page.

>If you specify a value for *nCodePage* that is not supported, Visual FoxPro displays an error message. You can use GETCP( ) for *nCodePage* to display the Code Page dialog box, allowing you to specify a code page for the imported file.

>If you omit AS *nCodePage* and Visual FoxPro cannot determine the code page of the imported file, Visual FoxPro copies the contents of the imported file and, as it copies the data, automatically converts the data to the current Visual FoxPro code page. If you omit AS *nCodePage* and Visual FoxPro can determine the code page of the imported file, Visual FoxPro automatically converts the data in the imported file from the data's code page to the current Visual FoxPro code page. Use CPCURRENT( ) to determine the current Visual FoxPro code page.

>If *nCodePage* is 0, Visual FoxPro assumes the code page of the imported file is the same as the current Visual FoxPro code page and no code page conversion occurs.

Remarks

Most software packages store their data in file formats that cannot be opened directly in Visual FoxPro. IMPORT creates a new Visual FoxPro table from data stored in file formats that Visual FoxPro cannot directly read.

A new table is created with the same name as the file from which the data is imported. A .dbf extension is assigned to the newly created table.

See Also

APPEND FROM, COPY TO, EXPORT, GETCP( )

_INCLUDE System Variable

Specifies a default header file included with user-defined classes, forms, or form sets.

Syntax

_INCLUDE = *HeaderFileName*

Arguments

HeaderFileName

>Specifies a default header file of predefined compile-time constants automatically included with user-defined classes, forms, or form sets. If your header file is in a directory other than the current default directory, include a path with the header file name. Contains the empty string by default.

Remarks

You can also specify the default header file with the **Default Include File** item in the **File Locations** tab of the **Options** dialog box.

See Also

CREATE CLASS, CREATE FORM, File Locations Tab, Options Dialog Box, #INCLUDE

Increment Property

Specifies how much the value in the Spinner control increases or decreases when you click the up or down arrow. Available at design time and run time.

Syntax

*Spinner.*Increment[= *nIncrement*]

Arguments

nIncrement
Specifies the number to add to the Spinner when the up button is clicked and the number to subtract from the Spinner when the down button is clicked. The default is 1.00.

Applies To

Spinner

See Also

RangeLow Event

IncrementalSearch Property

Specifies whether a control supports an incremental search for keyboard steering. Available at design time and run time.

Syntax

*Control.*IncrementalSearch[= *lExpr*]

Arguments

lExpr
The settings for the IncrementalSearch property are:

Setting	Description
True (.T.)	(Default) Supports incremental search.
False (.F.)	Does not support incremental search.

Remarks

An example of an incremental search is if you are searching for the word "ELASTIC," you can type E-L-A, and so on. As you type, Visual FoxPro incrementally searches for the combination of letters you have typed to match the word you are looking for. Otherwise, it finds the first word that starts with an E, then the first word that starts with an L, and so on.

Note that the setting of the _DBLCLICK system variable determines how long to wait for the next letter to be typed. You may need to adjust the value of _DBLCLICK to make incremental searching work properly.

Applies To

ComboBox, ListBox

See Also

ComboBox, _DBLCLICK, ListBox

INDBC( ) Function

Returns true (.T.) if the specified database object is in the current database; otherwise returns false (.F.).

Syntax

INDBC(*cDatabaseObjectName*, *cType*)

Returns

Logical

Arguments

cDatabaseObjectName
Specifies the name of a named connection, field, index, table, or SQL view for which INDBC( ) returns a logical value indicating whether or not the object is in the current database.

cType
Specifies the database object type of *cDatabaseObjectName*. The following table lists the values for *cType* and the corresponding database object type.

cType	Database object type
CONNECTION	Named connection
FIELD	Field
INDEX	Index
TABLE	Table
VIEW	SQL View

The CONNECTION, FIELD, INDEX, TABLE, and VIEW settings cannot be abbreviated.

Remarks

A database must be open and current when INDBC( ) is issued; otherwise Visual FoxPro generates an error message.

Example

In the following example, a temporary database named `mydbc` is created, and a temporary table named `mytable` is added to the database. INDBC( ) is used to determine if the new table is in the database. The database and table are closed and erased.

```
CLOSE DATABASES
CREATE DATABASE mydbc  && Creates a new database
CREATE TABLE mytable (field1 C(10)) && Automatically added to database

? 'MyTable in the database? '
?? INDBC('mytable', 'TABLE')  && Returns .T.

CLOSE DATABASES
DELETE DATABASE mydbc DELETETABLES
```

See Also

ADBOBJECTS( ), CREATE DATABASE, DELETE DATABASE, OPEN DATABASE, SET DATABASE

_INDENT System Variable

Included for backward compatibility. Use the Report Designer instead.

INDEX Command

Creates an index file to display and access table records in a logical order.

Syntax

INDEX ON *eExpression* TO *IDXFileName* I TAG *TagName* [OF *CDXFileName*]
    [FOR *lExpression*]
    [COMPACT]
    [ASCENDING I DESCENDING]
    [UNIQUE I CANDIDATE]
    [ADDITIVE]

Arguments

eExpression

Specifies an index expression that can include the name of a field or fields from the current table. An index key based on the index expression is created in the index file for each record in the table. Visual FoxPro uses these keys to display and access records in the table.

> **Note** Do not use a variable, an array element, or a field or field expression from a table in another work area for *eExpression*. If you access an index that contains a variable or field that no longer exists or cannot be located, Visual FoxPro generates an error message. Memo fields cannot be used alone in index file expressions; they must be combined with other character expressions.

> If you include a field prefaced by a table alias or work area letter in the index expression, Visual FoxPro generates an error message. Even though you can optimize FOR clauses with Rushmore technology if aliased fields are included, it is still highly recommended that you avoid using aliased fields when creating indexes. In several cases (USE ... AGAIN, SQL queries, and so on), a different alias is automatically assigned to a table and the index might not be properly updated or used.

> For more information on Rushmore technology, see "Understanding Rushmore Technology" in Chapter 15, "Optimizing Applications," in the *Microsoft Visual FoxPro 6.0 Programmer's Guide*.

If you attempt to build an index with a key that varies in length, the key will be padded with spaces. Variable-length index keys aren't supported in Visual FoxPro.

It is possible to create an index key with 0 length. For example, a 0-length index key is created when the index expression is a substring of an empty memo field. A 0-length index key generates an error message. When Visual FoxPro creates an index, it evaluates fields in the first record in the table. If a field is empty, it may be necessary to enter some temporary data in the field in the first record to prevent a 0-length index key.

The length of an index key for an .idx index must be between 1 and 100 characters. The length of an index key for a .cdx index must be between 1 and 240 characters.

TO *IDXFileName*

Creates an .idx index file. The index file is given the default extension .idx, which you can override by including a different extension or by changing the default index extension in the Visual FoxPro configuration file. Standard Windows rules for naming files, which include long file names, must be observed when creating index files.

TAG *TagName* [OF *CDXFileName*]

Creates a compound index file. A compound index file is a single index file that consists of any number of separate tags (index entries). Each tag is identified by its unique tag name. Tag names must begin with a letter or an underscore and can consist of any combination of up to 10 letters, digits, or underscores. The number of tags in a compound index file is limited only by available memory and disk space.

Multiple-entry compound index files are always compact. It isn't necessary to include COMPACT when creating a compound index file. Names of compound index files are given a .cdx extension.

Two types of compound index files can be created: structural and non-structural.

If you exclude the optional OF *CDXFileName* clause from TAG *TagName*, you create a *structural compound index file*. A structural compound index file always has the same base name as the table and is automatically opened when the table is opened.

If a table's structural compound index file cannot be located or is deleted or renamed, a dialog box appears when you try to open the table. If you choose the default Cancel push button, the table isn't opened. Choosing Ignore opens the table and removes the flag in the table's header that indicates an associated structural compound index file is present.

> **Tip** To reassociate a structural compound index that has become dissociated from its table, issue the following command:

```
USE TableName INDEX CDXFileName
```

If you include the optional OF *CDXFileName* clause after TAG *TagName,* you create a *non-structural compound index file*. Unlike a structural compound index file, a non-structural compound index file must be explicitly opened with SET INDEX or the INDEX clause in USE.

If a compound index file has already been created and opened, issuing INDEX with TAG *TagName* adds a tag to the compound index file.

CDXFileName is the name of the dissociated structural compound index. Be sure to reindex the table if it has been modified since the structural compound index was dissociated.

FOR *lExpression*
:   Specifies a condition whereby only records that satisfy the filter expression *lExpression* are available for display and access; index keys are created in the index file for just those records matching the filter expression.

    Rushmore optimizes an INDEX ... FOR *lExpression* command if *lExpression* is an optimizable expression. For best performance, use an optimizable expression in the FOR clause.

    For more information, see the SET OPTIMIZE Command, later in this language reference, and "Understanding Rushmore Technology" in Chapter 15, "Optimizing Applications," in the *Microsoft Visual FoxPro 6.0 Programmer's Guide*.

COMPACT
:   Creates a compact .idx file.

ASCENDING

Specifies an ascending order for the .cdx file. By default, .cdx tags are created in ascending order (you can include ASCENDING as a reminder of the index file's order). A table can be indexed in reverse order by including DESCENDING.

DESCENDING

Specifies a descending order for the .cdx file. You can't include DESCENDING when creating .idx index files. You can, however, specify a descending order for an .idx index file with SET INDEX and SET ORDER.

UNIQUE

Specifies that only the first record encountered with a particular index key value is included in an .idx file or a .cdx tag. UNIQUE can be used to prevent the display of or access to duplicate records. All records added with duplicate index keys are excluded from the index file. Using the UNIQUE option of INDEX is identical to executing SET UNIQUE ON before issuing INDEX or REINDEX.

When a UNIQUE index or index tag is active and a duplicate record is changed in a manner that changes its index key, the index or index tag is updated. However, the next duplicate record with the original index key cannot be accessed or displayed until you reindex the file using REINDEX.

CANDIDATE

Creates a candidate structural index tag. The CANDIDATE keyword can be included only when creating a structural index tag; otherwise Visual FoxPro generates an error message.

A candidate index tag prevents duplicate values in the field or combination of fields specified in the index expression *eExpression*. The term "candidate" refers to the type of index; because candidate indexes prevent duplicate values, they qualify as a "candidate" to be a primary index.

Visual FoxPro generates an error if you create a candidate index tag for a field or combination of fields that already contain duplicate values.

For additional information about candidate and primary index tags, see "Setting a Primary or Candidate Index" in Chapter 7, "Working with Tables," in the *Microsoft Visual FoxPro 6.0 Programmer's Guide*.

ADDITIVE

Keeps open any previously opened index files. If you omit the ADDITIVE clause when you create an index file or files for a table with INDEX, any previously opened index files (except the structural compound index) are closed.

Remarks

Records in a table that has an index file are displayed and accessed in the order specified by the index expression. The physical order of the records in the table isn't changed by an index file.

If SET TALK is ON, Visual FoxPro reports how many records are indexed during the indexing process. The record interval displayed during indexing can be specified with SET ODOMETER.

Use DISPLAY STATUS to display more information about open index files. This information includes the names of all open index files, their types (structural, .cdx, .idx), their index expressions, their collation sequences, and the name of the master index file or master tag.

The number of index files (.idx or .cdx) you can open is limited only by memory and system resources. In Visual FoxPro, FoxPro for Windows, and FoxPro for MS-DOS, the total number of files you can open is determined by the FILES setting in the MS-DOS Config.sys configuration file. For more information on the FILES setting, see your MS-DOS manual.

Index Types   Visual FoxPro lets you create two types of index files:

- Compound .cdx index files containing multiple index entries called tags.

- .idx index files containing one index entry.

You can also create a structural compound index file, which is automatically opened with the table.

> **Tip**   Because structural compound index files are automatically opened when the table is opened, they are the preferred index type.

Include COMPACT to create compact .idx index files. Compound index files are always compact.

Index Order and Updating   Only one index file (the master index file) or tag (the master tag) controls the order in which the table is displayed or accessed. Certain commands (SEEK, for example) use the master index file or tag to search for records. However, all open .idx and .cdx index files are updated as changes are made to the table. You can designate the master index file or tag with the INDEX clause of USE or with SET INDEX and SET ORDER.

User-Defined Functions   Although an index expression can contain a user-defined function, you should not use user-defined functions in an index expression. User-defined functions in an index expression increase the time it takes to create or update the index. Also, index updates may not occur when a user-defined function is used for an index expression.

If you use a user-defined function in an index expression, Visual FoxPro must be able to locate the user-defined function. When Visual FoxPro creates an index, the index expression is saved in the index file, but only a reference to the user-defined function is included in the index expression.

Examples

Example 1 opens the `customer` table and creates an index file named `complist`, which displays and processes records in the alphabetic order of the `company` field.

In Example 2, the `customer` table is again opened and an index file named `citycomp` is created from a substring of the first five characters of the `city` field and the first six characters of the `company` field. When this index file is used, records in the table are ordered primarily according to the `city` field and secondarily according to the `company` field.

In Example 3, index tags are created. The first tag is a structural compound index tag for `address`. The second tag is created in a non-structural index file named `custcdx`.

```
* Example 1
CLOSE DATABASES
OPEN DATABASE (HOME(2) + 'Data\testdata')
USE Customer      && Open customer table
INDEX ON company TO complist
CLEAR
DISPLAY STATUS

* Example 2
CLOSE DATABASES
OPEN DATABASE (HOME(2) + 'Data\testdata')
USE Customer       && Open customer table
INDEX ON SUBSTR(city,1,5) + SUBSTR(company,1,6) TO citycomp
CLEAR
DISPLAY STATUS

* Example 3
CLOSE DATABASES
OPEN DATABASE (HOME(2) + 'Data\testdata')
USE Customer       && Open customer table
INDEX ON address TAG address
INDEX ON company TAG company OF custcdx
CLEAR
DISPLAY STATUS
```

See Also

ALTER TABLE, CDX( ), COPY INDEXES, COPY TAG, DELETE TAG, FOR( ), INDEXSEEK( ), KEY( ), MDX( ), NDX( ), ORDER( ), REINDEX, SET COLLATE, SET INDEX, SET ODOMETER, SET ORDER, SET TALK, SET UNIQUE, SORT, SYS(14), SYS(21), SYS(22), SYS(2021), TAG( ), TAGCOUNT( ), USE

INDEXSEEK( ) Function

Without moving the record pointer, searches an indexed table for the first occurrence of a record whose index key matches a specified expression.

Syntax

INDEXSEEK(*eExpression* [, *lMovePointer* [, *nWorkArea* | *cTableAlias*
   [, *nIndexNumber* | *cIDXIndexFileName* | *cTagName*]]])

Returns

Logical

Arguments

eExpression
   Specifies the index key expression for which you want INDEXSEEK( ) to search.

lMovePointer
   Specifies if the record pointer is moved to the matching record. If *lMovePointer* is true (.T.) and a matching record exists, the record pointer is moved to the matching record. If *lMovePointer* is true (.T.) and a matching record doesn't exist, the record pointer isn't moved. If *lMovePointer* is false (.F.) or is omitted, the record pointer isn't moved even if a matching record exists.

nWorkArea
   Specifies the work area number of the table that is searched for the index key.

cTableAlias
   Specifies the alias of the table that is searched. If you omit *nWorkArea* and *cTableAlias*, the table in the currently selected work area is searched.

nIndexNumber
   Specifies the number of the index file or tag that is used to search for the index key. *nIndexNumber* refers to the index files as they are listed in USE or SET INDEX. Open .IDX files are numbered first in the order in which they appear in USE or SET INDEX. Tags in the structural .cdx file (if one exists) are then numbered in the order in which they were created. Finally, tags in any open independent .cdx files are numbered in the order in which they were created. For more information about index numbering, see the SET ORDER Command, later in this language reference.

cIDXIndexFileName
   Specifies an .idx file that is used to search for the index key.

cTagName
   Specifies a tag of a .cdx file that is used to search for the index key. The tag name can be from a structural .cdx file or any open independent .cdx file.

     Note The .idx file takes precedence if duplicate .idx file and tag names exist.

Remarks

INDEXSEEK( ) returns true (.T.) if a match is found; otherwise false (.F.) is returned. You can use INDEXSEEK( ) only with a table with an index order set, and you can search only for an index key. The match must be exact unless SET EXACT is set to OFF.

INDEXSEEK( ) provides a fast way to search for records without moving the record pointer. Because the record pointer isn't moved, rules and triggers aren't executed. If INDEXSEEK( ) returns true (.T.) indicating that a matching record is found, you can execute INDEXSEEK( ) again with the second parameter *lMovePointer* set to true (.T.) to move to the matching record.

See Also

INDEX, KEYMATCH( ), LOCATE, SEEK, SEEK( )

IndexToItemID Method

Returns an index for a given item ID.

Syntax

[*nItemID =*] *Control*.IndexToItemID(*nIndex*)

Arguments

nItemID
    Specifies a unique identification number.

nIndex
    Specifies a number that represents the position that an item is displayed in a control.

Remarks

Each item added to a ComboBox or ListBox has two identification numbers assigned to it:

- The *nItemID*, a unique identification number.

- The *nIndex*, an integer corresponding to the order in which items are displayed by the control: The first item in the list corresponds to *nIndex* = 1.

Initially, as items are added to the control, these two numbers are identical. But as items are sorted, removed, and added, these numbers are no longer identical.

Use the IndexToItemID method to return the *nItemID* number for a particular item in the control when you know its *nIndex* number.

Applies To

ComboBox, ListBox

See Also

AddItem Method, AddListItem Method, ItemIDToIndex Method

Init Event

Occurs when an object is created.

Syntax

PROCEDURE *Object*.Init
[LPARAMETERS Param1, Param2,...]

Arguments

Param1, Param2...
  Parameters are optional, but if parameters are passed, you must include an
  LPARAMETERS or PARAMETERS statement that lists each parameter. Otherwise,
  Visual FoxPro generates an error.

Remarks

For form sets and other container objects, the Init events for all the contained objects are
triggered before the container's Init event, so you can access the contained objects within
the container's Init event. The Init event for each contained object occurs in the order it
was added to the container object.

To prevent a control or an Active Document from being created, return false (.F.) from
the Init event. The Destroy event will not be triggered. For example, the following code
returns false (.F.) if the Invoice table is not available:

```
PROCEDURE INIT
  IF NOT FILE("INVOICE.DBF")
  ERROR 'Initialization Failed: File not found'
  RETURN .F.
  ELSE
  USE INVOICE IN 0 AGAIN
  THIS.WorkArea = SELECT()
  ENDIF
ENDPROC
```

Applies To

ActiveDoc Object, CheckBox, ComboBox, CommandButton, CommandGroup, Container
Object, Control Object, Cursor, Custom, DataEnvironment, EditBox, Form, FormSet,
Grid, Image, Label, Line, ListBox, OLE Bound Control, OLE Container Control,
OptionButton, OptionGroup, Page, PageFrame, ProjectHook Object, Relation, Shape,
Spinner, TextBox, Timer, ToolBar

See Also

AddObject Method, CREATEOBJECT( ), Load Event

InitialSelectedAlias Property

Specifies an alias associated with a Cursor object as the current alias when the data environment is loaded. Available at design time; read-only at run time.

Syntax

DataEnvironment.InitialSelectedAlias[= *cText*]

Settings

cText
    Specifies an alias name associated with a Cursor object.

Remarks

Mimics the behavior of SELECT.

Applies To

DataEnvironment

See Also

Alias Property, SELECT

INKEY( ) Function

Returns a number corresponding to the first mouse click or key press in the type-ahead buffer.

Syntax

INKEY([*nSeconds*] [, *cHideCursor*])

Returns

Numeric

Arguments

nSeconds
    Specifies how many seconds INKEY( ) waits for a keystroke. If *nSeconds* isn't included, INKEY( ) immediately returns a value for a keystroke. INKEY( ) waits indefinitely for a keystroke if *nSeconds* is 0.

cHideCursor
    Shows or hides the cursor, or checks for a mouse click. To show the cursor, include S in *cHideCursor*. To hide the cursor, include H in *cHideCursor*. If both S and H are included in *cHideCursor*, the last character in *cHideCursor* takes precedence.

By default, INKEY( ) doesn't detect a mouse click. To check for a mouse click, include M in *cHideCursor*. If M is included in *cHideCursor*, INKEY( ) returns the value 151 for a single mouse click. Refer to the second example in the following table to see how you can check for a double click.

To check for a mouse click and show the cursor, include both M and S. To check for a mouse click and hide the cursor, include H and M.

When a keyboard macro is assigned to a key or key combination, you can include E in *cHideCursor* to expand the keyboard macro. When E is included, INKEY( ) returns a value corresponding to the first keystroke assigned to the keyboard macro. You can return successive values for each keystroke in a macro by repeatedly executing INKEY( ) with E included. If you omit E, INKEY( ) returns the value for the key or key combination that triggers the keyboard macro.

Any characters other than H, M, S, and E in *cHideCursor* are ignored.

The following table lists INKEY( ) function return values for keys alone and in combination with the SHIFT, CTRL, and ALT keys. A dash (–) indicates that the key combination returns no value.

Key	Alone	SHIFT	CTRL	ALT
F1	28	84	94	104
F2	–1	85	95	105
F3	–2	86	96	106
F4	–3	87	97	107
F5	–4	88	98	108
F6	–5	89	99	109
F7	–6	90	100	110
F8	–7	91	101	111
F9	–8	92	102	112
F10	–9	93	103	113
F11	133	135	137	139
F12	134	136	138	140
1	49	33	–	120
2	50	64	–	121
3	51	35	–	122

(continued)

(continued)

Key	Alone	SHIFT	CTRL	ALT
4	52	36	–	123
5	53	37	–	124
6	54	94	–	125
7	55	38	–	126
8	56	42	–	127
9	57	40	–	128
0	48	41	–	19
a	97	65	1	30
b	98	66	2	48
c	99	67	3	46
d	100	68	4	32
e	101	69	5	18
f	102	70	6	33
g	103	71	7	34
h	104	72	127	35
I	105	73	9	23
j	106	74	10	36
k	107	75	11	37
l	108	76	12	38
m	109	77	13	50
n	110	78	14	49
o	111	79	15	24
p	112	80	16	25
q	113	81	17	16
r	114	82	18	19
s	115	83	19	31
t	116	84	20	20

(continued)

Key	Alone	SHIFT	CTRL	ALT
u	117	85	21	22
v	118	86	22	47
w	119	87	23	17
x	120	88	24	45
y	121	89	25	21
z	122	90	26	44
INS	22	22	146	162
HOME	1	55	29	151
DEL	7	7	147	163
END	6	49	23	159
PAGE UP	18	57	31	153
PAGE DOWN	3	51	30	161
UP ARROW	5	56	141	152
DOWN ARROW	24	50	145	160
RIGHT ARROW	4	54	2	157
LEFT ARROW	19	52	26	155
ESC	27	–/27	–*/27	–*/1
ENTER	13	13	10	–/166
BACKSPACE	127	127	127	14
TAB	9	15	148/*	*
SPACEBAR	32	32	32/–	57

* Keystroke reserved by Windows.

Remarks

INKEY( ) returns 0 if a key isn't pressed. If there are several keys in the type-ahead buffer, INKEY( ) returns the value of the first key entered in the buffer.

See Also

_DBLCLICK, KEYBOARD, KeyPress Event, LASTKEY( ), ON KEY, READKEY( ), SET TYPEAHEAD

INLIST( ) Function

Determines whether an expression matches another expression in a set of expressions.

Syntax

INLIST(*eExpression1*, *eExpression2* [, *eExpression3* ...])

Returns

Logical or null value

Arguments

eExpression1

Specifies the expression INLIST( ) searches for in the set of expressions.

eExpression2 [, *eExpression3* ...]

Specifies the set of expressions to search. You must include at least one expression (*eExpression2*), and can include up to 24 expressions (*eExpression2*, *eExpression3*, and so on).

All the expressions in the set of expressions must be of the same data type.

Remarks

INLIST( ) returns true (.T.) if it finds the expression in the set of expressions; otherwise INLIST( ) returns false (.F.). The null value is returned if *eExpression1* is the null value. The null value is also returned if *eExpression1* is not the null value, *eExpression1* does not match another expression, and at least one of the other expressions is the null value.

Example

In this example, INLIST( ) determines the quarter of the year for the current month. The current month is stored to the variable gcMonth. Each CASE statement uses INLIST( ) to determine whether the contents of gcMonth can be found in a list of month names. The name of the quarter returned is stored to the variable gcReporTitle.

```
SET TALK ON
STORE CMONTH(DATE( )) TO gcMonth
DO CASE
   CASE INLIST(gcMonth,'January','February','March')
      STORE 'First Quarter' TO gcReporTitle
   CASE INLIST(gcMonth,'April','May','June')
      STORE 'Second Quarter' TO gcReporTitle
   CASE INLIST(gcMonth,'July','August','September')
      STORE 'Third Quarter' TO gcReporTitle
   OTHERWISE
      STORE 'Fourth Quarter' TO gcReporTitle
ENDCASE
WAIT WINDOW gcReporTitle
```

See Also

BETWEEN( )

INPUT Command

Included for backward compatibility. Use the TextBox control instead.

InputMask Property

Specifies how data is entered and displayed in a control. Available at design time and run time.

Syntax

Control.InputMask[= *cMask*]

Settings

cMask

The settings for the InputMask property are:

Setting	Description
X	Any character can be entered.
9	Digits and signs, such as a minus (–) sign can be entered.
#	Digits, blanks, and signs can be entered.
$	Displays the current currency symbol (specified with SET CURRENCY) in a fixed position.
$$	Displays a floating currency symbol that is always adjacent to the digits in the spinner or text box.
*	Asterisks are displayed to the left of the value.
.	A period specifies the decimal point position.
,	Commas can be included to separate digits to the left of the decimal point.

Remarks

This property is in contrast to the Format property in which a behavior for the entire input field is specified. You can mix several Format codes, but they always affect everything in the input field.

Applies To

Column, ComboBox, Spinner, TextBox

See Also

DynamicInputMask Property, Format Property

INSERT Command

Included for backward compatibility. Use APPEND or INSERT – SQL instead.

INSERT – SQL Command

Appends a record to the end of a table that contains the specified field values.

Syntax

INSERT INTO *dbf_name* [(*fname1* [, *fname2*, ...])]
    VALUES (*eExpression1* [, *eExpression2*, ...])

– or –

INSERT INTO *dbf_name* FROM ARRAY *ArrayName* | FROM MEMVAR

Arguments

INSERT INTO *dbf_name*

Specifies the name of the table to which the new record is appended. *dbf_name* can include a path and can be a name expression.

If the table you specify isn't open, it is opened exclusively in a new work area and the new record is appended to the table. The new work area isn't selected; the current work area remains selected.

If the table you specify is open, INSERT appends the new record to the table. If the table is open in a work area other than the current work area, it isn't selected after the record is appended; the current work area remains selected.

[(*fname1* [, *fname2* [, ...]])]

Specifies the names of the fields in the new record into which the values are inserted.

VALUES (*eExpression1* [, *eExpression2* [, ...]])

Specifies the field values inserted into the new record. If you omit the field names, you must specify the field values in the order defined by the table structure. If SET NULL is ON, INSERT – SQL attempts to insert null values into any fields not specified in the VALUES clause.

FROM ARRAY *ArrayName*

Specifies the array whose data is inserted into the new record. The contents of the elements of the array, starting with the first element, are inserted into the corresponding fields of the record. The contents of the first array element are inserted into the first field of the new record; the contents of the second array element are inserted into the second field, and so on.

Any default values for fields are ignored when you include the FROM ARRAY clause.

FROM MEMVAR

Specifies that the contents of variables are inserted into fields with the same names as the variables. If a variable doesn't exist with the same name as the field, the field is left empty.

Remarks

The new record contains the data listed in the VALUES clause or contained in the specified array or variables. The record pointer is positioned on the new record.

Examples

The following example opens the `employee` table and adds one record.

```
USE employee
INSERT INTO employee (emp_no, fname, lname, officeno) ;
    VALUES (3022, "John", "Smith", 2101)
```

The following example opens the `customer` table in the `testdata` database. The contents of the current record are scattered to variables, and the table's structure is copied to a new table named `cust2`. INSERT – SQL is used to insert a new record in the `cust2` table, and BROWSE is issued to display the new record.

```
CLOSE DATABASES
CLEAR

OPEN DATABASE (HOME(2) + 'Data\testdata')
USE Customer      && Open customer table
* Scatter current record to memory variables
SCATTER MEMVAR

* Copy structure of current table to example table
COPY STRUCTURE TO cust2

* Insert record from memory variable
INSERT INTO cust2 FROM MEMVAR

SELECT CUST2
BROWSE

* Close and delete example table
USE
DELETE FILE cust2.dbf
```

See Also

CREATE QUERY, CREATE TABLE – SQL, MODIFY QUERY, SELECT – SQL

INSMODE( ) Function

Returns the current insert mode, or sets the insert mode on or off.

Syntax

INSMODE([*lExpression*])

Returns

Logical

Arguments

lExpression

Turns the insert mode on or off. INSMODE(.T.) turns the insert mode on and INSMODE(.F.) turns it off. A logical value corresponding to the insert mode setting before INSMODE(.T.) or INSMODE(.F.) was issued is returned.

Remarks

If you omit the optional argument and the insert mode is on (characters are inserted before the cursor), INSMODE( ) returns true (.T.). If the insert mode is off (characters are overwritten at the insertion point), INSMODE( ) returns false (.F.).

Example

The example below uses INSMODE( ) to set the insert mode on, and then toggles the insert mode to the opposite state.

```
SET TALK ON
=INSMODE(.T.)  && Set insert mode on
? INSMODE( )
= INSMODE(!INSMODE( ))  && Toggle insert mode to opposite state
? INSMODE( )
```

See Also

CAPSLOCK( ), NUMLOCK( )

Instancing Property

Specifies how a server in a project can be instantiated. Available at design time and run time.

Syntax

Object.Instancing[= *nExpression*]

Settings

nExpression

Specifies how the server can be instantiated. The following table lists the values for *nExpression* with a description of each.

Settings	FoxPro.h constant	Description
1	SERVERINSTANCE_SINGLEUSE	(Default) Allows you to create an instance of the class both inside Visual FoxPro and outside of Visual FoxPro using Automation.
		Each request for an instance of the class by an automation client outside of the project causes a separate copy of the automation server to start.
2	SERVERINSTANCE_NOTCREATABLE	Allows you to create instances of the class only inside Visual FoxPro.
3	SERVERINSTANCE_MULTIUSE	Allows you to create an instance of the class both inside Visual FoxPro and outside of Visual FoxPro using Automation.
		Each request for an instance of the class by an automation client outside of the project causes an already running copy of the automation server to be provided as the source for the new instance.

Applies To

Server Object

See Also

GETOBJECT( ), ServerClass Property, ServerClassLibrary Property

INT( ) Function

Evaluates a numeric expression and returns the integer portion of the expression.

Syntax

INT(*nExpression*)

Returns

Numeric

Arguments

nExpression

Specifies the numeric expression for which INT( ) returns the integer portion.

Example

```
CLEAR
? INT(12.5)  && Displays 12
? INT(6.25 * 2)  && Displays 12
? INT(-12.5)  && Displays -12
STORE -12.5 TO gnNumber
? INT(gnNumber)  && Displays -12
```

See Also

CEILING( ), FLOOR( ), ROUND( )

IntegralHeight Property

Specifies that the height of an EditBox or ListBox control is automatically adjusted so the last item in the control is properly displayed. Specifies that the height of a TextBox control is adjusted to accommodate one line of text. Available at design time; read-only at run time.

Syntax

Object.IntegralHeight[= *lExpr*]

Arguments

lExpr

One of the following:

lExpr	Description
True (.T.)	The height an EditBox or ListBox control is adjusted as necessary so the last item in the control is properly displayed. The height of a TextBox is adjusted to accommodate one line of text.
False (.F.)	(Default) The height of an EditBox or ListBox isn't adjusted, allowing the last item in the control to be improperly displayed. The height of a TextBox isn't adjusted to accommodate one line of text.

Remarks

The last line of text in an EditBox or ListBox control might be partially displayed if the control isn't the proper height. For example, the height of the control may be such that only the top half of the last item is displayed in the control. Set IntergralHeight to true (.T.) to automatically adjust the height of the control so the last item in the control is always properly displayed.

For a TextBox, set IntergralHeight to true (.T.) to ensure that the control automatically adjusts its height when its FontSize property is changed.

When the IntegralHeight property is set to true (.T.), the value of the Height property might not match the actual height of the control.

Applies To

EditBox, ListBox, TextBox

See Also

Height Property

InteractiveChange Event

Occurs when the user changes the value of a control using the keyboard or the mouse.

Syntax

PROCEDURE *Control*.InteractiveChange
[LPARAMETERS *nIndex*]

Arguments

nIndex
    Uniquely identifies a control if it is in a control array.

Remarks

This event occurs each time the object's value changes interactively. For example, as a user types in a text box, the InteractiveChange event is triggered after each keystroke.

Applies To

CheckBox, ComboBox, CommandGroup, EditBox, ListBox, OptionGroup, Spinner, TextBox

See Also

Click Event

Interval Property

Specifies the number of milliseconds between calls to a Timer control's Timer event. Available at design time and run time.

Syntax

Timer.Interval[= *nTime*]

Arguments

nTime
    Specifies the number of milliseconds between Timer events. The default value is 0, which prevents the Timer event from firing.

Remarks

For more information about the Interval property, see "Initializing a Timer Control" in Chapter 10, "Using Controls," in the *Microsoft Visual FoxPro 6.0 Programmer's Guide.*

Applies To

Timer

See Also

Reset Method, Timer Event

ISALPHA( ) Function

Determines whether the leftmost character in a character expression is alphabetic.

Syntax

ISALPHA(*cExpression*)

Returns

Logical

Arguments

cExpression
> Specifies the character expression that ISALPHA( ) evaluates. Any characters after the first character in *cExpression* are ignored.

Remarks

ISALPHA( ) returns true (.T.) if the leftmost character in the specified character expression is an alphabetic character; otherwise ISALPHA( ) returns false (.F.).

Example

```
CLOSE DATABASES
OPEN DATABASE (HOME(2) + 'Data\testdata')
USE Customer      && Open customer table
CLEAR

DISPLAY contact
? ISALPHA(contact)  && Displays .T.
DISPLAY maxordamt
? ISALPHA(cust_id)  && Displays .F.
```

See Also

ISLOWER( ), ISUPPER( ), LOWER( ), UPPER( )

ISBLANK( ) Function

Determines whether an expression is blank.

Syntax

ISBLANK(*eExpression*)

Returns

Logical

Arguments

eExpression

Specifies the expression that ISBLANK( ) evaluates. *eExpression* can be a field in a table, a variable or array element, or an expression.

For a field, ISBLANK( ) returns true (.T.) if the field contains the following values.

Type	Contents
Character	Empty string, spaces, or no value (newly appended blank record or cleared with BLANK)
Numeric	No value (newly appended blank record or cleared with BLANK)
Float	No value (newly appended blank record or cleared with BLANK)
Date	Blank date ({ / / }) or no value (newly appended blank record or cleared with BLANK)
DateTime	Blank datetime ({ / / : : }) or no value (newly appended blank record or cleared with BLANK)
Logical	No value (newly appended blank record or cleared with BLANK)
Memo	Empty (no memo contents)
General	Empty (no OLE object)
Picture	Empty (no picture)

Remarks

ISBLANK( ) returns true (.T.) if the expression *eExpression* is blank; otherwise, ISBLANK( ) returns false (.F.).

APPEND BLANK and BLANK are used to create a blank record. BLANK can also be used to clear data from fields in a record. ISBLANK( ) can determine if a field is blank.

Note that Currency, Integer and Double type expressions are never blank, and ISBLANK( ) always returns false (.F.) for these data types.

ISBLANK( ) differs from EMPTY( ) and ISNULL( ). For example, EMPTY( ) returns true (.T.) if a character expression contains any combination of null values, spaces, tabs, carriage returns, or line feeds; ISBLANK( ) returns true (.T.) if a character expression contains only the empty string or spaces.

Example

In the following example, a table named mytable is created and a blank record is appended. ISBLANK( ) returns true (.T.) because myfield is blank. A value is placed in myfield, and ISBLANK( ) returns false (.F.) because myfield is no longer blank.

```
CREATE TABLE mytable FREE (myfield C(20))
APPEND BLANK   && Add new blank record
CLEAR

? ISBLANK(myfield)   && Displays .T.
REPLACE myfield WITH 'John Smith'   && Insert a value in the field
? ISBLANK(myfield)   && Displays .F.
```

See Also

APPEND, BLANK, EMPTY( ), ISNULL( ), LEN( )

ISCOLOR( ) Function

Determines whether a computer can display color.

Syntax

ISCOLOR( )

Returns

Logical

Remarks

ISCOLOR( ) returns true (.T.) if the computer has color capability (whether or not a color monitor is actually being used). If the computer doesn't provide color support, ISCOLOR( ) returns false (.F.).

See Also

Colors Overview, SET DISPLAY, SYS(2006) – Current Graphics Card

ISDIGIT( ) Function

Determines whether the leftmost character of the specified character expression is a digit (0 through 9).

Syntax

ISDIGIT(*cExpression*)

Returns

Logical

Arguments

cExpression
   Specifies the character expression that ISDIGIT( ) tests. Any characters after the first character in *cExpression* are ignored.

Remarks

ISDIGIT( ) returns true (.T.) if the leftmost character of the specified character expression is a digit (0 through 9); otherwise, ISDIGIT( ) returns false (.F.).

Example

```
CLOSE DATABASES
OPEN DATABASE (HOME(2) + 'Data\testdata')
USE orders  && Open Orders table
CLEAR

DISPLAY cust_id
? ISDIGIT(cust_id)  && Displays .F.
DISPLAY order_dsc
? ISDIGIT(ALLTRIM(STR(order_dsc)))  && Displays .T.
```

See Also

ISALPHA( )

ISEXCLUSIVE( ) Function

Returns true (.T.) if a table or database is opened for exclusive use; otherwise, returns false (.F.).

Syntax

ISEXCLUSIVE([*cTableAlias* | *nWorkArea* | *cDatabaseName* [, *nType*]])

Returns

Logical

Arguments

cTableAlias

Specifies the alias of the table for which the exclusive use status is returned.
Visual FoxPro generates an error message if you specify a table alias that
doesn't exist.

nWorkArea

Specifies the work area of the table for which the exclusive use status is
returned. ISEXCLUSIVE( ) returns false (.F.) if a table isn't open in the work
area you specify.

cDatabaseName

Specifies the name of the database for which the exclusive use status is returned.

nType

Specifies whether the exclusive status is returned for a table or a database. The
following table lists the values for *nType* and the corresponding status returned.

nType	Exclusive Status Returned
1	Table
2	Database

To determine the exclusive status for a database, you must include *nType* with a
value of 2.

Remarks

ISEXCLUSIVE( ) returns a value for the table open in the currently selected work area
if you omit the optional *cTableAlias*, *nWorkArea*, or *cDatabaseName* arguments.

A table is opened for exclusive use by including the EXCLUSIVE keyword in USE,
or by setting SET EXCLUSIVE to ON before the table is opened.

A database is opened for exclusive use by including the EXCLUSIVE keyword in
OPEN DATABASE.

Example

In the following example, the ISEXCLUSIVE( ) function verifies that the table was
opened for exclusive use. The table is not reindexed since the one in the current work
are was not opened for exclusive use.

```
cExclusive = SET('EXCLUSIVE')
SET EXCLUSIVE OFF
SET PATH TO (HOME(2) + 'data\')
OPEN DATA testdata  && Opens the test databsase
```

```
USE customer     && Not opened exclusively
USE employee IN 0 EXCLUSIVE     && Opened exclusively in another work area
IF ISEXCLUSIVE( )
   REINDEX  && Can only be done if table opened exclusively
ELSE
   WAIT WINDOW 'The table has to be exclusively opened'
ENDIF
SET EXCLUSIVE &cExclusive
```

See Also

OPEN DATABASE, SET EXCLUSIVE, USE

ISFLOCKED( ) Function

Returns the table lock status.

Syntax

ISFLOCKED([*nWorkArea* | *cTableAlias*])

Returns

Logical

Arguments

nWorkArea
Specifies the work area number of the table for which the lock status is returned. If you omit *cTableAlias* and *nWorkArea*, the lock status is returned for the table open in the current work area.

cTableAlias
Specifies the alias of the table for which the lock status is returned. An "Alias not found" error message is generated if you specify an alias of a table that isn't open.

Remarks

ISFLOCKED( ) returns a logical true (.T.) if the table is locked; otherwise a logical false (.F.) is returned. ISFLOCKED( ) is similar to SYS(2011), but returns a logical value which does not require localization for international applications.

See Also

FLOCK( ), ISRLOCKED( ), LOCK( ), RLOCK( ), SYS(2011) – Current Lock Status

ISHOSTED( ) Function

Returns a logical value indicating if an Active Document is hosted in an Active Document container.

Syntax

ISHOSTED( )

Returns

Logical

Remarks

ISHOSTED( ) returns true (.T.) if an Active Document is hosted in an Active Document container such as Microsoft Internet Explorer. ISHOSTED( ) returns False (.F.) if an Active Document isn't hosted in an Active Document container, for example, the Active Document is running in an interactive Visual FoxPro session or within the Visual FoxPro runtime.

See Also

GETHOST( )

ISLEADBYTE( ) Function

Returns true (.T.) if the first byte of the first byte in a character expression is the lead byte of a double-byte character.

Syntax

ISLEADBYTE(*cExpression*)

Returns

Logical

Arguments

cExpression
Specifies the character expression that ISLEADBYTE( ) evaluates. Any bytes after the first byte in the first character in *cExpression* are ignored.

Remarks

ISLEADBYTE( ) returns true (.T.) if the first byte of the first character in a character expression is the lead byte in a double-byte character. If ISLEADBYTE( ) returns false (.F.), the character being tested is a single-byte character.

This function is useful for manipulating double-byte character sets for languages such as Hiragana and Katakana.

ISALPHA( ), ISDIGIT( ), ISLOWER( ), ISUPPER( )

ISLOWER( ) Function

Determines whether the leftmost character of the specified character expression is a lowercase alphabetic character.

Syntax

ISLOWER(*cExpression*)

Returns

Logical

Arguments

cExpression

Specifies the character expression that ISLOWER( ) tests. ISLOWER( ) ignores any characters after the first character in *cExpression*.

Remarks

ISLOWER( ) returns true (.T.) if the leftmost character in the specified character expression is a lowercase alphabetic character; otherwise, ISLOWER( ) returns false (.F.).

Example

```
CLEAR
? ISLOWER('redmond')   && Displays .T.
? ISLOWER('Redmond')   && Displays .F.
```

See Also

ISALPHA( ), ISUPPER( ), LOWER( ), UPPER( )

ISMOUSE( ) Function

Returns true (.T.) if mouse hardware is present.

Syntax

ISMOUSE( )

Remarks

ISMOUSE( ) returns true (.T.) if mouse hardware is present; otherwise it returns false (.F.).

Example

The following example displays a true value (.T.) if mouse hardware is present; otherwise, it displays false (.F.).

```
CLEAR
? 'Mouse hardware present?'
?? ISMOUSE( )
```

See Also

MCOL( ), MDOWN( ), MROW( ), SYSMETRIC( )

ISNULL( ) Function

Returns true (.T.) if an expression evaluates to a null value; otherwise, ISNULL( ) returns false (.F.).

Syntax

ISNULL(*eExpression*)

Returns

Logical

Arguments

eExpression
   Specifies the expression to evaluate.

Remarks

Use ISNULL( ) to determine if the contents of a field, memory variable, or array element contains a null value, or if an expression evaluates to a null value.

Example

In the following example, ISNULL( ) is used to check for a null value.

```
STORE .NULL. TO mNullvalue  && Store a null value to a memory variable

CLEAR
? mNullvalue  && Display the value of the memory variable
? ISNULL(mNullvalue)  && Returns .T., indicating a null value
? TYPE('mNullvalue')    && Returns L, indicating a logical value
? (mNullvalue = .NULL.)  && Returns .NULL., bad test for null values
```

See Also

NVL( ), SET NULL

ISREADONLY( ) Function

Determines whether a table is opened read-only.

Syntax

ISREADONLY([*nWorkArea* | *cTableAlias*])

Returns

Logical

Arguments

nWorkArea | *cTableAlias*

Returns the read-only status for a table open in another work area. *nWorkArea* specifies the work area number and *cTableAlias* specifies the table or work area alias. ISREADONLY( ) returns false (.F.) if a table isn't open in the work area you specify.

If you don't specify a work area number or a table or work area alias, the read-only status is returned for the table open in the current work area.

Remarks

ISREADONLY( ) returns true (.T.) if a table is opened read-only; otherwise, ISREADONLY( ) returns false (.F.).

A table can be opened read-only by including the NOUPDATE option when opening the table with USE, by checking the Read Only check box when opening the table from the Open dialog box, or by assigning MS-DOS read-only attributes to the table.

A cursor created with the SELECT – SQL command is always read-only.

Example

```
CLOSE DATABASES
OPEN DATABASE (HOME(2) + 'data\testdata')
USE customer    NOUPDATE  && Open customer table read-only

CLEAR
? ISREADONLY('customer')  && Returns .T.
```

See Also

USE

ISRLOCKED( ) Function

Returns the record lock status.

Syntax

ISRLOCKED([*nRecordNumber*, [*nWorkArea* | *cTableAlias*]])

Returns

Logical

Arguments

nRecordNumber

Specifies the number of the record for which the lock status is returned. If *nRecordNumber* is omitted, the record lock status is returned for the current record.

nWorkArea

Specifies the work area number of the table for which the record lock status is returned. If you omit *cTableAlias* and *nWorkArea*, the record lock status is returned for the table open in the current work area.

cTableAlias

Specifies the alias of the table for which the record lock status is returned.

Remarks

ISRLOCKED( ) returns a logical true (.T.) if the record is locked; otherwise a logical false (.F.) is returned.

See Also

FLOCK( ), ISFLOCKED( ), LOCK( ), RLOCK( ), SYS(2011) – Current Lock Status

ISUPPER( ) Function

Determines whether the first character in a character expression is an uppercase alphabetic character.

Syntax

ISUPPER(*cExpression*)

Returns

Logical

Arguments

cExpression

Specifies the character expression that ISUPPER( ) evaluates. Any characters after the first character in *cExpression* are ignored.

Remarks

ISUPPER( ) returns true (.T.) if the first character in a character expression is an uppercase alphabetic character; otherwise, ISUPPER( ) returns false (.F.).

Example

```
? ISUPPER('Redmond')   && Displays .T.
? ISUPPER('redmond')   && Displays .F.
```

See Also

ISALPHA( ), ISLOWER( ), LOWER( ), UPPER( )

Item Method

Returns an object reference to a specified file, project, or server in a files, projects, or servers collection.

Syntax

Object.Item(*nIndex*)

nIndex

A number that specifies a file, project, or server in a files, projects, or servers collection. An "Invalid subscript reference" error is generated if *nIndex* is greater than the number of files, projects, or servers in a collection.

Remarks

Use the Name property with the Item property to determine the name of a file, project, or server and the directory in which it is contained.

Applies To

Files Collection, Projects Collection, Servers Collection

See Also

Name Property

ItemBackColor, ItemForeColor Properties

Specifies the background or foreground color used to display the text of items in a ComboBox or ListBox control. Available at design time and run time.

Syntax

Control.ItemBackColor[= *nColor*]

– or –

Control.ItemBackColor = RGB(*nRedValue*, *nGreenValue*, *nBlueValue*)
Control.ItemForeColor[= *nColor*]

– or –

Control.ItemForeColor = RGB(*nRedValue*, *nGreenValue*, *nBlueValue*)

Arguments

nColor

Specifies an integer that represents the color of the text.

> **Note** In the Properties window, you can double-click any of the color properties to display the Color dialog box. You can choose or define colors from this dialog box. The red, green, and blue intensities that correspond to the color you choose become the settings for these properties after you close the Color dialog box.

For more information, see the color table in "BackColor, ForeColor Properties," earlier in this language reference.

Applies To

ComboBox, ListBox

See Also

BackColor, ForeColor Properties, SelectedItemBackColor, SelectedItemForeColor Properties

ItemData Property

Uses an index to reference a one-dimensional array that contains the same number of items as a ComboBox or ListBox control's List property setting. Not available at design time; read/write at run time.

Syntax

Control.ItemData(*nIndex*)[= *nData*]

Arguments

nIndex
> Specifies the index of the item to store or retrieve. The *nIndex* corresponds to the display order of the items in the list.

nData
> The number to store or retrieve from the ItemData list.

Remarks

Use the ItemData property to associate a specific number with each item in a combo box or list box. You can then use these numbers in code to identify the items in the list. For example, you can use an identification number to identify each employee name in a list box. When you fill the list box, also fill the corresponding elements in the ItemData array with the employee numbers.

> **Note** When you insert an item into a list with the AddItem method, an item is automatically allocated in the ItemData array as well. However, the value is not initialized; it retains the value that was in that position before you added the item to the list. When you use the ItemData property, be sure to set each element's value when adding new items to a list.

> Also note that the value of the ItemData property is only accurate for combo boxes or list boxes containing less than 60 items.

Applies To

ComboBox, ListBox

See Also

AddItem Method, ItemIDToIndex Method, List Property, ListItemID Property, NewItemID Property, RemoveItem Method, Selected Property, TopItemID Property

ItemIDData Property

Uses a unique identification number to reference a one-dimensional array that contains the same number of items as a ComboBox or ListBox control's List property setting. Not available at design time; read/write at run time.

Syntax

Control.ItemIDData(*nItemID*)[= *nData*]

Arguments

nItemID
> Specifies the item ID, a unique identification number.

nData
> The number to store or retrieve from the ItemIDData list.

Remarks

Use the ItemIDData property to associate a specific number with each item in a combo box or list box. You can then use these numbers in code to identify the items. For example, you can use an identification number to identify each employee name in a list box. When you fill the list box, also fill the corresponding elements in the ItemIDData array with the employee numbers.

> **Note** When you insert an item into a list with the AddItem method, an item is automatically allocated in the ItemIDData array as well. However, the value is not initialized; it retains the value that was in that position before you added the item to the list. When you use the ItemIDData property, be sure to set each element's value when adding new items to a list. This is the same array that is accessed by the ItemData Property.

Applies To

ComboBox, ListBox

See Also

IndexToItemID Method, List Property, ListItemID Property, NewItemID Property, RemoveItem Method, Selected Property, TopItemID Property

ItemIDToIndex Method

Returns the value of *nIndex*, the position of an item in a control's list.

Syntax

[*nIndex =*]*Control*.ItemIDToIndex(*nItemID*)

Arguments

nItemID
    The unique identification number associated with that item.

Remarks

Each item added to a combo box or list box has two numbers assigned to it:

- The *nItemID*, a unique identification number.

- The *nIndex*, an integer corresponding to the order in which items are displayed by the control. The first item in the list corresponds to *nIndex* = 1.

Initially, as items are added to the control, these two numbers are identical. But as items are sorted, removed, and added, these numbers are no longer identical.

Use the ItemIDToIndex method to retrieve the *nIndex* number for a particular item in the control's list when you know its *nItemID* number.

Applies To

ComboBox, ListBox

See Also

AddItem Method, AddListItem Method, IndexToItemID Method, ListItemID Property, List Property, ListCount Property

ItemTips Property

Specifies whether item tips are displayed for items in a combo box or list box. Available at design time; read/write at run time.

Syntax

Control.ItemTips[= *lExpression*]

Arguments

lExpression
The settings for the ItemTip property are:

Setting	Description
True (.T.)	Item tips are displayed for items in a combo box or list box.
False (.F.)	(Default) Item tips are not displayed for items in a combo box or list box.

Remarks

An item tip is a small window that displays an entire combo box or list box item when the mouse pointer is positioned over the item. Set this property to true (.T.) whenever items in a ComboBox or ListBox control are longer than the width of the control.

Applies To

ComboBox, ListBox

See Also

ItemData Property

JOIN Command

Included for backward compatibility. Use SELECT – SQL instead.

JUSTDRIVE( ) Function

Returns the drive letter from a complete path.

Syntax

JUSTDRIVE(*cPath*)

Returns

Character

Arguments

cPath
    Specifies the complete path name for which you want only the drive.

See Also

ADDBS( ), DEFAULTEXT( ), FILE( ), FORCEEXT( ), FORCEPATH( ), JUSTEXT( ), JUSTFNAME( ), JUSTPATH( ), JUSTSTEM( )

JUSTEXT( ) Function

Returns the three-letter extension from a complete path.

Syntax

JUSTEXT(*cPath*)

Returns

Character

Arguments

cPath
    Specifies the name, which may include the full path, of the file for which you want only the extension.

See Also

ADDBS( ), DEFAULTEXT( ), FILE( ), FORCEEXT( ), FORCEPATH( ), JUSTDRIVE( ), JUSTFNAME( ), JUSTPATH( ), JUSTSTEM( )

JUSTFNAME( ) Function

Returns the file name portion of a complete path and file name.

Syntax

JUSTFNAME(*cFileName*)

Returns

Character

Arguments

cFileName
Specifies the name, which may include the full path, of the file for which you want only the file name.

See Also

ADDBS( ), DEFAULTEXT( ), FILE( ), FORCEEXT( ), FORCEPATH( ), JUSTDRIVE( ), JUSTEXT( ), JUSTPATH( ), JUSTSTEM( )

JUSTPATH( ) Function

Returns the path portion of a complete path and file name.

Syntax

JUSTPATH(*cFileName*)

Returns

Character

Arguments

cFileName
Specifies the full name (including path) of the file for which you want only the path.

See Also

ADDBS( ), DEFAULTEXT( ), FILE( ), FORCEEXT( ), FORCEPATH( ), JUSTDRIVE( ), JUSTEXT( ), JUSTFNAME( ), JUSTSTEM( )

JUSTSTEM( ) Function

Returns the stem name (the file name before the extension) from a complete path and file name.

Syntax

JUSTSTEM(*cFileName*)

Returns

Character

Arguments

cFileName

Specifies the name (including path) of the file for which you want only the stem.

See Also

ADDBS( ), DEFAULTEXT( ), FILE( ), FORCEEXT( ), FORCEPATH( ), JUSTDRIVE( ), JUSTEXT( ), JUSTFNAME( ), JUSTPATH( )

KEY( ) Function

Returns the index key expression for an index tag or index file.

Syntax

KEY([*CDXFileName*,] *nIndexNumber* [, *nWorkArea* | *cTableAlias*])

Returns

Character

Arguments

CDXFileName

Specifies the name of a compound index file. KEY( ) returns the index key expressions of the .cdx file's index tag. The compound index file you specify can be the structural compound index file automatically opened with the table, or it can be an independent compound index file.

nIndexNumber

Specifies which index key expression to return.

USE and SET INDEX both support an index file list that lets you open multiple indexes for a table. Any combination of single-entry .idx index files, structural compound index files, or independent compound index files can be included in the index file list.

The numeric expression *nIndexNumber* specifies which index expression to return from the open index files. KEY( ) returns index expressions from open index files in the following order as *nIndexNumber* increases from 1 to the total number of open single-entry .idx files and structural compound and independent compound index tags:

1. Index expressions from single-entry .idx index files (if any are open) are returned first. The order in which the single-entry index files are included in USE or SET INDEX determines how the index expressions are returned.

2. Index expressions for each tag in the structural compound index (if one is present) are returned next. The index expressions are returned from the tags in the order in which the tags are created in the structural compound index.

3. Index expressions for each tag in any open independent compound indexes are returned last. The index expressions are returned from the tags in the order in which the tags are created in the independent compound indexes.

The empty string is returned if *nIndexNumber* is greater than the total number of open single-entry .idx files and structural compound and independent compound index tags.

nWorkArea

Specifies the work area number of the table whose index key expressions you want KEY( ) to return.

If a table isn't open in the work area you specify, KEY( ) returns the empty string.

cTableAlias

Specifies the alias of the table whose index key expressions you want KEY( ) to return.

If no table has the alias you specify, Microsoft Visual FoxPro generates an error message.

If you omit *nWorkArea* and *cTableAlias*, the index key expressions are returned for the table open in the current work area.

Remarks

An index key expression is specified when an index tag or index file is created with INDEX. The index key expression determines how a table is displayed and accessed when the index tag or index file is opened as the master controlling index tag or file.

For more information on creating index tags, index files, and index key expressions, see the INDEX Command, earlier in this language reference.

Example

The following example opens the `customer` table in the `testdata` database. FOR ... ENDFOR is used to create a loop in which KEY( ) is used to display the index expression of each index tag in the `customer` structural index. The name of each structural index tag is displayed with its index expression.

```
CLOSE DATABASES
OPEN DATABASE (HOME(2) + 'Data\testdata')
USE Customer      && Open customer table
CLEAR

FOR nCount = 1 TO 254
   IF !EMPTY(TAG(nCount))  && Checks for tags in the index
   ? TAG(nCount) + ' '  && Display tag name
   ?? KEY(nCount)  && Display index expression
   ELSE
      EXIT  && Exit the loop when no more tags are found
   ENDIF
ENDFOR
```

See Also

INDEX, REINDEX, SET INDEX, SYS(14) – Index Expression, USE

KEYBOARD Command

Places the specified character expression in the keyboard buffer.

Syntax

KEYBOARD *cKeyboardValue*
   [PLAIN] [CLEAR]

Arguments

cKeyboardValue

Specifies the character expression that is placed in the keyboard buffer. The character expression can be a character string, a key label, a set of key labels, or a user-defined function that returns a character expression.

If *cKeyboardValue* is a key label, it must be enclosed in braces and quotes.
For example:

```
KEYBOARD '{CTRL+LEFTARROW}'
```

For a listing of key labels, see the ON KEY LABEL Command, later in this language reference.

The keyboard buffer can be filled with up to 128 characters. Once the keyboard buffer is full, additional characters are ignored.

PLAIN

If you have keyboard macros defined or active ON KEY LABEL commands, you can include PLAIN to bypass these key assignments. PLAIN fills the keyboard with the literal key character, not the key assignment.

For example, if you have assigned a command to the A key with ON KEY LABEL and A is included in *cKeyboardValue*, use PLAIN to place the letter A in the keyboard buffer. The ON KEY LABEL command assigned to A isn't executed.

CLEAR
> Empties the keyboard buffer before the keyboard buffer is filled with *cKeyboardValue*.

Remarks

Use KEYBOARD to place characters in the keyboard buffer. The characters remain in the buffer until Visual FoxPro looks for keyboard input. At that point, the characters are read and acted upon as if they were entered directly from the keyboard.

You can use KEYBOARD to create self-running demonstration systems that showcase your applications.

See Also

CHRSAW( ), ON KEY LABEL, PLAY MACRO, SET FUNCTION

KeyboardHighValue, KeyboardLowValue Properties

Specifies the highest or lowest value that can be entered into a Spinner control text box using the keyboard. Available at design time and run time.

Syntax

Spinner.KeyboardHighValue[= *nHigh*]
Spinner.KeyboardLowValue[= *nLow*]

Arguments

nHigh
> Specifies the highest value that can be entered. The default value for *nHigh* is 2,147,483,647.

nLow
> Specifies the lowest value that can be entered. The default value for *nLow* is –2,147,483,647.

Applies To

Spinner

See Also

SpinnerHighValue, SpinnerLowValue Properties

KEYMATCH( ) Function

Searches an index tag or index file for an index key.

Syntax

KEYMATCH(*eIndexKey* [, *nIndexNumber* [, *nWorkArea* | *cTableAlias*]])

Returns

Logical

Arguments

eIndexKey

Specifies the index key that KEYMATCH( ) searches for. The index keys in an index file or index tag are determined by the index expression. An index expression is specified when an index file or index tag is created with INDEX. KEY( ) and SYS(14) can be used to return the index expressions for index files and index tags. For more information on creating index files, index expressions, and index keys, see the INDEX Command, earlier in this language reference.

If you don't include any of the optional parameters, KEYMATCH( ) searches the master index file or master index tag for the index key you specify. If a master index file or index tag isn't in effect (for example, you've issued SET ORDER TO without any parameters to place the table in physical record order), Visual FoxPro generates an error message.

nIndexNumber

Specifies which index file or index tag is searched. *nIndexNumber* is typically an integer that starts at 1 and is increased by 1 to search additional index tags.

If *nIndexNumber* is 1, the master single-entry .idx index file or master index tag (if one is present) is searched.

As *nIndexNumber* increases, subsequent tags in the structural compound index (if one is present) are searched. The tags are searched in the order in which the tags were created in the structural compound index.

As *nIndexNumber* continues to increase and all the tags in the structural compound index have been searched, tags in any open independent compound indexes are then searched. The tags are searched in the order in which the tags were created in the independent compound indexes.

An error message is generated if *nIndexNumber* is greater than the total number of open single-entry .idx files and structural compound and independent compound index tags.

nWorkArea | cTableAlias
>Searches index files or tags open in another work area. *nWorkArea* specifies the work area number and *cTableAlias* specifies the table alias. If you omit the work area and alias, KEYMATCH( ) searches index files or tags open for the table in the current work area.

>If no table has the alias you specify, Visual FoxPro generates an error message.

Remarks

KEYMATCH( ) searches an index tag or index file for a specific index key and returns true (.T.) if the index key is found; otherwise, KEYMATCH( ) returns false (.F.). KEYMATCH( ) can be used to prevent duplicate index keys.

KEYMATCH( ) returns the record pointer to the record on which it was originally positioned before KEYMATCH( ) was issued.

See Also

INDEX, INDEXSEEK( ), KEY( ), SET INDEX, SYS(14), USE

KeyPress Event

Occurs when the user presses and releases a key.

Syntax

PROCEDURE *Object.*KeyPress
LPARAMETERS [*nIndex,*] *nKeyCode, nShiftAltCtrl*

– or –

LPARAMETERS *nKeyCode, nShiftAltCtrl*

Arguments

You must include an LPARAMETERS or PARAMETERS statement in the event procedure and specify a name for each parameter.

nIndex
>Uniquely identifies a control if it is in a control array.

nKeyCode
>Contains a number which identifies the key pressed. For a list of codes for special keys and key combinations, see the INKEY( ) Function, earlier in this language reference.

nShiftAltCtrl

Sets a bit if a modifier key is held down while the key identified in *nKeyCode* is pressed.

The valid modifier keys are the SHIFT, CTRL, and ALT keys.

The values returned in *nShiftAltCtrl* for individual modifier keys are listed in the following table.

Modifier key values for *nShiftAltCtrl*

Key	Value
SHIFT	1
CTRL	2
ALT	4

This parameter is the sum of the bits, with the least-significant bits corresponding to the SHIFT key (bit 0), the CTRL key (bit 1), and the ALT key (bit 2).

These bits correspond to the values 1, 2, and 4, respectively. This parameter indicates the state of these keys. Some, all, or none of the bits can be set, indicating that some, all, or none of the keys is pressed. For example, if both CTRL and ALT are pressed, the value of *nShiftAltCtrl* is 6.

Remarks

The object with the focus receives the event.

A form can receive the KeyPress event in three special cases:

- The form contains no controls, or none of its controls is visible and enabled.
- The form's KeyPreview property is set to true (.T.). The form receives the KeyPress event first and then the control with focus receives the event.
- If a control on the form cannot process a keystroke (for example, when Tab is pressed to move the focus to the next control).

A KeyPress event is useful for intercepting keystrokes entered in a control. It enables you to immediately test keystrokes for validity or to format characters as they are typed. Use the KeyPreview property to create global keyboard-handling routines.

The KeyPress event does not occur for any combination of keys with the ALT key.

Applies To

CheckBox, ComboBox, CommandButton, EditBox, Form, ListBox, OptionButton, Spinner, TextBox

See Also

INKEY( ), KeyPreview Property

KeyPreview Property

Specifies whether a form's KeyPress event intercepts the KeyPress events of a control. Available at design time and run time.

Syntax

Object.KeyPreview[= *lExpr*]

Arguments

lExpr

The settings for the KeyPreview property are:

Setting	Description
True (.T.)	The form receives KeyPress events first and then the active control receives KeyPress events.
False (.F.)	(Default) The active control receives Keypress events; the form doesn't.

Remarks

The KeyPreview property is used to allow the form to handle KeyPress events before the active control processes them.

You can use this property to create a keyboard-handling procedure for a form. For example, when an application uses function keys, you can process the keystrokes at the form level rather than writing code for each control that can receive keystroke events.

If a form has no visible and enabled controls, it automatically receives all keyboard events.

Applies To

Form, Page, _SCREEN, ToolBar

See Also

Enabled Property, KeyPress Event, Visible Property

LABEL Command

Prints labels from a table file and a label definition file.

Syntax

LABEL [FORM *FileName1* | FORM ?],
    [ENVIRONMENT]
    [*Scope*]
    [FOR *lExpression1*]
    [WHILE *lExpression2*]
    [NOCONSOLE]
    [NOOPTIMIZE]
    [PDSETUP]
    [PREVIEW [NOWAIT]]
    [NAME *ObjectName*]
    [TO PRINTER [PROMPT] | TO FILE *FileName2*]

Arguments

FORM *FileName1*

Specifies the name of a label definition file whose labels you want to print. The default extension for a label definition file is .lbx. If the label definition file is on a drive or volume other than the default or in a directory other than the current directory, you must also specify the drive designator and directory.

FORM ?

Displays the Open dialog box from which you can choose an existing label file.

ENVIRONMENT

Included for backward compatibility with 2.x labels. To restore the data environment associated with a Visual FoxPro label, set the data environment AutoOpenTables property to true (.T.), which is the default. To make sure that the label environment is closed when the label is finished printing, set the data environment AutoCloseTables property to true (.T.), which is also the default.

When you create or modify labels, you can save the current Visual FoxPro data environment with the label definition file. Saving the Visual FoxPro data environment places additional records in the label definition table for all open tables and index files, the index order, and any relationships between the tables.

Scope

Specifies a range of records. Only the records that fall within the range are printed. The scope clauses are: ALL, NEXT *nRecords*, RECORD *nRecordNumber*, and REST. For more information on scope clauses, see "Scope Clauses" or "Overview of the Language," in Help. Commands that include *Scope* operate only on the table in the active work area.

The default scope for LABEL is ALL records.

FOR *lExpression1*

Specifies a condition whereby only the records that satisfy the logical condition *lExpression1* are printed. This argument allows you to filter out records you don't want to print.

Rushmore optimizes a query created with LABEL ... FOR if *lExpression1* is an optimizable expression. For best performance, use an optimizable expression in the FOR clause.

For more information, see the SET OPTIMIZE Command, later in this language reference, and "Understanding Rushmore Technology" in Chapter 15, "Optimizing Applications," in the *Microsoft Visual FoxPro 6.0 Programmer's Guide*.

WHILE *lExpression2*

Specifies a condition whereby records are printed for as long as the logical expression *lExpression2* evaluates to true (.T.).

NOCONSOLE

Suppresses the display of label output to the main Visual FoxPro window or to a user-defined window when labels are being printed or sent to a file.

NOOPTIMIZE

Disables Rushmore optimization of LABEL.

For more information, see the SET OPTIMIZE Command, later in this language reference, and "Understanding Rushmore Technology" in Chapter 15, "Optimizing Applications," in the *Microsoft Visual FoxPro 6.0 Programmer's Guide*.

PDSETUP

Loads a printer driver setup.

In Visual FoxPro, you can include PDSETUP to use a printer driver setup for printing character-based labels created in FoxPro for MS-DOS. PDSETUP is ignored when you print graphics-based labels created in Visual FoxPro.

PREVIEW [NOWAIT]

Displays the labels in a preview window before printing, but doesn't print the labels. To print the labels, you must issue LABEL again without the PREVIEW clause.

In Visual FoxPro, you can include the optional NOWAIT clause so that at run time Visual FoxPro does not wait for the page preview window to be closed before continuing program execution. Instead, Visual FoxPro continues program execution while the page preview window is open.

NAME *ObjectName*

Specifies an object variable name for the data environment of a label. The data environment and the objects in the data environment have properties and methods, for example AddObject, that need to be set or called at run time. The object variable provides access to these properties and methods. If you don't specify a NAME, Visual FoxPro uses as a default the name of the label file that can be referenced in the code associated with the events.

TO PRINTER [PROMPT]

Sends a label to the printer. You can include the optional PROMPT clause to display the Print dialog box before printing starts.

TO FILE *FileName2*

Sends character-based labels created in FoxPro for MS-DOS to the text file specified with *FileName2*. The file that is created when you include TO FILE has the default extension .TXT.

Remarks

Label definition files are created with MODIFY LABEL or CREATE LABEL.

If LABEL is issued without any additional arguments, the Open dialog box appears, displaying a list of existing label files to choose from.

See Also

CREATE LABEL, MODIFY LABEL

Label Control

Creates a label that displays text.

Syntax

Label

Remarks

A Label control is a graphical control that displays text that can't be changed directly. However, because a Label control has a full set of properties, events, and methods that other controls have, the Label control can respond to events and can be changed dynamically at run time.

To assign an access key to a label, include a backslash and a less-than sign (\<) in the caption immediately preceding the character you want to designate as the access key. When the label is displayed, the character is underlined. Pressing the access key for a label activates the next control in the tab order. Use the TabIndex property to assign a tab order to a label.

Captions are displayed differently depending on the object.

256 is the maximum number of characters for the Caption property for a Label control.

For additional information about creating Label controls, see Chapter 10, "Using Controls," in the *Microsoft Visual FoxPro 6.0 Programmer's Guide*.

Properties

Alignment	Application	AutoSize
BackColor	BackStyle	BaseClass
BorderStyle	Caption	Class
ClassLibrary	ColorScheme	ColorSource
Comment	DisabledBackColor	DisabledForeColor
DragIcon	DragMode	Enabled
FontBold	FontCondense	FontExtend
FontItalic	FontName	FontOutline
FontShadow	FontSize	FontStrikeThru
FontUnderline	ForeColor	Height
HelpContextID	Left	MouseIcon
MousePointer	Name	OLEDragMode
OLEDragPicture	OLEDropEffects	OLEDropHasData Property
OLEDropMode	Parent	ParentClass
RightToLeft	TabIndex	Tag
ToolTipText	Top	Visible
WhatsThisHelpID	Width	WordWrap

Events

Click	DblClick	Destroy
DragDrop	DragOver	Error
Init	MiddleClick Event	MouseDown
MouseMove	MouseUp	MouseWheel
OLECompleteDrag	OLEDragDrop	OLEDragOver
OLEGiveFeedBack	OLESetData	OLEStartDrag
RightClick	UIEnable	

Methods

AddProperty	CloneObject	Drag
Move	OLEDrag	ReadExpression
ReadMethod	ResetToDefault	SaveAsClass
UIEnable	WriteExpression	WriteMethod
ZOrder		

See Also

CREATE CLASS, CREATE FORM, DEFINE CLASS

LASTKEY( ) Function

Returns an integer corresponding to the last key pressed.

Syntax

LASTKEY( )

Returns

Numeric

Remarks

The values returned by LASTKEY( ) are the same as the values returned by INKEY( ). See the INKEY( ) Function, earlier in this language reference, for a list of keys and their return values.

LASTKEY( ) is updated when you move between controls.

See Also

CHRSAW( ), INKEY( ), READKEY( )

LastModified Property

Contains the date and time of the last modification made to a file in a project. Read-only at design time and run time.

Syntax

Object.LastModified

Remarks

The LastModified property contains a DateTime value indicating when the file was last modified.

Applies To

File Object

See Also

FDATE( ), FTIME( )

Left Property

Specifies the distance between the left edge of a control or form and its container object. Available at design time and run time.

Syntax

Object.Left[= *nDist*]

Arguments

nDist

Specifies the distance between the left edge of an object or form and the left edge of its container object.

The default container for a form is the main Visual FoxPro window.

Remarks

The Left property specifies how far from the object's zero position the object is located. For example, if a form is contained within the Visual FoxPro main window, the zero position is immediately to the right of the main window's left border. If a toolbar is docked to the left of the main window, the zero position is immediately to the right of the toolbar. In Visual FoxPro for Macintosh, if the form is on the desktop (not contained within the Visual FoxPro main window), the zero position is the left edge of the screen.

Use Left, Top, Height, and Width properties for operations based on an object's external dimensions, such as moving or resizing. Use the ScaleMode property to change the unit of measurement.

Note The Left property is read-only when it applies to a control contained in a Column object.

Example

The following example demonstrates how the Left property is used to position controls on a form. The AddObject method is used to add a Line control and three command buttons to a form, and the Left property specifies the horizontal placement of each control on the form.

```
frmMyForm = CREATEOBJECT('Form')  && Create a form
frmMyForm.Closable = .F.  && Disable the window pop-up menu

frmMyForm.AddObject('shpLine','Line')  && Add a Line control to the form
frmMyForm.AddObject('cmdCmndBtn1','cmdMyCmndBtn1')  && Up Cmnd button
frmMyForm.AddObject('cmdCmndBtn2','cmdMyCmndBtn2')  && Down Cmnd button
frmMyForm.AddObject('cmdCmndBtn3','cmdMyCmndBtn3')  && Quit Cmnd button
```

```
frmMyForm.shpLine.Visible = .T.  && Make Line control visible
frmMyForm.shpLine.Top = 20  && Specify Line control row
frmMyForm.shpLine.Left = 125  && Specify Line control column

frmMyForm.cmdCmndBtn1.Visible =.T.  && Up Command button visible
frmMyForm.cmdCmndBtn2.Visible =.T.  && Down" Command button visible
frmMyForm.cmdCmndBtn3.Visible =.T.  && Quit Command button visible

frmMyForm.SHOW  && Display the form
READ EVENTS  && Start event processing

DEFINE CLASS cmdMyCmndBtn1 AS COMMANDBUTTON  && Create Command button
   Caption = 'Slant \<Up'  && Caption on the Command button
   Left = 50  && Command button column
   Top = 100  && Command button row
   Height = 25  && Command button height

   PROCEDURE Click
      ThisForm.shpLine.Visible = .F.  && Hide the Line control
      ThisForm.shpLine.LineSlant ='/'  && Slant up
      ThisForm.shpLine.Visible = .T.  && Show the Line control
ENDDEFINE

DEFINE CLASS cmdMyCmndBtn2 AS CommandButton  && Create Command button
   Caption = 'Slant \<Down'  && Caption on the Command button
   Left = 200  && Command button column
   Top = 100  && Command button row
   Height = 25  && Command button height

   PROCEDURE Click
      ThisForm.shpLine.Visible = .F.  && Hide the Line control
      ThisForm.shpLine.LineSlant ='\'  && Slant down
      ThisForm.shpLine.Visible = .T.  && Show the Line control
ENDDEFINE

DEFINE CLASS cmdMyCmndBtn3 AS CommandButton  && Create Command button
   Caption = '\<Quit'  && Caption on the Command button
   Cancel = .T.  && Default Cancel Command button (Esc)
   Left = 125  && Command button column
   Top = 150  && Command button row
   Height = 25  && Command button height

   PROCEDURE Click
      CLEAR EVENTS  && Stop event processing, close form
ENDDEFINE
```

Applies To

CheckBox, ComboBox, CommandButton, CommandGroup, Container Object, Control Object, Custom, EditBox, Form, Grid, Image, Label, Line, ListBox, OLE Bound Control, OLE Container Control, OptionButton, OptionGroup, PageFrame, _SCREEN, Shape, Spinner, TextBox, Timer, ToolBar

See Also

Height Property, Move Method, ScaleMode Property, Top Property, Width Property

LEFT( ) Function

Returns a specified number of characters from a character expression, starting with the leftmost character.

Syntax

LEFT(*cExpression*, *nExpression*)

Returns

Character

Arguments

cExpression
Specifies the character expression from which LEFT( ) returns characters.

nExpression
Specifies the number of characters returned from the character expression. If *nExpression* is greater than the length of *cExpression*, all of the character expression is returned. The empty string is returned if *nExpression* is negative or 0.

LEFT( ) is identical to SUBSTR( ) with a starting position of 1.

Example

```
CLEAR
? LEFT('Redmond, WA', 4)   && Displays Redm
```

See Also

AT( ), LTRIM( ), RIGHT( ), RTRIM( ), SUBSTR( )

LEFTC( ) Function

Returns a specified number of characters from a character expression, starting with the leftmost character.

Syntax

LEFTC(*cExpression*, *nExpression*)

Returns

Character

Arguments

cExpression
Specifies the character expression from which LEFTC( ) returns characters.

nExpression
Specifies the number of characters returned from the character expression. If *nExpression* is greater than the length of *cExpression*, all of the character expression is returned. The empty string is returned if *nExpression* is negative or 0.

Remarks

LEFTC( ) is designed for expressions containing double-byte characters. If the expression contains only single-byte characters, LEFTC( ) is equivalent to LEFT( ).

LEFTC( ) returns a specified number of characters from a character expression containing any combination of single-byte and double-byte characters.

LEFTC( ) is identical to SUBSTRC( ) with a starting position of 1.

This function is useful for manipulating double-byte character sets for languages such as Hiragana and Katakana.

See Also

AT_C( ), LEFT( ), RIGHTC( ), SUBSTRC( )

LeftColumn Property

Contains the number of the left-most column being displayed by a Grid control. Read-only at design time and run time.

Syntax

Grid.LeftColumn

Remarks

Use the LeftColumn property to determine which columns are not visible to the user. For example, if LeftColumn = 3, columns 1 and 2 are not visible.

Applies To

Grid

See Also

ActiveColumn Property, ActiveRow Property, ColumnOrder Property, RelativeColumn Property, RelativeRow Property

LEN( ) Function

Returns the number of characters in a character expression.

Syntax

LEN(*cExpression*)

Returns

Numeric

Arguments

cExpression
    Specifies the character expression for which LEN( ) returns the number of characters.

Remarks

Use LEN( ) to determine the length of a character expression.

Example

The following example opens the `customer` table in the `testdata` database. LEN( ) is used to display the widths of the `cust_id` and `contact` fields.

```
CLOSE DATABASES
OPEN DATABASE (HOME(2) + 'Data\testdata')
USE Customer       && Open customer table

CLEAR
? 'Width of contact field: '
?? LEN(contact)
? 'Width of cust_id field: '
?? LEN(cust_id)
```

See Also

FSIZE( ), TXTWIDTH( )

LENC( ) Function

Returns the number of characters in a character expression or memo field.

Syntax

LENC(*cExpression*)

Returns

Numeric

Arguments

cExpression

Specifies the character expression for which LENC( ) returns the number of characters.

Remarks

LENC( ) is designed for expressions containing double-byte characters. If the expression contains only single-byte characters, LENC( ) is equivalent to LEN( ).

LENC( ) returns the number of characters in a character expression or memo field containing any combination of single-byte and double-byte characters.

This function is useful for manipulating double-byte character sets for languages such as Hiragana and Katakana.

See Also

LEN( )

LIKE( ) Function

Determines if a character expression matches another character expression.

Syntax

LIKE(*cExpression1*, *cExpression2*)

Returns

Logical

Arguments

cExpression1

Specifies the character expression that LIKE( ) compares with *cExpression2*. *cExpression1* can contain the wildcards such as * and ?. The question mark (?) matches any single character in *cExpression2* and the asterisk (*) matches any number of characters. You can mix any number of wildcards in any combination in *cExpression1*.

cExpression2

Specifies the character expression LIKE( ) compares with *cExpression1*. *cExpression2* must match *cExpression1* letter for letter in order for LIKE( ) to return true (.T.).

Remarks

LIKE( ) returns true (.T.) if *cExpression1* matches *cExpression2*; otherwise, it returns false (.F.).

SET COMPATIBLE determines how LIKE( ) evaluates *cExpression1* and *cExpression2*. If SET COMPATIBLE is set to ON or DB4, *cExpression1* and *cExpression2* have all trailing blanks removed before they are compared. If SET COMPATIBLE is set to OFF or FOXPLUS, any trailing blanks in *cExpression1* and *cExpression2* are used in the comparison.

Example

In the following example, all product names in the products table with the first two letters "Ch" are displayed.

```
CLOSE DATABASES
OPEN DATABASE (HOME(2) + 'Data\testdata')
USE products  && Open Products table

CLEAR
? 'All product names with first two letters Ch:'
?
SCAN FOR LIKE('Ch*', prod_name)
    ? prod_name
ENDSCAN
USE
```

See Also

$, AT( ), ATC( ), OCCURS( ), RAT( ), SET COMPATIBLE

LIKEC( ) Function

Determines whether a character expression matches another character expression.

Syntax

LIKEC(*cExpression1*, *cExpression2*)

Returns

Logical

Arguments

cExpression1

Specifies the character expression that LIKEC( ) compares with *cExpression2*. *cExpression1* can contain wild cards such as * and ?. A question mark (?) matches any single character in *cExpression2* and an asterisk (*) matches any number of characters. You can mix any number of wild cards in any combination in *cExpression1*.

cExpression2

Specifies the character expression LIKEC( ) compares with *cExpression1*. *cExpression2* must match *cExpression1* character for character in order for LIKE( ) to return true (.T.).

Remarks

LIKEC( ) is designed for expressions containing double-byte characters. If the expression contains only single-byte characters, LIKEC( ) is equivalent to LIKE( ).

LIKEC( ) determines if a character expression matches another character expression. LIKEC( ) returns true (.T.) if *cExpression1* matches *cExpression2*; otherwise, it returns false (.F.).

SET COMPATIBLE determines how LIKEC( ) compares blanks in *cExpression1* and *cExpression2*. If SET COMPATIBLE is set to ON or DB4, all trailing blanks are removed from *cExpression1* and *cExpression2* before they are compared. If SET COMPATIBLE is set to OFF or FOXPLUS, any trailing blanks in *cExpression1* and *cExpression2* are used in the comparison.

This function is useful for manipulating double-byte character sets for languages such as Hiragana and Katakana.

See Also

AT_C( ), ATCC( ), LIKEC( ), RATC( )

Line Control

Creates a control that displays a horizontal, vertical, or diagonal line.

Syntax

Line

Remarks

A Line control is a graphical control that displays a horizontal, vertical, or diagonal line that can't be changed directly. However, because a Line control has a full set of properties, events, and methods that other controls have, the Line control can respond to events and can be changed dynamically at run time.

For additional information about creating lines, see "Form Designer" in Help, and Chapter 10, "Using Controls," in the *Microsoft Visual FoxPro 6.0 Programmer's Guide*.

Properties

Application	BaseClass	BorderColor
BorderStyle	BorderWidth	Class
ClassLibrary	ColorSource Property	Comment
DragIcon	DragMode	DrawMode
Enabled	Height	HelpContextID
Left	LineSlant	MousePointer
Name	OLEDragMode	OLEDragPicture
OLEDropEffects	OLEDropHasData Property	OLEDropMode
Parent	ParentClass	Tag
Top	Visible	WhatsThisHelpID
Width		

Events

Click	DblClick	Destroy
DragDrop	DragOver	Error
Init	MiddleClick Event	MouseDown
MouseMove	MouseUp	MouseWheel
OLECompleteDrag	OLEDragDrop	OLEDragOver
OLEGiveFeedBack	OLESetData	OLEStartDrag
RightClick	UIEnable	

Methods

AddProperty	CloneObject	Drag
Move	OLEDrag	ReadExpression
ReadMethod	ResetToDefault	SaveAsClass
WriteExpression	WriteMethod	ZOrder

Example

The following example demonstrates how a Line control can be added to a form and how you can use the LineSlant property to specify the direction in which the line slants.

The AddObject method is used to add a Line control to a form. Three command buttons are added to the form, allowing you to change the direction in which the line slants or to close the form.

```
frmMyForm = CREATEOBJECT('Form')  && Create a Form
frmMyForm.Closable = .F.  && Disable the Control menu box

frmMyForm.AddObject('shpLine','Line')  && Add a Line control to the form
frmMyForm.AddObject('cmdCmndBtn1','cmdMyCmndBtn1')  && Up Cmnd button
frmMyForm.AddObject('cmdCmndBtn2','cmdMyCmndBtn2')  && Down Cmnd button
frmMyForm.AddObject('cmdCmndBtn3','cmdMyCmndBtn3')  && Quit Cmnd button

frmMyForm.shpLine.Visible = .T.  && Make Line control visible
frmMyForm.shpLine.Top = 20  && Specify Line control row
frmMyForm.shpLine.Left = 125  && Specify Line control column

frmMyForm.cmdCmndBtn1.Visible =.T.  && Up Command button visible
frmMyForm.cmdCmndBtn2.Visible =.T.  && Down" Command button visible
frmMyForm.cmdCmndBtn3.Visible =.T.  && Quit Command button visible

frmMyForm.SHOW  && Display the form
READ EVENTS  && Start event processing

DEFINE CLASS cmdMyCmndBtn1 AS COMMANDBUTTON  && Create Command button
   Caption = 'Slant \<Up'  && Caption on the Command button
   Left = 50  && Command button column
   Top = 100  && Command button row
   Height = 25  && Command button height

   PROCEDURE Click
      ThisForm.shpLine.Visible = .F.  && Hide the Line control
      ThisForm.shpLine.LineSlant ='/'  && Slant up
      ThisForm.shpLine.Visible = .T.  && Show the Line control
ENDDEFINE

DEFINE CLASS cmdMyCmndBtn2 AS CommandButton  && Create Command button
   Caption = 'Slant \<Down'  && Caption on the Command button
   Left = 200  && Command button column
   Top = 100  && Command button row
   Height = 25  && Command button height

   PROCEDURE Click
      ThisForm.shpLine.Visible = .F.  && Hide the Line control
      ThisForm.shpLine.LineSlant ='\'  && Slant down
      ThisForm.shpLine.Visible = .T.  && Show the Line control
ENDDEFINE
```

```
DEFINE CLASS cmdMyCmndBtn3 AS CommandButton  && Create Command button
   Caption = '\<Quit'  && Caption on the Command button
   Cancel = .T.  && Default Cancel Command button (Esc)
   Left = 125  && Command button column
   Top = 150  && Command button row
   Height = 25  && Command button height

   PROCEDURE Click
      CLEAR EVENTS  && Stop event processing, close Form
ENDDEFINE
```

See Also

CREATE CLASS, CREATE FORM, DEFINE CLASS

Line Method

Draws a line on a Form object.

Syntax

Object.Line(*nXCoord2*, *nYCoord2*)

– or –

Object.Line(*nXCoord1*, *nYCoord1*, *nXCoord2*, *nYCoord2*)

Arguments

nXCoord1, *nYCoord1*
   Specifies the coordinates of the starting point of the line. The unit of measurement is specified by the ScaleMode property of the form.

nXCoord2, *nYCoord2*
   Specifies the coordinates of the endpoint of the line.

Remarks

The width of the line drawn depends on the setting of DrawWidth property. The way a line is drawn on the background depends on the setting of the DrawMode and DrawStyle properties. After the Line method runs, the CurrentX and CurrentY properties are set to *nXCoord2, nYCoord2*.

Applies To

Form, _SCREEN

See Also

CurrentX, CurrentY Properties, DrawMode Property, DrawStyle Property, DrawWidth, Property, ScaleMode Property

LINENO( ) Function

Returns the line number of a line being executed in a program relative to the first line of the main program.

Syntax

LINENO([1])

Returns

Numeric

Arguments

1

Returns the line number relative to the first line of the current program or procedure. If you omit the 1 argument, the line number is returned relative to the first line of the main program.

Remarks

Program lines are counted starting from the top of the program. Comment lines, continuation lines, and blank lines are included in the line number count. If a program is suspended during execution, LINENO( ) returns the number of the program line at which program execution was suspended. LINENO( ) returns 0 if a program is canceled.

By default, line numbers are returned relative to the beginning of the main program. If a procedure is called, line numbering continues from the top of the calling program.

LINENO( ) is useful for debugging programs. You can set a breakpoint to stop program execution at a specific line number by issuing the following command in the Debug window:

```
LINENO( ) = nExpression
```

Program execution is suspended when the value of LINENO( ) is equal to *nExpression*.

Example

The following example is part of a simple error-handling routine.

```
ON ERROR DO bug_proc WITH LINENO( )
BRWS  && Causes an error
ON ERROR

*** Bug_Proc error handler ***
```

```
PROCEDURE bug_proc
PARAMETERS gnBadLine
WAIT WINDOW 'Error occurred at line: ' + ALLTRIM(STR(gnBadLine))
RETURN
```

See Also

ERROR( ), MESSAGE( ), PROGRAM( ), SYS(16) – Executing Program File Name

LineSlant Property

Specifies which way a line slants, from upper left to lower right or lower left to upper right. Available at design time and run time.

Syntax

Line.LineSlant[= *cSlant*]

Arguments

cSlant

The settings for the LineSlant property are:

Setting	Description
\	(Default) Line slants from upper left to lower right.
/	Line slants from lower left to upper right.

Example

The following example demonstrates how to use the LineSlant property to specify the direction in which a Line control slants.

A Line control is added to a form. Three command buttons are added to the form, allowing you to change the direction in which the line slants or to close the form.

```
frmMyForm = CREATEOBJECT('Form')  && Create a Form
frmMyForm.Closable = .F.  && Disable the Control menu box

frmMyForm.AddObject('shpLine','Line')  && Add a Line control to the form
frmMyForm.AddObject('cmdCmndBtn1','cmdMyCmndBtn1')  && Up Cmnd button
frmMyForm.AddObject('cmdCmndBtn2','cmdMyCmndBtn2')  && Down Cmnd button
frmMyForm.AddObject('cmdCmndBtn3','cmdMyCmndBtn3')  && Quit Cmnd button

frmMyForm.shpLine.Visible = .T.  && Make Line control visible
frmMyForm.shpLine.Top = 20  && Specify Line control row
frmMyForm.shpLine.Left = 125  && Specify Line control column
```

```
frmMyForm.cmdCmndBtn1.Visible =.T.  && Up Command button visible
frmMyForm.cmdCmndBtn2.Visible =.T.  && Down" Command button visible
frmMyForm.cmdCmndBtn3.Visible =.T.  && Quit Command button visible

frmMyForm.SHOW  && Display the form
READ EVENTS  && Start event processing

DEFINE CLASS cmdMyCmndBtn1 AS COMMANDBUTTON  && Create Command button
    Caption = 'Slant \<Up'  && Caption on the Command button
    Left = 50  && Command button column
    Top = 100  && Command button row
    Height = 25  && Command button height

    PROCEDURE Click
        ThisForm.shpLine.Visible = .F.  && Hide the Line control
        ThisForm.shpLine.LineSlant ='/'  && Slant up
        ThisForm.shpLine.Visible = .T.  && Show the Line control
ENDDEFINE

DEFINE CLASS cmdMyCmndBtn2 AS CommandButton  && Create Command button
    Caption = 'Slant \<Down'  && Caption on the Command button
    Left = 200  && Command button column
    Top = 100  && Command button row
    Height = 25  && Command button height

    PROCEDURE Click
        ThisForm.shpLine.Visible = .F.  && Hide the Line control
        ThisForm.shpLine.LineSlant ='\'  && Slant down
        ThisForm.shpLine.Visible = .T.  && Show the Line control
ENDDEFINE

DEFINE CLASS cmdMyCmndBtn3 AS CommandButton  && Create Command button
    Caption = '\<Quit'  && Caption on the Command button
    Cancel = .T.  && Default Cancel Command button (Esc)
    Left = 125  && Command button column
    Top = 150  && Command button row
    Height = 25  && Command button height

    PROCEDURE Click
        CLEAR EVENTS  && Stop event processing, close Form
ENDDEFINE
```

Applies To

Line

See Also

DrawMode Property, DrawStyle Property

LinkMaster Property

Specifies the parent table linked to the child table displayed in a Grid control. Available at design time; read/write at run time.

Syntax

Grid.LinkMaster[= *cName*]

Arguments

cName
> Specifies the alias of the parent table that drives the display of the child table in a Grid control.

Remarks

Use the LinkMaster property to set up a one-to-many relationship between the parent, or primary, table of the Form, and the table referenced by the Grid's RecordSource property.

Applies To

Grid

See Also

ChildOrder Property, RelationalExpr Property

LIST Commands

Continuously displays table or environment information.

Syntax

LIST
    [FIELDS *FieldList*]
    [*Scope*] [FOR *lExpression1*] [WHILE *lExpression2*]
    [OFF]
    [NOCONSOLE]
    [NOOPTIMIZE]
    [TO PRINTER [PROMPT] | TO FILE *FileName*]

– or –

LIST FILES
    [ON *Drive*]
    [LIKE *FileSkeleton*]
    [TO PRINTER [PROMPT] | TO FILE *FileName*]

– or –

LIST MEMORY
    [LIKE *FileSkeleton*]
    [NOCONSOLE]
    [TO PRINTER [PROMPT] | TO FILE *FileName*]

– or –

LIST STATUS
    [NOCONSOLE]
    [TO PRINTER [PROMPT] | TO FILE *FileName*]

– or –

LIST STRUCTURE
    [IN *nWorkArea* | *cTableAlias*]
    [NOCONSOLE]
    [TO PRINTER [PROMPT] | TO FILE *FileName*]

Remarks

These LIST commands are identical to the DISPLAY commands except for the following differences:

- The scope for LIST defaults to ALL records.

- LIST doesn't prompt you after filling the main Microsoft Visual FoxPro window or a user-defined window with information.

- LIST doesn't display records flagged for deletion when SET DELETED is ON.

For more information about the LIST commands, see the corresponding commands in the DISPLAY Command, earlier in this language reference.

See Also

DISPLAY, DISPLAY FILES, DISPLAY MEMORY, DISPLAY STATUS, DISPLAY STRUCTURE, SET DELETED

LIST CONNECTIONS Command

Continuously displays information about the named connections in the current database.

Syntax

LIST CONNECTIONS
    [TO PRINTER [PROMPT] | TO FILE *FileName*]
    [NOCONSOLE]

Arguments

TO PRINTER [PROMPT]
    Directs output from LIST CONNECTIONS to a printer.

In Visual FoxPro, you can include the optional PROMPT clause to display a Print dialog box before printing starts. Place PROMPT immediately after TO PRINTER.

TO FILE *FileName*

Directs output from LIST CONNECTIONS to the file specified with *FileName*. If the file already exists and SET SAFETY is ON, Visual FoxPro displays a prompt asking if you want to overwrite the file.

NOCONSOLE

Suppresses output to the main Visual FoxPro window or to the active user-defined window.

Remarks

The information displayed includes the names of named connections, datasources, and connection strings in the current database. Use DBGETPROP( ) to return additional information about connections in the current database.

Example

The following example assumes an ODBC data source called MyFoxSQLNT is available, and the user ID for the data source is "sa." The testdata database is opened, and a connection named Myconn is created. LIST CONNECTIONS is used to list the named connections in the database.

```
CLOSE DATABASES
OPEN DATABASE (HOME(2) + 'data\testdata')

CREATE CONNECTION Myconn DATASOURCE "MyFoxSQLNT" USERID "sa"
CLEAR

LIST CONNECTIONS  && Lists named connections in the database
```

See Also

CREATE CONNECTION, DELETE CONNECTION, DBGETPROP( ), DISPLAY CONNECTIONS, RENAME CONNECTION

LIST DATABASE Command

Continuously displays information about the current database.

Syntax

LIST DATABASE
    [TO PRINTER [PROMPT] | TO FILE *FileName*]
    [NOCONSOLE]

Arguments

TO PRINTER [PROMPT]

Directs output from LIST DATABASE to a printer.

In Visual FoxPro, you can include the optional PROMPT clause to display a Print dialog box before printing starts. Place PROMPT immediately after TO PRINTER.

TO FILE *FileName*

Directs output from LIST DATABASE to the file specified with *FileName*. If the file already exists and SET SAFETY is ON, Visual FoxPro displays a prompt asking if you want to overwrite the file.

NOCONSOLE

Suppresses output to the main Visual FoxPro window or to the active user-defined window.

Remarks

Use DBGETPROP( ) to return additional information about the current database.

Example

This example creates a database named people. A table named friends is created and is automatically added to the database. DISPLAY TABLES is used to display the tables in the database, and LIST DATABASES is used to list information about the tables in the database.

```
CREATE DATABASE people
CREATE TABLE friends (FirstName C(20), LastName C(20))
CLEAR
DISPLAY TABLES   && Displays tables in the database

LIST DATABASE    && Lists table information
```

See Also

DISPLAY DATABASE

LIST DLLS Command

Continuously displays information about shared library functions registered in Visual FoxPro with DECLARE – DLL.

Syntax

LIST DLLS
    [TO PRINTER [PROMPT] | TO FILE *FileName*]
    [NOCONSOLE]

Arguments

TO PRINTER [PROMPT]

Directs output from LIST DLLS to a printer.

In Visual FoxPro, you can include the optional PROMPT clause to display a Print dialog box before printing starts. Place PROMPT immediately after TO PRINTER.

TO FILE *FileName*

Directs output from LIST DLLS to the file specified with *FileName*. If the file already exists and SET SAFETY is ON, Visual FoxPro displays a prompt asking if you want to overwrite the file.

NOCONSOLE

Suppresses output to the main Visual FoxPro window or the active user-defined window.

See Also

DECLARE – DLL, DISPLAY DLLS

LIST OBJECTS Command

Continuously displays information about an object or a group of objects.

Syntax

LIST OBJECTS
  [LIKE *cObjectSkeleton*]
  [TO PRINTER [PROMPT] | TO FILE *FileName*]
  [NOCONSOLE]

Arguments

LIKE *cObjectSkeleton*

Displays information about a subset of objects. *cObjectSkeleton* is an object specification skeleton that supports wildcards (* and ?). For example, to continuously display all objects that begin with A, use the following command:

```
LIST OBJECTS LIKE A*
```

TO PRINTER [PROMPT]

Directs output from LIST OBJECTS to a printer.

You can include the optional PROMPT clause to display a Print dialog box before printing starts. Place the PROMPT keyword immediately after TO PRINTER.

TO FILE *FileName*

Directs output from LIST OBJECTS to the disk file specified with *FileName*. If the file already exists and SET SAFETY is ON, Visual FoxPro displays a prompt asking if you want to overwrite the file.

NOCONSOLE

Suppresses output to the main Visual FoxPro window or to the active user-defined window.

Remarks

LIST OBJECTS displays the following information about all existing objects:

- Properties and their values.

- Methods.

- Member objects and the class or subclass on which they are based.

- Class or subclass on which objects are based.

- Class hierarchy for the objects.

LIST OBJECTS fills the entire main Visual FoxPro window without pausing.

Example

The following example uses DEFINE CLASS and CREATEOBJECT( ) to create two custom classes named FormChild and FormGrandChild from the Visual FoxPro Form base class. LIST OBJECTS lists information about the objects and their properties.

```
CLEAR
frmMyForm = CREATEOBJECT("FormGrandChild")

LIST OBJECTS LIKE frm*
RELEASE frmMyForm

DEFINE CLASS FormChild AS FORM
ENDDEFINE

DEFINE CLASS FormGrandChild AS FormChild
ENDDEFINE
```

See Also

DISPLAY OBJECTS

LIST PROCEDURES Command

Continuously displays the names of stored procedures in the current database.

Syntax

LIST PROCEDURES
    [TO PRINTER [PROMPT] | TO FILE *FileName*]
    [NOCONSOLE]

Arguments

TO PRINTER [PROMPT]

Directs the information returned from LIST PROCEDURES to a printer.

You can include PROMPT to display a Print dialog box before printing starts. Place the PROMPT keyword immediately after TO PRINTER.

TO FILE *FileName*

Directs output from LIST PROCEDURES to the disk file specified with *FileName*. If the file already exists and SET SAFETY is ON, Visual FoxPro displays a prompt asking if you want to overwrite the file.

NOCONSOLE

Suppresses output to the main Visual FoxPro window or to the active user-defined window.

Remarks

Stored procedures are created with MODIFY PROCEDURES.

Example

The following example opens the `testdata` database and uses LIST PROCEDURES to list the stored procedures (if any) in the database.

```
CLOSE DATABASES
OPEN DATABASE (HOME(2) + 'data\testdata')

CLEAR

LIST PROCEDURES  && Lists stored procedures in the database
```

See Also

APPEND PROCEDURES, COPY PROCEDURES, CREATE DATABASE, DISPLAY DATABASE, DISPLAY PROCEDURES, MODIFY PROCEDURE

List Property

A character string array used to access the items in a ComboBox or ListBox control. Not available at design time; read/write at run time.

Syntax

Control.List(*nRow* [, *nCol*])[= *cChar*]

Arguments

nRow

Specifies the row of the item to be retrieved using the display order. For example, *nRow* = 3 specifies the third row shown in the list.

nCol

Specifies the column of the item to be retrieved using the display order. For example, *nCol* = 2 specifies the second column shown in the list. If *nCol* is not specified, the List property retrieves the first column by default. Only specify *nCol* for ComboBox and ListBox controls that have more than one column.

Remarks

The List property works in conjunction with the ListCount property; enumerating a list from 1 to ListCount returns all items in the list.

You cannot use array functions with the List property. However, if you set the RowSourceType property to 5 (Array) and set the RowSource property to the array of values to be contained in the list, you can use array functions on the array specified in the RowSource property.

Note When RowSourceType is set to 0 or 1, add items to a combo box or list box using the AddItem method. To remove items, use the RemoveItem method. To keep items in alphabetic order, set the control's Sorted property to true (.T.) before adding items to the list.

Example

In the following example, ListCount is used to cycle through all the of the items specified by the List property of the combo box or list box.

The following example creates a list box. The source of the items that appear in the list box items is an array; the array is specified with the RowSourceType and RowSource properties.

The MultiSelect property for the list box is set to true (.T.), allowing you to make multiple selections from the list box. The ListCount property is used within a FOR ... ENDFOR loop to display the item or items you choose in the list box. The Selected property is used to determine the items you chose, and the List property is used to return the items.

```
CLEAR

DIMENSION gaMyListArray(10)
FOR gnCount = 1 to 10  && Fill the array with letters
   STORE REPLICATE(CHR(gnCount+64),6) TO gaMyListArray(gnCount)
ENDFOR

frmMyForm = CREATEOBJECT('Form')  && Create a Form
frmMyForm.Closable = .F.  && Disable the Control menu box

frmMyForm.Move(150,10)  && Move the form

* Add "Quit" command button and list box control
frmMyForm.AddObject('cmbCommand1','cmdMyCmdBtn')
frmMyForm.AddObject('lstListBox1','lstMyListBox')
```

```
* && Specifies an array containing listbox items
frmMyForm.lstListBox1.RowSourceType = 5
frmMyForm.lstListBox1.RowSource = 'gaMyListArray'

frmMyForm.cmbCommand1.Visible =.T.  && "Quit" Command button visible
frmMyForm.lstListBox1.Visible =.T.  && "List Box visible

frmMyForm.SHOW  && Display the form
READ EVENTS  && Start event processing

DEFINE CLASS cmdMyCmdBtn AS CommandButton  && Create Command button
   Caption = '\<Quit'  && Caption on the Command button
   Cancel = .T.  && Default Cancel Command button (Esc)
   Left = 125  && Command button column
   Top = 210  && Command button row
   Height = 25  && Command button height

   PROCEDURE Click
      CLEAR EVENTS  && Stop event processing, close Form
      CLEAR  && Clear main Visual FoxPro window
ENDDEFINE

DEFINE CLASS lstMyListBox AS ListBox  && Create ListBox control
   Left = 10  && List Box column
   Top = 10  && List Box row
   MultiSelect = .T.  && Allow selecting more than 1 item

PROCEDURE Click
   ACTIVATE SCREEN
   CLEAR
   ? "Selected items:"
   ? "---------------"
   FOR nCnt = 1 TO ThisForm.lstListBox1.ListCount
      IF ThisForm.lstListBox1.Selected(nCnt)  && Is item selected?
         ? SPACE(5) + ThisForm.lstListBox1.List(nCnt)  && Show item
      ENDIF
   ENDFOR

ENDDEFINE
```

Applies To

ComboBox, ListBox

See Also

AddItem Method, IndexToItemID Method, ItemIDToIndex Method, ListCount Property, ListItem Property, ListItemID Property, RowSource, RowSourceType, Sorted Property

LIST TABLES Command

Displays without pausing all tables and information about the tables contained in the current database.

Syntax

LIST TABLES
    [TO PRINTER [PROMPT] | TO FILE *FileName*]
    [NOCONSOLE]

Arguments

TO PRINTER [PROMPT]
    Directs the information returned from LIST TABLES to a printer.

    You can include PROMPT to display a Print dialog box before printing starts. Place the PROMPT keyword immediately after TO PRINTER.

TO FILE *FileName*
    Directs output from LIST TABLES to the disk file specified with *FileName*. If the file already exists and SET SAFETY is ON, Visual FoxPro displays a prompt asking if you want to overwrite the file.

NOCONSOLE
    Suppresses output to the main Visual FoxPro window or to the active user-defined window.

Remarks

The information returned includes the table names and paths and is a subset of the information shown using LIST STATUS. However, the information displayed using LIST TABLES contains only table-related information and displays the information regardless of whether the tables are open.

Example

The following example opens the `customer` table in the `testdata` database. LIST TABLES is used to list information about the tables in the database.

```
CLOSE DATABASES
SET PATH TO (HOME(2) + 'data\')  && Sets path to database
OPEN DATABASE testdata  && Open testdata database
CLEAR

LIST TABLES  && Lists information about tables in the database
```

See Also

ADD TABLE, CLOSE DATABASES, CREATE DATABASE, DISPLAY TABLES, OPEN DATABASE, REMOVE TABLE

LIST VIEWS Command

Displays without pausing information about SQL views in the current database.

Syntax

LIST VIEWS
    [TO PRINTER [PROMPT] | TO FILE *FileName*]
    [NOCONSOLE]

Arguments

TO PRINTER [PROMPT]
    Directs the information returned from LIST VIEWS to a printer.

    You can include PROMPT to display a Print dialog box before printing starts. Place
    the PROMPT keyword immediately after TO PRINTER.

TO FILE *FileName*
    Directs output from LIST VIEWS to the disk file specified with *FileName*. If the file
    already exists and SET SAFETY is ON, Visual FoxPro displays a prompt asking if
    you want to overwrite the file.

NOCONSOLE
    Suppresses output to the main Microsoft Visual FoxPro window or to the active
    user-defined window.

Remarks

LIST VIEWS displays the names of SQL views in the current database, and indicates if the
SQL views are based on local or remote tables. Use DBGETPROP( ) to return additional
information about SQL views in the current database.

SQL views are created with CREATE SQL VIEW.

Example

The following example opens the `testdata` database. CREATE SQL VIEW is used to
create a local SQL view named `myview`. The View Designer is displayed, allowing you to
specify tables and conditions for the SQL view. After you save the SQL view you create,
information about the SQL views in the database is listed.

```
CLOSE DATABASES
OPEN DATABASE (HOME(2) + 'data\testdata')
CREATE SQL VIEW myview

CLEAR

LIST VIEWS
```

See Also

CREATE DATABASE, CREATE SQL VIEW, DBGETPROP( ), DISPLAY DATABASE, DISPLAY VIEWS

ListBox Control

Creates a list box.

Syntax

ListBox

Remarks

A list box displays a list of items from which you can select one or more items. A list box is similar to a combo box; however, a combo box initially displays a single item.

For additional information about creating ListBox controls, see "Form Designer" in Help, and Chapter 10, "Using Controls," in the *Microsoft Visual FoxPro 6.0 Programmer's Guide*.

Properties

Application	BaseClass	BorderColor
BoundColumn	BoundTo	Class
ClassLibrary	ColorScheme	ColorSource
ColumnCount	ColumnLines	ColumnWidths
Comment	ControlSource	DisabledBackColor
DisabledForeColor	DisabledItemBackColor	DisabledItemForeColor
DisplayValue	DragIcon	DragMode
Enabled	FirstElement	FontBold
FontCondense	FontExtend	FontItalic
FontName	FontOutline	FontShadow
FontSize	FontStrikeThru	FontUnderLine
Height	HelpContextID	IncrementalSearch
IntegralHeight	ItemBackColor	ItemData

ItemForeColor	ItemIDData	ItemTips
Left	List	ListCount
ListIndex	ListItem	ListItemID
MouseIcon	MousePointer	MoverBars
MultiSelect	Name	NewIndex
NewItemID	NullDisplay	NumberOfElements
OLEDragMode	OLEDragPicture	OLEDropEffects
OLEDropHasData Property	OLEDropMode	Parent
ParentClass	Picture	RightToLeft
RowSource	RowSourceType	Selected
SelectedID	SelectedItemBackColor	SelectedItemForeColor
Sorted	SpecialEffect	StatusBarText
TabIndex	TabStop	Tag
TerminateRead	ToolTipText	Top
TopIndex	TopItemID	Value
Visible	WhatsThisHelpID	Width

Events

Click	DblClick	Destroy
DragDrop	DragOver	Error
ErrorMessage	GotFocus	Init
InteractiveChange	KeyPress	LostFocus
Message	MiddleClick Event	MouseDown
MouseMove	MouseUp	MouseWheel
OLECompleteDrag	OLEDragDrop	OLEDragOver
OLEGiveFeedBack	OLESetData	OLEStartDrag
ProgrammaticChange	RangeHigh	RangeLow
RightClick	UIEnable	Valid
When		

Methods

AddItem	AddListItem	AddProperty
Clear	CloneObject	Drag
IndexToItemID	ItemIDToIndex	Move
OLEDrag	ReadExpression	ReadMethod
Refresh	RemoveItem	RemoveListItem
Requery	ResetToDefault	SaveAsClass
SetFocus	WriteExpression	WriteMethod
ZOrder		

Example

The following example creates a ListBox control. The source of the items that appear in the list box is an array specified with the RowSourceType and RowSource properties.

The MultiSelect property for the list box is set to true (.T.), allowing you to make multiple selections from the list. The item or items you choose are displayed by using the ListCount, Selected, and List properties (which determine the number of items in the list and the items you chose).

```
CLEAR

DIMENSION gaMyListArray(10)
FOR gnCount = 1 to 10   && Fill the array with letters
    STORE REPLICATE(CHR(gnCount+64),6) TO gaMyListArray(gnCount)
NEXT

frmMyForm = CREATEOBJECT('Form')  && Create a Form
frmMyForm.Closable = .f.  && Disable the Control menu box

frmMyForm.Move(150,10)  && Move the form

frmMyForm.AddObject('cmbCommand1','cmdMyCmdBtn')  && Add "Quit" Command button
frmMyForm.AddObject('lstListBox1','lstMyListBox')  && Add ListBox control

frmMyForm.lstListBox1.RowSourceType = 5  && Specifies an array
frmMyForm.lstListBox1.RowSource = 'gaMyListArray' && Array containing listbox items

frmMyForm.cmbCommand1.Visible =.T.  && "Quit" Command button visible
frmMyForm.lstListBox1.Visible =.T.  && "List Box visible

frmMyForm.SHOW  && Display the form
READ EVENTS  && Start event processing
```

```
DEFINE CLASS cmdMyCmdBtn AS CommandButton  && Create Command button
   Caption = '\<Quit'  && Caption on the Command button
   Cancel = .T.  && Default Cancel Command button (Esc)
   Left = 125  && Command button column
   Top = 210  && Command button row
   Height = 25  && Command button height

   PROCEDURE Click
      CLEAR EVENTS  && Stop event processing, close Form
      CLEAR  && Clear main Visual FoxPro window
ENDDEFINE

DEFINE CLASS lstMyListBox AS ListBox  && Create ListBox control
   Left = 10  && List Box column
   Top = 10  && List Box row
   MultiSelect = .T.  && Allow selecting more than 1 item

PROCEDURE Click
   ACTIVATE SCREEN
   CLEAR
   ? "Selected items:"
   ? "----------------"
   FOR nCnt = 1 TO ThisForm.lstListBox1.ListCount
      IF ThisForm.lstListBox1.Selected(nCnt)  && Is item selected?
         ? SPACE(5) + ThisForm.lstListBox1.List(nCnt) && Show item
      ENDIF
   ENDFOR

ENDDEFINE
```

See Also

CREATE CLASS, CREATE FORM, DEFINE CLASS

ListCount Property

Contains the number of items in the list portion of a ComboBox or ListBox control. Not available at design time; read-only at run time.

Syntax

Control.ListCount

Example

The following example creates a list box. The source of the items that appear in the list box items is an array; the array is specified with the RowSourceType and RowSource properties.

ListCount is used to cycle through all of the items specified by the List property of the ComboBox or ListBox.

The MultiSelect property for the list box is set to true (.T.), allowing you to make multiple selections from the list box. The ListCount property is used within a FOR ... ENDFOR loop to display the item or items you choose in the list box. The Selected and List properties are used to determine the items you chose.

```
CLEAR

DIMENSION gaMyListArray(10)
FOR gnCount = 1 to 10  && Fill the array with letters
    STORE REPLICATE(CHR(gnCount+64),6) TO gaMyListArray(gnCount)
ENDFOR

frmMyForm = CREATEOBJECT('Form')  && Create a Form
frmMyForm.Closable = .f.  && Disable the Control menu box

frmMyForm.Move(150,10)  && Move the form

frmMyForm.AddObject('cmbCommand1','cmdMyCmdBtn')  && Add "Quit" Command button
frmMyForm.AddObject('lstListBox1','lstMyListBox')  && Add list box control

frmMyForm.lstListBox1.RowSourceType = 5  && Specifies an array
frmMyForm.lstListBox1.RowSource = 'gaMyListArray' && Array containing listbox items

frmMyForm.cmbCommand1.Visible =.T.  && "Quit" Command button visible
frmMyForm.lstListBox1.Visible =.T.  && "List Box visible

frmMyForm.SHOW  && Display the form
READ EVENTS  && Start event processing

DEFINE CLASS cmdMyCmdBtn AS CommandButton  && Create Command button
    Caption = '\<Quit'  && Caption on the Command button
    Cancel = .T.  && Default Cancel Command button (Esc)
    Left = 125  && Command button column
    Top = 210  && Command button row
    Height = 25  && Command button height

    PROCEDURE Click
       CLEAR EVENTS  && Stop event processing, close Form
       CLEAR  && Clear main Visual FoxPro window
ENDDEFINE

DEFINE CLASS lstMyListBox AS ListBox  && Create ListBox control
    Left = 10  && List Box column
    Top = 10  && List Box row
    MultiSelect = .T.  && Allow selecting more than 1 item
```

```
PROCEDURE Click
   ACTIVATE SCREEN
   CLEAR
   ? "Selected items:"
   ? "---------------"
   FOR nCnt = 1 TO ThisForm.lstListBox1.ListCount
      IF ThisForm.lstListBox1.Selected(nCnt)  && Is item selected?
         ? SPACE(5) + ThisForm.lstListBox1.List(nCnt) && Show item
      ENDIF
   ENDFOR

ENDDEFINE
```

Applies To

ComboBox, ListBox

See Also

AddItem Method, List Property, ListItemID Property, RemoveItem Method

ListIndex Property

Specifies the index number of the selected item in a ComboBox or ListBox control. Not available at design time; read/write at run time.

Syntax

Control.ListIndex[= *nIndex*]

Settings

nIndex
   The settings for the ListIndex property are:

Setting	Description
0	(Default) Indicates no items selected. For a combo box, this means that the user has entered a value not in the list.
1 ... ListCount	The index of the selected item.

Remarks

The following displays the string of the selected item.

```
? List(MyList.ListIndex)
```

You can return the same value by using the control's Value property.

Applies To

ComboBox, ListBox

See Also

AddItem Method, AddListItem Method, IndexToItemID Method, ItemIDToIndex Method, List Property, ListItem Property, RemoveItem Method, Value Property

ListItem Property

A character string array used to access the items in a ComboBox or ListBox control by item ID. Not available at design time; read/write at run time.

Syntax

Control.ListItem(*nItemID*)[= *cChar*]

Settings

nItemID
    Specifies the item to retrieve using the item's unique ID.

Remarks

The ListItem property works in conjunction with the ListCount property; enumerating a list from 1 to ListCount returns all items in the list. Use the List property to retrieve items in the order they are displayed; use the ListItem property to retrieve items according to their item ID.

> **Note** To add items to a combo box or list box, use the AddItem or AddListItem method. To remove items, use the RemovetItem method or the RemoveListItem method. To keep items in alphabetic order, set the control's Sorted property to true (.T.) before adding items to the list.

Applies To

ComboBox, ListBox

See Also

AddItem Method, AddListItem Method, IndexToItemID Method, ItemIDToIndex Method, ListCount Property, List Property, ListItemID Property

ListItemID Property

Specifies the unique ID number for the selected item in a ComboBox or ListBox control. Not available at design time; read/write at run time.

Syntax

Control.ListItemID[= *nItemID*]

Settings

nItemID

The settings and interpretations for the ListItemID property are:

Setting	Description
–1	Indicates no items selected. For a combo box, it means that the user has entered a value not in the list.
1 (or any number greater than 1)	The item ID of the selected item.

Remarks

If an item is removed from a list using the RemoveListItem method, all remaining items retain their unique identification numbers. When an item is added to a list using the AddItem method, and the Sorted property is set to false (.F.), *nItemID* is assigned the lowest number available. When an item is added to a list using the AddListItem method, and the Sorted property is set to false (.F.), you can assign any number to *nItemID*.

Applies To

ComboBox, ListBox

See Also

AddItem Method, AddListItem Method, IndexToItemID Method, ItemIDToIndex Method, ListCount Property, List Property, ListItem Property, RemoveItem Method, RemoveListItem Method

_LMARGIN System Variable

Included for backward compatibility. Use the Report Designer instead.

LOAD Command

Included for backward compatibility. Use SET LIBRARY instead.

Load Event

Occurs just before an object is created.

Syntax

PROCEDURE *Object*.Load
[LPARAMETERS *nIndex*]

Arguments

nIndex
>   Uniquely identifies a control if it is in a control array.

Remarks

The Load event occurs first for the form set and then for the contained forms. The Load event occurs before the Activate and GotFocus events.

To prevent a form from being created, return false (.F.) from the Load event; the Destroy event will not be executed.

Applies To

Form, FormSet

See Also

Activate Event, GotFocus Event, Unload Event

LOADPICTURE( ) Function

Creates an object reference for a bitmap, icon, or Windows meta file.

Syntax

LOADPICTURE([*cFileName*])

Returns

Object

Arguments

cFileName
>   Specifies the bitmap (.bmp), icon (.ico), or Windows metafile (.wmf) file for which an object reference is created. If *cFileName* is omitted, the null picture is returned. You can include GETPICT( ) as *cFileName* to display the Open dialog from which you can choose a bitmap (.bmp) file.

Remarks

Many presentation properties of ActiveX controls require an object reference for their settings. For example, the ActiveX Outline control supports the PictureOpen property that requires an object reference for its setting.

See Also

GETPICT( ), SAVEPICTURE( )

LOCAL Command

Creates local variables and variable arrays.

Syntax

LOCAL *VarList*

– or –

LOCAL [ARRAY] *ArrayName1(nRows1* [, *nColumns1*])
   [, *ArrayName2(nRows2* [, *nColumns2*])] ...

Arguments

VarList
> Specifies one or more local variables to create.

[ARRAY] *ArrayName1* (*nRows1* [, *nColumns1*])
   [, *ArrayName2* (*nRows2* [, *nColumns2*])] ...
> Specifies one or more local arrays to create. See the DIMENSION Command, earlier in this language reference, for a description of each argument.

Remarks

Local variables and variable arrays can be used and modified only within the procedure or function in which they are created, and cannot be accessed by higher- or lower-level programs. Local variables and arrays are released once the procedure or function containing the local variables and arrays completes execution.

Variables and arrays created with LOCAL are initialized to false (.F.). Any variable or array you wish to declare as local must be declared local prior to assigning it a value. Visual FoxPro generates an error message if you assign a value to a variable or array and later declare it local with LOCAL.

Local variables can be passed by reference.

You cannot abbreviate LOCAL because LOCAL and LOCATE have the same first four letters.

See Also

DIMENSION, FUNCTION, LPARAMETERS, PARAMETERS, PARAMETERS( ), PRIVATE, PUBLIC, RELEASE

LOCATE Command

Sequentially searches the table for the first record that matches the specified logical expression.

Syntax

LOCATE FOR *lExpression1*
    [*Scope*]
    [WHILE]
    [NOOPTIMIZE]

Arguments

FOR *lExpression1*

Sequentially searches the current table for the first record that matches the logical expression *lExpression1*.

Rushmore optimizes a query created with LOCATE FOR if *lExpression1* is an optimizable expression. For best performance, use an optimizable expression in the FOR clause.

For more information, see the SET OPTIMIZE Command, later in this language reference, and "Understanding Rushmore Technology" in Chapter 15, "Optimizing Applications," in the *Microsoft Visual FoxPro 6.0 Programmer's Guide*.

Scope

Specifies a range of records to locate. Only the records that fall within the range are located. The scope clauses are: ALL, NEXT *nRecords*, RECORD *nRecordNumber*, and REST. For more information on scope clauses, see "Scope Clauses" or "Overview of the Language," in Help. Commands that include *Scope* operate only on the table in the active work area.

The default scope for LOCATE is ALL records.

WHILE *lExpression2*

Specifies a condition whereby records are searched for as long as the logical expression *lExpression2* evaluates to true (.T.).

NOOPTIMIZE

Disables Rushmore optimization of LOCATE.

For more information, see the SET OPTIMIZE Command, later in this language reference, and "Understanding Rushmore Technology" in Chapter 15, "Optimizing Applications," in the *Microsoft Visual FoxPro 6.0 Programmer's Guide*.

Remarks

The table doesn't have to be indexed.

If LOCATE finds a matching record, you can use RECNO( ) to return the number of the matching record. If a matching record is found, FOUND( ) returns true (.T.), and EOF( ) returns false (.F.). If SET TALK is ON, the record number of the matching record is displayed.

After LOCATE finds a matching record, you can issue CONTINUE to search the remainder of the table for additional matching records. When CONTINUE is executed, the search process resumes, starting with the record immediately following the matching record. You can issue CONTINUE repeatedly until the end of the scope or the end of the table is reached.

If a match isn't found, RECNO( ) returns the number of records in the table plus 1, FOUND( ) returns false (.F.), and EOF( ) returns true (.T.).

LOCATE and CONTINUE are specific to the current work area. If another work area is selected, the original search process can be continued when the original work area is reselected.

Example

In the following example, records for customers from Germany are located. The total count is then displayed.

```
CLOSE DATABASES
OPEN DATABASE (HOME(2) + 'Data\testdata')
USE customer  && Open Customer table
SET TALK OFF

STORE 0 TO gnCount

LOCATE FOR ALLTRIM(UPPER(customer.country)) = 'GERMANY'
DO WHILE FOUND( )
   gnCount = gnCount + 1
   ? company
   CONTINUE
ENDDO

? 'Total companies Germany: '+ LTRIM(STR(gnCount))
```

See Also

CONTINUE, EOF( ), FIND, FOUND( ), INDEXSEEK( ), RECNO( ), SEEK, SEEK( ), SET OPTIMIZE

LOCFILE( ) Function

Locates a file on disk and returns the file name with its path.

Syntax

LOCFILE(*cFileName* [, *cFileExtensions*] [, *cFileNameCaption*])

Returns

Character

Arguments

cFileName

Specifies the name of the file to locate. If *cFileName* includes only a file name, LOCFILE( ) searches the Visual FoxPro default directory or folder first. If the file isn't found in the default directory or folder, the Microsoft Visual FoxPro path is then searched. Use SET PATH to specify the Visual FoxPro path.

If *cFileName* includes a path and a file name, the specified location is searched. If the file can't be found in the specified location, LOCFILE( ) searches the Visual FoxPro default directory or folder and then the Visual FoxPro path.

If the file is located, LOCFILE( ) returns the file name and path.

cFileExtensions

Specifies file extensions for the file to locate. If the file name you specify with *cFileName* doesn't include an extension, Visual FoxPro applies the file extensions listed in *cFileExtensions* to the file name and searches for the file again.

cFileExtensions also specifies the file name extensions of the files displayed in the Open dialog box when the file you specified can't be located.

cFileExtensions can take a variety of forms:

- If *cFileExtensions* contains a single extension (for example, PRG), only files with that extension are displayed.

- *cFileExtensions* can also contain wildcards (* and ?). All files with extensions that meet the wildcard criteria are displayed. For example, if *cFileExtensions* is ?X?, all files with the extension .fxp, .exe, or .txt are displayed.

- In Visual FoxPro for Windows, *cFileExtensions* can contain a file description followed by a file extension or a list of file extensions separated with commas. The file description appears in the Files of Type list box. Separate the file description from the file extension or list of file extensions with a colon (:). Separate multiple file descriptions and their file extensions with a semicolon (;).

  For example, if *cFileExtensions* is "Text:TXT" the file description "Text" appears in the Files of Type list box and all files with a .txt extension are displayed.

If *cFileExtensions* is "Tables:DBF; Files:TXT,BAK" the file descriptions "Tables" and "Files" appear in the Files of Type list box. When "Tables" is chosen from the Files of Type list box, all files with a .dbf extension are displayed. When "Files" is chosen from the Files of Type list box, all files with .txt and .bak extensions are displayed.

cFileNameCaption
Specifies the text you want to use to prompt the user. The text appears to the left of the textbox in which you enter the file name. If omitted, "File name:" is displayed.

For a list of Visual FoxPro file extensions and corresponding creator types, see "File Extensions and File Types" in Help.

Remarks

The Open dialog box is displayed if the file can't be located in the default directory or folder, the Visual FoxPro path, or a specified location. The Open dialog box can be used to locate the file. When a file is chosen from the Open dialog box, the file name is returned with the file's path.

If you exit the Open dialog box by choosing Cancel, pressing ESC, or choosing Close from the Control menu, Visual FoxPro generates an error message and LOCFILE( ) doesn't return a value.

See Also

FILE( ), GETFILE( ), GETPICT( ), PUTFILE( ), SET PATH

LOCK( ) Function

Attempts to lock one or more records in a table.

Syntax

LOCK([*nWorkArea* | *cTableAlias*]
 | [*cRecordNumberList*, *nWorkArea* | *cTableAlias*])

Returns

Logical

Arguments

nWorkArea | *cTableAlias*
Attempts a lock on the current record in a table open in a specific work area. *nWorkArea* specifies the work area number and *cTableAlias* specifies the table alias. If you don't specify a work area or table alias, LOCK( ) attempts to lock the current record in the table in the current work area.

cRecordNumberList

Specifies a list of one or more record numbers which you must include to attempt to lock multiple records. SET MULTILOCKS must be ON and you must include the work area or alias of the table for which you are attempting to place multiple record locks.

LOCK( ) attempts to lock all of the records you specify. The record numbers specified with *cRecordNumberList* are separated by commas. For example, to attempt record locks on the first four records in a table, *cRecordNumberList* must contain 1,2,3,4.

You can also lock multiple records by moving the record pointer to the record you would like to lock, issuing LOCK( ) or RLOCK( ) and then repeating these steps for each additional record.

In Visual FoxPro, you can specify 0 as a record number. Specifying 0 lets you attempt to lock the table header.

Important Keep the table header locked for as short a time as possible because other users cannot add records to the table when the table header is locked.

Release the table header lock with UNLOCK RECORD 0, UNLOCK or UNLOCK ALL.

If all the records specified in *cRecordNumbers* are successfully locked, LOCK( ) returns true (.T.). If even one of the records specified with *cRecordNumbers* can't be locked, LOCK( ) returns false (.F.) and none of the records are locked. However, any existing record locks remain in place. Multiple record locking is an additive process. Placing additional record locks doesn't release locks on other records.

The maximum number of records that can be locked in each work area is approximately 8,000. It is always faster to lock the entire table rather than even a small number of records.

Remarks

LOCK( ) is identical to RLOCK( ).

If the lock or locks are successfully placed, LOCK( ) returns true (.T.). Locked records are available for both read and write access to the user who placed the locks; they are available for read-only access to all other users on the network.

Executing LOCK( ) doesn't guarantee that the record lock or locks will be successfully placed. A record lock can't be placed on a record already locked by another user or in a table locked by another user. If the record lock or locks can't be placed for any reason, LOCK( ) returns false (.F.).

By default, LOCK( ) makes one attempt to lock a record. Use SET REPROCESS to automatically retry a record lock when the first attempt fails. SET REPROCESS determines the number of lock attempts or the length of time during which lock attempts are made when the initial lock attempt is unsuccessful. For more information, see the SET REPROCESS Command, later in this language reference.

SET MULTILOCKS determines whether you can lock multiple records in a table. If SET MULTILOCKS is OFF (the default), you can lock only a single record in a table. When SET MULTILOCKS is ON, you can lock multiple records in a table. For more information, see the SET MULTILOCKS Command, later in this language reference.

Unlocking Records   A table record can be unlocked only by the user who placed the lock. You can release record locks by issuing UNLOCK, closing the table, or exiting Visual FoxPro.

UNLOCK can be used to release record locks in the current work area, a specific work area, or in all work areas. For more information, see the UNLOCK Command, later in this language reference.

Switching SET MULTILOCKS from ON to OFF or from OFF to ON implicitly performs UNLOCK ALL — all record locks in all work areas are released.

Tables can be closed with USE, CLEAR ALL, or CLOSE DATABASES.

For more information about record and file locking and sharing tables on a network, see Chapter 17, "Programming for Shared Access," in the *Microsoft Visual FoxPro 6.0 Programmer's Guide*.

Example

The following example locks and unlocks the first four records in the customer and employee tables.

```
CLOSE DATABASES
OPEN DATABASE (HOME(2) + 'data\testdata')
SET REPROCESS TO 3 AUTOMATIC
STORE '1,2,3,4' TO gcRecList
gcOldExc = SET('EXCLUSIVE')
SET EXCLUSIVE OFF
SELECT 0
USE employee  && Open Employee table
SELECT 0
USE customer  && Open Customer table
? LOCK('1,2,3,4', 'customer')  && Lock 1st 4 records in customer
? RLOCK(gcRecList, 'employee')  && Lock 1st 4 records in employee
UNLOCK IN customer
UNLOCK IN employee
SET EXCLUSIVE &gcOldExc
```

See Also

CLEAR, CLOSE, FLOCK( ), RLOCK( ), SET MULTILOCKS, SET REPROCESS, UNLOCK, USE

LockScreen Property

Determines whether a form batches all changes to property settings for its contained objects. Available at design time and run time.

Syntax

Object.LockScreen[= *lExpr*]

Arguments

lExpr

The settings for the LockScreen property are:

Setting	Description
True (.T.)	The form's contained objects reflect changes in property settings only when LockScreen is reset to false (.F.) rather than as soon as the changes are made.
False (.F.)	(Default) The form's contained objects reflect changes in property settings as soon as the changes are made.

Remarks

Set LockScreen to true (.T.) to reduce annoying screen refreshes when presentation properties such as BackColor, FontName, and so on are changed during run time.

The LockScreen property does not prevent changes to the form from being reflected immediately. For example, even if LockScreen is set to true, the form is moved if you call its Move method.

> **Note** If you set LockScreen to false (.F.), the form's contained controls are repainted immediately.

Applies To

Form, _SCREEN, ToolBar

See Also

Paint Event

LOG( ) Function

Returns the natural logarithm (base *e*) of the specified numeric expression.

Syntax

LOG(*nExpression*)

Returns

Numeric

Arguments

nExpression

Specifies the numeric expression for which LOG( ) returns the value of x in the equation $e^x = nExpression$. *nExpression* must be greater than 0.

Remarks

The base for the natural logarithm is the constant e. The number of decimal places returned in the result is specified with SET DECIMALS.

Example

```
CLEAR
? LOG(1)  && Displays 0.00
STORE EXP(2) TO gneSquare
? LOG(gneSquare)  && Displays 2.00
```

See Also

EXP( ), LOG10( ), SET DECIMALS

LOG10( ) Function

Returns the common logarithm (base 10) of the specified numeric expression.

Syntax

LOG10(*nExpression*)

Returns

Numeric

Arguments

nExpression

Specifies the numeric expression for which LOG10( ) returns the value of x in the equation $10^x = nExpression$. *nExpression* must be greater than 0.

Remarks

The base for the common logarithm is 10. The number of decimal places returned in the result is specified with SET DECIMALS.

Example

```
CLEAR
? LOG10(10)  && Displays 1.00
STORE 100 TO gnBaseTen
? LOG10(gnBaseTen)  && Displays 2.00
? LOG10(gnBaseTen^2)  && Displays 4.00
```

See Also

EXP( ), LOG( ), SET DECIMALS

LOOKUP( ) Function

Searches a table for the first record with a field matching the specified expression.

Syntax

LOOKUP(*ReturnField*, *eSearchExpression*, *SearchedField* [, *cTagName*])

Returns

Character, Numeric, Currency, Float, Integer, Double, Date, DateTime, or Logical

Arguments

ReturnField
> Specifies the field whose contents LOOKUP( ) returns when the search is successful. If the search is unsuccessful, LOOKUP( ) returns an empty character string of the same length and data type as *ReturnField*.

eSearchExpression
> Specifies the search expression. The search expression is usually the contents of a field in the table, or it can correspond to the index expression of the active index or compound index tag.

SearchedField
> Specifies the field to search. If the table doesn't have an active index, LOOKUP( ) performs a sequential search through the field specified with *SearchedField*.
>
> If an index file or index tag is open whose index key expression is the search field you specify, LOOKUP( ) uses the index file or index tag to perform a faster search.

cTagName
> Specifies the name of a compound index tag for LOOKUP( ) to use in the search. A compound index search is the fastest search LOOKUP( ) can perform.

Remarks

If the search is successful, LOOKUP( ) moves the record pointer to the matching record and returns the contents of a specified field in the record.

If the search expression isn't found, LOOKUP( ) returns a blank character string the same length and data type as *ReturnField*. The record pointer is positioned at the end of the file.

If LOOKUP( ) is used to search a parent table, record pointers in all related child tables are moved to the related records.

This function can't be optimized with Rushmore.

Example

In the following example, LOOKUP( ) uses the index tag company to search for the first occurrence of the string "Ernst Handel." If the search is successful, LOOKUP( ) returns the contents of the contact field and @ ... SAY displays the return value.

```
CLOSE DATABASES
OPEN DATABASE (HOME(2) + 'data\testdata')
USE customer ORDER company  && Open Customer table
CLEAR
@ 2,2 SAY LOOKUP(contact, 'Ernst Handel', company, 'company')
```

See Also

FIND, INDEX, LOCATE, SEEK, SEEK( )

LostFocus Event

Occurs when an object loses the focus.

Syntax

PROCEDURE *Object*.LostFocus
[LPARAMETERS *nIndex*]

Arguments

nIndex
Uniquely identifies a control if it is in a control array.

Remarks

The timing of this event occurs depends on the type of object:

- A control loses the focus by user action, such as tabbing to or clicking another control, or by changing the focus in code using the SetFocus method. A Grid loses the focus when a user presses CTRL+TAB in Microsoft Windows or CONTROL+TAB on the Macintosh to exit the Grid.

- A form loses the focus when the form has no controls, all its controls have their Enabled and Visible properties set to false (.F.), or another form gets the focus.

For forms, the LostFocus event occurs before the Deactivate event.

Applies To

CheckBox, ComboBox, CommandButton, Container Object, Control Object, EditBox, Form, ListBox, OLE Bound Control, OLE Container Control, OptionButton, Spinner, TextBox

See Also

Deactivate Event, Enabled Property, GotFocus Event, Visible Property

LOWER( ) Function

Returns a specified character expression in lowercase letters.

Syntax

LOWER(*cExpression*)

Returns

Character

Arguments

cExpression
Specifies the character expression LOWER( ) converts.

Remarks

LOWER( ) converts all uppercase letters (A–Z) in the character expression to lowercase (a-z). All other characters in the character expression remain unchanged.

Example

```
STORE 'FOX' TO gcName
CLEAR
? LOWER(gcName)  && Displays fox
```

See Also

ISALPHA( ), ISLOWER( ), ISUPPER( ), PROPER( ), UPPER( )

LPARAMETERS Command

Assigns data passed from a calling program to local variables or arrays.

Syntax

LPARAMETERS *ParameterList*

Arguments

ParameterList
Specifies the local variable or array names to which the data is assigned.

Parameters within *ParameterList* are separated by commas. There must be at least as many parameters in the LPARAMETERS statement as in the DO ... WITH statement. If more variables or arrays are listed in the LPARAMETERS statement than are passed by DO ... WITH, the remaining variables or arrays are initialized to false (.F.). A maximum of 27 parameters can be passed.

You can use PARAMETERS( ) to determine the number of parameters passed to the most recently executed program, procedure, or user-defined function.

Remarks

LPARAMETERS creates local variables or arrays within a called program, procedure, or user-defined function. Use PARAMETERS to create private variables or arrays.

LPARAMETERS must be the first executable statement in the called program, procedure, or user-defined function if you pass values, variables, or arrays to the program, procedure, or user-defined function.

By default, DO ... WITH passes variables and arrays to procedures by reference. When a value is changed in the called procedure, the new value is passed back to the associated variable or array in the calling program. If you want to pass a variable or array to a procedure by value, enclose the variable or array in parentheses in the DO ... WITH parameter list. Any changes made to the parameter in the called procedure are not passed back to the calling program.

Variables are by default passed by reference to a procedure and by value to a user-defined function. Use SET UDFPARMS TO REFERENCE to pass variables to a user-defined function by reference.

See Also

DO, FUNCTION, LOCAL, PARAMETERS, PARAMETERS( ), PRIVATE, PROCEDURE, PUBLIC, SET UDFPARMS

LTRIM( ) Function

Returns the specified character expression with leading blanks removed.

Syntax

LTRIM(*cExpression*)

Returns

Character

Arguments

cExpression
    Specifies the character expression whose leading blanks LTRIM( ) removes.

Remarks

This function is especially useful for removing the leading blanks that are inserted when you use STR( ) to convert a numeric value to a character string.

Example

```
STORE 'Redmond' TO gcCity
STORE 'Washington' TO gcState
CLEAR
```

```
? gcCity, gcState  && Displays Redmond Washington
? gcCity, LTRIM(gcState)  && Displays Redmond Washington
```

See Also

ALLTRIM( ), LEFT( ), RIGHT( ), RTRIM( ), SUBSTR( ), TRIM( )

LUPDATE( ) Function

Returns the date on which a table was last updated.

Syntax

LUPDATE([*nWorkArea* | *cTableAlias*])

Returns

Date

Arguments

nWorkArea | *cTableAlias*

Returns the last update to a table open in another work area. *nWorkArea* specifies the work area number and *cTableAlias* specifies the table alias. LUPDATE( ) returns the date of the last update to the table in the currently selected work area if you omit *nWorkArea* and *cTableAlias*.

If no table is open in the work area you specify, LUPDATE( ) returns a blank date. If no table has the alias you specify, Visual FoxPro generates an error message.

Remarks

This function is useful in update procedures.

Note that in earlier versions of Visual FoxPro, the last two digits of the year a table was last updated is stored in the table header. Because only the last two digits are stored, you cannot determine the century in which the table was updated; it always defaults to the 20th century.

In Visual FoxPro 6.0, LUPDATE( ) queries Windows to determine the date a table was last updated, allowing you to determine the century in which the table was updated. However, the last two digits of the year the table was last updated are still stored in the table header.

Example

```
CLOSE DATABASES
OPEN DATABASE (HOME(2) + 'data\testdata')
USE customer  && Open Customer table

CLEAR
? LUPDATE( )  && Displays date of last update
```

See Also

DIR, FDATE( ), FTIME( )

_MAC System Variable

Contains true (.T.) if the user is using FoxPro for Macintosh or Microsoft Visual FoxPro for Macintosh.

Syntax

_MAC = *lExpression*

Remarks

_MAC contains false (.F.) for any other platform version of FoxPro (Visual FoxPro for Windows, FoxPro for Windows, FoxPro for MS-DOS, or FoxPro for UNIX).

The value contained in _MAC cannot be changed with STORE or =.

See Also

_DOS, _UNIX, VERSION( ), _WINDOWS

MacDesktop Property

Specifies whether a form is placed in the main Visual FoxPro window.

Syntax

Object.MacDesktop[= *nValue*]

Arguments

nValue
The settings for the MacDesktop property are:

Setting	Description
0	(Default) Automatic. The form is contained in the Visual FoxPro main window according to the setting established with the SET MACDESKTOP command. If SET MACDESKTOP is set to ON, the form exists at the level of the Macintosh desktop; if set to OFF, the form is contained within the Visual FoxPro main window.
1	Macintosh Desktop. The form exists at the level of the Macintosh desktop, and can be moved and resized independently of the main Visual FoxPro window.
2	Visual FoxPro Desktop. The form is contained in the Visual FoxPro main window and cannot be moved outside it.

Remarks

Setting the MacDesktop property enables you to override for individual forms the setting established with the SET MACDESKTOP command. SET MACDESKTOP affects user-defined windows (forms) and system windows such as the Browse, View, and Form Designer windows. By default, user-defined windows behave according to the SET MACDESKTOP setting.

The MacDesktop property enables you to control whether your applications resemble Macintosh applications or Windows applications.

Applies To

Form

See Also

SET KEYCOMP

MainClass Property

Contains the name of an ActiveDoc class set as the main program in a project. Read-only.

Syntax

Object.MainClass

Remarks

An ActiveDoc class can be set as the main program in a project by right-clicking the ActiveDoc class and choosing **Set Main** from the shortcut menu. Only classes based on the ActiveDoc base class can be set as the main program. (A program or form can also be set as the main program.) Use the MainFile property to determine the .vcx visual class library that contains the ActiveDoc class set as the main program.

MainClass contains the empty string if the main program is not set to an ActiveDoc class.

Use the SetMain method to change the main file and main class.

Applies To

Project Object

See Also

MainFile Property, SetMain Method

MainFile Property

Contains the name and path of the file set as the main program in a project. Read-only.

Syntax

Object.MainFile

Remarks

MainFile contains the empty string if a main program has not been set for a project. A program, form, or ActiveDoc class can be set as the main program in a project by right-clicking the program, form, or ActiveDoc class and choosing **Set Main** from the shortcut menu. You can also use the SetMain method to programmatically specify a main program for a project.

If an ActiveDoc class is set as the main program, MainFile contains the name and path of the .vcx visual class library containing the class. Use the MainClass property to determine the ActiveDoc class set as the main program in the project.

Applies To

Project Object

See Also

MainClass Property, SetMain Method

Margin Property

Specifies the margin width created in the text portion of the control. Available at design time and run time.

Syntax

Control.Margin[= *nValue*]

Arguments

nValue
　　Specifies the margin created in the text portion of the control.

Remarks

Use the Margin property to specify the position of text on the control. The Margin property creates a margin in the interior portion of the control; it doesn't affect the size of the control.

Applies To

ComboBox, EditBox, Spinner, TextBox

See Also

Alignment Property

MAX( ) Function

Evaluates a set of expressions and returns the expression with the maximum value.

Syntax

MAX(*eExpression1*, *eExpression2* [, *eExpression3* ...])

Returns

Character, Numeric, Currency, Double, Float, Date, or DateTime

Arguments

eExpression1, *eExpression2* [, *eExpression3* ...]
Specify the expressions from which you want MAX( ) to return the expression with the highest value. All the expressions must be of the same data type.

Example

The following example uses APPEND BLANK to create a table with 10 records containing random values, then uses MIN( ) and MAX( ) to display the maximum and minimum values in the table.

```
CLOSE DATABASES
CREATE TABLE Random (cValue N(3))
FOR nItem = 1 TO 10  && Append 10 records.
   APPEND BLANK
   REPLACE cValue WITH 1 + 100 * RAND( )  && Insert random values
ENDFOR

CLEAR
LIST  && Display the values
gnMaximum = 1  && Initialize minimum value
gnMinimum = 100  && Initialize maximum value
SCAN
   gnMinimum = MIN(gnMinimum, cValue)
   gnMaximum = MAX(gnMaximum, cValue)
ENDSCAN
? 'The minimum value is: ', gnMinimum  && Display minimum value
? 'The maximum value is: ', gnMaximum  && Display maximum value
```

CALCULATE, MIN( ), SELECT – SQL

MaxButton Property

Specifies whether a form has a Maximize button. Available at design time and run time.

Syntax

Object.MaxButton[= *lExpr*]

Arguments

lExpr

The settings for the MaxButton property are:

Setting	Description
True (.T.)	(Default) The form has a Maximize button.
False (.F.)	The form doesn't have a Maximize button.

Remarks

A Maximize button enables a user to enlarge a form to full-screen size.

A Maximize button automatically becomes a Restore button when a window is maximized. Minimizing, or restoring, a window automatically changes the Restore button back to a Maximize button.

The settings you specify for MaxButton, MinButton, BorderStyle, and ControlBox are not reflected in the form's appearance until run time.

Maximizing a form at run time triggers the Resize event.

> **Note** The WindowState property reflects the current state of the window. If you set the WindowState property to 2 (Maximized), the form is maximized independently of whatever settings are in effect for the MaxButton and BorderStyle properties.

Applies To

Form, _SCREEN

See Also

BorderStyle Property, ControlBox Property, MinButton Property, Resize Event, TitleBar Property, WindowState Property

MaxHeight Property

Determines the maximum height to which a form can be sized. Available at design time and run time.

Syntax

Object.MaxHeight[= *nHeight*]

Arguments

nHeight

The maximum height, in the unit of measurement specified by the ScaleMode property of the form.

Remarks

When the user sizes a form by choosing either the **Size** command from the Control menu or by dragging the borders of the form, the form doesn't exceed the height specified in the MaxHeight property setting.

The default setting for the MaxHeight property is –1; no maximum height is specified.

Applies To

Form, _SCREEN

See Also

ScaleMode Property

MaxLeft Property

Specifies the distance a maximized form is from the left edge of the main Visual FoxPro window. Available at design time and run time.

Syntax

Object.MaxLeft[= *nMaxLeft*]

Arguments

nMaxLeft

Specifies the distance from the left edge of the main Visual FoxPro window to the left edge of the maximized form, in the unit of measurement specified by the ScaleMode property of the form.

Remarks

Use the MaxLeft property to ensure that a maximized form doesn't get moved too far to the left in the main Visual FoxPro window at run time.

Applies To

Form, _SCREEN

See Also

MaxTop Property, MaxWidth Property, MinHeight Property, Scalemode Property

MaxLength Property

Specifies the maximum length (in characters) that can be entered in an EditBox or TextBox control. Available at design time and run time.

Syntax

Control.MaxLength[= *nMaxLength*]

Arguments

nMaxLength
> The maximum number of characters that can be entered in an edit box or text box. If *nMaxLength* is set to 0, there is no limit to the number of characters that can be entered into an edit box. The number of characters that can be entered into a text box when *nMaxLength* is set to 0 is determined by the size of the text box and its data type.

Remarks

Use MaxLength to limit the amount of text a user can enter in an edit box or text box. MaxLength only applies for a text box when MaxLength is greater than 0, the text box does not use the InputMask property, and its Value property is of character type.

Applies To

EditBox, TextBox

See Also

SelLength Property

MaxTop Property

Specifies the distance a maximized form is from the top edge of the main Visual FoxPro window. Available at design time and run time.

Syntax

Object.MaxTop[= *nMaxTop*]

Arguments

nMaxTop

Specifies the distance from the top edge of the main Visual FoxPro window to the top edge of the maximized form, in the unit of measurement specified by the ScaleMode property of the form.

Remarks

This property is ignored in Visual FoxPro for the Macintosh.

Use the MaxTop property to ensure that a maximized form doesn't get moved too close to the top of the main Visual FoxPro window at run time.

Applies To

Form, _SCREEN

See Also

MaxLeft Property, MaxWidth Property, MinHeight Property, MinWidth Property, Scalemode Property

MaxWidth Property

Specifies the maximum width a form can be resized to. Available at design time and run time.

Syntax

Object.MaxWidth[= *nMaxWidth*]

Arguments

nMaxWidth

Specifies the maximum width a form can be resized to, in the unit of measurement specified by the ScaleMode property of the form.

Remarks

When the user sizes a form by choosing either the **Size** command from the Control menu or dragging the borders of the form, the form doesn't exceed the width specified in the MaxWidth property setting.

The default for the MaxWidth property setting is –1; no maximum width is specified.

Applies To

Form, _SCREEN

See Also

MaxHeight Property, MinHeight Property, MinWidth Property, ScaleMode Property

MCOL( ) Function

Returns the column position of the mouse pointer in the main Visual FoxPro window or a user-defined window.

Syntax

MCOL([*cWindowName* [, *nScaleMode*]])

Returns

Numeric

Arguments

cWindowName

Specifies the name of the window whose mouse-pointer column position MCOL( ) returns.

If you omit *cWindowName* and there is no active user-defined window, MCOL( ) returns the mouse pointer's column position in the main Visual FoxPro window. If you omit *cWindowName* and there is an active user-defined window, MCOL( ) returns the mouse pointer's column position in the active user-defined window. MCOL( ) returns –1 if the mouse pointer is positioned outside the user-defined window or if no mouse driver is loaded and there is no output window.

nScaleMode

Specifies the unit of measurement for the value MCOL( ) returns. The settings for *nScaleMode* are:

nScaleMode	Description
0	(Default) Foxels. A foxel is equivalent to the average height and width of a character based on the current font of the form in which an object is contained. Foxels are useful in developing cross-platform applications for character-based and graphical platforms.
3	Pixels. A pixel is the smallest element that can be displayed on a screen or printer. Pixels are screen-dependent.

See Also

AMOUSEOBJ( ), COL( ), GridHitTest Method, INKEY( ), ISMOUSE( ), MROW( ), ROW( ), WCOLS( ), WROWS( )

MD | MKDIR Command

Creates a new directory or subdirectory on disk.

Syntax

MD *cPath* | MKDIR *cPath*

Arguments

cPath

Specifies a directory or a path (with a drive designator and directories).

If *cPath* is a directory without a drive designator, the directory is created as a subdirectory of the current Microsoft Visual FoxPro default directory.

Remarks

Visual FoxPro generates an error message if you attempt to create a directory that already exists.

Example

The following example uses MKDIR to create a new directory named `mytstdir`, then CHDIR is used to change to the new directory. GETDIR( ) is used to display the directory structure, and then RMDIR is used to remove the newly created directory. GETDIR( ) is used to display the directory structure again.

```
SET DEFAULT TO HOME( )  && Restore Visual FoxPro directory

MKDIR mytstdir  && Create a new directory
CHDIR mytstdir  && Change to the new directory
= GETDIR( )  && Display the Select Directory dialog box
SET DEFAULT TO HOME( )  && Restore Visual FoxPro directory
RMDIR mytstdir  && Remove the new directory
= GETDIR( )  && Display the Select Directory dialog box
```

See Also

CD | CHDIR, DIRECTORY, DIRECTORY( ), GETDIR( ), HOME( ), RD | RMDIR, SET DEFAULT, SET PATH, SYS(5) – Default Drive, SYS(2003) – Current Directory, SYS(2004) – Visual FoxPro Start Directory

MDIForm Property

Included for backward compatibility. Use the ShowWindow Property instead.

MDOWN( ) Function

Included for backward compatibility. Use the Click, MouseDown, MouseUp, and RightClick events instead.

MDX( ) Function

Returns the name of the open .cdx compound index file that has the specified index position number.

Syntax

MDX(*nIndexNumber* [, *nWorkArea* | *cTableAlias*])

Returns

Character

Arguments

nIndexNumber

Specifies which compound index file name to return. If the table has a structural compound index file and *nIndexNumber* is 1, the name of the structural compound index file (which is always the same as the name of the table) is returned. If *nIndexNumber* is 2, the name of the first compound index file specified with USE or SET INDEX is returned. If *nIndexNumber* is 3, the second compound index file name is returned, and so on. If *nIndexNumber* is greater than the number of open compound index files, an empty string is returned.

If the table doesn't have a structural compound index file and *nIndexNumber* is 1, the name of the first compound index file specified with USE or SET INDEX is returned. If *nIndexNumber* is 2, the second compound index file name is returned, and so on. If *nIndexNumber* is greater than the number of open compound index files, an empty string is returned.

nWorkArea

Specifies the work area number for compound index files open in work areas other than the current one. If you omit this optional argument, names of compound index files are returned for the current work area.

cTableAlias

Specifies the table alias for compound index files open in work areas other than the current one. If you omit this optional argument, names of compound index files are returned for the current work area.

Remarks

MDX( ) is identical to CDX( ).

Index files can be opened for a table with the INDEX clause of the USE command or with SET INDEX. A structural compound index file is automatically opened with its table. MDX( ) ignores any .idx index files specified with USE or with SET INDEX.

Use TAG( ) to return tag names from a compound index file; use NDX( ) to return the name of an open .idx index file.

In Visual FoxPro for Windows, when SET FULLPATH is ON, MDX( ) returns the path to the .cdx file with the .cdx file name. When SET FULLPATH is OFF, MDX( ) returns the drive the .cdx file resides on with the .cdx file name.

See Also

CDX( ), INDEX, NDX( ), SET INDEX, SET FULLPATH, SYS(14) – Index Expression, TAG( ), USE

MDY( ) Function

Returns the specified date or datetime expression in month-day-year format with the name of the month spelled out.

Syntax

MDY(*dExpression* | *tExpression*)

Returns

Character

Arguments

dExpression
Specifies the date expression to return in month-day-year format.

tExpression
Specifies the datetime expression to return in month-day-year format.

Remarks

If SET CENTURY is OFF, the character expression is returned in a month dd, yy format. If SET CENTURY is ON, the format is month dd, yyyy.

Example

The following example creates a user-defined function that returns a date with the corresponding weekday.

```
SET CENTURY OFF

CLEAR
? Longdate({^1998-02-16})   && Displays Monday, February 16, 98

SET CENTURY ON
? Longdate({^1998-02-16})   && Displays Monday, February 16, 1998

*** LongDate ***

FUNCTION longdate
PARAMETERS gdDate
RETURN CDOW(gdDate) + ', ' + MDY(gdDate)
```

See Also

DMY( ), SET CENTURY, SET DATE

MEMLINES( ) Function

Returns the number of lines in a memo field.

Syntax

MEMLINES(*MemoFieldName*)

Returns

Numeric

Arguments

MemoFieldName

Specifies the name of the memo field. If the memo field is in a table that isn't open in the current work area, preface the memo field name with the table alias and a period.

Remarks

The number of lines in a memo field is determined by the current value of SET MEMOWIDTH.

Example

The following example scans three records in the employee table and uses MEMLINES( ) to determine whether or not there is data in the notes memo field and when page breaks should occur. The last_name data for the record appears, along with the notes (if there is data in the memo field) or a message indicating that there are no notes for that record.

```
CLOSE DATABASES
CLEAR
SET TALK OFF
CLOSE DATABASES
OPEN DATABASE (HOME(2) + 'Data\testdata')
USE employee  && Open Employee table

SET MEMOWIDTH TO 65
gnLine = 1
GOTO 2
SCAN NEXT 3
   gnMemoSize = MEMLINES(notes)
   IF gnMemoSize = 0
      STORE .T. TO glNoMemo
      STORE 1 TO gnMemoSize
   ELSE
      STORE .F. TO glNoMemo
   ENDIF
```

```
      IF gnLine + gnMemoSize > 65
         EJECT
         gnLine = 1
      ENDIF
      @ gnLine,2 SAY 'Last Name: '+ last_name
      gnLine = gnLine +1
      @ gnLine ,2 SAY 'Notes: '
      ?? IIF(glNoMemo, 'No notes ',notes)
      gnLine = gnLine + gnMemoSize + 2
      IF gnLine > 24
         gnLine = 1
         CLEAR
      ENDIF
ENDSCAN
```

See Also

ALINES( ), MLINE( ), SET MEMOWIDTH

MEMORY( ) Function

Returns the amount of memory available to run an external program.

Syntax

MEMORY( )

Returns

Numeric

Remarks

In Visual FoxPro, MEMORY( ) always returns 640.

MEMORY( ) is similar to SYS(12), with two exceptions:

- MEMORY( ) returns the amount of available memory in kilobytes; SYS(12) returns the amount of memory in bytes.

- MEMORY( ) returns a numeric expression. SYS(12) returns its value as a character string.

See Also

SYS(12) – Available Memory in Bytes, SYS(1001) – Visual FoxPro Memory

MemoWindow Property

Included for backward compatibility. Use an EditBox control instead.

MENU Command

Included for backward compatibility. Use the Menu Designer instead.

MENU( ) Function

Returns the name of the active menu bar as an uppercase character string.

Syntax

MENU( )

Returns

Character

Remarks

MENU( ) returns an empty string if no menu is active. Use the Menu Designer to create a menu and activate it.

Example

The following example uses MENU( ) to pass the name of a menu bar to a procedure. The current system menu bar is saved to memory with SET SYSMENU SAVE, and all system menu titles are removed with SET SYSMENU TO.

Several system menu titles are created with DEFINE PAD. When you choose a menu title, MENU( ) passes the name of the Microsoft Visual FoxPro system menu bar, _MSYSMENU, to the choice procedure. The choice procedure displays the name of the menu title you chose and the name of the system menu bar. If you choose the Exit menu, the original Visual FoxPro system menu is restored.

```
*** Save this program as MENUEXAM.PRG in the default VFP directory.***
CLEAR
SET SYSMENU SAVE
SET SYSMENU TO
DEFINE PAD padSys OF _MSYSMENU PROMPT '\<System' COLOR SCHEME 3 ;
   KEY ALT+S, ''
DEFINE PAD padEdit OF _MSYSMENU PROMPT '\<Edit' COLOR SCHEME 3 ;
   KEY ALT+E, ''
DEFINE PAD padRecord OF _MSYSMENU PROMPT '\<Record' COLOR SCHEME 3 ;
   KEY ALT+R, ''
DEFINE PAD padWindow OF _MSYSMENU PROMPT '\<Window' COLOR SCHEME 3 ;
   KEY ALT+W, ''
DEFINE PAD padReport OF _MSYSMENU PROMPT 'Re\<ports' COLOR SCHEME 3 KEY ALT+P, ''
DEFINE PAD padExit OF _MSYSMENU PROMPT 'E\<xit' COLOR SCHEME 3 ;
   KEY ALT+X, ''
```

```
ON SELECTION MENU _MSYSMENU ;
   DO choice IN menuexam WITH PAD(), MENU()
PROCEDURE choice
PARAMETER gcPad, gcMenu
WAIT WINDOW 'You chose ' + gcPad + ;
   ' from menu ' + gcMenu NOWAIT
IF gcPad = 'PADEXIT'
   SET SYSMENU TO DEFAULT
ENDIF
```

See Also

ACTIVATE MENU, CREATE MENU, DEFINE MENU

MENU TO Command

Included for backward compatibility. Use the Visual FoxPro Menu Designer instead.

Message Event

Included for backward compatibility. Use the StatusBarText property instead.

MESSAGE( ) Function

Returns either the current error message as a character string or the contents of the program line that caused the error.

Syntax

MESSAGE([1])

Returns

Character

Arguments

1

If MESSAGE( ) is used in an ON ERROR routine, include this argument to return the program source code that caused the error. If the program source code isn't available, MESSAGE(1) returns one of the following:

- The entire program line if the line is macro substituted.

- A command if the line contains a command without any additional clauses.

- A command followed by three dots (...) if the line contains a command and additional clauses.

Remarks

Unlike ERROR( ), MESSAGE( ) isn't reset by RETURN or RETRY.

Example

The following example displays output from MESSAGE( ) and MESSAGE(1).

```
ON ERROR DO Errhand

*** The next line should generate an error ***

USE Nodatabase
ON ERROR        && restore system error handler
PROCEDURE Errhand
? 'Line of code with error: ' + MESSAGE(1)
? 'Error number: ' + STR(ERROR( ))
? 'Error message: ' + MESSAGE( )
```

See Also

ERROR( ), ON ERROR

MESSAGEBOX( ) Function

Displays a user-defined dialog box.

Syntax

MESSAGEBOX(*cMessageText* [, *nDialogBoxType* [, *cTitleBarText*]])

Returns

Numeric

Arguments

cMessageText

Specifies the text that appears in the dialog box. Use a carriage return (CHR(13)) in *cMessageText* to move a portion of the message to the next line in the dialog box. The height and width of the dialog box is increased as necessary to contain *cMessageText*.

nDialogBoxType

Specifies the buttons and icons that appear in the dialog box, the default button when the dialog box is displayed, and the behavior of the dialog box.

In the following tables, the dialog box button values 0 to 5 specify the buttons that appear in the dialog box. The icon values 16, 32, 48, and 64 specify the icon that appears in the dialog box. The default values 0, 256, and 512 specify which button in the dialog box is the default button. The default button is selected when the dialog box is displayed.

Omitting *nDialogBoxType* is identical to specifying a value of 0 for *nDialogBoxType*.

Value	Dialog box buttons
0	OK button only
1	OK and Cancel buttons
2	Abort, Retry, and Ignore buttons
3	Yes, No, and Cancel buttons
4	Yes and No buttons
5	Retry and Cancel buttons

Value	Icon
16	Stop sign
32	Question mark
48	Exclamation point
64	Information (i) icon

Value	Default button
0	First button
256	Second button
512	Third button

nDialogBoxType can be the sum of up to three values — one value from each of the preceding tables. For example, if *nDialogBoxType* is 290 (2+32+256), the specified dialog box has the following characteristics:

- Abort, Retry, and Ignore buttons.

- The message box displays the question mark icon.

- The second button, Retry, is the default.

cTitleBarText
 Specifies the text that appears in the title bar of the dialog box. If you omit *cTitleBarText*, the title "Microsoft Visual FoxPro" appears in the title bar.

Remarks

The value MESSAGEBOX( ) returns indicates which button in the dialog box was chosen. In dialog boxes with a Cancel button, pressing ESC to exit the dialog box returns the same value (2) as choosing Cancel.

Note that the shortest abbreviation for this function is MESSAGEB( ).

The following table lists the values MESSAGEBOX( ) returns for each button.

Return value	Button
1	OK
2	Cancel
3	Abort
4	Retry
5	Ignore
6	Yes
7	No

Example

The following example displays a user-defined dialog box. The message "Record not found. Would you like to search again?" is displayed as the caption in the user-defined dialog box, and "My Application" is displayed in the title bar.

The user-defined dialog box contains Yes and No buttons and the question mark icon, and the second button (No) is the default button. When you choose one of the buttons, your choice is displayed.

```
cMessageTitle = 'My Application'
cMessageText = 'Record not found. Would you like to search again?'
nDialogType = 4 + 32 + 256
*   4 = Yes and No buttons
*   32 = Question mark icon
*   256 = Second button is default

nAnswer = MESSAGEBOX(cMessageText, nDialogType, cMessageTitle)

DO CASE
    CASE nAnswer = 6
        WAIT WINDOW 'You chose Yes'
    CASE nAnswer = 7
        WAIT WINDOW 'You chose No'
ENDCASE
```

See Also

WAIT

MiddleClick Event

Occurs when the user clicks the middle mouse button on a three-button mouse over a control.

Syntax

PROCEDURE *Control*.MiddleClick
    [LPARAMETERS *nIndex*]

Arguments

nIndex
    Uniquely identifies a control if it is in a control array.

Applies To

CheckBox, ComboBox, CommandButton, CommandGroup, Container, Control, EditBox, Form, Grid, Header, Image, Label, Line, ListBox, OptionButton, OptionGroup, Page, PageFrame, Shape, Spinner, TextBox, ToolBar

See Also

Click Event, DblClick Event, DragDrop Event, DragOver Event, DropDown Event, Enabled Property, KeyPress Event, MouseDown Event, MouseMove Event, MouseUp Event, Scrolled Event, Undock Event

MIN( ) Function

Evaluates a set of expressions and returns the expression with the minimum value.

Syntax

MIN(*eExpression1*, *eExpression2* [, *eExpression3* ...])

Returns

Character, Numeric, Currency, Double, Float, Date, or DateTime

Arguments

eExpression1, *eExpression2* [, *eExpression3* ...]
    Specify the set of expressions from which you want MIN( ) to return the expression with the lowest value. All the expressions must be of the same type.

Example

The following example uses APPEND BLANK to create a table with 10 records containing random values, then uses MIN( ) and MAX( ) to display the maximum and minimum values in the table.

```
CLOSE DATABASES
CREATE TABLE Random (cValue N(3))
FOR nItem = 1 TO 10  && Append 10 records,
   APPEND BLANK
   REPLACE cValue WITH 1 + 100 * RAND( )  && Insert random values
ENDFOR

CLEAR
LIST  && Display the values
gnMaximum = 1  && Initialize minimum value
gnMinimum = 100  && Initialize maximum value
SCAN
   gnMinimum = MIN(gnMinimum, cValue)
   gnMaximum = MAX(gnMaximum, cValue)
ENDSCAN
? 'The minimum value is: ', gnMinimum  && Display minimum value
? 'The maximum value is: ', gnMaximum  && Display maximum value
```

See Also

CALCULATE, MAX( )

MinButton Property

Specifies whether a form has a Minimize button. Available at design time and run time.

Syntax

Object.MinButton[= *lExpr*]

Arguments

lExpr

The settings for the MinButton property are:

Setting	Description
True (.T.)	(Default) The form has a Minimize button.
False (.F.)	The form doesn't have a Minimize button.

Remarks

A Minimize button enables users to minimize a Form window to an icon.

The settings you specify for MaxButton, MinButton, BorderStyle, and ControlBox are not reflected in the Form's appearance until run time.

In Microsoft Windows version 3.0 or later, an MDI child form is displayed with a Minimize button regardless of the setting of MinButton. However, if MinButton is set to false (.F.), it doesn't respond to clicks, and the corresponding **Minimize** command isn't on the form's Control-box menu.

Minimizing a form to an icon at run time generates a Resize event.

> **Note**   The WindowState property reflects the current state of the window. If you set the WindowState property to 1 (Minimized), the Form is minimized independently of whatever settings are in effect for the MinButton and BorderStyle properties.

Applies To

Form, _SCREEN

See Also

BorderStyle Property, ControlBox Property, MaxButton Property, TitleBar Property, WindowState Property

MinHeight Property

Specifies the minimum height that a form can be resized to. Available at design time and run time.

Syntax

*Object.*MinHeight[= *nHeight*]

Arguments

nHeight
   The minimum height that the form can be resized to, in the unit of measurement specified by the ScaleMode property of the form.

Remarks

When the user sizes a form by choosing either the **Size** command from the Control menu or by dragging the borders of the form, the form doesn't become any shorter than the height specified in the MinHeight property setting.

The default setting for the MinHeight property setting is –1; no minimum height is specified.

Applies To

Form, _SCREEN

See Also

MaxHeight Property, MaxWidth Property, MinWidth Property, ScaleMode Property

MINUTE( ) Function

Returns the minute portion from a DateTime expression.

Syntax

MINUTE(*tExpression*)

Returns

Numeric

Arguments

tExpression
Specifies the DateTime expression from which the minute portion is returned.

Example

The following example displays the minute portion of the current time and the minute portion of a specific time.

```
CLEAR
? MINUTE(DATETIME( ))
? MINUTE({^1998-02-16 10:42a})  && Displays 42
```

See Also

CTOT( ), DATE( ), DATETIME( ), DTOT( ), HOUR( ), SEC( ), SECONDS( ), SET SECONDS, TIME( )

MinWidth Property

Specifies the minimum width that a form can be resized to. Available at design time and run time.

Syntax

Object.MinWidth[= *nWidth*]

Arguments

nWidth
The minimum width that the form can be resized to, in the unit of measurement specified by the ScaleMode property of the Form.

Remarks

When the user sizes a Form by choosing either the **Size** command from the Control menu or by dragging the borders of the form, the Form cannot be made any narrower than the width specified in the MinWidth property setting.

The default setting for the MinWidth property is –1; no minimum width is specified.

Applies To

Form, _SCREEN

See Also

MaxHeight Property, MaxWidth Property, MinHeight Property, ScaleMode Property

MLINE( ) Function

Returns a specific line from a memo field as a character string.

Syntax

MLINE(*MemoFieldName, nLineNumber* [, *nNumberOfCharacters*])

Returns

Character

Arguments

MemoFieldName

Specifies the name of the memo field from which MLINE( ) returns a line. If the memo field is in a table open in a noncurrent work area, preface the memo field name with a period and the table alias.

nLineNumber

Specifies the number of the line to be returned from the memo field. An empty string is returned if *nLineNumber* is negative, 0, or greater than the number of lines in the memo field.

nNumberOfCharacters

Specifies the number of characters from the beginning of the memo field after which MLINE( ) returns the specified line.

The _MLINE system variable is typically used for *nNumberOfCharacters*. _MLINE is automatically adjusted each time MLINE( ) is called.

In recursive procedures that return lines from large memo fields, you can obtain the best performance by including _MLINE as *nNumberOfCharacters*.

Remarks

MLINE( ) trims any trailing spaces from the line specified with *nLineNumber*.

The length and number of the lines in a memo field are determined by the current value of SET MEMOWIDTH (the default line length is 50 characters). If a carriage return is encountered, no additional characters are returned. The current _WRAP setting determines how the memo field line is displayed.

When searching a memo field for a character string, you can use ATLINE( ) or
ATCLINE( ) to return the line number of the line in which the character string is found.
Use this line number in MLINE( ) to return the contents of the line from the memo field.

Example

In the following example, two methods are used to return lines from a memo field.
Two loops use MLINE( ) to return lines from the memo field. Note the improvement in
performance in the second loop when the system variable _MLINE is used in MLINE( ).

```
CLEAR
SET TALK OFF
SET MEMOWIDTH TO 50
CLOSE DATABASES
CREATE TABLE tmemo (name c(10), notes m)
APPEND BLANK                  && Add a record
WAIT WINDOW 'Filling memo field - takes several seconds' NOWAIT
*** Fill the memo field  ***
FOR gnOuterLoop = 1 TO 5          && loop 5 times
   FOR gnAlphabet = 65 TO 75   && letters A to H
      REPLACE notes WITH REPLICATE(CHR(gnAlphabet), 10) ;
         + CHR(13) ADDITIVE
   NEXT
NEXT

*** Display all lines from the memo field ***

STORE MEMLINES(notes) TO gnNumLines    && Number of lines in memo field
STORE SECONDS( ) TO gnBegin      && Beginning time
FOR gnCount = 1 TO gnNumLines    && Loop for # of lines in memo field
   ? MLINE(notes, gnCount)       && Display each line
NEXT
? STR(SECONDS( ) - gnBegin, 4, 2) + ' seconds'   && Total time

*** Preferable method using _MLINE in MLINE( ) ***
*** Display all lines from the memo field ***

WAIT 'Press a key to see the preferred method' WINDOW
CLEAR
STORE 0 TO _MLINE             && Reset _MLINE to zero
STORE SECONDS( ) TO gnBegin      && Beginning time
FOR count = 1 TO gnNumLines      && Loop for # of lines in memo field
   ? MLINE(notes, 1, _MLINE)     && Display each line
NEXT
? STR(SECONDS( ) - gnBegin, 4, 2) + ' seconds'   && Total time
SET TALK ON
CLOSE DATABASES
ERASE tmemo.dbf
ERASE tmemo.fpt
```

See Also

ALINES( ), ATCLINE( ), ATLINE( ), COPY MEMO, MEMLINES( ), _MLINE, MODIFY MEMO, SET MEMOWIDTH, _WRAP

_MLINE System Variable

Contains the memo field offset for the MLINE( ) function.

Syntax

_MLINE = *nNumberOfCharacters*

Arguments

nNumberOfCharacters

Specifies the memo field offset. For more information about the use of _MLINE and an example of its use, see the MLINE( ) Function, earlier in this language reference.

Remarks

MLINE( ) returns one line of text from a memo field. MLINE( ) stores the location of its memo field offset to the _MLINE system variable. Use _MLINE as the second numeric argument in the MLINE( ) function to increase the performance of MLINE( ).

The startup default value for _MLINE is 0. Be sure to reset _MLINE to 0 before using _MLINE again with the MLINE( ) function.

See Also

ALINES( ), MEMLINES( ), MLINE( ), SET MEMOWIDTH

MOD( ) Function

Divides one numeric expression by another numeric expression and returns the remainder.

Syntax

MOD(*nDividend*, *nDivisor*)

Returns

Numeric

Arguments

nDividend

Specifies the dividend. The number of decimal places in *nDividend* determines the number of decimal places in the return value.

nDivisor
>   Specifies the divisor. A positive number is returned if *nDivisor* is positive, and a negative number is returned if *nDivisor* is negative.

Remarks

The modulus function MOD( ) and the % operator return identical results.

Example

```
CLEAR
? MOD(36,10)  && Displays 6
? MOD((4*9), (90/9))  && Displays 6
? MOD(25.250,5.0)  && Displays 0.250
? IIF(MOD(YEAR(DATE( )), 4) = 0, 'Summer Olympics this year';
    , 'No Summer Olympics this year')
```

See Also

% Operator

Modify Method

Opens a file in a project for modification in the appropriate designer or editor.

Syntax

Object.Modify([*cClassName*])

Arguments

cClassName
>   Specifies the name of the visual class to open for modification when *Object* is a .vcx visual class library.

Remarks

The Modify method returns true (.T.) if the file is successfully opened for modification; otherwise false (.F.) is returned.

The QueryModifyFile event occurs before the file is opened. If the QueryModifyFile event returns false (.F.), the file isn't opened and the Modify method returns false (.F.). If the QueryModifyFile method returns true (.T.), the file is opened and the Modify method returns true (.T.).

Applies To

File Object

See Also

Add Method, Remove Method, QueryModifyFile Event

MODIFY CLASS Command

Opens the Class Designer, allowing you to modify an existing class definition or create a new class definition.

Syntax

MODIFY CLASS *ClassName* [OF *ClassLibraryName1*]
    [AS *cBaseClassName* [FROM *ClassLibraryName2*]]
    [METHOD MethodName] [NOWAIT] [SAVE]

Arguments

ClassName
    Specifies the name of the class definition to modify or create.

OF *ClassLibraryName1*
    Specifies the name of the .vcx visual class library containing the class definition. If you are creating a new class definition and the .vcx visual class library already exists, the class definition is added to it.

    A .vcx file extension is assumed for the visual class library. Be sure to include the file extension if the visual class library you specify has a file extension other than .vcx.

    If the .vcx visual class library you specify is currently in the SET CLASSLIB search list, the visual class library is removed from the search list.

AS *cBaseClassName*
    Specifies the class on which the class definition is based. *cBaseClassName* can be any of the Visual FoxPro base classes except Column, Cursor, DataEnvironment, Header, Page, and Relation. You can also specify a user-defined class for *cBaseClassName* if you include the FROM *ClassLibraryName2* clause that specifies the name of the .vcx visual class library containing the user-defined class.

    If you omit AS *cBaseClassName*, the class definition is based on the Visual FoxPro FormSet base class.

FROM *ClassLibraryName2*
    Specifies the name of the .vcx visual class library containing the user-defined class specified with *cBaseClassName*.

METHOD *MethodName*
    Specifies an event or method for which the Code window is opened in the Class Designer. The METHOD clause lets you immediately begin editing event or method code in the Class Designer.

MethodName supports the Visual FoxPro object syntax. For example, to immediately edit the Click event code for a text box named txtFirstName in the class named MyClass in a visual class library named MyClassLibrary, use the following command:

```
MODIFY CLASS MyClass OF MyClassLibrary;
    METHOD txtFirstName.Click
```

If you only include an event or method name in the METHOD clause, the Code window is opened for the class's event or method. For example, to immediately edit the Click event code for a class named MyClass in a visual class library named MyClassLibrary, use the following command:

```
MODIFY CLASS MyClass OF MyClassLibrary METHOD Click
```

NOWAIT

Continues program execution after the Class Designer is opened. The program doesn't wait for the Class Designer to be closed, but continues execution on the program line immediately following the line that contains MODIFY CLASS NOWAIT. If you omit NOWAIT when MODIFY CLASS is issued in a program, the Class Designer is opened and program execution pauses until the Class Designer is closed.

NOWAIT is effective only from within a program. It has no effect on MODIFY CLASS when issued from the Command window. If NOWAIT is included with the METHOD clause, be sure to place NOWAIT before the METHOD clause or NOWAIT will be ignored.

SAVE

Leaves the Class Designer open after another window is activated. If you omit SAVE, the Class Designer is closed when another window is activated. Including SAVE has no effect when issued from the Command window.

Remarks

Use MODIFY CLASS to modify an existing class definition or to create a new class definition and save it in a .vcx visual class library. You can open the .vcx visual class library with SET CLASSLIB, allowing you to access the class definitions within the .vcx visual class library.

See Also

ADD CLASS, CREATE CLASS, CREATE CLASSLIB, RELEASE CLASSLIB, SET CLASSLIB

MODIFY COMMAND Command

Opens an editing window so you can modify or create a program file.

Syntax

MODIFY COMMAND [*FileName* | ?]
    [NOEDIT]
    [NOMENU]
    [NOWAIT]
    [RANGE *nStartCharacter*, *nEndCharacter*]
    [[WINDOW *WindowName1*]
    [IN [WINDOW] *WindowName2* | IN SCREEN]]
    [AS *nCodePage*]
    [SAME]
    [SAVE]

Arguments

FileName

Specifies the file name for the program to open or create. If you don't specify an extension for a new program file, Visual FoxPro automatically assigns a .prg extension. MODIFY COMMAND supports a file skeleton that contains the asterisk (*) and question mark (?) wildcards. An editing window is opened for each program whose file name matches the file skeleton.

If you omit the file name, an editing window opens for a file initially named Prog1.prg. When you close the editing window, you can save the file with a different name.

?

Displays the Open dialog box. Choose one of the existing programs or enter the name of a new program to create.

NOEDIT

Specifies that the program file can't be changed, but can be viewed and copied to the Clipboard.

NOMENU

Removes the Format menu title from the Visual FoxPro system menu bar, preventing changes to font, font size, line spacing, and indentation.

NOWAIT

Continues program execution after the editing window is opened. The program doesn't wait for the editing window to be closed, but continues execution on the program line immediately following the line that contains MODIFY COMMAND NOWAIT. If you omit NOWAIT when MODIFY COMMAND is used in a program, an editing window is opened and program execution pauses until the editing window is closed.

NOWAIT is effective only from within a program. It has no effect on MODIFY COMMAND when issued from the Command window.

An implicit NOWAIT occurs if you open more than one editing window with a single MODIFY COMMAND command. For example:

```
MODIFY COMMAND *.PRG.
```

RANGE *nStartCharacter, nEndCharacter*

Specifies a range of characters selected when the editing window is opened. Characters are selected starting at the position specified with *nStartCharacter* up to (but not including) the character position of *nEndCharacter*. If *nStartCharacter* is equal to *nEndCharacter*, no characters are selected, and the cursor is placed at the position specified with *nStartCharacter*.

WINDOW *WindowName1*

Specifies a window whose characteristics the editing window takes on. For example, if the window is created with the FLOAT option of DEFINE WINDOW, the editing window can be moved. The window need not be active or visible, but it must be defined.

IN [WINDOW] *WindowName2*

Specifies a parent window in which the editing window is opened. The editing window doesn't assume the characteristics of the parent window and cannot be moved outside the parent window. If the parent window is moved, the editing window moves with it.

The parent window must first be defined with DEFINE WINDOW, and must be visible, to access the editing window.

IN SCREEN

Explicitly opens the editing window in the main Visual FoxPro window, after it has been placed in a parent window. An editing window is placed in a parent window by including the IN WINDOW clause.

AS *nCodePage*

Automatically converts accented characters in a program file created on another Visual FoxPro platform. The numeric expression *nCodePage* specifies the code page of the Visual FoxPro platform on which the program file was created. The file is saved in this code page unless you choose Save As from the File menu to save the file in a different code page.

SAME

Prevents the editing window from coming forward as the active window. If the editing window is hidden, it is displayed but doesn't become the active window.

SAVE

Leaves the editing window open after another window is activated. If you omit SAVE, the editing window is closed when another window is activated. Including SAVE has no effect when issued from the Command window.

Remarks

When modifications are made to a program file, the updated file is written to disk. In Visual FoxPro, a backup file with a .bak extension is created if you select the Make Backup Copy check box on the Edit Properties dialog box, which appears when you choose Properties from the Edit menu.

The built-in Visual FoxPro editor is used unless you specify an external editor with TEDIT in your configuration file.

See Also

*, &&, DO, MODIFY FILE, NOTE

MODIFY CONNECTION Command

Displays the Connection Designer, allowing you to interactively modify an existing named connection stored in the current database.

Syntax

MODIFY CONNECTION [*ConnectionName* | ?]

Arguments

ConnectionName
Specifies the name of the connection to modify.

?
Displays the Open dialog box from which you can choose an existing named connection to modify.

Remarks

If you omit the optional arguments, the Open dialog box is displayed, allowing you to specify an existing named connection to modify. The Connection Designer is displayed after you choose a named connection to modify.

Example

The following example assumes an ODBC data source called MyFoxSQLNT is available, and the user ID for the data source is "sa." The testdata database is opened, and a connection named Myconn is created. MODIFY CONNECTION is used to displays the Connection Designer so you can modify the connection.

```
CLOSE DATABASES
OPEN DATABASE (HOME(2) + 'data\testdata')
```

```
CREATE CONNECTION Myconn DATASOURCE "MyFoxSQLNT" USERID "sa"

MODIFY CONNECTION Myconn && Displays named connections in the database
```

See Also

CREATE CONNECTION, DELETE CONNECTION, OPEN DATABASE, RENAME CONNECTION

MODIFY DATABASE Command

Opens the Database Designer, allowing you to interactively modify the current database.

Syntax

MODIFY DATABASE [*DatabaseName* | ?]
    [NOWAIT] [NOEDIT]

Arguments

DatabaseName
    Specifies the name of the database to modify.

?
    Displays the Open dialog box from which you can specify the name of the database to modify.

NOWAIT
    Continues program execution after the Database Designer is opened. The program doesn't wait for the Database Designer to be closed, but continues execution on the program line immediately following the line that contains MODIFY DATABASE NOWAIT. If you omit NOWAIT when MODIFY DATABASE is issued in a program, the Database Designer is opened and program execution pauses until the Database Designer is closed.

    NOWAIT is effective only from within a program. It has no effect on MODIFY DATABASE when issued from the Command window.

NOEDIT
    Prevents changes to the database.

Remarks

For more information about interactively modifying a database with the Database Designer, see "Database Designer" and "Database Designer Toolbar" in Help, and Chapter 3, "Collecting Tables into a Database," in the *User's Guide* in Help.

Example

The following example displays the Database Designer with the tables in the `testdata` database.

```
CLOSE DATABASES
SET PATH TO (HOME(2) + 'data\')        && Sets path to database

MODIFY DATABASE testdata  && Open testdata database
```

See Also

ADD TABLE, CLOSE DATABASES, CREATE DATABASE, DBC( ), DBGETPROP( ), DBSETPROP( ), DELETE DATABASE, DISPLAY TABLES, OPEN DATABASE, REMOVE TABLE

MODIFY FILE Command

Opens an editing window so you can modify or create a text file.

Syntax

MODIFY FILE [*FileName* | ?]
    [NOEDIT]
    [NOMENU]
    [NOWAIT]
    [RANGE *nStartCharacter*, *nEndCharacter*]
    [[WINDOW *WindowName1*]
    [IN [WINDOW] *WindowName2* | IN SCREEN]]
    [AS *nCodePage*]
    [SAME]
    [SAVE]

Arguments

FileName

    Specifies the file name for the text file. If you don't specify an extension for a new text file, Visual FoxPro automatically assigns a .txt extension. MODIFY FILE supports a file skeleton that can contain the asterisk (*) and question mark (?) wildcards. An editing window is opened for each text file whose name matches the file skeleton.

    If you omit the file name, an editing window opens for a file initially named FILE1. When you close the editing window, you can save the file with a different name.

?

    Displays the Open dialog box, from which you can choose a text file.

NOEDIT

    Specifies that the text file can't be changed, but can be viewed and copied to the Clipboard.

NOMENU

Removes the Format menu title from the Visual FoxPro system menu bar, preventing changes to font, font size, line spacing, and indentation.

NOWAIT

Continues program execution after the editing window is opened. The program doesn't wait for the editing window to be closed, but continues execution on the program line immediately following the line that contains MODIFY FILE NOWAIT. If you omit NOWAIT when MODIFY FILE is issued in a program, the editing window is opened and program execution pauses until the editing window is closed.

NOWAIT is effective only from within a program. It has no effect on MODIFY FILE when issued from the Command window.

An implicit NOWAIT occurs if you open more than one editing window with a single MODIFY FILE command. For example:

```
MODIFY FILE *.TXT
```

RANGE *nStartCharacter*, *nEndCharacter*

Specifies a range of characters selected when you open an editing window. Characters are selected starting at the position specified with *nStartCharacter* up to (but not including) the character position of *nEndCharacter*. If *nStartCharacter* is equal to *nEndCharacter*, no characters are selected, and the cursor is placed at the position specified with *nStartCharacter*.

WINDOW *WindowName1*

Specifies a window whose characteristics the editing window takes on. For example, if the window is created with the FLOAT option of DEFINE WINDOW, the editing window can be moved. The window need not be active or visible, but it must be defined.

IN [WINDOW] *WindowName2*

Specifies a parent window in which the editing window is opened. The editing window doesn't assume the characteristics of the parent window and cannot be moved outside the parent window. If the parent window is moved, the editing window moves with it.

The parent window must first be defined with DEFINE WINDOW, and must be visible in order to access the editing window.

IN SCREEN

Explicitly opens the editing window in the main Visual FoxPro window, after it has been placed in a parent window. An editing window is placed in a parent window by including the IN WINDOW clause.

AS *nCodePage*

Automatically converts accented characters in a text file created on another Visual FoxPro platform. The numeric expression *nCodePage* specifies the code page of the Visual FoxPro platform on which the text file was created. The file is saved in this code page unless you choose Save As from the File menu to save the file in a different code page.

SAME

Prevents the editing window from coming forward as the active window. If the editing window is hidden, it is displayed but doesn't become the active window.

SAVE

Leaves the editing window open after another window is activated. If you omit SAVE, the editing window is closed when another window is activated. Including SAVE has no effect when issued from the Command window.

Remarks

When modifications are made to a text file, the updated file is written to disk. In Visual FoxPro, a backup file with a .bak extension is created if you select the Make Backup Copy check box on the Edit Properties dialog box, which appears when you choose Properties from the Edit menu. In previous versions of FoxPro, a backup file with a .bak extension is created if you select the Backup check box in the Preferences dialog box, which appears when you choose Preferences from the Edit menu.

The Visual FoxPro editor is used unless you specify an external editor with TEDIT in your configuration file.

See Also

*, &&, DO, MODIFY COMMAND, NOTE

MODIFY FORM Command

Opens the Form Designer so you can modify or create a Form.

Syntax

MODIFY FORM
    [*FormName* | ?] [METHOD MethodName]
    [NOENVIRONMENT] [NOWAIT] [SAVE]
    [[WINDOW *WindowName1*]
    [IN [WINDOW] *WindowName2* | IN SCREEN]]

Arguments

FormName

Specifies the file name for the Form. If you don't specify an extension for the file name, Visual FoxPro automatically assigns an .scx extension.

?

Displays the Open dialog box from which you can choose an existing Form or enter the name of a new Form to create.

METHOD *MethodName*

Specifies an event or method for which the Code window is opened in the Form Designer. The METHOD clause lets you immediately begin editing event or method code in the Form Designer.

MethodName supports the Visual FoxPro object syntax. For example, to immediately edit the Click event code for a text box named txtFirstName in a form named frmAddress, use the following command:

```
MODIFY FORM frmAddress METHOD txtFirstName.Click
```

If you only include an event or method name in the METHOD clause, the Code window is opened for the form's event or method. For example, to immediately edit the Click event code for a form named frmAddress, use the following command:

```
MODIFY FORM frmAddress METHOD Click
```

NOENVIRONMENT

Included for backward compatibility with 2.x screens, preventing the environment saved with the screen from being restored.

In Visual FoxPro, the data environment associated with a Visual FoxPro form is restored by setting the data environment AutoOpenTables property to true (.T.), which is the default. To make sure that the form environment is closed when the form is releases, set the data environment AutoCloseTables property to true (.T.), which is also the default.

When you create or modify forms, you can save the current Visual FoxPro data environment with the form definition file. Saving the Visual FoxPro data environment places additional records in the form definition table for all open tables and index files, the index order, and any relationships between the tables.

NOWAIT

Continues program execution after the Form Designer has been opened. The program doesn't wait for the Form Designer to be closed, but continues execution on the program line immediately following the line that contains MODIFY FORM NOWAIT. If you omit NOWAIT, when MODIFY FORM is issued in a program the Form Designer is opened and program execution pauses until the Form Designer is closed.

NOWAIT is effective only from within a program. It has no effect on MODIFY FORM when issued from the Command window. If NOWAIT is included with the METHOD clause, be sure to place NOWAIT before the METHOD clause or NOWAIT will be ignored.

SAVE

When issued in a program, leaves the Form Designer open after another window is brought forward. Including the SAVE option has no effect when issued from the Command window.

WINDOW *WindowName1*

Specifies a window whose characteristics the Form Designer takes on. For example, if the window is created with the FLOAT option of DEFINE WINDOW, the Form Designer can be moved. The window need not be active or visible, but it must be defined.

The Form Designer has a default size that can be larger than the window from which it takes its characteristics. In this case, the Form Designer still assumes the characteristics of the window in which it is placed. The upper-left corner of the Form Designer is placed at the same coordinates as the upper-left corner of the window, and extends beyond the window's borders.

IN [WINDOW] *WindowName2*

Specifies a parent window in which the Form Designer is opened. The Form Designer doesn't assume the characteristics of the parent window and cannot be moved outside the parent window. If the parent window is moved, the Form Designer moves with it.

The parent window must first be defined with DEFINE WINDOW, and must be visible, to access the Form Designer.

IN SCREEN

Specifies that the Form Designer is explicitly opened in the main Visual FoxPro window, after the Form Designer has been placed in a parent window. The Form Designer is placed in a parent window by including the IN WINDOW clause.

Remarks

Issuing MODIFY FORM without any arguments displays the Open dialog box. You can save the form with a different name when you close the Form Designer.

Example

The following example opens the stop watch (SWATCH.SCX) control sample in the Form Designer.

```
MODIFY FORM (HOME(2) + 'solution\controls\timer\swatch.scx')
```

See Also

COMPILE FORM, CREATE FORM, DO FORM

MODIFY GENERAL Command

Opens editing windows for general fields in the current record.

Syntax

MODIFY GENERAL *GeneralField1* [, *GeneralField2* ...]
    [NOMODIFY]
    [NOWAIT]
    [[WINDOW *WindowName1*]
    [IN [WINDOW] *WindowName2* | IN SCREEN]]

Arguments

GeneralField1 [, *GeneralField2* ...]

Specify the names of the general fields to open. To open an editing window for a general field in a table open in a noncurrent work area, include the table alias with the field name. You can open multiple general fields in the current record by including a list of general fields separated by commas.

NOMODIFY

Specifies that the OLE object contained in the general field can't be changed, but can be viewed and copied to the Clipboard.

NOWAIT

Continues program execution after the general field editing window is opened. The program doesn't wait for the editing window to be closed, but continues execution on the program line immediately following the line that contains MODIFY GENERAL NOWAIT. If you omit NOWAIT when MODIFY GENERAL is issued in a program, an editing window is opened and program execution pauses until the editing window is closed.

NOWAIT is effective only from within a program. It has no effect on MODIFY GENERAL when issued from the Command window.

WINDOW *WindowName1*

Specifies a window whose characteristics the general field editing window takes on. For example, if the window is created with the FLOAT option of DEFINE WINDOW, the general field editing window can be moved. The window need not be active or visible, but it must be defined.

IN [WINDOW] *WindowName2*

Specifies a parent window in which the general field editing window is opened. The general field window doesn't assume the characteristics of the parent window and cannot be moved outside the parent window. If the parent window is moved, the general field window moves with it.

The parent window must first be defined with DEFINE WINDOW, and must be visible, to access the general field window.

IN SCREEN

Explicitly opens the general field window in the main Visual FoxPro window, after it has been placed in a parent window. A general field editing window is placed in a parent window by including the IN WINDOW clause.

Remarks

When an editing window is open, you can insert, modify, or delete an OLE object.

For additional information about OLE objects in Visual FoxPro, see "Adding OLE Objects to Tables" in Chapter 16, "Adding OLE," in the *Microsoft Visual FoxPro 6.0 Programmer's Guide*.

See Also

@ ... SAY – Pictures & OLE Objects, APPEND GENERAL

MODIFY LABEL Command

Opens the Label Designer so you can create or modify a label.

Syntax

MODIFY LABEL [*FileName* | ?]
    [[WINDOW *WindowName1*]
    [IN [WINDOW] *WindowName2* | IN SCREEN]]
    [NOENVIRONMENT]
    [NOWAIT]
    [SAVE]

Arguments

FileName

Specifies the file name for the label. If you don't specify an extension for the file name, Visual FoxPro automatically assigns an .lbx extension. If the file you specify doesn't exist or can't be found, a new label file is created.

?

Displays the Open dialog box, from which you can choose an existing label or enter the name of a new label to create.

WINDOW *WindowName1*

Specifies a window whose characteristics the Label Designer takes on. For example, if the window is created with the FLOAT option of DEFINE WINDOW, the Label Designer can be moved. The window doesn't have to be active or visible, but it must be defined.

The Label Designer has a default size that can be larger than the window from which it takes its characteristics. In this case, the Label Designer still assumes the characteristics of the window in which it is placed. The upper-left corner of the Label Designer is placed at the same coordinates as the upper-left corner of the window, and extends beyond the window's borders.

IN [WINDOW] *WindowName2*

Specifies a parent window in which the Label Designer is opened. The Label Designer doesn't assume the characteristics of the parent window and cannot be moved outside the parent window. If the parent window is moved, the Label Designer moves with it.

The parent window must first be defined with DEFINE WINDOW, and must be visible to access the Label Designer.

IN SCREEN

Explicitly opens the Label Designer in the main Visual FoxPro window, after it has been placed in a parent window. A Label Designer is placed in a parent window by including the IN WINDOW clause.

NOENVIRONMENT

Included for backward compatibility with 2.x labels, preventing the environment saved with the label.

In Visual FoxPro, the data environment associated with a Visual FoxPro label is restored by setting the data environment AutoOpenTables property to true (.T.), which is the default. To make sure that the label environment is closed when the label is finished printing, set the data environment AutoCloseTables property to true (.T.), which is also the default.

When you create or modify labels, you can save the current Visual FoxPro data environment with the label definition file. Saving the Visual FoxPro data environment places additional records in the label definition table for all open tables and index files, the index order, and any relationships between the tables.

NOWAIT

Continues program execution after the Label Designer is opened. The program doesn't wait for the Label Designer to be closed, but continues execution on the program line immediately following the line that contains CREATE LABEL NOWAIT. If you omit NOWAIT when CREATE LABEL is issued in a program, a Label Designer is opened and program execution pauses until the Label Designer is closed.

Including the NOWAIT option has no effect on the CREATE LABEL command when issued from the Command window.

SAVE

Leaves the Label Designer open after another window is activated. If you omit SAVE, the Label Designer is closed when another window is activated. Including SAVE has no effect when issued from the Command window.

See Also

CREATE LABEL, LABEL

MODIFY MEMO Command

Opens an editing window for a memo field in the current record.

Syntax

MODIFY MEMO *MemoField1* [, *MemoField2* ...]
    [NOEDIT]
    [NOMENU]
    [NOWAIT]
    [RANGE *nStartCharacter*, *nEndCharacter*]
    [[WINDOW *WindowName1*]
    [IN [WINDOW] *WindowName2* | IN SCREEN]]
    [SAME]
    [SAVE]

Arguments

MemoField1 [, *MemoField2* ...]

Specifies the names of the memo fields to edit. To open an editing window for a memo field in a table open in another work area, include the table alias with the field name.

NOEDIT

Specifies that the memo field opened can't be changed, but can be viewed and copied to the Clipboard.

NOMENU

Removes the Format menu title from the Visual FoxPro system menu bar, preventing changes to font, font size, line spacing, and indentation.

NOWAIT

Continues program execution after the editing window is opened. The program doesn't wait for the editing window to be closed, but continues execution on the program line immediately following the line that contains MODIFY MEMO NOWAIT. If you omit NOWAIT when MODIFY MEMO is issued in a program, an editing window is opened and program execution pauses until the editing window is closed.

NOWAIT is effective only from within a program. It has no effect on MODIFY MEMO when issued from the Command window.

RANGE *nStartCharacter, nEndCharacter*

Specifies a range of characters selected when the editing window is opened. Characters are selected starting at the position specified with *nStartCharacter* up to (but not including) the character position of *nEndCharacter*. If *nStartCharacter* is equal to *nEndCharacter*, no characters are selected, and the cursor is placed at the position specified with *nStartCharacter*.

WINDOW *WindowName1*

Specifies a window whose characteristics the editing window takes on. For example, if the window is created with the FLOAT option of DEFINE WINDOW, the editing window can be moved. The window need not be active or visible, but it must be defined.

IN [WINDOW] *WindowName2*

Specifies a parent window in which the editing window is opened. The editing window doesn't assume the characteristics of the parent window and cannot be moved outside the parent window. If the parent window is moved, the editing window moves with it.

The parent window must first be defined with DEFINE WINDOW, and must be visible, to access the editing window.

IN SCREEN

Explicitly opens the editing window in the main Visual FoxPro window, after it has been placed in a parent window. An editing window is placed in a parent window by including the IN WINDOW clause.

SAME

Prevents the editing window from coming forward as the active window. If the editing window is hidden, it is displayed but doesn't become the active window.

SAVE

Leaves the editing window open after another window is activated. If you omit SAVE, the editing window is closed when another window is activated. Including SAVE has no effect when issued from the Command window.

Remarks

In the editing window, you can view or change the contents of the memo field.

In a table opened for shared access on a network, the current record is automatically locked when editing begins on one of its memo fields.

Note Syntax coloring in memo field editing windows is disabled in distributed run-time applications.

To enable syntax coloring in an editing window during development

1. Right-click the editing window and choose **Properties** from the shortcut menu.

2. Select the **Syntax coloring** check box.

Example

The following example opens the notes memo field for the first record in employee in an editing window with a highlighted range.

```
CLOSE DATABASES
OPEN DATABASE (HOME(2) + 'data\testdata')
USE employee  && Opens Employee table

MODIFY MEMO notes NOEDIT RANGE 1,10  && First 10 characters selected
USE
```

See Also

CLOSE MEMO

MODIFY MENU Command

Opens the Menu Designer so you can modify or create a menu system.

Syntax

MODIFY MENU [*FileName* | ?]
    [[WINDOW *WindowName1*]
    [IN [WINDOW] *WindowName2* | IN SCREEN]]
    [NOWAIT]
    [SAVE]

Arguments

FileName

Specifies the file name for the menu. If you don't specify an extension for the file name, Visual FoxPro automatically assigns an .mnx extension.

?

Displays the Open dialog box, from which you can choose an existing menu file or enter the name of a new menu to create.

WINDOW *WindowName1*

Specifies a window whose characteristics the Menu Designer takes on. For example, if the window is created with the FLOAT option of DEFINE WINDOW, the Menu Designer can be moved. The window need not be active or visible, but it must be defined.

IN [WINDOW] *WindowName2*

Specifies a parent window in which the Menu Designer is opened. The Menu Designer doesn't assume the characteristics of the parent window and cannot be moved outside the parent window. If the parent window is moved, the Menu Designer moves with it.

The parent window must first be defined with DEFINE WINDOW, and must be visible, to access the Menu Designer.

IN SCREEN

Explicitly opens the Menu Designer in the main Microsoft Visual FoxPro window, after it has been placed in a parent window. The Menu Designer is placed in a parent window by including the IN WINDOW clause.

NOWAIT

Continues program execution after the Menu Designer is opened. The program doesn't wait for the Menu Designer to be closed, but continues execution on the program line immediately following the line that contains MODIFY MENU NOWAIT. If you omit NOWAIT when MODIFY MENU is issued in a program, the Menu Designer is opened and program execution pauses until the Menu Designer is closed.

NOWAIT is effective only from within a program. It has no effect on MODIFY MENU when issued from the Command window.

If you issue MODIFY MENU from the Command window without a menu name and include NOWAIT, the Open dialog is not displayed. The New Menu dialog lets you specify the type of menu (standard or shortcut) created.

SAVE

Leaves the Menu Designer open after another window is activated. If you omit SAVE, the Menu Designer is closed when another window is activated. Including SAVE has no effect when issued from the Command window.

Remarks

For more information on creating menus, see "Creating a Menu System" in Chapter 11, "Designing Menus and Toolbars," in the *Microsoft Visual FoxPro 6.0 Programmer's Guide*.

See Also

DEFINE BAR, DEFINE MENU, DEFINE PAD, DEFINE POPUP, SET SYSMENU

MODIFY PROCEDURE Command

Opens the Visual FoxPro text editor, allowing you to create new stored procedures for the current database, or modify existing stored procedures in the current database.

Syntax

MODIFY PROCEDURE

Remarks

A database must be open before you can create or modify stored procedures. Stored procedures are typically specified in Delete, Insert, or Update triggers created for a database with CREATE TRIGGER.

Stored procedures in the current database can be executed like other Visual FoxPro procedures in an open procedure file or program. See the PROCEDURE Command, later in this language reference, for a description of the order and location in which Visual FoxPro searches for procedures.

Example

The following example opens the testdata database and uses MODIFY PROCEDURE to open the Visual FoxPro text editor, allowing you to create new stored procedures or modify existing stored procedures.

```
CLOSE DATABASES
OPEN DATABASE (HOME(2) + 'Data\testdata')

MODIFY PROCEDURE  && Opens the Visual FoxPro text editor
```

See Also

CREATE TRIGGER, DISPLAY PROCEDURES, OPEN DATABASE, PROCEDURE

MODIFY PROJECT Command

Opens the Project Manager so you can modify or create a project file.

Syntax

MODIFY PROJECT [*FileName* | ?]
    [IN SCREEN] [NOWAIT] [SAVE]
    [NOSHOW] [NOPROJECTHOOK]

Arguments

FileName

Specifies the file name for the project. If you don't specify an extension for the file name, Visual FoxPro automatically assigns a .pjx extension.

?

Displays the Open dialog box from which you can open an existing project file or enter the name of a new project to create.

IN SCREEN

Explicitly opens the Project Manager in the main Visual FoxPro window, after it has been placed in a parent window. The Project Manager is placed in a parent window by including the IN WINDOW clause.

NOWAIT

Continues program execution after the Project Manager is opened. The program doesn't wait for the Project Manager to be closed, but continues execution on the program line immediately following the line that contains MODIFY PROJECT NOWAIT. If you omit NOWAIT when MODIFY PROJECT is issued in a program, the Project Manager is opened and program execution pauses until the Project Manager is closed.

NOWAIT is effective only from within a program. It has no effect on MODIFY PROJECT when issued from the Command window.

SAVE

Leaves the Project Manager open after another window is activated. If you omit SAVE, the Project Manager is closed when another window is activated. Including SAVE has no effect when issued from the Command window.

NOSHOW

Specifies that the Project Manager is hidden (its Visible property is set to false (.F.)) when it is opened. To display the Project Manager, set the Project Manager's Visible property to true (.T.). NOSHOW allows you to manipulate a project before displaying it in the Project Manager. Note that to avoid confusion with the NOSHADOW keyword, you cannot abbreviate NOSHOW to less than five characters.

NOPROJECTHOOK

Specifies that a ProjectHook object isn't created when the Project Manager is opened. Include NOPROJECTHOOK for projects that will not be manipulated programmatically through the Project Manager hooks. Note that a Project object is still created whenever a project file (.pjx) is opened.

Remarks

In a project, you specify all the source files that are required for a final application, and then Visual FoxPro makes sure the generated application is based on the latest source files.

A project file is a table that keeps track of all the source files such as programs, forms, menus, libraries, reports, labels, tables, indexes, and format files. A project also keeps track of all the dependencies, references, and connections among the files.

Note Shared libraries (.fll, .mlb, .dll, and CFM files) cannot be included in projects.

A project file has a .pjx file name extension and an associated memo file with a .pjt extension.

Issuing MODIFY PROJECT without any arguments displays the Open dialog box.

For information on the Project Manager, see Chapter 13, "Compiling an Application," in the *Microsoft Visual FoxPro 6.0 Programmer's Guide*.

See Also

BUILD APP, BUILD EXE, BUILD PROJECT, COMPILE, CREATE PROJECT

MODIFY QUERY Command

Opens the Query Designer so you can modify or create a query.

Syntax

MODIFY QUERY [*FileName* | ?]
    [[WINDOW *WindowName1*]
    [IN SCREEN]
    [NOWAIT]
    [SAVE]
    [AS *nCodePage*]

Arguments

FileName

Specifies the file name for the query. If you don't specify an extension for the file name, Visual FoxPro automatically assigns a .qpr extension.

?

Displays the Open dialog box from which you can choose an existing query or enter the name of a new query to create.

WINDOW *WindowName1*

Specifies a window whose characteristics the Query Designer takes on. For example, if the window is created with the FLOAT option of DEFINE WINDOW, the Query Designer can be moved. The window need not be active or visible, but it must be defined.

IN SCREEN

Explicitly opens the Query Designer in the main Visual FoxPro window, after it has been placed in a parent window. The Query Designer is placed in a parent window by including the IN WINDOW clause.

NOWAIT

Continues program execution after the Query Designer is opened. The program doesn't wait for the Query Designer to be closed, but continues execution on the program line immediately following the line that contains MODIFY QUERY NOWAIT. If you omit NOWAIT when MODIFY QUERY is issued in a program, the Query Designer is opened and program execution pauses until the Query Designer is closed.

NOWAIT is effective only from within a program. It has no effect on MODIFY QUERY when issued from the Command window.

SAVE

Leaves the Query Designer open after another window is activated. If you omit SAVE, the Query Designer is closed when another window is activated. Including SAVE has no effect when issued from the Command window.

AS *nCodePage*

Specifies the code page of the query. Include AS *nCodePage* if the query was created with a code page other than the current Visual FoxPro code page. When the query is opened, Visual FoxPro automatically converts the query to the current Visual FoxPro code page. You can use GETCP( ) for *nCodePage* to display the Code Page dialog box, allowing you to specify a code page for the query.

The query is saved in its original code page when it is closed.

If you omit the AS *nCodePage* clause or *nCodePage* is 0, the query is not converted to the current Visual FoxPro code page. If you specify a value for *nCodePage* that is not supported, Visual FoxPro generates an error message.

In Visual FoxPro, queries can be added to a project, and you can specify the query's code page from within the Project Container. The Project Container keeps track of the query's code page. However, if you use MODIFY QUERY to open a query outside of the Project Container, you should include AS *nCodePage* to specify the query's code page.

Remarks

For more information about creating queries, see "Creating a Query" in Chapter 4, "Retrieving Data," in the *User's Guide* in Help.

Issuing MODIFY QUERY without any arguments displays the Open dialog box. If you choose New from this dialog box, the name QUERY1 is assigned to the query. You can save the query with a different name when you exit the Query Designer.

After you have created a query, the query is stored as a Visual FoxPro program file with a .qpr extension. You can execute a query program with DO, but you must include the .qpr extension with the query file name.

See Also

CREATE QUERY, DO, GETCP( )

MODIFY REPORT Command

Opens the Report Designer so you can modify or create a report.

Syntax

MODIFY REPORT [*FileName* | ?]
    [[WINDOW *WindowName1*]
    [IN [WINDOW] *WindowName2* | IN SCREEN]]
    [NOENVIRONMENT]
    [NOWAIT]
    [SAVE]

Arguments

FileName
    Specifies the file name for the report. If you don't specify an extension for the file name, Visual FoxPro automatically assigns an .frx extension.

?
    Displays the Open dialog box from which you can choose an existing report file or enter the name of a new report to create.

WINDOW *WindowName1*
    Specifies a window whose characteristics the Report Designer takes on. For example, if the window is created with the FLOAT option of DEFINE WINDOW, the Report Designer can be moved. The window need not be active or visible, but it must be defined.

IN [WINDOW] *WindowName2*
    Specifies a parent window in which the Report Designer is opened. The Report Designer doesn't assume the characteristics of the parent window and cannot be moved outside the parent window. If the parent window is moved, the Report Designer moves with it.

The parent window must first be defined with DEFINE WINDOW, and must be visible, to access the Report Designer.

IN SCREEN

Explicitly opens the Report Designer in the main Visual FoxPro window, after it has been placed in a parent window. The Report Designer is placed in a parent window by including the IN WINDOW clause.

NOENVIRONMENT

Included for backward compatibility with 2.x reports; prevents the environment saved with the report.

In Visual FoxPro, the data environment associated with a Visual FoxPro report is restored by setting the data environment AutoOpenTables property to true (.T.), which is the default. To make sure that the report environment is closed when the report is finished printing, set the data environment AutoCloseTables property to true (.T.), which is also the default.

When you create or modify reports, you can save the current Visual FoxPro data environment with the report definition file. Saving the Visual FoxPro data environment places additional records in the report definition table for all open tables and index files, the index order, and any relationships between the tables.

NOWAIT

Continues program execution after the Report Designer is opened. The program doesn't wait for the Report Designer to be closed, but continues execution on the program line immediately following the line that contains MODIFY REPORT NOWAIT. If you omit NOWAIT when MODIFY REPORT is issued in a program, the Report Designer is opened and program execution pauses until the Report Designer is closed.

NOWAIT is effective only from within a program. It has no effect on MODIFY REPORT when issued from the Command window.

SAVE

Leaves the Report Designer open after another window is activated. If you omit SAVE, the Report Designer is closed when another window is activated. Including SAVE has no effect when issued from the Command window.

Remarks

Issuing MODIFY REPORT without any arguments displays the Open dialog box. If you choose New from this dialog box, the name REPORT1 is assigned to the report file. You can save the report file with a different name when you close the Report Designer.

For more information on creating and modifying reports, see Chapter 7, "Designing Reports and Labels," in the *User's Guide* in Help.

See Also

_ASCIICOLS, _ASCIIROWS, CREATE REPORT, REPORT

MODIFY SCREEN Command

Included for backward compatibility. Use MODIFY FORM instead.

MODIFY STRUCTURE Command

Displays the Table Designer, allowing you to modify the structure of a table.

Syntax

MODIFY STRUCTURE

Remarks

In previous versions of FoxPro, MODIFY STRUCTURE opens the Table Structure dialog box.

If a table isn't open in the currently selected work area, the Open dialog box is displayed, allowing you to choose a table to modify.

Changes you can make to a table's structure include adding and deleting fields; modifying field names, sizes, and data types; adding, deleting, or modifying index tags; and specifying null value support for fields.

You can also modify the structure of a table using the interface. For more information, see "Modifying Tables" in Chapter 2, "Creating Tables and Indexes," in the *User's Guide* in Help.

> **Caution** Changing a field from one data type to another may not transfer the contents of the field correctly, or at all. For example, if you convert a field of date type to a numeric type, the field contents do not transfer.

Visual FoxPro automatically makes a backup copy of the current table before you change the table's structure. When the modifications are complete, the data contained in the backup copy of the table is appended to the newly modified table structure. If the table has a memo field, a memo backup file is also created. The table backup file has a .bak extension, and the memo backup file has a .tbk extension.

If you accept the structure changes and then interrupt the data-copying process, the new file will not contain all the records in the original table.

Remember that Visual FoxPro creates a .bak file for the original table file and, if the table has a memo field, a .tbk copy of the original memo file. If you have any problems with MODIFY STRUCTURE, you can delete the new file or files and rename the .bak file and .tbk file, if any, to the original file extensions (.dbf and .fpt).

When you modify the structure of a table that has a memo field, the blocksize of the memo file is set to the current blocksize setting. You can specify the memo file blocksize with SET BLOCKSIZE.

See Also

ALTER TABLE – SQL, CREATE, CREATE TABLE – SQL, SET BLOCKSIZE

MODIFY VIEW Command

Displays the View Designer, allowing you to modify an existing SQL view.

Syntax

MODIFY VIEW *ViewName* [REMOTE]

Arguments

ViewName
    Specifies the name of the view to modify.

REMOTE
    Specifies that the view is a remote view that uses remote tables. If you omit
    REMOTE, you can modify a view using local tables.

Remarks

SQL views are created with CREATE SQL VIEW.

See Also

CREATE SQL VIEW, OPEN DATABASE

MODIFY WINDOW Command

Modifies a user-defined window or the main Visual FoxPro window.

Syntax

MODIFY WINDOW *WindowName* | SCREEN
    [FROM *nRow1, nColumn1* TO *nRow2, nColumn2*
    | AT *nRow3, nColumn3* SIZE *nRow4, nColumn4*]
    [FONT *cFontName* [, *nFontSize*]]
    [STYLE *cFontStyle*]
    [TITLE *cTitleText*]
    [HALFHEIGHT]
    [DOUBLE | PANEL | NONE | SYSTEM]
    [CLOSE | NOCLOSE]
    [FLOAT | NOFLOAT]
    [GROW | NOGROW]
    [MINIMIZE | NOMINIMIZE]
    [ZOOM | NOZOOM]
    [ICON FILE *FileName1*]

[FILL FILE *FileName2*]
[COLOR SCHEME *nSchemeNumber*
| COLOR *ColorPairList*]

Arguments

WindowName
Specifies which user-defined window to modify. The window you specify must first be created with DEFINE WINDOW.

SCREEN
Specifies the main Visual FoxPro window as the window to modify. Do not abbreviate SCREEN or Visual FoxPro generates an error message. To return the main Visual FoxPro window to its startup configuration, issue the following command without any additional clauses:

```
MODIFY WINDOW SCREEN
```

> **Tip** Use MODIFY WINDOW SCREEN NOCLOSE to prevent accidentally terminating Visual FoxPro prematurely.

For more information about the MODIFY WINDOW clauses, see the DEFINE WINDOW Command, earlier in this language reference.

Remarks

MODIFY WINDOW changes the attributes of an existing user-defined window (a window created with DEFINE WINDOW) or the main Visual FoxPro window. MODIFY WINDOW can't be used to change the attributes of Visual FoxPro system windows (such as the Command window and Browse window).

Use MODIFY WINDOW to change the location, default font, title, border, controls, icon, wallpaper, and color of a user-defined window or the main Visual FoxPro window. You can change any of these attributes by including the optional clauses for the MODIFY WINDOW command. (Note that if you change colors, you must use CLEAR to apply the color changes.)

For example, include the FROM and TO or AT and SIZE clauses to specify a new location or size for a user-defined window or the main Visual FoxPro window. To prevent a user-defined window or the main Visual FoxPro window from being moved, include the NOFLOAT keyword.

Example

The following example changes the contents of the title bar of the main Visual FoxPro window.

```
MODIFY WINDOW SCREEN TITLE 'My Application'
```

See Also

DEFINE WINDOW, _SCREEN

MONTH( ) Function

Returns the number of the month for a given Date or DateTime expression.

Syntax

MONTH(*dExpression* | *tExpression*)

Returns

Numeric

Arguments

dExpression

Specifies the Date expression for which you want MONTH( ) to return the month number.

tExpression

Specifies the DateTime expression for which you want MONTH( ) to return the month number.

Remarks

MONTH( ) returns a number from 1 through 12. January is month 1, and December is month 12.

Example

```
CLEAR
? DATE( )  && Displays today's date
? MONTH(DATE( ))  && Displays the month number
STORE {^1998-05-03} TO gdBuy
STORE MONTH(gdBuy + 31) TO gdMonth
? gdMonth  && Displays 6
```

See Also

CMONTH( ), DAY( ), SYS( ) Functions Overview, YEAR( )

MOUSE Command

Performs the equivalent of clicking, double-clicking, or moving the mouse, or performs a drag operation.

Syntax

MOUSE [CLICK | DBLCLICK] [AT *nRow1, nColumn1*]
| DRAG TO *nRow2, nColumn2, nRow3, nColumn3 ...*]

[PIXELS]
[WINDOW *cWindowName*]
[LEFT | MIDDLE | RIGHT]
[SHIFT] [CONTROL] [ALT]

Arguments

CLICK | DBLCLICK

Specifies that the mouse is clicked or double-clicked. If you omit the AT clause, the mouse is clicked or double-clicked at the current mouse pointer position.

AT *nRow1, nColumn1*

Specifies where the mouse is clicked, double-clicked, or the position to which the mouse pointer is moved. If you omit CLICK or DBLCLICK, the mouse pointer is moved to the position specified with *nRow1, nColumn1*.

Unless you specify a WINDOW, the position specified by *nRow1, nColumn1* is relative to the main Microsoft Visual FoxPro window, and the position is determined by the font of the main Visual FoxPro window. Most fonts can be displayed in a wide variety of sizes, and some are proportionally spaced. A row corresponds to the height of the current font; a column corresponds to the average width of a letter in the current font.

You cannot use the AT clause to choose a Visual FoxPro menu title.
Use SYS(1500) – Activate a System Menu Item instead to choose a menu title.

DRAG TO *nRow2, nColumn2, nRow3, nColumn3* ...]

Specifies that the mouse pointer is dragged to a position or a set of positions.

When the mouse pointer is dragged, a mouse button is pressed and held down until the mouse pointer reaches the destination position; then the mouse button is released. If you omit the LEFT, MIDDLE, and RIGHT clauses, the left (primary) mouse button is pressed and held down by default.

The DRAG clause accepts multiple sets of *nRow, nColumn* coordinates, allowing the mouse pointer to be dragged to several positions.

If CLICK or DBLCLICK is included, the mouse is clicked or double-clicked at its current position; then the mouse pointer is dragged to the specified position.

PIXELS

Specifies that the position you include in the AT and DRAG TO clause is in pixels.

If PIXELS is omitted, the position is determined by the font of the main Visual FoxPro window or the window specified with *cWindowName*. Most fonts can be displayed in a wide variety of sizes, and some are proportionally spaced. A row corresponds to the height of the current font; a column corresponds to the average width of a letter in the current font.

WINDOW *cWindowName*

Specifies the window to which the coordinates in the AT and DRAG TO clauses are relative. If you don't include WINDOW and the name of an active window, the coordinates in the AT and DRAG TO clauses are relative to the main Visual FoxPro window.

To specify a system window or a toolbar, enclose the entire system window or toolbar name in quotation marks.

LEFT | MIDDLE | RIGHT

Specifies which mouse button is pressed when the mouse is clicked, double-clicked, or dragged. If you omit the LEFT, MIDDLE, and RIGHT clauses, the MOUSE commands acts as if you had clicked the left (primary) mouse button.

[SHIFT] [CONTROL] [ALT]

Specifies a key that is pressed when the mouse is clicked, double-clicked, or dragged. In Visual FoxPro for Windows, SHIFT specifies the SHIFT key, CONTROL specifies the CTRL key, and ALT specifies the ALT key.

You can specify any combination of SHIFT, CONTROL, and ALT.

Remarks

MOUSE is typically used to automate interactive application testing or to create demonstration programs.

Example

In the following example, the first command clicks the mouse at row and column 3 of the main Visual FoxPro window. The second command clicks the mouse at row and column 3 of the main Visual FoxPro window, and then drags the mouse pointer to the tenth row and column of the main Visual FoxPro window. The third command drags the mouse pointer from its current position to row and column 20. The fourth command double-clicks the mouse at its current position, and then drags the mouse pointer to row and column 30. The last command drags the mouse pointer from its current position to row and column 10, then to row and column 20, and then to row and column 30.

```
MOUSE CLICK AT 3,3
MOUSE CLICK AT 3,3 DRAG TO 10,10
MOUSE DRAG TO 20,20
MOUSE DBLCLICK DRAG TO 30,30
MOUSE DRAG TO 10,10,20,20,30,30
```

See Also

MCOL( ), MDOWN( ), MROW( ), SYS(1500) – Activate a System Menu Item

MouseDown Event

Occurs when the user presses a mouse button.

Syntax

PROCEDURE *Object.*MouseDown
[LPARAMETERS *nIndex, nButton, nShift, nXCoord, nYCoord*]

– or –

LPARAMETERS *nButton, nShift, nXCoord, nYCoord*

Arguments

You must include an **LPARAMETERS** or **PARAMETERS** statement in the event
procedure and specify a name for each parameter. Visual FoxPro passes the MouseDown
event four of five parameters in the following order:

nIndex
Contains a number which uniquely identifies a control if it is in a control array.
The *nIndex* parameter is passed only when the control is part of a control array.

nButton
Contains a number that specifies which button was pressed to trigger the event:
1 (left), 2 (right), or 4 (middle).

nShift
Contains a number specifying the state of modifier keys when the mouse is pressed.
The valid modifier keys are the SHIFT, CTRL, and ALT keys.

The values returned in *nShift* for individual modifier keys are listed in the following
table.

Modifier key values for *nShift*

Windows key	Value
SHIFT	1
CTRL	2
ALT	4

If more than one modifier key is held down when the mouse is pressed, the *nShift*
argument contains the sum of the values for the modifier keys. For example, if the user
holds CTRL while pressing the mouse button, the *nShift* argument contains 2. But if
the user holds CTRL+ALT while pressing the mouse button, the *nShift* argument
contains 6.

nXCoord, nYCoord

> Contains the current horizontal (*nXCoord*) and vertical (*nYCoord*) position of the mouse pointer within the form. These coordinates are expressed in terms of the form's coordinate system in the unit of measurement specified by the *ScaleMode* property of the form.

Remarks

Use a MouseDown procedure to specify actions to occur when a given mouse button is pressed. Unlike the Click and DblClick events, you can use the MouseDown event to distinguish between the left, right, and middle mouse buttons. You can also write code for mouse-keyboard combinations that use the modifier keys.

> **Note**   You can use a MouseMove event to respond to an event caused by moving the mouse. The *nButton* argument for MouseDown and MouseUp differs from the *nButton* argument used for MouseMove. For MouseDown or MouseUp, the *nButton* argument indicates exactly one button per event; for MouseMove, it indicates the current state of all buttons.

Applies To

CheckBox, ComboBox, CommandButton, CommandGroup, Container Object, Control Object, EditBox, Form, Grid, Header, Image, Label, Line, ListBox, OptionButton, OptionGroup, Page, PageFrame, Shape, Spinner, TextBox, ToolBar

See Also

Click Event, DblClick Event, MiddleClick Event, MouseMove Event, MousePointer Property, MouseUp Event, MouseWheel Event

MouseIcon Property

Specifies the mouse pointer icon displayed when the mouse pointer is positioned over an object. Available at design time and run time.

Syntax

Object.MouseIcon[= *cFileName*]

Arguments

cFileName

> Specifies the file that is displayed when the mouse pointer is positioned over the object. You can specify a mouse icon (.ico) file, a mouse cursor (.cur) file, or an animated mouse cursor (.ani) file.

Remarks

To display the mouse icon, set the MousePointer property to 99 (Custom).

Applies To

CheckBox, ComboBox, CommandButton, CommandGroup, Container Object, Control Object, EditBox, Form, Grid, Image, Label, Line, ListBox, OLE Bound Control, OLE Container Control, OptionButton, OptionGroup, _SCREEN, Shape, Spinner, TextBox, ToolBar

See Also

MousePointer Property

MouseMove Event

Occurs when the user moves the mouse over an object.

Syntax

PROCEDURE *Object*.MouseMove, [LPARAMETERS *nIndex*, *nButton*, *nShift*, *nXCoord*, *nYCoord*]

– or –

LPARAMETERS *nButton*, *nShift*, *nXCoord*, *nYCoord*

Arguments

You must include an LPARAMETERS or PARAMETERS statement in the event procedure and specify a name for each parameter. Visual FoxPro passes the MouseMove event four or five parameters in the following order:

nIndex
> Contains a number which uniquely identifies a control if it is in a control array. The *nIndex* parameter is passed only when the control is in a control array.

nButton
> Contains a number that specifies which mouse button was being held down as the mouse was moved, as listed in the following table:

Mouse button values for *nButton*

Windows	*nButton* Value
Left mouse button	1
Right mouse button	2
Middle mouse button	4

If more than one mouse button is held down as the mouse is moved, *nButton* contains the sum of the values for the mouse buttons. For example, if both the left and right mouse buttons are pressed, the value of *nButton* is 3.

nShift

Contains a number specifying the state of modifier keys when the mouse is moved. In Visual FoxPro for Windows, the valid modifier keys are the SHIFT, CTRL, and ALT keys.

The values returned in *nShift* for individual modifier keys are listed in the following table.

Modifier key values for *nShift*

Windows key	Value
SHIFT	1
CTRL	2
ALT	4

If more than one modifier key is held down when the mouse is pressed, the *nShift* argument contains the sum of the values for the modifier keys. For example, in Visual FoxPro for Windows, if the user holds CTRL while pressing the mouse button, the *nShift* argument contains 2. But if the user holds CTRL+ALT while pressing the mouse button, the *nShift* argument contains 6.

nXCoord, nYCoord

Contains the current horizontal (*nXCoord*) and vertical (*nYCoord*) position of the mouse pointer within the form. These coordinates are always expressed in terms of the form's coordinate system, in the unit of measurement specified in the ScaleMode property setting.

The MouseMove event is triggered continually as the mouse pointer moves across objects.

Note You can use MouseDown and MouseUp events to respond to events caused by pressing and releasing mouse buttons.

The *nButton* parameter for MouseMove differs from the *nButton* parameter for MouseDown and MouseUp. For MouseMove, the *nButton* parameter indicates the current state of all buttons; a single MouseMove event can indicate that some, all, or no buttons are pressed. For MouseDown or MouseUp, the *nButton* parameter indicates exactly one button per event.

Avoid moving a window inside a MouseMove event procedure; it can cause cascading events and generate run-time errors, such as a stack overflow. MouseMove events are triggered when the window moves underneath the pointer. A MouseMove event can be triggered even if the mouse is stationary.

Applies To

CheckBox, Column, ComboBox, CommandButton, CommandGroup, Container Object, Control Object, EditBox, Form, Grid, Header, Image, Label, Line, ListBox, OptionButton, OptionGroup, Page, PageFrame, Shape, Spinner, TextBox, ToolBar

See Also

Click Event, DblClick Event, MiddleClick Event, MousePointer Property, MouseDown Event, MouseUp Event, MouseWheel Event

MousePointer Property

Specifies the shape of the mouse pointer when the mouse is over a particular part of an object at run time. Available at design time and run time.

Syntax

Object.MousePointer[= *nType*]

Arguments

nType
    The settings for the MousePointer property are:

Setting	Description
0	(Default) Shape determined by the object.
1	Arrow.
2	Cross. A cross-hair pointer.
3	I-Beam.
4	Icon. A small white square within a black square.
5	Size. A four-pointed arrow pointing north, south, east, west.
6	Size NE SW. A double arrow pointing northeast and southwest.
7	Size NS. A double arrow pointing north and south.
8	Size NW SE. A double arrow pointing northwest and southeast.
9	Size WE. A double arrow pointing west and east.
10	Up Arrow.
11	Hourglass.
12	No Drop.
13	Hide Pointer.
14	Arrow.

Note   When you set the MousePointer property using the property sheet, the drop-down list displays the settings names used in Visual FoxPro for Windows.

Remarks

You can use the MousePointer property to indicate changes in functionality as the mouse pointer passes over controls on a form or dialog box. You can set the MousePointer property to 11 (Hourglass or Wristwatch) to indicate that the user should wait for a process to finish.

Applies To

CheckBox, ComboBox, CommandButton, CommandGroup, Container Object, Control Object, EditBox, Form, Grid, Image, Label, Line, ListBox, OLE Bound Control, OLE Container Control, OptionButton, OptionGroup, _SCREEN, Shape, Spinner, TextBox, ToolBar

See Also

MouseMove Event

MouseUp Event

Occurs when the user releases a mouse button.

Syntax

PROCEDURE *Object*.MouseUp
[LPARAMETERS *nButton, nShift, nXCoord, nYCoord*]

– or –

LPARAMETERS *nIndex, nButton, nShift, nXCoord, nYCoord*

Arguments

You must include an LPARAMETERS or PARAMETERS statement in the event procedure and specify a name for each parameter. Visual FoxPro passes the MouseUp event four of five parameters in the following order.

nIndex
    Contains a number which uniquely identifies a control if it's in a control array.

nButton
    In Visual FoxPro for Windows, contains a number that specifies which button was released to trigger the event: 1 (left), 2 (right), or 4 (middle).

nShift
    Contains a number specifying the state of modifier keys when the mouse is released. In Visual FoxPro for Windows, the valid modifier keys are the SHIFT, CTRL, and ALT keys.

The values returned in *nShift* for individual modifier keys are listed in the following table.

Modifier key values for *nShift*

Windows key	Value
SHIFT	1
CTRL	2
ALT	4

If more than one modifier key is held down when the mouse is released, the *nShift* argument contains the sum of the values for the modifier keys. For example, in Visual FoxPro for Windows, if the user holds CTRL while releasing the mouse button, the *nShift* argument contains 2. But if the user holds CTRL+ALT while releasing the mouse button, the *nShift* argument contains 6.

nXCoord, nYCoord

Contains the current horizontal (*nXCoord*) and vertical (*nYCoord*) position of the mouse pointer within the form. These coordinates are always expressed in terms of the form's coordinate system in the unit of measurement specified by the *ScaleMode* property of the form.

Remarks

Use a MouseUp procedure to specify actions to occur when a given mouse button is released. Unlike the Click and DblClick events, the MouseUp event allows you to distinguish between the left, right, and middle mouse buttons. You can also write code for mouse-keyboard combinations that use the modifier keys.

You can use a MouseMove procedure to respond to an event caused by moving the mouse.

Note The *nButton* argument for MouseDown and MouseUp differs from the *nButton* argument used for MouseMove. For MouseDown or MouseUp, the *nButton* argument indicates exactly one button per event; for MouseMove, it indicates the current state of all buttons.

Applies To

CheckBox, ComboBox, CommandButton, CommandGroup, Container Object, Control Object, EditBox, Form, Grid, Header, Image, Label, Line, ListBox, OptionButton, OptionGroup, Page, PageFrame, Shape, Spinner, TextBox, ToolBar

See Also

Click Event, DblClick Event, MiddleClick Event, MouseDown Event, MouseMove Event, MousePointer Property, MouseWheel Event, ScaleMode Property

MouseWheel Event

Occurs when the user rotates the mouse wheel on a mouse device that has a wheel.

Syntax

PROCEDURE *Object.*MouseWheel
LPARAMETERS [*nIndex,*] *nDirection, nShift, nXCoord, nYCoord*

Arguments

You must include an LPARAMETERS or PARAMETERS statement in the event procedure and specify a name for each parameter. Visual FoxPro passes the MouseWheel event four or five parameters in the following order.

nIndex

Contains a number which uniquely identifies a control if it is in a control array. The *nIndex* parameter is passed only when the control is in a control array.

nDirection

Contains a mouse device dependent number that indicates the direction the mouse wheel is rotated. A negative value indicates the mouse wheel is rotated backwards; a positive value indicates the mouse wheel is rotated forwards.

nShift

Contains a number specifying the state of modifier keys when the mouse wheel is rotated. The valid modifier keys are the SHIFT, CTRL, and ALT keys.

The values returned in *nShift* for individual modifier keys are listed in the following table.

Value	Key
1	SHIFT
2	CTRL
4	ALT

If more than one modifier key is held down when the mouse wheel is rotated, the *nShift* argument contains the sum of the values for the modifier keys. For example, if the user holds CTRL while rotating the mouse wheel, the *nShift* argument contains 2. But if the user holds CTRL+ALT while rotating the mouse wheel, the *nShift* argument contains 6.

nXCoord, nYCoord

Contains the current horizontal (*nXCoord*) and vertical (*nYCoord*) position of the mouse pointer within the form. These coordinates are always expressed in terms of the form's coordinate system, in the unit of measurement specified in the ScaleMode property setting.

Applies To

CheckBox, Column, ComboBox, CommandButton, CommandGroup, Container Object, Control Object, EditBox, Form, Grid, Header, Image, Label, Line, ListBox, OptionButton, OptionGroup, Page, PageFrame, Shape, Spinner, TextBox, ToolBar

See Also

Click Event, MiddleClick Event, MousePointer Property, MouseDown Event, MouseUp Event

Movable Property

Specifies whether an object can be moved at run time by the user. Available at design time; read-only at run time.

Syntax

Object.Movable[= *lExpr*]

Arguments

lExpr

The settings for the Movable property are:

Setting	Description
True (.T.)	(Default) The object can be moved. For forms in Visual FoxPro for Windows, the Move command is added to the Control menu.
False (.F.)	The object cannot be moved. For grid columns, you cannot move the column by direct manipulation. However, the column can be moved if you change the column's ColumnOrder property or move another column on top of it.

Applies To

Column, Form, _SCREEN, ToolBar

See Also

Sizable Property

Move Method

Moves an object.

Syntax

Object.Move (*nLeft* [, *nTop* [, *nWidth* [, *nHeight*]]])

Arguments

nLeft
> Specifies the horizontal coordinate for the left edge of the object. *nLeft* is a single-precision value.

nTop
> Specifies the vertical coordinate for the top edge of the object. *nTop* is a single-precision value.

nWidth
> Specifies the new width of the object. *nWidth* is a single-precision value.

nHeight
> Specifies the new height of the object. *nHeight* is a single-precision value.

Remarks

Only the *nLeft* argument is required. However, to include any other arguments, you must also include all arguments in the syntax before the argument you want to include. For example, you cannot specify *nWidth* without specifying *nLeft* and *nTop*. Any trailing arguments that are unspecified remain unchanged.

Moving a Form on the screen or moving a control on a form is always relative to the origin (0,0), which is the upper-left corner. When moving controls in a container, the coordinate system of the container is used.

Applies To

CheckBox, ComboBox, CommandButton, CommandGroup, Container Object, Control Object, EditBox, Form, Grid, Image, Label, Line, ListBox, OLE Bound Control, OLE Container Control, OptionButton, OptionGroup, PageFrame, _SCREEN, Shape, Spinner, TextBox, ToolBar

See Also

Top Property, Width Property

MOVE POPUP Command

Moves a user-defined menu created with DEFINE POPUP to a new location.

Syntax

MOVE POPUP *MenuName* TO *nRow1*, *nColumn1* | BY *nRow2*, *nColumn2*

Arguments

MenuName

Specifies the menu to move.

In Visual FoxPro, you cannot move the system menu.

TO *nRow1*, *nColumn1*

Moves the menu to a location, specified by *nRow1*, *nColumn1*, in a user-defined window or in the main Visual FoxPro window.

BY *nRow2*, *nColumn2*

Moves the menu to a location relative to its current position. *nRow2* specifies the number of rows to move the menu (down if *nRow2* is positive, up if negative). The numeric expression *nColumn2* specifies the number of columns to move the menu (to the right if *nColumn2* is positive, to the left if negative).

Remarks

A menu can be moved to a specific position or relative to its current position. If a menu has been defined, it can be moved; it doesn't have to be active or visible.

Example

The following example defines and activates a menu, then moves and changes its size.

```
CLOSE DATABASE
CLEAR
DEFINE POPUP popMovIn FROM 2,2 TO 7, 14 PROMPT FILES LIKE *.PRG ;
   TITLE 'Programs'
ACTIVATE POPUP popMovIn NOWAIT
=CHRSAW(2)
MOVE POPUP popMovIn BY 5,5        && Move menu down
=CHRSAW(2)
SIZE POPUP popMovIn BY 5,5        && Enlarge the menu
=CHRSAW(2)
SIZE POPUP popMovIn BY -5,-5      && Shrink the menu
=CHRSAW(2)
MOVE POPUP popMovIn BY -5,-5      && Move menu up
=CHRSAW(2)
DEACTIVATE POPUP popMovIn
RELEASE POPUP popMovIn
```

See Also

ACTIVATE POPUP, DEFINE POPUP, SIZE POPUP

MOVE WINDOW Command

Moves a user-defined window created with DEFINE WINDOW, or a Visual FoxPro system window (such as the Command window or Browse window) to a new location.

Syntax

MOVE WINDOW *WindowName* TO *nRow1, nColumn1*
    | BY *nRow2, nColumn2* | CENTER

Arguments

WindowName
    Specifies the name of the window to move.

TO *nRow1, nColumn1*
    Moves the window to a location, specified by *nRow1, nColumn1*, in the main Visual FoxPro window or in a user-defined window.

BY *nRow2, nColumn2*
    Moves a window to a location relative to its current position. The numeric expression *nRow2* specifies the number of rows to move the window (down if *nRow2* is positive, up if negative). The numeric expression *nColumn2* specifies the number of columns to move the window (to the right if *nColumn2* is positive, to the left if negative).

CENTER
    Centers a window in the main Visual FoxPro window or in its parent window.

Remarks

A window can be moved to a specific position or relative to its current position. If a window is defined, it can be moved; it doesn't have to be active or visible.

To move a system window and or a toolbar (in Visual FoxPro), enclose the entire system window or toolbar name in quotation marks. For example, to move the Report Controls toolbar (when it isn't docked) in Visual FoxPro, issue the following command:

```
MOVE WINDOW "Report Controls" BY 1,1
```

Example

In the following example, after the window named wEnter is defined and activated, the window is moved.

```
DEFINE WINDOW wEnter FROM 10,4 TO 15,54 SYSTEM ;
    TITLE "Nomadic Window"
ACTIVATE WINDOW wEnter
WAIT WINDOW 'Press any key to move the window'
```

```
MOVE WINDOW wEnter TO 20,15
WAIT WINDOW 'Press any key to center the window'
MOVE WINDOW wEnter CENTER
WAIT WINDOW 'Press any key to release the window'
RELEASE WINDOW wEnter
```

See Also

ACTIVATE WINDOW

Moved Event

Occurs when an object is moved to a new position or a container object's Top or Left property settings have been changed programmatically.

Syntax

PROCEDURE *Object*.Moved

Remarks

Occurs when an object is moved to a new position or when the settings for the Top or Left properties have been changed in code.

Applies To

Column, Container Object, Control Object, Form, Grid, OLE Bound Control, OLE Container Control, PageFrame, ToolBar

See Also

ColumnOrder Property, Left Property, Top Property

MoverBars Property

Specifies whether mover bars are displayed on a ListBox control. Available at design time; read/write at run time.

Syntax

ListBox.MoverBars[= *lExpr*]

Arguments

lExpr
    The settings for the MoverBars property are:

Setting	Description
True (.T.)	Mover bars are displayed. Users can interactively re-order the contents of the control.
False (.F.)	(Default) Mover bars are not displayed.

Remarks

The MoverBars property is only available if the RowSourceType property is set to 0 (None) or 1 (Value).

Applies To

ListBox

See Also

RowSourceType Property, ScrollBars Property

MRKBAR( ) Function

Determines whether a menu item on a user-defined or Microsoft Visual FoxPro system menu is marked.

Syntax

MRKBAR(*cMenuName*, *nMenuItemNumber* | *cSystemMenuItemName*)

Returns

Logical

Arguments

cMenuName

Specifies the name of the menu containing the menu item. The menu can be a Visual FoxPro system menu (such as _MFILE, MEDIT, or _MDATA).

nMenuItemNumber

Specifies the number of a menu item in a user-defined menu. A menu item's number is specified when the menu item is created with DEFINE BAR.

cSystemMenuItemName

Specifies the name of a Visual FoxPro system menu item. For example, the following command displays a logical value specifying if the New menu item on the File menu is marked.

```
? MRKBAR('_MFILE', _MFI_NEW)
```

Remarks

Use SET MARK OF to mark or unmark a menu item.

If the specified menu item is marked, MRKBAR( ) returns true (.T.); otherwise, MRKBAR( ) returns false (.F.).

For an example of using MRKBAR( ), see the CNTBAR( ) Function, earlier in this language reference.

See Also

MRKPAD( ), SET MARK OF, SET MARK TO

MRKPAD( ) Function

Determines whether a menu title on a user-defined menu bar or on the Visual FoxPro system menu bar is marked.

Syntax

MRKPAD(*cMenuBarName*, *cMenuTitleName*)

Returns

Logical

Arguments

cMenuBarName
>   Specifies the name of the menu bar containing the menu title.

cMenuTitleName
>   Specifies the name of the menu title.

Remarks

Use SET MARK OF to mark or unmark a menu title.

If the specified menu title is marked, MRKPAD( ) returns true (.T.); otherwise, MRKPAD( ) returns false (.F.).

Example

The following program example, named MARKPAD.PRG, uses MRKPAD( ) to toggle the mark character of a menu title when you choose it.

The current system menu bar is first saved to memory with SET SYSMENU SAVE, and all the system menu items are removed with SET SYSMENU TO.

Several system menu items are created with DEFINE PAD. When you choose a menu item, the `choice` procedure is executed. `choice` displays the name of the menu item you choose and the name of the menu bar. SET MARK OF is used with MRKPAD( ) to display or remove the menu item's mark character. If you choose the Exit menu, the original Visual FoxPro system menu is restored.

```
*** Name this program MARKPAD.PRG ***
CLEAR
SET SYSMENU SAVE
SET SYSMENU TO
SET MARK OF MENU _MSYSMENU TO CHR(4)
PUBLIC glMarkPad
glMarkPad = .T.
```

```
DEFINE PAD padSys OF _MSYSMENU PROMPT '\<System'  COLOR SCHEME 3 ;
   KEY ALT+S, ''
DEFINE PAD padEdit OF _MSYSMENU PROMPT '\<Edit'  COLOR SCHEME 3 ;
   KEY ALT+E, ''
DEFINE PAD padRecord OF _MSYSMENU PROMPT '\<Record'  COLOR SCHEME 3 ;
   KEY ALT+R, ''
DEFINE PAD padWindow OF _MSYSMENU PROMPT '\<Window'  COLOR SCHEME 3 KEY ALT+W, ''
DEFINE PAD padReport OF _MSYSMENU PROMPT 'Re\<ports' COLOR SCHEME 3 ;
   KEY ALT+P, ''
DEFINE PAD padExit OF _MSYSMENU PROMPT 'E\<xit'  COLOR SCHEME 3 ;
   KEY ALT+X, ''
ON SELECTION MENU _MSYSMENU ;
   DO choice IN markpad WITH PAD( ), MENU( )

PROCEDURE choice
PARAMETER gcPad, gcMenu
WAIT WINDOW 'You chose ' + gcPad + ;
   ' from menu ' + gcMenu NOWAIT
SET MARK OF PAD (gcPad) OF _MSYSMENU TO ;
   ! MRKPAD('_MSYSMENU', gcPad)
glMarkPad= ! glMarkPad
IF gcPad = 'PADEXIT'
   SET SYSMENU TO DEFAULT
ENDIF
```

See Also

MRKBAR( ), SET MARK OF

MROW( ) Function

Returns the row position of the mouse pointer in the main Visual FoxPro window or in a user-defined window.

Syntax

MROW([*cWindowName* [, *nScaleMode*]])

Returns

Numeric

Arguments

cWindowName
> Specifies the name of a window whose mouse-pointer row position MROW( ) returns.

nScaleMode

Specifies the unit of measurement for the value MROW( ) returns. The settings for *nScaleMode* are:

nScaleMode	Description
0	(Default) Foxels. A foxel is equivalent to the average height and width of a character based on the current font of the form in which an object is contained. Foxels are useful in developing cross-platform applications for character-based and graphical platforms.
3	Pixels. A pixel is the smallest element that can be displayed on a screen or printer. Pixels are screen-dependent.

Remarks

MROW( ) returns the main Visual FoxPro window row position of the mouse pointer if there is no active user-defined window and you omit the optional argument.

MROW( ) returns the mouse-pointer row coordinate relative to the active user-defined window if there is an active user-defined window and you omit the optional argument. MROW( ) returns a value of –1 if the mouse pointer is positioned outside the user-defined window or if no mouse driver is loaded and there is no output window.

See Also

AMOUSEOBJ( ), COL( ), GridHitTest Method, ISMOUSE( ), MCOL( ), ROW( ), WCOLS( ), WROWS( )

MTON( ) Function

Returns a Numeric value from a Currency expression.

Syntax

MTON(*mExpression*)

Returns

Numeric

Arguments

mExpression

Specifies a Currency expression whose value MTON( ) returns. *mExpression* must evaluate to a valid Currency value or Visual FoxPro generates an error.

Currency values are created by placing a dollar sign ($) prefix immediately before a Numeric value.

Remarks

MTON( ) returns a Numeric value with four decimal places.

Example

The following example creates a currency type variable named gyMoney. TYPE( ) displays Y, indicating the variable is a currency type. MTON( ) is used to convert the variable to a numeric type, and TYPE( ) now displays N, indicating the variable is a numeric type after the conversion.

```
STORE $24.95 TO gyMoney  && Creates a currency type memory variable
CLEAR
? "gyMoney is type: "
?? TYPE('gyMoney')  && Displays Y, currency type value

gyMoney = MTON(gyMoney)     && Converts gyMoney to a numeric value
? "gyMoney is now type: "
?? TYPE('gyMoney')  && Displays N, numeric type value
```

See Also

NTOM( )

MultiSelect Property

Specifies whether a user can make multiple selections in a ListBox control and how the multiple selections can be made. Available at design time; read/write at run time.

Syntax

ListBox.MultiSelect[= *nChoice*]

Arguments

nChoice
The settings for the MultiSelect property are:

Setting	Description
0	(Default) Multiple selection isn't allowed.
1	Multiple selection is allowed. To select multiple items in a ListBox control, hold the CTRL key down while clicking the items.

Remarks

Set MultiSelect to true (.T.) to enable a user to select multiple items in a list. You can use the Selected property to determine which items are selected.

Example

The following example creates a ListBox. The MultiSelect property for the list box is set to true (.T.), allowing you to make multiple selections from the list box. The source of the items that appear in the list box items is an array; the array is specified with the RowSourceType and RowSource properties.

The ListCount property is used within a FOR ... ENDFOR loop to display the item or items you choose in the list box. The Selected property is used to determine the items you chose, and the List property is used to return the items.

```
CLEAR

DIMENSION gaMyListArray(10)
FOR gnCount = 1 to 10  && Fill the array with letters
    STORE REPLICATE(CHR(gnCount+64),6) TO gaMyListArray(gnCount)
ENDFOR

frmMyForm = CREATEOBJECT('Form')  && Create a Form
frmMyForm.Closable = .f.  && Disable the Control menu box

frmMyForm.Move(150,10)  && Move the form

frmMyForm.AddObject('cmbCommand1','cmdMyCmdBtn')  && Add "Quit" Command button
frmMyForm.AddObject('lstListBox1','lstMyListBox')  && Add ListBox control

frmMyForm.lstListBox1.RowSourceType = 5  && Specifies an array
frmMyForm.lstListBox1.RowSource = 'gaMyListArray' && Array containing listbox items

frmMyForm.cmbCommand1.Visible =.T.  && "Quit" Command button visible
frmMyForm.lstListBox1.Visible =.T.  && "List Box visible

frmMyForm.SHOW  && Display the form
READ EVENTS  && Start event processing

DEFINE CLASS cmdMyCmdBtn AS CommandButton  && Create Command button
    Caption = '\<Quit'  && Caption on the Command button
    Cancel = .T.  && Default Cancel Command button (Esc)
    Left = 125  && Command button column
    Top = 210  && Command button row
    Height = 25  && Command button height

    PROCEDURE Click
        CLEAR EVENTS  && Stop event processing, close Form
        CLEAR  && Clear main Visual FoxPro window
ENDDEFINE

DEFINE CLASS lstMyListBox AS ListBox  && Create ListBox control
    Left = 10  && List Box column
    Top = 10  && List Box row
    MultiSelect = .T.  && Allow selecting more than 1 item
```

```
PROCEDURE Click
   ACTIVATE SCREEN
   CLEAR
   ? "Selected items:"
   ? "---------------"
   FOR nCnt = 1 TO ThisForm.lstListBox1.ListCount
      IF ThisForm.lstListBox1.Selected(nCnt)  && Is item selected?
         ? SPACE(5) + ThisForm.lstListBox1.List(nCnt) && Show item
      ENDIF
   ENDFOR

ENDDEFINE
```

Applies To

ListBox

See Also

AddItem Method, Clear Method, List Property, ListCount Property, NewItemID Property, RemoveItem Method, Selected Property, TopItemID Property

MWINDOW( ) Function

Returns the name of the window over which the mouse pointer is positioned.

Syntax

MWINDOW([*cWindowName*])

Returns

Character, Logical

Arguments

cWindowName
   Specifies a window name. If the mouse pointer is positioned over the specified window, MWINDOW( ) returns true (.T.); otherwise, MWINDOW( ) returns false (.F.).

Remarks

If you omit the optional window name, MWINDOW( ) returns the name of the window over which the mouse pointer is positioned, or an empty string if the mouse pointer is positioned over the main Visual FoxPro window or over any other window that is not part of Visual FoxPro.

See Also

MCOL( ), MDOWN( ), MROW( ), WONTOP( ), WOUTPUT( )

Name Property

Specifies the name used to reference an object in code. Available at design time; read/write at run time.

Syntax

Object.Name[= *cName*]

Arguments

cName
Specifies the name used to reference the object in code.

Remarks

The default name for new objects is the type of object plus a unique integer. For example, the first new Form object is Form1, and the third text box you create on a Form is Text3.

> **Note** If the object is the first object in the object hierarchy (that is, the outermost container object), use the object variable to reference the object instead of the Name property.

For a Project object, the Name property contains the name and path to the project, and is read-only at design time and run time.

For a File object, the Name property contains the name and path to the file, and is read-only at design time and run time.

Applies To

ActiveDoc Object, CheckBox, Column, ComboBox, CommandButton, CommandGroup, Container Object, Control Object, Cursor, Custom, DataEnvironment, EditBox, File Object, Form, FormSet, Grid, Header, Image, Label, Line, ListBox, OLE Bound Control, OLE Container Control, OptionButton, OptionGroup, Page, PageFrame, Project Object, ProjectHook Object, Relation, _SCREEN, Shape, Spinner, TextBox, Timer, ToolBar

See Also

Caption Property, NewIndex Property, NewItemID Property, ServerName Property, TypeLibName Property

NavigateTo Method

Navigates in an Active Document container to a specified location.

Syntax

Object.NavigateTo(*cTarget* [, *cLocation* [, *cFrame*]])

Arguments

cTarget
> Specifies the URL to navigate to. *cTarget* can be a URL or a document supported by the Active Document container such as Microsoft Internet Explorer. The NavigateTo method isn't executed if *cTarget* is not supported by the Active Document container.

cLocation
> Specifies a location to navigate to within the URL or document specified with *cTarget*.

cFrame
> Specifies a frame to navigate to within the URL or document specified with *cTarget*.

Remarks

If the NavigateTo method is executed in a hosted Visual FoxPro Active Document, the Active Document host navigates to the specified location.

If the NavigateTo method is executed outside of a hosted Visual FoxPro Active Document, then the application that is registered as supporting Active Documents (such as Microsoft Internet Explorer) is started. For example, if you execute the NavigateTo method from the Command window or a Visual FoxPro program (.prg), your registered Active Document container is started and it navigates to the specified location.

Note that a new instance of your registered Active Document container is started each time you execute the NavigateTo method outside of a hosted Visual FoxPro Active Document. Use the Hyperlink Button Foundation Class to navigate to a URL from a Visual FoxPro application without starting a new instance of your registered Active Document container.

Applies To

Hyperlink Object

See Also

GoBack Method, GoFoward Method

NDX( ) Function

Returns the name of an open index (.IDX) file for the current or specified table.

Syntax

NDX(*nIndexNumber* [, *nWorkArea* | *cTableAlias*])

Returns

Character

Arguments

nIndexNumber
> Specifies which .idx file name to return. USE and SET INDEX both support an index file list that lets you open .idx files for a table. The order of the file names

in this index file list determines which .idx file name NDX( ) returns. For example, if *nIndexNumber* is 1, NDX( ) returns the name of the first .idx file in the index file list; if *nIndexNumber* is 2, NDX( ) returns the second .idx file name, and so on. NDX( ) ignores names of compound index (.cdx) files in the index file list.

NDX( ) returns an empty string if *nIndexNumber* is greater than the number of .idx files in the index file list.

nWorkArea

Specifies the work area number for .IDX files open in a work area other than the current one. NDX( ) returns an empty string if no table is open in the work area you specify. If you omit *nWorkArea*, NDX( ) returns the names of .idx files open with the table in the current work area.

cTableAlias

Specifies the table alias for .idx files open in a work area other than the current one. If no table has the alias you include, Visual FoxPro generates an error message. If you omit *cTableAlias*, NDX( ) returns the names of .idx files open with the table in the current work area.

Remarks

The CDX( ) and MDX( ) functions can be used to return the names of open compound (.cdx) index files.

In Visual FoxPro for Windows, when SET FULLPATH is ON, NDX( ) returns the path to the .idx file with the .idx file name. When SET FULLPATH is OFF, NDX( ) returns the drive the .idx file resides on with the .idx file name.

See Also

CDX( ), INDEX, MDX( ), SET FULLPATH, SET INDEX, SYS(14) – Index Expression, TAG( ), USE

NewIndex Property

Specifies the index of the item most recently added to a ComboBox or ListBox control. Not available at design time; read-only at run time.

Syntax

Control.NewIndex

Remarks

The NewIndex property is especially useful when adding items to a sorted list.

Applies To

ComboBox, ListBox

See Also

Caption Property, NewItemID Property, Name Property

NewItemID Property

Specifies the item ID of the item most recently added to a ComboBox or ListBox control. Not available at design time; read-only at run time.

Syntax

[*Form.*]*Control*.NewItemID

Remarks

For more information about the differences between using an item ID or an index, see "AddItem Method" or "AddListItem Method," earlier in this language reference.

Applies To

ComboBox, ListBox

See Also

AddItem Method, AddListItem Method, Clear Method, ItemData Property, List Property, ListCount Property, MultiSelect Property, NewIndex Property, RemoveItem Method, Selected Property, TopItemID Property

NEWOBJECT( ) Function

Creates a new class or object directly from a .vcx visual class library or program.

Syntax

NEWOBJECT(*cClassName* [, *cModule* [, *cInApplication*
    [, *eParameter1, eParameter2, ...*]]])

Returns

Object

Arguments

cClassName

Specifies the class or object from which the new class or object is created.

OLE objects are created with the following syntax for *cClassName*:

ApplicationName.Class

For example, to create a Microsoft Excel worksheet (which supports Automation), you can use the following syntax:

oExcelSheet = NEWOBJECT('Excel.Sheet')

cModule

Specifies a .vcx visual class library or Visual FoxPro program (.prg, .mpr, .app, .exe, and so on) containing the class or object specified with *cClassName*. The default is a .vcx visual class library; you must include an extension if you specify a program.

> **Note** A class library can have an alias. To specify a class or object from a class library with an alias, include the class library alias followed by a period and the object name.

If *cModule* is omitted, or is the empty string or the null value, Visual FoxPro searches for the class or object in the following order:

1. Visual FoxPro base classes.

2. User-defined class definitions in memory in the order they were loaded.

3. Classes in the current program.

4. Class libraries opened with SET CLASSLIB.

5. Classes in procedure files opened with SET PROCEDURE.

6. Classes in the Visual FoxPro program execution chain.

7. The OLE registry if SET OLEOBJECT is ON.

cInApplication

Specifies the Visual FoxPro application (.exe, or .app) containing the .vcx visual class library you specify with *cClassLibName*. You must include an extension for the application. *CInApplication* is ignored if *cModule* is omitted, or if *cInApplication* is the empty string or the null value.

eParameter1, eParameter2, ...

Specifies optional parameters that are passed to the Init event procedure for the class or object.

Remarks

NEWOBJECT( ) allows you to create a new class or object without opening a .vcx visual class library or procedure file.

Use = or STORE to assign the object reference returned by NEWOBJECT( ) to a variable or array element. If an object assigned to a variable or array element is released, the variable or array element contains the null value. Use RELEASE to remove the variable or array element from memory.

See Also

Class Designer, CREATE CLASS, CREATE CLASSLIB, CREATEOBJECT( ), DEFINE CLASS, NewObject Method

NewObject Method

Adds a new class or object to an object directly from a .vcx visual class library or program.

Syntax

Object.NEWOBJECT(*cObjectName*, *cClassName* [, *cModule* [, *cInApplication*
[, *eParameter1*, *eParameter2*, ...]]])

cObjectName
Specifies the name used to reference the newly added class or object.

cClassName
Specifies the class or object from which the new class or object is added.

cModule
Specifies a .vcx visual class library or Visual FoxPro program (.prg, .mpr, .app, .exe, and so on) containing the class or object specified with *cClassName*. The default is a .vcx visual class library; you must include an extension if you specify a program.

> **Note** A class library can have an alias. To specify a class or object from a class library with an alias, include the class library alias followed by a period and the object name.

If *cModule* is omitted, or is the empty string or the null value, Visual FoxPro searches for the class or object in the following order:

1. Visual FoxPro base classes.

2. User-defined class definitions in memory in the order they were loaded.

3. Classes in the current program.

4. Class libraries opened with SET CLASSLIB.

5. Classes in procedure files opened with SET PROCEDURE.

6. Classes in the Visual FoxPro program execution chain.

7. The OLE registry if SET OLEOBJECT is ON.

cInApplication
Specifies the Visual FoxPro application (.exe or .app) containing the .vcx visual class library you specify with *cClassLibName*. You must include an extension for the application. *CInApplication* is ignored if *cModule* is omitted, or if *cInApplication* is the empty string or the null value.

eParameter1, *eParameter2*, ...
Specifies optional parameters that are passed to the Init event procedure for the class or object.

Remarks

The NEWOBJECT method allows you to add a new class or object to an object without opening a .vcx visual class library or procedure file.

Applies To

Column, CommandGroup, Container Object, Custom, DataEnvironment, Form, FormSet, Grid, OptionGroup, Page, PageFrame, _SCREEN, ToolBar

See Also

AddProperty Method, Class Designer, CREATE CLASS, CREATE CLASSLIB, CREATEOBJECT( ), DEFINE CLASS, NEWOBJECT( )

NoDataOnLoad Property

Causes the view associated with a Cursor to activate without downloading data. Available at design time; read/write at run time.

Syntax

DataEnvironment.Cursor.NoDataOnLoad[= *lExpr*]

Arguments

lExpr
> The settings for the NoDataOnLoad property are:

Setting	Description
True (.T.)	The view associated with the Cursor is opened without downloading data.
False (.F.)	(Default) The view associated with the Cursor is opened with data.

Remarks

> **Note** When the Cursor object is accessed using CURSORSETPROP( ), the NoDataOnLoad property is read-only at run time.

Use the NoDataOnLoad property to ensure that the FormSet or Form associated with the view loads quickly (it can be time-consuming to download data from a backend server). You can use REQUERY( ) in conjunction with NoDataOnLoad to download data into the active view once the Form is loaded.

The NoDataOnLoad property mimics the behavior of the NODATA clause of USE.

Applies To

Cursor

See Also

REQUERY( ), USE

NORMALIZE( ) Function

Converts a character expression, supplied by a user, into a form that can be compared with Visual FoxPro function return values.

Syntax

NORMALIZE(*cExpression*)

Returns

Character

Arguments

cExpression
    Specifies the character expression to normalize.

Remarks

NORMALIZE( ) returns a character string from the character expression *cExpression* with the following changes:

- The character expression is converted to uppercase. However, embedded strings are not changed. An example of an embedded string is "Hello" in the character expression "LEFT('Hello',1)."

- Any abbreviated Visual FoxPro keywords in the character expression are expanded to their full length.

- Any –> operators separating aliases from field names are converted to periods.

- The syntax of any Visual FoxPro commands or functions within the character expression is checked, although the expression is not evaluated. If the syntax is incorrect, Visual FoxPro generates a syntax error. NORMALIZE( ) does not check for the existence of any fields, tables, memory variables, user-defined functions, or other references in the character expression.

For example, a user may enter an index expression like the following in the Expression Builder:

```
UPPE(cust->lname) + UPPE(cust->fname)
```

While this is a valid Visual FoxPro index key expression, it's difficult to compare this to the return values from a Visual FoxPro function like KEY( ). NORMALIZE( ) returns the following character string for the expression above:

```
UPPER(CUST.LNAME) + UPPER(CUST.FNAME)
```

This can be easily compared to the value returned by a function like KEY( ), allowing you, in this example, to determine if an index or index tag with the user-supplied index expression already exists.

See Also

EVALUATE( ), ISUPPER( ), PROPER( ), UPPER( )

NOTE Command

Indicates the beginning of a nonexecuting comment line in a program file.

Syntax

NOTE [*Comments*]

Arguments

Comments
    Specifies the comment.

Remarks

Place a semicolon (;) at the end of each comment line that continues on a following line.

Example

```
NOTE  Initialize the page number;
   variable.
STORE 1 to gnPageNum
* Set up the loop
DO WHILE gnPageNum <= 25  && loop 25 times
   gnPageNum = gnPageNum + 1
ENDDO  && DO WHILE gnPageNum <= 25
```

See Also

&&, *, MODIFY COMMAND, MODIFY FILE

NTOM( ) Function

Returns a Currency value with four decimal places from a numeric expression.

Syntax

NTOM(*nExpression*)

Returns

Currency

Arguments

nExpression

Specifies a numeric expression whose Currency value NTOM( ) returns. If
nExpression has more than four decimal places, it is rounded to four decimal places.
If *nExpression* has less than four decimals places, it is padded with zeros until four
decimal places are created.

Example

The following example creates a numeric type variable named gnNumeric. TYPE( )
displays N, indicating the variable is a numeric type. NTOM( ) is used to convert the
variable to a currency type, and TYPE( ) now displays Y, indicating the variable is a
currency type after the conversion.

```
STORE 24.95 TO gnNumeric  && Creates a numeric type memory variable
CLEAR
? "gnNumeric is type: "
?? TYPE('gnNumeric')  && Displays N, numeric type value

gnNumeric= NTOM(gnNumeric)     && Converts gnNumeric to a currency value
? "gnNumeric is now type: "
?? TYPE('gnNumeric')  && Displays Y, currency type value
```

See Also

MTON( )

NullDisplay Property

Specifies the text that is displayed to indicate null values. Available at design time and
run time.

Syntax

Object.NullDisplay[= *cNullText*]

Arguments

cNullText

Specifies the text that is displayed for null values. .NULL. is the default value.

Remarks

This property changes the null display for individual objects only. To change null display
for all objects, use SET NULLDISPLAY.

Applies To

ComboBox, EditBox, ListBox, Spinner, TextBox

See Also

CREATE TABLE – SQL, SET NULLDISPLAY

NumberOfElements Property

Specifies how many items in an array are used to fill the list portion of a ComboBox or ListBox control. Available at design time and run time.

Syntax

[*Form.*]*Control.*NumberOfElements[= *nTotal*]

Arguments

nTotal
 Specifies the number of elements that a list can contain.

Remarks

Available only when the ListSourceType property is set to 5 (Array) and the ColumnCount property is set to 1.

NumberOfElements is useful to limit the number of elements in an array that are displayed in a list. The number of elements used for the list begins with the FirstElement property setting and includes the number of elements specified in the NumberOfElements property setting.

Applies To

ComboBox, ListBox

See Also

FirstElement Property

NUMLOCK( ) Function

Returns the current mode of the NUM LOCK key or sets the mode of the NUM LOCK key on or off.

Syntax

NUMLOCK([*lExpression*])

Returns

Logical

Arguments

lExpression
 Turns the NUM LOCK key on or off. If *lExpression* is true (.T.), the NUM LOCK key is turned on; if *lExpression* is false (.F.), the NUM LOCK key is turned off. NUMLOCK( ) returns a logical value corresponding to the NUM LOCK key setting before NUMLOCK(.T.) or NUMLOCK(.F.) is issued.

Remarks

NUMLOCK( ) returns true (.T.) if the NUM LOCK key is on (pressing a key on the numeric keypad returns a number), or false (.F.) if NUM LOCK is off (pressing a key on the numeric keypad moves the cursor).

Example

In the following example, the equal sign (=) is used to execute NUMLOCK( ) without returning a value.

```
gcOldLock = NUMLOCK( )  && Save original setting
WAIT WINDOW 'Press a key to turn Num Lock on'
= NUMLOCK(.T.)  && Turn Num Lock on
WAIT WINDOW 'Press a key to turn Num Lock off'
= NUMLOCK(!NUMLOCK( ))  && Toggle Num Lock to the opposite value
WAIT WINDOW 'Press a key to restore original Num Lock setting'
= NUMLOCK(gcOldLock)     && Return to original setting
```

See Also

CAPSLOCK( ), INSMODE( )

NVL( ) Function

Returns a non-null value from two expressions.

Syntax

NVL(*eExpression1*, *eExpression2*)

Returns

Character, Date, DateTime, Numeric, Currency, Logical, or the null value

Arguments

eExpression1, *eExpression2*
> NVL( ) returns *eExpression2* if *eExpression1* evaluates to a null value. NVL( ) returns *eExpression1* if *eExpression1* is not a null value. *eExpression1* and *eExpression2* may be any data type. NVL( ) returns .NULL. if both *eExpression1* and *eExpression2* both evaluate to the null value.

Remarks

Use NVL( ) to remove null values from calculations or operations where null values are not supported or are not relevant.

Example

The following example creates a memory variable named glMyNull that contains the null value. NVL( ) is used to return a non-null value from glMyNull and another expression.

```
STORE .NULL. TO glMyNull  && A memory variable containing the null value
CLEAR
? NVL(.T., glMyNull)  && Displays .T.
? NVL(glMyNull, glMyNull)  && Displays .NULL.
```

See Also

ISNULL( ), SET NULL

Object Property

Provides access to the Automation server properties and methods for an OLE object. Not available at design time. Depending on the Automation server, the properties for the OLE object may be read-only or read/write at run time.

Syntax

OLEObject.Object[*.Property*] [*= eValue*]

– or –

OLEObject.Object[*.Method*]

Arguments

Property
  Specifies a property the Automation server supports for the OLE object.

eValue
  Specifies a value for a property the Automation server supports for the OLE object.

Method
  Specifies a method the Automation server supports for the OLE object

Remarks

For information about the properties and methods supported by the Automation server, see the documentation for the OLE enabled application that created the object. For example, if the OLE object is a Microsoft Excel worksheet, see the Excel documentation for the properties and methods supported by Excel (an OLE enabled application).

Applies To

OLE Bound Control, OLE Container Control

See Also

CREATEOBJECT( ), GETOBJECT( )

Objects Collection

An array to access objects in an Application object.

Syntax

ApplicationObject.Objects(*nIndex*)

Arguments

nIndex
Uniquely identifies an object in the Application object. Note that *nIndex* might not correspond to the order in which the objects were created.

Remarks

The Objects collection can be used to determine the current objects for an Application object. The Column, Container, Control, Custom, Form, FormSet, Page, and Toolbar objects have collections, and these collections may appear in the Debug window.

Applies To

Application Object, _VFP System Variable

See Also

Forms Property

OBJNUM( ) Function

Included for backward compatibility. Use the TabIndex property for controls instead.

OBJTOCLIENT( ) Function

Returns a position or dimension of a control or object relative to its form.

Syntax

OBJTOCLIENT(*ObjectName*, *nPosition*)

Returns

Numeric

Arguments

ObjectName
Specifies the name of the control or object for which the form position is returned.

nPosition

Specifies which form position or dimension of the control or object is returned. The following table lists the values for *nPosition* and the corresponding position or dimension returned.

nPosition	Position or dimension
1	Top
2	Left
3	Width
4	Height

Remarks

OBJTOCLIENT( ) returns the position or dimension of a control or object relative to the client area of the form on which it resides. For example, a control or object can be placed on a page in a page frame, and the page frame is placed on a form. The Top, Left, Width, and Height properties return the position or dimension of a control or object relative to the page on which it is placed. However, you can use OBJTOCLIENT( ) to determine the position or dimension of a control or object relative to the form on which the page is placed.

The value returned by OBJTOCLIENT( ) is in pixels.

Example

The following example uses OBJTOCLIENT( ) to display the positions and dimensions of two check boxes relative to the form they're placed on. The Top, Left, Width, and Height properties are also used to display the positions and dimensions of the two check boxes relative to the page frame on which they're placed.

A command button and a page frame are placed on a form. The PageCount property is used to specify the number of pages on the page frame. The Tabs property is set to true (.T.) to specify that the page frame has tabs for each page. Check boxes are placed on each page in different positions.

When a check box is clicked, the Click procedure for the check box is executed. If the check box is checked, the Top, Left, Width, and Height properties are used to display the positions and dimensions of the check box relative to the page frame, and OBJTOCLIENT( ) is used to display the positions and dimensions of the check box relative to the form. If the check box is unchecked, the main Microsoft Visual FoxPro window is cleared.

```
CLEAR
STORE _DBLCLICK TO gnDblClick  && Save double-click value
STORE 0.05 TO _DBLCLICK  && Make double-click unlikely
```

```
frmMyForm = CREATEOBJECT('Form')  && Create a form
frmMyForm.Closable = .f.  && Disable the window pop-up menu

frmMyForm.Move(150,10)  && Move the form

frmMyForm.AddObject('cmbCommand1','cmdMyCmdBtn')  && Add Command button
frmMyForm.AddObject('pgfPageFrame1','pgfMyPageFrame')  && Add PageFrame
frmMyForm.pgfPageFrame1.Page1.AddObject('chkCheckBox1','chkMyCheckBox1')
frmMyForm.pgfPageFrame1.Page2.AddObject('chkCheckBox2','chkMyCheckBox2')

frmMyForm.cmbCommand1.Visible =.T.  && "Quit" Command button visible
frmMyForm.pgfPageFrame1.Visible =.T.  && PageFrame visible
frmMyForm.pgfPageFrame1.Page1.chkCheckBox1.Visible =.T.
frmMyForm.pgfPageFrame1.Page2.chkCheckBox2.Visible =.T.

frmMyForm.SHOW  && Display the form
READ EVENTS  && Start event processing

DEFINE CLASS cmdMyCmdBtn AS CommandButton  && Create Command button
    Caption = '\<Quit'  && Caption on the Command button
    Cancel = .T.  && Default Cancel Command button (Esc)
    Left = 125  && Command button column
    Top = 210  && Command button row
    Height = 25  && Command button height

    PROCEDURE Click
        CLEAR EVENTS  && Stop event processing, close Form
        CLEAR  && Clear main Visual FoxPro window
        STORE gnDblClick TO _DBLCLICK  && Restore double-click value
ENDDEFINE

DEFINE CLASS pgfMyPageFrame AS PageFrame  && Create PageFrame
    Left = 10  && PageFrame  column
    Top = 10  && PageFrame  row
    Height = 175  && PageFrame  height
    Width = 350  && PageFrame  height
    PageCount = 2  && 2 Pages on the PageFrame
    Tabs = .T.  && Tabs visible
ENDDEFINE

DEFINE CLASS chkMyCheckBox1 AS CheckBox  && Create first Check Box
    Top = 0
    Width = 200
    Caption = 'Display Position'
```

```
PROCEDURE Click
   DO CASE
      CASE ThisForm.pgfPageFrame1.Page1.chkCheckBox1.Value = 0
         ACTIVATE SCREEN
         CLEAR
      CASE ThisForm.pgfPageFrame1.Page1.chkCheckBox1.Value = 1
         ACTIVATE SCREEN
         CLEAR
         ? 'Positions relative'
         ? 'to PageFrame:'
         ?
         ? 'Top: '
         ?? ALLTRIM(STR;
            (ThisForm.pgfPageFrame1.Page1.chkCheckBox1.Top))
         ? 'Left: '
         ?? ALLTRIM(STR;
            (ThisForm.pgfPageFrame1.Page1.chkCheckBox1.Left))
         ? 'Width: '
         ?? ALLTRIM(STR;
            (ThisForm.pgfPageFrame1.Page1.chkCheckBox1.Width))
         ? 'Height: '
         ?? ALLTRIM(STR;
            (ThisForm.pgfPageFrame1.Page1.chkCheckBox1.Height))
         ?
         ? 'Positions relative'
         ? 'to Form:'
         ?
         ? 'Top: '
         ?? ALLTRIM(STR(OBJTOCLIENT;
            (ThisForm.pgfPageFrame1.Page1.chkCheckBox1,1)))
         ? 'Left: '
         ?? ALLTRIM(STR(OBJTOCLIENT;
            (ThisForm.pgfPageFrame1.Page1.chkCheckBox1,2)))
         ? 'Width: '
         ?? ALLTRIM(STR(OBJTOCLIENT;
            (ThisForm.pgfPageFrame1.Page1.chkCheckBox1,3)))
         ? 'Height: '
         ?? ALLTRIM(STR(OBJTOCLIENT(ThisForm.pgfPageFrame1.Page1.chkCheckBox1,4)))
   ENDCASE
ENDDEFINE

DEFINE CLASS chkMyCheckBox2 AS CheckBox  && Create second Check Box
   Top = 30
   Left = 175
   Width = 200
   Caption = 'Display Position'
```

```
PROCEDURE CLICK
   DO CASE
      CASE ThisForm.pgfPageFrame1.Page2.chkCheckBox2.Value = 0
         ACTIVATE SCREEN
         CLEAR
      CASE ThisForm.pgfPageFrame1.Page2.chkCheckBox2.Value = 1
         ACTIVATE SCREEN
         CLEAR
         ? 'Positions relative'
         ? 'to PageFrame:'
         ?
         ? 'Top: '
         ?? ALLTRIM(STR(ThisForm.pgfPageFrame1.Page2.chkCheckBox2.Top))
         ? 'Left: '
         ?? ALLTRIM(STR;
             (ThisForm.pgfPageFrame1.Page2.chkCheckBox2.Left))
         ? 'Width: '
         ?? ALLTRIM(STR;
             (ThisForm.pgfPageFrame1.Page2.chkCheckBox2.Width))
         ? 'Height: '
         ?? ALLTRIM(STR;
             (ThisForm.pgfPageFrame1.Page2.chkCheckBox2.Height))

         ?
         ? 'Positions relative'
         ? 'to Form:'
         ?
         ? 'Top: '
         ?? ALLTRIM(STR(OBJTOCLIENT;
             (ThisForm.pgfPageFrame1.Page2.chkCheckBox2,1)))
         ? 'Left: '
         ?? ALLTRIM(STR(OBJTOCLIENT;
             (ThisForm.pgfPageFrame1.Page2.chkCheckBox2,2)))
         ? 'Width: '
         ?? ALLTRIM(STR(OBJTOCLIENT;
             (ThisForm.pgfPageFrame1.Page2.chkCheckBox2,3)))
         ? 'Height: '
         ?? ALLTRIM(STR(OBJTOCLIENT;
             (ThisForm.pgfPageFrame1.Page2.chkCheckBox2,4)))
   ENDCASE
ENDDEFINE
```

See Also

Height Property, Left Property, Top Property, Width Property

OBJVAR( ) Function

Included for backward compatibility. Use the Name property for controls instead.

OCCURS( ) Function

Returns the number of times a character expression occurs within another character expression.

Syntax

OCCURS(*cSearchExpression*, *cExpressionSearched*)

Returns

Numeric

Arguments

cSearchExpression
Specifies a character expression that OCCURS( ) searches for within *cExpressionSearched*.

cExpressionSearched
Specifies the character expression OCCURS( ) searches for *cSearchExpression*.

Remarks

OCCURS( ) returns 0 (zero) if *cSearchExpression* isn't found within *cExpressionSearched*.

Example

```
STORE 'abracadabra' TO gcstring
CLEAR
? OCCURS('a', gcstring)   && Displays 5
? OCCURS('b', gcstring)   && Displays 2
? OCCURS('c', gcstring)   && Displays 1
? OCCURS('e', gcstring)   && Displays 0
```

See Also

$, INLIST( )

OEMTOANSI( ) Function

Included for backward compatibility. Use the GETCP( ) Function instead.

OLDVAL( ) Function

Returns original field values for fields that have been modified but not updated.

Syntax

OLDVAL(*cExpression* [, *cTableAlias* | *nWorkArea*])

Returns

Character, Currency, Date, DateTime, Double, Float, Integer, Logical, Numeric, or Memo

Arguments

cExpression
>   Specifies an expression whose original value OLDVAL( ) returns from a table or a
>   remote data source. *cExpression* is typically a field or an expression consisting of
>   a set of fields from the table or remote data source.

cTableAlias
>   Specifies the alias of the table or cursor from which the original field values are
>   returned.

nWorkArea
>   Specifies the work area of the table or cursor from which the original field values
>   are returned.

Remarks

OLDVAL( ) returns original field values for records in a Visual FoxPro table or cursor
that has row or table buffering enabled with CURSORSETPROP( ).

If a table in a database or a cursor has validation rules, OLDVAL( ) does not require that
row or table buffering be enabled in order to return original field values.

If the record pointer is moved to a different record when row buffering is enabled, or if
TABLEUPDATE( ) is issued to commit changes to the record, or there is some other
action that causes an update, such as ending a transaction, the fields are updated and the
original field values are no longer available.

The data type of the value OLDVAL( ) returns is determined by the expression you
specify with *cExpression*.

The original field values are returned for the table or cursor open in the currently selected
work area if OLDVAL( ) is issued without the optional *cTableAlias* or *nWorkArea*
arguments.

Example

The following example demonstrates how you can use OLDVAL( ) to return original
field value for a field in a buffered table. A table named `employees` is created and
INSERT – SQL is used insert the value "Smith" into the `cLastName` field.

MULTILOCKS is set to ON, a requirement for table buffering. CURSORSETPROP( ) is used to set the buffering mode to optimistic table buffering (5).

The original value of the cLastName field (Smith) is displayed and then the cLastName field is modified with REPLACE. The new value of the cLastName field (Jones) is displayed. The original value of the cLastName field (Smith) is displayed with OLDVAL( ). TABLEUPDATE( ) is then used to commit changes to the table. The updated value of the cLastName field (Jones) is then displayed.

```
CLOSE DATABASES
CLEAR

* Create new table and add blank record
CREATE TABLE employee (cLastName C(10))
APPEND BLANK

* Insert initial value
INSERT INTO employee (cLastName) VALUES ("Smith")

* Enable and set table buffering
SET MULTILOCKS ON  && Allow table buffering
=CURSORSETPROP("Buffering", 5, "employee" )  && Enable table buffering

* Display initial value
=MESSAGEBOX("Original cLastName value: "+ cLastName, 0, "Results")

* Change record value and display results
REPLACE cLastName WITH "Jones"
=MESSAGEBOX("Modified cLastName value: "+ cLastName, 0, "Results")

* Store the old value of the field to cTemp variable and display results
cTemp=OLDVAL("cLastName", "employee")
=MESSAGEBOX("Original cLastName value: "+ cTemp, 0, "Results")

* Update table and display final value
=TABLEUPDATE(.T.)
=MESSAGEBOX("Final cLastName value: "+ cLastName, 0, "Results")

* Close and delete example table file
USE
DELETE FILE employee.dbf
```

See Also

CURVAL( ), GETFLDSTATE( ), TABLEREVERT( ), TABLEUPDATE( ), CURSORSETPROP( )

OLE Bound Control

Creates an OLE bound control.

Syntax

OLEBoundControl

Remarks

On a form or report, an OLE bound control lets you display the contents of an OLE object (such as from Microsoft Word or Microsoft Excel) in a General field of a table.

Unlike OLE container controls, insertable OLE objects do not have their own set of events. Also, OLE bound controls, unlike OLE container controls, are bound to a General field in a Visual FoxPro table.

For additional information about OLE objects in Visual FoxPro, see Chapter 16, "Adding OLE," in the *Microsoft Visual FoxPro 6.0 Programmer's Guide*.

Properties

Application	AutoActivate	AutoSize
BaseClass	ClassLibrary	Class
Comment	ControlSource	DocumentFile
DragIcon	DragMode	Enabled
Height	HelpContextId	HostName
Left	MousePointer	Name
Object	OLEClass	OLELCID Property
OLETypeAllowed	ParentClass	Sizable
Stretch	TabIndex	TabStop
Tag	Top	Value
Visible	WhatsThisHelpID	Width

Events

Destroy	DragDrop	DragOver
Error	GotFocus	Init
LostFocus	Moved	Resize
UIEnable		

Methods

AddProperty	CloneObject	DoVerb
Drag	Move	Refresh
ResetToDefault	SaveAsClass	SetFocus
ZOrder		

See Also

APPEND GENERAL, CREATE FORM, CREATE CLASS, CREATEBINARY( ), DEFINE CLASS, MODIFY GENERAL, OLE Container Control

OLE Container Control

Creates an OLE container control.

Syntax

OLEControl

Remarks

An OLE container control lets you add OLE objects to your applications. OLE objects include ActiveX Controls (.ocx files) and insertable OLE objects created in other applications such as Microsoft Word and Microsoft Excel. Unlike ActiveX Controls (.ocx files), insertable OLE objects do not have their own set of events. OLE container controls, unlike OLE bound controls, are not bound to a General field in a Visual FoxPro table.

Note that the type of ActiveX control placed in an OLE container control determines the properties, events, and methods available for the ActiveX control

For additional information about OLE objects in Visual FoxPro, see Chapter 16, "Adding OLE," in the *Microsoft Visual FoxPro 6.0 Programmer's Guide*.

Properties

Align	Application	AutoActivate
AutoSize	AutoVerbMenu	BaseClass
Cancel	Class	ClassLibrary
Comment	ControlSource	Default
DocumentFile	DragIcon	DragMode
Enabled	Height	HelpContextID

HostName	Left	MouseIcon
MousePointer	Name	Object
OLEClass	OLELCID	OLETypeAllowed
Parent	ParentClass	Sizable
Stretch	TabIndex	TabStop
Tag	Top	Visible
WhatsThisHelpID	Width	

Events

Destroy	DragDrop	DragOver
Error	GotFocus	Init
LostFocus	Moved	Resize
UIEnable		

Methods

AddProperty	CloneObject	DoVerb
Drag	Move	Refresh
ResetToDefault	SaveAsClass	SetFocus
ShowWhatsThis	Zorder	

Example

The following example adds an OLE Container control to a form, and uses the OleClass and DocumentFile properties to specify Microsoft Excel as the Automation server and a Microsoft Excel worksheet as the file to edit.

The DocumentFile property specifies a worksheet named Book1.xls in the EXCEL directory on drive C. This example will not work properly if the file and directory specified in the DocumentFile property do not exist; it may be necessary to modify the DocumentFile property to specify an existing directory and worksheet file.

* The DoVerb method is used to activate the worksheet for editing.

```
frmMyForm = CREATEOBJECT('Form')  && Create a Form
frmMyForm.Closable = .F.  && Disable the window pop-up menu

frmMyForm.AddObject('cmdCommand1','cmdMyCmdBtn')  && Add Command button
frmMyForm.AddObject("oleObject","oleExcelObject")  && Add OLE object
```

```
frmMyForm.cmdCommand1.Visible=.T.  && Display the "Quit" Command button

frmMyForm.oleObject.Visible=.T.  && Display the OLE control
frmMyForm.oleObject.Height = 50  && OLE control height

frmMyForm.Show  && Display the Form

frmMyForm.oleObject.DoVerb(-1)  && -1 for Edit

READ EVENTS  && Start event processing

DEFINE CLASS oleExcelObject as OLEControl
   OleClass ="Excel.Sheet"  && Server name
   DocumentFile = "C:\EXCEL\BOOK1.XLS"  && This file must exist
ENDDEFINE

DEFINE CLASS cmdMyCmdBtn AS CommandButton  && Create Command button
   Caption = '\<Quit'  && Caption on the Command button
   Cancel = .T.  && Default Cancel Command button (Esc)
   Left = 125  && Command button column
   Top = 210  && Command button row
   Height = 25  && Command button height

   PROCEDURE Click
      CLEAR EVENTS  && Stop event processing, close form
ENDDEFINE
```

See Also

ActiveX Controls Overview, APPEND GENERAL, CREATE FORM, CREATE CLASS, CREATEBINARY( ), DEFINE CLASS, MODIFY GENERAL, OLE Bound Control

OLEClass Property

Returns the named class ID of an OLE object. Read-only at design time and run time for an existing object, but can be set for an object when creating it.

Syntax

Control.OLEClass[= *cName*]

Arguments

cName
> The named class ID of the object. This is the registered name of the application that was used to create the object or will be invoked if the object is activated.

Remarks

You set OLEClass property of an OLE container object using the Insert Object dialog box when you initially add an OLE container to a form, or in code when creating an OLE object as part of a class definition. This property is also set when you create OLE objects using the APPEND GENERAL command.

The OLEClass property of an object specifies the application that is used to create or edit the OLE object. To specify the actual contents of the object, set its DocumentFile property.

Example

The following example adds an OLE Container control to a form, and uses the OleClass and DocumentFile properties to specify Microsoft Excel as the Automation server and an Excel worksheet as the file to edit.

```
Define class foo as form
    add object oleXLSheet1 as oleXLSheet
EndDefine

Define class oleXLSheet as OLECONTROL
    oleclass = "Excel.Sheet"
    documentfile="C:\msoffice\Excel\mysheet.xls"
    oletypeallowed = 1  && Embedded
EndDefine
```

Applies To

OLE Bound Control, OLE Container Control

See Also

APPEND GENERAL, CREATEOBJECT( ), DocumentFile Property

OLECompleteDrag Event

Occurs when data is dropped on the drop target or the OLE drag-and-drop operation is canceled.

Syntax

PROCEDURE *Object*.OLECompleteDrag
LPARAMETERS *nEffect*

Arguments

nEffect
> A value passed from the OLEDragDrop event, corresponding to the action performed when data is dropped on the drop target. The following table lists the values for *nEffect* with a description of each action.

nEffect	Foxpro.h constant	Description
0	DROPEFFECT_NONE	Drop target did not accept the data or the drop operation was canceled.
1	DROPEFFECT_COPY	Data was copied from the drag source to the drop target.
2	DROPEFFECT_MOVE	Data was moved from the drag source to the drop target.
4	DROPEFFECT_LINK	Data was linked from the drag source to the drop target.

Remarks

OLECompleteDrag is a drag source event, and is the last event to occur during an OLE drag-and-drop operation. Including NODEFAULT prevents a text move from deleting the text.

This event allows the drag source to determine the action performed on the data on the drop target. The drop target can set *nEffect* in its OLEDragDrop event and the drag source can perform the appropriate action based on the value of *nEffect*. For example, if the data was moved to the drop target, the drag source should remove the data from itself.

Applies To

CheckBox, ComboBox, CommandButton, CommandGroup, Container Object, Control Object, EditBox, Form, Grid, Image, Label, Line, ListBox, OptionButton, OptionGroup, Page, PageFrame, Shape, Spinner, TextBox, ToolBar

See Also

OLE Drag-and-Drop Overview, OLEDragDrop Event, OLEDropMode Property

OLEDrag Method

Starts an OLE drag-and-drop operation.

Syntax

PROCEDURE *Object*.OLEDrag
LPARAMETERS *lDetectDrag*

Arguments

lDetectDrag
Specifies when the OLEStartDrag event is executed. If *lDetectDrag* is false (.F.), the OLEStartDrag event is immediately executed. If *lDetectDrag* is true (.T.), the OLEStartDrag event is executed after the user has pressed the mouse button for a sufficient period of time to indicate that a drag operation is occurring, or the mouse is moved a sufficient distance while the mouse button is pressed, again indicating that a drag operation is occurring.

If you don't specify a value for *lDetectDrag*, true (.T.) is automatically returned.

Remarks

OLEDrag is a drag source method.

Applies To

CheckBox, ComboBox, CommandButton, CommandGroup, Container Object, Control Object, EditBox, Form, Grid, Image, Label, Line, ListBox, OptionButton, OptionGroup, Page, PageFrame, Shape, Spinner, TextBox, ToolBar

See Also

OLE Drag-and-Drop Overview, OLEDragMode Property, OLEStartDrag Event

OLEDragDrop Event

Occurs when data is dropped on a drop target and the drop target's OLEDropMode property is set to 1 – Enabled.

Syntax

PROCEDURE *Object*.OLEDragDrop
LPARAMETERS *oDataObject*, *nEffect*, *nButton*, *nShift*,
   nXCoord, *nYCoord*

Arguments

oDataObject

An object reference to OLE drag-and-drop DataObject, used with the GetData and GetFormat methods to return data and data formats in the DataObject.

nEffect

A value passed to the OLECompleteDrag event, indicating the action performed when data is dropped on the drop target. *nEffect* is initially a value that indicates the OLE drag-and-drop operations supported by the drag source. Within the OLEDragDrop event you can change the value of *nEffect* which is passed to the OLECompleteDrag event. If you change the value of *nEffect*, be sure to include NODEFAULT in the event code to prevent the default behavior. The following table lists the values for *nEffect* that you can pass to the OLECompleteDrag event with a description of each action.

nEffect	Foxpro.h constant	Description
0	DROPEFFECT_NONE	Drop target did not accept the data or the drop operation was canceled.
1	DROPEFFECT_COPY	Data was copied from the drag source to the drop target.
2	DROPEFFECT_MOVE	Data was moved from the drag source to the drop target.
4	DROPEFFECT_LINK	Data was linked from the drag source to the drop target.

nButton
> Contains a number that specifies which mouse button was released to drop the data on the target: 1 (left), 2 (right), or 4 (middle).

nShift
> Contains a number specifying the state of modifier keys when the mouse was released to drop the data on the drop target. The valid modifier keys are the SHIFT, CTRL, and ALT keys. The values returned in *nShift* for individual modifier keys are listed in the following table.

nShift	Modifier key
1	SHIFT
2	CTRL
4	ALT

> If more than one modifier key is held down when the mouse is pressed, the *nShift* argument contains the sum of the values for the modifier keys. For example, if the user holds CTRL while releasing the mouse button, the *nShift* argument contains 2. But if the user holds CTRL+ALT while releasing the mouse button, the *nShift* argument contains 6.

nXCoord, *nYCoord*
> Contains the horizontal (*nXCoord*) and vertical (*nYCoord*) position of the mouse pointer within the Form when the mouse button was released to drop the data on the drop target. These coordinates are expressed in terms of the Form's coordinate system in the unit of measurement specified by the *ScaleMode* property of the Form.

Remarks

OLEDragDrop is a drop target event that only occurs when the OLEDropMode property for the control or object is set to 1 – Enabled. This event does not occur if the OLEDropMode property is set to 0 – Disabled or 2 – Pass to Container.

If you perform your own drop processing in the OleDragDrop event, include NODEFAULT to prevent the default drop from occuring. In this case, you must then set the resulting *nEffect* value.

Applies To

CheckBox, ComboBox, CommandButton, CommandGroup, Container Object, Control Object, EditBox, Form, Grid, Image, Label, Line, ListBox, OptionButton, OptionGroup, Page, PageFrame, ProjectHook Object, Shape, Spinner, TextBox, ToolBar

See Also

OLE Drag-and-drop Overview, OLECompleteDrag Event, OLEDropMode Property

OLEDragMode Property

Specifies how a drag operation is initiated. Available at design time and run time.

Syntax

Object.OLEDragMode[= *nValue*]

Arguments

nValue

Specifies how the control or object handles OLE drag operations. The following table lists the settings for *nValue*.

Setting	Description
0	Manual (Default).
	Visual FoxPro does not initiate the OLE drag operation when you attempt to drag data. You must call the OLEDrag method to begin the drag operation.
	Setting OLEDragMode to 0 provides backward compatibility (no OLE drag support) for existing applications if you do not include additional drag operation coding.
1	Automatic
	Visual FoxPro allows automatically initiates a drag operation when you attempt to drag data.

Remarks

OLEDragMode is a drag source property. If the DragMode property for a control or object is set to 1 – Automatic, the control or object cannot act as an OLE drag source. This provides backward compatibility for previous drag-and-drop support in earlier versions of Visual FoxPro.

Note that OLEDragMode property is read-only for the Grid control.

Applies To

CheckBox, ComboBox, CommandButton, CommandGroup, Container Object, Control Object, EditBox, Form, Grid, Image, Label, Line, ListBox, OptionButton, OptionGroup, Page, PageFrame, Shape, Spinner, TextBox, ToolBar

See Also

DragMode Property, OLE Drag-and-Drop Overview, OLEDrag Method, OLEStartDrag Event

OLEDragOver Event

Occurs when data is dragged over a drop target and the drop target's OLEDropMode property is set to 1 – Enabled.

Syntax

PROCEDURE *Object*.OLEDragOver
LPARAMETERS *oDataObject*, *nEffect*, *nButton*, *nShift*,
    nXCoord, *nYCoord*, *nState*

Arguments

oDataObject

An object reference to OLE drag-and-drop DataObject, used with the GetData and GetFormat methods to return data and data formats in the DataObject.

nEffect

A value passed to the OLEGiveFeedback event, indicating the action performed if data is dropped on the drop target. *nEffect* is initially a value that indicates the OLE drag-and-drop operations supported by the drag source. The following table lists the values for *nEffect* with a description of each action.

nEffect	Foxpro.h constant	Description
0	DROPEFFECT_NONE	Drop target doesn't accept the data or the drop operation is canceled.
1	DROPEFFECT_COPY	Data is copied from the drag source to the drop target.
2	DROPEFFECT_MOVE	Data is moved from the drag source to the drop target.
4	DROPEFFECT_LINK	Data is linked from the drag source to the drop target.

nButton

Contains a number that specifies which mouse button is pressed when data is dragged over a drop target: 1 (left), 2 (right), or 4 (middle).

nShift

Contains a number specifying the state of modifier keys when data is dragged over a drop target. The valid modifier keys are the SHIFT, CTRL, and ALT keys. The values returned in *nShift* for individual modifier keys are listed in the following table.

nShift	Modifier key
1	SHIFT
2	CTRL
4	ALT

If more than one modifier key is held down when the mouse is pressed, the *nShift* argument contains the sum of the values for the modifier keys. For example, if the user holds CTRL while releasing the mouse button, the *nShift* argument contains 2. But, if the user holds CTRL+ALT while releasing the mouse button, the *nShift* argument contains 6.

nXCoord, nYCoord

Contains the horizontal (*nXCoord*) and vertical (*nYCoord*) position of the mouse pointer within the Form when data is dragged over a drop target. These coordinates are expressed in terms of the Form's coordinate system in the unit of measurement specified by the *ScaleMode* property of the Form.

nState

Contains a number specifying the direction in which the data is dragged-into the control or object, within the control or object, or out of the control or object. The values for *nState* are listed in the following table.

nState	Description
0	Data is dragged into the control or object. The OLEDropEffects and OLEDropHasData properties can be set when *nState* is zero.
1	Data is dragged out of the control or object.
2	Data is dragged within the control or object.

Remarks

OLEDragOver is a drop target event that only occurs when the OLEDropMode property for the control or object is set to 1 – Enabled. This event does not occur if the OLEDropMode property is set to 0 – Disabled or 2 – Pass to Container.

Note that you should avoid creating wait states in the OLEDragOver event with commands and functions such as WAIT WINDOW and MESSAGEBOX( ).

Applies To

CheckBox, ComboBox, CommandButton, CommandGroup, Container Object, Control Object, EditBox, Form, Grid, Image, Label, Line, ListBox, OptionButton, OptionGroup, Page, PageFrame, ProjectHook Object, Shape, Spinner, TextBox, ToolBar

See Also

OLE Drag-and-Drop Overview, OLEGiveFeedBack Event, OLEDropEffects Property, OLEDropHasData Property, OLEDropMode Property

OLEDragPicture Property

Specifies the picture displayed under the mouse pointer during an OLE drag-and-drop operation. Available at design time and run time.

Syntax

Object.OLEDragPicture[= *cFileName*]

Arguments

cFileName

Specifies the file name and path of the graphic to display when an OLE drag-and-drop operation occurs. The graphics file you specify can be of type .bmp, .dib, .jpg, .gif, .ani, .cur, or .ico.

The graphics file is typically a translucent or outline representation of the object being dragged. To create a translucent representation of the object, use a black-and-white checkerboard mask file (.msk).

Remarks

OLEDragPicture is a drag source property. The picture is displayed when the mouse pointer is positioned over the form containing the drag source.

Applies To

CheckBox, ComboBox, CommandButton, CommandGroup, Container Object, Control Object, EditBox, Form, Grid, Image, Label, Line, ListBox, OptionButton, OptionGroup, Page, PageFrame, Shape, Spinner, TextBox, ToolBar

See Also

OLE Drag-and-Drop Overview

OLEDropEffects Property

Specifies the type of drop operations an OLE drop target supports. Available at design time and run time.

Syntax

Object.OLEDropEffects[= *nDropEffect*]

Arguments

nDropEffect

Specifies the type of drop operations an OLE drop target supports. The following table lists the values for *nDropEffect* with a description of each.

nDropEffect	Foxpro.h constant	Description
0	DROPEFFECT_NONE	Drop target does not accept the data as a drop target.
1	DROPEFFECT_COPY	Data can be copied to the drop target.
2	DROPEFFECT_MOVE	Data can be moved to the drop target.
4	DROPEFFECT_LINK	Data can be linked to the drop target.

A drop can support multiple drop operations by adding multiple values together for *nDropEffect*. For example, if *nDropEffect* is 3, the drop target supports both copy and move drop operations (3 = 1 (copy) + 2 (move)).

Remarks

OLEDropEffects is a drop target property, and should be set in the OLEDragOver event.

Applies To

CheckBox, ComboBox, CommandButton, CommandGroup, Container Object, Control Object, EditBox, Form, Grid, Image, Label, Line, ListBox, OptionButton, OptionGroup, Page, PageFrame, ProjectHook Object, Shape, Spinner, TextBox, ToolBar

See Also

OLE Drag-and-Drop Overview, OLEDragOver Event, OLEDropHasData Property

OLEDropHasData Property

Specifies how a drop operation is managed. Available at run time and read-only at design time.

Syntax

Object.OLEDropHasData[= *nDropEffect*]

Arguments

nDropEffect
Specifies how the drop operation is managed. The following table lists the values for *nDropEffect* with a description of each.

nDropEffect	Foxpro.h constant	Description
−1	DROPHASDATA_VFPDETERMINE	Default. Visual FoxPro automatically determines if the DataObject contains data in a format that can be dropped on the drop target.
		If the DataObject contains data in a proper format for the drop target, the data is dropped on the drop target. Visual FoxPro handles the mouse pointer and notification of the drag source.
		If the data isn't in the proper format for the drop target, Visual FoxPro displays the No Drop mouse pointer, the drop operation is canceled, and the drag source is notified that the drop operation was canceled.
0	DROPHASDATA_NOTUSEFUL	The DataObject does not contain data in a format that can be dropped on the drop target, and the No Drop mouse pointer is displayed.
1	DROPHASDATA_USEFUL	The DataObject contains data in a format that can be dropped on the drop target.

Remarks

OLEDropHasData is a drop target property and should be set in the OLEDragOver event. Use GetFormat in the OLEDragOver event to determine if the DataObject contains data in the proper format for the drop target. If the data is in the proper format for the drop target, set OLEDropHasData to 1.

Applies To

CheckBox, ComboBox, CommandButton, CommandGroup, Container Object, Control Object, EditBox, Form, Grid, Image, Label, Line, ListBox, OptionButton, OptionGroup, Page, PageFrame, ProjectHook Object, Shape, Spinner, TextBox, ToolBar

See Also

OLE Drag-and-Drop Overview, OLEDragOver Event, OLEDropEffects Property

OLEDropMode Property

Specifies how a drop target manages OLE drop operations. Available at design time and run time.

Syntax

Object.OLEDropMode[= *nValue*]

Arguments

nValue

Specifies how the control or object handles OLE drop operations. The following table lists the settings for *nValue*.

nValue	Foxpro.h constant	Description
0	DROP_DISABLED	Disabled (Default).
		Data cannot be dropped onto the control or object, and no drop target events occur. The No Drop mouse pointer is displayed when the mouse pointer is positioned over the control or object.
		Setting OLEDropMode to 0 provides backward compatibility (no OLE drop support) for existing applications.
1	DROP_ENABLED	Enabled.
		Visual FoxPro allows the dropping of data onto the control or object, and drop target events occur.
2	DROP_PASSTOCONTAINER	Pass to Container.
		The control or object behaves as if it is disabled for OLE drop operations, and the data is dropped on the container for the control or object.
		The container's OLEDropMode property must be set to 1 or 2 to accept the data. The No Drop mouse pointer is displayed if the container's OLEDropMode property is set to 0.

Remarks

OLEDropMode is a drop target property. If the DropMode property for a control or object is set to 0 – Disabled, the control or object cannot act as an OLE drop source. This provides backward compatibility for previous drag-and-drop support in earlier versions of Visual FoxPro.

If the Enabled property of a control or object is set to false (.F.), you cannot drop data on the control or object. For drop operations, the No Drop mouse pointer is displayed when the Enabled property of a control or object is set to false (.F.).

Applies To

CheckBox, ComboBox, CommandButton, CommandGroup, Container Object, Control Object, EditBox, Form, Grid, Image, Label, Line, ListBox, OptionButton, OptionGroup, Page, PageFrame, ProjectHook Object, Shape, Spinner, TextBox, ToolBar

See Also

Enabled Property, OLE Drag-and-Drop Overview

OLEDropTextInsertion Property

Specifies if you can drop text in the middle of a word in the text box portion of a control.

Syntax

*Object.*OLEDropTextInsertion[= *lExpression*]

Arguments

lExpression
    The settings for the OLEDropTextInsertion property are:

Setting	Description
0	(Default) Text can be dropped into a word.
1	Text can only be dropped before or after a word.

Remarks

The OLEDropMode property of a control must be set to 1 – Enabled to drop text in the text box portion of the control.

Applies To

ComboBox, EditBox, Spinner, TextBox

See Also

OLE Drag-and-Drop Overview, OLEDropMode Property

OLEGiveFeedback Event

Occurs after every OLEDragOver event. Allows the drag source to specify the type of OLE drag-and-drop operation and the visual feedback.

Syntax

PROCEDURE *Object*.OLEGiveFeedback
LPARAMETERS *nEffect, eMouseCursor*

Arguments

nEffect

The action performed when data is dropped on the drop target. The value of *nEffect* is set by the drop target in its OLEDragOver event. The following table lists the values for *nEffect* with a description of each action.

nEffect	Foxpro.h constant	Description
0	DROPEFFECT_NONE	Drop target cannot accept the data.
1	DROPEFFECT_COPY	Drop results in a copy.
2	DROPEFFECT_MOVE	Drop results in a move.
4	DROPEFFECT_LINK	Drop results in a link.

eMouseCursor

Specifies the mouse pointer displayed during the OLE drag-and-drop operation. *eMouseCursor* can be a character or numeric value. *eMouseCursor* is an output parameter and is set to zero on entry into event.

If *eMouseCursor* is a character value, it's assumed that the character value is the name of a graphics file of type .ani, .cur, or .ico. If *eMouseCursor* is a numeric value, the value specifies the mouse pointer displayed. The following table lists the numeric values for *eMouseCursor* with a description of each mouse pointer.

eMouseCursor	Foxpro.h constant	Description
0	MOUSE_DEFAULT	(Default)
		Shape determined by the object.
1	MOUSE_ARROW	Arrow.
2	MOUSE_CROSSHAIR	Cross.
		A cross-hair pointer.
3	MOUSE_IBEAM	I-Beam.
4	MOUSE_ICON_POINTER	Icon.
		A small white square within a black square.

(continued)

eMouseCursor	Foxpro.h constant	Description
5	MOUSE_SIZE_POINTER	Size.
		A four-pointed arrow pointing north, south, east, west.
6	MOUSE_SIZE_NE_SW	Size NE SW.
		A double arrow pointing northeast and southwest.
7	MOUSE_SIZE_N_S	Size NS.
		A double arrow pointing north and south.
8	MOUSE_SIZE_NW_SE	Size NW SE.
		A double arrow pointing northwest and southeast.
9	MOUSE_W_E	Size WE.
		A double arrow pointing west and east.
10	MOUSE_UP_ARROW	Up Arrow.
11	MOUSE_HOURGLASS	Hourglass.
12	MOUSE_NO_DROP	No Drop.
13	MOUSE_HIDE_POINTER	Hide Pointer.
14	MOUSE_ARROW2	Arrow.
15	MOUSE_ARROW_HOURGLASS	Arrow and hourglass.
16	MOUSE_ARROW_QUESTION	Arrow and question mark.

Remarks

OLEGiveFeedback is a drag source event that lets you provide visual feedback to the user. You can change the mouse cursor to indicate the operation that occurs when the mouse is positioned over the drag source or the drop target. Including NODEFAULT has no effect on the behavior of this method.

Note that you should avoid creating wait states in the OLEGiveFeedback event with commands and functions such as WAIT WINDOW and MESSAGEBOX( ).

Applies To

CheckBox, ComboBox, CommandButton, CommandGroup, Container Object, Control Object, EditBox, Form, Grid, Image, Label, Line, ListBox, OptionButton, OptionGroup, Page, PageFrame, ProjectHook Object, Shape, Spinner, TextBox, ToolBar

See Also

OLE Drag-and-Drop Overview, OLEDragOver Event

OLELCID Property

Contains a numeric value indicating the Locale ID for an OLE Bound control or an OLE Container control. Read-only at design time and run time.

Syntax

Control.OLELCID

Remarks

The Locale ID value is determined by the value of the DefOLELCID property for the form or the main Visual FoxPro window when an OLE Bound control or an OLE Container control is placed on the form or the main Visual FoxPro window.

If the form or the main Visual FoxPro window's DefOLELCID property is zero when the OLE Bound control or OLE Container control is placed on the form or the main Visual FoxPro window, the control uses the current Visual FoxPro Locale ID (LCID). Use SYS(3004) to determine the current Visual FoxPro Locale ID. Use the DefOLELCID property to specify a Locale ID for a form.

See SYS(3005), later in this language reference, for a listing of Locale IDs.

> **Note** The OLELCID property only affects the language of the user interface, which OLE controls display, and not the language of the Automation commands. The Automation command language is affected only by the Global LocaleID, set with SYS(3005).

Applies To

OLE Bound Control, OLE Container Control

See Also

DefOLELCID Property, SYS(3005) – Set Locale ID

OLERequestPendingTimeout Property

Specifies how long after an Automation request is made before a busy message is displayed. Read/write at run time.

Syntax

ApplicationObject.OLERequestPendingTimeout[= *nMilliseconds*]

Arguments

nMilliseconds
Specifies the number of milliseconds that must elapse before a busy message is displayed when an Automation request is pending. The busy message is displayed when a mouse or keyboard event occurs. The default value for *nMilliseconds* is 5,000 milliseconds.

If *nMilliseconds* is 0, a busy message isn't displayed when an Automation request is pending and a mouse or keyboard event occurs.

Applies To

Application Object, _VFP System Variable

See Also

OLEServerBusyRaiseError Property, OLEServerBusyTimeout Property

OLEServerBusyRaiseError Property

Specifies whether an error message is displayed when an Automation request is rejected. Read/write at run time.

Syntax

*ApplicationObject.*OLEServerBusyRaiseError[= *lExpression*]

Arguments

lExpression
One of the following settings:

Setting	Description
.T. (True)	An error doesn't occur and a busy message is not displayed when the number of milliseconds specified by the OLEServerBusyTimeout property have elapsed.
.F. (False)	(Default) An error occurs and a busy message is displayed when the number of milliseconds specified by the OLEServerBusyTimeout property have elapsed.

Applies To

Application Object, _VFP System Variable

See Also

OLERequestPendingTimeout Property, OLEServerBusyTimeout Property

OLEServerBusyTimeout Property

Specifies how long an Automation request is retried while a server is busy. Read/write at run time.

Syntax

*ApplicationObject.*OLEServerBusyTimeout[= *nMilliseconds*]

Arguments

nMilliseconds
Specifies the number of milliseconds for which an Automation request is retried before a server busy message is displayed.

Applies To

Application Object, _VFP System Variable

See Also

OLERequestPendingTimeout Property, OLEServerBusyRaiseError Property

OLESetData Event

Occurs on a drag source when a drop target calls the GetData method and there is no data in a specified format in the OLE drag-and-drop DataObject.

Syntax

PROCEDURE *Object.*OLESetData
LPARAMETERS *oDataObject, eFormat*

Arguments

oDataObject
An object reference to OLE drag-and-drop DataObject, used with the SetData method to place data in the DataObject.

eFormat
A numeric or character value that indicates the format of the data the GetData method requests. The drag source uses this value to determine the format of the data to place in the DataObject. See the "GetData Method," earlier in this language reference, for a table that lists the numeric or character values for each data format and a description of each format.

Remarks

OLESetData is a drag source event. Including NODEFAULT has no effect on the behavior of this method.

The OLESetData event occurs when the GetData method is executed and there is no data in the DataObject in the format specified in the GetData method. Within the OLESetData event you can place data in the DataObject in the specified format with the SetData method. This technique is called "delay rendering" and allows you to put data on the DataObject only when it is requested.

Applies To

CheckBox, ComboBox, CommandButton, CommandGroup, Container Object, Control Object, EditBox, Form, Grid, Image, Label, Line, ListBox, OptionButton, OptionGroup, Page, PageFrame, Shape, Spinner, TextBox, ToolBar

See Also

GetData Method, OLE Drag-and-Drop Overview, OLESetData Event, SetData Method

OLEStartDrag Event

Occurs when the OLEDrag method is called.

Syntax

PROCEDURE *Object*.OLEStartDrag
LPARAMETERS *oDataObject, nEffect*

Arguments

oDataObject
  An object reference to OLE drag-and-drop DataObject. You can call any of the DataObject methods from within the OLEStartDrag event.

nEffect
  The OLE drag operations supported by the drag source. The following table lists the values for *nEffect* with a description of each action. *nEffect* is an output parameter and is set to three on entry into event, so you should provide the value for *nEffect* in this event. For example, to allow only copy operations, set *nEffect* to 1 (DROPEFFECT_COPY).

nEffect	Foxpro.h constant	Description
0	DROPEFFECT_NONE	Drag source did not support any drag operations.
1	DROPEFFECT_COPY	Drag source supports Copy operations.
2	DROPEFFECT_MOVE	Drag source supports Move operations (the default).
4	DROPEFFECT_LINK	Drag source supports link operations.

A drag source can support multiple drag operations by adding multiple values together for *nEffect*. For example, if *nEffect* is 3, the drag source supports both copy and move drag operations (3 = 1 (copy) + 2 (move)).

Remarks

OLEStartDrag is a drag source event. Including NODEFAULT has no effect on the behavior of this method.

Applies To

CheckBox, ComboBox, CommandButton, CommandGroup, Container Object, Control Object, EditBox, Form, Grid, Image, Label, Line, ListBox, OptionButton, OptionGroup, Page, PageFrame, Shape, Spinner, TextBox, ToolBar

See Also

OLE Drag-and-Drop Overview, OLEDrag Method, OLEDragMode Property

OLETypeAllowed Property

Returns the type of OLE object (embedded or linked) contained in a control. Read-only at design time and run time.

Syntax

*Control.*OLETypeAllowed[= *nValue*]

Arguments

nValue

Returns a value that indicates the type of OLE object (embedded or linked) contained in a control. Possible values are 0 (Linked), 1 (Embedded), −1 (an OLE Bound control that does not contain an OLE object), and −2 (ActiveX control (.ocx)).

Remarks

OLETypeAllowed is only useful when you specify a setting for the DocumentFile property.

Note   You can set the OLETypeAllowed property in code to create a linked OLE object using the DEFINE CLASS command.

Applies To

OLE Bound Control, OLE Container Control

See Also

DEFINE CLASS, DocumentFile Property

ON BAR Command

Specifies a menu or menu bar that is activated when you choose a specific menu item from a menu.

Syntax

ON BAR *nMenuItemNumber* OF *MenuName1*
    [ACTIVATE POPUP *MenuName2*
    | ACTIVATE MENU *MenuBarName*]

Arguments

nMenuItemNumber OF *MenuName1*

Specifies the menu item number and menu of the menu item that activates another menu or menu bar. Each item in a menu can have another menu or menu bar assigned to it.

A menu item with a menu or menu bar assigned to it has an arrow placed to the right of the menu item. The arrow indicates that choosing that menu item activates an additional menu or menu bar. An additional space for the cascading submenu arrow is placed to the right of each item if you define the menu with DEFINE POPUP ... MARGIN. If you create the menu without the MARGIN clause, the cascading submenu arrow might overwrite the last character of the menu item.

ACTIVATE POPUP *MenuName2*

Specifies the name of the menu to activate when the menu item is chosen. Use ON BAR without ACTIVATE POPUP to release a menu from a menu item.

ACTIVATE MENU *MenuBarName*

Specifies the name of the menu bar to activate when the menu item is chosen. Use ON BAR without ACTIVATE MENU to release a menu bar from a menu item.

Remarks

A menu that displays and activates another menu is called a cascading submenu. Use ON SELECTION BAR or ON SELECTION POPUP to execute a command when an item is chosen from a menu.

The menus and menu bar can be user-defined (created with DEFINE POPUP and DEFINE MENU) or part of the Visual FoxPro menu system.

Example

The following example demonstrates a system of cascading submenus. A menu bar named mnuDinner is created with two menu bar titles. Each title uses ON PAD to activate the menu named popMainCourse or popDessert. The menus named popMainCourse and popDessert each have additional menus named popBurger, popPizza and popPie assigned to their item lists with three ON BAR commands. The popOlives and popPie items have additional menus assigned with two ON BAR commands.

When you make a selection, ON SELECTION POPUP ALL executes a procedure named yourchoice that activates a window and displays your choice. The choice is determined with POPUP( ) and PROMPT( ), which return the name of the menu and the contents (text) of the menu item.

```
DEFINE WINDOW wOrder FROM 10,0 TO 13,39
DEFINE MENU mnuDinner
DEFINE PAD padOne OF mnuDinner PROMPT '\<Main Course' KEY ALT+M, ''
DEFINE PAD padTwo OF mnuDinner PROMPT '\<Dessert'   KEY ALT+D, ''
ON PAD padOne OF mnuDinner ACTIVATE POPUP popMainCourse
ON PAD padTwo OF mnuDinner ACTIVATE POPUP dessert
DEFINE POPUP popMainCourse MARGIN MESSAGE ;
   'We have burgers and pizza today'
DEFINE BAR 1 OF popMainCourse PROMPT '\<Hamburgers'
DEFINE BAR 2 OF popMainCourse PROMPT '\<Pizza'
ON BAR 1 OF popMainCourse ACTIVATE POPUP burger
ON BAR 2 OF popMainCourse ACTIVATE POPUP pizza
DEFINE POPUP burger MARGIN MESSAGE ;
   'What would you like on your burger?'
DEFINE BAR 1 OF burger PROMPT '\<Ketchup'
DEFINE BAR 2 OF burger PROMPT '\<Mustard'
DEFINE BAR 3 OF burger PROMPT '\<Onions'
DEFINE BAR 4 OF burger PROMPT '\<Pickles'
DEFINE POPUP pizza MARGIN MESSAGE ;
   'Here are the available toppings'
DEFINE BAR 1 OF pizza PROMPT '\<Anchovies'
DEFINE BAR 2 OF pizza PROMPT '\<Green Peppers'
DEFINE BAR 3 OF pizza PROMPT '\<Olives'
DEFINE BAR 4 OF pizza PROMPT '\<Pepperoni'
ON BAR 3 OF pizza ACTIVATE POPUP olives
DEFINE POPUP olives MARGIN
DEFINE BAR 1 OF olives PROMPT '\<Black' MESSAGE 'Black olives?'
DEFINE BAR 2 OF olives PROMPT '\<Green' MESSAGE 'Green olives?'
DEFINE POPUP dessert MARGIN MESSAGE 'Our dessert offerings'
DEFINE BAR 1 OF dessert PROMPT '\<Brownies'
DEFINE BAR 2 OF dessert PROMPT '\<Cookies'
DEFINE BAR 3 OF dessert PROMPT '\<Ice Cream'
DEFINE BAR 4 OF dessert PROMPT '\<Pie'
ON BAR 4 OF dessert ACTIVATE POPUP pie
DEFINE POPUP pie MARGIN MESSAGE 'What kind of pie?'
DEFINE BAR 1 OF pie PROMPT '\<Blueberry'
DEFINE BAR 2 OF pie PROMPT '\<Cherry'
DEFINE BAR 3 OF pie PROMPT '\<Peach'
DEFINE BAR 4 OF pie PROMPT '\<Rhubarb'
ON SELECTION POPUP ALL DO yourchoice
ACTIVATE MENU mnuDinner
PROCEDURE yourchoice
ACTIVATE WINDOW wOrder
CLEAR
```

```
DO CASE
   CASE POPUP( ) = 'BURGER'
      @ 0,0 SAY 'A ' + POPUP( ) + ' order:'
      @ 1,0 SAY 'You ordered a burger with ' + LOWER(PROMPT( ))
   CASE POPUP( ) = 'PIZZA'
      @ 0,0 SAY 'A ' + POPUP( ) + ' order:'
      @ 1,0 SAY 'You ordered a pizza with ' + LOWER(PROMPT( ))
   CASE POPUP( ) = 'OLIVES'
      @ 0,0 SAY 'A ' + POPUP( ) + ' order:'
      @ 1,0 SAY 'You ordered a pizza with ' ;
         + LOWER(PROMPT( )) + ' olives'
   CASE POPUP( ) = 'DESSERT'
      @ 0,0 SAY 'A ' + POPUP( ) + ' order:'
      @ 1,0 SAY 'You ordered ' + LOWER(PROMPT( )) + ' for dessert'
   CASE POPUP( ) = 'PIE'
      @ 0,0 SAY 'A ' + POPUP( ) + ' order:'
      @ 1,0 SAY 'You ordered ' + LOWER(PROMPT( )) + ' pie'
ENDCASE
WAIT WINDOW
DEACTIVATE WINDOW wOrder
RETURN
```

See Also

ACTIVATE MENU, DEFINE BAR, DEFINE MENU, DEFINE POPUP,
ON SELECTION BAR, ON SELECTION POPUP

ON ERROR Command

Specifies a command that executes when an error occurs.

Syntax

ON ERROR
   [*Command*]

Arguments

Command

Specifies the Microsoft Visual FoxPro command to execute. After the command
executes, program execution resumes on the line immediately following the line that
caused the error. However, if the error-handling procedure includes RETRY, the
program line that caused the error is executed again.

If the command specifies a procedure to execute when an error occurs, you can use
ERROR( ), MESSAGE( ), LINENO( ), and PROGRAM( ) to pass the error number,
the error message, the program line number, and the program name to the procedure.
This information can be used to correct the cause of the error.

Remarks

When an error occurs during program execution, Visual FoxPro executes the command you specify with ON ERROR. Typically, ON ERROR uses DO to execute an error-handling procedure.

Use ON ERROR without a command to restore the default Visual FoxPro error handler.

ON ERROR procedures cannot be nested. If ON ERROR is issued within an ON ERROR procedure, the default Visual FoxPro error handler is restored.

Example

```
ON ERROR DO errhand WITH ;
   ERROR( ), MESSAGE( ), MESSAGE(1), PROGRAM( ), LINENO( )
*** The next line should cause an error ***
USE nodatabase

ON ERROR   && restore system error handler
PROCEDURE errhand
PARAMETER merror, mess, mess1, mprog, mlineno
CLEAR
? 'Error number: ' + LTRIM(STR(merror))
? 'Error message: ' + mess
? 'Line of code with error: ' + mess1
? 'Line number of error: ' + LTRIM(STR(mlineno))
? 'Program with error: ' + mprog
```

See Also

AERROR( ), COMRETURNERROR( ), DO, ERROR( ), FUNCTION, LINENO( ), MESSAGE( ), PROGRAM( ), PROCEDURE, RETRY

ON ESCAPE Command

Specifies a command that executes when you press the ESC key during program or command execution.

Syntax

ON ESCAPE
   [*Command*]

Arguments

Command
   Specifies the Visual FoxPro command to execute. After the command executes, program execution resumes on the line immediately following the program line that was executing when you pressed ESC. However, if a procedure specified with ON ESCAPE includes RETRY, the program line that was executing when you pressed ESC executes again.

Remarks

Typically, ON ESCAPE uses DO to execute a procedure.

If both ON ESCAPE and ON KEY are in effect and you press ESC, Visual FoxPro executes the command specified with ON ESCAPE.

Use ON ESCAPE without a command to cause no command to execute when ESC is pressed (the default).

Note Visual FoxPro doesn't execute an ON ESCAPE routine if SET ESCAPE is OFF.

Example

The following example sets up an infinite loop but defines an ON ESCAPE routine to exit it.

```
SET ESCAPE ON

ON ESCAPE DO stopit
WAIT WINDOW 'Press ESC to stop loop' NOWAIT
glMoreLoop = .T.

DO WHILE glMoreLoop
ENDDO
RETURN

PROCEDURE stopit
glMoreLoop = .F.
RETURN
```

See Also

INKEY( )

ON EXIT BAR Command

Included for compatibility with dBASE.

ON EXIT MENU Command

Included for compatibility with dBASE.

ON EXIT PAD Command

Included for compatibility with dBASE.

ON EXIT POPUP Command

Included for compatibility with dBASE.

ON KEY Command

Included for backward compatibility. Use ON KEY LABEL instead.

ON KEY = Command

Included for backward compatibility. Use ON KEY LABEL instead.

ON KEY LABEL Command

Specifies a command that executes when you press a specific key or key combination or click the mouse button.

Syntax

ON KEY [LABEL *KeyLabelName*] [*Command*]

Arguments

LABEL *KeyLabelName*
> Specifies the key label name assigned to the key. The *KeyLabelName* is the letter or digit on the key or a special name assigned to the key. The following table lists the special key label names.

Visual FoxPro key label assignments

For this key	Specify this *KeyLabelName* value
←	LEFTARROW
→	RIGHTARROW
↑	UPARROW
↓	DNARROW
HOME	HOME
END	END
PAGE UP	PGUP

Visual FoxPro key label assignments *(continued)*

For this key	Specify this *KeyLabelName* value
PAGE DOWN	PGDN
DEL	DEL
BACKSPACE	BACKSPACE
SPACEBAR	SPACEBAR
INS	INS
TAB	TAB
SHIFT+TAB	BACKTAB
ENTER	ENTER
F1 to F12	F1, F2, F3 ...
CTRL+F1 to CTRL+F12	CTRL+F1, CTRL+F2 ...
SHIFT+F1 to SHIFT+F12	SHIFT+F1, SHIFT+F2 ...
ALT+F1 to ALT+F12	ALT+F1, ALT+F2, ALT+F3 ...
ALT+0 to ALT+9	ALT+0, ALT+1, ALT+2 ...
ALT+A to ALT+Z	ALT+A, ALT+B, ALT+C ...
CTRL+LEFT ARROW	CTRL+LEFTARROW
CTRL+RIGHT ARROW	CTRL+RIGHTARROW
CTRL+HOME	CTRL+HOME
CTRL+END	CTRL+END
CTRL+PAGE UP	CTRL+PGUP
CTRL+PAGE DOWN	CTRL+PGDN
CTRL+A TO CTRL+Z	CTRL+A, CTRL+B, CTRL+C ...
CTRL+0	CTRL+0
RIGHT MOUSE BUTTON	RIGHTMOUSE
LEFT MOUSE BUTTON	LEFTMOUSE
MOUSE BUTTON	MOUSE
ESC	ESC

Command

Specifies the command that executes when you press the specified key or key combination or click the mouse button.

You can include parameter or parameter expressions with the command that you assign to the key, as in the following example:

```
ON KEY LABEL ALT+V WAIT WINDOW "Version: " + VERSION()
```

You can include variables in the assignment, but they must be public. For example:

```
PUBLIC message
message = "Default drive: " + SYS(5)
ON KEY LABEL ALT+D WAIT WINDOW message
```

Remarks

ON KEY LABEL typically uses DO to execute a procedure.

ON KEY LABEL executes the command immediately during the execution of READ, BROWSE, EDIT, CHANGE, and user-defined menus. If a program is executing when you press the key or click the mouse button, Visual FoxPro executes the current program line and then executes the ON KEY LABEL command. Any ON KEY LABEL key assignments created in a program remain in effect after the program is run. You can also create key assignments in the Command window.

To restore the behavior of a specific key to normal, issue ON KEY LABEL *KeyLabelName*. To restore all keys to their default behavior, issue ON KEY.

Tip To prevent recursive calls during the execution of an ON KEY LABEL procedure, include PUSH KEY CLEAR early in the procedure to disable all active ON KEY LABEL commands. Issue POP KEY at the end of the procedure to enable the ON KEY LABEL commands.

The ON KEY LABEL key assignments aren't in effect in the Visual FoxPro system menu bar, system menus, dialog boxes, alerts, and so on. The key assignments are effective in the Visual FoxPro system windows — the Visual FoxPro text editor, the Command window, the Trace window, and so on.

Unlike ON KEY, there can be multiple active ON KEY LABEL commands. For example, you can assign a command to each of the arrow keys and a mouse button.

Executing an ON KEY LABEL resets PARAMETERS( ) to 0. For more information, see the PARAMETERS( ) Function, later in this language reference.

In Visual FoxPro, certain events cannot be trapped because they are under the control of Windows. In particular, ON KEY LABEL MOUSE, ON KEY LABEL LEFTMOUSE, and ON KEY LABEL RIGHTMOUSE are not executed when you click a Windows control such as a Control menu, scroll bar, or the like. Also, CTRL+0 is supported in ON KEY LABEL in Visual FoxPro, allowing you to redefine the key combination used to enter a null value into a field.

Note that ON KEY LABEL operates outside of the scope of a form; the KeyPress event can be used within forms to execute code when a key is pressed.

Example

The following example displays a message when an arrow key is pressed.

```
CLEAR
PUBLIC msg
msg = CHR(13) + CHR(13) + "Press F9 to " + ;
   restore default key definition."

ON KEY LABEL RIGHTARROW Wait Window "Right Arrow " + msg NOWAIT

ON KEY LABEL LEFTARROW Wait Window "Left Arrow " + msg NOWAIT

ON KEY LABEL UPARROW Wait Window "Up Arrow " + msg NOWAIT

ON KEY LABEL DNARROW Wait Window "Down Arrow " + msg NOWAIT

* Press F9 to clear the ON KEY LABEL assignments

ON KEY LABEL F9 ON KEY
```

See Also

INKEY( ), KeyPress Event, ON( ), POP KEY, PUSH KEY

ON PAD Command

Specifies the menu or menu bar that is activated when you choose a specific menu title.

Syntax

ON PAD *MenuTitleName* OF *MenuBarName1*
    [ACTIVATE POPUP *MenuName*
    | ACTIVATE MENU *MenuBarName2*

Arguments

MenuTitleName OF *MenuBarName1*
    Specifies the menu title to which a menu or menu bar is assigned.

ACTIVATE POPUP *MenuName*
    Specifies the menu to activate when the menu title is chosen. Use ON PAD *MenuTitleName* OF *MenuBarName1* without ACTIVATE POPUP to release a menu from a menu title.

    If you specify the system menu bar _MSYSMENU for *MenuBarName1*, *MenuName* cannot specify a menu that is created with the DEFINE POPUP PROMPT clause.

ACTIVATE MENU *MenuBarName2*
> Specifies the name of the menu bar to activate when the menu title is chosen. Use ON PAD *MenuTitleName* OF *MenuBarName1* without ACTIVATE MENU to release a menu bar from a menu name.

Remarks

Use ON SELECTION PAD to execute a command when a menu title is chosen.

See Also

ACTIVATE MENU, DEFINE MENU, ON SELECTION MENU, ON SELECTION PAD

ON PAGE Command

Specifies a command that executes when printed output reaches a specified line number in a report or when you issue EJECT PAGE.

Syntax

ON PAGE
> [AT LINE *nLineNumber* [*Command*]]

Arguments

AT LINE *nLineNumber* [*Command*]
> Specifies the command to execute at the designated line number. The specified command executes when _PLINENO, the system variable that keeps track of the current line number in a report, becomes greater than the line number specified with *nLineNumber*. The command specified with ON PAGE also executes when you issue EJECT PAGE. For more information, see the EJECT PAGE Command, earlier in this language reference.

Remarks

ON PAGE typically uses DO to execute a procedure for handling page breaks, headers, and footers.

Executing ON PAGE without the AT LINE clause clears the ON PAGE command.

See Also

EJECT PAGE

ON READERROR Command

Included for backward compatibility. Use the Valid event instead.

ON SELECTION BAR Command

Specifies a command that executes when you choose a specific menu item.

Syntax

ON SELECTION BAR *nMenuItemNumber* OF *MenuName*
    [*Command*]

Arguments

nMenuItemNumber OF *MenuName* [*Command*]
    Specifies the menu item's bar number, the menu name, and the command to execute
    for the specified menu item.

Remarks

Typically, ON SELECTION BAR uses DO to execute a procedure or program. When you
create and activate a menu, place ON SELECTION BAR between DEFINE POPUP and
ACTIVATE POPUP.

You can also use ON SELECTION BAR with a Visual FoxPro system menu.

Use ON SELECTION POPUP to execute a command when you choose any menu item
on a menu. Use ON BAR to activate a menu or menu bar when you choose a specific
menu item.

Use ON SELECTION BAR *nMenuItemNumber* OF *MenuName* without a command to
release a command assigned to a menu item.

See Also

DEFINE BAR, DEFINE POPUP, ON BAR, ON SELECTION POPUP

ON SELECTION MENU Command

Specifies a command that executes when you choose any menu title on a menu bar.

Syntax

ON SELECTION MENU *MenuBarName* | ALL
    [*Command*]

Arguments

MenuBarName
    Specifies the name of the menu bar to which you assign a command. The command
    executes when you choose any menu title from the menu bar. You can specify the
    name of a user-defined menu bar created with DEFINE MENU or the Microsoft
    Visual FoxPro system menu bar _MSYSMENU.

ALL

Executes a command when you choose any menu title from any menu bar.

Command

Specifies the command to execute when you choose a menu title. Use ON SELECTION MENU without a command to release a command assigned to a menu bar.

Remarks

When you create and activate a menu bar, place ON SELECTION MENU between DEFINE MENU and ACTIVATE MENU.

Use ON SELECTION PAD to execute a command when you choose a specific menu item. ON SELECTION PAD takes precedence over ON SELECTION MENU. Use ON PAD to activate a menu or menu bar when you choose a specific menu title.

Use ON SELECTION MENU without a command to release a command assigned to a menu bar.

Example

In the following example, ON SELECTION MENU is used to execute a procedure when a menu title is chosen from the Visual FoxPro system menu bar.

The current system menu bar is saved to memory with SET SYSMENU SAVE and all system menu titles are removed with SET SYSMENU TO.

DEFINE PAD creates several system menu titles. When you choose a menu title, the choice procedure assigned to the menu bar with ON SELECTION MENU executes. The choice procedure displays the name of the menu title you choose and the name of the menu bar. If you choose the Exit menu title, the original Visual FoxPro system menu is restored.

```
*** Name this program ONMENU.PRG ***
CLEAR
SET SYSMENU SAVE
SET SYSMENU TO
DEFINE PAD padSys OF _MSYSMENU PROMPT '\<System' COLOR SCHEME 3 ;
   KEY ALT+S, ''
DEFINE PAD padEdit OF _MSYSMENU PROMPT '\<Edit' COLOR SCHEME 3 ;
   KEY ALT+E, ''
DEFINE PAD padRecord OF _MSYSMENU PROMPT '\<Record' COLOR SCHEME 3 ;
   KEY ALT+R, ''
DEFINE PAD padWindow OF _MSYSMENU PROMPT '\<Window' COLOR SCHEME 3 ;
   KEY ALT+W, ''
DEFINE PAD padReport OF _MSYSMENU PROMPT 'Re\<ports' COLOR SCHEME 3 KEY ALT+P, ''
DEFINE PAD padExit OF _MSYSMENU PROMPT 'E\<xit' COLOR SCHEME 3 ;
   KEY ALT+X, ''
```

```
ON SELECTION MENU _MSYSMENU ;
   DO choice IN onmenu WITH PAD( ), MENU( )
PROCEDURE choice
PARAMETER gcPad, gcMenu
WAIT WINDOW 'You chose ' + gcPad + ;
   ' from menu ' + gcMenu NOWAIT
IF gcPad = 'PADEXIT'
   SET SYSMENU TO DEFAULT
ENDIF
```

See Also

ACTIVATE MENU, DEFINE MENU, ON PAD, ON SELECTION PAD

ON SELECTION PAD Command

Specifies a command that executes when you choose a specific menu title on a menu bar.

Syntax

ON SELECTION PAD *MenuTitleName* OF *MenuBarName*
  [*Command*]

Arguments

MenuTitleName OF *MenuBarName*
  Specifies the menu title name to which the command is assigned.

Command
  Specifies the Visual FoxPro command to execute when you choose the specified menu title.

Remarks

When you choose the specified menu title, Visual FoxPro executes the command you specify with ON SELECTION PAD. Typically, ON SELECTION PAD uses DO to execute a procedure or program when you choose a specific menu title from the menu bar. When you create and activate the menu bar, place ON SELECTION PAD between DEFINE MENU and ACTIVATE MENU.

Use ON SELECTION MENU to execute a command when you choose any menu title on a menu bar. Use ON PAD to activate a menu or menu bar when you choose a specific menu title on a menu bar.

Use ON SELECTION PAD without a command to release a command assigned to the menu title.

See Also

ACTIVATE MENU, DEFINE MENU, DEFINE PAD, ON PAD, ON SELECTION MENU

ON SELECTION POPUP Command

Specifies a command that executes when you choose any menu item from a specified menu or from all menus.

Syntax

ON SELECTION POPUP *MenuName* | ALL
    [*Command*]

Arguments

MenuName
    Specifies the menu to which the command is assigned.

ALL
    If you include ALL instead of a menu name, Visual FoxPro executes the command when you choose a menu item from any menu.

Command
    Specifies the command to execute when you choose a menu item.

Remarks

When you choose any menu item from a menu, Visual FoxPro executes the command you specify with ON SELECTION POPUP. When you create and activate the menu, place ON SELECTION POPUP between DEFINE POPUP and ACTIVATE POPUP.

Use ON SELECTION BAR to execute a command when you choose a specific menu item. ON SELECTION BAR takes precedence over ON SELECTION POPUP. Use ON BAR to activate a menu or menu bar when you choose a specific menu item.

Use ON SELECTION POPUP without a command to release a command assigned to a menu item with a previous ON SELECTION POPUP.

See Also

ACTIVATE POPUP, DEFINE BAR, DEFINE POPUP, ON BAR

ON SHUTDOWN Command

Specifies a command that executes when you try to exit Visual FoxPro, or Microsoft Windows.

Syntax

ON SHUTDOWN [*Command*]

Arguments

Issue ON SHUTDOWN without *Command* to release the current ON SHUTDOWN command.

Remarks

The command you specify in ON SHUTDOWN is executed if you try to exit Visual FoxPro. If you try to exit Microsoft Windows while Visual FoxPro is open, control is returned to Visual FoxPro and the command you specify in ON SHUTDOWN is executed.

The ON SHUTDOWN command is typically a DO command that executes a routine to display a dialog box. The dialog box asks if you are sure you want to exit the current application and Visual FoxPro. If you want to exit the application, the routine can close open files, clean up the Visual FoxPro environment and then execute QUIT. If you don't want to exit the current application, the routine can return control back to the application.

See Also

QUIT

ON( ) Function

Returns the command assigned to each of these event-handling commands: ON ERROR, ON ESCAPE, ON KEY LABEL, or ON PAGE.

Syntax

ON(*cONCommand* [, *KeyLabelName*])

Returns

Character

Arguments

cONCommand

Specifies one of the event-handling commands. Here are the commands and corresponding character expressions to use with ON( ):

Command	*cONCommand*
ON ERROR	ERROR
ON ESCAPE	ESCAPE
ON KEY LABEL	KEY
ON PAGE	PAGE

For example, to return the command currently assigned to ON ERROR, use the following:

```
? ON('ERROR')
```

KeyLabelName

Used in ON KEY LABEL to specify a key or key combination to which the command is assigned. Specify KEY in *cONCommand* and the key label name of the key or key combination in *KeyLabelName*. For a complete list of key label names, see the ON KEY LABEL Command, earlier in this language reference.

For example, to return the command currently assigned to the F7 function key with ON KEY LABEL, use the following:

```
? ON('KEY', 'F7')
```

Remarks

When an event occurs that is trapped by one of the event-handling commands, the command assigned by the event-handling command executes. ON( ) returns the command you assigned to an event-handling command. ON( ) returns an empty string if a command isn't currently assigned to the event-handling command you specify.

Example

The following example uses ON( ) to display ON ERROR and ON KEY LABEL settings.

```
ON ERROR DO errorhand
ON KEY LABEL CTRL+F2 WAIT WINDOW 'You pressed ^F2'
ON KEY LABEL ALT+Z DISPLAY MEMORY
CLEAR
? ON('ERROR')  && Displays DO errorhand
? ON('KEY', 'CTRL+F2')  && Displays WAIT WINDOW 'You pressed ^F2'
? ON('KEY', 'ALT+Z')  && Displays DISPLAY MEMORY
ON ERROR
ON KEY LABEL CTRL+F2
ON KEY LABEL ALT+Z
```

See Also

INKEY( ), LASTKEY( ), ON ERROR, ON ESCAPE, ON KEY, ON KEY LABEL, ON PAGE, ON READERROR, READKEY( )

OneToMany Property

When moving through records in the parent table, specifies whether the record pointer remains on the same parent record until the record pointer of the child table moves through all related records. Available at design time; read-only at run time.

Syntax

Object.DataEnvironment.Relation.OneToMany[= *lExpr*]

Arguments

lExpr

The settings for the OneToMany property are:

Setting	Description
True (.T.)	The record pointer remains on the same parent record until the record pointer of the child table moves through all related records.
False (.F.)	(Default) The parent table's record pointer moves to the specified record and the child table's record pointer moves to the first related record.

Remarks

The OneToMany property can be used to specify the record pointer movement in a simple parent-child table relationship. To specify the record pointer movement in a more complex relationship (for example, a grandparent-parent-child relationship), use SET SKIP in the Init method for the Form or report.

When OneToMany is set to true (.T.), it mimics the behavior of SET SKIP.

Applies To

Relation

See Also

SET SKIP

OPEN DATABASE Command

Opens a database.

Syntax

OPEN DATABASE [*FileName* | ?]
    [EXCLUSIVE | SHARED]
    [NOUPDATE]
    [VALIDATE]

Arguments

FileName

Specifies the name of the database to open. If you don't specify an extension for the file name, Pro automatically assigns a .dbc extension. If you omit *FileName*, the Open dialog box is displayed. You can specify a path name as part of the database name.

Note Pro will not recognize a path name properly if a disk or directory name contains an exclamation point (!).

?

Displays the Open dialog box from which you can choose an existing database or enter the name of a new form to create.

EXCLUSIVE

Opens the database in exclusive mode. If you open the database exclusively, other users cannot access it and will receive an error if they try to gain access. If you do not include EXCLUSIVE or SHARED, the current SET EXCLUSIVE setting determines how the database is opened.

SHARED

Opens the database in shared mode. If you open the database for shared use, other users have access to it. If you do not include EXCLUSIVE or SHARED, the current SET EXCLUSIVE setting determines how the database is opened.

NOUPDATE

Specifies that no changes can be made to the database. In other words, the database is read-only. If you omit NOUPDATE, the database is opened with read/write access.

Tables contained in the database are not affected by NOUPDATE. To prevent changes to a table in the database, include NOUPDATE in USE when you open the table.

VALIDATE

Specifies that Pro ensures that references in the database are valid. Pro checks to see that tables and indexes referenced in the database are available on disk. Visual FoxPro also checks to see that referenced fields and index tags exist in the tables and indexes.

Remarks

While the database is open, all tables contained in it are available. However, the tables are not implicitly opened. You must open them with USE.

When USE executes, Visual FoxPro looks for the table within the current database. If the table isn't found, Visual FoxPro then looks for a table outside the database. This means that if a table in a database has the same name as a table outside the database, the table in the database is found first.

You cannot open a database that has been opened exclusively by another user.

Example

In the following example, OPEN DATABASE is used to open the testdata database. DISPLAY DATABASE is used to display information about the tables in the database.

```
CLOSE DATABASES
SET PATH TO (HOME(2) + 'Data\')    && Sets path to database

OPEN DATABASE testdata  && Open testdata database
DISPLAY DATABASE  && Displays table information
```

See Also

ADD TABLE, CLOSE DATABASES, CREATE DATABASE, DBUSED( ), DISPLAY DATABASE, FREE TABLE, LIST DATABASE, REMOVE TABLE

OpenTables Method

Programmatically opens the tables and views associated with the data environment.

Syntax

DataEnvironment.OpenTables

Arguments

DataEnvironment
    Specifies the data environment associated with the form, form set, or report.

Remarks

The OpenTables method loads the data environment tables when the AutoOpenTables property of the data environment is set to false (.F.), or if the data environment has been unloaded using the CloseTables method.

Applies To

DataEnvironment

See Also

AfterCloseTables Event, AutoOpenTables Property, BeforeOpenTables Event, CloseTables Method

OpenViews Property

Determines the type of views associated with a form set, form, or report's data environment that are opened automatically. Available at design time; read-only at run time.

Syntax

DataEnvironment.OpenViews[= *nExpression*]

Arguments

nExpression
    The settings for the OpenViews property are:

Setting	Description
0	(Default) Local and Remote. Both local and remote views for the data environment for the form set, form, or report are opened automatically.
1	Local only. Only local views for the data environment for the form set, form, or report are opened automatically.

(continued)

(continued)

Setting	Description
2	Remote only. Only remote views for the data environment of the form set, form, or report are opened automatically.
3	None. No views are opened for the data environment of the form set, form, or report.

Remarks

The OpenViews property applies when the AutoOpenTables property is set to true (.T.) or the OpenTables method is executed.

Applies To

DataEnvironment

See Also

AutoOpenTables Property, OpenTables Method

OpenWindow Property

Included for backward compatibility. Use an EditBox control instead.

OptionButton Control

Creates a single option button.

Syntax

OptionButton

Remarks

A single option button can be added only to a group of option buttons.

For more information about creating a group of option buttons, see the "OptionGroup Control," later in this language reference, and Chapter 10, "Using Controls," in the *Microsoft Visual FoxPro 6.0 Programmer's Guide*.

Properties

Alignment	Application	AutoSize
BackColor	BackStyle	BaseClass
Caption	Class	ClassLibrary

ColorScheme	ColorSource	Comment
ControlSource	DisabledBackColor	DisabledForeColor
DisabledPicture	DownPicture	DragIcon
DragMode	Enabled	FontBold
FontCondense	FontExtend	FontItalic
FontName	FontOutline	FontShadow
FontSize	FontStrikeThru	FontUnderLine
ForeColor	Height	HelpContextID
Left	MousePointer	Name
OLEDragMode	OLEDragPicture	OLEDropEffects
OLEDropHasData Property	OLEDropMode	Parent
ParentClass	Picture	RightToLeft
SpecialEffect	StatusBarText	Style
TabIndex	TabStop	Tag
TerminateRead	ToolTipText	Top
Value	Visible	WhatsThisHelpID
Width		

Events

Click	DblClick	Destroy
DragDrop	DragOver	Error
ErrorMessage	GotFocus	Init
KeyPress	LostFocus	Message
MiddleClick Event	MouseDown	MouseMove
MouseUp	MouseWheel	OLECompleteDrag
OLEDragDrop	OLEDragOver	OLEGiveFeedBack
OLESetData	OLEStartDrag	RightClick
Valid	When	

Methods

AddProperty	CloneObject	Drag
Move	OLEDrag	ReadExpression
ReadMethod	Refresh	ResetToDefault
SaveAsClass	SetFocus	WriteExpression
WriteMethod	ZOrder	

See Also

CREATE FORM, CREATE CLASS, DEFINE CLASS, OptionGroup Control

OptionGroup Control

Creates a group of option buttons.

Syntax

OptionGroup

Remarks

Option button groups are containers that contain option buttons. A group of option buttons let you make a choice from a set of buttons. Choosing an option button makes your choice current and releases a previous choice. A bullet next to the option button indicates the current choice. For example, option buttons can be used to direct output to a file, a printer, or a window.

For additional information about creating groups of option buttons, see Chapter 10, "Using Controls," in the *Microsoft Visual FoxPro 6.0 Programmer's Guide*.

Properties

Application	AutoSize	BackColor
BackStyle	BaseClass	BorderColor
BorderStyle	ButtonCount	Buttons
Class	ClassLibrary	Comment
ColorSource Property	ControlSource	DragIcon
DragMode	Enabled	Height
HelpContextID	Left	MouseIcon

MousePointer	Name	OLEDragMode
OLEDragPicture	OLEDropEffects	OLEDropHasData Property
OLEDropMode	Parent	ParentClass
SpecialEffect	TabIndex	Tag
TerminateRead	Top	Value
Visible	WhatsThisHelpID	Width

Events

Click	DblClick	DragDrop
DragOver	Error	ErrorMessage
Init	InteractiveChange	Message
MiddleClick Event	MouseDown	MouseMove
MouseUp	MouseWheel	OLECompleteDrag
OLEDragDrop	OLEDragOver	OLEGiveFeedBack
OLESetData	OLEStartDrag	ProgrammaticChange
RightClick	UIEnable	Valid
When		

Methods

AddObject	AddProperty	CloneObject
Drag	Move	OLEDrag
ReadExpression	ReadMethod	Refresh
RemoveObject	ResetToDefault	SaveAsClass
SetAll	WriteExpression	WriteMethod
ZOrder		

Example

The following example creates an OptionGroup control and places the control on a form. The OptionGroup control has three buttons, and depending on the option button you click, a circle, ellipse, or square is displayed. The Buttons and Caption properties are used to specify the text displayed next to each option button.

The Shape control is used to create the circle, ellipse, and square. The OptionGroup control's Click event uses a DO CASE ... ENDCASE structure and the Value property to display the appropriate shape when you click an option button.

```
frmMyForm = CREATEOBJECT('Form')  && Create a Form
frmMyForm.Closable = .F.  && Disable the Control menu box

frmMyForm.AddObject('cmdCommand1','cmdMyCmndBtn')  && Add Command button
frmMyForm.AddObject('opgOptionGroup1','opgMyOptGrp') && Add Option Group
frmMyForm.AddObject('shpCircle1','shpMyCircle')  && Add Circle Shape
frmMyForm.AddObject('shpEllipse1','shpMyEllipse')  && Add Ellipse Shape
frmMyForm.AddObject('shpSquare','shpMySquare')  && Add Box Shape

frmMyForm.cmdCommand1.Visible =.T.  && "Quit" Command button visible

frmMyForm.opgOptionGroup1.Buttons(1).Caption = "\<Circle"
frmMyForm.opgOptionGroup1.Buttons(2).Caption = "\<Ellipse"
frmMyForm.opgOptionGroup1.Buttons(3).Caption = "\<Square"
frmMyForm.opgOptionGroup1.SetAll("Width", 100) && Set Option group width
frmMyForm.opgOptionGroup1.Visible = .T.  && Option Group visible
frmMyForm.opgOptionGroup1.Click  && Show the circle

frmMyForm.SHOW  && Display the form
READ EVENTS  && Start event processing

DEFINE CLASS opgMyOptGrp AS OptionGroup  && Create an Option Group
   ButtonCount = 3  && Three Option buttons
   Top = 10
   Left = 10
   Height = 75
   Width = 100

   PROCEDURE Click
      ThisForm.shpCircle1.Visible = .F.  && Hide the circle
      ThisForm.shpEllipse1.Visible = .F.  && Hide the ellipse
      ThisForm.shpSquare.Visible = .F.  && Hide the square

      DO CASE
         CASE ThisForm.opgOptionGroup1.Value = 1
            ThisForm.shpCircle1.Visible = .T. && Show the circle
         CASE ThisForm.opgOptionGroup1.Value = 2
            ThisForm.shpEllipse1.Visible = .T.  && Show the ellipse
         CASE ThisForm.opgOptionGroup1.Value = 3
            ThisForm.shpSquare.Visible = .T.  && Show the square
      ENDCASE
ENDDEFINE

DEFINE CLASS cmdMyCmndBtn AS CommandButton  && Create Command button
   Caption = '\<Quit'  && Caption on the Command button
   Cancel = .T.  && Default Cancel Command button (Esc)
   Left = 125  && Command button column
   Top = 210  && Command button row
   Height = 25  && Command button height
```

```
   PROCEDURE Click
      CLEAR EVENTS  && Stop event processing, close Form
ENDDEFINE

DEFINE CLASS shpMyCircle AS SHAPE  && Create a circle
   Top = 10
   Left = 200
   Width = 100
   Height = 100
   Curvature = 99
   BackColor = RGB(255,0,0)  && Red
ENDDEFINE

DEFINE CLASS shpMyEllipse AS SHAPE  && Create an ellipse
   Top = 35
   Left = 200
   Width = 100
   Height = 50
   Curvature = 99
   BackColor = RGB(0,128,0)  && Green
ENDDEFINE

DEFINE CLASS shpMySquare AS SHAPE  && Create a square
   Top = 10
   Left = 200
   Width = 100
   Height = 100
   Curvature = 0
   BackColor = RGB(0,0,255)  && Blue
ENDDEFINE
```

See Also

CREATE FORM, CREATE CLASS, DEFINE CLASS, OptionButton Control

Order Property

Specifies the controlling index tag for a Cursor object. Available at design time and run time.

Syntax

*DataEnvironment.Cursor.*Order[= *cTagName*]

Arguments

cTagName
   Specifies an existing index tag for a table.

Remarks

If the ChildOrder property of a relation object is set, the Order property is ignored.

Use the Order property to specify the order in which records are displayed or accessed. Setting the Order property changes the index order and moves the record pointer to the first record in the cursor.

Applies To

Cursor

See Also

ChildOrder Property, INDEX, SET ORDER

ORDER( ) Function

Returns the name of the controlling index file or tag for the current or specified table.

Syntax

ORDER([*nWorkArea* | *cTableAlias* [, *nPath*]])

Returns

Character

Arguments

nWorkArea
Specifies the work area of a table whose controlling index file name or controlling tag name ORDER( ) returns.

cTableAlias
Specifies a table alias whose controlling index file name or controlling tag name ORDER( ) returns.

nPath
Specifies that the drive and directory are returned along with the single-entry or compound index file name. The numeric expression *nPath* can have any value.

Remarks

A table can have several index files open simultaneously. However, only one single-entry index file (the controlling index file) or tag from a compound index file (the controlling tag) controls the order in which the table is displayed or accessed. Certain commands, such as SEEK, use the controlling index file or controlling tag to search for records. This function returns the name of the controlling index file or controlling tag.

USE and SET INDEX both support opening more than one index with an index file list. A controlling index file or controlling tag can be designated in this index file list. SET ORDER can also be used to designate a controlling index or controlling tag.

By default, ORDER( ) returns the controlling index file name or controlling tag name for the current work area. ORDER( ) returns the empty string if an order has not been set (SET ORDER TO is issued or there is no controlling index file or tag).

Example

The following example displays index tags and files.

```
CLOSE DATABASES
OPEN DATABASE (HOME(2) + 'Data\testdata')
USE customer ORDER cust_id && Opens Customer table
? ORDER( )  && Displays CUST_ID
? ORDER('customer', 1)  && Displays CUSTOMER.CDX
```

See Also

INDEX, SET INDEX, SET ORDER, USE

OS( ) Function

Returns the name and version number of the operating system under which Microsoft Visual FoxPro is running.

Syntax

OS([1 | 2])

Returns

Character

Arguments

1

Specifies that the name and version number of the operating system is returned.

2

Specifies that a character string indicating if the operating system supports DBCS (double-byte character sets) is returned If DBCS is supported, the character string "DBCS" is returned, otherwise the empty string is returned.

Remarks

If the optional 1 or 2 argument is omitted, the underlying operating system name and its version number is returned.

Example

```
? OS( )
? OS(1)
? OS(2)
```

See Also

DISKSPACE( ), GETENV( ), VERSION( )

PACK Command

Permanently removes all records marked for deletion in the current table and reduces the size of a memo file associated with the table.

Syntax

PACK [MEMO] [DBF]

Arguments

MEMO

Removes unused space from the memo file but doesn't remove records marked for deletion from the table. Information in memo fields is stored in an associated memo file. A memo file has the same name as the table and an .fpt extension.

DBF

Removes records marked for deletion from the table but doesn't affect the memo file.

Remarks

When you use PACK, Microsoft Visual FoxPro copies all records not marked for deletion to a temporary table. After PACK is finished executing, Visual FoxPro deletes the original table from disk and renames the temporary table with the original table name. If you press ESC to interrupt PACK, the temporary table is deleted, and the original table remains unchanged. The original table is also recovered if you run out of disk space while PACK is executing.

When you issue PACK without the MEMO and DBF clauses, PACK affects both the table and the memo file.

PACK requires exclusive use of the table. For more information about opening a table exclusively on a network, see the SET EXCLUSIVE Command, later in this language reference.

If the current table has one or more indexes open, PACK rebuilds the index files.

> **Caution** Be careful to mark only records that you no longer need. There is no way to retrieve deleted records after using PACK.

See Also

DELETE – SQL, DELETE, DELETED( ), RECALL, SET EXCLUSIVE

PACK DATABASE Command

Removes records marked for deletion from the current database.

Syntax

PACK DATABASE

Remarks

A database contains records marked for deletion after a table or view is removed from the database, or if the structure of a table in the database is modified.

The database must be opened exclusively, and no table or view in the database can be open.

Example

In the following example, PACK DATABASE is used to pack the testdata database, removing records marked for deletion.

```
CLOSE DATABASES
SET PATH TO (HOME(2) + 'data\')  && Sets path to database
OPEN DATABASE testdata  && Open the database
PACK DATABASE && Pack the current database
```

See Also

CLOSE DATABASES, DELETE DATABASE, MODIFY DATABASE, OPEN DATABASE, SET DATABASE, VALIDATE DATABASE

PAD( ) Function

Returns as an uppercase character string the menu title most recently chosen from a menu bar, or returns a logical value indicating if a menu title is defined for an active menu bar.

Syntax

PAD([cMenuTitle [, cMenuBarName]])

Returns

Character or Logical

Arguments

cMenuTitle
Specifies the name of a menu title in a menu bar. Include this argument to test if the menu title is defined for an active menu bar. A logical true (.T.) is returned if the menu title is defined; otherwise a logical false (.F.) is returned.

cMenuBarName

Specifies the name of the menu bar containing the menu title *cMenuTitle*. If *cMenuBarName* is omitted, the menu title is assumed to be in the currently active menu bar.

Remarks

A menu bar must be defined and active for PAD( ) to return a menu title. Menu bars are created and activated with DEFINE MENU and ACTIVATE MENU.

You can also use PAD( ) with the Visual FoxPro system menu bar.

PAD( ) (issued without any of its optional arguments) returns an empty string if a menu bar isn't defined and active or you issue PAD( ) from the Command window.

Example

In this example, PAD( ) is used to pass a menu title to a procedure.

The current Visual FoxPro system menu bar is saved to memory with SET SYSMENU SAVE , and all system menu titles are removed with SET SYSMENU TO.

Several system menu titles are created with DEFINE PAD. When a menu title is chosen, PAD( ) is used to pass the menu title to the procedure named choice. choice displays the menu title chosen and the name of the menu bar. If you choose the Exit menu title, the original Visual FoxPro system menu is restored.

```
*** Name this program PADEXAM.PRG ***
CLEAR
SET SYSMENU SAVE
SET SYSMENU TO
DEFINE PAD padSys OF _MSYSMENU PROMPT '\<System' COLOR SCHEME 3 ;
   KEY ALT+S, ''
DEFINE PAD padEdit OF _MSYSMENU PROMPT '\<Edit' COLOR SCHEME 3 ;
   KEY ALT+E, ''
DEFINE PAD padRecord OF _MSYSMENU PROMPT '\<Record' COLOR SCHEME 3 ;
   KEY ALT+R, ''
DEFINE PAD padWindow OF _MSYSMENU PROMPT '\<Window' COLOR SCHEME 3 ;
   KEY ALT+W, ''
DEFINE PAD padReport OF _MSYSMENU PROMPT 'Re\<ports' COLOR SCHEME 3 KEY ALT+P, ''
DEFINE PAD padExit OF _MSYSMENU PROMPT 'E\<xit' COLOR SCHEME 3 ;
   KEY ALT+X, ''
ON SELECTION MENU _MSYSMENU ;
   DO choice IN padexam WITH PAD( ), MENU( )
PROCEDURE choice
PARAMETERS gcPad, gcMenu
WAIT WINDOW 'You chose ' + gcPad + ;
   ' from menu ' + gcMenu NOWAIT
IF gcPad = 'PADEXIT'
   SET SYSMENU TO DEFAULT
ENDIF
```

See Also

ACTIVATE MENU, BAR( ), DEFINE PAD, DEFINE MENU, MENU( ), ON PAD,
ON SELECTION PAD, PROMPT( )

PADL( ) | PADR( ) | PADC( ) Functions

Returns a string from an expression, padded with spaces or characters to a specified
length on the left or right sides, or both.

Syntax

PADL(*eExpression*, *nResultSize* [, *cPadCharacter*])

– or –

PADR(*eExpression*, *nResultSize* [, *cPadCharacter*])

– or –

PADC(*eExpression*, *nResultSize* [, *cPadCharacter*])

Returns

Character

Arguments

eExpression
Specifies the expression to be padded. This expression can be any expression type
except a logical or currency expression or a general or picture field.

nResultSize
Specifies the total number of characters in the expression after it is padded.

cPadCharacter
Specifies the value to use for padding. This value is repeated as necessary to pad
the expression to the specified number of characters.

If you omit *cPadCharacter*, spaces (ASCII character 32) are used for padding.

Remarks

PADL( ) inserts padding on the left, PADR( ) inserts padding on the right, and PADC( )
inserts padding on both sides.

Example

```
STORE 'TITLE' TO gcString
CLEAR
? PADL(gcString, 40, '=')
? PADR(gcString, 40, '=')
? PADC(gcString, 40, '=')
```

See Also

ALLTRIM( ), LEFT( ), LTRIM( ), RIGHT( ), STUFF( ), TRIM( )

_PADVANCE System Variable

Included for backward compatibility. Use the Report Designer instead.

Page Object

Creates a page in a page frame.

Syntax

Page

Remarks

Pages allow you to create tabbed forms or dialogs. A set of pages is contained in a page frame.

You can refer to a page within a page frame by name as in this example:

```
myFrame.MyPage1
```

You can also refer to a page by its index number with the PAGES keyword. This is consistent with the control collections in other Visual FoxPro containers.

```
myFrame.PAGES(2).Enabled = .T.
```

This index does not necessarily equal the PageOrder property. You may have three pages with PageOrders of 2, 3, and 5. You can refer to these pages as follows:

```
myFrame.PAGES(1)
myFrame.PAGES(2)
myFrame.PAGES(3)
```

Only the active page is refreshed when the Refresh method occurs for the form on which the page is located.

For additional information about creating pages and page frames, see "Adding Page Frames to a Form" in Chapter 10, "Using Controls," in the *Microsoft Visual FoxPro 6.0 Programmer's Guide*.

Properties

ActiveControl	Application	BackColor
BackStyle	BaseClass	Caption
Class	ClassLibrary	ColorSource
Comment	ControlCount	Controls
DragIcon	DragMode	Enabled
FontBold	FontCondense	FontExtend
FontItalic	FontName	FontOutline
FontShadow	FontSize	FontStrikeThru
FontUnderline	ForeColor	HelpContextID
MouseIcon	MousePointer	Name
OLEDragMode	OLEDragPicture	OLEDropEffects
OLEDropHasData	OLEDropMode	PageOrder
Parent	ParentClass	Picture
Tag	ToolTipText	WhatsThisHelpID

Events

Activate	Click	DblClick
Deactivate	Destroy	DragDrop
DragOver	Error	Init
MiddleClick Event	MouseDown	MouseMove
MouseUp	MouseWheel	OLECompleteDrag
OLEDragDrop	OLEDragOver	OLEGiveFeedBack
OLESetData	OLEStartDrag	RightClick

Methods

AddObject	AddProperty	CloneObject
Drag	OLEDrag	ReadExpression
ReadMethod	Refresh	RemoveObject
ResetToDefault	SaveAsClass	SetAll
WriteExpression	WriteMethod	ZOrder

See Also

CREATE FORM, CREATE CLASS, DEFINE CLASS, PageFrame Control

PageCount Property

Specifies the number of pages contained in a page frame. Available at design time and run time.

Syntax

PageFrame.PageCount[= *nPages*]

Arguments

nPages
    Specifies the number of pages contained in a page frame.

Remarks

The minimum value for the PageCount property setting is 0, and the maximum value is 99.

> **Caution** If you decrease the PageCount property setting (for example, if you change the setting from 3 to 2), all pages that exceed the new setting and the objects they contain are lost.

Applies To

PageFrame

See Also

ButtonCount Property, ControlCount Property, FormCount Property, Page Object

PageFrame Control

Creates a page frame to contain pages.

Syntax

PageFrame

Remarks

A page frame is a container object that contains pages. Pages, in turn, can contain controls. Note that for a page frame to be visible, it must be added to a form.

The page frame defines global characteristics of the page: size and positioning, borderstyle, which page is active, and so on.

The page frame determines the location of the pages and how much of each page is visible. Pages are positioned at the top left corner of the page frame. If the page frame is moved, the pages move with the page frame.

A page frame contains the individual pages which by default are named Page1, Page2, Page3, and so on.

Note that only the active page is refreshed when the Refresh method occurs for the Form on which the page is located.

For additional information about creating pages and page frames, see "Adding Page Frames to a Form" in Chapter 10, "Using Controls," in the *Microsoft Visual FoxPro 6.0 Programmer's Guide*.

Properties

ActivePage	Application	BaseClass
BorderColor	BorderWidth	Class
ClassLibrary	ColorSource Property	Comment
DragIcon	DragMode	Enabled
HelpContextID	Height	Left
MouseIcon	MousePointer	Name
OLEDragMode	OLEDragPicture	OLEDropEffects
OLEDropHasData Property	OLEDropMode	PageCount
PageHeight	Pages	PageWidth
Parent	ParentClass	RightToLeft
SpecialEffect	TabIndex	Tabs
TabStop	TabStretch	TabStyle
Tag	Top	Visible
WhatsThisHelpID	Width	

Events

Click	DblClick	Destroy
DragDrop	DragOver	Error
Init	MiddleClick Event	MouseDown

MouseMove	MouseUp	MouseWheel
Moved	OLECompleteDrag	OLEDragDrop
OLEDragOver	OLEGiveFeedBack	OLESetData
OLEStartDrag	Resize	RightClick
UIEnable		

Methods

AddObject	AddProperty	CloneObject
Drag	Move	OLEDrag
ReadExpression	ReadMethod	Refresh
RemoveObject	ResetToDefault	SaveAsClass
SetAll	WriteExpression	WriteMethod
ZOrder		

See Also

CREATE FORM, CREATE CLASS, DEFINE CLASS, Page Object

PageHeight Property

Specifies the height of a page. Read-only at design time and run time.

Syntax

PageFrame.PageHeight[= *nHeight*]

Arguments

nHeight

Specifies the height of the page in the unit of measurement specified by the ScaleMode property of the form.

Applies To

PageFrame

See Also

PageWidth Property, Page Object, ScaleMode Property

_PAGENO System Variable

Contains the current page number.

Syntax

_PAGENO = *nCurrentPageNumber*

Arguments

nCurrentPageNumber
Specifies a numeric value from 1 to 32,767 for the current page number. _PAGENO, _PBPAGE and _PEPAGE work in unison. If _PAGENO is set (or incremented) such that it falls outside the range of _PBPAGE to _PEPAGE, no pages are printed.

Remarks

_PAGENO contains a numeric value that determines the current page number. The startup default is 1. _PAGENO allows you to print page numbers in streaming output without defining, initializing, and incrementing a memory variable for that purpose.

See Also

ON PAGE, _PBPAGE, _PEPAGE, _PLENGTH, _PLINENO

PageOrder Property

Specifies the relative order of pages in a page frame. Available at design time and run time.

Syntax

Page.PageOrder[= *nOrder*]

Arguments

nOrder
Specifies the relative order of a page in a page frame.

Remarks

If a page frame contains five pages and you want the third page displayed last, set the PageOrder property of the third page to 5. The PageOrder setting for the fourth page becomes 3, the PageOrder setting for the fifth page becomes 4, and so on.

Note PageOrder settings don't have to be sequential. Also, the PageOrder must be less than or equal to the number of pages in a page frame.

Applies To

Page

See Also

Activate Event, Deactivate Event, PageFrame Control, ZOrder Method

Pages Property

An array used to access individual pages in a page frame. Available at run time only.

Syntax

PageFrame.Pages(*Index*).Property[= *Expr*]

Arguments

Index
> Represents the index of the page you want to access.

Expr
> Specifies a property value for the page contained in a page frame.

Applies To

PageFrame

See Also

Buttons Property, Page Object, PageCount Property

PageWidth Property

Specifies the width of the page. Available at design time; read-only at run time.

Syntax

PageFrame.PageWidth[= *nWidth*]

Arguments

nWidth
> Specifies the width of the page in the unit of measurement specified by the ScaleMode property of the form.

Remarks

The PageWidth property setting is the same as the Width property setting unless the page frame contains more than one page and the pages are stacked.

Applies To

PageFrame

See Also

PageHeight Property, Page Object, ScaleMode Property

Paint Event

Occurs when a form or toolbar is repainted.

Syntax

PROCEDURE *Object*.Paint

Remarks

A form or toolbar is repainted when part or all of the form or toolbar is exposed after it has been moved or sized, or after a window that was covering the form or toolbar has been moved.

Using a Refresh method in a Resize event forces repainting of the entire object every time a user resizes the form or toolbar.

Using a Paint event for certain tasks can cause a cascading event. In general, avoid using a Paint event for the following:

- Moving or sizing a form or control.

- Changing any variables that affect size or appearance, such as setting an object's BackColor property.

- Calling the Refresh method.

> **Note** A Resize event may be more appropriate for some of these tasks.

Applies To

Form, ToolBar

See Also

Circle Method, ClipControls Property, Line Method, Print Method, PSet Method, Refresh Method, Resize Event

Panel Property

Specifies the active panel in a Grid control. Available at design time; read/write at run time. Available only if the Partition property is set to a value greater than 0.

Syntax

Grid.Panel[= *nSide*]

Arguments

nSide

The settings for the Panel property are:

Setting	Description
0	Left panel is active.
1	(Default) Right panel is active.

Applies To

Grid

See Also

PanelLink Property, Partition Property

PanelLink Property

Specifies whether the left and right panels of a Grid control are linked when the grid is split. Available at design time; read/write at run time. Available only if the Partition property is set to a value greater than 0.

Syntax

Grid.PanelLink[= *lExpr*]

Arguments

lExpr

The settings for the PanelLink property are:

Setting	Description
True (.T.)	(Default) The left and right panels of the grid are linked when the grid is split.
False (.F.)	The left and right panels of the grid are not linked when the grid is split.

If PanelLink is set to true (.T.), both panels of the grid are affected when the following properties are set: HeaderHeight, DeleteMark, GridLineColor, GridLines, GridLineWidth, Highlight, RecordMark, RowHeight, and ScrollBars.

If PanelLink is set to false (.F.), the Panel property setting determines which panel the following properties are set on: HeaderHeight, DeleteMark, GridLineColor, GridLines, GridLineWidth, HighLight, RecordMark, RowHeight, and ScrollBars.

Applies To

Grid

See Also

DeleteMark Property, GridLineColor Property, GridLines Property,
GridLineWidth Property, HeaderHeight Property, Highlight Property, Panel Property,
Partition Property, RecordMark Property, RowHeight Property, ScrollBars Property

PARAMETERS Command

Assigns data passed from a calling program to private variables or arrays.

Syntax

PARAMETERS *ParameterList*

Arguments

ParameterList

Specifies the variable or array names to which the data is assigned.

Parameters within *ParameterList* are separated by commas. There must be at least as
many parameters in the PARAMETERS statement as in the DO ... WITH statement.
If more variables or arrays are listed in the PARAMETERS statement than are passed
by DO ... WITH, the remaining variables or arrays are initialized to false (.F.).
A maximum of 27 parameters can be passed.

PARAMETERS( ) returns the number of parameters that were passed to the most
recently executed routine.

Remarks

When PARAMETERS is used with DO ... WITH, it must be the first executable statement
in the called program, procedure, or user-defined function.

By default, DO ... WITH passes variables and arrays to procedures by reference. When a
value is changed in the called procedure, the new value is passed back to the associated
variable or array in the calling program. If you want to pass a variable or array to a
procedure by value, enclose the variable or array in parentheses in the DO ... WITH
parameter list. Any changes made to the parameter in the called procedure are not passed
back to the calling program.

Variables are by default passed by reference to a procedure and by value to a user-defined
function. Use SET UDFPARMS TO REFERENCE to pass variables to a user-defined
function by reference.

Example

The following example passes parameters to an error-handling routine.

```
ON ERROR DO errhand WITH ERROR( ), MESSAGE( ), ;
   MESSAGE(1),PROGRAM( ),LINENO( )
USE nodatabase
ON ERROR      && restores system error-handling routine
```

```
PROCEDURE errhand
PARAMETERS gnError, gcMess, gnMess1, gcProg, gnLineNo
? 'Error number: ' + LTRIM(STR(gnError))
? 'Error message: ' + gcMess
? 'Line of code with error: ' + gnMess1
? 'Line number of error: '+ LTRIM(STR(gnLineNo))
? 'Program with error: ' + gcProg
```

See Also

DO, LOCAL, LPARAMETERS, PARAMETERS( ), PRIVATE, PUBLIC, SET UDFPARMS

PARAMETERS( ) Function

Returns the number of parameters passed to the most recently called program, procedure, or user-defined function.

Syntax

PARAMETERS( )

Returns

Numeric

Remarks

PARAMETERS( ) is useful for determining how many parameters are passed to a program, procedure, or user-defined function.

Note The value returned by PARAMETERS( ) is reset every time a program, procedure, or user-defined function is called or when ON KEY LABEL is executed. Unlike PARAMETERS( ), the PCOUNT( ) function does not get reset, so PCOUNT( ) may be preferable in most programming situations.

Examples

Example 1 calls a procedure and displays in a wait window the number of parameters passed.

Example 2 uses a procedure to display the average of 4 values.

```
* Example 1
DO testpar WITH 1,2,3

PROCEDURE testpar
PARAMETERS gn1,gn2,gn3
gcMessage = 'PARAMETERS( ) ='+ALLTRIM(STR(PARAMETERS( )))
WAIT WINDOW (gcMessage)
RETURN
```

```
* Example 2
SET TALK OFF
gnVal1 = 10
gnVal2 = 20
gnVal3 = 30
gnVal4 = 15
gnMin = getavg(gnVal1, gnVal2, gnVal3, gnVal4)
? 'Average value is '
?? gnMin

* This user-defined function permits up to 9 parameters to be passed.
* It uses the PARAMETERS( ) function to determine how many
* were passed and returns the average value.

FUNCTION getavg
PARAMETERS gnPara1,gnPara2,gnPara3,gnPara4,gnPara5, ;
   gnPara6,gnPara7,gnPara8,gnPara9
IF PARAMETERS( ) = 0
   RETURN 0
ENDIF
gnResult = 0
FOR gnCount = 1 to PARAMETERS( )
   gcCompare = 'gnPara' +(STR(gnCount,1))
   gnResult = gnResult + EVAL(gcCompare)
ENDFOR
gnResult = gnResult / (gnCount - 1)
RETURN gnResult
```

See Also

DO, FUNCTION, LPARAMETERS, LOCAL, PARAMETERS, PCOUNT( ), PRIVATE, PROCEDURE, PUBLIC, SET UDFPARMS

Parent Object Reference

References the container object of a control. Not available at design time; read-only at run time.

Syntax

Control.Parent

Remarks

Use the Parent keyword to access the properties, methods, or controls of a control's container object. You can also use the Parent object reference to access the container object of a page or form.

The Parent keyword is useful in an application in which you pass controls as arguments. For example, you can pass a control variable to a general procedure and use the Parent object reference to access its container object.

You can also use the Parent object reference for objects in a control class that have been placed on an unknown form.

Applies To

ActiveDoc Object, CheckBox, Column, ComboBox, CommandButton, CommandGroup, Container, Control, Custom, EditBox, Form, Grid, Header, Image, Label, Line, ListBox, OLE Bound Control, OLE Container Control, OptionButton, OptionGroup, Page, PageFrame, Project Object, ProjectHook Object, Separator, Shape, Spinner, TextBox, Timer, ToolBar

See Also

BaseClass Property

ParentAlias Property

Specifies the alias name of the parent table. Read-only at design time and at run time.

Syntax

DataEnvironment.Relation.ParentAlias[= *cAliasName*]

Arguments

cAliasName
Specifies the alias name of the parent table in the relation.

Remarks

The ParentAlias property setting must be the same name as the Alias property setting for the Cursor object that represents the parent table.

Applies To

Relation

See Also

Alias Property, ChildAlias Property

ParentClass Property

Returns the name of the class on which the object's class is based. Read-only at design time and run time.

Syntax

Object.ParentClass

Remarks

In the Class Designer, the ParentClass property contains the name of the class on which the subclass's class is based.

Applies To

ActiveDoc Object, CheckBox, Column, ComboBox, CommandButton, CommandGroup, Container Object, Control Object, Custom, EditBox, Form, FormSet, Grid, Header, Image, Label, Line, ListBox, OLE Bound Control, OLE Container Control, OptionButton, OptionGroup, Page, PageFrame, ProjectHook Object, _SCREEN, Shape, Spinner, TextBox, Timer, ToolBar

See Also

Parent Property

Partition Property

Specifies whether a Grid control is split into two panels and specifies where the split is relative to the left edge of the grid. Available at design time; read/write at run time.

Syntax

Grid.Partition[= *nSplit*]

Arguments

nSplit
Specifies the position where the grid splits into two panels. If *nSplit* is 0, the grid isn't split.

Remarks

Note that the SplitBar property takes precedence over the Partition property.

Applies To

Grid

See Also

Panel Property, PanelLink Property, SplitBar Property

PasswordChar Property

Determines whether the characters entered by a user or placeholder characters are displayed in a TextBox control; determines the character used as a placeholder. Available at design time and run time.

Syntax

TextBox.PasswordChar[= *cCharString*]

Arguments

cCharString
   Specifies the characters displayed in a text box.

Remarks

Use this property to create a password field in a dialog box. Although you can use any character, most applications use the asterisk (*), ANSI character 42.

This property does not affect the Value property setting; it contains exactly what the user types or what was set from code. Set PasswordChar to an empty string ("") to display the actual text. The default setting is an empty string.

You can assign any string to this property, but only the first character is significant; all others are ignored.

Applies To

TextBox

See Also

Format Property, InputMask Property, Value Property

PAYMENT( ) Function

Returns the amount of each periodic payment on a fixed-interest loan.

Syntax

PAYMENT(*nPrincipal*, *nInterestRate*, *nPayments*)

Returns

Numeric

Arguments

nPrincipal
   Specifies the beginning principal of the loan.

nInterestRate

Specifies the fixed interest rate per period. If monthly payments are made on the loan but the interest rate is annual, divide the annual interest rate by 12.

nPayments

Specifies the total number of payments to be made on the loan.

Remarks

PAYMENT( ) assumes a constant periodic interest rate and assumes that payments are made at the end of each period.

Example

```
STORE 100000 to gnPrincipal   && $100,000 beginning principal
STORE .105/12 TO gnInterest   && 10.5% annual interest rate
STORE (20*12) TO gnPayments   && 20 years of monthly payments
CLEAR
? PAYMENT(gnPrincipal, gnInterest, gnPayments)   && Displays 998.38
```

See Also

CALCULATE, FV( ), PV( )

_PBPAGE System Variable

Included for backward compatibility. Use the Report Designer instead.

PCOL( ) Function

Returns the current column position of the printer's print head.

Syntax

PCOL( )

Returns

Numeric

Remarks

The value PCOL( ) returns is relative to the current setting of the left printer margin. You can set the left margin with SET MARGIN or by storing a value to the system memory variable _PLOFFSET.

PCOL( ) is especially useful for relative addressing of printed text.

You can use the $ operator in place of PCOL( ).

Example

```
CLEAR
@ PROW( ), PCOL( )+12 SAY 'Contact person'
@ PROW( ), $+12 SAY 'Contact person'
```

See Also

COL( ), ROW( ), PROW( )

_PCOLNO System Variable

Included for backward compatibility. Use the Report Designer instead.

_PCOPIES System Variable

Included for backward compatibility. Use the Report Designer instead.

PCOUNT( ) Function

Returns the number of parameters passed to the current program, procedure, or user-defined function.

Syntax

PCOUNT( )

Returns

Numeric

Remarks

PCOUNT( ) is useful for determining how many parameters are passed to the current program, procedure, or user-defined function.

Examples

Example 1 calls a procedure and displays in a wait window the number of parameters passed.

Example 2 uses a procedure to display the average of 4 values.

```
* Example 1
DO testpar WITH 1,2,3

PROCEDURE testpar
PARAMETERS gn1,gn2,gn3
```

```
gcMessage = 'PCOUNT( ) ='+ALLTRIM(STR(PCOUNT( )))
WAIT WINDOW (gcMessage)
RETURN

* Example 2
SET TALK OFF
gnVal1 = 10
gnVal2 = 20
gnVal3 = 30
gnVal4 = 15
gnMin = getavg(gnVal1, gnVal2, gnVal3, gnVal4)
? 'Average value is '
?? gnMin

* This user-defined function permits up to 9 parameters to be passed.
* It uses the PCOUNT( ) function to determine how many
* were passed and returns the average value.

FUNCTION getavg
PARAMETERS gnPara1,gnPara2,gnPara3,gnPara4,gnPara5, ;
   gnPara6,gnPara7,gnPara8,gnPara9
IF PCOUNT( ) = 0
   RETURN 0
ENDIF
gnResult = 0
FOR gnCount = 1 to PARAMETERS( )
   gcCompare = 'gnPara' +(STR(gnCount,1))
   gnResult = gnResult + EVAL(gcCompare)
ENDFOR
gnResult = gnResult / (gnCount - 1)
RETURN gnResult
```

See Also

DO, FUNCTION, LPARAMETERS, LOCAL, PARAMETERS, PARAMETERS( ),
PRIVATE, PROCEDURE, PUBLIC, SET UDFPARMS

_PDRIVER System Variable

Included for backward compatibility. Use the TO FILE ASCII argument in REPORT.

_PDSETUP System Variable

Included for backward compatibility. Use the TO FILE ASCII argument in REPORT.

_PECODE System Variable

Included for backward compatibility. Use the Report Designer instead.

_PEJECT System Variable

Included for backward compatibility. Use the Report Designer instead.

PEMSTATUS( ) Function

Returns an attribute for a property, event, method, or object.

Syntax

PEMSTATUS(*oObjectName* | *cClassName*, *cProperty* | *cEvent* | *cMethod* | *cObject*, *nAttribute*)

Returns

Character or Logical

Arguments

oObjectName

Specifies the object for which a property, event, method, or object attribute is returned. *oObjectName* can be any expression that evaluates to an object, such as an object reference, an object memory variable, or an object array element. If *oObjectName* is a container object such as a form, you can determine attributes for objects within the container object.

cClassName

Specifies the class for which a property, event, or method attribute is returned.

cProperty

Specifies the property for which an attribute is returned.

cEvent

Specifies the event for which an attribute is returned.

cMethod

Specifies the method for which an attribute is returned.

cObject

Specifies the object for which an attribute is returned. For example, you can use the AddObject method to add an object to a container object, and then use PEMSTATUS( ) to return information about the object added to the container object.

nAttribute

A numeric value that specifies which property, event, or method attribute is returned.

The following table lists the values for *nAttribute* and the corresponding property, event, or method attribute.

nAttribute	Property, event, or method attribute
0	Changed (properties only). A logical true (.T.) is returned if the property value has changed from its original, default value; otherwise a logical false (.F.) is returned.
1	Read-only (properties only). A logical true (.T.) is returned if the property is read-only; otherwise a logical false (.F.) is returned.
2	Protected. A logical true (.T.) is returned if the property, event, or method is a protected; otherwise a logical false (.F.) is returned.
3	Type. A character string is returned indicating if *cProperty*, *cEvent*, *cMethod* or *cObject* is a property, event, method or object. Property, Event, Method, or Object is returned.
4	User-defined. A logical true (.T.) is returned if the property, event, or method is a user-defined property, event, or method; otherwise a logical false (.F.) is returned.
5	Defined property, event, method, or object. A logical true (.T.) is returned if the property, event, method, or object exists for *oObjectName* or *cClassName*, otherwise a logical false (.F.) is returned.
6	Inherited property, event, method, or object. A logical true (.T.) is returned if the property, event, method, or object for *oObjectName* or *cClassName* was inherited from another object or class, otherwise a logical false (.F.) is returned.

Remarks

Calling PEMSTATUS( ) more than twice in a single Visual FoxPro command may cause a form to become inactive. Separate the command into several commands each containing a single PEMSTATUS( ) function.

See Also

CREATE FORM, GETPEM( ), SYS(1269) – Property Information, SYS(1270) – Object Location, SYS(1271) – Object's .SCX File, SYS(1272) – Object Hierarchy

_PEPAGE System Variable

Included for backward compatibility. Use the Report Designer instead.

PI( ) Function

Returns the numeric constant pi.

Syntax

PI( )

Returns

Numeric

Remarks

The numeric constant pi (3.141592) is the ratio of the circumference of a circle to its diameter.

The number of decimal places displayed in the value returned by PI( ) is determined by SET DECIMALS.

Example

```
CLEAR
? PI( ) && Displays 3.14
STORE 2.30 TO gnRadius
STORE PI( ) * gnRadius^2 TO gnArea
? gnArea  && Displays 16.6190
```

See Also

SET DECIMALS

Picture Property

Specifies the graphics file to be displayed on the control. Available at design time and run time.

Syntax

Control.Picture[= *cFileName*]

Arguments

cFileName
    Specifies a .bmp, .gif, .jpg or, .ico file.

Remarks

The setting for this property is a path to a .bmp, .gif, .jpg or, .ico file.

Note If you set the Picture property at design time and the file you specify does not exist, Microsoft Visual FoxPro displays an error message, but the property remains set to the file you specified. Visual FoxPro ignores the Picture property at run time if it is set to a file that does not exist.

Graphics are centered on the control. For CommandButton controls, the Style property must be set to 0 (Standard) for the bitmap to be displayed on the control; for CheckBox and OptionButton controls, the Style property must be set to 1 (Graphical).

For CommandButton and OptionButton controls, the specified bitmap is used whether a button is available, selected, or unavailable. You can specify a different bitmap for each button state using the DownPicture and DisabledPicture properties.

Applies To

CheckBox, CommandButton, Container Object, Control Object, Custom, Form, Image, OptionButton, Page, _SCREEN

See Also

DisabledPicture Property, DownPicture Property, Style Property

PLAY MACRO Command

Executes a keyboard macro.

Syntax

PLAY MACRO *MacroName*
    [TIME *nDelay*]

Arguments

MacroName
    Specifies the name of the keyboard macro to play.

TIME *nDelay*
    Specifies the time interval between the delivery of each keystroke in a keyboard macro. The delay time must be between 0 and 10 seconds. *nDelay* can evaluate to a number with a decimal fraction. For example, if you specify *nDelay* equal to 1.5, keystrokes from the macro will be played with a one-and-a-half-second delay between each keystroke.

Remarks

You can save a series of keystrokes as a keyboard macro by choosing Macros from the Tools menu. PLAY MACRO plays this series of keystrokes. Playing keyboard macros within programs lets you create self-running demo programs.

If you issue PLAY MACRO from the Command window, it executes immediately. If PLAY MACRO is issued in a program, execution is delayed until the program executes a command that allows keyboard input. Examples of commands that wait for input are @ ... GET, BROWSE, CHANGE, and EDIT.

If a series of PLAY MACRO commands is pending in a program, Visual FoxPro doesn't execute the commands in the order in which they are issued. Macros are played in reverse order — the first PLAY MACRO executes last, the last PLAY MACRO executes first — in their bottom-to-top order within the program.

See Also

CLEAR MACROS, ON KEY LABEL, RESTORE MACROS, SAVE MACROS

_PLENGTH System Variable

Included for backward compatibility. Use the Report Designer instead.

_PLINENO System Variable

Included for backward compatibility. Use the Report Designer instead.

_PLOFFSET System Variable

Included for backward compatibility. Use the Report Designer instead.

Point Method

Returns the red-green-blue (RGB) color of the specified point on a form.

Syntax

*Object.*Point ([*nXCoord, nYCoord*])

Arguments

nXCoord
  Specifies the horizontal coordinate of the point, in the units specified in the ScaleMode property setting of the form.

nYCoord
  Specifies the vertical coordinate of the point, in the units specified in the ScaleMode property setting of the form.

Remarks

If *nXCoord* or *nYCoord* is outside of the form, the Point method returns –1.

Applies To

Form, _SCREEN

See Also

Circle Method, Line Method, Print Method, PSet Method

POP KEY Command

Restores ON KEY LABEL assignments that were placed on the stack with PUSH KEY.

Syntax

POP KEY
   [ALL]

Arguments

ALL
   Clears all current key assignments defined with ON KEY LABEL and clears all key
   assignments defined with ON KEY LABEL from the stack.

Remarks

POP KEY, when used with PUSH KEY, lets you save a set of key assignments created
with ON KEY LABEL commands, make changes to the key assignments with more
ON KEY LABEL commands, and then restore the original key assignments.

For more information on placing ON KEY LABEL commands on the stack, see the
PUSH KEY Command, later in this language reference.

See Also

ON KEY LABEL, ON( ), PUSH KEY

POP MENU Command

Restores the specified menu bar definition that was placed on the stack with
PUSH MENU.

Syntax

POP MENU *MenuBarName*
   [TO MASTER]

Arguments

MenuBarName
   Specifies the name of the menu bar whose definition is pulled off the stack. The
   specified menu bar can be user-defined or the Visual FoxPro system menu bar.

TO MASTER
   Restores the first menu bar definition pushed onto the stack, and then clears the stack.

Remarks

When used with PUSH MENU, POP MENU lets you save a menu bar definition, make changes to the menu bar definition, and then restore the menu bar definition to its original state.

Menu bars are placed on and removed from the stack in last-in, first-out order.

Example

In the following example, the system menu bar definition is pushed to the stack and then modified. The original system menu definition is then restored by popping it off the stack.

```
PUSH MENU _MSYSMENU
SET SYSMENU TO _MFILE, _MEDIT
POP MENU _MSYSMENU
```

See Also

ACTIVATE MENU, DEFINE MENU, POP POPUP, PUSH MENU, PUSH POPUP

POP POPUP Command

Restores the specified menu definition that was placed on the stack with PUSH POPUP.

Syntax

POP POPUP *MenuName*

Arguments

MenuName

Specifies the name of the menu whose definition is pulled off the stack. The menu can be a user-defined menu created with DEFINE MENU or a Visual FoxPro system menu.

Remarks

When used with PUSH POPUP, POP POPUP lets you save a menu definition, make changes to the menu definition, and then restore the menu definition to its original state.

Menu definitions are placed on and removed from the stack in a last-in, first-out order.

Example

In the following example, a menu named popExam is created. menu definition is pushed to the stack and then one of the menu items is modified. The original menu definition is then restored by popping it off the stack.

```
DEFINE POPUP popExam FROM 5,5
DEFINE BAR 1 OF popExam PROMPT 'One'
DEFINE BAR 2 OF popExam PROMPT 'Two'
```

```
DEFINE BAR 3 OF popExam PROMPT 'Three'
DEFINE BAR 4 OF popExam PROMPT 'Four'
ACTIVATE POPUP popExam NOWAIT

PUSH POPUP popExam
WAIT 'Popup pushed' WINDOW
RELEASE BAR 2 OF popExam
WAIT 'This is the modified popup' WINDOW

POP POPUP popExam
WAIT 'Popup popped, original popup restored' WINDOW
DEACTIVATE POPUP popExam
RELEASE POPUP popExam
```

See Also

ACTIVATE POPUP, DEFINE POPUP, POP MENU, PUSH MENU, PUSH POPUP

POPUP( ) Function

Returns as a string the name of the active menu, or a logical value indicating if a menu has been defined.

Syntax

POPUP([cMenuName])

Returns

Character or Logical

Arguments

cMenuName
Returns a logical value indicating if *cMenuName* has been defined. POPUP( ) returns true (.T.) if the menu you specify has been defined; otherwise POPUP( ) returns false (.F.).

Remarks

POPUP( ) returns the name of the active menu as a character string if you omit the optional *cMenuName* argument. A menu must be defined and active for POPUP( ) to return its name. Menus are created and activated with DEFINE POPUP and ACTIVATE POPUP. The menu can also be a Visual FoxPro system menu. POPUP( ) returns an empty string if a menu isn't defined and active or you issue POPUP( ) from the Command window.

See Also

ACTIVATE POPUP, BAR( ), DEFINE BAR, DEFINE POPUP,
ON SELECTION POPUP

_PPITCH System Variable

Included for backward compatibility. Use the Report Designer instead.

_PQUALITY System Variable

Included for backward compatibility. Use the Report Designer instead.

_PRETEXT System Variable

Specifies a character expression to preface text merge lines.

Syntax

_PRETEXT = *cExpression*

Remarks

With SET TEXTMERGE you can merge text within a program. You can output lines of text, the contents of variables, and the results of expressions and functions to the screen, a window, a printer, a text file, or a low-level file.

If you store a character expression to _PRETEXT, the character expression is added to the beginning of the output text line. To facilitate program indentation, you can store a tab or tabs to _PRETEXT.

See Also

\ | \\, SET TEXTMERGE, _TEXT

PRIMARY( ) Function

Returns true (.T.) if an index tag is a primary index tag; otherwise, returns false (.F.).

Syntax

PRIMARY([*nIndexNumber*] [, *nWorkArea* | *cTableAlias*])

Returns

Logical

Arguments

nIndexNumber
Specifies the number of the index tag for which PRIMARY( ) returns the primary status. PRIMARY( ) returns the primary status in the following order as *nIndexNumber*

increases from 1 to the total number of structural compound and independent compound index tags.

1. Primary status for each tag in the structural compound index (if one is present) are returned first. The primary status is returned for the tags in the order the tags are created in the structural index.

2. Primary status for each tag in any open, independent compound indexes are returned next. The primary status is returned for the tags in the order in which the tags are created in the independent compound indexes.

If you omit *nIndexNumber*, PRIMARY( ) checks the master controlling index tag to see if it's a primary index tag. If there is no master controlling index tag, PRIMARY( ) returns false (.F.).

nWorkArea

Specifies the work area of the index tag specified with *nIndexNumber*.

cTableAlias

Specifies the work area of the index tag specified with *nIndexNumber*.

If you omit *nWorkArea* and *cTableAlias*, PRIMARY( ) checks the index tag in the currently selected work area to see if it's a primary index tag.

Example

The following example opens the customer table in the database. FOR ... ENDFOR is used to create a loop in which the primary status of each index tag in the customer structural index is checked. The name of each structural index tag is displayed with its primary status.

```
CLOSE DATABASES
SET PATH TO (HOME(2) + 'Data\')&& Sets path to database
OPEN DATABASE testdata  && Open testdata database
USE Customer  && Open customer table

FOR nCount = 1 TO 254
   IF !EMPTY(TAG(nCount))  && Checks for tags in the index
   ? TAG(nCount)  && Display tag name
   ? PRIMARY(nCount)   && Display primary status
   ELSE
      EXIT  && Exit the loop when no more tags are found
   ENDIF
ENDFOR
```

See Also

ALTER TABLE – SQL, CANDIDATE( ), CREATE TABLE – SQL, INDEX

Print Method

Prints a character string on a form.

Syntax

[*FormSet.*] *Object*.Print [(*cText*)]

Arguments

cText

Specifies the character string to print. If you omit *cText*, a blank line is printed.

cText is printed on the form starting at the position specified by the CurrentX and CurrentY properties. When a carriage return is included, CurrentX is increased by the width of *cText* (same as the value returned by TextWidth) and CurrentY remains unchanged.

When the Print method is finished, the CurrentX and CurrentY properties are set to the point immediately after the last character printed.

Applies To

Form, _SCREEN

See Also

CurrentX, CurrentY Properties, TextHeight Method, TextWidth Method

PRINTJOB ... ENDPRINTJOB Command

Activates the settings for print job system variables.

Syntax

PRINTJOB
    Commands

ENDPRINTJOB

Arguments

Commands

Specifies the Visual FoxPro commands that are executed until the print job is completed.

Remarks

PRINTJOB ... ENDPRINTJOB initializes the printer and certain system variables that affect printed output. It can send control codes to the printer, eject a page from the printer before and/or after a print job, initialize the printer column number, and control the number of copies printed.

PRINTJOB performs these tasks:

- Sends starting printer control codes, stored in the system variable _PSCODE, to the printer. For more information on printer control codes, see "System Variables Overview," later in this language reference, and your printer manual.

- Ejects a page if the system variable _PEJECT is set to BEFORE or to BOTH.

- Sets the system variable _PCOLNO to 0. _PCOLNO stores the printer column number.

ENDPRINTJOB performs these tasks:

- Sends ending printer control codes, stored in the system variable _PECODE, to the printer. You can reset the printer to the configuration it had before PRINTJOB was issued.

- Ejects a page if the system variable _PEJECT is set to AFTER or to BOTH.

- Loops back to PRINTJOB to print another copy of the report if the _PCOPIES system variable is set to a value higher than 1 (the default). The value of the system variable _PCOPIES determines the number of copies. When the number of copies printed equals the value of _PCOPIES, Visual FoxPro exits the loop. Program control then begins with the command immediately following ENDPRINTJOB.

PRINTJOB and ENDPRINTJOB may be executed only from within a program. You may not nest PRINTJOB ... ENDPRINTJOB commands.

See Also

ON PAGE, System Variables Overview

PRINTSTATUS( ) Function

Returns true (.T.) if the printer or print device is online; otherwise, false (.F.) is returned.

Syntax

PRINTSTATUS( )

Returns

Logical

Remarks

PRINTSTATUS( ) is similar to SYS(13), except SYS(13) returns READY instead of true (.T.) or OFFLINE instead of false (.F.).

In Visual FoxPro, PRINTSTATUS( ) always returns true (.T.) if the printer is connected through the Windows Control Panel.

Example

```
? PRINTSTATUS( )
*** Program Example ***
STORE PRINTSTATUS( ) TO glReady
IF NOT glReady
   WAIT 'Make sure printer is attached and turned on!' WINDOW
ELSE
   WAIT 'Printer is ready!' WINDOW
ENDIF
```

See Also

SET DEVICE, SET PRINTER, SYS(13) – Printer Status

PRIVATE Command

Hides specified variables or arrays that were defined in a calling program from the current program.

Syntax

PRIVATE *VarList*

– or –

PRIVATE ALL
[LIKE *Skeleton* | EXCEPT *Skeleton*]

Arguments

VarList
Specifies the variables or arrays to be declared private.

ALL LIKE *Skeleton*
Causes PRIVATE to hide all variables and arrays whose names match *Skeleton*, which can contain the question mark (?) and asterisk (*) wildcards.

ALL EXCEPT *Skeleton*
Causes PRIVATE to hide all variables or arrays unless their names match *Skeleton*, which can contain the question mark (?) and asterisk (*) wildcards.

Remarks

The hiding of variables created in higher-level programs enables variables of the same name as the private variables to be manipulated in the current program without affecting the values of the hidden variables. Once the program containing PRIVATE has completed execution, all variables and arrays that were declared private are again available.

PRIVATE doesn't create variables; it simply hides variables declared in higher-level programs from the current program.

Example

```
*** Program example demonstrating PRIVATE ***
SET TALK OFF
val1 = 10
val2 = 15

DO down
? val1, val2  && Displays 10, 100

PROCEDURE down
PRIVATE val1
val1 = 50
val2 = 100
? 'Val1  Val2'
? val1, val2  && Displays 50, 100
RETURN
```

See Also

DIMENSION, FUNCTION, LOCAL, LPARAMETERS, PARAMETERS, PARAMETERS( ), PROCEDURE, PUBLIC

PRMBAR( ) Function

Returns the text of a menu item.

Syntax

PRMBAR(*MenuName*, *nMenuItemNumber*)

Returns

Character

Arguments

MenuName
   Specifies the menu name.

nMenuItemNumber
   Specifies the number of the menu item whose text PRMBAR( ) returns. For example, if *nMenuItemNumber* is 1, the text of the first menu item is returned; if *nMenuItemNumber* is 2, the text of the second menu item is returned, and so on. The expression must be at least 1 and no greater than the number of menu items in the menu.

Remarks

Menus are created with DEFINE POPUP, which creates the menu, and DEFINE BAR, which creates the menu items in the menu. PRMBAR( ) also works with a Visual FoxPro system menu. PRMBAR( ) returns the text that appears on the menu item. The menu doesn't have to be active.

If a menu item was created using the backslash and less-than characters (\<) to create an access key, or a backslash (\) to disable the menu item, PRMBAR( ) returns only the menu item text; it doesn't include these special characters. PRMBAR( ) returns an empty string when a menu item is a separator created with the backslash and dash (\-) characters.

See Also

CNTBAR( ), GETBAR( ), DEFINE BAR, DEFINE POPUP, MRKBAR( ), PRMPAD( )

PRMPAD( ) Function

Returns the text of a menu title.

Syntax

PRMPAD(*MenuBarName*, *MenuTitleName*)

Returns

Character

Arguments

MenuBarName
Specifies the name of the menu bar containing the menu title.

MenuTitleName
Specifies the menu title.

Remarks

Menu bars are created with DEFINE MENU, which creates the menu bar, and DEFINE PAD, which creates the menu titles in the menu bar. PRMPAD( ) also works with the Visual FoxPro menu system. A menu bar doesn't have to be active for PRMPAD( ) to return the text for a menu title.

If a menu title was created using the backslash and less-than characters (\<) to create an access key, or a backslash (\) to disable the menu title, PRMPAD( ) returns only the text of the menu title; it doesn't include the special characters.

Example

In the following example, a menu bar named mnuExample is created with three menu titles. The access key and disabled option designators aren't returned from the menu titles named titleTwo and titleThree. The menu bar is activated to show the menu titles and is cleared from the screen and from memory when a menu title is chosen.

```
CLEAR
SET TALK OFF
STORE 'mnuExample' TO gcPopName

DEFINE MENU mnuExample BAR AT LINE 1
DEFINE PAD titleOne OF mnuExample PROMPT 'This will be returned'
DEFINE PAD titleTwo OF mnuExample PROMPT '\<As will this'
DEFINE PAD titleThree OF mnuExample PROMPT '\And this, too'

=messagebox( PRMPAD('mnuExample', 'titleOne') )
=messagebox( PRMPAD('mnuExample', 'titleTwo') )
=messagebox( PRMPAD(gcPopName, 'titleThree') )

ACTIVATE MENU mnuExample
DEACTIVATE MENU mnuExample
RELEASE MENU mnuExample
```

See Also

CNTBAR( ), GETBAR( ), DEFINE BAR, DEFINE POPUP, MRKPAD( ), PRMBAR( )

PROCEDURE Command

Identifies the beginning of a procedure in a program file.

Syntax

PROCEDURE *ProcedureName*
   Commands
   [RETURN [*eExpression*]]

ENDPROC

Arguments

ProcedureName
   Specifies the name of the procedure to create.

Remarks

PROCEDURE is a statement within a program file that specifies the beginning of each procedure in the program file and defines the procedure name. Procedure names must begin with a letter or underscore and may contain any combination of letters, numbers, and underscores.

In Visual FoxPro for Windows, procedure names can be up to 254 characters long.

Comments can be placed on the same line after PROCEDURE and ENDPROC. These comments are ignored during compilation and program execution.

The PROCEDURE statement is followed by a series of commands that make up the procedure. You can include RETURN anywhere in the procedure to return control to the calling program or to another program, and to define a value returned by the procedure. If you do not include a RETURN command, an implicit RETURN is automatically executed when the function quits. If the RETURN command does not include a return value (or if an implicit RETURN is executed), Visual FoxPro assigns .T. (True) as the return value.

The procedure ends with the ENDPROC command. This command is optional; the procedure quits when it encounters another PROCEDURE command, a FUNCTION command, or the end of the program file.

Note You cannot have normal executable program code included in a program file after procedures; only procedures, user-defined functions, and class definition can follow the first PROCEDURE or FUNCTION command in the file.

When you execute a procedure with DO *ProcedureName*, Visual FoxPro searches for the procedure in a specific order. Visual FoxPro searches:

1. The program containing DO *ProcedureName*.

2. The current database.

3. The procedure files opened with SET PROCEDURE.

4. Programs in the execution chain. It searches program files beginning with the most recently executed program and continuing back to the first executed program.

5. A stand-alone program file. If a program file with the same name as the file name specified with DO is found, Visual FoxPro executes the program. If a matching program file name isn't found, Visual FoxPro generates an error message.

Include the IN clause in DO to execute a procedure in a specific file.

By default, parameters are passed to procedures by value. For information on passing parameters to procedures by reference, see the SET UDFPARMS Command, later in this language reference. A maximum of 27 parameters can be passed to a procedure. Parameters can be passed to a procedure by including a PARAMETERS or LPARAMETERS statement in the procedure, or by placing a list of parameters immediately after PROCEDURE *ProcedureName*. Enclose the list of parameters in a set of parentheses, and separate the parameters with commas.

Example

The following example illustrates how a procedure can be called to accomplish a discrete task such as making an entry in a log file. The procedure opens the log file (which is assumed to exist in the example), constructs an entry based in information passed in parameters, writes the entry out, and closes the file. The procedure is called with a DO command similar to the one at the top of the program.

```
DO MakeLogEntry WITH "Logged in", "jsmith"

PROCEDURE MakeLogEntry
   PARAMETERS message, username
   pnHandle = FOPEN("LOG2.TXT",2)    && Assume the file exists
   pnSize = FSEEK(pnHandle,0,2)      && Move to end of file
   logEntry = dtoc(date())+","+time()+","+username+","+message
   =FPUTS(pnHandle, logEntry)
   =FCLOSE(pnHandle)  && Close file
ENDPROC
```

The following example shows how a procedure can be called to return a value.

```
SET CENTURY ON
? longdate(({^1998-02-16}))  && Displays Monday, February 16, 1998

PROCEDURE longdate
   PARAMETER mdate
   RETURN CDOW(mdate) + ", " + MDY(mdate)
ENDPROC
```

See Also

FUNCTION, LPARAMETERS, LOCAL, PARAMETERS, PARAMETERS( ),
PRIVATE, PUBLIC, RETURN, SET PROCEDURE, SET UDFPARMS

ProgID Property

Contains the registered PROGID (Programmatic Identifier) for a server in a project.
Read-only at design time and run time.

Syntax

Object.ProgID

Remarks

A PROGID is created in the Windows registry for a server when you build an
executable file (.exe) or dynamic link library (.dll) from a project.

Applies To

Server Object

See Also

CLSID Property, CREATEOBJECTEX( ), TypeLibCLSID Property,
TypeLibDesc Property, TypeLibName Property

PROGRAM( ) Function

Returns the name of the program currently executing, the current program level, or the name of the program executing when an error occurred.

Syntax

PROGRAM([*nLevel*])

Returns

Character or Numeric

Arguments

nLevel

Specifies how many program levels back the program name is to be found. This parameter can range from 0 to the program nesting depth. A program can execute another program which can execute another program, and so on. Programs may be nested to 128 levels.

If you specify 0 or 1 for *nLevel*, PROGRAM( ) returns the name of the master program (the highest-level program). If *nLevel* exceeds the program nesting depth, PROGRAM( ) returns an empty string.

If you specify –1 for *nLevel*, PROGRAM( ) returns as a numeric value the current program level. PROGRAM(–1) always returns zero when issued from the Command window.

Remarks

PROGRAM( ) helps your program recover from errors. It is similar to SYS(16).

If used without an argument, PROGRAM( ) returns the name of the currently executing program.

Example

```
ON ERROR DO errhand WITH PROGRAM( )
*** The next line should generate an error ***
USE nodatabase
ON ERROR    && Returns to system default error-handling routine
PROCEDURE errhand
PARAMETERS gcProgram
WAIT 'An error occurred in the program ' + gcProgram WINDOW
```

See Also

DO, INENO( ), MESSAGE( ), SYS(16) – Executing Program File Name

ProgrammaticChange Event

Occurs when the value of a control is changed in code.

Syntax

PROCEDURE *Control*.ProgrammaticChange
[LPARAMETERS *nIndex*]

Arguments

nIndex
    Uniquely identifies a control if it is in a control array.

Applies To

CheckBox, ComboBox, CommandGroup, EditBox, ListBox, OptionGroup, Spinner, TextBox

See Also

Caption Property, Style Property

Projects Collection

A collection of project objects.

Syntax

Projects

Remarks

A projects collection provides access to project objects, allowing you to manipulate a project and files and servers within the project.

Items in projects collection can be referenced by index number or by name. For example, the following code rebuilds the most recently opened project:

```
_VFP.Projects(1).Build( )
```

The following code rebuilds the project named MyProject:

```
_VFP.Projects('MyProject.pjx').Build( )
```

For more information about the projects collection, see "Project Manager Hooks" in Chapter 32, "Application Development and Developer Productivity," in the *Microsoft Visual FoxPro 6.0 Programmer's Guide*.

Properties

Count

Methods

Item

See Also

File Object, Files Collection, Project Object, ProjectHook Object, Server Object, Servers Collection

Project Object

Instantiated when a project is created or opened.

Syntax

Project

Remarks

A project object is instantiated when you issue CREATE PROJECT, MODIFY PROJECT, BUILD APP, BUILD DLL, BUILD EXE, or BUILD PROJECT.

Note that the project object and its properties and methods are not available in the ProjectHook object Init event. Project object property values you set or methods you invoke in the ProjectHook object Init event are ignored.

Note that a project object is a COM object, so assigning a project object reference to a memory variable creates a memory variable of class "Unknown Type."

For more information about projects, see "Project Manager Hooks" in Chapter 32, "Application Development and Developer Productivity," in the *Microsoft Visual FoxPro 6.0 Programmer's Guide*.

Properties

Application	AutoIncrement	BaseClass
BuildDateTime	Debug	Encrypted
HomeDir	Icon	MainClass
MainFile	Name	Parent
ProjectHook	ProjectHookClass	ProjectHookLibrary
SCCProvider	ServerHelpFile	ServerProject
TypeLibCLSID	TypeLibDesc	TypeLibName
VersionComments	VersionCompany	VersionCopyright
VersionDescription	VersionLanguage	VersionNumber
VersionProduct	VersionTrademarks	Visible

Methods

Build	CleanUp	Close
Refresh	SetMain	

See Also

ActiveProject Property, File Object, Files Collection, Projects Collection, ProjectHook Object, Server Object, Servers Collection

ProjectHook Object

Instantiated whenever a project is opened, providing programmatic access to project events.

Syntax

ProjectHook

Remarks

A ProjectHook object is a Visual FoxPro base class that is instantiated by default whenever a project is opened. (You can include the NOPROJECTHOOK clause in CREATE PROJECT and MODIFY PROJECT to prevent a ProjectHook object from being instantiated for the project.)

The ProjectHook object allows programmatic access to events that occur in a project. For example, you can execute code whenever a file is added to a project. Note that you can specify a default project hook class for new projects in the Projects tab, of the Options dialog box or you can specify a default project hook class for an individual project in the Project Information dialog box. At runtime, you can use the ProjectHook property to specify a project hook class for a project as in the following example:

```
MODIFY PROJECT MyProject
_VFP.Projects('MyProject.pjx').ProjectHook = ;
   NewObject('MyProjectHook', 'MyClass.vcx')
```

A ProjectHook base class can be created with CREATE CLASS, CREATEOBJECT( ), or NEWOBJECT( ).

For more information about projects, see "Project Manager Hooks" in Chapter 32, "Application Development and Developer Productivity," in the *Microsoft Visual FoxPro 6.0 Programmer's Guide*.

Properties

Application	BaseClass	Class
ClassLibrary	Comment	Name
OLEDropEffects	OLEDropHasData	OLEDropMode
Parent	ParentClass	Tag

Events

AfterBuild	BeforeBuild	Destroy
Error	Init	OLEDragDrop
OLEDragOver	OLEGiveFeedBack	QueryAddFile
QueryModifyFile	QueryRemoveFile	QueryRunFile

Methods

AddProperty	ReadExpression	ReadMethod
ResetToDefault	SaveAsClass	WriteExpression

See Also

CREATE CLASS, CREATEOBJECT( ), File Object, Files Collection, NEWOBJECT( ),
ProjectHook Property, Projects Collection, Project Object, Server Object,
Servers Collection

ProjectHook Property

An object reference to the ProjectHook object instantiated for a project.

Syntax

Object.ProjectHook[= *oProjectHookClass*]

Arguments

oProjectHookClass
Specifies a class based on the Visual FoxPro ProjectHook base class. By default,
contains an object reference to the default ProjectHook class specified in the Project
tab of the Project Information dialog box.

Remarks

The ProjectHook property contains the null value if it has not been assigned a class based
on the ProjectHook base class or the project doesn't have a default ProjectHook class
(specified in the **Project** tab of the Project Information dialog box). Assigning the null

value to ProjectHook property releases the ProjectHook object, but doesn't affect the default ProjectHook class for the project.

For more information about projects, see "Project Manager Hooks" in Chapter 32, "Application Development and Developer Productivity," in the *Microsoft Visual FoxPro 6.0 Programmer's Guide*.

Applies To

Project Object

See Also

ProjectHook Object, ProjectHookClass Property, ProjectHookLibrary Property

ProjectHookClass Property

The default ProjectHook class for a project.

Syntax

Object.ProjectHookClass[= *cClassName*]

Arguments

cClassName

Specifies the default ProjectHook class for a project. Before you can specify a ProjectHook class for a project, specify the .vcx visual class library containing the ProjectHook class with the ProjectHookLibrary property.

To delete the default ProjectHook class for a project, set the ProjectHookClass or ProjectHookLibrary property to the empty string.

Remarks

You can also specify the default ProjectHook class for a project in the Project tab of the Project Information dialog box.

Changing the ProjectHookClass property doesn't instantiate the new ProjectHook object. The change takes effect the next time the project is opened. To change the current ProjectHook object, use the ProjectHook property.

For more information about projects, see "Project Manager Hooks" in Chapter 32, "Application Development and Developer Productivity," in the *Microsoft Visual FoxPro 6.0 Programmer's Guide*.

Applies To

Project Object

See Also

ProjectHook Object, ProjectHook Property, ProjectHookLibrary Property

ProjectHookLibrary Property

The .vcx visual class library containing the default ProjectHook class for a project.

Syntax

Object.ProjectHookLibrary[= *cLibraryName*]

Arguments

cLibraryName

Specifies a .vcx visual class library that contains a class based on the ProjectHook base class. After you specify the .vcx visual class library with this property, use the ProjectHookClass property to specify the default class for the project.

To delete the default ProjectHook class for a project, set the ProjectHookLibrary or ProjectHookClass property to the empty string.

Remarks

You can also specify the default ProjectHook class for a project in the Project Tab of the Project Information dialog box.

Changing the ProjectHookLibrary property doesn't instantiate the new ProjectHook object. The change takes effect the next time the project is opened. To change the current ProjectHook object, use the ProjectHook property.

For more information about projects, see "Project Manager Hooks" in Chapter 32, "Application Development and Developer Productivity," in the *Microsoft Visual FoxPro 6.0 Programmer's Guide*.

Applies To

Project Object

See Also

ProjectHook Object, ProjectHook Property, ProjectHookClass Property

PROMPT( ) Function

Returns the text for a menu title chosen from a menu bar or for a menu item chosen from a menu.

Syntax

PROMPT( )

Returns

Character

Remarks

PROMPT( ) returns the text of the menu title last chosen from a menu bar or the menu item last chosen from a menu. The menu bar or menu can be user-defined or a Visual FoxPro system menu bar or menu. If a menu bar or menu isn't active or you press ESC to exit a menu bar or menu, PROMPT( ) returns an empty string.

A menu bar is created with DEFINE MENU, and each menu title in the menu bar is created with DEFINE PAD. A menu is created with DEFINE POPUP, and the menu items in the menu are created with DEFINE BAR.

MENU( ) and POPUP( ) can be used to return the name of the menu bar or menu from which the menu title or menu item is chosen.

See Also

BAR( ), DEFINE BAR, DEFINE MENU, DEFINE PAD, DEFINE POPUP, POPUP( ), PRMBAR( )

PROPER( ) Function

Returns from a character expression a string capitalized as appropriate for proper names.

Syntax

PROPER(*cExpression*)

Returns

Character

Arguments

cExpression
    Specifies the character expression from which PROPER( ) returns a capitalized character string.

Example

```
STORE 'Visual FoxPro' TO gcExpr1
CLEAR
? PROPER(gcExpr1)  && Displays "Visual Foxpro"
STORE 'VISUAL FOXPRO' TO gcExpr2
? PROPER(gcExpr2)  && Displays "Visual Foxpro"
```

See Also

LOWER( ), UPPER( )

PROW( ) Function

Returns the current row number of the printer's print head.

Syntax

PROW( )

Returns

Numeric

Remarks

If you issue EJECT, Visual FoxPro resets PROW( ) to 0.

PROW( ) is especially useful for relative addressing of printed text.

Example

In the following example, the two commands return the same result. You can use the $ operator in place of PCOL( ). Both $ and PCOL( ) return the current column position of the printer.

```
@ PROW( ), PCOL( ) + 12 SAY 'Contact person'
@ PROW( ), $+12 SAY 'Contact person'
```

See Also

@ ... SAY, COL( ), PCOL( ), ROW( )

PRTINFO( ) Function

Returns the current specified printer setting.

Syntax

PRTINFO(*nPrinterSetting* [, *cPrinterName*])

Returns

Numeric

Arguments

nPrinterSetting
Specifies which Visual FoxPro printer setting is returned.

The following tables list the printer setting return values.

> **Note**   If PRTINFO(2) returns –1 or a value other than those listed in the table below, use PRTINFO(3) and PRTINFO(4) to return the paper size.

If *nPrinterSetting* equals 1 (PRT_ORIENTATION in FOXPRO.H), PRTINFO( )
returns the paper orientation:

Return values	Setting
−1	Information not available
0	Portrait
1	Landscape

If *nPrinterSetting* equals 2 (PRT_PAPERSIZE in FOXPRO.H), PRTINFO( ) returns
the paper size:

Return values	Setting
−1 or a value other than those listed below	Information not available. Use *nPrinterSetting* = 3 and *nPrinterSetting* = 4 to determine the paper size.
1	Letter, 8 1/2 x 11 in
2	Letter Small, 8 1/2 x 11 in
3	Tabloid, 11 x 17 in
4	Ledger, 17 x 11 in
5	Legal, 8 1/2 x 14 in
6	Statement, 5 1/2 x 8 1/2 in
7	Executive, 7 1/4 x 10 1/2 in
8	A3, 297 x 420 mm
9	A4, 210 x 297 mm
10	A4, Small 210 x 297 mm
11	A5, 148 x 210 mm
12	B4, 250 x 354 mm
13	B5, 182 x 257 mm
14	Folio, 8 1/2 x 13 in
15	Quarto, 215 x 275 mm
16	10 x 14 in
17	11 x 17 in
18	Note, 8 1/2 x 11 in
19	Envelope #9, 3 7/8 x 8 7/8 in

(continued)

(continued)

Return values	Setting
20	Envelope #10, 4 1/8 x 9 1/2 in
21	Envelope #11, 4 1/2 x 10 3/8 in
22	Envelope #12, 4 1/2 x 11 in
23	Envelope #14, 5 x 11 1/2 in
24	C size sheet
25	D size sheet
26	E size sheet
27	Envelope DL, 110 x 220 mm
28	Envelope C5, 162 x 229 mm
29	Envelope C3, 324 x 458 mm
30	Envelope C4, 229 x 324 mm
31	Envelope C6, 114 x 162 mm
32	Envelope C65, 114 x 229 mm
33	Envelope B4, 250 x 353 mm
34	Envelope B5, 176 x 250 mm
35	Envelope B6, 176 x 125 mm
36	Envelope, 110 x 230 mm
37	Envelope Monarch, 3 7/8 x 7.5 in
38	6 3/4 Envelope, 3 5/8 x 6 1/2 in
39	US Std Fanfold, 14 7/8 x 11 in
40	German Std Fanfold, 8 1/2 x 12 in
41	German Legal Fanfold, 8 1/2 x 13 in

If *nPrinterSetting* equals 3 (PRT_PAPERLENGTH in FOXPRO.H), PRTINFO( ) returns the paper length in .1mm increments.

If *nPrinterSetting* equals 4 (PRT_PAPERWIDTH in FOXPRO.H), PRTINFO( ) returns the paper width in .1mm increments.

If *nPrinterSetting* equals 5 (PRT_SCALE in FOXPRO.H), PRTINFO( ) returns the factor by which printed output is scaled.

If *nPrinterSetting* equals 6 (PRT_COPIES in FOXPRO.H), PRTINFO( ) returns the number of copies to print.

If *nPrinterSetting* equals 7 (PRT_DEFASOURCE in FOXPRO.H), PRTINFO( ) returns the default paper source:

Return values	Setting
1	Upper bin
2	Lower bin
3	Middle bin
4	Manual feed
5	Envelope bin
6	Manual feed envelope
7	Auto select
8	Tractor feed
9	Small format
10	Large format
11	Large capacity
14	Cassette

If *nPrinterSetting* equals 8 (PRT_PRTQUAL in FOXPRO.H), PRTINFO( ) returns a positive value indicating the horizontal resolution in dots per inch (DPI), or a negative value indicating the print quality:

Return values	Setting
−1	Draft
−2	Low
−3	Medium
−4	High

If *nPrinterSetting* equals 9 (PRT_COLOR in FOXPRO.H), PRTINFO( ) returns a value indicating if a color printer renders color or monochrome output:

Return values	Setting
1	Color
2	Monochrome

If *nPrinterSetting* equals 10 (PRT_DUPLEX in FOXPRO.H), PRTINFO( ) returns the duplex mode:

Return values	Setting
1	Simplex printing
2	Vertical duplex
3	Horizontal duplex

If *nPrinterSetting* equals 11 (PRT_YRESOLUTION in FOXPRO.H), PRTINFO( ) returns the vertical resolution in dots per inch (DPI). −1 is returned if this information is not available.

If *nPrinterSetting* equals 12 (PRT_TTOPTION in FOXPRO.H), PRTINFO( ) returns a value that indicates how TrueType fonts are printed:

Return values	Setting
1	Print as bitmapped graphics
2	Download as soft fonts
3	Substitute device fonts

If *nPrinterSetting* equals 13 , PRTINFO( ) returns a value that indicates if output is collated:

Return values	Setting
0	No collation
1	Collated

cPrinterName
Specifies the name of the printer for which information is returned. If *cPrinterName* is omitted, information is returned for the default printer.

Remarks

Visual FoxPro printer settings are set in the Page Setup dialog box. Choose Page Setup from the File menu to display the Visual FoxPro Page Setup dialog box.

See Also

GETPRINTER( ) ,PRINTSTATUS( ), SET DEVICE, SET PRINTER, SYS(13) – Printer Status, SYS(1037) – Page Setup Dialog Box

_PSCODE System Variable

Included for backward compatibility. Use the Report Designer instead.

PSet Method

Sets a point on a form or the main Visual FoxPro window to the foreground color.

Syntax

[*FormSet.*]*Object*.PSet([*nXCoord*, *nYCoord*])

Arguments

nXCoord
> Specifies the horizontal coordinate of the point to set, in the unit of measurement specified by the ScaleMode property of the form.

nYCoord
> Specifies the vertical coordinate of the point to set, in the unit of measurement specified by the ScaleMode property of the form.

Remarks

The size of the point drawn depends on the DrawWidth property. When DrawWidth is set to 1, the PSet method sets a single pixel to the specified color. When DrawWidth is set to a value greater than 1, the point is centered on the specified coordinates. The way the point is drawn depends on the setting of the DrawMode and DrawStyle properties.

When the PSet method is called, the CurrentX and CurrentY properties are set to the point specified by the arguments.

Applies To

Form, _SCREEN

See Also

CurrentX, CurrentY Properties, DrawMode Property, DrawStyle Property, DrawWidth Property, ForeColor Property

_PSPACING System Variable

Included for backward compatibility. Use the Report Designer instead.

PUBLIC Command

Defines global variables or arrays.

Syntax

PUBLIC *MemVarList*

– or –

PUBLIC [ARRAY] *ArrayName1(nRows1* [, *nColumns1*])
   [, *ArrayName2(nRows2* [, *nColumns2*])] ...

Arguments

MemVarList
   Specifies one or more memory variables to be initialized and designated as global.

[ARRAY] *ArrayName1 (nRows1* [, *nColumns1*])
   [, *ArrayName2 (nRows2* [, *nColumns2*])] ...
   Specifies one or more arrays to be initialized and designated as global. See the
   DIMENSION Command, earlier in this language reference, for a description of
   each argument.

Remarks

Global variables and arrays can be used and modified from any program you execute
during the current Visual FoxPro session.

Variables and arrays created with PUBLIC are initialized false (.F.) except for the public
variables FOX and FOXPRO, which are initialized true (.T.). The public variables FOX
and FOXPRO can be used to conditionally execute code based on the product you are
running.

Any Variable or array you create in the Command window is automatically public.

Any Variable or array you wish to declare as public must be declared public prior to
assigning it a value.

Visual FoxPro generates a syntax error if, within a program, you assign a value to a
variable or array and later declare it public with PUBLIC.

Example

```
SET TALK OFF
PUBLIC val1,val2
val1 = 10
val2 = 15
```

```
DO down
? val1
? val2

RELEASE ALL  && Releases private variables only
DISPLAY MEMORY LIKE val?
RELEASE val1,val2  && Public variables must be released explicitly
DISPLAY MEMORY LIKE val?
PROCEDURE down
PRIVATE val1
val1 = 50
val2 = 100
? val1
? val2
RETURN
```

See Also

DIMENSION, FUNCTION, LOCAL, LPARAMETERS, PARAMETERS, PARAMETERS( ) ,PRIVATE, PROCEDURE ,RELEASE

PUSH KEY Command

Places all current ON KEY LABEL command settings on a stack in memory.

Syntax

PUSH KEY
    [CLEAR]

Arguments

CLEAR
    Clears all current key assignments from memory.

Remarks

PUSH KEY, when used with POP KEY, lets you save key assignments defined with ON KEY LABEL commands, change these assignments, and then restore the previous assignments.

For example, you may want to use a new set of ON KEY LABEL commands when you open a Browse window. Before you open the Browse window, use PUSH KEY to save the current ON KEY LABEL key assignments in memory. You can then add or change ON KEY LABEL assignments specifically for the Browse window. After you close the Browse window, your previous ON KEY LABEL key assignments can be restored from memory with POP KEY.

ON KEY LABEL settings are placed on and removed from the stack in a last-in, first-out order.

DISPLAY STATUS and LIST STATUS show the current key assignments defined with ON KEY LABEL commands.

See Also

ON KEY LABEL, ON( ), POP KEY

PUSH MENU Command

Places a menu bar definition in a stack of menu bar definitions in memory.

Syntax

PUSH MENU *MenuBarName*

Arguments

MenuBarName
Specifies the name of the menu bar whose definition is placed on the stack. The menu bar can be user-defined or the Visual FoxPro system menu bar.

Remarks

When used with POP MENU, PUSH MENU lets you save a menu bar definition, make changes to the menu bar definition, and then restore the menu bar definition to its original state.

Menu bar definitions are placed on and removed from the stack in last-in, first-out order.

Example

In the following example, the Visual FoxPro system menu bar is pushed to the stack and then modified. The original system menu bar is then restored by popping it off the stack.

```
WAIT WINDOW 'Press a key to push the system menu bar'
PUSH MENU _MSYSMENU
WAIT WINDOW 'Press a key to change the system menu bar'
SET SYSMENU TO _MFILE, _MEDIT
WAIT WINDOW 'Press a key to restore the system menu bar'
POP MENU _MSYSMENU
```

See Also

ACTIVATE MENU, DEFINE MENU

PUSH POPUP Command

Places a menu definition on a stack of menu definitions in memory.

Syntax

PUSH POPUP *MenuName*

Arguments

MenuName
> Specifies the name of the menu whose definition is placed on the stack.
> The menu can also be a Visual FoxPro system menu.

Remarks

When used with POP POPUP, PUSH POPUP lets you save a menu definition, make changes to the menu definition, and then restore the menu definition to its original state.

Menu definitions are placed on and removed from the stack in last-in, first-out order.

Example

In the following example, a menu named popExam is created. The menu definition is pushed to the stack and then modified. The original menu is then restored by popping it off the stack.

```
DEFINE POPUP popExam FROM 5,5
DEFINE BAR 1 OF popExam PROMPT 'One'
DEFINE BAR 2 OF popExam PROMPT 'Two'
DEFINE BAR 3 OF popExam PROMPT 'Three'
DEFINE BAR 4 OF popExam PROMPT 'Four'
ACTIVATE POPUP popExam NOWAIT
PUSH POPUP popExam
WAIT 'Original Popup' WINDOW
RELEASE BAR 2 OF popExam
WAIT 'Modified Popup. Original Popup is pushed to a stack.' WINDOW
POP POPUP popExam
WAIT 'Original Popup restored' WINDOW
DEACTIVATE POPUP popExam
RELEASE POPUP popExam
```

See Also

ACTIVATE POPUP, DEFINE POPUP

PUTFILE( ) Function

Invokes the Save As dialog box and returns the file name you specify.

Syntax

PUTFILE([*cCustomText*] [, *cFileName*] [, *cFileExtensions*])

Returns

Character

Arguments

cCustomText

Specifies custom text to appear in the Save As dialog box. In Windows 3.x, the text appears as the dialog box title. In Windows95, the custom text replaces the File Name label.

Note that under Windows 95, long captions may be truncated.

cFileName

Specifies the default file name displayed in the text box.

cFileExtensions

Specifies file name extensions. Only file names with the specified extension are displayed in the scrollable list of the Save As dialog box when the All Files check box is cleared. The first extension in *cFileExtensions* is automatically appended to the file name entered if an extension isn't included with the file name. For a list of Visual FoxPro file extensions and corresponding creator types, see "File Extensions and File Types" in Help.

The character expression *cFileExtensions* can take one of the following forms:

- *cFileExtensions* can contain a single extension, such as PRG, and only file names with that extension are displayed.

- *cFileExtensions* can contain a list of file name extensions separated by semicolons. For example, if you include PRG;FXP, Visual FoxPro displays all file names with the extensions .prg and .fxp.

- If file names have the same root name but different extensions (for example, Customer.prg and Customer.fxp), Visual FoxPro displays only the file name with the extension that appears first in *cFileExtensions*.

- *cFileExtensions* can contain a list of file name extensions separated by vertical bars, such as PRG|FXP. In such a case, Visual FoxPro displays all file names with listed extensions, even if the files have the same root name.

- If *cFileExtensions* contains only a semicolon (;), Visual FoxPro displays all file names that don't have an extension.

- If *cFileExtensions* is an empty string, Visual FoxPro displays the names of all files in the current directory or folder.

- If *cFileExtensions* contains MS-DOS wildcards, such as the question mark (?) and asterisk (*), Visual FoxPro displays all file names with extensions that meet the wildcard criteria. For example, if *cFileExtensions* is ?X?, all file names with the extensions .fxp, .exe, .txt, and so on, are displayed.

Remarks

Use PUTFILE( ) to choose an existing file name or specify a new file name. PUTFILE( ) returns the file name with its path. If you don't enter a file name, PUTFILE( ) returns the default file name (specified with *cFileName*) and extension (specified by *cFileExtensions*). If you choose Cancel or press ESC, PUTFILE( ) returns an empty string. You can use the file name that PUTFILE( ) returns to name a file and save it to disk.

Example

The following example creates a delimited data file from any existing table the user chooses. GETFILE( ) is used to find and open a table and PUTFILE( ) is used to return the name of the target file.

```
gcTableName = GETFILE('DBF', 'Open Table:')
USE (gcTableName)
gcDelimName = ALIAS( ) + '.DLM'
gcDelimFile = PUTFILE('Delimited file:', gcDelimName, 'DLM')
IF EMPTY(gcDelimFile)  && Esc pressed
   CANCEL
ENDIF
COPY TO (gcDelimFile) DELIMITED&& Create delimited file
MODIFY FILE (gcDelimFile) NOEDIT
```

See Also

FILE( ), GETEXPR, GETFILE( ), GETPICT( ), LOCFILE( )

PV( ) Function

Returns the present value of an investment.

Syntax

PV(*nPayment*, *nInterestRate*, *nTotalPayments*)

Returns

Numeric

Arguments

nPayment

Specifies the periodic payment amount. *nPayment* can evaluate to a positive or negative number. PV( ) assumes that the payments are made at the end of each period.

nInterestRate

Specifies the periodic interest rate. If the interest rate of an investment is annual and the payments are made monthly, divide the annual interest rate by 12.

nTotalPayments

Specifies the total number of payments.

Remarks

PV( ) computes the present value of an investment based on a series of equal periodic payments at a constant periodic interest rate.

Example

```
STORE 500 to gnPayment  && Periodic payments made monthly
STORE .075/12 TO gnInterest  && 7.5% annual interest rate
STORE 48 TO gnPeriods  && Four years (48 months)
CLEAR
? PV(gnPayment, gnInterest, gnPeriods)  && Displays 20679.19
```

See Also

CALCULATE, FV( )

_PWAIT System Variable

Included for backward compatibility. Use the Report Designer instead.

QueryAddFile Event

Occurs just before a file is added to a project.

Syntax

PROCEDURE *Object*.QueryAddFile
[LPARAMETERS *cFileName*]

Arguments

cFileName

Contains the name of the file to add to the project. *cFileName* is passed to the QueryAddFile event after the Add method is executed, you choose **Add** in the Project Manager, or you choose **Add File** from the **Project** menu.

Remarks

Include NODEFAULT in the QueryAddFile event to prevent a file from being added to the project.

Applies To

ProjectHook Object

See Also

Add Method, QueryModifyFile Event, QueryRemoveFile Event, QueryRunFile Event

QueryModifyFile Event

Occurs just before a file is modified in a project.

Syntax

PROCEDURE *Object*.QueryModifyFile
[LPARAMETERS *oFile*, *cClassName*]

Arguments

oFile
Contains an object reference to the file to modify. *oFile* is passed to the QueryModifyFile event after the Modify method is executed, you choose **Modify** in the Project Manager, or you choose **Modify File** from the **Project** menu.

cClassName
Contains the name of the class to modify if the file is a .vcx visual class library.

Remarks

Include NODEFAULT in the QueryModifyFile event to prevent a file from being modified in the project.

Applies To

ProjectHook Object

See Also

Modify Method, QueryAddFile Event, QueryRemoveFile Event, QueryRunFile Event

QueryRemoveFile Event

Occurs just before a file is removed from a project.

Syntax

PROCEDURE *Object*.QueryRemoveFile
[LPARAMETERS *oFile*, *cClassName*, *lDeleteFile*]

Arguments

oFile
Contains an object reference to the file to remove from the project. *oFile* is passed to the QueryRemoveFile event after the Remove method is executed, you choose **Remove** in the Project Manager, or you choose **Remove File** from the **Project** menu.

cClassName
Contains the name of the class to remove if the file is a .vcx visual class library.

lDeleteFile
Contains a logical value that indicates if the file is to be deleted from disk as well as the project. *lDeleteFile* contains false (.F.) if Remove (remove from project) is chosen in the dialog that is displayed when you attempt to remove a file from a project. *lDeleteFile* contains true (.T.) if Delete (remove from project and delete from disk) is chosen in the dialog.

Remarks

Include NODEFAULT in the QueryRemoveFile event to prevent a file from being removed from the project.

Applies To

ProjectHook Object

See Also

QueryAddFile Event, QueryModifyFile Event, QueryRunFile Event, Remove Method

QueryRunFile Event

Occurs just before a file is executed or a report or label is previewed in a project.

Syntax

PROCEDURE *Object*.QueryRunFile
[LPARAMETERS *oFile*]

Arguments

oFile

Contains an object reference to the file to execute or preview. *oFile* is passed to the QueryRunFile event after the Run method is executed, you choose **Run** or **Preview** in the Project Manager, or you choose **Run File** or **Preview File** from the Project menu.

Remarks

Include NODEFAULT in the QueryRunFile event to prevent a file from being executed or previewed.

Applies To

ProjectHook Object

See Also

QueryAddFile Event, QueryModifyFile Event, QueryRemoveFile Event, Run Method

QueryUnload Event

Occurs before a form is unloaded.

Syntax

PROCEDURE *Form*.QueryUnload

Remarks

The QueryUnload event occurs before the Destroy event. The ReleaseType property is set prior to the QueryUnload event being called.

The QueryUnload event occurs when CLEAR WINDOWS, RELEASE WINDOWS, or QUIT is executed in code, or when the user double-clicks the window pop-up menu icon or chooses Close from the window pop-up menu on a form.

Note The QueryUnload event does not occur if you issue the RELEASE command on the form in code or invoke the form's Release method.

Issuing NODEFAULT in the QueryUnload event procedure prevents the form from unloading.

Applies To

Form

See Also

CLEAR, ControlBox Property, DEFINE CLASS, Destroy Event, QUIT, RELEASE, Release Method, RELEASE WINDOWS, ReleaseType Property, Unload Event

QUIT Command

Ends the current Visual FoxPro session and returns control to the operating system.

Syntax

QUIT

Remarks

In Visual FoxPro for Windows, you are returned to Windows.

> **Caution** Always use QUIT to terminate a Visual FoxPro session. If you turn the computer off without issuing QUIT, open files may be damaged and data lost, and temporary work files that would normally be deleted may be left on disk.

See Also

CANCEL, RESUME, RUN, SUSPEND

Quit Method

Ends an instance of Visual FoxPro.

Syntax

ApplicationObject.Quit( )

Remarks

Call the Quit( ) method to return control to the application that created the instance of Visual FoxPro.

Applies To

Application Object, _VFP System Variable

See Also

QUIT

RAND( ) Function

Returns a random number between 0 and 1.

Syntax

RAND([*nSeedValue*])

Returns

Numeric

Arguments

nSeedValue

Specifies the seed value that determines the sequence of values RAND( ) returns.

RAND( ) returns the same sequence of random numbers if you use the same seed value for *nSeedValue* the first time you issue RAND( ) followed by subsequent RAND( ) function calls without *nSeedValue*.

If *nSeedValue* is negative the first time you issued RAND( ), a seed value from the system clock is used. To achieve the most random sequence of numbers, issue RAND( ) initially with a negative argument and then issue RAND( ) without an argument.

If you omit *nSeedValue*, RAND( ) uses a default seed value of 100,001.

Example

The first example below uses RAND( ) to create a table with 10 records containing random values, then uses MIN( ) and MAX( ) to display the maximum and minimum values in the table.

The second example below displays a random number that falls between two values, 1 and 10.

```
CLOSE DATABASES
CREATE TABLE Random (cValue N(3))
FOR nItem = 1 TO 10   && Append 10 records,
    APPEND BLANK
    REPLACE cValue WITH 1 + 100 * RAND( )  && Insert random values
ENDFOR

CLEAR
LIST  && Display the values
gnMaximum = 1  && Initialize minimum value
gnMinimum = 100  && Initialize maximum value
SCAN
    gnMinimum = MIN(gnMinimum, cValue)
    gnMaximum = MAX(gnMaximum, cValue)
ENDSCAN
? 'The minimum value is: ', gnMinimum  && Display minimum value
? 'The maximum value is: ', gnMaximum  && Display maximum value

CLEAR
gnLower = 1
gnUpper = 10

? INT((gnUpper - gnLower + 1) * RAND( ) + gnLower)
```

See Also

EXP( ), PI( )

RangeHigh Event

For a spinner or text box, occurs when the control loses the focus. For a combo box or list box, occurs when the control receives the focus.

Syntax

PROCEDURE *Object*.RangeHigh
[LPARAMETERS *nIndex*]

Arguments

nIndex
    Uniquely identifies a control if it is in a control array.

Remarks

A RangeHigh event can return a numeric value to Microsoft Visual FoxPro through a RETURN statement. For a spinner or a text box with a numeric value, if the value returned to Visual FoxPro is less than the value entered in the control, the control retains the focus. For a combo box or list box, the value returned to Visual FoxPro specifies which item in the control is initially selected, For example, if 2 is returned to Visual FoxPro, the second item in the control is initially selected.

Applies To

ComboBox, ListBox, Spinner, TextBox

See Also

KeyboardHighValue, KeyboardLowValue Properties, RangeLow Event, RETURN, SpinnerHighValue, SpinnerLowValue Properties

RangeLow Event

For a spinner or text box, occurs when the control loses the focus. For a combo box or list box, occurs when the control receives the focus.

Syntax

PROCEDURE *Object*.RangeLow
[LPARAMETERS *nIndex*]

Arguments

nIndex
    Uniquely identifies a control if it is in a control array.

Remarks

A RangeLow event can return a numeric value to Visual FoxPro through a RETURN statement. For a spinner or a text box with a numeric value, if the value returned to Visual FoxPro is greater than the value entered in the control, the control retains the focus. For a combo box or list box, the value returned to Visual FoxPro specifies which item in the control is initially selected, For example, if 2 is returned to Visual FoxPro, the second item in the control is initially selected.

Applies To

ComboBox, ListBox, Spinner, TextBox

See Also

KeyboardHighValue, KeyboardLowValue Properties, RangeHigh Event, RETURN, SpinnerHighValue, SpinnerLowValue Properties

RAT( ) Function

Returns the numeric position of the last (rightmost) occurrence of a character string within another character string.

Syntax

RAT(*cSearchExpression*, *cExpressionSearched* [, *nOccurrence*])

Returns

Numeric

Arguments

cSearchExpression
Specifies the character expression that RAT( ) looks for in *cExpressionSearched*. The character expression can refer to a memo field of any size.

cExpressionSearched
Specifies the character expression that RAT( ) searches. The character expression can refer to a memo field of any size.

nOccurrence
Specifies which occurrence, starting from the right and moving left, of *cSearchExpression* RAT( ) searches for in *cExpressionSearched*. By default, RAT( ) searches for the last occurrence of *cSearchExpression* (*nOccurrence* = 1). If *nOccurrence* is 2, RAT( ) searches for the next to last occurrence, and so on.

Remarks

RAT( ), the reverse of the AT( ) function, searches the character expression in *cExpressionSearched* starting from the right and moving left, looking for the last occurrence of the string specified in *cSearchExpression*.

RAT( ) returns an integer indicating the position of the first character in *cSearchExpression* in *cExpressionSearched*. RAT( ) returns 0 if *cSearchExpression* isn't found in *cExpressionSearched*, or if *nOccurrence* is greater than the number of times *cSearchExpression* occurs in *cExpressionSearched*.

The search performed by RAT( ) is case-sensitive.

Example

```
STORE 'abracadabra' TO string
STORE 'a' TO find_str
CLEAR
? RAT(find_str,string)    && Displays 11
? RAT(find_str,string,3)  && Displays 6
```

See Also

AT( ), ATCLINE( ), ATLINE( ), LEFT( ), OCCURS( ), RATLINE( ), RIGHT( ), SUBSTR( )

RATC( ) Function

Returns the numeric position of the last occurrence of a character expression or memo field within another character expression or memo field.

Syntax

RATC(*cSearchExpression*, *cExpressionSearched* [, *nOccurrence*])

Returns

Numeric

Arguments

cSearchExpression
Specifies the character expression that RATC( ) looks for in *cExpressionSearched*.

cExpressionSearched
Specifies the character expression that RATC( ) searches. The character expressions *cSearchExpression* and *cExpressionSearched* can be memo fields of any size.

nOccurrence
Specifies which occurrence, starting from the right and moving left, of *cSearchExpression* RATC( ) searches for in *cExpressionSearched*. By default, RATC( ) searches for the last occurrence of *cSearchExpression* (*nOccurrence* equals 1). If *nOccurrence* is 2, RATC( ) searches for the next to last occurrence, and so on.

Remarks

RATC( ) is designed for expressions containing double-byte characters. If the expression contains only single-byte characters, RATC( ) is equivalent to RAT( ).

RATC( ) returns the numeric position of the last occurrence of a character expression or memo field within another character expression or memo field. The character expressions or memo fields can contain any combination of single-byte and double-byte characters.

RATC( ) is the reverse of the AT_C( ) function: it searches from right to left.

RATC( ) returns an integer indicating the position of the first character in *cSearchExpression* in *cExpressionSearched*. RATC( ) returns 0 if *cSearchExpression* isn't found in *cExpressionSearched*, or if *nOccurrence* is greater than the number of times *cSearchExpression* occurs in *cExpressionSearched*.

The search performed by RATC( ) is case-sensitive.

This function is useful for manipulating double-byte character sets for languages such as Hiragana and Katakana.

See Also

AT_C( ), LEFTC( ), RAT( ), RIGHTC( ), SUBSTRC( )

RATLINE( ) Function

Returns the line number of the last occurrence of a character expression within another character expression or memo field, counting from the last line.

Syntax

RATLINE(*cSearchExpression*, *cExpressionSearched*)

Returns

Numeric

Arguments

cSearchExpression
Specifies the character expression that RATLINE( ) looks for in *cExpressionSearched*.

cExpressionSearched
Specifies the character expression that RATLINE( ) searches. The character expressions *cSearchExpression* and *cExpressionSearched* can be memo fields of any size.

Use MLINE( ) to return the line containing *cSearchExpression*.

> **Tip** RATLINE( ) offers a convenient way to search memo fields.

Remarks

RATLINE( ), the reverse of the ATLINE( ) function, searches a character expression *cExpressionSearched*, starting with the last character in *cExpressionSearched*, for the occurrence of *cSearchExpression*.

If the search is successful, RATLINE( ) returns the number of the line where the match occurs. If the search is unsuccessful, RATLINE( ) returns 0.

The search performed by RATLINE( ) is case-sensitive.

> **Caution** The line number that RATLINE( ) returns is determined by the value of SET MEMOWIDTH, even if *cExpressionSearched* isn't a memo field. For more information, see the SET MEMOWIDTH Command, later in this language reference.

Example

In the following example, RATLINE( ) returns the line number for the last line in the notes memo field containing the word "graduated." MLINE( ) uses this value to return the contents of the line.

```
CLOSE DATABASES
OPEN DATABASE (HOME(2) + 'data\testdata')
USE employee  && Opens Employee table
STORE 'graduated' TO gcString
STORE MLINE(notes, RATLINE(gcString, notes)) TO gnFileLine
? gnFileLine
```

See Also

AT( ), ATCLINE( ), ATLINE( ), LEFT( ), MLINE( ), OCCURS( ), RAT( ), RIGHT( ), SUBSTR( )

RD | RMDIR Command

Removes a directory or folder from disk.

Syntax

RD *cPath* | RMDIR *cPath*

Arguments

cPath
  Specifies the name and location of the directory or folder to remove from disk.

Remarks

Visual FoxPro generates an error message if you attempt to remove a directory or folder that is not empty.

Example

The following example uses MKDIR to create a new directory named mytstdir, then CHDIR is used to change to the new directory. GETDIR( ) is used to display the directory structure, and then RMDIR is used to remove the newly created directory. GETDIR( ) is used to display the directory structure again.

```
SET DEFAULT TO HOME( )  && Restore Visual FoxPro directory
MKDIR mytstdir  && Create a new directory
CHDIR mytstdir  && Change to the new directory
= GETDIR( )  && Display the Select Directory dialog box
SET DEFAULT TO HOME( )  && Restore Visual FoxPro directory
RMDIR mytstdir  && Remove the new directory
= GETDIR( )  && Display the Select Directory dialog box
```

See Also

CD | CHDIR, GETDIR( ), HOME( ), MD | MKDIR, SET DEFAULT, SET PATH, SYS(5) – Default Drive, SYS(2003) – Current directory, SYS(2004) – Visual FoxPro Start Directory

RDLEVEL( ) Function

Included for backward compatibility. Use the Form Designer instead of READ.

READ EVENTS Command

Starts event processing.

Syntax

READ EVENTS

Remarks

When READ EVENTS is issued, Visual FoxPro starts event processing.

Issue CLEAR EVENTS to stop event processing. When CLEAR EVENTS is issued, program execution continues with the line immediately following READ EVENTS.

Note that only one READ EVENTS can be active at a time. If a READ EVENTS is in effect, any subsequent READ EVENTS commands have no effect.

See Also

CLEAR Command, Form Designer

READ Command

Included for backward compatibility. Use the Form Designer instead.

READ MENU Command

Included for backward compatibility. Use the Menu Designer to create menus.

ReadActivate Event

Included for backward compatibility with READ. Use the Form Designer instead of READ.

ReadBackColor, ReadForeColor Properties

Included for backward compatibility with READ. Use the Form Designer instead of READ.

ReadCycle Property

Included for backward compatibility with READ. Use the Form Designer instead of READ.

ReadDeactivate Event

Included for backward compatibility with READ. Use the Form Designer instead of READ.

ReadExpression Method

Returns the expression entered for a property value in the Properties window. Available at design time and run time.

Syntax

Object.ReadExpression(*cPropertyName*)

Arguments

cPropertyName
Specifies the name of the property to return the expression from.

Applies To

ActiveDoc, CheckBox, Column, ComboBox, CommandButton, CommandGroup, Cursor, Custom, DataEnvironment, EditBox, Form, FormSet, Grid, Header, Image, Label, Line, ListBox, OLE Bound Control, OLE Container Control, OptionButton, OptionGroup, Page, PageFrame, ProjectHook Object, Relation, Shape, Spinner, TextBox, Timer, ToolBar

See Also

WriteExpression Method

READKEY( ) Function

Included for backward compatibility with READ. Use the Form Designer instead of READ.

ReadLock Property

Included for backward compatibility with READ. Use the Form Designer instead of READ.

ReadMethod Method

Returns the text of the specified method. Available at design time and run time.

Syntax

Control.ReadMethod(*cMethod*)

Arguments

cMethod
    Specifies the name of a method.

Applies To

ActiveDoc, CheckBox, Column, ComboBox, CommandButton, CommandGroup, Cursor, Custom, DataEnvironment, EditBox, Form, FormSet, Grid, Header, Image, Label, Line, ListBox, OLE Bound Control, OLE Container Control, OptionButton, OptionGroup, Page, PageFrame, ProjectHook Object, Relation, Shape, Spinner, TextBox, Timer, ToolBar

See Also

ReadExpression Method, WriteExpression Method, WriteMethod Method

ReadMouse Property

Included for backward compatibility with READ. Use the Form Designer instead of READ.

ReadObject Property

Included for backward compatibility with READ. Use the Form Designer instead of READ.

ReadOnly Property

Specifies whether the user can edit a control, specifies whether a table or view associated with a Cursor object allows updates, or contains a value the indicates if a file in a project can be edited. Available at design time; read/write at run time.

Syntax

[*Form.*]*Control.*ReadOnly[= *lExpr*]
*DataEnvironment.Cursor.*ReadOnly[= *lExpr*]
Project.Files.Item(*nItem*).ReadOnly

Settings

lExpr

The settings for the ReadOnly property are:

Setting	Description
True (.T.)	The user cannot edit the control.
	The table or view associated with the Cursor object cannot be modified.
False (.F.)	(Default) The user can edit the control.
	The table or view associated with the Cursor object can be modified.

Remarks

Note When the Cursor is accessed using CURSORSETPROP( ), the ReadOnly property is read-only at run time.

The ReadOnly property differs from the Enabled property because when ReadOnly is set to true (.T.), the user can still move to the control.

For Cursors, ReadOnly mimics the NOUPDATE clause of USE.

For combo box controls, the ReadOnly property cannot be set to true (.T.) when the Style property is set to 2 – Drop-down List.

For a file in a project, the ReadOnly property contains a logical value that indicates if the file can be edited. If ReadOnly is true (.T.), the file can be edited; otherwise the file cannot be edited. Read-only at design time and run time.

Applies To

CheckBox, Column, ComboBox, Cursor, EditBox, File Object, Grid, Spinner, TextBox

See Also

Enabled Property, USE

ReadSave Property

Included for backward compatibility with READ. Use the Form Designer instead of READ.

ReadShow Event

Included for backward compatibility with READ. Use the Form Designer instead of READ.

ReadTimeout Property

Included for backward compatibility with READ. Use the Form Designer instead of READ.

ReadValid Event

Included for backward compatibility with READ. Use the Form Designer instead of READ.

ReadWhen Event

Included for backward compatibility with READ. Use the Form Designer instead of READ.

RECALL Command

Unmarks records marked for deletion in the selected table.

Syntax

RECALL
  [*Scope*] [FOR *lExpression1*] [WHILE *lExpression2*]
  [NOOPTIMIZE]

Arguments

Scope
  Specifies a range of records to recall. Only the records that fall within the range specified are recalled. The scope clauses are: ALL, NEXT *nRecords*,

RECORD *nRecordNumber*, and REST. For more information on scope clauses, see "Scope Clauses" and "Overview of the Language," in Help.

The default scope for RECALL is the current record (NEXT 1).

FOR *lExpression1*

Specifies that only the records for which *lExpression1* evaluates to true (.T.) are recalled. This option allows you to filter out undesired records.

Rushmore optimizes a RECALL FOR if *lExpression1* is an optimizable expression. For best performance, use an optimizable expression in the FOR clause.

For more information, see the SET OPTIMIZE Command, later in this language reference, and "Understanding Rushmore Technology" in Chapter 15, "Optimizing Applications," in the *Microsoft Visual FoxPro 6.0 Programmer's Guide*.

WHILE *lExpression2*

Specifies a condition whereby records are recalled for as long as *lExpression2* evaluates to true (.T.).

NOOPTIMIZE

Prevents Rushmore optimization of RECALL

For more information, see the SET OPTIMIZE Command, later in this language reference, and "Understanding Rushmore Technology" in Chapter 15, "Optimizing Applications," in the *Microsoft Visual FoxPro 6.0 Programmer's Guide*.

Remarks

You can use RECALL to recover records, provided you have not issued PACK or ZAP.

Caution Once a file has been packed, all records marked for deletion are gone forever.

You can mark records for deletion by issuing DELETE or DELETE – SQL, or by choosing Delete Records from the Table menu when a Browse or Edit window is active. You can recall records by issuing RECALL, or by choosing Recall Records from the Record menu when a Browse or Edit window is active.

Example

The following example opens the customer table in the testdata database. DELETE – SQL is used to mark all records for deletion where the country field contains USA. All the records marked for deletion are displayed. RECALL ALL is used to unmark all the records marked for deletion.

```
CLOSE DATABASES
OPEN DATABASE (HOME(2) + 'data\testdata')
USE customer  && Opens Customer table

DELETE FROM customer WHERE country = 'USA'  && Mark for deletion
CLEAR
LIST FIELDS company, country FOR DELETED( ) && List marked records
RECALL ALL  && Unmark all records marked for deletion
```

See Also

DELETE, DELETE – SQL, PACK, SET DELETED, ZAP

RECCOUNT( ) Function

Returns the number of records in the current or specified table.

Syntax

RECCOUNT([*nWorkArea* | *cTableAlias*])

Returns

Numeric

Arguments

nWorkArea

Specifies the work area number for a table open in another work area.

RECCOUNT( ) returns 0 if a table isn't open in the work area you specify.

cTableAlias

Specifies the table alias for a table open in another work area.

Remarks

The value RECCOUNT( ) returns isn't affected by SET DELETED and SET FILTER.

RECCOUNT( ) without the optional arguments *nWorkArea* or *cTableAlias* returns the number of records in the table in the currently selected work area.

Example

In the following example, Microsoft Visual FoxPro compares the available disk space with the amount needed to sort `customer`.

```
*** Check DISKSPACE before a SORT ***

CLOSE DATABASES
OPEN DATABASE (HOME(2) + 'Data\testdata')
USE customer  && Opens Customer table

*** Get size of table header ***

gnTableHead = HEADER( )

*** Calculate size of table ***

gnFileSize = gnTableHead + (RECSIZE( ) * RECCOUNT( ) + 1)
IF DISKSPACE( ) > (gnFileSize * 3)
   WAIT WINDOW 'Sufficient diskspace to sort.'
```

```
ELSE
   WAIT WINDOW 'Insufficient diskspace. Sort cannot be done.'
ENDIF
```

See Also

RECNO( ), RECSIZE( )

RECNO( ) Function

Returns the current record number in the current or specified table.

Syntax

RECNO([*nWorkArea* | *cTableAlias*])

Returns

Numeric

Arguments

nWorkArea

Specifies the work area number for a table open in another work area. RECNO( ) returns 0 if a table isn't open in the work area you specify.

cTableAlias

Specifies the table alias for a table open in another work area.

Remarks

The current record is the record on which the record pointer is positioned.

RECNO( ) returns negative numbers for records appended in a table buffer.

RECNO( ) returns a value that is one greater than the number of records in the table if the record pointer is positioned beyond the last record in the table. RECNO( ) returns 1 if the record pointer is positioned before the first record in the table or the table has no records. If a table has no records, EOF( ) always returns true (.T.).

RECNO( ) issued without the optional arguments *nWorkArea* or *cTableAlias* returns the current record number for the table in the currently selected work area.

If you have issued SEEK unsuccessfully in an indexed table, you can specify 0 for *nWorkArea* to use "soft seek" logic to return the record number of the closest matching record. RECNO(0) returns 0 if a close match cannot be found. Visual FoxPro generates an error message if you issue GO RECNO(0) when a close match isn't found.

Example

The following example searches the customer table for a company name, and, if the company name isn't found, uses RECNO(0) to return the closest matching company.

```
CLOSE DATABASES
OPEN DATABASE (HOME(2) + 'data\testdata')
USE customer  && Opens Customer table
SET ORDER TO company
SEEK 'Ernst'
IF FOUND( )
   DISPLAY company, contact
ELSE
   GOTO RECNO(0)
   CLEAR
   ? 'Closest matching company is ' + company
   ? 'Record number: ' + ALLTRIM(STR(RECNO( )))
ENDIF
```

See Also

GO | GOTO, RECCOUNT( ), RECSIZE( ), SEEK, SKIP

RecordMark Property

Specifies whether the record selector column is displayed in a Grid control. Available at design time; read/write at run time.

Syntax

Grid.RecordMark[= *lExpr*]

Arguments

lExpr
   The settings for the RecordMark property are:

Setting	Description
True (.T.)	(Default) The record selector column is displayed in a Grid.
False (.F.)	The record selector column is not displayed in a Grid.

Applies To

Grid

See Also

ScrollBars Property

RecordSource Property

Specifies the source of data to which the Grid control is bound. Available at design time; read/write at run time.

Syntax

Grid.RecordSource[= *cName*]

Arguments

cName
> *cName* is typically the alias name of a cursor or the name of a table. The RecordSource property specifies the main cursor that the grid is bound to.

Remarks

If you specify a record source for a grid, you can specify the contents of individual columns in the grid by setting their ControlSource property. If you do not set the ControlSource property for a column in the grid, the column displays the next available undisplayed field of the grid's record source.

Applies To

Grid

See Also

ControlSource property, Order Property, RecordMark Property, RecordSourceType Property

RecordSourceType Property

Specifies how the data source that populates the Grid control is opened. Available at design time and read/write at run time.

Syntax

Grid.RecordSourceType[= *nType*]

Arguments

nType
> The settings for the RecordSourceType property are:

Setting	Description
0	Table. Automatically opens the table specified in the RecordSource property setting.
1	(Default) Alias. Treats the record source as specified.

(continued)

Setting	Description
2	Prompt. The user is prompted for the record source at run time. If a database is open, the user can choose one of the tables it contains as a record source.
3	Query (.qpr). The RecordSource property setting specifies a .qpr file.
4	SQL Statement. The SQL statement is specified in the RecordSource property.

Applies To

Grid

See Also

RecordSource Property

RECSIZE( ) Function

Returns the size (width) of a table record.

Syntax

RECSIZE([*nWorkArea* | *cTableAlias*])

Returns

Numeric

Arguments

nWorkArea
  Specifies the work area number for a table open in another work area. RECSIZE( ) returns 0 if a table isn't open in the work area you specify.

cTableAlias
  Specifies the table alias for a table open in another work area.

Remarks

RECSIZE( ) issued without the optional arguments *nWorkArea* or *cTableAlias* returns the record size for the table in the currently selected work area.

Example

In the following example, Microsoft Visual FoxPro compares the available disk space with the amount needed to sort customer.

```
*** Check DISKSPACE before a SORT ***

CLOSE DATABASES
OPEN DATABASE (HOME(2) + 'Data\testdata')
USE customer  && Opens Customer table
```

```
*** Get size of table header ***

gnTableHead = HEADER( )

*** Calculate size of table ***

gnFileSize = gnTableHead + (RECSIZE( ) * RECCOUNT( ) + 1)
IF DISKSPACE( ) > (gnFileSize * 3)
   WAIT WINDOW 'Sufficient diskspace to sort.'
ELSE
   WAIT WINDOW 'Insufficient diskspace. Sort cannot be done.'
ENDIF
```

See Also

RECCOUNT( ), FSIZE( )

Refresh Method

Repaints a form or control and refreshes any values, or refreshes a project's visual display.

Syntax

[*Form.*]*Object.*Refresh

– or –

*Project.*Refresh([*lUpdateSCCStatus*])

Arguments

lUpdateSCCStatus

For a project, specifies if the source control status for each file under source control is updated. If *lUpdateSCCStatus* is true (.T.), the source control status for each file in the project under source control is updated. If *lUpdateSCCStatus* is false (.F.) or omitted, the source control status for each file isn't updated. *lUpdateSCCStatus* is ignored if no files in the project are under source control.

Remarks

Generally, painting a form or control is handled automatically while no events are occurring. Use the Refresh method when you want to update the form or control immediately.

Use Refresh to force a complete repaint of a form or control, and to update the value of a control. The Refresh method is useful when you want a form to be displayed while another form is loading or when you want to update the contents of a control. To update the contents of a combo box or a list box, use the Requery method.

Note When a form is refreshed, all controls on the form are also refreshed. When a page frame is refreshed, only the active page is refreshed.

For projects, executing the Refresh method refreshes a project's visual display with any changes made to the project. For example, after programmatically adding files to the project with the Add method, you can execute the Refresh method to display the newly added files in the project.

Applies To

CheckBox, Column, ComboBox, CommandButton, CommandGroup, Container Object, Control Object, EditBox, Form, FormSet, Grid, Header, ListBox, OLE Bound Control, OLE Container Control, OptionButton, OptionGroup, Page, PageFrame, Project Object, _SCREEN, Spinner, TextBox, ToolBar

See Also

Paint Event, Requery Method

REFRESH( ) Function

Refreshes data in an updatable SQL view.

Syntax

REFRESH([*nRecords* [, *nRecordOffset*]] [, *cTableAlias* | *nWorkArea*])

Returns

Numeric

Arguments

nRecords
> Specifies the number of records to refresh. If *nRecords* is 1 or you omit *nRecords*, only the current record is refreshed. If *nRecords* is 0, no records are refreshed.

nRecordOffset
> Specifies the number of records before the current record where the refresh begins. For example, if the current record is record 10 and *nRecordOffset* is 4, record refresh begins with record 6. If *nRecordOffset* is 0 or you omit *nRecordOffset*, the refresh begins with the current record.

cTableAlias
> Specifies the alias of the remote SQL view in which records are refreshed.

nWorkArea
> Specifies the work area of the table or cursor in which records are refreshed. If you omit *nWorkArea* and *cTableAlias*, records are refreshed in the remote SQL view in the currently selected work area.

Remarks

REFRESH( ) returns the number of records refreshed.

The records are refreshed with data from the tables from which the SQL view is created. Records are refreshed in the SQL view open in the currently selected work area.

REFRESH( ) cannot refresh locked or buffered records, and the records must have unique primary keys. If a record in a table does not have a primary key value, the corresponding record in the SQL view is marked for deletion.

> **Tip** Calling the REFRESH( ) function can result in a significant impact on performance, because the function reexecutes the query on which the view is based. Therefore, do not call this function more than necessary.

See Also

CREATE SQL VIEW, CURSORGETPROP( ), CURSORSETPROP( )

REGIONAL Command

Creates regional variables and arrays.

Syntax

#REGION *nRegionNumber*
REGIONAL *VarList*

Arguments

#REGION *nRegionNumber*

Creates a region. Regional variables must be declared before they are used in a program. Note that #REGION is a compiler directive, not a command. *nRegionNumber* specifies a region number 0 through 31.

REGIONAL *VarList*

Declares the variables for the region created with the #REGION directive. *VarList* is a list of variables and arrays separated by commas.

During program compilation, if another identically named regional variable has already been compiled when a regional declaration is encountered, the second occurrence of the variable name is made unique to ensure there is no conflict with the previously declared regional variable.

A variable's name is made unique by padding the regional variable's name out to 10 characters with underscores and the current region number. This substitution takes place entirely during program compilation and has no effect on execution speed.

When a variable name is modified, use DISPLAY MEMORY to display the modified variable name. To monitor the variable in the Debug window, use its modified variable name. Since the Trace window uses the original program source code, the original variable name (not the modified name created by the compiler) appears in the Trace window.

Remarks

Variables or arrays with identical names will not interfere with each other if their values are protected within a "region." Regional variables are similar to private variables.

Example

In the following example, two sets of regional variables are created. In region 1, the variables gcA, gcB, gcC, and gcD are created, and the character string "One" is stored to each. In region 2, the variables gcC, gcD, gcE and gcF are created, and the character string "Two" is stored to each. The variables gcC and gcD are common to both regions.

The output from DISPLAY MEMORY is then shown. The names of variables gcC and gcD are modified in the second region. gcC becomes GCC_____2, and gcD becomes GCD_____2. All the variables are private and can be accessed by lower-level programs.

```
#REGION 1
REGIONAL gcA,gcB,gcC,gcD
STORE 'One' to gcA,gcB,cgC,gcD
#REGION 2
REGIONAL gcC,gcD,gcE,gcF      && gcC and gcD are common to both regions
STORE 'Two' to gcC,gcD,gcE,gcF
DO showmemory

PROCEDURE showmemory
DISPLAY MEMORY LIKE g*
```

See Also

PRIVATE, PUBLIC, STORE

REINDEX Command

Rebuilds open index files.

Syntax

REINDEX [COMPACT]

Arguments

COMPACT
    Converts regular single index (.idx) files to compact .idx files.

Remarks

Index files become outdated when you open a table without opening its corresponding index files and make changes to the index files' key fields. When index files become outdated, you can update them by reindexing.

REINDEX updates all index files open in the selected work area. Visual FoxPro recognizes each index file type (compound index (.cdx) files, structural .cdx files, and single index (.idx) files) and reindexes accordingly. It updates all tags in .cdx files, and updates structural .cdx files, which automatically open with the table.

Any index files created with the UNIQUE keyword of the INDEX command or with SET UNIQUE ON retain their UNIQUE status when reindexed.

To REINDEX outdated index files, issue these commands:

```
USE TableName INDEX OutdatedIndexNames
REINDEX
```

Example

In the following example, ISEXCLUSIVE( ) verifies that the customer table was opened for exclusive use. The table is not reindexed since the one in the current work area was not opened for exclusive use.

```
cExclusive = SET('EXCLUSIVE')
SET EXCLUSIVE OFF
SET PATH TO (HOME(2) + 'Data\')
OPEN DATA testdata  && Opens the test databsase
USE Customer      && Not opened exclusively
USE Employee IN 0 EXCLUSIVE    && Opened exclusively in another work area

IF ISEXCLUSIVE( )
   REINDEX  && Can only be done if table opened exclusively
ELSE
   WAIT WINDOW 'The table has to be exclusively opened'
ENDIF

SET EXCLUSIVE &cExclusive
```

See Also

INDEX, SET INDEX, SET EXCLUSIVE, SET UNIQUE, SYS( ) Functions Overview, USE

Relation Object

Created when you establish relationships from within the Data Environment Designer for a form, form set, or report.

Syntax

Relation

Remarks

The Relation object allows you to determine or specify how two tables are related.

Setting a Relation object property at run time generates an error. For a new property setting to take effect, you must call the CloseTables and OpenTables methods for the data environment.

For more information about the data environment for Forms and FormSets, see "Setting the Data Environment" in Chapter 9, "Creating Forms," in the *Microsoft Visual FoxPro 6.0 Programmer's Guide*.

For more information about the data environment for reports, see Chapter 12, "Adding Queries and Reports," in the *Microsoft Visual FoxPro 6.0 Programmer's Guide*.

Properties

Application	ChildAlias	ChildOrder
Comment	Name	OneToMany
ParentAlias	RelationalExpr	Tag

Events

Destroy	Error	Init

Methods

AddProperty	ReadExpression	ReadMethod
ResetToDefault	WriteExpression	

See Also

Cursor Object, DataEnvironment Object

RELATION( ) Function

Returns a specified relational expression for a table open in a specific work area.

Syntax

RELATION(*nRelationNumber* [, *nWorkArea* | *cTableAlias*])

Returns

Character

Arguments

nRelationNumber

Specifies which relation is returned. For example, if *nRelationNumber* is 3, RELATION( ) returns the relational expression for the third relation created.

nWorkArea

Specifies the work area for a table open in another work area. If a table isn't open in the work area you specify, RELATION( ) returns the empty string.

cTableAlias

Specifies the table alias for a table open in another work area.

Remarks

RELATION( ) by default returns relational expressions for the table in the currently selected work area. It returns the empty string if no relations exist. For additional information about creating relations between tables, see the SET RELATION Command, later in this language reference.

DISPLAY STATUS and LIST STATUS display relational expressions. Issue MODIFY DATABASE to display the Database Designer, allowing you to view and modify relations between tables in the current open database. Issue SET to display the Data Session window, allowing you to view and modify relations between free tables.

Example

In the following example, tables are opened and orders set, and then the relations are displayed using RELATION( ).

```
CLOSE DATABASES
OPEN DATABASE (HOME(2) + 'Data\testdata')
USE customer IN 0 ORDER cust_id  && Opens Customer table
USE employee IN 0 ORDER emp_id   && Opens Customer table
USE orders IN  0 ORDER order_id  && Opens Customer table
```

```
SELECT orders
SET RELATION TO emp_id INTO employee
SET RELATION TO cust_id INTO customer ADDITIVE
? RELATION(1)   && Displays CUST_ID
? RELATION(2)   && Displays EMP_ID
? RELATION(3)   && Displays empty string
```

See Also

DISPLAY STATUS, MODIFY DATABASE, LIST STATUS, SET, SET RELATION, SET RELATION OFF, TARGET( )

RelationalExpr Property

Specifies the expression based on fields in the parent table that relates to an index in the child table joining the two tables. For the Grid control, available at design time; read/write at run time. For the Relation object, available at design time; read-only at run time.

Syntax

Object.RelationalExpr[= *cExpr*]

Arguments

cExpr
Specifies any Visual FoxPro expression, typically one that matches the child table's current index as specified by the ChildOrder property.

Applies To

Grid, Relation

See Also

ChildOrder Property, LinkMaster Property, SET RELATION

RelativeColumn Property

Specifies the active column in the visible portion of a Grid control. Not available at design time and read-only at run time.

Syntax

Grid.RelativeColumn[= *nColumn*]

Arguments

nColumn
Specifies the active column in a Grid control.

Remarks

Use the RelativeColumn property to determine the relative position of the active column in a grid. For example, if you scroll through a grid so that the first column is no longer visible, but the active column is the first visible column in the grid, RelativeColumn is set to 1. To determine the absolute position of the active column in a grid, use the ActiveColumn property.

Applies To

Grid

See Also

ActiveColumn Property, ActiveRow Property, RelativeRow Property

RelativeRow Property

Specifies the active row in the visible portion of a Grid control. Not available at design time; read-only at run time.

Syntax

Grid.RelativeRow[= *nRow*]

Arguments

nRow
    Specifies the active row in a Grid control.

Remarks

Use the RelativeRow property to determine the relative position of the active row in a grid. For example, if you scroll through a grid so that the first row is no longer visible, but the active row is the first visible row in the grid, RelativeRow is set to 1. To determine the absolute position of the active row in a grid, use the ActiveRow property.

Applies To

Grid

See Also

ActiveColumn Property, ActiveRow Property, RelativeColumn Property

RELEASE Command

Removes variables and arrays from memory.

Syntax

RELEASE *MemVarList*

– or –

RELEASE ALL [EXTENDED]

– or –

RELEASE ALL [LIKE *Skeleton* | EXCEPT *Skeleton*]

Arguments

RELEASE *MemVarList*
> Specifies the variables and arrays released from memory. Separate the variables and array names with commas.

RELEASE ALL
> Releases from memory all variables and arrays.

EXTENDED
> When issued in a program, specifies that all public variables are released. RELEASE ALL does not release public variables when issued in a program.

LIKE *Skeleton* | EXCEPT *Skeleton*
> Releases from memory all variables and arrays that match the specified skeleton, or all variables and arrays except those that match the specified skeleton. *Skeleton* can include the wildcards ? and *. RELEASE ALL LIKE and RELEASE ALL EXCEPT do not release public variables when issued in a program.

See Also

CLEAR MEMORY, DIMENSION, PRIVATE, PUBLIC, STORE

RELEASE BAR Command

Removes a specified menu item or all menu items on a menu from memory.

Syntax

RELEASE BAR *nMenuItemNumber* OF *MenuName* | ALL OF *MenuName*

Arguments

nMenuItemNumber OF MenuName
> Specifies a menu item in a user-defined menu to remove from memory. To remove a menu item from a Microsoft Visual FoxPro system menu, include the internal Visual FoxPro system menu item name in *nMenuItemNumber*. For more information, see "System Menu Names," later in this language reference.

ALL OF *MenuName*
> Specifies that every menu item on a user-defined menu is removed from memory. ALL cannot be used to remove menu items from a Visual FoxPro system menu.

See Also

DEFINE BAR, RELEASE PAD

RELEASE CLASSLIB Command

Closes .vcx visual class libraries containing class definitions.

Syntax

RELEASE CLASSLIB *ClassLibraryName1* | ALIAS *AliasName1*
    [, *ClassLibraryName2* | ALIAS *AliasName2* ...]
    [IN *APPFileName* | *EXEFileName*]

Arguments

ClassLibraryName1 | ALIAS *AliasName1*
    Specifies the name or alias of a visual class library file to close.

ClassLibraryName2 | ALIAS *AliasName2* ...
    Specifies the names or aliases of additional visual class library files to close.

IN *APPFileName* | *EXEFileName*
    Specifies a Visual FoxPro application file (.app) or executable file (.exe) containing the visual class library.

Remarks

.vcx visual class libraries are opened with SET CLASSLIB. Once the library is open, the class definitions within the visual class library are available to programs and from the Command window.

To close all open visual class libraries, issue SET CLASSLIB TO without any additional arguments.

Example

The following example uses CREATE CLASSLIB to create a visual class library named myclslib. A class named myform based on the Visual FoxPro Form base class is created and is stored in the myclslib visual class library. SET CLASSLIB is used to open the myclslib visual class library so that classes within it can be used. RELEASE CLASSLIB is then used to close the myclslib visual class library.

```
CREATE CLASSLIB myclslib     && Creates a new .VCX visual class library
CREATE CLASS myform OF myclslib AS "Form"  && Creates new class
SET CLASSLIB TO myclslib ADDITIVE     && Opens MyClsLib.VCX
RELEASE CLASSLIB myclslib
```

See Also

ADD CLASS, CREATE CLASS, CREATE CLASSLIB, MODIFY CLASS, REMOVE CLASS, RENAME CLASS, SET CLASSLIB

RELEASE LIBRARY Command

Removes a single external API library from memory.

Syntax

RELEASE LIBRARY *LibraryName*

Arguments

LibraryName
Specifies the name of the API library to remove from memory.

Remarks

Issue SET LIBRARY TO to remove all API libraries from memory. An external API routine library is loaded into memory with SET LIBRARY. For more information on API routine libraries, see the SET LIBRARY Command, later in this language reference.

See Also

SET LIBRARY

RELEASE MENUS Command

Removes user-defined menu bars from memory.

Syntax

RELEASE MENUS [*MenuBarNameList* [EXTENDED]]

Arguments

MenuBarNameList
Specifies the menu bars to be released from memory. Separate the menu bar names with commas.

EXTENDED
Releases a menu bar and all its subordinate menus, menu titles, menu items, and all associated ON SELECTION BAR, ON SELECTION MENU, ON SELECTION PAD, and ON SELECTION POPUP commands.

Remarks

An active menu bar must first be deactivated with DEACTIVATE MENU before it can be released from memory.

If RELEASE MENUS is issued without any additional arguments, all user-defined menu bars are removed from memory.

See Also

DEFINE MENU

Release Method

Releases a form or form set from memory.

Syntax

Object.Release

Remarks

The Release method is useful when a form or form set is created with the DO FORM command and there is no variable by which to reference the form or form set.

You can use the forms collection of the Screen object to find the form or form set and call its Release method.

Applies To

Form, FormSet, _SCREEN

See Also

DO FORM

RELEASE PAD Command

Removes a specific menu title or all menu titles from memory.

Syntax

RELEASE PAD *MenuTitleName* OF *MenuBarName* | ALL OF *MenuBarName*

Arguments

MenuTitleName OF *MenuBarName*
Specifies the menu title to remove from memory.

You can remove a menu title from the Visual FoxPro system menu bar by specifying its name in *MenuTitleName*. For example, the command RELEASE PAD _MEDIT OF _MSYSMENU removes the Edit menu title from the Visual FoxPro system menu bar.

ALL OF *MenuBarName*
> Specifies that every menu title in a user-defined menu bar is removed from memory. The ALL clause cannot be used to remove menu titles from the Visual FoxPro system menu bar.

Example

The following example removes the Window menu title from the system menu bar.

```
PUSH MENU _MSYSMENU
RELEASE PAD _MSM_WINDO OF _MSYSMENU  && Removes Window menu title

WAIT WINDOW 'Press a key to restore the default menu'
POP MENU _MSYSMENU  && Restore default Visual FoxPro menu system
```

See Also

DEFINE PAD, RELEASE BAR, System Menu Names

RELEASE POPUPS Command

Removes a specific menu or all menus from memory.

Syntax

RELEASE POPUPS [*MenuNameList* [EXTENDED]]

Arguments

MenuNameList
> Specifies the menus to release from memory. Separate the menu names with commas.

> Visual FoxPro system menus that appear under the Visual FoxPro system menu bar can also be released. To release a Visual FoxPro system menu, include the internal name of the system menu (_MFILE, _MEDIT, _MDATA, and so on). Use SET SYSMENU TO DEFAULT to restore the default system menu bar and system menus.

EXTENDED
> Releases a menu, its items, and all commands associated with ON SELECTION POPUP and ON SELECTION BAR.

Remarks

An active menu must be deactivated with DEACTIVATE POPUP before it can be released from memory.

If RELEASE POPUPS is issued without any additional arguments, all user-defined menus are removed from memory.

See Also

DEFINE POPUP, System Menu Names

RELEASE PROCEDURE Command

Closes procedure files opened with SET PROCEDURE.

Syntax

RELEASE PROCEDURE *FileName1* [, *FileName2* ...]

Arguments

FileName1 [, *FileName2* ...]
Specifies the name of the procedure file or a set of procedure files to close.

Remarks

Procedure files are opened with SET PROCEDURE. Once the file is open, the procedures within the file are available to programs and from the Command window.

To close all open procedure files, issue SET PROCEDURE TO without any additional arguments.

See Also

SET PROCEDURE

RELEASE WINDOWS Command

Removes user-defined windows or Visual FoxPro system windows from memory.

Syntax

RELEASE WINDOWS [*WindowNameList*]

Arguments

WindowNameList
Specifies the windows released from memory. *WindowNameList* can include both user-defined windows and Visual FoxPro system windows. Separate the window names with commas.

If *WindowNameList* isn't included, the active user-defined window is released.

RELEASE WINDOWS can be used to remove Visual FoxPro system windows from the main Visual FoxPro window from or a parent, user-defined window.

The following list includes system windows that can be released from the main Visual FoxPro window or from a parent window.

- Command

- Debug

- Trace

- View

To release a system window and or a toolbar (in Visual FoxPro), enclose the entire system window or toolbar name in quotation marks. For example, to release the Report Controls toolbar in Visual FoxPro, issue the following command:

```
RELEASE WINDOW "Report Controls"
```

Use ACTIVATE WINDOW to place a system window in the main Visual FoxPro window or in a user-defined window.

See Also

ACTIVATE WINDOW, DEFINE WINDOW

ReleaseType Property

Returns an integer that determines how a Form object is released. Not available at design time; read-only at run time.

Syntax

Object.ReleaseType

Arguments

The settings for the ReleaseType property are:

Setting	Description
0	Variable released.
1	Close menu command or close box.
2	Exit Visual FoxPro.

Remarks

The ReleaseType property is set prior to the QueryUnload event being called.

Applies To

Form, _SCREEN

See Also

QueryUnload Event, Unload Event

Remove Method

Removes a file from its files collection and project.

Syntax

Object.Remove( )

Remarks

The Remove method returns true (.T.) if the file is successfully removed from the project; otherwise false (.F.) is returned. Note that a warning isn't displayed when you use the Remove method to remove files from a project, including files that are under source code control.

The QueryRemoveFile event occurs before the file is removed from its Files collection and project. If the QueryRemoveFile event returns false (.F.), the file isn't removed from its Files collection and project and the Remove method returns false (.F.). If the QueryRemoveFile method returns true (.T.), the file is removed from its Files collection and project and the Remove method returns true (.T.).

Applies To

File Object

See Also

Add Method, Modify Method, QueryRemoveFile Event

RemoveFromSCC Method

Removes a file in a project from source code control.

Syntax

Object.RemoveFromSCC( )

Remarks

The RemoveFromSCC method returns true (.T.) if the file is successfully removed from source code control; otherwise false (.F.) is returned.

Applies To

File Object

See Also

AddToSCC Method, CheckIn Method, CheckOut Method, GetLatestVersion Method, UndoCheckOut Method

REMOVE CLASS Command

Removes a class definition from a .vcx visual class library.

Syntax

REMOVE CLASS *ClassName* OF *ClassLibraryName*

Arguments

ClassName
Specifies the name of the class definition to remove from the visual class library.

OF *ClassLibraryName*
Specifies the name of the .vcx visual class library containing the class definition to remove. If no file extension is included in *ClassLibraryName*, a .vcx extension is assumed.

Remarks

Exercise care when removing class definitions — the class definition you remove may be a parent class on which other classes are based.

See Also

ADD CLASS, CREATE CLASS, CREATE CLASSLIB, MODIFY CLASS, RELEASE CLASSLIB, RENAME CLASS, SET CLASSLIB

REMOVE TABLE Command

Removes a table from the current database.

Syntax

REMOVE TABLE *TableName* | ?
    [DELETE] [RECYCLE]

Arguments

TableName
Specifies the table to remove from the current database.

?
Displays the Remove dialog box from which you can choose a table in the current database to remove.

DELETE
Specifies that the table is removed from the database and from disk.

Caution Any table deleted from disk with this clause cannot be retrieved. Even if SET SAFETY is ON, you are not warned before the table is deleted from disk.

RECYCLE
> Specifies that the table isn't immediately deleted from disk and is placed in the Microsoft Windows Recycle Bin.

Remarks

When a table is removed from the database, it becomes a free table and can be added to another database. Tables are added to a database with ADD TABLE.

When REMOVE TABLE is issued, all primary indexes, default values, and validation rules associated with the table are also removed. If SET SAFETY is ON, Visual FoxPro displays a prompt asking if you are sure you want to remove the table from the database.

> **Important** REMOVE TABLE affects other tables in the current database if those tables have rules or relations associated with the table being removed. The rules and relations are no longer valid when the table is removed from the database.

Example

The following example creates two databases named `mydbc1` and `mydbc2`, and a table named table1. The table is added to `mydbc1` when it is created. The table is then closed and removed from `mydbc1`. ADD TABLE is then used to add the table to `mydbc2`. RENAME TABLE is used to change the name of the table from `table1` to `table2`.

```
CREATE DATABASE mydbc1
CREATE DATABASE mydbc2
SET DATABASE TO mydbc1
CREATE TABLE table1 (cField1 C(10), n N(10))  && Adds table to mydbc1
CLOSE TABLES    && A table must be closed to remove it from a database
REMOVE TABLE table1
SET DATABASE TO mydbc2
ADD TABLE table1
RENAME TABLE table1 TO table2
```

See Also

ADD TABLE, CLOSE DATABASES, CREATE DATABASE, FREE TABLE, OPEN DATABASE

RemoveItem Method

Removes an item from a combo box or list box.

Syntax

Control.RemoveItem(*nIndex*)

Arguments

nIndex
> Specifies an integer corresponding to the order in which items are displayed in the control. For the first item in a list box or combo box, *nIndex* = 1.

Applies To

ComboBox, ListBox

See Also

AddItem Method, Clear Method, RemoveListItem Method

RemoveListItem Method

Removes an item from a combo box or list box.

Syntax

Control.RemoveListItem(*nItemId*)

Arguments

nItemId
Specifies an integer representing the unique ID of the item in the control.

Applies To

ComboBox, ListBox

See Also

AddItem Method, Clear Method

RemoveObject Method

Removes a specified object from a container object at run time.

Syntax

Object.RemoveObject(*cObjectName*)

Arguments

cObjectName
Specifies the name of an object to remove. If the object does not exist, an error occurs.

Remarks

When an object is removed, it disappears from the screen and can no longer be referenced.

Applies To

Column, CommandGroup, Container Object, Custom, DataEnvironment, Form, FormSet, Grid, OptionGroup, Page, PageFrame, _SCREEN, ToolBar

See Also

AddObject Method, RemoveItem Method, RemoveListItem Method

RENAME Command

Changes the name of a file to a new name.

Syntax

RENAME *FileName1* TO *FileName2*

Arguments

FileName1 TO *FileName2*

Specifies the file name to change and the new file name. Include a file extension for each file. If the file extensions are not included, the default extension .dbf is assumed. If you rename a free table that has an associated .fpt memo file, be sure to rename the memo file. Include a period (.) after the file name to rename a file that doesn't have an extension.

Do not use RENAME to change the name of a table in a database; RENAME does not change the name of the table in the database. Use RENAME TABLE to change the name of a table in a database.

Include paths with either or both file names if the files are not on the default path. If *FileName1* and *FileName2* are in different directories or folders, *FileName1* is moved into the directory or folder of *FileName2*.

When you issue RENAME, *FileName2* cannot already exist and *FileName1* must exist and cannot be open.

FileName1 and *FileName2* can contain wildcard characters such as * and ?. For example, to rename all program files with the extension .prg in the current directory or folder to backup files with extension .bak, issue RENAME *.prg TO *.bak.

See Also

COPY FILE, COPY TO, RENAME CLASS, RENAME TABLE

RENAME CLASS Command

Renames a class definition contained in a .VCX visual class library.

Syntax

RENAME CLASS *ClassName1* OF *ClassLibraryName* TO *ClassName2*

Arguments

ClassName1

Specifies the name of the class definition that is renamed.

OF *ClassLibraryName*
> Specifies the name of the .vcx visual class library containing the class definition to rename. If you don't specify a file extension in *ClassLibraryName*, Visual FoxPro automatically assigns a .vcx extension.

TO *ClassName2*
> Specifies the new name of the class definition.

Remarks

Visual FoxPro does not update other class definitions within the visual class library that reference the renamed class definition — be careful when renaming class definitions.

Example

The following example uses CREATE CLASSLIB to create a visual class library named myclslib. A class named myform based on the Visual FoxPro Form base class is created with CREATE CLASS and is stored in the myclslib visual class library. RENAME CLASS is used to change the class name from myform to yourform.

```
CREATE CLASSLIB myclslib      && Creates a new .VCX visual class library
CREATE CLASS myform OF myclslib AS "Form"  && Creates new class
RENAME CLASS myform OF myclslib TO yourform  && Change class name
```

See Also

ADD CLASS, CREATE CLASS, MODIFY CLASS, RELEASE CLASSLIB, REMOVE CLASS, SET CLASSLIB

RENAME CONNECTION Command

Renames a named connection in the current database.

Syntax

RENAME CONNECTION *ConnectionName1* TO *ConnectionName2*

Arguments

ConnectionName1
> Specifies the name of the connection to be renamed.

ConnectionName2
> Specifies the new name of the connection.

Remarks

The database containing the named connection must be opened exclusively and must be current before the connection can be renamed. To open a database for exclusive use, include EXCLUSIVE in OPEN DATABASE.

Example

The following example assumes an ODBC data source called MyFoxSQLNT is available, and the user ID for the data source is "sa." The testdata database is opened, and a connection named Myconn1 is created. DISPLAY CONNECTIONS is used to display the named connections in the database.

RENAME CONNECTION is then used to change the newly created connection name to Myconn2. DISPLAY CONNECTIONS is used again to display the connection with its new name. The newly renamed connection is then removed from the database with DELETE CONNECTION.

```
CLOSE DATABASES
OPEN DATABASE (HOME(2) + 'Data\testdata')
CREATE CONNECTION Myconn1 DATASOURCE "MyFoxSQLNT" USERID "sa"

CLEAR
DISPLAY CONNECTIONS  && Displays named connections in the database
RENAME CONNECTION Myconn1 TO Myconn2
DISPLAY CONNECTIONS  && Displays connection with new name

DELETE CONNECTION Myconn2  && Removes the connection just renamed
```

See Also

DELETE CONNECTION, DBGETPROP( ), DISPLAY CONNECTIONS, LIST CONNECTIONS, MODIFY CONNECTION, OPEN DATABASE

RENAME TABLE Command

Renames a table in the current database.

Syntax

RENAME TABLE *TableName1* TO *TableName2*

Arguments

TableName1
　　Specifies the name of the table to be renamed.

TableName2
　　Specifies the new name of the table.

Remarks

You cannot use RENAME TABLE to change the name of a free table; use RENAME instead.

Example

The following example creates two databases named `mydbc1` and `mydbc2`, and a table named table1. The table is added to `mydbc1` when it is created. The table is then closed and removed from `mydbc1`. ADD TABLE is then used to add the table to `mydbc2`. RENAME TABLE is used to change the name of the table from `table1` to `table2`.

```
CLOSE DATABASES
CREATE DATABASE mydbc1
CREATE DATABASE mydbc2
SET DATABASE TO mydbc1
CREATE TABLE table1 (cField1 C(10), n N(10))  && Adds table to mydbc1
CLOSE TABLES       && A table must be closed to remove it from a database
REMOVE TABLE table1
SET DATABASE TO mydbc2
ADD TABLE table1
RENAME TABLE table1 TO table2
```

See Also

ADD TABLE, CLOSE DATABASES, CREATE DATABASE, COPY FILE, COPY TO, OPEN DATABASE, RENAME

RENAME VIEW Command

Renames a SQL view in the current database.

Syntax

RENAME VIEW *ViewName1* TO *ViewName2*

Arguments

ViewName1
Specifies the name of the SQL view to be renamed.

ViewName2
Specifies the new name of the SQL view.

Remarks

The database containing the SQL view must be opened exclusively and must be current before the SQL view can be renamed. To open a database for exclusive use, include EXCLUSIVE in OPEN DATABASE.

Example

The following example opens the `testdata` database. CREATE SQL VIEW is used to create a local SQL view named `myview` which is created from a SELECT – SQL statement that selects all records from the `customer` table. RENAME VIEW is used to change the name of the view from `myview` to `yourview`.

The View Designer is displayed, allowing modify the newly renamed SQL view. After the View Designer is closed, the SQL view is erased.

```
CLOSE DATABASES
OPEN DATABASE (HOME(2) + 'Data\testdata')

CREATE SQL VIEW myview AS SELECT * FROM customer  && Create the view
RENAME VIEW myview TO yourview  && Change the view name
MODIFY VIEW yourview  && Open the View designer
DELETE VIEW yourview  && Delete the view
```

See Also

CREATE SQL VIEW, DELETE VIEW, DISPLAY VIEWS, LIST VIEWS, MODIFY VIEW, OPEN DATABASE, RENAME VIEW, SELECT – SQL, USE

REPLACE Command

Updates table records.

Syntax

REPLACE *FieldName1* WITH *eExpression1* [ADDITIVE]
    [, *FieldName2* WITH *eExpression2* [ADDITIVE]] ...
    [*Scope*] [FOR *lExpression1*] [WHILE *lExpression2*]
    [IN *nWorkArea* | *cTableAlias*]
    [NOOPTIMIZE]

Arguments

FieldName1 WITH *eExpression1* [, *FieldName2* WITH *eExpression2* ...]
    Specifies that the data in *FieldName1* be replaced with the value of the expression *eExpression1*; that the data in *FieldName2* be replaced with the value of the expression *eExpression2*; and so on.

    When the expression value is longer than the width of a numeric field, REPLACE forces the value to fit by carrying out the following steps:

    1. First, REPLACE truncates decimal places and rounds the remaining decimal portion of the field.

    2. If the value still doesn't fit, REPLACE stores the field contents using scientific notation.

    3. If the value still doesn't fit, REPLACE replaces the field contents with asterisks.

ADDITIVE
    Appends to the end of the memo fields replacements to memo fields. ADDITIVE applies to replacements in memo fields only. If you omit ADDITIVE, the memo field is overwritten with the value of the expression.

Scope

Specifies a range of records to replace. Only the records that fall within the range are replaced. The scope clauses are: ALL, NEXT *nRecords*, RECORD *nRecordNumber*, and REST. For more information on scope clauses, see "Scope Clauses" and "Overview of the Language," in Help.

The default scope for REPLACE is the current record (NEXT 1).

FOR *lExpression1*

Specifies that the designated fields be replaced only in records for which *lExpression1* evaluates to true (.T.). Including FOR lets you conditionally replace records, filtering out those you don't want replaced.

Rushmore optimizes REPLACE FOR if *lExpression1* is an optimizable expression. For best performance, use an optimizable expression in the FOR clause.

For more information, see the SET OPTIMIZE Command, later in this language reference, and "Understanding Rushmore Technology" in Chapter 15, "Optimizing Applications," in the *Microsoft Visual FoxPro 6.0 Programmer's Guide*.

WHILE *lExpression2*

Specifies a condition whereby fields are replaced for as long as the logical expression *lExpression2* evaluates to true (.T.).

IN *nWorkArea*

Specifies the work area of the table in which records are updated.

IN *cTableAlias*

Specifies the alias of the table in which records are updated.

If you omit *nWorkArea* and *cTableAlias*, records are updated in the table in the currently selected work area.

NOOPTIMIZE

Prevents Rushmore optimization.

For more information, see the SET OPTIMIZE Command, later in this language reference, and "Understanding Rushmore Technology" in Chapter 15, "Optimizing Applications," in the *Microsoft Visual FoxPro 6.0 Programmer's Guide*.

Remarks

REPLACE replaces data in a field with the value in an expression. Fields in unselected work areas must be prefaced with their alias.

Note If the IN clause is omitted, no replacement occurs if the record pointer is at the end of the file in the current work area and you specify a field in another work area.

Example

The following example creates a table with 10 records. REPLACE is used to place random values into a field. MIN( ) and MAX( ) displays the maximum and minimum values in the table.

```
CLOSE DATABASES
CREATE TABLE Random (cValue N(3))
FOR nItem = 1 TO 10   && Append 10 records,
   APPEND BLANK
   REPLACE cValue WITH 1 + 100 * RAND( )   && Insert random values
ENDFOR

CLEAR
LIST   && Display the values
gnMaximum = 1   && Initialize minimum value
gnMinimum = 100   && Initialize maximum value
SCAN
   gnMinimum = MIN(gnMinimum, cValue)
   gnMaximum = MAX(gnMaximum, cValue)
ENDSCAN
? 'The minimum value is: ', gnMinimum   && Display minimum value
? 'The maximum value is: ', gnMaximum   && Display maximum value
```

See Also

GATHER, INSERT – SQL, SCATTER

REPLACE FROM ARRAY Command

Updates data in fields with values from a variable array.

Syntax

REPLACE FROM ARRAY *ArrayName*
    [FIELDS *FieldList*]
    [*Scope*]
    [FOR *lExpression1*]
    [WHILE *lExpression2*]
    [NOOPTIMIZE]

Arguments

ArrayName
    Specifies the name of the array whose values replace the field data.

FIELDS *FieldList*

Specifies that only the fields in *FieldList* be replaced by the contents of the array. Fields in unselected work areas must be prefaced with their table alias.

Scope

Specifies a range of records to replace with the contents of the array. Only the records that fall within the range are replaced. Replacement occurs until the end of the scope or the end of the array is reached.

The scope clauses are: ALL, NEXT *nRecords*, RECORD *nRecordNumber*, and REST. For more information on scope clauses, see "Scope Clauses" and "Overview of the Language," in Help.

The default scope for REPLACE FROM ARRAY is the current record (NEXT 1).

FOR *lExpression1*

Specifies that fields be replaced only in records for which *lExpression1* evaluates to true (.T.). Including FOR lets you conditionally replace records, filtering out those you don't want. Replacement occurs in each record for which *lExpression1* is true (.T.), or until the end of the array is reached.

Rushmore optimizes REPLACE FROM ARRAY FOR if *lExpression1* is an optimizable expression. For best performance, use an optimizable expression in the FOR clause.

For more information, see the SET OPTIMIZE Command, later in this language reference, and "Understanding Rushmore Technology" in Chapter 15, "Optimizing Applications," in the *Microsoft Visual FoxPro 6.0 Programmer's Guide*.

WHILE *lExpression2*

Specifies a condition whereby fields in records are replaced by the contents of the array for as long as the logical expression *lExpression2* evaluates to true (.T.).

NOOPTIMIZE

Prevents Rushmore optimization.

For more information, see the SET OPTIMIZE Command, later in this language reference, and "Understanding Rushmore Technology" in Chapter 15, "Optimizing Applications," in the *Microsoft Visual FoxPro 6.0 Programmer's Guide*.

Remarks

Memo and general fields are ignored in REPLACE FROM ARRAY. To import data into these fields, use GATHER and APPEND GENERAL.

Starting with the first element, the elements of the array replace the corresponding fields of the record. The first array element replaces the first field of the record, the second array element replaces the second field, and so on.

If the array has fewer elements than the table has fields, the additional fields are ignored. If the array has more elements than the table has fields, the additional array elements are ignored.

> **Note** No replacement occurs if the record pointer is at the end of the file in the current work area and you specify a field in another work area.

See Also

APPEND FROM ARRAY, APPEND GENERAL, COPY TO ARRAY, GATHER, REPLACE, SCATTER, SET OPTIMIZE

REPLICATE( ) Function

Returns a character string that contains a specified character expression repeated a specified number of times.

Syntax

REPLICATE(*cExpression*, *nTimes*)

Returns

Character

Arguments

cExpression
Specifies the character expression that is replicated.

nTimes
Specifies the number of times the character expression is replicated.

Remarks

In Visual FoxPro, the maximum length of the resulting character string is restricted by the amount of available memory.

Example

```
CLEAR
? REPLICATE('HELLO ',4) && Displays HELLO HELLO HELLO HELLO
```

See Also

SPACE( )

REPORT Command

Displays or prints a report under the control of a report definition file created with MODIFY REPORT or CREATE REPORT.

Syntax

REPORT FORM *FileName1* | ?
    [ENVIRONMENT]
    [*Scope*] [FOR *lExpression1*] [WHILE *lExpression2*]
    [HEADING *cHeadingText*]
    [NOCONSOLE]
    [NOOPTIMIZE]
    [PLAIN]
    [RANGE *nStartPage* [, *nEndPage*]]
    [PREVIEW [[IN] WINDOW *WindowName* | IN SCREEN]
    [NOWAIT]]
    [TO PRINTER [PROMPT] | TO FILE *FileName2* [ASCII]]
    [NAME *ObjectName*]
    [SUMMARY]

Arguments

FileName1
    Specifies the name of the report definition file to print.

?
    Displays the Open dialog box, from which you can choose a report file.

ENVIRONMENT
    Included for backward compatibility with 2.x reports. To restore the data environment associated with a Visual FoxPro report, set the data environment AutoOpenTables property to true (.T.), which is the default. To make sure that the report environment is closed when the report is finished printing, set the data environment AutoCloseTables property to true (.T.), which is also the default.

    For reports converted from earlier versions of FoxPro, including ENVIRONMENT opens and restores all the tables and relations in the Data Environment even if AutoOpenTables is set to false (.F.).

    When you create or modify reports, you can save the current Visual FoxPro data environment with the report definition file. Saving the Visual FoxPro data environment places additional records in the report definition table for all open tables and index files, the index order, and any relationships between the tables.

Scope
    Specifies a range of records to include in the report. Only the records that fall within the range are included in the report.

The scope clauses are: ALL, NEXT *nRecords*, RECORD *nRecordNumber*, and REST. For more information on scope clauses, see "Scope Clauses" and "Overview of the Language," in Help.

The default scope for REPORT is ALL records.

FOR *lExpression1*

Prints data only in those records for which *lExpression1* evaluates to true (.T.). Including FOR lets you filter out the records you don't want to print.

Rushmore optimizes REPORT FOR if *lExpression1* is an optimizable expression. For best performance, use an optimizable expression in the FOR clause.

For more information, see the SET OPTIMIZE Command, later in this language reference, and "Understanding Rushmore Technology" in Chapter 15, "Optimizing Applications," in the *Microsoft Visual FoxPro 6.0 Programmer's Guide*.

WHILE *lExpression2*

Specifies a condition whereby data is printed for as long as the logical expression *lExpression2* evaluates to true (.T.).

HEADING *cHeadingText*

Specifies text for an additional heading to be placed on each page of the report. The PLAIN clause takes precedence if you include both HEADING and PLAIN.

NOCONSOLE

Suppresses the echoing of a report to the main Visual FoxPro window or to a user-defined window when the report is being printed or sent to a file.

NOOPTIMIZE

To prevent Rushmore optimization of REPORT, include NOOPTIMIZE.

For more information, see the SET OPTIMIZE Command, later in this language reference, and "Understanding Rushmore Technology" in Chapter 15, "Optimizing Applications," in the *Microsoft Visual FoxPro 6.0 Programmer's Guide*.

PLAIN

Specifies that a page heading appears only at the beginning of the report.

RANGE *nStartPage* [, *nEndPage*]

Specifies a range of pages to print. *nStartPage* specifies the first page printed; *nEndPage* specifies the last page printed. If *nEndPage* is omitted, the last page printed defaults to 9,999.

PREVIEW [[IN] WINDOW *WindowName* I IN SCREEN]

Displays the report in page preview mode instead of sending the report to the printer. To print a report, you must issue REPORT with TO PRINTER.

System variables are ignored when you include PREVIEW.

You can include the optional WINDOW or IN WINDOW clause to specify a window in which the report is previewed. *WindowName* can be the name of a window created with DEFINE WINDOW. If you include the WINDOW clause, the preview assumes the characteristics (title, size, and so on) of the window you specify with *WindowName*. If you include the IN WINDOW clause, the report is previewed in the window you specify with *WindowName*.

You can include the optional IN SCREEN clause to specify that the report preview window is contained in the main Visual FoxPro window and cannot be moved outside it.

You can include the optional NOWAIT clause so that at run time Visual FoxPro does not wait for the page preview window to be closed before continuing program execution. Instead, Visual FoxPro continues program execution while the page preview window is open.

In a distributed application, be sure that the View menu is available. If the Print Preview toolbar is closed, it cannot be restored unless the View menu is available.

TO PRINTER [PROMPT]
Sends a report to the printer.

In Visual FoxPro, you can include the optional PROMPT clause to display a printer settings dialog box before printing starts. The printer settings that you can adjust depend on the currently installed printer driver. Place PROMPT immediately after TO PRINTER.

TO FILE *FileName2* [ASCII]
Specifies the text file to which you send a report. The current printer driver is used when the report is sent to the text file. The file created when you include TO FILE has the default extension .txt.

You can include the optional ASCII clause to create an ASCII text file from the report definition file. Without the ASCII clause, PostScript and other printer codes are written to the text file. Any graphics, lines, rectangles, or rounded rectangles in the report definition do not appear in the ASCII text file.

The number of columns and rows on each page in the ASCII text file is determined by the contents of the _ASCIICOLS and _ASCIIROWS system variables. The default values for _ASCIICOLS and _ASCIIROWS are 80 columns and 63 rows respectively. These values correspond to a standard portrait page.

NAME *ObjectName*
Specifies an object variable name for the data environment of a report. The data environment and the objects in the data environment have properties and methods, for example AddObject, that need to be set or called at run time. The object variable provides access to these properties and methods. If you don't specify a NAME, Visual FoxPro uses as a default the name of the report file that can be referenced in the code associated with the events.

SUMMARY

Suppresses detail line printing. Only totals and subtotals are printed.

Remarks

The default extension for a report definition file is .frx. If the report definition file is not in the default directory or folder, the path must also be included with the file name.

See Also

_ASCIICOLS, _ASCIIROWS, CREATE REPORT, DataEnvironment Object, MODIFY REPORT

Requery Method

Requeries the row source to which the ListBox or ComboBox control is bound.

Syntax

Control.Requery

Remarks

Use the Requery method to ensure a control contains the most recent data. The Requery method requeries the RowSource property and updates the list with the new values.

Applies To

ComboBox, ListBox

See Also

RowSource Property

REQUERY( ) Function

Retrieves data again for a SQL view.

Syntax

REQUERY([*nWorkArea* | *cTableAlias*])

Arguments

nWorkArea
    Specifies the work area in which the SQL view is open.

cTableAlias
    Specifies the alias of the SQL view. If you omit *nWorkArea* and *cTableAlias*, the data for the SQL view open in the currently selected work area is retrieved.

Returns

Numeric

Remarks

REQUERY( ) returns 1 if the data is successfully retrieved; otherwise, it returns 0.

REQUERY( ) is typically used to refresh a SQL view when data has changed on the data source.

See Also

CREATE SQL VIEW, SELECT – SQL, USE

RequestData Method

Creates an array containing data from a table open in an instance of Visual FoxPro.

Syntax

ApplicationObject.RequestData([*nWorkArea* | *cTableAlias*] [, *nRecords*])

Returns

Array

Arguments

nWorkArea
Specifies the work area number of the table from which data is stored in the array.
If you omit *cTableAlias* and *nWorkArea*, data from the table open in the current work
area is stored in the array.

cTableAlias
Specifies the alias of the table from which data is stored in the array.

nRecords
Specifies the number of records stored in the array, starting from the current record.
If *nRecords* is omitted and sufficient memory is available, all records, starting from
the current record, are stored in the array.

Remarks

Use the RequestData method to retrieve data from an instance of Visual FoxPro.

Example

The following example, run from within Visual FoxPro, creates a second instance of
Visual FoxPro. The Customer table is opened in the second instance of Visual FoxPro.

An array containing data from the Customer table is created in the first instance of Visual FoxPro, and the contents of the array is displayed. The array contains data from the first 5 records in the Customer table. The second instance of Visual FoxPro is then closed.

```
oNewInstance = CREATEOBJECT('VisualFoxPro.Application')
oNewInstance.DoCmd "USE (HOME(2) + 'Data\Customer')"
aCustomerArray = oNewInstance.RequestData('Customer',5)
DISPLAY MEMORY LIKE aCustomerArray
oNewInstance.DoCmd('QUIT')
```

Applies To

Application Object, _VFP System Variable

See Also

DataToClip Method

Reset Method

Resets the Timer control so that it starts counting from 0.

Syntax

Timer.Reset

Applies To

Timer

See Also

Interval Property, Timer Event

ResetToDefault Method

Restores a property, event, or method to its Visual FoxPro default setting. Available at run time and design time.

Syntax

[*Form*.]*Object*.ResetToDefault(*cPropertyName*
    | *cEventName* | *cMethodName*)

Arguments

cPropertyName
    Specifies the name of the property to reset to the Visual FoxPro default setting.

cEventName
    Specifies the name of the event to reset. All user-defined code in the event is deleted.

cMethodName
> Specifies the name of the method to reset. All user-defined code in the method is deleted.

Remarks

ResetToDefault returns a property to the setting it had when first created. For example, if you have changed the font of a command button, calling this method for the caption resets the font to its default (Arial).

ResetToDefault removes all user-defined code from an event or method at design time.

Applies To

ActiveDoc, CheckBox, Column, ComboBox, CommandButton, CommandGroup, Container Object, Control Object, Cursor, Custom, DataEnvironment, EditBox, Form, FormSet, Grid, Header, Image, Label, Line, ListBox, OLE Bound Control, OLE Container Control, OptionButton, OptionGroup, Page, PageFrame, ProjectHook Object, Relation, _SCREEN, Shape, Spinner, TextBox, Timer, ToolBar

See Also

GETPEM( )

Resizable Property

Specifies whether a Column object can be sized at run time by the user. Available at design time; read/write at run time.

Syntax

Column.Resizable[= *lExpr*]

Arguments

lExpr
> The settings for the Resizable property are:

Setting	Description
True (.T.)	The Column object is sizable.
False (.F.)	(Default) The Column object cannot be sized by the user.

Applies To

Column

See Also

Width Property

Resize Event

Occurs when an object is resized.

Syntax

PROCEDURE *Object*.Resize
[LPARAMETERS *nIndex*]

Arguments

nIndex
Uniquely identifies a control if it is in a control array.

Remarks

Resize can be triggered interactively. Resize can be triggered in code by setting the Height and the Width properties. For a Column, Resize can be triggered in code by setting the Column's Width property.

Applies To

Column, Container Object, Control Object, Form, Grid, OLE Bound Control, OLE Container Control, PageFrame, ToolBar

See Also

Height Property, Paint Event, Width Property

RESTORE FROM Command

Retrieves variables and variable arrays saved in a variable file or a memo field and places them into memory.

Syntax

RESTORE FROM *FileName* | MEMO *MemoFieldName*
    [ADDITIVE]

Arguments

FileName
Specifies the variable file from which the variables and arrays are restored. Variable files are assigned a .mem extension.

MEMO *MemoFieldName*
Specifies the memo field from which variables and arrays are restored.

ADDITIVE

Prevents any variables or arrays currently in memory from being erased. If the number of variables or arrays being added with ADDITIVE plus the number of existing variables exceeds the variable limit, Microsoft Visual FoxPro brings as many variables and arrays as possible into memory from the variable file or memo field.

If you restore a variable or array that has the same name as an existing variable or array, the value in the existing variable or array is overwritten with the value of the restored variable or array.

Remarks

When RESTORE FROM is issued in a program, all PUBLIC and PRIVATE variables and arrays are restored as PRIVATE; all LOCAL variables and arrays are restored as LOCAL. If RESTORE is issued in the Command window, PUBLIC and PRIVATE variables and arrays are restored as PUBLIC; LOCAL variables and arrays are restored as LOCAL.

RESTORE FROM clears any variables or arrays currently in memory unless you include the ADDITIVE keyword. RESTORE FROM does not affect system variables.

Note that object type variables cannot be restored from a variable file or memo field.

Example

In the following example, two variables are created. They are saved to a variable file and restored without clearing the existing variables.

```
gnVal1 = 50
gcVal2 = 'Hello'
SAVE TO temp
CLEAR MEMORY

gdVal3 = DATE( )
RESTORE FROM temp ADDITIVE
CLEAR
DISPLAY MEMORY LIKE g*
```

See Also

DIMENSION, PUBLIC, PRIVATE, RELEASE, SAVE TO, STORE

RESTORE MACROS Command

Restores to memory keyboard macros saved in a keyboard macro file or memo field.

Syntax

RESTORE MACROS
    [FROM *FileName* | FROM MEMO *MemoFieldName*]

Arguments

FROM *FileName*

Specifies the macro file from which macros are restored. Macro files have an .fky extension, and this extension is assumed if you don't specify one. If you have assigned a different extension to the file, you must include this extension in *FileName*.

FROM MEMO *MemoFieldName*

Specifies the memo field from which macros are restored.

Remarks

Use SAVE MACRO to store keyboard macros to a keyboard macro file or a memo field.

By default, restoring macros from a file or memo field is additive — the restored macros are appended to the existing set of macros in memory. If a macro name in the file or memo field is the same as an existing macro name, the macro in the file or memo field overwrites the existing macro.

If issued without a file name or memo field name, RESTORE MACROS clears all macros from memory and restores the default macros. The default macros are restored from the keyboard macro file named Default.fky. If Default.fky cannot be found, Visual FoxPro restores the F2 through F9 keys to the standard Visual FoxPro startup settings.

See Also

CLEAR, PLAY MACRO, SAVE MACROS

RESTORE SCREEN Command

Restores the main Visual FoxPro window or a user-defined window previously saved to the screen buffer, a variable, or an array element.

Syntax

RESTORE SCREEN
    [FROM *VarName*]

Arguments

FROM *VarName*

Specifies the name of a variable or array element from which you want to restore the screen or window image.

Remarks

Use SAVE SCREEN to place the current main Visual FoxPro window or active user-defined window in the screen buffer, a variable, or an array element.

Variables or array elements containing stored screen or window images have an S data type when you view the variables or array elements with DISPLAY or LIST MEMORY. The main Visual FoxPro window or user-defined windows saved to variables or array elements can also be saved to and restored from variable files with SAVE TO and RESTORE FROM.

If issued without the FROM clause, RESTORE SCREEN restores the main Visual FoxPro window or user-defined window from the screen buffer.

See Also

RESTORE FROM, SAVE SCREEN, SAVE TO

RESTORE WINDOW Command

Restores to memory window definitions and window statuses saved to a window file or memo field.

Syntax

RESTORE WINDOW *WindowNameList* | ALL
FROM *FileName* | FROM MEMO *MemoFieldName*

Arguments

WindowNameList
Specifies one or more windows to be restored. Separate the window names with commas.

ALL
Restores all window definitions in the window file or memo field.

FROM *FileName*
Specifies the window file from which windows are restored. A window file has a .win extension. If the file was given another extension when it was saved, you must include this extension in *FileName*.

FROM MEMO *MemoFieldName*
Specifies the memo field from which the windows are restored.

Remarks

Use SAVE WINDOW to store window definitions in a window file or in a memo field.

Any windows in memory with the same names as those restored are overwritten. A window's status (hidden, active, and so on) when it is saved is preserved when it is restored.

Example

In the following example, a window named wOutput1 is defined and saved to a variable. All windows are cleared and the window named wOutput1 is restored and activated.

```
CLEAR
DEFINE WINDOW wOutput1 FROM 2,1 TO 13,75 TITLE 'Output' ;
   CLOSE FLOAT GROW ZOOM
SAVE WINDOW wOutput1 TO temp
CLEAR WINDOWS
RESTORE WINDOW wOutput1 FROM temp
ACTIVATE WINDOW wOutput1
WAIT "The window wOutput1 has been restored" WINDOW
RELEASE WINDOW wOutput1
```

See Also

ACTIVATE WINDOW, DEFINE WINDOW, SAVE WINDOWS

RESUME Command

Continues execution of a suspended program.

Syntax

RESUME

Remarks

Use SUSPEND to suspend program execution. The suspended program restarts at the line where execution was suspended.

SUSPEND and RESUME are valuable debugging tools. You can suspend a program to examine the current status of the Visual FoxPro environment, including memory variables, window, menu bar, or menu definitions.

> **Important** To prevent commands that are executed when a program is suspended from interfering with subsequent program output, issue CLEAR to clear the main Visual FoxPro window or the active user-defined window before you resume program execution.

See Also

CANCEL, CLEAR, RETURN, SUSPEND

RETRY Command

Reexecutes the previous command.

Syntax

RETRY

Remarks

RETRY returns control to the calling program and reexecutes the last line executed in the program. RETRY is similar to RETURN, except RETURN executes the next line in the calling program.

RETRY is useful in error-handling routines. It is frequently used to reexecute a command until a record- or file-locking function succeeds in locking the record or file. You can use SET REPROCESS to control retries of a record- or file-locking function. SET REPROCESS is preferable in most network situations.

See Also

ON ERROR, RETURN, SET REPROCESS

RETURN Command

Returns program control to a calling program.

Syntax

RETURN [*eExpression* | TO MASTER | TO *ProcedureName*]

Arguments

eExpression
    Specifies an expression returned to the calling program. If you omit RETURN or the return expression, true (.T.) is automatically returned to the calling program.

TO MASTER
    Returns control to the highest-level calling program.

TO *ProcedureName*
    Specifies the procedure to which control is returned.

Remarks

RETURN terminates execution of a program, procedure, or function and returns control to the calling program, the highest-level calling program, another program, or the Command window.

Visual FoxPro releases PRIVATE variables when RETURN is executed.

RETURN is usually placed at the end of a program, procedure, or function to return control to a higher-level program. However, an implicit RETURN is executed if you omit RETURN.

Example

In the following example, the function longdate returns a character string that is suitable for printing from a date.

```
SET CENTURY ON
? longdate({^1998-02-16})  && Displays Monday, February 16, 1998

FUNCTION longdate
PARAMETER mdate
RETURN CDOW(mdate) + ', ' + MDY(mdate)
```

See Also

DO, FUNCTION, LPARAMETERS, PARAMETERS, PARAMETERS( ), PRIVATE, PROCEDURE, PUBLIC

RGB( ) Function

Returns a single color value from a set of red, green, and blue color components.

Syntax

RGB(*nRedValue*, *nGreenValue*, *nBlueValue*)

Arguments

nRedValue
> Specifies the intensity of the red color component. *nRedValue* can range from 0 to 255. Zero is the minimum color intensity; 255 is the maximum color intensity.

nGreenValue
> Specifies the intensity of the green color component. *nGreenValue* can range from 0 to 255.

nBlueValue
> Specifies the intensity of the blue color component. *nBlueValue* can range from 0 to 255.

Remarks

The value returned by RGB( ) can be used to set color properties such as BackColor and ForeColor.

Example

The following example uses RGB( ) to change the background color of a Form to blue.

```
goMyForm = CREATEOBJECT('FORM')  && Create a form
goMyForm.Show  && Display the form
WAIT WINDOW 'Press a key to change the form color'
goMyForm.BackColor=RGB(0,0,255)  && Change the form background color
WAIT WINDOW 'Press a key to release the form'
RELEASE goMyForm  && Release the form from memory
```

See Also

GETCOLOR( ), RGBSCHEME( )

RGBSCHEME( ) Function

Returns an RGB color pair or an RGB color pair list from a specified color scheme.

Syntax

RGBSCHEME(*nColorSchemeNumber* [, *nColorPairPosition*])

Returns

Character

Arguments

nColorSchemeNumber

Specifies the number of the color scheme for which you want a complete RGB color listing. RGBSCHEME( ) returns 10 RGB color pairs.

nColorPairPosition

Returns a single RGB color pair from a color scheme. *nColorPairPosition* specifies the position of the RGB color pair in the color scheme. For example, if *nColorPairPosition* is 4, the fourth RGB color pair is returned.

Remarks

Use SCHEME( ) to return a traditional color pair or a color pair list from a color scheme. RGB color pairs use numeric values to specify colors. Traditional color pairs use letters to specify colors.

Example

The following displays the third RGB color pair from color scheme number 4.

```
CLEAR
? RGBSCHEME(4,3)
```

See Also

Colors Overview, RGB( ), SCHEME( )

RIGHT( ) Function

Returns the specified number of rightmost characters from a character string.

Syntax

RIGHT(*cExpression*, *nCharacters*)

Returns

Character

Arguments

cExpression

Specifies the character expression whose rightmost characters are returned.

nCharacters

Specifies the number of characters returned from the character expression. RIGHT( ) returns the entire character expression if *nCharacters* is greater than the length of *cExpression*. RIGHT( ) returns an empty string if *nCharacters* is negative or 0.

Remarks

Characters are returned beginning with the last character on the right and continuing for a specified number of characters.

Example

```
CLEAR
? RIGHT('Redmond, WA', 2)  && Displays WA
```

See Also

AT( ), LEFT( ), LTRIM( ), RAT( ), RTRIM( ), SUBSTR( ), TRIM( )

RIGHTC( ) Function

Returns the specified number of rightmost characters from a character string.

Syntax

RIGHTC(*cExpression*, *nCharacters*)

Returns

Character

Arguments

cExpression

Specifies the character expression whose rightmost characters are returned.

nCharacters

Specifies the number of characters returned from the character expression. RIGHTC( ) returns the entire character expression if *nCharacters* is greater than the length of *cExpression*. RIGHTC( ) returns an empty string if *nCharacters* is negative or 0.

Remarks

RIGHTC( ) is designed for expressions containing double-byte characters. If the expression contains only single-byte characters, RIGHTC( ) is equivalent to RIGHT( ).

Characters are returned beginning with the last character on the right and continuing for *nCharacters*.

This function is useful for manipulating double-byte character sets for languages such as Hiragana and Katakana.

See Also

AT_C( ), LEFTC( ), RATC( ), RIGHTC( ), SUBSTRC( )

RightClick Event

Occurs when the user clicks the right (secondary) mouse button over a control in Microsoft Windows.

Syntax

PROCEDURE *Control*.RightClick
   [LPARAMETERS *nIndex*]

Arguments

nIndex

Uniquely identifies a control if it is in a control array.

Applies To

CheckBox, ComboBox, CommandButton, CommandGroup, Container, Control, EditBox, Form, Grid, Header, Image, Label, Line, ListBox, OptionButton, OptionGroup, Page, PageFrame, Shape, Spinner, TextBox, ToolBar

See Also

Click Event, DblClick Event, DragDrop Event, DragOver Event, DropDown Event, Enabled Property, KeyPress Event, MouseDown Event, MouseMove Event, MouseUp Event, Scrolled Event, Undock Event

RightToLeft Property

Ignored unless you are running a Middle Eastern version of Microsoft Windows. Specifies the reading order of text in controls and the display of streaming output on forms. Available at design time; read/write at run time.

Syntax

Object.RightToLeft[= *lExpression*]

Arguments

lExpression

The settings for the RightToLeft property are:

Setting	Description
True (.T.)	(Default) Text is entered and displayed in controls in a right to left reading order. Streaming output (for example, text displayed with ? or ??) is displayed on forms in a right-to-left reading order.
False (.F.)	Text is entered and displayed in controls in a left-to-right reading order. Streaming output is displayed on forms in a left-to-right reading order.

Remarks

Use the Alignment property to specify the orientation of text in check boxes and option buttons.

Applies To

CheckBox, ComboBox, CommandButton, EditBox, Form, Grid, Label, ListBox, OptionButton, PageFrame, _SCREEN, Spinner, TextBox

See Also

Alignment Property

RLOCK( ) Function

Attempts to lock a table record or records.

Syntax

RLOCK([*nWorkArea* | *cTableAlias*]
| [*cRecordNumberList*, *nWorkArea* | *cTableAlias*])

Returns

Logical

Arguments

nWorkArea | cTableAlias

Specifies the work area number or table alias for a table open in another work area. If you don't specify a work area or alias, RLOCK( ) attempts to lock the current record in the table in the currently selected work area.

cRecordNumberList

Specifies that RLOCK( ) attempts to lock multiple records. The character expression *cRecordNumberList* specifies one or more record numbers, separated by commas, that RLOCK( ) attempts to lock. For example, to attempt record locks on the first four records in a table, *cRecordNumberList* should contain 1, 2, 3, 4.

To lock multiple records, you must have SET MULTILOCKS on and you must include the work area number (*nWorkArea*) or alias (*cTableAlias*) of the table in which you attempt to lock multiple records.

You can also lock multiple records by moving the record pointer to the record you would like to lock, issuing RLOCK( ) or LOCK( ) and then repeating this process for additional records.

In Visual FoxPro, you can specify 0 as a record number. Specifying 0 lets you attempt to lock the table header.

> **Important** Keep the table header locked for as short a time as possible because other users cannot add records to the table when the table header is locked.

Release the table header lock with UNLOCK RECORD 0, UNLOCK, or UNLOCK ALL.

If all the records specified in *cRecordNumberList* are successfully locked, RLOCK( ) returns true (.T.). If one or more of the records specified in *cRecordNumberList* cannot be locked, RLOCK( ) returns false (.F.) and locks none of the records. In either case, existing record locks remain in place. Multiple record locking is an additive process — placing additional record locks doesn't release existing record locks.

From a performance perspective, it is always faster to lock the entire table than to lock even a small number of records.

Remarks

RLOCK( ) is identical to LOCK( ).

If the lock or locks are successfully placed, RLOCK( ) returns true (.T.). Locked records are available for both read and write access by the user who placed the locks and for read-only access to all other users on the network.

Executing RLOCK( ) doesn't guarantee that the attempted record lock or locks are successfully placed. A record lock cannot be placed on a record already locked by another user or in a table locked by another user. If the record lock or locks cannot be placed for any reason, RLOCK( ) returns false (.F.).

By default, RLOCK( ) makes one attempt to lock a record. Use SET REPROCESS to automatically retry a record lock when the first attempt fails. SET REPROCESS controls the number of lock attempts or the length of time lock attempts are made when the initial lock attempt is unsuccessful. For more information about SET REPROCESS and table locking, see the SET REPROCESS Command, later in this language reference.

SET MULTILOCKS determines whether you can lock multiple records in a table. If SET MULTILOCKS is off (the default), you can lock only a single record in a table. If SET MULTILOCKS is on, you can lock multiple records in a table. For more information, see the SET MULTILOCKS Command, later in this language reference.

A table record can be unlocked only by the user who placed the lock. Record locks can be released by issuing UNLOCK, closing the table, or exiting Visual FoxPro.

UNLOCK can be used to release record locks in the current work area, a specific work area or in all work areas. For more information, see the UNLOCK Command, later in this language reference.

Switching SET MULTILOCKS from ON to OFF or from OFF to ON implicitly performs UNLOCK ALL. All record locks in all work areas are released.

To close tables, use USE, CLEAR ALL, or CLOSE DATABASES.

For more information about record and file locking and sharing tables on a network, see Chapter 17, "Programming for Shared Access," in the *Microsoft Visual FoxPro 6.0 Programmer's Guide*.

Example

The following example locks and unlocks the first four records in the `customer` and `employee` tables.

```
CLOSE DATABASES
OPEN DATABASE (HOME(2) + 'Data\testdata')
SET REPROCESS TO 3 AUTOMATIC
STORE '1,2,3,4' TO gcRecList
gcOldExc = SET('EXCLUSIVE')
SET EXCLUSIVE OFF
SELECT 0
USE employee  && Open Employee table
SELECT 0
USE customer  && Open Customer table
? LOCK('1,2,3,4', 'customer')  && Lock 1st 4 records in customer
? RLOCK(gcRecList, 'employee')  && Lock 1st 4 records in employee
UNLOCK IN customer
UNLOCK IN employee
SET EXCLUSIVE &gcOldExc
```

See Also

CLEAR, CLOSE, FLOCK( ), LOCK( ), SET MULTILOCKS, SET RELATION, SET REPROCESS, UNLOCK, USE

_RMARGIN System Variable

Included for backward compatibility. Use the Report Designer instead.

ROLLBACK Command

Cancels any changes made during the current transaction.

Syntax

ROLLBACK

Remarks

ROLLBACK restores the original tables, table memo files, and index files to the state they were in before the transaction began.

When you modify records in a database that is part of a transaction, other users on the network do not have access (read or write) to the records until you end the transaction.

When other users on the network try to access records you have modified, they must wait until you end your transaction. They receive the message "Record not available ... please wait" until the records become available. Because of this, it is important to keep the length of the transaction to a minimum or conduct the transaction during times when others do not need access.

ROLLBACK undoes any changes made during the current transaction. If the transaction is nested, only the modifications made since the previous BEGIN TRANSACTION are undone. Program execution continues with the next statement.

If any record or file locks were placed, they are released.

Example

In the following example, the customer table in the testdata database is opened. Optimistic table buffering is set for the customer table. The contents of the cust_id and company fields are displayed, and then the contents of the company field is replaced within the buffered data.

BEGIN TRANSACTION is issued to start a transaction. A TABLEUPDATE is used to write the changes to the table. The new contents are displayed, and ROLLBACK is issued to restore the original contents of the company field. The cust_id and company fields are displayed again with the company field containing its original values.

```
CLOSE DATABASES
CLEAR

* Transactions are only supported within a DBC
OPEN DATABASE (HOME(2) + 'Data\testdata')
```

```
SET MULTILOCKS ON      && Required for buffering

USE customer
=CURSORSETPROP("Buffering",5)
? 'The original company field'
LIST FIELDS cust_id, company NEXT 5
REPLACE ALL company WITH "***" && Change field contents

BEGIN TRANSACTION
   =TABLEUPDATE(.T.)
   GO TOP
   ? 'The modified company field'
   LIST FIELDS cust_id, company NEXT 5
ROLLBACK        && Restore original field contents

=TABLEREVERT(.T.)
GO TOP
? 'The restored company field'
LIST FIELDS cust_id, company NEXT 5
```

See Also

BEGIN TRANSACTION, END TRANSACTION, TXNLEVEL( )

ROUND( ) Function

Returns a numeric expression rounded to a specified number of decimal places.

Syntax

ROUND(*nExpression*, *nDecimalPlaces*)

Returns

Numeric

Arguments

nExpression

Specifies the numeric expression whose value is to be rounded.

nDecimalPlaces

Specifies the number of decimal places *nExpression* is rounded to.

If *nDecimalPlaces* is negative, ROUND( ) returns a whole number containing zeros equal in number to *nDecimalPlaces* to the left of the decimal point. For example, if *nDecimalPlaces* is –2, the first and second digits to the left of the decimal point in the value are 0.

Remarks

The value ROUND( ) returns has the same number of decimal places as *nDecimalPlaces*. ROUND( ) ignores the number of decimal places specified by SET DECIMALS.

Example

```
SET DECIMALS TO 4
SET FIXED ON      && Fix decimal display
CLEAR

? ROUND(1234.1962, 3) && Displays 1234.1960
? ROUND(1234.1962, 2) && Displays 1234.2000
? ROUND(1234.1962, 0) && Displays 1234.0000
? ROUND(1234.1962, -1)  && Displays 1230.0000
? ROUND(1234.1962, -2)  && Displays 1200.0000
? ROUND(1234.1962, -3)  && Displays 1000.0000

SET FIXED OFF  && Restore start up defaults
SET DECIMALS TO 2
```

See Also

INT( ), SET DECIMALS

ROW( ) Function

Included for backward compatibility. Use the CurrentY property.

RowHeight Property

Specifies the height of the rows in a Grid control. Available at design time; read/write at run time.

Syntax

Grid.RowHeight[= *nHeight*]

Arguments

nHeight
   Specifies the height of all the rows in a Grid control.

Remarks

If RowHeight is set to –1 (Auto), it automatically resizes the rows to fit the current FontSize property setting.

Applies To

Grid

See Also

FontSize Property

RowSource Property

Specifies the source of the values in a ComboBox or ListBox control. Available at design time and run time.

Syntax

Control.RowSource[= *cName*]

Arguments

cName
    Specifies the source of the values.

Remarks

The source of the values can be a comma-delimited list of values, a table, a SQL statement that creates a cursor or a table, a query, an array, a comma-delimited list of fields (which may be prefaced by a period and the table alias), a file skeleton (such as *.dbf or *.txt), a table's field names, or a menu. Use the RowSourceType property to set the type of row source.

You can use RowSource to specify multiple columns for a ComboBox or ListBox control at design time. To specify multiple columns, set RowSourceType to 1 (Value) and specify the RowSource values (separated by a comma) as follows:

```
Col1Row1,Col2Row1,Col1Row2,Col2Row2,,Col2Row3
```

To specify an alias for the table containing the columns, use the following syntax:

```
Alias.Col1Row1,Col2Row1,Col1Row2,Col2Row2,,Col2Row3
```

The values you specify fill the control, by row, up to the number of columns that are specified by the ColumnCount property. The preceding example assumes that ColumnCount is set to 2. As shown in the preceding example, there will be no value in column 1, row 3 because there are two successive commas with no value entered between them preceding column 2, row 3.

Example

The following example creates a list box. The source of the items that appear in the list box items is an array; the name of the array is specified with the RowSource property.

The RowSourceType property is set to 5 (array) to specify that an array is the source for the items in the list box.

The MultiSelect property for the list box is set to true (.T.), allowing you to make multiple selections from the list box. The item or items you choose in the list box are displayed by using the ListCount, Selected and List properties to determine the number of items in the list box and the items you chose.

```
CLEAR

DIMENSION gaMyListArray(10)
FOR gnCount = 1 to 10  && Fill the array with letters
   STORE REPLICATE(CHR(gnCount+64),6) TO gaMyListArray(gnCount)
NEXT

frmMyForm = CREATEOBJECT('Form')  && Create a Form
frmMyForm.Closable = .f.  && Disable the Control menu box

frmMyForm.Move(150,10)  && Move the form

frmMyForm.AddObject('cmbCommand1','cmdMyCmdBtn')  && Add "Quit" Command button
frmMyForm.AddObject('lstListBox1','lstMyListBox')  && Add ListBox control

frmMyForm.lstListBox1.RowSourceType = 5  && Specifies an array
frmMyForm.lstListBox1.RowSource = 'gaMyListArray' && Array containing listbox items

frmMyForm.cmbCommand1.Visible =.T.  && "Quit" Command button visible
frmMyForm.lstListBox1.Visible =.T.  && "List Box visible

frmMyForm.SHOW  && Display the form
READ EVENTS  && Start event processing

DEFINE CLASS cmdMyCmdBtn AS CommandButton  && Create Command button
   Caption = '\<Quit'  && Caption on the Command button
   Cancel = .T.  && Default Cancel Command button (Esc)
   Left = 125  && Command button column
   Top = 210  && Command button row
   Height = 25  && Command button height

   PROCEDURE Click
      CLEAR EVENTS  && Stop event processing, close Form
      CLEAR  && Clear main Visual FoxPro window
ENDDEFINE

DEFINE CLASS lstMyListBox AS ListBox  && Create ListBox control
   Left = 10  && List Box column
   Top = 10  && List Box row
   MultiSelect = .T.  && Allow selecting more than 1 item
```

```
PROCEDURE Click
   ACTIVATE SCREEN
   CLEAR
   ? "Selected items:"
   ? "----------------"
   FOR nCnt = 1 TO ThisForm.lstListBox1.ListCount
      IF ThisForm.lstListBox1.Selected(nCnt)  && Is item selected?
         ? SPACE(5) + ThisForm.lstListBox1.List(nCnt) && Show item
      ENDIF
   ENDFOR

ENDDEFINE
```

Applies To

ComboBox, ListBox

See Also

ColumnCount Property, RecordSource Property, RowSourceType Property

RowSourceType Property

Specifies the type of source for the values in a control. Available at design time and run time.

Syntax

*Control.*RowSourceType[= *nSource*]

Arguments

nSource

The settings for the RowSourceType property are:

Setting	Description
0	(Default) None. When the default value is used, fill the list at run time using the AddItem or AddListItem method.
1	Value. Populated by a comma-delimited list.
2	Alias. Use the ColumnCount property to select fields in the table.
3	SQL Statement. A SQL SELECT command that creates a cursor or a table.
4	Query (.qpr). Specify a file name with a .qpr extension.
5	Array. Set the columns property to display multiple dimensions.
6	Fields. A comma delimited list of fields. The fields may be prefaced by the table alias and a period.

(continued)

Setting	Description
7	Files. List is populated from the current directory. Specify file skeleton (such as *.dbf or *.txt) or mask in the RowSource property.
8	Structure. Fields from the table specified in RowSource.
	Note that when RowSourceType is set to 8, if the RowSource property is empty the currently selected table is used as the source of the values in a ComboBox or ListBox control. Otherwise, the RowSource property specifies the alias of the table, the name of the table, or the name of the database used as the source of the values in a ComboBox or ListBox control.
9	Pop-up. Included for backward compatibility.

For more information about using each of the RowSourceType settings, see "Using List Boxes and Drop-Down List Boxes" in Chapter 10, "Using Controls," in the *Microsoft Visual FoxPro 6.0 Programmer's Guide.*

Example

The following example creates a list box. The source of the items that appear in the list box items is an array; the name of the array is specified with the RowSource property. The RowSourceType property is set to 5 (array) to specify that an array is the source for the items in the list box.

The MultiSelect property for the list box is set to true (.T.), allowing you to make multiple selections from the list box. The item or items you choose in the list box are displayed by using the ListCount, Selected and List properties to determine the number of items in the list box and the items you chose.

```
CLEAR

DIMENSION gaMyListArray(10)
FOR gnCount = 1 to 10  && Fill the array with letters
   STORE REPLICATE(CHR(gnCount+64),6) TO gaMyListArray(gnCount)
NEXT

frmMyForm = CREATEOBJECT('Form')  && Create a Form
frmMyForm.Closable = .f.  && Disable the Control menu box

frmMyForm.Move(150,10)  && Move the form

frmMyForm.AddObject('cmbCommand1','cmdMyCmdBtn')  && Add "Quit" Command button
frmMyForm.AddObject('lstListBox1','lstMyListBox')  && Add ListBox control
```

```
frmMyForm.lstListBox1.RowSourceType = 5   && Specifies an array
frmMyForm.lstListBox1.RowSource = 'gaMyListArray' && Array containing listbox items

frmMyForm.cmbCommand1.Visible =.T.   && "Quit" Command button visible
frmMyForm.lstListBox1.Visible =.T.   && "List Box visible

frmMyForm.SHOW   && Display the form
READ EVENTS   && Start event processing

DEFINE CLASS cmdMyCmdBtn AS CommandButton   && Create Command button
   Caption = '\<Quit'   && Caption on the Command button
   Cancel = .T.   && Default Cancel Command button (Esc)
   Left = 125   && Command button column
   Top = 210   && Command button row
   Height = 25   && Command button height

   PROCEDURE Click
      CLEAR EVENTS   && Stop event processing, close Form
      CLEAR   && Clear main Visual FoxPro window
ENDDEFINE

DEFINE CLASS lstMyListBox AS ListBox   && Create ListBox control
   Left = 10   && List Box column
   Top = 10   && List Box row
   MultiSelect = .T.   && Allow selecting more than 1 item

PROCEDURE Click
   ACTIVATE SCREEN
   CLEAR
   ? "Selected items:"
   ? "----------------"
   FOR nCnt = 1 TO ThisForm.lstListBox1.ListCount
      IF ThisForm.lstListBox1.Selected(nCnt)   && Is item selected?
         ? SPACE(5) + ThisForm.lstListBox1.List(nCnt) && Show item
      ENDIF
   ENDFOR

ENDDEFINE
```

Applies To

ComboBox, ListBox

See Also

RowSource Property

RTOD( ) Function

Converts radians to degrees.

Syntax

RTOD(*nExpression*)

Returns

Numeric

Arguments

nExpression
Specifies the numeric expression representing radians that RTOD( ) converts to degrees.

Remarks

RTOD( ) converts the value (in radians) of a numeric expression to an equivalent value in degrees.

RTOD( ) is useful for working with the Visual FoxPro trigonometric functions COS( ), SIN( ), and TAN( ).

Use DTOR( ) to convert degrees to radians.

Example

```
CLEAR
? RTOD(ACOS(0))  && Displays 90.00
STORE -1 to gnArcAngle
? RTOD(ACOS(gnArcAngle))  && Displays 180.00
? RTOD(ACOS(SQRT(2)/2)) && Displays 45.00
```

See Also

COS( ), DTOR( ), SIN( ), TAN( )

RTRIM( ) Function

Returns a character string that results from removing the trailing blanks from a character expression.

Syntax

RTRIM(*cExpression*)

Returns

Character

Arguments

cExpression

Specifies the character expression from which trailing blanks are trimmed.

Remarks

RTRIM( ) can be used to ensure that blanks are removed from data entered by a user. RTRIM( ) is identical to TRIM( ).

Example

```
CLOSE DATABASES
OPEN DATABASE (HOME(2) + 'Data\testdata')
USE customer  && Opens Customer table
CLEAR
? 'The contact for '+ RTRIM(company) + ' is ' + contact
```

See Also

ALLTRIM( ), LTRIM( ), TRIM( )

RUN | ! Command

Executes external operating commands or programs.

Syntax

RUN [/N] *MS-DOSCommand* | *ProgramName*

– or –

! [/N] *MS-DOSCommand* | *ProgramName*

Arguments

MS-DOSCommand

Specifies the MS-DOS command to execute. See your MS-DOS documentation for more information about available MS-DOS commands.

ProgramName

Specifies the program or application to run. You can specify a Windows-based or an MS-DOS-based program or application.

/N

Specifies NOWAIT. Include the letter N to execute another Windows-based application.

Remarks

You can issue RUN from within the Command window or from within a program.

Important   To use RUN, you must have the operating system file Command.com in the current directory, or it must be located where the MS-DOS COMSPEC parameter can find it. For more information on COMSPEC, see your MS-DOS documentation.

Caution   Do not use RUN to run disk reorganization programs such as CHKDSK from within Visual FoxPro. These programs modify the contents of your disk in a manner that may prevent Visual FoxPro from operating properly.

RUN and Visual FoxPro   When RUN is used to run programs outside of Visual FoxPro, it searches for programs in a slightly different manner from FoxPro for MS-DOS.

If the program you specify in RUN doesn't have an extension, Visual FoxPro first look along the MS-DOS path for a Program Information File (PIF) with the name you specify. A PIF lets you run a non-Windows program under Windows. You can specify parameters for the program, whether the program is run in a window or on the full screen, the amount of memory allocated for the program, and so on.

If the PIF is found, the program specified in the PIF is executed with the PIF parameters. If a PIF isn't found, the MS-DOS path is then searched for an executable file with the name you specify.

When a PIF isn't found, Visual FoxPro uses Foxrun.pif, a PIF installed in the Visual FoxPro directory. Foxrun.pif is configured to run the program in a window. You can modify Foxrun.pif to run programs in another configuration.

Foxrun.pif   Foxrun.pif allows you to execute MS-DOS and Windows programs and commands from within Visual FoxPro. Foxrun.pif must be in the same directory as Vfp6.exe in Visual FoxPro.

/N means NOWAIT. Include the letter N to execute another Windows-based application. For example, the following statement opens the Windows Character Map accessory:

```
! /N CHARMAP.EXE
```

The following example opens the Windows color picker from the Windows Control Panel:

```
! /N CONTROL COLOR
```

A Windows-based application executed with RUN /N or ! /N behaves the same way the application does when you open it through the Windows Explorer or by selecting Run from the Start menu. You can switch between the application and Visual FoxPro or FoxPro for Windows using the standard Windows operations.

You can include an optional numeric value immediately after /N to specify how the Windows-based application is opened. Do not include any spaces between /N and the numeric value. The following table lists the numeric value you can include and describes the state of the Windows-based application when opened.

Value	Application attributes
1	Active and normal size
2	Active and minimized
3	Active and maximized
4	Inactive and normal size
7	Inactive and minimized

Running MS-DOS Programs in Visual FoxPro By default, Foxrun.pif runs the specified external MS-DOS program in a window. While the MS-DOS program or command is running, the title of the window is FoxPro Run Command. In Visual FoxPro, the FoxPro Run Command window is closed after the external program or command is finished executing.

You can use the Windows PIF editor to customize Foxrun.pif. You can edit the PIF to specify if the Inactive FoxPro Run Command window is left open or is closed (the default in Visual FoxPro) with the Close Window on Exit check box. You can also open external programs in a full screen by selecting Full Screen; allocate memory for the program; and so on.

Memory Considerations By default, Foxrun.pif allocates a minimum of 256K of memory for running an external command or program. If you do not have 256K of free conventional memory, Visual FoxPro displays an error message. To correct this, try one or both of the following:

- Close applications and files to free up additional memory.

- Edit Foxrun.pif to reduce the amount of memory required in the KB Required text box.

If the external command requires more than 256K, MS-DOS displays an error message in the FoxPro Run Command window. To correct this, edit your Foxrun.pif to increase the amount of memory required in the KB Required text box.

See Also

GETENV( ), _SHELL

Run Event

Occurs when an Active Document is ready to run user code.

Syntax

PROCEDURE *ActiveDoc*.Run
LPARAMETERS *cHyperlinkTarget*

Arguments

cHyperlinkTarget

cHyperlinkTarget is a parameter that is passed to the Run event from a URL (Universal Resource Locator) when HTTP (Hypertext Transfer Protocol) is used to run an Active Document. The parameter is passed as character data, and is appended in the URL to the name of the Active Document with a pound sign (#). For example, the following URL passes the character string "TargetString" to the Run event in an Active Document named MyActiveDoc:

```
Http://MyServer/MyActiveDoc.APP#TargetString
```

Note that the pound sign (#) is passed as the first character to *cHyperlinkTarget*. You can use SUBSTR( ) to remove the leading pound sign, as in the following Run event code:

```
LPARAMETERS cHyperLinkTarget
cNewTarget = SUBSTR(cHyperLinkTarget, 2, LEN(cHyperLinkTarget))
```

Remarks

The Run event should be the starting point for your Active Document application. Typically, the Run event contains code that executes your menu code, executes the main form in the application, and contains READ EVENTS to start event processing.

You can put setup code in your Active Document's Init event, but if the code takes too long to execute, the Active Document container may generate a time out error. If you do put setup code in the Init event, it should not require user interaction or create a user interface.

Applies To

ActiveDoc Object

See Also

Init Event, SUBSTR( )

Run Method

Runs or previews a file in a project.

Syntax

Object.Run( )

Remarks

The Run method returns true (.T.) if the file is successfully run or previewed; otherwise false (.F.) is returned. Labels and reports are previewed by the Run method.

The QueryRunFile event occurs before the file is run or previewed. If the QueryRunFile event returns false (.F.), the file isn't run or previewed and the Run method returns false (.F.). If the QueryRunFile method returns true (.T.), the file is run or previewed and the Run method returns true (.T.).

Applies To

File Object

See Also

QueryAddFile Event, QueryModifyFile Event, QueryRunFile Event, QueryRemoveFile Event

_RUNACTIVEDOC System Variable

Specifies an application that launches an Active Document.

Syntax

_RUNACTIVEDOC = *ProgramName*

Arguments

ProgramName
> Specifies the name of an application used to launch an Active Document. If your Active Document launch application is in a directory other than the current default directory, include a path with the application name.

Remarks

_RUNACTIVEDOC contains the name of an application that can be used to specify launch options for an Active Document. The application specified in _RUNACTIVEDOC is executed when you choose the **Run Active Document** option from the **Tools** menu. _RUNACTIVEDOC contains RUNACTD.PRG by default.

You can also specify a launch application for Active Documents with the **ActiveDoc Launcher** option on the **File Locations** tab in the **Options** dialog box.

An Active Document can be run in four different ways:

- Hosted in an Internet browser such as Microsoft Internet Explorer using the Visual FoxPro runtime.

- Standalone (unhosted) using the Visual FoxPro runtime.

- Hosted in an Internet browser using the Visual FoxPro debugger.

- Standalone using Visual FoxPro debugger.

See Also

Active Documents, File Locations Tab, Options Dialog Box, SYS(4204) – Active Document Debugging

_SAMPLES System Variable

Contains the path of the directory in which the Microsoft Visual FoxPro samples are installed.

Syntax

_SAMPLES[= cPath]

Arguments

cPath
Specifies the complete path to the directory containing the Visual FoxPro samples.

Remarks

By default, _SAMPLES contains the path of the directory containing the Visual FoxPro samples. Visual FoxPro samples are installed when you perform a **Full** installation of the MSDN (Microsoft Developer's Network) library, or you perform a **Custom** installation of the MSDN library and you specify to install the Visual FoxPro samples. If you don't install the Visual FoxPro samples, _SAMPLES contains the empty string.

The path that _SAMPLES contains is read from an MSDN registry key in the Windows Registry. If this registry key doesn't exist (for example, if you didn't install the samples), _SAMPLES contains the empty string.

You can also specify a path to the samples directory with the **Samples Directory** item in the File Locations tab of the **Options** dialog box. If you use the **Options** dialog box to specify a path to the samples directory, _SAMPLES contains the path you specify. If you choose **Set As Default**, the path is saved for subsequent Visual FoxPro sessions.

HOME(2) returns the path contained in _SAMPLES.

See Also

HOME( )

SAVE MACROS Command

Saves a set of keyboard macros to a keyboard macro file or to a memo field.

Syntax

SAVE MACROS TO *FileName* | TO MEMO *MemoFieldName*

Arguments

TO *FileName*
Specifies the file to which the macros are saved. Keyboard macro file names can contain a maximum of eight characters and must begin with a letter or an underscore; they cannot begin with a number. The subsequent characters can be any combination of

letters, numbers, and underscores. The file is assigned an .fky extension. If you assign an extension other than .fky, you must include that extension in RESTORE MACROS.

TO MEMO *MemoFieldName*
Specifies the memo field to which the macros are saved. The table containing the memo field must be open; however, it does not have to be in the selected work area. To save macros to a table in another work area, include the table's alias when specifying the memo field.

Remarks

When you quit Visual FoxPro, the macros you have created are lost unless you use SAVE MACROS to store them to a keyboard macro file or to a memo field.

Example

The following example saves the current set of macros to a file called Mymacros.fky.

```
SAVE MACROS TO mymacros
```

See Also

CLEAR, PLAY MACRO, RESTORE MACROS

SAVE SCREEN Command

Saves an image of the main Visual FoxPro window or an active user-defined window to the screen buffer, a variable, or an array element.

Syntax

SAVE SCREEN [TO *VarName*]

Arguments

TO *VarName*
Specifies the variable or array element to which the screen or window image is saved.

Remarks

Use RESTORE SCREEN to redisplay images saved to the screen buffer, a variable, or an array element.

Variables or array elements containing an image of the main Visual FoxPro window or user-defined window have an S data type when you view the variables or array elements with DISPLAY or LIST MEMORY.

If issued without the TO *VarName* clause, SAVE SCREEN saves the main Visual FoxPro window or user-defined window to the screen buffer.

See Also

RESTORE FROM, RESTORE SCREEN, SAVE TO

SAVE TO Command

Stores current variables and arrays to a variable file or memo field.

Syntax

SAVE TO *FileName* | MEMO *MemoFieldName*
    [ALL LIKE *Skeleton* | ALL EXCEPT *Skeleton*]

Arguments

FileName
    Specifies the variable file in which the variables and arrays are saved. The default extension for a variable file is .mem.

MEMO *MemoFieldName*
    Specifies the memo field in which the variables and arrays are saved.

ALL LIKE *Skeleton*
    Specifies that all variables and arrays which match the specified *Skeleton* be saved. The skeleton can include the question mark (?) and asterisk (*) wildcards.

ALL EXCEPT *Skeleton*
    Specifies that all variables and arrays except those that match the specified *Skeleton* be saved. The skeleton can include the question mark (?) and asterisk (*) wildcards.

Remarks

Use RESTORE FROM to place variables and arrays back into memory from a variable file or memo field. Note that object type variables cannot be saved to a variable file or memo field.

The variable file or memo field is marked with the current code page.

Example

In the following example, two variables are created. They are saved to a variable file and restored without clearing the existing variables.

```
gnVal1 = 50
gcVal2 = 'Hello'

SAVE TO temp
CLEAR MEMORY

gdVal3 = DATE( )
RESTORE FROM temp ADDITIVE
CLEAR
DISPLAY MEMORY LIKE g*
```

See Also

PRIVATE, PUBLIC, RELEASE, RESTORE FROM

SAVE WINDOWS Command

Saves all or specified window definitions to a window file or memo field.

Syntax

SAVE WINDOWS *WindowNameList* | ALL
    TO *FileName* | TO MEMO *MemoFieldName*

Arguments

WindowNameList
    Specifies one or more windows to be saved. Separate the window names with commas.

ALL
    Saves all window definitions to the window file or memo field.

TO *FileName*
    Specifies the window file to which the window definitions are saved.

    If you don't specify an extension when naming the file, the default extension of .win is assigned. If you specify another extension when you save the window definitions to a file, you must include the extension when you restore the window definitions from the file.

TO MEMO *MemoFieldName*
    Specifies the memo field to which the window definitions are saved. The table containing the memo field must be open; however, it does not have to be in the currently selected work area. To save window definitions to a table in another work area, include the table's alias when specifying the memo field.

Remarks

Use RESTORE WINDOW to restore window definitions from a window file or memo field. The status of each window is also saved. For example, if a window is hidden when it is saved to a file or memo field, it remains hidden when it is restored.

Example

In the following example, a window named wOutput1 is created, and the window definition is saved to the file Temp.win. All windows are cleared and wOutput1 is restored from the file and activated.

```
CLEAR
DEFINE WINDOW wOutput1 FROM 2,1 TO 13,75 TITLE 'Output' ;
   CLOSE FLOAT GROW ZOOM
ACTIVATE WINDOW wOutput1
@ 1,1 SAY 'This is the contents of the window'
```

```
SAVE WINDOWS wOutput1 TO temp
CLEAR WINDOWS
WAIT WINDOW 'The window has been saved - Press a key'

RESTORE WINDOW wOutput1 FROM temp
ACTIVATE WINDOW wOutput1
WAIT WINDOW 'The window has been restored - Press a key'

DEACTIVATE WINDOW wOutput1
RELEASE WINDOW wOutput1
DELETE FILE temp.win
```

See Also

DEFINE WINDOW, RESTORE SCREEN, RESTORE WINDOW, SAVE SCREEN

SaveAs Method

Saves an object as an .scx file.

Syntax

Object.SaveAs(*cFileName* [, *oObjectName*])

Arguments

cFileName
Specifies the .scx file to which you want to save the object.

oObjectName
Specifies a reference to a DataEnvironment object.

Remarks

Use the SaveAs method to create a form or form set and save it as an .scx file. The SaveAs method is only available during an interactive Visual FoxPro session.

When you use the SaveAs method, all the properties, events, and methods associated with the object are stored as as well. Note that only objects created from Visual FoxPro base classes can be saved. User-defined classes cannot be saved. See the DEFINE CLASS Command, earlier in this language reference, for a listing of Visual FoxPro base classes.

Applies To

DEFINE CLASS, Form, FormSet, _SCREEN

See Also

SaveAsClass Method, SET CLASSLIB

SaveAsClass Method

Saves an instance of an object as a class definition in a class library.

Syntax

Object.SaveAsClass.(*ClassLibName*, *ClassName* [, *Description*])

Arguments

ClassLibName
Specifies the name of the .vcx file in which to store the class definition.

ClassName
Specifies the name assigned to the class.

Description
Specifies the optional description for the class.

Remarks

When you use the SaveAsClass method, all the properties, events, and methods associated with the object are stored as part of the class definition.

Applies To

ActiveDoc, CheckBox, ComboBox, CommandButton, CommandGroup, Container Object, Control Object, Custom, EditBox, Form, FormSet, Grid, Image, Label, Line, ListBox, OLE Bound Control, OLE Container Control, OptionButton, OptionGroup, PageFrame, ProjectHook Object, _SCREEN, Shape, Spinner, TextBox, Timer, ToolBar

See Also

SaveAs Method, SET CLASSLIB

SAVEPICTURE( ) Function

Creates a bitmap (.bmp) file from a picture object reference.

Syntax

SAVEPICTURE(*oObjectReference*, *cFileName*)

Returns

Logical

Arguments

oObjectReference
Specifies a picture object reference from which SAVEPICTURE( ) creates a bitmap file.

cFileName

Specifies the name of the bitmap file that SAVEPICTURE( ) creates. If *cFileName* includes a path, the file is created in the directory specified in the path. If a file with the same name already exists, it is overwritten without warning, even if SET SAFETY is ON. An error message is displayed if the file you specify does not exist.

Remarks

Picture object references are typically created with LOADPICTURE( ). However, certain properties (such as the PictureOpen property for the OLE Outline control) use a default picture object reference which can be used to create a bitmap file.

See Also

LOADPICTURE( )

ScaleMode Property

Specifies the unit of measurement for the coordinates of an object when using graphics methods or when positioning controls. Available at design time and run time.

Syntax

Object.ScaleMode = *nMode*

Arguments

nMode

The settings for the ScaleMode property are:

Setting	Description
0	Foxels (A Visual FoxPro term. Equivalent to the maximum height and average width of a character in the current font.)
3	Pixels (default; smallest unit of monitor or printer resolution)

Remarks

If you create a custom visual class for cross-platform use, be sure that the ScaleMode property for Forms in the visual class is set to pixels.

Applies To

Form, _SCREEN, ToolBar

See Also

DrawMode Property, DrawStyle Property

SCAN ... ENDSCAN Command

Moves the record pointer through the currently selected table and executes a block of commands for each record that meets the specified conditions.

Syntax

SCAN [NOOPTIMIZE]
    [*Scope*] [FOR *lExpression1*] [WHILE *lExpression2*]
       [*Commands*]
    [LOOP]
    [EXIT]
ENDSCAN

Arguments

NOOPTIMIZE

Prevents Rushmore optimization of SCAN.

For more information, see the SET OPTIMIZE Command, later in this language reference, and "Understanding Rushmore Technology" in Chapter 15, "Optimizing Applications," in the *Microsoft Visual FoxPro 6.0 Programmer's Guide*.

Scope

Specifies a range of records to be scanned. Only the records within the range are scanned. The scope clauses are: ALL, NEXT *nRecords*, RECORD *nRecordNumber*, and REST. For more information on scope clauses, see "Scope Clauses" in Help.

The default scope for SCAN is all records (ALL).

FOR *lExpression1*

Executes commands only for records for which *lExpression1* evaluates to true (.T.). Including the FOR clause lets you filter out records you don't want scanned.

Rushmore optimizes a query created with SCAN ... FOR if *lExpression1* is an optimizable expression. For best performance, use an optimizable expression in the FOR clause.

For more information, see the SET OPTIMIZE Command, later in this language reference, and "Understanding Rushmore Technology" in Chapter 15, "Optimizing Applications," in the *Microsoft Visual FoxPro 6.0 Programmer's Guide*.

WHILE *lExpression2*

Specifies a condition whereby the commands are executed for as long as *lExpression2* evaluates to true (.T.).

Commands

Specifies the Visual FoxPro commands to be executed.

LOOP

Returns control directly back to SCAN. LOOP can be placed anywhere between SCAN and ENDSCAN.

EXIT

Transfers program control from within the SCAN ... ENDSCAN loop to the first command following ENDSCAN. EXIT can be placed anywhere between SCAN and ENDSCAN.

ENDSCAN

Indicates the end of the SCAN procedure.

Remarks

SCAN automatically advances the record pointer to the next record that meets the specified conditions and executes the block of commands.

You can place comments after ENDSCAN on the same line. The comments are ignored during program compilation and execution.

Example

The following example uses a SCAN ... ENDSCAN loop to display all the companies in Sweden.

```
CLOSE DATABASES
OPEN DATABASE (HOME(2) + 'Data\testdata')
USE customer  && Opens Customer table
CLEAR

SCAN FOR UPPER(country) = 'SWEDEN'
   ? contact, company, city

ENDSCAN
```

See Also

DO CASE ... ENDCASE, DO WHILE ... ENDDO, FOR ... ENDFOR

SCATTER Command

Copies data from the current record to a set of variables or to an array.

Syntax

SCATTER
[FIELDS *FieldNameList*
| FIELDS LIKE *Skeleton* | FIELDS EXCEPT *Skeleton*] [MEMO]
TO *ArrayName* | TO *ArrayName* BLANK | MEMVAR | MEMVAR BLANK
| NAME *ObjectName* [BLANK]

Arguments

FIELDS *FieldNameList*

Specifies the fields to be transferred to the variables or to the array. All fields are transferred if you omit FIELDS *FieldNameList*. The field list can contain memo fields if you follow the field list with the MEMO keyword. SCATTER always ignores general and picture fields, even if you include MEMO.

FIELDS LIKE *Skeleton* | FIELDS EXCEPT *Skeleton*

You can selectively transfer fields to variables or an array by including the LIKE or EXCEPT clause or both. If you include LIKE *Skeleton*, fields that match *Skeleton* are transferred to the variables or the array. If you include EXCEPT *Skeleton*, all fields except those that match *Skeleton* are transferred to the variables or the array.

Skeleton supports wildcard characters. For example, to transfer all fields that begin with the letters A and P to the variables or the array, use:

```
SCATTER FIELDS LIKE A*,P* TO myarray
```

The LIKE clause can be combined with the EXCEPT clause:

```
SCATTER FIELDS LIKE A*,P* EXCEPT PARTNO* TO myarray
```

MEMO

Specifies that the field list includes a memo field or memo fields. By default, memo fields are ignored in SCATTER.

You must have sufficient memory to scatter large memo fields to variables or to an array. Visual FoxPro generates an error message if you lack sufficient memory. If a memo field is too large to fit in memory, neither it nor any additional memo fields in the field list are scattered. If a memo field isn't scattered, its variable or array element is set to false (.F.).

TO *ArrayName*

Specifies the array to which the record contents are copied. Starting with the first field, SCATTER copies in sequential order the contents of each field into each element of the array.

Extra array elements are left unchanged if the array you specify has more elements than the number of fields. A new array is automatically created if the array doesn't already exist or if it has fewer elements than the number of fields. The array elements have the same size and data types as the corresponding fields.

TO *ArrayName* BLANK

Creates an array with empty elements which are the same size and type as the fields in the table.

MEMVAR

Scatters the data to a set of variables instead of to an array. SCATTER creates one variable for each field in the table and fills each variable with data from the corresponding field in the current record, assigning to the variable the same name, size, and type as its field.

A variable is created for each field in the field list if a field list is included.

Preface the variable name with the M. qualifier to reference a variable that has the same name as a field in the current table.

> **Important** Do not include TO with MEMVAR. Visual FoxPro creates an array named MEMVAR if you include TO.

MEMVAR BLANK

Creates a set of empty variables. Each variable is assigned the same name, data type and size as its field. If a field list is included, a variable is created for each field in the field list.

NAME *ObjectName* [BLANK]

Creates an object whose properties have the same names as fields in the table. If the BLANK keyword is not included, the values of each of the object's properties are the contents of the fields in the table. If the BLANK keyword is included, the properties are empty (see the EMPTY( ) Function, earlier in this language reference, for a description of what the empty properties contain, based on the corresponding field type). Properties are not created for general fields in the table.

To reference a property in an object that has the same name as an open table, preface the property name with the M. qualifier. For example:

```
USE customer
SCATTER NAME customer

? customer.company  && Returns the table value
? M.customer.company  && Returns the object property value
```

Remarks

SCATTER and COPY TO ARRAY are similar. COPY TO ARRAY copies multiple records into an array while SCATTER copies just one record into an array or a set of variables. SCATTER automatically creates the array or variables if they don't already exist.

Use GATHER to copy variables or array elements to table records.

Examples

Example 1

This example uses SCATTER to create a set of variables based on the fields in the test table. Each field is then assigned a value and a new blank record is added to the table. The data is copied to the table using the GATHER command.

```
CREATE TABLE Test FREE ;
    (Object C(10), Color C(16), SqFt n(6,2))

SCATTER MEMVAR BLANK
m.Object="Box"
m.Color="Red"
m.SqFt=12.5
APPEND BLANK
GATHER MEMVAR
BROWSE
```

Example 2

This example uses SCATTER along with the NAME clause to create an object with properties based on the fields in the table. The object's properties are then assigned values and a new blank record is added to the table. The data is copied to the new record using GATHER with the NAME clause.

```
CREATE TABLE Test FREE ;
    (Object C(10), Color C(16), SqFt n(6,2))

SCATTER NAME oTest BLANK
oTest.Object="Box"
oTest.Color="Red"
oTest.SqFt=12.5
APPEND BLANK
GATHER NAME oTest
RELEASE oTest
BROWSE
```

See Also

ALINES( ), APPEND FROM ARRAY, COPY TO ARRAY, DECLARE, DIMENSION, GATHER

SCCProvider Property

The name of the source code control provider for a project. Read-only.

Syntax

Object.SCCProvider

Remarks

You can specify a source code control provider for new projects in the Projects tab of the Options dialog box. The SCCProvider property contains the empty string if a project isn't under source control.

For more information about implementing source code control for projects, see "Working with Source Control Software in Visual FoxPro" in Chapter 29, "Developing in Teams," in the *Microsoft Visual FoxPro 6.0 Programmer's Guide*.

Applies To

Project Object

See Also

SCCStatus Property

SCCStatus Property

Contains a numeric value indicating the source control status of a file in a project. Read-only at design time and run time.

Syntax

Object.SCCStatus

Remarks

The following table lists the values the SCCStatus property can contain:

Value	FoxPro.h constant	Description
0	SCCFILE_NOTCONTROLLED	File is not source controlled.
1	SCCFILE_NOTCHECKEDOUT	File is in source control but is not checked out.
2	SCCFILE_CHECKEDOUTCU	File is checked out to the current user.
3	SCCFILE_CHECKEDOUTOU	File is checked out to someone other than the current user.
4	SCCFILE_MERGECONFLICT	File has a merge conflict.
5	SCCFILE_MERGE	File has been merged without conflict.
6	SCCFILE_CHECKEDOUTMU	File is checked out to multiple users.

Applies To

File Object

See Also

SCCProvider Property

_SCCTEXT System Variable

Specifies a Visual FoxPro conversion program that handles translating Visual FoxPro binary files into text equivalents and back.

Syntax

_SCCTEXT = *cProgramName*

Arguments

cProgramName

Specifies a source control conversion program. If your source control conversion program is in a directory other than the current default directory, include a path with the program name.

You can also specify a source control conversion program in your configuration file by including a line using this syntax:

```
_SCCTEXT = cProgramName
```

Remarks

By default, _SCCTEXT contains Scctext.prg, a Visual FoxPro conversion program that handles translating Visual FoxPro binary files into text equivalents and back. These text files are used as the basis for comparing and merging versions of Visual FoxPro binary files through a source control application.

See Also

Projects Tab, Options Dialog Box

SCHEME( ) Function

Returns a color pair list or a single color pair from a specified color scheme.

Syntax

SCHEME(*nSchemeNumber* [, *nColorPairNumber*])

Returns

Character

Arguments

nSchemeNumber

Specifies the number of the color scheme for which you want a complete color-pair list. SCHEME( ) returns ten color pairs.

nColorPairNumber

Specifies the position of one color pair in the color scheme, and SCHEME( ) returns only this color pair. For example, if *nColorPairNumber* is 4, SCHEME( ) returns the fourth color pair from the color scheme.

Example

The following example returns the third color pair from color scheme number 4:

```
? SCHEME(4,3)
```

See Also

Colors Overview

SCOLS( ) Function

Returns the number of columns available in the main Microsoft Visual FoxPro window.

Syntax

SCOLS( )

Returns

Numeric

Remarks

The value returned by SCOLS( ) depends on the current display mode. Display modes can be changed with SET DISPLAY.

See Also

COL( ), ROW( ), SET DISPLAY, SROWS( ), WCOLS( ), WROWS( )

_SCREEN System Variable

Specifies properties and methods for the main Visual FoxPro window.

Syntax

_SCREEN.*PropertyName* [= *eValue*]

– or –

_SCREEN.*MethodName*

Arguments

PropertyName

Specifies a property for the main Visual FoxPro window.

eValue

Specifies a value for the property.

MethodName

Specifies a method to execute for the main Visual FoxPro window.

Remarks

_SCREEN allows the main Visual FoxPro window to be manipulated as an object. Events procedures cannot be created for _SCREEN. _SCREEN is an object type system variable.

Properties

ActiveControl	ActiveForm	Application
AutoCenter	BackColor	BaseClass
BorderStyle	BufferMode	Caption
Class	ClassLibrary	ClipControls
Closable	Comment	ControlBox
ControlCount	Controls	CurrentX
CurrentY	DataSession	DataSessionID
DefOLELCID Property	Desktop	DrawMode
DrawStyle	DrawWidth	Enabled
FillColor	FillStyle	FontBold
FontItalic	FontName	FontOutline
FontShadow	FontSize	FontStrikeThru
FontUnderline	Forecolor	FormCount
Forms	HalfHeightCaption	Height
HelpContextID	Icon	KeyPreview
Left	LockScreen	MaxButton
MaxHeight	MaxLeft	MaxTop
MaxWidth	MDIForm	MinButton
MinHeight	MinWidth	MousePointer
Movable	Name	ParentClass
Picture	ReleaseType	RightToLeft
ScaleMode	ShowTips	TabIndex
TabStop	Tag	Top
Visible	Width	WindowState
WindowType		

Methods

AddObject	AddProperty	Box
Circle	Cls	Draw
Hide	Line	Move
Point	Print	Pset
Refresh	Release	RemoveObject
SaveAs	SaveAsClass	SetAll
Show	TextHeight	TextWidth
ZOrder		

Example

The following example demonstrates the use of _SCREEN to customize the main Visual FoxPro window.

```
* Local variables to store current settings
Local oldScreenLeft
Local oldScreenTop
Local oldScreenHeight
Local oldScreenWidth
Local oldScreenColor
WITH _Screen
   oldScreenLeft=.Left        && Save current position and size
   oldScreenTop=.Top
   oldScreenHeight=.Height
   oldScreenWidth=.Width
   oldScreenColor = .Backcolor
   .LockScreen=.T.        && Disable screen redraw
   .BackColor=rgb(192,192,192)   && Change the background to grey
   .BorderStyle=2        && Change the border to double
   .Closable=.F.         && Remove window control buttons
   .ControlBox=.F.
   .MaxButton=.F.
   .MinButton=.T.
   .Movable=.T.
   .Height=285
   .Width=550
   .Caption="Custom Screen"    && Set a caption
   .LockScreen=.F.        && Enable screen redraw
ENDWITH
```

```
=MESSAGEBOX("Return to normal  ",48,WTITLE())
With _Screen
    .Left = oldScreenLeft      && Reset original
    .Top = oldScreenTop        && position and size
    .Height = oldScreenHeight
    .Width  = oldScreenWidth
    .BackColor=oldScreenColor      && Change background to white
    .LockScreen=.T.        && Disable screen redraw
    .BorderStyle=3         && Change border to sizeable
    .Closable=.T.          && Reset window control buttons
    .ControlBox=.T.
    .MaxButton=.T.
    .MinButton=.T.
    .Movable=.T.
    .Caption="Microsoft Visual FoxPro"  && Reset the caption
    .LockScreen=.F.        && Enable screen redraw
Endwith
```

See Also

MODIFY WINDOW, Form Object

SCROLL Command

Scrolls an area of the main Visual FoxPro window or a user-defined window up, down, left, or right.

Syntax

SCROLL *nRow1*, *nColumn1*, *nRow2*, *nColumn2*, *nRowsScrolled*
  [, *nColumnsScrolled*]

Arguments

nRow1, *nColumn1*, *nRow2*, *nColumn2*

Specifies the rectangular region where scrolling occurs in the main Visual FoxPro window or in the active user-defined window. *nRow1*, *nColumn1* specifies the upper-left corner of the region, and *nRow2*, *nColumn2* specifies the lower-right corner.

nRowsScrolled

Specifies the number of rows up or down to scroll inside the rectangular region. If the numeric expression *nRowsScrolled* is positive, Visual FoxPro scrolls up the number of rows. If *nRowsScrolled* is negative, Visual FoxPro scrolls down the number of rows. If *nRowsScrolled* is 0 and you omit *nColumnsScrolled*, Visual FoxPro clears the rectangular region.

nColumnsScrolled

Specifies the number of columns left or right to scroll inside the rectangular region. If the numeric expression *nColumnsScrolled* is positive, Visual FoxPro scrolls to the right the number of columns. If *nColumnsScrolled* is negative, Visual FoxPro scrolls to the left the number of columns. If you include both *nRowsScrolled* and *nColumnsScrolled*, Visual FoxPro scrolls the area diagonally.

Example

The following command scrolls a small rectangular region:

```
CLEAR
@ 4, 1 FILL TO 10, 8 COLOR GR+/B
WAIT WINDOW 'Press key to scroll left top corner'

SCROLL 0, 0, 5, 5, -2, 1
```

See Also

MOVE WINDOW

ScrollBars Property

Specifies the type of scroll bars an edit box, form, or grid has. Available at design time; read/write at run time.

Syntax

[*Form*.]*Control*.ScrollBars[= *nType*]

Arguments

nType

For an edit box, the settings are:

Setting	Description
0	None
2	(Default) Vertical

For a form, the ScrollBars property settings are:

Setting	Description
0	(Default) None
1	Horizontal
2	Vertical
3	Both vertical and horizontal

For a grid, the ScrollBars property settings are:

Setting	Description
0	None
1	Horizontal
2	Vertical
3	(Default) Both vertical and horizontal

Remarks

If enabled, the scroll bars are displayed automatically when the form, grid, or edit box contains more information than can be displayed in the space provided. The Scrollbars property setting is evaluated for a form when the form is instantiated.

If an Active Document displays a form that has scroll bars, the scroll bars are displayed on the form when the viewport size is smaller than the size of a rectangle enclosing all the controls on the form.

The Scrollbars property is ignored for _SCREEN.

Applies To

EditBox, Form, Grid

See Also

ContinuousScroll Property, DoScroll Method, Scrolled Event

Scrolled Event

Occurs in a Grid control or form when the horizontal or vertical scroll bars are clicked or a scroll box is moved.

Syntax

PROCEDURE *Object*.Scrolled
LPARAMETERS [*nIndex*], *nDirection*

Arguments

nIndex
   Uniquely identifies a control if it is in a control array.

nDirection
   Specifies how the user scrolled through the contents of a Grid control or a form. The possible values are:

Value	User scrolled using...
0	UP ARROW key
1	DOWN ARROW key
2	Vertical scroll bar in area above the scroll box
3	Vertical scroll bar in area below the scroll box
4	LEFT ARROW key
5	RIGHT ARROW key
6	Horizontal scroll bar in area to the left of the scroll box
7	Horizontal scroll bar in area to the right of the scroll box

Remarks

The Scrolled event also occurs for a grid if you call the DoScroll method from within a program. The Scrollbars property determines if a form has scroll bars.

Avoid creating wait states (for example, WAIT WINDOW) within the Scrolled event because screen painting problems can occur when the grid or form is scrolled.

Applies To

Form, Grid

See Also

ActiveColumn Property, ActiveRow Property, DoScroll Method, RelativeColumn Property, RelativeRow Property, ScrollBars Property

SEC( ) Function

Returns the seconds portion from a DateTime expression.

Syntax

SEC(*tExpression*)

Returns

Numeric

Arguments

tExpression
　　Specifies the DateTime expression from which SEC( ) returns the second. If *tExpression* contains only a date and not a time, Visual FoxPro adds the default time of midnight (12:00:00 A.M.) to *tExpression*.

Example

The following example displays the second portion of the current time and the second portion of a specific time.

```
CLEAR
? SEC(DATETIME( ))
? SEC({^1998-08-21 10:42:16am})  && Displays 16
```

See Also

DATETIME( ), SET SECONDS

SECONDS( ) Function

Returns the number of seconds that have elapsed since midnight.

Syntax

SECONDS( )

Returns

Numeric

Remarks

SECONDS( ) returns a numeric value in decimal format, with a resolution of 1 millisecond. If you are running Windows NT, resolution is 10 milliseconds.

Example

```
CLEAR
? SECONDS( )
? SECONDS( )/(60 * 60)
```

See Also

SYS(2) – Seconds Since Midnight, TIME( )

Seconds Property

Specifies whether the seconds portion of a DateTime value is displayed in a text box. Available at design time and run time.

Syntax

Object.Seconds[= *nValue*]

Arguments

nValue
    One of the following settings:

Setting	Description
0	Off. The seconds portion of the DateTime value is not displayed.
1	On. The seconds portion of the DateTime value is displayed.
2	(Default) The SET SECONDS setting determines if the seconds portion of the DateTime value is displayed. If SET SECONDS is ON, the seconds portion of the DateTime value is displayed. If SET SECONDS is OFF, the seconds portion of the DateTime value is not displayed.

Remarks

The Seconds property setting is ignored if the DateFormat property is set to Short or Long.

Applies To

TextBox

See Also

Century Property, DateFormat Property, DateMark Property, Hours Property, SET SECONDS, StrictDateEntry Property

SEEK Command

Searches a table for the first occurrence of a record whose index key matches a general expression, then moves the record pointer to the matching record.

Syntax

SEEK *eExpression*
    [ORDER *nIndexNumber* | *IDXIndexFileName*
    | [TAG] *TagName* [OF *CDXFileName*]
    [ASCENDING | DESCENDING]]
    [IN *nWorkArea* | *cTableAlias*]

Arguments

eExpression
    Specifies the index key for which SEEK searches. *eExpression* can be null.

ORDER *nIndexNumber*
    Specifies the number of the index file or tag that is used to search for the index key. *nIndexNumber* refers to the index files as they are listed in USE or SET INDEX. Open .idx files are numbered first in the order in which they appear in USE or SET INDEX. Tags in the structural .cdx file (if one exists) are then numbered in the order in which they were created. Finally, tags in any open independent .cdx files are numbered in the order in which they were created. See the SET ORDER Command, later in this language reference, for more information about index numbering.

ORDER *IDXIndexFileName*
> Specifies an .idx file that is used to search for the index key.

ORDER [TAG] *TagName* [OF *CDXFileName*]
> Specifies a tag of a .cdx file that is used to search for the index key. The tag name can be from a structural .cdx file or any open independent .cdx file.
>
> If identical tag names exist in open independent .cdx files, use OF *CDXFileName* to specify the .cdx file containing the tag.
>
> **Note** The .idx file takes precedence if duplicate .idx file and tag names exist.

ASCENDING
> Specifies that the table is searched in ascending order.

DESCENDING
> Specifies that the table is searched in descending order.

IN *nWorkArea*
> Specifies the work area number of the table that is searched.

IN *cTableAlias*
> Specifies the alias of the table that is searched.
>
> If you omit IN *nWorkArea* and IN *cTableAlias*, the table in the currently selected work area is searched.

Remarks

You can use SEEK only with indexed tables, and you can search only on the index key. The match must be exact unless SET EXACT is set to OFF.

If SEEK finds a record with a matching index key, RECNO( ) returns the record number of the matching record, FOUND( ) returns true (.T.), and EOF( ) returns false (.F.).

If a matching key isn't found, RECNO( ) returns the number of records in the table plus 1, FOUND( ) returns false (.F.), and EOF( ) returns true (.T.).

If SET NEAR is on, the record pointer is positioned immediately after the record with the closest index key. If SET NEAR is off, the record pointer is positioned at the end of the file. In either case, RECNO() returns the record number of the closest record.

Example

In the following example, customer is opened and indexed on the company field. SEEK is used to find the index key expression that matches the value contained in the variable gcSeekVal.

```
CLOSE DATABASES
OPEN DATABASE (HOME(2) + 'Data\testdata')
USE customer ORDER company  && Opens Customer table
```

```
SET EXACT OFF
STORE 'B' TO gcSeekVal

SEEK gcSeekVal

IF FOUND( )
   DISPLAY FIELDS company, contact
ENDIF
```

See Also

EOF( ), FOUND( ), INDEX, INDEXSEEK( ), LOCATE, RECNO( ), SEEK( ),
SET EXACT, SET NEAR

SEEK( ) Function

Searches an indexed table for the first occurrence of a record whose index key matches
a specified expression. Returns a logical value indicating if the search was successful.

Syntax

SEEK(*eExpression* [, *nWorkArea* | *cTableAlias*
   [, *nIndexNumber* | *cIDXIndexFileName* | *cTagName*]])

Returns

Logical

Arguments

eExpression
Specifies the index key expression for which you want SEEK( ) to search.

nWorkArea
Specifies the work area number of the table that is searched for the index key.

cTableAlias
Specifies the alias of the table that is searched.

If you omit *nWorkArea* and *cTableAlias*, the table in the currently selected work area
is searched.

nIndexNumber
Specifies the number of the index file or tag that is used to search for the index key.
nIndexNumber refers to the index files as they are listed in USE or SET INDEX. Open
.idx files are numbered first in the order in which they appear in USE or SET INDEX.
Tags in the structural .cdx file (if one exists) are then numbered in the order in which
they were created. Finally, tags in any open independent .cdx files are numbered in the
order in which they were created. For more information about index numbering, see
the SET ORDER Command, later in this language reference.

cIDXIndexFileName

> Specifies an .idx file that is used to search for the index key.

cTagName

> Specifies a tag of a .cdx file that is used to search for the index key. The tag name can be from a structural .cdx file or any open independent .cdx file.

> > **Note** The .idx file takes precedence if duplicate .idx file and tag names exist.

Remarks

You can use SEEK( ) only with a table with an index order set, and you can search only for an index key. The match must be exact unless SET EXACT is set to OFF.

If a match is found, SEEK( ) returns true (.T.), and the record pointer moves to the matching record. If no match is found, SEEK( ) returns false (.F.) and the record pointer moves to the end of the file. Issuing SEEK( ) is equivalent to issuing SEEK and FOUND( ) in succession.

If you omit the *nIndexNumber*, *IDXIndexFileName*, and *cTagName* arguments, SEEK( ) uses the master controlling index or index tag to search for the index key.

Example

```
CLOSE DATABASES
OPEN DATABASE (HOME(2) + 'Data\testdata')
USE customer ORDER cust_id  && Opens Customer table
? SEEK('CHOPS')  && Returns .T., record found
```

See Also

EOF( ), FOUND( ), INDEXSEEK( ), LOCATE, SEEK, SET ORDER

SELECT Command

Activates the specified work area.

Syntax

SELECT *nWorkArea | cTableAlias*

Arguments

nWorkArea

> Specifies a work area to activate. If *nWorkArea* is 0, the lowest-numbered unused work area is activated.

cTableAlias

> Specifies a work area containing an open table to activate. *cTableAlias* is the alias of the open table. You can also include a letter from A through J for *cTableAlias* to activate one of the first ten work areas.

Remarks

By default, work area number 1 is active when you start Visual FoxPro.

Note Fields in tables open in any work area can be included in Visual FoxPro commands and functions. Use the following formats to access fields in a table open in a work area other than the current one: *alias.field* or *alias -> field*.

Example

The following example demonstrates ways of selecting work areas.

```
CLOSE DATABASES
OPEN DATABASE (HOME(2) + 'Data\testdata')

SELECT 1        && Work area 1
USE customer  && Opens Customer table

SELECT 2        && Work area 2
USE orders    && Opens Orders table

SELECT customer      && Work area 1
BROWSE

SELECT B        && Work area 2
BROWSE
```

See Also

ALIAS( ), SELECT( ), USE

SELECT – SQL Command

Retrieves data from one or more tables.

Syntax

SELECT [ALL | DISTINCT] [TOP *nExpr* [PERCENT]]
    [*Alias.*] *Select_Item* [AS *Column_Name*]
    [, [*Alias.*] *Select_Item* [AS *Column_Name*] ...]
FROM [FORCE]
[*DatabaseName!*]*Table* [[AS] *Local_Alias*]
    [[INNER | LEFT [OUTER] | RIGHT [OUTER] | FULL [OUTER] JOIN
        DatabaseName!]*Table* [[AS] *Local_Alias*]
        [ON *JoinCondition* …]]
[[INTO *Destination*]
    | [TO FILE *FileName* [ADDITIVE] | TO PRINTER [PROMPT]
    | TO SCREEN]]
[PREFERENCE *PreferenceName*]
[NOCONSOLE]

[PLAIN]

[NOWAIT]

[WHERE *JoinCondition* [AND *JoinCondition* ...]

    [AND | OR *FilterCondition* [AND | OR *FilterCondition* ...]]]]

[GROUP BY *GroupColumn* [, *GroupColumn* ...]]

[HAVING *FilterCondition*]

[UNION [ALL] *SELECTCommand*]

[ORDER BY *Order_Item* [ASC | DESC] [, *Order_Item* [ASC | DESC] ...]]

Arguments

SELECT

    Specifies the fields, constants, and expressions that are displayed in the query results.

ALL

    By default, displays all the rows in the query results.

DISTINCT

    Excludes duplicates of any rows from the query results.

        Note You can use DISTINCT only once per SELECT clause.

TOP *nExpr* [PERCENT]

    Specifies that the query result contains a specific number of rows or a percentage of rows in the query result. You must include an ORDER BY clause when you include the TOP clause. The ORDER BY clause specifies the columns on which the TOP clause determines the number of rows to include in the query result.

    You can specify from 1 to 32,767 rows. Rows with identical values for the columns specified in the ORDER BY clause are included in the query result. Therefore, if you specify 10 for *nExpr*, the query result can contain more than 10 rows if there are more than 10 rows with identical values for the columns specified in the ORDER BY clause.

    If the PERCENT keyword is included, the number of rows returned in the result is rounded up to the next highest integer. Permissible values for *nExpr* when the PERCENT keyword is included are 0.01 to 99.99.

Alias.

    Qualifies matching item names. Each item you specify with *Select_Item* generates one column of the query results. If two or more items have the same name, include the table alias and a period before the item name to prevent columns from being duplicated.

    Select_Item specifies an item to be included in the query results. An item can be one of the following:

- The name of a field from a table in the FROM clause.

- A constant specifying that the same constant value is to appear in every row of the query results.

- An expression that can be the name of a user-defined function.

AS *Column_Name*

> Specifies the heading for a column in the query output. This option is useful when *Select_Item* is an expression or contains a field function and you want to give the column a meaningful name. *Column_Name* can be an expression but cannot contain characters (for example, spaces) that aren't permitted in table field names.

FROM

> Lists the tables containing the data that the query retrieves. If no table is open, Visual FoxPro displays the Open dialog box so you can specify the file location. Once open, the table remains open once the query is complete.

> FORCE specifies that tables are joined in the order in which they appear in the FROM clause. If FORCE is omitted, Visual FoxPro attempts to optimize the query. However, the query might be executed faster by including the FORCE keyword to disable the Visual FoxPro query optimization.

DatabaseName!

> Specifies the name of a non-current database containing the table. You must include the name of database containing the table if the database is not the current database. Include the exclamation point (!) delimiter after the database name and before the table name.

[AS] *Local_Alias*

> Specifies a temporary name for the table named in *Table*. If you specify a local alias, you must use the local alias in place of the table name throughout the SELECT statement.

> INNER JOIN specifies that the query result contains only rows from a table that match one or more rows in another table.

> LEFT [OUTER] JOIN specifies that the query result contains all rows from the table to the left of the JOIN keyword and only matching rows from the table to the right of the JOIN keyword. The OUTER keyword is optional; it can be included to emphasize that an outer join is created.

> RIGHT [OUTER] JOIN specifies that the query result contains all rows from the table to the right of the JOIN keyword and only matching rows from the table to the left of the JOIN keyword. The OUTER keyword is optional; it can be included to emphasize that an outer join is created.

> FULL [OUTER] JOIN specifies that the query result contains all matching and non matching rows from both tables. The OUTER keyword is optional; it can be included to emphasize that an outer join is created.

> ON *JoinCondition* specifies the conditions for which the tables are joined.

INTO *Destination*

Specifies where to store the query results. If you include the INTO clause and the TO clause in the same query, the TO clause is ignored. If you don't include the INTO clause, query results are displayed in a Browse window. You can also use TO to direct query results to the printer or a file.

Destination can be one of the following clauses:

- ARRAY *ArrayName*, which stores query results in a memory variable array. The array isn't created if the query selects 0 records.

- CURSOR *CursorName* [NOFILTER], which stores query results in a cursor. If you specify the name of an open table, Visual FoxPro generates an error message. After SELECT is executed, the temporary cursor remains open and is active but is read-only. Once you close this temporary cursor, it is deleted. Cursors may exist as a temporary file on the drive or volume specified by SORTWORK.

  Include NOFILTER to create a cursor that can be used in subsequent queries. In previous versions of Visual FoxPro, it was necessary to include an extra constant or expression as a filter to create a cursor that could be used in subsequent queries. For example, adding a logical true as a filter expression created a query that could be used in subsequent queries:

  ```
  SELECT *, .T. FROM customers INTO CURSOR myquery
  ```

  Including NOFILTER can reduce query performance because a temporary table is created on disk. The temporary table is deleted from disk when the cursor is closed.

- DBF | TABLE *TableName*
  [DATABASE *DatabaseName* [NAME *LongTableName*]] stores query results in a table. If you specify a table that is already open and SET SAFETY is set to OFF, Visual FoxPro overwrites the table without warning. If you don't specify an extension, Visual FoxPro gives the table a .DBF extension. The table remains open and active after SELECT is executed.

  Include DATABASE *DatabaseName* to specify a database to which the table is added. Include NAME *LongTableName* to specify a long name for the table. Long names can contain up to 128 characters and can be used in place of short file names in the database.

TO FILE *FileName*

If you include a TO clause but not an INTO clause, you can direct query results to an ASCII text file named *FileName*, to the printer, or to the main Visual FoxPro window.

ADDITIVE appends query output to the existing contents of the text file specified in TO FILE *FileName*.

TO PRINTER [PROMPT] directs query output to a printer. Use the optional PROMPT clause to display a dialog box before printing starts. In this dialog box, you can adjust printer settings. The printer settings that you can adjust depend on the currently installed printer driver. Place PROMPT immediately after TO PRINTER.

TO SCREEN directs query output to the main Visual FoxPro window or to an active user-defined window.

PREFERENCE *PreferenceName*

Saves the Browse window's attributes and options for later use, if query results are sent to a Browse window. PREFERENCE saves the attributes, or preferences, indefinitely in the FOXUSER resource file. Preferences can be retrieved at any time.

Issuing SELECT with a PREFERENCE *PreferenceName* for the first time creates the preference. Issuing SELECT later with the same preference name restores the Browse window to that preference state. When the Browse window is closed, the preference is updated.

If you exit a Browse window by pressing CTRL+Q+W, changes you've made to the Browse window are not saved to the resource file.

NOCONSOLE

Prevents display of query results sent to a file, the printer, or the main Visual FoxPro window.

PLAIN

Prevents column headings from appearing in the query output that is displayed. You can use PLAIN whether or not a TO clause is present. If an INTO clause is included, PLAIN is ignored.

NOWAIT

Continues program execution after the Browse window is opened and query results are directed to it. The program doesn't wait for the Browse window to be closed, but continues execution on the program line immediately following the SELECT statement.

When TO SCREEN is included to direct output to the main Visual FoxPro window or to a user-defined window, output pauses when the main Visual FoxPro window or user-defined window is full of query results. Press a key to see the next set of query results. If NOWAIT is included, the query results are scrolled off the main Visual FoxPro window or the user-defined window without pausing for a key press. NOWAIT is ignored if included with the INTO clause.

WHERE

Tells Visual FoxPro to include only certain records in the query results. WHERE is required to retrieve data from multiple tables.

JoinCondition

>specifies fields that link the tables in the FROM clause. If you include more than one table in a query, you should specify a join condition for every table after the first.

>You must use the AND operator to connect multiple join conditions. Each join condition has the following form:

>*FieldName1 Comparison FieldName2*

>*FieldName1* is the name of a field from one table, *FieldName2* is the name of a field from another table, and *Comparison* is one of the following operators:

Operator	Comparison
=	Equal
==	Exactly equal
LIKE	SQL LIKE
<>, !=, #	Not equal
>	More than
>=	More than or equal to
<	Less than
<=	Less than or equal to

>When you use the = operator with strings, it acts differently depending on the setting of SET ANSI. When SET ANSI is set to OFF, Visual FoxPro treats string comparisons in a manner familiar to Xbase users. When SET ANSI is set to ON, Visual FoxPro follows ANSI standards for string comparisons. See the SET ANSI and SET EXACT Commands, later in this language reference, for additional information about how Visual FoxPro performs string comparisons.

>The WHERE clause supports the ESCAPE operator for the *JoinCondition,* allowing you to perform meaningful queries on data containing the SELECT – SQL % and _ wildcard characters.

>The ESCAPE clause lets you specify that a SELECT – SQL wildcard character be treated as a literal character. In the ESCAPE clause you specify a character, which when placed immediately before the wildcard character, indicates that the wildcard character be treated as a literal character.

FilterCondition

>specifies the criteria that records must meet to be included in the query results. You can include as many filter conditions as you like in a query, connecting them with the AND or OR operator. You can also use the NOT operator to reverse the value of a logical expression, or use EMPTY( ) to check for an empty field.

FilterCondition can take any of the forms in the following examples:

Example 1

Example 1 displays *FilterCondition* in the form of *FieldName1 Comparison FieldName2*

```
customer.cust_id = orders.cust_id
```

Example 2

Example 2 displays *FilterCondition* in the form of *FieldName Comparison Expression*

```
payments.amount >= 1000
```

Example 3

Example 3 displays *FilterCondition* in the form of *FieldName Comparison* ALL (*Subquery*)

When the filter condition includes ALL, the field must meet the comparison condition for all values generated by the subquery before its record is included in the query results.

```
company < ALL ;
```

```
(SELECT company FROM customer WHERE country = "UK")
```

Example 4

Example 4 displays *FilterCondition* in the form of *FieldName Comparison* ANY | SOME (*Subquery*)

When the filter condition includes ANY or SOME, the field must meet the comparison condition for at least one of the values generated by the subquery.

```
company < ANY ;
```

```
(SELECT company FROM customer WHERE country = "UK")
```

Example 5

Example 5 displays *FilterCondition* in the form of *FieldName* [NOT] BETWEEN *Start_Range* AND *End_Range*

This example checks to see whether the values in the field are within a specified range of values.

```
customer.postalcode BETWEEN 90000 AND 99999
```

Example 6

Example 6 displays *FilterCondition* in the form of [NOT] EXISTS (*Subquery*)

This example checks to see whether at least one row meets the criterion in the subquery. When the filter condition includes EXISTS, the filter condition evaluates to true (.T.) unless the subquery evaluates to the empty set.

```
EXISTS ;

(SELECT * FROM orders WHERE customer.postalcode =    orders.postalcode)
```

Example 7

Example 7 displays *FilterCondition* in the form of *FieldName* [NOT] IN *Value_Set*

When the filter condition includes IN, the field must contain one of the values before its record is included in the query results.

```
customer.postalcode NOT IN ("98052","98072","98034")
```

Example 8

Example 8 displays *FilterCondition* in the form of *FieldName* [NOT] IN (*Subquery*)

Here, the field must contain one of the values returned by the subquery before its record is included in the query results.

```
customer.cust_id IN ;

(SELECT orders.cust_id FROM orders WHERE orders.city="Seattle")
```

Example 9

Example 9 displays *FilterCondition* in the form of *FieldName* [NOT] LIKE *cExpression*

```
customer.country NOT LIKE "UK"
```

This filter condition searches for each field that matches *cExpression*.

You can use the percent sign (%) and underscore (_) wildcards as part of *cExpression*. The percent sign represents any sequence of unknown characters in the string. An underscore represents a single unknown character in the string.

GROUP BY *GroupColumn* [, *GroupColumn* ...]
    Groups rows in the query based on values in one or more columns. *GroupColumn* can be the name of a regular table field, a field that includes a SQL field function, or a numeric expression indicating the location of the column in the result table (the leftmost column number is 1).

HAVING *FilterCondition*

Specifies a filter condition which groups must meet to be included in the query results. HAVING should be used with GROUP BY. It can include as many filter conditions as you like, connected with the AND or OR operators. You can also use NOT to reverse the value of a logical expression.

FilterCondition cannot contain a subquery.

A HAVING clause without a GROUP BY clause acts like a WHERE clause. You can use local aliases and field functions in the HAVING clause. Use a WHERE clause for faster performance if your HAVING clause contains no field functions. Note that the HAVING clause should appear before an INTO clause or a syntax error occurs.

[UNION [ALL] *SELECTCommand*]

Combines the final results of one SELECT with the final results of another SELECT. By default, UNION checks the combined results and eliminates duplicate rows. Use parentheses to combine multiple UNION clauses.

ALL prevents UNION from eliminating duplicate rows from the combined results.

UNION clauses follow these rules:

- You cannot use UNION to combine subqueries.

- Both SELECT commands must have the same number of columns in their query output.

- Each column in the query results of one SELECT must have the same data type and width as the corresponding column in the other SELECT.

- Only the final SELECT can have an ORDER BY clause, which must refer to output columns by number. If an ORDER BY clause is included, it affects the entire result.

ORDER BY *Order_Item*

Sorts the query results based on the data in one or more columns. Each *Order_Item* must correspond to a column in the query results and can be one of the following:

- A field in a FROM table that is also a select item in the main SELECT clause (not in a subquery).

- A numeric expression indicating the location of the column in the result table. (The leftmost column is number 1.)

ASC specifies an ascending order for query results, according to the order item or items, and is the default for ORDER BY.

DESC specifies a descending order for query results.

Query results appear unordered if you don't specify an order with ORDER BY.

Remarks

SELECT is a SQL command that is built into Visual FoxPro like any other Visual FoxPro command. When you use SELECT to pose a query, Visual FoxPro interprets the query and retrieves the specified data from the tables. You can create a SELECT query from within:

- The Command window
- A Visual FoxPro program (as with any other Visual FoxPro command)
- The Query Designer

When you issue SET TALK ON and execute SELECT, Visual FoxPro displays the length of time the query took to execute and the number of records in the results. _TALLY contains the number of records in the query results.

SELECT does not respect the current filter condition specified with SET FILTER.

A *subquery*, referred to in the following arguments, is a SELECT within a SELECT and must be enclosed in parentheses. You can have up to two subqueries at the same level (not nested) in the WHERE clause (see that section of the arguments). Subqueries can contain multiple join conditions.

When you create query output, columns are named according to the following rules:

- If a select item is a field with a unique name, the output column name is the field's name.
- If more than one select item has the same name, an underscore and a letter are appended to the column name. For example, if a table called Customer has a field called STREET, and a table called Employees also has a field called STREET, output columns are named *Extension*_A and *Extension*_B (STREET_A and STREET_B). For a select item with a 10-character name, the name is truncated to add the underscore and letter. For example, DEPARTMENT would become DEPARTME_A.
- If a select item is an expression, its output column is named EXP_A. Any other expressions are named EXP_B, EXP_C, and so on.
- If a select item contains a field function such as COUNT( ), the output column is named CNT_A. If another select item contains SUM( ), its output column is named SUM_B.

User-Defined Functions with SELECT   Although using user-defined functions in the SELECT clause has obvious benefits, you should also consider the following restrictions:

- The speed of operations performed with SELECT may be limited by the speed at which such user-defined functions are executed. High-volume manipulations involving user-defined functions may be better accomplished by using API and user-defined functions written in C or assembly language.

- You can assume nothing about the Visual FoxPro input/output (I/O) or table environment in user-defined functions invoked from SELECT. In general, you don't know which work area is selected, the name of the current table, or even the names of the fields being processed. The value of these variables depends on where precisely in the optimization process the user-defined function is invoked.

- It isn't safe to change the Visual FoxPro I/O or table environment in user-defined functions invoked from SELECT. In general, the results are unpredictable.

- The only reliable way to pass values to user-defined functions invoked from SELECT is by the argument list passed to the function when it is invoked.

- If you experiment and discover a supposedly forbidden manipulation that works correctly in a certain version of FoxPro, there is no guarantee it will continue to work in later versions.

Apart from these restrictions, user-defined functions are acceptable in the SELECT clause. However, don't forget that using SELECT might slow performance.

The following field functions are available for use with a select item that is a field or an expression involving a field:

- AVG(*Select_Item*), which averages a column of numeric data.

- COUNT(*Select_Item*), which counts the number of select items in a column. COUNT(*) counts the number of rows in the query output.

- MIN(*Select_Item*), which determines the smallest value of *Select_Item* in a column.

- MAX(*Select_Item*), which determines the largest value of *Select_Item* in a column.

- SUM(*Select_Item*), which totals a column of numeric data.

You cannot nest field functions.

Joins Visual FoxPro supports ANSI SQL '92 Join syntax, allowing you to create queries that link the rows in two or more tables by comparing the values in specified fields. For example, an inner join selects rows from two tables only when the values of the joined fields are equal. Visual FoxPro supports nested joins.

Because SQL is based on mathematical set theory, each table can be represented as a circle. The ON clause that specifies the join conditions determines the point of overlap which represents the set of rows that match. For an inner join, the overlap occurs within the interior or "inner" portion of the two circles. An outer join includes not only those matched rows found in the inner cross section of the tables, but also the rows in the outer part of the circle to the left, or right, of the intersection.

Important Keep the following information in mind when creating join conditions:

- If you include two tables in a query and don't specify a join condition, every record in the first table is joined with every record in the second table as long as the filter conditions are met. Such a query can produce lengthy results.

- Be careful when using, in join conditions, functions such as DELETED( ), EOF( ), FOUND( ), RECCOUNT( ), and RECNO( ), which support an optional alias or work area. Including an alias or work area in these functions might yield unexpected results. SELECT doesn't use your work areas; it performs the equivalent of USE ... AGAIN. Single-table queries that use these functions without an optional alias or work area will return proper results. However, multiple-table queries that use these functions — even without an optional alias or work area — might return unexpected results.

- Use caution when joining tables that contain empty fields because Visual FoxPro matches empty fields. For example, if you join on CUSTOMER.ZIP and INVOICE.ZIP, and CUSTOMER contains 100 empty zip codes and INVOICE contains 400 empty zip codes, the query output contains 40,000 extra records resulting from the empty fields. Use the EMPTY( ) function to eliminate empty records from the query output.

For additional information about joins, see "Defining and Modifying Join Conditions" in Chapter 8, "Creating Views," in the *Microsoft Visual FoxPro 6.0 Programmer's Guide*.

Examples

The following examples illustrate the use of user-defined functions with SELECT – SQL:

Example 1

Example 1 displays the names of all companies in `customer` (one field from one table).

```
CLOSE ALL
CLOSE DATABASES
OPEN DATABASE (HOME(2) + 'data\testdata')

SELECT customer.company ;
   FROM customer
```

Example 2

Example 2 displays the contents of three fields from two tables and joins the two tables based on the `cust_id` field. It uses local aliases for both tables.

```
CLOSE ALL
CLOSE DATABASES
OPEN DATABASE (HOME(2) + 'data\testdata')

SELECT a.company, b.order_date, b.shipped_on ;
   FROM customer a, orders b ;
   WHERE a.cust_id = b.cust_id
```

Example 3

Example 3 displays only records with unique data in the specified fields.

```
CLOSE ALL
CLOSE DATABASES
OPEN DATABASE (HOME(2) + 'data\testdata')

SELECT DISTINCT a.company, b.order_date, b.shipped_on ;
   FROM customer a, orders b ;
   WHERE   a.cust_id = b.cust_id
```

Example 4

Example 4 displays the country, postalcode, and company fields in ascending order.

```
CLOSE ALL
CLOSE DATABASES
OPEN DATABASE (HOME(2) + 'data\testdata')

SELECT country, postalcode, company ;
   FROM customer ;
   ORDER BY country, postalcode, company
```

Example 5

Example 5 stores the contents of fields from two tables in a third table.

```
CLOSE ALL
CLOSE DATABASES
OPEN DATABASE (HOME(2) + 'data\testdata')

SELECT a.company, b.order_date, b.shipped_on ;
   FROM customer a, orders b ;
   WHERE a.cust_id = b.cust_id ;
   INTO TABLE custship.dbf
BROWSE
```

Example 6

Example 6 displays only records with an order date earlier than 02/16/1994.

```
CLOSE ALL
CLOSE DATABASES
OPEN DATABASE (HOME(2) + 'data\testdata')

SELECT a.company, b.order_date, b.shipped_on ;
   FROM customer a, orders b ;
   WHERE a.cust_id = b.cust_id ;
   AND b.order_date < {^1994-02-16}
```

Example 7

Example 7 displays the names of all companies from `customer` with a postal code that matches a postal code in the `orders` table.

```
CLOSE ALL
CLOSE DATABASES
OPEN DATABASE (HOME(2) + 'data\testdata')

SELECT company FROM customer a WHERE ;
   EXISTS (SELECT * FROM orders b WHERE a.postalcode = b.postalcode)
```

Example 8

Example 8 displays all records from `customer` having a company name that begins with an uppercase C and is an unknown length.

```
CLOSE ALL
CLOSE DATABASES
OPEN DATABASE (HOME(2) + 'data\testdata')

SELECT * FROM customer a WHERE a.company LIKE "C%"
```

Example 9

Example 9 displays all records from `customer` having a country name that begins with an uppercase U and is followed by one unknown character.

```
CLOSE ALL
CLOSE DATABASES
OPEN DATABASE (HOME(2) + 'data\testdata')

SELECT * FROM customer a WHERE a.country LIKE "U_"
```

Example 10

Example 10 displays the names of all cities in `customer` in uppercase and names the output column `CityList`.

```
CLOSE ALL
CLOSE DATABASES
OPEN DATABASE (HOME(2) + 'data\testdata')

SELECT UPPER(city) AS CityList FROM customer
```

Example 11

Example 11 demonstrates how you can perform a query on data that contains percentage signs (%). A backslash (\) is placed before the percentage sign to indicate that it should be treated as a literal, and the backslash is specified as the escape character in the ESCAPE clause.

Because the sample tables included with Visual FoxPro do not contain the percentage sign character, this query returns no results.

```
CLOSE ALL
CLOSE DATABASES
OPEN DATABASE (HOME(2) + 'data\testdata')
SELECT * FROM customer;
WHERE company LIKE "%\%%" ESCAPE "\"
```

Example 12

Example 12 demonstrates how you can perform a query on data that contains underscores (_). A backslash (\) is placed before the underscore to indicate that it should be treated as a literal, and the backslash is specified as the escape character in the ESCAPE clause.

Because the sample tables included with Visual FoxPro do not contain the underscore character, this query returns no results.

```
CLOSE ALL
CLOSE DATABASES
OPEN DATABASE (HOME(2) + 'data\testdata')
SELECT * FROM customer;
WHERE company LIKE "%\_%" ESCAPE "\"
```

Example 13

In example 13, the Escape character uses itself as a literal. The dash is both the escape character and a literal. The query returns all rows where the company name contains a percentage sign followed by a dash.

Because the sample tables included with Visual FoxPro do not contain the percentage sign character, this query returns no results.

```
CLOSE ALL
CLOSE DATABASES
OPEN DATABASE (HOME(2) + 'data\testdata')
SELECT * FROM customer;
WHERE company LIKE "%-%--%" Escape "-"
```

See Also

CREATE QUERY, CREATE TABLE – SQL, INSERT – SQL, MODIFY QUERY, SET ANSI, SET EXACT, SET PATH, _TALLY

SELECT( ) Function

Returns the number of the currently selected work area or the highest-numbered unused work area.

Syntax

SELECT([0 | 1 | *cTableAlias*])

Returns

Numeric

Arguments

0

Specifies that SELECT( ) return the number of the current work area.

1

Specifies that SELECT( ) return the highest-numbered unused work area.

cTableAlias

Specifies the alias of the table for which SELECT( ) returns the work area.

Remarks

SELECT( ) returns the number of the current work area if SET COMPATIBLE is set to OFF. If SET COMPATIBLE is set to ON, SELECT( ) returns the number of the unused work area with the highest number.

A work area can be selected (activated) with SELECT.

Example

```
CLOSE DATABASES
SET COMPATIBLE ON
OPEN DATABASE (HOME(2) + 'data\testdata')

SELECT 0  && Unused work area
USE customer  && Opens Customer table

SELECT 0  && Unused work area
USE orders  && Opens Orders table

CLEAR
? SELECT( )  && Returns 3, lowest available work area
```

See Also

ALIAS( ), SELECT, SET COMPATIBLE

Selected Property

Specifies whether an item is selected in a combo box or list box. Not available at design time; read/write at run time.

Syntax

[*Form.*]*Control*.Selected(*nIndex*)[= *lExpr*]

Arguments

nIndex
Specifies the index of an item in a combo box or list box.

lExpr
The settings for the Selected property are:

Setting	Description
True (.T.)	The item is selected.
False (.F.)	(Default) The item isn't selected.

Remarks

The Selected property is particularly useful where users can make multiple selections. You can quickly check which items in a list are selected. You can also use this property to select or deselect items in a list from within a program. To check whether the third item in a list box is selected, issue the following:

```
IF MyList.Selected(3)
   WAIT WINDOW "It's selected!"
ELSE
   WAIT WINDOW "It's not!"
ENDIF
```

Example

The following example creates a list box. The source of the items that appear in the list box items is an array; the name of the array is specified with the RowSource property. The RowSourceType property is set to 5 (array) to specify that an array is the source for the items in the list box.

The MultiSelect property for the list box is set to true (.T.), allowing you to make multiple selections from the list box. The item or items you choose in the list box are displayed by using the ListCount, Selected and List properties to determine the number of items in the list box and the items you chose.

```
CLEAR

DIMENSION gaMyListArray(10)
FOR gnCount = 1 to 10  && Fill the array with letters
    STORE REPLICATE(CHR(gnCount+64),6) TO gaMyListArray(gnCount)
NEXT

frmMyForm = CREATEOBJECT('Form')  && Create a Form
frmMyForm.Closable = .f.  && Disable the window pop-up menu

frmMyForm.Move(150,10)  && Move the form

frmMyForm.AddObject('cmbCommand1','cmdMyCmdBtn')  && Add "Quit" Command button
frmMyForm.AddObject('lstListBox1','lstMyListBox')  && Add ListBox control

frmMyForm.lstListBox1.RowSourceType = 5  && Specifies an array
frmMyForm.lstListBox1.RowSource = 'gaMyListArray' && Array containing listbox items

frmMyForm.cmbCommand1.Visible =.T.  && "Quit" Command button visible
frmMyForm.lstListBox1.Visible =.T.  && "List Box visible

frmMyForm.SHOW  && Display the form
READ EVENTS  && Start event processing

DEFINE CLASS cmdMyCmdBtn AS CommandButton  && Create Command button
    Caption = '\<Quit'  && Caption on the Command button
    Cancel = .T.  && Default Cancel Command button (Esc)
    Left = 125  && Command button column
    Top = 210  && Command button row
    Height = 25  && Command button height

    PROCEDURE Click
        CLEAR EVENTS  && Stop event processing, close Form
        CLEAR  && Clear main Visual FoxPro window
ENDDEFINE

DEFINE CLASS lstMyListBox AS ListBox  && Create ListBox control
    Left = 10  && List Box column
    Top = 10  && List Box row
    MultiSelect = .T.  && Allow selecting more than 1 item

PROCEDURE Click
    ACTIVATE SCREEN
    CLEAR
    ? "Selected items:"
    ? "---------------"
    FOR nCnt = 1 TO ThisForm.lstListBox1.ListCount
        IF ThisForm.lstListBox1.Selected(nCnt)  && Is item selected?
            ? SPACE(5) + ThisForm.lstListBox1.List(nCnt) && Show item
        ENDIF
    ENDFOR

ENDDEFINE
```

Applies To

ComboBox, ListBox

See Also

AddItem Method, Clear Method, List Property, ListCount Property, ListItemID Property, MultiSelect Property, NewItemID Property, RemoveItem Method, RemoveListItem Method, SelectedID Property, TopItemID Property

SelectedBackColor, SelectedForeColor Properties

Specifies the background or foreground color for the selected text. Available at design time and run time.

Syntax

Control.SelectedBackColor[= *nColor*]

– or –

Control.SelectedBackColor = RGB(*nRedValue, nGreenValue, nBlueValue*)
Control.SelectedForeColor[= *nColor*]

– or –

Control.SelectedForeColor = RGB(*nRedValue, nGreenValue, nBlueValue*)

Arguments

nColor

Specifies a single number to represent the color.

> **Note** In the Properties window, you can double-click any of the color properties to display the Color dialog box. You can choose or define colors from this dialog box. The red, green, and blue intensities that correspond to the color you choose become the settings for these properties after you close the Color dialog box.

For more information, see the color table in "BackColor, ForeColor Properties," earlier in this language reference.

Applies To

ComboBox, EditBox, Spinner, TextBox

See Also

BackColor, ForeColor Properties, RGB( ), SelectedItemBackColor, SelectedItemForeColor Properties

SelectedID Property

Specifies whether an item is selected in a combo box or list box. Not available at design time; read/write at run time.

Syntax

Control.SelectedID(*nItemID*)[= *lExpr*]

Arguments

nItemID
Specifies the item ID of an item in a combo box or ListBox.

lExpr
The settings for the SelectedID property are:

Setting	Description
True (.T.)	The item is selected.
False (.F.)	(Default) The item isn't selected.

Remarks

The SelectedID property is particularly useful where users can make multiple selections. You can quickly check which items in a list are selected. You can also use this property to select or deselect items in a list using code. To check whether the third item in a ListBox is selected, issue the following:

```
IF MyList.SelectedID(3)
   WAIT WINDOW "It's selected!"
ELSE
   WAIT WINDOW "It's not!"
ENDIF
```

Applies To

ComboBox, ListBox

See Also

AddItem Method, Clear Method, List Property, ListCount Property, ListItemID Property, MultiSelect Property, NewItemID Property, RemoveItem Method, RemoveListItem Method, Selected Property, TopItemID Property

SelectedItemBackColor, SelectedItemForeColor Properties

Specifies the background or foreground color for the selected item in a combo box or list box. Available at design time and run time.

Syntax

Control.SelectedItemBackColor[= *nColor*]

– or –

Control.SelectedItemBackColor RGB(*nRedValue, nGreenValue, nBlueValue*)
Control.SelectedItemForeColor[= *nColor*]

– or –

Control.SelectedItemForeColor RGB(*nRedValue, nGreenValue, nBlueValue*)

Arguments

nColor
Specifies a single number to represent the color.

> **Note** In the Properties window, you can double-click any of the color properties to display the Color dialog box. You can choose or define colors from this dialog box. The red, green, and blue intensities that correspond to the color you choose become the settings for these properties after you close the Color dialog box.

For more information, see the color table in "BackColor, ForeColor Properties," earlier in this language reference.

Applies To

ComboBox, ListBox

See Also

BackColor, ForeColor Properties, RGB( ), SelectedBackColor, SelectedForeColor Properties

SelectOnEntry Property

Specifies whether text in a column cell, edit box, or text box selected when the user moves to it. Available at design time and run time.

Syntax

Object.SelectOnEntry[= *lExpr*]

Arguments

The settings for the SelectOnEntry property are:

Setting	Description
True (.T.)	(Default for columns) The text is selected.
False (.F.)	(Default for edit and text boxes) The text isn't selected

Remarks

If the Highlight property is set to true (.T.), you can use it in conjunction with the SelectOnEntry property to determine if the entire text appears selected. If you set the Highlight property to false (.F.), the SelectOnEntry property is ignored.

Applies To

Column, EditBox Control, TextBox Control

See Also

Highlight Property, HighlightRow Property

SelLength Property

Returns the number of characters the user selects in a text-entry area of a control, or specifies the number of characters to select. Not available at design time; read/write at run time.

Syntax

[*Form*.]*Control*.SelLength[= *nLength*]

Arguments

nLength
Specifies the number of characters selected. Selected text appears highlighted. The valid range of settings is 0 to the total number of characters in the control. Setting SelLength to less than 0 causes a run-time error.

Remarks

Use this property with the SelStart and SelText properties for tasks such as:

- Setting the insertion point within a string of characters.
- Establishing an insertion range that limits where the insertion point can go.
- Selecting a specific group of characters (substrings) in a control.
- Clearing text.

When working with these properties, be aware of the following behaviors:

- Setting SelLength to less than 0 causes a run-time error.
- Setting SelStart to greater than the text length sets the property to the existing text length. Changing SelStart changes the selection to an insertion point and sets SelLength to 0.
- Setting SelText to a new value sets SelLength to 0 and replaces the selected text with the new string.

Applies To

ComboBox, EditBox, Spinner, TextBox

See Also

SelStart Property, SelText Property

SelStart Property

Returns the starting point of a text selection made by the user in a text-entry area of a control, or indicates the position of the insertion point if no text is selected. Also, specifies the starting point of a text selection in a text-entry area of a control. Not available at design time; read/write at run time.

Syntax

[*Form.*]*Control*.SelStart[= *nStart*]

Arguments

nStart

Specifies the starting point of text selected or indicates the position of the insertion point if no text is selected. Selected text appears shaded. The valid range of settings is 0 to the total number of characters in the edit area of the control.

Remarks

Use this property with the SelLength and SelText properties for tasks such as:

- Setting the insertion point within a string of characters.
- Establishing an insertion range that limits where the insertion point can go.

- Selecting a specific group of characters (substrings) in a control.

- Clearing text.

When working with these properties, be aware of the following behaviors:

- Setting SelLength to less than 0 causes a run-time error.

- Setting SelStart to greater than the text length sets the property to the existing text length. Changing SelStart changes the selection to an insertion point and sets SelLength to 0.

- Setting SelText to a new value sets SelLength to 0 and replaces the selected text with the new string.

Applies To

ComboBox, EditBox, Spinner, TextBox

See Also

SelLength Property, SelText Property

SelText Property

Returns the text that the user selected in a text-entry area of a control, or returns an empty string ("") if no characters are selected. Specifies the string containing the selected text. Not available at design time; read/write at run time.

Syntax

[*Form.*]*Control*.SelText[= *cString*]

Arguments

cString
Specifies the string containing the selected text or consists of an empty string if no characters are selected. Selected text appears shaded.

Remarks

Use this property with the SelLength and SelStart properties for tasks such as:

- Setting the insertion point within a string of characters.

- Establishing an insertion range that limits where the insertion point can go.

- Selecting a specific group of characters (substrings) in a control.

- Clearing text.

When working with these properties, be aware of the following behaviors:

- Setting SelLength to less than 0 causes a run-time error.

- Setting SelStart to greater than the text length sets the property to the existing text length. Changing SelStart changes the selection to an insertion point and sets SelLength to 0.

- Setting SelText to a new value sets SelLength to 0 and replaces the selected text with the new string.

Applies To

ComboBox, EditBox, Spinner, TextBox

See Also

SelLength Property, SelStart Property

Separator Object

Creates a Separator object that places space between controls in a toolbar.

Syntax

Separator

Remarks

Controls in a toolbar are placed immediately next to each other unless you include a Separator between the controls. A Separator is a special object that adds space between the controls and creates a group of controls.

For additional information about creating toolbars and separators, see Chapter 11, "Designing Menus and Toolbars," in the *Microsoft Visual FoxPro 6.0 Programmer's Guide*.

Properties

Application	BaseClass	Class
ClassLibrary	Comment	Enabled
Name	Parent	ParentClass
Tag		

Events

Destroy	Error	Init

Methods

AddProperty	ReadExpression	ReadMethod
ResetToDefault	SaveAsClass	WriteExpression
ZOrder		

See Also

CREATE CLASS, CREATE FORM, DEFINE CLASS, Toolbar Object

Server Object

An object reference to a server in a project.

Syntax

Server

Remarks

A server object is created and instantiated for each server in a project after building an executable file (.exe) or dynamic link library (.dll) from the project. The server object provides an object reference to a server in the project, and allows you to determine information about the server and manipulate it through the server object properties.

A project's servers collection is composed of all the server objects in the project.

Note that a server object is a COM object, so assigning a server object reference to a memory variable creates a memory variable of class "Unknown Type."

Properties

CLSID	Description	HelpContextID
Instancing	ProgID	ServerClass
ServerClassLibrary		

See Also

File Object, Files Collection, Project Object, Projects Collection, ProjectHook Object, Servers Collection

ServerClass Property

Contains the name of a server class in a project. Read-only at design time and run time.

Syntax

Object.ServerClass

Remarks

The names of server classes in a project are also displayed in the Server tab of the **Project Information** dialog box.

Automation servers are created in Visual FoxPro by adding classes defined as OLEPUBLIC to a project, and then building an executable file (.exe) or dynamic link library (.dll) from the project. You can have as many OLEPUBLIC classes as you want in the project and they can be defined in program files (.prg) or class libraries (.vcx).

For information about creating custom Automation servers, see "Creating Automation Servers" in Chapter 16, "Adding OLE," in the *Microsoft Visual FoxPro 6.0 Programmer's Guide*.

Applies To

Server Object

See Also

CREATE CLASS, DEFINE CLASS, ServerClassLibrary Property

ServerClassLibrary Property

Contains the name of the class library or program containing a server class. Read-only at design time and run time.

Syntax

Object.ServerClassLibrary

Remarks

The name of the class library or program containing the server class is also displayed in the Server tab of the **Project Information** dialog box.

Automation servers are created in Visual FoxPro by adding classes defined as OLEPUBLIC to a project, and then building an executable file (.exe) or dynamic link library (.dll) from the project. You can have as many OLEPUBLIC classes as you want in the project and they can be defined in program files (.prg) or class libraries (.vcx).

For information about creating custom Automation servers, see "Creating Automation Servers" in Chapter 16, "Adding OLE," in the *Microsoft Visual FoxPro 6.0 Programmer's Guide*.

Applies To

Server Object

See Also

CREATE CLASS, DEFINE CLASS, ServerClass Property

ServerHelpFile Property

The help file for the type library created for server classes in a project.

Syntax

Object.ServerHelpFile[= *cHelpFileName*]

Arguments

cHelpFileName
  Specifies the name of the help file for the type library. By default, *cHelpFileName* contains the empty string.

Remarks

The help file for a type library is typically used to provide information about properties or methods in server classes when the type library is viewed in a class or object browser. Visual FoxPro includes the Class Browser, which allows you to view type library information.

A type library is created when you build a .dll or .exe that contains server classes. If you specify a help file for the type library with the ServerHelpFile property, you can provide help for the properties or methods in the server classes from within a class or object browser.

Applies To

Project Object

See Also

HelpContextID Property, Server Object, Servers Collection, ServerProject Property

ServerName Property

Contains the full path and file name for an Automation server. Read-only at run time.

Syntax

ApplicationObject.ServerName

Remarks

The ServerName property allows you to determine the directory from which an in-process .dll or an out-of-process .exe Automation server was started, facilitating referencing of other files in distributed applications. You can also use ServerName to determine the directory from which a Visual FoxPro .exe application was started.

The ServerName property for a development version of Visual FoxPro started in an interactive session contains the same value as the FullName property.

Applies To

Application Object, _VFP

See Also

FullName Property, StartMode Property

ServerProject Property

The name of the project containing server classes.

Syntax

Object.ServerProject[= *cName*]

Arguments

cName
Specifies the name of the project containing server classes. The default value is the name of the project containing the server classes, or, identically, the value of the Name property for the project.

Remarks

The ServerProject name you specify is the first section of the ProgID (Programmatic Identifier) that uniquely identifies the server. For example, if you set the ServerProject property to "MyApplication" and the server has an OLEPublic class named "Server1," you access the Server1 class with the syntax "MyApplication.Server1."

This property corresponds to the Project name item on the Server tab of the Project Information dialog box.

Applies To

Project Object

See Also

Name Property, Server Object, Servers Collection, ServerHelpFile Property

Servers Collection

A collection of server objects.

Syntax

Servers

Remarks

A Servers collection provides access to server objects, allowing you to manipulate servers within the project.

For more information about the servers collection and projects, see "Project Manager Hooks" in Chapter 32, "Application Development and Developer Productivity," in the *Microsoft Visual FoxPro 6.0 Programmer's Guide*.

For information about creating custom Automation servers, see "Creating Automation Servers" in Chapter 16, "Adding OLE," in the *Microsoft Visual FoxPro 6.0 Programmer's Guide*.

Properties

Count

Methods

Item

See Also

File Object, Files Collection, Project Object, Projects Collection, ProjectHook Object, Server Object

SET Command

Opens the Data Session window.

Syntax

SET

Remarks

The Data Session window provides an easy way to open tables, establish relations, or set or change many Microsoft Visual FoxPro options.

See Also

SET VIEW

SET ALTERNATE Command

Directs screen or printer output created with ?, ??, DISPLAY, or LIST to a text file.

Syntax

SET ALTERNATE ON | OFF

– or –

SET ALTERNATE TO [*FileName* [ADDITIVE]]

Arguments

ON

Directs output to the text file.

OFF

(Default) Disables output to the text file.

TO *FileName*

Creates the text file, which is assigned the default extension .txt unless you include a different extension with the file name.

If you use SET ALTERNATE TO without *FileName*, the last file you created using SET ALTERNATE TO *FileName* is closed.

ADDITIVE

Appends output to the end of the file specified with *FileName*. If you omit ADDITIVE, the contents of the file are overwritten.

See Also

CLOSE, SET PRINTER

SET ANSI Command

Determines how comparisons between strings of different lengths are made with the = operator in Visual FoxPro SQL commands.

Syntax

SET ANSI ON | OFF

Arguments

ON

Pads the shorter string with the blanks needed to make it equal to the longer string's length. The two strings are then compared character for character for their entire lengths. Consider this comparison:

```
'Tommy' = 'Tom'
```

The result is false (.F.) if SET ANSI is on because when padded, 'Tom' becomes 'Tom ' and the strings 'Tom ' and 'Tommy' don't match character for character.

The == operator uses this method for comparisons in Visual FoxPro SQL commands.

OFF

Specifies that the shorter string not be padded with blanks. The two strings are compared character for character until the end of the shorter string is reached. Consider this comparison:

```
'Tommy' = 'Tom'
```

The result is true (.T.) when SET ANSI is off because the comparison stops after 'Tom.'

Remarks

SET ANSI determines whether the shorter of two strings is padded with blanks when a SQL string comparison is made. SET ANSI has no effect on the == operator; when you use the == operator, the shorter string is always padded with blanks for the comparison.

SET ANSI is scoped to the current data session.

SET ANSI and the Query Designer   Visual FoxPro builds a SELECT – SQL command in the Query Designer when you create a query. When creating Join and Filter conditions, if you choose the Equal or Exactly Like options, the = or == operator is included in the generated SELECT. The SET ANSI setting can affect the results of queries you create and perform in the Query Designer.

String Order   In SQL commands, the left-to-right order of the two strings in a comparison is irrelevant — switching a string from one side of the = or == operator to the other doesn't affect the result of the comparison.

See Also

CREATE QUERY, MODIFY QUERY, SELECT – SQL, SET DATASESSION, SET EXACT

SET ASSERTS Command

Specifies if ASSERT commands are evaluated or ignored.

Syntax

SET ASSERTS ON | OFF

Arguments

ON

Specifies that Visual FoxPro executes ASSERT commands.

OFF

Specifies that Visual FoxPro ignores ASSERT commands.

Remarks

ASSERTS is set to OFF if you choose the Ignore All button in the message box following an assert.

See Also

ASSERT

SET AUTOSAVE Command

Determines whether Visual FoxPro flushes data buffers to disk when you exit a READ or return to the Command window.

Syntax

SET AUTOSAVE ON | OFF

Arguments

ON
Specifies that buffers be flushed to disk whenever you exit a READ or return to the Command window.

OFF
Specifies that buffers be flushed to disk only if five minutes have elapsed since the last flush occurred, and only when you exit a READ or return to the Command window.

OFF is the default for SET AUTOSAVE.

Remarks

Flushing buffers may reduce the chance of data loss if your computer loses power.

SET AUTOSAVE is scoped to the current data session.

See Also

FFLUSH( ), FLUSH, SET DATASESSION

SET BELL Command

Turns the computer bell on or off and sets the bell attributes.

Syntax

SET BELL ON | OFF

– or –

SET BELL TO [cWAVFileName]

Arguments

ON
(Default) Turns the bell on.

OFF
Turns the bell off.

TO *cWAVFileName*

Specifies a waveform sound to play when the bell is rung. *cWAVFileName* can include a path to the waveform sound.

Issue SET BELL TO without *cWAVFileName* to restore the default waveform sound.

Remarks

SET BELL enables or disables the sounding of the bell during editing when you reach the end of a field or enter invalid data.

Example

In the following example, the waveform sound file Ding.wav is played.

```
SET BELL TO 'C:\WINDOWS\DING.WAV'
?? CHR(7)
```

SET BLOCKSIZE Command

Specifies how Visual FoxPro allocates disk space for the storage of memo fields.

Syntax

SET BLOCKSIZE TO *nBytes*

Arguments

nBytes

Specifies the block size in which disk space for memo fields is allocated. If *nBytes* is 0, disk space is allocated in single bytes (blocks of 1 byte). If *nBytes* is an integer between 1 and 32, disk space is allocated in blocks of *nBytes* bytes multiplied by 512. If *nBytes* is greater than 32, disk space is allocated in blocks of *nBytes* bytes.

If you specify a block size value greater than 32, you can save substantial disk space.

Remarks

The default value for SET BLOCKSIZE is 64. To reset the block size to a different value after the file has been created, set it to a new value and then use COPY to create a new table. The new table has the specified block size.

SET BLOCKSIZE is scoped to the current data session.

See Also

COPY FILE, MODIFY STRUCTURE, PACK, SET DATASESSION

SET BORDER Command

Included for backward compatibility. Use the BorderStyle Property instead.

SET BROWSEIME Command

Specifies if the Input Method Editor is opened when you navigate to a text box in a Browse window.

Syntax

SET BROWSEIME ON | OFF

Arguments

ON
> (Default for Taiwan region and People's Republic of China Windows) Opens the Input Method Editor when you navigate to a text box in a Browse window.

OFF
> (Default for Korean Windows) The Input Method Editor isn't opened when you navigate to a text box in a Browse window.

Remarks

SET BROWSEIME corresponds to the Browse IME control check box on the General tab of the Options dialog box.

This command has no effect if you are not working in a DBCS environment.

See Also

IMEMode Property, IMESTATUS( )

SET BRSTATUS Command

Included for backward compatibility. Use the StatusBarText Property instead.

SET CARRY Command

Determines whether Visual FoxPro carries data forward from the current record to a new record created with INSERT, APPEND, and BROWSE.

Syntax

SET CARRY ON | OFF

– or –

SET CARRY TO [*FieldList* [ADDITIVE]]

Arguments

ON
> Brings data from all fields in all work areas forward from the current record to a new record.

OFF

(Default) Prevents data from all fields from being passed to a new record.

TO [*FieldList* [ADDITIVE]]

FieldList specifies the fields from which data is carried forward. Separate the field names with commas.

ADDITIVE specifies that the fields in the field list be added to the current set of fields being carried forward.

Issuing SET CARRY TO implicitly performs SET CARRY ON.

Use SET CARRY TO without *FieldList* to restore the default setting (all fields are carried forward).

Remarks

Use SET CARRY to enable data to be carried forward from the current record to a new record or to prevent data from being carried forward. Fields that generally remain unchanged during an editing session can be brought forward for each new record. For example, a field containing the current date can be brought forward for each new record so a new date doesn't have to be entered again. Note that the contents of Memo and General type fields are not carried forward.

SET CARRY affects only the table open in the currently selected work area.

SET CARRY is scoped to the current data session.

See Also

INSERT, SET DATASESSION

SET CENTURY Command

Determines whether Microsoft Visual FoxPro displays the century portion of date expressions and how Visual FoxPro interprets dates that specify only 2 digit years.

Syntax

SET CENTURY ON | OFF | TO [*nCentury* [ROLLOVER *nYear*]]

Arguments

ON

Specifies a four-digit year in a format that includes 10 characters (including date delimiters).

Note To provide year 2000 compliance, it's recommended that you always set SET CENTURY to ON. For more information about year 2000 compliance, see "Year 2000 Date Support" in Chapter 33, "Programming Improvements," in the *Microsoft Visual FoxPro 6.0 Programmer's Guide*.

OFF

(Default) Specifies a two-digit year in a format that includes eight characters and assumes the twentieth century for date calculations.

TO *nCentury*

A number from 1 to 99 that specifies the current century. When a date has a two digit year, *nCentury* determines in which century the year occurs. The ROLLOVER value determines whether the year is in *nCentury* or the century following *nCentury*.

ROLLOVER *nYear*

A number from 0 to 99 that specifies the year equal to and above which is the current century and below which is the next century. The default value for *nYear* is the last two digits of the current year plus 50 years — if the current year is 1998, *nYear* is 48, the last two digits of 2048 (1998 + 50).

Note that the rollover value only determines the century for a date entered without a century portion — an ambiguous date format that is not recommended.

For example, if the current year is 1998 and *nYear* is the default (48), any date entered without a century portion and a year of 48 or greater is considered to be in the current century (the 20th century). Any date entered without a century portion but with a year before 48 is considered to be in the next century (the 21st century).

Remarks

Use SET CENTURY to specify how date variables and functions are displayed.

Issue SET CENTURY TO without any additional arguments to restore the default century to the current century and ROLLOVER to the default value of the current year plus 50 years. In Visual FoxPro 5.0, issuing SET CENTURY TO without any additional arguments sets the century to 19 and ROLLOVER to zero.

SET CENTURY is scoped to the current data session. New data sessions are initialized to the default values as specified above, ignoring the value of SET CENTURY for the current data session.

See Also

DATE( ), SET DATASESSION, SET STRICTDATE, SET SYSFORMATS, YEAR( )

SET CLASSLIB Command

Opens a .vcx visual class library containing class definitions.

Syntax

SET CLASSLIB TO *ClassLibraryName* [IN *APPFileName* | *EXEFileName*]
    [ADDITIVE] [ALIAS *AliasName*]

Arguments

TO *ClassLibraryName*

Specifies the name of the .vcx visual class library to open. If *ClassLibraryName* does not include a fully qualified path, Visual FoxPro first searches for the visual class library in the default Visual FoxPro directory, and then in the directories in the Visual FoxPro path. The default Visual FoxPro directory is specified with SET DEFAULT, and the Visual FoxPro search path is specified with SET PATH.

Issuing SET CLASSLIB TO without *ClassLibraryName* closes all open visual class libraries. Use RELEASE CLASSLIB to close an individual visual class library.

IN *APPFileName | EXEFileName*

Specifies a Visual FoxPro application file (.app) or executable file (.exe) containing the visual class library.

ADDITIVE

Opens the .vcx visual class library without closing any currently open .vcx visual class libraries. If this clause is omitted, all open .vcx visual class libraries are closed.

ALIAS *AliasName*

Specifies an alias for the visual class library. The visual class library can be referenced by its alias. For example, the following commands open a .vcx visual class library named MyClass, assign it the alias MyCntrls, and then create a control named MyButton.

```
SET CLASSLIB TO MyClass ALIAS MyCntrls
mMyButton = CREATEOBJ('MyCntrls.MyButton')
```

Remarks

When CREATEOBJECT( ), ADD OBJECT in DEFINE CLASS, or the AddObject method is issued, Visual FoxPro searches for the class definition defining the object specified in these commands in the following locations and order:

1. The Visual FoxPro base classes.

2. Class definitions in memory in the order they are loaded.

3. Class definitions in the current program.

4. Class definitions in the .vcx class libraries opened with SET CLASSLIB.

5. Class definitions in procedure files opened with SET PROCEDURE.

6. Class definitions in the Visual FoxPro program execution chain.

7. The OLE Registry if SET OLEOBJECT is set to ON.

If the class definition containing the object cannot be located, Visual FoxPro generates an error message.

Example

The following example uses CREATE CLASSLIB to create a visual class library named `myclslib`. A class named `myform` based on the Visual FoxPro Form base class is created and is stored in the `myclslib` visual class library. SET CLASSLIB is used to open the `myclslib` visual class library so that classes within it can be used.

```
CREATE CLASSLIB myclslib      && Creates a new .VCX visual class library
CREATE CLASS myform OF myclslib AS "Form"  && Creates new class
SET CLASSLIB TO myclslib ADDITIVE     && Opens MyClsLib.VCX
```

See Also

ADD CLASS, AddObject Method, CREATE CLASS, CREATE CLASSLIB, CREATEOBJECT( ), MODIFY CLASS, RELEASE CLASSLIB, SET PROCEDURE, SET OLEOBJECT

SET CLEAR Command

Included for backward compatibility. Use the Refresh Method instead.

SET CLOCK Command

Determines whether Visual FoxPro displays the system clock and specifies the clock location on the main Visual FoxPro window.

Syntax

SET CLOCK ON | OFF | STATUS

– or –

SET CLOCK TO [*nRow, nColumn*]

Arguments

ON
> Displays the clock in the upper-right corner of the main Visual FoxPro window.

OFF
> (Default) Removes the clock from the status bar or from the main Visual FoxPro window.

STATUS
> Displays the clock in the graphical status bar. Issue SET STATUS BAR ON to display the graphical status bar.

TO [*nRow*, *nColumn*]

Using row and column coordinates, specifies where the clock is displayed in the main Visual FoxPro window. Use SET CLOCK TO without the coordinates to display the clock in its default position in the upper-right corner of the main Visual FoxPro window.

If you place the clock in the graphical status bar with SET CLOCK STATUS and you specify a location in the main Visual FoxPro window with TO *nRow*, *nColumn*, Visual FoxPro removes the clock from the graphical status bar and places it at the location you specify.

See Also

SET BRSTATUS, SET HOURS, SET STATUS

SET COLLATE Command

Specifies a collation sequence for character fields in subsequent indexing and sorting operations.

Syntax

SET COLLATE TO *cSequenceName*

Arguments

cSequenceName

Specifies a collation sequence. The following collation sequence options are available.

Options	Language
DUTCH	Dutch
GENERAL	English, French, German, Modern Spanish, Portuguese, and other Western European languages
GERMAN	German phone book order (DIN)
ICELAND	Icelandic
MACHINE	Machine (the default collation sequence for earlier FoxPro versions)
NORDAN	Norwegian, Danish
SPANISH	Traditional Spanish
SWEFIN	Swedish, Finnish
UNIQWT	Unique Weight

Note When you specify the SPANISH option, "ch" is a single letter that sorts between "c" and "d," and "ll" sorts between "l" and "m."

If you specify a collation sequence option as a literal character string, be sure to enclose the option in quotation marks:

```
SET COLLATE TO "SWEFIN"
```

MACHINE is the default collation sequence option and is the sequence Xbase users are familiar with. Characters are ordered as they appear in the current code page.

GENERAL may be preferable for U.S. and Western European users. Characters are ordered as they appear in the current code page. In FoxPro versions earlier than 2.5, you may have used UPPER( ) or LOWER( ) on character fields when you created indexes. In FoxPro versions later than 2.5, you can instead specify the GENERAL collation sequence option and omit the UPPER( ) conversion.

If you specify a collation sequence option other than MACHINE and if you create an .idx file, a compact .idx is always created.

Use SET("COLLATE") to return the current collation sequence.

If you include the following line in your Visual FoxPro configuration file, a collation sequence is specified when you start Visual FoxPro:

```
COLLATE = cSequenceName
```

This is identical to issuing the following command:

```
SET COLLATE TO cSequenceName
```

Remarks

SET COLLATE enables you to order tables containing accented characters for any of the supported languages. Changing the setting of SET COLLATE doesn't affect the collating sequence of previously opened indexes. Visual FoxPro automatically maintains existing indexes, providing the flexibility to create many different types of indexes, even for the same field.

For example, if an index is created with SET COLLATE set to GENERAL, and the SET COLLATE setting is later changed to SPANISH, the index retains the GENERAL collation sequence.

SET COLLATE is scoped to the current data session.

For additional information on code pages and Visual FoxPro's international support, see "Code Pages Supported by Visual FoxPro" in Chapter 18, "Developing International Applications," in the *Microsoft Visual FoxPro 6.0 Programmer's Guide*.

For more information on configuring Visual FoxPro, see Chapter 3, "Configuring Visual FoxPro," in the *Installation Guide*, in Help.

See Also

IDXCOLLATE( ), SET DATASESSION

SET COLOR OF Command

Included for backward compatibility. Use SET COLOR OF SCHEME instead.

SET COLOR OF SCHEME Command

Specifies the colors of a color scheme or copies one color scheme to another color scheme.

Syntax

SET COLOR OF SCHEME *nScheme1* TO
    [SCHEME *nScheme2* | *ColorPairList*]

Arguments

nScheme1
> Specifies the number of the color scheme you want to change. This can be a value from 1 through 24.
>
> > **Note** In Visual FoxPro, color schemes 13 through 15 are reserved for internal use. Do not use these color schemes.

TO [SCHEME *nScheme2*]
> Specifies the number of a color scheme to which color scheme *nScheme1* is changed.

TO [*ColorPairList*]
> Specifies up to 10 color pairs you would like to change in your color scheme. You can selectively change colors in a color scheme by including a comma for each color pair that you don't want to change. For example, to change the third color pair in color scheme 1 to bright white and blue and leave the rest of the color settings unchanged, use this command:
>
> ```
> SET COLOR OF SCHEME 1 TO , , W+/B*
> ```
>
> A color pair can also be specified with a set of six RGB (red, green, and blue) color values separated by commas. To change the third color pair in color scheme 1 to bright white and blue and leave the rest of the color settings unchanged, you can use this command:
>
> ```
> SET COLOR OF SCHEME 1 TO , , RGB(255,255,255,0,0,255)
> ```

Remarks

Not all interface elements can be controlled by color schemes — system windows, such as the View and Command windows, the system menu bar, and so on are always controlled by the Control Panel color settings. Issuing SET COLOR OF SCHEME *nScheme1* TO without including an optional clause restores the colors from the current color scheme.

For more information about color sets and color schemes, see "Colors Overview," earlier in this language reference.

See Also

Colors Overview, CREATE COLOR SET, SET COLOR SET

SET COLOR SET Command

Loads a previously defined color set.

Syntax

SET COLOR SET TO [*ColorSetName*]

Arguments

ColorSetName
    Specifies the color set to load.

Remarks

You can create color sets with SET COLOR OF SCHEME and save them with CREATE COLOR SET.

If you issue SET COLOR SET without an optional clause, the current color set remains loaded.

For more information about color sets, see "Colors Overview," earlier in this language reference.

See Also

Colors Overview, CREATE COLOR SET, SET COLOR OF SCHEME

SET COLOR TO Command

Included for backward compatibility. Use SET COLOR OF SCHEME instead.

SET COMPATIBLE Command

Controls compatibility with Microsoft FoxBASE+ and other Xbase languages.

Syntax

SET COMPATIBLE FOXPLUS | OFF | DB4 | ON
    [PROMPT | NOPROMPT]

Arguments

FOXPLUS | OFF

(Default) These two keywords can be used interchangeably. Each allows programs created in FoxBASE+ to run in Microsoft Visual FoxPro without changes.

DB4 | ON

These two keywords can be used interchangeably. Including either keyword affects the behavior of the commands and functions listed below.

PROMPT | NOPROMPT

These options determine whether Visual FoxPro displays a dialog box when you open a dBASE table containing a memo field.

Include the PROMPT option to display the Convert Memos dialog box. If you open a dBASE table containing a memo field, Visual FoxPro by default displays the Convert Memos dialog box, which enables you to convert the dBASE memo file to a Visual FoxPro format. You must convert the memo file to a Visual FoxPro format to open the table in Visual FoxPro. You can later convert the memo file to a dBASE format by including the TYPE FOXPLUS option in the COPY command.

If you include NOPROMPT, the Convert Memos dialog box is not displayed when you open a dBASE table containing a memo field. The dBASE memo file is automatically converted to a Visual FoxPro format.

Remarks

Commands and functions affected by SET COMPATIBLE include LIKE( ), PLAY MACRO, SELECT( ), and STORE (when STORE is used with arrays).

SET COMPATIBLE doesn't create compatibility with other Xbase commands, functions, or features not supported in Visual FoxPro. For example, it doesn't allow you to open a report form created in other Xbase products with the Report Designer.

The following table lists the commands affected by SET COMPATIBLE.

Commands

@ ... GET with a RANGE clause	@ ... SAY with CHR(7)
@ ... SAY scrolling	@ ... SAY when STATUS is ON
ACTIVATE SCREEN	ACTIVATE WINDOW
APPEND MEMO	DECLARE
DIMENSION	GO	GOTO with SET TALK ON
FSIZE( )	INKEY( )
LASTKEY( )	LIKE( )
Menu commands	PLAY MACRO

READ with an @ ... GET VALID clause	Nested READs
READ	RUN | !
SET COLOR TO	SET BORDER
SET FIELDS	SET MESSAGE
SET MEMOWIDTH	SET PRINTER TO \<file\>
STORE	SUM
TRANSFORM( ) with a numeric PICTURE clause	SELECT( )
SYS(2001, "COLOR")	

See Also

SET KEYCOMP

SET CONFIRM Command

Specifies whether the user can exit a text box by typing past the last character in the text box.

Syntax

SET CONFIRM ON | OFF

Arguments

ON

Specifies that the user cannot exit a text box by typing past the last character in the text box. To exit the text box, the user can press ENTER, TAB, or any of the arrow keys to move from a text box to another control.

SET CONFIRM ON also affects menu items and menu titles created with DEFINE BAR and DEFINE PAD. If the user types the first letter of the menu item or menu title, the item or title is selected but is not chosen. To choose the menu item or title when it is selected, the user should press ENTER or the SPACEBAR.

OFF

Specifies that the user can exit a text box by typing past the last character in the text box. The insertion point, when it reaches the last character in a text box, moves to the next control, and the bell is sounded (if SET BELL is set to ON).

OFF is the default value of SET CONFIRM.

SET CONFIRM OFF also affects menu items and menu titles. If SET CONFIRM is set to OFF, the user can choose an item from a menu or a menu title in a menu bar by pressing the key corresponding to the first letter of the menu item or title. (When SET CONFIRM is set to ON, this action only selects the menu item or title.)

Remarks

SET CONFIRM has no effect on access keys for menu items and menu titles. If a menu item or menu title is created with an access key, the menu item or title can be chosen by pressing the corresponding access key.

You can create text boxes using the Form Designer.

SET CONFIRM is scoped to the current data session.

See Also

TextBox Control, SET DATASESSION

SET CONSOLE Command

Enables or disables output to the main Visual FoxPro window or to the active user-defined window from within programs.

Syntax

SET CONSOLE ON | OFF

Arguments

ON

(Default) Sends all output to the main Visual FoxPro window or to the active user-defined window.

OFF

Suppresses output to the main Visual FoxPro window or to the active user-defined window.

Remarks

SET CONSOLE is set to ON when you are using Visual FoxPro interactively, and it cannot be changed to OFF from the Command window. You can change the setting to OFF only from within a program.

SET CONSOLE affects some interactive Visual FoxPro dialog boxes. For example, if SET CONSOLE is set to OFF and you issue BROWSE when no table is open, Visual FoxPro displays an error message. If SET CONSOLE is set to ON in the same circumstances, Visual FoxPro displays the Open dialog box.

SET CONSOLE doesn't affect output from @ ... SAY. Output from @ ... SAY is controlled by the SET DEVICE setting.

Important An error always sets SET CONSOLE to ON. Use SYS(100) to check the SET CONSOLE setting before the error occurred. For more information, see "SYS(100) – Console Setting," later in this language reference.

See Also

SYS( ) Functions Overview

SET COVERAGE Command

Turns code coverage on or off or specifies a text file to which code coverage information is directed.

Syntax

SET COVERAGE TO [*FileName* [ADDITIVE]]

Arguments

TO *FileName*
> Specifies the name of a text file to which code coverage information is directed. Issue SET COVERAGE TO without a file name to close the text file.

> If the file you specify doesn't exist, Visual FoxPro automatically creates and opens it.

ADDITIVE
> Appends the code coverage information to the end of the text file specified with *FileName*. If you omit ADDITIVE, the code coverage information replaces the contents of the text file.

Remarks

You can also set code coverage options in the Coverage dialog box online topic.

For more information about the Visual FoxPro Coverage Profiler, see "Coverage Profiler Application" in Chapter 32, "Application Development and Developer Productivity," in the *Microsoft Visual FoxPro 6.0 Programmer's Guide*.

See Also

_COVERAGE, SET EVENTTRACKING

SET CPCOMPILE Command

Specifies the code page for compiled programs.

Syntax

SET CPCOMPILE TO [*nCodePage*]

Arguments

nCodePage
> Specifies the compilation code page with *nCodePage*.

For additional information on code pages and Visual FoxPro's international support, see "Code Pages Supported by Visual FoxPro" in Chapter 18, "Developing International Applications," in the *Microsoft Visual FoxPro 6.0 Programmer's Guide*.

Issue SET CPCOMPILE TO without *nCodePage* to reset the compilation code page to the current code page. Use CPCURRENT( ) to determine the current code page.

Remarks

Use SET CPCOMPILE to compile programs for a specific code page. The code page you specify with SET CPCOMPILE is used for programs compiled automatically by Visual FoxPro, programs compiled from the Compile dialog, and programs compiled with the COMPILE command. However, you can include the AS clause in the COMPILE command to override the code page you specify with SET CPCOMPILE.

See Also

COMPILE, CPCURRENT( )

SET CPDIALOG Command

Specifies whether the Code Page dialog box is displayed when a table is opened.

Syntax

SET CPDIALOG ON | OFF

Arguments

ON
> (Default) Displays the Code Page dialog box when you open a table and the following conditions are true:

- The table is opened exclusively.

- The table is not marked with a code page.

OFF
> Does not display the Code Page dialog box when a table is opened.

Remarks

The Code Page dialog box allows you to specify a code page for tables created in earlier FoxPro versions and other products that create Visual FoxPro tables. The table is marked with the code page you choose.

When creating an application, issue SET CPDIALOG ON to ensure that the tables included in your application are marked with the proper code page. In your completed application, be sure that SET CPDIALOG is OFF.

You can also interactively specify whether the Code Page dialog box is displayed with the Prompt for Code Page check box in the Data tab of the Options dialog box. The Options dialog box is displayed by choosing Options from the Tools menu.

Note For additional information on code pages and Visual FoxPro's international support, see "Code Pages Supported by Visual FoxPro" in Chapter 18, "Developing International Applications," in the *Microsoft Visual FoxPro 6.0 Programmer's Guide*.

See Also

CPCURRENT( ), CPCONVERT( ), CPDBF( ), GETCP( ), USE

SET CURRENCY Command

Defines the currency symbol and specifies its position in the display of numeric, currency, float, and double expressions.

Syntax

SET CURRENCY TO [*cCurrencySymbol*]

– or –

SET CURRENCY LEFT | RIGHT

Arguments

cCurrencySymbol
Specifies a character string representing the currency symbol; can be one to nine characters long. Issue SET CURRENCY TO without *cCurrencySymbol* to reset the currency symbol to the default dollar sign ($).

LEFT
(Default) Positions the currency symbol to the left of the currency value.

RIGHT
Positions the currency symbol to the right of the currency value.

Remarks

The currency symbol is displayed in output created with @ ... SAY and in text boxes created with @ ... GET when the $ code is included in the FUNCTION or PICTURE clause.

SET CURRENCY is scoped to the current data session.

Example

The following example displays the DM currency symbol on either side of the currency value. If you use PICTURE to display the currency symbol, be sure to include @ before the dollar sign.

```
STORE SET('CURRENCY') TO gcCurrPosit
STORE 1234.56 TO gnDollarAmnt
CLEAR
SET CURRENCY TO 'DM'
```

```
@ 2,2 SAY gnDollarAmnt PICTURE '@$99,999.99'
IF gcCurrPosit = 'LEFT'
   SET CURRENCY RIGHT
ELSE
   SET CURRENCY LEFT
ENDIF
@ 4,2 SAY gnDollarAmnt FUNCTION '$99,999.99'
```

See Also

SET DATASESSION, SET DECIMALS, SET SEPARATOR, SET SYSFORMATS

SET CURSOR Command

Determines whether the insertion point is displayed when Visual FoxPro waits for input.

Syntax

SET CURSOR ON | OFF

Arguments

ON

(Default) Causes the insertion point to be displayed during a pending @ ... GET, @ ... EDIT, WAIT, or INKEY( ).

OFF

Prevents the insertion point from being displayed during a pending @ ... GET, @ ... EDIT, WAIT, or INKEY( ).

Remarks

SET CURSOR, similar to SYS(2002), enables you to turn the insertion point on or off.

See Also

INKEY( ), SET( ), SYS(2002) – Turn Insertion Point On or Off, WAIT

SET DATABASE Command

Specifies the current database.

Syntax

SET DATABASE TO [*DatabaseName*]

Arguments

DatabaseName

Specifies the name of an open database to be made the current database. If you omit *DatabaseName*, no open database is made the current database.

Remarks

Many databases can be open at the same time, but only one can be the current database. Commands and functions that manipulate open databases, such as ADD TABLE and DBC( ), operate on the current database.

The current database can also be specified by choosing an open database from the Database drop-down list on the Standard toolbar.

Visual FoxPro may automatically open databases when a query or a Form is executed.

SET DATABASE is scoped to the current data session.

Example

The following example creates two databases named `mydbc1` and `mydbc2`, and a table named `table1`. SET DATABASE is used to make `mydbc1` the current database, and `table1` is added to `mydbc1` when it is created. The table is then closed and removed from `mydbc1`. SET DATABASE is used to make `mydbc1` the current database, and ADD TABLE is then used to add the table to `mydbc2`. RENAME TABLE is used to change the name of the table from `table1` to `table2`.

```
CREATE DATABASE mydbc1
CREATE DATABASE mydbc2
SET DATABASE TO mydbc1
CREATE TABLE table1 (cField1 C(10), n N(10))  && Adds table to mydbc1
CLOSE TABLES     && A table must be closed to remove it from a database
REMOVE TABLE table1
SET DATABASE TO mydbc2
ADD TABLE table1
RENAME TABLE table1 TO table2
```

See Also

ADD TABLE, CLOSE DATABASES, DBC( ), DBGETPROP( ), DBSETPROP( ), DELETE DATABASE, DISPLAY TABLES, MODIFY DATABASE, OPEN DATABASE, REMOVE TABLE, SET DATASESSION

SET DATASESSION Command

Activates the specified form's data session.

Syntax

SET DATASESSION TO [*nDataSessionNumber*]

Arguments

nDataSessionNumber
    Specifies a form's data session to activate. If you omit *nDataSessionNumber*, data session 1 (the Global data session) is activated.

Remarks

By default, data session 1, the Global data session, is active when you start Visual FoxPro.

A form's DataSession property determines whether the form has its own unique data session when the form is created. If a form's DataSession property is set to true (.T.), the form has its own data session; otherwise, a data session is not created for the form. You can use the form's read-only DataSessionId property to determine the form's data session number.

A data session is closed when the form that created the data session is released.

SET DATASESSION is typically used to debug forms, and should not be issued when a form is active.

The following SET commands scope to the current data session:

SET Commands

SET ANSI	SET AUTOSAVE
SET BLOCKSIZE	SET CARRY
SET CENTURY	SET COLLATE
SET CONFIRM	SET CURRENCY
SET DATABASE	SET DATE
SET DECIMALS	SET DELETED
SET DELIMITERS	SET EXACT
SET EXCLUSIVE	SET FIELDS
SET FIXED	SET HOURS
SET LOCK	SET MARK TO
SET MEMOWIDTH	SET MULTILOCKS
SET NEAR	SET NULL
SET POINT	SET REPROCESS
SET SAFETY	SET SECONDS
SET SEPARATOR	SET SYSFORMATS
SET TALK	SET UNIQUE

See Also

AUSED( ), CREATE FORM, DataSession Property, DataSessionId Property

SET DATE Command

Specifies the format for the display of Date and DateTime expressions.

Syntax

SET DATE [TO] AMERICAN | ANSI | BRITISH | FRENCH | GERMAN
| ITALIAN | JAPAN | TAIWAN | USA | MDY | DMY | YMD | SHORT | LONG

Remarks

Here are the settings and the resulting date formats:

Setting	Format
AMERICAN	mm/dd/yy
ANSI	yy.mm.dd
BRITISH/FRENCH	dd/mm/yy
GERMAN	dd.mm.yy
ITALIAN	dd-mm-yy
JAPAN	yy/mm/dd
TAIWAN	yy/mm/dd
USA	mm-dd-yy
MDY	mm/dd/yy
DMY	dd/mm/yy
YMD	yy/mm/dd
SHORT	Short date format determined by the Windows Control Panel short date setting.
LONG	Long date format determined by the Windows Control Panel long date setting. Note that when SET DATE is set to LONG, dates before {^1601-01-01} that are converted to character strings are returned as the empty date.

The default date setting is AMERICAN.

The SET DATE setting also determines how the date appears in datetime expressions.

If DATE is set to SHORT or LONG, the SET CENTURY, SET MARK, SET HOURS, and SET SECONDS settings are ignored.

SET DATE is scoped to the current data session.

See Also

DATE( ), DATETIME( ), SET CENTURY, SET DATASESSION, SET MARK TO, SET SYSFORMATS

SET DEBUG Command

Makes the Debug and Trace windows either available or unavailable from the Visual FoxPro menu system.

Syntax

SET DEBUG ON | OFF

Arguments

ON

> (Default) Makes the Debug and Trace windows either available or unavailable from the Visual FoxPro menu system.

OFF

> Makes the Debug and Trace windows unavailable from the Visual FoxPro system menu. However, when SET DEBUG is set to OFF, you can open the Debug window with SET ECHO ON or ACTIVATE WINDOW DEBUG, and you can open the Trace window with SET STEP ON or ACTIVATE WINDOW TRACE.

Remarks

For more information on using the Trace and Debug windows, see Chapter 14, "Testing and Debugging Applications," in the *Microsoft Visual FoxPro 6.0 Programmer's Guide*.

See Also

CLEAR DEBUG, DEBUG, SET ECHO

SET DEBUGOUT Command

Directs debugging output to a file.

Syntax

SET DEBUGOUT TO [*FileName* [ADDITIVE]]

Arguments

FileName

> Specifies the name of the file to which debugging output is directed. If the file you specify doesn't exist, it is automatically created. If the file you specify already exists, its contents are overwritten unless you include the ADDITIVE clause.

> Issue SET DEBUGOUT TO to stop direction of debugging output to the file and close the file.

ADDITIVE

> Specifies that debugging output is appended to the end of the file specified with *FileName*.

Remarks

Debugging output that is directed to the file includes ASSERT messages, output from the DEBUGOUT command, and events that are specified with SET EVENTLIST or in the Event Tracking Dialog Box. See the Event Tracking dialog box topic for more information about specifying events to track interactively.

See Also

ASSERT, DEBUG, DEBUGOUT, SET EVENTLIST, SET EVENTTRACKING

SET DECIMALS Command

Specifies the number of decimal places displayed in numeric expressions.

Syntax

SET DECIMALS TO [*nDecimalPlaces*]

Arguments

nDecimalPlaces
> Specifies the minimum number of decimal places to display. The default is two decimal places. The maximum number of decimal places is 18; the minimum is zero.

Remarks

SET DECIMALS specifies the minimum number of decimal places used to display the results of division, multiplication, and trigonometric and financial functions.

SET DECIMALS is scoped to the current data session.

See Also

SET DATASESSION, SET FIXED, SET SYSFORMATS

SET DEFAULT Command

Specifies the default drive and directory.

Syntax

SET DEFAULT TO [*cPath*]

Arguments

cPath
> Specifies one of the following:

- A drive designator.

- A drive designator with a directory name.

- A child directory name.

- Any of the above using Microsoft MS-DOS shorthand notation (\ or ..).

Remarks

SET DEFAULT changes the default directory to the directory you specify.

Microsoft Visual FoxPro searches for a file in the default Visual FoxPro directory. The default directory is the one from which you start Visual FoxPro. However, you can specify a different default directory in your Visual FoxPro configuration file or in a startup program. If Visual FoxPro cannot find a file in the default directory, it then searches the Visual FoxPro path if one has been specified. Use SET PATH to specify the Visual FoxPro path.

If you create a file and don't specify where to place it, the file is placed in the default Visual FoxPro directory.

When you quit Visual FoxPro, you are returned to Windows. When you exit Windows, you are returned to the drive and directory that you started Windows from.

> **Tip** SYS(5) returns the default drive. SYS(2003) returns the default directory with no drive designator. SYS(5) + SYS(2003) returns the default drive and the directory.

You can change the default drive to drive A using either of the following commands:

```
SET DEFAULT TO A
SET DEFAULT TO A:
```

You can specify a specific directory:

```
SET DEFAULT TO A:\sales
SET DEFAULT TO C:\sales\data
```

You can specify a child directory. If the root directory on drive C is the default Visual FoxPro directory, issue the following command to change the default directory to C:\Sales:

```
SET DEFAULT TO sales
```

You can use MS-DOS shorthand notation. If the current directory is C:\Sales\Data, issue the following command to make the root directory the default directory:

```
SET DEFAULT TO \
```

You can also move the default directory one directory toward the root directory with the following command:

```
SET DEFAULT TO ..
```

See Also

CD | CHDIR, MD | MKDIR, RD | RMDIR, SET PATH, SYS(5) – Default Drive, SYS(2003) – Current Directory

SET DELETED Command

Specifies whether Visual FoxPro processes records marked for deletion and whether they are available for use in other commands.

Syntax

SET DELETED ON | OFF

Arguments

ON

Specifies that commands which operate on records (including records in related tables) using a scope ignore records marked for deletion.

OFF

(Default) Specifies that records marked for deletion can be accessed by commands that operate on records (including records in related tables) using a scope.

Remarks

Queries that use DELETED( ) to test the status of records can be optimized using Rushmore technology if the table is indexed on DELETED( ).

For more information on optimizing queries, see "Understanding Rushmore Technology" in Chapter 15, "Optimizing Applications," in the *Microsoft Visual FoxPro 6.0 Programmer's Guide*.

You can mark records for deletion by issuing DELETE – SQL or DELETE, or by choosing Delete Records... from the Table menu from within a Browse or Edit window.

You can recall records by issuing RECALL or by choosing Recall Records... from the Table menu from within a Browse or Edit window.

> **Important** SET DELETED is ignored if the default scope for the command is the current record or you include a scope of a single record. INDEX and REINDEX always ignore SET DELETED and index all records in the table.

SET DELETED is scoped to the current data session.

See Also

DELETE, DELETE – SQL, DELETED( ), PACK, RECALL, SET DATASESSION

SET DELIMITERS Command

Included for backward compatibility. Use the Format Property instead.

SET DEVELOPMENT Command

Causes Visual FoxPro to compare the creation date and time of a program with those of its compiled object file when the program is run.

Syntax

SET DEVELOPMENT ON | OFF

Arguments

ON

> (Default) Specifies that Visual FoxPro recompile the source program before it executes if it is more current than its compiled object program. This option ensures that the most current version of a program is executed.

OFF

> Specifies that Visual FoxPro not compare the source and compiled versions of the program. If SET DEVELOPMENT is set to OFF, you might not always be executing the most current version of a program.

Remarks

The most current version of a program modified with the Visual FoxPro editor invoked with MODIFY COMMAND is always executed, regardless of the SET DEVELOPMENT setting.

SET DEVELOPMENT needs to be set to ON only when programs are modified outside of Visual FoxPro. Using an external editor — for example, a terminate-and-stay-resident (TSR) editor — may require you to issue CLEAR PROGRAM before you execute the modified program. For more information, see the CLEAR PROGRAM Command, earlier in this language reference. Use SET DEVELOPMENT OFF for optimum performance.

When SET DEVELOPMENT is set to ON, program execution can be canceled during a READ. The Cancel command on the Program menu is available when SET DEVELOPMENT is ON and a READ is active. Choosing Cancel during the READ cancels program execution. If SET DEVELOPMENT is set to OFF, the Cancel command on the Program menu is unavailable during a READ.

SET DEVELOPMENT also determines whether the Trace window is opened when an error occurs within a Form that is running. If SET DEVELOPMENT is ON, the Trace window is opened with the program line that caused the error selected. If SET DEVELOPMENT is OFF, the Trace window is not opened when an error occurs in a Form.

See Also

COMPILE, MODIFY COMMAND, MODIFY FILE

SET DEVICE Command

Directs output from @ ... SAY to the screen, a printer, or a file.

Syntax

SET DEVICE TO SCREEN | TO PRINTER [PROMPT] | TO FILE *FileName*

Arguments

TO SCREEN
Directs @ ... SAY output to the main Visual FoxPro window or to the active user-defined window.

TO PRINTER [PROMPT]
Directs @ ... SAY output to the printer. A page eject is issued when the coordinates in @ ... SAY specify a location on the page higher than the location specified by the coordinates in the previous @ ... SAY.

You can include the optional PROMPT clause to display a dialog box before printing starts. In this dialog box, the user can adjust printer settings, including the number of copies to print and page numbers. The currently installed printer driver determines which printer settings the user can adjust. Place PROMPT immediately after TO PRINTER.

TO FILE *FileName*
Specifies a file to which @ ... SAY sends output.

Remarks

@ ... SAY output can be sent to the main Visual FoxPro window, the active user-defined window, the printer, or a file.

See Also

SYS(101) – Device Setting

SET DISPLAY Command

Enables you to change the current display mode on monitors that support different modes.

Syntax

SET DISPLAY TO CGA | EGA25 | EGA43 | VGA25 | VGA50

Arguments

CGA
>   Switches the font size for the main Visual FoxPro window to 9-point.

EGA25
>   Switches the font size for the main Visual FoxPro window to 9-point and the main Visual FoxPro window size to 25 lines.

EGA43
>   Switches the font size for the main Visual FoxPro window to 7-point and the main Visual FoxPro window size to 50 lines.

VGA25
>   Switches the font size for the main Visual FoxPro window to 9-point and the main Visual FoxPro window size to 25 lines.

VGA50
>   Switches the Visual FoxPro window to a size of 50 lines with a 7-point font size.

Remarks

SET DISPLAY changes the font size for the main Visual FoxPro window. The size of the main Visual FoxPro window is increased if necessary to accommodate the number of lines required by the option you specify. If the graphical status bar appears when you issue SET DISPLAY, it is turned off.

Visual FoxPro generates an error message if an option isn't supported by your video hardware.

The SET MESSAGE line is reset to the last line of the main Visual FoxPro window whenever SET DISPLAY is issued.

See Also

SET MESSAGE, SYS(2006) – Current Graphics Card

SET DOHISTORY Command

Included for backward compatibility. Use the Trace Window instead.

SetData Method

Places data in the OLE drag-and-drop DataObject. Available at run time only.

Syntax

oDataObject.SetData(*eData* [, *nFormat* | *cFormat*])

Arguments

eData

Specifies the data placed on the DataObject. If you omit the optional *nFormat* and *cFormat* arguments, Visual FoxPro places the data on the DataObject in the CF_TEXT and CFSTR_OLEVARIANT formats. If *eData* is an array, precede *eData* with an ampersand (@). An array is placed on the DataObject in the CFSTR_OLEVARIANTARRAY format. An error is generated if *eData* is an object reference or a general field, or the array contains an object reference.

nFormat | *cFormat*

Specifies the format of the data placed on the DataObject. The following table lists the values for some common data formats with a description of each format. You can specify a user-defined format with *cFormat*. In this case, *eData* must be of character type or a binary type created with CREATEBINARY( ).

Data format*	cFormat	*nFormat*	Description
CF_TEXT	1	Text format.
CF_OEMTEXT	7	Text format containing characters in the OEM character set.
CF_UNICODETEXT	13	Unicode text format, available only under Windows NT.
CF_FILES or CF_HDROP	15	A handle that identifies a list of files, such as a set of files dragged from the Windows Explorer.
CFSTR_OLEVARIANTARRAY	"OLE Variant Array"	An array. Multiple values can be transferred in a single drag-and-drop operation with this format.
		For example, this format can be used to drag a set of items in a list box to another list box. *(continued)*

(continued)

Data format* | cFormat	nFormat	Description
CFSTR_OLEVARIANT	"OLE Variant"	A variant. All data types in Visual FoxPro are represented as variants. This format can be used to drag and drop Visual FoxPro data without losing the data type.
CFSTR_VFPSOURCEOBJECT	"VFP Source Object"	A reference to the Visual FoxPro drag source object.

* Defined in FOXPRO.H.

Remarks

The SetData method can only be executed in the OLEStartDrag event.

Applies To

DataObject Object

See Also

ClearData Method, CREATEBINARY( ), GetData Method, GetFormat Method, OLE Drag-and-Drop Overview, OLEStartDrag Event, SetFormat Method

SET ECHO Command

Opens the Trace window for program debugging. Included for backward compatibility. Use the Trace window instead.

Syntax

SET ECHO ON | OFF

Arguments

ON

Displays the source code for the program that is executing in the Trace window. The line currently executing is highlighted.

OFF

(Default) Closes the Trace window in FoxPro versions earlier than 2.0. From within a program, the Trace window can be closed with DEACTIVATE WINDOW TRACE.

Remarks

You can also use the Trace window to set breakpoints, which suspend program execution.

For more information about the Trace window, see "Trace Window" in Help, and Chapter 14, "Testing and Debugging Applications," in the *Microsoft Visual FoxPro 6.0 Programmer's Guide*.

See Also

RESUME, SET STEP, SUSPEND

SET ESCAPE Command

Determines whether pressing the ESC key interrupts program and command execution.

Syntax

SET ESCAPE ON | OFF

Arguments

ON

(Default) Allows command and program execution to be interrupted when the user presses ESC.

If the user presses ESC during the execution of a command or program while the insertion point is in the Command window, the following message appears:

*** INTERRUPTED ***

If the user presses ESC during command or program execution, processing completes at the current program line, and an alert appears with the following three options:

- (Default) Choose Cancel to immediately stop program execution and return to the Command window.

- Choose Suspend to pause program execution and return to the Command window. This option is useful for debugging a program. Choosing Resume from the Program menu or issuing RESUME in the Command window restarts the program at the line at which it was paused.

- Choose Ignore to continue program execution at the line at which it was paused.

OFF

Prevents command and program execution from being interrupted when the user presses ESC.

See Also

ON ESCAPE, ON KEY LABEL

SET EVENTLIST Command

Specifies events to track in the Debug Output Window or in a file specified with SET EVENTTRACKING.

Syntax

SET EVENTLIST TO [*EventName1* [, *EventName2* ...] [ADDITIVE]]

Arguments

EventName1 [, *EventName2* ...]
> Specifies the names of the events to track. You can include any number of event names separated by commas.

ADDITIVE
> Specifies that the events *EventName1*, *EventName2* ... are added to the set of events currently being tracked. If ADDITIVE is omitted, only the events *EventName1*, *EventName2* ... are tracked.

Remarks

Issue SET EVENTLIST TO without any event names to remove all events from the set of events being tracked. You can also specify events to track in the Event Tracking dialog box.

See Also

SET DEBUGOUT, SET EVENTTRACKING

SET EVENTTRACKING Command

Turns event tracking on or off or specifies a text file to which event tracking information is directed.

Syntax

SET EVENTTRACKING ON | OFF | PROMPT
TO [*FileName* [ADDITIVE]]

Arguments

ON
> Turns event tracking on and directs event tracking information to the text file specified with *FileName*.

OFF
> Turns event tracking off and stops directing event tracking information to the text file.

PROMPT

Displays the Event Tracking dialog box, allowing the user to specify which events are tracked.

TO *FileName*

Specifies the name of a text file to which event tracking information is directed. SET EVENTTRACKING must be ON to direct event tracking information to a text file. Issue SET EVENTTRACKING TO without a file name to close the text file.

If the file you specify doesn't exist, Microsoft Visual FoxPro automatically creates and opens it.

ADDITIVE

Appends the event tracking information to the end of the text file specified with *FileName*. If you omit ADDITIVE, the event tracking information replaces the contents of the text file.

Remarks

Use SET EVENTLIST or the Event Tracking dialog box to specify the events that are tracked.

See Also

SET COVERAGE, SET EVENTLIST

SET EXACT Command

Specifies the rules Visual FoxPro uses when comparing two strings of different lengths.

Syntax

SET EXACT ON | OFF

Arguments

ON

Specifies that expressions must match character for character to be equivalent. Any trailing blanks in the expressions are ignored for the comparison. For the comparison, the shorter of the two expressions is padded on the right with blanks to match the length of the longer expression.

OFF

(Default) Specifies that, to be equivalent, expressions must match character for character until the end of the expression on the right side is reached.

Remarks

The SET EXACT setting has no effect if both strings are the same length.

String Comparisons

Visual FoxPro has two relational operators that test for equality. The = operator performs a comparison between two values of the same type. This operator is suited for comparing character, numeric, date, and logical data.

However, when you compare character expressions with the = operator, the results might not be exactly what you expect. Character expressions are compared character for character from left to right until one of the expressions isn't equal to the other, or until the end of the expression on the right side of the = operator is reached (SET EXACT OFF), or until the ends of both expressions are reached (SET EXACT ON).

The == operator can be used when an exact comparison of character data is needed. If two character expressions are compared with the == operator, the expressions on both sides of the == operator must contain exactly the same characters, including blanks, to be considered equal. The SET EXACT setting is ignored when character strings are compared using ==.

The following table shows how the choice of operator and the SET EXACT setting affect comparisons. (An underscore represents a blank space.)

Comparison	= EXACT OFF	= EXACT ON	== EXACT ON or OFF
"abc" = "abc"	Match	Match	Match
"ab" = "abc"	No match	No match	No match
"abc" = "ab"	Match	No match	No match
"abc" = "ab_"	No match	No match	No match
"ab" = "ab_"	No match	Match	No match
"ab_" = "ab"	Match	Match	No match
"" = "ab"	No match	No match	No match
"ab" = ""	Match	No match	No match
"_" = ""	Match	Match	No match
"" = "_"	No match	Match	No match
TRIM("_") = ""	Match	Match	Match
"" = TRIM("_")	Match	Match	Match

SET EXACT is scoped to the current data session.

See Also

SET ANSI

SET EXCLUSIVE Command

Specifies whether Visual FoxPro opens table files for exclusive or shared use on a network.

Syntax

SET EXCLUSIVE ON | OFF

Arguments

ON

(The default for the global data session.) Limits accessibility of a table opened on a network to the user who opened it. The table isn't accessible to other users on the network. Unlike FLOCK( ), SET EXCLUSIVE ON also prevents all other users from having read-only access. A file can also be opened on a network for exclusive use by including the EXCLUSIVE clause with the USE command. It isn't necessary to perform record or file locking on a table opened for exclusive use.

Opening a table for exclusive use ensures that the file can't be changed by other users. For some commands, execution isn't possible until a table is opened for exclusive use. These commands are INSERT, INSERT BLANK, MODIFY STRUCTURE, PACK, REINDEX, and ZAP.

OFF

(The default for a private data session.) Allows a table opened on a network to be shared and modified by any user on the network.

For additional information about record and file locking and sharing tables on a network, see Chapter 17, "Programming for Shared Access," in the *Microsoft Visual FoxPro 6.0 Programmer's Guide*.

Remarks

Changing the setting of SET EXCLUSIVE doesn't change the status of previously opened tables. For example, if a table is opened with SET EXCLUSIVE set to ON, and SET EXCLUSIVE is later changed to OFF, the table retains its exclusive-use status.

SET EXCLUSIVE is scoped to the current data session.

See Also

FLOCK( ), RLOCK( ), SET DATASESSION, USE

SET FDOW Command

Specifies the first day of the week.

Syntax

SET FDOW TO [*nExpression*]

Arguments

nExpression

Specifies the first day of the week. The following table lists the values *nExpression* can assume and the corresponding first day of the week.

nExpression	Day of the week
1	Sunday
2	Monday
3	Tuesday
4	Wednesday
5	Thursday
6	Friday
7	Saturday

If you omit *nExpression*, the first day of the week is reset to Sunday (1).

Remarks

The first day of the week can also be set with the Week Starts On list box in the Regional tab of the Options dialog.

Example

```
STORE SET('FDOW') TO gnFdow  && Save current value
SET FDOW TO 1  && Sets first day of the week to Sunday, the default
SET FDOW TO 7  && Sets first day of the week to Saturday
SET FDOW TO &gnFdow  && Restore original day
```

See Also

CDOW( ), DAY( ), DOW( ), SET FWEEK, SYS( ) Functions Overview, WEEK( )

SET FIELDS Command

Specifies which fields in a table can be accessed.

Syntax

SET FIELDS ON | OFF | LOCAL | GLOBAL

– or –

SET FIELDS TO [[*FieldName1* [, *FieldName2* ...]]
    | ALL [LIKE *Skeleton* | EXCEPT *Skeleton*]]

Arguments

ON
> Specifies that only the fields in the field list can be accessed.

OFF
> (Default) Specifies that all the fields in the current table can be accessed.

LOCAL
> Specifies that only the fields in the current work area listed in the fields list can be accessed.

GLOBAL
> Specifies that all fields in the field list, including fields in other work areas, can be accessed.
>
> SET FIELDS GLOBAL lets you access fields in other work areas without issuing SET COMPATIBLE TO DB4.

TO [*FieldName1* [, *FieldName2* ...]]
> Specifies the names of fields that can be accessed in the current table. You must include an alias with the field name in the following cases:
>
> - When the field is in a table that is open in a work area other than the currently selected work area.
>
> - When the field names are the same in two or more tables.
>
> You can include fields from tables that are open in other work areas if the fields are prefaced with their table aliases. However, these fields cannot be accessed unless you issue SET FIELDS GLOBAL or SET COMPATIBLE DB4.
>
> The field list can contain statements for creating calculated fields. A calculated field contains read-only data created with an expression. This expression can take any form, but it must be a valid FoxPro expression. Calculated fields cannot be accessed unless you issue SET FIELDS GLOBAL or SET COMPATIBLE DB4.

The format of the statement you use to create a calculated field is:

```
<calculated field name> = <expr>
```

This example creates a calculated field called LOCATION:

```
CLOSE DATABASES
USE customer
SET FIELDS TO LOCATION = ALLTRIM(city) + ', ' + state
```

CITY and STATE are the names of fields from the selected table.

ALL

Allows access to all the fields in the current table.

ALL LIKE *Skeleton* | **EXCEPT** *Skeleton*

You can selectively access fields by including the LIKE or EXCEPT clause or both. If you include LIKE *Skeleton*, you can access fields that match *Skeleton*. If you include EXCEPT *Skeleton*, you can access all fields except those that match *Skeleton*.

The skeleton *Skeleton* supports wildcards such as * and ?. For example, to access fields that begin with the letters A and P, issue the following:

```
SET FIELDS TO ALL LIKE A*,P*
```

The LIKE clause can be combined with the EXCEPT clause:

```
SET FIELDS TO ALL LIKE A*,P* EXCEPT PARTNO*
```

Remarks

SET FIELDS TO is additive — issuing SET FIELDS TO with a field list adds the specified fields to those that are currently accessible.

Issuing SET FIELDS TO implicitly performs SET FIELDS ON. Issuing SET FIELDS TO without any additional arguments implicitly performs SET FIELDS OFF. Issue SET FIELDS TO without including either a field list or ALL to remove all fields from the field list for the current table.

SET FIELDS is scoped to the current data session.

See Also

SET FILTER, SET DATASESSION

SET FILTER Command

Specifies a condition that records in the current table must meet to be accessible.

Syntax

SET FILTER TO [*lExpression*]

Arguments

lExpression

Specifies the condition that records must satisfy.

If the current table is indexed on a field or fields specified in *lExpression*, Visual FoxPro Rushmore technology will optimize queries based on the field or fields.

Remarks

Once SET FILTER is issued, only the records that satisfy the condition specified by the logical expression *lExpression* are available in the table. All commands that access the table respect the SET FILTER condition. A separate filter can be set for every open table.

The condition specified by SET FILTER isn't evaluated until the record pointer is moved in the table.

Issuing SET FILTER TO without *lExpression* turns off the filter for the current table.

SELECT – SQL does not respect the current filter condition.

See Also

FILTER( ), SELECT – SQL

SET FIXED Command

Specifies if the number of decimal places used in the display of numeric data is fixed.

Syntax

SET FIXED ON | OFF

Arguments

ON

Uses the SET DECIMALS setting to determine the number of decimal places displayed in results. The default number of decimal places is 2.

OFF

(Default) Allows the number of decimal places displayed in results to depend on the specific constants, variables, and operators used in a numeric expression. The contents of fields are displayed with the declared number of decimal places.

Remarks

SET FIXED is scoped to the current data session.

See Also

SET DECIMALS, SET DATASESSION

SET FORMAT Command

Included for backward compatibility. Use the Format Property instead.

SET FULLPATH Command

Specifies if CDX( ), DBF( ), MDX( ), and NDX( ) return the path in a file name.

Syntax

SET FULLPATH ON | OFF

Arguments

ON

> (Default) Specifies that CDX( ), DBF( ), MDX( ), and NDX( ) return the drive designator, path, and file name.

OFF

> Specifies that only the drive designator and file name are returned.

See Also

CDX( ), DBF( ), MDX( ), NDX( )

SET FUNCTION Command

Assigns an expression (keyboard macro) to a function key or key combination.

Syntax

SET FUNCTION *nFunctionKeyNumber* | *KeyLabelName* TO [*eExpression*]

Arguments

nFunctionKeyNumber

> Specifies the number of the function key assigned to the macro. For example, use SET FUNCTION 2 to specify the F2 function key.

KeyLabelName

> Specifies a key combination, including a function key, to which to assign the macro. Visual FoxPro supports key combinations that include function keys. You can use the CTRL or SHIFT key in combination with a function key to create additional programmable keys. For a list of key label expressions, see the ON KEY LABEL Command, earlier in this language reference.

TO [*eExpression*]
>Specifies the series of keystrokes stored to the function key or key combination. Visual FoxPro interprets a semicolon (;) in the expression as a carriage return.

>Function key definitions can be cleared with CLEAR MACROS.

See Also

CLEAR MACROS, FKLABEL( ), FKMAX( ), ON KEY LABEL

SET FWEEK Command

Specifies the requirements for the first week of the year.

Syntax

SET FWEEK TO [*nExpression*]

Arguments

nExpression
>Specifies a value which determines the requirements for the first week of the year. The following table lists the values *nExpression* can assume and the corresponding requirements for the first week of the year:

nExpression	First week requirement
1	(Default) The first week contains January 1st.
2	The larger half (four days) of the first week is in the current year.
3	The first week has seven days.

>If you omit *nExpression*, the first week of the year is reset to 1 (the first week contains January 1st).

Remarks

The first week of the year can also be set with the First Week of Year list box in the Regional tab of the Options dialog.

Example

```
STORE SET('FWEEK') TO gnFweek  && Save current value
SET FWEEK TO 1  && First week contains January 1st
SET FWEEK TO 3  && First week has seven days
SET FWEEK TO &gnFweek  && Restore original setting
```

See Also

CDOW( ), DAY( ), DOW( ), SET FDOW, SYS( ) Functions Overview, WEEK( )

SetFormat Method

Places a data format in the OLE drag-and-drop DataObject. Available at run time only.

Syntax

oDataObject.SetFormat(*nFormat* | *cFormat*)

Arguments

nFormat | *cFormat*
> Specifies the format of the data placed on the DataObject. The following table lists the values for some common data formats with a description of each format. You can also create your own format by specifying a unique character string for *cFormat*.

Data format*	cFormat	*nFormat*	Description
CF_TEXT	1	Text format.
CF_OEMTEXT	7	Text format containing characters in the OEM character set.
CF_UNICODETEXT	13	Unicode text format, available only under Windows NT.
CF_FILES or CF_HDROP	15	A handle that identifies a list of files, such as a set of files dragged from the Windows Explorer.
CFSTR_OLEVARIANTARRAY	"OLE Variant Array"	An array. Multiple values can be transferred in a single drag-and-drop operation with this format.
		For example, this format can be used to drag a set of items in a list box to another list box.
CFSTR_OLEVARIANT	"OLE Variant"	A variant. All data types in Visual FoxPro are represented as variants. This format can be used to drag and drop Visual FoxPro data without losing the data type.
CFSTR_VFPSOURCEOBJECT	"VFP Source Object"	A reference to the Visual FoxPro drag source object.

* Defined in FOXPRO.H.

Remarks

You can place a data format in the DataObject before placing the corresponding data on the DataObject. If you place a data format in the DataObject without corresponding data and invoke the GetData method in the OLEDragDrop event, the OLESetData event is executed for the drag source. The drag source can then place the data on the DataObject with the SetData method in the OLESetData event.

OLE drag-and-drop performance can be improved by placing just the data formats on the DataObject when a large amount of data is placed on the DataObject, when using data formats that aren't natively supported by Visual FoxPro, or when using a large number of formats.

The SetFormat method can only be executed in the OLEStartDrag and OLESetData events.

Applies To

DataObject Object

See Also

ClearData Method, GetData Method, GetFormat Method, OLE Drag-and-Drop Overview, OLEDragDrop Event, OLESetData Event, OLEStartDrag Event, SetData Method

SET HEADINGS Command

Determines whether column headings are displayed for fields and whether file information is included when TYPE is issued to display the contents of a file.

Syntax

SET HEADINGS ON | OFF

Arguments

ON

(Default) Specifies that the field names are displayed.

If TYPE is issued to display the contents of a file, Visual FoxPro inserts a formfeed, the path and name of the file, and the date at the beginning of the displayed output.

OFF

Specifies that the field names are not displayed.

If TYPE is issued to display the contents of a file, Visual FoxPro does not insert additional information about the file at the beginning of the displayed output.

Remarks

SET HEADINGS specifies whether a field name appears as a column heading above each field in the output of AVERAGE, CALCULATE, DISPLAY, LIST, and SUM.

See Also

AVERAGE, CALCULATE, DISPLAY, LIST, SUM, TYPE

SET HELP Command

Enables or disables Microsoft Visual FoxPro online Help or specifies a Help file.

Syntax

SET HELP ON | OFF

– or –

SET HELP TO [*FileName*]

Arguments

ON

(Default) Displays the Help window when you press F1 or issue HELP in the Command window.

OFF

Makes Visual FoxPro online Help unavailable.

TO [*FileName*]

Specifies a Help file that is displayed when you press F1 or issue HELP. You can specify a .Dbf-style Help file, a Winhelp (.hlp) file, or an HTML (.chm) help file.

If you issue SET HELP TO without including a file name, Visual FoxPro looks for the MSDN Help file Msdnvs98.col. In Visual FoxPro 6.0, issuing SET HELP TO with a Help file name doesn't close any open Help windows.

Remarks

Use SET HELP to provide a tailored online Help file within a custom application or to switch between the different Help files in Visual FoxPro. For more information, see Part 7, "Creating Help Files," in the *Microsoft Visual FoxPro 6.0 Programmer's Guide*.

If you install the MSDN (Microsoft Developer's Network) library when you install Visual FoxPro, the default help file is the MSDN Help file Msdnvs98.col.

If you perform a complete installation of the MSDN (Microsoft Developer's Network) library, or you perform a custom installation of the MSDN library and you specify to install the Visual FoxPro documentation, the Visual FoxPro Help file, Foxhelp.chm, is installed.

If you don't install the MSDN library, no help file is installed.

You can also use the **Help File** option on the File Locations tab of the Options dialog box to interactively specify a Help file.

See Also

HELP, SET HELPFILTER, SET TOPIC

SET HELPFILTER Command

Enables Visual FoxPro to display a subset of .dbf-style Help topics in the Help window.

Syntax

SET HELPFILTER [AUTOMATIC] TO [*lExpression*]

Arguments

AUTOMATIC
Automatically removes the criteria specified with SET HELPFILTER after the Help window is closed. Including AUTOMATIC is identical to issuing SET HELPFILTER TO immediately after the Help window is closed. You must place AUTOMATIC directly before TO *lExpression*.

lExpression
Specifies a logical expression used to filter Help topics. Only topics for which *lExpression* evaluates to true (.T.) are displayed. *lExpression* typically contains a name of a field in the help table.

Remarks

You can only set a filter for .dbf-style Help only. You cannot set a filter for graphical Help. For more information, see Part 7, "Creating Help Files," in the *Microsoft Visual FoxPro 6.0 Programmer's Guide*.

See Also

HELP, SET HELP, SET TOPIC

SET HOURS Command

Sets the system clock to a 12- or 24-hour time format.

Syntax

SET HOURS TO [12 | 24]

Arguments

TO 12
(Default) Specifies a 12-hour format.

TO 24
Specifies a 24-hour format.

Remarks

Use SET HOURS TO without 12 or 24 to return to the default 12-hour format.

TIME( ) always returns a value in 24-hour format and isn't affected by SET HOURS. The value returned by DATETIME( ) is determined by the current SET HOURS setting.

SET HOURS is scoped to the current data session.

See Also

DATETIME( ), SECONDS( ), SET CLOCK, SET SYSFORMATS, TIME( )

SET INDEX Command

Opens one or more index files for use with the current table.

Syntax

SET INDEX TO [*IndexFileList* | ?]
    [ORDER *nIndexNumber* | *IDXIndexFileName*
    | [TAG] *TagName* [OF *CDXFileName*] [ASCENDING | DESCENDING]]
    [ADDITIVE]

Arguments

IndexFileList

Specifies one or more index files to open. Use commas to separate multiple index files in the list. The index file list can contain any combination of .idx and .cdx index file names; you don't have to include the file name extensions unless another .idx or .cdx file exists with the same name.

The first index file in the index file list becomes the controlling index file, which controls how records are accessed and displayed. The records are displayed and accessed in physical record order if the first index file is a .cdx file and SET ORDER TO TAG has not been issued.

?

Displays the Open dialog box from which you can open a single .idx file.

ORDER *nIndexNumber*

Specifies a controlling index file or tag. The numeric expression *nIndexNumber* specifies the index files as they appear in the index file list.

.Idx files are numbered first in the order in which they appear in the index file list. Tags in the structural .cdx file (if one exists) are numbered in the order in which the tags were created. Finally, tags in any independent .cdx files are numbered in the order in which they were created. See the SET ORDER Command, later in this language reference, for a further discussion of the numbering of index files and tags.

If *nIndexNumber* is 0, records in the table are displayed and accessed in physical record order, but the index files remain open. ORDER 0 enables you to update open index files while accessing records in physical order. ORDER with no additional arguments is identical to ORDER 0.

Visual FoxPro generates an error message if *nIndexNumber* is greater than the number of .idx files and .cdx file tags.

ORDER *IDXIndexFileName*
Specifies an .idx file as the controlling index file.

ORDER [TAG] *TagName* [OF *CDXFileName*]
Specifies a tag (*TagName*) of a .cdx file to be the controlling tag. The tag name can be from the structural .cdx file or any open independent .cdx file.

If tags with the same name exist in open independent .cdx files, use OF *CDXFileName* to specify the .cdx file the tag is in.

ASCENDING | DESCENDING
Specifies whether table records are displayed and accessed in ascending or descending order. The index files or tags aren't changed in any way; only the order in which the records are displayed and accessed is changed. Include the ASCENDING or DESCENDING clause immediately after the ORDER clause.

ADDITIVE
Specifies that previously opened index files, except for a structural compound index, are left open when you issue SET INDEX to open an additional index file or files for a table. Without ADDITIVE, the previously opened files would be closed.

Remarks

Records in a table that has an index file or files open can be displayed and accessed in an order determined by one of the index files. Both single index (.idx) and compound (.cdx) index files can be opened with SET INDEX. If a table has a structural .cdx file, the file is opened automatically when the table is opened.

Only one .idx file (the controlling index file) or tag from a .cdx file (the controlling tag) controls the order in which records in the table are displayed or accessed. Certain commands (SEEK, for example) use the controlling index file or tag to search for records.

Issuing SET INDEX TO without additional arguments closes all open index files (except a structural .cdx file) in the current work area.

See Also

CLOSE INDEXES, INDEX, SET ORDER, USE

SET INTENSITY Command

Included for backward compatibility. Use SET COLOR OF SCHEME instead.

SET KEY Command

Specifies access to a range of records based on their index keys.

Syntax

SET KEY TO [*eExpression1* | RANGE *eExpression2* [, *eExpression3*]]
    [IN *cTableAlias* | *nWorkArea*]

Arguments

eExpression1
> Allows access to a set of records with identical index keys. *eExpression1* is a single index key value. All records with index keys that match *eExpression1* are accessible.

RANGE *eExpression2* [, *eExpression3*]
> Allows access to a set of records with index keys that fall within a range of index key values. *eExpression2* allows access to records with index keys equal to or greater than *eExpression2*. *eExpression3* (preceded by a comma) allows access to records with index keys equal to or less than *eExpression3*. Including both *eExpression2* and *eExpression3* (separated by a comma) allows access to records with index keys equal to or greater than *eExpression2* and equal to or less than the *eExpression3*.
>
> For example, the CUSTOMER table includes a character field containing postal codes. If the table is indexed on the postal code field, you can specify a range of postal codes with SET KEY.
>
> In the following example, only records with postal codes falling within the range of 40000 to 43999 appear in a Browse window:

```
CLOSE DATABASES
USE customer
SET ORDER TO postalcode
SET KEY TO RANGE '40000', '43999'
BROWSE
```

IN *cTableAlias* | *nWorkArea*
> Allows access to a range of records for a table open in a specific work area. *cTableAlias* specifies the work area alias and *nWorkArea* specifies the work area number. If no table has the alias you specify, Visual FoxPro generates an error message. If you omit the work area alias and number, SET KEY operates on the table in the currently selected work area.

Remarks

Use SET KEY to limit the range of records you can access in a table. The table must be indexed, and the index key value or values you include must be the same data type as the index expression of the master index file or master tag.

Issue SET KEY TO without any additional arguments to restore access to all records in the table.

See Also

INDEX, KEY( ), SET FILTER

SET KEYCOMP Command

Controls Visual FoxPro keystroke navigation.

Syntax

SET KEYCOMP TO DOS | WINDOWS

Remarks

SET KEYCOMP determines the keystrokes and keystroke combinations you use to move through the Visual FoxPro interface by accessing controls such as buttons, list boxes, menus, and so on. The effect of SET KEYCOMP depends on the control.

Use SET KEYCOMP when you want to use keystrokes that are familiar to you.

To navigate in Microsoft Windows using MS-DOS keystrokes, issue the following:

```
SET KEYCOMP TO DOS
```

You can specify the DOS or WINDOWS (default) option.

You can specify a startup SET KEYCOMP setting in your Visual FoxPro configuration file, Config.fpw. For example, the following line, when placed in your configuration file, has the effect of SET KEYCOMP TO DOS:

```
KEYCOMP = DOS
```

This section describes how the DOS and WINDOWS options affect Visual FoxPro.

Default buttons

DOS	The default button in a dialog box has the focus; its appearance does not change. It is chosen when you press CTRL+ENTER.
WINDOWS	The default button in a dialog box can change appearance when you move among controls. It can be dimmed, or it has the focus (is surrounded by a bold border) to indicate it is the current default. It is chosen when you press ENTER. Pressing ENTER always performs the default button's action.
	For an illustration of how the default button changes appearance in a dialog box, issue SET KEYCOMP TO WINDOWS, choose Open from the File menu, and then press TAB to move through the Open dialog box.

Access keys

DOS	An access key for a control is a single key. If you aren't in a control that has keyboard steering (a combo box or a list box), you can press the access key to choose it.
WINDOWS	An access key for a control can be a single key or a key combination. If the current control has keyboard steering (a combo box or a list box), you can press ALT plus the access key to choose the control. To choose other controls, you can press the access key or ALT plus the access key.

Combo boxes

DOS	When a combo box has the focus, you can open it by pressing ENTER or the SPACEBAR. Keyboard steering within a combo box is not available until the combo box is open.
WINDOWS	When a combo box has the focus, you can open it by pressing the SPACEBAR, ALT+UP ARROW, or ALT+DOWN ARROW. Keyboard steering within a combo box is available when the combo box has the focus, and when it is open. For example, a selected combo box contains a list of available drives. If drives A, B, and C are available and drive B is currently displayed, you can choose drive C without opening the combo box by pressing C or the DOWN ARROW key. Drive C is chosen and you move to the next control.

Option buttons

DOS	Press the TAB key when a group of option buttons is selected to move among the option buttons.
WINDOWS	Press the TAB key when a group of option buttons is selected to move from the option buttons to the next control. To move among a set of option buttons, press the UP ARROW and DOWN ARROW keys.

Browse window

DOS	A field is not selected upon entry into the field.
WINDOWS	A field is automatically selected upon entry into the field.

See Also

SET COMPATIBLE

SET LIBRARY Command

Opens an external API (application programming interface) library file.

Syntax

SET LIBRARY TO [*FileName* [ADDITIVE]]

Arguments

FileName
Specifies the file name of the API library or procedure file to open.

Visual FoxPro assume an .fll extension for libraries. If the library has an .fll extension, you don't have to include the extension with the file name. If a library has an extension other than .fll, you must include the extension with the file name.

Important   When using SET LIBRARY, be aware of the following:

- You cannot use API libraries built for one platform on another platform. For example, libraries created for FoxPro for MS-DOS cannot be used in Visual FoxPro; libraries created for Visual FoxPro cannot be used in FoxPro for MS-DOS.

- You cannot use API libraries built for one version on another version. For example, you cannot use libraries built for FoxPro version 2.6 in Visual FoxPro. You must recompile and link.

Visual FoxPro assumes a .prg extension for a procedure file.

When you execute a procedure with DO *ProcedureName*, Visual FoxPro searches for the procedure in the following files in this order:

1. The file containing DO *ProcedureName*.

2. A procedure file opened with SET PROCEDURE (if one is set).

3. The programs in the execution chain. Visual FoxPro searches program files beginning with the most recently executed program and continuing back to the first executed program.

4. A procedure file opened with SET LIBRARY (if one is set).

5. A stand-alone program file. If Visual FoxPro finds a program file with the same name as the file name specified with DO, the program is executed. If it doesn't find a matching program file name, Visual FoxPro generates an error message.

ADDITIVE
Opens additional API libraries. Include ADDITIVE after the file name in successive SET LIBRARY commands.

Visual FoxPro ignores ADDITIVE when you use SET LIBRARY to open a procedure file.

Remarks

Use SET LIBRARY to open external Application Program Interface (API) libraries or a procedure file.

API routine libraries extend the capabilities of the Visual FoxPro language and user interface. Once an external API library is opened, you can use the API functions as if they were Visual FoxPro functions. Use DISPLAY STATUS or LIST STATUS to display the library's available functions.

You can use existing API libraries or create your own API libraries.

In Visual FoxPro, the preferred way to register functions in shared libraries is to use the DECLARE – DLL command.

To remove all API libraries from memory, use SET LIBRARY TO without including *FileName* or ADDITIVE. To remove an individual library from memory, use RELEASE LIBRARY *LibraryName*.

If you specify a procedure file, the procedures within the procedure file are made available to all programs and are also available interactively through the Command window.

> **Note** The ability of Visual FoxPro to open a procedure file with SET LIBRARY provides compatibility with dBASE IV. Using SET LIBRARY to open a procedure file will close all open API libraries. Using SET LIBRARY to open API libraries will close a procedure file opened with SET LIBRARY. Use SET PROCEDURE to open a procedure file and prevent API libraries from being closed.

For additional information about procedure files, see the PROCEDURE and SET PROCEDURE Commands, in this language reference.

See Also

CALL, DISPLAY STATUS, LIST, LOAD, RELEASE

SET LOCK Command

Enables or disables automatic file locking in certain commands.

Syntax

SET LOCK ON | OFF

Arguments

ON

Specifies that the commands listed below automatically lock the table when they execute. This provides read-only access to other users on the network and ensures that you are using the most current data.

OFF

(Default) Enables shared access of tables with commands listed below. Use SET LOCK OFF if you don't need the most current information from a table.

Remarks

Visual FoxPro doesn't place a lock on a file when executing commands that require read-only access to a table. These commands include the following:

Commands

AVERAGE	CALCULATE
COPY TO	COPY TO ARRAY
COUNT	DISPLAY (with a scope)
INDEX	JOIN (both files)
LIST	LABEL
REPORT	SORT
SUM	TOTAL

While they are executed, these commands don't change the contents of a table, and access to the table is available to other users on the network. Thus, the table can be changed while you are executing one of these commands. For example, you might begin printing a report by using REPORT before another user changes a record included in the report. Your report now contains outdated information.

SET LOCK is scoped to the current data session.

See Also

FLOCK( ), LOCK( ), RLOCK( ), SET DATASESSION, SET MULTILOCKS

SET LOGERRORS Command

Determines whether Visual FoxPro sends compilation error messages to a text file.

Syntax

SET LOGERRORS ON | OFF

Arguments

ON

(Default) Specifies that a compilation error message log file be created with the same name as the compiled program and an .err extension. If a log file with the same name already exists, it is overwritten.

OFF

Specifies that a compilation error message log file is not created when a program is compiled.

Remarks

Use SET LOGERRORS to save compilation error messages to a text file when programs are compiled.

If a log file exists with the same name as the compiled program, and if the program compiles without error, the log file is deleted.

See Also

COMPILE

SET MACKEY Command

Specifies a key or key combination that displays the Macro Key Definition dialog box.

Syntax

SET MACKEY TO [KeyLabelName]

Arguments

KeyLabelName

Specifies the key or key combination that displays the Macro Key Definition dialog box. See the ON KEY LABEL Command, earlier in this language reference, for the key labels to use.

Remarks

Use SET MACKEY to change the default key combination for displaying the Macro Key Definition dialog box. Choose Macros from the Tools menu to display this dialog box.

See Also

CLEAR, ON KEY LABEL, PLAY MACRO, RESTORE MACROS, SAVE MACROS

SET MARGIN Command

Sets the left printer margin and affects all output directed to the printer.

Syntax

SET MARGIN TO *nColumns*

Arguments

nColumns

Specifies the left margin in columns. The default is 0 columns; the maximum is 256.

Remarks

If you use SET MARGIN to adjust the left margin, the value specified with SET MARGIN is stored to the system variable _PLOFFSET. You can also set the left margin by storing a value directly to _PLOFFSET.

The value of the system variable _LMARGIN also affects the left margin setting.

Important The left margin setting specified in SET MARGIN doesn't affect reports created with the Report Designer and then run with REPORT. Although _PLOFFSET is adjusted during the running of a report created with the Report Designer, it is reset to its original value after the report is run. The Left Margin setting in the Page Setup dialog box of the Report Designer determines the offset from the left edge of the paper. Choose Page Setup from the File menu to display the Page Setup dialog when the Report Designer is open.

See Also

_LMARGIN, _PLOFFSET

SET MARK OF Command

Specifies a mark character for menu titles or menu items, or displays or clears the mark character.

Syntax

SET MARK OF MENU *MenuBarName1*
    TO *lExpression1*

– or –

SET MARK OF POPUP *MenuName1*
    TO *lExpression3*

– or –

SET MARK OF BAR *nMenuItemNumber* OF *MenuName2*
    TO *lExpression4*

Arguments

MENU *MenuBarName1*
    Specifies the name of the menu bar for which the mark character is specified, displayed or cleared.

- TO *lExpression1* Displays or clears the mark character for every menu title on the menu bar. If the logical expression *lExpression1* evaluates to true (.T.), the mark character is displayed beside every menu title. The mark character is cleared from every menu name if *lExpression1* evaluates to false (.F.).

POPUP *MenuName1*
Specifies the name of the menu for which the mark character is specified, displayed, or cleared.

- TO *lExpression3* Displays or clears the mark characters for all the menu items.
  If *lExpression3* evaluates to true (.T.), the mark characters are displayed.
  If *lExpression3* evaluates to false (.F.), the mark characters are cleared.

BAR *nMenuItemNumber* OF *MenuName2*
Specifies the number of the menu item (and the name of the menu containing the menu item) for which the mark character is specified, displayed, or cleared.

- TO *lExpression4* Displays or clears the mark character for the menu item.
  If *lExpression4* evaluates to true (.T.), the mark character is displayed.
  If *lExpression4* evaluates to false (.F.), the mark character is cleared.

Remarks

You cannot specify a mark character for menu titles or menu items. The mark character is always a check mark (✓). However, you can use SET MARK OF to display or clear the check mark for menu titles or menu items.

You cannot mark menu items created with any of the DEFINE POPUP PROMPT clauses (FIELD, FILES, or STRUCTURE).

Use MRKPAD( ) to determine if a menu title has a mark character displayed, and use MRKBAR( ) to determine if a menu item has a mark character displayed.

For an example using SET MARK OF, see the CNTBAR( ) Function, earlier in this language reference.

See Also

CNTBAR( ), CNTPAD( ), DEFINE BAR, DEFINE MENU, DEFINE PAD, DEFINE POPUP, MRKBAR( ), MRKPAD( )

SET MARK TO Command

Specifies a delimiter for the display of date expressions.

Syntax

SET MARK TO [*cDelimiter*]

Arguments

cDelimiter
Specifies the character you want to use as the date delimiter.

Remarks

SET MARK TO specifies the character that separates the month, day, and year in displayed dates.

Use SET MARK TO without *cDelimiter* to reset the delimiter to the default forward slash (/).

SET MARK TO is scoped to the current data session.

See Also

SET DATASESSION, SET DATE, SET SYSFORMATS

SET MEMOWIDTH Command

Specifies the displayed width of memo fields and character expressions.

Syntax

SET MEMOWIDTH TO *nColumns*

Arguments

nColumns
> Specifies a width between 8 and 8192 columns. The default width for output is 50 columns. If you issue SET COMPATIBLE ON or SET COMPATIBLE DB4, the default width is changed to 80 columns. If you specify a value for *nColumns* greater than 8192, width is set to 8192.

Remarks

SET MEMOWIDTH specifies the width of output sent to the main Microsoft Visual FoxPro window or a user-defined window by commands such as ? | ??, DISPLAY, or LIST. It affects the output width of memo fields and character expressions longer than 8192 characters. It also affects the values returned by the ATCLINE( ), ATLINE( ), MEMLINE( ), and MLINE( ) functions.

Note that for ? and ?? the displayed width will not exceed 256 characters.

If output is directed to the main Visual FoxPro window, the width of the output is determined by the font for the main Visual FoxPro window. If output is directed to a user-defined window, the width of the output is determined by the font for the user-defined window.

SET MEMOWIDTH is scoped to the current data session.

See Also

ATCLINE( ), ATLINE( ), MEMLINES( ), MLINE( ), SET DATASESSION

SET MESSAGE Command

Defines a message for display in the main Visual FoxPro window or in the graphical status bar, or specifies the location of messages for user-defined menu bars and menu commands.

Syntax

SET MESSAGE TO [*cMessageText*]

– or –

SET MESSAGE TO [*nRow* [LEFT | CENTER | RIGHT]]

– or –

SET MESSAGE WINDOW [*WindowName*]

Arguments

TO [*cMessageText*]
Specifies the message to display.

TO [*nRow* [LEFT | CENTER | RIGHT]]
Specifies the placement of messages in the main Visual FoxPro window. *nRow* specifies the row on which messages are displayed. If *nRow* is 0, no messages are displayed.

LEFT, CENTER, and RIGHT specify the horizontal screen placement of messages.

Visual FoxPro ignores a message location specified with SET MESSAGE when the graphical status bar is displayed.

WINDOW [*WindowName*]
Specifies the window in which messages are displayed. To remove a message from the window and display it on the screen, issue SET MESSAGE WINDOW.

Remarks

SET MESSAGE lets you create a message. It also lets you specify where to display messages created with DEFINE BAR, DEFINE MENU, DEFINE PAD, or DEFINE POPUP.

By default, messages are placed on the last line of the main Visual FoxPro window if the character-based status bar is displayed. If the graphical status bar is displayed, messages are placed in the status bar.

The SET MESSAGE line is reset to the last line of the main Visual FoxPro window whenever SET DISPLAY is issued.

SET MESSAGE TO without any arguments places messages in the graphical status bar.

See Also

SET DISPLAY, SET STATUS, SET STATUS BAR

SET MULTILOCKS Command

Determines whether you can lock multiple records using LOCK( ) or RLOCK( ).

Syntax

SET MULTILOCKS ON | OFF

Arguments

ON

Allows you to attempt locking a set of records. Include a set of record numbers in LOCK( ) or RLOCK( ) to try to lock multiple records.

OFF

(Default) Allows you to attempt locking a single record with LOCK( ) or RLOCK( ).

Remarks

When a table is opened for shared use on a network, you can attempt to lock more than one record in a table file. The SET MULTILOCKS setting determines whether you can attempt to lock either a single record or a set of records. Records can be locked with the LOCK( ) or RLOCK( ) function.

Note Switching SET MULTILOCKS from ON to OFF or from OFF to ON implicitly issues UNLOCK ALL — all record locks in all work areas are released.

SET MULTILOCKS is scoped to the current data session.

MULTILOCKS must be ON to before row or table buffering can be enabled with CURSORSETPROP( ). See the CURSORSETPROP( ) Function, earlier in this language reference, for additional information about row and table buffering.

If you select the Enable Data Buffering check box in the Work Area Properties dialog box (which is displayed when you choose the Properties button in the Data Session window), MULTILOCKS is automatically set to ON for the current data session. However, clearing the Enable Data Buffering check box does not set MULTILOCKS to OFF for the current data session.

For more information about record and file locking and sharing tables on a network, see the LOCK( ) and RLOCK( ) Functions, earlier in this language reference, and Chapter 17, "Programming for Shared Access," in the *Microsoft Visual FoxPro 6.0 Programmer's Guide*.

See Also

CURSORSETPROP( ), LOCK( ), RLOCK( ), SET DATASESSION

SET NEAR Command

Determines where the record pointer is positioned after FIND or SEEK unsuccessfully searches for a record.

Syntax

SET NEAR ON | OFF

Arguments

ON

Positions the record pointer on the closest matching record if a record search using FIND or SEEK is unsuccessful. With this setting, RECNO( ) returns the record number of the closest matching record, FOUND( ) returns false (.F.), and EOF( ) returns false (.F.).

OFF

(Default) Positions the record pointer at the end of the table if a record search using FIND or SEEK is unsuccessful. With this setting, RECNO( ) returns the number of records in the table plus 1, FOUND( ) returns false (.F.), and EOF( ) returns true (.T.).

Remarks

A search is unsuccessful when no record meets the search criteria.

Issuing RECNO( ) with an argument of 0 returns the record number of the closest matching record if a search is unsuccessful, regardless of the setting of SET NEAR.

SET NEAR is scoped to the current data session.

See Also

EOF( ), FIND, FOUND( ), RECNO( ), SEEK, SET DATASESSION

SET NOCPTRANS Command

Prevents translation to a different code page for selected fields in an open table.

Syntax

SET NOCPTRANS TO [*FieldName1* [, *FieldName2* ...]]

Arguments

TO [*FieldName1* [, *FieldName2* ...]]
Specifies the fields that should not be translated to another code page.

Issue SET NOCPTRANS TO without a set of fields to return to the default translation (established by the CODEPAGE configuration item) for all character and memo fields in a table. Use SET("NOCPTRANS") to return the fields specified in the last SET NOCPTRANS command you issued. Use the CHR( ) function to ensure that individual characters don't get translated.

Remarks

Because Microsoft Visual FoxPro can be configured to automatically translate character and memo fields into other code pages, the SET NOCPTRANS command is available to prevent the automatic translation of fields containing binary data. For example, a memo field may contain a Microsoft Word document. When you access the Word document, you would like the document in its original, untranslated form. Use SET NOCPTRANS to specify that the memo field not be translated.

You don't need to use SET NOCPTRANS to access binary data if the character or memo field containing the binary data has not been translated. You can ensure that character and memo fields are not translated by omitting the CODEPAGE configuration item from your Visual FoxPro configuration file.

For additional information on code pages and Visual FoxPro's international support, see "Code Pages Supported by Visual FoxPro" in Chapter 18, "Developing International Applications," in the *Microsoft Visual FoxPro 6.0 Programmer's Guide*.

See Also

CPCONVERT( ), CPCURRENT( ), CPDBF( ), MODIFY COMMAND, MODIFY FILE

SET NOTIFY Command

Enables or disables the display of certain system messages.

Syntax

SET NOTIFY ON | OFF

Arguments

ON
    (Default) Enables the display of certain system messages.

OFF
    Disables the display of certain system messages.

Remarks

Examples of system messages that SET NOTIFY affects are

- "Expression is valid" in the Expression Builder dialog box.

- "Do Canceled," which appears when program execution is canceled.

System messages are displayed in the graphical (not the character-based) status bar at the bottom of the main Visual FoxPro window.

See Also

SET MESSAGE, WAIT

SET NULL Command

Determines how null values are supported by the ALTER TABLE, CREATE TABLE and INSERT – SQL commands.

Syntax

SET NULL ON | OFF

Arguments

ON

Specifies that all columns in a table created with ALTER TABLE and CREATE TABLE will allow null values. You can override null value support for columns in the table by including the NOT NULL clause in the columns' definitions.

Also, specifies that INSERT – SQL will insert null values into any columns not included in the INSERT – SQL VALUE clause. INSERT – SQL will insert null values only into columns that allow null values.

> **Note** If you add support for null values to one or more columns in a table, the limit on the number of columns for that table is reduced from 255 to 254.

OFF

(Default) Specifies that all columns in a table created with ALTER TABLE and CREATE TABLE will not allow null values. You can designate null value support for columns in ALTER TABLE and CREATE TABLE by including the NULL clause in the columns' definitions.

Also specifies that INSERT – SQL will insert blank values into any columns not included in the INSERT – SQL VALUE clause.

Remarks

SET NULL affects only how null values are supported by ALTER TABLE, CREATE TABLE and INSERT – SQL. Other commands are unaffected by SET NULL. SET NULL is scoped to the current data session.

Example

The following example demonstrates how SET NULL affects support for null values. The first table, employee, is created with SET NULL ON, so its fields support null values.

REPLACE is used to place a null value in the cLastName field. The second table, staff, is created with SET NULL OFF, so its fields do not support null values. REPLACE is used to place zero in the cLastName field.

```
CLOSE DATABASES
SET NULL ON          && Fields will support null values
CREATE TABLE employee (cLastName C(20), ySalary Y(12,2))
APPEND BLANK         && Add a new blank record
REPLACE cLastName WITH .NULL.  && cLastName supports null values

SET NULL OFF         && Fields will not support null values
CREATE TABLE staff (cLastName C(20), ySalary Y(12,2))
APPEND BLANK         && Add a new blank record
REPLACE cLastName WITH 0   && Doesn't support null values
```

See Also

ALTER TABLE, CREATE TABLE, INSERT – SQL, ISNULL( ), NVL( ), SET DATASESSION

SET NULLDISPLAY Command

Specifies the text displayed for null values.

Syntax

SET NULLDISPLAY TO [*cNullText*]

Arguments

cNullText
> Specifies the text that is displayed for null values. If *cNullText* is omitted, the default null value text, .NULL., is restored and displayed for null values.

Remarks

By default, Visual FoxPro displays .NULL. for null values in objects, Browse windows, DISPLAY output, LIST output, and so on. Use SET NULLDISPLAY to change the default null value text to a different character string. SET NULLDISPLAY changes the default null value text for all objects for which the NullDisplay property is the empty string.

Use the NullDisplay property to change the default null value text to a different character string for an individual object.

See Also

CREATE TABLE – SQL, NullDisplay Property

SET ODOMETER Command

Specifies the reporting interval of the record counter for commands that process records.

Syntax

SET ODOMETER TO [*nRecords*]

Arguments

TO [*nRecords*]

Specifies the reporting interval in number of records. The value of *nRecords* can range from 1 to 32,767 records. The default value is 100 records.

Remarks

Use SET ODOMETER to change the interval at which commands display information about the number of records processed.

For example, COPY TO displays the number of records that are copied to a new file while the command is executing. The record counter can be turned off by issuing SET TALK OFF.

See Also

SET TALK, _TALLY

SET OLEOBJECT Command

Specifies whether Visual FoxPro searches the OLE Registry when an object cannot be located.

Syntax

SET OLEOBJECT ON | OFF

Arguments

ON

(Default) Specifies that Visual FoxPro searches the OLE Registry when an object cannot be located.

OFF

Specifies that Visual FoxPro does not search the OLE Registry when an object cannot be located.

Remarks

When an object is created with CREATEOBJECT( ) or GETOBJECT( ),
Visual FoxPro searches for the object in the following locations and order:

1. The Visual FoxPro base classes.

2. Class definitions in memory in the order they are loaded.

3. Class definitions in the current program.

4. Class definitions in the .vcx class libraries opened with SET CLASSLIB.

5. Class definitions in procedure files opened with SET PROCEDURE.

6. Class definitions in the Visual FoxPro program execution chain.

7. The OLE Registry.

When Visual FoxPro searches for an object, the OLE Registry is searched last.
Visual FoxPro loads OLE support before it searches the OLE Registry, increasing the
amount of memory required by Visual FoxPro and reducing the amount of memory
available to other applications.

If you are developing an application that does not require OLE support, issue SET
OLEOBJECT OFF to prevent Visual FoxPro from searching the OLE Registry when
an object cannot be located.

SET OLEOBJECT does not affect OLE objects in Forms or General fields.
Visual FoxPro always loads OLE support when a Form containing an OLE object is
opened for modification or is instantiated, or a table with a general field is opened.

Because GETOBJECT( ) activates an OLE object, Visual FoxPro generates an error
when GETOBJECT( ) is issued and SET OLEOBJECT is OFF.

See Also

CREATEOBJECT( ), GETOBJECT( )

SET OPTIMIZE Command

Enables or disables Rushmore optimization.

Syntax

SET OPTIMIZE ON | OFF

Arguments

ON
    (Default) Enables Rushmore optimization.

OFF
    Disables Rushmore optimization.

Remarks

Visual FoxPro uses a technology called Rushmore to optimize data retrieval. Table commands that support a FOR clause use Rushmore technology to enhance their performance. When you issue a command that is optimizable, Rushmore determines which records match the FOR criterion. The command is executed on records in the table that match the Rushmore record set.

In rare cases, you should disable Rushmore optimization. If a command that benefits from Rushmore optimization modifies a query's index keys, the Rushmore record set may become outdated. You can disable Rushmore optimization to ensure that you have the most current information from the table.

You can use SET OPTIMIZE to globally enable or disable Rushmore technology. Every command that uses Rushmore has a NOOPTIMIZE clause you can include to disable Rushmore optimization for the command.

For more information, see "Understanding Rushmore Technology" in Chapter 15, "Optimizing Applications," in the *Microsoft Visual FoxPro 6.0 Programmer's Guide*.

Below are the commands whose performance is optimized by Rushmore:

Commands

AVERAGE	BLANK	BROWSE
CALCULATE	CHANGE	COPY TO
COPY TO ARRAY	COUNT	DELETE
DISPLAY	EDIT	EXPORT
INDEX	LABEL	LIST
LOCATE	RECALL	REPLACE
REPLACE FROM ARRAY	REPORT	SCAN
SORT	SUM	TOTAL

See Also

INDEX, SET ORDER

SET ORDER Command

Designates a controlling index file or tag for a table.

Syntax

SET ORDER TO
    [*nIndexNumber* | *IDXIndexFileName* | [TAG] *TagName* [OF *CDXFileName*]
    [IN *nWorkArea* | *cTableAlias*]
    [ASCENDING | DESCENDING]]

Arguments

nIndexNumber

Specifies the number of the controlling index file or tag. *nIndexNumber* refers to the index files as they are listed in USE or SET INDEX. Open .idx files are numbered first in the order in which they appear in USE or SET INDEX. Tags in the structural .cdx file (if one exists) are then numbered in the order in which they were created. Finally, tags in any open independent .cdx files are numbered in the order in which they were created.

The following example illustrates how different index file types and tags are numbered. (The file names are for illustration only and don't necessarily exist.) A table named `video.dbf` is opened with three indexes (`title.idx`, `costs.cdx`, and `rating.idx`) in the first work area with this command:

```
USE video INDEX title.idx, costs.cdx, rating.idx IN 1
```

The `video` table has a structural compound index file (`video.cdx`) with two tags, `NUMBERSOLD` and `YEARSOLD`. The structural .cdx file is automatically opened when `video` is opened.

Since .idx files are numbered first, issue SET ORDER TO 1 to make `title.idx` the controlling index and SET ORDER TO 2 to make `rating.idx` the controlling index:

```
SET ORDER TO 1
Controlling index: C:\VFP\TITLE.IDX
SET ORDER TO 2
Controlling index: C:\VFP\RATING.IDX
```

The `video.cdx` are numbered next:

```
SET ORDER TO 3
Controlling index: C:\VFP\VIDEO.CDX  Tag: NUMBERSOLD
SET ORDER TO 4
Controlling index: C:\VFP\VIDEO.CDX  Tag: YEARSOLD
```

Finally, the tags in the independent file, `costs.cdx`, are numbered:

```
SET ORDER TO 5
Controlling index: C:\VFP\COSTS.CDX  Tag: RENTALCOST
SET ORDER TO 6
Controlling index: C:\VFP\COSTS.CDX  Tag: BUYCOST
```

nIndexNumber can also be 0. If you issue SET ORDER TO 0, all index files remain open and are updated when records are added, deleted or modified. However, the records in the table are displayed and accessed in record number order and not in an indexed order. Issuing SET ORDER TO without additional arguments is identical to issuing SET ORDER TO 0.

If *nIndexNumber* is greater than the number of .idx files and .cdx file tags, Visual FoxPro generates an error message.

IDXIndexFileName
Specifies an .idx file as the controlling index file.

[TAG] *TagName* [OF *CDXFileName*]
Specifies a tag of a .cdx file as the controlling tag. The tag name can be from a structural .cdx file or any open independent .cdx file.

If identical tag names exist in open independent .cdx files, use OF *CDXFileName* to specify the .cdx file containing the tag.

> **Note** The .idx file takes precedence if duplicate .idx file and tag names exist.

IN *nWorkArea* | *cTableAlias*
Designates a controlling index file or tag for a table open in a work area other than the currently selected work area. *nWorkArea* specifies the work area number and *cTableAlias* specifies the alias for a table.

ASCENDING | DESCENDING
Displays and allows access to table records in ascending or descending order. Including ASCENDING or DESCENDING doesn't change the index file or tag in any way.

Remarks

A table can have many index files open simultaneously. However, only one single-index (.idx) file (the controlling index file) or tag from a compound index (.cdx) file (the controlling tag) determines the order in which the records in a table are displayed or accessed. SET ORDER lets you designate the controlling index file or tag. Certain commands (SEEK, for example) use the controlling index file or tag to search for records.

You can open index files with a table by including the INDEX clause in the USE command. If a table has an associated structural .cdx file, that file is automatically opened with the table. After a table has been opened, you can open and close index files for the table using SET INDEX.

By default, SET ORDER designates the controlling index or controlling tag for the table open in the currently selected work area.

See Also

INDEX, ORDER( ), SET INDEX

SET PALETTE Command

Specifies whether the Visual FoxPro default color palette is used.

Syntax

SET PALETTE ON | OFF

Arguments

ON
(Default) Restores the default Visual FoxPro color palette.

OFF

Replaces the Visual FoxPro default color palette with color palettes from the .bmp graphics and OLE objects.

Remarks

OLE objects and .bmp graphics can contain color palettes that determine how the graphics and objects appear when they are displayed. The color palette of the first graphic or object displayed is used for all subsequent graphics or objects. Since a single color palette is used for all the graphics and objects, the colors of some of the graphics and objects may be changed in an unexpected manner.

The default Visual FoxPro color palette is designed to improve the display appearance of multiple .bmp graphics and OLE objects.

See Also

@ ... SAY, MODIFY GENERAL

SET PATH Command

Specifies a path for file searches.

Syntax

SET PATH TO [*Path*]

Arguments

TO [*Path*]

Specifies the directories you want Visual FoxPro to search. Use commas or semicolons to separate the directories.

Note Visual FoxPro will not recognize a path name properly if a disk or directory name contains an exclamation point (!).

On all FoxPro platforms, functions that return path information, such as CURDIR( ), DBF( ), and SYS(2003), use Microsoft MS-DOS path-naming conventions in their return values.

Remarks

Issue SET PATH TO without *Path* to restore the path to the default directory. Use SET DEFAULT to specify the default directory and CURDIR( ) to return the current default directory.

SET PATH is not scoped to the current data session; changes you make to the default path using the SET PATH command affect all data sessions.

See Also

CD | CHDIR, GETFILE( ), LOCFILE( ), MD | MKDIR, RD | RMDIR, SET DEFAULT, SET DATASESSION

SET PDSETUP Command

Loads a printer driver setup or clears the current printer driver setup.

Syntax

SET PDSETUP TO [[*cPrinterDriverSetup* [, *Parameter1*[, *Parameter2* ...]]]
    [WITH *Parameter3* [, *Parameter4* ...]]]

Arguments

cPrinterDriverSetup
    Specifies the name of the printer driver setup to load.

    When you load a printer driver setup, the name of the setup is stored in the
    _PDSETUP system variable, and a special variable array, _PDPARMS, can be
    created. (_PDPARMS is discussed in detail under the WITH clause in this topic.)

    If the printer driver setup name you specify with *cPrinterDriverSetup* doesn't exist
    in your resource file, the current printer driver setup application is executed so you
    can create a setup with this name. If the current printer driver setup application is
    Genpd.app, the Printer Setup Editing dialog box appears so you can create the setup.

    If the setup name begins with a dash (–), the _GENPD program won't be executed,
    but the name following the dash is stored in _PDSETUP.

    If you issue SET PDSETUP TO without *cPrinterDriverSetup*, the current printer driver
    setup is cleared, the empty string is stored in _PDSETUP, and the _PDPARMS array is
    cleared from memory.

Parameter1 [, *Parameter2* ...]
    Specifies any number of optional parameters. These parameters are passed to the
    printer setup interface application and can be of any type (character, numeric, logical,
    and so on). The first line in your printer setup interface application must be an
    LPARAMETERS or PARAMETERS statement to accept the parameters passed
    from SET PDSETUP.

    If you are using Genpd.app, don't include these optional parameters. Genpd.app
    doesn't accept parameters passed from SET PDSETUP, so including them generates
    an error.

WITH *Parameter3* [, *Parameter4* ...]
    Creates the special _PDPARMS printer array. Each parameter you specify with
    Parameter3, *Parameter4*, and so forth becomes an element in _PDPARMS. The first
    parameter (*Parameter3*) is stored to the first element of _PDPARMS, the second
    parameter (*Parameter4*) is stored to the second element, and so on. These parameters
    may be of any type (character, numeric, logical, and the like).

If you are using Genpd.app, any parameters you include are overwritten by the application.

Remarks

In Visual FoxPro, a printer driver setup is used when you print character-based reports created in FoxPro for MS-DOS.

A printer driver setup consists of a combination of settings, including the printer driver program and information such as page orientation, default font size and font style, margins, and so on. Printer driver setups are stored in your FoxPro for MS-DOS resource file, Foxuser.dbf, and can be created interactively and assigned a name in the Printer Setup Editing dialog box.

A printer driver setup can also be loaded or cleared with the _PDSETUP system variable.

When you issue SET PDSETUP, the current printer setup interface application is executed. The interface application is passed the name of the printer driver setup included in SET PDSETUP. The interface application can also be specified with the _GENPD system variable. The default interface application is Genpd.app, the printer setup interface application included with FoxPro for MS-DOS.

See Also

_GENPD, _PDRIVER, _PDSETUP, SET PRINTER

SET POINT Command

Determines the decimal point character used in the display of numeric and currency expressions.

Syntax

SET POINT TO [*cDecimalPointCharacter*]

Arguments

cDecimalPointCharacter
  Specifies the character for the decimal point.

Remarks

Use SET POINT to change the decimal point from the default, which is a period (.). Issue SET POINT TO without *cDecimalPointCharacter* to reset the decimal point to a period. Although you can set the displayed decimal point to a different character, you must use a period as the decimal point in calculations.

SET POINT is scoped to the current data session.

Example

```
gnX = 1.25
gcNewPoint = '_'
SET POINT TO gcNewPoint
? gnX
SET POINT TO        && Reset the decimal point to a period (.)
? gnX
```

See Also

SET DATASESSION, SET DECIMALS, SET FIXED, SET SEPARATOR,
SET SYSFORMATS

SET PRINTER Command

Enables or disables output to the printer, or routes output to a file, port, or network printer.

Syntax

SET PRINTER ON [PROMPT] | OFF

– or –

SET PRINTER FONT *cFontName* [, *cFontSize*]
    [STYLE *cFontStyle*]

– or –

SET PRINTER TO [*FileName* [ADDITIVE] | *PortName*]

– or –

SET PRINTER TO [DEFAULT | NAME *WindowsPrinterName*]

– or –

SET PRINTER TO NAME *ServerName**PrinterName*

Arguments

ON [PROMPT]

Enables output to the printer. Output formatted with @ ... SAY isn't routed to the printer when SET PRINTER is set to ON. Use SET DEVICE TO PRINTER to direct output from @ ... SAY to the printer.

You can include PROMPT to display a dialog box before printing starts. In this dialog box you can adjust printer settings. The currently installed printer driver determines which printer settings you can adjust.

OFF

(Default) Disables output to the printer.

FONT *cFontName* [, *cFontSize*]

Specifies a default font for printer output. *cFontName* specifies the name of the font, and *cFontSize* specifies the point size. For example, the following command specifies 16-point Courier font as the default printer font:

```
SET PRINTER FONT 'Courier', 16
```

If the font you specify is not available, a font with similar font characteristics is substituted.

STYLE *cFontStyle*

Specifies a default font style for printer output. If you omit the STYLE clause, the normal font style is used.

If the font style you specify is not available, a font style with similar characteristics is substituted.

The font styles you can specify with *cFontStyle* are as follows:

Character	Font style
B	Bold
I	Italic
N	Normal
O	Outline
Q	Opaque
S	Shadow
–	Strikeout
T	Transparent
U	Underline

You can include more than one character to specify a combination of font styles. For example, the following command specifies 16-point Courier Bold Italic:

```
SET PRINTER FONT 'Courier', 16 STYLE 'BI'
```

TO [*FileName* [ADDITIVE] | *PortName*]

Specifies a file or port to which output is directed.

In Visual FoxPro, use SET PRINTER TO NAME instead to specify a printer.

FileName specifies a file name to which output is directed. If you include ADDITIVE, output is appended to the existing contents of the file. If you omit ADDITIVE, the existing contents of the file are overwritten.

PortName sends output to a different local printer.

TO [DEFAULT | NAME *WindowsPrinterName*]

Sends printer output to the default Windows printer or to a specific Windows printer. Windows printer names are stored in Win.ini.

You can use GETPRINTER( ) or APRINTERS( ) to determine the names of the currently installed printers. For example, the following command displays the Windows Print Setup dialog box and makes printer you select the printer to which printed output is directed:

```
SET PRINTER TO NAME GETPRINTER( )
```

TO NAME *ServerName**PrinterName*

Supported only under Windows NT. Spools printer output to a network printer.

ServerName is the network name assigned to your print server. This name is assigned by the network administrator and must be unique.

PrinterName is a name assigned to the printer and is also assigned by the network administrator.

Remarks

Use SET PRINTER TO with the specified arguments to direct output to a file, a port for a different local printer, or a network printer.

Use SET PRINTER TO without an argument to reset output to the default MS-DOS PRN print utility.

When you direct output to a network printer, output prints or collects in a print spooler until a new SET PRINTER command is issued. For additional information about printing on your network, consult your network documentation.

See Also

APRINTERS( ), GETPRINTER( ), PRINTSTATUS( ), SET DEVICE

SET PROCEDURE Command

Opens a procedure file.

Syntax

SET PROCEDURE TO [*FileName1* [, *FileName2*, ...]]
    [ADDITIVE]

Arguments

FileName1 [, *FileName2*, ...]

Specifies the sequence in which files are to be opened. SET PROCEDURE can take more than one file name, allowing you to open several procedure files at once. This option allows you to create stand-alone libraries of functions and specify them separately.

ADDITIVE

Opens additional procedure files without closing currently open procedure files.

Remarks

Issuing SET PROCEDURE TO without any file names closes all open procedure files. Use RELEASE PROCEDURE to close individual files.

When you execute a procedure, the procedure files are searched if the procedure isn't located in the currently executing program.

For more information about procedure files, see the PROCEDURE and DO Commands, earlier in this language reference.

See Also

PROCEDURE, RELEASE PROCEDURE

SET READBORDER Command

Determines whether borders are placed around text boxes created with @ ... GET.

Syntax

SET READBORDER ON | OFF

Arguments

ON

Places a single-line border around all text boxes created with @ ... GET. If SET READBORDER is set to ON when the first text box is created, all subsequent text boxes created in the same READ level also have borders.

OFF

(Default) Specifies that a border isn't placed around text boxes created with @ ... GET. If SET READBORDER is set to OFF when the first text box is created, all subsequent text boxes created in the same READ level do not have borders.

Remarks

SET READBORDER specifies whether single-line borders are placed around text boxes created with @ ... GET.

Example

In the following example, the first three text boxes created with @ ... GET have borders. The third text box has a border, even though SET READBORDER was SET to OFF before it was created. The fourth text box does not have a border, since READBORDER was SET to OFF and it is encompassed in a different READ from the first three text boxes.

```
SET READBORDER ON
@ 2,2 GET gnW DEFAULT 1    && 1st READ
@ 4,2 GET gnX DEFAULT 1    && 1st READ
SET READBORDER OFF
@ 6,2 GET gnY DEFAULT 1    && 1st READ
READ
@ 8,2 GET gnZ DEFAULT 2    && 2nd READ
READ
```

See Also

READ, READ EVENTS

SET REFRESH Command

Determines whether and how often a Browse window is updated with changes made to records by other users on the network.

Syntax

SET REFRESH TO *nSeconds1* [, *nSeconds2*]

Arguments

TO *nSeconds1* [, *nSeconds2*]

Specifies whether and how often updates are made. *nSeconds1* specifies the number of seconds between updates to a Browse or memo-editing window. *nSeconds1* can be a value from 0 to 3,600; the default value is 0 seconds. When *nSeconds1* is a nonzero value and other users change records you are viewing, those records are updated when the refresh interval elapses. The records you are viewing aren't updated if *nSeconds1* is 0.

Microsoft Visual FoxPro buffers portions of tables in memory on your workstation. *nSeconds2* specifies how often these local data buffers are updated with current data from the network. *nSeconds2* is the number of seconds between data buffer updates. You can specify a value between 0 and 3,600; the default value is 5. The buffers are never refreshed if *nSeconds2* is set to 0.

If you specify a value for *nSeconds1* other than 0 but don't include *nSeconds2*, *nSeconds2* is set to the same value as *nSeconds1*. However, *nSeconds2* is set to 5 if you specify 0 for *nSeconds1* and don't include *nSeconds2*.

Performance can be improved by increasing the value of *nSeconds2*.

Remarks

Because tables can be opened for shared use on a network, it is possible that records you are viewing in a Browse window are being edited by other users on the network.

SET REFRESH affects records displayed in a Browse window opened with BROWSE, CHANGE, or EDIT. Memo fields opened for editing in a Browse window are also updated.

SET REFRESH can also be used to specify how often data buffered locally on your workstation is updated.

See Also

BROWSE, CHANGE, EDIT, MODIFY MEMO

SET RELATION Command

Establishes a relationship between two open tables.

Syntax

SET RELATION TO
    [*eExpression1* INTO *nWorkArea1* | *cTableAlias1*
    [, *eExpression2* INTO *nWorkArea2* | *cTableAlias2* ...]
    [IN *nWorkArea* | *cTableAlias*]
    [ADDITIVE]]

Arguments

eExpression1

    Specifies the relational expression that establishes a relationship between the parent and child tables. The relational expression is usually the index expression of the controlling index of the child table.

    The index for the child table can be a single-entry (.idx) index, a multiple-entry structural compound (.cdx) index, or an independent compound index. If the index is compound, specify the proper index tag to order the child table. SET ORDER can be used to specify the index tag that orders the child table.

    For example, consider the `customer` and `orders` tables described in the Remarks section below. Suppose the child `orders` table has been indexed and ordered on the customer number with this command:

```
SET ORDER TO TAG cust_id
```

    To relate the `customer` and `orders` tables on customer number, select the work area containing the `customer` parent table or include the IN clause to specify the parent table's work area or alias, and issue SET RELATION, specifying the index expression with the following relational expression:

```
SET RELATION TO cust_id INTO orders
```

    The child table must be indexed unless the relational expression is numeric. Visual FoxPro displays an error message if you issue SET RELATION with a non-numeric relational expression and the child table isn't ordered with an index.

If *eExpression1* is numeric, it is evaluated when the record pointer in the parent table is moved. The record pointer in the child table is then moved to record number *eExpression1*.

INTO *nWorkArea1* | *cTableAlias1*

Specifies the work area number (*nWorkArea1*) or table alias (*cTableAlias1*) of the child table.

eExpression2 **INTO** *nWorkArea2* | *cTableAlias2* ...

Specifies a relational expression (*eExpression2*) and a child table or tables to establish an additional relationship between the parent table and child tables. From a single SET RELATION command, you can create multiple relations between a single parent table and various child tables. Precede each relation by a comma.

nWorkArea2 specifies a work area number and *cTableAlias2* specifies a table alias for the child table.

IN *nWorkArea*

Specifies the work area of the parent table.

IN *cTableAlias*

Specifies the alias of the parent table.

The IN clause allows you to create a relationship without first selecting the parent table's work area. If you omit *nWorkArea* and *cTableAlias*, the parent table must be open in the currently selected work area.

ADDITIVE

Preserves all existing relationships in the current work area and creates the specified relationship. If you omit ADDITIVE, any relationships in the current work area are broken and the specified relationship is created.

Remarks

Before you can establish a relationship, one table (the parent table) must be open, and the other table (the child table) must be open in another work area.

Related tables typically have a common field. For example, suppose a table named customer contains customer information. It has fields for name, address, and a unique customer number. A second table named orders contains order information. It too has a field for the customer number, along with fields for dates and shipping information.

SET RELATION relates these two tables on their common field — the customer number field. To set the relation, the child table must be indexed on the common field. After you set the relation, whenever you move the record pointer to a record with a given customer number in the parent customer table, the record pointer in the child orders table moves to the record with the same customer number. If a matching record can't be found in the child table, the record pointer in the child table is positioned at the end of the table.

Issue SET RELATION TO with no arguments to remove all relationships in the currently selected work area. SET RELATION OFF can be used to remove a specific parent-child relationship.

See Also

INDEX, RELATION( ), SET ORDER, SET RELATION OFF, SET SKIP, TARGET( )

SET RELATION OFF Command

Breaks an established relationship between the parent table in the currently selected work area, and a related child table.

Syntax

SET RELATION OFF INTO *nWorkArea* | *cTableAlias*

Arguments

INTO *nWorkArea* | *cTableAlias*
Specifies the child table's work area number or table alias.

See Also

RELATION( ), SELECT, SET RELATION, SET SKIP, TARGET( )

SET REPROCESS Command

Specifies how many times and for how long Visual FoxPro attempts to lock a file or record after an unsuccessful locking attempt.

Syntax

SET REPROCESS TO *nAttempts* [SECONDS] | TO AUTOMATIC

Arguments

TO *nAttempts* [SECONDS]
Specifies the number of times Visual FoxPro attempts to lock a record or file after an initial unsuccessful attempt. The default value is 0, the maximum value is 32,000.

SECONDS specifies that Visual FoxPro attempts to lock a file or record for *nAttempts* seconds. It's available only when *nAttempts* is greater than zero.

For example, if *nAttempts* is 30, Visual FoxPro attempts to lock a record or file up to 30 times. If you also include SECONDS (SET REPROCESS TO 30 SECONDS), Visual FoxPro continuously attempts to lock a record or file for up to 30 seconds.

A system message ("Waiting for lock ... ") appears if SET STATUS is set to ON.

If an ON ERROR routine is in effect and attempts by a command to lock the record or file are unsuccessful, the ON ERROR routine is executed. However, if a function attempts the lock, an ON ERROR routine isn't executed and the function returns false (.F.).

If an ON ERROR routine isn't in effect, a command attempts to lock the record or file, and the lock can't be placed, an appropriate alert appears (for example, "Record is in use by another"). If a function attempts to place the lock, the alert isn't displayed and the function returns false (.F.).

If *nAttempts* is 0 (the default value) and you issue a command or function that attempts to lock a record or file, Visual FoxPro tries to lock the record or file indefinitely. Visual FoxPro displays the system message, "Attempting to lock... Press Escape to Cancel," while attempting to lock the record or file. The lock is placed and the system message is cleared if the record or file becomes available for locking while you wait. If a function attempted to place the lock, the function returns true (.T.).

If you press ESC in response to the system message, an appropriate alert appears (for example, "Record is in use by another"). If a function attempts to place the lock, the alert isn't displayed and the function returns false (.F.).

If an ON ERROR routine is in effect and a command is attempting to lock the record or file, the ON ERROR routine takes precedence over additional attempts to lock the record or file. The ON ERROR routine is immediately executed. Visual FoxPro does not attempt additional record or file locks and does not display the system message.

If *nAttempts* is –1, Visual FoxPro attempts to lock the record or file indefinitely. You can't cancel the locking attempts by pressing the ESC key, and an ON ERROR routine isn't executed.

Setting *nAttempts* to –2 is equivalent to using the TO AUTOMATIC clause.

Visual FoxPro displays the "Waiting for lock ... " system message only if SET STATUS is set to ON.

If a lock has been placed by another user on the record or file you are attempting to lock, you must wait until the user releases the lock.

TO AUTOMATIC

Specifies that Visual FoxPro attempts to lock the record or file indefinitely (equivalent to setting *nAttempts* to -2). This clause is similar to setting *nAttempts* to –1, except that it includes the facility to quit the attempt to lock a record or file.

The "Attempting to lock ... Press Escape to Cancel" system message appears while Visual FoxPro attempts to lock the record or file. The lock is placed and the system message is cleared if the record or file becomes available for locking while you wait. If a function is used to place the lock, the function returns true (.T.).

If an ON ERROR routine isn't in effect and you press ESC in response to the system message, an appropriate alert appears (for example, "Record is in use by another"). If a function attempts to place the lock, the alert isn't displayed and the function returns false (.F.).

If an ON ERROR routine is in effect and ESC is pressed, the ON ERROR routine is executed. If a function attempts to place the lock, an ON ERROR routine isn't executed and the function returns false (.F.).

For more information about record and file locking and sharing tables on a network, see Chapter 17, "Programming for Shared Access," in the *Microsoft Visual FoxPro 6.0 Programmer's Guide*.

Remarks

The first attempt to lock a record or file isn't always successful. Frequently, a record or file is locked by another user on the network. SET REPROCESS determines whether Visual FoxPro makes additional attempts to lock the record or file when the initial attempt is unsuccessful. You can specify either how many times additional attempts are made or for how long the attempts are made. An ON ERROR routine affects how unsuccessful lock attempts are handled.

SET REPROCESS is scoped to the current data session.

See Also

FLOCK( ), SET DATASESSION

SET RESOURCE Command

Updates or specifies a resource file.

Syntax

SET RESOURCE ON | OFF

– or –

SET RESOURCE TO [*FileName*]

Arguments

ON
> (Default) Specifies that changes made to the Visual FoxPro environment are saved to the resource file.

OFF
> Specifies that changes made to the Visual FoxPro environment are not saved to the resource file.

TO [*FileName*]
> Specifies that changes made to the Visual FoxPro environment are saved to a resource file (*FileName*) other than the default FOXUSER.DBF resource file.
>
> Issue SET RESOURCE TO without a resource file name to open the default Foxuser.dbf resource file. Issuing SET RESOURCE TO performs an implicit SET RESOURCE ON.

Remarks

The resource file is a Visual FoxPro table that contains information on system and user-defined resources such as keyboard macros, preferences, system window locations and sizes, diary entries, and so on.

See Also

SYS(2005) – Current Resource File

SET SAFETY Command

Determines whether Visual FoxPro displays a dialog box before overwriting an existing file, or whether table or field rules, default values, and error messages are evaluated when changes are made in the Table Designer or with ALTER TABLE.

Syntax

SET SAFETY ON | OFF

Arguments

ON

(Default) Specifies that a dialog box is displayed before you overwrite an existing file. The dialog box gives you the option of overwriting the existing file.

For the Table Designer, specifies that table or field rules, default values, and error messages are evaluated when you save changes to a table's structure. Data validation occurs for new or modified validation rules after you save the table structure changes. If a validation rule contains a UDF (user-defined function), the UDF isn't evaluated and the validation rule is ignored.

For ALTER TABLE, table or field rules, default values, and error messages are evaluated when ALTER TABLE changes the table's structure. Data validation occurs for new or modified validation rules when ALTER TABLE changes the table's structure. If a validation rule contains a UDF (user-defined function), the UDF isn't evaluated and the validation rule is ignored.

OFF

Specifies that a dialog box isn't displayed before an existing file is overwritten. Note that for in-process .dll automation servers the default setting of SET SAFETY is OFF.

For the Table Designer, specifies that table or field rules, default values, and error messages are not evaluated when you save changes to a table's structure. However, data validation occurs for new or modified validation rules after you save the table structure changes.

For ALTER TABLE, table or field rules, default values, and error messages are not evaluated when ALTER TABLE changes the table's structure. Data validation does not occur for new or modified validation rules after ALTER TABLE changes the table's structure.

Remarks

SET SAFETY is scoped to the current data session.

See Also

ALTER TABLE – SQL, MODIFY STRUCTURE, SET DATASESSION, SET TALK

SET SECONDS Command

Specifies whether seconds are displayed in the time portion of a DateTime value.

Syntax

SET SECONDS ON | OFF

Arguments

ON

(Default) Specifies that seconds are displayed in DateTime values.

OFF

Specifies that seconds are not displayed in DateTime values.

Remarks

SET SECONDS is scoped to the current data session.

Example

The following example demonstrates the effect of the SET SECONDS setting on the time value returned by DATETIME( ). When SET SECONDS is ON, the time value is displayed with the seconds portion. When SET SECONDS is OFF, the time value is displayed without the seconds portion.

```
SET SECONDS ON
CLEAR
? DATETIME( )  && Displays time value with the seconds portion

SET SECONDS OFF  && Displays time value without the seconds portion
? DATETIME( )
```

See Also

CTOT( ), DATE( ), DATETIME( ), DTOT( ), HOUR( ), MINUTE( ), SEC( ), SECONDS( ), SET SECONDS, TIME( )

SET SEPARATOR Command

Included for backward compatibility. Use the Windows Control Panel instead.

SET SKIP Command

Creates a one-to-many relationship among tables.

Syntax

SET SKIP TO [*TableAlias1* [, *TableAlias2*] ...]

Arguments

TO *TableAlias1* [, *TableAlias2*] ...

Specifies the aliases of multiple child tables. These are used to create a one-to-many relationship with a parent table. Use commas to separate the aliases. In commands that support a scope (DISPLAY, LIST, and so on), records in the parent table are repeated for each corresponding record in the child table.

Use SET SKIP TO without additional arguments to remove the one-to-many relationship from the parent table open in the currently selected work area. Any one-to-one relationships remain in effect. One-to-one relationships can be removed with SET RELATION TO.

Remarks

Using SET RELATION, you can establish relations between tables open in different work areas. When the record pointer is moved in the parent table, the record pointer in the child table moves to the first corresponding record. The relational expression in SET RELATION determines where the record pointer moves in the child table. A one-to-one relation is created — for each record in the parent table, the record pointer moves to the first matching record in the child table. If a matching record can't be found in the child table, the record pointer in the child table moves to the end of the table.

Frequently, a child table contains multiple records that correspond to one record in the parent table. SET SKIP lets you establish a one-to-many relationship between one record in the parent table and multiple records in the child table. When you skip through the parent table, the record pointer remains on the same parent record until the record pointer moves through all related records in the child table.

To establish a one-to-many relationship, first create the relationship between the parent and child table with SET RELATION. Then, issue SET SKIP to create a one-to-many relationship.

Example

This example below finds all occurrences in three tables where each item in the first field are the same. It does this by using scanning the first table which has a relation into a second, which table has a relation into a third. The first table then does a SET SKIP for the other two tables. A SET SKIP on the second table has no effect. It affects only the table being scanned (replaced, etc.). In the example, eight matches are found.

```
CLOSE DATABASES
* Creates parent table with values a and b in Name field
CREATE TABLE Parent FREE (Name C(1), Val C(10))
INSERT INTO Parent VALUES ('a', 'Parent.a1')
INSERT INTO Parent VALUES ('b', 'Parent.b1')

SELECT 0     && Child1 will have two a's and two b's
CREATE TABLE Child1 FREE (Name1 C(1), Val C(10))
INSERT INTO Child1 VALUES ('a', 'Child1.a1')
INSERT INTO Child1 VALUES ('b', 'Child1.b1')
INSERT INTO Child1 VALUES ('b', 'Child1.b2')
INSERT INTO Child1 VALUES ('a', 'Child1.a2')
INDEX ON Name1 TAG tagName   && The tag name is irrelevant

SELECT 0  && Child2 will have two a's and two b's
CREATE TABLE Child2 FREE (Name2 C(1), Val C(10))
INSERT INTO Child2 VALUES ('b', 'Child1.b1')
INSERT INTO Child2 VALUES ('b', 'Child1.b2')
INSERT INTO Child2 VALUES ('a', 'Child1.a1')
INSERT INTO Child2 VALUES ('a', 'Child1.a2')
INDEX ON Name2 TAG tagName      && The tag name is irrelevant

SELECT Child1
SET RELATION TO Name1 INTO Child2
SELECT Parent
SET RELATION TO Name INTO Child1
SET SKIP TO Child1, Child2  && Parent gets both skips.
         && Otherwise, only four record triplets
         && would be listed.
SCAN ALL  && There will be eight triplets: four a's and four b's
   ? Parent.Val, Child1.Val, Child2.Val
ENDSCAN
```

See Also

RELATION( ), SET RELATION, SKIP

SET SKIP OF Command

Enables or disables a menu, menu bar, menu title, or menu item for user-defined menus or the Microsoft Visual FoxPro system menu.

Syntax

SET SKIP OF MENU *MenuBarName1 lExpression1*

– or –

SET SKIP OF PAD *MenuTitleName* OF *MenuBarName2 lExpression2*

– or –

SET SKIP OF POPUP *MenuName1 lExpression3*

– or –

SET SKIP OF BAR *nMenuItemNumber* | *SystemItemName* OF *MenuName2 lExpression4*

Arguments

MENU *MenuBarName1 lExpression1*

Enables or disables the Visual FoxPro system menu bar or user-defined menu bar created with DEFINE MENU. For example, the Visual FoxPro system menu bar _MSYSMENU can be disabled with this command:

```
SET SKIP OF MENU _MSYSMENU .T.
```

It can be enabled with this command:

```
SET SKIP OF MENU _MSYSMENU .F.
```

PAD *MenuTitleName* OF *MenuBarName2 lExpression2*

Enables or disables a Visual FoxPro system menu title or a user-defined menu title created with DEFINE PAD. For example, the Visual FoxPro Edit menu title can be disabled with this command:

```
SET SKIP OF PAD _MSM_EDIT OF _MSYSMENU .T.
```

The menu title can be enabled with this command:

```
SET SKIP OF PAD _MSM_EDIT OF _MSYSMENU .F.
```

POPUP *MenuName1 lExpression3*

Enables or disables a Visual FoxPro system menu or a user-defined menu created with DEFINE POPUP. For example, the Visual FoxPro Edit menu can be disabled with this command:

```
SET SKIP OF POPUP _MEDIT .T.
```

The menu can be enabled with this command:

```
SET SKIP OF POPUP _MEDIT .F.
```

BAR *nMenuItemNumber* | *SystemItemName* **OF** *MenuName2 lExpression4*

Enables or disables a menu item on a Visual FoxPro system menu or a user-defined menu item created with DEFINE BAR. For example, the New command on the Visual FoxPro File menu can be disabled with this command:

```
SET SKIP OF BAR _MFI_NEW OF _MFILE .T.
```

where *SystemItemName* specifies the menu command `_MFI_NEW`, *MenuName2* specifies the menu `_MFILE`, and *lExpression4* specifies the logical expression `.T.`. The menu command can be enabled with this command:

```
SET SKIP OF BAR _MFI_NEW OF _MFILE .F.
```

Use *nMenuItemNumber* to specify a menu item created with DEFINE BAR.

Remarks

For a complete listing of the internal names of Visual FoxPro system menu components, see "System Menu Names," later in this language reference. You can also use SYS(2013) to return the system menu internal names.

If the logical expression *lExpression* evaluates to true (.T.), the menu, menu bar, menu name, or menu item included in SET SKIP OF is disabled, appears dimmed, and can't be selected. If *lExpression* evaluates to false (.F.), the menu, menu bar, menu name, or menu item is enabled and can be selected.

See Also

CREATE MENU, DEFINE BAR, DEFINE MENU, DEFINE PAD, DEFINE POPUP, System Menu Names Overview, SKPBAR( )

SET SPACE Command

Determines whether a space is displayed between fields or expressions when you use the ? or ?? command.

Syntax

SET SPACE ON | OFF

Arguments

ON

(Default) Inserts a space between fields and expressions.

OFF

Removes all spaces between fields or expressions and runs them together.

See Also

? | ??

SET STATUS Command

Displays or removes the character-based status bar.

Syntax

SET STATUS ON | OFF

Arguments

ON

> If SET STATUS is ON, the character-based status bar is displayed showing the name of the program currently executing (if any) the alias of the active table, the current record pointer position, the number of records in the table, and the state of the Insert, NumLock and CapsLock keys. The record or file lock status is also shown in the status bar when the table is opened for shared use. The status bar is updated each time you execute a command that changes status information.

OFF

> (Default) Issue SET STATUS OFF to remove the status bar.

See Also

SET STATUS BAR, StatusBarText Property

SET STATUS BAR Command

Displays or removes the graphical status bar.

Syntax

SET STATUS BAR ON | OFF

Arguments

ON

> Issue SET STATUS BAR ON to display the graphical status bar.

OFF

> (Default) Issue SET STATUS BAR OFF to remove the graphical status bar.

See Also

SET STATUS, StatusBarText Property

SET STEP Command

Opens the Trace window and suspends program execution for debugging.

Syntax

SET STEP ON

Arguments

ON
Opens the Trace window and suspends program execution.

Remarks

SET STEP is used to debug programs. You can insert SET STEP ON in a program at the point where you'd like to execute individual commands.

For information about the "Trace Window," see Chapter 14, "Testing and Debugging Applications," in the *Microsoft Visual FoxPro 6.0 Programmer's Guide.*

You can pass parameters to a program and then trace its execution by following these steps:

8. Open the Trace window.

9. From the Trace window's Program menu, choose Open and select the program to trace.

10. Set a breakpoint on the first executable line of the program.

11. In the Command window, DO the program WITH the parameters.

See Also

SET ECHO

SET STRICTDATE Command

Specifies if ambiguous Date and DateTime constants generate errors.

Syntax

SET STRICTDATE TO [0 | 1 | 2]

Arguments

0
Specifies that strict date format checking is off. This setting provides compatibility with earlier versions of Visual FoxPro. 0 is the default setting for the Visual FoxPro runtime and ODBC driver. When STRICTDATE is set to 0, invalid Date and DateTimes evaluate to the empty date.

1

Specifies that all Date and DateTime constants be in the strict date format. Any Date or DateTime constant that is not in the strict format or evaluates to an invalid value generates an error, either during compilation, at runtime, or during an interactive Visual FoxPro session. 1 is the default setting for an interactive Visual FoxPro session.

2

Identical to setting STRICTDATE to 1, but also generates a compilation error (2033 – CTOD and CTOT can produce incorrect results) whenever CTOD( ) and CTOT( ) functions appear in code.

Because the values returned by CTOD( ) and CTOT( ) rely on SET DATE and SET CENTURY to interpret the date string they contain, they are prone to year 2000 noncompliance errors. Use DATE( ) and DATETIME( ) with the optional numeric arguments to create Date and DateTime constants and expressions.

This setting is most useful during debugging sessions to trap for code that may contain year 2000 compliance errors.

Remarks

Note that the StrictDateEntry property isn't affected by the setting of SET STRICTDATE.

For more information about strict date formats, see "Year 2000 Date Support" in Chapter 33, "Programming Improvements," in the *Microsoft Visual FoxPro 6.0 Programmer's Guide*.

See Also

COMPILE, CTOD( ), CTOT( ), SET LOGERRORS, StrictDateEntry Property

SET SYSFORMATS Command

Specifies whether Visual FoxPro for Windows system settings are updated with the current Microsoft Windows system settings.

Syntax

SET SYSFORMATS ON | OFF

Arguments

ON

Specifies that the Visual FoxPro system settings are updated when the Windows system settings are changed. SET SYSFORMAT ON is identical to choosing the Use System Settings check box on the International tab of the Options dialog. Note that issuing SET SYSFORMAT ON changes the SET DATE setting to SHORT.

The settings are used for the duration of the current data session, or, if issued during the default data session, for the duration of the Visual FoxPro session.

OFF

(Default) Specifies that the Visual FoxPro system settings are not updated when the Windows system settings are changed. The Visual FoxPro default settings are not restored.

Remarks

The Windows system settings are specified in International option of the Windows Control Panel.

When SET SYSFORMATS is ON, the following SET commands can be used to override the current system settings. However, changing the Windows system settings when SET SYSFORMATS is ON overrides these SET commands:

- SET CENTURY
- SET CURRENCY
- SET DATE
- SET DECIMALS
- SET HOURS
- SET MARK TO
- SET POINT
- SET SEPARATOR

When Visual FoxPro is started, the Visual FoxPro system settings are the default settings of these SET commands. To use the Windows system settings when Visual FoxPro is started, place the following line in your Visual FoxPro Config.fpw configuration file:

```
SYSFORMATS = ON
```

SET SYSFORMATS is scoped to the current data session.

See Also

SET CENTURY, SET CURRENCY, SET DATASESSION, SET DATE, SET DECIMALS, SET HOURS, SET MARK TO, SET POINT, SET SEPARATOR

SET SYSMENU Command

Enables or disables the Visual FoxPro system menu bar during program execution, and allows you to reconfigure it.

Syntax

SET SYSMENU ON | OFF | AUTOMATIC
    | TO [*MenuList*]
    | TO [*MenuTitleList*]
    | TO [DEFAULT] | SAVE | NOSAVE

Arguments

ON

> Enables the main Visual FoxPro menu bar during program execution when Visual FoxPro is waiting for keyboard input during commands such as BROWSE, READ, and MODIFY COMMAND.

OFF

> Disables the main Visual FoxPro menu bar during program execution.

AUTOMATIC

> Makes the main Visual FoxPro menu bar visible during program execution. The menu bar is accessible and menu items are enabled and disabled as appropriate for the current command.

> AUTOMATIC is the default setting.

TO [*MenuList*]
TO [*MenuTitleList*]

> Specifies a subset of menus or menu titles for the main Visual FoxPro menu bar. The menu or menu title list can contain any combination of menus or menu titles separated by commas. The internal names for the menus and menu titles are listed in the System Menu Names topic.

> For example, the following command removes all menus from the main Visual FoxPro menu bar except the File and Window menus:

```
SET SYSMENU TO _MFILE, _MWINDOW
```

> Use RELEASE BAR to specify the menu items available in the menus.

TO [DEFAULT]

> Restores the main menu bar to its default configuration. If you have modified the main menu bar or its menus, issue SET SYSMENU TO DEFAULT to restore it. You can specify a default configuration with SET SYSMENU SAVE.

SAVE

> Makes the current menu system the default configuration. If you modify the menu system after issuing SET SYSMENU SAVE, you can restore the previous configuration by issuing SET SYSMENU TO DEFAULT.

NOSAVE

> Resets the menu system to the default Visual FoxPro system menu. However, the default Visual FoxPro system menu is not displayed until you issue SET SYSMENU TO DEFAULT.

Remarks

SET SYSMENU controls the main Visual FoxPro menu bar during program execution and lets you selectively remove menu titles and menus from and restore them to the main Visual FoxPro menu system.

Issuing SET SYSMENU TO without additional arguments disables the main Visual FoxPro menu bar.

See Also

System Menu Names, POP MENU, PUSH MENU, RELEASE, SYS(2013) – System Menu Name String

SET TALK Command

Determines whether Visual FoxPro displays command results.

Syntax

SET TALK ON | OFF | WINDOW [*WindowName*] | NOWINDOW

Arguments

ON
> (Default) Allows talk to be sent to the main Visual FoxPro window, the system message window, the graphical status bar, or a user-defined window. If SET TALK is set to OFF and is then changed to ON, the talk is directed to the same location it was sent to before you issued SET TALK OFF.

OFF
> Prevents talk from being sent to the main Visual FoxPro window, the system message window, the graphical status bar, or a user-defined window. Note that for in-process .dll automation servers the default setting of SET TALK is OFF.

WINDOW [*WindowName*]
> *WindowName* specifies a user-defined window to which talk is directed. You must create the user-defined window before directing talk to it. Talk is directed to the Visual FoxPro system window if the window you specify doesn't exist.

NOWINDOW
> Directs talk to the main Visual FoxPro window.

Remarks

Some table processing commands return information, or "talk," about their status while they execute. These commands include:

Commands

APPEND FROM	AVERAGE	CALCULATE
COPY TO	COUNT	DELETE
INDEX	PACK	REINDEX
REPLACE	SELECT – SQL	SORT
SUM	TOTAL	

Talk can be directed to the main Visual FoxPro window, the graphical status bar, or a user-defined window. Talk can also be turned off.

The SET TALK reporting interval can be specified with SET ODOMETER. The default value for SET ODOMETER is 100. Note that execution speed can be degraded when SET TALK is set to ON, because the main Visual FoxPro window or user-defined window must be frequently updated. If you just need the total number of records processed by a command, you can issue SET TALK OFF and display the _TALLY system variable once the command has completed executing.

SET TALK is scoped to the current data session.

See Also

DEFINE WINDOW, SET DATASESSION, SET NOTIFY, SET ODOMETER, SYS(103) – Talk Setting, _TALLY

SET TEXTMERGE Command

Enables or disables the evaluation of fields, variables, array elements, functions, or expressions that are surrounded by text-merge delimiters, and lets you specify text-merge output.

Syntax

SET TEXTMERGE
   [ON | OFF]
   [TO [*FileName*] [ADDITIVE]]
   [WINDOW *WindowName*]
   [SHOW | NOSHOW]

Arguments

ON

Specifies that any fields, variables, array elements, functions, or expressions surrounded by the text-merge delimiters be evaluated and output when placed after \ or \\, or between TEXT and ENDTEXT.

The following short program example demonstrates how the contents of the variable gcTodayDate and the DATE( ) and TIME( ) functions are evaluated when SET TEXTMERGE is set to ON. The variable gcTodayDate, DATE( ), and TIME( ) are evaluated because they are enclosed by the text-merge delimiters and SET TEXTMERGE is set to ON.

```
CLEAR
SET TALK OFF
STORE 'Today is: ' TO gcTodayDate
SET TEXTMERGE ON
```

```
\<<gcTodayDate>>
\\<<DATE( )>>
\The time is:
\\ <<TIME( )>>
```

Here is the output from the program above when run on January 1:

```
Today is: 01/01/1998
The time is: 10:55:19
```

OFF

(Default) Specifies that any fields, variables, array elements, functions, or expressions be literally output along with the text-merge delimiters surrounding them. Note the difference in output when SET TEXTMERGE is set to OFF in the previous example:

```
CLEAR
SET TALK OFF
STORE 'Today is: ' TO gcTodayDate
SET TEXTMERGE OFF
\<<gcTodayDate>>
\\<<DATE( )>>
\The time is:
\\ <<TIME( )>>
```

Here is the output from this program:

```
<<gcTodayDate>><<DATE( )>>
The time is: <<TIME( )>>
```

TO [*FileName*]

Specifies that output from \, \\, and TEXT ... ENDTEXT be directed to a text file rather than the main Visual FoxPro window, which is the default. You can also direct the output to a text file by including *FileName*. If a file with that name doesn't exist, a new file is created. If a file with the same name already exists and SET SAFETY is set to ON, you are given the option of overwriting the existing file.

The text file is opened as a low-level file, and its file handle is stored to the _TEXT system variable. You can close the file by issuing SET TEXTMERGE TO without additional arguments. If the file handle of another file was previously stored in _TEXT, that file is closed.

ADDITIVE

Specifies that output from \, \\, and TEXT ... ENDTEXT be appended to an existing file keyword.

For more information on directing text-merge output to a file, see the _TEXT System Variable, later in this language reference.

WINDOW *WindowName*

Specifies that output from \, \\, and TEXT ... ENDTEXT be directed to a user-defined window rather than the main Visual FoxPro window, which is the default. *WindowName* specifies the name of the window to which you want to direct output. The window must be created with DEFINE WINDOW before output can be sent to it. The window doesn't have to be active or visible.

SHOW | NOSHOW

(Default) SHOW displays text-merge output.

NOSHOW suppresses display of text-merge output.

By default, output generated by \, \\, and TEXT ... ENDTEXT is sent to the main Visual FoxPro window or an active user-defined window.

Remarks

The \, \\, and TEXT ... ENDTEXT commands are used to merge text with the contents of tables, variables, array elements, and the results of functions and expressions. If a field, variable, array element, function, or expression is surrounded by text-merge delimiters (by default, << and >>), it can be evaluated and merged with text. This text-merge capability lets you produce letters, programs, and templates that create programs.

SET TEXTMERGE determines how fields, variables, array elements, functions, or expressions surrounded by text-merge delimiters are evaluated. It also lets you direct text-merge output to the main Visual FoxPro window, a user-defined window, or a file.

Memo fields can be used to nest merged text. If a memo field contains field names, variables, array elements, functions, or expressions surrounded by the current text-merge delimiters, these are evaluated and output with the contents of the memo field. The memo field name must also be enclosed in text-merge delimiters.

See Also

\ | \\, _PRETEXT, SET TEXTMERGE DELIMITERS, _TEXT

SET TEXTMERGE DELIMITERS Command

Specifies the text-merge delimiters.

Syntax

SET TEXTMERGE DELIMITERS
  [TO *cLeftDelimiter* [, *cRightDelimiter*]]

Arguments

TO *cLeftDelimiter* [, *cRightDelimiter*]
> Specifies the delimiters. If you specify only one delimiter with *cLeftDelimiter*, both the left and right delimiters are set to *cLeftDelimiter*. If you specify both delimiters with *cLeftDelimiter* and *cRightDelimiter*, the left delimiter is set to *cLeftDelimiter* and the right delimiter is set to *cRightDelimiter*.

Remarks

With SET TEXTMERGE DELIMITERS, you can specify a set of text-merge delimiters other than the default delimiters, which are double angle brackets (<< and >>). The current delimiters can be displayed with DISPLAY STATUS.

If you issue SET TEXTMERGE DELIMITERS without any additional arguments, the default delimiters are restored.

For more information about text-merge delimiters, see the SET TEXTMERGE Command, earlier in this language reference.

See Also

\ | \\, _PRETEXT, SET TEXTMERGE, _TEXT

SET TOPIC Command

Specifies the Help topic or topics to open when you invoke the Visual FoxPro Help system.

Syntax

SET TOPIC TO [*cHelpTopicName* | *lExpression*]

Arguments

cHelpTopicName
> Specifies the name of the Help topic you want to display.

lExpression
> A logical expression that is the basis for opening a specific topic or topics.

Remarks

For more information on creating your own Help system, see Part 7, "Creating Help Files," in the *Microsoft Visual FoxPro 6.0 Programmer's Guide*.

See Also

HELP, SET HELP, SET HELPFILTER, SET TOPIC ID

SET TOPIC ID Command

Specifies the Help topic to display when you invoke the Visual FoxPro Help system. The Help topic is based on the topic's context ID.

Syntax

SET TOPIC ID TO *nHelpContextID*

Arguments

nHelpContextID
Specifies the Help topic to display, based on a numerical context ID. *nHelpContextID* is a context number in the MAP section of the Help project file.

See Also

HELP, SET HELP, SET TOPIC

SET TRBETWEEN Command

Enables or disables tracing between breakpoints in the Trace window.

Syntax

SET TRBETWEEN ON | OFF

Arguments

ON
Specifies that every line of program code be displayed and highlighted in the Trace window as it is executed. Issuing SET TRBETWEEN ON is identical to enabling the Trace Between Breaks command in the Trace window's Program menu.

OFF
(Default) Specifies that only the last line at which program execution was paused be highlighted in the Trace window. Issuing SET TRBETWEEN OFF is identical to disabling the Trace Between Breaks command.

Remarks

The Trace window displays the source code for a program as the program executes. The executing program line is highlighted. When the Trace window is open, you can set breakpoints that cause program execution to stop.

The Trace window can also be opened by issuing ACTIVATE WINDOW TRACE, SET ECHO ON, or SET STEP ON.

See Also

ACTIVATE WINDOW, SET ECHO, SET STEP

SET TYPEAHEAD Command

Specifies the maximum number of characters that can be stored in the type-ahead buffer.

Syntax

SET TYPEAHEAD TO *nCharacters*

Arguments

nCharacters
Specifies the maximum number of characters to store in the type-ahead buffer.

No characters are held in the type-ahead buffer if you issue SET TYPEAHEAD TO 0. This statement deactivates INKEY( ) and ON KEY.

Remarks

The type-ahead buffer can store as many as 32,000 characters until the they are ready to be processed. The default value for SET TYPEAHEAD is 20.

See Also

INKEY( ), ON KEY

SET UDFPARMS Command

Specifies if Microsoft Visual FoxPro passes parameters to a user-defined function (UDF) by value or by reference.

Syntax

SET UDFPARMS TO VALUE | REFERENCE

Arguments

TO VALUE
Specifies that a variable be passed to a user-defined function by value. When a variable is passed by value, the variable's value can be changed in the user-defined function, but the variable's original value in the calling program isn't changed.

TO REFERENCE
Specifies that a variable be passed to a user-defined function by reference. When a variable is passed by reference and the user-defined function changes the value of the passed variable, the variable's original value in the calling program is also changed.

Remarks

By default, variables are passed to a user-defined function by value. (Variables passed to procedures with DO ... WITH are passed by reference.)

You can force parameters to be passed to a UDF by value or reference, regardless of the setting of SET UDFPARMS. Enclose a variable in parentheses to force the variable to be passed by value. Preface the variable with an @ symbol to force the variable to be passed by reference.

Tip Entire arrays can be passed to a procedure or user-defined function. The entire array is passed if you issue SET UDFPARMS TO REFERENCE or preface the array name with @. The first element of the array is passed by value if you issue SET UDFPARMS TO VALUE or enclose the array name by parentheses. Array elements are always passed by value.

Example

The following example illustrates the difference between passing variables by value and by reference.

```
*** Pass variable by value ***
CLEAR
SET TALK OFF
WAIT 'Press a key to pass by value' WINDOW
SET UDFPARMS TO VALUE
STORE 1 TO gnX

*** The value of gnX is unchanged ***
@ 2,2 SAY 'UDF value: ' + STR(plusone(gnX))
@ 4,2 SAY 'Value of gnX: ' + STR(gnX)

*** Pass variable by reference ***
WAIT 'Press a key to pass by reference' WINDOW
CLEAR
SET UDFPARMS TO REFERENCE
STORE 1 TO gnX
*** The value of gnX is changed ***
@ 2,2 SAY 'UDF value: ' + STR(plusone(gnX))
@ 4,2 SAY 'Value of X: ' + STR(gnX)
SET UDFPARMS TO VALUE

*** This is a UDF that adds one to a number ***
FUNCTION plusone
PARAMETER gnZ
gnZ = gnZ + 1
RETURN gnZ
*** End of UDF ***
```

The following is the above example with variables passed by value and reference through the use of parentheses and @, respectively.

```
*** Pass variable by value ***
CLEAR
SET TALK OFF
```

```
WAIT 'Press a key to pass by value' WINDOW
STORE 1 TO gnX
@ 2,2 SAY 'UDF value: ' + STR(plusone((gnX)))
@ 4,2 SAY 'Value of gnX: ' + STR(gnX)

*** Pass variable by reference ***
WAIT 'Press a key to pass by reference' WINDOW
CLEAR
STORE 1 TO gnX
@ 2,2 SAY 'UDF value: ' + STR(plusone(@gnX))
@ 4,2 SAY 'Value of gnX: ' + STR(gnX)

*** This is a UDF that adds one to a number ***
FUNCTION plusone
PARAMETER gnZ
gnZ = gnZ + 1
RETURN gnZ
*** End of UDF ***
```

See Also

DO, LPARAMETERS, PARAMETERS, PARAMETERS( ), PROCEDURE

SET UNIQUE Command

Specifies whether records with duplicate index key values are maintained in an index file.

Syntax

SET UNIQUE ON | OFF

Arguments

ON

Specifies that any record with a duplicate index key value not be included in the index file. Only the first record with the original index key value is included in the index file.

OFF

(Default) Specifies that records with duplicate index key values be included in the index file.

Remarks

An index file retains its SET UNIQUE setting when you issue REINDEX. For more information, see the INDEX and REINDEX Commands, earlier in this language reference.

SET UNIQUE is scoped to the current data session.

See Also

INDEX, REINDEX, SET DATASESSION

SET VIEW Command

Opens or closes the Data Session window or restores the Visual FoxPro environment from a view file.

Syntax

SET VIEW ON | OFF

– or –

SET VIEW TO *FileName* | ?

Arguments

ON

Opens the Data Session window.

OFF

(Default) Closes the Data Session window.

TO *FileName*

Restores the Visual FoxPro environment to the state it was in when the view file specified with *FileName* was created. View files are created with CREATE VIEW.

?

Displays the Open dialog box, from which you can open a view file.

Remarks

For more information on view files, see the CREATE VIEW Command, later in this language reference.

See Also

CREATE VIEW, SET

SET WINDOW OF MEMO Command

Included for backward compatibility. Use the TextBox Control instead.

SET( ) Function

Returns the status of various SET commands.

Syntax

SET(*cSETCommand* [, 1 | *cExpression* | 2 | 3])

Returns

Character, Numeric

Arguments

cSETCommand

A character expression specifying the SET command for which you want information returned. The current setting of the specified command is returned as a character or numeric string.

1 | *cExpression* | 2 | 3

Specifies that additional information about a SET command be returned. 1 and *cExpression* are identical; *cExpression* can be any expression that evaluates to a character type value.

Including an argument doesn't return additional information for all SET commands, just those listed with 1, 2, or 3 in the following table.

SET command	Value returned
ALTERNATE	ON or OFF
ALTERNATE, 1	*FileName*
BELL, 1	*cWAVFileName*
CENTURY	ON or OFF
CENTURY, 1	*nCentury*
CENTURY, 2	ROLLOVER *nYear*
CLOCK	ON or OFF
CLOCK, 1	*nRow* and *nColumn*
COMPATIBLE	ON or OFF
COMPATIBLE, 1	PROMPT or NOPROMPT
COVERAGE,1	*FileName*
CURRENCY	LEFT or RIGHT
CURRENCY, 1	*cCurrencySymbol*
DATE	AMERICAN, ANSI, BRITISH/FRENCH, GERMAN, ITALIAN, JAPAN, USA, MDY, DMY, or YMD
DATE, 1	Date Ordering: 0 – MDY 1 – DMY 2 – YMD
DELIMITERS	ON or OFF

(continued)

(continued)

SET command	Value returned
DELIMITERS, 1	*cDelimiters*
EVENTTRACKING	ON or OFF
EVENTTRACKING, 1	*FileName*
FIELDS	ON or OFF
FIELDS, 1	*FieldName1*, *FieldName2*, ...
FIELDS, 2	LOCAL or GLOBAL
HELP	ON or OFF
HELP, 1	*FileName*
KEY	*eExpression2*, *eExpression3*
KEY, 1	*eExpression2*
KEY, 2	*eExpression3*
MESSAGE	*nRow*
MESSAGE, 1	*cMessageText*
MOUSE	ON or OFF
MOUSE, 1	*nSensitivity*
PRINTER	ON or OFF
PRINTER, 1	*FileName* or *PortName*
PRINTER, 2	Default Windows printer name
PRINTER, 3	Default Visual FoxPro printer name (specified in the Visual FoxPro Print or Print Setup dialog boxes)
RESOURCE	ON or OFF
RESOURCE, 1	*FileName*
TALK	ON or OFF
TALK, 1	WINDOW, NOWINDOW or *WindowName*
TEXTMERGE	ON or OFF
TEXTMERGE, 1	*cLeftDelimiter* and *cRightDelimiter*
TOPIC	*cHelpTopicName*	*lExpression*
TOPIC, 1	*nContextID*

Remarks

SET( ) recognizes the four character abbreviation for all Visual FoxPro SET keywords (with the exception of HELPFILTER, which can be abbreviated to five characters). For example, STAT and PRIN can be used for SET STATUS and SET PRINTER, respectively.

The SET( ) function is identical to SYS(2001).

See Also

DISPLAY STATUS, LIST, SET, SYS(2001) – SET Command Status

SetAll Method

Assigns a property setting on all, or a certain class of, controls in a Container object.

Syntax

Container.SetAll(*cProperty*, *Value* [, *cClass*])

Arguments

cProperty
Specifies the property to be set.

Value
Specifies the new setting for the property. The data type of *Value* depends on the property being set.

cClass
Specifies the class name (the class on which the object is based, not the Visual FoxPro base class for the object).

Remarks

Use the SetAll method to set a property for all, or a certain class of, controls in a Container. For example, to set the BackColor property on all the Column objects in a Grid control to red, issue the following:

```
Form1.Grid1.SetAll("BackColor", RGB(255, 0, 0), "Column")
```

You can also set the properties for objects that are contained by other objects within the container. To set the ForeColor property of the Headers that are contained by each Column object contained in a Grid control to green, issue the following:

```
Form1.Grid1.SetAll("ForeColor", RGB(0, 255, 0), "Header")
```

Example

The following example uses the SetAll method with the DynamicBackColor property to specify the background colors for the records in a Grid control. If the number of a record displayed in the Grid is even, the record's DynamicBackColor is white, otherwise its DynamicBackColor is green.

A Grid control is placed on a form, and the `customer` table is opened and its contents displayed in the grid. The Caption property is used to specify a different header caption (Customer ID) for the CUST_ID field. A command button is placed on the form to close the form.

```
CLOSE ALL  && Close tables and databases
OPEN DATABASE (HOME(2) + 'Data\testdata')

USE customer  IN 0  && Opens Customer table

frmMyForm = CREATEOBJECT('Form')  && Create a form
frmMyForm.Closable = .f.  && Disable the window pop-up menu

frmMyForm.AddObject('cmdCommand1','cmdMyCmdBtn')  && Add Command button
frmMyForm.AddObject('grdGrid1','Grid')  && Add Grid control

frmMyForm.grdGrid1.Left = 25  && Adjust Grid position

frmMyForm.grdGrid1.SetAll("DynamicBackColor", "IIF(MOD(RECNO( ), 2)=0, RGB(255,255,255),
   RGB(0,255,0))", "Column")  && Alternate white and green records

frmMyForm.grdGrid1.Visible = .T.  && Grid control visible
frmMyForm.cmdCommand1.Visible =.T.  && "Quit" Command button visible
frmMyForm.grdGrid1.Column1.Header1.Caption = 'Customer ID'

frmMyForm.SHOW  && Display the form
READ EVENTS  && Start event processing

DEFINE CLASS cmdMyCmdBtn AS CommandButton  && Create Command button
   Caption = '\<Quit'  && Caption on the Command button
   Cancel = .T.  && Default Cancel Command button (Esc)
   Left = 125  && Command button column
   Top = 210  && Command button row
   Height = 25  && Command button height

   PROCEDURE Click
      CLEAR EVENTS  && Stop event processing, close form
      CLOSE ALL  && Close table and database
ENDDEFINE
```

Applies To

Column, CommandGroup, Container Object, Form, FormSet, Grid, OptionGroup, Page, PageFrame, _SCREEN, ToolBar

See Also

SaveAs Method, SaveAsClass Method

SETFLDSTATE( ) Function

Assigns a field or deletion state value to a field or record in a table or cursor.

Syntax

SETFLDSTATE(*cFieldName* | *nFieldNumber*, *nFieldState*
    [, *cTableAlias* | *nWorkArea*])

Returns

Logical

Arguments

cFieldName | *nFieldNumber*

Specifies the name or the number of the field for which the edit or deletion status is assigned. The field number *nFieldNumber* corresponds to the position of the field in the table or cursor structure. DISPLAY STRUCTURE or FIELD( ) can be used to determine a field's number.

To set the deletion status for the record, include 0 as the field number.

nFieldState

Specifies a value for the field or deletion status. The following table lists the field or deletion state value and the corresponding edit or deletion status:

nFieldState	Edit or deletion status
1	Field has not been edited or deletion status has not changed.
2	Field has been edited or deletion status has changed.
3	Field in an appended record has not been edited or deletion status has not changed for the appended record.
4	Field in an appended record has been edited or deletion status has changed for the appended record.

cTableAlias

Specifies the alias of the table or cursor in which the edit or deletion status is assigned.

nWorkArea

Specifies the work area of the table or cursor in which the edit or deletion status is assigned. The field or deletion state value is assigned for the table or cursor open in the currently selected work area if SETFLDSTATE( ) is issued without the optional *cTableAlias* or *nWorkArea* arguments.

Remarks

Visual FoxPro uses field state values to determine which fields in tables or cursors are updated. SETFLDSTATE( ) lets you control which fields Visual FoxPro attempts to update, regardless of which fields have been edited in the table or cursor.

Example

The following example demonstrates how you can use SETFLDSTATE( ) to change the field status. MULTILOCKS is set to ON, a requirement for table buffering. The `customer` table in the `testdata` database is opened, and CURSORSETPROP( ) is then used to set the buffering mode to optimistic table buffering (5).

GETFLDSTATE( ) is issued to display a value (1) corresponding to the unmodified state of the `cust_id` field before it is modified. The `cust_id` field is modified with REPLACE, and GETFLDSTATE( ) is issued again to display a value (2) corresponding to the modified state of the `cust_id` field.

SETFLDSTATE( ) is used to change the field status of the `cust_id` field back to 1 (unmodified). GETFLDSTATE( ) is issued again and displays 1, corresponding to the state of the `cust_id` field assigned by SETFLDSTATE( ). TABLEREVERT( ) is used to return the table to its original state.

```
CLOSE DATABASES
SET MULTILOCKS ON  && Must be on for table buffering
SET PATH TO (HOME(2) + 'Data\')    && Sets path to database
OPEN DATABASE testdata  && Open testdata database
USE Customer     && Open customer table
= CURSORSETPROP('Buffering', 5, 'customer')  && Enable table buffering

CLEAR
? GETFLDSTATE('cust_id')  && Displays 1, not modified
REPLACE cust_id    WITH '***'  && Changes field contents
? GETFLDSTATE('cust_id')  && Returns 2, field modified
= SETFLDSTATE('cust_id', 1)  && Change the field status
? GETFLDSTATE('cust_id')  && Displays 1, not modified
= TABLEREVERT(.T.)  && Discard all table changes
```

See Also

DELETED( ), DISPLAY STRUCTURE, FIELD( ), GETFLDSTATE( )

SetFocus Method

Assigns the focus to a control.

Syntax

*Control.*SetFocus

Remarks

You cannot assign the focus to a control if the control's Enabled or Visible property is set to false (.F.), or the control's When event returns false (.F.). If the Enabled or Visible property has been set to false (.F.), you must first set it to true (.T.) before the control can receive the focus from the SetFocus method.

Once a control has the focus, any user input is directed to that control.

Applies To

CheckBox, Column, ComboBox, CommandButton, Container Object, Control Object, EditBox, Grid, ListBox, OLE Bound Control, OLE Container Control, OptionButton, Page Object, Spinner, TextBox

See Also

Enabled Property, GotFocus Event, LostFocus Event, Visible Property

SetMain Method

Sets the main file in a project.

Syntax

*Object.*SetMain([*cFileName* [, *cActiveDocClass*]])

Arguments

cFileName
Specifies a file in the project to set as the main file. The main file can be a program, form, or a visual class library containing an Active Document class. Be sure to include the file extension in *cFileName*. If *cFileName* is omitted or is the empty string, no file in the project is set as the main file.

cActiveDocClass
Specifies an Active Document class to set as the main file. To specify an Active Document class as the main file, *cFileName* must be the name of the visual class library containing the Active Document class.

Remarks

The SetMain method returns true (.T.) if the file or Active Document class you specify is set as the main file. False (.F.) is returned if the file or Active Document class you specify isn't in the project or the file you specify isn't the proper file type.

The main file is a program (.prg file), form (.scx file), or Active Document class that serves as the execution starting point for a compiled application, and from which other components of your application are called. Typically, the main file sets the application's operational environment, runs menu programs or forms to display the application's interface, and establishes the event loop of the application with the READ EVENTS command. You must designate a main file in the Project Manager before you can create an application (.app) or executable file (.exe) from the project.

Note Specifying a file or Active Document class as the main file in a project also sets the project's MainFile and MainClass properties.

Applies To

Project Object

See Also

MainClass Property, MainFile Property

SetVar Method

Creates a variable and stores a value to the variable for an instance of the Visual FoxPro application automation server.

Syntax

ApplicationObject.SetVar(*cVariableName*, *eValue*)

Arguments

cVariableName
Specifies the name of the variable to create.

eValue
Specifies the value stored to the variable. If the variable specified with *cVariableName* already exists, the new value is store to the variable.

Remarks

While the DoCmd method can be used to set a variable to a character value, the SetVar method should be used to set a variable to other data types.

Applies To

Application Object, _VFP System Variable

See Also

DoCmd Method, Eval Method, STORE

SetViewPort Method

Sets the values of the ViewPortLeft and ViewPortTop properties for a form.

Syntax

Object.SetViewPort(*nLeft*, *nTop*)

Arguments

nLeft
Specifies the value of the ViewPortLeft property for the form.

nTop
Specifies the value of the ViewPortTop property for the form.

Remarks

The SetViewPort method returns true (.T.) if the ViewPortLeft and ViewPortTop properties are successfully set; otherwise false (.F.) is returned. The SetViewPort method is ignored for forms that do not contain scroll bars.

The unit of measurement for the ViewPortLeft and ViewPortTop properties is determined by the form's ScaleMode property setting – pixels (the default) or foxels.

Applies To

Form

See Also

ScaleMode Property, ScrollBars Property, ViewPortLeft Property, ViewPortHeight Property, ViewPortTop Property, ViewPortWidth Property

Shape Control

Creates a Shape control that displays a box, circle, or ellipse.

Syntax

Shape

Remarks

A Shape control is a graphical control that displays a box, circle, or ellipse that can't be changed directly. However, because a Shape control has a full set of properties, events, and methods that other controls have, the Shape control can respond to events and can be changed dynamically at run time.

The Curvature property determines what shape is displayed and can vary from 0 to 99. 0 specifies no curvature and creates square corners; 99 specifies maximum curvature and creates circles and ellipses.

For additional information about creating shapes, see "Form Designer" in Help, and Chapter 10, "Using Controls," in the *Microsoft Visual FoxPro 6.0 Programmer's Guide*.

Properties

Application	BackColor	BackStyle
BaseClass	BorderColor	BorderStyle
BorderWidth	Class	ClassLibrary
ColorScheme	ColorSource	Comment
Curvature	DragIcon	DragMode
DrawMode	Enabled	FillColor
FillStyle	Height	HelpContextID
Left	MouseIcon	MousePointer
Name	OLEDragMode	OLEDragPicture
OLEDropEffects	OLEDropHasData Property	OLEDropMode
Parent	ParentClass	SpecialEffect
Tag	ToolTipText	Top
Visible	WhatsThisHelpID	Width

Events

Click	DblClick	Destroy
DragDrop	DragOver	Error
Init	MiddleClick Event	MouseDown
MouseMove	MouseUp	MouseWheel
OLECompleteDrag	OLEDragDrop	OLEDragOver
OLEGiveFeedBack	OLESetData	OLEStartDrag
RightClick	UIEnable	

Methods

AddProperty	CloneObject	Drag
Move	OLEDrag	ReadExpression

ReadMethod	ResetToDefault	SaveAsClass
ShowWhatsThis	WriteExpression	WriteMethod
ZOrder		

Example

The following example demonstrates how the Shape control can be used to display a circle, ellipse, or square on a form.

A form is created, and a set of option buttons and a command button are placed on the form. When you click one of the option buttons, the corresponding shape is displayed on the form. The Visible property is set to true (.T.) to display a shape; it is set to false (.F.) to hide the shape before another shape is displayed. The Height, Width, and Curvature properties of each shape determine the type of shape (circle, ellipse, or square) created.

```
frmMyForm = CREATEOBJECT('Form')  && Create a Form
frmMyForm.Closable = .F.  && Disable the Control menu box

frmMyForm.AddObject('cmdCommand1','cmdMyCmndBtn')  && Add Command button
frmMyForm.AddObject('opgOptionGroup1','opgMyOptGrp') && Add Option Group
frmMyForm.AddObject('shpCircle1','shpMyCircle')  && Add Circle Shape
frmMyForm.AddObject('shpEllipse1','shpMyEllipse')  && Add Ellipse Shape
frmMyForm.AddObject('shpSquare','shpMySquare')  && Add Box Shape

frmMyForm.cmdCommand1.Visible =.T.  && "Quit" Command button visible

frmMyForm.opgOptionGroup1.Buttons(1).Caption = "\<Circle"
frmMyForm.opgOptionGroup1.Buttons(2).Caption = "\<Ellipse"
frmMyForm.opgOptionGroup1.Buttons(3).Caption = "\<Square"
frmMyForm.opgOptionGroup1.SetAll("Width", 100) && Set Option group width
frmMyForm.opgOptionGroup1.Visible = .T.  && Option Group visible
frmMyForm.opgOptionGroup1.Click  && Show the circle

frmMyForm.SHOW  && Display the form
READ EVENTS  && Start event processing

DEFINE CLASS opgMyOptGrp AS OptionGroup  && Create an Option Group
   ButtonCount = 3  && Three Option buttons
   Top = 10
   Left = 10
   Height = 75
   Width = 100

   PROCEDURE Click
      ThisForm.shpCircle1.Visible = .F.  && Hide the circle
      ThisForm.shpEllipse1.Visible = .F.  && Hide the ellipse
      ThisForm.shpSquare.Visible = .F.  && Hide the square
```

```
        DO CASE
           CASE ThisForm.opgOptionGroup1.Value = 1
              ThisForm.shpCircle1.Visible = .T. && Show the circle
           CASE ThisForm.opgOptionGroup1.Value = 2
              ThisForm.shpEllipse1.Visible = .T.  && Show the ellipse
           CASE ThisForm.opgOptionGroup1.Value = 3
              ThisForm.shpSquare.Visible = .T.  && Show the square
        ENDCASE
ENDDEFINE

DEFINE CLASS cmdMyCmndBtn AS CommandButton  && Create Command button
   Caption = '\<Quit'  && Caption on the Command button
   Cancel = .T.  && Default Cancel Command button (Esc)
   Left = 125  && Command button column
   Top = 210  && Command button row
   Height = 25  && Command button height

   PROCEDURE Click
      CLEAR EVENTS  && Stop event processing, close Form
ENDDEFINE

DEFINE CLASS shpMyCircle AS Shape  && Create a circle
   Top = 10
   Left = 200
   Width = 100
   Height = 100
   Curvature = 99
   BackColor = RGB(255,0,0)  && Red
ENDDEFINE

DEFINE CLASS shpMyEllipse AS Shape  && Create an ellipse
   Top = 35
   Left = 200
   Width = 100
   Height = 50
   Curvature = 99
   BackColor = RGB(0,128,0)  && Green
ENDDEFINE

DEFINE CLASS shpMySquare AS Shape  && Create a square
   Top = 10
   Left = 200
   Width = 100
   Height = 100
   Curvature = 0
   BackColor = RGB(0,0,255)  && Blue
ENDDEFINE
```

See Also

CREATE CLASS, CREATE FORM, DEFINE CLASS

_SHELL System Variable

Specifies a program shell.

Syntax

_SHELL = *cCommand*

Remarks

The _SHELL system memory variable is used to prevent access to the Command window while a program is running in Visual FoxPro. The DO command with the name of a program to execute is usually stored to _SHELL.

You can also specify a command to execute when Visual FoxPro is started by placing the SHELL configuration item in your Visual FoxPro configuration file.

The following example demonstrates how _SHELL typically can be used.

1. A startup program named Mystart.prg is used to launch another program named Myapp.prg. Mystart.prg stores the command to run Myapp.prg to _SHELL. This starts Myapp.prg. Before Visual FoxPro displays the Command window, _SHELL is checked for a command. If _SHELL contains a command, it is executed and Visual FoxPro then stores the empty string to _SHELL.

2. After the initialization code in Myapp.prg is successfully executed, the command to launch Myapp.prg is stored again to _SHELL. Visual FoxPro does not execute the command or store the empty string to _SHELL, and access to the Command window is prevented. (The Command window cannot be accessed when _SHELL contains anything but the empty string).

3. Before Myapp.prg finishes execution, it stores the empty string to _SHELL to restore access to the Command window.

```
*** MYSTART.PRG ***
...
_SHELL = "DO MYAPP.PRG"

*** MYAPP.PRG ***
*** Initialization Code ***
...
*** Initialization Code successfully completed? ***
_SHELL = "DO MYAPP.PRG" && Prevents access to Command window
...
*** Clean up Code ***
_SHELL = ""
```

See Also

DO, RUN | !, _STARTUP System Variable

SHOW GET Command

Included for backward compatibility. Use the Refresh method to redisplay a control after changing the control's properties.

SHOW GETS Command

Included for backward compatibility. Use the Refresh method to redisplay all controls on a form or formset after changing the control's properties.

SHOW MENU Command

Displays one or more user-defined menu bars without activating them.

Syntax

SHOW MENU *MenuBarName1* [, *MenuBarName2* ...] | ALL
    [PAD *MenuTitleName*]
    [SAVE]

Arguments

MenuBarName1 [, *MenuBarName2* ...]
    Specifies the name of one or more menu bars to display.

ALL
    Displays all currently defined menu bars.

PAD *MenuTitleName*
    Specifies a menu title to be highlighted on a menu bar.

SAVE
    Retains an image of the specified menu bars without activating them. You can clear the menu bar images with CLEAR.

Remarks

The menu bars are displayed but can't be used. Before they can be displayed, you must first create the menu bars with DEFINE MENU.

Example

```
CLEAR
DEFINE MENU mnuExample BAR AT LINE 2
DEFINE PAD padConv OF mnuExample PROMPT '\<Conversions' COLOR SCHEME 3 ;
    KEY ALT+C, ''
```

```
DEFINE PAD padCard OF mnuExample PROMPT 'Card \<Info' COLOR SCHEME 3 ;
   KEY ALT+I, ''
SHOW MENU mnuExample
```

See Also

ACTIVATE MENU, CREATE MENU, DEFINE MENU

Show Method

Displays a form and determines whether the form is modal or modeless.

Syntax

[*FormSet.*]*Object*.Show([*nStyle*])

Arguments

nStyle

Determines how a form is shown. The following values are valid:

Value	Description
1	Modal. No user input (keyboard or mouse) can occur in any other form or in the menu until the modal form is hidden or released. The program must hide or release a modal form (usually in response to some user action) before further user input can occur. Although other forms in your application are disabled when a modal form is displayed, other applications are not.
2	(Default) Modeless. Code that occurs after the Show method is run as it is encountered.

If you omit *nStyle*, the form is shown in the style specified by the WindowType property.

Remarks

The Show method sets a form or form set's Visible property to true (.T.) and makes the form the active object. If a form's Visible property is already set to true (.T.), the Show method makes it the active object.

If a form set is activated, the last active form in the form set also becomes active. If no form is active, the form that was added to the FormSet class definition first is made active.

Forms contained within a form set retain their Visible property setting. If a form's Visible property is set to false (.F.), the Show method for the form set does not show the form.

Applies To

Form, FormSet, _SCREEN, ToolBar

See Also

Activate Event, Hide Method, Visible Property, WindowType Property

SHOW OBJECT Command

Included for backward compatibility. Use the Refresh method to redisplay a control after changing the control's properties.

SHOW POPUP Command

Displays one or more menus defined with DEFINE POPUP without activating them.

Syntax

SHOW POPUP *MenuName1* [, *MenuName2* ...] | ALL
    [SAVE]

Arguments

MenuName1 [, *MenuName2* ...]
    Specifies the name of one or more menus to display.

ALL
    Displays all currently defined menus.

SAVE
    Retains an image of the specified menus without activating them. The menu images can be cleared with CLEAR.

Remarks

The menus are displayed but can't be used. Before they can be shown, the menus must first be created with DEFINE POPUP.

See Also

ACTIVATE POPUP, DEFINE POPUP

SHOW WINDOW Command

Displays one or more user-defined windows or Visual FoxPro system windows without activating them.

Syntax

SHOW WINDOW *WindowName1* [, *WindowName2* ...] | ALL | SCREEN
    [IN [WINDOW] *WindowName3*]
    [REFRESH]
    [TOP | BOTTOM | SAME]
    [SAVE]

Arguments

WindowName1 [, *WindowName2* ...]

Specifies the name of one or more windows to display.

ALL

Displays all user-defined windows.

SCREEN

Displays the main Visual FoxPro window when it is hidden. You can also choose Screen from the Window menu to display the main Visual FoxPro window. You can hide the main Visual FoxPro window by clicking its close box or issuing DEACTIVATE WINDOW SCREEN, HIDE WINDOW SCREEN, or RELEASE WINDOW SCREEN.

IN [WINDOW] *WindowName3*

Displays the window inside a parent window specified with *WindowName3*. The window doesn't assume the characteristics of the parent window. A window displayed inside a parent window can't be moved outside the parent window. If the parent window is moved, the child window moves with it.

The parent window specified with *WindowName3* must first be created with DEFINE WINDOW.

IN SCREEN

Explicitly displays the window in the main Visual FoxPro window instead of in another window. Windows are placed in the main Visual FoxPro window by default.

REFRESH

Redraws a Browse window. This option is useful on a network to ensure that you are browsing the most current version of a table. The work area for the Browse window table is selected.

Memo-editing windows are refreshed with changes made to the memo field by other users on a network. SET REFRESH determines the interval between memo-editing-window refreshes. Refer to SET REFRESH for additional information on how data is refreshed in tables opened for shared use on a network.

TOP

Places the specified window in front of all other windows.

BOTTOM

Places the specified window behind all other windows.

SAME

Places the specified window back into a stack of windows in the same position the window occupied before it was deactivated. SAME affects only windows that have been previously displayed or activated and then cleared from the main Visual FoxPro window with DEACTIVATE WINDOW.

SAVE

Keeps an image of the window in the main Visual FoxPro window or in another window after the window is released. Normally, windows are removed from the main Visual FoxPro window after they are released. The window image can be cleared from the main Visual FoxPro window or a window with CLEAR.

Remarks

SHOW WINDOW controls the display and front-to-back screen placement of windows. If a window is hidden or hasn't been activated, SHOW WINDOW displays the window without activating it. If one or more windows are currently displayed, SHOW WINDOW lets you change the front-to-back order of the windows.

You can also display system windows, such as the Command window.

In Visual FoxPro, you can use SHOW WINDOW to display the Visual FoxPro toolbars. Use HIDE WINDOW to remove a toolbar from the FoxPro window. Toolbars must be active before they can be displayed. The following table lists the Visual FoxPro toolbars names to use in SHOW WINDOW and HIDE WINDOW. Enclose the toolbar name in quotation marks.

Toolbar Names

Color Palette	Database Designer	Form Controls
Form Designer	Layout	Print Preview
Query Designer	Report Controls	Report Designer
Standard	View Designer	

To show a system window, enclose the entire system window name in quotation marks.

You can't specify where output is directed to user-defined windows with SHOW WINDOW. Use ACTIVATE WINDOW to direct output to a user-defined window created with DEFINE WINDOW.

Example

The following example, a window named wOutput1 is created and displayed. Since SHOW WINDOW is used to display the window, output can't be directed to the window until it is activated.

```
CLEAR
DEFINE WINDOW wOutput1 FROM 2,1 TO 13,75 TITLE 'Output' ;
   CLOSE FLOAT GROW ZOOM
SHOW WINDOW wOutput1
```

See Also

ACTIVATE WINDOW, DEFINE WINDOW

ShowDoc Event

Occurs when you navigate to an Active Document.

Syntax

PROCEDURE *Object*.ShowDoc

Remarks

The ShowDoc event occurs when you navigate to an Active Document, either by opening the Active Document or by returning to the Active Document from its container's cache or history list. Unlike the Init event, the ShowDoc event doesn't occur until after the Active Document is fully sited in its container.

The ShowDoc event doesn't occur when the Active Document's container is minimized or when the container is restored to its original size.

Applies To

ActiveDoc Object

See Also

HideDoc Event, Init Event

ShowTips Property

Determines whether ToolTips are shown for the controls on the specified Form object or the specified ToolBar object. Available at design time and run time.

Syntax

Object.ShowTips = *lExpr*

Arguments

lExpr
Determines whether ToolTips are shown for the specified control. The settings for the ShowTips property are:

Setting	Description
True (.T.)	(Default for the ToolBar object) ToolTips are displayed when a user places the mouse on a control.
False (.F.)	(Default for the Form object) ToolTips are not displayed when a user places the mouse on a control.

Remarks

You can specify the text that appears in each ToolTip using the ToolTipText property.

Applies To

Form, _SCREEN, ToolBar

See Also

ToolTipText Property

ShowWhatsThis Method

Displays the Whats This Help topic specified for an object with the WhatsThisHelpID property.

Syntax

Object.ShowWhatsThis

Arguments

Object
> Specifies the object for which the Whats This Help topic is displayed.

Remarks

The ShowWhatsThis method is automatically called when the F1 key is pressed. If the WhatsThisHelp property is set to true (.T.), the Whats This Help topic for the object, specified with the WhatsThisHelpID property, is displayed. If the WhatsThisHelp property is set to false (.F.), the Help topic for the object, specified with the HelpContextID property, is displayed.

Applies To

CheckBox, ComboBox, CommandButton, CommandGroup, Container Object, Control Object, EditBox, Form, Grid, Image, Label, Line, ListBox, OLE Bound Control, OLE Container Control, OptionButton, OptionGroup, Shape, Spinner, TextBox, Timer, ToolBar

See Also

WhatsThisButton Property, WhatsThisMode Method, WhatsThisHelp Property, WhatsThisHelpID Property

ShowWindow Property

Specifies whether a form or toolbar is a top-level form or a child form. Available at design time; read-only at run time.

Syntax

Form.ShowWindow[= *nExpr*]

Arguments

nExpr

The settings for the ShowWindow property are:

Setting	Description
0	In Screen (Default). The form is a child form that is placed in the main Visual FoxPro window.
1	In Top-Level Form. The form is a child form of the active top-level form, which can be the main Visual FoxPro window or another top-level form. Use this setting if you want the child form to be placed inside the active top-level form.
	If *nExpr* is set to 1 when the top-level form is the main Visual FoxPro window, Visual FoxPro automatically resets *nExpr* to 0.
2	As Top-Level Form. The form is a top level form in which child forms can be placed. Note that a top level form is always modeless, regardless of the WindowType property setting.

Remarks

A child form is a form contained within another form. Child forms cannot be moved outside the bounds of their parent form; when minimized, they appear at the bottom of their parent form. If a parent form is minimized, the child forms are also minimized.

A top-level form is an independent, modeless form without a parent form, and is used to create an SDI (single document interface) application or to serve as the parent for other child forms. Top-level forms work at the same level as other Windows applications, and can appear in front of or behind them. Top-level forms appear on the Windows taskbar.

The Desktop property determines the behavior of a child form. If the Desktop property is set to true (.T.) the child form is not constrained to the borders of its parent form and can be moved anywhere on the Windows desktop. The child form doesn't appear in the Windows taskbar.

Applies To

Form, ToolBar

See Also

ACTIVATE WINDOW, AlwaysOnTop Property, Desktop Property

SIGN( ) Function

Returns a numeric value of 1, –1, or 0 if the specified numeric expression evaluates to a positive, negative, or 0 value.

Syntax

SIGN(*nExpression*)

Returns

Numeric

Arguments

nExpression

Specifies the numeric expression SIGN( ) evaluates. SIGN( ) returns 1 if *nExpression* evaluates to a positive number, –1 if *nExpression* evaluates to a negative number, and 0 if *nExpression* evaluates to 0.

Example

```
STORE 10 TO gnNum1
STORE -10 TO gnNum2
STORE 0 TO gnZero
CLEAR
? SIGN(gnNum1)   && Displays 1
? SIGN(gnNum2)   && Displays -1
? SIGN(gnZero)   && Displays 0
```

See Also

ABS( )

SIN( ) Function

Returns the sine of an angle.

Syntax

SIN(*nExpression*)

Returns

Numeric

Arguments

nExpression

Specifies an angle whose sine SIN( ) returns. *nExpression* can assume any value and the value returned by SIN( ) ranges between –1 and 1.

Note *nExpression* is specified in radians. Use DTOR( ) to convert an angle from degrees to radians. The number of decimal places displayed by SIN( ) can be specified with SET DECIMALS.

Example

```
CLEAR
? SIN(0)  && Displays 0.00
? SIN(PI( )/2)  && Displays 1.00
? SIN(DTOR(90))  && Displays 1.00
```

See Also

ACOS( ), COS( ), DTOR( ), RTOD( ), SET DECIMALS

Sizable Property

Specifies whether an object can be sized. Available at design time; read/write at run time.

Syntax

Object.Sizable = *lExpr*

Arguments

lExpr
> The settings for the Sizable property are as follows:

Setting	Description
True (.T.)	(Default) You can size the object.
False (.F.)	You cannot size the object.

Remarks

For bound and unbound OLE controls, Sizable affects the OLE object that the control contains. If Sizable is set to true (.T.) and you activate the OLE object, you can size it larger or smaller than the OLE control. If the AutoSize property is set to true (.T.), the OLE control automatically resizes to fit the new size of the OLE object when you deactivate it.

> **Note** To make a Form sizable, set the BorderStyle property to 3.

Applies To

OLE Bound Control, OLE Container Control, ToolBar

See Also

AutoSize Property, BorderStyle Property

SizeBox Property

Specifies whether a form has a size box. Available at design time; read/write at run time.

Syntax

Object.SizeBox = *lExpr*

Arguments

lExpr

The settings for the SizeBox property are as follows:

Setting	Description
True (.T.)	(Default) A size box appears in the lower-right corner of the form if the form's BorderStyle property is set to 3 (the default).
False (.F.)	No size box appears in the form.

Remarks

The SizeBox provides a way for users to resize a form using the mouse. The size box can appear in a form only if the form's BorderStyle property is set to 3 (Sizable Border), which is the default for new forms.

Applies To

Form

See Also

BorderStyle Property, ZoomBox Property

SIZE POPUP Command

Changes the size of a menu created with DEFINE POPUP.

Syntax

SIZE POPUP *MenuName* TO *nRow1, nColumn1* | BY *nRow2, nColumn2*

Arguments

MenuName

Specifies the name of the menu whose size you want to change.

TO *nRow1, nColumn1*

Changes the size of a menu to a specific size. *nRow1* and *nColumn1* specify the new row and column coordinates, respectively, of the lower-right corner of the menu.

BY *nRow2, nColumn2*

> Changes the size of a menu relative to its current size. *nRow2* and *nColumn2* specify the change in size of the menu in rows and columns, relative to the current row and column coordinates of the lower-right corner of the menu.

Remarks

If a user-defined menu has been created, its size can be changed; it doesn't have to be active or visible.

Example

This example creates a menu containing files with a .prg extension and moves, enlarges, and shrinks the menu before closing it.

```
CLEAR
DEFINE POPUP popMovIn FROM 2,2 TO 7, 14 PROMPT FILES LIKE *.PRG ;
   TITLE 'Programs'
ACTIVATE POPUP popMovIn NOWAIT
=CHRSAW(2)
MOVE POPUP popMovIn BY 5,5      && Move popup down
=CHRSAW(2)
SIZE POPUP popMovIn BY 5,5   && Enlarge the popup
=CHRSAW(2)
SIZE POPUP popMovIn BY -5,-5  && Shrink the popup
=CHRSAW(2)
MOVE POPUP popMovIn BY -5,-5   && Move popup up
=CHRSAW(2)
DEACTIVATE POPUP popMovIn
RELEASE POPUP popMovIn
```

See Also

ACTIVATE POPUP

SIZE WINDOW Command

Changes the size of a window created with DEFINE WINDOW or a Visual FoxPro system window.

Syntax

SIZE WINDOW *WindowName* TO *nRow1, nColumn1* | BY *nRow2, nColumn2*

Arguments

WindowName

> Specifies the name of the window whose size you want to change.

> To change the size of a system window, enclose the entire system window name in quotation marks.

For example, to increase the size of the Command window by 1 row and 1 column, issue the following command:

```
SIZE WINDOW 'Command Window' BY 1,1
```

You can only change the size of the Command, Debug, and Trace windows.

TO *nRow1, nColumn1*

Changes the size of a window to a specific size. *nRow1* and *nColumn1* specify the new row and column coordinates, respectively, of the lower-right corner of the window relative to the upper-left corner of the window.

BY *nRow2, nColumn2*

Changes the size of a window relative to its current size. *nRow2* and *nColumn2* specify the change in size of the window in rows and columns, relative to the current row and column coordinates of the lower-right corner of the window.

Remarks

If a user-defined window has been created, its size can be changed; it doesn't have to be active or visible.

See Also

ACTIVATE WINDOW, DEFINE WINDOW, ZOOM WINDOW

SKIP Command

Moves the record pointer forward or backward in a table.

Syntax

SKIP
    [*nRecords*]
    [IN *nWorkArea* | *cTableAlias*]

Arguments

nRecords

Specifies the number of records to move the record pointer.

Issuing SKIP without *nRecords* advances the record pointer to the next record. The record pointer moves toward the end of the file *nRecords* records if *nRecords* evaluates to a positive number. The record pointer moves toward the beginning of the file *nRecords* records if *nRecords* evaluates to a negative number.

If the record pointer is positioned on the last record of a table and SKIP with no arguments is executed, RECNO( ) returns a value 1 greater than the number of records in the table and EOF( ) returns true (.T.). If the record pointer is positioned on the first record of a table and SKIP –1 is executed, RECNO( ) returns 1 and BOF( ) returns true (.T.).

IN *nWorkArea | cTableAlias*
>   Moves the record pointer in a table in a specific work area. *nWorkArea* specifies the
>   work area number and *cTableAlias* specifies a table or work area alias.

Remarks

If the table has a master controlling index tag or index file, SKIP moves the record pointer
to the record determined by the index sequence.

Example

```
CLOSE DATABASES
OPEN DATABASE (HOME(2) + 'data\testdata')
USE customer  && Opens Customer table
CLEAR

SKIP 4 IN 'customer'
? RECNO('customer')  && Displays 5
GO BOTTOM
SKIP -5
? RECNO( )
```

See Also

GO | GOTO, SET SKIP

SKPBAR( ) Function

Determines if a menu item is enabled or disabled with SET SKIP OF.

Syntax

SKPBAR(*cMenuName, MenuItemNumber*)

Returns

Logical

Arguments

cMenuName
>   Specifies the name of the menu that contains the item.

MenuItemNumber
>   Specifies the number of the menu item whose status (enabled or disabled) SKPBAR( )
>   returns. The menu item number is assigned when the menu item is created with
>   DEFINE BAR.

Remarks

SKPBAR( ) returns true (.T.) if the menu item is disabled, and false (.F.) if the menu item
is enabled.

See Also

DEFINE BAR, SET SKIP OF, SKPPAD( )

SKPPAD( ) Function

Determines whether a menu title is enabled or disabled with SET SKIP OF.

Syntax

SKPPAD(*cMenuBarName*, *cMenuTitleName*)

Returns

Logical

Arguments

cMenuBarName
Specifies the name of the menu bar that contains the menu title.

cMenuTitleName
Specifies the name of the menu title whose status (enabled or disabled) SKPPAD( ) returns.

Remarks

SKPPAD( ) returns true (.T.) if the menu title is disabled, and false (.F.) if the menu title is enabled.

See Also

DEFINE BAR, SET SKIP OF, SKPBAR( )

SORT Command

Sorts records in the currently selected table and outputs the sorted records to a new table.

Syntax

SORT TO *TableName*
ON *FieldName1* [/A | /D] [/C]
   [, *FieldName2* [/A | /D] [/C] ...]
   [ASCENDING | DESCENDING]
   [*Scope*] [FOR *lExpression1*] [WHILE *lExpression2*]
   [FIELDS *FieldNameList*
   | FIELDS LIKE *Skeleton*
   | FIELDS EXCEPT *Skeleton*]
   [NOOPTIMIZE]

Arguments

TableName

Specifies the name of the new table containing the sorted records. Visual FoxPro assumes a .dbf file name extension for tables. A .dbf extension is automatically assigned if the file name you include doesn't have an extension.

ON *FieldName1*

Specifies the field in the currently selected table on which the sort is based. The contents and data type of the field determine the order of the records in the new table. By default, the sort is done in ascending order. You can't sort on memo or general fields.

The following example sorts a table on the cust_id field. The customer table is opened and sorted, creating a new table named temp. The records in temp are ordered by the cust_id field.

```
CLOSE DATABASES
OPEN DATABASE (HOME(2) + 'data\testdata')
USE customer  && Opens Customer table
CLEAR
LIST FIELDS company, cust_id NEXT 3
SORT TO temp ON cust_id
USE temp
LIST FIELDS company, cust_id NEXT 3
WAIT WINDOW 'Now sorted on CUST_ID' NOWAIT
```

You can include additional field names (*FieldName2*, *FieldName3*) to further order the new table. The first field *FieldName1* is the primary sort field, the second field *FieldName2* is the secondary sort field, and so on.

[/A | /D] [/C]

For each field you include in the sort, you can specify an ascending or descending sort order. /A specifies an ascending order for the field. /D specifies a descending order. /A or /D can be included with any type of field.

By default, the field sort order for character fields is case sensitive. If you include the /C option after the name of a character field, case is ignored. You can combine the /C option with the /A or /D option. For example, /AC or /DC.

In the following example, a new table named clients is created. The orders table is sorted on the order_date field in ascending order and the freight field in descending order.

```
USE orders
SORT TO clients ON order_date/A,freight/D
```

ASCENDING

Specifies an ascending order for all fields not followed by /D.

DESCENDING

Specifies a descending order for all fields not followed by /A.

If you omit either ASCENDING or DESCENDING, the sort order is ascending by default.

Scope

Specifies a range of records to sort. The scope clauses are: ALL, NEXT *nRecords*, RECORD *nRecordNumber*, and REST.

The default scope for SORT is ALL records.

FOR *lExpression1*

Specifies that only the records in the current table for which the logical condition *lExpression1* evaluates to true (.T.) are included in the sort. Including FOR lets you conditionally sort records, filtering out undesired records.

Rushmore optimizes a SORT ... FOR command if *lExpression1* is an optimizable expression. For best performance, use an optimizable expression in the FOR clause.

A discussion of expressions that Rushmore can optimize appears in Chapter 15, "Optimizing Applications," in the *Microsoft Visual FoxPro 6.0 Programmer's Guide*.

WHILE *lExpression2*

Specifies a condition whereby records from the current table are included in the sort for as long as the logical expression *lExpression2* evaluates to true (.T.).

FIELDS *FieldNameList*

Specifies fields from the original table to include in the new table that SORT creates. If you omit the FIELDS clause, all fields from the original table are included in the new table.

FIELDS LIKE *Skeleton*

Specifies that fields from the original table that match the field skeleton *Skeleton* are included in the new table that SORT creates.

FIELDS EXCEPT *Skeleton*

Specifies that all fields except those that match the field skeleton *Skeleton* are included in the new table that SORT creates.

The field skeleton *Skeleton* supports wildcards. For example, to specify that all fields that begin with the letters A and P are included in the new table, use the following:

```
SORT TO mytable ON myfield FIELDS LIKE A*,P*
```

The LIKE clause can be combined with the EXCEPT clause:

```
SORT TO mytable ON myfield FIELDS LIKE A*,P* EXCEPT PARTNO*
```

NOOPTIMIZE

Disables Rushmore optimization of SORT.

For more information, see the SET OPTIMIZE Command, earlier in this language reference, and "Understanding Rushmore Technology" in Chapter 15, "Optimizing Applications," in the *Microsoft Visual FoxPro 6.0 Programmer's Guide*.

Remarks

One or more specified fields in the current table determine the order in which the records appear in the new table.

> **Important** Be sure you have enough disk space for the new table and the temporary work files created during the sort. The disk space needed to perform a sort can be as much as three times the size of the source table. The amount of available disk space can be determined with DISKSPACE( ) and SYS(2020). If you run out of disk space during a sort, Visual FoxPro displays an error message, and the temporary work files are deleted.

Character-type fields that contain numbers and spaces might not sort in the order you expect. Numeric fields fill from right to left, with empty spaces to the left. In contrast, character fields fill from left to right, with empty spaces to the right.

For example, if two records in a table contain a character field with 1724 in one record and 18 in the other, and the table is sorted on this field in ascending order, the record containing 1724 appears before the record containing 18. This is because Visual FoxPro reads each character in the character fields from left to right, and because 17 (in 1724) is less than 18 (in 18), it puts 1724 first. To avoid this problem, always precede lower numbers with leading zeros (0018) or make the field numeric.

See Also

COPY FILE, DISKSPACE( ), INDEX, SYS(2020) – Default Disk Size

Sorted Property

Specifies whether the items in the list portion of a ComboBox or ListBox control are automatically sorted alphabetically. Available at design time and run time.

Syntax

[*Form.*]*Control*.Sorted[= *lExpr*]

Arguments

lExpr
The settings for the Sorted property are as follows:

Setting	Description
True (.T.)	List items are sorted alphabetically (case-sensitive). Visual FoxPro handles almost all necessary string processing to maintain alphabetic order, including changing the index numbers for items as required when items are added or removed from the list.
False (.F.)	(Default) List items are not sorted alphabetically.

Remarks

The Sorted property is only available if the RowSourceType property is set to 0 (None) or 1 (Value).

Note that once the items are sort alphabetically, setting the Sorted property to false (.F.) doesn't restore the items to their original order. To restore the original order, set the control's RowSource property to itself, as in the following example:

```
MyForm.MyCombo1.Rowsource = MyForm.MyCombo1.Rowsource
```

Applies To

ComboBox, ListBox

See Also

AddItem Method, List Property, ListCount Property, ListItemID Property, RemoveItem Method, RowSource Property, RowSourceType Property

SOUNDEX( ) Function

Returns a phonetic representation of the specified character expression.

Syntax

SOUNDEX(*cExpression*)

Returns

Character

Arguments

cExpression
Specifies the character expression SOUNDEX( ) evaluates.

Remarks

SOUNDEX( ) returns a four-character string. By comparing the results SOUNDEX( ) returns for two character expressions, you can determine if the two expressions are phonetically similar, indicating that they sound alike. This can be useful when searching for duplicate records in a table.

SOUNDEX( ) isn't case sensitive and generally disregards vowels.

Example

```
CLEAR
? SOUNDEX('Smith') = SOUNDEX('Smyth')  && Displays .T.
? SOUNDEX('Computer')  && Displays C513
```

See Also

DIFFERENCE( )

SPACE( ) Function

Returns a character string composed of a specified number of spaces.

Syntax

SPACE(*nSpaces*)

Returns

Character

Arguments

nSpaces
Specifies the number of spaces that SPACE( ) returns. The maximum value of *nSpaces* is limited only by memory in Microsoft Visual FoxPro.

See Also

PADC( ) | PADL( ) | PADR( ), REPLICATE( )

Sparse Property

Specifies whether the CurrentControl property affects all cells or only the active cell in a Column object. Available at design time; read/write at run time.

Syntax

Column.Sparse [= *lExpr*]

Arguments

lExpr
The settings for the Sparse property are as follows:

Setting	Description
True (.T.)	(Default) Only the Column's active cell uses the CurrentControl property setting to accept and display data. The other cells use the TextBox control if the current control for the cells is not the container object or a command button. The other cells remain empty if the current control for the cells is the container object or a command button.
False (.F.)	All cells in the Column object use the CurrentControl property setting to display data; the active cell accepts data.

Applies To

Column

See Also

Bound Property, CurrentControl Property, DynamicCurrentControl Property

SpecialEffect Property

Specifies different format options for a control. Available at design time and run time. SpecialEffect is ignored for command buttons.

Syntax

[*Form.*]*Control.*SpecialEffect = *nExpr*

Arguments

nExpr

For a PageFrame control, Container object, or Control object, the settings for the SpecialEffect property are as follows:

Setting	Description
0	Raised. The control appears to be raised from the form.
1	Sunken. The control appears to be set into the form.
2	Flat.

Note For a PageFrame control, SpecialEffect is available only if the Tabs Property is set to false (.F.). Also, the BorderColor property for a PageFrame applies only when n*Expr* is set to 2 (Flat).

For all other controls, the settings for the SpecialEffect property are as follows:

Setting	Description
0	(Default for all controls and objects except the Container object.) 3D. Border of control is raised to simulate a 3-dimensional look.
1	Plain. Control appears without a 3-dimensional border.
2	Flat (Available for the Container object only.).

Note If the Height property is set to a value too small, the 3D setting has no effect.

Applies To

CheckBox, ComboBox, CommandButton, CommandGroup, Container Object, Control Object, EditBox, ListBox, OptionButton, OptionGroup, PageFrame, Shape, Spinner, TextBox

See Also

BackColor, ForeColor Properties, SelectedItemBackColor, SelectedItemForeColor Properties

_SPELLCHK System Variable

Specifies a spelling checker program for the Visual FoxPro text editor.

Syntax

_SPELLCHK = *ProgramName*

Arguments

ProgramName

Specifies a spelling checker program. If your spelling checker program is in a directory other than the current default directory, include a path with the program name.

You can also specify a spelling checker program in your Visual FoxPro configuration file. Include the line:

```
_SPELLCHK = ProgramName
```

Remarks

By default, _SPELLCHK uses Spellchk.app. If you rename Spellchk.app or move it to another directory, store the new spelling checker program name and its path in _SPELLCHK.

See Also

MODIFY COMMAND, MODIFY FILE, MODIFY MEMO

Spinner Control

Creates a spinner.

Syntax

Spinner

Remarks

A spinner allows a user to choose from a range of numeric values by 'spinning' through the values by clicking the up or down arrows on the spinner or by typing a value into the spinner box.

The KeyBoardHighValue and SpinnerHighValue properties specify the maximum numeric values that can be entered from the keyboard into the spinner box and by clicking the arrow buttons on the spinner.

The KeyBoardLowValue and SpinnerLowValue properties specify the minimum numeric values that can be entered from the keyboard into the spinner box and by clicking the arrow buttons on the spinner.

For additional information about creating spinners, see "Form Designer" in Help, and Chapter 10, "Using Controls," in the *Microsoft Visual FoxPro 6.0 Programmer's Guide*.

Properties

Alignment	Application	BackColor
BaseClass	BorderColor	BorderStyle
Class	ClassLibrary	ColorScheme
ColorSource	Comment	ControlSource
DisabledBackColor	DisabledForeColor	DragIcon
DragMode	Enabled	FontBold
FontCondense	FontExtend	FontItalic
FontName	FontOutline	FontShadow
FontSize	FontStrikeThru	FontUnderline
ForeColor	Format	Height
HelpContextID	HideSelection	Increment
InputMask	KeyboardHighValue	KeyboardLowValue
Left	Margin	MouseIcon
MousePointer	Name	NullDisplay
OLEDragMode	OLEDragPicture	OLEDropEffects
OLEDropHasData Property	OLEDropMode	OLEDropTextInsertion
Parent	ParentClass	ReadOnly
RightToLeft	SelectedBackColor	SelectedForeColor
SelectOnEntry	SelLength	SelStart
SelText	SpecialEffect	SpinnerHighValue
SpinnerLowValue	StatusBarText	TabIndex
TabStop	Tag	TerminateRead
Text	ToolTipText	Top
Value	Visible	WhatsThisHelpID
Width		

Events

Click	DblClick	Destroy
DownClick	DragDrop	DragOver
Error	ErrorMessage	GotFocus
Init	InteractiveChange	KeyPress
LostFocus	Message	MiddleClick Event
MouseDown	MouseMove	MouseUp
MouseWheel	OLECompleteDrag	OLEDragDrop
OLEDragOver	OLEGiveFeedBack	OLESetData
OLEStartDrag	ProgrammaticChange	RangeHigh
RangeLow	RightClick	UIEnable
UpClick	Valid	When

Methods

AddProperty	CloneObject	Drag
Move	OLEDrag	ReadExpression
ReadMethod	Refresh	ResetToDefault
SaveAsClass	SetFocus	ShowWhatsThis
WriteExpression	WriteMethod	ZOrder

See Also

CREATE CLASS, CREATE FORM, DEFINE CLASS

SpinnerHighValue, SpinnerLowValue Properties

Specifies the highest or lowest value that can be entered into a Spinner control by clicking the up and down arrows. Available at design time and run time.

Syntax

Spinner.SpinnerHighValue[= *nHigh*]
Spinner.SpinnerLowValue[= *nLow*]

Arguments

nHigh

Specifies the highest value that can be entered into a spinner with the up arrow.

nLow

Specifies the lowest value that can be entered into a spinner with the down arrow.

Applies To

Spinner

See Also

KeyboardHighValue, KeyboardLowValue Properties

SplitBar Property

Specifies whether the split bar is displayed in a Grid control. Available at design time; read-only at run time.

Syntax

Grid.SplitBar[= *lExpr*]

Arguments

lExpr

One of the following:

lExpr	Description
True (.T.)	(Default) The split bar is displayed in a Grid control, allowing you to split the Grid into two separate panes.
False (.F.)	The split bar isn't displayed in a Grid control, preventing you from splitting the Grid into separate panes.

Remarks

Note that the SplitBar property takes precedence over the Partition property.

Applies To

Grid Control

See Also

GridLines Property, Partition Property

SQL Commands Overview

Visual FoxPro supports Structured Query Language (SQL) commands. Visual FoxPro's SQL commands make use of Rushmore technology to optimize performance, and a single SQL command can be used to replace multiple Visual FoxPro commands.

Visual FoxPro supports the following SQL commands:

SELECT – SQL

Specifies the criteria on which a query is based and issues the query. Visual FoxPro interprets the query and retrieves the specified data from the table(s). The SELECT command is built into Visual FoxPro like any other Visual FoxPro command. You can create a SELECT command query in these areas:

- In the Command window.

- In a Visual FoxPro program (like any other Visual FoxPro command).

- In the Query Designer.

ALTER TABLE – SQL

Modifies an existing table. You can modify the name, type, precision, scale, null value support, and referential integrity rules for each field in the table.

CREATE CURSOR – SQL

Creates a temporary table. Each field in the temporary table is defined with a name, type, precision, scale, null value support, and referential integrity rules. These definitions can be obtained from the command itself or from an array.

CREATE TABLE – SQL

Creates a table. Each new table field is defined with a name, type, precision, scale, null value support, and referential integrity rules. These definitions can be obtained from the command itself or from an array.

DELETE – SQL

Marks records in a table for deletion using SQL syntax.

INSERT – SQL

Appends a new record to the end of an existing table. The new record contains data listed in the INSERT command or from an array.

UPDATE – SQL

Updates records in a table. The records can be updated based on the results of a SELECT – SQL statement.

See Also

CREATE CURSOR – SQL, CREATE QUERY, CREATE TABLE – SQL, DELETE – SQL, INSERT – SQL, MODIFY QUERY, SELECT – SQL, UPDATE – SQL

SQLCANCEL( ) Function

Requests cancellation of an executing SQL statement.

Syntax

SQLCANCEL(*nConnectionHandle*)

Returns

Numeric

Arguments

nConnectionHandle
Specifies the active connection handle whose SQL statement is to be cancelled.

Remarks

SQLCANCEL( ) returns 1 if the SQL statement is successfully cancelled, –1 if there is a connection level error, and –2 if there is an environment level error.

SQLCANCEL( ) cancels the execution of SQLCOLUMNS( ), SQLEXEC( ), SQLMORERESULTS( ), and SQLTABLES( ) in asynchronous mode. Use SQLSETPROP( ) to establish asynchronous mode.

Example

The following example assumes SQLCONNECT( ) is successfully issued, and its return value is stored to a memory variable named gnConnHandle.

SQLEXEC( ) is used to sends a SQL statement to the data source and return the results to a cursor. SQLCANCEL( ) is issued to stop the query.

```
= SQLSETPROP(gnConnHandle, 'asynchronous', .T.)  && To stop SQLEXEC( )
= SQLEXEC(gnConnHandle, 'SELECT * FROM authors')
= SQLCANCEL(gnConnHandle)  && Wrong select statement, cancel
```

See Also

AERROR( ), SQLCOLUMNS( ), SQLEXEC( ), SQLMORERESULTS( ), SQLSETPROP( ), SQLTABLES( )

SQLCOLUMNS( ) Function

Stores a list of column names and information about each column for the specified data source table to a Visual FoxPro cursor.

Syntax

SQLCOLUMNS(*nConnectionHandle*, *TableName*
    [, "FOXPRO" | "NATIVE"] [, *CursorName*])

Returns

Numeric

Arguments

nConnectionHandle
Active connection handle.

TableName
Specifies the name of the table from which the column names are returned. *TableName* can contain the wildcard characters ? and *. The question mark (?) matches any single character and the asterisk (*) matches any number of characters.

FOXPRO | NATIVE
Specifies the format for the column information in the result set. Be sure to enclose FOXPRO or NATIVE in quotation marks. The NATIVE format option stores column information for tables in the same format as the data source. The FOXPRO format option stores the column information in the same format as that used for the Visual FoxPro table or cursor that would be created if you imported the data source table into Visual FoxPro. If you omit FOXPRO or NATIVE, the format option defaults to FOXPRO.

The following table shows the columns in the result set for the FOXPRO format.

Column name	Description
Field_name	Column name
Field_type	Column data type
Field_len	Column length
Field_dec	Number of decimal places

The following table shows the columns in the result set for the NATIVE format. In NATIVE format, depending on the data source, additional columns not listed in the following table may be included in the result set.

Column name	Description
Table_qualifier	Table qualifier identifier
Table_owner	Table owner identifier
Table_name	Table identifier
Column_name	Column identifier
Data_type	Column data type
Type_name	Column data type name

(continued)

(continued)

Column name	Description
Precision	Precision of the column
Length	Transfer size of the data
Scale	Scale of the column
Radix	Base for Numeric type
Nullable	Supports null values
Remarks	Description of the column

If the table you specify with *TableName* doesn't exist and the format is set to NATIVE, SQLCOLUMNS( ) returns true (.T.) and creates an empty table or cursor. If the table you specify with *TableName* doesn't exist and the format is set to FOXPRO, SQLCOLUMNS( ) returns false (.F.).

CursorName
Specifies the name of the Visual FoxPro cursor for the result set. If you don't include a cursor name, Visual FoxPro uses the default name SQLRESULT.

Remarks

SQLCOLUMNS( ) returns 1 if the cursor is successfully created, 0 if SQLCOLUMNS( ) is still executing, –1 if a connection level error occurs, and –2 if an environment level error occurs.

SQLCOLUMNS( ) is one of the four functions that you can execute either synchronously or asynchronously. The Asynchronous setting of SQLSETPROP( ) determines if these functions execute synchronously or asynchronously. In asynchronous mode, you must call SQLCOLUMNS( ) repeatedly until a value other than false (.F.) (still executing) is returned.

Example

The following example assumes SQLCONNECT( ) is successfully issued, and its return value is stored to a memory variable named gnConnHandle. SQLCOLUMNS( ) is used to create a cursor named MyCursor containing information about the columns in the authors table.

```
= SQLCOLUMNS(gnConnHandle, 'authors', 'FOXPRO', 'MyCursor')
```

See Also

AERROR( ), SQLGETPROP( ), SQLSETPROP( ), SQLTABLES( )

SQLCOMMIT( ) Function

Commits a transaction.

Syntax

SQLCOMMIT(*nConnectionHandle*)

Returns

Numeric

Arguments

nConnectionHandle
    Specifies the connection handle to the data source returned by SQLCONNECT( ).

Remarks

Use SQLCOMMIT( ) to commit a transaction. SQLCOMMIT( ) returns 1 if the transaction is successfully committed; otherwise, it returns –1. If SQLCOMMIT( ) returns –1, you can use AERROR( ) to determine why the transaction could not be committed.

If manual transactions are in effect (the SQLSETPROP( ) Transactions property is set to Manual), you can send multiple updates to remote tables and commit all the updates with SQLCOMMIT( ).

Updates can be rolled back with SQLROLLBACK( ).

Example

The following example assumes SQLCONNECT( ) is successfully issued, and its return value is stored to a memory variable named gnConnHandle. SQLSETPROP( ) is used to set the Transactions property to 2 (Manual), allowing you to use SQLCOMMIT( ) and SQLROLLBACK( ).

The authors table is modified with SQLEXEC( ), and the changes to the table are committed with SQLCOMMIT( ).

```
= SQLSETPROP(gnConnHandle, 'Transactions', 2)  && Manual transactions
= SQLEXEC(gnConnHandle, "INSERT INTO authors (au_id, au_lname);
   VALUES ('aupoe', 'Poe')")  && Modify the authors table
= SQLCOMMIT(gnConnHandle)  && Commit the changes
```

See Also

AERROR( ), BEGIN TRANSACTION, END TRANSACTION, SQLCONNECT( ), SQLROLLBACK( ), SQLSETPROP( )

SQLCONNECT( ) Function

Establishes a connection to a data source.

Syntax

SQLCONNECT([*DataSourceName, cUserID, cPassword | cConnectionName*])

Returns

Numeric

Arguments

DataSourceName
Specifies the name of a data source as defined in your Odbc.ini file.

cUserID
Specifies a user identifier used to log on to the data source.

cPassword
Specifies the password to the data source.

cConnectionName
Specifies a named connection created with CREATE CONNECTION.

Remarks

SQLCONNECT( ) returns a positive non-zero numeric handle if you successfully connect to the data source. You should store this handle in a memory variable and use the variable in subsequent function calls that require a connection handle. SQLCONNECT( ) returns –2 if the connection cannot be made.

If SQLCONNECT( ) is issued without any of its additional arguments, the Select Connection or Data Source dialog box can be displayed, allowing you to choose a data source.

> **Note** The ODBC login dialog must be disabled to support SQL pass through with Microsoft Transaction Server. Use SQLSETPROP(*cConnectionHandle*, 'DispLogin', 3) to disable the ODBC login dialog (*cConnectionHandle* is the connection handle returned by SQLCONNECT). The ODBC login dialog can also be disabled in the Connection Designer.

Example

The following example assumes an ODBC data source called MyFoxSQLNT is available, and the user ID for the data source is "sa." SQLCONNECT( ) is issued, and its return value is stored to a variable named gnConnHandle.

If you successfully connect to the data source, SQLCONNECT( ) returns a positive number, a dialog is displayed and SQLDISCONNECT( ) is used to disconnect from the data source.

If you cannot connect to the data source, SQLCONNECT( ) returns a negative number and a message is displayed.

```
STORE SQLCONNECT('MyFoxSQLNT', 'sa') TO gnConnHandle
IF gnConnHandle <= 0
   = MESSAGEBOX('Cannot make connection', 16, 'SQL Connect Error')
ELSE
   = MESSAGEBOX('Connection made', 48, 'SQL Connect Message)
   = SQLDISCONNECT(gnConnHandle)
ENDIF
```

See Also

AERROR( ), CREATE CONNECTION, SQLDISCONNECT( ), SQLGETPROP( ), SQLEXEC( ), SQLSETPROP( ), SQLSTRINGCONNECT( )

SQLDISCONNECT( ) Function

Terminates a connection to a data source.

Syntax

SQLDISCONNECT(*nConnectionHandle*)

Returns

Numeric

Arguments

nConnectionHandle
Specifies the connection handle to the data source returned by SQLCONNECT( ).
Specify 0 for *nConnectionHandle* to terminate all active connections.

Remarks

SQLDISCONNECT( ) returns 1 if the connection is successfully terminated, –1 if there is a connection level error, and –2 if there is an environment level error.

SQLDISCONNECT( ) terminates a connection to a data source. You must supply the connection handle that SQLCONNECT( ) returned when you established the connection.

Note If you execute SQLDISCONNECT( ) within an asynchronous function sequence or during a transaction, SQLDISCONNECT( ) generates an error.

Example

The following example assumes an ODBC data source called MyFoxSQLNT is available, and the user ID for the data source is "sa." SQLCONNECT( ) is issued, and its return value is stored to a variable named gnConnHandle.

If you successfully connect to the data source, SQLCONNECT( ) returns a positive number, a dialog is displayed and SQLDISCONNECT( ) is used to disconnect from the data source.

If you cannot connect to the data source, SQLCONNECT( ) returns a negative number and a message is displayed.

```
STORE SQLCONNECT('MyFoxSQLNT', 'sa') TO gnConnHandle
IF gnConnHandle <= 0
   = MESSAGEBOX('Cannot make connection', 16, 'SQL Connect Error')
ELSE
   = MESSAGEBOX('Connection made', 48, 'SQL Connect Message)
   = SQLDISCONNECT(gnConnHandle)
ENDIF
```

See Also

AERROR( ), SQLCONNECT( ), SQLSTRINGCONNECT( )

SQLEXEC( ) Function

Sends a SQL statement to the data source, where the statement is processed.

Syntax

SQLEXEC(*nConnectionHandle*, [*cSQLCommand*, [*CursorName*]])

Returns

Numeric

Arguments

nConnectionHandle
Specifies the connection handle to the data source returned by SQLCONNECT( ).

cSQLCommand
Specifies the SQL statement passed to the data source.

The SQL statement can contain a parameterized WHERE clause which creates a parameterized view. All parameters in the WHERE clause must be defined before SQLEXEC( ) is issued. For example, if the parameters are variables, the variables must be created and initialized before SQLEXEC( ) is issued.

For additional information about creating parameterized views, see Chapter 8, "Creating Views," in the *Microsoft Visual FoxPro 6.0 Programmer's Guide*.

CursorName
Specifies the name of the Visual FoxPro cursor to which the result set is sent. If you don't include a cursor name, Visual FoxPro uses the default name SQLRESULT.

For multiple result sets, new cursor names are derived by appending an incremented number to the name of the first cursor.

Remarks

SQLEXEC( ) returns the number of result sets if there is more than one. SQLEXEC( ) returns 0 if it is still executing and returns 1 when it has finished executing. SQLEXEC( ) returns –1 if a connection level error occurs.

If SQLEXEC( ) is used to execute a SQL statement prepared with SQLPREPARE( ), only the connection handle argument *nConnectionHandle* is required. The *cSQLCommand* and *CursorName* arguments should be omitted.

If the SQL statement generates one result set, SQLEXEC( ) stores the result set to the specified Visual FoxPro cursor. If the SQL statement generates two or more result sets and SQLSETPROP( ) is set to 1 (batch mode), you can name each result set by setting the SQLSETPROP( ) BatchMode option to 0 and changing the cursor name each time you call SQLMORERESULTS( ).

SQLEXEC( ) is one of the four functions that you can execute either synchronously or asynchronously. The Asynchronous setting of SQLSETPROP( ) determines whether these functions execute synchronously or asynchronously. In asynchronous mode, you must call SQLEXEC( ) repeatedly until it returns a value other than 0 (still executing).

Example

The following example assumes SQLCONNECT( ) is successfully issued, and its return value is stored to a memory variable named gnConnHandle.

SQLEXEC( ) is used to execute a query that returns all the information in the authors table into a cursor named MyCursor.

```
= SQLSETPROP(gnConnHandle, 'asynchronous', .F.)
= SQLEXEC(gnConnHandle, 'SELECT * FROM authors', 'MyCursor')
```

See Also

AERROR( ), SQLCANCEL( ), SQLGETPROP( ), SQLMORERESULTS( ), SQLPREPARE( ), SQLSETPROP( )

SQLGETPROP( ) Function

Returns current or default settings for an active connection.

Syntax

SQLGETPROP(*nConnectionHandle*, *cSetting*)

Returns

Character, Numeric, or Logical

Arguments

nConnectionHandle
>Specifies the connection handle to the data source returned by SQLCONNECT( ). If you specify 0 for *nConnectionHandle*, SQLGETPROP( ) returns the environment setting.

cSetting
>Specifies the setting. See the SQLSETPROP( ) Function, later in this language reference, for a list of the settings you can specify.

Remarks

If a connection level error occurs, –1 is returned. If an environment level error occurs, –2 is returned.

Example

The following example uses SQLCONNECT( ) to display the connection dialog box. Choose a datasource and the example will display the results using SQLGETPROP( ) with the DataSource *cSetting*.

```
* Clear environment
CLOSE ALL
CLEAR ALL
CLEAR

* Display the Select Connection or Data Source dialog box
* to choose a connection
nHandle=SQLCONNECT()

* Test connection, report results
IF nHandle > 0
   cSource= SQLGETPROP(nHandle, "datasource")
   =MESSAGEBOX("Current Data Source = "+cSource,0,"Connection Results")
ELSE
   =MESSAGEBOX("Connection Error = " + ;
   ALLTRIM(STR(nHandle)),0,"Connection Results")
ENDIF
=SQLDISCONNECT(nHandle)
```

See Also

AERROR( ), SQLCONNECT( ), SQLSETPROP( )

SQLMORERESULTS( ) Function

Copies another result set to a Visual FoxPro cursor if more result sets are available.

Syntax

SQLMORERESULTS(*nConnectionHandle*)

Returns

Numeric

Arguments

nConnectionHandle
   Specifies the connection handle to the data source returned by SQLCONNECT( ).

Remarks

SQLMORERESULTS( ) determines if more result sets are available from a SQL statement executed with SQLEXEC( ) in non-batch mode. If more result sets are available, they are copied to a Visual FoxPro cursor, one set at a time.

SQLMORERESULTS( ) returns 0 if the SQL statement is still executing, returns 1 if it is finished executing, and returns 2 if no more data is found. In non-batch mode, SQLMORERESULTS( ) should be called after each successful SQLEXEC( ) call until SQLMORERESULTS( ) returns 2 (no more data found). The setting of the SQLSETPROP( ) batch mode option determines whether SQLEXEC( ) executes a SQL statement in batch or non-batch mode.

SQLMORERESULTS( ) returns –1 if a connection level error occurs, and returns –2 if an environment level error occurs.

SQLMORERESULTS( ) is one of the four functions that you can execute either synchronously or asynchronously. The asynchronous setting of SQLSETPROP( ) determines if these functions execute synchronously or asynchronously. In asynchronous mode, you must call SQLMORERESULTS( ) repeatedly until it returns a value other than 0 (still executing).

Example

The following example assumes SQLCONNECT( ) is successfully issued, and its return value is stored to a memory variable named gnConnHandle. SQLSETPROP( ) is used to set the BatchMode property to false (.F.) so the individual result sets can be retrieved.

SQLMORERESULTS( ) is issued twice to create two cursors containing the results of the SQLEXEC( ) query. SET is used to display the View window and the cursors created by SQLEXEC( ).

```
= SQLSETPROP(gnConnHandle, 'BatchMode', .F.)  && Individual result sets
= SQLEXEC(gnConnHandle, 'SELECT * FROM authors; SELECT * FROM titles')
= SQLMORERES(gnConnHandle)  && First result set
= SQLMORERES(gnConnHandle)  && Second result set
```

See Also

AERROR( ), SQLCANCEL( ), SQLCONNECT( ), SQLEXEC( ), SQLGETPROP( ), SQLSETPROP( )

SQLPREPARE( ) Function

Prepares a SQL statement for remote execution by SQLEXEC( ).

Syntax

SQLPREPARE(*nConnectionHandle*, *cSQLCommand*, [*CursorName*])

Returns

Numeric

Arguments

nConnectionHandle

Specifies the connection handle to the data source returned by SQLCONNECT( ).

cSQLCommand

Specifies the SQL statement passed to the data source.

The SQL statement can contain a parameterized WHERE clause which creates a parameterized view. All parameters in the WHERE clause must be defined before SQLPREPARE( ) is issued. For example, if the parameters are variables, the variables must be created and initialized before SQLPREPARE( ) is issued.

For additional information about creating parameterized views, see Chapter 8, "Creating Views," in the *Microsoft Visual FoxPro 6.0 Programmer's Guide*.

CursorName

Specifies the name of the Visual FoxPro cursor to which the result set is sent. If you don't include a cursor name, Visual FoxPro uses the default name SQLRESULT.

For multiple result sets, new cursor names are derived by appending an incremented number to the name of the first cursor.

Remarks

SQLPREPARE( ) sends the SQL statement to the data source where it is compiled for faster execution. After the SQL statement is compiled, it can be executed with SQLEXEC( ). If SQLEXEC( ) is used to execute a SQL statement prepared with SQLPREPARE( ), only the connection handle is required in SQLEXEC( ).

Example

```
gcAuthor = 'Smith'
= SQLPREPARE(gnConnHandle, 'SELECT * FROM authors; WHERE au_lname = ?gcAuthor')
= SQLEXEC(gnConnHandle)

…

gcAuthor = 'Jones'
= SQLEXEC(gnConnHandle)
```

See Also

SQLCONNECT( ), SQLEXEC( )

SQLROLLBACK( ) Function

Cancels any changes made during the current transaction.

Syntax

SQLROLLBACK(*nConnectionHandle*)

Returns

Numeric

Arguments

nConnectionHandle
　　Specifies the connection handle to the data source returned by SQLCONNECT( ).

Remarks

SQLROLLBACK( ) returns 1 if the transaction is successfully rolled back; otherwise, it returns −1. If SQLROLLBACK( ) returns −1, you can use AERROR( ) to determine why the transaction could not be rolled back.

If manual transactions are in effect (the SQLSETPROP( ) transaction property is set to manual), you can send multiple updates to remote tables. The updates can all be rolled back with SQLROLLBACK( ).

Updates can be committed with SQLCOMMIT( ).

Example

The following example assumes SQLCONNECT( ) is successfully issued, and its return value is stored to a memory variable named gnConnHandle. SQLSETPROP( ) is used to set the Transactions property to 2 (manual), allowing you to use SQLCOMMIT( ) and SQLROLLBACK( ).

The authors table is modified with SQLEXEC( ), and the changes to the table are cancelled with SQLROLLBACK( ).

```
= SQLSETPROP(gnConnHandle, 'Transactions', 2)  && manual
= SQLEXEC(gnConnHandle, "INSERT INTO authors (au_id, au_lname); VALUES ('aupoe', 'Poe')")
= SQLROLLBACK(gnConnHandle)
```

See Also

AERROR( ), SQLCOMMIT( ), SQLCONNECT( ), SQLSETPROP( )

SQLSETPROP( ) Function

Specifies settings for an active connection.

Syntax

SQLSETPROP(*nConnectionHandle*, *cSetting* [, *eExpression*])

Returns

Numeric

Arguments

nConnectionHandle
Specifies the connection handle to the data source returned by SQLCONNECT( ).

cSetting
Specifies the setting. The following table lists the values for *cSetting*.

Setting	Description
Asynchronous	Specifies whether result sets are returned synchronously (false (.F.), the default), or asynchronously (true (.T.)).
	Read/Write.
BatchMode	Specifies whether SQLEXEC( ) returns result sets all at once (true (.T.), the default), or individually with SQLMORERESULTS( ) (false (.F.)).
	Read/Write.
ConnectBusy	Contains true (.T.) if a shared connection is busy; otherwise contains false (.F.).
	Read-Only.
ConnectString	The login connection string.
ConnectTimeOut	Specifies the time to wait (in seconds) before returning a connection time-out error. If you specify 0, the wait is indefinite and a time-out error is never returned. ConnectTimeOut can be 0 to 600. The default is 15.
	Read/Write.

(continued)

Setting	Description
DataSource	The name of the data source as defined in the ODBC.INI file.
	Read/Write.
DispLogin	Contains a numeric value that determines when the ODBC Login dialog box is displayed. DispLogin may assume the following values:
	1 or DB_PROMPTCOMPLETE (from FOXPRO.H). 1 is the default.
	2 or DB_PROMPTALWAYS (from FOXPRO.H).
	3 or DB_PROMPTNEVER (from FOXPRO.H).
	If 1 or DB_PROMPTCOMPLETE is specified, Visual FoxPro displays the ODBC Login dialog box only if any required information is missing.
	If 2 or DB_PROMPTALWAYS is specified, the ODBC Login dialog box is always displayed, allowing you to change settings before connecting.
	If 3 or DB_PROMPTNEVER is specified, the ODBC Login dialog box isn't displayed and Visual FoxPro generates an error if the required login information isn't available.
	Read/Write.
DispWarnings	Specifies if error messages are displayed (true (.T.)) or are not displayed (false (.F.), the default).
	Read/Write.
IdleTimeout	The idle timeout interval in seconds. Active connections are deactivated after the specified time interval. The default value is 0 (wait indefinitely).
	Read/Write.
ODBChdbc	The internal ODBC connection handle which may be used by external library files (FLL files) to call ODBC.
	Read-Only.
ODBChstmt	The internal ODBC statement handle which may be used by external library files (FLL files) to call ODBC.
	Read-Only.
PacketSize	The size of the network packet used by the connection. Adjusting this value can improve performance. The default value is 4096 bytes (4K).
	Read/Write

(continued)

(continued)

Setting	Description
Password	The connection password.
	Read-Only.
QueryTimeOut	Specifies the time to wait (in seconds) before returning a general time-out error. If you specify 0 (the default), the wait is indefinite and a time-out error is never returned. QueryTimeOut can be 0 to 600.
	Read/Write.
Transactions	Contains a numeric value that determines how the connection manages transactions on the remote table. Transactions may assume the following values:
	1 or DB_TRANSAUTO (from FOXPRO.H). 1 is the default. Transaction processing for the remote table is automatically handled.
	2 or DB_TRANSMANUAL (from FOXPRO.H). Transaction processing is handled manually through SQLCOMMIT( ) and SQLROLLBACK( ).
	Read/Write.
UserId	The user identification.
	Read-Only.
WaitTime	The amount of time in milliseconds that elapses before Visual FoxPro checks if the SQL statement has completed executing. The default is 100 milliseconds.
	Read/Write.

eExpression
Specifies the value for the setting you designate with *cSetting*. If you omit *eExpression*, the default value is restored for the setting.

Remarks

SQLSETPROP( ) returns 1 if it is successful; otherwise, it returns −1 if a connection level error occurs or −2 if an environment level error occurs.

Use SQLSETPROP( ) to specify settings at the connection level. To specify Visual FoxPro default settings at the environment level, include 0 as the connection handle.

The ConnectTimeOut option can be set only at the Visual FoxPro level and has no equivalent at the connection level. You can set all other options at either the connection or the Visual FoxPro level. Each option set at the Visual FoxPro level serves as a default value for subsequent connections.

Use SQLGETPROP( ) to return the current value for a specified setting.

Note The ODBC login dialog must be disabled to support SQL pass through with Microsoft Transaction Server. Use SQLSETPROP(*cConnectionHandle*, 'DispLogin', 3) to disable the ODBC login dialog. The ODBC login dialog can also be disabled in the Connection Designer.

Example

SQLSETPROP( ) is used to set the packet size for the current connection.

```
* Clear environment
CLOSE ALL
CLEAR ALL
CLEAR

* Display the Select Connection or Datasource dialog box
* to choose a connection
nHandle=SQLCONNECT( )

* Test connection, report results
IF nHandle > 0
   * Set PacketSize
   nSet=SQLSETPROP(nHandle, "PacketSize", 2048 )
   * Test setting and display results
   IF nSet > 0
      =MESSAGEBOX("PacketSize was set to 2048",0,"Connection Results")
   ELSE
      =MESSAGEBOX("Error setting PacketSize",0,"Connection Results")
   ENDIF
ELSE
   =MESSAGEBOX("No Connection",0,"Connection Results")
ENDIF
=SQLDISCONNECT(nHandle)
```

See Also

AERROR( ), SQLGETPROP( )

SQLSTRINGCONNECT( ) Function

Establishes a connection to a data source through a connection string.

Syntax

SQLSTRINGCONNECT([*cConnectString*])

Returns

Numeric

Arguments

cConnectString

Specifies the data source connection string required by some ODBC drivers. Visual FoxPro passes the connection string to the ODBC driver. For more information about data source connection strings, see your ODBC driver documentation.

If SQLSTRINGCONNECT( ) is issued without *cConnectString*, the SQL Data Sources dialog box is displayed, allowing you to choose a data source.

Remarks

SQLSTRINGCONNECT( ) returns a positive non-zero numeric handle if you successfully connect to the data source. You should store this handle in a memory variable and use the variable in subsequent function calls that require a connection handle.

Example

The following example assumes an ODBC data source called MyFoxSQLNT is available, and the user ID for the data source is "sa," and the password is "FOXPRO." SQLSTRINGCONNECT( ) is issued, and its return value is stored to a variable named gnConnHandle.

If you successfully connect to the data source, SQLSTRINGCONNECT( ) returns a positive number, a dialog is displayed and SQLDISCONNECT( ) is used to disconnect from the data source.

If you cannot connect to the data source, SQLSTRINGCONNECT( ) returns a negative number and a message is displayed.

```
STORE SQLSTRINGCONNECT('dsn=MyFoxSQLNT;uid=sa;pwd=FOXPRO');
   TO gnConnHandle
IF gnConnHandle < 0
   = MESSAGEBOX('Cannot make connection', 16, 'SQL Connect Error')
ELSE
   = MESSAGEBOX('Connection made', 48, 'SQL Connect Message')
   = SQLDISCONNECT(gnConnHandle)
ENDIF
```

See Also

AERROR( ), SQLCONNECT( ), SQLDISCONNECT( )

SQLTABLES( ) Function

Stores the names of tables in a data source to a Visual FoxPro cursor.

Syntax

SQLTABLES(*nConnectionHandle* [, *cTableTypes*] [, *cCursorName*])

Returns

Numeric

Arguments

nConnectionHandle
Specifies the connection handle to the data source returned by SQLCONNECT( ).

cTableTypes
Specifies one or more table types. Valid table types are 'TABLE,' 'VIEW,' 'SYSTEM TABLE,' or any valid data source-specific table type identifier. *cTabletypes* must be in upper-case. If you include a list of table types, separate the table types with commas.

All table names in the data source are selected if you omit *cTableTypes* or if *cTableTypes* is the empty string.

The table type you specify must be delimited with single quotation marks. The following example demonstrates how to specify the 'VIEW' and 'SYSTEM TABLE' table types as a string literal.

```
? SQLTABLES(handle, "'VIEW', 'SYSTEM TABLE'", "mydbresult")
```

cCursorName
Specifies the name of the Visual FoxPro cursor to which the result set is sent. If you don't include a cursor name, Visual FoxPro uses the default name SQLRESULT.

The following table shows the columns in the cursor.

Column name	Description
TABLE_QUALIFIER	Table qualifier identifier
TABLE_OWNER	Table owner identifier
TABLE_NAME	The table name as it appears in the data dictionary
TABLE_TYPE	The table type as it appears in the data dictionary
REMARKS	A description of the table

Remarks

SQLTABLES( ) returns 1 if the cursor is successfully created, 0 if SQLTABLES( ) is still executing, –1 if a connection level error occurs, and –2 if an environment level error occurs.

SQLTABLES( ) is one of the four functions that you can execute either synchronously or asynchronously. The setting of the SQLSETPROP( ) asynchronous option determines if these functions execute synchronously or asynchronously. In asynchronous mode, you must call SQLTABLES( ) repeatedly until it returns a value other than false (.F.), meaning the function is still executing.

Example

The following example assumes an ODBC data source called MyFoxSQLNT is available, and the user ID for the data source is "sa." SQLCONNECT( ) is issued, and its return value is stored to a variable named gnConnHandle.

If you cannot connect to the data source, SQLCONNECT( ) returns a negative number and a message is displayed.

If you successfully connect to the data source, SQLCONNECT( ) returns a positive number and a dialog is displayed. SQLTABLES( ) is used to create a cursor named mycursor that contains information about tables in the data source. LIST is used to display information about the tables.

```
STORE SQLCONNECT('MyFoxSQLNT', 'sa') TO gnConnHandle
IF gnConnHandle < 0
   = MESSAGEBOX('Cannot make connection', 16, 'SQL Connect Error')
ELSE
   = MESSAGEBOX('Connection made', 48, 'SQL Connect Message')
   STORE SQLTABLES(gnConnHandle, 'TABLE', 'mycursor') TO nTables
   IF nTables = 1
      SELECT mycursor
      LIST
   ENDIF
ENDIF
```

See Also

AERROR( ), SQLCOLUMNS( ), SQLCONNECT( ), SQLGETPROP( ), SQLSETPROP( )

SQRT( ) Function

Returns the square root of the specified numeric expression.

Syntax

SQRT(*nExpression*)

Returns

Numeric

Arguments

nExpression
Specifies the numeric expression SQRT( ) evaluates. *nExpression* cannot be negative.

Remarks

The number of decimal places in the value returned by SQRT( ) is the larger of the current decimal place setting and the number of decimal places contained in *nExpression*. The current decimal place setting is specified with SET DECIMALS.

Example

```
CLEAR
? SQRT(4)  && Displays 2.00
? SQRT(2*SQRT(2))  && Displays 1.68
```

See Also

SET DECIMALS

SROWS( ) Function

Returns the number of rows available in the main Visual FoxPro window.

Syntax

SROWS( )

Returns

Numeric

Remarks

In Visual FoxPro for Windows, the value returned by SROWS( ) depends on the current display mode. The display mode can be changed with SET DISPLAY.

Example

```
CLEAR
? SROWS( )
```

See Also

COL( ), ROW( ), SCOLS( ), SET DISPLAY, WCOLS( ), WROWS( )

StartMode Property

Contains a numeric value that indicates how an instance of Visual FoxPro was started. Read-only at run time.

Syntax

ApplicationObject.StartMode

Remarks

The following table lists the numeric values the StartMode property can contain and how the instance of Visual FoxPro was started.

Value	Description
0	A development version of Visual FoxPro was started in an interactive session.
1	Visual FoxPro was started as an application object. For example, the following command creates an instance of Visual FoxPro as an application object: `oMyObject = CREATEOBJECT('VisualFoxPro.Application')`
2	Visual FoxPro was started as an out-of-process .exe automation server.
3	Visual FoxPro was started as an in-process .dll automation server.
4	Visual FoxPro was started as a distributable .app or .exe file.

For additional information about using Visual FoxPro to create custom automation servers, see Chapter 16, "Adding OLE," in the *Microsoft Visual FoxPro 6.0 Programmer's Guide*.

Applies To

Application Object, _VFP System Variable

See Also

CREATEOBJECT( ), ServerName Property, SYS(2335) – Unattended Server Mode

_STARTUP System Variable

Specifies the name of the application that runs when you start Visual FoxPro.

Syntax

_STARTUP = *ProgramName*

Arguments

ProgramName

Specifies the application that is run when you start Visual FoxPro. You must include _STARTUP in your Visual FoxPro configuration file.

You can also specify a command or program to run when Visual FoxPro starts by including one of the following in your configuration file:

```
COMMAND = cVisualFoxProCommand
```

– or –

```
COMMAND = DO ProgramName
```

A startup application specified with _STARTUP always runs before a command or program specified with COMMAND in your configuration file.

Remarks

_STARTUP contains Vfp6strt.app by default. You can also specify a startup application in the **Files Location** tab of the **Options** dialog.

See Also

DO

StatusBar Property

Specifies the text displayed in the status bar of an instance of Visual FoxPro. Read/write at run time.

Syntax

ApplicationObject.StatusBar[= *cMessageText*]

Arguments

cMessageText
    Specifies the text displayed in the status bar.

Applies To

Application Object, _VFP System Variable

See Also

SET MESSAGE

StatusBarText Property

Specifies the text displayed in the status bar when a control has the focus. Available at design time and run time.

Syntax

[*Form.*]*Control*.StatusBarText[= *cText*]

Arguments

cText
    Specifies the text that describes the control with the focus.

Applies To

CheckBox, ComboBox, CommandButton, EditBox, Grid, ListBox, OptionButton, Spinner, TextBox

See Also

Caption Property

STORE Command

Stores data to a \variable, to an array, or to an array element.

Syntax

STORE *eExpression* TO *VarNameList | ArrayNameList*

– or –

VarName | ArrayName = eExpression

Arguments

eExpression

Specifies an expression whose value is stored to the variable, array, or array element. If the variable doesn't exist, it is created and initialized to *eExpression*. An array must be previously defined with DIMENSION. STORE replaces the value in an existing variable, array, or array element with the new value.

VarNameList

Specifies a list of variables or array elements to which *eExpression* is stored. Separate the names or array elements with commas.

ArrayNameList

Specifies a list of names of existing arrays to which *eExpression* is stored. Separate array names with commas.

STORE initializes every element in the arrays to the specified value if SET COMPATIBLE is OFF. STORE stores the specified value to memory variables of the specified names if SET COMPATIBLE is ON, overwriting any existing arrays that have those names.

Remarks

An alternative to STORE is the equal sign (=) assignment operator. The variable, array, or array element must be on the left side of the equal sign and its value on the right side.

Dates can be stored directly to variables, arrays, or array elements by using braces:

```
STORE {^1998-12-25} TO gdXMas
```

For more information about creating Date and DateTime values, see "Year 2000 Date Support" in Chapter 33, "Programming Improvements," in the *Microsoft Visual FoxPro 6.0 Programmer's Guide*.

The maximum number of variables or arrays you can create is listed in "System Capacities," in Help. The limit can be increased or decreased in your Visual FoxPro configuration file. For more information on configuring Visual FoxPro, refer to Chapter 3, "Configuring Visual FoxPro," in the *Installation Guide*, in Help.

Example

```
STORE DATE( ) TO gdDate
STORE 50 TO gnNumeric
STORE 'Hello' TO gcCharacter
STORE .T. TO glLogical
STORE $19.99 TO gyCurrency

DIMENSION gaMyArray(2,2)
SET COMPATIBLE OFF
STORE 2 TO gaMyArray

CLEAR
DISPLAY MEMORY LIKE g*
```

See Also

DIMENSION, SET COMPATIBLE

STR( ) Function

Returns the character equivalent of a specified numeric expression.

Syntax

STR(*nExpression* [, *nLength* [, *nDecimalPlaces*]])

Returns

Character

Arguments

nExpression
Specifies the numeric expression STR( ) evaluates.

nLength
Specifies the length of the character string STR( ) returns. The length includes one character for the decimal point and one character for each digit to the right of the decimal point.

STR( ) pads the character string it returns with leading spaces if you specify a length larger than the number of digits to the left of the decimal point. STR( ) returns a string of asterisks, indicating numeric overflow, if you specify a length less than the number of digits to the left of the decimal point.

If *nExpression* is of numeric or float type, STR( ) returns a value using scientific notation if *nLength* is less than the number of digits in *nExpression*. If *nExpression* is an integer, STR( ) returns a string of asterisks, indicating numeric overflow, if *nLength* is less than the number of digits in *nExpression*.

If *nLength* isn't included, the length of the character string defaults to 10 characters.

nDecimalPlaces

Specifies the number of decimal places in the character string STR( ) returns. You must include *nLength* to specify the number of decimal places.

If you specify fewer decimal places than are in *nExpression*, the return value is rounded.

If *nDecimalPlaces* isn't included, the number of decimal places defaults to zero.

See Also

VAL( )

STRCONV( ) Function

Converts character expressions between single-byte, double-byte, UNICODE, and locale-specific representations.

Syntax

STRCONV(*cExpression*, *nConversionSetting* [, *nLocaleID*])

Returns

Character

Arguments

cExpression

Specifies the character expression that STRCONV( ) converts.

nConversionSetting

Specifies the type of conversion. The following table lists the values of *nConversionSetting* and the type of conversion performed.

nConversionSetting	Conversion
1	Converts single-byte characters in *cExpression* to double-byte characters.
2	Converts double-byte characters in *cExpression* to single-byte characters.
3	Converts double-byte Hiragana characters in *cExpression* to double-byte Katakana characters.
4	Converts double-byte Katakana characters in *cExpression* to double-byte Hiragana characters.
5	Converts double-byte characters to UNICODE (wide characters).
6	Converts UNICODE (wide characters) to double-byte characters.
7	Converts *cExpression* to locale-specific lowercase.
8	Converts *cExpression* to locale-specific uppercase.

nLocaleID
> Specifies the Locale ID to use for the conversion. If *nLocaleID* is invalid or not supported on the machine, the error "Invalid locale ID" is generated. If *nLocaleID* is omitted, the system locale ID is used by default.

Remarks

This function is useful for manipulating double-byte character sets for languages such as Hiragana and Katakana.

See Also

CHRTRANC( ), IMESTATUS( ), ISLEADBYTE( )

Stretch Property

Specifies how an image is sized to fit inside a control. Available at design time and run time.

Syntax

[*Form.*]*Control*.Stretch[= *nType*]

Arguments

nType
> The settings for the Stretch property are as follows:

Setting	Description
0	(Default) Clip. The image is clipped to fit the control.
1	Isometric. The image resizes to fit the control while maintaining its original proportions.
2	Stretch. The image resizes to fit the control, but does not maintain its original proportions.

Applies To

Image, OLE Bound Control, OLE Container Control

See Also

Autosize Property, Sizable Property

StrictDateEntry Property

Specifies whether date and DateTime values must be entered in a specific, strict format in a text box. Available at design time and run time.

Syntax

Object.StrictDateEntry[= *nValue*]

Arguments

nValue

One of the following settings:

Setting	Description
0	Loose. Dates and DateTime values can be entered in a loosely formatted manner. The order in which the days, months, and years are entered is determined by the DateFormat property or SET DATE.
	Spaces, backslashes, periods, hyphens, and the current date delimiter (specified with the DateMark property or SET MARK) can be used to delimit date values. If the year is omitted from a date, the current year is used for the date.
	A caret (^) can be included as the first character in a date to specify year-month-day date ordering, overriding the order specified by the DateFormat property or SET DATE.
	A comma or a space can be used to delimit the date from the time in a DateTime value. When entering just an hour in a DateTime value, the colon can be omitted if the year is included in the date or a comma is used to separate the date from the time.
	Note If an invalid date or DateTime value is entered, an error message is not displayed and the text box value is set to an empty date or DateTime value. You can test for an invalid date in the Valid event.
1	(Default) Strict. Provides compatibility with previous versions of Visual FoxPro.
	Dates in date and DateTime values must be entered in a strict 99/99/99 format when CENTURY is set to OFF, or a 99/99/9999 format when CENTURY is set to ON. 99 represents days, months, and years, and 9999 represents years including the century. The order in which the days, months, and years are entered is determined by the DateFormat property or SET DATE.

Remarks

The following table lists valid date and DateTime values you can enter in a text box when StrictDateEntry is set to 0 (Loose).

Date or DateTime value	Description
12 31	December 31st of the current year.
12 31 98 14	December 31st of 1998, 2 P.M.
12 31, 14	December 31st of the current year, 2 P.M.
12 - 31 - 98, 2p	December 31st of 1998, 2 P.M. Note the extra spaces between the hyphen delimiters.

(continued)

Date or DateTime value	Description
^98-12-31, 2p	December 31st of 1998, 2 P.M. Caret (^) specifies year-month-day date ordering, overriding the order specified by the DateFormat property or SET DATE.
^/12/31	December 31st of the current year. Caret (^) specifies year-month-day date ordering, overriding the order specified by the DateFormat property or SET DATE.

Applies To

TextBox

See Also

Century Property, DateFormat Property, DateMark Property, Hours Property, Seconds Property, SET CENTURY, SET DATE, SET MARK TO, SET STRICTDATE

STRTOFILE( ) Function

Writes the contents of a character string to a file.

Syntax

STRTOFILE(*cExpression, cFileName* [, *lAdditive*])

Returns

Numeric

Arguments

cExpression
Specifies the character string that is written to the file. *cExpression* can be a literal character string, an expression that evaluates to a character string, or a character type variable, array element, or field.

cFileName
Specifies the name of the file to which the character string is written. Include a path with the file name if the file is in a directory other than the current default directory. If the file you specify does not exist, Visual FoxPro automatically creates it.

lAdditive
Specifies if the character string is appended to the end of the file. If *lAdditive* is true (.T.), the character string is appended to the end of the file.

If *lAdditive* is false (.F.) (the default), the file is overwritten with the character string. You are asked if you want to overwrite an existing file if SET SAFETY is set to ON. If SET SAFETY is set to OFF, the file is overwritten without warning.

Remarks

STRTOFILE( ) returns the number of bytes written to the file.

See Also

FILETOSTR( ), FWRITE( )

STRTRAN( ) Function

Searches a character expression or memo field for occurrences of a second character expression or memo field, and then replaces each occurrence with a third character expression or memo field.

Syntax

STRTRAN(*cSearched, cSearchFor* [, *cReplacement*]
    [, *nStartOccurrence*] [, *nNumberOfOccurrences*])

Returns

Character

Arguments

cSearched

    Specifies the character expression that is searched. *cSearched* can be a memo field.

cSearchFor

    Specifies the character expression that is searched for in *cSearched*. The search is case-sensitive. *cSearchFor* can be a memo field.

cReplacement

    Specifies the character expression that replaces every occurrence of *cSearchFor* in *cSearched*. If you omit *cReplacement*, every occurrence of *cSearchFor* is replaced with the empty string.

nStartOccurrence

    Specifies which occurrence of *cSearchFor* is the first to be replaced. For example, if *nStartOccurrence* is 4, replacement begins with the fourth occurrence of *cSearchFor* in *cSearched* and the first three occurrences of *cSearchFor* remain unchanged. The occurrence where replacement begins defaults to the first occurrence of *cSearchFor* if you omit *nStartOccurrence*.

nNumberOfOccurrences

    Specifies the number of occurrences of *cSearchFor* to replace. If you omit *nNumberOfOccurrences*, all occurrences of *cSearchFor*, starting with the occurrence specified with *nStartOccurrence*, are replaced.

Remarks

You can specify where the replacement begins and how many replacements are made. STRTRAN( ) returns the resulting character string.

Example

```
STORE 'abracadabra' TO gcString
? STRTRAN(gcString, 'a', 'z')  && Displays zbrzczdzbrz
? STRTRAN(gcString, 'a', 'q', 2, 3)  && Displays abrqcqdqbra
```

See Also

STUFF( )

STUFF( ) Function

Returns a character string created by replacing a specified number of characters in a character expression with another character expression.

Syntax

STUFF(*cExpression*, *nStartReplacement*, *nCharactersReplaced*, *cReplacement*)

Returns

Character

Arguments

cExpression
Specify the character expression in which the replacement occurs.

nStartReplacement
Specifies the position in *cExpression* where the replacement begins.

nCharactersReplaced
Specifies the number of characters to be replaced. If *nCharactersReplaced* is 0, the replacement string *cReplacement* is inserted into *cExpression*.

cReplacement
Specifies the replacement character expression. If *cReplacement* is the empty string, the number of characters specified by *nCharactersReplaced* are removed from *cExpression*.

Example

```
STORE 'abcdefghijklm' TO gcString1
STORE '12345' TO gcString2
CLEAR
? STUFF(gcString1, 4, 0, gcString2)     && insert
? STUFF(gcString1, 4, 3, gcString2)     && replace
```

```
? STUFF(gcString1, 4, 6, '')        && delete
? STUFF(gcString1, 4, 1, gcString2)     && replace and insert
? STUFF(gcString1, 4, 4, gcString2)     && replace and delete
? STUFF(gcString1, 4, LEN(gcString1), gcString2)   && replace, delete rest
```

See Also

LEFT( ), PADC( ) | PADL( ) | PADR( ), RIGHT( ), STRTRAN( ), SUBSTR( )

STUFFC( ) Function

Returns a character string created by replacing a specified number of characters in a character expression with another character expression.

Syntax

STUFFC(*cExpression*, *nStartReplacement*, *nCharactersReplaced*, *cReplacement*)

Returns

Character

Arguments

cExpression
Specify the character expression in which the replacement occurs.

nStartReplacement
Specifies the character position in *cExpression* where the replacement begins.

nCharactersReplaced
Specifies the number of characters to be replaced. If *nCharactersReplaced* is 0, the entire replacement string *cReplacement* is inserted into *cExpression*.

cReplacement
Specifies the replacement character expression. If *cReplacement* is the empty string, the number of characters specified by *nCharactersReplaced* are removed from *cExpression*.

Remarks

STUFFC( ) is designed for expressions containing double-byte characters. If the expression contains only single-byte characters, STUFFC( ) is equivalent to STUFF( ).

STUFFC( ) returns a character string created by replacing a specified number of characters in a character expression with another character expression. The character expressions can consist of any combination of single-byte and double-byte characters.

This function is useful for manipulating double-byte character sets for languages such as Hiragana and Katakana.

See Also

LEFTC( ), RIGHTC( ), STUFF( ), SUBSTRC( )

Style Property

Specifies the style of a control. Available at design time and run time.

Syntax

[*Form.*]*Control.*Style[= *nType*]

Arguments

nType

For ComboBox controls, the settings for the Style property are as follows:

Setting	Description
0	Drop-down Combo. Includes a drop-down list and an edit area. The user can select from the list or enter characters in the edit area.
2	Drop-down List. The user must select from the drop-down list.

Follow these guidelines in deciding which setting to choose:

- Set Style to 0 (Dropdown Combo) to give the user a list of choices and also enable the user to enter a selection in the edit area. Style 0 saves space on the Form because the list portion closes when the user makes a selection.

- Set Style to 2 (Dropdown List) to display a fixed list of choices from which the user can select one. The list portion closes when the user selects an item.

For CheckBox and OptionButton controls, the settings for the Style property are as follows:

Setting	Description
0	Standard.
1	Graphical. The button appears like a command button. It can contain both graphics and text. When the button contains both, the text is always centered at the bottom of the button.

For CommandButton controls, the settings for the Style property are as follows:

Setting	Description
0	Standard
1	Invisible

For TextBox controls, the settings for the Style property are:

Setting	Description
0	(Default) Normal.
1	Included for backward compatibility with the FoxPro version 2.x @ ... SAY command. The TextBox is read-only and cannot receive the focus.

Applies To

CheckBox, ComboBox, CommandButton, OptionButton, TextBox

See Also

Click Event, DblClick Event

SUBSTR( ) Function

Returns a character string from the given character expression or memo field.

Syntax

SUBSTR(*cExpression*, *nStartPosition* [, *nCharactersReturned*])

Returns

Character

Arguments

cExpression
Specifies the character expression or memo field from which the character string is returned.

StartPosition
Specifies the position in the character expression or memo field *cExpression* from where the character string is returned. The first character of *cExpression* is position 1.

If TALK is SET ON and *nStartPosition* is greater than the number of characters in *cExpression*, Visual FoxPro generates an error message. If TALK is SET OFF, the empty string is returned.

nCharactersReturned
Specifies the number of characters to return from *cExpression*. If you omit *nCharactersReturned*, characters are returned until the end of the character expression is reached.

Remarks

SUBSTR( ) returns a character string from a character expression or memo field, starting at a specified position in the character expression or memo field and continuing for a specified number of characters.

When using SUBSTR( ) with memo fields in a SELECT – SQL command, include the PADR( ) function in SUBSTR( ) so that empty or variable length memo fields produce consistent results when converted to character strings.

SUBSTR( ) will not return a value for a memo field when issued in the Debug window. To return a value in the Debug window, place the memo field name within ALLTRIM( ), and place ALLTRIM( ) within SUBSTR( ).

Example

```
STORE 'abcdefghijklm' TO mystring
CLEAR
? SUBSTR(mystring, 1, 5)  && Displays abcde
? SUBSTR(mystring, 6)  && Displays fghijklm
```

See Also

AT( ), LEFT( ), PADR( ), RIGHT( ), STRTRAN( ), STUFF( )

SUBSTRC( ) Function

Returns a character string from the given character expression or memo field.

Syntax

SUBSTRC(*cExpression*, *nStartPosition* [, *nCharactersReturned*])

Returns

Character

Arguments

cExpression
Specifies the character expression or memo field from which the character string is returned.

nStartPosition
Specifies the position in the character expression or memo field *cExpression* from where the character string is returned. The first character of *cExpression* is position 1.

If TALK is set to ON and *nStartPosition* is greater than the number of characters in *cExpression*, Visual FoxPro generates an error message. If TALK is set to OFF, the empty string is returned.

nCharactersReturned
Specifies the number of characters to return from *cExpression*. If you omit *nCharactersReturned*, characters are returned until the end of the character expression is reached.

Remarks

SUBSTRC( ) is designed for expressions containing double-byte characters. If the expression contains only single-byte characters, SUBSTRC( ) is equivalent to SUBSTR( ).

SUBSTRC( ) returns a character string from the given character expression or memo field. The character expression or memo field can contain any combination of single-byte and double-byte characters.

SUBSTRC( ) will not return a value for a memo field when issued in the Debug window. To return a value in the Debug window, place the memo field name within ALLTRIM( ), and place ALLTRIM( ) within SUBSTRC( ).

This function is useful for manipulating double-byte character sets for languages such as Hiragana and Katakana.

See Also

AT_C( ), LEFTC( ), RIGHTC( ), STUFFC( ), SUBSTR( )

SUM Command

Totals all or specified numeric fields in the currently selected table.

Syntax

SUM [*eExpressionList*]
    [*Scope*] [FOR *lExpression1*] [WHILE *lExpression2*]
    [TO *MemVarNameList* | TO ARRAY *ArrayName*]
    [NOOPTIMIZE]

Arguments

eExpressionList
    Specifies one or more fields or field expressions to total. If you omit the field expression list, all numeric fields are totaled.

Scope
    Specifies a range of records to include in the total. The scope clauses are: ALL, NEXT *nRecords*, RECORD *nRecordNumber*, and REST. For more information on scope clauses, see "Scope Clauses" and "Overview of the Language," in Help.

    The default scope for SUM is ALL records.

FOR *lExpression1*
    Specifies that only the records for which the logical condition *lExpression1* evaluates to true (.T.) are included in the total. Including FOR lets you conditionally total records, filtering out undesired records.

Rushmore optimizes a SUM ... FOR command if *lExpression1* is an optimizable expression. For best performance, use an optimizable expression in the FOR clause.

For more information on Rushmore optimization, see the SET OPTIMIZE Command, earlier in this language reference, and "Using Rushmore to Speed Data Access" in Chapter 15, "Optimizing Applications," in the *Microsoft Visual FoxPro 6.0 Programmer's Guide*.

WHILE *lExpression2*

Specifies a condition whereby records from the current table are included in the total for as long as the logical expression *lExpression2* evaluates to true (.T.).

TO *MemVarNameList*

Stores each total to a variable. If you specify a variable in *MemVarNameList* that doesn't exist, Visual FoxPro automatically creates it. Separate the variable names in the list with commas.

TO ARRAY *ArrayName*

Stores totals to a variable array. If the array you specify in SUM doesn't exist, Visual FoxPro automatically creates it. If the array exists and is too small to contain all the totals, the size of the array is automatically increased to accommodate the totals.

NOOPTIMIZE

Disables Rushmore optimization of SUM.

For more information, see the SET OPTIMIZE Command, earlier in this language reference, and "Using Rushmore to Speed Data Access" in Chapter 15, "Optimizing Applications," in the *Microsoft Visual FoxPro 6.0 Programmer's Guide*.

Example

The following example displays the totals of the in_stock and on_order fields in the products table, along with a sum of the two totals.

```
CLOSE DATABASES
OPEN DATABASE (HOME(2) + 'data\testdata')
USE products   && Opens Products table

SUM in_stock, on_order, in_stock+on_order ;
   TO gnInStock, gnOnOrder, gnUnits

CLEAR
?
? 'Total in stock : ', gnInStock   && Displays 3119.00
? 'Total on order: ', gnOnOrder   && Displays 780.00
? 'Total # units : ', gnUnits   && Displays 3899.00
```

See Also

AVERAGE, CALCULATE, COUNT

SUSPEND Command

Pauses program execution and returns to interactive Visual FoxPro.

Syntax

SUSPEND

Remarks

While a program is paused, you can execute intervening commands, check variable values, open the Trace and Debug windows, and so on.

All variables created while the program is paused are PRIVATE.

Use RESUME to restart execution of a suspended program. Program execution continues with the line following the line containing SUSPEND.

See Also

CANCEL, RESUME

SYS( ) Functions Overview

Returns Microsoft Visual FoxPro system information.

Syntax

SYS( )

Returns

Character

Remarks

Visual FoxPro SYS( ) functions return character values that contain useful system information.

To get help for a SYS( ) function

- Highlight the SYS( ) function in the Command window or in a program and press the F1 key.

The following table shows what each SYS( ) function returns:

Function	Information returned
SYS(0)	Network machine information
SYS(1)	Julian system date
SYS(2)	Seconds since midnight
SYS(3)	Legal file name
SYS(5)	Default drive or volume

(continued)

Function	Information returned
SYS(6)	Current printer device
SYS(7)	Current format file
SYS(9)	Visual FoxPro serial number
SYS(10)	String from Julian day number
SYS(11)	Julian day number
SYS(12)	Available memory in bytes
SYS(13)	Printer status
SYS(14)	Index expression
SYS(15)	Character translation
SYS(16)	Executing program file name
SYS(17)	Processor in use
SYS(18)	Current control
SYS(20)	Transform German text
SYS(21)	Controlling index number
SYS(22)	Controlling tag or index name
SYS(23)	FoxPro EMS memory usage
SYS(24)	EMS memory limit
SYS(100)	Console setting
SYS(101)	Device setting
SYS(102)	Printer setting
SYS(103)	Talk setting
SYS(1001)	Visual FoxPro memory
SYS(1016)	User object memory use
SYS(1023)	Enable Help diagnostic mode
SYS(1024)	Disable Help diagnostic mode
SYS(1037)	Page Setup Dialog Box
SYS(1269)	Property Information
SYS(1270)	Object Location
SYS(1271)	Object's .scx File

(continued)

(continued)

Function	Information returned
SYS(1272)	Object Hierarchy
SYS(1500)	Activate a system menu item
SYS(2000)	File name wildcard match
SYS(2001)	SET command status
SYS(2002)	Turn insertion point on or off
SYS(2003)	Current directory
SYS(2004)	Visual FoxPro start directory
SYS(2005)	Current resource file
SYS(2006)	Current graphics card
SYS(2007)	Checksum value
SYS(2010)	CONFIG.SYS file settings
SYS(2011)	Current lock status
SYS(2012)	Memo field block size
SYS(2013)	System menu name string
SYS(2014)	Minimum path
SYS(2015)	Unique procedure name
SYS(2016)	SHOW GETS WINDOW name
SYS(2017)	Display startup screen
SYS(2018)	Error message parameter
SYS(2019)	Configuration file name and location
SYS(2020)	Default disk size
SYS(2021)	Filtered index expression
SYS(2022)	Disk cluster (block) size
SYS(2023)	Temporary Path
SYS(2029)	Table type
SYS(2333)	ActiveX Dual Interface Support
SYS(2334)	Automation Server Invocation Mode
SYS(2335)	Unattended Server Mode
SYS(3004)	Return Locale ID

(continued)

Function	Information returned
SYS(3005)	Set Locale ID
SYS(3006)	Set Language and Locale IDs
SYS(3050)	Set Buffer Memory Size
SYS(3051)	Set Lock Retry Interval
SYS(3052)	Override SET REPROCESS Locking
SYS(3053)	ODBC Environment Handle
SYS(3054)	Rushmore Optimization Level
SYS(3055)	FOR and WHERE Clause Complexity
SYS(3056)	Read Registry Settings
SYS(4204)	Active Document Debugging Support

SYS(0) – Network Machine Information

SYS(0) returns network machine information when using Visual FoxPro in a network environment.

Syntax

SYS(0)

Returns

Character

Remarks

Machine information must first be assigned by the network software and the network shell must be loaded.

If machine information has not been assigned or the network shell hasn't been loaded, SYS(0) returns a character string consisting of 15 spaces, a number sign (#) followed by another space, and then 0. Consult your network documentation for further information on defining machine information.

SYS(0) returns 1 when using Visual FoxPro in a stand-alone environment.

SYS(0) returns the machine name and user name.

See Also

SYS( ) Functions Overview

SYS(1) – Julian System Date

Returns the current system date as a Julian day number character string.

Syntax

SYS(1)

Returns

Character

Remarks

The value returned by SYS(1) is valid in the U.S.A. You can get Visual FoxPro versions for any system date after September 14, 1752, and before December 31, 9999.

Example

```
? SYS(1)
? SYS(10,VAL(SYS(1)))
```

See Also

CDOW( ), CTOD( ), DATE( ), DATETIME( ), DAY( ), DOW( ), DTOC( ), SYS( ) Functions Overview, SYS(10) – String from Julian Day Number, SYS(11) – Julian Day Number

SYS(2) – Seconds Since Midnight

Returns the number of seconds elapsed since midnight.

Syntax

SYS(2)

Returns

Character

Example

```
? TIME( )
? SYS(2)
```

See Also

DATETIME( ), SECONDS( ), SYS( ) Functions Overview, TIME( )

SYS(3) – Legal File Name

Returns a legal file name that can be used to create temporary files.

Syntax

SYS(3)

Returns

Character

Remarks

SYS(3) may return a non-unique name when issued successively on a fast computer. Use SUBSTR(SYS(2015), 3, 10) to create unique, legal eight character file name.

See Also

FILE( ), SYS( ) Functions Overview, SYS(2015) – Unique Procedure Name

SYS(5) – Default Drive

Returns the current Visual FoxPro default drive.

Syntax

SYS(5)

Returns

Character

Remarks

This function returns the current Visual FoxPro default drive. Use SET DEFAULT to specify a default drive.

Example

```
IF _DOS OR _WINDOWS
   SET DEFAULT TO C:
ENDIF
? SYS(5)
```

See Also

DRIVETYPE( ), SET DEFAULT, SYS( ) Functions Overview

SYS(6) – Current Printer Device

Returns the current print device.

Syntax

SYS(6)

Returns

Character

Remarks

This function returns the current SET PRINTER TO setting.

Example

```
? SYS(6)
SET PRINTER TO output.txt
? SYS(6)
```

See Also

SET PRINTER, SYS( ) Functions Overview

SYS(7) – Current Format File

Returns the name of the current format file.

Syntax

SYS(7 [, *nWorkArea*])

Returns

Character

Arguments

nWorkArea
    Specifies the work area number for which SYS(7) returns the format file name.
    The format file name for the current work area is returned if you omit *nWorkArea*.

Remarks

A format file is opened with SET FORMAT. The empty string is returned if a format file isn't open for the work area you specify.

See Also

SET FORMAT, SYS( ) Functions Overview

SYS(9) – Visual FoxPro Serial Number

Returns your Visual FoxPro serial number.

Syntax

SYS(9)

Returns

Character

See Also

SYS( ) Functions Overview, VERSION( )

SYS(10) – String from Julian Day Number

Converts a Julian day number to a character string.

Syntax

SYS(10, *nJulianDayNumber*)

Returns

Character

Remarks

SYS(10) returns a Character-type date from a Julian day number *nJulianDayNumber*.

Example

```
? SYS(1)
? SYS(10,VAL(SYS(1)))
```

See Also

CDOW( ), CTOD( ), DATE( ), DATETIME( ), DAY( ), DOW( ), DTOC( ),
SYS( ) Functions Overview, SYS(1) – Julian System Date, SYS(11) – Julian Day Number

SYS(11) – Julian Day Number

Converts a date expression or character string in date format to a Julian day number.

Syntax

SYS(11, *dExpression* | *tExpression* | *cExpression*)

Returns

Character

Remarks

SYS(11) returns a Julian day number from a date expression *dExpression*, a datetime expression *tExpression*, or a character expression *cExpression* in a date format. The day number is returned as a character string.

Example

```
? SYS(11, {^1998-06-06})
? SYS(11,'06/06/1998')
```

See Also

CDOW( ), CTOD( ), DATE( ), DATETIME( ), DAY( ), DOW( ), DTOC( ), SYS( ) Functions Overview, SYS(10) – String from Julian Day Number

SYS(12) – Available Memory in Bytes

Returns the amount of memory below 640K that is available to execute an external program.

Syntax

SYS(12)

Returns

Character

Remarks

In Visual FoxPro, SYS(12) always returns 655,360.

SYS(12) is similar to MEMORY( ), with two exceptions:

- SYS(12) returns the amount of available memory in bytes. MEMORY( ) returns available memory in kilobytes.

- SYS(12) returns a character string. MEMORY( ) returns a numeric value.

See Also

MEMORY( ), RUN | !, SYS( ) Functions Overview, SYS(23) – FoxPro EMS Memory Usage, SYS(24) – EMS Memory Limit, SYS(1001) – Visual FoxPro Memory, SYS(1016) – User Object Memory Use

SYS(13) – Printer Status

Returns the status of the printer.

Syntax

SYS(13)

Returns

Character

Remarks

OFFLINE is returned if the printer isn't ready. READY is returned if the printer is ready.

If the printer is connected to a COM port, SYS(13) returns READY if the printer returns Clear To Send Data or Data Set Ready.

If the printer is connected to a parallel port, SYS(13) returns OFFLINE if the printer returns Out of Paper, I/O Error, Time Out, Printer Busy, or Printer Not Selected.

Example

```
IF SYS(13) = 'OFFLINE'
   WAIT WINDOW 'Printer is offline'
ENDIF
```

See Also

PRINTSTATUS( ), SET PRINTER, SYS( ) Functions Overview

SYS(14) – Index Expression

Returns index expression of an open single-entry .idx index file or index expressions for tags in compound .cdx index files.

Syntax

SYS(14, *nIndexNumber* [, *nWorkArea* | *cTableAlias*])

Returns

Character

Arguments

nIndexNumber
  Specifies which index expression to return from the open index files or tags. SYS(14) returns index expressions from open index files and tags in the following order as *nIndexNumber* increases from 1 to the total number of open single-entry files and structural compound and independent compound index tags:

1. Index expressions from single-entry index files (if any are open) are returned first. The order the single-entry index files are included in USE or SET INDEX determines the order the index expressions are returned.

2. Index expressions for each tag in the structural compound index (if one is present) are returned next. The index expressions are returned from the tags in the order that the tags were created in the structural index.

3. Index expressions for each tag in any open independent compound indexes are returned last. The index expressions are returned from the tags in the order that the tags were created in the independent compound indexes.

The empty string is returned if *nIndexNumber* is greater than the total number of open single-entry files and structural compound and independent compound index tags.

nWorkArea | cTableAlias
Specifies a work area number or work area alias. If you omit *nWorkArea* and *cTableAlias*, index expressions are returned from index files open in the current work area. If a table doesn't have the alias you specify, Visual FoxPro generates an error message.

Remarks

An index expression is specified when an index file or tag is created with INDEX. The index expression determines how a table is displayed and accessed when an index file or tag is used to order the table.

For more information on index expressions and creating index files and tags, see the INDEX Command, earlier in this language reference. SYS(14) is similar to the KEY( ) function.

USE and SET INDEX both support an index file name list that lets you open index files for a table. Any combination of single-entry index files, structural compound or independent compound index file names can be included in the index file list.

See Also

CDX( ), KEY( ), INDEX, MDX( ), NDX( ), REINDEX, SET INDEX, SET ORDER, SYS( ) Functions Overview, TAG( )

SYS(15) – Character Translation

Included for backward compatibility. Use SET COLLATE instead.

SYS(16) – Executing Program File Name

Returns the file name of the program being executed.

Syntax

SYS(16 [, *nProgramLevel*])

Returns

Character

Arguments

nProgramLevel

Indicates from how many levels back the program name is fetched. This value can range from 1 to the depth at which programs are nested.

If *nProgramLevel* is 0 or 1, SYS(16) returns the name of the main program (the program first executed). The name of the currently executing program is returned if *nProgramLevel* is omitted. The empty string is returned if *nProgramLevel* is greater than the program nesting depth.

Remarks

This option is useful for recovering from errors. SYS(16) is similar to PROGRAM( ). However, SYS(16) returns a path with the program name; whereas PROGRAM( ) returns just the program name.

If a procedure or function is being executed, SYS(16) returns the name of the file containing the procedure or function after the procedure or function name.

When the executing program is part of an application (.app), SYS(16) returns only the name of the program — the path isn't returned with the program name.

Example

The program nesting is returned in the following short program example:

```
STORE 1 TO gnX
DO WHILE LEN(SYS(16,gnX)) != 0
   ? SYS(16,gnX)
   STORE gnX+1 TO gnX
ENDDO
```

See Also

LINENO( ), ON ERROR, PROGRAM( ), SYS( ) Functions Overview

SYS(17) – Processor in Use

Returns the central processing unit (CPU) being used.

Syntax

SYS(17)

Returns

Character

Remarks

This function returns the type of central processing unit you are using: 80386, 80486, and so on.

Example

```
? 'Processor in use: ', SYS(17)
```

See Also

SYS( ) Functions Overview

SYS(18) – Current Control

Included for backward compatibility. Use the ActiveControl property instead.

SYS(20) – Transform German Text

Included for backward compatibility. Use SET COLLATE instead.

SYS(21) – Controlling Index Number

Returns, as a character string, the index position number of the master controlling .cdx compound index tag or .idx index file for the currently selected work area.

Syntax

SYS(21)

Returns

Character

Remarks

The index position number is determined by the order in which the .idx index files and .cdx compound index tags are specified in USE and SET INDEX.

You can use SET INDEX, SET ORDER, and USE to specify which .idx index file or .cdx compound index tag is the master controlling index file or tag. For more information on specifying a master controlling index or tag, see the SET INDEX, SET ORDER, and USE Commands, in this language reference.

"0" is returned if there isn't a master controlling .cdx compound index tag or .idx index file (for example, SET ORDER TO is issued to display and access the table in natural record order).

See Also

CDX( ), KEY( ), INDEX, MDX( ), NDX( ), REINDEX, SET INDEX, SET ORDER, SYS( ) Functions Overview, SYS(22) – Controlling Tag or Index Name, TAG( ), USE

SYS(22) – Controlling Tag or Index Name

Returns the name of the master controlling .cdx compound index tag or .idx index file for a table.

Syntax

SYS(22 [, *nWorkArea*])

Returns

Character

Remarks

You can use SET INDEX, SET ORDER, and USE to specify which .idx index file or .cdx compound index tag is the master controlling index file or tag. For more information on specifying a master controlling index or tag, see the SET INDEX, SET ORDER, and USE Commands, in this language reference.

The empty string is returned if there isn't a master controlling .cdx compound index tag or .idx index file (for example, SET ORDER TO is issued to display and access the table in natural record order).

nWorkArea
    Specifies the work area number of the table for which SYS(22) returns the name of the master controlling .cdx compound index tag or .idx index file.

See Also

CDX( ), KEY( ), INDEX, MDX( ), NDX( ), REINDEX, SET INDEX, SET ORDER, SYS( ) Functions Overview, SYS(21) – Controlling Index Number, TAG( )

SYS(23) – FoxPro EMS Memory Usage

Returns the amount of EMS memory (in 16K segments) that is currently being used by the Standard (16-bit) version of FoxPro for MS-DOS.

Syntax

SYS(23)

Returns

Character

Remarks

Zero is returned if no EMS memory is in use.

SYS(23) always returns 0 in the Extended (32-bit) version of FoxPro for MS-DOS and Visual FoxPro.

See Also

SYS( ) Functions Overview, SYS(12) – Available Memory in Bytes, SYS(24) – EMS Memory Limit, SYS(1001) – Visual FoxPro Memory, SYS(1016) – User Object Memory Use

SYS(24) – EMS Memory Limit

Returns the EMS limit set in your FoxPro for MS-DOS configuration file.

Syntax

SYS(24)

Returns

Character

Remarks

SYS(24) returns 0 in the Standard version of FoxPro for MS-DOS if an EMS limit is not included in your configuration file.

SYS(24) always returns 0 in the Extended (32-bit) version of FoxPro for MS-DOS and Visual FoxPro.

For complete information on this configuration setting, see Chapter 3, "Configuring Visual FoxPro," in the *Installation Guide*, in Help.

See Also

SYS( ) Functions Overview, SYS(12) – Available Memory in Bytes, SYS(23) – FoxPro EMS Memory Usage, SYS(1001) – Visual FoxPro Memory, SYS(1016) – User Object Memory Use

SYS(100) – Console Setting

Returns the current SET CONSOLE setting.

Syntax

SYS(100)

Returns

Character

Example

```
IF SYS(100) != 'ON'
    SET CONSOLE ON
ENDIF
```

See Also

SET CONSOLE, SYS( ) Functions Overview

SYS(101) – Device Setting

Returns the current SET DEVICE setting.

Syntax

SYS(101)

Returns

Character

Example

```
IF SYS(101) != 'SCREEN'
    SET DEVICE TO SCREEN
ENDIF
```

See Also

SET DEVICE, SYS( ) Functions Overview

SYS(102) – Printer Setting

Returns the current SET PRINTER setting.

Syntax

SYS(102)

Returns

Character

Example

```
IF SYS(102) != 'OFF'
   SET PRINTER OFF
ENDIF
```

See Also

SET PRINTER, SYS( ) Functions Overview

SYS(103) – Talk Setting

Returns the current SET TALK setting.

Syntax

SYS(103)

Returns

Character

Example

```
IF SYS(103) != 'ON'
   SET TALK ON
ENDIF
```

See Also

SET TALK, SYS( ) Functions Overview

SYS(1001) – Visual FoxPro Memory

Returns the total amount of memory available to the Visual FoxPro memory manager.

Syntax

SYS(1001)

Returns

Character

Remarks

In Visual FoxPro, SYS(1001) returns the virtual memory pool size, which is approximately four times the amount of physical memory.

See Also

SYS( ) Functions Overview, SYS(12) – Available Memory in Bytes, SYS(23) – FoxPro
EMS Memory Usage, SYS(24) – EMS Memory Limit, SYS(1016) – User Object
Memory Use

SYS(1016) – User Object Memory Use

Returns amount of memory being used by objects you define.

Syntax

SYS(1016)

Returns

Character

Remarks

User-defined objects include: user-defined windows, menu bars, menus, variables,
arrays, open tables, files opened with low-level file functions, and so on.

See Also

SYS( ) Functions Overview, SYS(12) – Available Memory in Bytes, SYS(23) – FoxPro
EMS Memory Usage, SYS(24) – EMS Memory Limit, SYS(1001) – Visual FoxPro
Memory

SYS(1023) – Enable Help Diagnostic Mode

Enables the Help diagnostic mode, allowing you to trap the HelpContextID passed to the
Visual FoxPro Help system.

Syntax

SYS(1023)

Returns

Character

Remarks

SYS(1023) is useful for debugging a custom Help system for your application. SYS(1023)
returns the empty string.

When the Help diagnostic mode is enabled with SYS(1023), a dialog box is displayed whenever you press F1 or issue HELP. The dialog box displays the HelpContextID to be passed to the Visual FoxPro Help system, and you are given the option of passing the HelpContextID to the Visual FoxPro Help system.

If you choose Yes, the HelpContextID is passed to the Visual FoxPro Help system and the corresponding Help topic (if available) is displayed. If you choose No, the HelpContextID is not passed to the Visual FoxPro Help system and the corresponding Help topic is not displayed.

Use SYS(1024) to disable the Help diagnostic mode and restore the default Visual FoxPro Help system processing.

See Also

HELP, HelpContextID Property, SET HELP, SYS(1024) – Disable Help Diagnostic Mode

SYS(1024) – Disable Help Diagnostic Mode

Disables the Help diagnostic mode enabled by issuing SYS(1023).

Syntax

SYS(1024)

Returns

Character

Remarks

Use SYS(1024) to disable the Help diagnostic mode enabled with SYS(1023) and restore the default Visual FoxPro Help system processing. SYS(1023) is used to debug a custom Help system for your application.

SYS(1024) returns the empty string.

See Also

HELP, HelpContextID Property, SET HELP, SYS(1023) – Enable Help Diagnostic Mode

SYS(1037) – Page Setup Dialog Box

Displays the Page Setup dialog box

Syntax

SYS(1037)

Returns

Character

Remarks

SYS(1037) displays the Page Setup dialog box, allowing you to make adjustments to printer settings such as the paper size and orientation. The settings you can adjust in this dialog depend on the printer you've installed.

SYS(1037) always returns the empty string.

See Also

GETPRINTER( ), PRINTSTATUS( ), SET DEVICE, SET PRINTER

SYS(1269) – Property Information

Returns a logical value that indicates whether a property setting has changed from its default setting or whether the property is read-only.

Syntax

SYS(1269, *oObjectName*, *cProperty*, *nPropertyAttribute*)

Returns

Logical

Arguments

oObjectName
   Specifies the object for which the property setting information is returned.

cProperty

Specifies the property for which SYS(1269) returns information.

nPropertyAttribute

Specifies the property attribute.

If *nPropertyAttribute* is 0, SYS(1269) returns true (.T.) if the property setting has changed from its default setting. SYS(1269) returns false (.F.) if the property setting has not been changed from its default value.

If *nPropertyAttribute* is 1, SYS(1269) returns true (.T.) if the property setting is read-only. SYS(1269) returns false (.F.) if the property setting is read/write.

Remarks

Use SYS(1269) to determine whether a property setting has been changed from its default value or is read-only before attempting to set the property programmatically.

See Also

CREATE FORM, GETPEM( ), PEMSTATUS( ), SYS(1270) – Object Location, SYS(1271) – Object's .SCX File, SYS(1272) – Object Hierarchy

SYS(1270) – Object Location

Returns a reference for an object at the specified point.

Syntax

SYS(1270 [, *nXCoord, nYCoord*])

Returns

Object, Logical

Arguments

nXCoord

Specifies the horizontal coordinate.

nYCoord

Specifies the vertical coordinate.

Remarks

If you omit the coordinates *nXCoord* and *nYCoord*, a reference to the object that is under the current mouse position is returned. If you include the coordinates *nXCoord* and *nYCoord*, a reference to the object at that location is returned.

False (.F.) is returned if no object is under the mouse pointer or located at the coordinates specified with *nXCoord* and *nYCoord*.

See Also

AMOUSEOBJ( ), CREATE FORM, GETPEM( ), PEMSTATUS( ), SYS(1269) – Property Information, SYS(1271) – Object's .SCX File, SYS(1272) – Object Hierarchy

SYS(1271) – Object's .SCX File

Returns the name of the .SCX file in which the specified instantiated object is stored.

Syntax

SYS(1271, *oObjectName*)

Returns

Character, Logical

Arguments

oObjectName
    Specifies the name of the object for which the .scx file is returned.

Remarks

SYS(1271) returns the name of the .scx file in which the specified instantiated object is stored.

SYS(1271) returns a logical false (.F.) if the object cannot be located in an .scx file (for example, if the object was created from the Command window).

See Also

CREATE FORM, GETPEM( ), PEMSTATUS( ), SYS(1269) – Property Information, SYS(1270) – Object Location, SYS(1272) – Object Hierarchy

SYS(1272) – Object Hierarchy

Returns the object hierarchy for a specified object. Not available at design time.

Syntax

SYS(1272, *oObjectName*)

Returns

Character

Arguments

oObjectName
    Specifies the name of the object for which the hierarchy is returned.

See Also

CREATE FORM, GETPEM( ), PEMSTATUS( ), SYS(1269) – Property Information, SYS(1270) – Object Location, SYS(1271) – Object's .SCX File

SYS(1500) – Activate a System Menu Item

Activates a Visual FoxPro system menu item.

Syntax

SYS(1500, *cSystemItemName*, *cMenuName*)

Returns

Character

Arguments

cSystemItemName

Specifies the name of the Visual FoxPro system menu item to activate.

cMenuName

Specifies the name of the Visual FoxPro system menu or submenu containing the menu item.

Remarks

See "System Menu Names," earlier in this language reference, for a list of Visual FoxPro menu and menu item names. You can also use SYS(2013) – System Menu Name String to display a list of Visual FoxPro menu and menu item names.

User-defined menu items and disabled system menu items cannot be activated with SYS(1500).

SYS(1500) returns the empty string.

Example

The following example uses SYS(1500) to paste a command into a program file.

```
_CLIPTEXT = "MESSAGEBOX('TEST')"  && Command to paste
MODIFY COMMAND myprog NOWAIT  && Open a program file
SYS(1500, '_MED_PASTE', '_MEDIT')  && Paste menu item
```

See Also

SYS(2013) – System Menu Name String, System Menu Names

SYS(2000) – File Name Wildcard Match

Returns the name of the first file that matches a file name skeleton.

Syntax

SYS(2000, *Skeleton* [, 1])

Returns

Character

Arguments

Skeleton

Specifies the file name skeleton. The file skeleton can contain the wildcards ? and *.

1

Returns the name of the next matching file.

Remarks

The empty string is returned if a matching file can't be found.

Example

```
? SYS(2000,'FOX.*')
? SYS(2000,'FOX.*',1)
```

See Also

LOCFILE( ), SYS( ) Functions Overview

SYS(2001) – SET ... Command Status

Returns the status of the specified SET commands.

Syntax

SYS(2001, *cSETCommand* [, 1 | 2])

Returns

Character

Arguments

cSETCommand

Specifies the SET command whose status SYS(2001) returns.

1 | 2

Some SET commands have two or more settings; for example, SET PRINTER ON, SET PRINTER OFF, and SET PRINTER TO *FileName*. Use SYS(2001) without 1 or 2 to return the ON or OFF switch setting. Use SYS(2001) with 1 or 2 to return the additional settings. See the SET( ) Function, earlier in this language reference, for a list of SET commands for which additional information is returned when 1 or 2 is included.

Remarks

SYS(2001) is identical to SET( ).

Example

```
? SYS(2001,'PRINTER')
? SYS(2001,'PRINTER',1)
```

See Also

SET( ), SYS( ) Functions Overview

SYS(2002) – Turn Insertion Point On or Off

Turns the insertion point on or off.

Syntax

SYS(2002 [, 1])

Returns

None

Remarks

SYS(2002) turns the insertion point off. SYS(2002, 1) turns the insertion point on. For more information about turning the insertion point on and off, see the SET CURSOR Command, earlier in this language reference.

See Also

INKEY( ), SET CURSOR, SYS( ) Functions Overview

SYS(2003) – Current Directory

Returns the name of the current directory on the default drive.

Syntax

SYS(2003)

Returns

Character

Remarks

You can use SYS(5) to determine the current drive.

See Also

SYS( ) Functions Overview

SYS(2004) – Visual FoxPro Start Directory

Returns the name of the directory from which Visual FoxPro was started.

Syntax

SYS(2004)

Returns

Character

Remarks

SYS(2004) returns the location of the Vfp6r.dll file in a distributed run time Visual FoxPro application.

Example

```
? 'Visual FoxPro launch directory: ', SYS(2004)
```

See Also

HOME( ), SET PATH, SYS( ) Functions Overview

SYS(2005) – Current Resource File

Returns the name of the current Visual FoxPro resource file.

Syntax

SYS(2005)

Returns

Character

Remarks

The Visual FoxPro resource file is a Visual FoxPro table that contains information on system and user-defined resources like keyboard macros, preferences, system window locations and sizes, diary entries, and so on.

The Visual FoxPro resource file defaults to Foxuser.dbf. Use SET RESOURCE to specify a different Visual FoxPro resource file.

Example

```
? 'Current resource file: ', SYS(2005)
```

See Also

SET RESOURCE, SYS( ) Functions Overview

SYS(2006) – Current Graphics Card

Returns the type of graphics card and monitor you are using.

Syntax

SYS(2006)

Returns

Character

Example

```
? 'Current graphics card/monitor: ', SYS(2006)
```

See Also

ISCOLOR( ), SET DISPLAY, SYS( ) Functions Overview

SYS(2007) – Checksum Value

Returns the checksum value of a character expression.

Syntax

SYS(2007, *cExpression*)

Returns

Character

Remarks

A checksum can be used to test the validity of data or to compare two character expressions.

cExpression
   Specifies the character expression for which SYS(2007) returns a checksum value.

See Also

SET RESOURCE, SYS( ) Functions Overview

SYS(2010) – CONFIG.SYS File Settings

Returns the files setting in CONFIG.SYS.

Syntax

SYS(2010)

Returns

Character

Remarks

In FoxPro for MS-DOS, SYS(2010) returns as a character string the files setting in your CONFIG.SYS configuration file.

In Visual FoxPro, SYS(2010) always returns 255.

Most Config.sys files contain a line specifying the maximum number of files that can be opened at the same time under MS-DOS. This line usually reads FILES=NNN, where NNN is a number. SYS(2010) returns this number.

A Config.sys configuration file doesn't have to have a files setting; furthermore, you need not have a Config.sys file. SYS(2010) returns the default MS-DOS files setting in either case.

The number returned by SYS(2010) isn't the number of files you can open in Visual FoxPro, FoxPro for Windows, and FoxPro for MS-DOS. MS-DOS opens files for its own use. Visual FoxPro and FoxPro for Windows also open files for their own internal use, and the number of these open files can vary throughout a FoxPro session. The files setting in your Config.sys file must be somewhat greater than the number of files you would like to open in Visual FoxPro.

For more information on the Config.sys configuration file, see your MS-DOS manual.

See Also

SYS( ) Functions Overview

SYS(2011) – Current Lock Status

Returns the record or table lock status for the current work area.

Syntax

SYS(2011)

Returns

Character

Remarks

Unlike the FLOCK( ), LOCK( ), and RLOCK( ) functions, SYS(2011) doesn't attempt to lock the table or record.

The character string returned by SYS(2011) is identical to the message displayed in the status bar (Exclusive, Record Unlocked, Record Locked ...).

SYS(2011) returns Exclusive only at the workstation that opened the table exclusively, and Record Locked only at the workstation that applied the record lock.

See Also

FLOCK( ), LOCK( ), RLOCK( ), SYS( ) Functions Overview

SYS(2012) – Memo Field Blocksize

Returns the memo field block size for a table.

Syntax

SYS(2012 [, *nWorkArea* | *cTableAlias*])

Returns

Character

Arguments

nWorkArea | cTableAlias

Specifies the work area number or table alias for the table for which the memo field block size is returned. *nWorkArea* specifies a work area number and *cTableAlias* specifies a table alias. If you do not specify a work area or alias, SYS(2012) returns the memo field block size for the table open in the currently selected work area.

SYS(2012) returns 0 if a table isn't open in the specified work area or the table doesn't have a memo field.

Remarks

For more information on specifying the memo field block size for a table, see the SET BLOCKSIZE Command, earlier in this language reference.

See Also

SET BLOCKSIZE

SYS(2013) – System Menu Name String

Returns a space-delimited character string containing the internal names of the Visual FoxPro menu system.

Syntax

SYS(2013)

Returns

Character

Remarks

SYS(2013) facilitates utilization of the Visual FoxPro system menu bar and system menus. The character string returned contains the name of the system menu bar, its menu titles, and the name of each item on the menus.

SYS(2013) returns the names of the menu titles and menu items for every FoxPro platform. See "System Menu Names," later in this language reference, for a listing of menu titles and menu items for Visual FoxPro 6.0.

See Also

DEFINE BAR, DEFINE MENU, DEFINE POPUP, SYS( ) Functions Overview, SYS(1500) – Activate a System Menu Item, System Menu Names

SYS(2014) – Minimum Path

Returns the minimum path relative to the current or specified directory for a specified file.

Syntax

SYS(2014, *cFileName* [, *Path*])

Returns

Character

Arguments

cFileName

Specifies the name of the file for which SYS(2014) returns the minimum path. If you omit *Path*, SYS(2014) returns the minimum path between the file and the current directory. You can change the current directory with SET DEFAULT.

Path

Specifies a directory for which SYS(2014) returns the minimum path between the specified directory and the file specified with *cFileName*.

Remarks

SYS(2014) can be used with FULLPATH( ) to make applications portable. That is, when given the location of the current program and the location of other files used by the program, FULLPATH( ) and SYS(2014) obtain the proper paths for these files. Once the files' paths are determined, the files can be accessed by the program.

See Also

FULLPATH( ), SET DEFAULT, SET PATH, SYS( ) Functions Overview

SYS(2015) – Unique Procedure Name

Returns a unique 10-character procedure name that begins with an underscore followed by a combination of letters and numbers.

Syntax

SYS(2015)

Returns

Character

Remarks

SYS(2015) can be used to create unique procedure or function names.

The name that SYS(2015) returns is created from the system date and system time. Calling SYS(2015) more than once during the same millisecond interval will return a unique character string.

See Also

SYS( ) Functions Overview, SYS(3) – Legal File Name

SYS(2016) – SHOW GETS WINDOW Name

Included for backward compatibility. Use the Refresh method instead of SHOW GETS.

SYS(2017) – Display Startup Screen

Included for backward compatibility. Use CREATE FORM instead.

SYS(2018) – Error Message Parameter

Returns the error message parameter for the most recent error.

Syntax

SYS(2018)

Returns

Character

Remarks

Certain error messages return additional information about the cause of the error. For example, if you reference a variable that doesn't exist, the name of the variable is included in the error message. SYS(2018) returns this additional information, called the error message parameter. Names of variables and files are common types of error message parameters.

Suppose you try to run a program named REPORTS, but the program doesn't exist. The text of the error message displayed is:

```
File REPORTS does not exist.
```

REPORTS is the error message parameter, and it is returned by SYS(2018):

```
? SYS(2018)
```

See Also

ERROR( ), MESSAGE( ), ON ERROR, SYS( ) Functions Overview

SYS(2019) – Configuration File Name and Location

Returns the name and location of the Visual FoxPro configuration file.

Syntax

SYS(2019)

Returns

Character

Remarks

The Visual FoxPro configuration file is named Config.fpw, and it isn't installed by default. You can create your own Config.fpw configuration file with MODIFY FILE.

If a configuration file can't be located, SYS(2019) returns an empty string.

The Visual FoxPro configuration file is typically located in the directory where Visual FoxPro is started, but can be located elsewhere. Visual FoxPro first looks for it in the startup directory. If the configuration file isn't located in the startup directory, the MS-DOS path is then searched. Two options let you tell Visual FoxPro where your configuration file is located and its name:

- You can create an MS-DOS environmental variable named FOXPROWCFG with the MS-DOS SET command, and you can store the location and name of your configuration file in FOXPROCFG. In FoxPro for MS-DOS, the MS-DOS environmental variable is named FOXPROCFG.

- When you start Visual FoxPro, you can also use the –C switch to designate a configuration file. Include the location and name of the configuration file immediately after –C.

For further information about the Visual FoxPro configuration file, see Chapter 3, "Configuring Visual FoxPro," in the *Installation Guide*, in Help.

See Also

MODIFY FILE, SYS( ) Functions Overview

SYS(2020) – Default Disk Size

Returns the total size in bytes of the default disk.

Syntax

SYS(2020)

Returns

Character

Remarks

The default disk can be specified with SET DEFAULT.

See Also

DISKSPACE( ), SET DEFAULT, SYS( ) Functions Overview

SYS(2021) – Filtered Index Expression

Returns the filter expression for an open single-entry index (.idx) file or filter expressions for tags in compound index (.cdx) files.

Syntax

SYS(2021, *nIndexNumber* [, *nWorkArea* | *cTableAlias*])

Returns

Character

Arguments

nIndexNumber

The numeric expression *nIndexNumber* specifies which filter expression to return from the open index files. SYS(2021) returns filter expressions from open index files in the following order as *nIndexNumber* increases from 1 to the total number of open single-entry .idx files and structural compound and independent compound index tags:

1. Filter expressions from single-entry .idx files (if any are open) are returned first. The order in which the single-entry .idx files are included in USE or SET INDEX determines the order in which the filter expressions are returned.

2. Filter expressions for each tag in the structural .cdx file (if one is present) are returned next. The filter expressions are returned from the tags in the order the tags were created in the structural index.

3. Filter expressions for each tag in any open independent .cdx files are returned last. The filter expressions are returned from the tags in the order the tags were created in the independent compound indexes.

The empty string is returned if *nIndexNumber* is greater than the total number of open single-entry .idx files and structural and independent .Cdx file tags.

nWorkArea

Specifies the work area number for a table open in another work area.

cTableAlias
> Specifies a table alias for a table open in another work area. If a table doesn't have the alias you specify, Visual FoxPro displays an error message.

Remarks

You can create filtered indexes in Visual FoxPro. If you include the optional FOR clause in INDEX, the index file acts as a filter on the table. Only records that match the filter expression *lExpression* in the FOR clause are available for display and access. Index keys are created in the index file for only those records matching the filter expression.

The empty string is returned if an index or index tag was created without a FOR clause.

USE and SET INDEX both support an index file name list that lets you open index files for a table. Any combination of single-entry .idx file names, structural .cdx file names, and independent .cdx file names may be included in the index file name list.

SYS(2021) returns filter expressions from index files open in the current work area unless you include a specific work area or alias.

See Also

CDX( ), KEY( ), INDEX, MDX( ), NDX( ), REINDEX, SET INDEX, SET ORDER, SYS( ) Functions Overview, TAG( )

SYS(2022) – Disk Cluster Size

Returns the cluster size in bytes of a specified disk.

Syntax

SYS(2022 [, *cDiskName*])

Returns

Character

Arguments

cDiskName
> Specifies a drive letter (A, B, C, ...) for a disk other than the current default disk.

See Also

SET DEFAULT, SYS( ) Functions Overview

SYS(2023) – Temporary Path

Returns the path on which Visual FoxPro stores its temporary files.

Syntax

SYS(2023)

Returns

Character

Remarks

You can specify the path on which temporary files are stored by including the special TMPFILES configuration item in your Visual FoxPro configuration file.

For additional information about the special TMPFILES configuration item, see Chapter 3, "Configuring Visual FoxPro," in the *Installation Guide*, in Help.

See Also

SYS( ) Functions Overview

SYS(2029) – Table Type

Returns a value corresponding to the table type.

Syntax

SYS(2029 [, *nWorkArea* | *cTableAlias*])

Returns

Character

Arguments

nWorkArea
Specifies the work area in which the table is open.

cTableAlias
Specifies the alias of the table. If you omit *nWorkArea* and *cTableAlias*, SYS(2029) returns a value for the table open in the currently selected work area.

Remarks

The following table lists the values returned by SYS(2029) and the corresponding table type:

Return value	Table type
0	No table open
3	Previous versions of FoxPro, FoxBASE+, dBASE III PLUS, and dBASE IV with no memo field
48	Visual FoxPro with or without a memo field
67	dBASE IV SQL table with no memo field
99	dBASE IV SQL System table with a memo field
131	FoxBASE+ and dBASE III PLUS table with a memo field
139	dBASE IV table with a memo field
203	dBASE IV SQL table with a memo field
245	Previous versions of FoxPro with a memo field

Example

The following example opens the customer table in the testdata database.

```
CLOSE DATABASES
OPEN DATABASE (HOME(2) + 'Data\testdata')
USE Customer      && Open customer table

CLEAR
DO CASE
   CASE SYS(2029) = '3'
      ? 'Previous versions of FoxPro'
   CASE SYS(2029) = '48'
      ? 'Visual FoxPro Table'
   CASE SYS(2029) = '67'
      ? 'dBASE IV SQL table, no memo fields'
   CASE SYS(2029) = '99'
      ? 'dBASE IV SQL System table with a memo field'
   CASE SYS(2029) = '131'
      ? 'FoxBASE+ table with a memo field'
   CASE SYS(2029) = '139'
      ? 'dBASE IV table with a memo field'
   CASE SYS(2029) = '203'
      ? 'dBASE IV SQL table with a memo field'
   CASE SYS(2029) = '245'
      ? 'Previous versions of FoxPro with a memo field'
ENDCASE
```

See Also

ALTER TABLE – SQL, CREATE, CREATE TABLE – SQL, USE

SYS(2333) – ActiveX Dual Interface Support

Enables or disables ActiveX dual interface (VTABLE binding) support.

Syntax

SYS(2333 [, 0 | 1 | 2])

Returns

Character

Arguments

0

Disables ActiveX dual interface support. If 0 or 1 is omitted, ActiveX dual interface support is disabled. 0 is the startup default for Visual FoxPro 6.0.

1

Enables ActiveX dual interface support. 1 is the startup default for Visual FoxPro 5.0.

2

Returns the current SYS(2333) setting (0 or 1).

Remarks

The ActiveX control dual interface (VTABLE binding) is an optimization supported by Visual FoxPro. If an ActiveX control doesn't use the dual interface, you can disable the optimization while using that control.

If an ActiveX control does not perform properly when the control is instantiated, issue SYS(2333) or SYS(2333, 0) before the control is instantiated to disable dual interface support for the control. After the control has been instantiated, issue SYS(2333, 1) to enable ActiveX dual interface support for any controls that are later instantiated.

See Also

ActiveX Controls Overview, OLE Container Control

SYS(2334) – Automation Server Invocation Mode

Returns a value indicating how a Visual FoxPro automation server method was invoked.

Syntax

SYS(2334)

Returns

Character

Remarks

The following table lists the values SYS(2334) returns for automation servers:

Return value	Invocation method
0	Unknown (for example, invoked from the INIT method which is neither VTable or IDispatch)
1	OLEPUBLIC method invoked via VTable binding
2	IDispatch

SYS(2334) also returns zero when executed from within a stand-alone executable (.exe). Use the StartMode property to determine how an instance of Visual FoxPro was started.

See Also

StartMode Property, SYS( ) Functions Overview

SYS(2335) – Unattended Server Mode

Enables or disables modal states for distributable Visual FoxPro .exe automation servers.

Syntax

SYS(2335 [, 0 | 1])

Returns

Character

Arguments

0

Enables unattended mode. When unattended mode is enabled, a Visual FoxPro error is generated whenever a modal state occurs. Your .exe automation server can trap for these errors with an ON ERROR routine.

1

(Default) Disables unattended mode. Modal states which require user intervention can occur. Unattended mode is disabled at startup.

Remarks

Use SYS(2335) to enable or disable modal states in Visual FoxPro .exe automation servers. Automation servers are created with the Project Manager. For additional information about using Visual FoxPro to create .exe automation servers, see Chapter 16, "Adding OLE," in the *Microsoft Visual FoxPro 6.0 Programmer's Guide*.

Modal states occur when dialogs or errors messages are displayed, requiring input from a user to exit the dialog or error message and continue program execution. Modal states can be undesirable in .exe servers that are deployed remotely, possibly without intervention from a user. Program execution is halted, and requires intervention for program execution to continue.

The following table lists some typical examples of modal states that can occur in an .exe server.

Modal State	Examples
WAIT command or MESSAGEBOX( ) function	Can occur in program code.
Visual FoxPro errors such as "File access is denied" or "Allowed DO nesting level exceeded"	Can occur in program code.
Open dialog boxes	Can occur when files included in a SQL statement cannot be located.
SQL Connection Login dialog box	Can occur after a connection cannot be established.

SYS(2335 ,0) should be executed as soon as possible in unattended .exe automation server program code because a modal state can occur anytime after program execution begins.

Note that SYS(2335) applies only to .exe automation servers for which the StartMode property equals two. Unattended mode is always enabled for in-process .dll automation servers (for which the StartMode property equals three).

Issuing SYS(2335) without an argument in a runtime application returns its current setting.

See Also

ON ERROR, StartMode Property, SYS( ) Functions Overview

SYS(3004) – Return Locale ID

Returns the Locale ID used by automation and ActiveX controls.

Syntax

SYS(3004)

Returns

Character

Remarks

SYS(3004) returns the current Visual FoxPro Locale ID (LCID), which is determined by the Visual FoxPro Language ID (LangID) and Sort ID.

The Locale ID determines the language in which automation and ActiveX controls exchange information. The default Visual FoxPro Locale ID is 1033, English.

For example, assume you have installed the German version of Microsoft Excel 5.0, which supports both English and German commands. In this case, the following example allows you to start and close the German version of Microsoft Excel 5.0:

```
oleExcel1 = CREATEOBJECT('Excel.Application')  && Starts Excel

? SYS(3005, 1033)  && English Locale ID
oleExcel.Quit  && Closes Excel with English command

oleExcel2 = CREATEOBJECT('Excel.Application')  && Starts Excel

? SYS(3005, 1031)  && German Locale ID
oleExcel.Beenden  && Closes Excel with German command
```

For a list of Visual FoxPro Locale IDs, see SYS(3005) – Set Locale ID. For additional information about Locale, Language, and Sort IDs, search MSDN.

See Also

DefOLELCID Property, OLELCID Property, SYS(3005) – Set Locale ID, SYS(3006) – Set Language and Locale IDs

SYS(3005) – Set Locale ID

Sets the Locale ID used by automation and ActiveX controls.

Syntax

SYS(3005, *nLocaleID*)

Returns

Character

Arguments

nLocaleID

Specifies the Locale ID. The following list contains the Locale IDs supported in Visual FoxPro:

nLocaleID	Language
1029	Czech
1031	German
1033	English (Default)

(continued)

nLocaleID	Language
1034	Spanish
1036	French
1040	Italian
1045	Polish
1046	Portuguese (Brazilian)
2070	Portuguese (Standard)

Remarks

SYS(3005) sets the global Locale ID (LCID). The Locale ID determines the language in which automation and ActiveX controls exchange information. The default Visual FoxPro Locale ID is 1033, English.

> **Note** Using the DefOLELCID Property is the preferred method for setting a Locale ID for a form or the main Visual FoxPro window. The automation command language is affected only by the Global LocaleID, set with SYS(3005). The DefOLELCID and OLELCID properties affect only the language of the user interface, which ActiveX controls display, and not the language of the automation commands.

For example, assume you have installed the German version of Microsoft Excel 5.0, which supports both English and German commands. In this case, the following example allows you to start and close the German version of Microsoft Excel 5.0:

```
oleExcel1 = CREATEOBJECT('Excel.Application')  && Starts Excel

? SYS(3005, 1033)  && English Locale ID
oleExcel.Quit  && Closes Excel with English command

oleExcel2 = CREATEOBJECT('Excel.Application')  && Starts Excel

? SYS(3005, 1031)  && German Locale ID
oleExcel.Beenden  && Closes Excel with German command
```

For additional information about Locale IDs, search MSDN.

See Also

DefOLELCID Property, OLELCID Property, SYS(3004) – Return Locale ID, SYS(3006) – Set Language and Locale IDs

SYS(3006) – Set Language and Locale IDs

Sets the Language ID and the Locale ID.

Syntax

SYS(3006, *nLanguageID*)

Returns

Character

Arguments

nLanguageID
    Specifies the Language ID.

Remarks

SYS(3006) sets the Visual FoxPro Language ID (LangID), and then sets the Locale ID (LCID) based on the Language ID and the current value of the Sort ID.

Note Using the DefOLELCID Property is the preferred method for setting a Locale ID for a form or the main Visual FoxPro window.

For additional information about Language, Locale, and Sort IDs, search MSDN.

See Also

DefOLELCID Property, OLELCID Property, SYS(3004) – Return Locale ID, SYS(3005) – Set Locale ID

SYS(3050) – Set Buffer Memory Size

Sets the foreground or background buffer memory size.

Syntax

SYS(3050, *nType*, [*nBuffMemSize*])

Returns

Character

Arguments

nType

Specifies the buffer. The following table lists the values for *nType* and the corresponding buffer:

nType	Buffer
1	Foreground
2	Background

nBuffMemSize

Specifies the maximum buffer memory size in bytes. If you specify a value for *nBuffMemSize* that is less than 256K bytes, Visual FoxPro sets the buffer memory size to 256K bytes.

Specify 0 for *nBuffMemSize* to return the buffer memory size to the Visual FoxPro startup value. The startup value depends on the amount of your computer's memory. If you omit *nBuffMemSize*, SYS(3050) returns the buffer memory size for the buffer specified with *nType*.

Remarks

SYS(3050) allows you to optimize Visual FoxPro performance by adjusting the amount of memory Visual FoxPro allocates for the foreground and background buffers. The foreground memory buffer is the memory available to Visual FoxPro when it is operating in the foreground as the currently active application. The background memory buffer is the memory available to Visual FoxPro when it is operating in the background when another application is the foreground application.

SYS(3050) returns a numeric value as a character string that indicates the maximum amount of memory Visual FoxPro allocates for the foreground or background buffers.

See Also

SYS(1001) – Visual FoxPro Memory

SYS(3051) – Set Lock Retry Interval

Specifies the time in milliseconds that Visual FoxPro waits before attempting to lock a record, table, memo, or index file after an unsuccessful locking attempt.

Syntax

SYS(3051, [*nWaitMilliseconds*])

Returns

Character

Arguments

nWaitMilliseconds

Specifies the wait time in milliseconds; can be a value from 100 to 1000 milliseconds.

Specify 0 for *nWaitMilliseconds* to return the lock attempt time interval to the Visual FoxPro default startup value (333 milliseconds). If you omit *nWaitMilliseconds*, SYS(3051) returns the current lock attempt time interval.

Remarks

SYS(3051) returns a numeric value as a character string that indicates the lock attempt time interval.

See Also

SET REPROCESS, SYS(3052) – Override SET REPROCESS Locking

SYS(3052) – Override SET REPROCESS Locking

Specifies whether Visual FoxPro uses the SET REPROCESS setting when attempting to lock an index or memo file.

Syntax

SYS(3052, *nFileType*, [*lHonorReprocess*])

Returns

Character

Arguments

nFileType

Specifies the type of file. The following table lists the values for *nType* and the corresponding file type:

nFileType	File type
1	Index
2	Memo

lHonorReprocess

Specifies whether Visual FoxPro uses the SET REPROCESS setting for unsuccessful lock attempts for index and memo files.

Specify true (.T.) to use the SET REPROCESS setting when Visual FoxPro attempts to lock files specified with *nFileType*. Specify false (.F.), the default, to override the SET REPROCESS setting when Visual FoxPro attempts to lock files specified with *nFileType*. When set to false, Visual FoxPro waits indefinitely for locks on the specified files; this option is the same as locking behavior in previous versions of FoxPro.

If you omit *lHonorReprocess*, SYS(3052) returns the current setting for the file type specified with *nFileType*.

Remarks

SYS(3052) provides additional control over file locking in Visual FoxPro. It's best to set *lHonorReprocess* to true (.T.) in order to reduce the risk of file lock contention if your application uses transaction processing.

SYS(3052) returns as a character string a numeric value of 0 (corresponding to false (.F.)) or 1 (corresponding to true (.T.)). If *lHonorReprocess* is included in SYS(3052), the value returned is identical to the logical value you specify for *lHonorReprocess*. If you omit *lHonorReprocess*, the value returned is the current setting for the file type specified with *nFileType*.

See Also

SET REPROCESS, SYS(3051) – Set Lock Retry Interval

SYS(3053) – ODBC Environment Handle

Returns the ODBC environment handle.

Syntax

SYS(3053)

Returns

Character

Remarks

If ODBC isn't loaded, SYS(3053) loads it and returns the ODBC environment handle.

The environment handle returned by SYS(3053) provides access to ODBC through ODBC API calls. Access to the ODBC API is available in Visual FoxPro through DECLARE – DLL, and through external Visual FoxPro API library routines.

Only one ODBC environment handle should be used at any time. A Visual FoxPro program using ODBC calls should use SYS(3053) to get the ODBC environment handle rather than reallocating and freeing the ODBC environment handle through ODBC API calls.

Exercise care when manipulating an ODBC environment handle. For further information about the ODBC API, search MSDN.

See Also

DECLARE – DLL, SET LIBRARY

SYS(3054) – Rushmore Optimization Level

Enables or disables display of Rushmore optimization levels for queries.

Syntax

SYS(3054, 0 | 1 | 11)

Returns

Character

Arguments

0

(Default) Disables the display of Rushmore optimization levels.

1

Enables the display of the Rushmore filter optimization levels.

11

Enables the display of Rushmore join optimization levels.

Remarks

SYS(3054) returns the parameter you include (0, 1, or 11) as a character string.

Use SYS(3054) to improve query performance by determining the extent to which the query is optimized by Rushmore technology.

Issue SYS(3054, 1) to display the Rushmore filter optimization level after a query is executed. The filter optimization level is displayed in the active window.

The following table lists the three levels of Rushmore optimization:

Optimization Level	Description
None	The query could not be optimized with Rushmore technology.
Partial	Some expressions in the query could be optimized with Rushmore technology. The index tags used for Rushmore optimization are listed.
Full	The query was fully optimized with Rushmore technology. The index tags used for Rushmore optimization are listed.

If SYS(3054,1) indicates that a query could not be optimized or could be optimized only partially, you can modify the query to take advantage of Rushmore optimization.

Issue SYS(3054, 11) to display the Rushmore join optimization level after a query is executed. The optimization level is displayed in the active window.

Issue SYS(3054, 0) to stop display of the Rushmore optimization level after a query is executed.

For more information about Rushmore technology and optimizing queries, see "Understanding Rushmore Technology" in Chapter 15, "Optimizing Applications," in the *Microsoft Visual FoxPro 6.0 Programmer's Guide*.

See Also

SELECT – SQL Command

SYS(3055) – FOR and WHERE Clause Complexity

Sets the complexity level of the FOR and WHERE clauses in commands and functions that support those clauses.

Syntax

SYS(3055 [, *nComplexity*])

Returns

Character

Arguments

nComplexity
Specifies the complexity level. The valid range for *nComplexity* is 320 to 2040. The default value is 320. If you specify an odd value, it is rounded down to the closest even integer.

Remarks

If you receive the error 1308 – Insufficient Stack Space or 1812 – SQL: Statement Too Long, you can increase the FOR and WHEN clause complexity to help prevent the error.

For example, calling TABLEUPDATE( ) for a local table or view that doesn't use key fields generates a long WHERE clause to find the update row. The default number of fields supported in the WHERE clause is 40. If you receive the error 1812 – SQL: Statement Too Long, you should either use a key field for the update or increase the complexity of the WHERE clause with SYS(3055). If you use SYS(3055), increase its value to 8 times the number of fields in the table:

```
= SYS(3055, 8 * MIN(40, FCOUNT( )))
```

If SYS(3055) is issued without the *nComplexity* argument, its current setting is returned.

The following commands and functions support the FOR or WHERE clauses:

APPEND FROM	APPEND FROM ARRAY	AVERAGE
BLANK	BROWSE	CALCULATE
CHANGE	COPY TO ARRAY	COPY TO
COUNT	DEFINE PAD	DELETE
DELETE – SQL	DISPLAY	EXPORT
FOR( )	INDEX	LABEL
LIST	LOCATE	RECALL
REPLACE	REPLACE FROM ARRAY	REPORT
SCAN ... ENDSCAN	SELECT – SQL	SORT
SUM	TABLEUPDATE( )	UPDATE – SQL

See Also

TABLEUPDATE( ), SYS( ) Functions Overview

SYS(3056) – Read Registry Settings

Forces Visual FoxPro to read its registry settings again and update itself with the current registry settings.

Syntax

SYS(3056 [,1])

Returns

Character

Arguments

1

> Include the 1 option to prevent SET command settings from being updated from the registry.

Remarks

Returns the empty string.

Visual FoxPro stores the settings in the Options dialog box in the Windows registry. Visual FoxPro reads these registry settings when it is started and uses these settings to configure itself. Only SET commands and registry settings for system variables containing file names and their paths are updated by SYS(3056).

The settings you specify in the Options dialog box are written to the registry when you choose **Set As Default**. Some of these settings include SET commands (such as SET BELL, SET CLOCK, and so on) that affect the Visual FoxPro environment. Registry settings can also be changed through the Windows API. For an example, see the Windows API section of Solution.app, located in the Visual Studio …\Samples\Vfp98\Solution directory.

> **Note** SYS(3056) does not update settings from Config.fpw, the Visual FoxPro configuration file.

See Also

Options Dialog Box

SYS(4204) – Active Document Debugging

Enables or disables debugging support for Active Documents in the Visual FoxPro debugger.

Syntax

SYS(4204 [, 0 | 1])

Returns

Character

Arguments

0

> Turns off Active Document hosting in Visual FoxPro, preventing you from debugging an Active Document in the debugger.

1

(Default) Turns on Active Document support in Visual FoxPro, allowing you to debug an Active Document in the debugger.

Remarks

Returns the empty string.

Use SYS(4204) to debug Active Documents within the Visual FoxPro debugger. Executing SYS(4204, 1) allows Visual FoxPro to act as an Active Document server so you can debug an Active Document. Executing SYS(4204, 0) turns off Active Document hosting.

Note You must add SET STEP ON in your Active Document code to open the debugger.

See Also

_RUNACTIVEDOC System Variable

SYSMETRIC( ) Function

Returns the size of the operating system's screen elements.

Syntax

SYSMETRIC(*nScreenElement*)

Returns

Numeric

Arguments

nScreenElement

Specifies a screen element. The following table shows values for *nScreenElement* and the corresponding screen element:

nScreenElement	Screen Element
1	Screen width
2	Screen height.
3	Width of sizable window frame
4	Height of sizable window frame
5	Width of scroll arrows on vertical scroll bar
6	Height of scroll arrows on vertical scroll bar
7	Width of scroll arrows on horizontal scroll bar

(continued)

nScreenElement	Screen Element
8	Height of scroll arrows on horizontal scroll bar
9	Height of window title
10	Width of non-sizable window frame
11	Height of non-sizable window frame
12	Width of DOUBLE or PANEL window frame
13	Height of DOUBLE or PANEL window frame
14	Scroll box width on horizontal scroll bar in text editing windows
15	Scroll box height on vertical scroll bar in text editing windows
16	Minimized window icon width
17	Minimized window icon height
18	Maximum insertion point width
19	Maximum insertion point height
20	Single-line menu bar height
21	Maximized window width
22	Maximized window height
23	Kanji window height
24	Minimum sizable window width
25	Minimum sizable window height
26	Minimum window width
27	Minimum window height
28	Window controls width
29	Window controls height
30	1 if mouse hardware present; otherwise 0
31	1 for Microsoft Windows debugging version; otherwise 0
32	1 if mouse buttons swapped; otherwise 0
33	Width of a button in a half-caption window's caption or title bar
34	Height of half-caption window caption area

Remarks

SYSMETRIC( ) returns the size of screen elements. Screen elements include menus, windows, window controls, and the insertion point. Values are returned in pixels unless otherwise noted and can vary for different displays, display drivers, and video hardware. For further information on screen elements, refer to the GetSystemMetrics function in the *Microsoft Windows Programmer's Reference*.

SYSMETRIC( ) enables you to determine the size of menus, windows, and window controls you create in Visual FoxPro. Windows and menus created with DEFINE WINDOW and DEFINE MENU use the same screen element sizes as the operating system's windows and menus.

See Also

FONTMETRIC( ), GETFONT( ), TXTWIDTH( ), WFONT( )

System Variables Overview

System variables are built-in variables that Visual FoxPro creates and maintains automatically. They are PUBLIC by default, but you can declare them PRIVATE.

Important The functionality of many system variables has been replaced by new features in Visual FoxPro. For details, see the description for each system variable.

The following table lists the five types of Visual FoxPro system variables and their designation in expressions:

Variable type	Description	Expression
C	Character	*cExpression*
D	Date	*dExpression*
L	Logical	*lExpression*
N	Numeric	*nExpression*
O	Object	*oExpression*

The following table lists all system variables — their types and default values:

Variable	Type	Default value
_ALIGNMENT	C	LEFT
_ASCIICOLS	N	80
_ASCIIROWS	N	63
_ASSIST	C	Empty string

(continued)

Variable	Type	Default value
_BEAUTIFY	C	Empty string
_BOX	L	.T.
_BROWSER	C	Browser.app
_BUILDER	C	Builder.app
_CALCMEM	N	0.0
_CALCVALUE	N	0.0
_CLIPTEXT	C	Empty string
_CONVERTER	C	Convert.app
_COVERAGE	C	Coverage.app
_CUROBJ	N	−1
_DBLCLICK	N	0.5
_DIARYDATE	D	Current date
_DOS	L	.T. in FoxPro for MS-DOS
_FOXDOC	C	Empty string
_GALLERY	C	Gallery.app
_GENGRAPH	C	Empty string
_GENHTML	C	Genhtml.prg
_GENMENU	C	Genmenu.prg
_GENPD	C	Empty string
_GENSCRN	C	Genscrn.prg
_GENXTAB	C	Empty string
_GETEXPR	C	Empty string
_INCLUDE	C	Empty string
_INDENT	N	0
_LMARGIN	N	0
_MAC	L	.T. in Visual FoxPro for Macintosh
_MLINE	N	0
_PADVANCE	C	FORMFEED

(continued)

(continued)

Variable	Type	Default value
_PAGENO	N	1
_PBPAGE	N	1
_PCOLNO	N	Current column
_PCOPIES	N	1
_PDRIVER	C	Empty string
_PDSETUP	C	Empty string
_PECODE	C	Empty string
_PEJECT	C	NONE
_PEPAGE	N	32767
_PLENGTH	N	66
_PLINENO	N	0
_PLOFFSET	N	0
_PPITCH	C	DEFAULT
_PQUALITY	L	.F.
_PRETEXT	C	Empty string
_PSCODE	C	Empty string
_PSPACING	N	1
_PWAIT	L	.F.
_RMARGIN	N	80
_RUNACTIVEDOC	C	Runactd.prg
_SCCTEXT	C	Scctext.prg
_SCREEN	O	FORM
_SHELL	C	Empty string
_SPELLCHK	C	Spellchk.app
_STARTUP	C	Empty string
_TABS	C	Empty string
_TALLY	N	0
_TEXT	C	–1

(continued)

Variable	Type	Default value
_THROTTLE	N	0
_TRANSPORT	C	Empty string
_TRIGGERLEVEL	N	0
_UNIX	L	.T. in FoxPro for UNIX
_VFP	O	Microsoft Visual FoxPro Application 6.0
_WINDOWS	L	.T. in Visual FoxPro for Windows
_WIZARD	C	Wizard.app
_WRAP	L	.F.

See Also

PUBLIC, PRIVATE, STORE

System Menu Names

The following tables list the internal names and user interface names for the
Visual FoxPro system menu bar, menu titles, menus, and menu items. With these
names you can use the Visual FoxPro system menu bar to create a menu system for
your own application.

The SYS(2013) function returns a space-delimited string containing these names.
You can also create a quick menu using the Menu Designer to see the internal system
menu names.

For more information on the system menu bar, see Chapter 11, "Designing Menus
and Toolbars," in the *Microsoft Visual FoxPro 6.0 Programmer's Guide*.

System Menu Names in Visual FoxPro

The internal name for the system menu bar itself in Visual FoxPro is _MSYSMENU.

System Menus

Menu titles	Internal name
File	_MSM_FILE
Edit	_MSM_EDIT
Data Session	_MSM_VIEW
Format	_MSM_TEXT
Tools	_MSM_TOOLS
Program	_MSM_PROG

(continued)

(continued)

Menu titles	Internal name
Window	_MSM_WINDO
Help	_MSM_SYSTM
File menu	_MFILE
New...	_MFI_NEW
Open...	_MFI_OPEN
Close	_MFI_CLOSE
Close All	_MFI_CLALL
1st Separator	_MFI_SP100
Save	_MFI_SAVE
Save As...	_MFI_SAVAS
Save As HTML...	_MFI_SAVASHTML
Revert	_MFI_REVRT
2nd Separator	_MFI_SP200
Import	_MFI_IMPORT
Export	_MFI_EXPORT
3rd Separator	_MFI_SP300
Page Setup...	_MFI_PGSET
Print Preview	_MFI_PREVU
Print...	_MFI_SYSPRINT
Send	_MFI_SEND
4th Separator	_MFI_SP400
Exit	_MFI_QUIT

Edit Menu – Visual FoxPro

Menu and items	Internal name
Edit menu	_MEDIT
Undo	_MED_UNDO
Redo	_MED_REDO
1st Separator	_MED_SP100
Cut	_MED_CUT

(continued)

Menu and items	Internal name
Copy	_MED_COPY
Paste	_MED_PASTE
Paste Special	_MED_PSTLK
Clear	_MED_CLEAR
2nd Separator	_MED_SP200
Select All	_MED_SLCTA
3rd Separator	_MED_SP300
Find...	_MED_FIND
Find Again	_MED_FINDA
Replace...	_MED_REPL
Go To Line...	_MED_GOTO
4th Separator	_MED_SP400
Insert Object...	_MED_INSOB
Object...	_MED_OBJ
Links...	_MED_LINK
Convert to Static	_MED_CVTST
5th Separator	_MED_SP500
Properties	_MED_PREF

View Menu

Menu and items	Internal name
View menu	_MVIEW
Toolbars...	_MVI_TOOLB

Tools Menu

Menu and items	Internal name
Tools menu	_MTOOLS
Wizards	_MTL_WZRDS
1st Separator	_MTL_SP100
Spelling...	_MTL_SPELL
Macros...	_MST_MACRO
Class Browser	_MTL_BROWSER

(continued)

(continued)

Menu and items	Internal name
Component Gallery	_MTL_GALLERY
Coverage Profiler	_MTL_COVERAGE
Beautify…	_MED_BEAUT
Run Active Document…	_MTI_RUNACTIVEDOC
2nd Separator	_MTL_SP200
Debugger	_MTL_DEBUGGER
3rd Separator	_MTL_SP400
Options…	_MTL_OPTNS

Program Menu

Menu and items	Internal name
Program item	_MPROG
Do…	_MPR_DO
Cancel	_MPR_CANCL
Resume	_MPR_RESUM
Suspend	_MPR_SUSPEND
1st Separator	_MPR_SP100
Compile…	_MPR_COMPL

Window Menu

Menu and items	Internal name
Window menu	_MWINDOW
Arrange All	_MWI_ARRAN
1st Separator	_MWI_SP100
Hide	_MWI_HIDE
Hide All	_MWI_HIDE
Show All	_MWI_SHOWA
Clear	_MWI_CLEAR
Cycle	_MWI_ROTAT
2nd Separator	_MWI_SP200
Command Window	_MWI_CMD
Data Session	_MWI_VIEW

Help Menu

Menu and items	Internal name
Help menu	_MSYSTEM
Microsoft Visual FoxPro Help Topics	_MST_HPSCH
1st Separator	_MST_SP100
Contents	_MST_MSDNC
Index	_MST_MSDNI
Search	_MST_MSDNS
Technical Support	_MST_TECHS
Microsoft on the Web	_HELPWEBVFPFREESTUFF
2nd Separator	_MST_SP200
About Microsoft Visual FoxPro...	_MST_ABOUT

See Also

SYS(2013) – System Menu Name String, SYS(1500) – Activate a System Menu Item

TabIndex Property

Specifies the tab order of controls on a page and the tab order of forms in a form set. Available at design time and run time.

Syntax

[*Object*.]*Control*.TabIndex[= *nOrder*]

Arguments

nOrder
    Specifies the tab order for the control.

Remarks

For controls on a form, a tab order is assigned based on the order in which the controls are added. Each new control is placed last in the tab order.

For a form in a form set, a tab order is assigned based on the order in which the form was added. The form with *nOrder* set to 1 is the first form that is active in the form set. When a user tabs from the last control on a form, the first control on the next form in the tab order gets the focus. If a form is not included in a form set, the TabIndex property is ignored.

You can make changes at design time using the Properties window or at run time using code. However, if you change the TabIndex setting of one control or form, be sure to change the TabIndex setting for all controls on the pages or forms in the form set. If you do not designate a tab order for all controls or forms, Microsoft Visual FoxPro assigns the tab order for the remaining controls and forms based on the order in which they are added and changed at run time, which can produce unintended results.

To ignore the tab order of a control or a form, set the TabStop property to false (.F.).

Applies To

CheckBox, ComboBox, CommandButton, CommandGroup, Container Object, Control Object, EditBox, Form, Grid, Label, ListBox, OLE Bound Control, OLE Container Control, OptionButton, OptionGroup, Page, PageFrame, _SCREEN, Spinner, TextBox

See Also

TabStop Property

TABLEREVERT( ) Function

Discards changes made to a buffered row or a buffered table or cursor and restores the OLDVAL( ) data for remote cursors and the current disk values for local tables and cursors.

Syntax

TABLEREVERT([*lAllRows* [, *cTableAlias* | *nWorkArea*]])

Returns

Numeric

Arguments

lAllRows

Determines whether all changes made to the table or cursor are discarded. If *lAllRows* is true (.T.) and table buffering is enabled, changes made to all records are discarded in the table or cursor. If *lAllRows* is false (.F.) and table buffering is enabled, only changes made to the current record in the table or cursor are discarded.

If row buffering is enabled, the value of *lAllRows* is ignored and the changes made to the current record in the table or cursor are discarded.

The default value for *lAllRows* is false (.F.).

cTableAlias

Specifies the alias of the table or cursor in which the changes are discarded.

nWorkArea

Specifies the work area of the table or cursor in which the changes are discarded.

Remarks

TABLEREVERT( ) returns the number of records for which changes were discarded.

Note On a network, the data currently on disk may differ from the data on disk when the table was opened or the cursor was created. Other users on the network may have changed the data after the table was opened or the cursor was created.

TABLEREVERT( ) cannot discard changes made to a table or cursor that does not have row or table buffering enabled. If you issue TABLEREVERT( ) and row or table buffering is not enabled, Visual FoxPro generates an error message. Use CURSORSETPROP( ) to enable or disable row and table buffering.

Changes are discarded in the table or cursor open in the currently selected work area if TABLEREVERT( ) is issued without the optional *cTableAlias* or *nWorkArea* arguments.

TABLEREVERT( ) does not return the record pointer to its original position.

Example

The following example demonstrates how you can use TABLEREVERT( ) to discard changes made to a buffered table. MULTILOCKS is set to ON, a requirement for table buffering. The customer table in the testdata database is opened, and CURSORSETPROP( ) is then used to set the buffering mode to optimistic table buffering (5).

The value of the cust_id field is displayed and then the cust_id field is modified with REPLACE. The new value of the cust_id field is displayed. TABLEREVERT( ) is then used to return the table to its original state (TABLEUPDATE( ) could be issued instead to commit the changes). The reverted value of the cust_id field is then displayed.

```
CLOSE DATABASES
SET MULTILOCKS ON  && Must be on for table buffering
SET PATH TO (HOME(2) + 'data\')     && Sets path to database
OPEN DATABASE testdata  && Open testdata database
USE Customer      && Open customer table
= CURSORSETPROP('Buffering', 5, 'customer')  && Enable table buffering

CLEAR
? 'Original cust_id value: '
?? cust_id  && Displays current cust_id value
REPLACE cust_id     WITH '***'  && Changes field contents
? 'New cust_id value: '
?? cust_id  && Displays new cust_id value
= TABLEREVERT(.T.)  && Discard all table changes
? 'Reverted cust_id value: '
?? cust_id  && Displays reverted cust_id value
```

See Also

CURSORSETPROP( ), CURVAL( ), OLDVAL( ), TABLEUPDATE( )

TABLEUPDATE( ) Function

Commits changes made to a buffered row or a buffered table or cursor.

Syntax

TABLEUPDATE([*nRows* [, *lForce*]] [, *cTableAlias* | *nWorkArea*]
[, *cErrorArray*])

Returns

Logical

Arguments

nRows

Specifies which changes made to the table or cursor are committed. If *nRows* is 0 and row or table buffering is enabled, only changes made to the current record in the table or cursor are committed.

If *nRows* is 1 and *table* buffering is enabled, changes made to all records are committed to the table or cursor. If *nRows* is 1 and *row* buffering is enabled, only changes made to the current record in the table or cursor are committed.

If *nRows* is 2, changes made to the table or cursor are committed in the same manner as when *nRows* is 1. However, an error doesn't occur when a change cannot be committed, and Visual FoxPro continues to process any remaining records in the table or cursor. If *cErrorArray* is included, an array containing error information is created when an error occurs.

The default value for *nRows* is 0.

lForce

Determines whether changes made to the table or cursor by another user on a network are overwritten. If *lForce* is true (.T.), any changes made to the table or cursor by another user on a network are overwritten.

If *lForce* is false (.F.), Visual FoxPro commits changes to the table or cursor, starting with the first record and continuing towards the end of the table or cursor. If a record modified by another user on the network is encountered, Visual FoxPro generates an error.

When Visual FoxPro generates the error, you can handle the error through an ON ERROR routine, and the ON ERROR routine can issue TABLEUPDATE( ) with *lForce* set to true (.T.) to commit changes to the record. Alternately, if a transaction is in progress, the ON ERROR routine can handle the error and then issue ROLLBACK to revert the table or cursor to its original state.

The default for *lForce* is false (.F.).

cTableAlias

Specifies the alias of the table or cursor in which the changes are committed. If you include a table or cursor alias, you must include the *lForce* argument.

nWorkArea

Specifies the work area of the table or cursor in which the changes are committed. If you include a work area, you must include the *lForce* argument.

cErrorArray

Specifies the name of an array created when *nRows* is 2 and changes to a record cannot be committed. The array contains a single column containing the record numbers of the records for which changes could not be committed. If you include an array name, you must include either a table or cursor alias *cTableAlias* or a work area number *nWorkArea*.

Note If an error other than a simple commit error occurs while updating records, the first element of *cErrorArray* will contain –1 and you can then use AERROR( ) to determine the why the changes could not be committed.

Remarks

TABLEUPDATE( ) returns true (.T.) if changes to all records are committed; otherwise, TABLEUPDATE( ) returns false (.F.). If you specify 0 or 1 for *nRow*, the record pointer remains on the record where changes could not be committed and can issue AERROR( ) to determine why the changes could not be committed.

TABLEUPDATE( ) cannot commit changes made to a table or cursor that does not have row or table buffering enabled. If you issue TABLEUPDATE( ) and row or table buffering is not enabled, Visual FoxPro generates an error message. However, TABLEUPDATE( ) can still commit changes to a table or cursor that has validation rules. Use CURSORSETPROP( ) to enable or disable row and table buffering.

Changes are committed to the table or cursor open in the currently selected work area if TABLEUPDATE( ) is issued without the optional *cTableAlias* or *nWorkArea* arguments.

If table buffering is used and multiple records are updated, TABLEUPDATE( ) moves the record pointer to the last record updated.

Note Calling TABLEUPDATE( ) for a local table or view that doesn't use key fields generates a long WHERE clause to find the update row. The default number of fields supported in the WHERE clause is 40. If you receive the error 1812 – SQL: Statement Too Long, you should either use a key field for the update or increase the complexity of the WHERE clause with SYS(3055). If you use SYS(3055), increase its value to 8 times the number of fields in the table:

```
= SYS(3055, 8 * MIN(40, FCOUNT( ))
```

Example

The following example demonstrates how you can use TABLEUPDATE( ) to commit changes made to a buffered table. A table named `employees` is created and INSERT – SQL is used insert the value "Smith" into the `cLastName` field.

MULTILOCKS is set to ON, a requirement for table buffering. CURSORSETPROP( ) is used to set the buffering mode to optimistic table buffering (5).

The original value of the cLastName field (Smith) is displayed and then the cLastName field is modified with REPLACE. The new value of the cLastName field (Jones) is displayed. TABLEUPDATE( ) is then used to commit changes to the table (TABLEREVERT( ) could be issued instead to discard the changes). The updated value of the cLastName field (Jones) is then displayed.

```
CLOSE DATABASES
CREATE TABLE employee (cLastName C(10))
SET MULTILOCKS ON  && Must be on for table buffering
= CURSORSETPROP('Buffering', 5, 'employee' )  && Enable table buffering
INSERT INTO employee (cLastName) VALUES ('Smith')

CLEAR
? 'Original cLastName value: '
?? cLastName  && Displays current cLastName value (Smith)

REPLACE cLastName WITH 'Jones'
? 'New cLastName value: '
?? cLastName  && Displays new cLastName value (Jones)

= TABLEUPDATE(.T.)  && Commits changes
? 'Updated cLastName value: '
?? cLastName  && Displays current cLastName value (Jones)
```

See Also

CURSORSETPROP( ), CURVAL( ), OLDVAL( ), TABLEREVERT( )

Tabs Property

Specifies whether a page frame has tabs. Available at design time and run time.

Syntax

PageFrame.Tabs[= *lExpr*]

Arguments

lExpr

The settings for the Tabs property are as follows:

Setting	Description
True (.T.)	(Default) The page frame has tabs.
False (.F.)	The page frame doesn't have tabs.

Remarks

Specify the text on the tabs by setting the Caption property of the page. The width of the tab is increased if the Caption width is greater than the default width of the tab. Shorter captions have no effect on tab width.

Applies To

PageFrame

See Also

Caption Property

_TABS System Variable

Included for backward compatibility. Use the Report Designer instead.

TabStop Property

Specifies whether a user can use the TAB key to move the focus to an object. Available at design time and run time.

Syntax

[*Object.*]*Control.*TabStop[= *lExpr*]

Arguments

lExpr
    Specifies whether an object is included in the tab order. The settings for the TabStop property are as follows:

Setting	Description
True (.T.)	(Default) The control or form is included in the tab order, as determined by the TabIndex property.
False (.F.)	The object is ignored in the tab order. For a control, when a user presses the TAB key, the focus skips a control that has its TabStop property set to false (.F.). For a form, when a user presses the TABkey on the last control on a form and the next form in the tab order has its TabStop property set to false (.F.), the focus moves to the first control on the same form. The focus does not move to the next form in the tab order.

Remarks

If TabStop property is set to false (.F.) for a control or form, the control or form is skipped when the TAB key is used to move through the tab order, but it can still receive the focus when the mouse is used.

Note The TabStop property is read-only when it applies to a control contained in a Column object.

Applies To

CheckBox, ComboBox, CommandButton, Container Object, Control Object, EditBox, Form, Grid, ListBox, OLE Bound Control, OLE Container Control, OptionButton, Page, PageFrame, _SCREEN, Spinner, TextBox

See Also

TabIndex Property

TabStretch Property

Specifies the behavior if the tabs do not fit on the page frame. Available at design time and run time. TabStretch is available only if Tabs is set to true (.T.).

Syntax

PageFrame.TabStretch[= *nSetting*]

Arguments

nSetting
The settings for the TabStretch property are as follows

Setting	Description
0	Stack. A second row of tabs is created.
1	(Default) Clip. The tabs are clipped as necessary.

Applies To

PageFrame

See Also

Tabs Property

TabStyle Property

Specifies whether the Page tabs in a page frame are justified or non-justified. Available at design time and run time.

Syntax

PageFrame.TabStyle[= *nStyle*]

Arguments

nStyle
One of the following:

nStyle	Description
0	(Default) Justified. The width of each page tab is adjusted to accommodate its caption. If necessary, the width of each page tab is increased so the page tabs span the entire width of the PageFrame.
	This setting is ignored if the TabStretch property is set to 1, Single Row.
1	Non-justified. The width of each page tab is not adjusted to accommodate its caption. The width of each page tab isn't adjusted so that the page tabs span the entire width of the PageFrame.
	This setting is ignored if the TabStretch property is set to 1, Single Row.

Applies To

PageFrame

See Also

TabStretch Property

Tag Property

Stores any extra data needed for your program. Available at design time and run time.

Syntax

*Object.*Tag[= *Expr*]

Arguments

Expr
Specifies any string.

Remarks

By default, the Tag property is set to an empty string (""). You can use this property to assign any string to an object without affecting it in any way. Unlike other properties, the value of the Tag property is not used by Visual FoxPro.

Applies To

ActiveDoc, CheckBox, ComboBox, CommandButton, CommandGroup, EditBox, Form, Grid, Image, Label, Line, ListBox, OLE Bound Control, OLE Container Control, OptionButton, OptionGroup, ProjectHook Object, _SCREEN, Shape, Spinner, TextBox, Timer

See Also

Comment Property

TAG( ) Function

Returns a tag name from an open, multiple-entry compound .CDX index file or the name of an open, single-entry .IDX index file.

Syntax

TAG([*CDXFileName,*] *nTagNumber* [, *nWorkArea* | *cTableAlias*])

Returns

Character

Arguments

CDXFileName

Specifies the name of the multiple-entry compound .cdx index file from which TAG( ) returns a tag name.

nTagNumber

Specifies a number corresponding to the order in which a tag was created in the compound index file. For example, if *nTagNumber* is 1, TAG( ) returns the name of the first tag created in the compound index file. If *nTagNumber* is 2, TAG( ) returns the name of the second tag created, and so on. TAG( ) returns the empty string when *nTagNumber* exceeds the number of tag names.

If you omit *CDXFileName*, TAG( ) returns compound index file tag names and single-entry index file names in a specific order as follows.

1. Names of single-entry index files are returned based on their order in the INDEX clause of USE or SET INDEX.

2. Tag names from the structural compound index file (if one exists for the table) are returned.

3. Tag names from other open compound index files are returned, again in the order in which the tags were created in the compound index files and in the order in which the compound index files are specified in the INDEX clause for USE or SET INDEX.

nWorkArea | *cTableAlias*

Returns tag names and index file names from files open in another work area. *nWorkArea* specifies a work area number and *cTableAlias* specifies a table alias. By default, tag names and index file names are returned from files in the current work area.

Remarks

Tags are index entries in multiple-entry compound .cdx index files created with INDEX.

Note Multiple-entry compound .cdx index files and single-entry .idx index files can be opened for a table with the INDEX clause in USE or with SET INDEX. A structural compound .cdx index file is automatically opened with its table.

Example

The following example opens the customer table in the testdata database. FOR ... ENDFOR is used to create a loop in which CDX( ) is used to display the name of each structural index.

```
CLOSE DATABASES
OPEN DATABASE (HOME(2) + 'data\testdata')
USE Customer     && Open customer table

CLEAR
FOR nCount = 1 TO 254
   IF !EMPTY(TAG(nCount))  && Checks for tags in the index
   ? CDX(nCount)      && Display .CDX names
   ELSE
      EXIT  && Exit the loop when no more tags are found
   ENDIF
ENDFOR
```

See Also

CDX( ), INDEX, MDX( ), NDX( ), SET INDEX, SYS(14) – Index Expression, USE

TAGCOUNT( ) Function

Returns the number of .cdx compound index file tags and open .idx single-entry index files.

Syntax

TAGCOUNT([*CDXFileName* [, *nExpression* | *cExpression*]])

Returns

Numeric

Arguments

CDXFileName

Specifies the name of a compound index file for which TAGCOUNT( ) returns the number of tags. If *CDXFileName* is omitted, TAGCOUNT( ) returns the number of tags in all .cdx compound index files and open .idx single-entry index files in the currently selected work area.

nExpression

Specifies the work area of the table for which TAGCOUNT( ) returns the number of tags for the .cdx compound index file.

cExpression

Specifies the alias of the table for which TAGCOUNT( ) returns the number of tags for the .cdx compound index file.

Remarks

Included for compatibility with dBASE.

See Also

INDEX, TAGNO( )

TAGNO( ) Function

Returns the index position for .cdx compound index file tags and open .idx single-entry index files.

Syntax

TAGNO([*IndexName* [, *CDXFileName* [, *nExpression* | *cExpression*]]])

Returns

Numeric

Arguments

IndexName

Specifies the name of a .cdx compound index file tag or an open .idx single-entry index file for which TAGNO( ) returns the index position.

CDXFileName

Specifies the name of a .cdx compound index file containing the name of the tag you specify with *IndexName*.

nExpression

Specifies the work area of the table for which TAGNO( ) returns the index position for .cdx compound index file tags and .idx single-entry index files.

cExpression

Specifies the alias of the table for which TAGNO( ) returns the index position for .cdx compound index file tags and .idx single-entry index files.

Remarks

TAGNO( ) returns 0 if a master index isn't set (the table is in natural record number order) and the optional parameters are omitted.

Included for compatibility with dBASE.

See Also

INDEX, TAGCOUNT( )

_TALLY System Variable

Contains the number of records processed by the most recently executed table command.

Syntax

_TALLY = *nRecords*

Arguments

nRecords
    Contains a numeric value indicating the number of records processed by the most
    recently executed table command.

Remarks

Certain table processing commands return information about their status ("talk") while
they execute. When such a command finishes executing, it displays the number of
records it processed (if SET TALK is ON), and stores this number to the _TALLY
system variable.

The following commands return status information:

APPEND FROM	AVERAGE	CALCULATE
COPY To	COUNT	DELETE
INDEX	PACK	REINDEX
REPLACE	SELECT – SQL	SORT
SUM	TOTAL	UPDATE

When you start Visual FoxPro, _TALLY is set to 0. Executing one of the commands
above replaces the _TALLY value with the number of records the command processed.

Example

This example uses SELECT to return the number of customers in the USA. The result
is automatically stored to _TALLY. The _TALLY value is displayed.

```
SELECT * FROM customer ;
   WHERE country = 'USA' ;
   INTO CURSOR temp
? _TALLY
```

See Also

SET ODOMETER, SET TALK

TAN( ) Function

This trigonometric function returns the tangent of an angle.

Syntax

TAN(*nExpression*)

Returns

Numeric

Arguments

nExpression

Specifies the angle in radians for which TAN( ) returns the tangent. To convert an angle from degrees to radians, use DTOR( ). The number of decimal places returned by TAN( ) can be specified with SET DECIMALS.

Example

```
CLEAR
? TAN(0)  && Displays 0.00
? TAN(PI( )/4)  && Displays 1.00
? TAN(PI( )*3/4)  && Displays -1.00
```

See Also

COS( ), DTOR( ), RTOD( ), SET DECIMALS, SIN( )

TARGET( ) Function

Returns the alias of a table that is the target for a relation as specified in the INTO clause of SET RELATION.

Syntax

TARGET(*nRelationshipNumber* [, *nWorkArea* | *cTableAlias*])

Returns

Character

Arguments

nRelationshipNumber

Specifies the number of a relationship. Include a number from 1 to the number of relationships out of the specified work area. The aliases of the target databases are returned (in no specific order) until *nRelationshipNumber* is greater than the number of relationships. When *nRelationshipNumber* is greater than the number of relationships, the empty string is returned.

nWorkArea | cTableAlias

Returns the alias of the target table in another work area. *nWorkArea* specifies a work area number and *cTableAlias* specifies a table alias. By default, the alias of the target table from the current work area is returned if you don't specify the work area or alias.

Example

In the following example, a relation is set on the field `order_id` from `orders` into `customer`. The TARGET( ) function is then used to return the alias of the target table.

```
CLOSE DATABASES
OPEN DATABASE (HOME(2) + 'Data\testdata')
USE orders IN 0 ORDER order_id
USE customer IN 0 ORDER cust_id
SELECT orders
SET RELATION TO cust_id INTO customer
? TARGET(1)  && Displays customer
? TARGET(2)  && Empty string
```

See Also

RELATION( ), SET RELATION

TerminateRead Property

Included for backward compatibility with READ.

Text Property

Contains the unformatted text entered in the textbox portion of a control. Not available at design time; read-only at run time.

Syntax

Object.Text

Remarks

Unlike the Value property, the value contained in the Text property is unformatted and is identical to the text entered in the control by the user.

The unformatted text contained in a control's Text property can differ from the control's Value property for the following reasons:

- The Value property may not be of Character type; it may contain a Date or Numeric value.

- For an edit box, the Value property may add line feeds to the text entered in the edit box, providing compatibility with previous versions. For this reason, using the

Text property is the preferred method for selecting text with the SelStart and SelLength properties.

- If the Format property for the control uses the R setting, input mask characters are removed from the Value property.

If the Style property for a combo box control is set to 2 (Drop-down List), the Text property contains the empty string because the ComboBox does not have a text box.

Applies To

ComboBox, EditBox, Spinner, TextBox

See Also

Format Property, SelStart Property, SelLength Property, Style Property, Value Property

TEXT ... ENDTEXT Command

Outputs lines of text, the results of expressions and functions, and the contents of variables.

Syntax

TEXT
TextLines

ENDTEXT

Arguments

TextLines

Specifies the text sent to the current output device. *TextLines* can consist of text, memory variables, array elements, expressions, functions or any combination of these.

Expressions, functions, memory variables, and array elements specified with *TextLines* are evaluated only if SET TEXTMERGE is ON and must be enclosed in the delimiters specified by SET TEXTMERGE DELIMITERS. If SET TEXTMERGE is OFF, the expressions, functions, memory variables, and array elements are output as literals along with their delimiters.

For example, today's date is output if SET TEXTMERGE is ON and a text line contains <<DATE( )>>. If SET TEXTMERGE is OFF, <<DATE( )>> is output literally.

If you place comments within TEXT and ENDTEXT or after \ or \\, the comments are also output.

Remarks

This structured programming command sends text lines placed between TEXT and ENDTEXT to the main Visual FoxPro window, a user-defined window, a printer, a text file, or a low-level file.

TEXT sends the text lines to the current output device. This continues until an ENDTEXT statement is encountered or until the program ends.

By default, output from TEXT ... ENDTEXT is sent to the main Visual FoxPro window or the active window. Issue SET CONSOLE OFF to suppress output to the main Visual FoxPro window or the active window. Use SET PRINTER to send output to a printer or a text file.

Output from TEXT ... ENDTEXT can also be sent to a low-level file created or opened with FCREATE( ) or FOPEN( ). If a file handle returned by FCREATE( ) or FOPEN( ) is stored to the _TEXT system variable, output is directed to the corresponding low-level file.

Example

The following example demonstrates how you can use SET TEXTMERGE, SET TEXTMERGE DELIMITERS, TEXT ... ENDTEXT, and the _TEXT system variable.

A low-level file called Names.txt is created and its file handle is stored in the _TEXT system variable. The program is exited if Names.txt can't be created. The customer table is opened, and the names of the first 10 contacts are output to Names.txt. Text and the results of functions are output to the text file.

The text file containing the names is then opened with MODIFY FILE.

```
CLEAR
CLOSE DATABASES
SET TALK OFF
SET TEXTMERGE ON     && Enable embedding of expressions and functions
STORE FCREATE('names.txt') TO _TEXT     && Create low-level file
IF _TEXT = -1  && Can't create low-level file then exit program
   WAIT WINDOW 'Cannot create an output file; press a key to exit'
   CANCEL
ENDIF

CLOSE DATABASES
OPEN DATABASE (HOME(2) + 'Data\testdata')
USE customer  && Opens Customer table

TEXT
        CONTACT NAMES
   <<DATE( )>>    <<TIME( )>>
ENDTEXT
WAIT WINDOW 'Press a key to generate the first ten names'
SCAN NEXT 10
   TEXT
     <<contact>>
   ENDTEXT
ENDSCAN
CLOSE ALL  && Close the text file and the table
MODIFY FILE names.txt
ERASE names.txt
```

See Also

FOPEN( ), _PRETEXT, SET TEXTMERGE, SET TEXTMERGE DELIMITERS, _TEXT

_TEXT System Variable

Directs output from the \ I \\ and TEXT ... ENDTEXT text merge commands to a low-level file.

Syntax

_TEXT = *nFileHandle*

Arguments

nFileHandle
> Specifies a numeric value that determines the low-level file to which output is directed.

Remarks

\ I \\ and TEXT ... ENDTEXT facilitate the merging of text with the contents of tables, memory variables, and the results of functions and expressions. Output generated by these text merge commands can be directed to the screen or a window or to a low-level file. The _TEXT system memory variable lets you direct text merge output from these commands to a low-level file.

To send output from the \ and \\ and TEXT ... ENDTEXT text merge commands to a low-level file, include the TO *FileName* clause in SET TEXTMERGE. The file handle of *FileName* is stored to _TEXT. If the file handle of another low-level file was previously stored in _TEXT, that low-level file is closed.

FCREATE( ) creates and opens low-level files and FOPEN( ) opens existing files. These functions return a positive file handle if the file is successfully created or opened. Storing this file handle to _TEXT directs any subsequent output from the \, \\ and TEXT ... ENDTEXT text merge commands to the file. Use STORE or = to store a file handle to _TEXT. You must open a low-level file with write privileges in order for it to accept output from the text merge commands.

You can close low-level files with FCLOSE( ) or CLOSE ALL. You can also use SET TEXTMERGE TO without a file name to close the low-level file whose handle is stored in _TEXT.

The startup default value of _TEXT is –1. If you are directing text merge output to a file whose file handle is stored in _TEXT, you can turn off the output to that file without closing the file by storing –1 to _TEXT. By storing different file handles and –1 to _TEXT, you can direct text merge output to alternate files.

Example

The following program demonstrates how to direct text merge output to alternate files.

```
SET TALK OFF
SET TEXTMERGE ON NOSHOW      && Enable text merge, no output to screen
SET TEXTMERGE DELIMITERS TO   && Default text merge delimiters <<,>>
SET TEXTMERGE TO date.txt    && Create and send output to date.txt
STORE _TEXT TO gcDateHandle   && Save date.txt's file handle
STORE -1 TO _TEXT            && Output off to date.txt; keep it open
SET TEXTMERGE TO time.txt    && Create and send output to time.txt
STORE _TEXT TO gcTimeHandle   && Save time.txt's file handle
*** Send the following text to time.txt ***
\The time is:
STORE gcDateHandle TO _TEXT    && Now direct output to date.txt
*** Send the following text to date.txt ***
\Today's date is:
STORE gcTimeHandle TO _TEXT    && Now direct output to time.txt
*** Output the time on the same line ***
\\ <<TIME( )>>
STORE gcDateHandle TO _TEXT    && Now direct output to date.txt
*** Output the date on the same line ***
\\ <<DATE( )>>
CLOSE ALL  && Close all files
TYPE date.txt  && See what's in this file...
WAIT WINDOW  && Pause
TYPE time.txt  && ...and what's in this file
ERASE date.txt
ERASE time.txt
```

See Also

\ | \\, FOPEN( ), FCLOSE( ), FCREATE( ), _PRETEXT, SET TEXTMERGE,
SET TEXTMERGE DELIMITERS

TextBox Control

Creates a text box.

Syntax

TextBox

Remarks

Creates a text box in which you can edit the contents of a memory variable, array element, or field. All standard Visual FoxPro editing features, such as cut, copy, and paste, are available in the text box. If the text box is used to edit a date or datetime value and the entire value is selected, you can press + or – to increment or decrement the value by one day.

Use the InputMask and Format properties to specify how values are entered and displayed in the text box.

For additional information about creating text boxes, see "Form Designer" in Help, and Chapter 10, "Using Controls," in the *Microsoft Visual FoxPro 6.0 Programmer's Guide*.

Properties

Alignment	Application	BackColor
BackStyle	BaseClass	BorderColor Property
BorderStyle	Century	Class
ClassLibrary	ColorScheme	ColorSource
Comment	ControlSource	DateFormat
DateMark	DisabledBackColor	DisabledForeColor
DragIcon	DragMode	Enabled
FontBold	FontCondense	FontExtend
FontItalic	FontName	FontOutline
FontShadow	FontSize	FontStrikeThru
FontUnderline	ForeColor	Format
Height	HelpContextID	HideSelection
Hours	IMEMode	InputMask
IntegralHeight	Left	Margin
MaxLength	MemoWindow	MouseIcon
MousePointer	Name	NullDisplay
OLEDragMode	OLEDragPicture	OLEDropEffects
OLEDropHasData	OLEDropMode	OLEDropTextInsertion
OpenWindow	Parent	ParentClass
PasswordChar	ReadOnly	RightToLeft
Seconds	SelectedBackColor	SelectedForeColor
SelectOnEntry	SelLength	SelStart
SelText	SpecialEffect	StatusBarText
StrictDateEntry	Style	TabIndex
TabStop	Tag	TerminateRead
Text	ToolTipText	Top
Value	Visible	WhatsThisHelpID
Width		

Events

Click	DblClick	Destroy
DragDrop	DragOver	Error
ErrorMessage	GotFocus	Init
InteractiveChange	KeyPress	LostFocus
Message	MiddleClick	MouseDown
MouseMove	MouseUp	MouseWheel
OLECompleteDrag	OLEDragDrop	OLEDragOver
OLEGiveFeedBack	OLESetData	OLEStartDrag
ProgrammaticChange	RangeHigh	RangeLow
RightClick	UIEnable	Valid
When		

Methods

AddProperty	CloneObject	Drag
Move	OLEDrag	ReadExpression
ReadMethod	Refresh	ResetToDefault
SaveAsClass	SetFocus	ShowWhatsThis
WriteExpression	WriteMethod	ZOrder

See Also

CREATE CLASS, CREATE FORM, DEFINE CLASS

TextHeight Method

Returns the height of a text string as it would be displayed in the current font.

Syntax

[*nHeight* =] [*FormSet.*]*Object*.TextHeight(*cText*)

Arguments

nHeight
    Returns a value in pixels specifying the height of the text string.

cText
    Specifies the character string for which the text height is determined.

Remarks

The TextHeight method determines the amount of vertical space required to display *cText*. The height returned includes the leading space above and below the character string, so you can use the height returned to calculate and position multiple lines of text within the form. If *cText* contains embedded carriage returns, the TextHeight method returns the cumulative height of the lines, including the leading space above and below each line.

Applies To

Form, _SCREEN

See Also

FontSize Property, ScaleMode Property, TextWidth Method

TextWidth Method

Returns the width of a text string as it would be displayed in the current font.

Syntax

[*nWidth =*] [*FormSet.*]*Object*.TextWidth(*cText*)

Arguments

nWidth
    Returns a value in pixels specifying the width of the text string.

cText
    Specifies the character string for which the text width is determined.

Remarks

The TextWidth method determines the amount of horizontal space required to display *cText*.

Applies To

Form, _SCREEN

See Also

FontSize Property, ScaleMode Property, TextHeight Method

THIS Object Reference

Provides a reference to the current object in event code or in a class definition.

Syntax

THIS.*PropertyName* | *ObjectName*

Arguments

PropertyName
   Specifies a property to set or get for the object.

ObjectName
   Specifies an object in the class.

Remarks

THIS provides a convenient way of referring to the current object when writing event-handling programs in a form. For example, this Click Event program for a command button sets the button's caption to the current time:

```
this.caption = time()
```

Using THIS instead of explicitly referring to the current object by name (for example, `thisform.command1.caption`) makes program code portable between objects, because it avoids the object's name, and automatically encapsulates the object's parent class.

THIS also allows you to reference a property or an object in a class definition. Methods in a class definition block can use THIS to specify a property or object that will exist when the class is created.

Because multiple instances of objects share the same method code, THIS always refers to the instance in which the code is executing. If there are multiple instances of an object, and one of the object's methods is called, THIS refers to the correct object.

Example

The following example creates a subclass called `MyForm`, based on the Form class. A method called ChangeBackColor is created. ChangeBackColor uses THIS to refer to `MyForm`.

```
DEFINE CLASS MyForm AS FORM
   CAPTION = "This Form"
   HEIGHT = 15
   WIDTH = 20

   PROCEDURE ChangeBackColor
   PARAMETER NewColor
      THIS.BACKCOLOR = NewColor
   ENDPROC
ENDDEFINE
```

See Also

THISFORM, THISFORMSET

THISFORM Object Reference

Provides a reference to the current form in form event code or in a class definition.

Syntax

THISFORM.*PropertyName* | *ObjectName*

Arguments

PropertyName
>   Specifies a property for the form.

ObjectName
>   Specifies an object in the form.

Remarks

THISFORM provides a convenient way of referring to the current form when writing event-handling programs in a form. For example, this Click Event program for a command button sets the button's caption to the current time:

```
thisform.command1.caption = time()
```

Using THISFORM instead of explicitly referring to the current form by name (for example, `form1.command1.caption`) makes program code portable between forms.

When creating class definitions, THISFORM also provides a means of referring to the current form within a method. THISFORM lets you reference an object on the form or property without using multiple Parent properties.

See Also

THIS, THISFORMSET

THISFORMSET Object Reference

Provides a reference to the current form set in event code or in a class definition.

Syntax

THISFORMSET.*PropertyName* | *ObjectName*

Arguments

PropertyName
>   Specifies a property for the form set.

ObjectName
>   Specifies an object in the form set.

Remarks

THISFORMSET provides a convenient way of referring to the current formset when writing event-handling programs in a form. Using THISFORMSET instead of explicitly referring to the current form by name (for example, `form1.command1.caption`) makes program code portable between forms.

When creating class definitions, THISFORMSET also provides a means of referring to the current formset within a method. THISFORMSET lets you reference an object on the form or property without using multiple Parent properties.

See Also

THIS, THISFORM

_THROTTLE System Variable

Specifies the execution speed of programs when the Trace window is open.

Syntax

_THROTTLE = *nSeconds*

Arguments

nSeconds
Specifies the delay in seconds between execution of each program line. The startup default value is 0, with no pause between execution of program lines. *nSeconds* can range from 0 to 5.5 seconds. For example, if *nSeconds* is 0.5 seconds, a 1/2-second delay occurs between execution of program lines.

Remarks

The Trace window, one of the debugging tools available in Visual FoxPro, displays a program's source code as the program executes. The Trace window highlights each line in the program when the line executes. The numeric value of _THROTTLE determines the delay between execution of each program line when the Trace window is open.

Note The Trace Between Breaks option on the Trace window's Program menu must be on for a delay to occur.

See Also

SET DEBUG, SET STEP

TIME( ) Function

Returns the current system time in 24-hour, eight-character string (hh:mm:ss) format.

Syntax

TIME([*nExpression*])

Returns

Character

Arguments

nExpression

The time returned includes hundredths of a second if *nExpression* is included. The numeric expression *nExpression* can be any value. However, the actual maximum resolution is about 1/18 second. Use SECONDS( ) for greater resolution.

See Also

CTOT( ), DATE( ), DATETIME( ), DTOT( ), HOUR( ), SEC( ), SECONDS( ), SET SECONDS, SYS(2) – Seconds Since Midnight

Timer Control

Creates a timer that can execute code at regular intervals.

Syntax

Timer

Remarks

The Timer control, invisible to the user, is useful for background processing. A typical use for the timer is checking the system clock to determine if it is time to run a program or application.

For additional information about creating timers, see Chapter 10, "Using Controls," in the *Microsoft Visual FoxPro 6.0 Programmer's Guide*.

Properties

Application	BaseClass	Class
ClassLibrary	Comment	Enabled
Height	Interval	Left
Name	Parent	ParentClass
Tag	Top	Width

Events

Destroy	Error	Init
Timer		

Methods

AddProperty	CloneObject	ReadExpression
ReadMethod	Reset	ResetToDefault
SaveAsClass	WriteExpression	WriteMethod

See Also

CREATE CLASS, CREATE FORM, DEFINE CLASS, Form Designer

Timer Event

Occurs when the number of milliseconds specified in the Interval property has elapsed.

Syntax

PROCEDURE *Timer.*Timer
[LPARAMETERS *nIndex*]

Arguments

nIndex
Uniquely identifies a control if it is in a control array.

Applies To

Timer

See Also

Interval Property, Reset Method

TitleBar Property

Specifies if a title bar appears at the top of a form.

Syntax

*Object.*TitleBar[= *nExpression*]

Arguments

nExpression
The settings for the TitleBar property are as follows:

Setting	Description
0	The title bar is not displayed.
1	(Default) The title bar is displayed.

Remarks

If the TitleBar property is set to 0, a title bar is not displayed and the window pop-up menu and the Minimize, Maximize, and Close buttons are not available.

Applies To

Form

See Also

Closable Property, MaxButton Property, MinButton Property, WhatsThisButton Property

ToolBar Object

Creates a custom toolbar.

Syntax

ToolBar

Remarks

Use the ToolBar object to create your own toolbars for your applications.

The following list describes the properties of a custom toolbar:

- Toolbars are always on top.

- Toolbars automatically dock when they are moved to the edge of the main Visual FoxPro window.

- When toolbars aren't docked, they have a half-height title bar.

- When the size of a toolbar is changed, the controls are arranged to fit.

- You can move a toolbar by clicking and dragging in any area of the toolbar that isn't a control.

- Many controls placed on the toolbar do not receive the focus when they're chosen.

- Access keys in controls placed in a toolbar are disabled.

Although any control can be placed on a toolbar, some controls, such as a list box, may be too large to fit properly in a docked toolbar. These controls can be programmatically removed from the toolbar when the toolbar is docked and replaced with a smaller version of the same control or a different control.

For additional information about creating toolbars, see Chapter 11, "Designing Menus and Toolbars," in the *Microsoft Visual FoxPro 6.0 Programmer's Guide*.

Properties

ActiveControl	Application	BackColor
BaseClass	Caption	Class
ClassLibrary	Comment	ColorSource Property
ControlBox	ControlCount	Controls
DataSession	DataSessionID	Docked
DockPosition	Enabled	ForeColor
Height	HelpContextID	KeyPreview
Left	LockScreen	MouseIcon
MousePointer	Movable	Name
Objects	OLEDragMode	OLEDragPicture
OLEDropEffects	OLEDropHasData	OLEDropMode
Parent	ParentClass	ScaleMode
ShowTips	ShowWindow	Sizable
Tag	Top	Visible
WhatsThisHelpID	Width	

Events

Activate	AfterDock	BeforeDock
Click	DblClick	Deactivate
Destroy	DragDrop	DragOver
Error	Init	MiddleClick Event
MouseDown	MouseMove	MouseUp
MouseWheel	Moved	OLECompleteDrag
OLEDragDrop	OLEDragOver	OLEGiveFeedBack
OLESetData	OLEStartDrag	Paint
Resize	RightClick	UnDock

Methods

AddObject	AddProperty	CloneObject
Dock	Hide	Move

NewObject	OLEDrag	ReadExpression
ReadMethod	Refresh	Release
RemoveObject	ResetToDefault	SaveAsClass
SetAll	Show	ShowWhatsThis
WriteExpression Method	ZOrder	

Example

The following example demonstrates how you can create a toolbar from the Toolbar class. Visual FoxPro rearranges the buttons when the toolbar is resized. When the ToolBar object is created, Visual FoxPro automatically places the controls from left to right in the order they are added to the class definition, ignoring the controls' Top and Left properties.

```
PUBLIC tbrDesktop
tbrDesktop = CREATEOBJ('mytoolbar')
tbrDesktop.SHOW

DEFINE CLASS myToolBar  AS Toolbar
   ADD OBJECT btnBold   AS CommandButton
   ADD OBJECT sep1       AS Separator
   ADD OBJECT btnItalics AS CommandButton

   btnBold.HEIGHT = 20
   btnBold.WIDTH = 50
   btnBold.Caption = "Bold"
   btnItalics.HEIGHT = 20
   btnItalics.WIDTH = 50
   btnItalics.Caption = "Italic"
   btnItalics.FontBold = .F.

   LEFT   = 1
   TOP = 1
   WIDTH = 25

   CAPTION = "Desktop Attributes"

   PROCEDURE Activate
   this.btnBold.FontBold = _SCREEN.FONTBOLD
   this.btnItalics.FontItalic = _SCREEN.FONTITALIC
   ENDPROC

   PROCEDURE btnBold.CLICK
   _SCREEN.FONTBOLD = !_SCREEN.FONTBOLD
   This.FontBold =_SCREEN.FONTBOLD
   ENDPROC
```

```
   PROCEDURE btnItalics.CLICK
   _SCREEN.FONTITALIC = !_SCREEN.FONTITALIC
   This.FontItalic = _SCREEN.FONTITALIC
   ENDPROC
ENDDEFINE
```

See Also

CREATE CLASS, CREATE FORM, DEFINE CLASS, Separator Object

ToolTipText Property

Specifies the text that appears as a ToolTip for a control. Available at design time and run time.

Syntax

Control.ToolTipText = *cText*

Arguments

cText
> Specifies the text to use for the ToolTip. The maximum number of characters you can specify for *cText* is 127.

Remarks

You can only set the ToolTipText property if the ShowTips property is set to true (.T.) for the form or toolbar that contains the control.

Applies To

CheckBox, ComboBox, CommandButton, EditBox, Grid, ListBox, OptionButton, Shape, Spinner, TextBox

See Also

ShowTips Property

Top Property

Specifies the distance between the top edge of a control or form and its container object. Available at design time and run time.

Syntax

Object.Top[= *nValue*]

Arguments

nValue

Specifies the distance between the top edge of an object or form and the top edge of its container object.

The default container for a form is the main Visual FoxPro window.

Remarks

The Top property specifies how far from the object's zero position the object is located. For example, if a form is contained within the Visual FoxPro main window, the zero position is immediately below the system menu, or if a toolbar is docked to the top of the main window, immediately below the toolbar.

Use the Left and Top and the Height and Width properties for operations based on an object's external dimensions, such as moving or resizing.

Note The Top property is read-only when it applies to a control contained in a Column object.

The unit of measurement used by the Top property is determined by the control's ScaleMode property setting.

Example

The following example demonstrates how the Top property is used to position controls on a form. The AddObject method is used to add a Line control and three command buttons to a form. The Top property specifies the vertical placement of each control on the form.

```
frmMyForm = CREATEOBJECT('Form')  && Create a Form
frmMyForm.Closable = .F.  && Disable the window pop-up menu

frmMyForm.AddObject('shpLine','Line')  && Add a Line control to the form
frmMyForm.AddObject('cmdCmndBtn1','cmdMyCmndBtn1')  && Up Cmnd button
frmMyForm.AddObject('cmdCmndBtn2','cmdMyCmndBtn2')  && Down Cmnd button
frmMyForm.AddObject('cmdCmndBtn3','cmdMyCmndBtn3')  && Quit Cmnd button

frmMyForm.shpLine.Visible = .T.  && Make Line control visible
frmMyForm.shpLine.Top = 20  && Specify Line control row
frmMyForm.shpLine.Left = 125  && Specify Line control column

frmMyForm.cmdCmndBtn1.Visible =.T.  && Up Command button visible
frmMyForm.cmdCmndBtn2.Visible =.T.  && Down" Command button visible
frmMyForm.cmdCmndBtn3.Visible =.T.  && Quit Command button visible

frmMyForm.SHOW  && Display the form
READ EVENTS  && Start event processing
```

```
DEFINE CLASS cmdMyCmndBtn1 AS COMMANDBUTTON  && Create Command button
   Caption = 'Slant \<Up'  && Caption on the Command button
   Left = 50  && Command button column
   Top = 100  && Command button row
   Height = 25  && Command button height

   PROCEDURE Click
      ThisForm.shpLine.Visible = .F.  && Hide the Line control
      ThisForm.shpLine.LineSlant ='/'  && Slant up
      ThisForm.shpLine.Visible = .T.  && Show the Line control
ENDDEFINE

DEFINE CLASS cmdMyCmndBtn2 AS CommandButton  && Create Command button
   Caption = 'Slant \<Down'  && Caption on the Command button
   Left = 200  && Command button column
   Top = 100  && Command button row
   Height = 25  && Command button height

   PROCEDURE Click
      ThisForm.shpLine.Visible = .F.  && Hide the Line control
      ThisForm.shpLine.LineSlant ='\'  && Slant down
      ThisForm.shpLine.Visible = .T.  && Show the Line control
ENDDEFINE

DEFINE CLASS cmdMyCmndBtn3 AS CommandButton  && Create Command button
   Caption = '\<Quit'  && Caption on the Command button
   Cancel = .T.  && Default Cancel Command button (Esc)
   Left = 125  && Command button column
   Top = 150  && Command button row
   Height = 25  && Command button height

   PROCEDURE Click
      CLEAR EVENTS  && Stop event processing, close Form
ENDDEFINE
```

Applies To

CheckBox, ComboBox, CommandButton, CommandGroup, Container Object, Control Object, Custom, EditBox, Form, Grid, Image, Label, Line, ListBox, OLE Bound Control, OLE Container Control, OptionButton, OptionGroup, PageFrame, _SCREEN, Shape, Spinner, TextBox, Timer, ToolBar

See Also

Left Property, Height Property, Move Method, ScaleMode Property, Width Property

TopIndex Property

Specifies the item that appears in the top-most position in a list. Not available at design time; read-only at run time.

Syntax

Control.TopIndex[= *nIndex*]

Arguments

nIndex
    Specifies the index of the item that appears in the top-most position in a list.

Remarks

The index of an item reflects its position in the list, which is relative to other items in the list and can change.

Applies To

ComboBox, ListBox

See Also

AddItem Method, Clear Method, List Property, ListCount Property, MultiSelect Property, NewItemID Property, RemoveItem Method, Selected Property, TopItemID Property

TopItemID Property

Specifies the item ID of the item that appears in the top-most position in a list. Not available at design time; read/write at run time.

Syntax

Control.TopIItemID[= *nItemID*]

Arguments

nItemID
    Specifies the item ID of the item that appears in the top-most position in a list.

Remarks

The default setting for the TopItemID property is 1, or the first item in the list.

Applies To

ComboBox, ListBox

See Also

AddItem Method, Clear Method, List Property, ListCount Property, MultiSelect Property, NewItemID Property, RemoveItem Method, Selected Property, TopIndex Property

TOTAL Command

Computes totals for numeric fields in the currently selected table.

Syntax

TOTAL TO *TableName*
ON *FieldName*
    [FIELDS *FieldNameList*]
    [*Scope*]
    [FOR *lExpression1*]
    [WHILE *lExpression2*]
    [NOOPTIMIZE]

Arguments

TableName
    Specifies the name of the table that will contain the totals. If the specified table doesn't exist, Visual FoxPro creates it. If the table exists and SET SAFETY is ON, Visual FoxPro asks if you would like to overwrite the existing table. If SET SAFETY is OFF, you aren't prompted, and the output table is overwritten.

FieldName
    Specifies the field on which the totals are grouped. The table must be sorted on this field, or an open index or index tag must have this field as its key expression.

FIELDS *FieldNameList*
    Specifies the fields to be totaled. Separate the field names in the list with commas. If you omit the FIELDS clause, all numeric fields are totaled by default.

Scope
    Specifies a range of records to total. The scope clauses are: ALL, NEXT *nRecords*, RECORD *nRecordNumber*, and REST. For more information on scope clauses, see "Scope Clauses" and "Overview of the Language," in Help.

    The default scope for TOTAL is ALL records.

FOR *lExpression1*
    Specifies a condition whereby only the records that satisfy the logical condition *lExpression1* are included in the totals.

    Rushmore optimizes a query created with TOTAL ... FOR if *lExpression1* is an optimizable expression. For best performance, use an optimizable expression in the FOR clause.

For more information, see the SET OPTIMIZE Command, earlier in this language reference, and "Understanding Rushmore Technology" in Chapter 15, "Optimizing Applications," in the *Microsoft Visual FoxPro 6.0 Programmer's Guide*.

WHILE *lExpression2*

Specifies a condition whereby records from the current table are included in the totals for as long as the logical expression *lExpression2* evaluates to true (.T.).

NOOPTIMIZE

Disables Rushmore optimization of TOTAL.

For more information, see the SET OPTIMIZE Command, earlier in this language reference, and "Understanding Rushmore Technology" in Chapter 15, "Optimizing Applications," in the *Microsoft Visual FoxPro 6.0 Programmer's Guide*.

Remarks

The table in the currently selected work area must be sorted or indexed. A separate total is calculated for each set of records with a common field value or unique index key value. The results are placed into records in a second table. One record is created in the second table for each common field value or unique index key value.

Numeric overflow can occur if the numeric fields in the second table aren't wide enough to contain the totals. Visual FoxPro conserves the most significant portions of the totals when numeric overflow occurs. When a field is too small to accept a total:

- Decimal places are truncated, and the remaining decimal portion of the total is rounded.

- If the total still doesn't fit, scientific notation is used if the total field contains seven or more digits.

- Finally, asterisks replace the field contents.

See Also

AVERAGE, CALCULATE, INDEX, SORT, SUM

TRANSFORM( ) Function

Returns a character string from an expression in a format determined by a format code.

Syntax

TRANSFORM(*eExpression*, [*cFormatCodes*])

Returns

Character

Arguments

eExpression
Specifies the character, currency, date, or numeric expression to format.

cFormatCodes
Specifies one or more format codes that determine how the expression is formatted.
The following table lists the available format codes.

Format Codes	Description
@C	CR is appended to positive currency or numeric values to indicate a credit.
@D	Date and DateTime values are converted to the current SET DATE format.
@E	Date and DateTime values are converted to a BRITISH date format.
@R	The transformation uses a format mask. The mask characters are not stored to the transformed value. Use only with character or numeric data. Mask characters include:
9 or #	Represents a character or number.
!	Converts lower-case letters to upper-case letters.
@T	Leading and trailing spaces are trimmed from character values.
@X	DB is appended to negative currency or numeric values to indicate a debit.
@Z	If 0, currency or numeric values are converted to spaces.
@(	Encloses negative currency or numeric values in parentheses.
@^	Converts currency or numeric values to scientific notation.
@0	Converts numeric or currency values to their hexadecimal equivalents. The numeric or currency value must be positive and less than 4,294,967,296.
@!	Converts an entire character string to uppercase.
@$	Adds the current currency symbol specified by SET CURRENCY to currency and numeric values. By default, the symbol is placed immediately before or after the value. However, the currency symbol and its placement (specified with SET CURRENCY), the separator character (specified with SET SEPARATOR) and the decimal character (specified with SET POINT) can all be changed.
X	Specifies the width of character values. For example, if *cFormatCodes* is 'XX', 2 characters are returned.
Y	Converts logical true (.T.) and false (.F.) values to Y and N, respectively.
!	Converts a lowercase character to uppercase in the corresponding position in a character string.
.	Specifies the decimal point position in currency and numeric values.
,	Separates digits to the left of the decimal point in currency and numeric values.

If you omit *cFormatCodes*, Visual FoxPro performs a default transformation on *eExpression*. The following table describes the transformation performed for each data type *eExpression* can assume:

Data Type	Transformation Description
Character	No transformation is performed.
Currency	Transformation is determined by the settings specified in the Regional tab of the Options dialog box.
Date	A DTOC( ) transformation is performed on the date.
DateTime	A TTOC( ) transformation is performed on the date time.
Logical	Logical true (.T.) and false (.F.) values are transformed to the character strings ".T." and ".F." respectively.
Numeric (includes Double, Float, or Integer data types)	Trailing zeros are removed from the decimal portion of a numeric value. If the numeric value is a whole number, a decimal point is not included in the transformed value (for example, 4.0 is transformed to 4). If the numeric value is less than one but greater than negative one, zero is included before the decimal point (for example, .4 is transformed to 0.4).
General	"Gen" is returned if the general field contains an object; "gen" is returned if the general field doesn't contain an object.
Memo	No transformation is performed.

Example

```
STORE 12.34 TO gnPrice
CLEAR
? TRANSFORM(gnPrice, '$$$$.99')   && Displays $12.34
```

See Also

DTOC( ), TTOC( ), InputMask Property

_TRANSPORT System Variable

Included for backward compatibility. Use the Visual FoxPro Converter instead.

_TRIGGERLEVEL System Variable

Contains a read-only numeric value indicating the current trigger procedure nesting level.

Syntax

_TRIGGERLEVEL = *nExpression*

Arguments

nExpression
Contains the current trigger procedure nesting level. _TRIGGERLEVEL contains 1 when the initial trigger procedure is executing. If a trigger procedure causes another trigger procedure to fire, _TRIGGERLEVEL is incremented by 1. _TRIGGERLEVEL contains 0 if a trigger procedure is not executing.

Remarks

Use CREATE TRIGGER to create a Delete, Insert, or Update trigger for a table. You can use APPEND PROCEDURES and MODIFY PROCEDURES to create stored procedures that are executed when a Delete, Insert, or Update trigger occurs.

_TRIGGERLEVEL contains a numeric value that is read-only. If you use STORE or = to assign a value to _TRIGGERLEVEL, the value is ignored.

See Also

APPEND PROCEDURES, CREATE TRIGGER, MODIFY PROCEDURE

TRIM( ) Function

Returns the specified character expression with all trailing blanks removed.

Syntax

TRIM(*cExpression*)

Returns

Character

Arguments

cExpression
Specifies the character expression from which TRIM( ) removes all trailing blanks.

Remarks

TRIM( ) is identical to RTRIM( ).

Example

```
CLOSE DATABASES
OPEN DATABASE (HOME(2) + 'Data\testdata')
USE customer  && Opens Customer table
CLEAR
? 'The contact for '+ TRIM(company) + ' is ' + contact
```

See Also

ALLTRIM( ), LTRIM( ), RTRIM( )

TTOC( ) Function

Converts a DateTime expression to a Character value of a specified format.

Syntax

TTOC(*tExpression* [, 1 | 2])

Returns

Character

Arguments

tExpression

Specifies a DateTime expression from which TTOC( ) returns a Character value. If *tExpression* contains only a time, Visual FoxPro adds the default date of 12/30/1899 to *tExpression*. If *tExpression* contains only a date, Visual FoxPro adds the default time of midnight (12:00:00 A.M.) to *tExpression*.

1

Specifies that TTOC( ) return a Character string in a format suitable for indexing. The character string has a 14 character yyyy:mm:dd:hh:mm:ss format that is not affected by the current settings of SET CENTURY or SET SECONDS.

2

Specifies that TTOC( ) return a Character string consisting of only the time portion of the DateTime expression. The settings of SET SECONDS and SET DATE specify if the seconds portion of the time is included in the character string. Note that if SET DATE is set to LONG or SHORT, the format of the character string is determined by the format of the Control Panel time setting.

Example

The following example creates a Datetime type variable named gtDtime. TYPE( ) displays T, indicating the variable is a Datetime type. TTOC( ) is used to convert the variable to a character type, and TYPE( ) now displays C, indicating the variable is a character type after the conversion.

```
STORE DATETIME( ) TO gtDtime  && Creates a Datetime type memory variable
CLEAR
? "gtDtime is type: "
?? TYPE('gtDtime')  && Displays T, Datetime type value

gtDtime = TTOC(gtDtime)     && Converts gtDtime to a character value
? "gtDtime is now type: "
?? TYPE('gtDtime')  && Displays C, character type value
```

See Also

DATE( ), DATETIME( ), HOUR( ), MINUTE( ), SEC( ), SECONDS( ), SET CENTURY,
SET DATE, SET SECONDS, TIME( ), TTOD( )

TTOD( ) Function

Returns a Date value from a DateTime expression.

Syntax

TTOD(*tExpression*)

Returns

Date

Arguments

tExpression

Specifies a date and time expression from which TTOD( ) returns a Date value.
tExpression must evaluate to a valid DateTime. If *tExpression* contains only a time,
Visual FoxPro adds the default date of 12/30/1899 to *tExpression* and returns this
default date.

Example

The following example creates a Datetime type variable named gtDtime. TYPE( )
displays T, indicating the variable is a Datetime type. TTOD( ) is used to convert the
variable to a date type, and TYPE( ) now displays D, indicating the variable is a date
type after the conversion.

```
STORE DATETIME( ) TO gtDtime  && Creates a Datetime type memory variable
CLEAR
? "gtDtime is type: "
?? TYPE('gtDtime')  && Displays T, Datetime type value

gtDtime = TTOD(gtDtime)     && Converts gtDtime to a date value
? "gtDtime is now type: "
?? TYPE('gtDtime')  && Displays D, character type value
```

See Also

DATE( ), DATETIME( ), HOUR( ), MINUTE( ), SEC( ), SECONDS( ), SET CENTURY, SET SECONDS, TIME( ), TTOC( )

TXNLEVEL( ) Function

Returns a numeric value indicating the current transaction level.

Syntax

TXNLEVEL( )

Returns

Numeric

Remarks

Use BEGIN TRANSACTION to create a transaction. Transactions are nested by issuing BEGIN TRANSACTION when another transaction is in progress. Transactions can be nested in this manner to five levels. Use TXNLEVEL( ) to determine the current transaction level.

TXNLEVEL( ) returns a value from 0 to 5. TXNLEVEL( ) returns 0 if a transaction is not in progress.

Example

In the following example, the customer table in the testdata database is opened. BEGIN TRANSACTION is issued to start a transaction, and TXNLEVEL( ) is used to display the transaction level (1). BEGIN TRANSACTION is issued again to start a nested transaction, and TXNLEVEL( ) displays 2 for the current transaction level.

```
CLOSE DATABASES
OPEN DATABASE (HOME(2) + 'Data\testdata')
USE Customer     && Open customer table
CLEAR

BEGIN TRANSACTION
   tLevel = ALLTRIM(STR(TXNLEVEL()))
   =MESSAGEBOX("Current Transaction: " + tLevel, 0, "Trasaction Level")
   BEGIN TRANSACTION
      tLevel = ALLTRIM(STR(TXNLEVEL()))
      =MESSAGEBOX("Current Transaction: " + tLevel, 0, ;
         "Trasaction Level")
   END TRANSACTION
END TRANSACTION
```

See Also

BEGIN TRANSACTION, END TRANSACTION, ROLLBACK

TXTWIDTH( ) Function

Returns the length of a character expression with respect to the average character width for a font.

Syntax

TXTWIDTH(*cExpression* [, *cFontName*, *nFontSize* [, *cFontStyle*]])

Returns

Numeric

Arguments

cExpression

Specifies a character expression for which TXTWIDTH( ) returns the length. If you include only *cExpression*, the length of the character expression is returned for the current font for the main Visual FoxPro window or the active output window. A non-proportional font always returns a value equal to the number of characters in *cExpression*.

Include the optional arguments *cFontName*, *nFontSize* and *cFontStyle* to determine the length of a character expression with a specific font, font point size, or font style.

cFontName

Specifies the name of the font. Include *cFontName* to return the length of a character expression with a specific font.

nFontSize

Specifies a number that corresponds to the point size of the font. Include *nFontSize* to return the length of a character expression with a specific point size.

cFontStyle

Specifies a special font style for the character expression. *cFontStyle* is a font style code specified by a character or a set of characters. The Normal font style is used if *cFontStyle* isn't included. Here are the characters for each font style:

Character	Font Style
B	Bold
I	Italic
N	Normal
O	Outline
Q	Opaque
S	Shadow

(continued)

(continued)

Character	Font Style
–	Strikeout
T	Transparent
U	Underline

You can include more than one character to specify a combination of font styles. For example, BI specifies a Bold Italic font style.

The following command displays a message in a Courier normal 24-point font, centered horizontally in the main Visual FoxPro window:

```
@ 25,(WCOLS( )-TXTWIDTH('Hello!','Courier ',24)* ;
   FONTMETRIC(6,'Courier ',24)/FONTMETRIC(6))/2  ;
   SAY 'Hello!' FONT 'Courier ',24
```

Remarks

TXTWIDTH( ) returns the number of characters a character expression *cExpression* occupies, based on the average character width of a specified font (the average character width of a font is called a foxel). Use FONTMETRIC(6) to determine the average character width of a font.

If you don't include a font in TXTWIDTH( ), the value returned by TXTWIDTH( ) is determined by the current font for the main Visual FoxPro window, as long as output is directed to the main Visual FoxPro window when TXTWIDTH( ) is issued. If output is being directed to a user-defined window, the value returned is determined by the window's current font.

See Also

FONTMETRIC( ), GETFONT( ), LEN( ), SYSMETRIC( ), WFONT( )

TYPE Command

Displays the contents of a file.

Syntax

TYPE *FileName1*
    [AUTO]
    [WRAP]
    [TO PRINTER [PROMPT] | TO FILE *FileName2*]
    [NUMBER]

Arguments

FileName1
Specifies the name of the file to display. The name must include a file extension.

AUTO
Turns automatic indentation on. When you also include WRAP, TYPE automatically indents wrapped text in each paragraph by the same amount it indents the first line of the paragraph. For example:

- Wrapped lines are aligned with the tab when a paragraph begins with a tab.

- Wrapped lines are aligned with the tab when a paragraph begins with a number (or other text) followed by a tab and text.

- Wrapped lines are indented by the same amount as the first line when the first line of a paragraph is indented with spaces.

WRAP
Enables wordwrap so that a word that is too long to fit at the end of a line is automatically moved to the next line.

TO PRINTER [PROMPT]
Directs output to the printer.

You can include the optional PROMPT clause to display a print dialog before printing starts. Place the PROMPT keyword immediately after TO PRINTER.

TO FILE *FileName2*
Directs output to the file specified with *FileName2*.

NUMBER
Places line numbers at the beginning of each line in the output.

Remarks

TYPE displays the contents of files. This display can be directed to the main Visual FoxPro window, the active user-defined window, a printer, or another file.

When SET HEADINGS is ON, Visual FoxPro inserts a formfeed, the path and name of the file, and the date at the beginning of output produced with TYPE. If SET HEADINGS is OFF, this information isn't included.

In FoxPro for MS-DOS, if a printer driver setup is loaded and you direct output from TYPE to a file or a printer, TYPE displays the file contents using the settings from the printer driver setup.

See Also

SET HEADINGS

Type Property

Contain a character indicating the file type of a file in a project. Available at design time and run time.

Syntax

Object.Type

Remarks

The following table list the values the Type property can contain and the corresponding file types.

Value	FoxPro.H Constant	File Type and Extension
d	FILETYPE_DATABASE	Database, .dbc
D	FILETYPE_FREETABLE	Free table, .dbf
Q	FILETYPE_QUERY	Query, .qpr
K	FILETYPE_FORM	Form, .scx
R	FILETYPE_REPORT	Report, .frx
B	FILETYPE_LABEL	Label, .lbx
V	FILETYPE_CLASSLIB	Visual class Library, .vcx
P	FILETYPE_PROGRAM	Program, .prg
L	FILETYPE_APILIB	Visual FoxPro dynamic link library, .fll
Z	FILETYPE_APPLICATION	Application, .app
M	FILETYPE_MENU	Menu, .mnx
T	FILETYPE_TEXT	Text file, varies
x	FILETYPE_OTHER	Other, varies

These values are stored in the Type field of the project's .pjx file.

Applies To

File Object

See Also

FileClass Property, FileClassLibrary Property

TYPE( ) Function

Evaluates an expression and returns the data type of its contents.

Syntax

TYPE(*cExpression*)

Returns

Character

Arguments

cExpression

Specifies the expression to be evaluated, which can be a variable, field, memo field, or any other expression. The expression must be passed as a character string; place quotation marks around the names of memory variables, fields, and so on. If you do not place quotation marks around the expression, the TYPE( ) function returns "U" (undefined expression).

Remarks

The following table lists the character values TYPE( ) returns and their corresponding data types:

Data type	Character returned
Character	C
Numeric (also float, double, and integer)	N
Currency	Y
Date	D
DateTime	T
Logical	L
Memo	M
Object	O
General	G
Screen (created with SAVE SCREEN)	S
Undefined type of expression	U

Example

```
CLOSE DATABASES
OPEN DATABASE (HOME(2) + 'Data\testdata')
USE customer  && Opens Customer table
nTest = 1.01
cTest = "String"

CLEAR
? TYPE('customer.contact')  && Displays C
? TYPE('(12 * 3) + 4')  && Displays N
? TYPE('DATE( )')  && Displays D
? TYPE('.F. OR .T.')  && Displays L
? TYPE('ANSWER=42')  && Displays U
? TYPE('$19.99')  && Displays Y
? TYPE('nTest')  && Displays N
? TYPE('cTest')  && Displays C
```

See Also

EVALUATE( )

TypeLibCLSID Property

The registry CLSID (Class Identifier) for a type library created for server classes in a project. Read-only.

Syntax

Object.TypeLibCLSID

Remarks

A type library is created and registered when you build a .dll or .exe from a project that contains server classes. Type libraries have a .tlb extension, and are placed in the same directory as the .dll or .exe that is built.

Applies To

Project Object

See Also

CLSID Property, ProgID Property, TypeLibDesc Property, TypeLibName Property

TypeLibDesc Property

The description for a type library created for server classes in a project.

Syntax

Object.TypeLibDesc[= *cTypeLibraryDescription*]

Arguments

cTypeLibraryDescription
Specifies the description for a type library created for server classes in a project.
By default, contains the name of the project containing the server classes appended
with "Type Library."

Remarks

A type library is created and registered when you build a .dll or .exe from a project that
contains server classes. Type libraries have a .tlb extension, and are placed in the same
directory as the .dll or .exe that is built.

This property corresponds to the Typelib description item on the Server tab of the Project
Information dialog box.

Applies To

Project Object

See Also

CLSID Property, ProgID Property, TypeLibCLSID Property, TypeLibName Property

TypeLibName Property

The name of the type library created for server classes in a project. Read-only.

Syntax

Object.TypeLibName

Remarks

A type library is created and registered when you build a .dll or .exe from a project that
contains server classes. Type libraries have a .tlb extension, and are placed in the same
directory as the .dll or .exe that is built.

Applies To

Project Object

See Also

CLSID Property, Name Property, ProgID Property, TypeLibCLSID Property, TypeLibDesc Property

UIEnable Event

Occurs for all objects contained within a page whenever the page is activated or deactivated.

Syntax

PROCEDURE *Object*.UIEnable
[LPARAMETERS *nIndex, lEnable*]

– or –

PROCEDURE *Object*.UIEnable
LPARAMETERS *lEnable*

Arguments

nIndex

Contains a number that uniquely identifies a control if it is in a control array. The *nIndex* parameter is passed only if the control is in a control array.

lEnable

Contains a logical value that specifies whether the page that the object is contained within is being activated or deactivated. If *lEnable* is true (.T.), the page that the object is contained within is being activated (becoming the active page). If *lEnable* is false (.F.), the page is being deactivated (becoming the inactive page).

Remarks

Use the UIEnable event to specify any action you want to occur for an object or control when the page that it is contained within is activated or deactivated.

The UIEnable event does not occur for pages when the form is initially activated. The UIEnable event occurs only when a page is programmatically or interactively activated or deactivated.

Applies To

CheckBox, ComboBox, CommandButton, CommandGroup, Container Object, Control Object, EditBox, Grid, Image, Label, Line, ListBox, OLE Bound Control, OLE Container Control, OptionGroup, PageFrame, Shape, Spinner, TextBox

See Also

Activate Event, Deactivate Event

UndoCheckOut Method

Discards any changes made to a file and checks the file back into source code control.

Syntax

Object.UndoCheckOut( )

Remarks

True (.T.) is returned if the changes to the file are successfully discarded and the file is checked back into source code control; otherwise a false (.F.) is returned.

Applies To

File Object

See Also

AddToSCC Method, CheckIn Method, CheckOut Method, GetLatestVersion Method, RemoveFromSCC Method

UnDock Event

Occurs when the toolbar is dragged from its docked position.

Syntax

PROCEDURE *ToolBar*.Undock
[LPARAMETERS *nIndex*]

Arguments

nIndex
Uniquely identifies a control if it is in a control array.

Applies To

ToolBar

See Also

AfterDock Event, BeforeDock Event, Dock Method

UNIQUE( ) Function

Included for compatibility with dBASE.

_UNIX System Variable

Contains true (.T.) if you are using FoxPro for UNIX.

Syntax

_UNIX = *lExpression*

Remarks

The _UNIX system variable contains true (.T.) if you are using FoxPro for UNIX. _UNIX contains false (.F.) if you are using a different platform version of FoxPro or Visual FoxPro.

The value contained in _UNIX cannot be changed with STORE or =.

See Also

_DOS, _MAC, VERSION( ), _WINDOWS

Unload Event

Occurs when an object is released.

Syntax

PROCEDURE *Object*.Unload
[LPARAMETERS *nIndex*]

Arguments

nIndex
  Uniquely identifies a control if it is in a control array.

Remarks

The Unload event is the last event to occur before a form set or form is released. Unload occurs after the Destroy event and after all the contained objects have been released.

The occurrence of this event depends on the type of object:

- Form objects are released in code when the object variable that refers to the form is released or when its form set is released.

- form set objects are released in code when the object variable that refers to the form set is released.

If a container object, such as a form set, contains objects, the Unload event for the container object occurs after the Unload events for the objects it contains. For example, a form set containing one form that contains one control (a CommandButton) is released in this order:

1. FormSet's Destroy event

2. Form's Destroy event

3. CommandButton's Destroy event

4. Form's Unload event

5. FormSet's Unload event

Applies To

Form, FormSet

See Also

Destroy Event

UNLOCK Command

Releases a record lock, multiple record locks, or a file lock from a table, or releases all record and file locks from all open tables.

Syntax

UNLOCK
    [RECORD *nRecordNumber*]
    [IN *nWorkArea* | *cTableAlias*]
    [ALL]

Arguments

RECORD *nRecordNumber*
    Releases the record lock on record number *nRecordNumber*. You can specify 0 for *nRecordNumber* to unlock a table header locked with LOCK(0) or RLOCK(0).

    Issuing UNLOCK RECORD *nRecordNumber* for a record in a table with a file lock releases the file lock.

IN *nWorkArea* | *cTableAlias*
    Releases a record lock (or locks) or a file lock from a table in a specific work area. *nWorkArea* specifies a work area number and *cTableAlias* specifies a table alias. If you don't include *nWorkArea* or *cTableAlias*, UNLOCK releases a record lock (or locks) or a file lock from the table in the currently selected work area.

ALL
    Releases all record and file locks in all work areas.

For more information about record and file locking and sharing tables on a network, see Chapter 17, "Programming for Shared Access," in the *Microsoft Visual FoxPro 6.0 Programmer's Guide*.

Remarks

Record and file locks can be removed from a table only by the user who issued the locks. UNLOCK cannot unlock a table opened for exclusive use.

A record lock (or locks) or a file lock is released from the table in the current work area if you issue UNLOCK without any additional arguments.

If relations are established between tables, releasing a record lock (or locks) or a file lock from one of the tables doesn't release locks from the related records or files. You must explicitly release the record or file locks in each of the related files. You can release all locks on any related tables by issuing UNLOCK ALL (this also releases locks in unrelated files).

Example

```
CLOSE DATABASES
SET REPROCESS TO 3 AUTOMATIC
STORE '1,2,3,4' TO gcRecList      && Lock records 1 through 4
gcOldExc = SET('EXCLUSIVE')       && Save the EXCLUSIVE setting
SET EXCLUSIVE OFF  && Allow sharing of tables

CLOSE DATABASES
OPEN DATABASE (HOME(2) + 'Data\testdata')
USE customer  && Opens Customer table
SELECT 0
USE employee  && Opens Employee table

? LOCK('1,2,3,4', 'customer')  && Lock the first 4 records in customer
? RLOCK(gcRecList, 'employee') && Lock the first 4 records in employee

UNLOCK IN customer
UNLOCK IN employee
SET EXCLUSIVE &gcOldExc  && Restore original EXCLUSIVE setting
```

See Also

FLOCK( ), LOCK( ), RLOCK( )

UpClick Event

Occurs when the up arrow on a control is clicked.

Syntax

PROCEDURE *Control*.UpClick
[LPARAMETERS *nIndex*]

Arguments

nIndex
> Uniquely identifies a control if it is in a control array.

Applies To

ComboBox, Spinner

See Also

DownClick Event

UPDATE – SQL Command

Updates records in a table with new values.

Syntax

UPDATE [*DatabaseName1!*]*TableName1*
SET *Column_Name1 = eExpression1*
> [, *Column_Name2 = eExpression2* ...]
> WHERE *FilterCondition1* [AND | OR *FilterCondition2* ...]]

Arguments

[*DatabaseName1!*]*TableName1*
> Specifies the table in which records are updated with new values.
>
> *DatabaseName1!* specifies the name of a non-current database containing the table. You must include the name of the database containing the table if the database is not the current one. Include the exclamation point (!) delimiter after the database name and before the table name.

SET *Column_Name1 = eExpression1*
> [, *Column_Name2 = eExpression2*]
> Specifies the columns that are updated and their new values. If you omit the WHERE clause, every row in the column is updated with the same value.

WHERE *FilterCondition1* [AND | OR *FilterCondition2* ...]]
> Specifies the records that are updated with new values.
>
> *FilterCondition* specifies the criteria that records must meet to be updated with new values. You can include as many filter conditions as you like, connecting them with the AND or OR operator. You can also use the NOT operator to reverse the value of a logical expression, or use EMPTY( ) to check for an empty field.

Remarks

UPDATE – SQL can only update records in a single table. Note that subqueries are supported in UPDATE – SQL.

Unlike REPLACE, UPDATE – SQL uses record locking when updating multiple records in a table opened for shared access. This reduces record contention in multiuser situations, but may reduce performance. For maximum performance, open the table for exclusive use or use FLOCK( ) to lock the table.

Example

The following example opens the customer table in the testdata database. UPDATE – SQL is used to set all of the values in the maxordamt field to 25.

```
CLOSE DATABASES

OPEN DATABASE (HOME(2) + 'Data\testdata')
USE Customer        && Open customer table

* Set and display amounts for customers
UPDATE customer SET maxordamt = 25
BROWSE FIELDS company,maxordamt
```

See Also

DELETE – SQL, GATHER, INSERT – SQL, REPLACE, SCATTER

UPDATE Command

Included for backward compatibility. Use UPDATE – SQL instead.

UPDATED( ) Function

Included for backward compatibility. Use the InteractiveChange or ProgrammaticChange events instead.

UPPER( ) Function

Returns the specified character expression in uppercase.

Syntax

UPPER(*cExpression*)

Returns

Character

Arguments

cExpression
    Specifies the character expression UPPER( ) converts to uppercase.

Remarks

Each lowercase letter (a–z) in the character expression is converted to uppercase (A–Z) in the returned string. All other characters remain unchanged.

Example

```
CLEAR
? UPPER('abcdefgh')  && Displays ABCDEFGH
```

See Also

ISLOWER( ), ISUPPER( ), LOWER( )

USE Command

Opens a table and its associated index files, or a SQL view.

Syntax

USE [[*DatabaseName!*]*Table* | *SQLViewName* | ?]
    [IN *nWorkArea* | *cTableAlias*]
    [ONLINE]
    [ADMIN]
    [AGAIN]
    [NOREQUERY [*nDataSessionNumber*]]
    [NODATA]
    [INDEX *IndexFileList* | ?
    [ORDER [*nIndexNumber* | *IDXFileName*
    | [TAG] *TagName* [OF *CDXFileName*]
        [ASCENDING | DESCENDING]]]]]
    [ALIAS *cTableAlias*]
    [EXCLUSIVE]
    [SHARED]
    [NOUPDATE]

Arguments

[*DatabaseName!*]*TableName*
    Specifies the name of the table to open. Because spaces are significant in file names in Microsoft Windows 95 and Windows NT, avoid using extraneous spaces in *TableName*. If a table name contains spaces, enclose the table name in quotation marks (" " or ' ').

    To open a table not in the current database, qualify the table name with the database name, using an exclamation point (!) to separate the database and tables names. If you don't qualify a table with a database name, Microsoft Visual FoxPro can open tables only in the current database. If the database name or table name or both contains spaces, enclose the database and table name in quotation marks (" " or ' ').

SQLViewName

Specifies the name of a SQL view in the current database to open. A SQL view is created with CREATE SQL VIEW. *SQLViewName* can also be the name of an offline view created with CREATEOFFLINE( ).

?

Displays the Use dialog, from which you can choose a table to open.

IN *nWorkArea*

Specifies the work area in which the table is opened. You can close a table in a specific work area by issuing USE with the IN clause and the work area number.

The IN clause supports 0 as a work area. Including 0 opens a table in the lowest available work area. For example, if tables are open in work areas 1 through 10, the following command opens the customer table in work area 11:

```
USE customer IN 0
```

IN *cTableAlias*

Specifies that the table is opened in the work area of a table that is currently open. The alias of the open table is specified with *cTableAlias*.

If you omit *nWorkArea* and *cTableAlias*, the table is opened in the currently selected work area.

ONLINE

Opens an offline view created with CREATEOFFLINE( ). Specify the name of the offline view in *SQLViewName*. Use TABLEUPDATE( ) to update data on the server.

The offline view must be opened exclusively. Include the EXCLUSIVE clause in USE or SET EXCLUSIVE to ON before opening the offline view with USE.

ADMIN

Opens an offline view created with CREATEOFFLINE( ), but does not update the data on the server with the changes made to the offline view. Opening an offline view with the ADMIN keyword allows you to make changes to the offline view without updating the data on the server.

AGAIN

To open a table concurrently in multiple work areas, you can do one of the following:

- Select another work area and issue USE with the table name and the AGAIN clause.

- Issue USE with the table name and the AGAIN clause, and specify a different work area with the IN clause.

When you open a table again in another work area, the table in the new work area takes on the attributes of the table in the original work area. For example, if a table is opened for read-only or exclusive access and is opened again in another work area, the table is opened for read-only or exclusive access in the new work area.

Index files opened for the original table are available for the table you open again if you don't open indexes when you open the table again. The index order is set to 0 in the work areas where the table is opened again.

You can open indexes that weren't opened with the original table. This sets the index order to 0 for the original table.

A table opened again is assigned the default alias of the work area. You can include an alias every time you open a table in multiple work areas as long as the aliases are unique.

In Visual FoxPro for Windows, opening a table again in another work area doesn't consume an additional file handle.

NOREQUERY [*nDataSessionNumber*]

Specifies that data from a remote SQL view is not downloaded again. NOREQUERY is available only for SQL views and is typically used when you open a SQL view again by including the AGAIN clause. Including the NOREQUERY clause increases performance for large data sets because the data does not need to be downloaded again.

nDataSessionNumber can be included to specify that data for a remote SQL view in a specific data session isn't downloaded again. If *nDataSessionNumber* is omitted, data isn't downloaded for the view open in the current data session.

For additional information about the NOREQUERY clause, see Chapter 8, "Creating Views," in the *Microsoft Visual FoxPro 6.0 Programmer's Guide*.

NODATA

Specifies that only the structure of a SQL view is downloaded. The SQL view's data isn't downloaded. NODATA provides the fastest method for determining a SQL view's structure.

For additional information about the NODATA clause, see Chapter 8, "Creating Views," in the *Microsoft Visual FoxPro 6.0 Programmer's Guide*.

INDEX *IndexFileList*

Specifies a set of indexes to open with the table. If a table has a structural compound index file, the index file is automatically opened with the table.

IndexFileList can contain any combination of names of single-entry .idx and compound .cdx index files. You don't have to include the file name extensions for index files unless an .idx and a .cdx index file in the index file list have the same name.

The first index file named in the index file list is the master controlling index file, which controls how records in the table are accessed and displayed. However, if the first index file is a .cdx compound index file, records in the table are displayed and accessed in physical record order.

INDEX ?

Displays the Open dialog with a list of available index files to choose from.

ORDER [*nIndexNumber*]

Specifies a master controlling single-entry .idx index file or compound .cdx index file tag other than the first index file or index tag specified in *IndexFileList*.

.Idx index files are numbered first, in the order in which they appear in the index file list. Tags in the structural compound index file (if one exists) are then numbered in the order in which the tags were created. Finally, tags in any independent compound index files are numbered in the order in which they were created. You can also use SET ORDER to specify the controlling index file or tag. See the SET ORDER Command, earlier in this language reference, for a further discussion of the numbering of index files and tags.

If *nIndexNumber* is 0, records in the table are displayed and accessed in physical record order, and the indexes remain open. Including ORDER 0 enables open index files to be updated while presenting the file in record number order. Including ORDER without *nIndexNumber* is identical to including ORDER 0.

ORDER [*IDXFileName*]

Specifies a single-entry .idx index file as the master controlling index file.

ORDER [TAG *TagName*] [OF *CDXFileName*]

Specifies a master controlling tag in a compound .cdx index file. The tag name can be from the structural compound index file or any open compound index file. If identical tag names exist in open compound index files, include OF *CDXFileName* and specify the name of the compound index file containing the desired tag.

ASCENDING

Specifies that the table records are accessed and displayed in ascending order.

DESCENDING

Specifies that the table records are accessed and displayed in descending order.

Including ASCENDING or DESCENDING doesn't change the index file or tag; it alters only the order in which records are displayed and accessed.

ALIAS *cTableAlias*

Creates an alias for the table. You can refer to a table by its alias in commands and functions that require or support an alias.

When a table is opened, it is automatically assigned an alias, which is the table name if ALIAS isn't included. You can create a different alias for the table by including ALIAS and a new alias. In Visual FoxPro, an alias can contain up to 254 letters, digits or underscores and must begin with a letter or an underscore. In other FoxPro versions, an alias can contain up to 10 letters, digits or underscores and must begin with a letter or an underscore.

A default alias is assigned automatically if you use AGAIN to open a single table simultaneously in multiple work areas and you don't specify an alias when you open the table in each work area.

A default alias is also assigned if a conflict occurs. For example:

```
CLOSE DATABASES
OPEN DATABASE (HOME(2) + 'Data\testdata')
ACTIVATE WINDOW View  && Open the Data Session Window
USE customer ALIAS orders IN 1     && Alias is ORDERS
USE orders IN 3     && Conflict; alias is C
```

EXCLUSIVE

Opens a table for exclusive use on a network. For more information on the exclusive use of tables, see the SET EXCLUSIVE Command, earlier in this language reference.

SHARED

Opens a table for shared use on a network. SHARED allows you to open a table for shared use even when EXCLUSIVE is set ON.

NOUPDATE

Prevents changes to the table and its structure.

Remarks

If USE is issued without a table name and a table file is open in the currently selected work area, the table is closed. Also, a table is closed when another table is opened in the same work area. You can't have more than one table open in a work area at one time.

Example

The following example opens three tables in three different work areas. The Data Session window is opened to show where the tables are open and to show the alias for each table.

```
CLOSE DATABASES
OPEN DATABASE (HOME(2) + 'Data\testdata')
ACTIVATE WINDOW View

USE customer IN 0  && Opens Customer table
USE employee IN 0  && Opens Employee table
USE products IN 0  && Opens Products table
```

See Also

CREATE, CREATE SQL VIEW, CREATE TABLE – SQL, CREATEOFFLINE( ), DBF( ), INDEX, USED( )

USED( ) Function

Determines if an alias is in use or a table is open in a specific work area.

Syntax

USED([*nWorkArea* | *cTableAlias*])

Returns

Logical

Arguments

nWorkArea | *cTableAlias*

Specifies a table's work area or alias. USED( ) returns a logical true (.T.) if a table is opened in the work area you specify with *nWorkArea*; otherwise a logical false (.F.) is returned. USED( ) returns a logical true (.T.) if an alias is in use with the alias you specify with *cTableAlias*; otherwise false (.F.) is returned.

If you omit *nWorkArea* and *cTableAlias*, USED( ) returns a logical true (.T.) if a table is open in the currently selected work; otherwise false (.F.) is returned.

Remarks

USED( ) can determine if an alias is in use or if a table is open in a specific work area.

Example

```
CLOSE DATABASES
OPEN DATABASE (HOME(2) + 'Data\testdata')
SELECT A
USE customer  && Opens Customer table
SELECT B
USE orders  && Opens Orders table
SELECT C
USE employee  && Opens Employee table
? USED('A')  && Displays .T.
? USED('B')  && Displays .T.
? USED(4)  && Displays .F.
```

See Also

ALIAS( ), SELECT( )

VAL( ) Function

Returns a numeric value from a character expression composed of numbers.

Syntax

VAL(*cExpression*)

Returns

Numeric

Arguments

cExpression
> Specifies a character expression composed of up to 16 numbers. Rounding occurs if more than 16 numbers are included in *cExpression*.

Remarks

VAL( ) returns the numbers in the character expression from left to right until a non-numeric character is encountered (leading blanks are ignored). VAL( ) returns 0 if the first character of the character expression isn't a number or a plus sign (+) or minus sign (–).

VAL( ) can be used to convert the character strings returned by the Visual FoxPro SYS( ) functions to numeric values.

Example

```
CLEAR
STORE '12' TO A
STORE '13' TO B
? VAL(A) + VAL(B)  && Displays 25.00
STORE '1.25E3' TO C
? 2 * VAL(C)  && Displays 2500.00
```

See Also

SET DECIMALS, STR( )

VARTYPE( ) Function

Returns the data type of an expression.

Syntax

VARTYPE(*eExpression* [, *lNullDataType*])

Returns

Character

Arguments

eExpression

Specifies the expression for which the data type is returned. VARTYPE( ) returns a single character indicating the data type of the expression. The following table lists the characters that VARTYPE( ) returns for each data type:

Character returned	Data type
C	Character or Memo
N	Numeric, Integer, Float, or Double
Y	Currency
L	Logical
O	Object
G	General
D	Date
T	DateTime
X	Null
U	Unknown

Note If *eExpression* is an array, the first element in the array is evaluated.

lNullDataType

Specifies if VARTYPE( ) returns the data type when *eExpression* contains the null value. If lNullDataType is true (.T.), VARTYPE( ) returns the data type of *eExpression*. If lNullDataType is false (.F.) or omitted, VARTYPE( ) returns 'X', indicating that *eExpression* contains the null value.

Remarks

VARTYPE( ) is similar to the TYPE( ) function, but VARTYPE( ) is faster and does not require quotation marks to enclose the expression for which the data type is returned.

VARTYPE( ) returns "U" if you specify a variable, field, object, or object property that doesn't exist. If there is no current active form, evaluating the ActiveForm property generates an OLE IDispatch error.

See Also

EVALUATE( ), TYPE( )

Valid Event

Occurs before a control loses the focus.

Syntax

PROCEDURE *Control*.Valid
[LPARAMETERS *nIndex*]

Arguments

nIndex
Uniquely identifies a control if it is in a control array.

Remarks

If the Valid event returns true (.T.), the control loses focus. If the Valid event returns false (.F.), the control does not lose focus.

The Valid event can also return a numeric value. Returning a numeric value has one of three effects:

- If 0 is returned, the control does not lose focus.

- If a positive value is returned, the value specifies the number of controls the focus advances. For example, if the Valid event returns 1, the next control gets the focus.

- If a negative value is returned, the value specifies the number of controls the focus moves back. For example, if the Valid event returns –1, the previous control gets the focus.

Applies To

CheckBox, ComboBox, CommandButton, CommandGroup, EditBox, Grid, ListBox, OptionButton, OptionGroup, Spinner, TextBox

See Also

LostFocus Event, When Event

VALIDATE DATABASE Command

Ensures that the locations of tables and indexes in the current database are correct.

Syntax

VALIDATE DATABASE
    [RECOVER]
    [NOCONSOLE]
    [TO PRINTER [PROMPT] | TO FILE *FileName*]

Arguments

RECOVER

> Displays dialogs that allow you to locate tables and indexes that are not in the locations contained in the database. VALIDATE DATABASE RECOVER must be issued in the Command window; issuing VALIDATE DATABASE RECOVER within a program generates an error message.

NOCONSOLE

> Suppresses error message output to the main Visual FoxPro window or to the active user-defined window.

TO PRINTER [PROMPT]

> Directs error message output from VALIDATE DATABASE to a printer.

> PROMPT displays a Print dialog box before printing starts. Place the PROMPT keyword immediately after TO PRINTER.

TO FILE *FileName*

> Directs error message output to the file specified with *FileName*. If the file already exists and SET SAFETY is ON, you are asked if you want to overwrite the file.

Remarks

VALIDATE DATABASE ensures that the database contains the proper locations of tables and indexes, that tables in the database contain the proper fields, and that index tags in the database exist.

VALIDATE DATABASE operates on the current database. The database must be opened for exclusive use by including the EXCLUSIVE keyword when you issue OPEN DATABASE.

Example

The following example opens the `testdata` database and uses VALIDATE DATABASE to ensure that the locations of tables and indexes in the database are correct.

```
CLOSE DATABASES
SET PATH TO (HOME(2) + 'Data\') && Sets path to database
OPEN DATABASE testdata EXCLUSIVE && Open testdata database

VALIDATE DATABASE
```

See Also

CREATE DATABASE, MODIFY DATABASE, OPEN DATABASE, USE

Value Property

Specifies the current state of a control. Available at design time and run time. Read-only for ComboBox and ListBox controls.

Syntax

[*Form.*]*Control.*Value[= *nSetting*]

Arguments

nSetting

For a CheckBox control, the settings for the Value property are:

Setting	Description
0	(Default) Unchecked.
1	Checked.
2	Mixed-value. This setting is only available in code.

For CommandGroup, ComboBox, EditBox, ListBox, OptionGroup, and Spinner controls, the setting for the Value property is the character string or numeric value that is currently selected.

For an OptionButton control, the settings for the Value property are:

Setting	Description
0	(Default) Indicates the button isn't selected.
1	Indicates the button is selected.

For a TextBox control, the setting for the Value property is the character string or numeric, date, datetime, currency, or logical value that is currently selected. The default setting is a character string.

Remarks

For the Grid control, the Value property is available only when the Grid control has the focus.

The Value property of a CommandGroup or OptionGroup control can be used to determine which button in the group caused an event. It is set to an integer that indicates which button in the group caused the event.

The Value property changes behavior when a control source is set for a control. When a control source is set, the Value property setting of a control is the data type of the variable or field referenced by the ControlSource property. If the data type is not valid for the given control, Visual FoxPro generates an error.

The following is a list of valid data types:

Control	Data Types allowed
CheckBox	Integer, Logical, Numeric
ComboBox	Character, Integer, Numeric
CommandGroup	Character, Integer, Numeric
EditBox	Character, Memo
Grid	Character, Numeric
ListBox	Character, Integer, Numeric
OptionButton	Integer, Logical, Numeric
OptionGroup	Character, Integer, Numeric
Spinner	Currency, Integer, Numeric
TextBox	Any data type

Applies To

CheckBox, ComboBox, CommandGroup, EditBox, Grid, ListBox, OptionButton, OptionGroup, Spinner, TextBox

See Also

Bound Property, ListIndex Property

VARREAD( ) Function

Included for backward compatibility in Visual FoxPro. Use the ControlSource or Name properties instead.

VERSION( ) Function

Returns information about the Visual FoxPro version you are using.

Syntax

VERSION(*nExpression*)

Returns

Character, Numeric

Arguments

nExpression

Specifies that VERSION( ) returns additional information about Visual FoxPro.
If you omit *nExpression*, VERSION( ) returns the Visual FoxPro version number.

The following table lists values for *nExpression* and the additional Visual FoxPro
information returned.

nExpression	Additional Visual FoxPro information returned
1	Visual FoxPro date and serial number.
2	Visual FoxPro version type: 0 – Run time version 1 – Standard Edition (earlier versions) 2 – Professional Edition (earlier versions)
3	Localized Visual FoxPro language. The following two character values indicate the language for which Visual FoxPro is localized: 00 – English 33 – French 34 – Spanish 39 – Italian 42 – Czech 48 – Polish 49 – German 55 – Portuguese 82 – Korean 86 – Simplified Chinese 88 – Traditional Chinese
4	The Visual FoxPro version number in a standard, easily parsed format. The standard format is "MM.00.YDDD.mm" where MM is the major release number, 00 is a fixed placeholder, YDDD is the four digit product date for the day the version was created, and mm is the incremental minor revision number. For the product date YDDD, Y is the year number in the 1990 decade, and DDD is the day number for that year. For example, 8001 corresponds to January 1, 1998.
5	The Visual FoxPro release version in the format "Mmm" where M is the major release number and mm is the incremental minor revision number. For example, VERSION(5) returns "600" in Visual FoxPro 6.0.

Remarks

Use VERSION( ) to conditionally execute version-specific portions of code.

VERSION( ), VERSION(1), VERSION(3), and VERSION(4) return character strings;
VERSION(2) returns a numeric value.

Example

```
CLEAR
? VERSION( )
? VERSION(1)
? VERSION(2)
? VERSION(3)
? VERSION(4)
? VERSION(5)
```

See Also

GETCP( ), GETENV( ), OS( )

Version Property

Returns the version number of an instance of Visual FoxPro as a character string. Read-only at run time.

Syntax

ApplicationObject.Version

Applies To

Application Object, _VFP System Variable

See Also

VERSION( )

VersionComments Property

The comments for a project.

Syntax

Object.VersionComments[= *cComments*]

Arguments

cComments
    Specifies the comments for a project. The default value is the empty string.

Remarks

The VersionComments property corresponds to the value of the **Comments** item in the EXE Version dialog box.

Applies To

Project Object

See Also

AGETFILEVERSION( ), VersionCompany Property, VersionCopyright Property, VersionDescription Property, VersionLanguage Property, VersionNumber Property, VersionProduct Property, VersionTrademarks Property

VersionCompany Property

The company name information for a project.

Syntax

Object.VersionCompany[= *cCompanyName*]

Arguments

cCompanyName
Specifies the company name information for a project. The default value is the empty string.

Remarks

The VersionCompany property corresponds to the value of the **Company Name** item in the EXE Version dialog box.

Applies To

Project Object

See Also

AGETFILEVERSION( ), VersionComments Property, VersionCopyright Property, VersionDescription Property, VersionLanguage Property, VersionNumber Property, VersionProduct Property, VersionTrademarks Property

VersionCopyright Property

The copyright information for a project.

Syntax

Object.VersionCopyright[= *cCopyRight*]

Arguments

cCopyRight
Specifies the copyright information for a project. The default value is the empty string.

Remarks

The VersionCopyRight property corresponds to the value of the **Legal Copyright** item in the EXE Version dialog box.

Applies To

Project Object

See Also

AGETFILEVERSION( ), VersionComments Property, VersionCompany Property, VersionDescription Property, VersionLanguage Property, VersionNumber Property, VersionProduct Property, VersionTrademarks Property

VersionDescription Property

The description for a project.

Syntax

Object.VersionDescription[= *cDescription*]

Arguments

cDescription
    Specifies the description for a project. The default value is the empty string.

Remarks

The VersionDescription property corresponds to the value of the **File Description** item in the EXE Version dialog box.

Applies To

Project Object

See Also

AGETFILEVERSION( ), VersionComments Property, VersionCompany Property, VersionCopyright Property, VersionLanguage Property, VersionNumber Property, VersionProduct Property, VersionTrademarks Property

VersionLanguage Property

The language information for a project.

Syntax

Object.VersionLanguage[= *nLanguage*]

Arguments

nLanguage
    Specifies the language ID for a project. FOXPRO.H contains a listing of the values for the primary and sub-language IDs that can be combined to create a valid language ID.

For example, the following code sets the VersionLanguage to United States English
(0x09 specifies English, 0x0400 specifies United States English) for the current
project:

```
Application.ActiveProject.VersionLanguage = 0x09 + 0x0400
```

Remarks

The VersionLanguage property corresponds to the value of the **Language ID** item in
the EXE Version dialog box.

Applies To

Project Object

See Also

AGETFILEVERSION( ), VersionComments Property, VersionCompany Property,
VersionCopyright Property, VersionDescription Property, VersionNumber Property,
VersionProduct Property, VersionTrademarks Property

VersionNumber Property

The build number for a project.

Syntax

Object.VersionNumber[= *cBuildNumber*]

Arguments

cBuildNumber
   Specifies a build number for a project. The standard format for a project build number
   is "MMMM.mmmm.bbbb" where MMMM is the major build number, mmmm is
   the minor build number, and bbbb is the build number. Separate each component
   of a project build number with a period (.). Each build number can be zero to four
   digits (numbers). Do not use letters in the build number. You can specify ".." for
   cBuildNumber to reset both the minor build number and the build number to zero.

   If the AutoIncrement property is set to true (.T.) and you build an executable (.exe)
   or dynamic link library (.dll) from the project, the build number has leading zeros
   removed from last portion (".bbbb") of the build number.

   The default value is the empty string.

Remarks

The VersionNumber property corresponds to the values of **Version Number** items in
the EXE Version dialog box.

Applies To

Project Object

See Also

AGETFILEVERSION( ), VersionComments Property, VersionCompany Property, VersionCopyright Property, VersionDescription Property, VersionLanguage Property, VersionProduct Property, VersionTrademarks Property

VersionProduct Property

The product name information for a project.

Syntax

Object.VersionProduct[= *cProductName*]

Arguments

cProductName
Specifies the product name information for a project. The default value is the empty string.

Remarks

The VersionProduct property corresponds to the value of the **Product Name** item in the EXE Version dialog box.

Applies To

Project Object

See Also

AGETFILEVERSION( ), VersionComments Property, VersionCompany Property, VersionCopyright Property, VersionDescription Property, VersionLanguage Property, VersionNumber Property, VersionTrademarks Property

VersionTrademarks Property

The trademarks information for a project.

Syntax

Object.VersionTrademarks[= *cTradeMarks*]

Arguments

cTradeMarks
Specifies the trademarks information for a project. The default value is the empty string.

Remarks

The VersionTrademarks property corresponds to the value of the **Legal Trademarks** item in the EXE Version dialog box.

Applies To

Project Object

See Also

AGETFILEVERSION( ), VersionComments Property, VersionCompany Property, VersionCopyright Property, VersionDescription Property, VersionLanguage Property, VersionNumber Property, VersionProduct Property

_VFP System Variable

References the Application object for the current instance of Visual FoxPro.

Syntax

_VFP.*PropertyName*[= *eValue*]

– or –

_VFP.*Method*

Arguments

PropertyName
    Specifies a property for the application object.

eValue
    Specifies a value for the property.

Method
    Specifies a method to execute for the application object.

Remarks

_VFP provides access to the Objects collection.

Properties

ActiveForm	Application	AutoYield
Caption	DefaultFilePath	Forms
FullName	Height	Left
Name	OLERequestPendingTimeout	OLEServerBusyRaiseError
OLEServerBusyTimeout	Parent	StartMode
StatusBar	Top	Version
Visible	Width	

Methods

DataToClip	DoCmd	Eval
Help	Quit	RequestData
SetVar		

See Also

Application Object, CREATEOBJECT( )

View Property

Specifies the type of view for a Grid control. Available at design time; read/write at run time.

Syntax

Grid.View[= *nType*]

Arguments

nType
   If the panes are not split (the Partition property is set to 0), the settings for the View property are:

Setting	Description
0	Browse
1	Change

If the panes are split, the settings for the View property are:

Setting	Description
0	Browse (left pane), Browse (right pane)
1	Browse (left pane), Change (right pane)
2	Change (left pane), Browse (right pane)
3	Change (left pane), Change (right pane)

Applies To

Grid

See Also

Panel Property, PanelLink Property, Partition Property

ViewPortHeight Property

Contains the viewport height for a form. Read-only at design time and run time.

Syntax

Object.ViewPortHeight

Remarks

The viewport is the rectangular area of a form displayed in the form's container. The form container controls the size of the viewport. If you change the size of a form's container, the viewport also changes size.

The viewport properties and methods are typically used for forms in Active Documents. If an Active Document displays a form that has scroll bars, the scroll bars are displayed on the form when the viewport size is smaller than the size of a rectangle enclosing the controls on the form.

The unit of measurement for the viewport height is determined by the form's ScaleMode property setting — pixels (the default) or foxels.

Applies To

Form Object

See Also

ScaleMode Property, SetViewPort Method, ViewPortLeft Property, ViewPortTop Property, ViewPortWidth Property

ViewPortLeft Property

Contains the left coordinate of the form that is visible in the viewport. Read-only at design time and run time.

Syntax

Object.ViewPortLeft

Remarks

The viewport is the rectangular area of a form displayed in the form's container. The form container controls the size of the viewport. If you change the size of a form's container, the viewport also changes size.

The viewport properties and methods are typically used for forms in Active Documents. If an Active Document displays a form that has scroll bars, the scroll bars are displayed on the form when the viewport size is smaller than the size of a rectangle enclosing the controls on the form.

Use the SetViewPort method to set the left and top coordinates of a form in an Active Document at run time.

The unit of measurement for the left coordinate of the form is determined by the form's ScaleMode property setting — pixels (the default) or foxels.

Applies To

Form Object

See Also

ScaleMode Property, SetViewPort Method, ViewPortHeight Property, ViewPortTop Property, ViewPortWidth Property

ViewPortTop Property

Contains the top coordinate of the form that is visible in the viewport. Read-only at design time and run time.

Syntax

Object.ViewPortTop

Remarks

The viewport is the rectangular area of a form displayed in the form's container. The form container controls the size of the viewport. If you change the size of a form's container, the viewport also changes size.

The viewport properties and methods are typically used for forms in Active Documents. If an Active Document displays a form that has scroll bars, the scroll bars are displayed on the form when the viewport size is smaller than the size of a rectangle enclosing the controls on the form.

Use the SetViewPort method to set the top and left coordinates of a form in an Active Document at run time.

The unit of measurement for the top coordinate of the form is determined by the form's ScaleMode property setting — pixels (the default) or foxels.

Applies To

Form Object

See Also

ScaleMode Property, SetViewPort Method, ViewPortHeight Property, ViewPortLeft Property, ViewPortWidth Property

ViewPortWidth Property

Contains the viewport width for a form. Read-only at design time and run time.

Syntax

Object.ViewPortWidth

Remarks

The viewport is the rectangular area of a form displayed in the form's container. The form container controls the size of the viewport. If you change the size of a form's container, the viewport also changes size.

The viewport properties and methods are typically used for forms in Active Documents. If an Active Document displays a form that has scroll bars, the scroll bars are displayed on the form when the viewport size is smaller than the size of a rectangle enclosing the controls on the form.

The unit of measurement for the viewport width is determined by the form's ScaleMode property setting — pixels (the default) or foxels.

Applies To

Form Object

See Also

ScaleMode Property, SetViewPort Method, ViewPortHeight Property, ViewPortLeft Property, ViewPortTop Property

Visible Property

Specifies whether an object is visible or hidden. Available at design time and run time.

Syntax

Object.Visible[= *lExpr*]

Arguments

lExpr
  The settings for the Visible property are:

Setting	Description
True (.T.)	The default in the Form Designer. The object is visible.
False (.F.)	The default in program code. The object is hidden.

Remarks

Setting the Visible property for the _SCREEN system variable has no effect in Visual FoxPro for Windows.

Even if the object is hidden, it can still be accessed in code.

To hide an object at startup, set the Visible property to false (.F.) at design time. If you set the Visible property in code, you can hide an object and display it at run time in response to a particular event.

When a form's Visible property is set to false (.F.), the form is hidden and the last-active form set, form, or other object becomes active. When a form's Visible property is set to true (.T.), the form becomes visible. Setting a form's Visible property to true (.T.) does not affect the form's Order property setting. The form does not become active when Visible is set to true (.T.). Use the Show method to activate a form and make it visible in the same step.

> **Note** If the Visible property of a form is set to false (.F.), the form isn't displayed, even if the form set's Visible property is set to true (.T.). However, if the form set's Visible property is set to false (.F.), all forms contained in the form set are invisible.

Example

The following example demonstrates how the Visible property is used to display controls after they have been added to a form with the AddObject method.

The AddObject method is used to add a Line control and three command buttons to the form. The Visible property is set to true (.T.) for the Line control and the command buttons, displaying them on the form. The Visible property is also used to hide the Line control before its slant direction is changed, and to display the Line control after its slant direction is changed.

```
frmMyForm = CREATEOBJECT('Form')  && Create a form
frmMyForm.Closable = .F.  && Disable the window pop-up menu

frmMyForm.AddObject('shpLine','Line')  && Add a Line control to the form
frmMyForm.AddObject('cmdCmndBtn1','cmdMyCmndBtn1')  && Up Cmnd button
frmMyForm.AddObject('cmdCmndBtn2','cmdMyCmndBtn2')  && Down Cmnd button
frmMyForm.AddObject('cmdCmndBtn3','cmdMyCmndBtn3')  && Quit Cmnd button

frmMyForm.shpLine.Visible = .T.  && Make Line control visible
frmMyForm.shpLine.Top = 20  && Specify Line control row
frmMyForm.shpLine.Left = 125  && Specify Line control column

frmMyForm.cmdCmndBtn1.Visible =.T.  && Up Command button visible
frmMyForm.cmdCmndBtn2.Visible =.T.  && Down" Command button visible
frmMyForm.cmdCmndBtn3.Visible =.T.  && Quit Command button visible
```

```
frmMyForm.SHOW  && Display the form
READ EVENTS  && Start event processing

DEFINE CLASS cmdMyCmndBtn1 AS COMMANDBUTTON  && Create Command button
   Caption = 'Slant \<Up'  && Caption on the Command button
   Left = 50  && Command button column
   Top = 100  && Command button row
   Height = 25  && Command button height

   PROCEDURE Click
      ThisForm.shpLine.Visible = .F.  && Hide the Line control
      ThisForm.shpLine.LineSlant ='/'  && Slant up
      ThisForm.shpLine.Visible = .T.  && Show the Line control
ENDDEFINE

DEFINE CLASS cmdMyCmndBtn2 AS CommandButton  && Create Command button
   Caption = 'Slant \<Down'  && Caption on the Command button
   Left = 200  && Command button column
   Top = 100  && Command button row
   Height = 25  && Command button height

   PROCEDURE Click
      ThisForm.shpLine.Visible = .F.  && Hide the Line control
      ThisForm.shpLine.LineSlant ='\'  && Slant down
      ThisForm.shpLine.Visible = .T.  && Show the Line control
ENDDEFINE

DEFINE CLASS cmdMyCmndBtn3 AS CommandButton  && Create Command button
   Caption = '\<Quit'  && Caption on the Command button
   Cancel = .T.  && Default Cancel Command button (Esc)
   Left = 125  && Command button column
   Top = 150  && Command button row
   Height = 25  && Command button height

   PROCEDURE Click
      CLEAR EVENTS  && Stop event processing, close form
ENDDEFINE
```

Applies To

CheckBox, Column, ComboBox, CommandButton, CommandGroup, Container Object, Control Object, EditBox, Form, FormSet, Grid, Image, Label, Line, ListBox, OLE Bound Control, OLE Container Control, OptionButton, OptionGroup, PageFrame, Project Object, _SCREEN, Shape, Spinner, TextBox, ToolBar

See Also

Show Method, ZOrder Method

VScrollSmallChange Property

Specifies the increment a form scrolls vertically when you click on a scroll arrow. Available at design time and run time.

Syntax

Object.VScrollSmallChange[= *nExpression*]

Arguments

nExpression

Specifies the increment for vertical scrolling. The unit of measure is determined by the Scalemode property setting. The default increment is 10 pixels when the Scalemode property is set to 3 – Pixels.

Applies To

Form

See Also

HScrollSmallChange Property, ScaleMode Property, ScrollBars Property

WAIT Command

Displays a message and pauses Microsoft Visual FoxPro execution until the user presses a key or click the mouse.

Syntax

WAIT
    [*cMessageText*]
    [TO *VarName*]
    [WINDOW [AT *nRow*, *nColumn*]]
    [NOWAIT]
    [CLEAR | NOCLEAR]
    [TIMEOUT *nSeconds*]

Arguments

cMessageText

Specifies a custom message to display. If you omit *cMessageText*, Visual FoxPro displays the default message. If *cMessageText* is an empty string (""), a message isn't displayed and Visual FoxPro waits until a key is pressed before continuing program execution.

TO *VarName*

Saves the key pressed to a variable or an array element. If the variable or an array element you specify with *VarName* doesn't exist, it is created. The empty string is stored in *VarName* if you press ENTER or a nonprintable key or key combination, or click the mouse.

WINDOW

Displays the message in a system message window located in the upper-right corner of the main Visual FoxPro window. The window can be temporarily hidden by pressing the CTRL or SHIFT key.

AT *nRow*, *nColumn*

In Visual FoxPro, specifies the position of the message window on the screen.

NOWAIT

Continues program execution immediately after the message is displayed. The program doesn't wait for the message to be removed from the main Visual FoxPro window, but continues executing on the program line immediately following the program line containing WAIT NOWAIT. If you omit NOWAIT, program execution pauses until the message is removed from the main Visual FoxPro window by pressing a key or clicking the mouse.

CLEAR

Removes a Visual FoxPro system window or a WAIT message window from the main Visual FoxPro window from within a program. For example, talk from indexing, sorting, and so on is directed to a Visual FoxPro system window if you issue SET TALK WINDOW. The window can be removed interactively if you press a key or move the mouse. Issue WAIT CLEAR to remove the window from within a program.

NOCLEAR

Specifies that a WAIT message window remains on the main Visual FoxPro window until WAIT CLEAR or another WAIT WINDOW command is issued, or a Visual FoxPro system message is displayed.

TIMEOUT *nSeconds*

Specifies the number of seconds that can elapse without input from the keyboard or the mouse before the WAIT is terminated. *nSeconds* specifies the number seconds (fractional seconds are permitted) that elapse. If TIMEOUT isn't the last clause in WAIT, Visual FoxPro generates a syntax error message.

Remarks

If a WAIT message is displayed in Visual FoxPro for Windows, pressing the SHIFT or CTRL keys hides all windows including the WAIT message.

See Also

ACCEPT

WBORDER( ) Function

Determines whether the active or specified window has a border.

Syntax

WBORDER([*WindowName*])

Returns

Logical

Arguments

WindowName

Specifies the name of the window for which WBORDER( ) returns a logical value.

WBORDER( ) returns a logical value for the active output window if you omit a window name.

Remarks

WBORDER( ) returns true (.T.) if the specified window has a border; otherwise WBORDER( ) returns false (.F.). By default, windows have borders. Include the NONE clause in DEFINE WINDOW to create a window without a border.

See Also

ACTIVATE WINDOW, DEFINE WINDOW

WCHILD( ) Function

Returns either the number of child windows in a parent window or the names of the child windows in the order in which they are stacked in the parent window.

Syntax

WCHILD([*WindowName*] [*nChildWindow*])

Returns

Character or Numeric

Arguments

WindowName

Specifies a window other than the active output window for which WCHILD( ) returns the number of child windows. The number of child windows in the specified window is returned if you include just a window name without the numeric expression *nChildWindow*.

If you include both *WindowName* and *nChildWindow*, WCHILD( ) returns the names of the child windows in the specified window. If you include both *WindowName* and *nChildWindow*, separate *WindowName* and *nChildWindow* with a comma.

You can also include the empty string in *WindowName* to specify the main Visual FoxPro window.

nChildWindow

Specifies a numeric expression included to return the names of child windows in the active output window when you omit *WindowName*.

The numeric expression *nChildWindow* can be 0 or any positive value. The name of the child window at the bottom of the stack of child windows in the current output window is returned if *nChildWindow* is 0.

If *nChildWindow* is a positive number, WCHILD( ) returns the name of the next child window in the window stack. The name of next child window in the stack is returned if you issue WCHILD( ) again with a positive number, and so on. The empty string is returned if WCHILD( ) is called more times than the number of child windows in the parent window. For more information on window stacking, see the ACTIVATE WINDOW Command, earlier in this language reference.

Note In Visual FoxPro for Windows, if the main Visual FoxPro window is active, all windows are children of the main Visual FoxPro window. In Visual FoxPro, toolbars that are not docked in the border of the main Visual FoxPro window are children of the main Visual FoxPro window. Issuing a series of WCHILD( ) functions with positive numbers returns the names of the active windows and toolbars.

If you include both *WindowName* and *nChildWindow*, separate *WindowName* and *nChildWindow* with a comma.

Remarks

You can create a window (the parent window) and place other windows (child windows) inside. Including the IN or IN WINDOW clause in DEFINE WINDOW creates a child window inside the parent window. A child window created and activated inside a parent window cannot be moved outside the parent window. If the parent window is moved, the child window moves with it.

The number of child windows in the active output window is returned if you issue WCHILD( ) without any arguments.

See Also

ACTIVATE WINDOW, DEFINE WINDOW, WPARENT( )

WCOLS( ) Function

Returns the number of columns within the active or specified window.

Syntax

WCOLS([*WindowName*])

Returns

Numeric

Arguments

WindowName

Specifies the window for which WCOLS( ) returns the number of columns. In Visual FoxPro, you can also specify the name of a toolbar. If you don't specify a window, the number of columns in the active output window is returned. If no window is active, WCOLS( ) returns the number of columns in the main Visual FoxPro window.

You can specify the name of a system window (the Command window, the Data Session window, a Browse window, and so on) in WCOLS( ) if the system window has been activated and is visible or hidden. In Visual FoxPro, you can specify the name of a toolbar (the Standard toolbar, the Color Palette toolbar, and so on) in WCOLS( ) if the toolbar has been activated and is visible or hidden. If you specify the name of a system window or toolbar that has not been activated, Visual FoxPro generates an error message. The Debug window is an exception. Once the Debug window has been opened, its name can be included in WCOLS( ) if it is visible, hidden or closed.

You can also include the empty string as the window name to return the number of columns in the main Visual FoxPro window.

The empty string can be used to specify the main Visual FoxPro window in functions such as WLCOL( ), WLROW( ), and WROWS( ), which return window locations or sizes.

Remarks

In Visual FoxPro, the value returned by WCOLS( ) depends on the font specified for the window. Many fonts can be displayed in a wide variety of sizes, and some are proportionally spaced. A column corresponds to the average width of a letter in the current font. For more information, see "Fonts Overview," earlier in this language reference.

Example

The following example centers a short output message in the last row of a window of unknown size.

```
CLEAR
DO SendMesg WITH 'Message', WCOLS( ), WROWS( ) -1

*** SendMesg ***

PROCEDURE SendMesg
PARAMETERS gcMsg, gnCol, gnRow
STORE (gnCol - LEN(gcMsg))/2 TO gnCol
@ gnRow, gnCol SAY gcMsg
RETURN
```

See Also

SCOLS( ), SROWS( ), WLCOL( ), WLROW( ), WROWS( )

WEEK( ) Function

Returns a number representing the week of the year from a Date or DateTime expression.

Syntax

WEEK(*dExpression* | *tExpression* [, *nFirstWeek*] [, *nFirstDayOfWeek*])

Returns

Numeric

Arguments

dExpression | *tExpression*

Specifies the Date or DateTime expression for which WEEK( ) returns the week of the year.

If you omit the optional *nFirstWeek* and *nFirstDayOfWeek* arguments, WEEK( ) uses Sunday as the first day of the week.

nFirstWeek

Specifies the requirements for the first week of the year. *nFirstWeek* may be one of the following values.

nFirstWeek	Description
0	WEEK( ) returns whatever week is currently selected in the First Week of Year list box on the International tab in the Options dialog box.
1	First week contains January 1st. This is the default when you omit *nFirstWeek*.
2	The larger half (four days) of the first week is in the current year.
3	First week has seven days.

nFirstDayOfWeek
> Specifies the first day of the week. *nFirstDayOfWeek* may be one of the following values.

nFirstDayOfWeek	Description
0	WEEK( ) returns whatever day is currently selected in the Week Starts on list box on the International tab in the Options dialog box.
1	Sunday. This is the default when you omit *nFirstDayOfWeek*, and is the first day of the week used in earlier FoxPro versions.
2	Monday
3	Tuesday
4	Wednesday
5	Thursday
6	Friday
7	Saturday

Remarks

WEEK( ) returns a number from 1 to 53 that represents the week of the year. For example, WEEK( ) returns 1 for the first week of the year, 2 for the second week of the year, and so on. Note that a week can be split between years — the first week of the year can be in the current year and the previous year.

Example

The following example displays the week of the year for today's date and for a specific date.

```
CLEAR
? WEEK(DATE( ))
? WEEK({^1998-02-16})  && Displays 8
```

See Also

CDOW( ), DAY( ), DOW( ), SET FDOW, SET FWEEK, SYS( ) Functions Overview

WEXIST( ) Function

Determines whether the specified user-defined window exists.

Syntax

WEXIST(*WindowName*)

Returns

Logical

Arguments

WindowName

Specifies the name of the user-defined window.

You can also specify the name of a Visual FoxPro system window (the Command window, the Data Session window, a Browse window, and so on), and in Visual FoxPro, the name of a toolbar. WEXIST( ) returns true (.T.) if the system window or toolbar you specify is visible or hidden. WEXIST( ) returns false (.F.) if the specified system window or toolbar is closed.

Two exceptions are the Command and Debug windows. Including the Command window's name in WEXIST( ) always returns a true value. If the Debug window has been opened, WEXIST( ) returns true, even if the Debug window is closed.

Remarks

WEXIST( ) returns true (.T.) if the user-defined window you specify has been created with DEFINE WINDOW; otherwise WEXIST( ) returns false (.F.). The specified window doesn't have to be active or visible for WEXIST( ) to return true (.T.), but it must exist.

Example

```
DEFINE WINDOW wScreen1 FROM 10,10 TO 20,69
DEFINE WINDOW wScreen2 FROM 1,0 TO 19,79
CLEAR

? WEXIST('wScreen1')  && Displays .T.
STORE 'wScreen2' TO gcWinName
? WEXIST('win_name')  && Displays .F.
? WEXIST(gcWinName)  && Displays .T.
RELEASE WINDOWS wScreen1, wScreen2
```

See Also

ACTIVATE WINDOW, DEFINE WINDOW, WONTOP( ), WOUTPUT( ), WVISIBLE( )

WFONT( ) Function

Returns the name, size, or style of the current font for a window in Visual FoxPro for Windows.

Syntax

WFONT(*nFontAttribute* [, *WindowName*])

Returns

Character and Numeric

Arguments

nFontAttribute

Specifies the font attribute you want to return.

If *nFontAttribute* is 1, WFONT( ) returns the name of the current font for the active or specified window.

If *nFontAttribute* is 2, WFONT( ) returns the font size.

If *nFontAttribute* is 3, WFONT( ) returns a code that identifies the font style.

The font style code is a character or set of characters that correspond to the current font style. For example, the current font style is Bold Italic if WFONT(3) returns BI.

The following table lists the codes for each font style:

Character	Font Style
B	Bold
I	Italic
N	Normal
O	Outline
Q	Opaque
S	Shadow
–	StrikeThru
T	Transparent
U	Underline

WindowName

Specifies the name of the window for which you want to determine the current font, font size, or font style. In Visual FoxPro, you can also include the name of a toolbar. Include the empty string to return the current font, font size, or font style for the main Visual FoxPro window.

WindowName can be the name of a user-defined window created with DEFINE WINDOW or a text- or memo-editing window.

You can also include the name of a system window (View, Trace, Debug, and so on). WFONT( ) can return font attributes only for a system window that has been opened and is currently visible or hidden. If the system window you specify is closed, Visual FoxPro generates an error message.

WFONT( ) returns the current font, font size or font style for the active output window if you omit *WindowName*.

Example

The following example creates a user-defined window called `wFontChar`. The window is activated and its font characteristics are displayed in the window. The font characteristics are then displayed for the main Visual FoxPro window.

```
CLEAR
DEFINE WINDOW wFontChar ;
    FROM 1,1 TO 3,35 ;
    FONT 'MS SANS SERIF',8 ;
    STYLE 'BI'  && Define window with font and style
ACTIVATE WINDOW wFontChar
? WFONT(1), WFONT(2), WFONT(3)  && wFontChar window
ACTIVATE SCREEN
?
?
?
? 'Font characteristics for the window wFontChar'
?
?
? WFONT(1,''), WFONT(2,''), WFONT(3,'')  && Main Visual FoxPro window
?
? 'Font characteristics for the main Visual FoxPro window'
WAIT WINDOW
RELEASE WINDOW wFontChar
CLEAR
```

See Also

FONTMETRIC( ), GETFONT( ), SYSMETRIC( ), TXTWIDTH( )

WhatsThisButton Property

Specifies whether the What's This button appears in a form's title bar. Read-only at run time.

Syntax

Form.WhatsThisButton[= *lExpr*]

Settings

lExpr
    One of the following:

Setting	Description
True (.T.)	Turns display of the What's This button on.
False (.F.)	(Default) Turns display of the What's This button off.

Remarks

The What's This button is not displayed in the form's title bar if the WhatsThisButton property is set to true (.T.) and any of the following are true:

- The form's WhatsThisHelp property is set to false (.F.).
- The form's BorderStyle property is set to 0 (None).
- The form's MinButton property is set to true (.T.).
- The form's MaxButton property is set to true (.T.).

Applies To

Form

See Also

BorderStyle Property, MaxButton Property, MinButton Property, ShowWhatsThis Method, TitleBar Property, WhatsThisMode Method, WhatsThisHelp Property, WhatsThisHelpID Property

WhatsThisHelp Property

Specifies whether context-sensitive Help uses What's This help or the Windows help file specified with SET HELP.

Syntax

Form.WhatsThisHelp[= *lExpr*]

Settings

lExpr
    One of the following:

Setting	Description
True (.T.)	The form uses one of the three What's This Help techniques to open the Windows help file specified with SET HELP and display the topic specified with the WhatsThisHelpID property.
False (.F.)	(Default) The form uses the F1 key to open the Windows help file specified with SET HELP. The Help topic specified with the HelpContextID property is displayed.

Remarks

The three What's This Help techniques are as follows:

1. A What's This button is displayed in the form title bar. When this button is clicked, the mouse pointer changes to an arrow with a question mark. The Help topic displayed when a control is clicked is specified with the WhatsThisHelpID property for the control.

2. The WhatsThisMode method is invoked, changing the mouse pointer changes to an arrow with a question mark. The Help topic displayed when a control is clicked is specified with the WhatsThisHelpID property for the control.

3. The ShowWhatsThis method is invoked for a control. The Help topic displayed is specified with the control's WhatsThisHelpID property.

Note that in Visual FoxPro 6.0, if Help is set to an HTML Help file (for example, Foxhelp.chm), the Help topic is displayed in the HTML Help viewer. If Help is set to a Windows Help file (for example, Foxhelp.hlp), the Help topic is displayed in a small popup window next to the control.

Applies To

Form

See Also

HelpContextID Property, SET HELP, ShowWhatsThis Method, WhatsThisButton Property, WhatsThisMode Method, WhatsThisHelpID Property

WhatsThisHelpID Property

Specifies a Help topic context ID to provide Whats This Help for an object. Available at design time and run time.

Syntax

Object.WhatsThisHelpID[= *nContextID*]

Settings

nContextID

Specifies the context ID number of a topic in a Help file. *nContextID* may be negative, zero, or positive. The following table lists the values for *nContextID* and what is displayed when the object is clicked with the question mark mouse pointer:

nContextID	Description
Negative	(Default, −1) Displays the Whats This Help popup with the message "No Help topic is associated with this item."
Zero	Visual FoxPro searches upward through the object's hierarchy for the first object with a positive WhatsThisHelpID property value. If an object with a positive WhatsThisHelpID property value is found, the Whats This Help topic is displayed. If an object with a positive WhatsThisHelpID property value isn't found, no Whats This Help topic is displayed.
Positive	Displays the Whats This Help topic corresponding to the context ID specified with *nContextID*. If no Help topic has the context ID specified with *nContextID*, the Whats This Help popup with the message "No Help topic is associated with this item" is displayed.

Applies To

CheckBox, ComboBox, CommandButton, CommandGroup, Container Object, Control Object, EditBox, Form, Grid, Header, Image, Label, Line, ListBox, OLE Bound Control, OLE Container Control, OptionButton, OptionGroup, Shape, Spinner, TextBox, Timer, ToolBar

See Also

HelpContextID Property, SET HELP, ShowWhatsThis Method, WhatsThisButton Property, WhatsThisHelp Property, WhatsThisMode Method

WhatsThisMode Method

Displays the Whats This Help question mark mouse pointer and enables Whats This Help mode.

Syntax

[*Form.*]*Object*.WhatsThisMode

Remarks

Calling the WhatsThisMode method changes the mouse pointer to an arrow with a question mark and enables Whats This Help mode. Clicking an object displays the Whats This Help topic specified by the WhatsThisHelpID property for the object. Pressing ESC disables the Whats This Help mode and returns the mouse pointer to it's original state.

Applies To

Form

See Also

HelpContextID Property, SET HELP, ShowWhatsThis Method, WhatsThisButton Property, WhatsThisHelp Property, WhatsThisHelpID Property

When Event

Occurs before a control receives the focus.

Syntax

PROCEDURE *Control*.When
[LPARAMETERS *nIndex*]

Parameters

nIndex
    Uniquely identifies a control if it is in a control array.

Remarks

If the When event returns true (.T.), the default control receives the focus. If the When event returns false (.F.), the control doesn't receive the focus. The order of events when a control gains the focus is:

1. When event

2. GotFocus event

For ListBox controls, the When event occurs each time a user moves the focus between items in the list by clicking on items or by moving the selection with the arrow keys.

For all other controls, the When event occurs when an attempt is made to move the focus to the control.

Applies To

CheckBox, ComboBox, CommandButton, CommandGroup, EditBox, Grid, ListBox, OptionButton, OptionGroup, Spinner, TextBox

See Also

GotFocus Event, Valid Event

Width Property

Specifies the width of an object. Available at design time and run time.

Syntax

[*Object.*]Width[= *nWidth*]

Settings

nWidth
    Specifies the width of an object.

Remarks

Use the Height, Width, Left, and Top properties for operations or calculations based on an object's total area, such as sizing or moving the object.

For forms and controls, the values for this property changes as the object is sized by the user or in code. Maximum settings of this property for all objects are system-dependent.

For forms, the Width property specifies the external width of the form, excluding the borders.

For controls, the Width property is measured from the center of the control's border so that controls with different border widths align correctly.

> **Note** The Width property is read-only when it applies to a control contained in a Column object.

The Width property is determined in the unit of measurement specified by the ScaleMode property setting.

Applies To

CheckBox, Column, ComboBox, CommandButton, CommandGroup, Container Object, Control Object, Custom, EditBox, Form, Grid, Image, Label, Line, ListBox, OLE Bound Control, OLE Container Control, OptionButton, OptionGroup, PageFrame, _SCREEN, Shape, Spinner, TextBox, Timer, ToolBar

See Also

Height Property, Left Property, Move Method, ScaleMode Property, Top Property

WindowList Property

Included for backward compatibility with READ. Use the Form Designer instead of READ.

WindowState Property

Specifies whether a form window is displayed as a maximized, minimized, or normal window at run time. Available at design time and run time.

Syntax

[*Object*.]WindowState[= *nState*]

Settings

nState
> The settings for the WindowState property are as follows:

Setting	Description
0	Normal
1	Minimized (minimized to an icon). If the main Visual FoxPro window is minimized when Visual FoxPro is exited, the main Visual FoxPro window isn't displayed before exiting. If you application displays a dialog before exiting, be sure to set _SCREEN.WindowState to 0 before displaying the dialog.
2	Maximized (enlarged to fill the screen)

Applies To

Form, _SCREEN

See Also

Height Property, Left Property, Top Property, Width Property

_WINDOWS System Variable

Contains true (.T.) if you are using Visual FoxPro for Windows.

Syntax

_WINDOWS = *lExpression*

Remarks

_WINDOWS contains false (.F.) if you are using a different platform version of FoxPro or Visual FoxPro.

The value contained in _WINDOWS cannot be changed with STORE or =.

See Also

_DOS, _MAC, _UNIX, VERSION( )

WindowType Property

Specifies how a form set or form behaves when it is shown or run with DO FORM. Available at design time and run time.

Syntax

Object.WindowType[= *nType*]

Settings

nType
For a form set, the settings for the WindowType property are as follows:

Setting	Description
0	Modeless.
1	Modal. No other forms can become active and the menu can be active. All forms in the form set are active.
2	Read. The form set behaves as if it were activated by the READ command. Execution stops on the Show method or DO FORM command. When the Form is deactivated, execution continues. (Included for backward compatibility, and available only for Forms converted from previous versions of FoxPro.)
3	Read Modal. The form set behaves as if it were activated by a READ command's MODAL clause. Program execution stops at the Show method or the DO FORM command. Any forms specified in the WindowList property are available, but other forms and the menu are not available. (Included for backward compatibility, and available only for forms converted from previous versions of FoxPro.)

For a form, the settings for the WindowType property are as follows:

Setting	Description
0	Modeless.
1	Modal. No other forms can become active and the menu is inactive. All forms in the form set are active.

Remarks

You cannot change the WindowType setting once the window has been displayed.

The Show method takes a parameter that can override the WindowType setting.

Note The WindowType setting of a form set overrides the individual WindowType settings of the forms it contains. For example, if the WindowType property for a form set is set to 0, all the forms contained in it are modeless, regardless of their individual WindowType property settings.

Applies To

Form, FormSet, _SCREEN

See Also

DO FORM, READ EVENTS, Show Method, WindowList Property

WITH ... ENDWITH Command

Specifies multiple properties for an object.

Syntax

WITH *ObjectName*
    [*.cStatements*]
ENDWITH

Arguments

ObjectName
    Specifies the name of the object. *ObjectName* can be the name of the object or a reference to the object.

.cStatements
    cStatements can consist of any number of Microsoft Visual FoxPro commands used to specify properties for *ObjectName*. Place a period before *cStatement* to denote that it is a property of *ObjectName*.

Remarks

WITH ... ENDWITH provides a convenient way to specify a number of properties for a single object. Note that you can also execute methods from within a WITH ... ENDWITH structure.

Example

The following example creates a custom class name Employee. After the Employee class has been created with CREATEOBJECT( ), WITH ... ENDWITH is used to set multiple properties for the class. The properties values are then displayed.

```
moemployee = CREATEOBJECT('employee')

WITH moemployee
    .First_Name = 'John'
    .Last_Name = 'Smith'
    .Address = '16 Maple Lane'
    .HireDate = {^1998-02-16}
ENDWITH

CLEAR
? moemployee.First_Name + ' '
?? moemployee.Last_Name
? moemployee.Address
? moemployee.HireDate

DEFINE CLASS employee AS CUSTOM
      First_Name = SPACE(20)
      Last_Name = SPACE(20)
      Address = SPACE(30)
      HireDate = {  -  -  }
ENDDEFINE
```

See Also

:: Scope Resolution Operator, ADD CLASS, CREATE CLASS, CREATE CLASSLIB, CREATEOBJECT( ), GETOBJECT( ), MODIFY CLASS, RELEASE CLASSLIB, SET CLASSLIB

_WIZARD System Variable

Contains the name of the Visual FoxPro wizard application.

Syntax

_WIZARD = *cProgramName*

Arguments

cProgramName
　　Specifies a wizard application. If your wizard application is in a directory other than the current Visual FoxPro default directory, include a path with the application name.

You can also specify a wizard application in your Visual FoxPro configuration file by including a line using the following syntax:

```
_WIZARD = cProgramName
```

Remarks

The _WIZARD system variable contains the name of the application that Visual FoxPro uses when you choose a wizard to run. By default, _WIZARD contains Wizard.app, installed in your Visual FoxPro directory. You can specify a different name for the wizard application.

See Also

System Variables Overview

WLAST( ) Function

Returns the name of the window that was active prior to the current window or determines whether the specified window was active prior to the current window.

Syntax

WLAST([*WindowName*])

Returns

Character or Logical

Arguments

WindowName

Specifies a window that WLAST( ) evaluates. In Visual FoxPro, you can also specify the name of a toolbar. WLAST( ) returns true (.T.) if the specified window was active prior to the current window; otherwise false (.F.) is returned. False (.F.) is also returned if the window you specify doesn't exist.

The name of the window that was active prior to the current window is returned if you omit *WindowName*.

Remarks

WLAST( ) returns the empty string if the window that was active prior to the current window is the Debug, Trace, or Command window. Program execution isn't affected by bringing these windows forward when you are debugging a program that uses WLAST( ).

See Also

ACTIVATE WINDOW, DEFINE WINDOW, WEXIST( ), WONTOP( ), WOUTPUT( ), WVISIBLE( )

WLCOL( ) Function

Returns the column coordinate of the upper-left corner of the active or specified window.

Syntax

WLCOL([*WindowName*])

Returns

Numeric

Arguments

WindowName

Specifies the window for which WLCOL( ) returns the column coordinate. In Visual FoxPro, you can also specify the name of a toolbar. If you omit *WindowName*, WLCOLS( ) returns the column coordinate of the active output window. You can also use the empty string for *WindowName* to specify the main Visual FoxPro window.

In Visual FoxPro, if no window is active, WLCOLS( ) returns the column coordinate of the main Visual FoxPro window relative to the Windows desktop.

If a system window (the Command window, the Data Session window, a Browse window, and so on) has been opened and is visible or hidden (its name appears on the Window menu), you can include its name in WLCOL( ). If you specify the name of a system window that is closed, Visual FoxPro generates an error message. The Debug window is an exception. Once the Debug window has been opened, its name can be included in WLCOL( ) if it is visible, hidden, or closed.

Remarks

The value returned by WLCOL( ) depends on the current video display mode, and is relative to the main Visual FoxPro window. The display mode can be changed with SET DISPLAY.

Windows can be positioned outside the main Visual FoxPro window. If the specified window is to the left of the main Visual FoxPro window, WCOL( ) returns a negative value. If the window's left border is to the right of the main Visual FoxPro window, WCOL( ) returns a positive value greater than the width of the main Visual FoxPro window.

See Also

SET DISPLAY, WCOLS( ), WLROW( ), WROWS( )

WLROW( ) Function

Returns the row coordinate of the upper-left corner of the active or specified window.

Syntax

WLROW([*WindowName*])

Returns

Numeric

Arguments

WindowName

Specifies the window for which WLROW( ) returns the row coordinate. In Visual FoxPro, you can also specify the name of a toolbar. If you omit *WindowName*, WLROW( ) returns the row coordinate of the active output window. You can also use the empty string for *WindowName* to specify the main Visual FoxPro window.

In Visual FoxPro, if no window is active, WLROW( ) returns the row coordinate of the main Visual FoxPro window relative to the Windows desktop.

If a system window (the Command window, the Data Session window, a Browse window, and so on) has been opened and is visible or hidden (its name appears on the Window menu), you can include its name in WLROW( ). If you specify the name of a system window that is closed, Visual FoxPro generates an error message. The Debug window is an exception. Once the Debug window has been opened, its name can be included in WLROW( ) if it is visible, hidden, or closed.

Remarks

The value returned by WLROW( ) depends on the current video display mode, and the row coordinate is relative to the main Visual FoxPro window. The display mode can be changed with SET DISPLAY.

Windows can be positioned off the main Visual FoxPro window. If the top of the window is above the main Visual FoxPro window, WLROW( ) returns a negative value. If the top of the window is below the bottom of the main Visual FoxPro window, WLROW( ) returns a positive value greater than the height of the main Visual FoxPro window.

See Also

SET DISPLAY, WCOLS( ), WLCOL( ), WROWS( )

WMAXIMUM( ) Function

Determines whether the active or specified window is maximized.

Syntax

WMAXIMUM([*WindowName*])

Arguments

WindowName

Specifies the name of the window WMAXIMUM( ) evaluates. You can specify the name of a Visual FoxPro system window (the Command window, the Data Session window, a Browse window, and so on).

If you omit *WindowName*, WMAXIMUM( ) returns a logical value for the active window. You can also use the empty string for *WindowName* to specify the main Visual FoxPro window.

Remarks

Windows can be enlarged to fill the window that contains them. In Visual FoxPro for Windows, the default container window is the main window.

A user-defined window created with DEFINE WINDOW can be maximized only if the ZOOM keyword is included in its definition.

WMAXIMUM( ) returns true (.T.) if the current or specified window is maximized; otherwise WMAXIMUM( ) returns false (.F.). In Visual FoxPro, you can include the name of a toolbar. However, WMAXIMUM( ) always returns false (.F.) for a toolbar because toolbars cannot be maximized.

See Also

DEFINE WINDOW, WMINIMUM( ), ZOOM WINDOW

WMINIMUM( ) Function

Determines whether the active or specified window is minimized.

Syntax

WMINIMUM([*WindowName*])

Returns

Logical

Arguments

WindowName

Specifies the name of the window WMINIMUM( ) evaluates. You can specify the name of a Visual FoxPro system window (the Command window, the Data Session window, a Browse window, and so on).

If you omit *WindowName*, WMINIMUM( ) returns a logical value for the active window. You can also include the empty string in *WindowName* to specify the main Visual FoxPro window.

Remarks

In Visual FoxPro for Windows, windows can be reduced to an icon.

A user-defined window created with DEFINE WINDOW can be minimized only if the MINIMIZE keyword is included in its definition.

WMINIMUM( ) returns true (.T.) if the current or specified window is minimized; otherwise it returns false (.F.). In Visual FoxPro, you can include the name of a toolbar. However, WMINIMUM( ) always returns false (.F.) for a toolbar because toolbars cannot be minimized.

See Also

DEFINE WINDOW, WMAXIMUM( ), ZOOM WINDOW

WONTOP( ) Function

Determines whether the active or specified window is in front of all other windows.

Syntax

WONTOP([*WindowName*])

Returns

Character or Logical

Arguments

WindowName

Specifies the name of the window WONTOP( ) evaluates. You can specify the name of a user-defined window created with DEFINE WINDOW or a system window (the Command window, the Data Session window, a Browse window, and so on). If you omit *WindowName*, WONTOP( ) returns the name of the frontmost window. You can also include the empty string in *WindowName* to specify the main Visual FoxPro window.

If the Debug, Trace, or Command window is frontmost and you don't specify a window name, WONTOP( ) returns the empty string. When you are debugging a program that uses WONTOP( ), program execution isn't affected by bringing these windows forward.

Remarks

WONTOP( ) returns true (.T.) if the specified window is frontmost. It returns false (.F.) if the window isn't frontmost or doesn't exist.

Example

The following example uses WONTOP( ) to display the name of the frontmost window. Before you run this program, open some windows (Browse windows, the Data Session window, and so on), then run the example.

```
IF NOT EMPTY(WONTOP( ))
   WAIT WINDOW 'Frontmost window: ' + WONTOP( )
ELSE
   WAIT WINDOW 'No windows are open'
ENDIF
```

See Also

ACTIVATE WINDOW, DEFINE WINDOW, WEXIST( ), WOUTPUT( ), WVISIBLE( )

WordWrap Property

Specifies whether a Label control expands vertically or horizontally to fit the text specified with its Caption property when the control is resized. Available at design time and run time.

Syntax

[*Form.*]*Label.*WordWrap[= *lExpr*]

Arguments

lExpr
    The settings for the WordWrap property are as follows:

Setting	Description
True (.T.)	The text wraps and the label expands or contracts vertically to fit the text and the size of the font. The horizontal size does not change.
False (.F.)	(Default) The text does not wrap and the label expands or contracts horizontally to fit the length of the text and vertically to fit the size of the font and the number of lines. The vertical size does not change.

Remarks

Use this property to determine how a label displays its contents. For example, a graph that changes dynamically might have a label containing text that also changes. To maintain a constant horizontal size for the label and allow for increasing or decreasing text, you would set the WordWrap property to true (.T.).

If you want a label to expand only horizontally, set WordWrap to false (.F.). If you do not want the label to change size, set AutoSize to false (.F.).

Note   If the WordWrap property is set to true (.T.), the AutoSize property is ignored.

Applies To

Label

See Also

AutoSize Property, Caption Property

WOUTPUT( ) Function

Determines whether output is being directed to the active or specified window.

Syntax

WOUTPUT([*WindowName*])

Returns

Logical and Character

Arguments

WindowName

Specifies the window WOUTPUT( ) evaluates for output. Output cannot be directed to a system window or toolbar. If you omit *WindowName*, WOUTPUT( ) returns the name of the window to which output is currently directed. You can also include the empty string in *WindowName* to specify the main Visual FoxPro window.

WOUTPUT( ) returns the empty string if output is being directed to the main Visual FoxPro window.

Remarks

WOUTPUT( ) returns true (.T.) if the specified user-defined window is the active output window. WOUTPUT( ) returns false (.F.) if the window you specify doesn't exist or is a system window. The last user-defined window activated with ACTIVATE WINDOW is the active output window.

Example

In the following example, a window is created and activated. WOUTPUT( ) is used to display the name of this active output window. The window is closed and removed from memory. If another window is active, its name is displayed. If another window isn't active, a message is displayed indicating that output is directed to the main Visual FoxPro window.

```
DEFINE WINDOW wOutput1 FROM 2,2 TO 12,32 TITLE 'Output Window'
ACTIVATE WINDOW wOutput1
WAIT WINDOW 'wOutput1 window: ' + WOUTPUT( )
RELEASE WINDOW wOutput1
IF EMPTY(WOUTPUT( ))
   WAIT WINDOW 'Output being directed to the main Visual FoxPro window'
ELSE
   WAIT WINDOW 'Output window: ' + WOUTPUT( )
ENDIF
```

See Also

ACTIVATE WINDOW, DEFINE WINDOW, WEXIST( ), WONTOP( ), WVISIBLE( )

WPARENT( ) Function

Returns the name of the parent window of the active or specified window.

Syntax

WPARENT([*WindowName*])

Returns

Character

Arguments

WindowName

Specifies a window whose parent window name WPARENT( ) returns. WPARENT( ) returns the empty string if the specified window doesn't have a parent window. If you omit *WindowName*, WPARENT( ) returns the name of the parent window of the active output window. WPARENT( ) returns the empty string if the active output window doesn't have a parent window.

Remarks

You can use DEFINE WINDOW to create a window and place it in a parent window. The child window becomes integrated with its parent window. For example, a child window defined and activated inside a parent window can't be moved outside the parent window. If the parent window is moved, the child window moves with it.

Example

The following example defines a parent and child window. It then uses WPARENT( ) to identify which window is the parent.

```
CLEAR ALL
CLEAR
DEFINE WINDOW wParent ;
   FROM 1,1 TO 20,20 ;
   TITLE 'wParent'      && Parent window
ACTIVATE WINDOW wParent
DEFINE WINDOW wChild ;
   FROM 1,1 TO 10,10 ;
   TITLE 'wChild' ;
   IN WINDOW wParent   && Child window
ACTIVATE WINDOW wChild
WAIT WINDOW 'The parent window is ' + WPARENT( )
RELEASE WINDOW wParent, wChild
```

See Also

ACTIVATE WINDOW, DEFINE WINDOW, WCHILD( )

_WRAP System Variable

Included for backward compatibility. Use the Report Designer instead.

WREAD( ) Function

Included for backward compatibility. Use the Form Designer instead.

WriteExpression Method

Writes an expression to a property. Available at design time and run time.

Syntax

Object.WriteExpression[*cPropertyName*, *cExpression*]

Arguments

cPropertyName
Specifies the name of the property to write the expression to.

cExpression
Specifies a character string that is written to the property sheet as an expression.

Applies To

ActiveDoc, CheckBox, Column, ComboBox, CommandButton, CommandGroup, Cursor, Custom, DataEnvironment, EditBox, Form, FormSet, Grid, Header, Image, Label, Line, ListBox, OLE Bound Control, OLE Container Control, OptionButton, OptionGroup, Page, PageFrame, ProjectHook Object, Relation, Shape, Spinner, TextBox, Timer, ToolBar

See Also

ReadExpression Method

WriteMethod Method

Writes the specified text to the specified method. Available at design time only.

Syntax

Control.WriteMethod(*MethodName*, *MethodText*)

Arguments

MethodName
    Specifies the name of the method to write the specified text to.

MethodText
    Specifies the text to write to the specified method to.

Remarks

This method will only set the method text for existing methods. If the object does not contain the method specified, Visual FoxPro generates an error.

Applies To

CheckBox, Column, ComboBox, CommandButton, CommandGroup, Custom, EditBox, Form, FormSet, Grid, Header, Image, Label, Line, ListBox, OLE Bound Control, OLE Container Control, OptionButton, OptionGroup, Page, PageFrame, Shape, Spinner, TextBox, Timer, ToolBar

See Also

ReadExpression Method, ReadMethod Method, WriteExpression Method

WROWS( ) Function

Returns the number of rows within the active or specified window.

Syntax

WROWS([*WindowName*])

Returns

Numeric

Arguments

WindowName

Specifies the window for which WROWS( ) returns the number of rows. In Visual FoxPro, you can also specify the name of a toolbar.

In Visual FoxPro, the value returned by WROWS( ) depends on the font specified for the window. Most fonts can be displayed in a wide variety of sizes, and some are proportionally spaced. A row corresponds to the height of the current font. For more information, see "Fonts Overview," earlier in this language reference.

You can specify the name of a system window (the Command window, the Data Session window, a Browse window, and so on) in WROWS( ) if the system window has been opened and is visible or hidden. If you specify the name of a system window that is closed, FoxPro generates an error message. The Debug window is an exception. Once the Debug window has been opened, its name can be included in WROWS( ) if it is visible, hidden, or closed.

You can also include the empty string in *WindowName* to return the number of rows in the main Visual FoxPro window.

The empty string can be used to specify the main Visual FoxPro window in functions such as WLCOL( ), WLROW( ), and WCOLS( ), which return window locations or sizes.

Remarks

If you don't specify a window name, the number of rows in the active output window is returned. If no window is active, the number of rows in the main Visual FoxPro window is returned.

See Also

SCOLS( ), SROWS( ), WCOLS( ), WLCOL( ), WLROW( )

WTITLE( ) Function

Returns the title assigned to the active or specified window.

Syntax

WTITLE([*WindowName*])

Returns

Character

Arguments

WindowName

Specifies a window whose title WTITLE( ) returns. The title assigned to the window with the TITLE clause is returned if you include the name of a user-defined window created with DEFINE WINDOW.

When you issue BROWSE WINDOW to open a Browse window in a user-defined window, WTITLE( ) returns the title of the user-defined window if the Browse window doesn't have a title. WTITLE( ) returns the title of the Browse window if the Browse window does have a title.

You can also use the empty string for *WindowName* to specify the main Visual FoxPro window.

Remarks

WTITLE( ) can be used to return a window's title, which appears in the top border of the window. The title is returned for the active window if you omit *WindowName*. WTITLE( ) returns the empty string if the Debug, Trace or Command window is active or output is being directed to the main Visual FoxPro window.

Window Names and Titles   Names are assigned to user-defined windows, system windows, toolbars (in Visual FoxPro), and Browse windows in the following manner:

User-defined windows are assigned names when they are created with DEFINE WINDOW. There is a distinction between user-defined window names and titles. By default, user-defined windows don't have titles. If the TITLE clause is included when the window is created, the specified title appears in the top border of the window, but isn't the name of the window.

By default, each system window, which is part of the Visual FoxPro interface, derives its name from the title of the window. Examples of system windows include the Command window, the Data Session window, and the Trace window. In Visual FoxPro, each toolbar derives its name from the title of the toolbar.

Program and editing windows and the Label and Report Designer windows derive their names from the name of the file being created or modified.

A Browse window derives its name from the title of the window. The name and title of the Browse window is assigned in one of three ways: either by the default title assignment of the table alias, or by the window title (if any exists), or by the Browse title (if any exists).

By default, the Browse window name is the table alias.

To specify a system window and toolbar names in commands and functions, enclose the entire system window or toolbar name in quotation marks. For example, to hide the Report Controls toolbar in Visual FoxPro, issue the following command:

```
HIDE WINDOW "Report Controls"
```

Additional Notes on Window Names   If you are unsure of the name assigned to a window, check the Window menu. All window names are listed at the bottom of the Window menu.

Two windows exist if you issue BROWSE WINDOW *WindowName*. The Browse window is a separate window and takes on the attributes of the specified user-defined window.

If a window is active when you issue BROWSE and you don't include the WINDOW clause, the Browse window takes on the attributes of the active window. You can override this behavior by including NORMAL in BROWSE.

You can include window names that contain spaces in commands and functions that accept window names, such as MOVE WINDOW, DEACTIVATE WINDOW, and WONTOP( ), by specifying the part of the window name that begins with the first non-space character and continuing until the last non-space character is encountered.

For example, a Browse window with the name Invoice Entry can be moved with this command:

```
MOVE WINDOW invoice BY 1,1
```

The names of user-defined windows cannot contain spaces, but the names of Browse and system windows can.

See Also

ACTIVATE WINDOW, DEFINE WINDOW, WEXIST( ), WLAST( ), WONTOP( ), WOUTPUT( ), WREAD( )

WVISIBLE( ) Function

Determines if the specified window has been activated and isn't hidden.

Syntax

WVISIBLE(*WindowName*)

Returns

Logical

Arguments

WindowName

Specifies the name of the window WVISIBLE( ) evaluates. In Visual FoxPro, you can also specify the name of a toolbar. You can also include the empty string in *WindowName* to specify the main Visual FoxPro window.

Remarks

WVISIBLE( ) returns true (.T.) if the specified window is shown or activated and isn't hidden. Windows are shown and activated with SHOW WINDOW and ACTIVATE WINDOW.

WVISIBLE( ) returns false (.F.) if the window has not been activated, has been hidden with HIDE WINDOW, has been deactivated with DEACTIVATE WINDOW, or doesn't exist.

See Also

ACTIVATE WINDOW, DEFINE WINDOW, WEXIST( ), WONTOP( ), WOUTPUT( )

YEAR( ) Function

Returns the year from the specified date or datetime expression.

Syntax

YEAR(*dExpression* | *tExpression*)

Returns

Numeric

Arguments

dExpression
Specifies a date expression from which YEAR( ) returns the year. *dExpression* can be a function that returns a date, or a Date-type memory variable, array element, or field. It can also be a literal date string, such as {^1998-06-06}.

tExpression
Specifies a datetime expression from which YEAR( ) returns the year.

Remarks

YEAR( ) always returns the year with the century. The CENTURY setting (ON or OFF) doesn't affect the returned value.

Example

```
CLEAR
? YEAR(DATE( ))
```

See Also

DATE( ), DATETIME( ), DOW( ), SET CENTURY

ZAP Command

Removes all records from a table, leaving just the table structure.

Syntax

ZAP
    [IN *nWorkArea* | *cTableAlias*]

Arguments

IN *nWorkArea*
Specifies the work area of the table in which all records are removed.

IN *cTableAlias*

> Specifies the alias of the table in which all records are removed.

> If you omit *nWorkArea* and *cTableAlias*, all records are removed in the table in the currently selected work area.

Remarks

Issuing ZAP is equivalent to issuing DELETE ALL followed by PACK, but ZAP is much faster.

If SET SAFETY is ON, Microsoft Visual FoxPro asks if you would like to remove the records from the current table.

Issuing ZAP does not cause a Delete trigger to occur. For more information about creating triggers for a table, see the CREATE TRIGGER Command, earlier in this language reference.

> **Caution**   Records zapped from the current table cannot be recalled.

See Also

CREATE TRIGGER, DELETE, PACK

ZoomBox Property

Specifies whether a form has a zoom box. Available at design time; read/write at run time.

Syntax

Object.ZoomBox = *lExpr*

Arguments

lExpr

> The settings for the ZoomBox property are as follows:

Setting	Description
True (.T.)	(Default) A zoom box appears in the upper-right corner of the form.
False (.F.)	No zoom box appears in the form.

Applies To

Form

See Also

BorderStyle Property, SizeBox Property

ZOOM WINDOW Command

Changes the size and position of a user-defined window or a Visual FoxPro system window.

Syntax

ZOOM WINDOW *WindowName* MIN | MAX | NORM
    [AT *nRow1, nColumn1* | FROM AT *nRow1, nColumn1*
    [SIZE AT *nRow2, nColumn2* | TO *nRow2, nColumn2*]]

Arguments

WindowName
    Specifies the name of the window whose size you want to change.

MIN
    Reduces the window to minimum size.

    In Visual FoxPro for Windows, the window is reduced to an icon.

    All system windows can be reduced to a minimum size in Visual FoxPro for Windows. Visual FoxPro system windows must be open in the main Visual FoxPro window or a user-defined window before they can be minimized.

    A user-defined window can be minimized after it is defined. It doesn't have to be activated before you change its size.

MAX
    Expands a window to fill the main Visual FoxPro window, the Windows desktop, or a user-defined window. If a child window is placed in a parent window and the child window is maximized, it fills the parent window. If any of the additional ZOOM WINDOW clauses (AT, SIZE, TO, or FROM) are included with MAX, MAX is ignored.

    Only user-defined windows defined with ZOOM can be expanded to maximum size.

NORM
    Returns a window to its original size after it has been minimized or maximized. NORM can also be used to move a window without changing its size. Use ZOOM WINDOW NORM without any additional clauses to return a minimized or maximized window to its original size and location.

AT *nRow1, nColumn1* | FROM *nRow2, nColumn2*
    You can specify the placement of a window by including the AT or FROM clause.

ZOOM WINDOW *WindowName* NORM AT AT *nRow1*, *nColumn1* restores a minimized or maximized window to its original size and places it at the specific location. The AT *nRow1*, *nColumn1* coordinates specify where the upper-left corner of the window is placed. A window's location can also be changed with MOVE WINDOW.

In Visual FoxPro for Windows, if NORM is included, the upper-left corner of the window is placed in the main Visual FoxPro window at the location specified with AT *nRow1*, *nColumn1*. If MIN is included, AT and FROM are ignored and the window is displayed as an icon in the lower portion of the main Visual FoxPro window. If MAX is included, AT and FROM are ignored and the window is expanded to fill the main Visual FoxPro window.

In Visual FoxPro for Windows, if the window is created with the IN DESKTOP clause, the upper-left corner of the window is placed in the Windows desktop at the location specified with AT *nRow1*, *nColumn1*. If MIN is included, AT and FROM are ignored and the window is displayed as an icon in the lower portion of the Windows desktop. If MAX is included, AT and FROM are ignored and the window is expanded to fill the Windows desktop.

SIZE AT *nRow2*, *nColumn2* | TO *nRow2*, *nColumn2*

You can also specify a window size for a window by including SIZE or TO. If SIZE is included, the window size is *nRow2* rows high and *nColumn2* columns wide. If the TO clause is included, the upper-left corner of the window remains in its current position and the lower-right corner of the window is placed at the position specified with *nRow2*, *nColumn2*.

Remarks

In Visual FoxPro for Windows, windows can be reduced to a minimum size, enlarged to fill the entire main Visual FoxPro window, or sized anywhere in between.

If you create a user-defined window with DEFINE WINDOW and the IN DESKTOP clause in Visual FoxPro for Windows, the window you create can be enlarged to fill the entire desktop.

In Visual FoxPro for Windows, windows can be zoomed directly from minimum to maximum size and vice versa.

When zooming a window, you can specify where to place the resized window in the main Visual FoxPro window or a user-defined window.

To zoom a system window, enclose the entire system window name in quotation marks. For example, to maximize the Command window, issue the following command:

```
ZOOM WINDOW 'Command Window' MAX
```

You can use ZOOM WINDOW to resize all system windows.

Example

In the following example, a Browse window is opened for the `customer` table. The Browse window is minimized. The Browse window is then returned to its default size. It is then minimized again at a specific location. The Browse window is then enlarged to a specific size and is maximized.

```
CLEAR ALL
CLEAR
CLOSE DATABASES
OPEN DATABASE (HOME(2) + 'Data\Testdata')
USE customer  && Opens Customer table
BROWSE NORMAL NOWAIT

IF _DOS OR _WINDOWS
   ZOOM WINDOW customer MIN
   WAIT WINDOW TIMEOUT 3 ;
      'MIN clause - This window will timeout. Please wait.'
ENDIF

ZOOM WINDOW customer NORM
WAIT WINDOW TIMEOUT 3 ;
   'NORM clause - This window will timeout. Please wait.'

IF _DOS OR _WINDOWS
   ZOOM WINDOW customer MIN AT 10,10
   WAIT WINDOW TIMEOUT 3 ;
      'MIN AT 10,10 clause - This window will timeout. Please wait.'
ENDIF

ZOOM WINDOW customer NORM AT 1,1 SIZE 22,25
WAIT WINDOW TIMEOUT 3 ;
   'NORM & SIZE clauses - This window will timeout. Please wait.'
ZOOM WINDOW customer NORM FROM 10,10 TO 22,70
WAIT WINDOW TIMEOUT 3 ;
   'NORM & TO clauses - This window will timeout. Please wait.'
ZOOM WINDOW customer MAX
WAIT WINDOW TIMEOUT 3 'MAX clause - This window will timeout. Please wait.'
CLEAR ALL
```

See Also

ACTIVATE WINDOW, DEFINE WINDOW, SIZE WINDOW

ZOrder Method

Places a specified form or control at the front or back of the z-order within its graphical level. Places a control contained by the ToolBar object at the front or back of the controls array that determines the order in which controls appear in the toolbar.

Syntax

[*Object.*]ZOrder([*nOrder*])

Arguments

nOrder

Specifies an integer indicating the position of the object relative to other objects. If you omit *nOrder*, the setting is 0.

Setting	Description
0	(Default) The object is positioned at the front of the z-order.
1	The object is positioned at the back of the z-order.

Remarks

There are two graphical layers associated with objects. The back layer is the drawing space, where the results of the graphics methods appear, and the front layer is the object layer. The contents of one layer covers the contents of the layer behind. The ZOrder method arranges objects only within the layer where the object appears.

Note For a Page object, the ZOrder method does not affect the PageOrder property setting. ZOrder only determines the Page that is on top and active.

For more information about using controls, see Chapter 10, "Using Controls," in the *Microsoft Visual FoxPro 6.0 Programmer's Guide*.

Applies To

CheckBox, ComboBox, CommandButton, CommandGroup, Container Object, Control Object, EditBox, Form, Grid, Image, Label, Line, ListBox, OLE Bound Control, OLE Container Control, OptionButton, OptionGroup, Page, PageFrame, _SCREEN, Shape, Spinner, TextBox, ToolBar

See Also

PageOrder Property

How to Be Sure
Your First Important Project
Isn't Your Last.

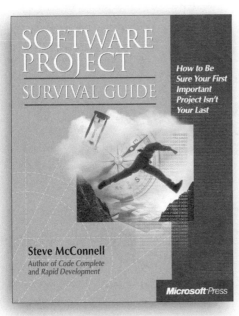

U.S.A.	**$24.99**
U.K.	£22.49
Canada	$34.99

ISBN 1-57231-621-7

Equip yourself with SOFTWARE PROJECT SUR-VIVAL GUIDE. It's for everyone with a stake in the outcome of a development project—and especially for those without formal software project management training. That includes top managers, executives, clients, investors, end-user representatives, project managers, and technical leads. Here you'll find guidance from the acclaimed author of the classics *Code Complete* and *Rapid Development*. Steve McConnell draws on solid research and a career's worth of hard-won experience to map the surest path to your goal—what he calls "one specific approach to software development that works pretty well most of the time for most projects." Get SOFTWARE PROJECT SURVIVAL GUIDE. And be sure of success.

***Microsoft*®** Press

Microsoft Press has titles to help everyone— from new users to seasoned developers—

Step by Step Series
Self-paced tutorials for classroom instruction or individualized study

Starts Here™ Series
Interactive instruction on CD-ROM that helps students learn by doing

Field Guide Series
Concise, task-oriented A–Z references for quick, easy answers— anywhere

Official Series
Timely books on a wide variety of Internet topics geared for advanced users

All User Training   All User Reference

Quick Course® Series
Fast, to-the-point instruction for new users

At a Glance Series
Quick visual guides for task-oriented instruction

Running Series
A comprehensive curriculum alternative to standard documentation books

Microsoft Press® products are available worldwide wherever quality computer books are sold. For more information, contact your book or computer retailer, software reseller, or local Microsoft Sales Office, or visit our Web site at mspress.microsoft.com. To locate your nearest source for Microsoft Press products, or to order directly, call 1-800-MSPRESS in the U.S. (in Canada, call 1-800-268-2222).

Prices and availability dates are subject to change.

start faster and go farther!

The wide selection of books and CD-ROMs published by Microsoft Press contain something for every level of user and every area of interest, from just-in-time online training tools to development tools for professional programmers. Look for them at your bookstore or computer store today!

Professional Select Editions Series
Advanced titles geared for the system administrator or technical support career path

Microsoft® Certified Professional Training
The Microsoft Official Curriculum for certification exams

Best Practices Series
Candid accounts of the new movement in software development

Microsoft Programming Series
The foundations of software development

Professional   Developers

Microsoft Press® Interactive
Integrated multimedia courseware for all levels

Strategic Technology Series
Easy-to-read overviews for decision makers

Microsoft Professional Editions
Technical information straight from the source

Solution Developer Series
Comprehensive titles for intermediate to advanced developers

Microsoft® Press

mspress.microsoft.com

Register Today!

Return this
Microsoft® Visual FoxPro® 6.0
Language Reference
registration card for
a Microsoft Press® catalog

U.S. and Canada addresses only. Fill in information below and mail postage-free. Please mail only the bottom half of this page.

1-57231-870-8   *MICROSOFT® VISUAL FOXPRO® 6.0*   *Owner Registration Card*
                              LANGUAGE REFERENCE

_____
NAME

_____
INSTITUTION OR COMPANY NAME

_____
ADDRESS

_____

_____
CITY   STATE   ZIP

Microsoft®*Press*
Quality Computer Books

For a free catalog of
Microsoft Press® products, call
1-800-MSPRESS

BUSINESS REPLY MAIL
FIRST-CLASS MAIL   PERMIT NO. 53   BOTHELL, WA

POSTAGE WILL BE PAID BY ADDRESSEE

NO POSTAGE
NECESSARY
IF MAILED
IN THE
UNITED STATES

MICROSOFT PRESS REGISTRATION
MICROSOFT® VISUAL FOXPRO® 6.0
LANGUAGE REFERENCE
PO BOX 3019
BOTHELL   WA   98041-9946